HISTORY OF THE CHURCH

V

HISTORY OF THE CHURCH

Edited by
HUBERT JEDIN
and
JOHN DOLAN

Volume V

REFORMATION AND COUNTER REFORMATION

by

ERWIN ISERLOH

JOSEPH GLAZIK

HUBERT JEDIN

Translated by

Anselm Biggs

and

Peter W. Becker

A Crossroad Book

THE SEABURY PRESS · NEW YORK

1980

The Seabury Press.

815 Second Avenue

New York, N.Y. 10017

Translated from the *Handbuch der Kirchengeschichte*

Vol. IV: *Reformation, Katholische Reform und Gegenreformation,* 2d edition

© Verlag Herder KG Freiburg im Breisgau 1967

English translation © 1980 by The Seabury Press, Inc.

Printed in the United States of America

Library of Congress Cataloging in Publication Data

Jedin, Hubert, 1900–   ed.

History of the church.

Translation of Handbuch der Kirchengenschichte.

"A Crossroad book."

Vols. 1, 3, and 4 previously issued under title:

Handbook of church history.

Includes bibliographies and indexes.

CONTENTS: [etc.]—v. 5. Iserloh, E., Glazik, J. and

Jedin, H.   Reformation and counter reformation.

1. Church history.   I. Dolan, John Patrick.   II. Title.

BR145.2.J413   1980   270   79-29649

ISBN 0-8164-0449-6 (v. 5)

CONTENTS

CONTENTS

PART TWO: CATHOLIC REFORM AND COUNTER REFORMATION

CONTENTS

PREFACE

This volume was originally intended to treat the Late Middle Ages together with the Reformation and the Catholic Reform. Such an arrangement would have much in its favor, since the historical dependence of the Reformation would have been much clearer. For if the Reformation was the revolutionary answer to the unrealized reform of the Church in the fourteenth and fifteenth centuries, the late medieval period belongs among the causes of the Reformation. These are discussed briefly in the present volume because it was decided not to deal with the Late Middle Ages and the Age of the Reformation in the same volume. Chapter 13, "Luther's Rejection of Humanism—Erasmus' Later Years," is thus deprived of a direct connection with the chapter "German Humanism," which is now the concluding chapter of volume IV. Nevertheless, the new arrangement, while dictated by technical necessity, is not without an objective basis. For the beginning of the Reformation, the discovery of America, the invention of printing, and other events occurring around A.D. 1500 so clearly inaugurated a new epoch that this has become standard in previous historical works and has, as a matter of fact, determined this one.

The chapters of this volume were produced over a period of about six years. Confident that all contributors could adhere to their agreement and seeking to fulfill its own pledge to the book trade and to the reader, Verlag Herder proceeded quite early with the typesetting and the preparation of page proofs. As a result the bibliography for Part II, in existence for some time, could only be brought into conformity with the most recent publications by means of the supplement given on pages 740–755.

The authors' views on the term "Counter Reformation," used in the title of the volume, is explained on pages 431–432.

Erwin Iserloh

PREFACE TO THE ENGLISH EDITION

The eminent German Jesuit theologian Hugo Rahner recently wrote that through this volume of the *Handbuch der Kirchengeschichte* one can learn that what took place over a thousand years ago—part of which was highly regarded down to the present day—was audaciously cut away by the Church of our day as antiquated historical ballast. A product of the stirring days of the Second Vatican Council, this volume of the history of the Church reflects many of the changes introduced by the Council, but its relationship to that great assembly is more causal than consequential. In a very special way it proves the verity of the old axiom that though history may not confer faith or virtue, it can clear away the misconceptions and misunderstandings that turn men against each other.

No other period in Christian history has witnessed a greater and more violent display of men turning against each other for the sake of a common religion than the events recounted in this volume. At the time the plans for this series on ecclesiastical history were being drawn up by its organizer and editor, Hubert Jedin, he wrote in the *Historisches Jahrbuch* that the history of the Reformation had as yet not been written, nor would it be written until the atmosphere was cleared of the accumulated bias and misconceptions that have continued to cloud both Catholic and Protestant interpretations of the event. Certainly the efforts of those who have produced this volume indicate a step in the right direction. As in the previous volumes, each contributor has been free to present his own scholarly opinions and thus there will be differences in the judgments of persons and events.

In addition to being the result of teamwork, this series has the merit of bringing into proper perspective many aspects of the reform movements that have long been the preserve of the specialist. The attention given the lesser known *personae dramatis,* the collaborators of Luther and his Catholic literary opponents, is an example of this, as is the detailed account of the spread of Lutheranism into Scandinavia and Slavic lands and of Calvinism into eastern Europe.

In a Rankean sense there are no great heroes and villains treated here. A proper balance between the role played by the papacy and the Church at large is consistently maintained. The authors are aware of the fact that historians are often wont to coin phrases—"Reformation" and "Counter Reformation" being examples—without always keeping in mind the disparate realities such terms may have represented in different periods of time. Luther, for example, in his most sensational and stirring attack on the papacy, *An Appeal to the Nobility of the German Nation,* did not use the term "Reformation;" rather he used the expression "improvement" (*Besserung*). The framers of the Augsburg Confession strongly attest to their catholicism. The term "Counter Reformation" in the sense of a common effort was not used until the nineteenth century and then by Leopold von Ranke in his *Deutsche Geschichte im Zeitalter der Reformation.*

In addition to providing the reader with a wide-ranging account of the reform movements, it is hoped that this volume will act as a moderating influence in the trend among certain church historians who emphasize particularism, if not literally parochialism, as the true approach to understanding the church, seemingly oblivious to the fact that the expression "church" was first used in a universal sense. Thus the book represents, in a real sense, a projection of the Pauline exhortation to the Ephesians:

σπουδάζοντες τηρεῖν τὴν ἑνότητα τοῦ πνεύματος ἐν τῷ συνδέσμῳ τῆς εἰρήνης.

John P. Dolan

LIST OF ABBREVIATIONS

AAug	*Analecta Augustiniana,* Rome 1905ff.
ADB	*Allgemeine deutsche Biographie,* 55 vols, Leipzig 1875–1910; Index Vol. 1912 (see NDB)
AElsKG	*Archiv für elsässische Kirchengeschichte,* ed. Gesellschaft für elsässische Kirchengeschichte, 1926ff.
AER	*The American Ecclesiastical Review,* Washington 1889ff.
AFP	*Archivum Fratrum Praedicatorum,* Rome 1931ff.
AFrH	*Archivum Franciscanum Historicum,* Florence–Quaracchi 1908ff.
AHPont	*Archivum Historiae Pontificiae,* Rome 1963ff.
AHSI	*Archivum historicum Societatis Iesu,* Rome 1932ff.
AHVNrh	*Annalen des Historischen Vereins für den Niederrhein, insbesondere das alte Erzbistum Köln,* Cologne 1855ff.
AIA	*Archivo Ibero-Americano,* Madrid 1914ff.
AkathKR	*Archiv für Katholisches Kirchenrecht,* (Innsbruck) Mainz 1857.
AKG	*Archiv für Kulturgeschichte,* (Leipzig) Münster and Cologne 1903ff.
Allen	*Opus Epistolarum Des. Erasmi Roterodami,* ed. P. S. Allen, 12 vols, Oxford 1906–58.
AMrhKG	*Archiv für mittelrheinische Kirchengeschichte,* Speyer 1949ff.
Ann. Eccl.	*Annales Ecclesiastici.*
Anthropos	*Anthropos. Internationale Zeitschrift für Völker-und Sprachenkunde,* Mödling 1906ff.
Antonianum	*Antonianum,* Rome 1926ff.
AÖG	*Archiv für österreichische Geschichte,* Vienna 1865ff.
ARC	*Acta reformationis catholicae ecclesiam concernentia saeculi XVI,* ed. G. Pfeil-schifter, 6 vols., Regensburg 1959ff.
ARG	*Archiv für Reformationsgeschichte,* (Leipzig) Gütersloh 1903ff.
ArSKG	*Archiv für schlesische Kirchengeschichte* I–VI Breslau 1936–41, VIIff. Hildesheim 1949ff.
ASR	*American Sociological Review,* Washington 1936ff.
ASRomana	*Archivio della Reale Societa Romana di Storia Patria,* Rome 1878–1934.
AstIIt	*Archivio storico Italiano,* Florence 1842ff.
BGDSL	*Beiträge zur Geschichte der deutschen Sprache und Literatur,* Halle 1874ff.
BRN	*Bibliotheca Reformatoria Neerlandica,* ed. S. Cramer and F. Pijper, 10 vols., Den Haag 1903–14.
BSLK	*Die Bekenntnisschriften der evangelisch-lutherischen Kirche,* ed. Deutschen Evangelischen Kirchenausschuss, Göttingen 1956.

BullPatr   *Bullarium Patronatus Portugalliae Regum in Ecclesiis Africae, Asia et Oceaniae* . . . , ed. L. M. Jordão et al., I–III Lisbon 1868–70.

BullRom   *Bullarium, Diplomatum et Privilegiorum Romanorum Pontificum*, ed. G. Tomassetti et al., Turin 1857ff.

BZThS   *Bonner Zeitschrift für Theologie und Seelsorge*, Düsseldorf 1924–31.

CA   *Confessio Augustana.*

Car   *Caritas*, Freiburg i. Br. 1896ff.

CCath   *Corpus Catholicorum*, founded by J. Gerving, Münster 1919ff.

CH   *Church History*, New York–Chicago 1932ff.

CHR   *The Catholic Historical Review*, Washington 1915ff.

CivCatt   *La Civiltà Cattolica*, Rome 1850ff. (1871–87 Florence).

Cl   *Luthers Werke in Auswahl*, ed. O. Clemen, E. Vogelsang, H. Rückert and E. Hirsch, 4 vols., Berlin 1966 and 4 suppl., Berlin 1959–66.

Coll   *Collectanea S. Congregationis de Propaganda Fide*, Rome 1893ff.

CollFr   *Collectanea Franciscana*, Rome 1931ff.

CR   *Corpus Reformatorum*, (Braunschweig) Berlin 1834ff.; Leipzig 1906ff.

CT   *Concilium Tridentinum. Diariorum, Actorum, Epistularum, Tractatuum nova Collectio*, edidit Societas Goerresiana promovendis inter Catholicos Germaniae Litterarum Studiis, Freiburg i. Br. 1901ff.

Dahlmann-Waitz   F. C. Dahlmann and G. Waitz, *Quellenkunde der Deutschen Geschichte*, 9th ed., ed. H. Haering, Leipzig 1931–32.

DG   *Dogmengeschichte.*

DHGE   *Dictionnaire d'Histoire et de géographie ecclésiastiques*, Paris 1912ff.

DSAM   *Dictionnaire de Spiritualité ascétique et mystique. Doctrine et Histoire*, Paris 1932ff.

DThC   *Dictionnaire de théologie catholique*, Paris 1930ff.

DVfLG   *Deutsche Vierteljahresschrift für Literaturwissenschaft und Geistesgeschichte*, Halle 1923ff.

EA   Erlanger Ausgabe der Werke Luthers, 1826ff.

ECarm   *Ephemerides Carmeliticae*, Florence 1947ff.

EE   *Estudios eclesiásticos*, Madrid 1922–36, 1942ff.

EHR   *English Historical Review*, London 1886ff.

EKL   *Evangelisches Kirchenlexikon. Kirchlich-theologisches Handwörterbuch*, Göttingen 1955ff.

Elit   *Ephemerides Liturgicae*, Rome 1887ff.

EThL   *Ephemerides Theologicae Lovanienses*, Bruges 1924ff.

Etudes   *Études*, Paris 1856ff. (to 1896: *Études religieuses*)

EvTh   *Evangelische Theologie*, Munich 1934ff.

FStud   *Franziskanische Studien*, (Münster) Werl 1914ff.

GGA   *Göttingische Gelehrte Anzeigen*, Berlin 1738ff.

GuL   *Geist und Leben. Zeitschrift für Aszese und Mystik* (to 1947:ZAM), Würzburg 1947ff.

HJ   *Historisches Jahrbuch der Görres-Gesellschaft*, (Cologne 1880ff.), 1950ff.

HM   *Historia Mundi*, founded by F. Kern, 10 vols., Bern–Munich 1952ff.

HPBl	*Historisch-politische Blätter für das katholische Deutschland,* 171 vols., Munich 1838–1923.
HS	*Hispania Sacra,* Madrid 1948ff.
HV	*Historische Vierteljahresschrift,* Leipzig 1898–1937.
HZ	*Historische Zeitschrift,* Munich 1859ff.
IusPont	*Ius Pontificium seu Ephemerides urbanae ad canonicas disciplinas spectantes,* Rome 1921ff.
Jb	*Jahrbuch.*
Jedin	H. Jedin, *History of the Council of Trent,* 2 vols., London 1957–1961.
JEH	*The Journal of Ecclesiastical History,* London 1950ff.
JLH	*Jahrbuch für Liturgik und Hymnologie,* Kassel 1955ff.
JLW	*Jahrbuch für Liturgiewissenschaft,* Münster 1921–41.
JThS	*The Journal of theological Studies,* London 1899ff.
KG	*Kirchengeschichte.*
KLK	*Katholisches Leben und Kämpfen im Zeitalter der Glaubensspaltung* (Münster 1927ff.)
KuD	*Kerygma und Dogma,* Göttingen 1955ff.
Kurtscheid F	B. Kurtscheid–F. A. Wilches, *Historia Iuris Canonici,* Tom. I: *Historia Fontium et scientiae Iuris Canonice,* Rome 1943.
Le Plat	J. Le Plat, *Monumentorum ad historiam Concilii Tridentini . . . spectantium amplissima collectio,* 7 vols., Louvain 1781–87.
LexCap	*Lexicon Capuccinum. Promptuarium Historico-Bibliographicum* (1525 to 1950), Rome 1951.
LJ	*Liturgisches Jahrbuch,* Münster 1951ff.
Lortz F	*Festgabe Joseph Lortz,* ed. E. Iserloh–P. Manus, 2 vols., Baden-Baden 1957.
LThK	*Lexikon für Theologie und Kirche,* Freiburg 1957ff.
LuJ	*Lutherjahrbuch.* Jahrbuch der Luthergesellschaft, 1919ff.
Luther	*Luther-Mitteilungen der Luthergesellschaft.*
MAH	*Mélanges d'archéologie et d'histoire,* Paris 1880ff.
Mai S	A. Mai, *Spicilegium Romanum,* 10 vols., Rome 1839–44.
Mansi	J. D. Mansi, *Sacrorum conciliorum nova et amplissima collectio,* 31 vols., Florence–Venice 1757–98; new edition & editions ed. L. Petit–J. B. Martin in 60 vols., Paris 1899–1927.
MCom	*Miscelánea Comillas,* Comillas/Santander 1943ff.
MHOMC	*Monumenta Historica Ordinis Minorum Capuccinorum,* 8 vols., Assisi–Rome 1937–60.
MHSI	*Monumenta Historica Societatis Iesu,* Madrid 1894ff.; Rome 1932ff.
MIÖG	*Mitteilungen des Instituts für österreichische Geschichtsforschung,* Innsbruck–Graz–Cologne 1880ff.
Mirbt	C. Mirbt, *Quellen zur Geschichte des Papsttums und des römischen Katholizismus,* 6th ed. prepared by K. Aland, I. Tübingen 1967.
Misc. Hist. Pont.	*Miscellanea Historiae Pontificiae.*
MiscMercati	*Miscellanea Giovanii Mercati* 6 vols., Rome 1946.
ML	*Mennonitisches Lexikon,* Frankfurt–Karlsruhe 1913–58ff.
MOP	*Monumenta ordinis Fratrum Praedicatorum historica,* 14 vols., Rome 1896–1904; Paris 1931ff.

MQR	*The Mennonite Quarterly Review*, Goshen, Ind. 1927ff.
MThZ	*Münchener Theologische Zeitschrift*, Munich, 1950ff.

NA	*Neues Archiv der Gesellschaft für ältere deutsche Geschichtskunde zur Beförderung einer Gesamtausgabe der Quellenschriften deutscher Geschichte des Mittelalters*, Hannover 1876ff.
NBD	*Nuntiaturberichte aus Deutschland, Abt. I (1534–59)*, ed. Preussischen historischen Institut in Rome, 12 vols., Gotha 1892ff.
NDB	*Neue Deutsche Biographie*, Berlin 1953ff.
NGG	*Nachrichten von der Gesellschaft der Wissenschaften zu Göttingen*, Berlin 1845–1940.
NKZ	*Neue kirchliche Zeitschrift*, Leipzig 1890ff.
NRTh	*Nouvelle Revue Théologique*, Tournai–Louvain–Paris 1879ff.
NZM	*Neue Zeitschrift für Missionswissenschaft*, Beckenried 1945ff.
NZSTh	*Neue Zeitschrift für systematische Theologie und Religionsphilosophie*, Berlin 1959ff.

OC	*Opera Calvini*, 59 vols., *CR* 29–87, Braunschweig–Berlin 1863–1900.
OrChrP	*Orientalia Christiana periodica*, Rome 1935ff.
OS	*Joannis Calvini opera selecta*, ed. P. Barth et al., 5 vols., Munich 1952–63.

Pastor	Ludwig von Pastor, *Geschichte der Päpste seit dem Ausgang des Mittelalters*, 16 vols., Freiburg i. Br. 1885ff. Eng.: *The History of the Popes from the Close of the Middle Ages*, 40 vols., St. Louis 1891–1953.

QFIAB	*Quellen und Forschungen aus italienischen Archiven und Bibliotheken*, Rome 1897ff.
QQ	*Quellen*.

RAM	*Revue d'ascétique et de mystique*, Toulouse 1920ff.
RE	*Realenzyklopädie für protestantische Theologie und Kirche*, founded by J. J. Herzog, ed. A. Hauck, 24 vols., Leipzig 1896–1913.
Reformata	*Reformanda Reformata Reformanda*, Festgabe for Hubert Jedin, ed. E. Iserloh and K. Repgen, 2 vols., Münster 1965.
RET	*Revista Espanola de teologia*, Madrid 1941ff.
RevSR	*Revue des Sciences Religieuses*, Strasbourg 1921ff.
RF	*Razon y Fe*, Madrid 1901ff.
RGG	*Die Religion in Geschichte und Gegenwart*, Tübingen 1909–13; 1927–32; 1956ff.
RGStT	*Reformationsgeschichtliche Studien und Texte*, founded by J. Greving, Münster 1906ff.
RH	*Revue historique*, Paris 1876ff.
RHE	*Revue d'histoire ecclésiastique*, Louvain 1900ff.
RHEF	*Revue d'histoire de l'Eglise de France*, Paris 1910ff.
RHM	*Revue d'histoire des missions*, Paris 1924ff.
RHPhR	*Revue d'histoire et de philosophie religieuses*, Strasbourg, 1921ff.
RQ	*Römische Quartalschrift für christliche Altertumskunde und für Kirchengeschichte*, Freiburg i. Br. 1887ff.
RSIt	*Rivista storica Italiana*, Naples 1884ff.
RSPhTh	*Revue des sciences philosophiques et théologiques*, Paris 1907ff.

RSR   *Recherches de science religieuse*, Paris 1910ff.

RSTI   *Rivista di storia della chiesa in Italia*, Rome 1947ff.

RTA   *Deutsche Reichstagsakten*, ed. Hist. Kommission bei der Bayerischen Akademie der Wissenschaften, n.s. 1519–24; I–IV Gotha 1882ff.; 1527–29; VII Stuttgart 1935-Reprints Göttingen 1956ff.

SAB   *Sitzungsberichte der Deutschen* (until 1944: *Preussischen*) *Akademie der Wissenschaften zu Berlin*. Philosophisch-historische Klasse, Berlin 1882ff.

SAH   *Sitzungsberichte der Heidelberger Akademie der Wissenschaften*, Philosophisch-historische Klasse, Heidelberg 1910ff.

SAM   *Sitzungsberichte der Bayerischen Akademie der Wissenschaften*, Philosophisch-historische Abteilung, Munich 1871ff.

SAW   *Sitzungsberichte der* (since 1947: *Österreichischen*) *Akademie der Wissenschaften in Wien*, Vienna 1831ff.

SC   *Scuola Cattolica*, Milan 1873ff.

Scholastik   *Scholastik*, Freiburg i. Br. 1926ff.

Schottenloher   K. Schottenloher, *Bibliographie zur deutschen Geschichte im Zeitalter der Glaubensspaltung 1517–85*, 6 vols., Leipzig 1933–40; Stuttgart 1956ff.; Vol 7: *Das Schrifttum von 1938–60*, Stuttgart 1966.

Scritt. ant.   *Scritture antiche* (Propaganda Archives)

SE   *Sacris Erudiri. Jaarboek voor Godsdienstwetenschapen*, Bruges 1948ff.

Sehling   E. Sehling, *Die evangelischen Kirchenordnungen des XVI. Jahrhunderts* I–V Leipzig 1902–13; VI–VIII, XI–XIII Tübingen 1955ff.

ST.A.   *Melanchthons Werke in Auswahl* (Studienausgabe), ed. R. Stupperich, 6 vols., Gütersloh 1951 ff.

StC   *Studia Catholica*, Roermond 1924ff.

StdZ   *Stimmen der Zeit* (Before 1914: *Stimmen aus Maria-Laach*), Freiburg i. Br. 1871ff.

Stegmüller M   F. Stegmüller, *Geschichte des Molinismus*, Bd I: *Neue Molinaschriften*, Münster 1935.

SteT   *Studi e Testi*, Rome 1900ff.

StL   *Staatslexikon*, ed. H. Sacher, Freiburg i. Br. 1926–32.

StMis   *Studia Missionalia*, Rome 1943ff.

SVRG   *Schriften des Vereins für Reformationsgeschichte*, Halle 1883ff.; Leipzig 1907ff.; Gütersloh 1951ff.

ThBl   *Theologische Blätter*, Leipzig 1922ff.

ThGl   *Theologie und Glaube*, Paderborn 1909ff.

ThLZ   *Theologische Literaturzeitung*, Leipzig 1878ff.

ThQ   *Theologische Quartalschrift*, Tübingen 1819ff.; Stuttgart 1946ff.

ThR NF   *Theologische Rundschau*, Tübingen 1897ff.

ThRv   *Theologische Revue*, Münster 1902ff.

ThStK   *Theologische Studien und Kritiken*, (Hamburg) Gotha 1828ff.

ThZ   *Theologische Zeitschrift*, Basel 1945ff.

TThZ   *Trierer Theologische Zeitschrift* (to 1944: *Pastor Bonus*), Trier 1888ff.

UB   *Urkundenbuch.*

WA   M. Luther, *Werke. Kritische Gesamtausgabe* (Weimar Edition), 58 vols., Weimar 1883–1948.

WABr   *D. Martin Luthers Werke, Briefwechsel*, 12 vols., Weimar 1930–67.

WADB   *D. Martin Luthers Werke, Die Deutsche Bibel*, Weimar 1906ff.
WATr   *D. Martin Luthers Werke, Tischreden*, 6 vols., Weimar 1912–21.
Walch   *Dr. Martin Luthers sämtliche Schriften*, ed. J. G. Walch, 23 vols., St. Louis, Mo. 1880–1910.
WW   *Werke.*
WZ   *Westfälische Zeitschrift, Zeitschrift für Vaterländische Geschichte*, Münster 1838ff.

Zam   *Zeitschrift für Aszese und Mystik* (since 1947: GuL), (Innsbruck, Munich) Würzburg 1926ff.
ZBKG   *Zeitschrift für bayerische Kirchengeschichte*, Gunzenhausen 1926ff.
ZblB   *Zentralblatt für Bibliothekswesen*, Leipzig 1884 ff.
ZBLG   *Zeitschrift für Bayerische Landesgeschichte*, Munich 1928ff.
ZE   *Zeitschrift für Ethnologie*, Berlin 1869ff.
ZGObrh   *Zeitschrift für die Geschichte des Oberrheins*, Karlsruhe 1851ff.
ZHTh   *Zeitschrift für die historische Theologie*, 45 vols., Leipzig–Gotha 1832–75.
ZKG   *Zeitschrift für Kirchengeschichte*, (Gotha) Stuttgart 1876ff.
ZKTh   *Zeitschrift für Katholische Theologie*, (Innsbruck) Vienna 1877ff.
ZMR   *Zeitschrift für Missionswissenschaft und Religionswissenschaft*, 34ff. Münster 1950ff. (*Zeitschrift für Missionswissenschaft*, 18–25 edb. 1928–35; *Zeitschrift für Missionswissenschaft*, 26–27 edb. 1935–37; *Missionswissenschaft und Religionswissenschaft*, 28–33 edb. 1938–41, 1947–49).
ZRGG   *Zeitschrift für Religions und Geistesgeschichte*, Marburg 1948ff.
ZSavRGkan *Zeitschrift der Savigny-Stiftung für Rechtsgeschichte*, Kanonistische Abteilung, Weimar 1911ff.
ZSKG   *Zeitschrift für Schweizer Kirchengeschichte*, Fribourg, 1907ff.
ZSTh   *Zeitschrift für systematische Theologie*, (Gütersloh) Berlin 1923ff.
ZThK   *Zeitschrift für Theologie und Kirche*, Tübingen 1891ff.
ZW   *Huldreich Zwinglis sämtliche Werke*, vols. 1–14 = *CR* 88–101, Berlin 1905; Leipzig 1908–35; Zürich 1959ff.

PART ONE

The Protestant Reformation

Martin Luther and the Coming of the Reformation (1517–1525)

CHAPTER 1

Causes of the Reformation

When we ask about the causes of the Reformation, we admit that this event of such tremendous importance was not the work of one man, such as Luther, and that it did not first begin with the ninety-five indulgence theses of 31 October 1517. Long before the outbreak of the Reformation things occurred, facts were provided, steps were taken, ideas were spread and emotions were stirred, which facilitated, made possible, provoked, and even made unavoidable the coming of a revolt against the Church—so unavoidable that we can speak of an inner historical necessity. This does not mean that it could not have happened differently. For in regard to historical causes it was in great measure a matter of facts in the realm of the spirit. But these have many facets, can combine in various ways, and can operate in different directions. Thus the same idea, the same word, and the same deed may be links in various series of causes. The *devotio moderna,* with its striving for inwardness and Christocentrism and the resulting criticism of the late medieval system of pilgrimages and relics,[1] is about equally oriented to the Catholic Reform and to the Reformation.

To establish historical necessity does not mean to make a pronouncement on truth or error. A thing can be significant—that is, it can fit into a larger context—without being true. Furthermore, historical blame does not also mean moral blame. Something which was said and done with the best intention and was also good in itself can turn out unfortunately and become "guilty" of an unhappy development. For ideas and facts act independently of the intention of those who express or perform them.

No one desired a reformation that would lead to a division in Western Christendom. The reformers wanted the reform of the one Church common to all. Because this reform in head and members was thwarted, the split occurred. Consequently the Reformation would be the revolu-

---

[1] *Imitatio Christi* I, 23, 25; III, 58, 9; IV, 1, 38.

tionary rejoinder to the failure of reform in the fourteenth and fifteenth centuries. The causes of this were all the conditions and attitudes in need of reform, in particular everything that stood in the way of the realizing of reform at the proper time. The causes must not be restricted to so-called abuses and bad Popes. For reform never means—and especially not at the end of the fifteenth century—a mere return to an original condition that is now unattainable and the removal of abuses which have crept in, but always an adaptation to new circumstances and an awakening of self to the needs of the hour.

Certainly the disgust of the time over the "wretched conditions," to use Zwingli's words, gave great impetus to the Reformation, but its enticing appeal was contributed by the circumstance that to the men of the new age it seemed to lead the way out of outmoded medieval attitudes and conditions, and promised to give man what he had long demanded or unconsciously yearned for in vain. Not by chance was the "freedom of the Christian man" the great shibboleth of the Reformation, laden with portents for the future and frequently misunderstood.

The so-called abuses were certainly no greater at the end of the fifteenth century than in the second half of the fourteenth century. But people put up with them much less easily, for they had become more alert, more aware, more critical, and in the good sense more demanding and hence more sensitive to the contradiction between ideal and reality, teaching and living, claim and achievement.

The fact that this augmented religious need, this greater maturity of the layman, was not sufficiently taken into account, or that an attitude typical of the Middle Ages, and at that time justified by circumstances, was not definitely put aside early, was consequently more disruptive than any failure, however regrettable, on the part of individuals.

Accordingly, a cause of the Reformation in the broader sense is the dissolution of the medieval order and of the fundamental attitudes proper to it or the failure to replace it at the proper time with new organizations in keeping with the times. Here must be mentioned first the disruption of the unity which embraced the totality of political, intellectual, and religious life. The one Church in the one Christendom, expressed in the unity effected through the counterbalancing of *Sacerdotium* and *Imperium,* was the most striking characteristic of the Middle Ages. The papacy itself contributed to severing this unity. For the sake of the independence and autonomy of the Church, it saw itself forced to weaken the power of the *Imperium.* For a while it seemed as though the Pope could also assume political leadership. But the more he exercised his fullness of authority on the secular political sphere, the more decidedly he encountered the justified resistance of a world becoming ever more strongly divided into nations and conscious of its autonomy. Soon, together with its unjustified claims, people were attacking the papacy itself, and its religious guidance was rejected along with its political leadership. It was frankly a warning signal that Boniface VIII, who replaced the traditional two-powers theory—that the secular and the spiritual power are autonomous and both come directly from God—with the monism of the Bull "Unam Sanctam, " became at Anagni in 1303 the captive of the modern national state, represented by Nogaret, and of the laicized democratic forces, symbolized by Sciarra Colonna.

The sequel was the so-called Avignon Exile of the Popes and their far-reaching dependence on France. The papacy seemed no longer to consider the interests of the Universal Church but all the more to be exploiting the nations of Europe in a thoroughly organized fiscal system.

Especially in Germany this charge would henceforth never cease to be heard. In France, Spain, and England the national state, which more and more dominated the territorial Church and made the Church's sources of income useful to itself, was able to a great extent to thwart the exportation of money. The Western Schism obscured the unity of the Church as expressed in the Pope to such a degree that not even saints knew who was the lawful Pope. Conciliarism seemed to be the only escape from the difficulty of the "damnable trinity" of Popes.

After the Council of Constance (1414–18), conciliarism was not overcome from within nor fundamentally but *via facti* and largely by political means. By means of concordats—agreements with states—the Popes sought to protect themselves against democratic currents and in addition to avoid the reform that was in many ways embarrassing for them. Indeed, when schism again loomed at the Council of Basel in 1437, the fate of the Church seemed, according to Haller, to have been handed entirely to the secular powers. The Pope had to pay dearly for recognition by the German princes, the Emperor, and the King of France and allow the state extensive power over the Church. The result was the territorial Church—the dependence of the Church on the secular powers, whether royal, princely, or city, with the possibility granted to these of interfering on a large scale in the life of the Church. Without this sovereignty over Church government it is difficult to conceive of the victory of the Reformation. The papal policy of concordats also brought it about that, in the course of the fifteenth century, the Popes, instead of stressing their proper religious mission in view of the secularization, became more and more princes among princes, with whom alliances could be made and against whom war could also be waged, as against any other prince. This entanglement in politics enabled Leo X to become the savior of the Reformation by neglecting for two years to proceed vigorously against Luther and thus capture the foxes while they were small, as Johannes Cochläus put it.

Also characteristic of the Middle Ages was a clericalism based on the monopoly of education by clerics and on the privileges of the clerical state. To the young and intellectually immature Germanic peoples the Church had to transmit not only the revelation of Jesus Christ but also the cultural treasures of antiquity. This led to a preponderance on the part of clerics, which went beyond their specific duty of religious leadership. The day had to come when medieval man attained his majority and was both able and willing on his own to distinguish between the treasures of faith and of culture held out to him. This required of the Church that at a given time she should relinquish all the fields of activity which she had assumed only in a subsidiary way and the rights not directly connected with her function, which was based on divine institution, and that she should make her religious mission all the clearer.

As consideration of the late Middle Ages has shown, this peaceful change did not take place. The movements in which the striving of the laity for independence was at stake involved revolutionary features. The Church maintained outdated claims, and the world—the individual as well as the state and society—had to extort its autonomy. Thus the process of secularization was carried out against the Church under the standards of subjectivism, nationalism, and laicism.

In the encounter with antiquity and through his own investigation and experience, man discovered realities which had not grown in the soil of Christianity or were self-evident and not in need of confirmation by authorities. The representatives of the new scholarship wanted indeed to be Christians also, but the more the Church seemed to identify herself with the old and the traditional, the more did the new, brought forward with all the fervor of the joy of discovery, have to act on her as critic. The circles of the humanists frequently produced an antischolastic, anticlerical, anti-Roman, and, in the final results, if not an antiecclesiastical, at least a nonecclesiastical atmosphere. If people did not take an aggressive attitude toward the Church, they still held aloof from her dogma, sacramental life, and prayer.

As immediate causes of the Reformation there must be mentioned the abuses among clergy and people, a far-reaching dogmatic uncertainty, and the venality of religious life. When abuses in the Church on the eve of the Reformation are discussed, one thinks especially of "bad Popes," in particular of Alexander VI. But perhaps the decay was even more dangerous in the reign of Leo X. He cannot be charged with the enormous misdeeds by which Alexander VI sullied the throne of Peter; instead he was guilty of shocking negligence, irresponsible frivolity, and prodigal love of pleasure. One does not find in him an awareness of duty and of the responsibility of the supreme shepherd of Christendom and a manner of life in conformity with this responsibility. The deterioration of the Christian is achieved not only in an openly wicked life, but also furtively and hence more dangerously in an inner wasting away, a slow loss of substance, an imperceptible secularization, and a confused lack of responsibility. In 1513 Leo X, scion of the Medici, took possession of his office and of Rome in a great festive display which, in the form of a Corpus Christi procession, was a grand exhibition of the Pope and his court. On a great placard could be read: "Once Venus reigned [i.e., Alexander VI], then Mars [i.e., Julius II], and now Pallas Athene takes the scepter." Humanists and artists thus saluted in the new Pope their patron and Maecenas, but they also proclaimed the frivolous worldliness and thoughtless unconcern which characterized the pontificate of Leo X, the pontificate in which Luther was to sound the prelude to the Reformation.

"Depravity has become so taken for granted that those soiled by it no longer notice the stench of sin." These words were uttered, not by an enemy of the Church, but by no less than the successor of Leo X, Pope Adrian VI, at his first consistorial allocution.

The situation of the clergy, high and low, was no better than that of the papacy. Here too we should not direct our attention exclusively to failures in a restricted moral sphere, such as clerical concubinage. In some areas concubinage was so widespread that parishioners were hardly seriously scandalized in this respect by the lives of their pastors. If only they had really been pastors! Certainly in the late Middle Ages there was holiness in the Church, and much sincere and loyal devotion to duty. But there were also many manifestations of neglect.

Without exaggeration it can be said that the Church appeared altogether as the property of the clergy, property intended to bring economic advantage and profit. In the establishing of positions the needs of divine worship and of the care of souls were often far less decisive than the desire to do a good work in order to gain for oneself and one's family a share in the treasures of grace. Consequently a person would, for example, erect an altar with a benefice for a priest to celebrate Mass. And so there existed revenue which sought a beneficiary. Considering the great number of positions, one could not be very selective in choosing candidates. Bishops and pastors did not regard themselves primarily as persons who held an office for whose exercise the necessary livelihood was provided. They regarded themselves as holders of a benefice in the sense of Germanic feudal law. This benefice was a profitable right to which were attached certain obligations of service. But these could be turned over to a poorly paid substitute, a vicar, a hireling, to whom the sheep did not belong, to paraphrase the Lord's words (John 10:12).

Thus to the detriment of the care of souls, several bishoprics or other pastoral offices could be united in one person. As late as 1556 Cardinal Alessandro Farnese, grandson of Paul III, possessed ten episcopal sees, twenty-six monasteries, and 133 other benefices—canonries, parishes, and chaplaincies. In the Netherlands the "vicars" who served in place of a nonresident benefice holder as canon, curial official, university professor, or administrator of a monastery have been estimated by R. R. Post at 30 to 50 percent. An especially pernicious aspect was that in Germany the episcopal sees and most abbacies were open to members of the nobility only. Thus they became the means of providing for younger children of noble families, who often never gave a thought to leading a clerical life or even engaging in the care of souls. What concerned them was a carefree existence, as enjoyable as possible. If a bishop seriously desired to improve the inner state of his diocese, he was in no position to do so, because he did not control his territory. For his jurisdiction was to a great extent limited, from above by many sorts of exemptions, and from below because most pastors were named by secular patrons, ecclesiastical corporations, and monasteries, and the archdeacons had usurped other episcopal rights.

The lower the religious spirit and zeal for the care of souls sank at the Roman Curia and in the rest of the clergy, the more unpleasant the pursuit of money became, and the preoccupation with financial matters heightened the scandal. At the Curia men sought to fill up the coffers by means of an elaborate system of fees, taxes, more or less voluntary contributions, and finally even indulgence offerings. The prodigal and worldly papal court, the extensive building activity, and the great expenses of war brought about a continuing need for money. It was certainly not accidental that the scandal of Tetzel's dealings in indulgences, which provided the immediate occasion for the outbreak of the Reformation, was connected with this concern for money.

The abuses described resulted in a far-reaching dissatisfaction with the Church, which more and more grew into a resentment and even a hatred of Rome. For a whole century people called for a reform of the Church in head and members but they were disappointed time and again. The *gravamina* of the German nation were expressed for the first time as early as 1455 by Dietrich von Erbach, Archbishop of Mainz. This listing of German grievances against the papacy was thereafter renewed again and again, but the less successful it was, the more it increased the anti-Roman feeling in Germany.

In his *An den christlichen Adel deutscher Nation* (*To the Christian Nobility of the German Nation*) Luther made these complaints his own and thereby became a national hero. Zwingli too knew how to exploit the dissatisfaction. He directed his disciples not to preach chiefly about doctrine but about the wretched conditions and the necessity of restoring righteousness.

The call for reform and the related opposition to the Church thus brought it about that many a person who had absolutely no involvement with their teaching acclaimed the reformers merely because they seemed to be bringing the long-desired reform. There was a great readiness for anything new that announced salvation. The ground was broken and fertile for catchwords that promised what had become urgent. But the explosive had also been accumulated and it was waiting for the word that would ignite it.

Deplorable as the abuses were—here pointed out rather than described in detail—and however much they contributed to the origin and success of the Reformation, they are not the most significant factors in this context. More decisive than the personal failings of Popes, priests, and laity is the question whether the truth given by Christ and the order established by him were attacked, whether the moral decay was an expression of a falling off in matters touching the essence of religion.

We must ask, "Precisely what were the strong and weak points of the Church as it entered the era of the Reformation?"[2] To what extent was the external religious activity, which was so rich and varied, a façade or a reality? In the many-colored picture of popular devotion, veneration of saints, pilgrimages, processions, Mass foundations, and so forth, how much was really genuine and to what extent did superstition, a desire for pious activity, or a mercenary spirit hold sway?

Another question to be asked is: Was this external practice based on a sound theological doctrine, explained by it, and illuminated by it? And special mention must be made here of an extensive dogmatic uncertainty as a manifestation of failure fraught with dire consequences. The areas of truth and error were not delineated with sufficient clarity. Men fancied themselves in accord with the Church, although positions had long been adopted that contradicted her teaching. Luther thought that he was still in the Church when he reviled the Pope as Antichrist, and in 1530 Melanchthon in the Augsburg Confession could still try to have people believe that in that teaching there was no opposition to the "Roman Church" and that persons were of different opinions merely in

---

[2] J. Lortz, *The Reformation, A Problem for Today* (Westminster, Md. 1964), p. 74.

reference to a few abuses.[3] (Article 21). Uncertainty was particularly great in regard to the concept of the Church. Because of the Western Schism—the last antipope, Felix V, had abdicated only in 1449—it was no longer generally clear that the papacy established by Jesus Christ was essential to the Church. Unable to ascertain who was the legitimate Pope, many people had stopped asking this question and had grown accustomed to getting along without a Pope. Great impetus was given to the Reformation by the fact that many felt Luther was merely bringing about the reform long due and did not notice at all, or only belatedly, that he was questioning essential doctrines of the Church.

If Luther became a reformer—not the least reason being that he was unable to reconcile his understanding of revelation, gained in severe and perilous religious struggles, with the theology and practice of his day—the cause lay especially in the fact that this theology was the one-sided doctrine of nominalism, while the depth and wealth of an Augustine or an Aquinas, and especially of Scripture, were lacking. Consequently nominalism, going back to William of Ockham and communicated to Luther in the shallow form of Gabriel Biel, who had given it a moralizing tendency, must be named among the decisive causes of the Reformation. Manifestations of failure showed themselves to be especially fateful in the theology and practice of the Mass. If the Mass, which occupied so much of the life of piety in the late Middle Ages, could in so short a time thereafter be abolished as the worst idolatry, must we not suppose that often it was performed only as an external ritual, something not really grasped, not performed from within?

In the lack of inner strength and life, which can be connected very closely with correctness and legalism, is also to be sought the reason why the Fifth Lateran Council (1512–17), referred to by Jedin as the last "papal reform effort clothed in the guise of a council" before the Reformation, was of only meager effectiveness. The new spirit was lacking. For of what use can one or another well-meant measure be? Nothing sheds more light on the situation than the fact that in 1514, together with the papal bull on the reform of the Church read at the ninth session of the Council, there was sent to Archbishop Albrecht of Magdeburg and Mainz the Curia's offer, which provided the immediate occasion for the Reformation: for a fee of 10,000 ducats the archbishop would be allowed to hold the two sees simultaneously, and for the financing of the fee, half of the indulgence offerings for Saint Peter's would be made over to him. "Theory and practice were in such glaring contradiction"![4]

---

[3] "Beschluss des 1. Teils," *BSLK*, 83c.
[4] A. Schulte, *Die Fugger in Romo* I (Leipzig 1904), 115.

A lack of seriousness and determination in the leaders, beginning with the Pope himself, condemned the Council to ineffectiveness. And so, after the many useless calls to reform and the many lost opportunities, a revolutionary confrontation, similar to that which actually occurred in the Reformation, was almost inevitable.

CHAPTER 2

Martin Luther: The Early Years

None of the suggested causes of the Reformation really "explains" it. The far-reaching deterioration of religious and moral strength, the want of precision in central questions of faith, and the lack of a sense of pastoral responsibility in the clergy, along with so many lost opportunities for reform and in view of widespread criticism of the Church, make an upheaval quite intelligible. But the fact that it occurred as it did, in what we know as the Reformation, depended to a great extent on Martin Luther himself and hence is steeped in the mystery of the human person. If every *individuum* is something "ineffable," this is especially so of Luther, whom Lortz characterizes as a "sea of energies, of impulses and perceptions and experiences."

If the reformer's image has remained controversial, this is so not only because a judgment on his person and work is bound up with a decision in regard to the Reformation's claim to truth. For one side he is the hero of the faith; for the other the archheretic, the destroyer of the Church's unity. Actually, however, the reason for the difficulty of assessing his person and work and of correctly portraying them is found in Luther himself. We have an abundance of writings from his pen and of his own testimony about himself and his aims. Even though an inner cohesion is not missing from all these statements and all of Luther's questions fit under a rather small number of viewpoints and are answered accordingly, nevertheless he was not a systematizer. He was far too dependent on his experience and will. This makes it even more difficult to grasp the richness and versatility of his being, and he often seems to be vacillating and contradictory. He experienced a profound change in developing from friar to reformer. Because his career was so intimately connected with experience, he was unable to look back without bias on earlier stages of his development. And so he himself had a decisive share in the origin of the "Luther legend," whose gradual deflation has occurred only in recent decades, thanks to the learned and painstaking study by men such as Otto Scheel.[1] Furthermore, everything that Luther wrote and

---

[1] *Martin Luther. Vom Katholizismus zur Reformation,* 2 vols. (Tübingen 1915–17; 3rd–4th ed., 1921–30).

said is a confession or realization which was paid for in his own experience and suffering and which he had to communicate to others. But again it was uttered in a distressing way, in which he did not shrink from violent language for the sake of clarity, and even the paradox became for him a suitable manner of expression. Luther always asserted things; a cautious consideration for and against seemed to him to be skepticism. No wonder he all too often succumbed to the hazards of his irascible temperament and his polemical ability. All this made it difficult to assess his character and his work, which to a great extent fashioned the German Reformation.

Home and Youth

Martin Luther was born at Eisleben on 10 November 1483. His peasant ancestors came from Mohra, on the western edge of the Thuringian forest. His father, Hans Luder, lacking hereditary title to land, had to earn his living in the copper mining industry. In 1484 he moved to Mansfeld, where by stubborn hard work he slowly rose from simple miner to partner in mining companies and small entrepreneur. The community repeatedly selected him as one of the board of four who had to defend the rights of the citizenry against the town council. Luther's youth in this aspiring lower-middle-class family of numerous children was thus marked by hardship, sobriety, and severity. How much it influenced the sensitive boy is clear from the fact that he often spoke of it in later life:

> At first my parents were poor. My father was a poor miner. My mother carried all the wood home on her back. It was in this way that they raised us. They endured hard work. Now the world no longer does it. [WA, Tr 3, 51, no. 2888a] My parents kept me in the strictest order, even to the point of intimidation. [WA, Tr 3, 416 no. 3566A]

In the parental home, of course, there prevailed a Catholic piety which, with its colorful customs, was a part of the world of peasants and miners, but which was also laden with superstition and apparitions of witches and devils. The ambitious father wanted a better career for his son and sent him quite early to the Latin school at Mansfeld (1488–97). Here, in addition to reading and writing, he especially learned Latin and ecclesiastical song. Even more severely and perhaps with more justice than Erasmus did, Luther later complained of his teachers' crudeness. He claims "to have been once flogged fifteen times in a morning for no fault" (WA, Tr 5, 254, no. 5571). This harsh upbringing at home and at school to a great extent fashioned the uncommonly sensitive youth's image of God. "From childhood I was so trained that I could not but turn pale and become terrified if I merely heard the name of Christ mentioned, for I was taught only to regard him as a stern and angry judge" (WA 40, I, 298).

In 1497, at the age of fourteen, Martin and a fellow student went to Magdeburg, to the school of the Brothers of the Common Life. Both there and at Eisenach, to which he transferred after a year (1498), he had to earn his bread, according to the custom of the time, as an itinerant singer, or "Partekenhengst," outside doors (WA 30, II, 576). At his "beloved city" of Eisenach he had a number of relatives. Especially in the Schalbe-Cotta family a warm, genuinely Christian environment embraced him.

University and Monastery

In the summer term of 1501 Luther entered the University of Erfurt and began the basic course in the liberal arts. He was enrolled in the Sankt Georgenburse. Manner of life and curriculum were determined for him. The arts faculty belonged entirely to the *via moderna,* the nominalist philosophy deriving from William of Ockham. Luther accordingly said later, "Sum enim Occamicae fractionis" (WA 6, 600). Following the course in the trivium—grammar, dialectic, rhetoric—he became a bachelor of arts in the fall of 1502. In this capacity he had to give lectures of his own while continuing his required courses. In addition to the quadrivium he had to attend lectures on cosmology, metaphysics, and ethics. Having become a master of arts on 7 January 1505, he could choose one of the special fields, theology, medicine, or law. His father's ambition destined him for the study of law, which he began on 20 May 1505. But on 20 June, for reasons not clear, he went home for a vacation. On his way back, on 2 July, a powerful electric storm took him by surprise at Stotternheim near Erfurt. Thrown to the ground by lightning striking very close to him, he cried out in great anguish, "Saint Anne, help me and I will become a monk!"

Despite the consternation of his friends and the extreme disapproval of his father, Luther fulfilled this vow, probably wrung from him by terror, and on 17 July entered the monastery of the Hermits of Saint Augustine of the Observance at Erfurt. Of the numerous monasteries in the city, this one may have recommended itself to him, apart from its serious asceticism, because of its Ockhamist bent, which offered Luther an organic continuation of his studies in the arts faculty.[2]

[2] L. Meier, "On the Ockhamism of Martin Luther at Erfurt," *AFrH* 43 (1950), 4–15; F. Benary, *Zur Geschichte der Stadt und Universität Erfurt am Ausgang des Mittelalters* (Gotha 1919), pp. 70f.

The choral office and the scriptural reading prescribed by the rule made the young Augustinian thoroughly familiar with the Bible. After a year's novitiate he was professed in September 1506, and only a few months later, on 3 April 1507, he was ordained a priest. Anxieties experienced during his first Mass, which almost caused him to flee from the altar, show to what a degree he was impressed by the overwhelming majesty of God and how little he was able to attend to and understand liturgical texts such as "clementissime Pater." This is important for a judgment on Luther's claim that in the monastery he had been taught "to expect forgiveness of sins and salvation through our works" (*WA* 40, III, 719). For the texts[3] that had been spoken at his reception as a novice and that he prayed daily from the missal were, in their constant assertion that man can do nothing of himself and that God supplies the will and the accomplishment, an impressive disavowal of all justification by works. At his reception the superior uttered the following prayers, among others:

> May God, who has begun this good work in you, bring it to completion. . . . O Lord, honor this servant with your blessing, so that by your help he may persevere in your Church and merit eternal life through Christ our Lord . . . that he may be always protected by the holiness which you infuse in him. . . .

But apparently this made no impression on Luther, for he was too much concerned with himself and his experiences.

Marked out to be a teacher of theology, Luther studied at his Order's *studium generale* in Erfurt, which was connected with the university. Here he again came under the influence of Ockhamism, as presented in the commentaries on Peter Lombard's *Sentences* by Peter d'Ailly and Gabriel Biel. At the same time he was lecturing in the liberal arts.[4] In the autumn of 1508 he obtained the post of lecturer in moral philosophy at the recently founded University of Wittenberg, and continued his study of theology there. In March 1509 he obtained the baccalaureate and, after that, delivered lectures on the Bible. Before he had reached the position of *sententiarius* he was transferred back to Erfurt, where he lectured on *The Sentences*. In the autumn of 1510 he became *baccalaureus formatus,* as he began the third book—that is, he had completed the requirements for the master's degree.

In his marginal notes on the text of Peter Lombard and those made at the same time on the writings of Saint Augustine we have the first

---

[3] O. Scheel, I, 281f.
[4] Luther is mentioned as a lecturer in an indulgence letter of 1508 for the Erfurt community (*RHE* 55 1960, 822).

theological observations from Luther's hand. In the notes on Augustine he shows himself to be an Ockhamist on the question of universals and in his concept of God. He interprets Augustine in this sense but at the same time regards himself as confirmed by him in his criticism of philosophy[5] and of philosophers. In their sterile disputations they were, according to Luther, relics of the Stoa (WA 9, 24), unwilling to admit the incompatibility of Aristotle with Catholic truth (WA 9, 27).

At the beginning of his comments on *The Sentences* Luther emphasizes that he does not intend to deny all usefulness of philosophy for theology, but that he would rather, with Peter Lombard, rely more on the doctors of the Church, especially Augustine, instead of seeking support in the discussions of the philosophers and the views in which they attack one another (WA 9, 29, 1). If we want to speak of divine things, we need only the word of God itself.[6] Otherwise we are groping in the dark, but the oversubtle philosophers will not admit to this. Whereas the master of *The Sentences* stresses with Augustine that our words lag behind our thoughts in regard to God, and our thoughts on the other hand are unable adequately to grasp God's being, the philosophers act as though everything could be comprehended and expressed by them (WA 9, 47, 25). To the opinions of the "highly esteemed doctors," who can claim only human traditions, Luther opposes Holy Scripture[7] and thereby first sounds the note of the principle of Scripture.

In these marginal notes Luther was already preoccupied with the questions that would later be so urgent for the reformer—original sin and the justification and sanctification of man by faith and charity. In relatively great detail he concerned himself with the problem of the relationship of the Holy Spirit and charity, discussed in the seventeenth distinction of Book I of *The Sentences.* He distinguished our love, *caritas creata,* from the Holy Spirit, *caritas increata.* The latter is the efficient cause of our love, but not its formal cause, not that whereby we love. This is not the Holy Spirit himself but rather his gift. In the actual order of salvation, however, created love is given and returned with the Holy Spirit.[8]

---

[5] ". . . totam philosophiam stultitiam esse etiam ratione convincit" (WA 9, 13); L. Grane, *Contra Gabrielem* (Copenhagen 1962), pp. 10–12. To what extent Luther in this criticism of Aristotle had forerunners in his own order is shown by A. Zumkeller, "Die Augustinertheologen Simon Fidati von Cascia (+1348) und Hugolin von Orvieto (+1373) und M. Luthers Kritik an Aristoteles," *ARG* 54(1963), 15–36.

[6] "Non relictus est hominum eloquiis de Dei rebus alius quam Dei sermo" (WA 9, 29).

[7] ". . . ego in ista opinione habeo scripturam . . . ideo dico cum Apostolo . . ." (WA 9, 46); ". . . credere oportet et verbis scripturae fidem profiteri et linguam illis aptare et non econtra" (WA 9, 84).

[8] "Primo sciendum, quod charitas (quidquid sit de possibili) de facto semper datur cum spiritu sancto et spiritus sanctus cum ea et in ea" (WA 9, 42).

Just as "for us Christ is faith, justice, grace, and sanctification,"[9] but at the same time these are created gifts, which become our own, so love is on the one hand the Holy Spirit and on the other hand the act of love which the Holy Spirit produces by means of our will. Hence Luther did not want to assume a specifically created *habitus* of love but only an actual created love, again and again produced in us by the Holy Spirit, who, as the principle of love, plays the role of *habitus*.

Luther did not accept from Peter Lombard the identification of supernatural charity with the person of the Holy Spirit, according to which he himself would be our love immediately. But he defended the master of *The Sentences* against the scholastics. He could not appreciate the reasons for their criticism of Lombard. Their intention was to preserve the distinction between creator and creature and to stress that the sinner needs a new disposition in order to enter upon the new relation and the new dealings with God. For Luther this is a chimera; the scholastics are simply determined by the teaching on *habitus* of that "rancid philosopher" Aristotle.[10] Hence he stood by the doctrine of the Ockhamists, who would have preferred most of all to do without habitual grace in order to eliminate in man every reason which might oblige God to make man happy.[11]

According to Luther, the love effected by the Holy Spirit is not only a good disposition in man; rather it makes "the entire person pleasing"— all its acts and attitudes. "It alone is virtue and makes all else virtue" (*WA* 9, 90); it is "the mistress of virtues and the queen of merits" (*WA* 9, 44, 6). But this love exists only in connection with faith and hope. On

---

[9] 1 Cor. 1:30. Already in the notes on Augustine occurs: "Ipse enim per fidem suae incarnationis est vita nostra, iustitia nostra et resurrectio nostra" (*WA* 9, 17).

[10] "Quia commentum illud de habitibus opinionem habet ex verbis Aristotelis rancidi philosophi. Alias bene posset dici quod spiritus sanctus est charitas concurrens seipso cum voluntate ad productionem actus amandi, nisi si forte determinatio ecclesiae in oppositum" (*WA* 9, 43); ". . . Augustinus hic loquitur de actu charitatis, qui nos deo jungit, habitus autem adhuc est spiritus sanctus" (*WA* 9, 44).

[11] Cf. E. Iserloh, *Gnade und Eucharistie*, p. 89. When R. Schwarz, *Fides, spes und caritas beim jungen Luther* (Berlin 1962), p. 40, maintains that "none of the Ockhamists consulted by Luther in his commentary on *The Sentences*—Ockham, d'Ailly, Biel—had assailed the scholastic *habitus*-idea as theologically inappropriate," he is mistaken. For Ockham emphasizes that the assuming of a supernatural created form obliges God to give eternal life to the one concerned and favors Pelagianism; *cf.* Iserloh, *op. cit.*, p. 217, footnotes 289 and 290. Biel too feels impelled to stress that ". . . Deus quem cumque beatificat, mere contingenter, libere et misericorditer beatificat ex gratia sua, non ex quacumque forma vel dono collato" (I *Sent.*, d. 17, q. 1, a. 2, concl. 3E). Hence against P. Vignaux, *Luther: Commentateur des Sentences* (Paris 1935), p.93, it must be affirmed that Luther's protest against the *habitus*-idea is an Ockhamist trait. On the other hand, Luther in *Contra Occam* stresses that *acceptatio* without *gratia iustificans* is impossible (*WA* 1, 227, 4).

the other hand, justifying faith is possible only in connection with love and hope.[12] But one in mortal sin also believes! Is this another faith and not the same, lacking only the form provided by love? Luther assumes two kinds of faith. Infused faith comes and departs with love and hence is identical with *fides formata*. *Fides informis,* on the contrary, is to be identified with *fides acquisita et naturaliter moralis*.[13] Accordingly, as supernatural virtues, faith, hope, and charity are inseparable. They are infused together. They are based on no habitus except the Holy Spirit himself, who effects them in us and in whom they must be constantly activated by us. Justifying faith, which makes us do what the law commands, is thus always a faith produced in love. All merit is preceded by grace, and in his rewards God crowns his own gifts.[14]

In regard to the preparation for the grace of justification, Luther, along with Peter Lombard, stresses against the theology of the Biel school that good will is already a gift of grace and that faith precedes it, not indeed in time but causally and by nature.[15] In his doctrine of original sin Luther turns somewhat sharply against Lombard, whose opinion "that original sin is tinder is not to be held" (WA 9, 75). Original sin consists in the deprivation of the supernatural justice of man's original state and is totally obliterated in baptism. Concupiscence remains as a punishment; it is the "tinder" which kindles sin and consists in the insubordination of the flesh. Reason, deprived of grace and virtue, can no longer restrain the flesh, whose nature it is to run wild, just as a horse whose reins are broken no longer submits. After baptism the state of concupiscence is weaker (*debilitatur*) but it is not eliminated. As a punishment man encounters the resistance of the flesh; he can control it and fulfill God's commands only with difficulty (WA 9, 73). Original sin is, to be sure, transmitted by means of procreation. Its cause, however, is not carnal desire but divine punishment. Against Peter Lombard Luther insists: "Even if the flesh were totally pure and were reproduced without carnal desire, still, by virtue of God's judgment on Adam, the soul would necessarily have to be devoid of the original justice, and hence it would be in original sin" (WA 9, 75). In these views Luther was still within the framework of the theology of his day. Of a particular pes-

---

[12] "Talis fides non est sine charitate et spe" (*WA,* 9, 72).

[13] ". . . sed sunt duae fides, infusa quae venit et recedit cum charitate" (*WA* 9, 90). "Dico certe et teneo quod tres theologicae sint inseparabiles. Et fides quae remanet cum peccato morali non est ea, quae possit martyrium obire et caetera. Sed est acquisita et naturaliter moralis . . ." (*WA* 9, 90).

[14] "Unde hic non simpliciter fides dicitur, sed (quae) per dilectionem operatur vel qua iustificati sumus . . . Nil deus in nobis praeter sua dona coronat" (*WA* 9, 72).

[15] *WA* 9, 72; cf. L. Grane, *Contra Gabrielem,* pp. 270f.

simism, based on his own struggles and sad experiences, and of a noteworthy dependence on Augustine there is hardly a trace.

Luther's Visit to Rome

Conflicts within his Order took Luther to Rome at this time. In 1510 Johann von Staupitz, the German vicar general of the Observant Augustinians, also became provincial of the Saxon province of the Conventual branch of the Order. In keeping with the desire of the Curia, Staupitz sought to unite the two branches, but seven houses of the Observance, including that at Erfurt, resisted, fearing a dilution of the reform through concessions made to the Conventuals. Luther's teacher, Johann Nathin, with Luther as his companion, was sent to the Curia as spokesman of the strict Observance, but very little was accomplished.

What was the significance of this encounter with Renaissance Rome for Luther's development into a reformer? Did he there perhaps receive the decisive impulse for his war against the Curia? Not at all. Luther's experience of Rome was like that of other devout pilgrims of the time. Sacred Rome, with its places of pilgrimage, so monopolized him that unfavorable impressions could scarcely make themselves felt.

> At Rome I was a fanatical saint; I hurried through all the churches and clefts and believed everything that is fabricated there. I suppose I celebrated one or ten Masses at Rome and was then almost sorry that my father and mother were still alive, for I should have been happy to rescue them from purgatory by my Masses and other excellent works and prayers. [1530: WA 31, I, 226]

"The main purpose of my journey to Rome," Luther explained later in one of his Table Talks, "was to fulfill my desire of making a complete confession from my youth and to become devout."[16] But he was disappointed in this expectation of being delivered from his inner distresses by a general confession in Rome. He found uneducated and, so he felt, unsympathetic confessors.

Doctor of Holy Scripture

When by the "Compact of Jena" a compromise was found for the conflict in the Augustinian Order which prevented the Observance being outvoted in the chapter, Luther no longer had any reason for opposition to Staupitz, and in the summer of 1511 the latter recalled him to Wittenberg. He now was to prepare to assume the post of professor of

---

[16] TR 3, 3582a; WA 47, 392; H. Boehmer, *Luthers Romfahrt*, pp. 159f.

Scripture, hitherto filled by Staupitz. In June 1512 Luther was appointed preacher in the Order and on 19 October he became a doctor of theology.

He was now qualified to take over the lectures on the Bible. This post, which he retained until his death, was to determine his lot and to push into the center of world interest the little university town of Wittenberg, lacking in every sort of tradition and "on the edge of civilization" (WA, Tr 2, 669, no. 2800b). His lectures, transmitted in autograph or in transcripts by his pupils, were in part discovered only at the turn of this century, but thereafter they were more and more taken into consideration, since they are the most important source for Luther's development into a reformer. They comprise his lectures on the Psalms (1513–15) and on the Epistles to the Romans (1515–16), the Galatians (1516–17), and the Hebrews (1517–18). With his arrangement of the lectures in glosses and *scholia* and his use of the fourfold sense of Scripture, Luther was within the framework of the traditional exegesis. But at the same time he appropriated the new humanistic linguistic studies, for example in his use of the *Psalterium Quincuplex* (1509) of Lefèvre d'Etaples (c. 1450–1536) and the latter's translation and exegesis of the Pauline Epistles (1512). Although these editions may actually have determined the choice of material for the lectures, more decisive is the fact that it was precisely the Psalms and the Pauline Epistles that were best qualified to bring out Luther's strongly experienced theology.

It was in his Order that Luther had been brought early and intensely into contact with Scripture. He bears witness to this in the Table Talks: In the monastery the friars gave him a Bible bound in red leather. He became so familiar with it that he knew what was on every page and could immediately open to any passage.

> If I had been permitted to keep this Bible, I would have become a better expert in Scripture [*localis biblicus*]. Already at that time no other study was as pleasing to me as that of Holy Scripture. I read the Physics of Aristotle with great repugnance, and my heart was on fire when finally I was allowed to return to the Bible. [WA, Tr 1, 44, no. 116] When I had entered the monastery, I began to read the Bible, to read it again and again, to the great amazement of Doctor Staupitz. [WA, Tr 3, 598, no. 3767]

Thus Luther attained a remarkable grasp of the Bible, which enabled him to quote it at length from memory. But more important than this formal mastery of Scripture was the personal relationship which he developed with it and as a consequence of which he could call it his bride. For him the Bible was not a cultural experience, as it was for some of the humanists, nor a theology·in contradistinction to the direct religious encounter with the word of God. To Luther there was no such separation.

> If you intend to become a Christian, take the word of Christ and understand that you will never finish learning it, and you will have to acknowledge with me that you do not yet know the ABC's. If it were worthwhile to boast, then I could also boast. For I have spent days and nights in this study, but I must remain a pupil. Every day I begin, like an elementary school pupil. [WA 29, 383]

The scholar J. Lortz comments:

> And yet, from the very beginning, this state of subjection is something totally different from the mere acceptance of a humble Christian. From the start it is an acquisition by the seeker, the wrestler, the fighter, by the giant Luther. This is decisive: he who so totally desired to be captured by the word of God was never a *listener* in the real sense. We will see that this fact overshadowed Luther's road to the end. Luther was subjectively inclined *from his very roots*.[17]

This strong subjectivism allowed Luther to throw an entirely new light on many pages of Scripture, but it also made him blind to other pages, apart from the fact that the reformer Luther would soon shunt off whole books of Scripture—the Epistle of Saint James and the Apocalypse—because they seemed to contradict his understanding of revelation.

The Lectures on the Psalms (1513–15)

The *Dictata super Psalterium,* the written version of the lectures on the Psalms which Luther delivered from August 1513 to October 1515, constitute the earliest comprehensive record of his views. Hence in recent decades they have been repeatedly discussed, but unanimity about their role in Luther's development into a reformer has not yet been achieved.

The young professor, relying on the *Psalterium Quincuplex* of Lefèvre d'Etaples, had a text of the psalter printed expressly for the use of students, with wide margins and considerable space between the lines. The edition was preceded by a preface written by him, and each psalm by an account of its content. Luther's personal copy, with its linear and marginal glosses, is preserved in the "Wolfenbüttel Psalter;" the detailed textual exegesis, the *scholia,* in a Dresden manuscript. Luther began to prepare the lectures for printing in the fall of 1516, but he got no

---

[17] J. Lortz, *Die Reformation in Deutschland,* I, 162.

farther than the earliest steps—Psalms 1, 4, and 22 to 24. Nevertheless, we encounter difficulty with the chronology of individual passages, for we do not know whether we are dealing with an expression of Luther's from the time of the lecture series or from the later revision.

Loyal to the exegetical tradition, Luther adhered to the fourfold sense of Scripture. In his view the literal sense was a reference to Christ as already manifested, but this Christ was seen in union with his mystical body. "What can be understood of Christ as the head can also be understood of the Church and of faith in him" (WA 4, 215; 3, 458). Hence assertions in regard to Christ can be applied allegorically or mystically to the Church and morally or tropologically to the Christian. Thus there is found in Luther a close connection of Christology, ecclesiology, and soteriology. But though the Church is obviously regarded as the body of Christ, and her function as an instrument of salvation in the administration of the Sacraments is important—above all in her preaching of the word of God—emphasis is placed on the identification of the Christian with Christ, based on the mystery of the mystical body. "Every scriptural passage that speaks of the advent of Christ in the flesh can appropriately, or rather must be understood of his spiritual advent through grace" (WA 4, 407; 4, 19). "Hence, as Christ was conceived by the Holy Spirit, so too every believer is justified and reborn without any human action by the grace of God alone and the operation of the Holy Spirit" (WA 3, 468).

God has revealed himself in Christ, the *opus Dei,* but he is still the hidden one, *Deus absconditus.* Though he cannot in any event be comprehended by us, he has concealed himself in a special manner in the Incarnation (WA 4, 7); indeed, in the wretched human figure on the cross he has hidden himself under the very opposite of his true form.[18] In the Crucified the contrast between God and man, heaven and earth, visible and invisible, present and future, spiritual and carnal, judgment and grace, justice and mercy, death and life, was intensified to the point of contradiction, but at the same time all contrasts were reduced in him to a higher unity.[19] By means of the Cross God kills in order to awaken to life, he destroys in order to save, he condemns in order to bless, he judges in order to pardon, in *opus alienum* he effects his *opus proprium* (WA 3, 246; 19ff.; 4, 87, 21ff.).

Christ's Cross and death are a judgment on sin; on the Cross Christ assumed our condemnation and rejection. However, God punishes, not to destroy, but to lead to life. God accomplishes marvels in his saints (Ps. 4:4), because he subjects Christ to every temptation of suffering

---

[18] "sub contrario" (WA 4, 449); "sub contrariis" (WA 4, 42).
[19] "Fere omnis contradictio hic conciliatur in Christo" (WA 3, 52).

and death and by this very means saves him. He embraces him the most powerfully where he abandons him the most. He leads him to salvation where he condemns him (*WA* 4, 87, 20ff.). Christ, who appears to be the most depraved and accursed, is blessed (*WA* 3, 63, 13ff.). Thus on the Cross is ended the tension between judge and redeemer, between divine anger and grace, and the unity of God's holy wrath and grace-bestowing love becomes visible.

What is now true of Christ by origin (*radicaliter*) and cause (*causaliter*), what happened to him as exemplar, is affirmed in the tropological sense of the Christian, who through his faith is included in salvation history. In fact,

> whoever will rightly understand the Apostle and the other Scriptures must interpret tropologically expressions such as truth, wisdom, virtue, salvation, righteousness. *Virtus* is the power whereby he makes us strong, through redemption we are saved, and through righteousness we are made just. Thus the works of God are the ways of God. In the literal sense everything is Christ; in the moral sense, it is faith in him. [*WA* 3, 458, 8–11]

The *opus Dei* Christ thus becomes the *opus Dei* faith in Christ. Christ is Sacrament, that is, a sign pointing beyond him; "he is our *abstractum,* we are his *concretum*" (*WA* 4, 173, 23), that is, Christ, so to speak, aspires after realization in the believer; "we must all be fashioned according to his example" (*WA* 4, 243, 15).

The applying of the work of salvation occurs in word and in Sacrament: the words of the Gospel are the "vehiculum" (*WA* 4, 229, 38) on which the truth comes to me. This word is not merely a communication but a living word; in it the judgment of God is continued through history, the cross is made contemporary with us. This cross, as the judgment and justice of God, means tropologically *humilitas* or, better, *humiliatio* and *fides.* In humility the just man becomes his own accuser (*WA* 3, 29, 16). Thus the divine summons to judgment becomes effective; we renounce our justice, acknowledge our sins, and admit that God is right, even when he seems to be unjust (*WA* 3, 465, 9).

> There will be no righteousness in us, and none arises, unless first righteousness is totally destroyed and our righteousness disappears. We do not get up unless we first fall. Otherwise, God's justice would become mockery and Christ would have died in vain. [*WA* 3, 31, 9ff.] It is reasonable that we should become unjust and sinners in order that God may be justified in his words . . . and thus the justice of Christ may all the more prevail in us. [*WA* 4, 383, 7ff.]

Thus "all our ardor must be directed to making our sins great and serious" (*WA* 3, 429, 3).

This self-judgment, the "crucifying of the flesh, is an effect of the word of God" (*WA* 4, 461, 37). It is no mere prerequisite of justification, but, as "humilitas fidei" (*WA* 3, 588, 8; 4, 90, 20; 127, 10; 226, 4; 231, 7, *et passim*), it is justification itself. "For not he who considers himself humble . . . but he who thinks himself to be abominable and worthy of damnation is just" (*WA* 3, 465, 6). Tropologically understood, judgment is the *humiliatio,* self-condemnation beneath God's word (*WA* 3, 465; 462), and justice is faith. For according to Romans (1:17), the justice of God is revealed in the Gospel and proceeds from faith to faith (*WA* 3, 466, 26; 463, 1). *Humilitas* and *fides* can be distinguished as concepts, but they are as inseparable as two sides of the same thing. "Self-condemnation is, as it were, the aspect made visible to the outside; faith is the inner side of justice."[20]

Judgment and justification must be understood as one, and judgment must be identified with the Gospel and with grace—for Luther this is the great marvel.

> It is amazing that grace or the law of grace, which is the same thing, can be judgment and justice. . . . No doubt, because he judges and justifies him who believes him. From this point of view, every word of God is judgment. [*WA* 3, 462, 23ff.]

Justification is not completed, however, it is a process. If we come to a standstill we cease to be good. We who are just are still in need of justification (*WA* 4, 364, 14) and never reach an end (*WA* 4, 296, 35). To advance means always to begin anew (*WA* 4, 350, 15; 334, 35). So far we are only redeemed as a result of hope. Justification is not visible; it is imparted only in faith. We who are saved "in spe" are not yet saved "in re" (*WA* 3, 453, 33). In this world we have not the "res" itself, but

---

[20] H. Bornkamm, "Zur Frage der Iustitia beim jungen Luther," *ARG* 52 (1961), 16–29 (especially p. 23); cf. *WA* 4, 383: "Quae [i.e., humilitas] est omnis veritas et omnis iustitia, et brevi verbo ipsa Crux Christi." Here breaks down the sharp distinction between an Augustinian mystical theology of *humilitas* in the first lecture series on the Psalms and in the lectures on Romans and a later and only then really reform theology of Luther of 1518–19, attempted by E. Bizer, *Fides ex auditu* (Neukirchen 1958) and A. Peters, "Luthers Turmerlebnis," *Neue ZSTh* 3 (1961), 203–236. The latter goes so far as to say that, up to the *Operationes in Psalmos* (1518–19), and in the works of edification even up to 1521, it was not easy for Luther "to divest himself of the Semipelagian remnants in the *humilitas* piety" (p. 217). All this so that the reform discovery can be a shattering "of the intellectual structure of Roman Catholic theology" (p. 236). L. Grane, on the other hand, holds it as proved "that Luther's line of thought is misunderstood when *humilitas* is regarded as a human achievement" (*Contra Gabrielem*, p. 295; cf. p. 321, footnote 3).

only evidence or signs of it, for faith is, of course, not the "res" itself, but the conviction of invisible realities (WA 3, 279, 30).

This antithesis of *res* and *spes* can be understood only against the background of Luther's Christology and doctrine of *absconditas*. In a gloss on Psalm 113 he says that Christ has two natures, one of which is manifest "in res," while the other is given only in faith and will be manifest "in re" only in the future (WA 4, 258, 27). The contrast between "in re" and "in spe" is, then, not that between "real" and "unreal" but between "manifest" and "hidden," between "visible" and "invisible." In this life we have Christ, salvation, justification, and so forth, not "in re"—that is, not in the brilliance of the final state—but in the hidden state of the "absconditas sub contraria specie." Hence the hidden reality is accessible to us only "in fide et spe." It must be our concern not to lose what has been given to us only in hope and not permit sin again to obtain power over us (WA 3, 364). For even after the forgiveness of guilt there remains much of what sin has done to us—weakness of the memory, blindness of the intellect, concupiscence or disorder in the will. Every sin derives from these three as its source. They are the remains of sin, which was itself remitted in baptism (WA 3, 453, 7ff.; 215, 28). Thus even the baptized remain in need of sanctification (WA 4, 211, 11).

In the earliest period of his monastic life Luther had learned by experience that "we fall again and again and are always unclean" (WA 4, 364, 9f.). In addition, the lectures on the Psalms are full of the recognition that the Christian, like Christ on the Cross, is closest to God in the depths of his abandonment by God (WA 3, 63); he is saved when he regards himself as lost, justified when he is dead (Rom. 6:7; WA 4, 90). Accordingly it is of no avail to be free from temptation, but rather one must accept it in faith in God, who "alone is just and justifies all in Christ" (WA 4, 299, 21; 417, 26).

The Lectures on the Epistle to the Romans (1515–16)

The ideas on judgment and justification expounded in the *Dictata super Psalterium* were further clarified and developed in the lectures delivered from November 1515 to September 1516 on the Epistle to the Romans. If Luther was already inclined to paradox in thought and expression, he was challenged by the language of this Pauline Epistle to thinking in paradoxes to a shocking extent. In the introduction to the *scholia* he thus formulated the fundamental idea of the lectures, the persistence of sin and the external character of justice:

The sum total of this Epistle is: to destroy, to extirpate, to annihilate all the wisdom and justice of the flesh . . . so far as may be done by the heart and the honest mind, and to plant, raise, and make sin grow. [WA 56, 157] For God wants to save us, not through our own, but through an external justice and wisdom, through a justice which does not come from us and grow out of us, but comes to us from elsewhere, which does not spring from our earth but from heaven. Thus one must teach a justice which comes entirely from without and is an exterior justice. Therefore, first our own justice, which abides in us, must be extirpated.
[WA 56, 158]

The question at issue is the acknowledgment that we are sinners, and in this sense we must "become sinners." By this sin, which Luther experienced as persisting and against which the baptized must struggle throughout life, was not meant actual sin but radical sin, which precedes all wicked individual acts—evil concupiscence. Its innermost nature is self-righteousness, self-complaisance, and selfishness. We have grown crooked and bent back upon ourselves (WA 56, 258, 304). This reference to self (WA 56, 356) threatens to gnaw away and ruin our best dispositions and actions. " 'You shall not covet,' that is, you shall direct nothing to yourself and seek nothing for yourself, but in all things live, act, and think for God alone" (WA 56, 356). Everything—knowledge, virtues, property—though it may be good in itself, is perverted because of this false reference. "Hence, if faith does not enlighten man and love does not free him, he cannot will or possess or do anything good; he can do only evil, even when he does good" (WA 56, 355). This evil concupiscence is for Luther not only the remains of sin, as it was in the lectures on the Psalms (WA 3, 453), and not only the tinder for new sins, but real sin. Luther reproached the scholastic theologians for "imagining that the totality of original sin as well as actual sin is taken away, as if they were certain things which one could remove from sight, as darkness is expelled by light" (WA 56, 273).

Guilt may be remitted, but sin as the perverted fundamental disposition of man is eliminated only by grace as a result of a slow process. Luther says that he was not aware of this in the struggles of the years behind him.

Therefore, I struggled with myself without knowing that forgiveness was indeed real but that there was no taking away of sin, except in hope; that is, that sin must be removed by the gift of grace, which begins to take it away so that henceforth it is no longer reckoned as sin. [WA 56, 274]

Whoever admits this sin as his own and "voluntarily acknowledges his damnation" has "satisfied God and is just." "This happens through faith, when man surrenders his intellect to the word of the Cross and renounces himself and abandons all things, dead to himself and to everything" (WA 56, 419, 12–16).

This persisting sin does not prevent a real unity of the believer with Christ, nor does it exclude the transfer to him of the justice of God in the sense of an objective justification. "Through his faith, which is Christ's faith, bound up to his death on the Cross and therein accepting the condemnation of his sin in God's sentence, he is transformed in his innermost being and justified before God."[21] Luther's oversubtle formulas and frequent recourse to the words *imputare, reputare,* and *nonimputatio* have led to the erroneous belief that Luther knew no justification of man in the sense of an inner transformation and real remission of sins. External justification does not mean that it remains merely external, but that it comes from without, is bestowed by God, is achieved not through man's strength but only through faith in God's word.[22] In fact Luther stresses that it is above all not a question of the elimination of individual sins but of the elimination of the old man and the creation of a new man. According to human speech, sins would be taken away, while the man remained. But for the Apostle it is quite different:

> It is man who is removed from sin, while sin persists as remains. . . . Grace and spiritual justice elevate man himself, transform him, and alienate him from sins, though they may leave the sin behind. [WA 56, 334] Hence Samuel also says, "You will become another man" [1 Sam. 10:6], that is, another human being. He does not say, "Your sins will be changed," but "You will first become another, and only when you have become another will your works be other." [WA 56, 335]

Justice does not result from righteous acting, as Aristotle teaches, but precedes it (WA 56, 172). As the official acts of the priest presuppose ordination, so the works of faith presuppose justification by faith (WA 56, 248). This grace of justification is not a habit or quality which adheres to man as whitewash adheres to the wall (WA 56, 354), but it is the state of being touched by the strength of God, by the Holy Spirit, who receives power over us and adjusts our whole existence toward God in faith, hope, and charity. To the extent that we allow ourselves to be actually seized upon by the Holy Spirit, we are just. Man is freed

[21] J. Lortz, "Luthers Römerbriefvorlesung," *TThZ* 71 (1962), 247.
[22] ". . . per solam fidem, qua Dei verbo creditur" (WA 56, 172).

from sin, actual and radical, when "he permits God to act and himself keeps still" (WA 56, 277). For the sake of this actualism and to exclude any disposal of grace by man separated from the Holy Spirit—this was Luther's wrong interpretation of scholasticism—he, like Ockham, rejected habitual grace. He saw Christians in danger of wishing to please God independent of Christ, as if they no longer needed Christ after they had received justifying grace (WA 56, 288). Life by faith is thus an ever new beginning, an ever new delivering of self to Christ. But it is also a continuous process, "a renewal of the spirit day by day and more and more (2 Cor. 4:16)" (WA 56, 443).

Luther regarded the justified man as a sick man in the presence of his physician, who promises health and has already begun to cure him. Christ, the good Samaritan, has "taken the half-dead man into the inn and begun to heal him after he has promised him complete health for eternal life." Meanwhile he denies him anything that could delay recovery.

> Is he thereby completely just? No; he is simultaneously a sinner and just [simul peccator et iustus]; a sinner in reality, but just by virtue of the consideration and the sure promise of God that he will redeem him from sin until he completely saves him. Accordingly, he is fully saved in hope [in spe], but in reality [in re] he is a sinner. Still, he possesses the first gift of justice in order that he may continue to seek, always in the awareness of being unjust. [WA 56, 272; cf. 56, 513]

"Iustus ex fide" then means not merely "I am just because of faith," but that justice is the object of faith. It is not visible and empirical ("non in re"). In fact it must remain concealed; like the divine glory in Christ, it must not become visible (WA 56, 171). It is established in me and aspires slowly to obtain dominion over me. "For our whole life is a time in which a person wants justice, but it is never completely attained; this occurs only in the life to come" (WA 56, 280). In a sense God already has the outcome before his eyes. He beholds man as just and does not impute his sins to him (WA 56, 272).

Luther thus distinguishes between justification, which is indivisible, like faith (WA 56, 249; 251), and sanctification, which proceeds slowly. In this lecture series, however, he does not yet speak of "double justice" but, following Romans 5:15, of grace and gift. Gratia means that whereby God justifies us, or rather that which has been given in Christ as the source, while donum signifies that which Christ infuses into us. "That expression, 'through the grace of this one man,' is to be understood of the personal grace of Christ, corresponding to the proper and personal sin of Adam, but the 'gift' is the justice which is given to us"

(WA 56, 318). Luther emphasizes that grace and gift are "one and the same" and does not further define the relationship between them. Even the relationship between *gratia operans,* the only efficient "first grace," and *gratia cooperans,* which knows growth and degree (WA 56, 379), is not explained. Especially obscure is the subject, which is flesh and spirit, just and sinner, which does the works of the law and of faith, which is passive in regard to the only efficient grace but nevertheless must believe, hope, and love, must even cooperate with grace and grow in it and become holy.

Whereas Paul, besides flesh and spirit, admits also the *nous,* the inner man, which can be carnal and spiritual, Luther knows only *caro* and *spiritus* and is tempted to identify them with man's body and spirit. "The same man is both spirit and flesh" (WA 56, 350). Luther compares this unity to that of the two natures in Christ, and in both cases the *communicatio idiomatum* is valid.

> But because one and the same man, as a whole, consists of flesh and spirit, Paul assigns both elements to the whole man, though they are opposed to one another and arise from mutually opposing parts of his being. Thus there results the common possession of properties [*communicatio Idiomatum*]—that one and the same man is spiritual and carnal, just and sinful, good and evil. As one and the same person of Christ is simultaneously dead and alive, simultaneously suffering and happy, simultaneously active and inactive, and so forth, because of the common possession of properties, even though neither of the two natures acquires what is proper to the other, but the most absolute contradiction persists between them [WA 56, 343].

According to this comparison the human person ought to be the bearer of *caro* and *spiritus;* though indeed it is inclined to evil, it is not so totally evil "that not even a remnant would remain which is oriented to the good, as becomes clear in our conscience" (WA 56, 237).

Thus man must work with the *donum;* or, better, the man seized by the divine Spirit, the *homo spiritualis,* must oppose concupiscence in order that sin, remaining in us, may destroy in us that which formerly prevailed over us (WA 56, 314), that man may endure it (WA 56, 346; 272) until the spirit removes it. Thus through *concupiscentia* man is a sinner, but because he asks for the justice of God (WA 56, 269) he is just. This is not something static, but an enduring process of improvement.

> One who goes to confession must not think that he is there ridding himself of his burden in order to be able to live calmly. He must

know that, in putting aside the burden, he is entering upon the service of God in war. . . . If anyone, therefore, is not determined to fight thereafter, why does he ask to be absolved and to be enrolled in the levy of Christ? [WA 56, 350].

If Luther is in many respects lacking in theological accuracy and care, he is exceedingly serious in regard to man's "being on the way" and to the "typically Pauline problem of being and becoming, of having and aspiring, of indicative and imperative" (O. Kuss). This led easily to the first indulgence thesis, according to which the entire life of a Christian should be a repentance.

The Lectures on the Epistle to the Galatians (1516–17)

After the Epistle to the Romans, Luther expounded the Epistle to the Galatians in the winter of 1516–17 (27 October to 13 March). These lectures have been preserved in only one student manuscript. In 1519 Luther or Melanchthon prepared the series for printing as a "Commentarius" (WA 2, 443–618; cf. WA 57, II, XVI). The Epistle to the Galatians was to occupy Luther quite often. It was "his letter," to which he had given himself in marriage: "It is my Katharina von Bora" (WA, Tr 2, 69, no. 146). In it Luther found confirmation of his concept of justification by faith, of the works of the law and the works of faith, of flesh and spirit, of continuing sin. "The wonderful new definition of righteousness" is as follows:

Righteousness is faith in Christ. . . . According to a saying of Jerome, the believer does not live by righteousness, but the just man lives by faith; that is, he does not live because he is just, but he is just because he believes. [WA 57, II, 69]

By faith we become "one with Christ." Faith is righteousness taken collectively ("universalis iustitia"). Thus every sin can be reduced to unbelief in Christ. To the objection that in that case faith suffices and I no longer need to do good and abandon evil, Luther retorts: In itself faith suffices, but no one has so great a faith that it cannot be increased. Hence works serve to increase faith. Moreover, they are to be done as a free service to the Lord Christ (WA 57, II, 70).

In connection with Galatians 2:17 the question is posed how the Apostle could deny that even believers in Christ are found to be sinners (Rom. 6:2, 10ff.). Luther replies:

All believers are just because of Christ, in whom they believe and to whom they begin to be conformed by the mortifying of the old man. Hence, what is not yet mortified is not imputed because of faith and the conformity begun. [WA 57, II, 74]

Accordingly justification is really instituted in me but is not yet completed. It is a process of becoming conformed to Christ. Sin persisting to the end is not imputed because God, so to speak, looks to the end, which is already anticipated in faith.

The Lectures on the Epistle to the Hebrews (1517–18)

The final lectures, those on the Epistle to the Hebrews, have also come down only in transcripts. Luther delivered them from the spring of 1517 to the spring of 1518, and so they fall in the period of the indulgence controversy and the first months of the reform struggle. Little of this is noticeable, however. Criticism of the external image of the Church is no more striking than in the preceding lectures. On the other hand, Luther's philological and humanist interests are much more prominent. Justification has a sharper Christological tone. Union with Christ is given to us in faith. Faith is the cement between the heart and the word of God; by faith they are joined in one spirit (WA 57, III, 157) and "man becomes like to the word of God, but the word is the Son of God; and so it finally comes about that everyone who believes in him is a son of God (John 1:12)" (WA 57, III, 151).

The idea of the death of Christ as *sacramentum* and *exemplum,* explained (WA 9, 18) in the marginal notes on Augustine's *De Trinitate* (IV, 3) and later quite frequently taken up again, among other things, in the lectures on Romans (WA 56, 321), was worked out in detail by Luther and brought into close connection with justification. Christ's passion is a divine sign (*sacramentum*) of death and the remission of sins.[23]

> Before Christ can become an example, man must grasp in firm faith that Christ suffered and died for him as a divine sign [*quo ad sacramentum*]. Hence they are badly mistaken who seek at once to obliterate sin by works and exertions of penance and begin, as it were, with the example, when they should begin with the Sacrament. [WA 57, III, 114]

Man must die with Christ in faith so that Christ can live and act and even rule in him. "Then, of themselves, works flow out from faith" (WA 57, III, 114). In the exegesis of Hebrews 10:19, the death of Christ and his entry into the glory of the Father are the sign and Sacrament[24] of the

---

[23] "Sacramentum passionis Christi est mors et remissio peccatorum" (WA 57, III, 222).
[24] ". . . significat et est sacramentum imitandi Christum" (WA 57, III, 222).

imitation of Christ. The death of Christ is the divine sign of the mortification of concupiscence,[25] even of its death, and his entry into heaven is the sign (sacramentum) "of the new life and the way on which we now seek and love what is heavenly" (WA 57, III, 223).

However, Christ is not only the model for our passover, not only our leader, but our helper, our ferryman. "For he will be borne on Christ's shoulders who rests on him in faith" (WA 57, III, 224). In the death of Christ God allowed the devil to have his way, but thereby death overreached itself against the divinity of Christ. In slaying him the devil was overcome and by death he could create nothing but life. "Thus God advances his work to completion through another's work" (WA 57, III, 128).

Just as Christ, by his union with the immortal Godhead, overcame death by dying, so the Christian, by the union contracted in faith with the immortal Christ, overcomes death by dying.[26] Justice is not done to this argument on the basis of the Anselmian doctrine of satisfaction. It must be understood in conformity with the patristic doctrine of redemption against the background of Philippians 2:7ff. Christ divested himself of his divine form, that is, "of justice . . . glory, peace, joy," and assumed what "is ours: sin, folly, perdition, humiliation, the Cross, sorrow, and so forth" (WA 57, III, 136), and thereby took away the power from all this from within. Because he thus became conformed to us lost men, we can be brought into likeness to him. He took our injustice upon himself and gave us his justice.

> Justice is grace itself, by which man is justified, that is, faith, hope, love, as expressed in Psalm 31:2: "Rescue me in your justice." . . . This justice is now that written of in Romans 1:17. It comes "from faith," as it is there written: In the Gospel "God's justice is revealed from faith into faith." This is wrongly interpreted as the justice of God, whereby he himself is just. Unless it is thus understood that faith so lifts up man's heart and by itself carries it over to God that "one spirit" (1 Cor. 6:17) is constituted from the heart and God, and the divine justice itself is the justice of the heart . . . just as in Christ the humanity became one and the same person through its union with the divine nature. [WA 57, III, 187f.]

According to this exegesis Christ would not communicate his justice

---

[25] According to Hirsch-Rucker, p. 251, "concupiscentiae," but WA 57, III, 222, follows the manuscript in reading "conscientiae."

[26] "Sicut enim Christus per unionem immortalis divinitatis moriendo mortem superavit, ita Christianus per unionem immortalis Christi (Quae fit per fidem in illum) etiam moriendo mortem superat, ac sic deus diabolum per ipsummet diabolum destruit et alieno opere suum perficit" (WA 57, III, 129).

to me, but an exchange of subjects would take place. Man would emerge from his own personality and put on the person of Christ, just as in Christ the human nature put on the divine person. Then the properties of Christ could be predicated of man in a *communicatio idiomatum.*

What is new in the lectures on Hebrews is the discussion of the relations of faith and Sacrament and the presentation of a relatively detailed doctrine of the Lord's Supper. As previously in the lectures on Romans (*WA* 56, 370), in the same words and with a reference to the same passage in Bernard of Clairvaux,[27] Luther maintains: "Faith in the remission of sins does not suffice if you do not believe with absolute certainty that *your* sins are remitted" (*WA* 57, III, 169). This granting of the foregiveness of sins to me personally is effected in the Sacraments. "Hence it is that no one obtains grace because he receives absolution or baptism or communion or anointing but because he believes he obtains grace through absolution, baptism, communion, or anointing" (*WA* 57, III, 169f.).

The statement quoted by Thomas Aquinas[28] from Augustine,[29] that the Sacrament operates by virtue of the word, and not because the word is uttered but because it is believed, is cited by Luther in a somewhat abridged form in which he stresses the necessity of the preparedness of the heart, that is, of faith, for the fruitful reception of the Sacrament. To present no obstacle is not enough.

> Even today a child is not baptized unless someone answer for him, "I believe." [*WA* 57, III, 170] The Sacraments of grace help no one, but rather they harm anyone who does not approach in full faith. No, faith is already a justifying grace. [*WA* 57, III, 191]

Especially urgent for Luther, as for the late medieval theologians, was the question of why there are Sacraments, if faith already justifies. "External word and sign are common to worthy and unworthy; they do not suffice unless we also savor Christ concealed in them" (*WA* 57, III, 200). When Luther stresses that "in the New Testament it is not the Sacrament but faith in the Sacrament that justifies" (*WA* 57, III, 206), he does not intend to deny the *opus operatum* nor to deny that the

---

[27] "Sermo in festo annuntiationis I," *PL* 183, 383. Bizer's remark that "Luther *now* disputes the idea of conscience in Bernard" (*Fides ex auditu,* p. 62) is misleading. As in the lectures on Romans, Luther here points out with Bernard that we do not have the conviction of conscience in regard to the remission of our sins from ourselves, but it is a gift of the Holy Spirit. Bizer's attempt to show in the lectures on Hebrews an advance from Luther's understanding of justice by faith turns out here as elsewhere to be contrived.

[28] *S. Th.* III, q. 60, a. 6.

[29] "In Ev. Ioan. tract.," 80; *PL,* 35, 1840.

Sacrament is effected independently of the worthiness of minister and recipient, but to emphasize that the mere sacramental reception without a spiritual reception, that is, without faith, is of no avail. But on the other hand, the mere spiritual reception, without the sacramental, does avail, according to what Augustine said: "Why do you make ready your stomach and your teeth? Believe! Then you have eaten."[30]

To be mindful of Christ's passion does not mean to take pity on him—even the pagans can do this—but to believe that Christ shed his blood for my sins. "For that means to drink and eat spiritually; by such faith to be plunged into Christ and incorporated into him" (WA 57, III, 209). For Luther the Eucharist is a testament—the bequest of the dying Christ. In it the remission of sins is promised to me. The testament became valid by the death of the testator. This death is the sacrifice of the New Covenant, offered once for all time (WA 57, III, 172; 217). "What is sacrificed by us daily is not so much a sacrifice as the memorial of that sacrifice, as he said: 'Do this in memory of me'" (WA 57, III, 217f.).

If we disregard the development in the lectures on the Psalms, which is difficult to determine because of the later revision, and keep in mind Luther's dependence on his current subject and the central ideas formed under its inspiration,[31] we can say that the exegetical lectures of 1513–18 are based on the same fundamental concept: justification through Jesus Christ, who assumed our weakness and gives us his justice in faith. Faith as communion with Christ, in whom we gradually overcome persisting sin, is a process which will be completed only with death.

Luther's Reform Understanding of *Iustitia Dei*

From 1532 Luther referred frequently in the *Table Talks* and in his lectures to an understanding, even an experience, which had given him an entirely new insight into the Gospel and, after hellish suffering, had opened to him the gate to the joy of paradise and to life and salvation.[32] In substance the understanding of the justice of God was involved. Until then he had been frightened when he read in Psalms 31(30):2 or

---

[30] "In Ev. Ioan. tract.," 25, 12; *PL*, 35, 1602.

[31] J. Lortz, "Luthers Römerbriefvorlesung," *loc. cit.*, pp. 150, 152.

[32] *Tr* III, no. 3232 a–c (Scheel, no. 235); *Enarr. Ps. 51* (1532), *WA* 40, II, 33 1f. (Scheel, no. 237); 444f. (Scheel, no. 245); *Tr* II, no. 1681 (Scheel, no. 238); *Tr* IV, no. 4007 (Scheel, no. 404); *Tr* V, no. 5247 (Scheel, no. 449); *Enarr. in genes.*, cap. 27, 38(1542), *WA* 43, 537 (Scheel, no. 460); *Tr* V, no. 5518 (Scheel, no. 474); *Tr* V, no. 5553 (Scheel, no. 476); *Enarr. in genes.*, cap. 42, 18–20 (1543), *WA* 44, 485 (Scheel, no. 490); introduction to Volume I of the Latin writings (1545), *WA* 54, 179–187 (Scheel, no. 511).

71(70):2 or Romans 1:17 the words the "justice of God." This expression had struck him like a flash of lightning. Then it had dawned on him, thanks to the illumination of the Holy Spirit, that the meaning was not punitive justice but the justice through which God makes us just in his grace. Thereupon, he says, "all of Holy Scripture and heaven itself was opened up" to him, who had previously hated the Psalms and Scripture because of this anixiety (WA 43, 537).

According to Luther's remark in early 1532, one of the *Table Talks* which was written down in almost identical words by Cordatus, Kumer, Schlaginhaufen, and Rorer, this can be described as follows:

> These words, just and justice, had the effect of lightning on my conscience. When I heard them I was horrified. If God is just, he will punish. However, thanks be to God, when I was once meditating in this tower and in my study over the words "the just man lives by faith" [Rom. 1:17] and "the justice of God," I thereupon thought: If we, as just, must live by faith and if the justice of God must bring about salvation in everyone who believes, then it must be not our merit but the mercy of God. In this way my spirit was lifted up. For the justice of God consists in our being justified and redeemed by Christ. And those words then became more pleasing to me. The Holy Spirit revealed Scripture to me in this tower. [*Tr* 3, no. 3232c]

As the place of this experience Luther specified the heated room (*hypocaustum*) in the tower of the Wittenberg monastery, which served as his study. For this reason it is referred to as the "tower experience."

More controversial is the time to which Luther attributed the experience, and on this depends its content. The dispute broke out over Luther's last and most detailed report of his experience in the introduction to Volume I of his Latin works in 1545. In it Luther intends to show the reader that in his earlier writings are found "many important concessions to the Pope," which he, Luther, "now regards and condemns as the greatest blasphemy and abomination" (WA 54, 179, 34ff.). It was, he says, quite difficult "to extricate himself from such errors" (WA 54, 183, 21ff.). Luther would like, so to speak, to ask his "Protestant" reader's leniency and to give him the theological keys to the correct idea. These keys are justification through faith in Christ and the justice of God as *iustitia passiva*. Both dawned on him only in a long, severe struggle. He shows this in two digressions, which he includes in the report of the external events, with allusion to the past by use of the pluperfect tense (WA 54, 183, 21–184, 3, and WA 54, 185, 12–186, 20). The second digression is as follows:

Meanwhile during the meeting with Miltiz and the Leipzig Disputation in that year 1519 I had returned to the explanation of the Psalms, confident that I was better prepared after having treated Saint Paul's Epistles to the Romans, Galatians, and Hebrews in lectures. I had been seized upon [captus fueram] by a certain wonderful desire to understand Paul in Romans. No lack of seriousness had hitherto stood in my way, but only a single statement in the first chapter: "The justice of God is revealed in the Gospel." I had, of course, conceived a hatred of this phrase, "justice of God," because, in conformity with the custom of all theologians, I had been taught to understand it philosophically as formal or active justice, whereby God is just and punishes sinners and the unjust.

Though as a friar I had led a blameless life, I felt myself to be a sinner before God, with a totally restless conscience, and I could not be confident that I had reconciled God by my satisfactions. Hence I did not love, but rather I hated the just God who punishes sinners. Thus I was angry with God, if not in secret blasphemy, at least in strong grumbling, and I said: It is not enough that wretched sinners and those lost forever because of original sin should be oppressed according to the law of the Old Covenant with every sort of calamity. No, God also intends to heap affliction upon affliction by the Gospel, while menacingly holding out to us his justice and his anger through the good tidings. And so I was frantic, upset and raving in conscience, and struggled relentlessly with that passage of Paul, filled with an ardent desire to know what Paul meant.

After days and nights of meditation God finally took pity on me and I noted the inner connection of the two passages: "The justice of God is revealed in the Gospel, as it is written, 'The just man lives by faith.'" Then I began to understand the justice of God as that by which the just man lives, thanks to the gift of God, that is, by faith; that the justice of God, which is revealed by the Gospel, is to be understood in the passive sense; that God in his mercy justifies us by faith, as it is written: "The just man lives by faith." At once I felt myself to be reborn and as though I had entered paradise through the opened gates. Holy Scripture immediately showed me another face. I then went through Scripture, as my memory presented it, and found a corresponding meaning in other passages. For example, the "work of God" is what God works in us; the "strength of God" is that whereby he makes us strong; the "wisdom of God" is that by which he makes us wise. In a similar manner are to be understood the "power of God," "salvation of God," "glory of God."

Just as great as was my hate with which I had previously encountered the phrase, "justice of God," so great was now my love with which I glorified it as the sweetest word of all. Thus did this Pauline passage really become for me a gate to paradise. Later I read Augustine's *De spiritu et litera,* and there I unexpectedly found that he too understood the justice of God in a similar manner, as that with which God clothes us by justifying us. And though this is said defectively and Augustine does not clearly develop everything concerning imputation, I was pleased that here the justice of God was taught as one whereby we are justified.

Better equipped by such reflections, I began for the second time to expound the Psalms. [*WA* 54, 185f.]

Luther established the point of time of his basic understanding with the remark that he had afterwards read Augustine's *De spiritu et litera.* But he had already quoted abundantly from this work at the beginning of his lecture on Romans (*WA* 56, 157; 172; 173; 191; 200; 202) in order to prove his idea of the *iustitia Dei passiva* in connection with Romans 1:17.[33] Hence we should have to place the reform understanding, so important for Luther, at the period of the first lectures on the Psalms and at the latest before Easter of 1515. On the other hand, Luther himself seems to indicate as the point of time the days before the beginning of the second lectures on the Psalms, the autumn of 1518.[34] For his account is fitted into the second reference to the second lectures on the Psalms. This does not mean that the events related could not

---

[33] *Scholion* on Romans 1:17: "On the other hand, by the justice of God one must not understand here that whereby he himself is just in himself but that whereby we are made just by him. This comes through faith in the Gospel. Hence the blessed Augustine says in the eleventh chapter of his book *De spiritu et litera:* 'Justice thus means the justice of God, because by the fact that he imparts it he makes men just'. . ." (*WA* 56, 172). Cf. *WA, Br* 1, 70. Bizer, who would like to assign Luther's new understanding of *Iustitia Dei* to 1518–19 at the earliest, supports himself by the thesis that, in the reading of *De spiritu et litera,* mentioned in retrospect in 1545, not the first but a second reading is involved (p. 10). But why does Luther already cite here in the lectures on Romans what he claimed to have found only in the alleged second reading? And from the letter to Spalatin of 19 October 1516 it is clear that Luther was at that time aware of the importance of Augustine's *De spiritu et litera* for a right understanding of justice (*WA, Br* 1, 10, 9f.). Cf. B. Lohse, "Die Bedeutung Augustins für den jungen Luther," *KuD* 11 (1965), 116–135.

[34] This date is accepted by, among others, H. Grisar (*Luther* I, 307) and P. J. Reiter (*Martin Luthers Umwelt, Charakter und Psychose,* II, 316). A. Gyllemkrok, *Rechtfertigung und Heiligung,* pp. 65ff., sees a reform trend in the lectures on Hebrews (1517–18). E. Bizer, *Fides ex auditu,* pp. 7 and 168, places the "experience" in the spring or summer of 1518, and according to K. Aland, *Der Weg zur Reformation,* p. 110, "the breakthrough to liberating clarity had been achieved in February–March 1518."

have occurred much earlier; in fact the double pluperfect, *redieram* and *captus fueram,* even demands this. Luther aims to show that his lectures on the Pauline Epistles had better equipped him for the lectures on the Psalms, and so, in describing his realization, he goes back beyond the beginning of the lectures on the Psalms. He certainly does not mean that he had lectured on this Epistle for a year without a correct understanding of Romans 1:17. In fact he there interpreted the justice meant in Romans 1:17 as that whereby God makes us just "per solam fidem, qua Dei verbo creditur" (*WA* 56, 172). In a letter of 8 April 1516 to the Augustinian Georg Spenlein, he developed his doctrine of the "justice of God, which is given to us most abundantly and gratuitously in Christ" (*WA, Br* 1, 35, 19), with the indication that he had fallen into error in this regard.[35] Accordingly, a basically new understanding had meanwhile become his. If Luther were specifying the year 1518–19, he must have been mistaken in regard to the time, as some scholars indeed hold.[36] Others assume 1518 as the correct date, but then they have to attribute a different content to the reform experience; H. Grisar, for example, regards it as the discovery of the assurance of salvation.[37] But there is none of this in the text. There is likewise no indication that "Luther discovered the word as the means of grace," which E. Bizer considers the content of the discovery.[38] But a person would be more likely to make a mistake in regard to the date rather than in regard to the substance of so decisive an experience. Nevertheless, as has been said, a glance back from 1545 does not compel us to accept 1518.

Are we to think of an experience in the sense of a realization flashing like lightning? The *Table Talks* give this impression, whereas the 1545

---

[35] "Fuisti tu apud nos in hac opinione, immo errore; fui et ego" (*WA, Br* 1, 35, 22). According to K. Aland, *Der Weg zur Reformation,* p. 13, "it is easy to incur the danger of interpreting the letter falsely and possibly of thinking that Luther is here announcing a new theological discovery, perhaps even that of Romans 1:17. But from the rest of the letter it is clear that in reality what is involved is a theological position other than that described in the *Praefatio* . . ." But the proof of this is not forthcoming.

[36] J. Ficker, *Luthers Vorlesung über den Römerbrief* (Leipzig, 4th ed. 1930), LXXII; F. Loofs, *Leitfaden zum Studium der Dogmengeschichte* (H1, 4th ed. 1906), p. 688; O. Scheel, *Martin Luther* II, 664, assumes an error in Luther's memory. K. Holl, *Luther,* p. 195, calls Luther's claim not to have obtained his understanding of *Iustitia Dei* until 1519 "an assertion which contradicts the known facts." A. Peters ("Luthers Turmerlebnis," *Neue ZSTh* 3 [1961], 203–236) distinguishes between the first appearance of the new exegetical insight, which is present in the *Dictata super Psalterium,* and the point "where Luther definitely succeeded in bringing the unfinished exegetical and dogmatic questions to a solution from this new start" (p. 211). This would have happened no earlier than 1518.

[37] *Luther* I, 316ff.; *Martin Luthers Leben und Werk,* pp. 94–99.

[38] *Fides ex auditu,* p. 7.

retrospect presents the new understanding rather as the result of long, stubborn, and quiet struggling with the meaning of Holy Scripture. Luther, in fact, expressly invites the reader to keep in mind that he, as Augustine says, was one of those who seek to advance themselves by writing and teaching and not one of those who suddenly rise from a nonentity to be everything, and who "at the first glance fathom all the meaning of Holy Scripture" (WA 54, 186). Accordingly, he means that he "has begun to understand." In another passage he says of himself: "I did not learn my theology all at once, but I had to dig deeper and deeper" (Tr 1, no. 352).

We certainly must not claim to find in the lectures any direct reference to a "tower experience." But we can inquire when Luther first made fruitful use in his exegesis of the new understanding, so revolutionary, so decisive for his self-knowledge and for his idea of Scripture. The answer must be in the *Dictata super Psalterium,* in the first series of lectures on the Psalms. In them the *scholia* of Psalms 1 and 4 must first be eliminated as the result of a later revision of the series for printing.

In the exegesis of Psalm 30(31):2, where the bitterly hated expression "In iustitia tua libera me" was to be explained for the first time, the new understanding of God's justice is not yet present. There is likewise no trace of the "thunder bolt" (Tr 4, no. 4007) by which Luther claimed to have been struck when reading this verse. In the exegesis of Psalm 71(72):2, which Luther tackled twice (WA 3, 464, 1–467, 4; 461, 20–463, 37), he clearly defines *iustitia Dei* as *fides Christi,* referring to Romans 1:17 (WA 463, 1; 466, 26). To his exegesis of Psalm 71:2 he adds as a general rule of hermeneutics:

> If one wishes to understand wisely the Apostle and the other Scriptures, one must explain tropologically all these concepts: truth, wisdom, virtue, salvation, justice, as that whereby he makes us strong, saved, just, wise, and so forth. Thus the works of God are the ways of God. In the literal sense everything is Christ; in the moral sense, everything is faith in Christ.[39]

Luther commented on Psalm 71 in the autumn of 1514. At that time, then, he would already have made use of his discovery, that *iustitia Dei* is not punitive justice but that of faith given us by God, not *iustitia activa* but *iustitia passiva.*[40]

---

[39] WA 3, 458. According to the evidence of the manuscript, this passage is incorrectly arranged. Cf. H. Bornkamm, *Zur Frage der Iustitia,* p. 22, footnote 10.

[40] This idea, used in the retrospect of 1545, is first found in Luther in 1525 in *De servo arbitrio* (WA 18, 768f.). According to E. Hirsch, *Luthers Studien* II (Gütersloh 1954), 18, it did not acquire a strict meaning in terminology until 1531 in the commentary on Genesis (WA 44, 485–487).

But there is hardly a trace of an immediately previous liberating discovery, of the "entry into paradise" after distressing anxiety. Certainly Luther speaks later of the "wonderful new definition of justice" (*WA* 57, II, 69) and of the fact that the Lord accomplishes marvels in his saints. But what about Luther's contention that until then Romans 1:17 had been understood by all doctors in the sense of punitive justice?[41] H. Denifle refuted this claim by means of an examination of some sixty commentaries on the Epistle to the Romans.[42] Of course the systematic theology—that is, the commentaries on *The Sentences*—and especially the piety of the age should be taken into consideration. For it is possible that a truth may exist in books without making any great impression or emerging into practical realization. In the *Dictata super Psalterium* Luther himself makes a reference to this distinction, remarking that the doctrine of Saint Paul, "the most profound theologian," on justice, which is not ours but God's grace, is "entirely unknown, perhaps not theoretically but definitely in practice," to contemporary theologians (*WA* 3, 21). But this reproach touches Luther too. The collects of the missal time and again put in his mouth expressions such as: "We who place no trust in our own justice" (Mass *Iustus ut palma*), "since we trust in none of our works" (Mass of Sexagesima Sunday), and "we who trust in your power." Obviously he had not pondered the content of these prayers.

Be that as it may, Luther's discovery in regard to *iustitia Dei* is fundamentally Catholic. And he accordingly "was struggling against a Catholicism that was no longer Catholic in the full sense of the word."[43] Luther routed, as religiously inadequate and not in accord with the Gospel, positions which had been handed down to him from late medieval practice and Ockhamist theology. The latter is not quite scholasticism; in fact it is not readily to be identified even with the teaching of William of Ockham himself. The *venerabilis inceptor* did indeed sharply stress human liberty alongside the divine sovereignty, but he no less unequivocally expounded that everything lies in the *acceptatio divina* and neither a naturally nor a supernaturally good work of man can bind God and limit his free choice of graces. Ockham's pupils had no longer been able to maintain this strong tension, exaggerated to paradox, between human freedom and divine caprice. With Gabriel Biel, who directly influenced Luther, they bent Ockham's

---

[41] *Enarr. in genes.*, cap. 27, 38: "Sic omnes Doctores hunc locum interpraetati fuerunt, excepto Augustino" (*WA* 43, 537); cf. the introduction of 1545 (*WA* 54, 185).

[42] H. Denifle, *Die abendländischen Schriftausleger bis Luther über Justitia Dei (Rom 1, 17) und Justificatio* (Mainz 1905).

[43] J. Lortz, *The Reformation: A Problem for Today*, p. 126; id., *Reformation in Deutschland* I, 176.

theses to conform with morality and understood a sentence such as "Facienti quod est in se, deus non denegat gratiam," which is not in the works of the Franciscan, to mean that man by himself can and must dispose himself for grace[44] and that there exists a synchronism, even a causality, between this disposition, effected by man's power, and the infusion of grace, in so far as God, on the basis of his arrangement, necessarily bestows the supernatural *habitus* on whoever loves him above all things *ex puris naturalibus*.[45] But in Catholic doctrine, according to Aquinas[46] as well as Augustine, every disposition—that is, every act directed toward God—which is answered by God with justifying grace, is already a work of prevenient grace, the gift of him who produces the will and the accomplishment (Phil. 2:13).

Luther's *Disputatio contra scholasticam theologiam* (WA 1, 224–228) of 4 September 1517 was an express and official confrontation with the Ockhamist school of theology. He attributed great importance to it and intended to make it available to far wider circles than would be the case in regard to the indulgence theses of 31 October.[47]

With the individual theses their opponents were named at the same time. They were Scotus, Ockham, Peter d'Ailly, and Gabriel Biel, and the last named was the chief opponent. He was cited most and was also dealt with in passages where the others were specified by name. The matter was taken from Biel's commentary on *The Sentences* and his *Collectorium*.

Luther first objected to any attempt to explain away Augustine's theses on the wickedness of man. Without grace man can will and do only evil (1–4). He has no liberty to turn in both directions (5), but, without grace, necessarily chooses the evil act (6), and to assume that man of his own power can love God above all things is a pretense (18). The *amor amicitiae* is a work of prevenient grace (20). Thus the initiative lies with God, and his choice and predestination constitute the sole disposition for grace (19). It is false to say that man eliminates obstacles when he does what lies in his power (33). Left to himself, he has neither right understanding nor good will (34).

There is no natural morality. Externally good works are sins because of our pride or our bad disposition (37–38). Hence we cannot become just through just works, but we must be just in order to be able to do

---

[44] E. Iserloh, *Gnade und Eucharistie*, pp. 129f.

[45] Gabriel Biel, III *Sent.*, q. un. a. 3, dub. 2 (Q): "Quia secundum legem ordinatam cuilibet facienti quod in se est et per hoc sufficienter disposito ad gratiae susceptionem Deus infundit gradiam . . ." Cf. L. Grane, *Contra Gabrielem*, pp. 242–261.

[46] *S. Th.* I–II, q. 112, a. 2: "Whatever can act as a preparation in man comes from the help of God moving the soul to the good."

[47] *WA, Br* I, 103; 106ff. For what follows cf. L. Grane, *Contra Gabrielem*.

just works. In connection with this attack on moral philosophy Luther turns in general against Aristotle and the use of logic and metaphysics in theology (43–53).

He then emphasizes that grace is not something in man; it determines his entire existence. It is always effective and is not to be separated from love of God, just as love of God is never without grace (54–56) and God cannot accept man without justifying grace (57). As early as the lectures on Romans, Biel's doctrine that man of his own power can love God above all things and fulfill the law in fact (*secundum substantiam facti*), even if not according to the mind of the lawgiver (*ad intentionem praecipientis*), had driven Luther to exclaim, "O fools, O piggish theologians!" (*WA* 56, 274). In the *Disputatio* too this is the chief reproach against scholastic theology. Just as one must not separate love and grace, so also the fulfilling of the law and grace. Grace requires no new work in addition to the observance of the law by natural strength, but it makes possible the spiritual fulfillment of the law (58–60).

For "not to kill" is not a sin because of the mere absence of the grace prescribed by God but because a false disposition—pride, anger, or greed—is at the basis of this external right conduct (61–63). To fulfill the law means to overcome hatred and greed, which inspire the external act, and the will, which rebels against the law (64–73). Only grace, or, better, "the child who is born to us," can do so (74). Only love, which is poured out in our heart by the Holy Spirit, can reconcile the will, which hates the law, with the law (85–90). At the end Luther once more turns on the Ockhamist understanding of the love of God. Grace does not facilitate the act of love, but rather makes it possible at all. We cannot by the same act love God for his own sake and creation for God's sake (94); that is, love of God and love of creature are irreconcilable (95). To love God above all else means to hate self and to know nothing except God (96).

Luther is here opposing a concept which, so to speak, sees man in a neutral zone where he is not challenged by God, does not face him in faith or in defiance, or where neither the anger nor the mercy of God is the power fundamentally determining him. In this disputation it is clear that the scholastic theology attacked by Luther is Ockhamism of the Biel type. With his stressing of prevenient grace, with his requiring of the grace of justification as the basis for *acceptatio divina,* and with his teaching that grace is not added as a condition to an already good natural activity but that it forms man's activity from the very beginning and leads to God, Luther contests what would have been censured by Thomism too and above all by Augustinianism. But at the same time Luther remains dominated by Ockhamism. And therefore he does not succeed, for example, in showing the relationship of the love of neighbor and of God and in seeing creation as an image of the divine nature.

CHAPTER 3

The Indulgence Controversy

History and Use of Indulgences

An indulgence is a remission of the temporal punishment of sins, granted by the Church and effective before God. The practice of indulgences in the Church, going back to the eleventh century, preceded the theological justification. Several factors contributed to the rise of indulgences. Private penance in the early Middle Ages brought about a connection in time between confession and absolution, whereby the subjective performance of penance followed reconciliation and the distinction between guilt and punishment became clearer. And in the atonements and commutations—that is, the adaptations whereby penitential works were adjusted to the circumstances and abilities of the penitent—it became evident that various kinds of penance could be substituted for one another and that the Church could decide such matters. Earlier the Church had already provided assistance outside the Sacrament in the penitential efforts of individuals by means of the intercession of martyrs and the official liturgical prayer. In the early medieval "absolutions" this aid acquired a more official form. These were prayers or benefits of the Church, which were to some extent connected with a summons to a particular work, such as the building of a church or participation in a crusade. Because it had been expressed by the bearer of the power of the keys, such an intercession was regarded as of special efficacy with God.

Whereas the atonement was concerned primarily with the canonical penalty, the absolution referred to the punishment in God's sight. The indulgence united them. But the indulgence differed from the atonement, because in the latter the substituted penitential work had to be equivalent, and also from the absolution, since this was not a judicial act. The indulgence, as a jurisdictional act, concerned the remission of ecclesiastical penance. But it was connected with prayer for the remission of the penalties for sin before God, a prayer which, because of its official character, one could be especially sure would be granted. The transition from a mildly administered atonement to an indulgence is naturally not clear. Still, the mitigation afforded by an indulgence was so well understood that even up to the thirteenth century it was regarded as a kindness toward the imperfect, a kindness that serious Christians were not to claim.

The theological justification of indulgences followed their use. The canonist Huguccio (d. 1210) was the first to describe an indulgence as a jurisdictional act relative to the penalties for sin before God. The question as to the source of the substitute for the remitted penance was answered after Hugh of Saint-Cher in 1230 with the doctrine of the *thesaurus ecclesiae,* of which the Church lawfully disposes. The more its efficacy was derived from the treasury of the Church, the more the indulgence became reserved to the Pope, who alone had power over this treasury, but the penitential work lost its significance in regard to the degree of the remission of punishment. If, besides, the punishments of sin were regarded as merely vindictive penalties, which as such had no meaning for the purification of man, then there was the further danger of disregarding man's susceptibility to the remission of penalties granted him and of neglecting pastoral responsibility for man's inner penitential spirit. Thus it was that the late Middle Ages saw a multiplication of indulgences and ever lighter works of indulgence and an unscrupulous financial exploitation of them.

The indulgence for the dead provided a special opportunity here. As early as the thirteenth century theologians and canonists had taught that indulgences could be applied to the dead,[1] and indulgence preachers had proclaimed such indulgences on their own authority.[2] We do not have genuine papal grants of indulgences for the dead until the middle of the fifteenth century, such as that of Calixtus III in 1457 for a crusade against the Muslims and that of Sixtus IV in 1476 for Saint-Pierre de Saintes.[3] An efficacy *per modum suffragii* was attributed to indulgences for the dead, but this did not keep many theologians and, above all, preachers of indulgences from ascribing to them an infallible effect and from teaching that they could be gained even by one in the state of mortal sin and hence that only the prescribed monetary contribution was necessary.[4] Thus the indulgence agent Raymond Peraudi explained the indulgence bull of Sixtus IV: "The method *per modum suffragii* does not derogate from the method of authority."[5] And in his twelfth "obelisk" against Luther's twenty-fifth thesis Eck asserted that "it [the phrase *per modum suffragii*] does not lessen, as Luther claims, but rather increases" (WA 1, 296). Despite the objections of several theologians, such as Cajetan, these views were prevalent around 1500, and indulgence preachers further exaggerated them in the pulpit. As early as

---

[1] E.g., Thomas, IV *Sent.,* d. 45, q. 2, a. 2, so. 2.

[2] N. Paulus, *Geschichte des Ablasses*, II, 167ff.

[3] Ibid., III, 380 ff.

[4] E.g., Raymond Peraudi; cf. Paulus, op. cit., III, 386.

[5] *ZKG*, 24 (1903), 225, footnote 1; WA 1, 582; cf. Paulus, op. cit., III, 384–386.

1482 there was submitted to the judgment of the Sorbonne a proposition which was identical in content with the notorious lampoon: "As soon as the money jingles in the chest, the soul springs out of Purgatory."[6]

The strong financial exploitation of indulgences by the Curia led to similar practices by the territorial lords. They aspired to a direct share in the financial results; otherwise they forbade the preaching of the indulgence. When in 1508 King Sigismund of Poland opposed the indulgence for Saint Peter's basilica, Julius II granted him two-thirds of the proceeds for the defense of the kingdom.[7] And even Duke Georg of Saxony, later to be so firmly opposed to Luther, was unwilling for financial and political reasons "to grant any favor," that is, he forbade the preaching of the indulgence in his territory. This "indulgence sovereignty" of the territorial lords, which signified a secularization of indulgences, was ridiculed on the eve of the Reformation by Thomas Murner in his *Narrenbeschwörung* (1512):

> Wil der Bapst ein Ablass geben
> So nympt der herr syn teil do neben;
> Wolt man im syn teil nit lon
> So miest der aplass blyben ston.[8]

The Trafficking in Indulgences by Albrecht of Mainz

In 1505 Pope Julius II (1503–13) had begun the rebuilding of Saint Peter's basilica, and in 1507, according to custom, he had announced a plenary indulgence to finance this immense building project. The indulgence had been renewed by Leo X (1513–21). Because of considerable resentment at the financial exploitation by the Curia, as well as the efforts of territorial lords to permit only the preaching of indulgences in which they would have a financial share or which would benefit the churches of their territories, the proclamation of an indulgence did not necessarily assure its being preached. But a special opportunity presented itself in the territories of the Archbishops of Mainz and Magdeburg, the Bishop of Halberstadt, and the Margrave of Brandenburg. In 1513 Albrecht of Brandenburg, a twenty-three-year-old youth, became Archbishop of Magdeburg and administrator of Halberstadt. And in the very next year the chapter of Mainz also postulated the easygoing

---

[6] Paulus, op. cit., III, 386.

[7] J. Hashagen, *Staat und Kirche vor der Reformation* (Essen 1931), p. 174.

[8] "If the Pope wants to grant an indulgence, then the prince wants to have his share. If one won't let him have his share, then the indulgence must be given up." T. Murner, *Deutsche Schriften* II, ed. M. Spanier (Berlin, 1926), 249.

prince as Archbishop-Elector of Mainz. For Albrecht proposed to pay personally the *servitia* and the pallium tax, which had fallen due now for the third time within one decade. They amounted to 14,000 ducats.[9] In addition there was owed a dispensation fee of 10,000 ducats, since, along with the great Mainz archbishopric, Albrecht wanted to retain his present sees of Magdeburg and Halberstadt—an illegal accumulation of pastoral benefices. The archbishop borrowed 29,000 Rhenish gold florins from the Fugger banking house, and the Curia itself indicated how this burden of debt could be paid. The archbishop was to undertake the preaching of the indulgence for Saint Peter's for eight years and be allowed to retain half the proceeds. Including the tax of 2,143 ducats which the Emperor had reserved for himself, Albrecht had to raise 26,143 ducats. Accordingly the indulgence had to raise 52,286 ducats if it was to achieve its goal.[10] Representatives of the Fuggers accompanied the indulgence preachers in order to take their share on the spot. Thus did the indulgence, which Leo X granted by the Bull "Sacrosanctis Salvatoris et Redemptoris" of 31 March 1513 become an "object of barter in a wholesale commercial transaction," as Lortz stigmatizes the deal. It is useless to inquire whether or not this was a formal case of simony. In shame we can only acknowledge with Meissinger that "the whole thing was a full-fledged scandal."

As papal agent for this indulgence, Archbishop Albrecht issued for his deputies and the indulgence preachers a comprehensive set of instructions, the *Instructio Summaria*.[11] Despite certain obscurities, the doctrine of indulgences contained in this is correct, but in its recourse to pious formulas and superlatives it resorts in practice to a commercialized extolling of the indulgence in order to realize the highest possible monetary profit. The remission of future sins was not promised, contrary to what Luther claimed in 1541 (*WA* 51, 538). But one could purchase a confession certificate, by virtue of which one could confess to any priest at any desired time in his later life sins reserved to the Pope. The indulgence preacher had to make it clear that a person did not need to confess at the moment of buying such a confession certificate, which procured for him, among other things, then and forever a share in the spiritual goods of the Church Militant.[12] Likewise, one could gain a plenary indulgence for the dead without contrition and confession but

[9] A. Schulte, *Die Fugger in Rom 1495–1523* I, 93–141; G. von Polnitz, *Jakob Fugger* (Tübingen 1949), I, 307–311, II, 324–327.

[10] Schulte, op. cit., I, 140.

[11] Text in W. Kohler, *Dokumente,* pp. 104–124.

[12] "Declaramus etiam, quod pro dictis duabus gratiis principalibus consequendis non est opus confiteri seu ecclesias aut altaria visitare, sed dumtaxat confessionale redimere" (W. Kohler, *Dokumente,* p. 116).

merely by the paying of the money.[13] And especially this indulgence was represented as "efficacissime" and "certissime," and sermons of a content such as that referred to in the lampoon mentioned above were thus abetted by it. The faithful were invited to postpone repentence, and the impression was strengthened that what was at stake was money rather than the salvation of souls.

On 22 January 1517, Johannes Tetzel (c. 1465–1519), a Leipzig Dominican, was appointed one of the two deputies for the preaching of the indulgence in the province of Magdeburg, and a high compensation was granted him.[14] He quickly took up the task. He is reported to have been active in Halle in March and at Jüterbog on 10 April; according to Luther's statement people flocked to him from Wittenberg also, as though they were "insane" and "possessed."[15] Frederick the Wise had not given leave for the preaching of the indulgence in Electoral Saxony, for he was unwilling to permit his subjects' money to profit Albrecht of Brandenburg, the rival of his dynasty, or to allow the pilgrimage to his Wittenberg Church of All Saints, so richly endowed with relics and indulgences, to suffer any falling off. The store of relics which the elector had assembled there, and the multitude of indulgences which he acquired for those venerating them,[16] show clearly that Frederick the Wise was in no sense an opponent of indulgences.

In regard to his personal life Tetzel provided no reason for any special complaints. He was not one of those indulgence preachers about whom not only Luther (WA 1, 588) but also Johann Eck himself, in his opinion on reform for the Pope, said that they paid off their prostitutes with indulgence certificates.[17] But he was one of those who, as Johannes Cochläus, Duke Georg of Saxony, and his court chaplain Hieronymus Emser complained, emphasized the money at the expense of contrition.[18]

As a confessor, Luther had occasion to deal with indulgence preaching and with the expectations and ideas it aroused in the minds of his

---

[13] ". . . nec opus est, quod contribuentes pro animabus in capsam sint corde contriti et ore confessi" (ibid., p. 116).

[14] H. Volz, Martin Luthers Thesenanschlag, p. 13.

[15] WA, TR 5, 76, no. 5346; WA 51, 539; WA 30, II, 282–284; WA, TR 5, 535, no. 6201.

[16] Even in 1516 Frederick the Wise requested from Rome an increase of the indulgences for his castle church. The relevant bull was not brought to Germany by von Miltitz until 1518, and it was delivered to the elector in 1519. The collection of relics was constantly added to until 1520. For 1518 Spalatin recorded 17,443 items, and for 1520 there were 18,970. In one visit an indulgence of 1,902,202 years, 270 days, and of 1,915,983 quarantines could be gained for each action; P. Kalkoff, Ablass und Reliquienverehrung an der Schlosskirche zu Wittenberg (Gotha 1907), pp. 65f.

[17] Acta reformationis catholicae I, 110.

[18] Paulus, op. cit., III, 483.

penitents. He had already directed criticism at indulgences in the lectures on the Psalms and on Romans,[19] and in a sermon usually assigned to 31 October 1516, he came out specifically against the indulgence Tetzel had preached on the Feast of Saint Matthias in 1517. He maintained that as a consequence of indulgences the people learned to flee and abhor the penalties of sin but not sin itself. It would be far better to admonish them to love the punishment and to embrace the Cross (WA 1, 141). In a sermon on the occasion of a church dedication, which he delivered in April 1517 or later, he came out against the "big show" of Tetzel's indulgence preaching. In this he emphasized that indulgences merely free from the conditions of private penance and not infrequently stand in the way of inner repentance. The genuine penitent, he said, did not wish to be freed from punishment by indulgences (WA 1, 98).

Luther presented his idea in detail in the treatise De indulgentiis (WA 1, 65–69). According to this, an indulgence is the remission of the satisfaction imposed in confession by the priest. In itself it does not lessen concupiscence nor does it increase love and grace. In Luther's opinion the faithful should be directed to genuine penance, that is, to inner conversion and the eradicating of radical sin. One cannot buy oneself off from it by an indulgence. Hence an indulgence is to be rejected if it provides the occasion for false security and spiritual laziness and does not promote the allaying of concupiscence and a longing for God. "We have to seek God's healing grace incessantly"—so runs the last sentence of this far too little noticed treatise. Till then Luther had regarded the indulgence doctrine expounded by Tetzel as the latter's private opinion and had ascribed its excesses to his charlatanry. But acquaintance with the Instructio Summaria of the Archbishop of Mainz showed him that Tetzel's sermons were based on official instructions. This may have induced him to turn to the prelates responsible—the Bishop of Brandenburg as local Ordinary and the Archbishop of Magdeburg and Mainz as the papal agent for the indulgence.

In a letter of 31 October 1517 to Albrecht of Mainz, Luther complained that the indulgence preachers "by deceiving stories and promises about indulgences lull the people into security and lack of fear" (WA, Br 1, 111). The archbishop should withdraw his Instructio and give other directions to the preachers; otherwise great shame and dishonor would ensue. From the accompanying theses he would be able to ascertain how unsettled the doctrine on the indulgence really was. The reference here was to the celebrated ninety-five theses. Luther actually sent them to the bishops directly concerned on the eve of All Saints. Only when these prelates did not reply, or replied in an unsatisfactory man-

[19] WA 3, 416; 424f.; WA 56, 417; 503.

ner, did he, as he maintained throughout his life, distribute them to learned men in and outside Wittenberg.[20] A posting of the theses at the Wittenberg castle church on 31 October 1517 is incompatible with these statements of Luther. Neither Luther himself nor any other of the numerous contemporary sources refers to such a move. Only after Luther's death did Melanchthon speak of a posting of the theses in his introduction to Volume II (1546) of the reformer's works, which has been proved to be very unreliable on other points also.[21]

Luther's Ninety-five Theses

Apart from numerous other inconsistencies, the posting of the theses on the eve of the titular feast of the castle church, in view of the great concourse of people attracted by the rich indulgences to be gained there, would have had the character of a public spectacle, despite the fact that the theses were written in Latin. But as he repeatedly insisted, Luther sought a discussion among scholars for a clarification of the doctrine of indulgences, thus far not officially defined.[22] The colleagues to whom Luther forwarded the theses after 31 October—Johann Lang in Erfurt, for example, on 11 November (WA, Br 1, 122)—passed them on. Thus in both longhand and print they acquired in a few weeks such a rapid and extensive distribution as no one, not even Luther, could have foreseen (WA, Br 1, 120; WA 51, 540).

"Our Lord and Master Jesus Christ in saying, 'Do penance . . .' (Mt. 4:17), desired that the whole life of the faithful should be a penance" (Thesis 1). Here is expressed Luther's anxiety lest the faithful be lulled into a false assurance of salvation. Rather they should be "admonished to follow Christ, their Head, through suffering, death, and hell" (Thesis 94; 92–95). Indulgence preachers who by "extravagant and unrestrained" words (Thesis 92) commend indulgences far beyond their value (Thesis 24; 73–80) promote a lazy peace (Thesis 95), at the expense of contrition and penance (Theses 39–41). In this connection Luther later wrote in his *Resolutions:* "See the danger! Indulgences are preached to the people in direct opposition to the truth of the Cross and the fear of God" (WA 1, 601). Indulgences are not to be rejected in principle (Thesis 71), but people are not to put their trust in them (Theses 49, 52, 32), and works of charity and prayer especially are

---

[20] WA 1, 528; WA, Br 1, 245; WA 51, 540; WA 54, 180; cf. B. Iserloh, *Luthers Thesenanschlag*, pp. 13–15.

[21] CR 6, 161f.; H. Boehmer, *Luthers Romfahrt* (Leipzig 1914), p. 8.

[22] WA, Br 1, 138; 152; WA 1, 311; 528. Cf. the heading of the theses: "Quare petit, ut qui non possunt verbis praesentes nobiscum disceptare, agunt id literis absentes" (WA 1, 233).

superior to them (Theses 41–47). In opposition to the *Instructio* and the indulgence preachers, who give the impression that only by means of indulgences do we obtain remission of the penalties of sin and a share in the goods of Christ and the Church, Luther overemphasizes that every Christian finds full remission of penalty and guilt in true contrition (Thesis 36) and, even without indulgences, has a share in all the treasures of Christ and the Church (Thesis 37). The true treasury of the Church is the Gospel of the glory and grace of God. (Thesis 62). Hence only enemies of Christ can, like the *Instructio,* forbid the preaching of the word of God in the churches during the time of indulgence preaching (Theses 53–55). In Theses 14 to 19 Luther stresses the uncertain character of the statements of theologians in regard to the souls in purgatory. In any case, the indulgence for the dead is granted only in the form of an intercession (Theses 26, 25), and so one must not speak of an infallible effect (Theses 27–29).

All these topics can be understood as orthodox, as legitimate criticism of abuses in the indulgence system, and as a contribution to the discussion of theological questions not yet defined. Even Luther's idea of the declaratory nature of absolution—that the Pope can remit guilt only by the declaration and the acknowledgment that it is remitted by God (Theses 6, 38)—was in line with contemporary nominalist theology, according to which the sacramental absolution does not cancel "guilt and eternal punishment, but only indicates a cancellation that has already taken place."[23]

Luther also stresses the intention of confessing as a condition of forgiveness by God (Theses 7, 38), and he even allows the Pope a right, efficacious with God, to reserve sins (Thesis 6). But he questions the nature of indulgences, especially according to the prevailing opinion of the time, when he restricts them to the remission of the canonical penalties (Theses 5, 11, 20, 21, 31) and does not concede that ecclesiastical penalties correspond to those imposed by God.[24] In the declaration of these theses, however, he repeatedly affirms that he does not desire to make claims but wishes to dispute and would willingly be corrected.[25]

Although, he says, the views of Thomas and Bonaventure are against him, no canon of law and no passage of Scripture is, and no doctrinal decision by the Church has yet been issued (WA 1, 568). Luther is convinced that he is within the limits of theological opinions that are defensible. That he was correct in this view is proved by the fact that his

---

[23] B. Poschmann, *Handbuch der Dogmengeschichte* IV, 3, 102.

[24] "Resolutiones . . . " concl. 36 (WA 1, 592).

[25] "Hanc disputo et doceri humiliter peto" (WA 1, 534); "Hanc disputo, nondum pertinaciter assero" (WA 1, 567).

Resolutions, or explanation of the theses, was submitted to his Ordinary, the Bishop of Brandenburg, whose *placet* it obtained (*WA* 1, 164).

If we are not satisfied merely to establish the facts, if we inquire historically and causally to determine what the theses were aiming at and what development lay imminent in them, then we will attribute to them a greater significance. In so inquiring we have to keep in mind that in the nominalist theology divine and human activity were already separated to a great extent, in the sense that God accepted the action of the Church only as an occasion for his own saving action, without actually entering into it. Luther pushed this separation of the human and the ecclesiastical from the divine so far that he no longer attributed to the ecclesiastical penalty or its remission even an interpretive significance with regard to the penalties for sin imposed by God. In my view this seems to be a root of Luther's proximate rejection of the hierarchical priesthood as a divine institution.

But this theological impact of the theses was not immediately effective. The secret of the inflammatory effect and rapid spread of the indulgence theses lies in their polemical and folksy tone. With them Luther touched long-smoldering questions, grievances, and resentments which had already often become vocal; he made himself the spokesman of many disillusioned hopes and of a widespread discontent. In Theses 80 to 91 he took up, as he himself said, "the quite pointed and critical objections of the laity" (Theses 30, 81), which were not to be "silenced by force" and not to be appeased by cheap excuses. Many contemporaries felt as Prior Johannes Fleck did when, on becoming acquainted with the theses, he said to his confreres, "This is the one who will do it" (*TR* 5, 177, no. 5480). And even such determined later opponents of Luther as Johannas Cochläus, Hieronymus Emser, and Duke Georg of Saxony hailed the theses. The Duke's councillor, Caesar Pflug, told him of a remark by Bishop Adolf VII of Merseburg to the effect that the prelate thought the theses "should be posted in many places" to warn the poor "against Tetzel's humbug."[26]

The rapid circulation of the theses was for Luther himself a proof that he had expressed what many had kept quiet about because of "fear of the Jews" (John 7:13; *WA, Br* 1, 152). But he deplored this turn because the theses had been intended, not for the people but for a few scholars, and because they contained some doubtful propositions (letter to Scheuerl of 5 March 1518). Hence he hastened to put his basic ideas on indulgences in writing for the people in the "Sermon on indulgences

---

[26] F. Gess, *Akten und Briefe zur Kirchenpolitik Herzog Georgs von Sachsen,* vol. I (1517 to 1524) (Leipzig 1905), p. 29.

and grace" in March 1518 (*WA* 1, 239–246). In 1518 alone thirteen printings of this appeared, an indication of the possibilities afforded to Luther and the Reformation by the printing press. At the same time, in his *Resolutiones disputationum de indulgentiarum virtute* Luther provided a detailed case for his indulgence theses, but this did not appear until August 1518 (*WA* 1, 530–628). In it Luther was concerned to protect himself against misunderstandings and distortions and to give his superiors—Leo X, Staupitz, and the Bishop of Brandenburg—a first-hand account of the motives for his action. In the accompanying letter to the Pope Luther alludes to the unprecedented success of his theses. He says that he deplores this because they were unsuited for a circulation of this sort. However, they cannot be withdrawn now ("revocare non possum"; *WA* 1, 529), and so he is issuing this explanation of them. In this way it should become clear that he is honestly concerned for the power of the Church and the respect due to her keys. At the end he wrote: "Therefore, most holy Father, I cast myself at the feet of Your Holiness and commit myself to you with all that I am and have" (*WA* 1, 529). In the *Protestatio* introducing the *Resolutiones* he affirmed: "I first of all declare that I intend to say and to assert nothing except what is contained primarily in Holy Scripture and then in the Church Fathers acknowledged and preserved by the Roman Church and in canon law and the papal decrees . . ." But he declined to be committed to the opinions of the theological schools: "Through this *Protestatio* of mine it is, so I hope, made sufficiently clear that I can err but that no one can make me out to be a heretic . . ." (*WA* 1, 530f.). The letters accompanying the *Resolutiones,* with their quite singular mixture of candid humility, prophetic self-assurance, and bold avowal, are not adequately characterized when they are referred to as "first-rate chess moves."[27] Be that as it may, they prove—especially if the posting of the theses did not take place—that there was a real possibility of binding the Wittenberg friar, zealously striving for the honor of God and the salvation of souls, to the Church and of making him productive in her.

Of course there was also required on the part of the bishops concerned and of the Pope an approximately equal measure of religious strength and of apostolic and pastoral responsibility. That such was unthinkable reveals the radical weakness of the Church of that time. In this failure in the sphere of what is proper to the priesthood rather than in all the abuses lies her part of the guilt for the Reformation.

[27] K. A. Meissinger, *Der Katholische Luther,* p. 162.

CHAPTER 4

Rome's Proceedings against Luther
and
the Leipzig Disputation

The first person affected by Luther's theses was Archbishop Albrecht of Mainz, who requested an opinion from his university at Mainz. The university returned an evasive reply and suggested that the matter be submitted to the Pope, since his authority was at stake. Even before this answer reached him, Albrecht informed his Magdeburg advisers on 13 December 1517 that he had sent the theses to the Pope and suggested that they should institute a *processus inhibitorius* whereby Luther would be summoned and called upon, under threat of punishment, to refrain in future from all attacks on indulgences in preaching, writing, and disputation. But apparently the advisers did not comply. The denunciation of Luther at Rome for spreading new doctrine was the archbishop's only strong weapon. He obviously did not want to be bothered further with the affair, and so his advisers shelved the *processus.*

The efforts of Tetzel and the Dominicans were more effective, but their activity only too easily created the impression that this was a case of a dispute between rival orders. In January 1518, at the chapter of the Saxon Dominican province in Frankfurt on the Oder, Tetzel debated either ninety-five or 106 theses—the sources differ—against Luther, drawn up by Konrad Wimpina, rector of the university. Here he frivolously defended the lampoon: "As soon as the money jingles in the chest, the soul springs out of purgatory." In fact he stressed that the soul would be freed even more quickly, for the money took time to fall.[1] But even he was outdone by his confrere Sylvester Prierias, the Pope's own theologian. According to Prierias, a preacher who taught this was no more blameworthy than a cook who makes food more attractive to a satiated stomach by adding condiments.[2]

Just as grave as this lack of religious seriousness was the thoughtlessness with which opinions of the schools were passed off as dogmas and their opponents were branded as heretics. The opinion so offensive to Luther, that the state of grace was not necessary for gaining indulgences for the dead, was put forth by Tetzel in Thesis 42 as a "Christian

[1] "Quisquis ergo dicit, non citius posse animam evolare, quam in fundo ciste denarius possit tinnire, errat" (N. Paulus, *Johannes Tetzel,* p. 174).
[2] N. Paulus, *Johannes Tetzel,* p. 147.

dogma."[3] It was for this reason that Cardinal Cajetan, in a treatise on indulgences of 20 November 1519, attacked preachers who pass off private opinions as teachings of the Church.[4] This arbitrary method of making dogmas out of questions still open to debate was a no less dangerous variation of the "theological vagueness" which was one of the most decisive causes of the Reformation.

The Dominican chapter agreed to denounce Luther at Rome of suspicion of heresy. This was done in March 1518, and, considering the great influence of the Preaching Friars at the Curia, it was not without danger for Luther.

Johannes Eck's rather hastily scribbled *Obelisci,* comments on the indulgence theses, were intended for the private use of Gabriel von Eyb, Bishop of Eichstätt. In March 1518 they came into Luther's hands through Wenceslas Link of Nürnberg but obtained about as little publicity as Luther's *Asterisci* did (*WA* 1, 281–314). In addition to his eagerly pursued amusements—the hunt, comedies, banquets—Leo X was fully occupied with plans for filling his always empty coffers, with the family politics of the House of Medici, and with at least one serious enterprise, the defense of Christendom against the Turkish threat; and so he was disinclined to take seriously the "squabble of monks" in Germany.[5] On 3 March 1518, Gabriel della Volta, general-designate of the Augustinians, was directed "to calm down the man" and to put out the rising flame in time. But nothing more than a fraternal admonition by Staupitz seems to have resulted. On the contrary, the Augustinian chapter meeting at Heidelberg in April and May of 1518 turned into a pro-Luther demonstration. Theses composed by Luther on original sin, grace, free will, and the power of the natural man for the good were debated under his direction, with his pupil Leonard Beier as *respondens.* The Heidelberg meeting showed that the German Augustinians were backing Luther. In addition, he was able to gain the support of several of the younger theologians, such as Martin Bucer, a Dominican, and Johannes Brenz, the future reformer of Württemberg.

On 17 May, the day after he returned to Wittenberg, Luther preached on John 16:2: "They are going to put you out of the synagogue." Who-

---

[3] "Non esse christianum dogma, quod redempturi pro amicis confessionalia, vel purgandis Iubileum, possint hec facere absque contritione, error" (N. Paulus, *Johannes Tetzel,* p. 175).

[4] *Opuscula* (Lyons 1558), 105a.

[5] ". . . ricae monachales . . ." cf. P. Kalkoff, *Zu Luthers römischem Prozess,* p. 15, footnote 2. According to the Dominican Matthew Bandello (d. 1562 as Bishop of Agen), Leo X is supposed to have said: "Che fra Martino haveva un belissimo ingegno e che coteste erano i invidie fratesche."

ever dies under an unjust excommunication is saved, even though he dies without the Sacraments. Excommunication can deprive one only of external membership in the Church, not of a share in heavenly treasures. At the same time Luther composed the very submissive accompanying letter to his *Resolutiones* for Leo X.

The Dominican general chapter at Rome became important for the start of the proceedings against Luther in May 1518, when Tetzel was promoted to doctor of theology by authorization of Leo X. In mid-June, at the Pope's request, Sylvester Prierias drew up an opinion, *In praesumptuosas Martini Lutheri conclusiones de potestate papae dialogus*. This hastily composed polemic rightly began with the authority of Church and Pope as the crucial point of controversy, but exaggerated the extent of the infallible doctrinal authority and made so slight a distinction between binding Church teaching and the practice of indulgences, or rather the views of theologians,[6] and was furthermore so biting in tone, that from the outset it rendered any "dialogue" impossible. The *Dialogus* was printed in June and attached to the notification with which, at the beginning of July, the Auditor of the *Camera Apostolica*, Ghinucci, cited Luther to Rome for hearings.

The summons reached the reformer on 7 August through Cardinal Cajetan, who had been at the Diet of Augsburg since 7 July in an effort to win the German estates for the Turkish war. The next day Luther requested the Elector Frederick the Wise to induce the Emperor to have the Pope allow the proceedings to take place in Germany. If Prierias had allegedly jotted down his *Dialogus* in three days, then Luther claimed to have prepared his *Responsio* (WA 1, 647–686) in two days. A work of poor quality, wrote Luther to Spalatin on 31 August 1518, did not deserve a more serious consideration. Thus Luther likewise failed to do justice to the gravity of the situation in style and content. "Both the Pope and a council can err" (WA 1, 656). Scripture, as Augustine writes, is without error. To be sure, up to now the Roman Church, Luther gratefully admits, has actually not deviated from the true faith in her decrees and has clung to the authority of the Bible and of the Fathers (WA 1, 662). Luther regards himself as bound by her decrees. He will not, however, submit to the opinions of the Thomists but will await the decision of Church or council in the question of indulgences (WA 1, 658).

Luther could not count on the good will of Maximilian I. For on 5 August the latter had pointed out to the Pope the danger to the unity of faith caused by Luther's appearance and had promised to back up in the

---

[6] "Qui circa indulgentias dicit, Ecclesiam Romanam non posse facere id, quod de facto facit, haereticus est" (F. Lauchert, *Die italienischen literarischen Gegner,* p. 11).

Empire the measures to be taken by the Church. Without respecting the period of time specified in the summons, Leo X on 23 August issued a brief for Cajetan at Augsburg: the legate was to summon Luther as a notorious heretic. If he should recant, he was to be graciously received. If he failed to appear voluntarily or refused to recant, Cajetan was to arrest him and send him to Rome. In the event that he was unable to arrest him, the legate received authority to declare Luther and his adherents excommunicated (WA 2, 23–25).

At the same time the request was made that Frederick the Wise should surrender the "son of wickedness" to Cajetan or to Rome. The elector exerted himself to have Luther's case dealt with by a court in Germany. From Cajetan he obtained a promise to deal with Luther at Augsburg "paternally" and to release him even if Luther refused to recant. The legate agreed to this concession for political reasons. On 27 August five of the electors—those of Trier and Saxony were not included—had pledged themselves to elect King Charles I of Spain as Maximilian's successor. The Elector Frederick had violently opposed the election of the Habsburg and had thus become a partisan of the Pope, who at any cost wanted to prevent the encirclement of the Papal State by the united Habsburg lands.

On 3 September Leo X announced in consistory his intention of bestowing the Golden Rose on Frederick the Wise. On 10 September the delivery of the distinction to the elector, together with rich indulgences for the Wittenberg castle church, was assigned to a papal notary and secret chamberlain, Karl von Miltitz, a young Saxon noble. But this mission was halted by the arrival of a message from Cajetan reporting Frederick the Wise's opposition to the election of Charles I, as well as his personal intervention in Luther's favor. The Curia agreed to the legate's arrangement about Luther's hearing in Augsburg, but in the brief "Dum nuper" of 11 September placed the responsibility on Cajetan by giving him judicial authority over Luther's case. He was to give the Wittenberg friar a careful interrogation, avoiding any disputation, and, in accord with his findings, acquit or condemn him.

At the end of September Luther received orders from his prince to appear before Cajetan at Augsburg. He arrived there on 7 October 1518. He first waited for the imperial safe-conduct and on 12 October and the two succeeding days went to Cajetan. If any contemporary theologian did, then Cajetan possessed the qualifications for gaining Luther for the Church. He had already written on indulgences in 1517, making it clear that the opinions of canonists and theologians on the subject were widely divergent.[7] At Augsburg in the weeks preceding

---

[7] *Opuscula* (Lyons 1562), 90–97a.

Luther's interrogation he had composed five more *quaestiones* on the subject.[8] He took the trouble to read Luther's writings, and his views on indulgences were moderate. Of course, for Cajetan an indulgence could not be a mere remission of ecclesiastical penalties; it must also free us from the penalties which we have incurred for our sins before the divine justice. Otherwise it would be a dangerous misleading of the faithful. To be concerned about indulgences was not a mark of imperfection. However, it was to be conceded to Luther that an alms is preferable to an indulgence and that anyone who neglects an obligatory alms for the sake of an indulgence commits a sin. Although indulgences for the dead are also based on the Church's power of the keys, they take effect only *per modum suffragii.*

A more detailed study of Luther's writings by Cajetan at Augsburg is attested by several treatises on the Sacrament of penance, excommunication, and purgatory. In a *quaestio* completed on 26 September 1518, Cajetan asks whether, for the fruitful reception of penance, the penitent must have the certainty of faith that he has obtained from God the forgiveness of his sins. After six affirmative arguments, mostly taken *verbatim* from Luther's sermon *De Poenitentia* (WA 1, 323f.), Cajetan stresses that the penitent need not necessarily have faith that he has actually been absolved, but he must believe that the grace of absolution is given to us through the Sacrament of penance.[9] Luther's requirement of the certainty of faith by the one receiving the Sacrament that his sins have been pardoned is regarded by Cajetan as unheard of and of great significance; for him it implies "the establishing of a new Church."[10] It is not the necessity of faith for a fruitful reception of the Sacrament that is questioned. Cajetan rejects the faith that is referred back to the recipient; that is, the uncertainty of faith that pardon has been obtained as the constitutive element in justification.

This "reflexive faith" (P. Hacker), together with the doctrine of the *thesaurus ecclesiae,* was the chief topic of the interrogation in Augsburg. According to Luther's description, he was received on 12 October "very graciously by the Lord Cardinal Legate, almost with too much deference" (WA 2, 7). Cajetan could not and would not engage in a disputation. He demanded recantation and a promise to keep the peace thereafter. In him Luther saw not the legate of the Church but the Thomist, a "member of the opposition," by whom he refused to let himself be

---

[8] Ibid., 97a–105a.

[9] "Non est necessarium ipsum poenitentem tunc habere fidem se esse absolutum, quamquam credere oporteat absolutionis beneficium per poenitentiae sacramentum conferri" (*Opuscula,* Lyons 1562, 109b).

[10] "Hoc enim est novam ecclesiam construere" (*Opuscula,* Lyons 1562, 111a). Cf. P. Hacker, *Das Ich im Glauben bei Martin Luther* (Graz 1966).

committed to "the hallucinations of scholastic opinions" (WA 2, 16). And so a heated dispute arose, nevertheless. The Cardinal demanded the withdrawal of Thesis 58, according to which the treasury of the Church is not identical with the merits of Christ and the saints. Luther refused and insisted upon the thesis: "That the merits of Christ are not the treasury of indulgences, but rather they have amassed it" (WA 2, 13), or, as he expressed it in the *Resolutiones:*

> . . . since Christ is the ransom and the Redeemer of the world, he is therefore truly the only treasury of the Church. But I deny, until shown otherwise, that he is the treasury of indulgences. [WA 1, 608]

It cannot be said that this decisive conversation foundered on hairsplitting distinctions. Luther wanted to make sure that access to the merits of Christ is not restricted to indulgences and even that an indulgence is not the closest and best route to them. But would not and could not the Cardinal concede this? Luther, however, saw a difference between the "treasury of indulgences" and the "treasury of the life-giving grace of God," between what is granted to us on the basis of the "cooperation of the power of the keys and of indulgences" and what we obtain only "through the Holy Spirit and on no account from the Pope" (WA 2, 12). Thus the fundamental difference lay in the concept of the Church. For Luther the Pope is "authority," to whom he subjects himself, as he does to political authority, on the basis of Romans 13:1, and not of Matthew 16:18, so long as such submission is pleasing to God (WA 2, 19f.). In the same breath Luther emphasized that he "awaited the Pope's judgment" and that "truth has power over the Pope too and he [Luther] no longer awaits any man's judgment where he has clearly recognized the judgment of God" (WA 2, 18).

More important for Luther, because it was of immediate significance for salvation, was the question of the certainty of faith in regard to justification proper as the presupposition for it. He claimed to have maintained against Cajetan that it is "an indispensable condition that man believe with firm conviction that he is justified and not to entertain any doubt that he will obtain grace" (WA 2, 13). Here, he says, has been found a new kind of theology and an error.

To these fundamental viewpoints in the case were added great differences in character and mentality. Cardinal Cajetan, a precise and objective Italian, was soon angered by the obstinate seriousness and presumptuous and passionate manner of this German friar, who fancied himself to be so important with his "curious speculations" and who felt, for his part, that he was not taken seriously and understood. According to *Table Talk* 3857 (May 1538), Cajetan shouted at Luther, "Do you think that the Pope cares for Germany?" To Karlstadt Luther wrote from Augsburg:

> Cajetan may be a renowned Thomist, but he is a vague, obscure, and unintelligible theologian or Christian and hence as qualified for judging, understanding, and giving sentence in this matter as an ass is for playing the harp. For that reason my affair is in so much greater danger in that it has such judges who are not only enemies and angered, but also unable to recognize and understand it. [WA, Br 1, 216]

When they separated on the third day, 14 October, Cajetan directed Luther not to come back until he had changed his mind, but at the same time he tried to influence him through Staupitz and Wenceslas Link. They induced Luther to excuse himself to Cajetan in a letter of 17 October for his haughty, biting, and disrespectful conduct and to promise not to treat further of indulgences, provided the others also observed silence. Luther still felt unable to retract, but he asked for a decision from the Pope on the unsettled questions so that the Church could definitely require retraction or faith. In a second letter, on 18 October, Luther announced his departure and also an appeal to the Pope suggested to him by higher authority. This appeal, "from the Pope poorly informed and from his judges to the Most Holy Father to be better informed," he had already registered before a notary and witnesses on 16 October. The doctrine of indulgences, he said, was in many respects unclear. Hence he considered disputation permissible and useful. He had undertaken one and subjected his controversial opinions to the judgment of the Church and of everyone who understood it better, above all, however, to that of the Most Holy Father and Lord, Pope Leo X. On the other hand, he had not been able to give the recantation which the "very learned and amiable Cajetan" demanded, because the points on which he erred had not been pointed out to him (WA 2, 28–33).

This appeal was posted at the Augsburg cathedral on 22 October, after Luther had left the city by night through a small gate in the wall. On 19 November a letter from Cajetan, dated 25 October, reached Frederick the Wise; the cardinal demanded the extradition or the expulsion of Luther. The elector should not, because of a miserable friar, stain the renown of his ancestors with dishonor (WA, Br 1, 235). Luther offered to emigrate for the sake of his prince (WA, Br 1, 245), who seems for the moment to have agreed to the plan or at least to have given it serious consideration. Spalatin advised against a headlong flight to France. But perhaps he had already thought of hiding Luther some-where in Saxony.[11]

In the Constitution "Cum Postquam,"[12] of 9 November 1518, Leo X rendered the binding doctrinal definition on indulgences which Luther had requested. It was based on a draft composed by Cajetan and its essence was: To render any evasion impossible it is here declared as the doctrine of the Roman Church that the Pope, by virtue of his power of the keys, can remit punishments of sin through an indulgence, by distributing the treasure of the merits of Christ and the saints. This indulgence is conceded to the living as absolution and to the dead by intercession. Cajetan published this bull at Linz an der Donau on 13 December. It was printed several times but had no lasting effect. Public opinion was already too strong against indulgences as a means of satisfy-ing curial avarice, and Luther, despite all protestations of submission to the Holy See, was prepared to retract only if convicted of error on the basis of Holy Scripture as he understood it.

Meanwhile, he had advanced another step. On 28 November, in the chapel of the Holy Body of Christ at Wittenberg, he registered his appeal to the council, soon and legitimately to be summoned in the Holy Spirit. This, he said, was above the Pope in matters of faith. In the text Luther followed the Sorbonne, which on 28 March 1518, in the controversy over the Gallican liberties, had likewise appealed to the council. The printing of his appeal was commissioned by Luther, but it was not intended for distribution; it was merely to be kept ready in the event of his excommunication. But as Luther several times asserts,[13] the edition was almost disposed of by the enterprising printer before the reformer had his hands on a copy.

An action of such great import, then, is supposed to have happened more or less by chance, contrary to Luther's intention. Must we not, then, accuse him of an irresponsible negligence? Or are we dealing with a diplomatic maneuver whereby Luther intended to present the Saxon court with a *fait accompli* without having acted contrary to its clear instructions? The case of the *Acta Augustana* was probably similar. Here, according to Luther, Spalatin's prohibition did not arrive until after the document, except for the last sheet, had already been distrib-uted (*WA, Br* 1, 263; 281). But Luther might have tempted fate in the sense that he left the decision in the balance in the secret hope that it

---

[11] I. Hoss, *Georg Spalatin*, p. 141.

[12] P. Kalkoff, "Die von Cajetan verfasste Ablassdekretale," *ARG*, 9 (1911f.), 142–171; N. Paulus, "Die Ablassdekretale Leos X. vom Jahre 1518," *ZKTh* 37 (1913), 394–400.

[13] Letter of 18 December 1518 to W. Link (*WA, Br* 1, 270) and of 20 December to Spalatin (*WA, Br* 1, 280f.).

would be determined in his favor by other factors. Doubtless he was much more anxious and more inwardly troubled than his often bold and decisive actions and noisy language lead one to suppose. We must allow that Luther perhaps often consciously made any retreat impossible and burned his bridges behind him, while in other cases he carried matters too far but then shrank from the ultimate consequences. When these, nevertheless, occurred, due to the inner or the external dynamics of the facts, he accepted them and even greeted them as God's will. Luther knew in what great demand his books and pamphlets were, and he had enough experience with printers to foresee what would happen in the printing of his appeal. Hence what he wrote to Wenceslas Link—that, to his great displeasure, the printer had distributed the appeal, that he had intended to keep the printed copy for himself but God had disposed otherwise[14]—is only superficially credible. Just as he had assured the Pope that the indulgence theses had been widely circulated against his will but that he could now no longer do away with them (WA 1, 529), so now he wrote to Spalatin in regard to the publication of his appeal to the council: "What has once happened I cannot undo" (WA, Br 1, 281).

In these weeks Luther again thought of emigrating. He was probably not only concerned not to burden his prince with his affairs but also aimed to obtain liberty of action and to be freed from the network of petty tactical considerations to which his connection with the Saxon court forced him again and again. At this very time (18 December 1518) he thus expressed himself to Wenceslas Link: "I do not know the source of these ideas. In my judgment the case has not yet begun and even less can the lords at Rome yet anticipate its end." And he even entertained misgivings "that the true Antichrist, to whom Paul refers, rules in the Roman Curia. Today I already believe it possible to prove that Rome is worse than the Turk" (WA, Br 1, 270).

The Curia confronted a twofold task: to render the heretic Luther harmless and to gain his prince as an ally on the tax for the campaign against the Turks and especially on the question of the imperial succession. It was still uncertain whether both goals could be pursued with all energy simultaneously, that is, whether Frederick the Wise would drop Luther. To clarify the matter—in other words, to investigate the attitude of the elector (WA, Br 1, 274)—was the commission entrusted to the papal chamberlain, Karl von Miltitz. In mid-November he was finally started on his way to Cajetan at Augsburg, with the Golden Rose, rich indulgences, and a bull excommunicating Luther. But he did not find the

---

[14] "Edidit impressor noster Appellationem mean ad concilium, multa et magna displicentia mea; sed actum est. Volui impressam apud me servare. Deus autem alia cogitat" (WA, Br 1, 270).

legate, by whose instructions he was supposed to be strictly bound. Hence he deposited the Golden Rose and the papal bulls with the Fuggers and in mid-December joined the electoral councillor Degenhard Pfeffinger, who was returning to the court of Frederick the Wise. En route he could not but ascertain how very much German sentiment favored Luther. But this did not cause the conceited, ambitious, and intellectually mediocre courtier to maintain his reserve. On the contrary, he boasted loudly of his alleged commissions and related Roman gossip, according to which the Pope did not think much of Tetzel or of Prierias.

On 28 December Miltitz reached Altenburg, the residence of Frederick the Wise. A short time earlier, on 8 December—or, according to the date which Kalkoff prefers,[15] on 18 December—the elector had finally replied to Cajetan, refusing to surrender or to expel his professor. Luther, he said, had not been convicted of heresy; on the contrary, he was open to correction and ready for a disputation. Thus had Frederick the Wise set himself up as Luther's protector, at the same time leaving the proceedings against him open. With this delaying tactic, the arrival of the pompous chamberlain, who, contrary to his instructions, was posing as mediator, was not unwelcome. Frederick brought about a meeting of Luther and Miltitz on 4 and 5 January 1519 which resulted in the following agreement: both parties were henceforth forbidden "to preach about, write about, or discuss the matter," and Miltitz would induce the Pope to appoint a bishop to designate the erroneous articles for Luther's recantation (WA, Br 294; 299). Frederick the Wise and Luther did not take the thoughtless officiousness of the "nuncio" very seriously but agreed to the "Miltitziad," because they thereby hoped to achieve their goal of having Luther's case dealt with in Germany, and they at least gained time. In agreement with the elector, Miltitz on 12 June offered the function of arbiter to Richard von Greiffenklau, Archbishop of Trier. In accord with his tactics of putting the blame for the increasing gravity of the situation on the Dominicans, Cajetan and Tetzel, Miltitz reprimanded Tetzel and declared that he would accuse him at Rome of immorality and unlawful personal acquisition of indulgence funds. The indulgence preacher withdrew entirely into the shadows and died on 11 August 1519.

His unprecedented and arbitrary action in bargaining with the friar Martin Luther, who had been declared a heretic by the Pope, ought to have brought down on Miltitz severe criticism from Cajetan and the Curia. But the death of Emperor Maximilian I on 12 January 1519 had created a new situation and was destined to be the prelude to what

---

[15] ZKG 27 (1906), 325ff.

Kalkoff calls the "greatest diplomatic campaign" of the age, to which everything else, including Luther's trial, had to give way. As early as 23 January 1519 Cajetan received from Leo X instructions to prevent the election of Charles of Spain by any means. Thus the good will of Frederick the Wise must be gained. Hence the intrigues of Miltitz, with no binding force, did not do the Curia any harm; he was at least catered to and temporarily found a willing ear for his frivolous optimism. Cajetan's own role was more difficult: to have to suppress the condemnatory judgment against Luther that was in his hands and to have to offer the imperial crown to the heretic's protector. The highly embellished reports made by Miltitz provided Leo X with a pretext for pretending in a brief of 29 March 1519 that Luther was prepared to recant and for extending to him a fatherly invitation. Before the Pope, the vicar of Christ, he could make the retraction from which he had been deterred at Augsburg only by Cajetan's severity and partisan favoring of Tetzel (WA, Br 364f.). If that was the way matters were, then the Pope had no further reason to be annoyed with Frederick the Wise for patronizing the heretic. His wooing of the elector reached its culmination in the message which Miltitz had to deliver eight days before the election.[16] The elector was urgently requested to exert himself for the election of the King of France. If the King's election was impossible, Frederick should himself accept the imperial crown. In return, the Pope would do anything in his power for him and would make one of his friends a cardinal.[17] In Rome at this time Luther was considered the friend of the elector. Thus this could have been a hint that he would be created a cardinal.

Out of concern for the Papal State and the position of the Medici in Italy, then, the Pope behaved as though Luther and his protectors had not been declared heretics. He dropped the proceedings for almost a year and gave the Lutheran movement time to strike deeper roots; he held back the bull of excommunication and instead offered the imperial crown and the red hat.

> If the Roman Court, despite the warnings of Cajetan, forgot, so to speak, the danger which threatened the whole Church from this Martin Luther Eleutherius and put aside the handling of this secular crisis in favor of the momentary exigencies of the papacy's Italian policy, this is perhaps the greatest proof of all that Luther and the opposition were correct when they reproached the Church of Christ for having degenerated into an institution of legal and wordly authority.[18]

[16] On 21 June; P. Kalkoff in ZKG 25 (1904), 413, footnote 3.
[17] Deutsche Reichstagsakten, Jüngere Reihe, I, ed. A. Kluckhohn (Gotha 1893), 824.

The Leipzig Disputation

Though political considerations caused the shelving of the proceedings against Luther, the controversy of intellects that he had stirred up was not to be easily appeased. Some theses which Luther's Wittenberg colleague Andreas von Karlstadt had composed against Eck's *Obelisci* afforded Eck the welcome opportunity in August 1518 to issue an invitation for a debate. In October the professor from Ingolstadt had had a relatively amicable conversation with Luther. They agreed to propose Erfurt and Leipzig to Karlstadt as places for the disputation. Karlstadt left the final choice to Eck, who in December asked the Leipzig theological faculty and Duke Georg of Saxony to permit the disputation there. The faculty and the local Ordinary, Bishop Adolf of Merseburg, were opposed, but Duke Georg eagerly favored it and was able to persuade the faculty to agree. That same month Eck had published twelve theses on penance, indulgences, the treasury of the Church, and purgatory. Ostensibly against Karlstadt, in reality they were against Luther and his view of the authority of the Pope and the Church. Thus, for example, Thesis 12 (later 13) stated: "It is false to assert that before the time of Silvester [314–355] the Roman Church did not yet have supremacy over the other churches."[19] Despite his understanding with Miltitz, Luther published opposing theses (*WA* 2, 160f.), and announced that he would participate in the disputation. With reference to Eck's counter-thesis 13, he claimed that the primacy of the Roman Church was demonstrated by forged papal decretals which were only four hundred years old. To the worried Spalatin he wrote:

> I hide much and hold back, for the sake of the elector and of the university, what, if I were elsewhere, I would spew forth onto the destroyer of Scripture and of the Church, onto Rome, or rather onto Babylon. It is impossible, my dear Spalatin, to deal with the truth of Scripture and the Church without wounding this monster. Do not expect, then, that I will be silent and calm, for otherwise you would have to want me to abandon theology entirely. [*WA, BR* 351]

Some days later, on 5 March, he assured Spalatin that it had never entered his mind to separate from the Apostolic See in Rome. He was agreed to its being called and being the lord of all. A person must also honor and bear with the Turks because of the power bestowed by God (*WA, Br* 1, 356). Hence at that time the papacy was for Luther only a

---

[18] R. Stadelmann, *Das Zeitalter der Reformation, Handbuch der Geschichte,* ed. Brandt–Meyer–Just, II (Constance 1954) 49.

[19] Against Luther's *Resolutiones,* concl. 22 (*WA* 1, 571).

ruling power like any secular authority. But this was not all. On March 13 he whispered to Spalatin[20] that in his study of the decretals for the disputation he had asked himself whether the Pope was not the Antichrist or at least his envoy, since in his decrees he so wretchedly crucified Christ, that is, the truth.

The disputation took place at the Pleissenburg at Leipzig and lasted from 27 June to 16 July 1519. Luther was admitted to it by the Duke of Saxony only at the last moment and through Eck's intervention. First Eck and Karlstadt debated on predestination. Then the controversy between Eck and Luther came to a climax on the problems of divine law, the papal primacy, and the authority of councils. According to Luther, councils could err and had erred; for example, the Council of Constance had been wrong in condemning Hus. Thereby was Scripture set up as the sole source of faith and *sola scriptura* as the formal principle of the Reformation. Luther no longer recognized a supreme ecclesiastical teaching authority which renders a binding interpretation of Scripture. In the disputation Eck's good memory and dialectical skill served him very well. If through his cold precision Eck risked driving his opponent to heretical conclusions and committing him to heresy, still Eck has the merit, granted the absence of dogmatic clarity in his day, of having made it clear that Luther implied, not reform, but an attack on the constitution of the Church.

CHAPTER 5

Luther's Reform Writings of 1520

After the Leipzig Disputation Luther rapidly became the hero and spokesman of the nation. He himself was filled with an apocalyptic spirit and imagined himself called to confront the Antichrist. This outlook gave his words their prophetic solemnity, urgency, and certainty. Knights, townsmen, and peasants, hardly qualified to grasp the reformer's essential religious concern, were carried along by the conviction that Luther would bring about the long-desired reform of Church and Empire. By reform was also understood the realization of one's own social and political aims. From everywhere students flocked to the University of Wittenberg. In 1518, at Luther's urging, the arts faculty had undergone reform in the direction of humanism, and Melanchthon was occupying the chair of Greek. In turn the students were active heralds of Lutheran doctrine to the remotest corner of the Empire.

[20] ". . . in aurem tibi loquor" (*WA, Br* 1, 359).

In addition, printing offered quite new possibilities for propaganda. As early as 1518 the humanist Johannes Froben at Basel had brought out a complete edition of Luther's Latin works in a large number of copies. New, enlarged editions appeared in 1520 at Strasbourg and Basel. At Basel in May 1520 and at Strasbourg in July collections of Luther's German works were made available and sold well. Occasionally Luther employed as many as three printers to make his works available. They were mostly controversial writings, called for by some event of the moment and hastily composed, assailing abuses or parrying an attack. But there were also many works of edification, testimonies to his own religious experiences and at the same time pastoral aids for the many who applied to him. Luther was fully conversant with the language of the people. He was often coarse and full of bitter mockery, never boring and ponderous like the involved disputations of scholastic theology.

The year 1520 brought the first climax in his journalistic activity. Deserving of special mention among his pastoral pieces at the end of 1519 are the sermons on the three Sacraments which alone Luther would henceforth regard as true Sacraments: that on penance (WA 2, 713–723), that on baptism (WA 2, 727–737), and that on the venerable Sacrament of the Holy and True Body of Christ and on fellowship (WA 2, 742–758). Whether Luther still held to the sacramental character of penance in the accepted sense is open to question. From the purely declaratory meaning of absolution, already stressed in the indulgence theses, he deduced that any lay person could grant absolution:

> As a result of number 9 it follows that in the Sacrament of penance and the remission of guilt a pope or bishop does no more than the lowliest priest; in fact, if no priest is at hand every Christian can do as much, even though only a woman or a child. If any Christian says to you, "God forgives you your sins . . ." and you are able to seize upon that word with a firm faith, then God is speaking to you and in the same faith you are indeed absolved. Thus everything rests entirely in the faith in God's word. [WA 2, 716]

In regard to baptism and the Eucharist, the "two foremost Sacraments in the Church," Luther stresses the subjective acquiring of the grace offered in them and their fruitful effect. The *opus operatum* must become *opus operantis* in faith; otherwise it only produces harm, just as the Cross of Christ became misfortune for the Jews. Luther rejected Spalatin's suggestion that he should write on the other Sacraments also, because, he said, there is no basis for them in Scripture: "For me there is no other Sacrament. For there only exists a Sacrament where there exists an express divine promise for the exercise of faith" (WA, Br 1, 595).

In the spring of 1520, at Spalatin's request, Luther replied to the charge that, by his teaching on justification by faith alone, he prejudiced works or even rendered them contemptible. In the long sermon "On good works," dealing with the relation of faith and works (WA 6, 202–276), he supplied the laity with copious advice for a good Christian life and activity. The most eminent of all works is faith (John 6:28). It is, however, not a good work in addition to others, but the source of all good works. These are fruits of faith, which "brings with it charity, peace, joy, and hope." The important thing is not the size of the external work; all that we do can become a good work, if only it has faith as its motivating cause. "For if justice exists in faith, it is clear that faith alone fulfills all commands and makes all their works justified" (WA 6, 211). If we possessed the living faith, "we would not need any law, but each of himself would do good works at all times" (WA 6, 213). But so long as we do not have this liberty of faith for good works, we need laws and admonitions, and, like children, we must be motivated to good works by ceremonies and promises. Faith, however, does not spring from the works, but is a gift of Christ.

> See! You must then form Christ in you and behold how in him God holds out his mercy to you and offers it without any merits being present in you, and from such a picture of his grace you must obtain faith and confidence in the remission of all your sins. Hence, faith does not begin with works, they do not create it, but it must flow from the blood, wounds, and death of Christ. [WA 6, 216]

Faith proves itself in daily life, in obedience to God's command. With that we have our hands full; there is no further need of works which we impose upon ourselves. The works imposed upon me "do not shine and glisten" as do the voluntary works of the "new saints." They are the more sublime and the better the less they "glisten" and "take place so quietly and secretly that no one but God alone is aware of them." In this first and perhaps most important treatise of the decisive year 1520—a treatise that was not heeded in accord with its significance—Luther was moving among the ideas of German mysticism, especially of Tauler. Through all the polemic it remains clear that he did not reject works as such, but only a piety of works that had become mechanical in many respects.

Not his doctrine of justification but his teaching on the Church led ever more clearly to the break. Luther had been struggling for some time with the idea of the Pope as Antichrist.[1] In February 1520 he

---

[1] Letter to W. Link of 18 December 1518 (WA, Br 1, 270).

became acquainted with Ulrich von Hutten's new edition of Lorenzo Valla's work on the alleged Donation of Constantine (1440). On the strength of this he wrote to Spalatin on 24 February: "I am so afraid that I have almost no doubts now that the pope is really the Antichrist whom the world is expecting according to the general opinion" (*WA, Br* 2, 48f.). At the same time there came into Luther's hands the *Epithoma responsionis ad Lutherum* (1519) of Sylvester Prierias, with its strong emphasis on papal primacy and infallibility. In May appeared the Franciscan Augustine Alveldt's *Super apostolica sede*, which was answered by Luther's pupil, Johannes Lonicer. When Alveldt thereupon published in German a revised edition of his work, Luther personally wrote a violent rejoinder: *Von dem Papsttum zu Rome wider den hochberühmten Romanisten zu Leipzig* (1520; *WA* 6, 285–324). In it Luther developed his doctrine of the Church: Christianity, as the congregation of all believers in Christ, is not a "corporal" collection but one "of hearts in one faith." This "spiritual unity" is of itself alone sufficient to constitute Christianity. Baptism and the Gospel are its signs in the world. This Christianity, which alone is the true Church, has no head on earth, "but only Christ in heaven is the head here and alone rules." Bishops are messengers and by divine disposition are all equal. Only by human arrangement is "one above another in the visible Church." Matthew 16:18 must be interpreted by Matthew 18:18. Then it is clear that the keys were given to Saint Peter, not for himself alone, but vicariously for the whole community. Accordingly, the Pope, permitted by God, must be endured in all patience, "as though the Turk were over us."

Luther felt that he would

> like kings, princes, and the whole nobility to intervene so that the road would be closed to the scoundrels of Rome. How has Roman greed gone so far that it monopolizes all institutions, bishoprics, and feudal holdings of our fathers? Who has ever heard or read of such an unspeakable robbery? [*WA* 6, 322]

If Luther was here touching the national resentment against the Curia, which had been so often expressed in the *gravamina* of the German nation, he unequivocally made himself the spokesman of these desires and complaints in the first of the three great statements of programs in the summer of 1520, *An den christlichen Adel deutscher Nation von des christlichen Standes Besserung*. On 7 June 1520 he wrote to Spalatin: "I am planning to issue a pamphlet, addressed to the Emperor Charles and the nobility of all Germany, against the tyranny and unworthiness of the Roman Curia" (*WA, Br* 2, 120). The introductory first part deals with razing the three walls behind which the "Romanists," that is, the Curia, are entrenched in order to avoid any reform. These are: (1) the spiritual power is superior to the secular; (2) only the Pope has the right to interpret Scripture; (3) only he can convoke a legitimate council. In contrast to this, Luther stresses the universal priesthood; he will recognize no other special priesthood.

> For all Christians belong to the true spiritual estate, and among them there is no distinction except that of function. . . . This is so because we have one baptism, one Gospel, one faith . . . which alone make the spiritual and Christian people. . . . For what emerges from baptism may boast that it has already been consecrated as priest, bishop, and pope, although it is not seemly for everyone to exercise such a function . . . . It follows that among lay persons, priests, princes, bishops, and, as they say, clergy and people of the world there is fundamentally no other distinction than that of function (service) or of work, and not that of station. [WA 6, 407f.]

If Pope and bishops have failed, then it is the duty of the so-called secular estates to provide a remedy:

> Therefore, when necessity requires and the pope is vexatious to Christendom, the first person who is able should, as a true member of the entire body, do what he can so that a legitimate and free council may take place. None can do this better than the secular sword, especially since they are now also fellow-Christians, fellow-priests, equally spiritual, equally powerful in all things, and must let their office and work, which they hold from God over everyone, operate freely where there is need and use. [WA 6, 413] Hence, dear Germans, let us wake up and fear God more than men, so that we may not share in guilt against all the poor souls who are so miserably lost through the infamous and diabolical rule of the Romans. [WA 6, 415]

There follows a list of accusations, especially against the "Roman greed and see of robbers." They culminate in the charge that Pope and Curia do not obey their own canon law (WA 6, 418). In the third part Luther develops in twenty-eight points a reform program, extending from the abolition of annates, reservations, celibacy, and the numerous feast days to the reform of universities and even the closing of brothels. All—nobles, peasants, and the poor in the cities—could here consider the redress of their grievances. What Luther had struggled with in his personal anxieties of conscience became in this treatise the concern of the nation. Accordingly, readers scrambled to obtain it. The sale— 4,000 copies in the first week—was unprecedented.

In the second great statement of program, *De captivitate Babylonica ecclesiae praeludium* (October 1520), one of Luther's few writings on systematic theology, he directed himself to theologians. Its occasion was a work by Alveldt, *Tractatus de communione sub utraque specie* (June 1520), but it went far beyond that and was a discussion of the sacramental doctrine of the Catholic Church. Luther admits only three valid Sacraments—baptism, penance, and communion—but they have been "brought by the Roman Court into a wretched prison." The Sacrament of the Eucharist is in a threefold captivity: the refusal of the other species, the doctrine of transubstantiation, and the concept of communion as a sacrifice. Luther does not claim that the second species should be given unconditionally and that the doctrine of transubstantiation is false, but he wants freedom to be preserved. It is Roman tyranny that forbids the chalice to the laity or makes an opinion of Aquinas an article of faith. Luther stresses the true presence of the body of Christ but he wants to leave open the "how." To him the presence of the body of Christ in, with, and under the bread, analogous to the imminence of the divinity in Christ's humanity, is very obvious.

On the other hand, the third prison of the Sacrament is a thoroughly impious abuse and a source of further, more deeply rooted evils. Luther here repeats ideas from the "Sermon on the New Covenant, that is, on the Mass" (1520). He demands a return to the "first and simple institution" of Christ, to his word. According to this, the Sacrament of the altar is a covenant, in which the remission of sins is granted to us. The words of the narrative of the institution are the essence and the power of the Mass and at the same time the totality and epitome of the whole Gospel.

> Behold, O sinful man, fit for damnation, From the genuine and undeserved love whereby I love you. . . . I promise you by these words, before you have merited and desired anything, forgiveness of all your sins and eternal life. And in order that you may entirely be sure of this irrevocable promise of mine I will yield my life and pour out my blood and confirm this promise by death itself and leave them both as a sign and memorial of this promise. As often as you make use of this, you should be mindful of me and esteem, praise, and thank this love and gentleness of mine toward you. [WA 6, 515]

Instead of accepting this bequest in faith, men have, according to Luther, made of it a sacrifice, a work, or, in other words, something which they give to God.

> For there should be no one so insane as to say that he does a good work who comes poor and needy and claims from the hand of the rich an alms of the divine promise through the hand of the priest

offered to all men. Hence, it is certain that the Mass is not a sacrifice. [*WA* 6, 523]

In Christ, the Lord of the Eucharist, Luther sees God simply and not the God-Man, the Mediator. Thus the Eucharist is meant by God for us and not, through Christ the Mediator, for the Father also. Hence Luther likewise sees no inner bond of the community's worship of praise and thanksgiving, the Eucharist, with the Sacrament.

> Therefore, these two are not to be confused—the Mass and prayer, the Sacrament and work, the covenant and the sacrifice. For the one comes to us from God through the priest's ministry and requires faith. The other comes from our faith to God through the priests and asks a favorable hearing. [*WA* 6, 526]

In these years of his attack on the late medieval sacramental practice Luther strongly emphasizes faith, whereby we answer the *verbum sacramenti,* the promise of Christ. In this the real presence, as the seal and pledge of the promise, moves into the background. But Luther holds to the traditional concept of the Sacrament, even when he says:

> And as the word is more important than the sign, so also is there more value to the covenant than to the Sacrament. For a man can have the word or the covenant and make use of it without the sign or the Sacrament. "Believe," says Augustine, "and you have eaten." [*WA* 6, 518]

For by the word is here meant the *verbum sacramenti* and by the Sacrament the *sacramentum tantum.* According to the scholastic teaching on the Sacraments, only the word transforms the sign into a Sacrament and the word is more important than the sign. According to Aquinas, the Sacrament produces its sanctifying effect when the sign touches the body and the word is believed (*Summa Theologiae* III, q. 60, a. 6). Accordingly, scholastic theology is acquainted with a *manducare spiritualiter Christum* in faith, whereas the mere sacramental reception without faith is a sin. Despite his polemic against the concepts *opus operatum* and *opus operantis,* Luther held to what was meant by them. The Sacrament is effected independently of the worthiness of the minister, who is an instrument acting in God's stead, and it produces fruit, though of opposite sorts, in the believer and the unbeliever.[2]

This polemic, with its vehement rejection of the sacrifice of the Mass and its denial of four Sacraments, not only assailed essential doctrines of faith but also amounted to an elimination of the very heart of the

---

[2] ". . . manet tamen semper idem sacramentum et testamentum, quod in credente operatur suum opus, in incredulo operatur alienum opus" (*WA* 6, 526).

Church's worship and the individual's piety. Thus it provoked scandal and contributed fundamentally to a clarification of positions. Many an old friend, such as Staupitz, recoiled in horror. Erasmus felt that before the appearance of this tract the break could have been healed, and Johann Glapion, the confessor of Emperor Charles V, was of the same opinion. The University of Paris issued a public protest against the polemic, and in 1521 King Henry VIII of England composed his *Assertio septem sacramentorum,* which gained for him the papal designation of *Defensor Fidei.* Thomas Murner, a Franciscan opponent of Luther, expected to turn public opinion against Luther merely by translating the *De Captivitate* into German without comment.

The third statement of program, *Von der Freiheit eines Christenmenschen* (November 1520), was written at the suggestion of Karl von Miltitz after the publication of "Exsurge Domine," the bull threatening excommunication, to convince the Pope of Luther's orthodoxy and good will. Hence in it polemic yields to a warm, popular exposition of the Christian ideal of life. The Christian is a free man, lord over all things and subject to no one, to the extent that he accepts by faith the Gospel, that is, the promises of Christ. But since "on earth there is only a beginning and a progressing," we have received only the first-fruits of the Spirit and thus, in addition, the commandments and laws of God must be observed. But man cannot become pious and saved through observing them, through works. For works do not make a man pious, but a good and pious man makes works good and pious. However, the commandments lead us to a recognition of sin and to contrition. "And so man is justified and lifted up by faith in the divine words, when he is humbled by fear of God's command and has arrived at self-knowledge" (*WA* 7, 34). The Christian furthermore submits to the law in order to serve his neighbor. Although he is entirely free, he must "willingly again make himself a servant in order to aid his neighbor . . . . Hence from faith flow love and desire for God and from love a free, willing, and joyful life of serving one's neighbor without recompense" (*WA* 7, 35f.). Thus the Christian is "a servant of all things and subject to everyone."

CHAPTER 6

The Excommunicated Friar before the Diet of Worms

With the election on 28 June 1519 of the King of Spain as Emperor Charles V, the Curia's consideration toward Frederick the Wise came to an end. But other political worries, financial distress, and above all his private entertainments deterred Leo X from an energetic pursuit of

Luther's case. It was not until February 1520 that the Roman proceedings entered a new stage. Under the presidency of two cardinals, the theologian Cajetan and the canonist Accolti, three committees in succession examined Luther's teaching. Johannes Eck played a decisive role in the third, which convened at the end of April. In December 1519 the Cardinal of Tortosa, Adrian of Utrecht, had advised that in the condemnation of Luther not a word should be changed from Luther's own formulation, and this suggestion was to a great extent followed. The opinions handed down by the University of Cologne on 30 August 1519, and by that of Louvain on 7 November, were used as supporting material. The last-named listed the objectionable propositions in Luther's own words, and six of these passed *verbatim* into the papal bull. The draft submitted by the third committee was discussed in consistory from 21 May to 1 June 1520, and was finally released as the Bull "Exsurge Domine," dated 15 June 1520.

The bull condemned forty-one propositions extracted from Luther's writings as "heretical, scandalous, false, offensive to pious ears, misleading to simple folk, and contrary to Catholic doctrine," without indicating under which category of this very broad gamut of censures the individual propositions fell. Hence it remained unclear where the area of opinions, dangerous but still open to discussion, ceased and heresy began. The condemnation of the latter was thereby deprived of real effect. Johannes Eck himself had to concede this three years later, when in his reform opinion for the Pope he asked for a new bull in which only the most serious errors would be refuted by full recourse to Holy Scripture. In "Exsurge Domine," he said, much remained obscure; some of the condemned propositions were so vague and insignificant that even scholars could not understand why they had been condemned.[1] This inadequacy of the bull was the more consequential in that it was "the sole authoritative papal intervention in the Lutheran affair right up to the Council of Trent."[2]

Luther was given sixty days to recant—the time to be counted from the publication of the bull in the Saxon bishoprics—and his writings that contained the offensive teachings were to be burned. The Italian humanist Girolamo Aleander[3] and Johannes Eck were deputed to pub-

---

[1] "Nam etsi in bulla priori multa fuerint damnata, tamen aliqua videbantur adeo obscura, immo quaedam adeo indifferentia, ut visum fuerit quandoque viris etiam doctissimis partem contrariam veriorem esse quam ea quae damnata fuerint" (*Acta Reformationis catholicae* I, ed. G. Pfeilschifter, Regensburg 1959, 143).

[2] H. Jedin, *A History of the Council of Trent* I (St. Louis 1957), 192.

[3] Born at Motta (Friuli) in 1480, he was, following his studies in the humanities, active as a teacher at the universities of Padua, Venice, Paris, and Orléans. In 1516 he entered the service of the Roman Curia, and in July 1519 he was made prefect of the Vatican

licize the bull and its threat of excommunication in Germany. On 17 July they were appointed nuncios and Eck was also made a protonotary.

In Germany, especially South Germany,[4] the promulgation of the bull ran into difficulties because the bishops were uninterested and feared that it would cause trouble. In Central Germany Eck encountered dangerous opposition. He had to learn at his own peril how very general the resentment against the Curia was. He was able to have the bull posted in Meissen on 21 September and in Merseburg and Brandenburg a few days later. But at Leipzig the university refused publication and the students rioted, while at Erfurt they stormed the printer's and threw the copies they seized into the river. On 3 October Eck sent the bull to the University of Wittenberg, where the matter was pigeonholed. No one wanted to do anything until the attitude of the elector, who was in the west, on his way to Charles V's coronation at Aachen, became known.

At this time Karl von Miltitz was again busy on Luther's behalf. He apparently begrudged Eck the role of papal nuncio and now intended, following Eck's ill luck with the proclamation of the bull, to come forth on his own again as peacemaker and acquire the credit of having achieved reconciliation. On 12 October 1520, at Lichtenburg an der Elbe, Miltitz induced Luther to send Leo X a letter asserting that he had never intended to attack the person of the Pope but had only meant to defend himself against his opponents. Like Tetzel in 1519, Johannes Eck was now to be made the scapegoat. To avoid the impression that Luther's letter had been instigated only by Eck's publication of the bull, the letter was to be predated 6 September. With it Luther was to convey to the Pope his homage in the form of a treatise. For this purpose *Von der Freiheit eines Christenmenschen* was composed, in which Luther aimed to offer "the sum total of a Christian life" (*WA* 7, 11).

Luther's letter to Leo X is a questionable document in so far as Luther, who on other occasions had already termed the Pope the Antichrist, designates him as "Most Holy Father" and "pious Leo" and wants to be regarded as one who has never undertaken anything bad against the person of the Pope and is so well disposed toward him that he desires and wishes the very best for him. But at the same time Luther

---

Library. The important but excessively ambitious humanist was spiritually concerned with the Catholic Reform only in his later years. From the autumn of 1536 he was a member of the great reform commission and a cardinal. He died in Rome on 1 February 1542.

[4] The bull, printed at Eck's expense, was not promulgated at Augsburg until 30 December 1520 (*ZKG* 37 [1918], 159). The Bishop of Freising did not issue the order of promulgation until 10 January 1521 (*Zeitschrift für Bücherfreunde*, NF, 9[1918], 198). Cf. Jedin, op. cit., I, 176ff.

engaged in wild ravings against the Roman Curia. It is worse than Sodom, Gomorrah, or Babylon; nothing but corruption has proceeded thence for years:

> The Roman See is through. God's anger has overtaken it without cessation. It is hostile to the general council. It refuses to be taught or to be reformed and yet cannot stop its mad and unchristian conduct. . . . That is why I have always regretted, O pious Leo, that you have become pope at this time, you who would surely be worthy to be pope in a better age. The Roman See is not worthy of you and the likes of you, but the evil spirit ought to be pope. . . . O most unfortunate Leo, who sit in the most perilous see, I truly speak the truth to you, for I desire your good. [WA 7, 5f.]

Like Saint Bernard, Luther presumes to teach the Pope. A recantation of his teaching, however, is out of the question: "But that I should disavow my teaching—it won't happen" (WA 7, 9).

This distinction between the Pope and the intrigues of the Curia or of Eck was also drawn in the two other writings Luther was composing during the second half of October: a polemic against Eck, *Von den neuen Eckischen Bullen und Lügen* (WA 6, 579–594), and the Latin rejoinder to "Exsurge Domine," *Adversus execrabilem Antichristi bullam* (WA 6, 597–612). Luther pretended, contrary to his own belief,[5] to doubt the authenticity of the bull. But whoever had composed it, he had no doubt, he said, that it came from Antichrist and hence he meant to treat it as the work of Antichrist:

> I defy you, Leo X, and you too, cardinals, and all other persons who are of importance at the Curia, and say to your face: If this bull really came forth under your name with your knowledge, I admonish you by virtue of the power which I, like all other Christians, have received through baptism: Repent and desist from such satanic blasphemies against God, and do so quickly. Otherwise you must know that I, with all other worshippers of Christ, regard the See of Rome as possessed by Satan and as the throne of Antichrist and will no longer obey or be bound to it, for it is the chief and mortal foe of Christ. If you persevere in this madness, I rather condemn you and hand you over, together with this bull and your decretals, to Satan for the destruction of the flesh that your spirit may be saved with us on the day of the Lord. In the name of him whom you persecute, Jesus Christ our Lord. [WA 6, 604]

At the end of the German version, *Wider die Bulle des Endchristes* (WA 6, 614–629), on the other hand, Luther completely drops the fiction of

---

[5] Cf. letter of 11 October 1520 to Spalatin (WA, Br 2, 195).

spuriousness: "If the pope will not repudiate and condemn the bull and punish Eck and his associates, who observe such a bull, then no one should be in doubt that he is the enemy of God, persecutor of Christ, destroyer of Christianity, and the real Antichrist" (WA 6, 629).

In the western part of the Empire, Aleander was more successful in promulgating the bull. On 28 September 1520, at Antwerp, he succeeded in inducing Charles V to issue an edict against heresy for his Burgundian hereditary lands. Lutheran writings were solemnly burned at Louvain on 8 October and at Liège on 15 October. The coronation of Charles V on 23 October brought Aleander into the Rhineland, where he found some opposition. On 29 October he visited Cologne. A number of princes and other personages were staying here after the coronation, including Frederick the Wise, who had remained here because of illness instead of going on to the coronation. At first Frederick declined to receive Aleander, but on 4 November the nuncio succeeded in speaking with the elector, demanding that he surrender Luther and burn his writings. Frederick thereupon consulted with Erasmus, who was also at Cologne. Erasmus expressed himself quite superficially but in a way that amused the elector. Luther, he said, had sinned on two points: he had struck the Pope on his crown and the friars in the belly. On 6 November the elector had his reply sent to Aleander. He had never made common cause with Luther's affair and would be greatly displeased if Luther had written anything improper against the Pope. But without doubt Luther would have been accommodating to the Archbishop of Trier as papal deputy if the latter had summoned him under a safe-conduct, and the same disposition was still to be expected of him. When the report of the elector's position reached Wittenberg, in consequence people were even less eager to heed the bull.

On 12 November Luther's books were burned in Cologne at the instigation of Aleander. However, Luther's adherents seem to have slipped so much waste paper and scholastic codices into the executioner's hands that few of Luther's writings were actually committed to the flames. This too indicates how unpopular the proceedings against Luther were. Just the same it became clear that Rome had begun to take the battle against the Lutheran heresy seriously, and not a few on both sides finally understood its importance.

On 2 or 3 December Spalatin visited Luther in Wittenberg and ascertained that he was determined to burn the papal bull together with some books of canon law if, as at Cologne and Liège, there was any move to burn his books at Leipzig also. Spalatin informed Frederick the Wise, but before the latter replied Luther proceeded to act. On 10 December a Latin notice composed by Melanchthon was posted at the parish church in Wittenberg: Whoever was devoted to seeking the truth of the

Gospel should be at the Holy Cross Chapel in front of the Elster Gate at nine o'clock, when the papal decretals and the books of the scholastics would be burned. There was no mention of the bull. The site was the city's knacker's yard, close to the Elbe, the usual place for such undertakings. Several volumes of canon law, a theological *Summa,* and writings of Eck and Emser were burned first. Then Luther approached the pyre and threw a small book into the flames, allegedly saying at the same time: "Quoniam tu turbasti sanctam veritatem Dei, conturbet te hodie Dominus in ignem istum."[6] That the slender volume contained the Bull "Exsurge" was probably not known to all of those present. But even as a burning of the canon law, this spectacle was an impressive challenge to the Curia. It was further underscored by a pamphlet of Luther, *Warum des Papstes und seiner Jünger Bücher verbrannt sind* (WA 7, 152–186). The Bull "Decet Romanum Pontificem" of 3 January 1521 now at last carried out the excommunication. On 8 February 1521 Aleander reported to Rome:

> All Germany is in an uproar. For nine-tenths "Luther" is the war-cry; for the rest, if they are indifferent to Luther, it is at least "Death to the Roman Curia," and everyone demands and shouts for a council.[7]

According to the medieval law of Church and state, when Luther was banned by the Church he should have been outlawed: that is, the excommunication should have been carried out by the secular arm. But in fact the Empire negotiated with Luther. This was due only in part to the election capitulation sworn to by Charles V on 3 July 1519, whereby no one might thereafter be outlawed without a previous hearing.[8] In these months Luther had become so truly the voice of the German nation, he had so made himself the advocate of its difficulties and wishes, that no one could have simply ignored him. But for this very reason a further enhancing of his already powerful prestige was to be feared from a public negotiation with the reformer. The papal nuncios sought to avoid this. Moreover, they did not want to let go unchallenged the lay powers' claim to act as judges in a matter of faith already decided by the Pope. In his discourse of 13 February 1521 Aleander stressed that it did not belong to the secular authority "to take cognizance of such matters concerning the faith."[9] Hence the mere fact of Luther's hearing—that the diet should of itself be involved with a question of religion instead

---

[6] Thus J. Luther harmonizes the slightly differing reports in "Noch einmal Luthers Worte bei der Verbrennung der Bannbulle," *ARG* 45 (1954), 260–265.

[7] T. Breiger, *Aleander und Luther,* p. 48.

[8] *RA* I, 873; K. Zeumer, *Quellensammlung,* no. 180, p. 311.

[9] *RA* II, 506.

of proceeding as a matter of course against the condemned heretic—was a new fact of great import.[10]

But on 28 November 1520 Charles V had promised Frederick the Wise that he would interrogate Luther. The elector was to bring him along to the Diet of Worms.[11] Because of Aleander's intervention this imperial promise was restricted to mean that the elector could bring Luther into the vicinity of Worms only after a recantation had been made.[12] The reply to this was a protest by Frederick the Wise, who maintained it was only fair to give Luther the possibility of defending himself; a condemnation of a German without trial could not but produce profound scandal. At the urging of the elector the diet on 19 February rejected a law for the suppression of Luther's writings, proposed by Aleander in person on 13 February in a three-hour speech, and requested the Emperor to summon Luther to Worms, out of regard for the excitement among the common people, and there to have him questioned by experts. This decision of the diet proved to be a compromise when it finally directed that there should be no discussion with Luther; he was only to be asked whether he was ready to repudiate his writings against the Church and the Christian faith.[13] In the summons, dated 6 March, that was sent to Wittenberg on 16 March with a safe-conduct, there was no further mention of a recantation. In this the heretic formally condemned by the Pope was addressed as follows:

> Honorable, dear, and pious one: After we and the estates of the Holy Empire, now assembled here, have taken up and reached the decision that because of the doctrines and books which for a time have come from you we wish to obtain information from you, and for this we have given you our and the Empire's assurance and safe-conduct so that you may come to us.[14]

Aleander did not admit defeat. He managed the publication on 26 March of an imperial mandate which had been prepared for some time, in which the confiscation of all of Luther's writings was commanded and the summons of Luther to Worms for a recantation was stated.[15] Perhaps Luther was by this means meant to be deterred from appearing at Worms; in any event, this was how he understood it (*WA, Br* 2, 298). There was anxiety in the entourage of the Elector of Saxony, but Luther himself was in high spirits, filled with the courage of a martyr, defiance,

---

[10] K. Repgen, *Die römische Kurie und der Westfälische Friede* I (Tübingen 1962), 35f.
[11] *RA* II, 450, 466ff.
[12] *RA* II, 468ff.
[13] *RA* II, 515f.
[14] *RA* II, 526.
[15] *RA* II, 531f.

and a proud self-assurance. En route to Worms he is supposed to have written: "Even though there were as many devils at Worms as tiles on the roofs, I still would go there" (WA, Tr 5, 65). He had just published the German version of the great Latin treatise on justification against the Bull "Exsurge Domine," *Grund und Ursach aller Artikel D. M. Luthers so durch römische Bulle unrechtlich verdammt sind* (WA 7, 308–457). In the introduction he points out that the prophets and champions of truth have always stood alone. "I do not say that I am a prophet, but I say that they have the more reason to fear that I am one, the more they scorn me and esteem themselves" (WA 7, 3, 313). Just before his departure for Worms he completed the *Antwort* (WA 7, 705–778) to the *Apologia* of the Italian Dominican Ambrose Catharinus as the second part of *De captivitate.* In it he defined precisely his teaching on the Church and the papacy: The Church is not limited as to place nor bound up with persons. She is where the Gospel is proclaimed and where baptism and communion are celebrated according to it. The papal Church is the demoniacal power described in Scripture as Antichrist, which lasts to the end of days and is to be fought, not with weapons, but with the word and the Spirit.

Full of such ideas and emotions, Luther, accompanied by Kaspar Sturm as imperial herald, began his journey to Worms on 2 April 1521. From Frankfurt on 14 April he wrote to Spalatin: "We will go to Worms in spite of all the gates of hell and the powers in the air" (WA, Br 2, 298). On 16 April, at ten o'clock in the morning, Luther entered Worms through crowded streets, in his little dray, attended by members of the nobility. The next day, at eight in the evening, he faced the Emperor and the diet in the episcopal palace. The conduct of the hearing was entrusted to Johann von der Ecken,[16] *officialis* of Richard von Greiffenklau, Archbishop of Trier, the prelate whom Frederick the Wise had wanted as arbiter in Luther's case in 1519.

Luther was asked whether he acknowledged as his the twenty books exhibited and published under his name and whether he was prepared "to disavow these books or anything in them." In a low voice, "as though he were frightened and shocked" (RA II, 863), he acknowledged them as his writings. With regard to recantation he asked for time to reflect, for it would be presumptuous and dangerous were he not to ponder carefully before giving his reply to such a question. This evasive answer need not have been either a tactical move or the result of temporary confusion. Luther, in whose summons there was no mention of a

---

[16] Born at Trier, he became, after studies at Bologna and Siena, a professor in the law faculty at Trier in 1506. From 1512 he was the archbishop's officialis, but he was not a priest and was scarcely trained in theology. He died at Esslingen on 2 December 1524.

recantation, may have counted on a discussion of faith and may not have been prepared for a simple disavowal without a previous refutation. On the next day, 18 April, he was again asked whether he was prepared to recant. He refused:

> If I do not become convinced by the testimony of Scripture or clear rational grounds—for I believe neither the pope nor councils alone, since it is obvious that they have erred on several occasions—I remain subjugated by the scriptural passages I have cited and my conscience held captive by the word of God. Therefore, I neither can nor will recant anything. For to act against conscience is difficult, noxious, and dangerous. May God help me. Amen.[17]

Sent back to his lodging, Luther there exclaimed, with outstretched arms and a joyful countenance: "I am through, I am through." The Emperor refused a further hearing but granted a delay of three days during which the estates could try to persuade Luther. Luther appeared before their special committee on 24 April in the lodging of the Archbishop of Trier. These discussions were also fruitless, and von Greiffenklau then made private efforts on Luther's behalf through Johannes Cochläus and the *officialis* Johann von der Ecken. The hopelessness of all these efforts became clear when on the next day Luther again denied the binding force of a conciliar decision. It was not only a question of *gravamina,* not of opposition to an ecclesiastical political view, not even simply of reform, but of fundamentally different concepts of the natur? of the Church. On the evening of 25 April Luther received the Emperor's decision: since all admonitions had been without effect, the Emperor, as protector of the Church, would now proceed against him.

The next day the reformer left Worms. Through a hint by his territorial prince he was prepared to be "seized and hidden" *(WA, Br* 2, 305) somewhere along the way. According to a secret instruction he did not travel from Eisenach directly to Gotha but took a detour via Mohra, where he visited his relatives. Then, on 4 May, in the vicinity of Burg Altenstein, he was kidnapped by prearrangement and taken to Wartburg castle.

The Edict of Worms was prepared by Aleander and on 8 May its draft was approved by the imperial ministers. But it was only on 25 May, when most of the estates had already dispersed, that, with some alterations, it was publicly read at the Emperor's residence. The Elector Joachim of Brandenburg accepted it in the name of the estates, and the

---

[17] *RA* II, 581f., 555. The turn of speech, "Here I stand; I cannot do otherwise," is an early legendary addition. Cf. K. Muller, "Luthers Schlussworte in Worms 1521," *Philotesia, Festschrift für P. Kleinert* (Berlin 1907), pp. 269–289.

Emperor signed it on 26 May. The edict enumerates Luther's erroneous teachings with reference to *De captivitate Babylonica*. It finds fault especially with his attacking the Council of Constance and his causing disturbance:

> By virtue of our imperial dignity, majesty, and authority, with the unanimous advice and consent of ourselves and of the electors, princes, and estates of the Holy Empire, here assembled, for an everlasting remembrance of this action and for the implementation . . . of the bull which our Holy Father, the Pope, as the proper judge of this matter, has issued, we have recognized and declared that the aforementioned Martin Luther is to be regarded by us and you, each and every one, as a member severed from the Church of God, an obstinate schismatic, and a manifest heretic.[18]

Luther's adherents and well-wishers were also to be be banned. It was forbidden to buy, sell, read, copy, or print his writings, which were to be burned or otherwise destroyed. And to prevent writings hostile to the faith, all books which "touch upon the Christian faith, slightly or to a great degree," must obtain the local Ordinary's authorization for printing.[19]

The edict was valid in law because the estates had allowed the Emperor to proceed against Luther in the event that Luther refused to recant.[20] Nevertheless, the manner of its publication and the fact that it had not been promulgated until after the diet recessed could give rise to doubts as to its authority and provide pretexts to those who lacked the will or the courage to execute it. Immediately after the diet the Emperor journeyed to Spain under the impression that war with France was impending, and he was to remain absent from Germany for nine years. Hence he could not lend personal emphasis to the Edict of Worms, while for his wars in the west, south, and east of the Empire he needed the aid of the pro-Luther estates against which he ought to have taken measures.

[18] *RA* II, 654.
[19] Ibid.
[20] N. Paulus in *HJ* 39 (1918f.), 269–277, against P. Kalkoff, *Die Entstehung des Wormser Edikts* (Leipzig 1913).

CHAPTER 7

Luther at the Wartburg and the Reform Movement in Wittenberg

Luther had just been the center of the Diet of Worms, thus actually of German public life; he had spoken before the Emperor and the imperial estates and had been cheered by the people. Now he was suddenly thrust into solitude. Until his tonsure had grown out and a suitable beard adorned "Junker Jörg," he could not show himself to anyone at the Wartburg except the servant who brought his meals. If the sudden loneliness following stormy events would have got on anyone's nerves, and if enormous tension would naturally be followed by profound depression, it can be imagined how much more the solitude of the Wartburg would take its toll of Luther, who was highly emotional, impulsive, and given to depression. And in fact these weeks and months—from 4 May 1521 to 6 March 1522—were for Luther a period of temptations and torment of conscience. He reproached himself for having started the fire and on the other hand for having been too weak before his judges. Prayer left him cold; the devil tormented him all the more with doubts and fears for his salvation. To Spalatin, who was his connection with the outside world, who transmitted his letters and gave his manuscripts to the printers, Luther wrote on 9 September 1521:

> It is time to pray with all strength against the devil; he is bringing so disastrous a tragedy over Germany. And I, who am afraid that the Lord may not grant it, am still snoring and too lazy to pray and to resist, so that I dislike myself beyond measure and am a burden to myself, perhaps because I am alone and you do not help me. [*WA, Br* 2, 388]

Furthermore, there were physical sufferings, including constipation, which were certainly not alleviated by immoderate eating and drinking due to emotional unrest. And his anxiety about the friends at Wittenberg who needed his counsel and comfort did not permit peace of mind.

Luther coped with all these difficulties and temptations by means of literary activities that were unusually energetic and prolific, as well as spontaneous and unrestrained. The Wartburg became his "Patmos" (*WA, Str* 3, no. 3814). He applied himself to the exegesis of Psalm 67 (68), which was followed later by an exposition of Psalms 21 (22) and 36 (37). He also finished his explanation of the "Magnificat" (*WA* 7, 544–601) and began to compose a book of sermons as an aid to parish priests and for family prayer. In *Von der Beichte, ob die der Papst Macht habe, zu gebieten* (*WA* 8, 138–185) he attacked compulsory confession, which he regarded as a torment of conscience.

> I regard private confession, like virginity and chastity, as a very precious and salutary thing. Oh, it should indeed be quite painful to all Christians if there were no private confession, and they should thank God with all their hearts that it is permitted and available. But it is a bad thing that the pope makes it a compulsory institution and puts it within the chains of precept, as he also does with chastity. [WA 8, 164]

If a person does not want to confess to a priest, he should open his soul to any man from whom he may expect help.

In *Ein Widerspruch D. Luthers* (WA 8, 247–254), Luther continued his controversy with Hieronymus Emser, "the goat of Leipzig." In it he again denied a special priestly state. The *Rationis Latomianae confutatio,* called by Melanchthon *Antilatomus,* was directed against the detailed justification of the Louvain faculty's judgment against Luther by Jacob Latomus. Employing a systematic method not usual with him, Luther here treated a central question of his theology, that of sin persisting: "When all sins have been washed away, there is still a remainder to be washed away" (WA 8, 57). He who has been pardoned is nothing but a "shackled robber."

> For the same movement of anger and of lust is in the pious and the godless, the same before grace and after grace, just as the same flesh before grace and after grace. But in grace it can do nothing, whereas without grace it has predominance. [WA 8, 91]
>
> [Sins are] entirely remitted but not yet all destroyed. For we believe that the remission of all sins has occurred without any doubt, but every day we have to work and to wait for the blotting out [*abolitio*] of all sins and their complete removal [*evacuatio*]. And those who labor at this do good works. See, this is my faith, for that is the Catholic faith. [WA 8, 96]

Luther's distinction between *gratia* and *donum* corresponds to this twofold process of remission and extirpation of sins, of justification and sanctification. "The law reveals two evils, an inner and an outer: the one, which we have laid upon ourselves, sins or the corruption of nature; the other, which God imposes, wrath, death, and damnation" (WA 8, 104). To these correspond two goods of the Gospel, *gratia et donum.* Grace obliterates wrath and brings God's favor and peace; the gift brings recovery from corruption. Grace is indivisible, "so that the person is really accepted and in him there is no further place for wrath. . . . Hence it is entirely impious to say that the baptized is still in sins or that not all sins have been entirely remitted"(WA 8, 107).

On the other hand, the inner healing and purification of man, which the gift effects and in which man must cooperate, is a slow process.

> All is forgiven by grace, but all is not yet healed by the gift. But the gift is infused, the leaven is mixed with the flour and is operating to purge out the sin which is already forgiven to the person. So long as this process lasts, we speak of sin, and it is sin by nature; but now a sin without wrath, without the law, a dead sin, a harmless sin, if you only remain constant in grace and the gift. In no respect is sin distinguished from sin in its nature, before grace or after grace. But it is distinguished in regard to its treatment. [WA 8, 107]

Even though, according to Luther, we "must separate grace and gift from each other" (WA 8, 107), yet they are oriented toward each other and the one is given for the sake of the other. Man, even as a person, is "not in God's good pleasure and has no grace except because of the gift which is operating in such a manner as to purge out sin" (WA 8, 107). Because sin still has to be purged out, "God does not save imagined but real sinners,"[1] and so man must not boast of his purity but "rather of the grace and gift of God, that he has a gracious God who does not impute these sins and in addition has given his gifts in order thereby to purge them out" (WA 8, 108).

If it is borne in mind that Luther is speaking concretely and existentially; that he is employing the concept "sin" analogously, as theology in general does; if, in addition, one does not, like Luther's theological opponents, start with a doctrine of redemption concerned merely with satisfaction and, correspondingly, does not regard the penalties of sin as purely vindictive; then these assertions of Luther are much more reconcilable with Catholic doctrine than is generally held, but in any case they compel the abandonment of the customary scheme of a purely external justification.

The University of Paris, invited to act as arbiter of the Leipzig Disputation, had maintained silence and so could long be counted as a secret partisan of Luther. Not until 15 April 1521 had it condemned as heretical 104 propositions of Luther, one-fourth of them from *De captivitate Babylonica.* Melanchthon came forward with an *Apologia* against the condemnation. Luther translated this and the Paris decree into German and added a foreword and an epilogue in which he specified his attack

---

[1] From here light is cast on the much quoted expression, astonishing in its paradoxical boldness, which Luther wrote to Melanchthon on 1 August 1521, during the printing of the *Antilatomus*: "Si gratiae praedicator es, gratiam non fictam, sed veram praedica; si vera gratia est, verum, non fictum peccatum ferto. Deus non facit salvos ficte peccatores. Esto peccator et pecca fortiter, sed fortius fide et gaude in Christo, qui victor est peccati, mortis et mundi . . . Sufficit, quod agnovimus per divitias gloriae Dei agnum, qui tollit peccatum mundi . . . Ora fortiter, etiam fortissimus peccator" (*WA, Br* 2, 372).

on the papacy as the decisive point of controversy. For he hurled at the Paris theologians the reproach that in all their articles they had not at all mentioned the most important—indulgences and the papacy.

> They are thinking of their appeal of 1517 to a council against the pope. The pope hurt them and they decided to take revenge. For that reason I do not want their voice; they do this for no love of truth. I have no desire to associate with these knaves who abandon their master in trouble, but not for God's sake. If I could do so with a clear conscience, I would again exalt the papacy to spite and hurt French perfidy. [WA 8, 293]

With this allusion to Gallican resentments Luther had skillfully parried the Sorbonne's thrust, rendering the accompanying filthy expressions quite unnecessary.

Luther was both violently angry and disdainful when he heard that Albrecht of Mainz, against his better judgment and out of mere avarice, had placed the treasury of relics of Halle on exhibition and was inviting all the faithful to visit it and make an offering, promising rich indulgences. He was even more furious, however, when Spalatin, at the instigation of Capito,[2] who despite his reform sentiments had entered the archbishop's service in 1519, prevented the publication of his tract *Wider den Abgott zu Halle.*

> I would rather destroy you and the elector himself and every creature. . . . It is fine of you that you are unwilling to see the divine calm destroyed; but that the everlasting peace of God is destroyed by that impious, temple-desecrating, pernicious action of that man—you will let that pass? By no means, Spalatin! By no means, elector! But for Christ's sheep this detestable wolf must be opposed with all force. [WA, Br 2, 402]

The tract did not appear but Luther sent the archbishop an ultimatum on 1 December 1521. In reply the cardinal-elector referred to himself as "stinking filth" and so drew in his horns that the reformer for his part was not certain whether he should praise him as honest or upbraid him for hypocrisy (WA, Br 2, 433f.). But to Capito, who wanted to advise him to observe diplomatic caution, Luther wrote pitilessly: "What has a Christian to do with a sycophant?" (WA, Br 2, 431). "You wish to have a Luther who will connive at all your doings if his hide is patted only with nice and endearing notes" (WA, Br 2, 433).

---

[2] Wolfgang Fabricius Capito, born at Hagenau in 1478, was in the serivce of Albrecht of Mainz from 10 February 1520. In 1523 he acquired the provostship of Sankt Thomas at Strasbourg through the good offices of the nuncio Aleander and then passed definitely to the Reformation. Together with Bucer he tried to mediate between Luther and Zwingli. He died at Strasbourg in 1541.

Monastic Vows and Freedom by the Gospel

Luther's absence from Wittenberg enabled others to come more energetically into the foreground and influence the course of the Reformation. To some extent they had an outlook different from his and had in common with him only an attitude of protest against the abuses in the old Church and the demand for reform. Furthermore, they had not suffered nearly so much under the criticized conditions nor struggled with the truth in painful experience as the Wittenberg friar had done. Thus they were more inclined toward a rapid external upheaval; they saw salvation in a change of form and not chiefly in a transformation of attitude. If Luther's critical writings, such as *An den christlichen Adel* and *De captivitate Babylonica,* were convincing, then a series of practical consequences could not but follow, especially in regard to the celebration of Mass, priestly celibacy, and monastic vows.

The Kemberg Provost Bartholomäus Bernhardi, a pupil of Luther's, had married his cook and hence was under indictment. Melanchthon had written in his defense, stressing that everyone may rid himself of a human regulation that endangers his conscience. Would this also be valid if a religious felt he could no longer fulfill the obligations he had assumed? Luther, unlike Karlstadt and Melanchthon, was not ready so quickly to reply in the affirmative. He distinguished between the priests' obligation of celibacy and monastic vows. With regard to vows he looked for a firm basis for the conscience, a "testimonium divinae voluntatis." Karlstadt's arguments had not convinced him and he was not sure whether by the same token one could also dispense oneself from divine precepts.[3] In his letter to Melanchthon of 9 September 1521 he wrote that he believed he had found the way to a solution in the expression "freedom by the Gospel" (*WA, Br* 2, 384). At the same time he sent to Wittenberg Latin theses for a disputation on the vows. These begin with the text from Romans 14:23, "Omne quod non est ex fide, peccatum est," henceforth to be quoted again and again (*WA* 8, 323).

Gabriel Zwilling, Luther's fellow Augustinian, had fewer scruples. In October he preached violently against the Mass and "monkery." Freedom from the vows was not enough for him. The monk should discard the habit and abandon his state. In November fifteen out of forty Augustinians left the Wittenberg friary. Luther learned of it and feared that not all of them had taken the step with a clear conscience. To help those who had decided to depart he set about composing a treatise on the

---

[3] "Imo ista ratio, quod melius est nubere quam uri, seu, ut peccatum fornicationis vitetur, matrimonium in peccato fidei fractae ineunt, quid est nisi ratio? Scripturam quaerimus et testimonium divinae volumtatis. Quis scit, si cras uratur, qui hodie uritur?" (Letter to Melanchthon of 1 August 1521. *WA, Br* 2, 371).

vows. On 11 November 1521 he wrote to Spalatin: "I have resolved now to take up the question of religious vows also and to free young people from this infernal celibacy" (*WA, Br* 2, 403). In the same month he had completed *De votis monasticis . . . iudicium* (*WA* 8, 573–669). Held back by Spalatin, this work did not appear until February 1522.

The dedicatory letter to his father, who had opposed Luther's embracing the monastic life, shows that in this piece he also wanted to settle with his own past. His vows, whereby he had removed himself from the paternal will imposed by God, were worthless, even impious. But now his conscience had become free and that meant freedom in superabundance. "Therefore, I am still a friar and at the same time not a friar; I am a new creature, not the pope's but Christ's (*WA* 8, 575). "And so I hope," he wrote to his father, "that the Lord has deprived you of a son in order to counsel through me many others of his sons" (*WA* 8, 576). On 18 December 1521 he wrote to Wenceslas Link: "I, however, shall continue in this state [*habitu*] and this way of life [*ritu*], unless this world changes" (*WA, Br* 2, 415).

Decisive for an evaluation of vows is freedom according to the Gospel: "For this freedom is of divine law. God has sanctioned it. Neither will he repudiate it nor can he accept anything against it nor permit man to infringe on it by any, even only a slight, statute" (*WA* 8, 613). Hence a vow contrary to freedom is null and void—for example, if it was made on the assumption that the religious life is necessary for justification and salvation, which indeed can be obtained only through faith in Christ (*WA* 8, 605). Furthermore, vows are to be made only with the provision that there is freedom to abandon religious life again. The vow should accordingly be: "I vow chastity as long as it shall be possible for me, but I can marry if I cannot preserve it" (*WA* 8, 633). If till now Luther had parried the argument that one may renounce a vow if one is unable to fulfill it with the remark that a complete observance of the commandments is impossible also, he now stressed that the married state makes possible the fulfilling of the precept of chastity. "But if I can observe the precepts of God and not the vow, then the vow must yield in order that the commandments may remain and that vow and precept may not be violated in unchastity" (*WA* 8, 632).

These ideas could not have been other than alluring to many religious. They made all the more sense to contemporaries because the prevalence of concubinage among the priests of the time made celibacy and the religious state seem to many unworthy of credence. Modern man was less able and ready than man of previous centuries to put up with such tension between ideal and reality. To Luther, however, it was a source of uneasiness that all too many, as a result of his cry of Christian liberty, were abandoning the monastic life. On 28 March 1522 he wrote to Johann Lang, his friend of many years, who had left the Erfurt Augustinian monastery, of which he had been prior:

> I note that many of our friars have departed for the same reason that induced them to enter—for the sake of the belly and of carnal freedom. Through them Satan intends to put out a great stench in opposition to the good odor of our word. But what are we to do? They are sluggards and seek only what is theirs; it is, then, preferable that they sin and perish without the monastic habit than in it. Otherwise, they will perish doubly if they are deprived of this life also. [WA, Br 2, 488]

Regulation of Community Worship

On 1 August 1521 Luther wrote to Melanchthon that, after his return from the Wartburg, he intended first of all to take up a regulating of the Eucharist in keeping with the institution by Christ. However, his followers in Wittenberg, especially Karlstadt and the Augustinian Gabriel Zwilling, would not wait for this. And so on their own responsibility they began to draw the conclusions from Luther's criticism of the Mass in De captivitate and other works. They constructed an "evangelical Mass," abolished private Masses, and took steps against the adoration of the Sacrament. On Michaelmas of 1521 Melanchthon and his students received the Sacrament under both species. Because of Zwilling's sermons the Augustinians ended private Masses on 13 October.[4] These novelties caused a sensation and ran into opposition. The elector was alarmed and appointed an investigating committee. Luther entered the controversy in November with De abroganda missa privata (WA 8, 411–476), which he then translated as Vom Missbrauch der Messe (WA 8, 482–536). In it he not only attacks the private Mass, as the title suggests, but the Sacrifice of the Mass in general. In a far more caustic and polemical manner he expounds ideas previously developed on the Mass as a covenant or legacy, as a gift to us, citing as a further argument the "once for all" text of Hebrews against the sacrificial character of the Mass.

> Tell us, you priests of Baal: Where is it written that the Mass is a sacrifice or where has Christ taught that consecrated bread and wine are to be offered? Do you not hear? Christ sacrificed himself once; he does not wish to be sacrificed thereafter by any other person. He wants us to recall his sacrifice. Why, then, are you so

---

[4] "Cessatum est a celebrandis missis in coenobio Augustianorum" (A. Burer to B. Rhenanus on 13 October 1521, in ARG 6 1908–1919, 193).

> bold that you make a sacrifice out of a memorial . . . your sacrific-
> ing means a shameful repetition of crucifixion. [WA, 8, 421, 493]
> Everyone knows on what the whole kingdom of priests is based
> and built: on celebrating Mass. In other words, on the grossest
> idolatry on earth, on shameful falsehood, on the perverted and
> godless abuse of the Sacrament, and on an unbelief that is more
> wicked than that of the pagans. [WA 8, 443, 520]

Radical though the language of this tract was, powerfully though it
called for a correction of the situation,[5] Luther himself still hesitated to
introduce a new liturgy. But this does not mean that he rejected the
procedure of the Augustinians and the ecclesiastical novelties at Wittenberg as a matter of course. Filled with anxiety and eager to learn
about the development at first hand, he secretly left the Wartburg on 2
December 1521 and went to Wittenberg, where he stayed 4-9 December. There on 3 December armed students and townsmen invaded
the parish church, drove the priests from the altars, and carried away the
missals. The next day a similar scene occurred in the Franciscan friary.
The friars were jeered and prevented from offering private Masses. The
city council feared there would be an attack on the monastery and had it
guarded during the night.

Despite this, Luther wrote to Spalatin: "All that I see and hear gives
me special delight. May the Lord strengthen the spirit of those who are
motivated by a good intention" (WA, Br 2, 410). But the atmosphere of
ferment disturbed him and he intended after his return to the Wartburg
to raise a warning voice against it.

At the same time, however, he discovered to his great wrath that
Spalatin, from a dread of agitation, had held up his tracts against religious vows and the Mass. Hence he wrote to Spalatin from the
Wartburg: "Is one, then, only to dispute unceasingly about the word of
God but always to refrain from action? . . . If nothing more is to be
done than what we have done until now, then nothing else ought to
have been taught either" (WA, Br 2, 412). But at the same time he sent
his friend the proclamation "Eine treue Vermahnung zu allen Christen,
sich zu hüten vor Aufruhr und Empörung" (WA 8, 676-687). According to this it is not the business of all ("omnes") to remedy abuses by
force. Luther proves the power of the unarmed word of God by point-

---

[5] "Cum ergo ex his omnibus probetur, missas non nisi Satanae operatione et communi
errore mundi in sacrificia versas esse adversus Evangelium et fidem et caritatem, quae
hac machina abolentur, tota fiducia abrogandae sunt universae nobis, qui Christiani esse
volumus, nec spectandum, quod pauci pio errore illis utantur sine perditione" (WA 8,
457). On 11 November 1521 Luther wrote to Spalatin: "Abrogationem missarum con-
firmo hoc, quem mitto, libro" (WA, Br 2, 403).

ing to his own fate: "Consider my activity. Have I not done more damage to the pope, bishops, priests, and monks, by my mouth alone, without any wielding of the sword, than all emperors, kings, and princes did previously with their might?" (WA 8, 683). He then warns against making the Gospel a matter of factions and forbids his adherents to call themselves "Lutherans." "How should it happen to a poor, stinking heap of maggots, such as I am, that the children of Christ should be called by my wretched name?" (WA 8, 685).

The Elector Frederick demanded that the city council punish the authors of the disturbances, but large segments of the townspeople rallied to protesters calling for the free preaching of the Gospel, the abolition of private Masses, the lay chalice, and the closing of public houses—"since they are maintained for excessive drinking"—and of whorehouses.[6] Repeatedly, once more expressly on 19 December, Frederick forbade unauthorized changes. People were to "leave the old customs alone"[7] until greater unanimity should be achieved. Nevertheless, on the fourth Sunday of Advent Karlstadt announced that on New Year's Day he would celebrate Mass with communion under both species, with the words of consecration intelligible and without the other ceremonies and the vestments.[8] Probably to forestall a prohibition by the Elector, he carried out the plan on Christmas. Before a large congregation he celebrated a "German Mass"; that is, he recited the words of institution in German and omitted the rest of the Canon along with the elevation. For the rite he wore secular dress. He pointedly omitted the preparatory confession of sins as unnecessary and administered communion under both species, passing the Host and the chalice into the communicants' hands. On 6 January the chapter of the German Augustinian Congregation declared that the friars were free to abandon the monastery. All who remained were to occupy themselves with preaching or teaching or earn their livelihood by means of a craft.[9] Begging was to be henceforth forbidden. On 11 January Zwilling sounded the call for an attack on images and the elimination of side altars, on the basis that images are forbidden by God's word (Ex. 20:4). On 19 January Karlstadt solemnized his own wedding.

Meanwhile there had appeared in Wittenberg the "Zwickau Prophets," the weavers Nikolaus Storch and Thomas Drechsel, and

---

[6] N. Muller, *Die Wittenberger Bewegung 1521 und 1522* (Leipzig 1911), pp. 161ff.

[7] Ibid., pp. 123ff.

[8] Ibid., pp. 125f.

[9] Ibid., pp. 147ff. "Quantum per nos stat, omnibus fratribus nostris Evangelicam et Christianam permittimus libertatem, Quantonus ii, qui nobiscum vivere, deserto corrupto vitae nostrae fuco, secundum puritatem Evangelicae doctrinae velint, possint" (p. 148).

Mark (Thomas) Stübner, a former pupil of Melanchthon. They prided themselves on being directly guided by the Holy Spirit. For them the "inner word" was decisive, and so they felt less in need of the written word. According to their dreams and visions, the entire order of the world would soon undergo a transformation and through the extermination of priests and the wicked the foundation would be laid for the Kingdom of God. If the possession of the Spirit was decisive, then the Sacraments were unimportant, and the meaning of infant baptism was questionable. For how could one receive the Spirit as a result of another's faith? Melanchthon, in whose house Stübner had taken up residence, was impressed by these doctrines but also disquieted. He wrote to Spalatin on 1 January 1522: "These opinions are surely not to be condemned and will probably cause difficulties for persons much more learned than I am and for the masses. Well, I was expecting that the devil would attack us in a weak spot" (CR I, 534).

Melanchthon did not venture to give a judgment and turned to Luther, who advised that the criterion of the spirits should be whether their manifestations were connected with frightening phenomena. For God is a consuming fire, and visions of the saints are fearful. "So apply this test and don't let them tell you about Jesus in his glory before you have seen the Crucified" (WA, Br 2, 425). Melanchthon must not let himself be impressed by talk against infant baptism. For no other recourse "is left to any of us except to accept another's faith," the faith whereby Christ believes for us.

> Why, the other's faith is our own faith . . . . To bring a child for baptism signifies nothing else than to present it into Christ's open hands of grace. Since he has proved to us by many examples that he accepts what is offered to him, why do we doubt here? [WA, Br 2, 426]

The Zwickau Prophets probably did not intervene directly in the situation at Wittenberg, but they supplied a new stimulus to Karlstadt, Zwilling, and the rigoristic elements among the citizenry. Under Karlstadt's influence the city council on 24 January 1522 issued the "Order of the City of Wittenberg." Among other things, this decreed the removal of images, the celebration of Mass according to Karlstadt's liturgy, and the combining of the spiritual revenues into a common social fund, the "common chest." The sequel was resentment and complaints by the orthodox canons to the elector. On the other hand, the "Order" was not radical enough for the fanaticism of the zealots; above all, it was not carried out quickly and decisively enough. In a document dated 27 January, "On abolishing images and that there should be no beggars among Christians," Karlstadt complained that three days after the enactment of the city order the images still had not been removed.[10] People took the law into their own hands and at the beginning of February there was an iconoclastic attack on the Wittenberg parish church.

These radical reform efforts spread to other localities in the electorate. Frederick the Wise was doubly anxious, for in the meantime a decree had been issued by the Imperial Governing Council (*Reichsregiment*) at Nürnberg on 22 January 1522 against the innovations in Electoral Saxony.[11] In this he and the Bishops of Meissen, Merseburg, and Naumburg were obliged "seriously and *ex officio*" to proceed against priests who in celebrating Mass deviated from the old usages or who married, and against monks who left their monastery. From 6 February the elector several times intimated to the people of Wittenberg—the last time on 17 February—that they were to observe ancient custom. But the collegiate chapter, the university, and the city council were no longer in control of the situation. In this emergency Melanchthon and the council turned to Luther and asked him to come back to Wittenberg.

Luther, probably on the strength of this, announced his coming in a letter to the elector: ". . . I have no more time; if God so wills, I intend to be there soon" (*WA, Br* 2, 449). Luther did not permit the misgivings and remonstrances of his prince to keep him any longer from a public return. He set out on 1 March and, on the way, wrote to Frederick the Wise again, on 5 March:

> In regard to my affair, most gracious Lord, I reply thus: Your gracious Highness [E.K.F.G.] knows or, if you don't, then let it be known to you herewith, that I have the Gospel, not from man, but only from heaven through our Lord Jesus . . . . Such is written to your gracious Highness that Your Highness may know that I am coming to Wittenberg under a far higher protection than that of the elector. And I have no intention of asking protection from your gracious Highness. Indeed, I believe, I wish rather to protect your gracious Highness more than your Highness could protect me. [*WA, Br* 2, 455]

Filled with this prophetic self-confidence, Luther entered Wittenberg on 6 March 1522. At the elector's request and for his protection against the Imperial Governing Council, Luther stated on 7 March and again on 12 March—in a new draft prepared in accord with an instruction of the Elector—that he had returned to Wittenberg without the elector's

---

[10] Printed in E. Sehling, *Die ev. Kirchenordnungen des 16. Jahrhunderts* I, 1 (Leipzig 1902), 697f.

[11] Ed. H. Lietzmann, Kleine Texte, 74 (Bonn 1911), 20.

"knowledge, will, favor, and permission" (*WA, Br* 2, 470). His feelings were expressed in letters of the succeeding days:

> Of necessity I have hurled myself alive into the very center of the raging of pope and emperor, to see if I could drive the wolf from the fold. Unprotected, except by heaven, I linger in the midst of my enemies, who according to human law have every right to kill me. [*WA, Br* 2, 476] I do not know Christ's thoughts; but I do know that in this business I have never been so courageous and of such proud spirit as I am now [*WA, Br* 2, 479].

Publicly his anger was directed, not at the Pope and the Emperor but at the fanatics and hotheads. In this he was following the wish of his prince and the latter's regard for the decree of the Imperial Governing Council, but especially his own dislike of tumult and violent revolution. From the first through the second Sunday in Lent 9–16 March he was daily in the pulpit of the parish church, wearing his habit and a newly trimmed tonsure. In these eight Lenten sermons (*WA* 10, III, 1–64) Luther denounced all who made a new law out of the freedom according to the Gospel and demanded regard for weak consciences. Then the Mass vestments and the elevation were resumed and, except for the abolition of private Masses, everything was as before. The directions in *De captivitate*, repeated by Luther in *Von beider Gestalt des Sakraments zu nehmen* (*WA* 10, II, 11–41), which was completed on 25 March 1522, remained in force. The priest should simply omit in the prayers and the Canon all words referring to sacrifice. Thus he could celebrate Mass according to the Gospel, while the common man would not notice anything to cause scandal. Karlstadt opposed this rescission of the reform and termed Luther and his adherents "neopapists." There ensued a violent scene between him and Luther. A polemic by Karlstadt, containing veiled attacks on Luther, was suppressed by the university (*WA, Br* 2, 509, 511).

Likewise in the 1523 liturgical regulations, the *Formula missae et communionis* (*WA* 12, 205–229), Luther still provided a Latin Mass, purified, however, of all allusions to sacrifice. Equally moderate was his German translation of the rites of baptism (*WA* 12, 42–48), also in 1523.

When the German Mass was already being celebrated in many places, not merely in Thomas Müntzer's Allstedt but also in Strasbourg, Nördlingen, Nürnberg, Basel, Zurich, and elsewhere, the Mass remained in Latin at Wittenberg. The political prudence of Frederick the Wise was surely decisive in this respect. As Spalatin stated, for example, only after Frederick's death was it possible "to drive the whole pope out of All Saints Church at Wittenberg."[12] But it was not only regard for his prince that made Luther hesitate to draw the practical consequences from his principles. There were also reasons within him, and they were of several kinds.

For Luther, forms of worship, prayers, rites, vestments, and vessels were "vain and external things," *adiaphora,* neither prescribed nor forbidden. If the Latin liturgy was not to be regarded as necessary for salvation, then neither was the German liturgy. To issue binding prescriptions on this matter meant to restrict the freedom of Christians and to lay unnecessary burdens on "poor consciences."

> I like it that now Mass is being celebrated by Germans in German. But that Karlstadt wants to make it a necessity, as though it had to be thus, is again too much. The Spirit cannot do otherwise, for always, always there is law, misery of conscience, and the creation of sins. [*WA* 18, 132]

Luther wanted to make it crystal clear that he was concerned for spiritual attitude, not for external conduct or form; for faith, not for works. Of course as a nominalist he underestimated the sign and had too little grasp of the power of images to illuminate or confuse the spirit. He saw only the road from the inside to the outside, whereby the spirit expresses itself in the body, and failed to understand that, on the other hand, the body aids the spirit into crystallization and even into existence.

Second, Luther demanded regard for "weak consciences." If he aimed first to change man's way of thinking and then to provide this with a suitable expression, he had to exercise patience. Of himself Luther relates that he needed three years of struggling to gain "faith"; *a fortiori* he had to allow time to simple folk and could not lead them into confusion and burdened consciences through precipitate changes not adequately prepared by preaching (*WA* 10, II, 25; *WA* 12, 212f.). Of course no compromise was to be made in regard to principles, but remedies could be quietly provided without the necessity of disturbing the common man (*WA* 10, II, 29).

Third, Luther's attachment to tradition and his feeling for form and organization caused him to delay. He was aware that the correct shape of the liturgy cannot be made but must grow. A mere translation of the texts was not enough; melody and text should constitute a unity.

---

[12] *RA* III, 21; F. Gess, *Akten und Briefe zur Kirchenpolitik Herzogs Georgs von Sachsen* I (Leipzig–Berlin 1905), 250ff; H. Barge, *Aktenstücke zur Wittenberger Bewegung* (Leipzig 1912), pp. 3–6.

> I should like very much to have a German Mass today. I am experimenting with it. But I should also want it to be of a genuinely German character. I do not stop people from translating the text into German and retaining the Latin tone or notes, but the result sounds neither right nor honest. Text and notes, stress, method, and style must proceed from the proper mother tongue and voice; otherwise, it is only imitation after the manner of apes. [WA 18, 123]

Finally, as a humanist and a teacher, Luther wanted to see the cultural value of the Latin language preserved. The young in particular should be trained in this language through the Latin liturgy. For them the *Formula missae,* or Latin liturgy, should be continued in use, even after the introduction of the German Mass (1526). In fact, if he had his way, he would celebrate Mass on Sundays in German, Latin, Greek, and Hebrew in turn (*WA* 19, 74).

Luther's Translation of the Bible

The most important literary product of the Wartburg period was the translation of the New Testament. After his secret visit to Wittenberg in December 1521, Luther, at the request of his friends, prepared it in about eleven weeks. He was intimately acquainted with the Vulgate, and in addition he had the Greek text edited by Erasmus—the second edition of 1519—with its translation into Latin and its copious exegesis. Considering the brief period of time and Luther's own knowledge of Greek—he had not undertaken serious study of this language until 1518—it can hardly be called a translation from the original.[13] To what extent he relied on the Greek text is difficult to say, but "in any case this much is certain: he sought to grasp the meaning of the basic text."[14] For the translation of the Old Testament, which was protracted to 1534, he called upon the services of linguistic specialists, and that project may fairly be regarded as teamwork.

There were German versions of the Bible before Luther. Between 1461 and 1522 fourteen High German and four Low German printed editions appeared, not counting German psalters, harmonizations of the

---

[13] I. Hoss, *Spalatin,* p. 242.

[14] H. Dibbelt, "Hatte Luthers Verdeutschung des NT den griechischen Text zur Grundlage?" *ARG* 38 (1941), 300–330; H. Bornkamm, "Die Vorlage zu Luthers Übersetzung des NT," *ThLZ* 72 (1947), 23–28; S. Kruger, "Zum Wortschatz des 18. Jahrhunderts: Fremdbegriff und Fremdwort in Luthers Bibelübersetzung," *BGDSL* 77 (1955), 402–464; H. -O. Burger, "Luther als Ereignis der Literaturgeschichte," *Luther Jb.* 24 (1957), 86–101; H. Bluhm, *Martin Luther—Creative Translator* (St. Louis, Mo. 1965).

Gospels, and books of pericopes. The last named in particular were familiar to Luther from the liturgy and his pastoral duties. It is an exaggeration to say that Luther was the first to give the Bible to the Germans, but in his German Bible he created a work which is unrivaled in accuracy of expression, in feeling for the language, and in literary force. Because Luther himself read the Scriptures "as though they had been written yesterday,"[15] because in fact he saw and heard sacred history as alive, message and German language could be blended into such unity that in its German dress the Bible remained a book to be listened to and the sacred text penetrated remarkably into ear and memory. This was, however, not only the fruit of Luther's power of expression, but also of an encounter, filled equally with painful struggle and joy, with God in his word. For Luther this was not only a testimony of the mighty saving action of God, it was itself the divine power. As no one else could, Luther was able to express by means of speech this living and impetuous power of God's word.

Luther translated the Bible when the process of fusing various German dialects into a uniform literary language was under way. On the fringe of the Empire, in the East German area of colonization, where immigration brought numerous dialects together, the prerequisites for the task were particularly favorable. "It is a Protestant legend that the reformer Luther created the new High German literary language,"[16] but he did accelerate the development toward a uniform speech by making use of the idiom of Saxon officialdom.

> I have no certain, special, proper speech in German, but use the common German speech in order that both, speakers of High and Low German, may be able to understand me. I speak the tongue of the Saxon chancery, which all princes and kings in Germany imitate; thus it is the commonest German speech. The Emperor Maximilian and the Elector Frederick have, therefore, pressed the Empire into a definite tongue, thereby absorbing all dialects into one language. [WA, Tr 2, no. 2758]

Certainly the translation of the Bible into a language is of great significance for revelation to the extent that this affects a new group of people. But it is likewise an event for that language, since it is challenged to develop potentialities thus far not realized. This became evident to an outstanding degree in Luther's translation. Even his Catholic opponents did not withhold recognition of his achievement. Although Hieronymus Emser (d. 1527), in his tract *Aus was Grund und Ursach*

---

[15] H. Bornkamm, *Luthers geistige Welt* (Gütersloh, 3 d ed. 1959), p. 266.
[16] Sermon of 22 March 1523 (WA 12, 444).

Luthers Dolmetschung über das Neue Testament dem gemeinen Mann billig verboten worden sei (1523), verified 1400 "heretical errors and lies" in Luther's New Testament, in his own translation of 1527 he largely adhered to Luther's text. Johannes Dietenberger (d. 1537) also, in his German Bible of 1534—which with fifty-eight editions of the complete Bible alone became the most used German Catholic Bible—made use of Luther's text. According to Johannes Cochläus (d. 1527), Luther's German version stirred the religious feeling of the people and awakened in the ordinary man a truly devouring hunger for the work of God.

But the reformer's impulsive nature, directed by experience, poses the question whether he reproduced the meaning of Holy Scripture in pure form. Because of his painful experience in wrestling with the meaning of *iustitia Dei,* he certainly put some of the emphases too strongly, and he occasionally overstepped the bounds of faithful translation. For example, he translated "justice of God" as "justice valid before God," and to Romans 3:26 and 3:28 he added the controversial "alone," which is quite in accord with the meaning but is not in Paul's text.[17]

More serious is the fact that Luther did not accept the Bible throughout as the word of God but for his part determined what was essential and thereby selected and put aside entire books, such as the Epistle of James and the Apocalypse. For him James was a "straw Epistle" (*WA, DB* 6, 10:7, 385), which he almost wanted to throw in the stove (*WA* 39, II, 199). But Luke 16 was for Luther a "Gospel right for priests and monks" (*WA* 10, III, 273), "one of the quarrelsome Gospels" (*WA* 29, 488), which "Satan cites as proof" (*WA* 12, 646). Christ must "be mastered *in suis verbis*" (*WA* 27, 296); "he must have himself led by the nose *suis verbis*" (*WA* 27, 279, 300); "we must not let ourselves be made fools of by Scripture" (*WA* 27, 303). In themselves these sentences can be understood as hermeneutical references in which Luther is calling attention to uncritical scriptural expressions or demanding that they be interpreted in their context. Thus he stated in the forty-first promotion thesis of 11 September 1535: "Scripture is not to be interpreted against but for Christ; hence either it must be referred to him or it must not be regarded as true Scripture" (*WA* 39, I, 47). But where do we stand if unsuitable doctrines or opponents are thereby driven from the field, as for example according to Thesis 49, "If opponents force Scripture against Christ, we shall force Christ against Scripture" (*WA* 39, I, 47)?

[17] H. -O. Burger, *loc. cit.,* p. 86; A. E. Berger, "Luther und die neuhochdeutsche Sprache," *Deutsche Wortgeschichte* 2 (1943), 37–132.
[18] H. Gerdes, "Überraschende Freiheiten in Luthers Bibelübersetzung," *Luther* 27 (1956), 71–80.
[19] Cf. W. von Loewenich, *Luther als Ausleger der Synoptiker* (Munich 1954), pp. 50ff.

With the touchstone of whether the books of Scripture "enhance Christ or not" (*WA, DB* 7, 385), everyone is in the last analysis left to his own personal judgment. When Luther referred both the fanatics and the orthodox who appealed to Scripture against him to its true meaning, then, ultimately, the reformer's personal experience of Christ decided the meaning of Scripture.

CHAPTER 8

The Reformers in Luther's Circle

Luther's protective custody at the Wartburg had shown that even without him the Reformation was alive; in fact, that without him its growth proceeded more impetuously. Even if Luther had been eliminated, it probably would no longer have been possible to wipe out the reform movement by force. It was not only the fanatics, Karlstadt and Müntzer, who in Luther's absence were trying to determine the form of the movement. In addition, in and outside Wittenberg there were a number of men who were working with Luther and in his spirit. On his return from the Wartburg it was clear that, while he no doubt played a decisive role, he was not the only one who would decide the shape of the new doctrine and of the church into which it was developing. Thus it could be seen at the outset that "Lutheranism" would be both more and less than what was embodied in Luther's person: less, because the sea of forces which he contained and the subjective nature of his prophetic function could not be institutionalized; more, because from the beginning his work was also carried by the formative and preserving force of others. Such helpers in Wittenberg, loyal and dedicated, even though to some extent of a different turn of mind, were Nikolaus von Amsdorf, Justus Jonas, Johannes Bugenhagen, Georg Spalatin, and, most important of all, Philip Melanchthon.

Nikolaus von Amsdorf (1483–1565) had been since 1507 a lecturer at the university and since 1508 a canon of the collegiate church of All Saints at Wittenberg. He joined Luther as early as 1517 and was thereafter one of his closest collaborators. He accompanied him to the Leipzig Disputation in 1519 and to the Diet of Worms in 1521 and assisted in the translation of the Bible. As a reformer he was active at Goslar, Einbeck, and Meissen, among other places, and especially at Magdeburg, where in 1524 he became senior minister. On 20 January 1542 Luther "ordained" him Protestant bishop of Naumburg, "without any chrism . . . oil, or incense" (*WA* 53, 231). In 1547 he had to give way to the Catholic Julius Pflug. He lived as a private scholar at Eisenach and took part in the founding of the University of Jena, which became the stronghold of Lutheran orthodoxy in opposition to "Philippist" Wittenberg. Amsdorf was averse to any compromise in the doctrines of justification and the Eucharist. Hence he was an opponent of the Wittenberg Accord of 1536, resisted the *Interim* of 1547, and came out against Melanchthon in the Synergist Controversy. If Melanchthon, and Georg Major (1502–74) after him, stressed the necessity of good works, if not for justification, at least for the preservation of faith and salvation, Amsdorf established against them the paradoxical opinion of the harmfulness of good works for the salvation of souls. He aimed by means of the Jena edition of Luther's works to transmit the latter's doctrine unadulterated to later generations. Hence he helped to canonize the reformer's theology in the sense of Lutheran orthodoxy and to stamp the latter with an inflexible intolerance.

The jurist Justus Jonas (1493–1555) had studied at Erfurt and Wittenberg and had joined the Erfurt humanist circle. An admirer of Erasmus, he discovered Scripture and the Fathers. From 1518 he was professor of canon law at Erfurt and in this capacity he was called to Wittenberg in 1521 and appointed provost of the castle church. He here changed to the theological faculty and gave exegetical lectures. He became one of Luther's chief collaborators and rendered valuable service in the translation of the Bible. He also put into German important writings of Luther and Melanchthon, including *De servo arbitrio, Loci communes,* and *Apologia Confessionis Augustanae.* His knowledge of law stood the Reformation in good stead on the occasion of church visitations, the setting up of the ecclesiastical organizations in Zerbst, Ducal Saxony, and Halle, and in the Wittenberg consistory. He later established the Reformation at Halle, where he became preacher in 1541 and senior minister in 1544. He accompanied Luther on his last journey in 1546, attended him at the hour of death, and delivered his eulogy at Eisleben.

Johannes Bugenhagen (1485–1558) was from Wollin in Pomerania and hence was known as Pomeranus. From 1504 he was headmaster in Treptow. In 1509, with no theological study, he was ordained a priest and in 1517 became lecturer in Scripture and patrology at the monastery school of Belbuck. Here he became acquainted with Luther's writings. At first shocked by the radicalism of *De captivitate Babylonica,* he was won by this very work, and in 1521 undertook the study of theology at Wittenberg. He was soon lecturing there on the Bible but did not obtain the doctorate in theology until 1533; in 1535 he was made a professor. Disregarding the chapter's right of presentation, the city council in 1523 elected him pastor of the parish church, and Luther announced the election from the pulpit. Bugenhagen had married the previous year. In a sense he created the model of the German Lutheran rectory and energetically stressed its blessings in *De coniugio episcoporum et diaconorum* (1525). As a gifted shepherd of souls, pastor rather than professor, he excelled Luther in his closeness to the people. He displayed more practical sense and did not share Luther's indifference to external forms. At Wittenberg he was even more in Luther's shadow than Melanchthon. His significance was more evident as the trail blazer of the Reformation in North Germany, where through numerous organizations of churches he laid the foundation for the local ecclesiastical structure. In addition to the years of cooperation and friendship, Bugenhagen was intimately bound to Luther as his adviser and confessor. He officiated at Luther's marriage in 1525, comforted him in sicknesses, temptations, and fits of depression, and in 1546 delivered his funeral sermon.

Georg Burckhardt (1484–1545) was from Spalt, near Nürnberg, and for that reason was known from 1502 as Spalatin. He studied the liberal arts at Erfurt, and here came under the spell of the humanist circle. In October 1502 he went with his teacher, Nikolaus Marschalk, to the newly founded University of Wittenberg and there became a master of arts in February 1503. He entered upon the study of law as his special field, but in 1504 he transferred to Erfurt, where Mutianus Rufus in Gotha became decisive for his life. Without completing his legal studies, in the fall of 1505 Spalatin accepted the post of instructor of the novices in the Cistercian monastery of Georgenthal, not far from Gotha. His turning to an ecclesiastical career probably derived chiefly from motives of economic security. As early as 1507, without any real theological preparation, he accepted the pastorate of Hohenkirchen and in 1508 had himself ordained a priest. At the end of that year he was called to Torgau to become tutor of the princes at the court of the Elector Frederick the Wise. From 1511 he was the teacher of the elector's nephews at Wittenberg and took over the direction of the library. In addition he worked on a Saxon chronicle and a history of his time.

Spalatin first came into contact with Luther in 1513–14, on the occasion of the Reuchlin controversy. There developed a friendship[1] which found expression in personal communications and in a lively correspondence—more than four hundred of Luther's letters to Spalatin have come down to us—and which reached its climax in 1521 in Luther's reform activity. The sequel to the encounter with Luther was a

[1] Spalatin's fascination with Luther is apparent from a letter of 2 May 1515, written by Johann Lang to Mutianus: "Eum Luther ipsum ut Apollinem Spalatinus noster veneraturque et consulit" (K. Gillert, *Der Briefwechsel des Conradus Mutianus,* Halle 1890 no. 490; cf. I. Hoss, *Spalatin,* p. 79).

growing interest in theological problems on the part of the humanist. In September 1516, with his appointment to the Elector's chancery, Spalatin entered the direct service of the court. In particular he had to be concerned with affairs of the university and of the ecclesiastical organization. With Luther, and soon with Melanchthon too, from 1517–18 he promoted the reform of studies in the direction of humanism and of the fostering of the biblical languages.

As private secretary, ecclesiastical adviser, and later court preacher, Spalatin acquired a powerful position in the confidence of the elector, which stood Luther in good stead in the critical years 1518–22. Frederick the Wise did not know the reformer personally; at least he had never spoken with him and for tactical reasons avoided his company. Spalatin acted as intermediary. With an eye for the politically acceptable and the possible, he exerted a moderating influence on Luther. Above all, he knew what could be expected of his prince, who was basically cautious and attached to the medieval Church organization, and how to communicate to him Luther's controversial views and actions. If he was unable to persuade the elector to Luther's views on indulgences and relics, Spalatin at least obtained the assurance that the Wittenberg professor could be certain of the elector's protection. This was decisive for the fate of Luther and of the Reformation. The Curia recognized the importance of Spalatin's influence on Luther's prince when in February 1518 it granted him extensive faculties for confession and the right to concede the indulgences attached to visiting the seven churches of Rome to corresponding exercises of devotion in the castle church.[2] In Rome it was as yet impossible to determine to what extent Spalatin supported Luther. Even in 1521 he still solicited benefices and took care to fulfill conscientiously his duties as the elector's priest and confessor. In keeping with his humanist's reserve, he drew the ultimate consequence of separation from the old Church much later than Luther. On the other hand, the reformer, in many respects insolently pugnacious and pressing his own affairs without regard for circumstances, understood how much he needed his diplomatically experienced friend. After receiving the papal summons he wrote to him on 8 August 1518: "I need your aid now most urgently, my Spalatin" (WA, Br 1, 188). But this did not prevent Luther in succeeding years from interfering time and again by biting statements and writings with the diplomatic activities of the prudent courtier and endangering their success. Just the same, Spalatin was able constantly to afford Luther effective protection. The

---

[2] WA, Br 1, 161f.; P. Kalkoff, Zu Luthers römischem Prozess (Gotha 1912), p. 74; Forschungen zu Luthers römischem Prozess (Rome 1905), p. 46; I. Hoss, Spalatin, pp. 127f.

elector did not need to acknowledge his Wittenberg professor publicly if he tended to his affairs only in a procrastinating manner.

Spalatin embodied a union of humanist culture with reform Christianity. Accordingly, he long sought to mediate between Luther and Erasmus. After the death of Frederick the Wise he accepted the pastorate of Altenburg in 1525 and here established his own household. But he continued to render service to the electoral Saxon court in religious negotiations, as at the diets of Speyer (1526) and Augsburg (1530) and in the compromise negotiations at Schweinfurt and Nürnberg in 1532. In 1527 he was named by the Elector Johann to the visitation commission and thereby obtained a prominent share in the organization of the Church government of the principality. The final years of quiet from 1540 were devoted to historical studies and to his congregation at Altenburg, where he died on 16 January 1545.

The most important of the men around Luther was Philip Melanchthon, originally Schwartzert (1497–1560). If his meeting Luther was the turning point in his life, for his part he had a strong influence on Luther and especially on the course of the Reformation, but he was always in the shadow of the greater and more active man. His relationship with Luther moved between intimate friendship and deep respect for a great achievement and groans over the "shameful servitude" (*CR* 6, 880) of Luther's irritable intolerance. He remained with Luther through all vicissitudes; even in serious crises and despite the allurement of honorable offers he could not bring himself to leave Wittenberg and the reformer's direct sphere of action.

Melanchthon was born at Bretten in Baden on 14 February 1497. The early death of his father served to enhance the influence of his great-uncle, Johann Reuchlin, on the course of his education. Directly or by means of his students, Reuchlin equipped the gifted youth with the ancient languages and introduced him into the world of Christian Platonism. After attending the Latin school at Pforzheim (1508–10) and earning his baccalaureate in the liberal arts at the University of Heidelberg (1511), Melanchthon transferred in 1512 to the University of Tübingen, where he became master of arts as early as January 1514. The great-nephew of the famous Hebraist was soon himself a celebrated teacher of classical literature and almost of necessity involved in the Reuchlin controversy. Reuchlin directed him to the field of theology, recommended the works of Jean Gerson and of Wessel Gansfort, and presented him with a New Testament, possibly Erasmus' Greek-Latin edition of 1516.

Quite early Melanchthon admiringly looked up to Erasmus as the master of linguistic elegance and humanist culture. Through Oecolampadius, whose friendship he gained at Tübingen, he probably came into contact with the great humanist. Beyond the distinction of his literary style, he was also won by Erasmus' ethically oriented humanism. For him Erasmus opened up the sources of Christian tradition, the works of the Fathers and their scriptural exegesis.

Despite some minor successes, the young scholar did not really make any great headway at Tübingen. Recommended by Reuchlin and with his encouragement, he accepted the chair of Greek and Hebrew at Wittenberg. In his inaugural lecture on 29 August 1518, "De corrigendis adulescentiae studiis," he advocated a scripturally oriented humanism:

> If we grasp the letter, we shall also comprehend the meaning of things. . . . And if we direct the mind to the sources, we shall begin to understand Christ, his commandments will enlighten us, and we shall be permeated by the blessed nectar of divine wisdom.[3]

Luther was won over to this humanism, which aimed by means of the languages of the Bible to unlock its content. He worked together with Melanchthon on the reform of studies, and the two were soon close friends. The friendship became even deeper when as early as 1518–19 the young humanist embraced Luther's reform ideas and devoted himself to theology. In the theses on the occasion of his obtaining the baccalaureate in theology on 9 September 1519 he proceeded further than Luther himself in his assault on the teaching of the Church.

Melanchthon never became a doctor of theology nor did he ever mount the pulpit. He was satisfied with being able to deliver theological lectures as a bachelor, without achieving full membership in the faculty. With great devotion he dedicated himself to exegetical lectures. We know of thirteen from the years 1518–22 alone, and these include three on Romans.[4] He regarded that epistle, along with the psalter, as the most outstanding book of the Bible, a guide to the understanding of the other books.[5] He gave eloquent expression to his enthusiasm for the new theology under the auspices of Saint Paul in his festive discourse of 25 January 1520, "In divi Pauli Doctrinam." The humanist, made rather for the scholar's study, even ventured into polemics. After the Leipzig Disputation, to which he had accompanied Luther, there ensued a sharp literary duel with Johannes Eck. And rather extensive polemics of 1521

---

[3] *CR*, 11, 23; *Studienausgabe* III, 40.

[4] *Studienausgabe* IV, 10f.

[5] *WA* 5, 24f. According to the preface of the Latin edition of Romans (Wittenberg 1520) this Epistle is "rerum theologicarum et summam et methodum continens."

attacked the Dominican Thomas Rodinus and the theologians of the Sorbonne.

Melanchthon's most valuable service to the young reform movement was a work he wrote during Luther's stay at the Wartburg, the *Loci communes rerum theologicarum seu hypotyposes theologicae* (1521). Employing his *Theologica institutio in epistolam Pauli ad Romanos* (CR 21, 49–60)—produced in connection with his lectures on Romans in 1519—and the *Rerum theologicarum capita seu loci* (CR 21, 11–48)—a discussion of the scholastic exegesis of "sentences"—and in conformity with the method developed in these treatises from the application of the rules of classical rhetoric to Scripture, Melanchthon listed the fundamental ideas or great essential subjects according to which the truths of revelation are to be arranged. This work made him the theologian of the Reformation, though the characterization of the *Loci* as the "first Protestant dogmatic theology" is applicable to the 1521 edition only in regard to its systematic presentation. The completeness expected of dogmatic theology is lacking. The doctrine of the Trinity and the Incarnation is excluded; only soteriology and ethics are treated. Melanchthon's concern is to grasp all of Scripture by means of the leading theological ideas which he acquired in his study of Romans—sin, law, grace, Gospel—to explain them as a unity, and to show their connection in salvation history. "The law shows sin; the Gospel, grace. The law proclaims sickness; the Gospel, the remedy" (CR 21, 139). Through the *Loci* Melanchthon aims to assist young students to a right understanding of Scripture and to stimulate them to the study of the Bible. The *Loci* are to be signposts or pole stars for "those wandering lost through the divine books" and to present the basic points of Scripture in outline (*hypotyposis*). The student is to be brought by means of a few ideas into direct contact with that "on which depends the totality of Christian doctrine" (CR 21, 82).

Without subjecting his humanism to a fundamental criticism, without even becoming entirely clear on the distinction between humanism and Reformation, as W. Maurer puts it, Melanchthon accepted radical theses of Luther's anthropology, such as man's inability to arrive at a natural knowledge of God and the lack of free will; saw in the law only a death-bringing law in contrast to the Gospel; and regarded only an ethics of faith as possible. But Melanchthon found himself in a serious crisis in 1521–22 because of the Wittenberg disturbances. He saw himself compelled to reexamine his theological ideas and to turn back more strongly to humanism and to the traditions of natural law of the Middle Ages. In the new editions of the *Loci,* from 1522, the door was again opened to a philosophical ethics. Fallen nature can know the *lex naturae,* and free will suffices for its external fulfillment. Thus the unbelieving man of the flesh can produce acts of virtue, which, while they do not lead to the justice of the heart, do make possible a civil justice (*iustitia civilis*). Now, too, the ceremonies of the Church and the enactments by authority are "good creations of God" and their disregard is a sin. If until this point Melanchthon was inclined to adjust everything, spiritual and secular, exclusively according to the Bible, now he begins to speak of a twofold justice, of a "justice of the spirit" and a "civil justice." Reason and tradition supply the norms for this natural ethics. Thus with Melanchthon there ensued a revival of the classical moral philosophy and even a sort of Protestant, humanist neo-Aristotelianism. This union of humanism and Reformation has been evaluated in differing ways up to our own day. The judgments range from Emanuel Hirsch's reproach that Melanchthon "heinously mutilated" Luther's doctrine of justification, to the conviction that he saved it. In between are those who speak of a synthesis[6] or of a juxtaposition and union[7] of humanism and Reformation in Melanchthon, of the hazards and at the same time of the blessings and fruitfulness of this amalgamation. In any case, it is due to him that the Reformation proceeded, not against but with the education of the age, and it was Melanchthon who, in the future, would largely determine the creed, ecclesiology, theology, and pedagogy of Lutheranism.

CHAPTER 9

The Pontificate of Adrian VI

Notwithstanding the Edict of Worms, the Reformation was able to spread without resistance. The German bishops took no steps, and the Pope, in accord with his character, was neither inclined nor fitted to introduce any effective measures of reform beyond the condemnation of Luther's doctrines. The Emperor was to be kept away from Germany for nine years by the wars with France and the necessity of establishing his authority in Spain. Furthermore, in his war on two fronts, against France and the Turks, he was dependent on the help of the very princes against whom he would have had to proceed if he enforced the Edict of Worms. Charles V's relations with Leo X were strained because of the Pope's pro-French policy and his having taken sides in the imperial election. However, it had become evident in the meantime that France was a threat rather than an effective help to the interests of the House of

[6] H. Bornkamm, "Melanchthons Menschenbild," in *Philipp Melanchthon. Forschungsbeiträge* (Göttingen 1961), pp. 76–70 (especially p. 90).
[7] W. H. Neuser, *Der Ansatz der Theologie Philipp Melanchthons* (Neukirchen 1957), p. 135.

Medici and the Papal State, whereas Spanish Naples was in a position to afford protection against the Muslim menace to the coasts. Indeed, if the Pope's anxiety in regard to the Turkish danger was serious, his place was at the side of the Emperor and not of the "Most Christian King" who was conspiring with the Turks. Finally, who but the Emperor was to master the Lutheran movement in Germany, so alarmingly described by Aleander? He showed himself to be obliging in this regard, and so Leo X inclined more and more to the imperial side. In May 1521 there emerged an alliance whose goal was to reestablish the rule of the Sforza at Milan and to deprive the French of Genoa. The Emperor promised aid against the enemies of the Catholic faith and was in turn promised imperial coronation in Italy together with help against Venice. Hence Italian politics were decisive, and the Pope was involved both as head of the House of Medici and as Prince of the Papal State.

The alliance was a success. As a result of a rising of the Milanese against the French, papal and imperial troops were able to occupy the city on 19 November 1521, and Francesco II Sforza assumed the government. But soon afterward, on 1 December, the Pope succumbed to malaria. This implied a serious upset in Italian politics and jeopardized the successes thus far gained in France.

But the change of pontificate seemed to assure especially favorable circumstances for cooperation between Emperor and Pope. The conclave, in which thirty-nine cardinals participated—only three of them non-Italians—was difficult. The cardinals, for the most part worldly and at enmity with one another, were a reflection of the Church and of Christendom. But on 9 January 1522 there occurred the completely unexpected election of the absent Cardinal Adrian of Utrecht, Bishop of Tortosa, in Spain. The disappointed Romans were enraged at the choice of the unknown "barbarian."

This Dutchman, the son of a carpenter, was born at Utrecht in 1459. Raised in the spirit of the *devotio moderna,* with a love of virtue and learning, he entered the University of Louvain in 1476. He there became a respected professor and dean of Sankt Peter. His commentary on the fourth book of *The Sentences* and his twelve *Quodlibeta* show him to have been a late scholastic deeply interested in canonical and moral and casuistic questions. In 1507 Emperor Maximilian I appointed him tutor of his grandson, the seven-year-old Archduke Charles. Thus Adrian entered the council of Margaret, Regent of the Netherlands, and in 1515 he was sent to Spain to assure Charles's succession to the throne. Ferdinand the Catholic annulled the will he had made in 1512, which had promised the Spanish crown to Charles's younger brother Ferdinand, raised in Spain and very popular there. After the death of King Ferdinand in 1516, Adrian, together with the great humanist Cardinal

Ximenes, conducted the regency for Charles until the new king was able to assume the government in Spain personally in 1517. Meanwhile Adrian had become Bishop of Tortosa in 1516 and inquisitor for Aragon and Navarre; he later became inquisitor for Castile and León also, and in January 1517 was made a cardinal. King Charles, in whose council Adrian had a seat, was unable to win the Spaniards. They complained of the arrogance of the Burgundians and the greed of the foreigners and they insisted on their liberties. Hence when Charles went to Germany in 1520, he turned over to the Cardinal as his representative a difficult assignment which proved to be too much for him. There was open revolt in Castile, and Adrian contrived to master it only with the aid of two coregents of Spanish blood. The news of the papal election reached him on January 22 at Vitoria, where he was instituting military measures for the defense of Navarre against France.

In a solemn statement on 8 March 1522, Adrian VI accepted the election. In it he emphasized his reliance on Christ, "who would endow him, though unworthy, with the strength necessary to protect the Church against the attacks of the Evil One, and to bring back the erring and deceived to the unity of the Church after the example of the Good Shepherd."[1] For his journey to Rome the Pope chose the sea route, to point up his independence of both France and the Empire. His departure was delayed and it was not until 5 August that he put to sea at Tarragona. He landed at Ostia on 28 August and a day later was in Rome.

In the meantime Belgrade had fallen to Sultan Suleiman, Hungary was defenseless before the threat of a Turkish invasion, and Rhodes, the last Christian outpost in the Mediterranean, was being besieged by superior forces. The Pope would be able to deal with the tasks imposed on him by this situation only if he succeeded in restoring the political and religious unity of Christendom. For this a reform of the Church was necessary and it had to begin with the Curia. Only thus could the Church win back confidence as a prerequisite for carrying out her functions as the regulating authority in the West.

To the Romans Adrian was a barbarian. At the time of the Pope's arrival a pestilence was raging in the Eternal City, and his coronation at Saint Peter's on 31 August was reduced to the simplest form. In his address in the consistory on 1 September Adrian asked the aid of the cardinals in his twofold concern: the uniting of the Christian princes for a war against the Turks and the reform of the Curia.[2] Evil, he said, had become so widespread that, to quote Saint Bernard, those covered with

[1] Pastor, *Geschichte der Päpste* IV, 2, 35; *The History of the Popes* IX, 49.
[2] A. Mercati, *Diarii,* 88, with footnote 47.

sins no longer noticed the stench of vice. The cardinals should set a good example for the rest of the clergy.

If the Pope's stern asceticism and piety—his daily celebration of Mass, for example, was unusual—impressed many people quite unfavorably, for most it was even more distressing that he was so stingy with favors. In the consistory of 26 March 1523 the Cardinal of Santa Croce requested the confirmation of the indults and privileges granted by Leo X. When on this occasion he recalled the unprecedented pleasure of the cardinals at having elevated him to the height of the papacy, Adrian replied that they had called him to suffering and prison. He had found an exhausted and impoverished Church and hence he owed them little. Actually they were his executioners.[3] The dull Dutch scholar apparently had no sympathy for the Italian way of life and the splendor of Renaissance art. When he set about abolishing superfluous offices and showing the door to the beneficiaries of Leo X's prodigal mode of life, the widespread consternation and aversion became bitter hatred. His predecessors had bequeathed to Adrian debts and empty coffers. In addition it was necessary to redeem valuables and works of art, including the Gobelins made after Raphael's designs, which had had to be pawned after the death of Leo X. Drastic economy measures were thus necessary, all the more if the Pope intended to renounce, within the scope of Church reform, the excessive fees which were causing so much bad feeling throughout the world. Adrian's thrift brought upon him the reputation of being a miser. The Romans forgave him this far less than they had pardoned the prodigality of his predecessor.

In addition, Adrian's activities were initially hindered by the plague, which in the fall became worse. On 1 October the Swiss Cardinal Schinner, one of his few reform-minded colleagues, fell victim to it. Against all warnings the Pope stayed in Rome, whereas the cardinals and most officials sought to get as far away as possible. It was only at the end of 1522 that the Curia could again be activated. Collaborators in the carrying out of reform were lacking. The difficulties of the few Dutch and Spaniards, whom the Pope trusted, were increased by the unfamiliar environment, and their ineptitude provoked further opposition. Disillusionment made the Pope even more suspicious of his retinue and even more lonely, and induced him to do much on his own. Added to this, the northerner's ponderous and pedantic methods produced even louder complaints about the slow course of business. Pastor sums it up: "A foreigner, surrounded by foreign confidants, the Dutch pope was unable to find his way about in the new world which confronted him in Rome."

---

[3] Ibid., 95.

The slower the reform of the Curia proceeded, the more difficult became the Pope's position in Germany. He saw himself compelled at the Diet of Nürnberg in 1522–23 to ask the estates to be patient. During the absence of Charles V the religious question was turned over to the Imperial Governing Council, which met at Nürnberg on 1 October 1521. It consisted of twenty-three representatives of the several imperial estates. One elector and two other princes—one secular and one spiritual—were to serve in it, changing every three months. With such organizational weakness consistent action and continuity were possible only with great difficulty. Despite these unpropitious conditions the Imperial Governing Council accomplished much that was useful and it especially sought to adjust the divergent interests to the "common good." The endeavor to coordinate criminal justice provided the basis for the *Carolina* (1532). For defense against the Turks it aimed to provide the Empire with a permanent revenue by means of an imperial toll, a withholding of annates, and a reform of the "common pfennig," an imperial tax established in 1495.

The commotion in Saxony and the fall of Belgrade to the Turks peremptorily showed the urgency of unifying the Empire and of exorcising the religious unrest by means of reform, and Adrian VI meant to extend a helping hand. To the Diet of Nürnberg, which had been summoned for 1 September 1522 but did not actually meet until 17 November, he sent Francesco Chieregati. The legate made known the Pope's agreement that annates and pallium fees should for the future be retained in Germany and spent on the Turkish war; but he also vigorously demanded German assistance for imperiled Hungary.[4] It was only on 10 December that the legate referred to the religious situation in Germany. The erroneous doctrine of Luther was, he said, more threatening than the Turkish danger, and the Pope demanded the implementation of the Edict of Worms.[5] The estates gave an evasive reply and showed little inclination to occupy themselves with this delicate question. Only Elector Joachim of Brandenburg, who did not arrive until 23 December, energetically urged the matter, with the support of the Archduke Ferdinand and the Archbishop of Salzburg. On 3 January 1523 the legate read aloud the documents forwarded to him, a brief and an instruction, in which the Pope, in view of the Turkish peril, deplored the religious danger produced by Luther. Worse even than his errors, said the Pope, was the fact that, despite papal condemnation and imperial edict, he had found patrons and adherents among the princes. It seemed incredible to the Pope that a

[4] *RA* III, no. 54.
[5] Ibid., no. 73.

nation so pious would let itself be led by an insignificant friar [*fraterculum*], who has apostatized from the Catholic faith, away from the path shown by the Saviour and his Apostles . . . almost as though only Luther were wise and possessed the Holy Spirit, whereas the Church . . . had been wandering about in the darkness of folly and on the road to ruin until Luther's new light had enlightened her.[6]

The Pope spoke in a similar vein in the instruction. Here, however, he not only deplored and condemned heresy and the schism in the Church produced by the Lutheran movement, but he also laid bare the deeper causes and with an unprecedented candor admitted the guilt of Curia and Church. At the same time he asked patience, since abuses so deeply rooted could not be eradicated at one stroke.

You are to say also that we frankly confess that God has allowed this punishment to overtake his Church because of the sins of men, and especially those of priests and prelates. . . . Holy Scripture loudly proclaims that the sins of the people have their source in the sins of the priesthood. . . . We are well aware that even in this Holy See much that is detestable has appeared for some years already—abuses in spiritual things, violation of the commandments—and that everything has been changed for the worst. Hence it is not to be wondered at that the sickness has been transmitted from the head to the members, from the popes to the prelates. All of us, prelates and clergy, have turned aside from the road of righteousness and for a long time now there has been not even one who did good [Psalm 13(14), 3]. Hence we must all give glory to God and humble ourselves before him. Everyone of us must consider why he has fallen and judge himself rather than be condemned by God on the day of his wrath. You must therefore promise in our name that we intend to exert ourselves so that, first of all, the Roman Court, from which perhaps all this evil took its start, may be improved. Then, just as from here the sickness proceeded, so also from here recovery and renewal may begin. We regard ourselves as all the more obliged to carry this out, because the whole world demands such a reform. . . . However, no one should be amazed that we do not liquidate all abuses at one blow. For the disease is deeply entrenched and of many shapes. Therefore, progress must be made step by step, and first of all the most serious and most dangerous evils must be dealt with by proper medicines, lest everything become still more chaotic through a

[6] Ibid., no. 75, pp. 401f.

premature reform. Aristotle rightly says that any sudden change in a community is dangerous.[7]

The Pope's confession of guilt, which must be regarded above all as a religious act and the prerequisite of inner reform in the Curia, and his appeal to the estates had no immediate decisive effect. Hans von der Planitz, a councilor of the Elector of Saxony, knew how to postpone the decision by referring it to a committee and at the same time directing attention to the lot of four Lutheran preachers in Nürnberg, whose arrest Chieregati had demanded. Finally, on 5 February 1523, the estates replied to the nuncio. Proceedings against Luther would evoke the most serious disturbances unless first the Roman Curia, from which, admittedly, the corruption had proceeded, was reformed and the *gravamina* of the German nation were remedied. The Pope, in agreement with the Emperor, should, as quickly as possible and at least within a year, convoke a free Christian council in a German city. Meanwhile the Elector of Saxony should see to it that Luther and his adherents neither wrote nor published anything else. The secular and ecclesiastical estates would during the same time guarantee the suppression of any inflammatory preaching and pledge themselves that nothing but the true, pure, authentic, and holy Gospel should be preached, according to the approved interpretation of the Church and the Fathers.[8]

These vague and procrastinating statements were the outcome of a diet at which the ecclesiastical estates predominated. If the discussion of the religious question was irksome to them anyway, they did not regard themselves as obligated by the Pope's cry for penance to reflection and energetic penitence but instead felt themselves offended and exposed.

The reaction of Luther and Melanchthon was equally irreligious. It was published in 1523 in their pamphlet *Deutung der zwei gräulichen Figuren, Papstesels zu Rom und Mönchskalbs zu Freiberg in Meissen gefunden* (WA 11, 369–385). Luther considered it not worth the trouble to acknowledge Adrian's good intentions. To him the Pope was "a *magister noster* from Louvain, a university in which such jackasses are crowned." It is Satan who speaks through the Pope.

In his concern for the Church, in which the Curia left him unaided, the Pope looked about for outside help. In December 1522 he asked his countryman Erasmus, whom he had known from his days at Louvain, to employ his scholarship and his stylistic gifts against the "new heretics." He could not render a greater service, the Pope said, to God, the fatherland, and Christendom. He also invited him to Rome, where he

---

[7] Ibid., no. 74, pp. 397f.
[8] Ibid., no. 82.

would have an ample supply of books at his disposal and would find an opportunity for contacts with scholars and pious men.[9] The prince of humanists had congratulated Adrian on his elevation and had dedicated to him his edition of Arnobius' commentary on the Psalms.[10] In a second letter he had offered his counsel to the Pope.[11] The latter asked the scholar to come to Rome or to make known his suggestions as soon as possible. The proper measures had to be found "in order to expel the dreadful malady from the midst of our nation, while it is still curable."[12] Erasmus warned against recourse to force and advised the Pope to surround himself with a circle of incorruptible and worthy men, free from personal animosity. But he declined for himself, pleading poor health. He could do more at Basel; if he should go to Rome and thus openly take sides, his writings would lose their influence.[13]

Unlike Erasmus, Johannes Eck was ready to do what he could for the Pope's reform work. He came to Rome in March 1523 to represent the interests of the Dukes of Bavaria, but he was able to join to this assignment the welfare of the Church and of Christendom. For the enhancing of the Bavarian Dukes' authority over the Church meant a guarantee against the unreliability of the episcopate. In his memoranda Eck called for the restoration of the conciliar system, whose decay was responsible for both the abuses in the Church and the revolt. A general council would not be achieved so quickly. Besides, for Eck the business of Luther was a German affair. He urgently insisted that a mere attack on error would do no good without a serious undertaking of Church renewal. With regard to reform in Rome, Eck called especially for a limitation of indulgences and the abolition of *commendam*.[14]

The Italian political situation had stabilized before the Pope's entry into Rome. A French countermove had been thwarted on 27 April 1522 by German mercenaries under Jörg von Frundsberg, and the French had lost Genoa. Charles V, convinced that God himself had arranged Adrian's election, wrote to the Pope that, united in harmony,

---

[9] Letter of 1 December 1522; P. S. Allen, *Opus epistularum D. Erasmi* V (Oxford 1924), 145–150. On Erasmus and Adrian VI see L. R. Halkin, "Adrien VI et la reforme de l'eglise," *EThL* 33 (1959), 534–542, 539ff.

[10] Cf. the foreword to the edition of Arnobius of 1 August 1522 (Allen, V, 99) and the letter of September 1522 to Adrian (Allen, V, 121f.). At the same time Erasmus wrote to John Fisher in regard to the Pope: "Is qualis olim fuerit novi, qualis futurus sit in magistratu tanto nescio. Illus unum scio, totus est scholasticus, nec admodum aequus bonis litteris" (Allen, V, 123).

[11] Letter of 22 December 1522 (Allen, V, 155f.).

[12] Letter of 23 January 1523 (Allen, V, 196ff.).

[13] Letter of 22 December 1522 (Allen, V, 155f.); of 22 March 1523 (Allen, V, 257–261).

[14] *Acta reformationis catholicae*, ed. G. Pfeilschifter, I (Regensburg 1959), 109–150.

they would accomplish great feats. Naturally he expected Adrian to join the league against Francis I. But the Pope, already under suspicion of being a partisan of his former pupil, had to maintain a strict neutrality if his efforts for peace among the princes of Europe for the sake of defense against the Turks were to be crowned with success. This endeavor to maintain his independence vis-à-vis Charles V and especially his tactless and importunate envoy led to a temporary estrangement from the Emperor, without gaining for the Pope the confidence of the French king.

On 21 December 1522, Rhodes fell to the Turks. The Pope's intensified exertions to unite the Christian princes for resistance or at least to arrange a truce were fruitless. All the more he sought by means of tithes and taxes to raise money himself for the Turkish war. In his distress he made concessions to the princes which contradicted his own principles. The disagreement with Charles V and the more flexible attitude of Francis I enabled Cardinal Soderini, a long-time partisan of France, to gain the Pope's confidence and to draw him into the twilight of partiality. A rising against the Emperor was to be contrived in Sicily, and Francis I intended to exploit it for an attack on North Italy. Soderini was arrested and thereafter Cardinal Giuliano de Medici exercised a decisive influence in the Curia. The Pope still tried to bring about peace. On 30 April 1523 he proclaimed a three-year truce for all of Christendom and stipulated the severest ecclesiastical penalties as its sanction. At the end of July he arranged the Peace of Venice with the Emperor.

This and Soderini's trial caused Francis I to show his true colors. In a very insulting letter he threatened the Pope with the fate of Boniface VIII.[15] He also stopped the transfer of money to Rome and readied troops for an invasion of Lombardy. Thus the Pope witnessed the collapse of his peace efforts. On 3 August 1523 he entered into a defensive alliance with the Emperor, with King Henry VIII of England, with Ferdinand of Austria, and with Milan, Florence, Genoa, Siena, and Lucca. In his disillusionment Adrian VI in a sense collapsed. He died on 14 September 1523, after a pontificate of less than thirteen months. This brief time and the unpropitiousness of the circumstances frustrated great hopes and fulfilled the Pope's melancholy inscription on his tomb: "Oh, how much depends upon the time in which the work of even the best man falls!"

---

[15] A. Mercati, op. cit., 107f.

The Struggle over the Concept of Christian Freedom

CHAPTER 10

The Knights' War

Luther's message *To the Christian Nobility of the German Nation on the Improvement of the Christian Estate* did not die out unheard. While the reformer had at this point taken up the complaints of the humanists and of the Free Knights and made himself the spokesman of national self-assertion against "the shameful and diabolical rule of the Romans" (*WA* VI, 415), conversely many people had become enthusiastic about Luther's religious message because they assured themselves it would mean the fulfillment of their economic, social, and political expectations. The revolt of the Free Knights in 1522–23 and the Peasants' War of 1524–25 indicated the connection of the religious movement with social and political currents.

The profound changes in the economic, social, and political situation at the beginning of the modern age had pushed the estate of the knights into the background. Its position was based on landed property and the feudal rights derived from it. The more a natural economy was replaced by a money economy, a person-oriented feudalism by the territorial and bureaucratic state, and the feudal levy by mercenaries with firearms and cannon, the more the knights, rendered militarily insignificant, were threatened with being crushed by the aspiring cities and princely power. On the other hand, they were no longer ready to support and represent the Empire. They shunned service and refused to pay the "common pfennig." They further undermined the authority of the Empire by violating the territorial peace. By means of private feuds and local conflicts they aimed to enhance their own power and wealth. They were in no way different from the cities and princes in exploiting the weakness of the central power for their own interests. Any of them who was unwilling to maintain himself in a state befitting his rank by more or less disguised brigandage and plundering expeditions had either to enter the service of a territorial prince or to try to raise himself to the position of a territorial prince. This last was possible almost exclusively at the expense of the ecclesiastical principalities. But their elimination meant a great loss for the nobility, which occupied virtually all the episcopal sees and canonicates in Germany. Hence by no means all the knights could be won for a "war on priests." Among those uninterested were extensive groups of Franconian knights who were variously related to ecclesiastical dignitaries.

Ulrich von Hutten (1488–1523) had publicized the "war on priests" since the end of 1520 from Ebernburg an der Nahe, where he had found asylum with Franz von Sickingen (1481–1523). It was not to end without "murderous struggle and the shedding of blood." From this time on Hutten wrote in German; he had his Latin dialogues published as "conversation booklets." His fiery and inspiring polemics gained him great influence over public opinion. But what continued to be literature to him became for Franz von Sickingen and other knights a disastrous and suicidal act.

Franz von Sickingen was born in 1481 at Ebernburg, the scion of a ministerial family of the Palatinate, which in 1488 became a direct imperial vassal. He claimed to have studied under Reuchlin. In 1504 he entered into his paternal inheritance and was successful in strengthening his position. He exploited mines and maintained a small force in his capacity as an official of the Palatinate and in the service of the Archbishop of Mainz. He distinguished himself from the robber knights of his day only through the style and the degree of his enterprises. Exploiting the situation of the Empire, he was able, in attacks on Worms, Metz, Frankfurt, Lorraine, and Hesse, to make himself a considerable political and financial power on the middle Rhine by means of extortion. Under the guise of the knightly ideals of the struggle for justice and the protection of the weak, he had the lower classes turn over to him their alleged and real legal titles and defended them with modern military means such as artillery and mercenaries.

Outlawed for breach of the territorial peace, he entered the service of France. But he was reconciled with Emperor Maximilian, advocated the election of Charles V, and in 1519 took part in the campaign against Ulrich of Württemberg. In this way he became friendly with Hutten and favored his national humanism. Accordingly he supported Reuchlin and forced the Dominicans of the upper Rhine to give way in the controversy with the great humanist. Von Sickingen's castles, as "inns of justice," became places of refuge for reformers such as Bucer, Oecolampadius, Aquila, and Schwebel. He espoused the cause of the Reformation in pamphlets such as *Sendbrieff zu Unterrichtung etlicher Artickel Christliches glaubens* (1522). But the religious question had little effect on him. He had as meager a grasp of the Lutheran doctrine of justification as Hutten had, much as they declared their desire to open a door to the Gospel. Instead they were influenced by the "struggle for German freedom and justice," as they understood it. At an assembly of knights at Landau on 13 August 1522 a "fraternal alliance" of the knights of the middle and upper Rhine, which also had connections with the Franconian nobility, elected von Sickingen their captain. Thereafter disputes were to be settled only by a special knights' court.

Thus assured, von Sickingen began preparations for a great raid against Richard von Greiffenklau, Archbishop of Trier. The challenge was issued on 27 August 1522, and the matter was at first a private affair. The archbishop was said to have designated two citizens of Trier to commit perjury and not to have paid the ransom agreed upon. But the chief reason alleged was that the Elector, as a partisan of Francis I of France, had, on the occasion of the imperial election, "acted against God, the imperial majesty, and the order and justice of the Holy Empire." Finally, the declaration of war spoke of the opening of the struggle as a campaign for the honor of Christ against the enemies and destroyers of the truth of the Gospel.

In the final analysis what was afoot was a grand-scale brigandage under the pretext of an appeal to ideals. The secularization of the archbishopric was supposed to enable von Sickingen to advance to princely status. But he was unable to mobilize groups of his own estate for this, and still less to separate the city of Trier from the archbishop. The promise to the archbishop's subjects to rescue them from the harsh anti-Christian law of priests and to conduct them to evangelical freedom did not prove very effective.

As a warrior, Richard von Greiffenklau was the equal of von Sickingen and knew how to make use of artillery at least as well as his opponent did. Von Sickingen captured Blieskastel and on 3 September 1522 the city of Sankt Wendel. His force is said to have consisted at that time of 600 cavalry and 7,000 infantry.[1] But he did not attempt to exploit his initial successes at once. While he was awaiting reinforcements the archbishop had time to put Trier into a state of defense and to mobilize defensive forces. When von Sickingen appeared before the city on 8 September he was unable to accomplish much and had to withdraw after an eight-day siege. The Archbishop of Trier, to whose aid the Landgrave of Hesse and the Elector Palatine came by virtue of the "agreement" of Oberwesel (1519), could now proceed to the offensive. In April 1523 he undertook a punitive expedition against von Sickingen. The latter had to retire to his castle of Landstuhl, where he vainly waited for reinforcements and at length was forced to capitulate on 7 May. The victorious princes found him, mortally wounded, behind the shattered walls of the castle, and a few hours later he died of his

---

[1] *RA* III (Gotha 1901), no. 148, p. 802; K. H. Rendenbach, *Die Fehde von Sickingens gegen Trier* (Berlin 1933), pp. 59f.

injuries. Not real power but a skillful and unscrupulous exploitation of the entangled political situation had conducted von Sickingen to success, but when he ran into determined opposition before Trier, he failed miserably. His cause was thereby stripped of its prestige, and the collapse of the knightly estate became clear.

In the summer of 1523 an army of the Swabian League under Baron Georg Truchsess von Waldburg took the field against the Franconian and Swabian knights to put an end to their brigandage and violations of the territorial peace. A cooperative defense by the knights did not materialize. The still bold and defiant resistance of individuals did not suffice when faced with superiority of numbers. In barely six weeks thirty-two castles were burned in the Odenwald and in Franconian Württemberg, and the knightly class was finished as a political force shaping the Empire. The winners were the territorial princes. Some of these saw in the Reformation a promoter of revolution, and this strengthened their will to fight against it.

CHAPTER 11

The "Fanatics" Karlstadt and Müntzer

Men like Melanchthon were so overshadowed by Luther that we are able only with difficulty to evaluate their personal achievement and their significance in the development and form of the Reformation. But there were others, such as Karlstadt and Müntzer, who so quickly ran afoul of Luther, and hence were isolated by him and turned into sectarians, that they were unable to develop and to make their full personal contribution to the reform movement. Neither of them was granted a long and consistent activity nor any possibility of lasting innovation. Only starting points can be examined and these allow no certain judgment. Furthermore, their image was, even in their lifetime, given a prejudiced stamp by the polemics of their opponents, notably Luther. The latter originated the word *Schwärmer,* "fanatics," for Karlstadt and Müntzer as well as for all factions which did not accord with his views, such as those of Zwingli and the Swiss. Only quite recently, and even today inadequately, has the trouble been taken to understand men such as Müntzer and Karlstadt from the basis of their own world of ideas. Thus the numerous works of Karlstadt, which, because they were frequently suppressed, have come down to us only in a few defective first printings, found no revised editions.[1]

Karlstadt

Andreas Rudolf Bodenstein was born around 1480 at Karlstadt am Main and is known by the name of his birthplace. He matriculated at Erfurt in 1499, but he was chiefly influenced not by Erfurt's nominalism but by the Thomism of Cologne, where he studied till the end of 1504. He then went to Wittenberg as a strict Thomist. He became a doctor of theology there in 1510 and was elected archdeacon of the Chapter of All Saints. He held lectures on Aristotle and Saint Thomas. In these he represented a scholastic position opposed to that of Martin Luther, who became doctor of theology in 1512 while Karlstadt was dean and was soon attracting attention by his lectures on the Psalms and Romans. In 1515 Karlstadt traveled to Italy and after a brief stay in Rome gained a doctorate of laws at Siena in 1516. He had thereby acquired the prerequisites for obtaining the provostship at Wittenberg.

From the beginning of 1517 he was preoccupied with Saint Augustine in preparation for a critical discussion of Luther's interpretation of that Father. Under the spell of Augustine's works, especially the anti-Pelagian writings, he became favorably inclined toward Luther. This is evident from Karlstadt's 151 theses on Augustine's theology of 26 April 1517, which were hailed by Luther as witnesses of the new theology (*WA, Br* 1, 94), and from his commentary on Augustine's *De spiritu et litera*. In the dedication to Johann Staupitz of 18 November 1517 Karlstadt relates that he had intended to forge from Augustine's works weapons against Luther, but he had been converted to the new theology.

> The truth thus revealed made me blush and filled me with awe at the same time. For I recognized that I had been made a fool of in a thousand scholastic theses—an ass at the mill, a blind man on the stone—that I had hitherto talked nonsense.[2]

In Karlstadt's commentary the most important question deals with justice and the fulfilling of the law. Of himself man cannot fulfill the law. Justice based on the law—that is, man's claim to fulfill the law by his own strength—is in the strict sense ungodliness, because man attributes to

---

[1] The list of printed works given by E. Freys and H. Barge (*ZblB,* 21 1904) cites sixty-eight writings in 156 printings. E. Hertzsch, *Karlstadts Schriften aus den Jahren 1523–25* (Halle 1956f.) has edited eight of these.
[2] E. Kahler, *Karlstadt und Augustin* (Halle 1952), p. 5.

himself what is God's.[3] It is the function of the law to lay bare man's inability and to testify that man cannot become just by the law or his own free will, but "only through the help of the Spirit and through God's gift" (p. 70). The law thus proves our weakness and indicates him, Christ, from whom we must obtain through faith the ability to do what the law commands (p. 71).

More so than Luther, Karlstadt sees justification as sanctification. Grace signifies a change affecting the whole man, qualifying him for good actions but for that very reason requiring of him also a strict moral conduct. If for Luther the tension between law and Gospel persisted and the law retained the function of disclosing and denouncing man's sin, Karlstadt did not rest content with the opposition of spirit and world, which he felt deeply, but taught, in conjunction with Augustine, that grace enables us to love and to fulfill the law.[4] Grace turns the hearer into a doer of the law. In grace, which is identified with love, Christ gives himself to us and through the Holy Spirit effects good works in us. "Christ himself makes us act; he himself makes his work our good works" (p. 18). The justice bestowed on us is only a deposit; we must take further pains with it.[5] In this life it does not acquire full perfection, and hence no man is without sin.[6]

Like law and grace, Scripture and the spirit are oriented to each other. If the law without grace is dead, and in fact brings death, then the letter is dead without the life-giving spirit (p. 34). Christ must enlighten the inner man for a right understanding of the external word. "Thus we direct our ears to the preacher and our eyes to the letters, but our heart only to God, creator of heaven and earth, who from within, as the true word, first breathes life into all works and touches the heart" (p. 27). It is incorrect to see in these Augustinian ideas a "devaluation of the external, the preached word."[7] The nominalist Luther was in more danger of undervaluing the external or of representing it as insignificant than Karlstadt was.

The profound difference between the two men was not apparent at first. Karlstadt's theses of May 1518, a confrontation with Eck's *Obelisci,*

---

[3] "Illa iustitia est proprie impietas, qua sibi tribuit homo, quod dei est" (ibid., p. 70).
[4] Thesis 85 of 26 April 1517: "Gratia facit nos legis dilectores et factores."
[5] "Nam facere iusticiam est incipere facere, est tendere ad iusticiam et operari" (E. Kahler, op. cit, p. 30).
[6] ". . . nullum hominem hic viventem inveniri sine peccato, hoc est, perfectam et ex omni parte absolutam iusticiam facere . . . non erit hic vita sine peccato, non erit hic ex omni parte absoluta iusticia" (ibid., p. 21).
[7] This is E. Kahler's interpretation (op. cit., p. 41). E. Wolf, "Gesetz und Evangelium in Luthers Auseinandersetzung mit den Schwärmern," *EvTh* 5 (1938), 96–109, sees here "the separating of letter and spirit as the principle of scriptural exegesis" (p. 103). Karlstadt "has no confidence in the word of God" (p. 105).

maintained the scriptural principle and the fallibility of a general council. They and the Leipzig Disputation, for which the theses were responsible, made the two Wittenberg professors appear in the eyes of the public as fighters for the same cause. Karlstadt was above all concerned about the relationship of divine grace and the human will. How little he undervalued the external word of Holy Scripture is made clear in his *De canonicis scripturis* of August 1520,[8] in which he opposed the rejection of the Epistle of James and insisted that sympathy or antipathy is no criterion for the evaluation of Scripture. He thereby criticized Luther, but not by name. For Karlstadt the authority of the canonical Scripture is absolute, standing above every human authority, papal and episcopal included.

When Johannes Eck added Karlstadt's name in the Bull "Exsurge Domine," threatening excommunication, Karlstadt replied with an "appeal"[9] to the general council. He made crystal clear his break with the Church in his treatise *Von päpstlicher Heiligkeit.*[10]

> If I preach the liberty of Christ to the laity, your excommunication and your malediction must be for me a refreshing dew . . . . All Christians are priests, for they are built on the rock which makes them priests. Christ is that specially chosen rock . . . . Hence it follows that faith in Christ makes all believers priests or pastors and that priests receive nothing new when they are ordained but are only chosen for the office and the ministry.[11]

Karlstadt spent May and June 1521 in Denmark as adviser to King Christian II in the latter's Reformation or, more correctly, in his legislative work against the clergy. But after the Edict of Worms he was no longer welcome at the court of the Dane, who was a brother-in-law of Charles V. When Karlstadt returned to Wittenberg in mid-June, Luther was at the Wartburg. Thus Karlstadt automatically moved more prominently into the foreground. In his treatise on the Eucharist, *Von den Emphahern, Zeichen, und Zusag des heiligen Sakramentes, Fleisch und Blut Christi*[12] he is more moderate than Luther. He does not yet demand the chalice for the laity and quite naturally maintains the real presence. On the other hand, he goes further in the attack on religious vows and celibacy.[13] In dispute at Wittenberg over the conformity of the

---

[8] Freys-Barge, nos. 34f.

[9] 19 October 1522; Freys-Barge, no. 45.

[10] 17 October 1520; Freys-Barge, no. 44.

[11] H. Barge, *Andreas Bodenstein von Karlstadt* (Leipzig 1905), I, 234.

[12] 24 June 1521; Freys-Barge, nos. 54–58.

[13] "Von Gelübden Unterrichtung" (1521; Freys-Barge, nos. 50–53); "Super coelibatu, monachatu et viduitate axiomata" (1521; Freys-Barge, nos. 59–62).

liturgy with Scripture, he maintains in contrast to Luther that private Masses are permissible in case of need. In any case they are to be preferred to a public Mass without communion under both species. Now Karlstadt held that "one who takes only the bread commits sin"[14] and, unlike Luther, did not allow communion under one species. Luther, however, saw unlawfulness in the Mass celebrated privately (WA, Br 2, 395) and wrote to Melanchthon on 1 August 1521: "I will never again celebrate a private Mass" (WA, Br 2, 372). It was not Karlstadt but Gabriel Zwilling and the Augustinians who took the initiative in introducing the reformed liturgy. Partly out of regard for Frederick the Wise, Karlstadt was more hesitant. He, much more than Luther, pressed for the practical consequences of the reform doctrines and the abolition of everything that in his view was opposed to the Gospel. To him, a realist, it was not possible, as it was to the nominalist Luther, to leave dialectical propositions unreconciled. He urged solutions, syntheses, and consequences, and on this are founded his rationalism as well as his mystical thinking.

Karlstadt intended, however, to realize his concept of a congregational Christianity quietly and with the cooperation of the city council. At a disputation on 17 October 1521, in which Karlstadt rejected transubstantiation while demanding the adoration of the sacramental bread, and allowing private Masses in case of necessity, for the sake of communion under both species, Melanchthon impetuously demanded: "Somebody has to make a start; otherwise nothing will happen." Karlstadt retorted: "Indeed, but without any tumult and without providing opponents with an opportunity for slander."[15]

Toward the close of the year he let himself be more and more driven to a change of liturgy by the turbulent pressure of radical elements in the population. Thus, disregarding the elector's regulations, on Christmas 1521 he celebrated the first "German Mass," a Mass with the account of the institution of the Eucharist in German and with communion under both species. He rejected liturgical vestments and let the laity touch with their hands the Eucharistic bread and the chalice to demonstrate that there was no need of a priestly class and that the laity are ministers of the liturgy. On 19 January 1522, in the presence of a group of professors and of Wittenberg councilors, he solemnized his marriage. He had a decisive influence on the Wittenberg city ordinance of 24 January 1522, and vigorously demanded the removal of images by the city council, thinking thus to forestall an iconoclastic outbreak. But in

[14] Thesis 10 of 19 July 1521; cf. E. Hertzsch, *Karlstadts Schriften*, p. 13; H. Barge, I, 290.
[15] H. Barge, I, 323.

fact through this pamphlet and his sermons he fostered radicalism in Wittenberg. When the electoral councilor Einsiedel called upon him for moderation, he expressly protested against the accusation of insurrection. "I pride myself on hating and shunning insurrection. God grant that my detractors do not in time stir up revolt, which will accomplish no good. I forbid revolt."[16]

Thinking that he had acted in accord with Luther, Karlstadt was deeply hurt by Luther's harsh criticism of him as a fanatic and author of disturbance. The pulpit was denied him (*WA, Br* 2, 478), as was any relationship with the community. A treatise in which he defended those of his reforms that Luther had annulled was censured by the university. This and the measures of restoration taken by Luther, the "neopapist," led to a deeper alienation and hastened Karlstadt's own development, which deviated ever more from the path of the Lutheran Reformation. His unpleasant experiences with his colleagues at the university strengthened his anticultural tendencies, which had been becoming more evident since the beginning of 1523. Condemning the new scriptural scholarship and its dogmatic posturing, he turned more and more to the laity, drawing the ultimate consequences of Luther's teaching on the universal priesthood. He stressed the laity's obligation to read the Bible and their right to interpret it. In *Eine Frage, ob auch jemand möge selig werden ohne die Fürbitte Mariens*[17] he would soon advocate the opinion that many craftsmen were more proficient in theology than priests. Once a prelate of high rank and an intellectually proud professor, thereafter he would live, without academic title or official dress, as "a new layman," like the peasants.

Physically too he took his leave of Wittenberg, taking personal charge in the summer of 1523 of the parish of Orlamünde, the revenues of which he drew as archdeacon of the All Saints collegiate chapter. Here he introduced the changes in the liturgy that had been annulled at Wittenberg, enriched the church singing with German translations of psalms, and preached daily to a great concourse of people.

In contrast to Luther, who attributed no importance to external form and regarded it as *adiaphoron,* Karlstadt felt compelled to press for the changing of what he regarded as wrong practices—expressions, ceremonies, images—because they seduced the people. "Not for my sake but for the sake of the sick and the weak, who are misled by such words and prevented from making progress and coming to God."[18] To wait in this matter, as Luther wanted to do, until the inner judgment was sound

---

[16] Letter of 4 February 1522, to Hugo von Einsiedel; cf. N. Müller, p. 181.
[17] 27 July 1523; Freys-Barge, nos. 106–109.
[18] "Dialogus oder ein gesprech-büchlein" (1524); Hertzsch, op. cit., II, 11.

would be like letting a child play with a sharp knife until he is intelligent enough to put it aside on his own. "We should take such dangerous things especially from the weak and snatch them out of their hands and pay no attention if they weep, scream, or curse."[19]

In Karlstadt's numerous treatises from this period the attack on infant baptism and on the real presence of Christ in the Eucharist are still in the background. To him it is far more urgent to introduce into his community—through thoughts of mysticism—union with the divine will, the "supreme virtue of composure," inner recollection and sanctification. These are the conditions *sine qua non* for being filled with God, a condition granted to the individual by means of divine illumination in conjunction with the word of Scripture.

> It is, of course, totally impossible that one should become God's friend or son without God's inner and secret revelation. It is equally impossible for one to accept God's external word and consider . . . it a word of the Bridegroom, unless God reveals himself previously or simultaneously in the external hearing with his bright and luminous ray so that one can hear who God is and what he wants.[20]

Karlstadt became the center of a religious movement that was not confined to Orlamünde. This gave the circles at Wittenberg no rest. In March 1524 the university called upon Karlstadt to fulfill his duties as archdeacon and professor and hence to return to Wittenberg. Luther pressed for a prohibition of his writings if he did not submit to the university's censorship. When the petitions and requests of Karlstadt and of the Orlamünde congregation, which claimed the right to choose its priest, were denied, Karlstadt renounced his office as pastor of Orlamünde and resigned the archdeaconry, because he could not reconcile any further celebrating of Mass with his conscience.[21]

In spite of this isolation by the Wittenberg circles, however, Karlstadt did not allow himself to be enticed by Müntzer to join the league for the annihilation of the godless. As early as 1522 he had urged moderation on Müntzer,[22] and now he expressly renounced any connection with him. Such alliances, he said, were contrary to the will of God, in whom alone one must place one's hope.[23] Similar ideas were expressed in the

---

[19] "Ob man gemach faren und des ergernüssen der schwachen verschonen soll" (1524); Hertzsch, op. cit., I 88.

[20] ". . . wie sich der glaub und unglaub gegen dem licht und finsternis . . . halten" (1524), fol. B4.

[21] *ARG* 11 (1914), 70f.

[22] *Thomas Müntzers Briefwechsel*, ed. H. Böhmer–P. Kirn (Leipzig 1931), p. 39.

[23] Ibid., p. 69.

open letter sent by the people of Orlamünde to those of Allstedt.[24] But this decisive withdrawal from Müntzer and the latter's efforts to restore the order of the Gospel by force if necessary did not save Karlstadt from the accusation of sedition. Luther denied to the people of Orlamünde the right of free election of their priest, a right which he himself had proclaimed.[25] He saw them infected by the fanaticism of Allstedt. Hence the *Letter to the Princes of Saxony* of July 1524 (WA 15, 210–221), in which Luther asked them to take steps and to forestall insurrection, although directed expressly against Müntzer also included Karlstadt by implication.

On 22 August 1524 Luther preached at Jena against the "Karlstadt fanaticism." Karlstadt was present and in the afternoon, in a conference with Luther, he explicitly protested against being identified with the "Allstedt spirit": "You do me violence and injustice in putting me with that murderous spirit. I solemnly declare before all these brethren that I have nothing to do with the spirit of revolt" (WA 15, 236). But he was unable to dissipate Luther's distrust. Even less suited to this purpose was the heated dispute which the people of Orlamünde had with the reformer two days later. Luther convinced the princes of the danger of mob spirit (WA 18, 86; 99), and on 18 September 1524, Karlstadt, with his family, was expelled from electoral Saxony.

He sought refuge in South Germany, but more than once had to move again. He went, among other places, to Strasbourg and Basel and finally, toward the end of December 1527, to Rothenburg ob der Tauber. In these troubled weeks and despite severe privations, he published eight works, including five treatises on communion. They had probably been partly written, or at least begun, in Orlamünde, but Karlstadt did not publish them until after his expulsion from Saxony. Hence they could not have been used as the alleged reason for his banishment.

Notwithstanding his numerous works on this subject, Karlstadt provides us with no coherent exposition of his teaching on the Eucharist. The reason for this is probably to be found in his restless ways and the adverse circumstances under which the treatises originated. In them he clearly and definitely denies the real presence, but the point of departure in this is not his understanding of the account of the institution of the Eucharist. His curious explanation of "this is my body" is secondary and does not play in his writings the role that could be expected, according to the literature. If for Luther the Mass is a derogation from the

---

[24] Ibid., p. 88.
[25] "Dass eine christliche Versammlung oder Gemeine Recht und Macht habe, alle Lehre zu erteilen und Lehrer zu berufen, ein- und abzusetzen" (1523) (WA 11, 408–416).

Cross of Christ, so for Karlstadt the bodily presence in the Sacrament is also. The Lord's promise to give us his body is a reference to his sufferings and death on the Cross. Here, and not in the Sacrament, occurs the remission of sins. If this were to refer to Christ in his glorified body, the clear relationship with his sacrificial death would disappear. In Karlstadt's view, there are only two modes of Christ's presence—the historical bloody form on the Cross and the glorified form in the splendors of heaven. Christ remains corporally in heaven "until he comes" at the end of time. Karlstadt cannot accept a mysterious descent into the bread: "There are no more than two advents—one in the form of the Cross and Passion here on earth, the other in glory. You must not invent a third, and you cannot add either of the two others to the Host."[26]

Because Karlstadt does not accept a sacramental presence and can understand the real presence of Christ's body only locally, he has to deny the real presence unless he is willing to admit that Christ abandons heaven or is omnipresent in the sense of Luther's doctrine of ubiquity. It now remained to bring this conviction of his—a sort of theological *a priori*—into harmony with the testimony of Scripture. This led to the contrived explanation, greatly ridiculed by Luther, that with the *touto* of the words of institution Christ pointed to the body in which he was present to the disciples.

> I have always reckoned that Christ pointed to his own body and hence said: This is that body of mine, which is given for you. For Christ did not point to the bread, and he did not say: This bread is my body, which is sacrificed for you. But they who say that the bread is the body speak on their own authority . . . . Listen: Jesus took the bread and gave thanks to God and broke it and gave it to his disciples and said that they should eat it in remembrance of him and placed directly in his word the cause and mode of the remembrance of him. That is, for the sake of a remembrance and hence that his disciples should recall that he surrendered his body for them.[27] Christ's body is not in the bread and his blood is not in the chalice. But we must eat the Lord's body in the remembrance or acknowledgment of his body, which he gave into the hands of the unjust for our sake, and drink from the chalice in the recognition of his blood, which Christ shed for us—in other words, we eat and drink in acknowledgment of Christ's death.[28]

Karlstadt's writings produced loud reverberations and were widely accepted. It was learned with alarm at Wittenberg that the banishment

[26] E. Hertzsch, op. cit., II, 42.
[27] "Dialogus" (Hertzsch, op. cit., II, 17).
[28] Ibid., II, 49.

of the fanatic from Saxony had in no way silenced him; in fact, in southwestern Germany and in Switzerland he was now even better known and esteemed. "You will not believe," wrote Luther to Wolfgang Stein on 11 October 1524, "how that man Karlstadt is succeeding in Switzerland, Prussia, Bohemia, and everywhere and is seeking a nest" (*WA, Br* 3, 456).

Luther took a position against Karstadt in his *Brief an die Christen zu Strassburg wider den Schwärmergeist* of December 1524 (*WA* 15, 391–397). In it he admits how difficult a struggle it was for him to accept belief in the real presence.

> I confess that if Doctor Karlstadt or anyone else had said to me five years ago that there is nothing but bread and wine in the Sacrament, he would have done me a great service. I have truly endured such severe temptations in this question, struggled and wrestled with myself, that I would have been glad to be out of it, for I realized that thereby I could have given the papacy the greatest blow . . . . But I am held captive, I cannot escape. The text is too powerfully present and cannot be driven from the mind by words. [*WA* 15, 394, 12–20]

In *Wider die himmlischen Propheten, von den Bildern und Sakrament* (*WA* 18, 62–214) he provided a detailed refutation. The first part was in print in December 1524. It attacks the new law of Karlstadt, his iconoclasm, his attitude toward authority, and his disregard of the external word. Luther castigates the spirit which can do nothing but "create more and more law, misery, conscience, and sin" (*WA* 18, 123). Karlstadt "makes for himself his own Moses" and "his own Christ" (*WA* 18, 117), just like the Pope, except that "the pope does so by precept, Doctor Karlstadt by prohibition." The Pope "compels and constrains one to do what is not commanded nor forced by God." Karlstadt "prevents and hinders one from allowing what is not forbidden nor hindered by God" (*WA* 18, 111). "But Christian freedom perishes just as readily when it must give up what is not forbidden as when it is forced to do what it is not obliged to do" (*WA* 18, 111).

Luther furthermore attacks the disparagement of the external word as opposed to the "spirit," of which one becomes aware in an "inner experience" and to which Scripture is only a confirmation. In the *Dialogus* Karlstadt had had the layman say: "For my part I would need no external evidence. I wish to have my evidence from the spirit in my inner self."[29] In the second part of *Wider die himmlischen Propheten,* which appeared at the end of January 1525, Luther discusses the doctrine of the Eucharist

---

[29] Ibid., II, 18.

in detail. He first of all stresses that, according to God's arrangement, the "external details," the "word of the Gospel given by the tongue" and the "material signs, such as baptism and the Eucharist," precede the imparting of the inner spirit. God "will give to no one either spirit or faith without the external word and sign" (WA 18, 136). Karlstadt, the mob agitator, casts it scornfully and mockingly to the winds and "wishes first to enter into the Spirit" (WA 18, 136). Luther wishes "to take the words simply as they are . . . and let the bread be the body of Christ" (WA 18, 147). Despite all his attempts at interpreting the words of institution, especially in regard to *touto,* Karlstadt is unable to quote a single scriptural text supporting his theory, but all the more he indulges reason, the "arch-whore and bride of the devil" (WA 18, 164). When he quotes Scripture, he wishes "not to honor the word of God with faith or to accept it according to the plain manner of speech, but to measure and master it with sophistical reasoning and pointed subtlety" (WA 18, 186f.). He shifts the center of gravity from word and Sacrament to the subject—to the remembering and proclaiming of Christ's death on the Cross. He thereby makes "what Christ promised a command and sets up a work in place of faith" (WA 18, 196). "But it is still worse and more insane that he attributes to such a memorial the power to justify as faith does," whereas "they who preach and proclaim must first be justified" (WA 18, 197f.).

Luther's words were unusually cutting. Throughout, Karlstadt is called an agitator who "stirs up the crazy mob," a fool or a lying spirit, even a prophet of the devil (WA 18, 152; 193; 142).

When the Peasants' War broke out in March 1525, Karlstadt was living at Rothenburg. Now, as before, he did not take part in the social-political disputes, but this did not prevent his being branded even more a fanatic, an iconoclast, an agitator, a murderer of souls, a sinful spirit. This extraordinary acidity in Luther's polemics greatly shocked many contemporaries, including Melanchthon, but especially all who had hitherto regarded Karlstadt as a partisan of the Wittenberg circle. People sided with Karlstadt at Strasbourg and in Switzerland, and he defended himself in three works. In these he sought to shore up his idea of the Eucharist, but otherwise he stressed a practical Christianity which had to produce the fruits of freedom and justice in good works. Caught between the two sides in the Peasants' War—"the ecclesiastical lords hunted me as game, the peasants . . . would have devoured me"[30]— Karlstadt had to leave Rothenburg on 30 or 31 May. He went to his mother in Karlstadt am Main but found no peace there and at last, crushed in spirit, he asked Luther from Frankfurt on 12 June 1525 to

[30] Ibid., II, 117.

obtain from the elector permission for him to return to Saxony. He intended "for the future not to write, preach, or teach any more" (WA, Br 3, 529). In his *Entschuldigung des falschen Namens des Aufruhrs* he again protested against the accusation of being an agitator. "In brief, I know that I am innocent of any share in Müntzer's revolt."[31] And in the *Erklärung wie Karlstadt seine Lehre von dem hochwürdigen . . . achtet und geachtet haben will* he maintained that in his writings on the Eucharist he aimed to question rather than to assert and that he was open to further correction.

Luther was satisfied with this virtual recantation and, happy "to purchase his silence by such a favor and mercy so that he might not cause more distress elsewhere through vengeance or final despair" (WA, Br 3, 572), he recommended that the elector allow Karlstadt to take up residence at Kemberg or in a nearby village. Thus Karlstadt managed to support himself as farmer and shopkeeper, wretchedly and under supervision, first at Segrehna, then at Bergwitz, and finally at Kemberg, until in the spring of 1529 he escaped the increasing spiritual constraint by flight to further misery. Via Holstein, East Friesland, Strasbourg, and Basel he went in May 1530 to Zwingli in Zurich. Here he supported himself as a proofreader in a print shop and then as deacon at the hospital. At the end of 1531 he obtained a pastorate at Altstätten in the Rheintal, but after Zwingli's death he had to give it up. He again sought refuge in Zurich until in June 1534 he at last found his final field of activity as preacher and professor in Basel. On 14 April 1534, Bullinger, preacher at the Grossmünster in Zurich, wrote to his friend Myconius at Basel; "You need have no fear that that man is such as Luther has described him. He is very good-natured, modest, humble, and in every respect irreproachable."[32] In contrast to his earlier hostility to scholarship and titles, at Basel Karlstadt again fostered the traditional disputations and obtaining of degrees. In other ways also, happy to have found an asylum after so much persecution and privation, in the service of the Swiss Reformed Church he seems to have given up "trying to impose his own earlier personal convictions."[33] He died of the plague at Basel on 24 December 1541.

Karlstadt was among the first who had to experience how severely Luther and the reformers, who appealed to their own consciences and their own understanding of Scripture, would proceed against those who made the same claim for themselves. With direct reference to Karlstadt and Müntzer, Luther had said that they should be confidently allowed to

---

[31] Ibid., II, 112; WA, 18, 440.
[32] Hertzsch, I, XVI.
[33] Barge; RE X, 80.

preach, for there had to be sects and the word of God had to be on the battlefield and fight there.

> Let the spirits confront and strike one another . . . for we who carry the word of God should not fight with the fist. . . . Our function is to preach and to endure, not to strike with fists and to defend ourselves [WA 15, 219].

How little prepared he was to live according to these precepts is clear from his attitude toward Karlstadt. It is true that formally Luther was consistent, since he had the princes use force against him, not because of his preaching but because of his "insurrection." But what does that amount to when one who maintained a different interpretation of the Gospel was branded as a fanatic and an agitator and thereby handed over to the secular authority for punishment?

Thomas Müntzer

Luther's opposition to Thomas Müntzer was even more bitter and more fundamental. Müntzer was from Stolberg in the Harz Mountains, but details of his youth are lacking. If, with H. Boehmer, we assume that ordinarily young men who were not well off matriculated only when they had reached the minimum age of about seventeen, required for the baccalaureate, then Müntzer's birth must be assigned to 1488 or 1489. For a Thomas Müntzer from Quedlinburg was enrolled at Leipzig on 16 October 1506, and we know that Müntzer's family lived in Quedlinburg. As late as 1512 we find him a student at Frankfurt an der Oder. Obviously his studies were unusually prolonged, but the reasons are unknown. In any event, Müntzer acquired an education that was superior to the ordinary student's. He was well read in the Church Fathers, the mystics, Joachim of Fiore, and, above all, Holy Scripture, for the sake of which he studied Greek and Hebrew. In letters he is addressed as master of arts and bachelor of theology. He was a priest of the diocese of Halberstadt[34] and before 1513 an assistant in Aschersleben and Halle; as such he took part in an "alliance" against Archbishop Ernst (1476–1513) of Magdeburg and Halberstadt, a brother of Frederick the Wise. Later (in 1516) he was a prior at the convent in Forse. He was staying at Leipzig in 1519 and perhaps met Luther on the occasion of the disputation. From the end of that year he was confessor at the convent of Beuditz, east of Naumburg. Here he had a slender income but much

---

[34] On 6 May 1514 the council of Altstadt Braunschweig presented "Thomam Munther Halber [stadensis] dyocesis presbiterum" for an altar benefice in Sankt Michaelskirche. Cf. *Thomas Müntzers Briefwechsel,* appendix no. 1, p. 129.

leisure for study. He occupied himself with Augustine, Tauler, Suso, Eusebius, and other writers and provided himself with the acts of the Councils of Constance and Basel.

In May 1520, on Luther's recommendation, Müntzer became vicar of the pastor Johann Sylvius Egranus at Sankt-Marien in Zwickau, and, when the pastor returned, he accepted the small Katharinenkirche in the same town, with a congregation of craftsmen and miners. A zealous and vehement preacher, filled with prophetic self-assurance and a mysticism of the Cross,[35] he came into conflict with the Franciscans. In the autumn he began to be influenced by Nikolaus Storch and the Zwickau prophets. His language became even more radical in his dealings with these spiritualist and Taborite circles, and he did not shrink from personal attacks, above all on the Erasmian Egranus, pastor of the main parish church.[36]

Müntzer disregarded a summons to appear before the bishop's *officialis* at Zeitz. Eventually the elector's local agent and the council intervened and deposed him on 16 April 1521. Müntzer fled the same night. His subsequent wanderings brought him several times to Bohemia. He preached at Prague and tried to gain adherents by means of a proclamation, the Prague Manifesto of 1 November 1521. This document provides our first concrete hold on his views. It is extant in four versions—two in German, one in Czech, one in Latin. The vernacular versions are especially oriented to the needs and desires of the common people.[37] Müntzer emphasizes the necessity of the sevenfold Holy Spirit, especially the Spirit of the fear of the Lord, for the exercise of faith. Without the Spirit we can neither hear nor recognize God. He fits the parts to the whole. Preachers who offer only the "cold" and the "naked" Scripture are thieves and robbers. They "steal the word of God from their neighbor's mouth" (140; 155). The priests give the people only the "dead words of Scripture" and "the sheep do not know that they should hear the living voice of God, that they should all have revelations" (147). For

> the hearts of men are the paper or parchment on which God, with his finger rather than with ink, inscribes his unchangeable will and eternal wisdom. Any man can read this writing, if he has a reason that is in any way developed [140].

[35] On 13 July 1520 he wrote to Luther: ". . . omnia propter Christum meum sunt mihi gratissima, graviora certamina mihi restant . . . Crux mea nondum integra . . . Opus meum non ago, sed Domini" (*WA, Br* 2, 140f.).
[36] Agricola then (before April 1521) wrote to Müntzer: ". . . Significaverunt nobis certe ii, qui tibi optime volunt, te abuti officio verbi. . . . Te nihil spirare nisi caedes et sanguinem" (*Thomas Müntzers Briefwechsel,* no. 21, p. 21).
[37] *Thomas Müntzers Briefwechsel,* appendix no. 6, A-D, pp. 139–159.

The true preacher should, according to First Corinthians 14, "have revelations, for otherwise he cannot preach the word" (141). God has not ceased to speak. Man must hear the word as now uttered by God and not as a historical report.

If the Church has been made a whore by scholars and priests, now, since God is separating the wheat from the weeds and has appointed Müntzer over the harvest, the "new, apostolic Church" is to begin, first in Bohemia and then everywhere else (150), a church, not of "priests and apes" (*Pfaffen und Affen*), but "of the elect friends of God," who learn to prophesy and thus "truly experience how friendly, in fact cordially, God delights to speak with all his elect" (142). The stressing of the gifts of the Holy Spirit, of the "living Spirit," the tension between the dead letter and the living and timely word of God, the summons to the carrying out of his demanding will, the doctrine of the Church of the elect, which is separated from the godless, and, finally, Müntzer's conviction of being the instrument of God's judgment—such are the special marks of this Prague Manifesto.

Müntzer did not find the anticipated reaction in Bohemia, and the ensuing difficult period up to the spring of 1523 is obscure. Müntzer stayed in his native Central Germany and seems, as can be inferred from a remark by Luther (*WA* 38, 213) and one of Müntzer's letters of 9 March 1523, to have been in the service of a convent at Halle.[38] He interpreted his sufferings and bitter poverty as a sign of election. Thus he wrote to his followers on 19 March 1523:

> In such tribulation the depths of the soul are cleansed. . . . No one can find God's mercy; he must be forsaken, as Isaiah 28:19 and 54:7 clearly says. . . . The Spirit cannot be given to any except the disconsolate [John 16:7]. Therefore, let my sufferings be equal to yours. Let all the weeds spring up as they wish; they must submit to the flail with the pure wheat. Accordingly, the living God is sharpening his scythe within me so that later I can cut the red poppies and the little blue flowers.[39]

The mystical self-annihilation leads to communion with God, which will in turn transform man's cause into God's cause.

At Easter of 1523 Müntzer was tentatively made pastor of the Johanniskirche at Allstedt, a small town of craftsmen and farmers. Here at Allstedt, where he gained the confidence of Johann Zeys, the official agent of the elector, and of the former pastor, he was able for the first time to carry out his ideas. His peaceful outlook and his pressing pas-

---

[38] O. Schiff in *ARG* 23 (1926), 287–293.
[39] *Thomas Müntzers Briefwechsel,* no. 38, p. 40.

toral concern are evident in his letter to the "brethren at Stolberg," in which he represents suffering and poverty in the Spirit as the prerequisite of the rule of Christ, as well as in his regulation of worship. In the "Deutsch Kirchenamt"—Matins, Lauds, and Vespers—and in the "Deutsch Evangelisch Messe" he created the first completely German liturgy, and in the "Ordnung und Berechnung des Deutschen Amtes zu Allstedt" he provided its theoretical justification. Müntzer intended to foster an intelligible liturgy in keeping with Scripture and thereby to serve the "deliverance of the poor, wretched, blind consciences of men." As the subject of the liturgy, the congregation must actively participate in it. Müntzer equaled Luther in linguistic content and surpassed him in fidelity to liturgical tradition and in a grasp of the religious needs of simple folk. With this emphatically pastoral attitude the "fanatic" Müntzer, like Karlstadt, was much more concerned about formal worship than Luther was. Luther was inspired by him to compose his hymns. Rendered self-sufficient as pastor at Allstedt, Müntzer ceased to court Wittenberg and even sharply criticized Luther and his friends for their hesitation about translating the liturgy into German. "They fear for their own skins and yet want to be preachers of faith and of the Gospel."[40]

In two doctrinal treatises at the end of 1523, *Von dem getichten Glauben* and *Protestation . . . Von dem rechtem Christenglauben und der Taufe,* Müntzer publicly declared war on Luther. In the *Protestation* he took up the problem of baptism for the first time, warning against overestimating the "external baptism." Nowhere, he said, do we read that Mary or the disciples of Christ were baptized with water. In John 3:5 and throughout the fourth Gospel, water is to be understood as the "movement of the Spirit," which effects the inner, true, and absolutely necessary baptism. The demand for adult baptism is not contained in this train of thought, and Luther and Melanchthon were wrong in making Müntzer the author of Anabaptism. He never practiced rebaptism, which came into use in Zurich only in 1525. Next to Tauler's mysticism of suffering, the spiritualist and chiliastic doctrines of Joachim of Fiore were Müntzer's sources: "The testimony of Abbot Joachim carries great weight with me" (*Von dem getichten Glauben*).

Müntzer was profoundly convinced that faith must prove itself in testimony before the world and that the Christian bears an active responsibility for the world and the fate of his neighbor. For him there was no division into two sides as there was for Luther. The will of God demanded an immediate and absolute realization in all spheres. But Müntzer still thought that the goal could be achieved by peaceful

---

[40] E. Sehling, *Die evgl. Kirchenordnungen* 1 (Leipzig 1902), 499.

means, especially by the preaching of the word of God. His first conflict with the political authorities did not originate in sociopolitical misunderstandings but because the Count of Mansfeld forbade his subjects to attend Müntzer's "heretical" Mass. From the pulpit Müntzer denounced him as a scoundrel and bloodsucker and in a statement of 22 September 1523,[41] which he signed as "destroyer of unbelievers." he reaffirmed his stand. The count was presuming to forbid the holy Gospel. "You should know that in such mighty and righteous matters I do not fear even the whole world." Even if Müntzer threatened, "do not snap, for otherwise the old garment will tear," he was still in no way presenting the picture of a rebel against the social order but that of a zealous man of God concerned about the irrevocable claims of the Gospel.

His "Sermon to the Princes," delivered at the Castle of Allstedt on 13 July 1524 in the presence of Frederick the Wise's brother, Duke Johann of Saxony, and the latter's son and heir, Prince Johann Friedrich, shows how unrevolutionary Müntzer was at the outset and how much he still hoped to achieve his goal along with the princes.[42] In it the Kingdom of God is no purely eschatological thing and the princes are not "heathen folk" with merely secular duties; rather, the Kingdom of God is to be realized in this world and time, if necessary by the sword of princes. The proved, unlettered faith of the elect cannot be established alongside the order of the world; it must create a new reality in human society. This is true especially of princes. The sword bestowed by God upon authority has no mere function of warding off or punishing evildoers but a positive, constructive task. The true ruler must take hold of authority by the roots.[43] Like the simple believer, the prince who supports the Gospel must also endure a "great cross and great tribulation." For the cross is the mark of the Christian and the pledge of victory. But if princes refuse to use their sword on behalf of the pious elect against the evil, then "the sword will be taken from them and given to the fervent people for the destruction of the godless."[44]

Even after this sermon, when Müntzer was still uncertain of the princes' reaction to his words, he sought to achieve his aims with them. He invited them to join the divine covenant with the people: "A contractual league, that is, regulated by agreed terms, must be made in such a form that the common man may join himself to the pious rulers for the

---

[41] *Thomas Müntzers Briefwechsel,* no. 44, pp. 47f.

[42] C. Hinrichs, *Thomas Müntzers Politische Schriften* (Halle 1950), pp. 5–28.

[43] Ibid., p. 24.

[44] Letter of 4 October 1523 to Frederick the Wise, *Briefwechsel,* no. 45, p. 50; cf. "Auslegung," *Politische Schriften,* p. 26.

sake of the Gospel alone."[45] Müntzer decried a social misconception of the sins of the league, as though there were a question of material relief.

Meanwhile, at the end of July Luther wrote his *Brief an die Fürsten zu Sachsen von dem aufrührerischen Geist* (WA 15, 210–221), in which he branded Müntzer as Satan and asked the princes "to check disorder and forestall revolution." He accused Müntzer of cowardice for having declined a hearing "in the corner," that is, before Luther at Wittenberg. Even after Müntzer had been questioned at Weimar on 1 August after the Allstedt council had abandoned him and his league and his printing press had been forbidden, he still thought at that time of a legal course with the princes, as is evident from his letter of 3 August 1524 to Frederick the Wise. But it soon became clear to him that the territorial authority had rejected him. He was unwilling to accept the fate of sitting down and awaiting their judgment like a dumb animal. And so, on the night of 7–8 August, he secretly left the city and went to Mühl-hausen.

But even the *Ausgedrückte Entblössung des falschen Glaubens,* printed at Nürnberg in October, which was a more radical version of the interpretation of the first chapter of Luke submitted to the prince at Weimar on 1 August, shows that for Müntzer not the social question but the religious quest for the true faith was absolutely predominant. Faith implies power to do the impossible. Before it can be achieved, the godless must be hurled from the seat of judgment and man must be made empty by suffering and the cross. Only then can the "power of the Most High" come upon him and the Holy Spirit overshadow him. Holy Scripture confirms faith and from it the road to faith is learned. But faith remains a "matter of letters" and does not become an actual, experienced faith so long as there is no contact with the always and eternally acting spirit. The "godless scriptural scholars" comport themselves "according to Scripture without the spirit of Scripture"; they "make Scripture a shameful cover which impedes the true nature of Christian faith." They would like "to bring the witness of the Spirit of Jesus to the university" and, by means of their monopoly of scriptural exegesis, keep the people dependent "with their stolen Scripture."

Thus for Müntzer the proud who must be toppled from the throne were, before the princes, the scriptural scholars, or rather the "scriptural thieves" with their "monkish idol," Luther. They deceived the people, claiming that the study of Scripture is necessary for salvation and at the same time preaching to the common man that he should permit himself

---

[45] Letter of 25 July 1524 to Hans Zeyss; *Briefwechsel,* no. 59, p. 76.

to be oppressed and exploited by tyrants, so that from mere anxiety about his daily bread he has no time for the study of Scripture.

Complaints about material needs are merely incidental. According to Müntzer's mysticism of the cross, man attains to the true faith only through external and inner suffering.

> Man must smash to pieces his stolen, bookish Christian faith by powerful and sublime sorrow and painful grief and by indispensable questioning. Thus man becomes very small and contemptible in his own eyes, and while the godless brag and become arrogant, the elect is swallowed up. Then he can glorify and magnify God and after keen grief he can rejoice with all his heart in God, his saviour. Then what is great must give way to the little and be confounded by it. If only the poor spurned peasants knew this, it would be very profitable to them.[46]

If God despises the "bigwigs," the "big heads with fine titles, such as the Church of godless now has," and takes the humble into his service, still the people are not yet ready. They "must first be quite severely punished." They need the right leader, "a servant of God, filled with his grace, in the spirit of Elias."[47] "Many must be awakened in order that, with a sublime zeal and in fervent seriousness, they may purge Christendom of godless rulers."[48] The new John must "by means of a tried and proved life, make known to others the Cross, understood since his youth, and shout into the wretched, desolate, confused hearts of the God-fearing, who are now beginning to be on the watch for the truth."[49]

At stake is religious renewal, the "movement of the Spirit," that man may resemble Christ "in his sufferings and life through the overshadowing of the Holy Spirit," whom the world mocks but who is given only to the poor in the Spirit.[50] Of course, if the genuine Christian government is to be realized in this world and against the mighty, then a regrouping of political and social conditions cannot be avoided.

Even in Allstedt Müntzer had intended to reply to Luther's *Brief an die Fürsten zu Sachsen von dem aufrührerischen Geist,* for on 3 August he wrote to Frederick the Wise that, because of the scandal given to many pious persons, Luther's slanderous letter should not remain unanswered.[51] But it is not known whether it was at Allstedt that he undertook the *Hochverursachte Schutzrede und Antwort wider das geistlose,*

[46] *Politische Schriften*, p. 46.
[47] Ibid., pp. 46f.
[48] Ibid.
[49] Ibid., p. 51.
[50] Ibid., p. 55.
[51] *Briefwechsel*, no. 64, pp. 84f.

sanftlebende Fleisch zu Wittenberg. In any event it was finished only at Mühlhausen—and presumably before 19 September, for in it no mention is made of the revolutionary events there, which ended on 27 September with Müntzer's banishment and flight to Nürnberg.

In this *Schutzrede* Müntzer rejects the charge of having incited "insurrection." He has shown the princes from Scripture that they should use the sword to prevent rebellion, though the princes are not the masters but the servants of the sword. They also are bound by the law. Luther, "father of obsequiousness," "flatterer," "Doctor Liar," attempts "to cover up for them with Christ in concocted validity." For Müntzer law and grace are one: "Christ in the Gospel has made known the Father's righteousness through his kindness." It is not right that Luther should practice the "patience of Christ" toward the great and demand the observance of the law by the little folk. "If the great wish to possess grace, they must also fulfill the law, and the little folk do not need merely to exercise patience but can compel the fulfilling of the law."[52] Thus Müntzer in the most decisive manner rejects the annulling of the law in favor of grace, that is, Luther's doctrine of justification. In fact he insinuates that this doctrine one-sidedly operates in favor of the class interests of the great. Accordingly he attacks Luther's denial of the freedom of the will:

> You claim to confide to God that you are a poor sinner and a poisonous snake, with your rotten humility. You have concocted this, with your fantastic imagination, from your Augustine— indeed a blasphemous thing, to look with scorn on men voluntarily."[53]

In Mühlhausen, Heinrich Pfeiffer had been active since the beginning of 1523, delivering sermons at the Nikolaikirche which were acquiring an increasingly strong political and social character. The townspeople's dissatisfaction with the council had blazed up again at the time of Müntzer's arrival, and Müntzer and Pfeiffer summarized the demands of the citizens in eleven articles drawn from Scripture. On 19 September open insurrection broke out, with the aim of establishing a new order of city regulations in accord with God's word. With the aid of the peasants the council contrived to put down the rising and on 29 September 1524 Pfeiffer and Müntzer were expelled. In October Müntzer was at Nürnberg, where he succeeded in getting his *Ausgedrückte Entblössung* and *Hochverursachte Schutzrede* printed. But both works were confiscated and he was banished. He went south and was in touch with the

---

[52] C. Hinrichs, *Luther und Müntzer* (Berlin 1952), p. 178.
[53] *Politische Schriften,* p. 95.

rebellious peasants in South Germany, with Oecolampadius at Basel, and with Hubmaier. As a result of an appeal by his followers, he returned to Mühlhausen in February 1525 and was made preacher at the Marienkirche. He now more and more assumed the traits of a social revolutionary, not only in regard to active opposition to a godless authority but also in the reorganization of the total order of life in Christendom to bring it into accord with divine justice.

In March 1525 Mühlhausen elected a new "perpetual council," which was supposed to introduce a new Christian government based only on the word of God: a Christian democracy under the decisive influence of the preachers. In it Pfeiffer, with his more practical social aims, seems to have had a greater appeal than Müntzer, who remained fundamentally foreign to the people with his preaching of the Kingdom of God. In the meantime the Thuringian peasants had rebelled, less because of Müntzer's agitation than as a result of the example set in South Germany. But Müntzer now urged his followers, as "God's servant against the impious," to join the Peasants' War "with the sword of Gideon." He interpreted the war theologically as a struggle for God's rule against every usurped authority.

> I say this to you: if you are unwilling to suffer for God's sake, you must be the devil's martyrs . . . . The entire German, French, and Italian lands are astir. . . . Therefore, do not let yourselves be frightened. God is with you. . . . You should have no fear of the great multitude; it is not your struggle, but the Lord's. It is not you who fight there.[54]

Müntzer accompanied the hordes of peasants in this "struggle of the Lord," not as a military leader but as a preacher who spurred their will to resist and sought assistance. Thus on 13 May 1525 he wrote to the people of Erfurt:

> Assist us as far as you can, with men and guns, so that we may fulfill what God himself has commanded [Ezekiel 39:4–18; Daniel 7:27; Ezekiel 34:25]. . . . If you now have a desire for the truth, join the dance with us. For we wish to step it lively, so as to repay the blasphemers of God exactly as they have treated poor Christendom.

Müntzer's personal participation in the Peasants' War was limited to three weeks and connected with only one episode—the Thuringian rising which was crushed in a massacre at Frankenhausen on 15 May

---

[54] Letter of 26 or 27 April 1525, to the people of Allstedt; *Briefwechsel,* no. 75, pp. 109ff.

1525. In this he had, however, an important part, in so far as he had swept the masses along in his optimism, counting on divine intervention and frustrating all negotiations. He was arrested in an attic and after cruel torture was executed outside Mühlhausen on 27 May. According to his farewell letter he felt that he had "not been correctly understood" by the people. They had "sought their self-interest more than the vindication of Christianity"[55] and had picked what suited them out of Müntzer's preaching on the realization of the divine will. Thus "a last token was given publicly that the revolutionary in the name and service of God was neither a 'peasant leader' nor a social agitator, that to him the truly important thing was not human rights and social progress but God's law and a Christianity subject to God in faith and life and mighty in spirit, which then, in obedience to God, cannot but give the right shape and order to the things of this world also."[56]

Müntzer's liturgical work survived his fall. His church offices and hymns continued to be sung and were revived in the Erfurt church office of 1525 and 1526. The Müntzer church order at Allstedt was maintained until the visitation of March 1533. According to what Bugenhagen reported in 1543, it was then being used in Wolfenbüttel along with others.[57]

If Christianity exists in tension between the preparatory historical realization of the kingship of God and its final completion in other ages, then Luther with a purely eschatological understanding and Müntzer with a narrow "now-and-here" identification represent the farthest extremes. It is thus not to be wondered at that each felt himself to be closer to "papistry" than to the other.

Posterity regarded Müntzer solely in the light of his connection with the Peasants' War, and overrated his influence on it. This can be traced back, not least of all, to the *Histori Thome Muntzers des anfengers der Döringischen uffrur*[58] of 1526, attributed to Melanchthon, and to Luther himself. Luther defamed Müntzer as a "murderous and bloodthirsty prophet" (*WA* 18, 367) and represented him as the "archdevil," "who rules at Mühlhausen and causes nothing but robbery, murder, and bloodshed" (*WA* 18, 357) or as the murderous spirit who, "using God's name, has spoken through the devil" (*WA* 18, 367). This image was constructed in detail by Melanchthon in his account of the teachings and deeds of the "madman" and was believed by future generations.

---

[55] *Briefwechsel*, no. 94.
[56] W. Elliger, *Thomas Müntzer* (Berlin 1960), pp. 59f.
[57] O. H. Brandt, *Thomas Müntzer*, p. 239; p. 31.
[58] Reprinted in *Thomas Müntzer. Sein Leben und seine Schriften*, ed. O. H. Brandt (Jena 1933), pp. 38-50; cf. H. Boehmer, *Studien zu Thomas Müntzer: Zur Feier des Reformationsfestes der Universität* (Leipzig 1922), pp. 3ff.

Confronted with the essential dissimilarity of men such as Luther on the one side and Karlstadt or Müntzer on the other—a difference not merely in methods but in intellectual and theological content, and also in the harshness with which they fought each other from the start—the question arises: What, then, are the characteristics of the "reform"? What did these men have in common, apart from their attack on the traditional ecclesiastical order?

CHAPTER 12

The Peasants' War

Not only the knights but the people thought that Luther and Zwingli meant the fulfillment of their social and political desires. The reformers had questioned spiritual authority and urged the common man to criticize and to express his opinion. Luther's written program had reached the people in many printings. In addition, short and easily understood pamphlets had made the reformers and especially Luther extraordinarily popular. The Bible had been handed to the peasant, who eagerly read it or had it read to him. Zwingli reported: "The house of every peasant is a school in which the New and the Old Testament, the sovereign art, can be read."[1]

The Bible should even be the guide of daily life. In this way the common man was trained to ponder over much that he had hitherto accepted as a matter of course, to form his own ideas. To use an expression of Eberlin von Günzburg, the peasant had become "smart."[2] He looked to Luther for the long-desired reform in which lay liberation from his political difficulties and the fulfillment of his social desires.

Luther himself, in works such as *An den christlichen Adel,* had encouraged such a "sensual" understanding of the Gospel, even if he had always warned that the Gospel would conquer, not through fist and sword but through its inherent divine strength. But why should the struggle against unbiblical human laws deal only with the hierarchy and the monasteries and not be directed also against the territorial lords, who were, besides, often identical with the bishops and abbots? In *Von weltlicher Obrigkeit, wieweit man ihr Gehorsam schuldig sei* (1523; *WA* 11, 245–280) Luther had resisted interferences on the part of the secular power in the ecclesiastical sphere, but at the same time he had

[1] *Werke* III, 361.
[2] P. Bockmann, "Der gemeine Mann in den Flugschriften der Reformation," *DVfLG* 22 (1944), 186–230.

directed heavy criticism at its worldly rule and had expressed his concern about an imminent judgment.

> The secular lords could no longer flay and scrape, impose a toll on some, a tax on others . . . and act as though they were rather brigands and knaves and their secular government was as much neglected as the rule of the spiritual tyrants. [WA 11, 265] And you must know that from the very beginning of the world an intelligent prince is an unusual bird, while even more rare is a pious prince. Usually they are the greatest fools or the worst knaves on earth. [WA 11, 267f.] People will not, cannot, do not intend to endure your tyranny and wantonness for long. Dear princes and lords, learn to judge yourselves accordingly; God will not endure longer. It is now no longer one world, as formerly, for the people as well as the beasts hunt and pursue you. Therefore, cease from your crimes and violence. [WA 11, 270]

In contrast to Luther, Zwingli approved active resistance to an ungodly authority. "If the eye is evil, it must be torn out and thrown away; the hand or foot must be cut off."[3] Accordingly, with the introduction of the Reformation at Zurich he had begun a reorganization of the political situation.

The sixteenth century brought a general amelioration of the peasants' economic status. It is incorrect to speak of a distress of the peasantry, of a special economic oppression. Rather one should speak of a new self-assurance, which was demanding a corresponding status in society and was more than ever resisting the limitation of peasant autonomy and of common holdings in pasture, forests, and water by the developing territorial states. Thus the leaders in the Peasants' War were not the poor of the village, the proletariat, but precisely the prosperous and respected farmers. They demanded their "ancient right" and, in addition, an incorporation on equal terms into civic life, as was their due according to divine justice.

At the same moment many cities were the scene of violent social conflicts, in which the socially inferior strata rose up against the governing bourgeoisie, journeymen and other craftsmen against patricians and masters. Not only peasants but all the poor common folk in city and country fought for their Christian, fraternal liberty and for their social and political status in society. The term "Peasants' War" does not do justice to this frequent cooperation of urban people and peasants.

For some decades before the peasant rising in much of Germany under the influence of the reform movement, local peasant insurrections had occurred again and again. Among these special importance

---

[3] *Werke* II, 344.

attaches to the "Armer Konrad," which seized Württemberg in 1514, and the "Bundschuh" movement of Southwest Germany. The latter flared up following the example of the nearby Swiss Confederation; it began in the district of Schlettstadt in 1483 and was active in the bishopric of Speyer in 1502, in the Breisgau in 1513, and along the upper Rhine in 1517. Its leader was Joss Fritz, a serf of the Bishop of Speyer. He demanded the abolition of serfdom, with all its payments and tithes, and of the seignorial monopoly of hunting and fishing. In particular there should be an end to clerical domination and to monasteries. Obedience should be rendered only to Emperor and Pope, and to no other lord. The *Reformation des Kaisers Siegmund,* of 1439, which came out in several new editions around the turn of the century, gave the "Bundschuh" its slogan:

> "Nothing but justice" appeared triumphantly on the standard of the confederates over the image of the crucified Saviour; to one side of him was to be seen a clog, to the other a kneeling peasant, weeping, and raising his hands to the Lord. "To lend a hand to justice" was the goal of the "Bundschuh."[4]

But all its undertakings were frustrated.

The Peasants' War affected extensive areas of Germany and penetrated deep into Thuringia and Saxony. But it was not a uniform and centrally directed undertaking. Rather, it was a group of individual movements, all of which caught fire on the same combustible material, made the same demands, and obtained their dangerous fundamental dynamic from the universal unrest or, better, fever of the age. The insurrection began in May–June 1524 with the rising of the peasants of Stühlingen in the southern part of the Black Forest. Here people did not appeal at first to the law of God and the Bible, but defended their old written law against the territorial authority of Count Sigmund.

In the former mercenary soldier Hans Müller the peasants found a leader who had experience in war and in speaking. His aim was a violent confrontation, and he looked around for allies, whom he expected to find in neighboring Waldshut. The municipality had refused to surrender to the Austrian governor their Zwinglian preacher, Balthasar Hubmaier; had again elected him as their pastor; and had expelled the Catholic priests from the city. Thus townspeople and peasants stood together against authority, and the affair of the peasants was connected with that of the Gospel.

The political situation prevented Archduke Ferdinand from resorting to energetic measures. The Turkish peril tied his hands in the East, while war with Francis I made it necessary to have consideration for

---

[4] G. Franz, *Der deutsche Bauernkrieg* (Darmstadt, 4th ed. 1956), p. 65.

Switzerland. Furthermore, Ulrich of Württemberg wanted to profit by Austria's embarrassment to recover his principality by means of French money, Swiss mercenaries, and the aid of the peasants. Hence there could be no thought of a quick, forcible suppression of the revolt. The unrest spread, but nothing decisive occurred during the winter. But the defeat of Francis I at Pavia on 24 February 1525 caused Ulrich's fighting force, consisting overwhelmingly of Swiss, to melt away before Stuttgart, just when victory seemed certain. His failure was also a defeat for the peasants.

Meanwhile the movement had spread to Swabia, Alsace, Franconia, Thuringia, Saxony, Tirol, and Carinthia. The Memmingen furrier Sebastian Lotzer drew up the platform in Swabia, the twelve "Chief Articles of the Whole Peasantry."[5] These demands of the peasants were presented by the Zwinglian preacher Christoph Schappeler as the Gospel. On the basis of numerous biblical passages the following points were demanded: free election of pastors; pure preaching; use of the great tithe as salary for pastors; abolition of the lesser tithe; an end of serfdom, since Christ redeemed all men and so they should be free; annulling of privileges connected with hunting and fishing. Demands made previously on the basis of old German law were now deduced from the Gospel. These articles were everywhere seized upon as a weapon.

At first the disturbances were not of a warlike character. The peasants did indeed band together, not for a war with arms but to back up their demands with demonstrations. Negotiations were arranged. It was precisely the fusing of social and economic demands with religious motives that led in many cases to the use of force, to the sacking of castles and monasteries. Nonpeasant elements also joined in. Since a single, strict leadership was lacking and the maintaining of a rather large number of men presented formidable problems, the revolt progressively deteriorated into general plundering.

The peasants' eyes were fixed on Luther, from whom they expected moral support. He sought at first to mediate. In April he wrote the *Ermahnung zum Frieden auf die zwölf Artikel der Bauernschaft in Schwaben* (WA 18, 291–334), in which he admonished the peasants not to misuse God's name: ". . . do not drag in the Christian name, I say, and do not make it a means of concealing your impatient, quarrelsome, unchristian projects" (WA 18, 314). The Christian, he said, should suffer injustice and not rise against authority. But he also admonished the lords

---

[5] A. Goetze, (ed.), *HV* 5 (1902), 9–15; G. Franz, *Quellen zur Geschichte des Bauernkrieges* (Munich 1963), pp. 174–179; A. Waas, *Die Bauern im Kampf um Gerechtigkeit* (Munich 1965), pp. 96ff.

not to misuse their secular power and to stop "oppressing and taxing" the peasants (WA 18, 293). "It is not the peasants who oppose you. God himself opposes you in order to punish your madness" (WA 18, 295).

But before this work appeared in print in May, Luther, affected by the war, which was being waged with an almost unbelievable harshness, and by what he regarded as Thomas Müntzer's abuse of the Gospel, called upon the princes to intervene pitilessly. In his *Wider die räuberischen und mörderischen Rotten der Bauern* (WA 18, 357–361) Luther saw the devil at work in the peasants; their overthrow was a service to God.

> A rebel is outlawed by God and the emperor, so that the first one who can and will slay him does what is right. For in regard to a public rebel every man is two things—supreme judge and executioner. . . . Therefore, whoever can should here slam, choke, stab, secretly or publicly, and bear in mind that there can be nothing more venomous, more pernicious, more diabolical than a rebel. It is just as though one had to kill a mad dog. Do not strike and you harm yourself and a great nation with you (WA 18, 358). And so, dear lords, save, rescue, help here. Have pity on the poor people. Stab, strike, slay here, whoever can. If you should perish in this, know that you can never die a more blessed death. For you will die in obedience to the divine word and command [Romans 13] and in the service of love, in order to rescue your neighbor from hell and from the devil's bonds. [WA 18, 361]

The princes carried this out, striking, stabbing, and slaying with pitiless cruelty. They would probably not have needed Luther's appeal. After initial successes—the Electors of Mainz and the Palatinate were compelled to accept the twelve articles—the peasant armies were soon overcome by the organized resistance of the princes because they lacked firm leadership and long-range planning. The commander of the Swabian League, Georg Truchsess von Waldburg, defeated the Upper Swabian peasants near Wurzach on 14 April, those of Württemberg near Böblingen on 12 May, and those of Franconia near Königshofen on 2 June and Ingolstadt on 4 June. After overwhelming the Hessian peasants, Philip of Hesse marched to Thuringia and, with Duke Georg of Saxony and the Duke of Braunschweig, annihilated a large army of some eight thousand peasants and townsmen near Frankenhausen. As their chaplain, Thomas Müntzer had fanned their spirit of resistance, leading them into battle with the Pentecost hymn, "Veni, Creator Spiritus." But the battle soon turned into a disorderly rout and a wild killing spree. Müntzer himself was found in an attic and executed. The Alsatian peasants were defeated by Duke Anton of Lorraine near Zabern on 17 May; those of the Palatinate near Pfeddersheim on 24

June. The capture of Salzburg by the Swabian League on 30 July marked the end of the peasants' revolt. All told, some one hundred thousand peasants had perished in battle or been cruelly slain; many were beheaded, run through, burned, or blinded. Settlements agreed upon with the peasants came to an end. All arrangements made with them by lords and princes had to be declared null and void at the demand of the Swabian League or of its general, Georg Truchsess von Waldburg.

The victors were the princes. Even more than the weakened petty nobility, peasants and townsmen were subjected to the power of their prince. Furthermore, the princes confiscated the property of destroyed or abandoned monasteries. To a great extent the Peasants' War meant the end of the Reformation as a popular movement. Luther was often regarded as sharing the responsibility for its attendant ferocity. He accepted these reproaches, even though in quite a different meaning, when in January 1533 he stated in one of his *Table Talks:*

> Preachers are the greatest of all slayers. For they urge the authorities to execute their office strictly and punish the wicked. In the revolt I slew all the peasants; all their blood is on my head. But I pass it on to our Lord God, who commanded me to speak thus. [*WA, Tr* III, no. 2911a.]

People took it amiss that on 13 June 1525, in the middle of these dreadful days, Luther married the former Cistercian nun, Katharina von Bora. Even Melanchthon was exasperated. No wonder Catholic controversialists, such as Johannes Cochläus, exploited it against the reformer. The common people, disillusioned, abandoned Luther in many cases and joined the Anabaptists and the sects or, indifferent, held themselves aloof. The Reformation had ceased to be a popular movement; or at least the Peasants' War greatly damaged Luther's popularity. His "heroic" period was over. The authorities more and more took charge of the Reformation and exploited it to incorporate their subjects into the modern state. Hereafter we can speak of the age of the Princes' Reformation.[6] The Christian congregation, enjoying free elections of pastors, was succeeded by the territorial Church.

[6] F. Lau, "Der Bauernkrieg und das angebliche Ende der lutherischen Reformation als spontaner Volksbewegung," *LuJ* 26 (1959), 109–134, regards the assertion that the age of churches directed by the authorities began with the Peasants' War as an "especially rigid" and "perhaps the most dangerous of Luther legends." In refutation he points to the Reformation of the North German cities between 1525 and 1530. But this refers to cities, and specifically to cities of North Germany, where the Peasants' War did not occur. Furthermore, the reform movement there was for the most part still in progress up to 1535, and no one will claim that the change to the Princes' Reformation occurred suddenly.

CHAPTER 13

Luther's Rejection of Humanism—Erasmus' Later Years

The relations between humanism and the Reformation were varied and close. Many of Luther's friends and collaborators—among them Melanchthon, Spalatin, and Justus Jonas—were humanists. Luther himself was in the grip of humanism and favorably disposed toward it, especially as a teacher and lover of the biblical languages. Ulrich Zwingli was a pupil of Erasmus and a humanist, and the other Swiss reformers bore a strong humanist stamp. Humanism had prepared the ground for the Reformation through its criticism of the Church and its urging of reform. Luther found his first response and enthusiastic followers in the sodalities, the humanist circles. Still, humanists such as Johannes Reuchlin rejected the Reformation. Others, including Willibald Pirckheimer, Conrad Peutinger, Ulrich Zasius, Mutianus Rufus, Christoph Scheurl, and Crotus Rubeanus, at first were favorably inclined toward it because they anticipated from it the long-demanded reform. But they backed away when it became clear that the Lutheran movement amounted to a revolutionary innovation which could only shatter the unity of the Church, and when in its sometimes tumultuous course it ran counter to the ideas of this cultural aristocracy.[1] The outstanding men of the older generation, especially, turned completely away from Luther again. If humanism, in its concern with and efforts for the text of the Bible and in its criticism of the Church, formally had much in common with the Reformation, still in its ethical optimism or moralism it was further away from the Reformation's basic principle—*sola fide* or *sola gratia*—than most contemporaries were aware.

This was especially true of Desiderius Erasmus. At the outbreak of the Reformation he had achieved the zenith of his influence, and everyone awaited his decision for or against Luther. But he held back. As late as May 1519 he wrote: "Luther is entirely unknown to me; I have still had no time to read his books."[2] He wanted "to stay away from all controversy, if possible, in order to be the more useful for the revival of scholarship."[3] Even after the publication of the Bull "Exsurge Domine" he saw the war against Luther as a case of "hatred of scholarship." Monks wanted to suppress it "so that they can rule with impun-

---

[1] C. Mutianus: "Ego phanaticos lapidatores non amo" (K. Gillert, *Der Briefwechsel des Conradus Mutianus* [Halle 1890], no. 620).

[2] Letter of 18 May 1519 to T. Wolsey (H. M. Allen, *Opus epistolarum Desiderii Erasmi Roterodami* III, no. 967, 78ff.); cf. the letter of 30 May 1519 to Luther (ibid., III, no. 980).

[3] Letter of 30 May 1519 to Luther (Allen, op. cit., III, no. 980, 37f.).

ity with their barbarism."[4] As regards Luther, it was only his loudness and pugnacity that Erasmus disliked. "Would that Luther had followed my advice and kept away from these subjects which cause hatred and insurrection!"[5] "His edge is so sharp that, even if all he had written were the purest truth, this business could not have a happy outcome."[6] To the Pope Erasmus wrote in September 1520 that he must not be regarded as a Lutheran just because he had not written against Luther. He declared that he had not the leisure for a thorough perusal of Luther's writings, and this task was beyond his talents and his education. In addition he was unwilling to challenge the position of the universities, which were already preoccupied with this, and, besides, he dreaded calling down the hatred of so many powerful men.[7] At Cologne in October 1520, asked by Frederick the Wise for his opinion of the controversy, he replied, according to Spalatin, with an equal amount of frivolity and *esprit:* Luther has sinned in two respects—he has struck at the Pope on his crown and the monks in their bellies.[8] Taken to task for this by the papal legate Aleander, Erasmus denied having said it.

From the desire to remain a spectator and perhaps to act as mediator at the opportune time, he avoided a decision, which he could no longer dodge in Louvain, by "fleeing" to Basel in the fall of 1521. From there he wrote to W. Pirckheimer: "The Lutherans threaten me publicly with invective, and the emperor is almost convinced that I am the source and the head of the whole Lutheran disturbance. And so I am in bad danger from both sides, whereas I have actually deserved well of all."[9]

When at the end of 1522 Ulrich von Hutten tried to induce Erasmus to come out clearly for the Reformation and at the same time sought support from him in his own difficult situation, Erasmus refused to see him for days. To the bitter reproaches of the mortally ill knight in his *Expostulatio cum Erasmo* (1523), that Eramus did not dare to draw the consequences because, in his insatiable ambition, he feared for his reputation among the great lords, Erasmus replied, "I remain on the outside. . . . I am not a party to any side. . . . By taking sides I mean total adherence to all that Luther has written. . . . But I love complete freedom and will not and cannot ever serve one side."[10]

---

[4] Letter of 9 September 1520 to G. Geldenhauer (Allen, op. cit., IV, no. 1141, 25f., 39).

[5] Allen, op. cit., IV, no. 1141, 10.

[6] Letter of July 5, 1521 (Allen, op. cit., IV, no. 1218, 5–7).

[7] Allen, op. cit., IV, no. 1143, 50–58; cf. the letter of 23 September 1521 (Allen, op. cit., IV, no. 1236).

[8] Cf. Allen, op. cit., IV, 370; *WA, TR* I, 55, no. 131.

[9] Letter of 30 March 1522 (Allen, op. cit., V, no. 1268, 76–79).

[10] "Spongia adversus adspergines Hutteni" (1523), *Opp.* X, 1650, BD.

Luther esteemed Erasmus for his services in regard to the biblical languages, without knowledge of which he could not conceive of any genuine theology.[11] He extravagantly glorified the humanist, greeted him as "our adornment and hope," and referred to himself as Erasmus' "little brother in Christ."[12] In *De servo arbitrio* Luther still emphasized the great service that Erasmus had rendered him in the field of linguistics: "I confess that I am much indebted to you and hence I sincerely honor and admire you" (*WA* 18, 786, 38ff.). But even so the reformer sensed early how incompatible he and Erasmus were spiritually, and he suspected in Erasmus the pagan of intellectual snobbery, to whom "human things are of greater importance than divine things."[13] But Luther was aware of what it would mean for his cause if Erasmus came out against him. If he was unable to gain him for his side, he hoped at least for his silence. Accordingly he wrote in April 1524: "If you are unwilling to contribute further, then at least be a mere spectator of our tragedy. But do not make common cause with our adversaries. Above all, do not publish anything against me, just as I will publish nothing against you."[14]

But by then Erasmus was already working on his *De libero arbitrio diatribe sive collatio.* Of course he took his time, but in September 1524 he informed King Henry VIII: "The die is cast: the book on free will has seen the light of day."[15] Clearly Erasmus had been hard pressed and had been reluctant to take a stand publicly. The choice of topic indicates what to the great humanist seemed especially imperiled—the dignity of man, who despite all dependence on grace is God's partner. In his reply Luther himself acknowledged that Erasmus had grasped the decisive point:

> You have really confined yourself to the essential point and—unlike all the others who have assailed me till now—you have not tackled me vainly with the ridiculous questions about papacy, purgatory, and indulgences. You, and you alone, have understood what is really at stake. You have seized the bull by the horns.[16]

Erasmus had been drawn into the dispute over free will some time earlier. In February 1523 he had had to defend himself against the charge of Pelagianism, which had been made by the Lutheran side as a result of his teaching on free will in the explication of Romans (1517).

---

[11] Letter of 29 March 1523 to Eobanus Hessus (*WA, Br* 2, 50).

[12] Letter of 28 March 1519 (*WA, Br* 1, 361, 363).

[13] Letter of 1 March 1517 to John Lang (*WA, Br* 1, 90, 19).

[14] *WA, Br* 3, 271; Allen, op. cit., V, no. 1443, 67–70.

[15] Allen, op. cit., V, no. 1493, 4.

[16] *De servo arbitrio, WA* 18, 786; in what follows cited by page and lines.

In it he marshaled arguments which he pursued in greater detail in *De libero arbitrio*,[17] seeing man between the Scylla and Charybdis of trust in his own works and an unbridled fatalism. He gathered Luther's teaching from the *Assertio* of 1520, the detailed rejoinder to the Bull "Exsurge Domine." In this the reformer had defended the thesis that "after sin free will is a mere word, and, when man acts according to what is inside him, he sins mortally."[18] In the dispute between Luther and Erasmus the point at issue was not moral freedom in general but the role of the human will in effecting salvation. Can man achieve salvation by himself, that is, can he freely accept or reject the grace offered? In Erasmus' view, Holy Scripture, the philosophers, and common sense testify that the will is free. Otherwise why would Scripture need to blame and to admonish or to praise obedience? God's justice and mercy make no sense unless there is some vestige of freedom of choice in man.

With Augustine, Erasmus would prefer not to rate the role of free will too high: "To my taste is the opinion of those who attribute something to free will but most to the grace of God."[19] Man needs prevenient and concurring grace. It is the source and not the mere accompaniment of the work, which it effects with free will. Against Karlstadt and Luther, Erasmus expounded a third view, which, while leaving room for free will, left no doubt that ultimately everything depends on the grace of God:

> Here we have to do with those who are very far removed from Pelagius, who attribute very much to grace and almost nothing to free will, but who nevertheless do not entirely abolish free will. They say that man cannot desire the good without a special grace [*gratia peculiaris*], that he cannot begin nor advance nor finish without the guiding and enduring aid of divine grace. Their view appears sufficiently probable, for it allows man the possibility of exerting himself but does not thereby leave him any possibility for boasting of his efforts. [30, 22–29]

Scriptural passages which speak of an absolute predestination and of a deliberate hardening of men's hearts by God are, according to Erasmus, to be interpreted prudently. In general he would prefer to make as few apodictic claims as possible.

> I take no delight in rigid claims and prefer to take the part of the skeptics where this is allowed by the sacrosanct authority of Scrip-

---

[17] Allen, op. cit., V, no. 1342.

[18] Art. 36 (*WA* 7, 142, 22).

[19] Cited by page and lines according to the edition by Johann von Walther (Leipzig 1910; reprinted 1935).

ture and the decisions of the Church, to which I gladly submit my judgment in all matters, regardless of whether I understand her regulations or not. [3, 15–20]

But quite apart from man's personal, intellectual, and spiritual make-up, the matter itself calls for a prudent restraint. In any event, the subjective appeal to the "evangelical spirit" (16, 18) affords no certainty. "What am I to do if various interpretations are adduced by several persons and each one swears that he has the Holy Spirit?" (17, 25f.). The self-assurance with which the reformers came forward and shoved aside the biblical exegesis of the Church Fathers was for Erasmus in striking contrast to the disagreements in their own camp. Consequently the meaning of Scripture could not be as clear as had been asserted. It was not in his nature to make over clear-cut claims. He knew too much about the ambiguity of life, he saw too clearly the false in the true and the true in the false, to commit himself unequivocally. He felt disturbed in an age which pressed so relentlessly for decision. What had previously been freely discussed was now not even to be yawned over. Actually out of love of truth he would prefer to remain undecided. "As a matter of fact, there are in Holy Scripture certain inaccessible passages which, in accord with God's will, we should not fathom more deeply and in which, if we nonetheless do seek to penetrate, increasing darkness encompasses us" (5, 17ff.). Many questions, "instead of being postponed till an ecumenical council, as is often demanded today, should be left for the time when mirror and mystery have been eliminated and we behold God face to face."[20] Above all, obscure and uncertain doctrines and even some passages of the Bible do not bear it well when they are held up to unlettered folk. Even supposing that

> it is true in some sense—which Wyclif taught and Luther has confirmed—that everything we do is done not out of free will but of pure necessity, what could be more inappropriate than publicly to advertise this paradox. . . . What weak person would thereafter continue to endure the lasting and laborious struggle against his own flesh? What evil person would thereafter still aspire to improve his life? [9, 20–10, 11]

Erasmus cannot conceive a Christian ethic without the freedom to choose the good and reject the evil, without man's being at least released to this freedom by grace. If the proof of this cannot be unambiguously demonstrated, then a pastoral and theological concern for the uneducated masses compels one to postulate this truth and forbids one to call it in question outside the discussions of scholars.

[20] Allen, op. cit., V, no. 1334, 231–234.

Luther did not reply to Erasmus at once. He was preoccupied with his fight "against the heavenly prophets" and with the peasant risings. But despite serious setbacks and so many disappointments he seems to have lost none of his certainty in his counterwork, *De servo arbitrio,* which finally appeared in December 1525. It is, he says, necessary to witness to the truth in God's word, without human and pedagogical considerations, even against the Church and her tradition as well as against the seemingly unquestionable judgment of human reason. Erasmus, he writes, seems to have missed the point that Holy Scripture contains only one doctrine—that God is God, that is, absolute and unlimited, and that man is man, that is, limited and dependent on God.

> He is God, for whose will neither cause nor reason has any importance that can be prescribed for him as rule or measure. He has nothing above or beyond himself, but his will is the rule for everything. If any rule or measure or cause or reason were to have any importance for his will, it could no longer be the will of God. For it is not because he has to will or has had to will thus that what he wills is right; on the contrary, because he himself wills it, therefore what happens must be right. Cause and reason are prescribed for the will of the creature but not for the will of the Creator. [712, 32–38]

Correspondingly, in things subordinated to him man is free and acts according to his own law. Differing from the *Assertio,* in *De servo arbitrio* Luther acknowledges a freedom of choice in the civil sphere.[21]

Whereas Erasmus took pains with nuances, Luther overemphasized to make as clear as possible his undoubtedly serious religious concern. In so doing he did not lack a consciousness of mission and self-assurance. Unfortunately he did not hesitate to revile his adversary and to reproduce the latter's views inaccurately when such a procedure facilitated his own argument. In his view Erasmus was an atheist, a scorner of Scripture and destroyer of Christianity, a hypocrite, blasphemer, and skeptic.[22] "A Christian must love assertions, however, or he is not a Christian" (603, 11).

> I say, this, therefore, in order that from now on you may stop accusing our cause of obstinacy and stubborness. For you thereby only make known that you cherish in your heart a Lucian or an-

---

[21] ". . . intelligamus hominem in duo regna distribui. Uno quo fertur suo arbitrio et consilio, absque praeceptis et mandatis Dei, puta in rebus inferioribus. Hic regnat et est dominus, ut in manu consilii sui relictus" (*WA,* 18, 672, 8–11).

[22] Cf. Erasmus' grievances in regard to Elector John of Saxony (Allen, op. cit., VI, no. 1670, 28–37) and Luther (ibid., no. 1688, 12–24).

other pig from the herd of Epicurus, who does not himself believe that there is a God and laughs privately at all who do believe and confess. Let us be "assertors" and find our joy in assertions and, for yourself, stick to your skeptics until Christ summons even you. The Holy Spirit is not a skeptic. In our hearts he has written, not doubtful opinions, but assertions, which are more certain and firmer than life itself and all experience. [605, 26–34]

For Luther Holy Scripture is clear in this matter; at the most it offers philological difficulties. Of course the inner clarity in the heart is the prerequisite for understanding. "Man needs the Spirit of God in order to understand Scripture or even only a part of it" (609, 11). It is by no means irreligious and impertinent, as Erasmus claims, "but, on the contrary, salutary and necessary for a Christian to know whether his will can accomplish anything or nothing for his salvation" (614, 2). "If we do not know this"—and revelation alone assists us in this—"then we know absolutely nothing about Christianity and are worse than all pagans" (614, 6f.). In this matter one should not be afraid of disturbance. "If God and antigod are struggling with each other, must there not be a disturbance throughout the world? To wish to calm this uproar is to wish to annul God's word and to forbid it" (626, 23–26). It is a question of "humiliating our arrogance and recognizing the grace of God" (632, 28).

But man is unable to humble himself completely until he knows that his salvation is totally beyond his resources, resolves, and exertions, beyond his will and his works, and depends entirely on the free judgment, the resolve, will, and work of another—namely, God. . . . But he who in no way doubts that everything depends upon the will of God, gives up all hope in himself, makes no choice but waits for the operation of God—he is closest to the grace of being saved. [632, 30; 633, 1]

Only those thus humbled and annihilated can be saved—those who believe not only in the unseen but in that which is most deeply concealed, "in contrast to the objective, to perception, and to experience."[23]

Thus God conceals his external goodness and mercy under eternal anger, his justice under injustice. . . . To be able to believe that he is just who, deliberately and without their being able to change it, makes men deserving of damnation—that is the highest degree of faith. [633, 14–18]

[23] "Non autem remotius absconduntur, quam sub contrario obiectu, sensu, experientia" (633, 9).

God, revealing himself, remains the hidden one; he even veils himself in the opposite. Luther wants the doctrine of the servile will understood in the context of this mystery of the *Deus absconditus*—that man is possessed either by evil or by the Spirit of God. Man always acts according to necessity, which is not the same as "forced." For external compulsion is not needed; one's desire or inclination, which cannot be changed by one's own strength, makes one act. If the will is changed by the Holy Spirit,

> it is in no sense free even then. It cannot do otherwise, so long as it is animated by the Spirit of God and grace. [635, 5f.] Thus the human will is placed in the middle, like a beast of burden. If God sits on it, it wills and goes where God wills . . . . If Satan sits on it, it wills and goes where Satan wills. And it is not within its free choice to run to one of the two riders or to seek him; rather, the riders themselves vie to hold on to him and to take possession of him.[24]

When Erasmus cited the tradition of the Church and the testimony of the saints against this unheard-of view, Luther countered with: "The Church is concealed and the saints are unknown. Whom are we to believe?" (652, 23). Only "Holy Scripture decides who is right" (653, 28). It is all the more true that "whoever denies that the Holy Scripture grants a clear insight deprives men of all light, of every possibility of enlightenment" (656, 10f.).

On this basis Luther set to work to refute Erasmus' arguments and to defend his own position. He ended with a eulogy of freely operating grace. The unfreedom of the will is a mark not only of fallen man but in general of man as a creature; even man reborn is unfree. At stake is the "powerless free will inherent in all men, which is nothing but clay, nothing but untilled land, precisely because it cannot will the good" (206, 4–6). But Luther is not depressed by this truth; it is for him the reason for a glad assurance of salvation.

> I do indeed confess concerning myself: if it could possibly happen, I would not desire that free will should be given me or that anything should be entrusted to me whereby I could exert myself for salvation . . . or would be compelled constantly to labor in the dark and to strike at the air. For my conscience will . . . never be certain and secure as to how much it would have to do in order to satisfy God. [783, 17–26]

---

[24] 635, 27–22; cf. A. Adam, "Die Herkunft des Lutherwortes vom menschlichen Willen als Reittier Gottes," *LuJ* 29 (1962), 25–34.

Because salvation is not subject to his will, and is promised as a result not of his work but of God's grace, Luther is sure that no devil can overcome him and snatch him away from God. Even though only a few may be saved, "not even one would be saved by the power of free will, but all would be lost together" (783, 35).

In view of the overwhelming majesty of God, who is pure will in the Ockhamist sense, there is no place for man's free action. If he is not to pine away out of dread, then he needs assurance at any cost. But where does he obtain the assurance of belonging to the few who cannot fail to be saved?

Erasmus was deeply hurt by Luther's violent and personally insulting manner. In his view Luther had "written in such a manner that no further place for friendship remained."[25] In his *Hyperaspistes diatribae* (1526–27) the great humanist again defended his standpoint. He once more showed that Scripture contains obscure passages and should by no means be discussed in all its parts in front of everyone at all times. He firmly protests Luther's insinuations:

> As though I taught that there could be a Christian piety without Christ! . . . Here, Luther, I appeal once more to your conscience. Are you not ashamed to scribble such elegies? You twist my words. . . . In whose books does the name of Christ appear oftener than in mine?[26]

After a struggle Erasmus had come out against the Reformation and had adhered to the teaching of the ancient Church in a question especially close to his humanist heart. His anger and indignation at Luther's reply were strong, but he continued to strive not to appear as belonging to one side. In the *Hyperaspistes,* addressed to Luther, he wrote:

> I have always hated factions. Hitherto I have sought to remain apart; I was unwilling to separate myself from the Catholic Church. . . . I have never abandoned her. . . . I have never wanted to call your church a Church. . . . I know that in the Church which you term "papist" there are many things which offend me, but I see them also in your church. But evils to which one is accustomed are more easily endured. And so I put up with this Church until I shall discover a better one, and she is equally obliged to put up with me until I have become better. It is not a bad policy to keep a middle course between two evils.[27]

[25] Allen, op. cit., VI, no. 1717, 42f.
[26] *Opp.* X, 1266, AB.
[27] *Opp.* X, 1257, C; F.

Even such an admission still demonstrates intellectual restraint, a fear about taking sides and maintaining a stand. Skepticism, even a great amount of dogmatism, also characterized the aging Erasmus. He was concerned, not about theology, but about the piety of the heart and about education. Just as he kept aloof from Luther's religious rigorism, so in the *Ciceronianus* (1528) he divorced himself from a pagan humanism which smacked more of Cicero than of Christianity. The more the religious factions fought among themselves, the more he wanted to bring them back to unity by means of a simple, practical, and scripturally inspired Christianity and by deemphasizing dogma and religious creed. In 1526 he wrote to Bishop Fabri of Vienna that partisans should be excluded from the schools and replaced by men "who do not deal with dogmatic controversies but impart to their students only that which contributes, without controversy, to piety and good morals . . . who, free from the study of details, teach the useful to the children."[28] He confronts the primacy of truth with the primacy of peace. In a letter to Jacob Sadoleto as late as 1530 he maintained that "If people had paid no attention to Luther in the beginning, this conflagration would not have occurred or certainly it would not have spread so."[29] Ultimately guilty, he held, were the friars who first shamelessly preached the indulgence and then attacked Luther when he came forward against it.

It was Erasmus' fate to be born into a time which relentlessly posed the question of truth and pressed for an answer, but to be himself cut out for anything but the role of a martyr.[30] His great friend Thomas More proved that partisanship could be combined with liberal thought, tolerance, and broadmindedness. But nothing better characterizes Erasmus' own failure than his inability to understand the martyrdom of the English chancellor: "If only he had never become involved in that dangerous business and had left the theological matter to theologians."[31]

If the aging Erasmus rejected the Reformation with a growing decisiveness and severity, this was not because of error and heresy but because it was *fatalis tumultus*—it led to unrest, immorality, intolerance, and the ruin of humanistic pursuits. When, under Oecolampodius, the Reformation was forcibly introduced at Basel and the Mass was abolished, Erasmus left for Freiburg im Breisgau in 1529 to find quiet

[28] Allen, op. cit., VI, no. 1690, 33–101.

[29] Ibid., VIII, no. 2315, 256f.

[30] "Non omnes ad martyrium satis habent roboris" (Allen, op. cit., IV, no. 1218, 32). Cf. J. Huizinga: "Erasmus was a man who was too prudent and too moderate to be heroic" (p. 225). Meanwhile, Huizinga and his generation have learned by experience that it is not left to our liking to be heroic or not.

[31] Letter of 24 August 1535 to B. Latomus (Allen, op. cit., XI, no. 3048, 59f.).

for his literary work. He aimed to restore the unity of the Church (*Liber de sarcienda ecclesiae concordia,* 1533) by a contemplation of the simplicity of the Apostolic Church. A return to Holy Scripture and a confinement to the basic truths of the Apostle's Creed (*Explanatio symboli,* 1533) would put an end to all controversies and enable the Church to rediscover her original spiritual purity (*De puritate ecclesiae christianae,* 1536). These ideas met with the approval of princes—those of the Lower Rhine for example—and found adherents among theologians such as G. Witzel, M. Bucer, and G. Cassander. But Erasmus' unwillingness for a decision and for a confession probably hurt rather than helped the unity of the Church he claimed to serve. "For nothing so fostered the ecclesiastical schism," says H. Jedin, "as the illusion that there was none." The budding starts of reform, present in the work of Erasmus and with roots in the Christian humanism of John Colet (1466–1519) and others, were not equal to the tempest of the Reformation and were rapidly destroyed by it.

It is especially as a teacher and catechist that Erasmus became significant in the inner reform of the Church.[32] As early as 1512, at the request of John Colet, he composed in his *Christiani Hominis Institutum* an elementary instruction, a sort of children's catechism in verse. In at least seventy printings this little work obtained a wide circulation. Once more at the request of an Englishman, the father of Queen Anne Boleyn, there came into print in 1533 a larger catechetical work, the *Explanatio Symboli . . . Decalogi praeceptorum et Dominicae precationis,* which in later editions was called the *Catechismus.* In its literary form the *Explanatio* is a dialogue between catechist and pupil. The first five of the six lessons deal with the Creed; the last with the commandments and the Lord's Prayer.

The Sacraments are explained only briefly, or, as he himself notes, "in passing."[33] In proportion to the size of the work the section on the Sacraments is briefer than in the *Institutum,* although it was the Sacraments that were so hotly disputed because of the Reformation and it was here precisely that the laity would have had need of a clear answer. There is no more unequivocal indication of how foreign to Erasmus were worship and Sacraments and how very much he dodged not

---

[32] But it seems to me that R. Padberg (*Erasmus als Katechet,* Freiburg 1956) is overestimating him when he terms Erasmus the "renewer of catechetical preaching" (p. 157) and says of the *Explanatio* that it provided "answer and clarity in the fullest sense for this hour of distress and danger" (p. 127).

[33] "Tantum obiter de sacramentis attigisse sat est" (*Opp.* V, 1176 E).

merely theological controversy but also the necessary religious avowal.[34] This appears especially in his treatment of the Eucharist. In the *Institutum* he had still spoken of the mystical food which under the image of bread and wine truly offers us the real presence of Christ.[35] In the *Explanatio,* on the other hand, we find:

> The Eucharist provides strength for the real combat. By it the power of faith is roused in us and we are filled with abundant grace by recalling the holy death, since in some mysterious way we renew that unique Sacrifice to which we owe our salvation.[36]

Not a word about the real presence. This is astonishing in view of the sharp denial of it by Oecolampadius at Basel, but at the same time understandable if we reflect that Erasmus inclined toward the ideas of this reformer because they "are simpler and more intelligible and raise less complicated questions."[37] He had, it is true, emphatically clung to the teaching of the ancient Church, but preferred that the "how" of the bodily presence should be undiscussed and so far as possible not doctrinally established. As a "return to the proclamation of the Bible and the Fathers,"[38] the fact here under consideration has not been sufficiently characterized. The effort to limit as far as possible the area of obligatory doctrine remained, therefore, a chief characteristic of the theology of Erasmus even at a time when in the Church it was finally realized that, in view of dogmatic vagueness, it was necessary to establish her doctrine and to apply the brake in the face of error.

In the *Institutum* the author had expressly declared his desire to receive the Sacraments of the Church at the hour of death.[39] But the prohibition of celebrating Mass and the risk of dying without the Sacraments did not restrain the priest Erasmus from returning in May 1535 to Protestant Basel when external calm had been restored there. In the

---

[34] Contrary to R. Padberg, who, precisely by means of the *Explanatio,* would like to refute the thesis of the neglect of sacramental theology by Erasmus, maintained by Lortz, Huizinga, and others. Cf. Padberg, op. cit., pp. 46, 56 (footnote 72), 110 (footnote 238).

[35] Mysticus ille cibus (Graeci dixere Synaxin)
Qui panis vinique palam sub imagine Christum
Ipsum praesentem vere exhibet intima nostra
Viscera coelesti saginet et educat esca
Inque Deo reddit vegetos, et reddit adultos.
                              (*Opp.* V, 1358 E).

[36] *Opp.* V, 1175f.

[37] Allen, op. cit., VIII, no. 2147, 32f.

[38] Padberg, op. cit., p. 107, footnote 221.

[39] *Opp.* V, 1359f.

treatise *De praeparatione ad mortem* (1534) he appears to have come to grips with the thought of dying in a non-Catholic environment. According to it, a sincere confession at the close of life is certainly beneficial, but if a priest cannot be had, one need not tremble in superstitious dread, for prayer and inner sorrow can also bring salvation.[40] A year later, on 11 July 1536, Erasmus died at Basel without priestly support. He was solemnly buried as a Protestant. To the end of his days he had thus given preference over truth to that peace which proved useful, not least for his own well-being and for *bonae litterae*.

[40] Ibid., 1310f., 1311 BC.

CHAPTER 14

Zwingli and the Beginnings of the Reformation in German Switzerland

The reform movement was not uniform in doctrine and ecclesiastical organization because in southwestern Germany, and above all in Switzerland, the Reformation was from the start essentially independent of Martin Luther and, under the influence of such important and individualistic men as Ulrich (Huldrych) Zwingli (1484–1531), Johannes Oecolampadius (1482–1531), Joachim Vadian (1483–1551), and Berchtold Haller (1492–1536), acquired a form of its own. And the Reformation was not uniform even in Switzerland. Every canton has its own Reformation history, although this did not prevent Zurich from acquiring a leading position because of its political importance and the surpassing figure of its reformer, Ulrich Zwingli. If the Wittenberg Reformation was under the auspices of the territorial principality, the stage of the Swiss Reformation was the republican urban and rural communities.

The Swiss Confederates, unconcerned for Emperor and Empire, had long been accustomed to regulate their own affairs at diets— *Tagsatzungen*—of their own. Following the Swabian War they had obtained their *de facto* independence of the Empire in the Peace of Basel (1499). Both as mercenaries in the papal service and on their own they had a great share in the struggle between France, Emperor, and Pope for Lombardy. The dream of obtaining for themselves a place among the great powers by acquiring northern Italy after the victory over the French at Novara came to a sudden end with the overwhelming defeat at Marignano in 1515.[1]

[1] E. Gagliardi, *Geschichte der Schweiz* I (Zurich, 2nd ed. 1934), 288–312.

The frequent military assistance given to the Pope had brought the Swiss a number of privileges and had led to a state church that was further developed than was elsewhere customary in the cities. The introduction of the Reformation by the authorities was thereby facilitated.

The Reformation first established itself at Zurich, where it was the accomplishment of Ulrich Zwingli. The third son in a family of ten children, he was born at Wildhaus in the county of Toggenburg on New Year's Day 1484. His father was the local cantonal president. Zwingli stressed his rustic origin—"I am a peasant, all peasant"—which stood him in good stead in his graphic, folksy speech. At the age of six he received his first instruction from his uncle, the pastor at Walensee. When he was ten he attended the Latin school at Basel and completed his early schooling with the humanist Wölfflin at Berne in 1497. He did his university studies at Vienna in 1498 and Basel in 1502. Humanism was flourishing in both places, but especially at Basel, with its circle of outspoken scholars.

At the university the *via antiqua* was decisive for Zwingli. Its combining of Thomistic scholasticism and humanism, of rationality and ethics, characterized him throughout life. He claims to have been shown the questionable nature of indulgences by his teacher, Thomas Wyttenbach (ZW 2, 145, 27). However, he did not take his formal study of theology very far. Scarcely had he begun it, after obtaining the degree of master of arts in the spring of 1506, when he was elected pastor of Glarus. Having received priestly ordination, he took charge of his parish on 19 September 1506. Zealous, he organized a pilgrimage and built a chapel for it. The care of souls, in which, aided by three or four chaplains, he had to attend to not many more than a thousand people, left him ample time for the study of the ancient authors, the Fathers, and the Vulgate. From 1513 he learned Greek on his own. At the same time he developed a passion for politics. His first literary works were patriotic fables in verse, in which he warned against the French King's recruiting of mercenaries. He often accompanied the Swiss to Lombardy as an army chaplain and was proud that his countrymen were honored by the Pope with the title of "Deliverers of the Church." For his services he received a pension from the Curia.

Zwingli's solemn appeal to the Confederates at Monza for unity and loyalty to the Pope was unable to prevent the catastrophe of Marignano. Because the "Frenchies" now established themselves in Glarus, he had to resign as army chaplain. On 1 November 1516 he obtained leave to go to Einsiedeln for three years and there was active as a priest in the management of the pilgrimage in the customary manner, and in the summer of 1517 he himself made a pilgrimage to the shrines at Aachen. At the same time he studied Erasmus' Greek New Testament and made his own copy of Paul's Epistles. In Zwingli's case there is no question of a struggle for the Gospel, as there was with Luther, or even of a reform understanding that deeply stirred him. If in 1523 he maintained in retrospect: "Before anyone in our area knew anything of Luther's name, I began to preach the Gospel of Christ in 1516 . . ." (ZW 2, 144, 32ff.), he was referring to reform preaching and criticism of abuses—something that was not new in Erasmus' circle. Zwingli did not take his obligation of celibacy very seriously. When in 1518 he was about to receive a call to become the priest of the cathedral at Zurich, it was urged against him that in Einsiedeln he had seduced the daughter of an official. In a "letter of confession" (ZW 7, 110–113), which in tone did not do justice to the matter and bears very little trace of a theology of the cross, Zwingli stated that she had been the easygoing daughter of a barber and that he had never dishonored a chaste maiden. If he had offended in this regard in Glarus, his sense of shame had caused him to do so in all secrecy. This previous history did not keep seventeen of the twenty-four canons from voting for him.

At his installation he explained to the canons his plan to preach on the text of the Gospel without regard to the order of pericopes. Despite opposition he began on 2 January 1519 with the first chapter of Saint Matthew.[2] In this way he had preached through the entire New Testament by 1525. He did not write out his sermons; at most his thoughts are sketched in one or another later essay.

Zwingli's keeping the indulgence preacher Samson out of Zurich cannot be taken as a reform activity, for the Pope had forbidden this Franciscan to appear again in Switzerland. Likewise, the manner in which in the spring of 1519 he dealt with the veneration of the saints did not go beyond the reform efforts customary among humanists. At that time he wrote, "I have forbidden the worship of the saints; I did not intend to root out entirely the invocation of the saints" (ZW 7, 181, 7). He merely attacked the addressing of the "Our Father" to the saints.

A closer acquaintance by Zwingli with Luther's works can be established from 1519. He circulated Luther's writings and saw in them a confirmation of the concept of the Gospel that he had independently gained since 1516. Luther's attitude on the occasion of the Leipzig Disputation deeply impressed him. The treatise *Von der Gewalt des Papstes* (WA 2, 183–240), which was printed by Froben at Basel in September, met with his approval. According to this work, Christ rules his kingdom from heaven. The papacy is not of divine law, and councils can err. Scripture alone can be the basis of faith. But when in the middle of 1520 Luther was threatened with excommunication, Zwingli found

---

[2] *Cf. Apologeticus Archeteles* (1522) in ZW 1, 284f.

fault with his inconsiderate and extravagant manner (*ZW* 7, 293, 9). Unwilling to jeopardize his own affairs by a relationship with the Wittenberg professor, the shrewd Swiss peasant kept aloof from him. He stressed that he was not Lutheran and that he had discovered the Gospel on his own.[3] In fact, as late as 1523 he claimed he had read little of Luther's books: "I do not wish to bear Luther's name. I have read very little of his teaching and have often intentionally maintained reserve in regard to his books just in order to satisfy the papists" (*ZW* 2, 147, 28).

At the end of 1519 Zwingli fell seriously ill of the plague. This experience contributed to his inner maturation but not to his conversion or even to his awakening as a reformer. He himself transferred the beginning of his preaching of the Gospel to 1516[4] and assigned his break with the papacy to the end of 1520. To ascribe the break to a religious shock or to a decisive theological understanding in these months is an invention.[5] Walther Köhler calls the preparatory notes made in the summer of 1520 for a lecture series on the Psalms for the coming winter "the oldest confession of faith of the reformer Ulrich Zwingli."[6] But if he first stresses that "In this lecture series on the psalms, Zwingli, if he ever delivered it, expounded Augustine's theology as a theology from faith alone, as a reform awareness of redemption," he also states that Zwingli did not move to entirely new paths. With selected citations from Augustine he expressed what was then in the air and what he himself had expressed earlier in marginal glosses to Augustine's writings. Forgiveness of sins and justification by faith received central significance, but at the same time the stressing of human cooperation and of the good will made free in grace showed full respect for the humanist legacy.

---

[3] *ZW* 2, 149, 34: "Also wil ich nit, das mich die Bapstler luterisch rennind; denn ich die leer Christi nit vom Luter gelernt hab, sunder uhs dem selbstwort gottes."

[4] At the end of 1521 he wrote: "I began the work on the Gospel five years ago" (*ZW* 7, 485, 3). "I learned the power and the meaning of the Gospel from reading John and the treatises of Augustine as well as from careful study of Paul's Epistles in the Greek text, which I copied with my own hand—this was eleven years ago, whereas you [Luther] came to power only eight years ago" (*ZW* 5, 712).

[5] F. Schmidt-Clausing, *Zwingli,* p. 47, would like to assume the petition of the Our Father, "forgive us our trespasses," as Zwingli's "reform passage." He quotes F. Blanke: "It must no longer be said that Zwingli's development, in contrast to Luther's, was without struggle, without inner shock. Instead, what Luther experienced in Romans 1:17 was brought home to Zwingli in Matthew 6:12. Both knew the sanctification of temptation, both knew the wonder of discovering the Gospel."

[6] W. Kohler, *Huldrych Zwingli* (Stuttgart, 2nd ed. 1952), p. 71; *id.* "Die Randglossen Zwinglis zum Röm in seiner Abscrift der paulinischen Briefe 1516/17, *"Festgabe Joh. Ficker* (1931), pp. 86–106.

The Break with the Church

Zwingli himself saw his break with the papacy in his refusal of the papal pension: "I rejected it in 1520 in a special letter" (ZW 2, 314, 13f.). This was entirely in harmony wiith the policy of neutrality which he always clearly professed. An intimate connection of political and reform activity was indeed to become altogether characteristic of his life's work.

At the beginning of his Zurich period he was still devoted to Cardinal Schiner and his anti-French policy, but he even more zealously put forward the idea of peace as held by Erasmus. He encouraged Christoph Froschauer to inaugurate his printery at Zurich with a German translation of the *Querela Pacis*. In May 1521 Zurich alone, of thirteen confederated cantons, rejected an alliance with France, and on 11 January Zurich issued a mandate whereby enlistment was threatened with prison. It is uncertain whether these measures were directly due to Zwingli. In any event he supported independence from foreign powers[7] as well as peace. He sought, with strong words but to no avail, to prevent the city council from allowing the cardinal to raise a levy of fifteen hundred men for the Pope's protection in July 1521. The fact that Schiner tried to lead the troops in the campaign against Milan and France, contrary to the agreement, and that the men, when recalled, had to wait for their wages greatly prejudiced the city against the Pope and contributed to the separation from the Roman Church. Zwingli's renunciation of the papal pension was demanded when he was unwilling to allow his right to take a stand against military support of the Pope to be questioned. The loss of fifty florins, painful in his indigent situation, was somewhat compensated by his admission to the ranks of the canons at the cathedral on 29 April 1521. He continued to perform his priestly duties until October 1522.

An apparently superficial occasion brought about Zwingli's major conflict with the Church. In the Lent of 1522 the printer Froschauer, with a group of citizens, had a dinner of sausages as a demonstration on behalf of the freedom of the Gospel. Zwingli was present but did not eat the sausage. This did not save him from an investigation instituted by the council and the episcopal authorities, for it was evident that offenses against the law of fasting, also seen on previous occasions, were connected with Zwingli's preaching. The matter seemed to proceed without difficulty. A conciliar report of 9 April was accepted, whereby until further notice no one was to eat meat in Lent without a special reason and permission. All malicious conversation regarding the eating

---

[7] "Fürsten Fürsten sein lassen und Eidgenossen bleiben" became his motto, according to Bullinger, *Reformationsgeschichte,* ed. J. J. Hottinger–H. H. Vögeli (Frauenfeld 1838, II, 1840), pp. 41f.

of meat and preaching was also forbidden. Zwingli was able to interpret this in his own favor. On 16 April he published as his first reform writing the Lenten sermon that he had preached on 23 March. It was entitled *Von Auswahl und Freiheit der Speisen* (ZW, 1, 88–136). In this he defended the freedom of the Christian: "If you like to fast, then fast. If you do not like to eat meat, then do not eat it, but let the Christian enjoy freedom" (ZW 1, 106, 15).

The Bishop of Constance and, even more so, his zealous vicar general, Doctor Johann Fabri of Leutkirch, were further alarmed. In letters to the council of Zurich and to the chapter of the cathedral they warned of the danger to the unity of the Church and of the destruction of her discipline. On 27 May 1522 complaint was made at the *Tagsatzung* at Lucerne that "now priests everywhere in the Confederation are preaching various things whereby indignation, dissension, and error in the Christian faith are springing up among the common people."[8] This probably induced Zwingli to direct to the Confederation in German the petition which on 2 July 1522 he had sent to the bishop in Latin. Ten other priests by their signatures supported the request for the freedom of preaching in accord with Scripture and for the abolition of the obligation of celibacy. All of them were probably already secretly married; in the spring of 1522 Zwingli had entered a secret marriage with Anna Reinhardt, a widow living in his neighborhood. This was not sanctioned until April 1524, shortly before the birth of their first child, by a public procession. Until then ample opportunity was provided for malicious talk.

In the 1522 petition to the Confederation the unhappy consequences of the widespread concubinage were described in detail and the results for the children were amply represented. This argument must have made an impression because of the large number of such illegitimate children. For at that time the Franciscan *Custos*, Sebastian Meyer, was able to maintain in a pamphlet, *Ernstliche Ermahnung Hugos von Landenberg*,[9] that in the bishopric of Constance an annual average of fifteen hundred children of priests were born and the fines imposed in this connection by the bishop brought him six thousand florins per year. Even if the figures are too high, there remains the fact that the wrong was widespread; there was likewise the sad circumstance that the episcopal curia exploited the moral transgressions of the clergy for financial gain.

---

[8] *Eidgenössische Abschiede* IV, 1a, 194.
[9] *Flugschriften aus den ersten Jahren der Reformation*, IV, 7, ed. K. Schottenloher (Leipzig 1911), pp. 305f.; O. Vasella, *Reform und Reformation in der Schweiz* (Münster 1958), pp. 28, 61.

The question of Church reform was focused more and more on that of preaching in accord with Scripture and of the principle of Scripture. On the occasion of conflicts between Zwingli and the religious of Zurich, the city council decided that for the future only the Gospel, Saint Paul, and the prophets should be preached. Hence the mandate of the Bishop of Constance of 10 August 1522—which complained that, despite the condemnation of Luther's heresy by Pope and Emperor, opinions were expressed in pulpits to the detriment of the Church and her organization and the secular authority was asked to assist the bishop in averting the danger—lagged behind current developments. On 19 August the clergy of the Zurich chapter recognized the principle of Scripture and decreed that for the future only that should be preached which could be demonstrated by the word of God. Zwingli now published his written defense, *Apologeticus Archeteles,* the "first and last" word (*ZW* 1, 256–327). It signified the break with the bishop. In sixty-nine controverted points the bishop's admonition was opposed with all the resources of scholarly argument, but basically it was the principle of Scripture that was involved.

> Holy Scripture must be the leader and teacher. Whoever uses it rightly must be able to do so with impunity, even if this gives very little comfort to the learned lords. Otherwise it will go badly for us, for a knowledge of Scripture is today no longer the prerogative of priests; it has become common property. [*ZW* 1, 262, 29ff.]

In September 1522 Zwingli issued in print an expanded version of a sermon against the argument that Scripture requires interpretation by means of the teaching authority and tradition. This was entitled *Von Klarheit und Gewissheit des Wortes Gottes* (*ZW* 1 338–384). The word of God does not need human supports; it imposes itself by its own impact. "The word of God cannot err . . . it is clear, does not get lost in darkness, teaches itself, reveals itself" (*ZW* 1, 382, 25ff.). Later, in view of the scriptural exegesis of the Anabaptists and on the occasion of the Marburg discussion with Luther, it would become evident how little Scripture by itself was able to maintain the unity of the Church. But Zwingli himself did not rely on the "pure Gospel." He called upon the arm of authority to impose it and, later, to curb the independence of the Anabaptists.

Until now, as a parish priest, he had to provide Mass and administer the Sacraments. On 10 October 1522, in a pulpit declaration, he resigned his office. The council then instituted a preaching position for him. Thus with no great stir he changed from Catholic priest into reform preacher.

Aided by the city council, Zwingli resolutely carried the Reformation further. He induced the city officials to send invitations to a religious colloquy at Zurich on 29 January 1523. The council, not the bishop, summoned the clergy of the territory. A "notification" was sent to "His Lordship of Constance" and his presence was suggested. A delegation named by the bishop and consisting of four gentlemen, headed by the vicar general, Johann Fabri, appeared. Fabri regarded himself as sent by his Gracious Lord, not to dispute "as a fencer, but to be a spectator or even an arbiter of peace" (ZW 1, 484, note 12). The other cantons of the Confederation had refused to participate. The basis of the disputation was Zwingli's sixty-seven theses, for which he later gave more detailed reasons in his extensive work, *Auslegen und Gründe der Schlussreden* (ZW 2, 14–457), a "collection of all opinions now in dispute" (ZW 2, 2, 2). Differing from Luther in his indulgence theses, Zwingli offered in the epilogue the comprehensive program of his Reformation. He could do so because he knew that, with the council, the ruling circles of the population were behind him. At issue on 29 January was not a disputation and even less a clarification of controversial questions, but the publication of a new order, whose validity was presupposed. In it[10] Christ alone is presented as authoritative for the individual and for all aspects of society. He is "the leader and captain promised and sent by God for all mankind" (6). The Church is "Christ's wife" (8). He who obeys Christ is "drawn to him by his Spirit and transformed into him" (13). What is strictly of a reform nature is expressed in the emphasis on "only the Gospel of Christ" (14), which is self-explanatory. Not by chance does the first article state that "whoever maintains that the Gospel is nothing without the ratification of the Church errs and blasphemes God" and the concluding proposition declare that "here no one should venture to dispute with sophistry and human trifles, but one should come to have Scripture for a judge." According to this principle the papacy, the Mass, the intercession of the saints, regulations concerning food, holy seasons and places, religious orders, celibacy, misuse of excommunication, and other things were repudiated (17–33). Also according to it Zwingli developed his doctrine of the state and justified in practice the ecclesiastical policy of the Zurich council. "The so-called spiritual power in its arrogated pomp is not based on Christ's teaching" (34). "On the other hand, the secular power has its authority and basis in Christ's teachings and practice." Christians must obey it, so long as it commands nothing that is opposed to God (37–38). It alone wields the sword and has the right to kill (40). The other articles deal with correct praying and singing, the forgiveness of sins, penitential works, indulgences, purgatory, the priestly office, and the manner of eradicating

[10] Text of the sixty-seven articles in ZW 1, 458–465.

abuses. To those who are lacking in judgment one should "offer no physical violence, unless they behave so contumaciously that one could not otherwise deal with them" (65).

There took part in the disputation in the Zurich city hall on 29 January 1523 not only the 212 men of the small and the great council but some four hundred other persons, in particular the clergy of the territory of Zurich.[11] When at the beginning Johann Fabri referred to the council contemplated by the Diet of Nürnberg as the competent tribunal for questions of faith, Zwingli successfully exploited Swiss self-assertion against both the Empire and Rome by stressing: "Here in this chamber is, without any doubt, a Christian gathering" (ZW 1, 495, 10). Persons cannot wait for a council. It is a utopia. "For Pope, bishops, prelates, and big Johnnies will not put up with a council at which the divine Scripture is declared purely and clearly" (ZW 1, 497, 11). In the explanation of article 64 Zwingli entirely rejected a council:

> Hence, devout Christians, not a council is needed but only the pure word of God. In it all things become bright and clear. . . . To cry out for councils is no different from crying out that the word of God should again be fettered and caught in the power of ostentatious bishops. [ZW 2, 449, 10ff.]

After a debate on the veneration of the saints the discussion returned to the subject that was decisive for the Zurich Reformation—that of the relations between Scripture and tradition, or the binding force of ecclesiastical laws. In the afternoon the council announced that Master Ulrich Zwingli should continue as before to proclaim the Holy Gospel and the orthodox divine Scripture according to the Spirit of God (ZW 1, 547, 12). "All other parish priests, persons entrusted with the care of souls, and preachers should preach nothing which they cannot justify by recourse to the Holy Gospels and the rest of the divine Scripture" (ZW 1, 547, 12). Thus was the principle of Scripture officially declared to be the basic law for all pastors, and the conclusions Zwingli deduced from it were fundamentally recognized. Moved and joyful, the reformer exclaimed; "Glory and thanksgiving to God, who wants his holy word to prevail in heaven and on earth" (ZW 1, 547, 27).

But people at Zurich still shrank from the practical consequences. In September 1523, probably because of an address by Zwingli, the chapter of the cathedral was reformed. The posts of canon and chaplain were

---

[11] There is no official protocol. We are informed of the process by the copy made by Erhard Hegenwald (ZW 1, 479–569) and the reports of the vicar general Faber in Latin to the Archduke Ferdinand and in German to "the lords of government at Innsbruck" (ed. J. G. Mayer, *Kath. Schweizer Blätter* 11 1895, 183–195).

limited to the number necessary for the "word of God and other Christian uses," and the ecclesiastical property was destined "for the common profit"—that is, the hiring of teachers and the care of the poor. For the overdue reform of the school system Zwingli outlined his pedagogical program in the *Lehrbüchlein*,[12] which, dedicated to his fifteen-year-old stepson, Gerald Meyer, is less a catechism than a mirror of the Christian citizen. The youth should be introduced to his duties in regard to God, self, and the community and learn to serve "the glory of God, the fatherland, and the good of all" (ZW 2, 547, 25). A patriotic spirit, motivated by Christianity and humanism, is the goal of education.

Clear encroachments into the sphere of worship, such as the abolition of images and of the Mass, had not yet been attempted. But as at Wittenberg two years earlier, radical elements now pushed to the fore at Zurich and in the neighboring areas. On 10 August 1523, perhaps on the initiative of Leo Jud, the first child was "baptized in the German language"[13] in the cathedral. At the same time Zwingli undertook work on the liturgical practice. He proceeded vary cautiously in his *Versuch über den Messkanon*[14] of 29 August 1523. Except for the readings the service continued to be in Latin, and rites such as the sign of the cross and the Mass vestments were retained. He changed only the Canon and wanted to eliminate whatever referred to the Mass as a sacrifice. When this was not possible because of regard for the "weak," people should stick with the old and be satisfied with a mental restriction. But this was not enough for the radical forces, headed by Konrad Grebel, and in October Zwingli directed against them his *Verteidigung des Büchleins von Messkanon* (ZW 2, 620–625). Similarly, in regard to images the adherents of the Reformation intended to effect both preaching in accord with Scripture and the elimination of idols. And when on 1 September 1523 Leo Jud preached expressly that, according to Holy Scripture, it was "right that idols should be removed from the churches," restraint was no longer possible. Altar images, statues, and crucifixes were wrecked, the lamps for the perpetual light were shattered, and holy water was ridiculed. But the council had to intervene because of the painful impression created and out of regard for the episcopal officials. Even Zwingli came out for punishment of the iconoclasts. Though he was basically in agreement with them—they were for the most part

---

[12] It appeared in August 1523 in Latin as *Quo pacto ingenui adolescentes formandi sint* (ZW 2, 536–551). The title *Lehrbüchlein* goes back to Jacob Ceporinus' translation of 1524. N. ed., *H. Zwingli: An den jungen Mann. Zwinglis Erziehungsschrift aus dem Jahre 1523*, ed. E. R. Rüsch (Zurich 1957).

[13] F. Schmidt-Clausing, *Zwingli als Liturgiker*, p. 49.

[14] De canone missae epicheresis (ZW 2, 556–608).

eventually to become Anabaptists—he was more prudent in his method of procedure.

The council called for a Second Disputation of Zurich[15] to meet 26–28 October 1523 for a clarification of the controverted questions. The bishops were not represented, and the other Swiss cantons, except Sankt Gallen and Schaffhausen, held aloof. On the first day Leo Jud spoke before some nine hundred participants against "images and idols." The next day Zwingli attacked the Mass as a sacrifice:

> It is a blasphemous undertaking, a very work of Antichrist, to make a sacrifice out of the tender body of the Lord and the blood of Christ and to take money for it. Christ our Redeemer gave us this only as a food and a memorial of his sufferings and his covenant. [ZW 2, 733, 9ff.]

A participant declared that "the measuring and the butchering" had already given him anxiety of conscience. For the future he would dispense the Sacrament under both species. In opposition to delaying tactics, Konrad Grebel demanded that an unequivocal stand be taken against the Sacrifice of the Mass and purgatory and called for the abolition of hosts, of the mingling of water with the wine, of the placing of the bread in the communicant's mouth, and of the communicating of themselves on the part of priests. There was virtual unanimity in regard to the rejection of the Sacrifice of the Mass, but many felt that the time had not yet come for thoroughgoing changes. The secular authority had the final word. The council issued a mandate[16] at the end of October. According to this, matters were to be left as they were for the moment. Images must not be removed, the Mass must not be abolished. And so seven months were to pass before the disappearance of images and a good eighteen months before an Evangelical Last Supper replaced the Mass. This yielding to the authority of the state procured for Zwingli the opposition of the radical groups and soon led to the founding of Anabaptist congregations. Meanwhile, on behalf of the authorities Zwingli wrote *Eine kurze und christliche Einleitung* (ZW 2, 630–663), a primer intended to prepare the clergy and congregations for the changes about to take place. According to this, representations of God are forbidden and the Mass is contrary to Scripture because Christ was sacrificed on the cross, once for all time. The Christian is free with regard to ceremonies but bound by the law emanating from the magistrates. Even when chaplains at the cathedral emphasized in December 1523 that they were tired of being upbraided as butchers of God and

---

[15] Acts in ZW 2, 671–803.
[16] *Actensammlung zur Geschichte der Züricher Reformation 1519–1533*, ed. E. Egli (Zurich 1879), no. 436.

refused to celebrate Mass any more, the hesitant regulation remained in force. "Although it is clear from Holy Scripture that the Mass is not a sacrifice, still there are so many weak and ignorant persons that one cannot suddenly abolish the Mass without giving scandal to the weak" (*ZW* 2, 812, 3ff.). However, the attitude of the council was determined not only by regard for the "weak" but even more by the critical political situation. A powerful movement in defense of the ancient faith was stirring in the rest of the Confederation. At the Lucerne *Tagsatzung* of January 1524 a united front against Zurich was formed and a mandate was issued forbidding any change of faith until the decision of a council. Zurich was to be invited to give up its doctrine.[17] The city declined to do so, calling the extravagant outbursts and the abuses of the Mass a result of misunderstanding of preaching in conformity with Scripture, and sought to shield itself by referring to the needed reform of the Church.

The attitude of the confederated cantons was, to be sure, not so uniform as the mandate of January 1524 made it seem. Bern, Basel, and Schaffhausen did not take a clear stand. Together with Fribourg the five interior cantons especially adopted a position of compromise in regard to the reform movement, which at that time meant that they rejected the principle of Scripture. In April 1524 they joined together for the unconditional defense of the ancient faith and in the Confederate Concordat of Faith of January 1525 they drew up an extensive reform program.[18]

Despite all the official reserve, the Reformation moved forward in Zurich. Like Zwingli in April 1524, the priests married. Processions and pilgrimages were abolished. On 15 June 1524 a conciliar mandate decreed "that images and idols should be removed with all propriety so that a place can be found for the word of God."[19] Images and relics disappeared from the churches without any spectacular iconoclasm. But the council opposed Zwingli's suggestion that now was the time to give up the Mass and celebrate a biblical Lord's Supper. The Latin Mass in the customary vestments continued until 1525, except that all sacrificial prayers were omitted. Zwingli proceeded all the more relentlessly against the Mass in his writings. Between December 1524 and March 1525 he composed his *Commentary on True and False Religion*,[20] the epilogue of a comprehensive exposition of his theology. In the section

---

[17] O. Vasella, op. cit., p. 67.

[18] *Eidgenössische Abschiede* IV, la, 572–578; O. Vasella, *Abt Theodul von Schlegel von Chur und seine Zeit* (Fribourg 1954), pp. 41f.

[19] *Actensammlung zur Geschichte der Züricher Reformation,* no. 544.

[20] *Commentarius de vera et false religione,* March 1525 (*ZW* 3, 628–911). German translation in *Zwingli Hauptschriften,* Vols. 9 and 10 (Zurich 1941–1963).

"On the Eucharist" he subjected the Mass and the worship of the Sacrament to the severest criticism.

> Why do we not bid all Mass priests to refrain from so horrible an affront to Christ? For if Christ must again be sacrificed every day, it follows that the sacrifice which he once offered on the cross does not suffice for all eternity. Is there a greater insult than this? All Masses must be immediately discontinued, and the Lord's Supper must be made use of in accord with Christ's institution. (ZW 3, 805, 15–20)

On 11 April 1525, Zwingli felt that the time had finally come for the decisive attack. With Leo Jud, Oswald Myconius, and two other priests he complained to the council, demanding the abolition of the Mass as idolatry. By means of his *Aktion oder Brauch des Nachtmahls* (ZW 4, 13–24), which he had just finished, he was able to demonstrate how he understood the celebration of the evangelical Lord's Supper. On the next day, Wednesday of Holy Week, the council, by a bare majority, decreed the abolition of the Mass. The last Mass was celebrated before a great crowd of people, "who wanted to have the Holy Sacrament administered to them according to the old custom, as before."[21] Therefore something that was still entirely alive was abolished by official decree. Even Zwingli had to be lectured by the secular authority in regard to his order of the Eucharistic liturgy. He wanted the *Gloria,* the *Credo,* and Psalm 113 to be alternated by the men and the women, but the council forbade it. It likewise did not concede to the Church the right of excommunication, which Zwingli wanted exercised by the congregation as an exclusion from the Eucharist. The Lord's Supper was first celebrated on Holy Thursday 1525 as a "thanksgiving and memorial of Christ's Passion." It is still celebrated in Zwinglian congregations according to the version prepared by Zwingli after Easter 1525, the *Ordnung der christlichen Kirche zu Zürich.* Provision was made for only four feasts: Easter, Pentecost, the Dedication, and Christmas. On Sundays only a service of the word of God, similar to the late medieval preaching service, the *pronaus,* was to take place.

> There was no community singing. Quite otherwise than Luther, the musically gifted Zwingli gave no psalms and hymns to those of his church. The organs remained silent. With the singsong of the Latin choral chant, which no one understood, what pertained to music entirely disappeared.[22]

---

[21] Gerald Edlibach, *Chronik,* ed. Jon. M. Usteri (Zurich 1847), p. 273.
[22] W. Köhler, op. cit., p. 123.

With the elimination of the Mass the Reformation finally achieved its break-through in Zurich. At the same time the creation of other institutions was necessitated by the destruction of the ancient ecclesiastical system. Zwingli had commissioned Leo Jud to prepare German rituals for baptism, marriage, and burial. The city council had issued a "Regulation for the Poor"[23] on 15 January 1525 which to a great extent disposed of ecclesiastical and monastic property. A substitute for the canon law on marriage and for the ecclesiastical matrimonial tribunals was urgently needed. Zwingli also left this important innovation in the hands of the council. On 10 May 1525 it announced the Zurich Order of the Matrimonial Tribunal,[24] which had been worked out by a commission in which Zwingli had played a decisive role. This was the first reform. Judicial power was entrusted to six matrimonial judges, two pastors as people acquainted with Scripture and two members each of the great and the small council. The only court of appeals was the city council. In the following year, 1526, the matrimonial tribunal was expanded into a tribunal of morals, which controlled the lives of the citizens by penal and preventive powers and kept watch over them by means of spies. The authority to punish lay with the council, to which a denunciation had to be made after three warnings. With the introduction in 1529 of the obligation of attending worship and the prohibition of attendance at Catholic Masses outside the territory, the city congregation completely controlled the lives of the citizens. In opposition to Zwingli's spiritualism and to his thesis of the inherent power of the Gospel, but at the same time also in consequence of it, the secular authority had seized control of ecclesiastical government. The church congregation had been absorbed into the civic community.

The founding of a theological school, decided on in 1523, could also move nearer to realization in 1525. To provide payment for the teaching personnel, the canonries at the cathedral were reduced from twenty-four to eighteen. Reuchlin's pupil Jakob Ceporinus was appointed professor of Hebrew in January 1525; after his early death he was succeeded by the former Franciscan, Konrad Pellikan. In place of the morning choral office, Zwingli, in association with Ceporinus, gave daily lectures on the Old Testament from 19 June in the cathedral at 8:00 A.M. "All pastors, preachers, canons, and chaplains and the older students"[25] had to attend. Zwingli himself gave to this hour of philological and theological exegesis of Scripture the name of prophecy. It

---

[23] Text in W. Oechsli, *Quellenbuch zur Schweizergeschichte,* Neue Folge (Zurich 1893), pp. 536–541.

[24] *Ordnung und ansehen* (= Weisung), *wie hynfür zu Zürich in der statt über eelich sachen gericht sol werden* (ZW 4, 182–187).

[25] H. Bullinger, *Reformationsgeschichte* I, 290.

served for the elementary and more advanced education of preachers and at the same time hastened the appearance of the "Zurich Bible." Until then Luther's translation of the New Testament had been reprinted in an adaptation using the Swiss dialect. Similarly the Pentateuch appeared in 1527 and soon afterwards came the other historical books and the sapiential books of the Old Testament. People qualified to put the prophetic books, still lacking in Luther's translation, into German were sought in Zurich itself. Zwingli and Leo Jud played the chief roles in this, and Jud also translated the so-called apocrypha. And so in March 1529, five years before Luther's Bible was finished, the complete "Zurich Bible" existed in six volumes. In 1531, the year of Zwingli's death, these six were united as one volume, the so-called Froschauer Bible. Holbein had contributed about half of the two hundred illustrations of this typographical masterpiece.

The Reformation in the Other Cantons of German Switzerland

From Zurich the reform movement was stimulated and fostered in northern and eastern Switzerland. Two laymen, the humanist-educated city physician Joachim Vadian (1483–1551) and the former theological student and later master saddler Johannes Kessler (1502–74), aided in the breakthrough in Sankt Gallen. At first both were under the influence of Erasmus. Vadian was gained for the Reformation by Zwingli. His helper, Kessler, had studied theology at Wittenberg and had then decided to earn his bread as an artisan. They recruited for the Reformation by means of their *Lesinen,* or lay Bible lessons. In 1524 the council put the city church at their disposal and ordered preaching in accord with Scripture. Vadian's election as mayor in 1526 assured the victory of the Reformation. Images, "idols," and altars were removed at night without disturbance and in 1527 an evangelical celebration of the Lord's Supper was introduced.

The Reformation was also established in Toggenburg by 1528. In Appenzell, adjacent to Sankt Gallen, pastors were able to induce their congregations to abolish the Mass as early as 1522. In the next year the community, influenced by the First Zurich Disputation, ordered its priests to preach in conformity with Scripture.

In the lordship of Thurgau the government was in the hands of the nine Catholic localities, which strongly opposed reform influences. In the adjoining northeast tip of the canton of Zurich, at Stammheim and Burg bei Stein, conflict occurred when the congregations, following the directions of the Zurich council, in 1524 ruthlessly removed images and burned them. While low justice here pertained to Zurich, high justice for crimes of witchcraft pertained to the *Landvogt* of Schwyz. He had the pastor of Burg arrested at Frauenfeld. When the peasants of Stammheim and Burg, who came together there, were unable to aid their pastor and their hunger grew together with their anger, they plundered the Ittinger Charterhouse, which was in the neighborhood, and put it to the torch. Under pressure from the nine localities, Zurich was induced to surrender the ringleaders to the *Tagsatzung* in Baden, which had three of them executed in the fall of 1524.

In 1522 Zwingli had installed Valenti Tschudi as pastor in Glarus and had dedicated the "epilogue" of 1523 to his former parish. But Tschudi clung to the unity of the Church and repudiated Zwingli. Hence the adherents of the Reformation did not succeed in achieving a majority in the local congregation until 1528.

In Graubünden (Grisons) the soul of the resistance to the innovations was not the Bishop of Chur, who was disliked on political and personal grounds, but the Abbot of Sankt Luzi at Chur, Theodulus Schlegel (1485–1529). When the cathedral chapter denounced the preacher Johannes Komander (1484–1557) as a heretic, the secular authorities gave him the opportunity to vindicate himself at the Religious Colloquy of Ilanz on 7–9 January 1520.[26] Abbot Schlegel was spokesman on the Catholic side. Komander was not banished and the Reformation was only temporarily halted.

The *Bundestag* soon left it to each area of the canton to choose its own faith. In the Ilanz Articles of June 1526 the episcopal territorial authority was considerably restricted and the regulation of the ecclesiastical situation was turned over to the congregations. Hence confessional allegiance in this canton developed along various lines. In the summer of 1528 the Mass was forbidden at Chur by the council. In 1529 Komander finally succeeded in protestantizing the city, except for the episcopal household. Abbot Schlegel was arrested in the course of a Protestant trial and executed on 23 January 1529, after horrible torture.

In Schaffhausen there was a scholarly circle of humanists around the city physician, Adelphi (John Müling) of Strasbourg, and the Abbot of All Saints, Michael von Eggendorf. These men read and circulated reform literature. But the Reformation found no stronger basis until 1522, when the Franciscan Sebastian Hofmeister, expelled from Lucerne, came to his native city, Schaffhausen, and preached against the papacy and ceremonies. He took part in the disputations at Zurich. His cause experienced a great success when Erasmus Ritter, called in from Rottweil against him by the Catholics, was soon himself converted to the Reformation. The council favored Hofmeister's activity but was unable to decide upon a reform mandate, as had been done at Zurich.

[26] O. Vasella, *Abt Theodul von Schlegel,* pp. 53–63.

In 1525 pressure from the Confederation brought about a setback. Hofmeister was banished and the retention of the Mass and of the *Salve Regina* was decreed. The Reformation could not be imposed until 1529.

In Basel humanism and the struggle of the city congregation against the episcopal government had prepared the ground for the Reformation, but on the other side the traditional forces thwarted a quick victory for it. Here the Reformation was under Luther's auspices rather than Zwingli's. The Alsatian Wolfgang Capito (1478–1541), from 1515 preacher at the cathedral, and the Franciscan Konrad Pellikan, *custos* at Basel from 1519, were already spreading Lutheran ideas. Luther's writings were zealously reprinted by the Basel publishers Johannes Froben and Adam Petri. Ostentatious violations of the fasting law and sermons against Church laws led to complaints to the council, which sought to bring calm by a mandate in May 1523. Preachers were urged to adhere to Holy Scripture but not to mention the teachings of Luther and other doctors.

Six months earlier Johannes Oecolampadius (1482–1531) had come to Basel for the second time. As early as 1520 he had come out for the Wittenberg reformer in the *Iudicium de Luthero.* Then in *Quod non sit onerosa christianis confessio paradoxon* (1521) he defended as an escape from his own scruples the view that one need confess only external sins. Thereafter he could no longer stay at the Birgittine monastery of Altomünster. He went to Basel in November 1522 in order to have his translations of Chrysostom printed. After Easter 1523 he began lectures on Isaiah and in the summer was appointed professor of Scripture. Around him gathered the groups of citizens who were inclined toward the Reformation, especially since, in addition to giving his lectures, he preached zealously in Sankt Martin, of which he was named pastor in February 1525. At first he restricted himself to preaching, but before the end of the year he instituted an evangelical celebration of the Lord's Supper. In the late autumn of 1524 he had had a detailed discussion of the question of the Eucharist with Zwingli. In the *Elleboron* (1525), an attack on J. Latomus' *De confessione secreta,* he developed a spiritualist concept of the Church and the Sacraments. Faith, not the Sacraments, bestows salvation. In the Eucharist the bread remains what it was. He developed this idea of a purely spiritual reception of the body of Christ in faith, for which the Sacrament is the sign, in *De genuina verborum Domini expositione liber* (1525) and in *Antisyngramma* (1526). He thereby set himself in opposition to Pirkheimer, Luther, and Brenz. He had several contacts with the Anabaptists in 1525–27, but came out against them in favor of infant baptism. He took a leading part in the disputations at Baden in 1526 and Bern in 1528. But at first he was unable to establish the Reformation at Basel against the council and the clergy of the city and the influence of Erasmus. In spite of the proclaiming of religious freedom on 29 February—"everyone is to allow the others to continue in his faith without any hatred"[27]—at Easter 1528 there occurred iconoclast outbreaks and protests against the tithe. The guilds opposed the chapter clergy and the council. In a petition to the council on 23 December 1528 they demanded "the abolishing of conflicting preaching and of the Mass."[28] The council tried to mediate and appointed a disputation for May. But the mob, once mobilized, could no longer be restrained. The cathedral was forced on 9 February and, as in other churches, crucifixes, images, and altars were destroyed. The council yielded to the terror. It excluded its Catholic members, had the iconoclasm carried to its completion by urban craftsmen, and in a mandate of 10 February 1529 forbade images and the Mass in the city and its territory.[29] The cathedral chapter fled to Neuenburg and in May established itself at Freiburg im Breisgau. Erasmus, professors of the university, the Carthusian and Dominican communities, and some others also left the city.

Oecolampadius, who was connected with the disturbances and was in fact regarded as their chief instigator, advised the council in the drawing up of the Reformation ordinance[30] of 1 April. In it the council, advised by the clergy in accord with Scripture, dealt with the proclaiming of the word of God, the celebrating of baptism and of the Lord's Supper, the problem of images, and the norms of public morality. In May 1529 Oecolampadius was chosen *antistos* (overseer) of the Church and pastor of the cathedral. He exerted himself at five synods in 1529–31 on behalf of Church doctrine and discipline. He wanted the synods to be controlled by a *presbyterium* of laymen and pastors in a certain independence of the city government, but he had as little success as Zwingli. The city council claimed the right to excommunicate and permitted no central excommunicating authority that would be competent for the entire city but only one for individual parish communities.

Bern was long undecided between the religious factions. The city had to have regard for the conservative rural congregations in its territory. And an outstanding personality was lacking.

Thomas Wyttenbach had done the preliminary work here, but his assistant and successor as canon at the cathedral, Berchtold Haller (1492–1536), is regarded as Bern's reformer. From 1521 Haller was in

---

[27] *Aktensammlung zur Geschichte der Basler Reformation* III, ed. P. Roth (Basel 1937), p. 60.

[28] Ibid., III, 291.

[29] "Adversarii me fontem omnis huius rei vocant" (E. Staehelin, *Briefe und Akten* II, 282, no. 636).

[30] *Aktensammlung* III, 473.

contact with Zwingli. The Franciscan Doctor Sebastian Meyer and Jörg Brunner, chaplain at the pilgrimage center of Kleinhöchstetten, worked for the Reformation at his side, but with more alacrity. The council sought by means of a mandate of 15 June 1523[31] to deal with the disturbances caused by their preaching against pilgrimages and the Mass. The spread of Lutheran teaching was forbidden, but at the same time the arranging of scripturally oriented preaching was fostered. Bern adhered to the mandate of January 1524, issued by the Lucerne *Tagsatzung* for the unconditional defense of the Catholic faith but rejected the Concordat of Faith of January 1525. In a mandate of 2 April the council expressly decreed the defense of the seven Sacraments, of the veneration of saints, of ceremonies, and of the religious life, out of regard for the frame of mind of the rural folk. Steps were taken against the marriage of priests, but on the other hand the nuns of Königsfelden were allowed to leave their convent. At the beginning of 1526 the situation in Bern was even more unfavorable for the Reformation. On 28 March the great council agreed to participate in the Disputation of Baden, called for 6 May and ordered Berchtold Haller to attend.

Johannes Eck had suggested to the Swiss such a disputation against Zwingli after the Regensburg meeting in June and July 1524. At that time the sacrificial character of the Mass was to be the special topic of discussion, and in 1525 the real presence was added as a controverted point. In a letter of 28 October 1525 Eck again offered his services for a disputation and noted that thus far Zwingli, with Luther, had rejected the Mass, but now he was breaking with him and, together with Oecolampadius, was seducing "many thousands into the detestable heresy . . . that they should not believe that in the venerable Sacrament are the true body and blood of Christ."[32] Thus the real presence was brought to the fore and related to the doctrinal opposition between Luther and Zwingli. It was shown that Zwingli surpassed in heresy the Wittenberg teacher who had already been outlawed and excommunicated. Zwingli declined to appear at the Disputation of Baden, which was dominated by the Catholic localities. Berchtold Haller held himself entirely aloof. Oecolampadius was the spokesman; he was pitted against Eck, Fabri, and Murner. The first two of the seven theses posted by Eck on the church doors read as follows: (1) Christ's true body and blood are present in the Sacrament of the altar; (2) they are really offered up in the Mass for the living and the dead.[33]

---

[31] A. Fluri (ed.), "Das erste gedruckte Berner Reformations-Mandat," *Schweizerisches Gutenbergmuseum* 14 (1928), 3–6.

[32] *Eidgenössische Abschiede* IV, 1a, 812; *Briefmappe* (*RST,* 21/2, Münster 1912), 1, 157.

[33] L. von Muralt, *Die Badener Disputation* (Leipzig 1926), pp. 100f.

The religious discussion was protracted from 21 May to 8 June 1526. The Catholic side claimed the victory, but the goal of this last effort to preserve the religious unity of the Swiss was thwarted. Even the reference to the doctrinal opposition between Luther and Zwingli did not convince the representatives of Basel and Bern that Holy Scripture did not suffice as a norm of faith and to move them to suppress the new teachings. The "Verdict of Basel"[34] was signed only by the nine Catholic cantons—Lucerne, Uri, Schwyz, Unterwalden, Zug, Glarus, Fribourg, Solothurn, and Appenzell—but not by Basel, Bern, and Schaffhausen. In it Zwingli was declared to have incurred excommunication. Preachers were solemnly bound to the Church's doctrine and worship, and the books of Luther and Zwingli were forbidden. An authority was to be instituted to see to it that persons expelled from one canton were not admitted to another. "The Baden Disputation was the Swiss parallel to the Diet of Worms and the Regensburg Assembly."[35]

On 21 May 1526, the very day on which the Baden Disputation began, the great council of Bern had bound itself under oath to make no change of faith without the consent of the officials. Haller, returning from Baden, was faced with the alternative of offering Mass again or of leaving Bern. He appealed to the council. When the citizenry took to the streets and demonstrated in his favor, he was relieved of his function as canon and hence of his obligation to a sacramental worship and installed as preacher. The elections of Easter 1527 finally brought victory to the new believers. They gained a majority in the great council and were able to prevail also in the small council. The Reformation mandate was renewed. Free preaching was allowed but all high-handed changes were forbidden. This increased the confusion, so it was decided to hold a religious colloquy on 15 November 1527. It was planned to form public opinion and to make an impression on the rural congregations by a pointed display. Eck refused to take part in a "sham disputation" to which the Confederation had not issued the invitation. The Catholic side was not officially represented, and so the disputation of 5–26 January 1528 acquired the character of a display which was to consolidate the decision already basically arrived at. Zwingli set out with about forty Zurich pastors and others from eastern Switzerland under an escort of three hundred armed men. Representatives arrived from the South German cities of Strasbourg, Augsburg, Memmingen, Lindau, Ulm, Constance, and so forth.

The ten theses drawn up by Berchtold Haller and his assistant Franz Kolb were largely a copy of the epilogue of the Ilanz Colloquy of 1526.

---

[34] *Eidgenössische Abschiede* IV, 1a, 935ff.; L. von Muralt, op. cit., pp. 134f.
[35] L. von Muralt, op. cit., p. 151.

The first was as follows: "The Holy Christian Church, whose only head is Christ, was born of the word of God; she continues in it and does not listen to the voice of a stranger" (ZW 6, 243, 10ff.). According to the fourth thesis it cannot be proved by Holy Scripture "that the body and blood of Christ are substantially and physically received in the bread of the Eucharist." The Mass is contrary to Scripture, as are also the invocation of saints, purgatory, office of the dead, lamps, candles, images, and celibacy. Not many of the clergy refused to sign at the end; a larger number added that they acquiesced in the decision of the council. A few days after the disputation, on 7 February 1528, the council issued a religious mandate. In it the Mass was abolished and a liturgy was introduced according to the Zurich model. The jurisdiction of the Bishop of Lausanne was repudiated and the direction of the Church was transferred to the council. The accession of Bern gave the reform movement in Switzerland a great boost. In 1536 Bern introduced the Reformation in Vaud, which it had conquered.

The expansion of the evangelical movement increased the tensions in the Confederation. Differing from Luther, Zwingli was willing to defend and propagate the faith by political means and even by arms. "Alive in Zwingli was the complete statesman, who understood the struggle for the faith as a power-struggle and was disposed to carry it out as such."[36]

Zurich pushed forward an expansion of the existing agreements in regard to citizenship. Bern entered into a treaty with Constance, and Sankt Gallen and Mühlhausen in Alsace soon followed. Basel joined in February 1529, and from there the connections continued on to Strasbourg. Such alliances took place in the first place, so Zwingli felt, "for the honor of God and the unlocking of his holy word." They were aimed directly against the Catholic cantons but no less against Austria. The answer to them was the "Christian Union," formed in April 1529. Incidents, such as the attack on the monastery of Sankt Gallen in the spring of 1529, undertaken under the protection of Zurich and the abbey's secularization, or the execution of an evangelical preacher in Schwyz, intensified the mood for war on both sides. Finally a war for the faith was decided on. When Zurich declared war on 8 June it disposed of imposing forces, estimated at more than twelve thousand in April. The addition of the troops of the allies raised this figure to a total of about thirty thousand, to which the Catholic side could oppose only nine thousand. It was desired to spare the reformer and "not allow him to fight . . . But he refused to stay at home. He sat on a charger and had a fine halberd over his shoulder. And so they moved on Kappel."[37] The

[36] W. Köhler, op. cit., p. 173.
[37] Die Chronik des Bernhard Wyss, 1519–1530, ed. G. Finsler (Bern 1901), 121, 1ff.

advance came to a halt there on 10 June. Zurich's allies urged negotiations. Zwingli advised: "Be firm and do not fear war" (*ZW* 10, 147, 2). But Bern in particular refused to take part. The community consciousness of the Confederates asserted itself and on 26 June the First Territorial Peace of Kappel[38] was concluded. The Catholic cantons had to give up their alliance with Ferdinand. Otherwise the terms were not clear and became the source of further conflict. Zwingli had demanded free, that is, Protestant preaching in the Catholic territories. In the peace it was stated "that, since no one is to be forced on account of the word of God, the cantons and their people are likewise not to be coerced." As the people of Zurich had no intention of allowing Catholic preaching and the Mass in their territory, the five cantons saw no reason to permit evangelical preaching. They understood the peace in the sense that each was allowed to persevere in its own faith.

[38] Text in Bullinger, *Reformationsgeschichte* II, 185–191.

CHAPTER 15

Anabaptists and Spiritualists

Even as early as the sixteenth century Anabaptism was often traced back to the Zwickau prophets, Karlstadt and Müntzer, or at least they are supposed to have influenced and substantially promoted it. Today it is known that, apart from an occasional contact with these Central German fanatics, the Anabaptists were an independent movement originating in the immediate circle of Zwingli at Zurich.[1] Attempts have also been made to establish connections with medieval sects, such as the Cathari, the Waldensians, the Bohemian Brethren, and others, but Leonhard von Muralt[2] and Walther Köhler have convincingly shown that Anabaptism was a "separate growth of the Reformation period,"[3] a religious and not a social revolutionary movement.

Anabaptists are distinguished from the fanatics by the conviction that the kingdom of God is to be realized in this world only in a small circle and must not be established by force. They are distinguished from the Spiritualists by the firm determination to form a visible community of

[1] Zwingli: "They went out from us but were not ours." (Quoted from W. Köhler, *Die Zürcher Täufer*, p. 63.)
[2] "Zum Problem Reformation und Täufertum," *Zwingliana*, 6(1934–37), 65–85; cf. H. S. Bender, "Die Zwickauer Propheten, Thomas Müntzer und die Täufer," *ThZ* 8(1952), 262–278.
[3] *Die Zürcher Täufer*, p. 48.

the reborn, which is recognized by the covenant sign of baptism, the celebration of the Lord's supper, and a penitential life and which is kept pure by a stern community discipline.

The Swiss Brethren and the South German Anabaptists

In 1523 the Zurich city council had introduced the Reformation. Above all, this meant preaching only "in accord with Scripture"; the liturgy should still remain unchanged. When Zwingli agreed to this prohibition of the evangelical Lord's Supper, zealous collaborators broke with him in order to form their own congregation, independent of any hierarchical authority and unencumbered by the mass of customary Christians. The leaders of this movement were Konrad Grebel (c. 1498–1526), son of a councilor, and Felix Mantz (c. 1500–27), whose father was a canon of the Zurich Cathedral. Both had received a humanist education. As Konrad Grebel wrote to Thomas Müntzer in September 1524, the decisive factor for them was the realization that the Church of the New Testament is not a church of everybody, but a community of the few, who have the right faith and lead a proper life. It is based on voluntary membership and stands as an antithesis to the people's church, which has surrendered itself to dependence on authority. "In human respect and all sorts of seductions there is a more serious and more pernicious error than there has ever been since the beginning of the world."[4] From this concept of the congregation arose the criticism of infant baptism. Only he who has experienced a penitential change of mind and believes personally can testify to this experience of salvation in baptism and be incorporated by it into the community. The question of correct baptism, the baptism of adults, thus became the distinguishing factor, and "rebaptizers" became the name given to the brethren by opponents. They themselves repudiated it, for they regarded infant baptism as no baptism at all.[5]

This new congregation wanted to make itself visible. Its members not only kept aloof from the state Church; they also took no part in civic life. Authority was recognized in accord with Romans 13:14. But the disciple of Christ was not to assume any military duty, for such would lead to a conflict of conscience. When in the fall of 1524 Grebel did not have his newly born son baptized, a conflict with the Zurich council resulted. Following a public disputation of 17 January 1525, the council decreed

---

[4] *Thomas Müntzers Briefwechsel,* ed. H. Böhmer–P. Kirn (Leipzig 1937), p. 93; H. Fast, *Der linke Flügel der Reformation,* p. 13.

[5] E.g., *Quellen zur Geschichte der Täufer in der Schweiz* I, 238; *Urkundliche Quellen zur Hess. Ref. Gesch.* IV, 57; *Quellen zur Geschichte der Täufer* V, 171.

expulsion from the city and canton for everyone who did not have his child baptized within eight days. Grebel and Mantz were forbidden to speak and their close friends, Wilhelm Reublin (Röubli), Ludwig Hätzer, Johannes Brotli, and Andreas Castelberger, were banished. Ready "to obey God rather than man" (Acts 5:29), those condemned met secretly on 21 January 1525, and on this occasion Grebel administered the baptism of faith to a former priest from the Grisons, Jörg of the House of Jacob, called Blaurock ("Blue Coat"). The latter then did the same for the brethren.[6] Thereupon, they retired to the peasant village of Zollikon, celebrated the Lord's Supper as a memorial and love feast, according to the apostolic model, and thus called into being the first Anabaptist congregation.

The Zurich council intervened here too. In the formation of a free Church of the Brethren it saw insurrection and it quelled it. This led to the spread of the Anabaptist movement into the rest of Switzerland and to South Germany. On 7 March 1526, when even torture was of no avail, the Zurich council decreed death by drowning for anyone who rebaptized. The Anabaptists displayed a great readiness to suffer. Konrad Grebel, who succumbed to the plague in the summer of 1526, had written in May 1525 to Vadian, the reformer, at Sankt Gallen: "I will bear witness to the truth by the loss of my property, even of my home, and that is all I have. I will bear witness to the truth by imprisonment, by outlawry, by death."[7]

On 5 January 1527 Felix Mantz was put to death by drowning and thus became the first martyr of Anabaptism. On the same day Jörg Blaurock was whipped on the exposed upper part of his body and driven from the city. He preached with great success in Tirol, but on 6 September 1527 he was burned after cruel torture. The indictment against him had mentioned abandonment of the priesthood and denial of infant baptism, of the Mass, of confession, and of prayer to Mary. The Anabaptist movement was almost completely wiped out in the canton of Zurich by ca. 1530.

But meanwhile it had obtained a foothold in South Germany, especially in Alsace, Baden, and Palatinate, Württemberg, and Tirol. Augsburg and Strasbourg became the chief centers. In November 1525 Michael Sattler, from Staufen im Breisgau, former prior of the monastery of Sankt Peter in the Black Forest, had been expelled from Zurich. He had gone to Württemberg, where he displayed a brisk activity. He presided at a meeting of Anabaptists on 24 February 1527, at Schleitheim near Schaffhausen, at which his Anabaptist profession of

[6] F. Blank, "Ort und Zeit der 1. Widertauf," *ThZ* 8(1952), 74.
[7] *Quellen zur Geschichte der Täufer in der Schweiz* I, 78f.

faith, the seven "Articles of Schleitheim," was adopted. This profession contained only the points of doctrine in which Anabaptism differed from the Reformation—baptism of faith, excommunication, common Lord's Supper, separation from the abominations of the world, pastoral office, nonresistance, and rejection of oaths.[8] Soon after the Schleitheim meeting Sattler was arraigned at Rottenburg am Neckar as a heretic and executed on 21 May 1527.

Wilhelm Reublin (ca. 1480–after 1559), expelled from Zurich in 1525, went to Waldshut, where he converted the pastor, Balthasar Hubmaier (1485–1528), and with him almost the entire city to Anabaptism; it had earlier been won for Zwingli's Reformation. Hubmaier wrote a pamphlet against Zwingli, *Vom christlichen Tauf' der Gläubigen* (*On the Christian Baptism of the Faithful*), which was very highly esteemed in Anabaptist circles. Because of his connection with the rebellious peasants he had to escape to Zurich at the end of 1525. He was imprisoned here but was able to obtain his release by abjuring Anabaptism. Later he again espoused the cause of Anabaptism; at Augsburg he baptized, among others, Hans Denck. In July 1526 he settled at Nikolsburg in Moravia, where various professions of faith were tolerated side by side. For a time Nikolsburg, because of Hubmaier's zeal, became the center of those sympathetic toward Anabaptism—within a year he published eighteen treatises on the true baptism, Church order, excommunication, the Lord's Supper, and so forth. He strongly emphasized congregational discipline. "Where it does not exist, there is surely also no Church, even though baptism with water and the Eucharist itself are preserved," he states in an inscription of his pamphlet *Von der brüderlichen Strafe* (*On Fraternal Punishment*). Contrary to Hans Hut (c. 1490–1527) and the rest of the Anabaptists, Hubmaier did not advocate complete nonresistance. He allowed the authority and the individual Christians to wield the sword and supported the Moravian nobles in their war against the attacking Turks. He justified this idea of his in the work *Vom Schwert* (*The Sword,* 1527). As Anabaptism gained an ever stronger hold in the Austrian lands, Ferdinand I applied energetic measures against it and demanded the surrender of Hubmaier. The latter's trial was less concerned with his reform and rebaptizing activities than with his seductive teaching at Waldshut, whereby he was accused of having caused insurrection and revolt among the common folk. He tried in vain to justify himself in his *Rechenschaft seines*

---

[8] Text in *Urkunden zur Geschichte des Bauernkrieges und der Wiedertäufer,* pp. 28–33; H. Fast, op. cit., pp. 62–70; cf. B. Jenny, *Das Schleitheimer Täuferbekenntnis* 1527 (Thayngen, Switzerland 1951).

Glaubens (*Accounting of His Faith*). On 10 March 1528 he was burned at the stake.

Hans Denck (c. 1500–27) worked a short while at Augsburg, following his baptism in May 1526. Here he baptized Hans Hut, a former adherent of Thomas Müntzer. Both introduced strongly spiritualistic and mystical elements into the Anabaptist movement. Difficulties with the leading Lutheran preacher, Urban Rhegius, over his doctrine of justification, predestination, and the ultimate sharing of all in salvation (the *apokatastasis panton* of Origenism), drove Denck from Augsburg. He went to Strasbourg in November 1526, where he met Michael Sattler and Ludwig Hätzer and, through disputations with Capito and Bucer, attracted attention. He had to leave Strasbourg too at Christmas 1526. He went to the Palatinate and worked successfully by word and writing in the Anabaptist congregations of Landau and Worms. Here he collaborated with Ludwig Hätzer and they gained the Lutheran preachers Kautz and Hilarius for their cause. But Kautz caused disturbances by posting theses and distributing pamphlets and was therefore expelled. Hätzer and Denck went to Worms but had to leave there also. In August 1527 Denck was at the "martyrs' synod" at Augsburg where Hans Hut and his theology of the imminent Parousia were at the center of the discussion. In view of the impending end of the world there was a desire to undertake a large-scale missionary activity, and Denck was dispatched to carry it out in the territory of Basel. Meanwhile there was a strong resurgence of persecution against the Anabaptists. Denck arrived at Basel in October 1527 but in mid-November he died of the plague in the house of a friendly humanist. Broken by persecution and setbacks, he seems to have regarded his work as an Anabaptist as ruined and to have turned to an individualistic spiritualism.

By virtue of an imperial decree of 4 January 1528[9] and of the recesses of the Imperial Diets of Speyer (1529) and Augsburg (1530), the Anabaptists fell under the law on heresy. They were persecuted on the charge of heresy and sedition by Catholic and often even more relentlessly by Protestant authorities and were put to death or banished. Nevertheless they could not be entirely suppressed.

The ideas common to Anabaptists can be noted as follows. They desired to reestablish the primitive community of Jerusalem. Only the elect, who were determined to lead a new life in the strictest imitation of the Lord and to testify to their conversion by the baptism of faith could belong to it. The life of the individual and of the congregation must be oriented to Scripture, preferably the New Testament. The

---

[9] Text in *Quellen zur Geschichte der Täufer* I, 3*f.

Spirit of God, which one knows with certainty, guarantees the correct understanding of its content. The real presence was denied, but great significance for the inner stability of the congregation was attached to the Lord's Supper as a memorial and love feast. As the "congregation of the saints" the community must be kept pure by strict application of excommunication, which is the sign of a legitimate Church. A well-developed awareness of their apostolate led to bustling missionary activity, which was powerfully influenced by the idea of the Second Coming. Only he who belongs to the covenant can expect grace at the time of judgment. While private property was everywhere retained, persons wanted to share goods and chattels with their brothers in voluntary charity. If community of property was required, this referred to common use, not acquisition. The brethren were basically prepared to render obedience to authority, even though real Christians need no authority as such. But, by appealing to the Sermon on the Mount, military service, oaths, and the death penalty were rejected. For the same reason an Anabaptist was not to assume any office of authority. Even when the brethren behaved peaceably and submissively, the authorities saw in them a threat to public order and safety. The Anabaptists met persecution with a great readiness for suffering, this being a mark of their election. Konrad Grebel wrote to Thomas Müntzer:

> Right-believing Christians are sheep in the midst of wolves, sheep for the slaughter. They must be baptized in anguish and distress, in sorrow, persecution, suffering, and death. They must prove themselves by fire and reach the fatherland of eternal rest not by slaying bodily enemies but by killing spiritual foes.[10]

The Moravian Brethren

In addition to the Swiss Brethren, who spread from Zurich throughout southwestern Germany as far as Hesse and Thuringia, the Hutterites (or Hutterian Brethren) are to be mentioned as a second group. The Hutterites of Moravia derived their name from Jakob Hutter (d. 1536). Born at Pustertal, he became leader and organizer of Tirolese Anabaptism after the death of Jörg Blaurock. To escape persecution in Tirol, he and his followers sought refuge in Moravia in 1529. There he came upon Anabaptist congregations which practiced a strict community of goods, following the ideal of the Apostolic congregation at Jerusalem. On this foundation Hutter in 1533–1535 built his consumption and production communes. Ulrich Stadler (d. 1540), director of the Hutte-

---

[10] *Thomas Müntzers Briefwechsel,* p. 97; H. Fast, op. cit., p. 20.

rite Brethren at Bucovice in Moravia, wrote in his treatise on community property: "Therefore, where there is property, where persons have it and seek it, . . . there persons are outside of Christ and his congregation and have also no 'Father in heaven.' " On the other hand, it is "true calm to place and surrender oneself thus to the service of the saints with all one's possessions and belongings."[11] One of the Moravian Hutterite Brethren was the Silesian Kaspar Braitmichel (d. 1573), chronicler of the Anabaptist movement. The *Geschichtsbuch* that he began is an important source for the Zurich beginnings for the history and self-evaluation of the Hutterite Brethren.[12]

The Anabaptists in the Netherlands and North Germany

The third group, the Anabaptists of the Netherlands and North Germany, goes back to Melchior Hofmann. In the Münster Anabaptist area the movement acquired a radical and even fantastic expression, which was especially prejudicial to the reputation of Anabaptists. However, Menno Simons succeeded in bringing Anabaptism in North Germany back to its originally peaceable character.

The furrier Melchior Hofmann (c. 1500–43), born at Schwäbisch Hall, had worked from 1523 as a Lutheran lay preacher in the Baltic provinces, Sweden, and North Germany. There he came into opposition to Luther and the Lutheran Reformation because of his fantastic scriptural exegesis, his ideas about the end of the world, and his spiritualistic doctrine of the Lord's Supper. Hofmann became acquainted with the Anabaptists at Strasbourg in 1529 and joined them in 1530. Like them, he demanded toleration and freedom of belief, strict sanctification of life, baptism of adults as the seal of the covenant with God, and nonviolence. But he differed from them in extravagant apocalyptic teaching and his Monophysite concept of the Incarnation. According to this, Christ received his flesh, not from, but out of Mary. For Hofmann the Bible was a secret revelation, which only he who was endowed with the Spirit, as with the key of David, knew how to interpret correctly. As a person so endowed, Hofmann believed he recognized the signs of the end of the world and that he was called to collect from Scripture the divine intentions and demands. He regarded himself as one of the two final witnesses announced in Apocalypse 11:3 and on several occasions proclaimed the end of the world. He had to leave Strasbourg repeatedly and worked in East Friesland (Emden) and Hol-

---

[11] H. Fast, op. cit., pp. 139f., 146.
[12] Ed. by A. J. F. Zieglschmid, *Die älteste Chronik der Hutterischen Brüder* (Ithaca, N.Y. 1943).

land. Through his impassioned eloquence he succeeded in gaining recognition of Anabaptism in Holland and in winning many adherents for the new "community of the covenant." They were later called "Melchiorites" or "Bontgenooten," (Members of the Covenant). The authorities at Amsterdam took measures against them, however, and Hofmann had to flee. His deputy, Volkertszoon, and eight other followers were beheaded at The Hague on 5 December 1531. After this the community operated as quietly as possible. Hofmann himself had given the directive not to baptize for two years and to limit activity to preaching and admonishing until the Lord set the hour. The Swiss Brethren regarded this as cowardice and disobedience to Christ's missionary command.

Jan Matthijs of Haarlem, a neophyte of Hofmann's, also rejected his prohibition to baptize and at the end of 1533 sent out twelve "apostles" to preach and baptize. Two of them, Bartel Boeckbinder and Willem Cuper, baptized in Friesland; among their neophytes was Obbe Philips, whom they appointed as elder. He in turn, some two years later (1536), baptized the former Catholic priest Menno Simons (d. 1567), who was to become the head of the group named for him, the Mennonites.

Hofmann, meanwhile, had been led once again to Strasbourg by his awareness of mission—that, as the new Elias, he had to cooperate in the second coming of Christ. An Anabaptist prophet from Friesland had prophesied to him that he would go to Strasbourg and, after an imprisonment of six months, would, at the Lord's return lead a victorious Anabaptist procession through the whole world. Finding himself left in peace for two months, he presented himself to the Strasbourg council to be arrested. The council complied with his wish in May 1533 and discussed his case on the occasion of the General Synod of Strasbourg, in which Martin Bucer participated. The "new Elias" was subsequently kept in prison until his death ten years later, under conditions that were at times downright shameful. Despite his experience, he clung to his apocalyptic hopes. For lack of paper he wrote his visions on linen cloths. Like many others of his numerous writings—more than thirty-five merely in the decade 1523–33—these were lost.

Melchior Hofmann, called by Samuel Cramer the "father of Dutch Anabaptism," belonged to the "peaceful, quiet Anabaptism," which renounced any recourse to force and demanded discipline and sanctification. But through his extravagant apocalyptic teaching and his warning of the imminence of the Last Judgment, and above all through his adherents, the Melchiorites—who emigrated from Holland to Westphalia in large numbers—he shared responsibility for the bloody tragedy of Anabaptism in Münster.

Bernhard Rothmann, a chaplain, born at Stadtlohn (c. 1495), had preached Lutheran doctrine at Münster since 1529. In 1531 he had visited Wittenberg and Strasbourg and in the latter city had met Anabaptists and the spiritualist, Kasper von Schwenckfeld. On his return he had established the Reformation at Münster. His church order and Eucharistic doctrine were influenced by Zwingli. From 1533 he was under the influence of the so-called "Wassenberg Preachers," who rejected the baptism of infants, leading to difficulties with the city council.

But, along with the Melchiorites, who had been pouring in since the summer of 1533, even more radical circles gained a footing in Münster. The Dutchmen Bartel Boeckbinder and Willem Cuper arrived on 5 January 1534 and administered rebaptism to Rothmann and other preachers. Rothmann continued the baptizing. At first the city council resisted and the prince-bishop arranged proceedings against the Anabaptists as rebels and agitators. But they succeeded in getting control of the city government and on 23 February 1534 brought about the election of an Anabaptist council. The internal government was, however, exercised by the Haarlem baker, Jan Matthijs, who wanted to do away with all opponents of Anabaptism. But the Münster cloth merchant Knipperdolling simply had them expelled.

Meanwhile, Bishop Franz von Waldeck had the city blockaded. The Anabaptists mobilized the entire population for defense of the city and to a great extent annulled the right of private property. When Jan Matthijs perished in a sortie, the tailor Jan Beuckelsz of Leiden (Jan van Leiden) came forward as his successor. He dissolved the Anabaptist council and instituted twelve elders as rulers of the tribes of Israel. In reality he did the ruling. After a military success on 31 May he had himself proclaimed king, not only of Münster but of the world. Bernhard Rothmann placed himself at the service of the Kingdom of Münster as court preacher and writer. Of the five works from the years 1533–35, the pamphlet *Von der Rache und Strafe des babylonischen Greuels* (On the Vengeance and Punishment of the Abomination of Babylon) aimed to induce the Anabaptists in the Netherlands to come to Münster and relieve the besieged city:

> Therefore, beloved brothers, prepare yourselves for the struggle, not only with the humble weapons of the Apostles for suffering [2 Cor. 10:4], but also with the glorious armor of David for vengeance, to exterminate with God's strength and help all the power of Babylon and godless existence.[13]

---

[13] H. Fast, op. cit., p. 360.

Communism was not so thoroughly established as among the Moravian Brethren. Production communism among the crafts resulted rather from military necessity, and the family remained together. Still, in June 1534, polygamy in the sense of the simultaneous marriage of one husband with several wives was introduced and all women without husbands were ordered to marry. Those of the banished "godless" who remained behind were obliged to contract a new marriage. The ability and ruthlessness of Jan van Leiden and the stubborness of the Anabaptists succeeded in holding the city for a year and four months, though famine appeared by the end of 1534. Even as treachery was opening up a way into the city for the besiegers, the Anabaptists were defending themselves so effectively with the courage of despair that they came near to inflicting defeat on the bishop's troops. Münster fell on 25 June 1535, and the bloodbath was frightful. Jan van Leiden, his representative Knipperdolling, and the royal councilor Bernhard Krechting were examined under torture for seven months, the king himself being conducted around the country on exhibition, until on 22 January 1536 they were tortured to death at Münster with glowing tongs and their corpses were exhibited in iron cages on the tower of the Lambert church. Thus did the kingdom of Münster, a repulsive "mixture of piety, hedonism, and thirst for blood," as von Ranke styles it, meet a dreadful end. In their striving to establish the Kingdom of God visibly in this world and to subject world and society forcibly to its dominion, the rebaptizers of Münster must be counted as belonging to the fanatics and not to the Anabaptists. For nonviolence and withdrawal into communities of brethren are the distinguishing characteristics of the latter.

But the kingdom of Münster seriously and enduringly injured their reputation. It remained for Menno Simons and the Philips brothers to restore Low German Anabaptism to its original character. The Philips brothers were illegitimate sons of a Catholic priest. In 1533 they were baptized by emissaries of Jan Matthijs at Leeuwarden in Friesland. Obbe (d. 1568), barber and surgeon by profession, and Dirk (1504–68), an ex-Franciscan, opposed the revolutionary Anabaptism of Münster and assumed the leadership of the peaceful wing of the Melchiorites, who were for a time called "Obbenites."

Obbe, appointed an Anabaptist preacher through the imposition of hands, ordained his brother Dirk as elder in the Dutch Anabaptist brotherhood. He did the same at Groningen in 1537 with Menno Simons, whom he had baptized a year earlier. But around 1540 Obbe withdrew from the Anabaptist movement. He accused it of falling into the visible and the external, doubted his own vocation or "mission," and advocated an individualistic spiritualism. His "confession" is an important source for the history of the Melchiorites and of Münster Anabaptism.[14]

In contrast to the spiritualism of his brother and of Sebastian Franck—he had come to a parting of the ways with the latter in the *Verantwortung und Reputation auf zwei Briefe*—[15] Dirk Philips concentrated on the congregation and wanted to set up in it a community of truly converted persons. For the sake of its purity and sanctity he required excommunication and a consequent avoidance of the excommunicated. He labored tirelessly in the Netherlands and North Germany. From 1550 his chief residence was at Danzig. He spread his ideas in numerous works, which he collected and published before his death in the *Enchiridion oder Handbüchlein christlicher Lehre*.[16] He thereby became the theologian and dogmatist of North German and Dutch Anabaptism. Clearer and more systematic than Menno Simons, with whom he collaborated for a long time, he in no sense achieved the latter's depth and breadth of influence because of his sharp, one-sided, and obstinate manner.

Menno Simons (1496–1561) worked for seven years in Friesland and North Holland after his ordination as an elder. He simultaneously displayed a prolific literary activity. His chief work, *Das Fundament der christlichen Lehre* (1539) deals with penance, faith, baptism, the Lord's Supper, the avoidance of the godless, and the mission, life, and teaching of preachers. At Emden in January 1544 Menno had a disputation with Johannes a Lasco who was working there as a reformer. They did not agree in regard to the Incarnation of Christ, infant baptism, and the vocation of preachers. Like Melchior Hofmann, Menno defended the opinion that Christ was born, not of, but in Mary, that he received his flesh, not through Mary, but through the Holy Spirit by virtue of a special creative act of God. After two years' activity at Cologne, his chief residence was in Holstein, and from here he toured the Baltic coast from Lübeck to Livonia.

In various controversies and in regard to rigorists Menno played a reconciling role; he was more and more concerned with peace and unity. Hotly disputed points among the Dutch Anabaptists were excommunication, mixed marriages with those who were not Anabaptists, and the avoidance of an apostate or infidel spouse, which in practice meant divorce. In *Eine wehmütige und christliche Entschuldigung und Verantwortung* (1552) Menno strongly protested against being identified with the Münster insurgents. He and his brethren, he said, were

---

[14] *BRN* VII, 121–138; H. Fast, op. cit., pp. 319–340.
[15] *BRN* X, 493–507; H. Fast, op. cit., pp. 171–188.
[16] *BRN* X.

against tumult and did not require community of goods. The charge of polygamy was a wicked calumny. People should not call them rebaptizers or destroyers or souls, for they rejected infant baptism as not a genuine Christian baptism, nor were they blasphemers of the Sacrament, when they did not believe that bread and wine are flesh and blood in substance. Menno repeatedly succeeded in escaping persecution. He died in 1561 at Wüstenfeld near Bad Oldesloe in Holstein. His importance lies in his having gathered together the peaceful Anabaptists of Holland and North Germany and, through his work and his writings, to have gradually brought men to distinguish between those of the Anabaptist persuasion and rebaptizers of the Münster movement. His teaching did not contain much sublime theological speculation. At the center of his doctrine stood rebirth, as the most basic demand of the Christian life. It is the work of God and grows from the seed of the divine word, but it has to show itself in a penitential life, in obedience to God's word and command. Only those truly reborn may belong to the congregation of Christ. Excommunication and the rejection of mixed marriages thus played a big role.

Although Menno Simons was not the founder of the Anabaptist community, which was already ten years old when he joined it, the name Mennonites became popular in the course of the sixteenth century to designate the Anabaptists of the Netherlands and Germany. In Germany it indeed served as a protective designation to distinguish Anabaptists from the "rebaptizers," whom imperial law threatened with death. In the seventeenth century Mennonite became the usual name for all groups of Anabaptists, except the Hutterites. In the independent Netherlands the Mennonites obtained a limited toleration. Since 1811 they have been united there with the "Algemene Doopsgezinde Societeit." Persecutions and the idea of isolation led to migration throughout the world and made the Mennonites pioneers in sparsely populated areas. Through their serious and simple way of life and their community solidarity they acquired great importance for the economic development of their localities. In turn this led to the point that, at least in Germany and the Netherlands, they abandoned the principle of separation more and more in favor of an active participation in social and cultural life.

Spiritualism

A striving toward spiritualization runs through all the reform movements of the fifteenth and sixteenth centuries. In opposition to the venality and materialism of piety, there was a demand for inwardness, for a more inward justice. But spiritualism obtains only where the external is absolutely regarded as unworthy or at least as unimportant. Proceeding from Neoplatonic assumptions, people adopted a dualism and set spirit in opposition to body, letter, and the visible Church with externals such as Sacrament, liturgy, and ecclesiastical discipline. Spiritualist traits are found in Erasmus and Zwingli and to a lesser degree in Luther; but in Luther in some respects these traits are more pronounced than in the fanatics, Karlstadt and Müntzer. Of the Anabaptists, Hans Denck was especially influenced by spiritualism and seems to have embraced it entirely at the end of his life. Under Denck's influence Ludwig Hätzer (c. 1500–1529) also became a spiritualist, as did Christian Entelder and Hans Bunderlin.

The most important representatives of spiritualism in the sixteenth century were Kaspar von Schwenckfeld (1489–1561) and Sebastian Franck (1499–1542). Schwenckfeld, a Silesian noble, was at first an adherent of Luther. As privy councilor for Frederick II of Liegnitz, he gained the latter for the Reformation and contributed powerfully to its spread in Silesia. He called for the life of the primitive Apostolic community. Hence the moral fruits of Christian life were decisive for him. Because of his spiritualist concept of the Lord's Supper and the suspicion of being an Anabaptist, he had to leave Silesia in 1529. He went to Strasbourg until 1533. During his stay there his doctrine acquired its peculiar form in the exchange of views and in disputes with reformers such as Capito and Bucer and with the various groups of Anabaptists, spiritualists, and fanatics. Bucer banished him to Augsburg, and from there he went to Ulm in 1535. Having run afoul of the Swiss also because of his Christology and having been condemned by the Lutheran assembly of theologians at Schmalkalden as a Sacramentarian and Anabaptist, he led a restless life for the next two decades, seeking shelter on the estates of noble families or in the houses of his adherents. Through his numerous writings, of which more than a hundred were printed while others were circulated in manuscript, he created for himself a large circle of readers, the members of which gave mutual edification and strengthened one another in their faith as they individually understood it. They had to separate themselves from the "Church of creatures." The true Church lives in dispersion; only God knows its members.

Human nature itself is a sin, which it is all-important to overcome, just as Christ made his human nature divine. His glorified flesh is the only everlasting food of believers. Matter cannot communicate spirit. Hence there is only the way from within to the external, and God cannot bind himself to external rites, Sacraments, or the written word, but only to man's inwardness.

I seek that we act precisely and constantly from within, with spirit, faith, and divine love for the improvement of men. They, on the contrary, seek to act from without, with ceremonies and Sacraments.[17]

It is not the Scripture that brings the Spirit, but the man filled with the Spirit who brings it to the Scripture. He "must bring the divine light to Scripture, the Spirit to the letter, the truth to the image, and the master to his work."[18]

Sebastian Franck (1499–1542) of Donauwörth was a priest. From 1526 to 1528 he functioned in evangelical congregations near Nürnberg. Then he relinquished his ecclesiastical position and busied himself as a writer in Nürnberg and Strasbourg. He was expelled from Strasbourg on a complaint by Erasmus, whom he had labeled a heretic. For a time he earned his living as a soap-boiler at Esslingen. From 1533 on he managed a printing press at Ulm, but he had to have most of his voluminous works printed elsewhere. They consisted of chronicles (*Türkenchronik*, 1531; *Chronika, Zeitbuch, und Geschichtsbibel*, 1531; *Germaniae Chronicon*, 1538), a cosmography, *Weltbuch* (1534), biblical exegesis, collections of proverbs, and translations. In 1539 he was expelled from Ulm and in 1540 he was condemned by the assembly of theologians at Schmalkalden because of withdrawal from the Church and contempt for the Bible and the office of preacher. He died at Basel in 1542

In his view "the visible Church of Christ was ruined and destroyed right after the Apostles."[19] Because external doctrine and Sacraments were defiled from that time on, God now allows everything to occur through the Spirit in his invisible Church which is dispersed among the pagans. Besides, God only intended the Sacraments for the Church for the time of her youth, as a doll for a child. Now one must "seek more serious things, such as faith, penance, self-denial."[20] Pagans and Turks also must be considered as brothers, even though they have never heard a letter of the story of Christ. What is important is that through the inner word they have experienced his power. Christ is the invisible word. His story is as meaningless as the external word of Holy Scripture, the "paper pope." The letter conceals the mystery. God must "awaken the dead and death-dealing letter to spirit and life in us."[21]

---

[17] "Unterschied zwischen Kaspar Schwenckfeld und der Predicanten leere" (1556). *Corpus Schwenckfeldianorum* XV, Doc. 989, p. 24; H. Fast, op. cit., p. 207.

[18] "Von der heiligen Schrift" (1551), *Corpus Schw.* XII, Doc. 780, p. 430.

[19] H. Fast, op. cit., p. 224.

[20] Ibid., p. 227.

[21] Ibid., p. 245.

Franck studied Church history as the history of heretics, in which the latter have to be regarded as the true Christians. "For Christians have been heretics to the whole world everywhere and always."[22] Franck accused the reformers of having given up the principle of the inwardness and freedom of faith, which had been present at the beginning of Protestantism. And, like Schwenckfeld, he fought with all the more vigor for toleration.

Spiritualists and Anabaptists, "the Reformation's left wing," became, because of their basic principles and in consequence of persecution, protagonists of such modern ideas as religious freedom, free Church membership, and separation of Church and state, ideas which of course acquired wider recognition only through the English Free Churchmanship and the French Revolution.[23]

[22] Ibid., p. 235
[23] R. H. Bainton, "Die täuferische Beitrag zur Geschichte," *Das Täufertum,* ed. Hershberger, pp. 299–308.

CHAPTER 16

The Catholic Literary Opponents of Luther and the Reformation

In view of Luther's extensive literary activity and of the many broadsides and pamphlets which he and his friends circulated widely among the people, thanks to the printing press, the question arises: What was done on the part of the ancient Church to counteract this? Did the defense likewise avail itself of the new means of publicity for forming public opinion and exert itself to keep in the Church or to win back for her the masses going over to Luther? And how successful was this? The number of theological writers who undertook the defense of the old Church was amazingly high,[1] especially if it is borne in mind how unpopular and burdensome this assignment was. It is only in recent decades that greater attention has been given to the Catholic controversialists and a beginning has been made of rendering their writings accessible in the *Corpus Catholicorum.* These throw much light on the question of the religious and theological force with which Luther was met. Furthermore, for a better understanding of the reformers, their partners in the discussion must be known. And, lastly, the writings of the pre-

[1] N. Paulus increased the number of German controversialists cited by J. Falk to more than 260: *Katholik* 73, 2 (1893), 213–223. F. Lauchert lists the number of "Luther's Italian literary opponents" at sixty-six.

Tridentine controversialists are important as preparations for the Council of Trent and for a correct evaluation of its theological achievement.

In order not to underestimate the works of the early opponents of Luther[2] it is necessary to delineate the difficulties of their task and the unfavorable conditions under which they had to accomplish it. It was necessary to recognize both the extent and the far-reaching importance of error and to fight it by presenting the truth. The first of these aims was not easy because of the extensive theological vagueness. Many regarded Luther as the one who would effect the long overdue reform and felt it was a question merely of the elimination of wrongs, abuses, and grievances that had permeated ecclesiastical life. As late as 1530 Melanchthon sought to have this view accepted at the Diet of Augsburg. In comparison, men who, like Johannes Eck, pinpointed heresy clearly, logically, and inexorably, could not but appear as zealots and disturbers of the peace.

Once heresy had been established, it was necessary to counteract it. Mere refutation was not enough, for the reform movement was not just the sum of individual errors. Like every heresy, it drew its life from the truth, from the partial truth which had hitherto been overlooked or belied in ecclesiastical practice. It had to be shown how the justified concern of the reformers had its place in the doctrine of the Church and that one was prepared to make it respected. All this demanded religious strength and theological vitality on the part of the Catholic writer. He had to sense the basic coherence of the truth and recognize the center which gives life to everything else and to which the peripheral has to be related time and again. Hence it was of decisive importance whether they were able to be detached enough from the opponent in order to achieve an independent presentation of Catholic doctrine. This, invariably, was not the case. For the most part they were mere counterwritings, and frequently these were not only limited in their direction against one specific reform pamphlet, but also they undertook to expound and refute these sentence by sentence. As late as 1524 Hieronymus Emser was disputing Luther and Zwingli in his writings in this medieval and rather cumbersome manner, even though he was convinced that they could "not be cured of their deeply rooted illness

---

[2] W. Koehler takes the easy way out when, in *Dogmengeschichte als Geschichte des christlichen Selbstbewusstseins. Das Zeitalter der Reformation* (Zurich 1951), p. 91, he expresses his judgment: "Facing the richness and the awareness of battle and of victory in the world of ideas in the Protestant line of Christian self-awareness, Catholicism was not only on the defensive but even in intellectual poverty. There was no dearth in number of disputants but the writings now assembled in the Corpus Catholicorum seem alarmingly like the threshing of straw."

by either arguments of reason or skills."[3] Luther had on his side the verve and the appeal of the new and the pathos of the criticism of abuses. He had the advantage of the offensive as Johannes Cochläus once stated, inasmuch as he "struck the first blow and was able to circulate his booklets in great numbers before a reply could be made by the opposition."[4]

It was all the more unfortunate, then, that the Catholic writers often did not get beyond a purely defensive method and permitted their adversary to dictate to them the course of action. Instead of taking up his fundamental points and refuting them from their center, attention was often concentrated on quite superficial details. Successes thus gained proved to be worthless, because the opponent had long since taken up new positions. In *De captivatate Babylonica* (1520) Luther described this situation to the point: "I am always ahead of them, and hence, while they, like illustrious victors, are celebrating triumphs over one of my alleged heresies, I meanwhile usher in a new one" (WA 6, 501). In addition, the defenders of the ancient Church were confronting a public opinion which had been heavy with anti-Roman sentiments for decades and was filled with a deep-rooted distrust of the Curia, feelings which Luther, with his great flair for publicity and even demagoguery, was able to utilize skillfully. On the other hand, his opponents operated in a tedious, clumsy, and pedantic fashion and found it doubly difficult to deal with a Reformation that had become a popular movement and was carried along by the appeal of the new.

Beyond the propitiousness of the moment and the greater talent for publicity, in the final analysis it was a question of a different method in theology. With Luther proclamation took the place of the systematic analysis of revelation by philosophical means, which was greatly removed from religious and liturgical life. The "for me," the personal experience of salvation, moved him and urged him to confess his knowledge-become-experience before men. As opposed to this, the prosaic and complicated method of scholasticism could only appear pale or faded. It took time before Catholic writers arrived at a theology which was primarily a proclamation and directly answered the needs of the hour.[5]

Frequently the men who felt called upon to defend the Church and who did not refuse their service were not theologians but humanists— men of letters or schoolmen and practical spiritual directors. Johannes

---

[3] *Canonis missae contra Huldricum Zwinglium defensio* (1524), A, III, c.

[4] *Von der heyligen Mess und Priesterweyhe* (Leipzig 1534), A, II, v.

[5] Cf. E. Feifel, *Grundzüge einer Theologie des Gottesdienstes* (Freiburg 1960), pp. 36ff.

Cochläus, for example, "was by calling a school master and philologist interested in editing ancient works, and a theologian only out of a sense of duty."[6] It was a sacrifice for him to engage in the conflict. He participated in it because, according to his own statement at the time of the Diet of Worms, the Catholic faith was more important to him than *belles lettres.*[7] Similarly, Hieronymus Emser saw himself faced with the task of leading a theological battle without being a theologian.

Scholastic theology had done little by way of preparation. How was the Mass to be defended, when the theology of the fourteenth and fifteenth centuries had not concerned itself with it practically at all and in regard to the Eucharist had been interested only in transubstantiation or in the cosmological questions connected with it? The unscriptural theology of nominalism, predominantly bogged down in problems of form, on which the criticism of Luther and of the Reformation had caught fire, provided a poor basis for defense. What was the very cause of the Reformation—the dogmatic vagueness and lack of religious depth and force in late scholastic theology—naturally also hamstrung any defense against it.

The principle of Scripture, relentlessly championed by Luther, placed the Catholic controversialists in the presence of a serious problem of methodology. Were they to abandon any appeal to tradition, to the Fathers, councils, and popes and be content with scriptural proof? Were they not to do so at least in practice in order to lend more force to their line of argument vis-a-vis the adherents of the Reformation? In principle they adhered to the view that "not only that which is expressly contained in the divine Scriptures and can be proved from them is to be believed and preserved,"[8] and considered tradition as the "living Gospel."[9] The more the Protestants contended among themselves over such central truths as the Eucharist, the Catholics pointed out that Scripture does not adequately interpret itself but needs a living *magisterium* for that purpose. In practice a few theologians were satisfied with scriptural proofs. Thus, for example, the *Scrutinium*[10] of the Franciscan Kaspar Schatzgeyer is almost a mere enumeration of scriptural passages on faith, grace, good works, the Mass, and so forth. But most Catholic writers, and especially the most outstanding among them, adhered to

[6] M. Spahn, *Johannes Cochlaeus* (Berlin 1898), p. 197.
[7] "Colloquium Cochlaei cum Luthero Wormatiae olim habitum" (1521), ed. by J. Greving, *Flugschriften aus den ersten Jahren der Reformation* IV (Leipzig 1911), 177–218 (especially p. 199).
[8] J. Eck, *Enchiridion,* p. 33b.
[9] S. Hosius, *Confutatio,* p. 292b.
[10] *Scrutinium divinae Scripturae pro conciliatione dissidentium dogmatum,* ed. U. Schmidt, *CCath* 5 (Münster 1922).

the traditional method. This did not stem merely from an embrace of dogmatic conviction or even less from inability to adjust to one's opponent and to follow him to the field of battle; it had its basis in the works of the Protestants themselves. Luther's contention that the idea of the Mass as a sacrifice had developed out of the ancient Christian offering of gifts, that before Gregory the Great private Masses were unknown, or that for twelve centuries the Church had known nothing about transubstantiation could not but stimulate his Catholic opponents to seek proof to the contrary in history. Even more than Luther, the other reformers, such as Melanchthon and Zwingli, appealed to the usage of the early Church and quoted the Church Fathers for this purpose. This not only justified the patristic argumentation of the Catholics but practically promoted it. But it also meant that it more and more acquired the character of an historical proof.[11]

Though at first the more peripheral questions of indulgences, vows, the veneration of saints, and the like formed the object of controversy, soon the basic problems—the doctrine of the Church, of authority, of the papal primacy, of justification, and of the Mass—preempted the stage. In the years 1522–26 there appeared a number of works in defense of the Mass. With its abolition, as idolatry, the reformers interfered the most profoundly and the most noticeably in the religious life of the people. Here the far-reaching effect of their teaching revealed itself most clearly.

The first, most indefatigable, best known, and also most hated adversary of the Reformation was Johannes Eck (1486–1543), diocesan priest and professor at Ingolstadt. At the Leipzig Disputation (1519) he had made plain Luther's abandonment of the idea of the Church. The same end was served by *De primatu Petri adversus Ludderum* (1520), which he submitted in Rome while working there from March until July of 1520 for the condemnation of Luther. Following several works on justification and penance—among others, *De poenitentia et confessione* (1522); *De purgatorio* (1523); *De satisfactione et aliis poenitentiae annexis* (1523)—he produced a "manual" in 1525, *Enchiridion locorum communium adversus Ludderanos,* as a counterpart of Melanchthon's *Loci communes* of 1521. In this he applies the scriptural and patristic proof to the questions in controversy and then seeks to refute the objections of his adversaries. More than ninety editions and translations prove the importance of the *Enchiridion.* When it turned out that, due to a dearth of Catholic sermon manuals, priests were using those of Protestants, Eck wrote five volumes of sermons in German on the liturgical cycles, the feasts of saints,

---

[11] P. Polman, *L'element historique dans la controverse religieuse du XVIe siecle* (Gembloux 1932), p. 310; cf. p. 320.

the Sacraments, and the commandments. At the request of his prince, Duke Wilhem II, he published a German Bible in 1537. He himself translated the Old Testament, with great accuracy, into "High German," that is, the South German dialect. For the New Testament he adopted Emser's translation. Eck endeavored to comply with the trend of the age—"to the sources"—by a careful regard for Scripture and the Fathers. But despite an abundance of citations his encounter with them was not creative. He was unable to make them sufficiently fruitful in a religious and theological sense. Keeping in mind the lack of dogmatic clarity in this period, it was to Eck's merit to have shown clearly and even caustically that Luther stood, not for reform, but for revolution and to have spurned any compromise at the expense of truth. At the same time, however, the question arises whether Eck sufficiently felt the responsibility for unity and was correspondingly concerned about his opponent, or whether in his zeal for the disputation he pushed him to heretical conclusions and committed him to error.

A tireless champion of the Catholic Church at the court of Duke Georg of Saxony was the latter's secretary and chaplain, Hieronymus Emser (1478–1527). Following the Leipzig Disputation he had criticized Luther's position regarding the Bohemians. Alluding to Emser's coat of arms, which displayed an ibex, Luther replied in an extremely harsh polemic, *Ad aegocerotem Emserianum* (1519), the prelude to a series of polemical exchanges between the "goat of Leipzig" and the "bull of Wittenberg." Emser's later writings also, which were directed against Karlstadt and Zwingli as well as Luther and were concerned with the defense of images, the Mass, and the priesthood, did not amount to more than a mere "refutation" of his adversary. In 1523 after Emser had attributed 1400 "heretical errors and lies" to Luther's New Testament, he himself, at the instigation of his duke, published his own translation of the New Testament in 1527, which closely followed Luther's text. Emser had been summoned from the carefree life of a humanist to defend the Church. He had not declined the task but had accepted it zealously. Still, he was not enough of a theologian and commanded too little religious respect to do full justice to it.

Emser's successor as Duke Georg's chaplain was Johannes Cochläus (1479–1552). Like many other adversaries of Luther, he had originally held a positive opinion of the reformer. But as of Luther's treatises of 1520, he became his decided opponent. With more than two hundred writings he sought to serve his Church over a thirty-year span in a tireless and selfless literary activity. He was not a theologian and never became one of any significance. He was too much the humanist to become a writer for the people, and his works were burdened with an excess of scholarship. Devoid of a sense of humor and thus all the more fierce in his wrath, he proved to the "many-headed Luther" his real and alleged contradictions. His *Commentaria de actis et scriptis Martini Lutheri* (Mainz 1549) had a powerful effect later on. As the first extensive biography of Luther, this work yielded important source material for the history of the Reformation, but it also carried a great deal of mud, which the malicious polemics on both sides had stirred up. The distortions presented in Cochläus' commentary on Luther determined the Catholic image of Luther into the twentieth century.

Johann Fabri (1478–1541) and Friedrich Nausea (c. 1490–1552) were able to work effectively against the Reformation and for the inner reform of the Church not only as authors but directly as successive bishops of Vienna. Fabri, humanist and jurist, came into the open against Luther only in 1521 as vicar general of Constance. In 1522 appeared his *Opus,* composed according to the scholastic method, a "work against some new doctrines of Martin Luther, which in every way contradict Christian teaching." In 1524 a Cologne Dominican published it under the new title, *Malleus in haeresim Lutheranam.* As coadjutor of Wiener Neustadt (from 1524), Fabri composed a number of works in German, the most important being the *Summarium* (1526), which had far more popular appeal. In picturesque language and with abundant references to Scripture he defended the teaching of the Church and pointed out the pernicious results of the Lutheran innovation, which had become especially clear in the Peasants' War. In the *Christliche underrichtung* (1528) he examined the "report of the visitors" (*WA* 26, 195–240) and showed how much Luther had "improved." Had he always taught in that manner, said Fabri, this great misfortune would not have fallen on Germany and the Church. This work shows that the Catholic controversialists still did not draw the full consequences from the break and in a sense were still running after their opponent instead of engaging in positive propaganda for their own cause. This is also the case when Fabri proves how Luther was actually dissenting from Huss and other heretics to whom he appealed,[12] and even contradicted himself.[13] As Bishop of Vienna (from 1530), Fabri published a series of sermons and writings in defense of the Mass and the priesthood, and *Über den Glauben und die guten Werke.* They were worthwhile works but they give little indication of the heated atmosphere of the age.

Fabri's coadjutor and successor, Friedrich Nausea, had been cathedral preacher and writer at Mainz since 1526. His *Centuriae IV homiliarum* appeared in Cologne in 1532. Following his summons to Vienna by Ferdinand I, he opposed the spread of the Reformation in sermons and

---

[12] *Wie sich Joh. Huss . . . . Lehren und Bücher mit M. Luther vergleichen* (1528).
[13] *Antilogiarum M. Lutheri Babylonia ex eiusdem libris—excerpta* (1530).

in his writings. In his works on parish visitations (*Pastoralium inquisitionum elenchi tres,* 1547), and on the education of candidates for the priesthood (*Isagogicon de Clericis ordinandis,* 1548), and in his *Catechismus catholicus* (1543), he left behind him polemics and can be regarded as a representative of the incipient inner reform of the Church.

Berthold Pürstinger of Chiemsee (1465–1543) had already resigned his episcopal see when in 1528 he wrote his *Tewtsche Theologey,* based on Scripture and closely related to Saint Thomas. It is considered the first work in German on dogmatic theology. His treatises on the Eucharist, the *Tewtsche Rational über das Ambt heiliger Mess* and the *Keligpuechl,* were directly concerned with defense against the Reformation. Whether he wrote the pamphlet *Onus ecclesiae* (1519; printed in 1524 and 1531) is disputed. It came out against the abuses of the age and called for Church reform in head and members.

Cologne and Louvain were the first universities to take a stand against Luther. On 7 November 1519 Louvain issued a *Condemnatio doctrinalis librorum Lutheri.* In 1521 the Louvain professor Jakob Latomus (c. 1475–1544), published *Articolorum doctrinae fratris Martini Lutheri . . . damnatio* against Luther. Luther later paid him the compliment that he was the "most distinguished writer against me."[14] Later works dealt with auricular confession (1525), the papal primacy (1526), and faith, good works, and religious vows (1530).

The Louvain professor and Dominican friar Eustachius van Zichem (d. 1538) brought out in 1521 a "brief refutation of Martin Luther's errors" and in 1523 a defense of the Sacraments and of the ecclesiastical hierarchy.[15] Johannes Driedo (c. 1480–1535), the third among the professors at Louvain, was one of the few contemporary controversialists who knew how to take up new questions and to seek new solutions without rancor and in loyalty to tradition. Hence his writings were still influential at Trent and in the grace controversy. In *De ecclesiasticis scripturis et dogmatibus libri IV* (1533) he discussed the methods and sources of theology; in *De captivitate et redemptione humani generis* (1534), the original state and the redemption of man. Important also for theological anthropology are his *Über die Vereinbarkeit von freiem Willen und Predestination* (1537, *Über Gnade und freien Willen* (1537), and *Über die christliche Freiheit* (1546). These three were published posthumously, the last only in the complete edition prepared by Ruard Tapper (1487–1559) in 1546. Tapper and his colleague at Louvain, Josse Ravesteyn (1506–70),

---

[14] *WA, Tr* I, 202; cf. II, 189, IV, 145, V, 75.

[15] *Errorum M. Luther brevis confutatio* and *Sacramentorum brevis elucidatio simulque nonulla perversa M. Luther dogmata excludens.* Reprinted in *Bibliotheca reformatoria neerlandica* III, ed. F. Pijper (The Hague 1905), 227–284, 295–373.

extend into the era of the Council of Trent. In 1544 Louvain University committed its professors to fifty-nine theses. In them it provided, in a carefully thought out-outline of the controverted teachings, a summary of the work thus far accomplished and essentially anticipated the constructing of the Tridentine decrees.[16]

From the University of Louvain came the influential controversialist Albert Pigge (1490–1542). With the doctrine of papal infallibility, expounded in *Hierarchiae ecclesiasticae assertio* (1538), he exerted influence up to modern times. The Council of Trent adopted his views on tradition but not those on justification. His writings *Über den freien Willen des Menschen* (1541) and on original sin in *Controversiarum praecipuarum . . . explicatio* (1541) were even put on the Index at Lisbon in 1624.

In England the first to take up the pen in reply to Luther's *De captivitate Babylonica* was King Henry VIII himself, probably assisted by Thomas More (1478–1535). For, in the face of such heresies, no one could "refrain from opposing them with all one's diligence and resources." In content and method his *Assertio septem sacramentorum* (1521) excelled the other early works of controversy. In 1522 it came out in two German translations, by H. Emser and T. Murner. Luther reacted angrily in his *Antwort deutsch auf König Heinrichs Buch* (1522; WA 10, II, 227–262). Ironically the royal "defender of the faith" had his own collaborators Thomas More and Bishop John Fisher (1469–1535) executed for their opposition to his headship of the Church in 1535. As humanists, both of them had profitably used the new interest in the Bible and the Fathers for the defense of the Church.

Zealous literary adversaries of Luther were found in the several Orders, especially in the ranks of the Dominicans and the Franciscans. The Dominicans had managed the trial against Luther and supplied the first writers against him. Silvester Prierias (1456–1523) was concerned, as *Magister sacri palatii* and censor, with Luther's indulgence theses and "quickly strode into the arena" (*WA, Tr* 3, 564, no. 3722) with his *Dialogus* of June 1518. His polemic was frivolous and clumsy. He showed little readiness to take up Luther's concern but clearly grasped and stressed that the Church, in both its ecclesiastical and papal authority, was in question. To Luther's *Responsio* (*WA* I, 647–868) Prierias gave a preliminary answer in his *Replica*.[17] Then, in the *Epitoma responsionis ad Lutherum* (1519; WA 6, 328–348), he announced a detailed discussion with Luther on the authority of the pope and the power of

---

[16] H. De Jongh, *L'ancienne faculte de theologie de Louvain* (Louvain 1911), pp. 81*–89; cf. H. Jedin, *Geschichte des Konzils von Trient* I, 326 (*History of the Council of Trent* I, 398f., 406f.).

[17] With a foreword by Luther given in print (*WA* II, 50–56).

indulgences. It appeared at Rome in 1520 under the title *Errata et argumenta Martini Lutheri recitata, detecta, repulsa. . . .* In it he expounded the monarchical constitution of the Church in a quite one-sided fashion. As vicar of Christ, the pope has not only the highest but the only ordinary power. He is *virtualiter* the Catholic Church and the source of all jurisdiction. A council has power only as assigned to it by the pope.[18] This chief polemic of Prierias gained little notice and Luther deigned it as unworthy of an answer.

Cardinal Thomas de Vio (1469–1534), commonly known as Cajetan, the most important theologian of the day, had already composed a treatise on indulgences (*De indulgentiis* of 8 December 1517) before obtaining a copy of Luther's theses and meeting him in person at Augsburg. In that city he wrote a number of essays on indulgences and penance, which he completed, after his return to Rome, with *De indulgentia plenaria concessa defunctis* of 20 November 1519. In this he strove for an objective solution to the difficulties, which he did not deny, and just as he denounced Luther's errors, so also did he blame the indulgence preachers, who talked too big and gave out their private opinions as the Church's teaching.[19] On the cardinal point of the controversy Cajetan in 1521 wrote *De divina institutione Pontificatus Romani* in reply to Luther's *Resolutio . . . de potestate Papae* of 1519 (WA 2, 183–240). He did not, however, mention his adversary by name nor did he lapse into a violently polemical tone so common at the time. His *opuscula* on the Eucharist (*De coena Domini,* 1525; *De sacrificio Missae,* 1531; *De communione,* 1531) stand out among the contemporary writings of others. Not only does he assert the unity of the Mass and the sacrifice of the cross; he is also able to establish it theologically. Christ is present "immolatitio modo," in the manner of sacrifice. The sacrifice is not repeated, but the unique sacrifice, offered once, continues to endure, and in repeated celebrations the everlasting sacrifice is rendered present. Hence, in the Mass Christ is the real priest and intrinsically the Mass is of infinite value. The faith and devotion of the participants are decisive for its fruitfulness. Here was an answer to Luther's objections to the Mass. But it was not heard in Germany and had little effect even on the Council of Trent.

In *De fide et operibus* (1532) Cajetan took up again the chief controversial point discussed with Luther at Augsburg in 1518—the certainty of

---

[18] "Si vero loquamur de authoritate concilii quae convenit omnibus collective sive collegialiter, eadem est authoritas pontificis et collegii: sed in pontifice est plena et ordinaria, in concilio autem est quantum placet papae, et commissa seu vicaria" (cap. 12, fol. LXXXI b; cf. F. Lauchert, *Die italienischen literarischen Gegner Luthers* (Freiburg 1912), p. 25).

[19] *Opuscula* (Lyons 1562), pp. 103ff.

faith versus reflexive faith. He attacked the confusing of a justifying faith with a subjective *credulitas;* he fought against the idea that it is supposedly not enough to receive the Sacrament with confidence in the merits of Christ, but rather that a person has to be certain of being justified, and that this certainty, only in a sense, establishes justification.[20]

Exceptionally noisy and pugnacious was Ambrosius Catharinus (c. 1484–1553), who assailed not only Luther but even his own confreres, Cajetan, Soto, and Spina. This "third of the Thomists," as Luther styled him (*WA* 7, 706), composed in 1520, at the command of his superiors, the comprehensive *Apologia pro veritate catholicae et apostolicae fidei* against Luther, and followed it up with the *Excusatio disputationis contra Martinum* even before being in possession of the reformer's vexed reply (*WA* 7, 705–778). The *Apologia* is basically concerned with Luther's *Resolutio Lutheriana . . . de potestate Papae* and, apart from the authority of the Church and the papal primacy, treats in some detail only penance and purgatory. The author's line of argument does not substantially go beyond Prierias; it is merely much more eloquent and clever, without being any less biting and polemical. He tried to establish that Luther was a heretic. After the *Excusatio* Ambrosius Catharinus took no further part in the dispute over faith until 1540, when his *Speculum haereticorum* appeared. In this he tried to unmask the true aims of the reformers, show the evil results of their doctrines, and call for the extirpation of the heresy.

In Germany the Dominican Jakob van Hoogstraeten (1460–1527) came forward against Luther. Ever since the Reuchlin controversy public opinion had been strongly prejudiced against him. When in the dedicatory epistle to his *Zerstörung der Kabala* in April 1519 he suggested that Leo X take energetic action against the disturbers of the Christian faith, without at all mentioning Luther, the latter reacted sharply against the "grand inquisitor" who lusted after the blood of his brothers but was himself the worst heretic (*WA* 2, 386f.). Hoogstraeten did not go in for cheap polemics. He traced Luther's sources and tried to refute him by Augustine in *Cum Divo Augustino colloquia contra enormes et perversos Lutheri errores* (1521–1522). In this he noted the doctrine of original sin and concupiscence as the stumbling block on which Luther had been shattered. Later works of controversy dealt with the veneration of saints, faith and works, and the liberty of the Christian.

As court preacher at Dessau, the Dominican Johannes Mensing (d. c.

---

[20] "Quod dicta credulitas apprehendit remissionem peccatorum" (cap. 3), *Opuscula,* p. 288.

1541)[21] published three treatises on the Mass in 1526, two sermons on the Catholic priesthood in 1527, and in 1529 an essay on the Blessed Sacrament, in particular on the doctrine of concomitance. He also produced an essay on the authority of the Church. He tried to show that the sacrifice of the cross was not confined to the restrictions of history. The very sacrifices of the Old Covenant obtained their efficacy from the cross and in them Christ was already sacrificed. In the New Covenant the sacrifice on the cross remains present before the heavenly Father and hence the priesthood of Christ is eternal. But Mensing does not explicitly draw the obvious conclusion—that the Mass is the representation before the heavenly Father of the ever present sacrifice of the cross. His *Antapologie* (1533–35) is the most important reply to the *Confessio Augustana* and its defense of the teaching of justification.

Johannes Faber (c. 1470–1530), long-time prior at Augsburg, was a close friend of Erasmus and, like him, opposed any strong action against Luther. He expressed this view in the brief *Iudicium in causa Lutheri* (1527) and even more clearly in a "Ratschlag," which appeared anonymously at Cologne at the end of 1520 and was attributed to Erasmus. It was only after the Diet of Worms of 1521 that Faber changed his mind and came out determinedly against the innovation.

More effective as a writer was Johann Fabri (1504–58), also active at Augsburg. But his works, including a *Katechismus* (1551), *Christlich-katholischer Unterricht* (1556), and a much read work on the Mass (1555), belong to the later phase of the controversy in connection with the Council of Trent. The same holds true of the work of Ambrosius Pelagus (1493–1561), except for his treatises of 1528–1529 on the Mass, directed against Oecolampadius.

The Dominican Johannes Dietenberger (c. 1475–1537) was recruited by Johannes Cochläus for the literary war against Luther. As prior at Frankfurt and Koblenz and as professor at Mainz, he composed some twenty polemical works based on the Bible. In 1534 he published a German Bible, which took over extensive parts of Emser's New Testament. For the Old Testament he used the Vulgate as basis. He tried to avoid the linguistic harshness of the pre-Luther translations and had frequent, if critical, recourse to Luther's Bible. His was the most popular Catholic translation of the Bible into German. It saw fifty-eight editions of the complete Bible, and in addition fourteen of the New Testament and twenty of the Psalter alone. In his last work, the German catechism of 1537, polemics disappear and Dietenberger's popular and deeply religious style attained its full expression.

---

[21] N. Paulus, *Die deutschen Dominikaner im Kampf gegen Luther* (Freiburg 1903), pp. 16–45; E. Iserloh, *Der Kampf um die Messe* (Münster 1952), pp. 46–52.

The controversialist writings of the Franciscans were in general more appealing to the people than the often overly scholastic counterparts composed by Dominicans. Augustin von Alveldt (c. 1480–after 1532), lecturer in theology at Leipzig, published in 1520 eight other works in addition to his *Super apostolica sede* to which Luther reacted violently with his *Von dem Papsttum zu Rom wider den hochberühmten Romanisten zu Leipzig* (WA 6, 285–324).

"Of all Luther's literary opponents, without any question the most quick-witted, the cleverest, and the most popular"[22] was the Strasbourg Franciscan Thomas Murner (1475–1537). He was already one of the favorite and most influential authors when he took up his pen against the religious novelties. Among his four works of 1520 against Luther, most deserving of mention is his *Christliche und brüderliche Ermahnung*. It defends the Mass against the *Sermon von dem Neuen Testament*. Genuinely fraternal in tone, it is both popular and deeply religious. Calumnies such as *Murnarr* and defamations later provoked Murner to give in further to his bent for satire and polemics. His satirical epic, *Vom Lutherischen Narren* (1522), is one of the very few Catholic writings of these years which to some extent equalled Luther in journalistic skill and even in poetic vigor. Expelled from Strasbourg, Murner went in 1525 to Lucerne. He took part in the Baden Disputation of 1526 and wrote against the Swiss reformers, among other works, *Kirchendieb und Ketzerkalender* (1527) and *Die gots heylige mess* (1528).

With his *Scrutinium divinae Scripturae* Kaspar Schatzgeyer (1463–1527), provincial of the South German Franciscan Observants, began a productive career in controversial theology that was to yield twenty-nine works in print and sixteen in manuscript. In a truly ironic spirit he tried to write "pro conciliatione dissidentium dogmatum" and did not become bogged down in mere polemics. Through arguments based on Scripture he approached the reformers on the plane of method. Better than anyone else he was able to present the Catholic teaching, especially on the Church and the Mass, in a way that not only refuted the error of the reformers but at the same time pointed out what was legitimate in their concern in the whole context of truth. Unfortunately, his voice could not make itself heard due to the noisy polemics and his premature death.

His confrere at Marburg, Nikolas (Ferber) Herborn (c. 1480–1535), had vainly fought in several polemics against the Reformation that was being carried out by the ex-Franciscan Francis Lambert of Avignon, acting on the orders of Philip of Hesse. Having fled to Cologne in 1527,

---

[22] W. Kawerau, *Murner und die deutsche Reformation* (Halle 1891), p. 1.

Herborn wrote a manual[23] against contemporary errors, dealing in popular form with almost all the truths of faith and demonstrating them from Scripture. Without attacking specific persons or books, he called attention to the points in controversy, extolled the Church, and depicted the sad consequences of the revolt.

In the effort to prove one's adversary wrong and to triumph over him instead of winning him back lay the danger of controversial theology. This biased polemical attitude was very plainly characterized by the Dutchman, Johann van Kampen, when in 1536 he wrote from Rome that the "four evangelists"—Fabri, Eck, Cochläus, and Nausea—would, he was convinced, "rather that three new Luthers should arise than that the one Luther should be converted."[24] The writer had been summoned to the service of Cardinal Contarini in Rome. Contarini, with Johannes Gropper, Julius Pflug, Michael Helding, Georg Witzel, and others, belonged to a group of theologians who displayed understanding for the religious aims of the Reformation and at first worked for both unity and reform. As so-called theologians of mediation,[25] they were, of course, often exposed to the charge of making compromises at the expense of the truth.

Gasparo Contarini (1483–1542), in his *Confutatio articulorum seu quaestionum Lutheranorum,* a refutation of the main points in the *Confessio Augustana,* complains that the Christians of his day, instead of confessing the faith and, with it, preserving love and humility, were dazzled by disputatiousness and were concerned with nothing but "defending their own viewpoint and refuting that of the opponent."[26] He himself took pains to be open-minded in regard to his opponent's motives and to do justice to him. Even before his elevation to the purple while still a layman in 1535, he defended the divine right of the papacy in *De potestate Pontificis.* In a comprehensive treatise on the Sacraments he refers to the reform position merely in brief remarks. At the Religious Colloquy of Regensburg both sides accepted the doctrine of twofold justice—the one inherent in us and imperfect; the other the justice of Christ imputed to us. The cardinal explained this in more detail in the *Epistola de iustificatione*[27] of 25 May 1541. But this concept was rejected in a consistory at Rome on 27 May 1541 and later at Trent.

As a student of Albert Pigge (Pighius), Johann Gropper (1503–1559)

---

[23] *Locorum communium, adversus huius temporis haereses Enchiridion* (1528), ed. P. Schlager, *CCath,* 12 (Münster 1927).

[24] *ZKG* 43 (1924), 217.

[25] On this inadequate term cf. J. Lortz, *Die Reformation in Deutschland* II (Freiburg, 4th ed. 1962), 216–219; W. Lipgens, *Kardinal J. Gropper* (Münster 1951), pp. 111–114.

[26] *CCath* 7 (Münster 1923), 17.

[27] Ibid., pp. 23–34.

of Cologne had already maintained the doctrine of a twofold justice in 1538 in his *Enchiridion Christianae Institutionis* and he later worked out the subject in full detail in his *Antididagma* (1544). If this "protagonist of the ancient faith,"[28] who preserved Cologne and hence Northwest Germany for the Church, could, like Contarini, be suspected of heresy, and if his *Enchiridion* was consigned to the Index under Clement VIII, then it is easy to see what external and inner danger those persons were courting who did not yet regard the doctrinal split as irreconcilable.

Julius Pflug (1499–1564) likewise fell under the reproach of doctrinal unreliability in a letter from Johannes Eck to Contarini.[29] As Bishop of Naumburg–Zeitz, he was already forced by circumstances, instead of attacking the reformers, to devote himself rather to the instruction of his poorly educated faithful and to gaining back Protestants who had for the most part been only superficially won to the new faith. Especially in his *Institutio Christiani Hominis* (1562), a "catechism in the service of unity of faith," Pflug displays himself as a pastor and a herald of the Gospel far more than as an apologist and controversialist.

Also primarily a preaching theologian was Michael Helding (1506–1561), Auxiliary Bishop of Mainz. Concern for catechetical instruction is the dominant motive in his series of sermons on several books of the Bible and in his sermons on the Mass (1548). His catechetical sermons, delivered in the Mainz cathedral from 1542 to 1544, were printed as *Catechismus, das ist Christliche Underweissung,* in 1551 and later, as a manual for parish priests.

Thus, during the years up to 1540, occurred the development of the literature of controversy from polemics to a positive presentation of the faith, from the *enchiridion,* a brief apologetically oriented compendium of dogma, expanding into a proclamation of the faith in great homiletic works, such as those of Eck (1530–39), Nausea (1542), and Hoffmeister (1547), and into catechisms.

The first German catechism before that of Dietenberger was composed in 1535 by Georg Witzel (1501–73). He had studied for a short time at Wittenberg under Luther and Melanchthon, but, nevertheless, in 1520 he was ordained a priest. In 1523 he married without a dispensation and became a Protestant. According to his own account he was led to this by the allurement of the new, the sad condition of the Church, but especially by "the great hope that everything might become much more Christian."[30] It was precisely on this last point that he was disil-

---

[28] H. Förster, *Reformbestrebungen Adolfs III. vom Schaumburg in der Kölner Kirchenprovinz* (Münster 1925), p. 11.

[29] Letter of 20 January 1542 (W. Friedensburg, *Briefwechsel*, p. 479).

[30] *Epistolarum . . . libri IV* (Leipzig 1537), IV, S. b 4 v.

lusioned. Soon "much in the evangelical Church, above all in regard to morals," began to offend him. In addition, an intensive study of the Church Fathers assured him that the Reformation was not in harmony with the apostolic tradition. He resigned as a pastor in 1531 and in his *Apologie* of 1533 publicly abandoned Luther. Therefore he and his family led an insecure life filled with privations, persecuted by Protestants and often treated with distrust by Catholics. But Witzel labored indefatigably for the reform and unity of the Church at religious conferences and at diets, with memoranda for the Emperors Ferdinand I and Maximilian II, the "Via regia," and in almost 150 writings.

His literary work served primarily for preaching, for the liturgy, and for catechetical instruction. Numerous and frequently printed were his lectures and sermons. His works on the history of the Church and of the liturgy sought to point out the usages of the ancient Church (*Typus ecclesiae*, 1540; Parts I–V, 1559) or aimed to defend the Mass (*Von der hl. Eucharisty odder Mess*, 1534 and later) and the liturgy (*Defensio Ecclesiasticae Liturgiae*, 1564, and other works). By means of translations of the missal, ritual, and breviary he tried to arouse an understanding of the liturgy and to make possible an active participation by the laity.[31] He warmly advocated German hymns. He probably worked on the *New Gesangbüchlein* (1537) of Michael Vehe (d. 1539), but he himself also published German hymnals (*Odae Christianae*, 1541). His *Catechismus Ecclesiae* (1535 and later) was the first in the German language and noteworthy as the first to provide a summary of biblical history. It was followed by other catechisms and catechetical works. Witzel's attempts at mediation were Erasmian in spirit.[32] By means of a serious moral reform and with the aid of a few concessions in dogmatically unimportant points, such as the lay chalice and clerical marriage, he hoped to overcome the religious split on the basis of the doctrine of the Fathers. Witzel's efforts were destined to have no penetrating success, and his rich literary legacy to have only a slight effect.

History followed other paths. It agreed that the Bishop of Ermland and papal legate at Trent, Cardinal Stanislaus Hosius (1504–1579), was right when he prevented the invitation of Witzel to Trent because of the latter's readiness to make concessions.[33] Hosius accepted the separation in faith as a melancholy fact and clearly pinpointed the doctrinal differ-

---

[31] *Psaltes Ecclesiasticus* (1550); *Ecclesiastica Liturgia. Wie sich der gemein Christen Lay der Latinischen Missen zur besserung sein selbst gebrauchen künde* (1545); *Verdeutschte Kyrchgesenge* (1546); *Täglichs lob Gottes* (1545).

[32] *Methodus Concordiae ecclesiasticae* (1537); *Dialogorum libri tres. Drey Gesprechbüchlein von der Religion sachen in itzigem ferlichen Zweispalt* (1539 and 1562); O. Clemen, "Reunionsvorschläge Witzels von 1540," *ARG* 10 (1912f.), 101–105.

[33] *Nuntiaturberichte*, section 2, I (Vienna 1897), 269f.

ences. By putting decisive emphasis on the divine authority of the Church, indivisible in essence, and on the truth entrusted to her and by pointing at the split within Protestantism he sought to closely tie the wavering to the Church and hoped in time to win back the schismatics. His *Confessio catholicae fidei* (1552–53) brought to a close the Catholic handbook literature. During its author's lifetime it saw thirty editions and translations.

The Reform in the German Principalities

CHAPTER 17

*The Confessional Leagues. The Imperial Diets of Nürnberg (1524)
and Speyer (1526)*

The reform movement was able to grow unhindered because the chief representatives of the old order, Emperor and Pope, were consuming their energies in war against each other. The Pope feared Habsburg power in Lombardy and Naples and supported France against the Emperor. The French King conspired with the Turks and urged them, after the fall of Belgrade, to invade Hungary, which, through the marriage of Ferdinand of Austria with Queen Anna, had become the outpost of Habsburg power. Hence Charles V was prevented from energetically tackling the internal problems of Germany. He and his brother Ferdinand, who had remained in the Empire, were not able to take measures against princes whose help they needed in the war against the Turks. Neither the Imperial Governing Council nor the Imperial Diets were able or even willing to implement the Edict of Worms. The Third Diet of Nürnberg, opening in January 1524, continued the policy of procrastination, declaring that the estates should, "as far as possible," act in accordance with the Edict of Worms. At the same time there was a new demand for a free general council on German territory, which should carry out Church reform and clarify the questions in dispute, "so that the good would not be suppressed with the evil and it would finally be discussed how each should behave in the future."[1] It was, however, fully understood that the summoning of the council would take time and that any delay would give further aid to the innovations. This induced especially the staunchly Catholic Bavarian Dukes to demand "a synod of the German nation."[2]

This idea of a national council for settling the religious question and redressing the grievances pointed out in the *gravamina* already had been broached in November 1523 at a conference in Salzburg of the representatives of the bishops of the Salzburg province.[3] The papal legate

[1] *RTA* IV, 604
[2] Ibid., 434.
[3] *ARC* I, 186f.

Lorenzo Campeggio saw in a national council the danger of the apostasy of the entire nation and determinedly rejected it. Just the same, the estates clung to their project and decided that, until the convoking of the general council, an assembly of the German nation should be held. It was to meet at Speyer on Martinmas on 11 November.[4] In Rome there was dismay over the attempt to reach a national ecclesiastical solution and a protest was lodged with the Emperor, who on 15 July forbade the Speyer assembly. A national council had about as little place in the universalism of Charles V as it had in the views of the Pope, and through the imperial veto it was temporarily shelved as a means of solving the Church problem.

But at the diet the legate Campeggio had realized that no implementation of the Edict of Worms could be expected from the Empire and that princes as strongly anti-Lutheran as the Bavarian Dukes had demanded a German ecclesiastical assembly in order to make possible a quick and thorough improvement of Church conditions. He endeavored to do justice to this concern by means of provincial councils or of similar particular boards appointed by the Church. He urged the founding of a league of the South German princes and the Rhenish bishops. In March–April 1524 he had requested permission from Clement VII for a special reform conference. And so on 8 May invitations were issued by the legate and the Archduke Ferdinand to the Bavarian Dukes Wilhelm and Ludwig and to twelve bishops of the Austrian and Bavarian territories to meet at Regensburg in order to discuss an anti-Lutheran front. In addition, the reform of the Church and the mutual grievances of the spiritual and the secular princes were to be the themes of the conference.

In the complaints the secular lords demanded that steps be taken not only in the struggle against Lutheranism but also that the reform and inner renewal of the Church should be seriously faced. The bishops, on the other hand, called for the full restoration of their rights of immunity and of jurisdiction. The princes, especially the Bavarian Dukes, sought to exercise, by means of prelates belonging to their territories, criminal justice against heretical or otherwise culpable clerics in the territories of those bishops who failed to take action.[5] The bishops, seeing in this a threat to their jurisdiction, demanded its complete restoration as a sine qua non of effective reform work.

The Regensburg Conference lasted from 27 June to 7 July. The negotiations were dominated by the secular princes, Archduke Ferdinand and the Bavarian Dukes. The bishops and their proxies had no

---

[4] *RTA* IV, 604.
[5] *ARC* I 159f.

other choice than to accept the decision of the Big Two and to declare their approval.[6] The resulting resentments naturally impaired the effectiveness of the conference results. These were contained in two decrees. In the Regensburg Agreement of 6 July 1524,[7] the implementation of the Edict of Worms was called for. Furthermore, attention was to be devoted to the preaching of the true Gospel by certified preachers and to the reform of the clergy. As to the celebration of Mass, the administration of the Sacraments, and the carrying out of other usages, persons should "adhere to what has laudably come down to us from the holy Fathers and our ancestors."[8] Hence stern measures were to be taken against the reception of the Eucharist without previous confession and against disregard of the laws of abstinence and fasting. Runaway religious and those living in concubinage were to be punished, and the circulation of heretical books was to be stopped by censorship and authorization to print, to be granted expressly. Study at Wittenberg was to be forbidden, and students were to be recalled from there within three months under the threat of confiscation of their benefices. Whoever had studied there should not be admitted to any offices or benefices. Penalties and banishments decreed in one territory should be enforced also in all others. In the event of uprisings the parties would assist one another. These regulations were concerned mainly with measures against Lutheranism, while the Regensburg Reform Order of 7 July 1524, proposed by Campeggio and issued by him, dealt especially with eliminating abuses within the Church and improving the conduct of priests.[9] "If the Regensburg formula had been given effect throughout Germany, as had been planned, the term 'reformation' would no longer have stood for something exclusively Lutheran and a national council would have been superfluous."[10]

But even the South German bishops represented at the conference were, from indolence and from concern about their jurisdiction, not overly inclined to put the Regensburg Reform Order into effect. It was, therefore, all the more difficult to move to action other bishops who had not been participants in it. Hence Campeggio's effort to make the Reform Order binding on the entire German Church by means of a decree was a failure, for the Rhenish ecclesiastical princes would not comply with an enactment in which they had not participated. Thus any decisive

[6] Ibid., 296.

[7] Ibid., 329–334.

[8] Ibid., 331.

[9] Ibid., 334–344. The German title under which it was published in Austria and Bavaria by the princes is as follows: "Ordnung und Reformation zu abstellung der Missbreuch: und aufrichtung aines erbern wesens: und wandls in der gaistlichkeit" (*ARC* I, 363).

[10] Jedin, I 174 (English trans. I, 218).

effectiveness was denied the Regensburg Conference, since one can speak of a league only in a very limited sense. Nevertheless, here the first official step toward Church reform was taken, which served also as the preliminary to forming confessional alliances.

In the succeeding year, on 19 July 1525, a union of princes of North Germany was established at Dessau, corresponding to the Regensburg Union. Influenced by the Peasants' War and convinced that its source was the new preaching, the Electors Joachim I of Brandenburg and Albrecht of Mainz and the Dukes Georg of Saxony and Eric I and Heinz II of Braunschweig-Wolfenbüttel formed an agreement, the League of Dessau, for resisting any peasant risings and for exterminating the Lutheran sect as the "root of this disturbance."

Philip of Hesse (1504–67) had put down the Peasants' War, together with his father-in-law, Georg of Saxony. They had the same aim—to strengthen their territorial authority following the unrest. But their differing attitudes toward the reform movement would not allow them to pursue the aim together. Converted by Melanchthon, Philip of Hesse was in 1524 the first German prince to embrace the Reformation. Luther's own prince, Frederick the Wise, on the other hand, did not receive communion according to the Lutheran rite until he lay on his death bed. At his death on 5 May 1525 he was succeeded by his brother, Johann the Steadfast, who came forward more openly and more energetically for the Reformation. On 6 May 1526 Philip of Hesse formed with him the League of Gotha-Thorgau, which was joined at Magdeburg on 12 June by the Princes Ernst and Franz of Braunschweig-Lüneburg, Philip of Braunschweig-Grubenhagen, Heinz of Mecklenburg, Wolfgang of Anhalt, and Albrecht of Mansfeld, and by the city of Magdeburg. Albrecht of Prussia, who had transformed the territory of the Teutonic Order into a secular principality which he held as a fief of Poland, also allied himself with Johann of Saxony. Thus in Germany, not only did differing religious views confront each other; they now had as their counterparts political power alignments, thereby deepening the split and bringing in their wake the danger of religious wars.

After the Peace of Madrid (14 January 1526), Charles V felt he was free to arrange the religious affairs of Germany according to his own views and to enforce the Edict of Worms. Accordingly, he issued instructions to the Archduke Ferdinand for a diet which was summoned to Speyer for 1 May but did not actually begin its deliberations until 25 June 1526. Charles decreed that in matters of faith nothing should be changed; everything should continue as before "until the council should take up and establish a unanimous, Christian, constant, and needed reformation, regulation, and order." In view of the change that had meanwhile occurred in the political situation—on 22 May 1526 the Pope had formed the League of Cognac with the Emperor's enemies, while the Turks were increasing their pressure on Ferdinand's lands— such an edict could only cripple the not very energetic efforts for reform on the Catholic side.

The evangelical estates, notably the cities, showed a high degree of self-assurance. On the cloaks and in the lodgings of the Saxons and Hessians was to be seen the slogan, "Verbum Dei manet in aeternum." In the courtyards of their inns their preachers recruited publicly for the new faith. According to one report, it was evident to all the people that they no longer belonged to the old faith, "for they no longer went to Mass, they observed no fast days, they made no distinction of foods."[11] Thus the ineffectiveness of the Edict of Worms became clear to everyone. A committee of secular and ecclesiastical princes, including Philip of Hesse, submitted an opinion relevant to the traditional cere- monies and the correcting of abuses. According to this, the seven Sac- raments and the Mass should be retained; but fees and Masses offered for money alone were to be abolished. To make it possible for the people to participate in a lively faith and an inner union with the Passion of Christ, the texts of the liturgy should be recited in German and explained. The lay chalice should be tolerated until a general council could give a decision and it would be better to allow priests to marry than to watch how they cohabited with persons of evil reputation to the general scandal and with injury to their souls.

The Archduke Ferdinand rejected the suggestions, appealing to the imperial instructions, according to which no break was to be made with the tradition of the Church until the council. But under the pressure of the political situation and the necessity of obtaining help from the es- tates against the Turks, he gave his consent to the Recess of the Diet of 27 August, just two days before the defeat of the Hungarians by the Turks at Mohacs. According to this, no innovations were to be under- taken in matters of the Christian faith and religion, in conformity with the imperial instruction. It was felt that the best means of establishing peace and unity was to hold, within a year or eighteen months, a free general council or at least a German national council. *Apropos* of the Edict of Worms, the estates were in agreement that, until the holding of the council, they, with their subjects, "should live, rule, and act in such a

---

[11] Cited from J. Janssen, *Geschichte des deutschen Volkes* III (Freiburg, 15th ed. 1891), 49; cf. W. Friedensburg, *Der Reichstag zu Speier 1526 im Zusammenhang der politischen und kirchlichen Entwicklung Deutschlands im Reformationszeitalter* (Berlin 1887), pp. 299ff.

way as each expects and trusts to be justifiable before God and the imperial majesty."[12]

Such procrastinating decrees could not but have a catastrophic effect on the old faith, the slighter the prospects became for an early convoking of the council. In itself the Recess of the Diet contained no acknowledgment of territorial churches or of a *ius reformandi* and gave no pretext for the suppression of Catholic worship and the confiscation of Church property. But *de facto* it abetted such measures and in the course of time was quoted as their justification.

[12] *Neue Sammlung der Reichstagsabschiede:* I. *Teil derer Reichstagsabschiede von dem Jahr 1495 bis auf das Jahr 1551* (Frankfurt/Main, 1747), pp. 273ff., sections 1–4, 11.

CHAPTER 18

Luther's Concept of the Church and Doctrine of the Two Kingdoms

In the mid-1520s the first German territorial princes and city governments adhered openly to the Reformation. Thereby the question was raised of what position they should occupy in the new ecclesiastical system and whether they should directly participate in constructing it. This construction proceeded slowly. Many of the old institutions had indeed ended, but Luther hesitated to create new ones. He long did without an order of worship and of Church organization, partly because he regarded all externals as indifferent and hence optional—for him rites and institutions were *adiaphora*[1]—partly because he felt that, like himself, everyone had to find justifying faith by a free decision of conscience; and could be led to this only by the preaching of the Gospel. One must not encroach upon this personal decision of faith by means of external reforms, and no one must be induced or compelled to take part in ceremonies whose inner meaning he does not grasp or again he would be legally mistaken.

Concept of the Church

Luther did not offer a new concept of the Church in the sense of determining a system. In the struggle against the Church of his day, which, as a self-sufficient and even a tyrannical institution, in his view took the place of salvation based on faith in Christ's Gospel, and against the

[1] "Libertas enim spiritus hic regnat, quae facit omnia indifferentia nulla necessaria, quaecumque corporalia et terrena sunt" (WA 7, 720, 11).

Anabaptists, who based the Gospel only on the subjectivity of man, Luther wanted to destroy what seemed to him to contradict the "true Church" and to stress what seemed hitherto dim. For him the Church was a self-evident precondition, without which the Christian would be nothing. Christ "wishes to hear the multitude, not me, not you, not a Pharisee running around by himself."[2]

But for Luther the Church was not the external authority that threatened him with excommunication, not the hierarchical organization and sacral institution, but the community of the true believers in Christ. Luther did not esteem the word "church," because he incorrectly derived it from "Curia."[3] He preferred "common of all Christians," "Christian community or assembly," "nation of believers," "community of the saints," that is, of the *fideles,* who in faith are certain of forgiveness for Christ's sake. But this community in faith is not to be understood in the sense of congregationalism. It is not produced by the voluntary amalgamation of believers, but "convened by the Holy Spirit in one faith."[4] The Gospel transmitted in word and Sacrament constitutes the Church. She is "creatura verbi." Wherever the Gospel is proclaimed in accord with Scripture, the true Church (*ecclesia spiritualis*) lives in the external church (*ecclesia manifesta*), as the soul in the body.[5]

Word and Sacrament are external signs for the existence of the true Church, which herself remains hidden.

> The signs whereby one can note externally where the same Church is in the world are baptism, Sacrament, and the Gospel.[6] A sign is actually necessary, and we have it—baptism, bread, and, the most important of all, the Gospel. These three are Christians' sign of recognition, voucher, and criterion. For, where you see baptism, bread, and Gospel, no matter where, no matter by whom directed, there you must not doubt is the Church.[7]

In this regard the word has precedence over the Sacrament.

> The Gospel is, even before the bread and baptism, the real, surest, and most excellent sign of the Church. For only by the Gospel and

---

[2] *Auslegung deutsch des Vaterunsers* (1519; WA 2, 114, 28).

[3] *Grosser Katechismus* II, 48; *Bekenntnisschriften,* p. 656.

[4] *Grosser Katechismus* II, 51; *Bekenntnisschriften,* p. 657.

[5] Because of baptism and the word of God, even the Roman Church was holy for Luther: "Nos et dicimus hodie Ecclesiam Romanam Sanctam . . . manent in Romana urbe, quamquam Sodoma periore, baptismus, vox Evangelii, textus, sacra scriptura, ministeria, nomen Christi, dei . . . Ecclesia ergo Romana est sancta, quia habet nomen sanctum dei, baptismum, verbum" (1531; WA 40, I, 68).

[6] *Vom Papsttum zu Rom* (1520; WA 6, 301, 3).

[7] *Ad librum . . . Ambrosii Catharini responsio* (1521; WA 7, 720, 34).

through the Gospel is the Church received, formed, nourished, attested, fashioned, fed, clothed, adorned, strengthened, armed, equipped, maintained. In brief, the entire life and being of the Church consists in the word of God.[8] In this must one certainly recognize the Christian community: where the pure Gospel is preached. [WA 11, 408] Hence in the Church nothing must be preached except the certain, pure, and agreed word of God. Where this is wanting there is no longer the Church. [WA 51, 518]

Luther's concern was not for the written but for the proclaimed word, and in that context about the word in the Church. But no special office is required for the proclamation, "for whatever comes forth from baptism may boast that it is already ordained priest, bishop, and pope" (WA 6, 408).

Gospel and Church know no jurisdictions; these are merely tyrannical human inventions. He who teaches the Gospel is pope and successor of Peter. He who does not teach it is Judas, Christ's betrayer. [WA 7, 721, 30]

Every baptized person has the right and duty "of teaching and spreading" the word of God (WA 11, 412, 6). Of course, "in order to avoid serious confusion in the people of God" (WA 12, 189, 23), not everyone should discharge this duty. Hence the community calls ministers, who act in its name.[9] Then

ordination is nothing other than . . . taking one out of the crowd—they all have the same power—and commanding him to carry out the same power for the others, just as when ten brothers, sons of the king and his heirs, selected one to administer the inheritance for them. [WA 6, 407; 6, 564, 6–17]

The promise in Matthew 16:18 refers "to no person but only to the Church, which is built in the Spirit on the rock, Christ, and not on the

---

[8] " . . . tota vita et substantia Ecclesiae est in verbo dei" (WA 7, 721, 12). "Verbum Dei est instrumentum, quo operans efficit istam creaturam ecclesiam" (WA 4, 189); " . . . cum Ecclesia verbo Dei nascatur, alatur, servetur et roboretur" (WA 12, 191, 16).

[9] Later, for example, in Von der Winkelmesse (1533; WA 38, 240, 24) and in Von den Konziliis und Kirchen (1539; WA 50, 647, 8), Luther admits an establishing of the office by Christ. According to Vom Abendmahl Christi, Bekenntnis (1528), the priestly function is an "order" or "class" instituted by God, like marriage and the office of secular authority (WA 26, 504, 30). We must not harmonize Luther's concepts in his first years as a reformer, in which he identified the universal priesthood with the spiritual function in general and admitted a preaching function only for practical reasons, with his teaching on an office instituted by Christ over and above that of all the baptized. He upheld this last after the Peasants' War in the conflict with the fanatics and in the process of constructing a national Church. Cf. inf., footnote 14.

pope and not on the Roman Church" (*WA* 7, 709, 26). For the rock foundation of Christianity must be holy and sinless. Since one cannot know this in regard to Peter,

> Christ alone must necessarily be the rock, since he alone is sinless and will certainly so continue, and with him his holy Church in the Spirit. [*WA* 7, 709, 30] Just as now the rock [Christ] is sinless, invisible, and spiritual and tangible only in faith, so also of necessity is the Church sinless, invisible, and spiritual, and tangible only in faith [*WA* 7, 710, 1].

In regard to its head and its true members the Church is invisible or, as Luther preferred to say, hidden. "The Church is hidden, the saints are unknown" (18, 652, 23). She has no earthly head, and Christ has no vicar, "but only Christ in heaven is her head here and alone rules" (*WA* 6, 297, 39; *WA, Br* 3, 210, 31). Of course, in carrying out the ruling of the Church in word and Sacrament he makes use of human ministers as mere tubes.[10] However, he alone knows his own, knows in whom his means of salvation are really effective and who really belongs to the Church. For us men there is only the standard of fraternal love. We have to consider every baptized person as a member of the Church of Christ who has not excluded himself. Thus there are many baptized unbelievers, who are outwardly "in the Church," but not "of the Church."[11] The Church indeed lives in the flesh, but

> just as the Church is not without food and drink in this life, and yet, according to Paul, the Kingdom of God does not consist in eating and drinking, so also the Church is not without place and body and yet body and place are not the Church nor do they pertain to her. [*WA* 7, 720, 1]
>
> All this is without importance and optional. Every place is suitable for the Christian, and no place is necessary to the Christian. Any person can be his shepherd, and no definite person is necessary to him. For liberty of spirit reigns here, which makes all this of no importance and lets nothing that is corporeal and earthly be indispensable. [*WA* 7, 720, 8]

Therefore, Luther would like "to abolish or change nothing which cannot be abolished or changed with a clear scriptural warrant" (*WA* 26, 167), and no one was more hateful to him than he who forcibly abolished voluntary and harmless ceremonies and made necessity out of freedom (*WA, Br* 4, 411, 15). On the other hand, he was confident that,

---

[10] *WA* 45, 521, 32.
[11] *WA* 5, 430, 34; 41, 521, 23.

with the preaching of the word of God, the necessary external form would grow "of itself."

> But where the word of God is pure and certain, then it must be everything: Kingdom of God, Kingdom of Christ, Holy Spirit, baptism, Sacrament, priestly function, preaching office, faith, love, cross, life and blessedness and everything that the Church should have. [WA 38, 237]

Luther developed his teaching on the Church in the struggle against the hierarchically established papal Church. In connection with an abbot's right of patronage he defended the fundamental principle: "That a Christian assembly or community has the right and power to review all doctrine and to summon, install, and depose teachers" (1523; WA 11, 408–416). But this congregational Christianity soon proved to be impracticable. Luther denied the right of free election of its pastor to Karlstadt's congregation at Orlamünde. The Peasants' War and the disturbances produced in the community by the fanatics, together with the various types of disorder in morality and discipline, showed that nothing could be accomplished without ecclesiastical discipline, Church organization, and especially tribunals above the local level. The practice of the late medieval territorial Church, with extensive control of churches, monasteries, and hospitals by territorial lords or city governments, and the theory of the state of emergency as developed by William of Ockham suggested the entrusting of the external direction of the Church to the authority that had become Lutheran. Luther had impeded this development, however, by his teaching on the hidden Church and the competence assigned by him to the congregation, and especially by his rigorous distinction or even separation of the secular and the spiritual power.

Doctrine of the Two Kingdoms

Luther elaborated his teaching on the two governments in view of the steps taken by Catholic princes against the Reformation (*Von weltlicher Oberkeit, wie weit man ihr Gehorsam schuldig sei,* 1523), in the struggle against the fanatics (*Wider die himmlischen Propheten,* 1525), and on the occasion of the Turkish war (*Vom Kriege wider die Türken,* 1529). This polemical situation resulted in exaggerations and one-sidedness which not even Luther could maintain to the end. This led in turn to contradictions, which make Luther's doctrine of the two kingdoms seem even today to be a "maze." The doctrine must be understood in relation to Luther's teaching on justification or his idea of law and Gospel. Just as the Christian is at the same time sinner and just, just as he is subject to the claim and jurisdiction of the law and at the same time has been acquitted by the Gospel, so too he belongs to the secular and to the spiritual government.

Luther felt obliged to stress the distinction between, or the separation of, the two governments on two counts. On the one side was the theocracy of the old Church, which, in his view, made the Gospel a law, that is, a political juridical order to be enforced by the sword; on the other was the anarchy of the fanatics, who denied the secular government in the name of the spiritual or understood evangelical freedom as freedom from any juridical order. The two governments must not be understood as the Kingdom of God and the Kingdom of the Devil. Instead, both come from God's love; they are two different ways in which God rules the world, even though in the secular government he acts only as *deus absconditus*. The secular government wields the sword. It is under the standard of power and the possibility of compulsion and has to maintain external order against the ceaseless anarchical threat from the world, against disruptive tendencies from within and without, the consequences of sin. Sin would have as its result the self-annihilation of creation, if God did not keep destructive forces in check by means of the state and other authorities. For

> the world cannot be ruled according to the Gospel; the word is too little esteemed. [*WA* 17, I, 149] On the other hand, emperors and kings do not have to wage wars, as Christians. Who knows whether they are Christians? Are they not usually the worst enemies of Christendom and of the faith? [*WA* 30, II, 130, 29]

The Christian contends against even the Turks, not with weapons, but with God's word, penance, and prayer. He enters the Turkish war, because "in his body and his property he is subject to the secular authority," which summons him to the struggle against the Turks (*WA* 30, II, 179, 16). If he falls under Turkish rule, then he is subject to it as to his superior, just as to a papal government, "for the Pope . . . is much worse than the Turk" (195, 15). But under no circumstances must the Christian permit himself to be misused for war against the Gospel or for persecution of Christians (197, 9). "The emperor is not the head of Christendom nor the shield of the Gospel and of the faith" (*WA* 30, II, 130, 27). As a secular master, he must wage war for the protection of his subjects.

The secular government is indeed from God, but it has no special relationship to salvation. It is not in the order of redemption but pertains to the order of preservation. The Christian does not actually need it, he is "extricated" by Christ (*WA* 11, 260, 5). "The Christian, to the extent that he is really a Christian, is free from all laws, is subject to no law, within or without" (*WA* 40, I, 235, 8). Even Christ rules him "with the mere word" (*WA* 12, 330, 30). From this it follows that "if all the world were really Christian, no prince, king, lord, sword, or law would be necessary or useful" (*WA* 11, 249f.). But "the world and the multitude is and continues to be non-Christian, even though all are baptized and are called Christians" (*WA* 11, 253). Therefore, to prevent the triumph of evil, law and compulsory order are necessary. The secular government assures the area in which the proclamation of the word and the administration of the Sacraments can take place. These are the tasks of the spiritual government, "by means of which men should become pious and just, so that by the same justice they may attain to eternal life" (*WA* 19, 629). Whether the Church of experience, *ecclesia large dicta* or *manifesta,* pertains to the secular government is not clear in Luther and is still controverted.[12]

Because, though justified, he is still a sinner, the Christian is subject to the secular government, or to the "Kingdom on the left," to which, in addition to *politia, oeconomia* pertains, that is, marriage, parenthood, and vocation. However, he is subject to it voluntarily, and out of love, consents to the arrangements prevailing there, and in them serves his brother. In fact, he can

> even serve God in power and should serve within, where the needs of the neighbor demand. [*WA* 11, 258] For the sword and power belong, as a special divine service, to Christians especially, in preference to all others on earth. [*WA* 11, 258]

In the Christian who takes an interest in the world, Christ's Kingdom is present in the world, even though the world's institutions, such as the state, do not thereby become Christian.

With regard to unjust authority there is, according to Luther, the right of nonviolent active resistance by means of public instruction or rebuke, and then of passive resistance and flight; otherwise, the Christian must endure injustice for God's sake. With regard to his equals and his subjects, in accord with Matthew 5:39 he should not resist evil for himself, and so he does not need the secular power and law; but for others, for example, as prince, father, and soldier, he should "seek revenge, right, protection, and aid" (*WA* 11, 259).

> Here there is no time to listen to the Gospel but rather to the law. [*WA* 40, I, 210] Christian and fraternal ways of acting do not pertain to the secular government . . . a Christian and evangelical

[12] For example, between P. Althaus, who seems to uphold the affirmation, and J. Heckel. Cf. the article "Zwei-Reiche-Lehre," *EKL* III, 1927–47, in which both expound their opposing interpretations.

character belongs only to the governing of consciences. [WA 24, 677] Two persons and two sorts of function thus devolve upon one man; he is at the same time a Christian and a prince, judge, lord, servant, maid. These are called vain worldlings, for they belong to the secular government. . . . You are a Christian for yourself, but in regard to your servant you are another. [WA 32, 390, 10ff.]

Although one may wield the secular sword, one must not have thoughts of vengeance, "for where the heart is pure, there everything is made right and well" (WA 32, 392, 14). Thus was the Sermon on the Mount removed from the sphere of the heart and a dangerous distinction made between "Christian person" and "secular person" or between personal morality and official morality. Only too easily was support provided for a wordly-wise recognition of an emancipated political reality.

Church Government

If Christ alone governs his Church by faith, charity, and the other gifts of the Holy Spirit (WA, Br 3, 210, 31) and she is therefore hidden, but if she is, on the other hand, no *civitas Platonica,* but has a visible side, the question arises: in what does this visible side find its order? Luther gave no systematic answer to this question. We have only scattered remarks of the reformer, occasioned by different polemical situations. It is certain that the constitution of the visible Church is not divine but is based on human regulations. But, is the external aspect of the Church to be attributed for this reason to the secular government, as P. Althaus maintains, or is it constructed according to proper ecclesiastical, even if human, law, which is itself based on principles arising from the spiritual government of Christ, as J. Heckel holds? Have the princes, as the secular authority, any competence in constructing the eccelesiastical system or are they only called to a special ministry as outstanding members of the Church?

As early as 1520 Luther had summoned the secular power, along with all the baptized, to the reform of the Church and of Christendom in his "Sermon von den guten Werken" (WA 6, 257, 32) and in *An den christ-lichen Adel deutscher Nation* (WA 6, 406; 409; 411). Because the spiritual authority had refused a thorough-going reform and in particular had opposed the convoking of a council, the secular power should carry out its function. It must protect its subjects from every iniquity, including the corruption of the spiritual power and its interference in the secular sphere. It must punish exploitation, brigandage, and adultery and, in so doing, not stop before Pope and bishops. As Christian authorities, "because now they are also fellow Christians, fellow priests, fellow ecclesiastics, fellow masters in all things" (WA 6, 413, 30), they should be concerned with the convoking of a council. In view of the refusal of the spiritual power, no one can do this "as well as the secular sword" (*WA* 6, 413, 29). The more Luther had to do with Protestant authorities, the more he stressed their obligation of crushing resistance to the Gospel and of forbidding the celebration of Mass, just as sacrilege and blasphemy were forbidden. "The secular power does not coerce belief but only defends it externally." It should not overcome heresy: "Bishops should do this, . . . not princes, . . . for heresy is something spiritual [*WA* 11, 268]. If heresy exists, let it be overcome by God's word, as is proper" (*WA* 11, 270). The secular authority must intervene if there is a breakdown of order and in cases of public blasphemy. "Our princes do not coerce to faith and the Gospel, but they prevent external outrages," wrote Luther to Spalatin on 11 November 1525 (*WA, Br* 3, 616, 18). But "assault, theft, murder, and adultery are not so pernicious as this abomination of the papist Mass" (*WA* 15, 777, 8). Hence "authority is bound to prevent such a public blasphemy" (*WA* 18, 36, 19). If this is true of authority in general, then, in addition, the prince, as a "brother in Christ" (*WA, Br* 2, 515, 23) or "as a Christian member" (521, 59), must cooperate in tasks within the Church, for example, in the appointing of a preacher.

Until 1525 Luther rarely called upon his territorial prince, though the latter was very well-disposed toward his affairs. The order of worship was not the prince's business. "What are we to ask of him? He can do no more than in secular matters" (*WA* 12, 649, 18). The renewal of the Church should be accomplished in the power of the word on the basis of the congregation. Luther expected the congregation to create an order at the proper time, that is, the institutions necessary for worship and for community life. Luther also thought of bishops, who governed several communities or were over several pastors (*WA* 6, 440, 29). They too should be appointed by the congregations. However, such an ordination begins only in the regulated public ministry of word and Sacrament. It is merely a ratification by the congregation. Of themselves, all have the same power, but for this very reason no one should on his own "call attention to himself, but rather he should let himself be summoned and brought forward in order that he may preach and teach in the place and at the command of the others."[13] If the papal bishops are not ready for such a call to office, then the leading members of the congregation, should, as Luther wrote to the Bohemians, "lay hands on suitable persons in the presence of the congregation, confirm them, and recommend them to the people and the Church." Thus would they be "bishops, ministers, or shepherds" (*WA* 12, 193, 38).

---

[13] *WA* 11, 412, 31; cf. *WA* 12, 189, 17–27.

The question is whether this call of individuals to the ministry of the word arises only from a practical need when the members of the congregation transfer their rights, so to speak, to an attorney (*WA* 6, 407, 29), as Luther more or less consistently maintained in the 1520s, or whether ordination must follow for the sake of the commission and hence is of divine law, which is the view of the *Confessio Augustana* (XXVIII, 20–22), of the *Apologia* (XIII, 7–13), and probably also of Luther himself later (*WA* 50, 663, 3).[14]

[14] Luther's concept of the office is still disputed because he is not consistent in regard to it. J. W. F. Hofling, *Grundsätze ev.-lutherischer Kirchen verfassung* (Erlangen, 3rd ed. 1853), regards Luther's idea as consistent but does not really go into Luther's expressions in his works against the fanatics. According to him, for Luther there was only one function which was given to the whole Church and is entrusted to a special class only for practical reasons. According to A. W. Dieckhoff, *Luthers Lehre von der Kirchlichen Gewalt* (Berlin 1865), two different versions of the doctrine of the spiritual office must be recognized in Luther. In the first period (1520–23) Luther identified the universal priesthood, that is, the same spiritual character of all Christians, with the spiritual office and justified the ministry of the special officials by the "transmission theory" (82–97). Later he stressed the autonomy of an office instituted by God, over and above the universal priesthood (149–159). According to W. Elert, *Morphologie des Luthertums* I (Munich, 2nd ed. 1958), in Luther "two apparently completely opposed ideologies confronted each other" (I, 299), when it was a question of understanding the necessity of the office—a "utilitarian" concept, which required the preaching office for the sake of "order," and another, which saw it based on divine institution. But Luther perceived no opposition between the two concepts (301). Elert probably saw "the danger of a relapse . . . imminent" in expressions of the later Luther, in which the distinction between clergy and laity again emerged (303), but still found the harmony of both ideologies in Luther's view of ordination. According to it, the congregation issued the call, but: "In such a call issued by men we may and should behold a divine call, if those calling are so authorized by God" (304). E. Sommerlath, "Amt und allgemeines Priestertum," *Schriften des Konvents Augsburgischen Bekenntnisses* 5 (Berlin 1953), 40ff., also perceives two "ideologies." "A complete adjustment" between them and "a theological clarification were probably never achieved" (41). Hence two lines will probably always have to be seen in Luther (50). W. O. Munter, *Die Gestalt der Kirche "nach göttlichem Recht"* (Munich 1941), and *Begriff und Wirklichkeit des geistlichen Amtes* (Munich 1955), and P. Brunner, "Vom Amt des Bischofs," *Schriften des Konvents Augsburigschen Bekenntnisses,* 9 (Berlin 1955), stress the divine establishment of the preaching office in addition to and even ahead of the universal priesthood. They have in mind especially the Lutheran creeds. But P. Brunner emphasizes that "Luther's views are not in opposition to these" (16, footnote 11). As proof he cites *Von den Konziliis und Kirchen* (1539). Finally, W. Brunotte, *Das geistliche Amt bei Luther* (Berlin 1959), investigates "whether Luther's concept of the spiritual office remained the same in the course of the years . . . , whether it is homogeneous in itself or unadjusted tensions prevail in it" (32). His conclusion is "the unity of Luther's concept" (112). But he admits that from 1520 to 1523 the full power and responsibility of the universal priesthood occupied much space, whereas the coordination of Church and spiritual office was discussed especially in the period from 1530 (112ff.). The claim that there are contradictions in Luther's teaching on the office he regards as "at least very questionable" (116).

Luther gave no further thought to other organs of the community. He agreed to ecclesiastical discipline and more than once inflicted excommunication as a shepherd of souls.[15] But he created no office for this. Organizing was not his forte. He preferred to let things grow. Above all, for him a Church order must never become a "necessary law" (WA 18, 72, 6). For Christian congregations can be formed only by the preaching of the Gospel, through faith and charity, not through a reform of rites. It is absolutely unnecessary that the same order be maintained everywhere. No doubt it is good that the liturgy be celebrated uniformly in one lordship or one city with its environs (WA 18, 73, 6). But a decreed Church order does not have the binding force of laws which oblige because of the obedience commanded by God toward superiors. For authorization to issue such laws is contained neither in the power of the keys nor in the pastoral office of bishops.[16] Human order in the Church is thus not a juridical order in the strict sense, binding in conscience and to be enforced under compulsion.

But this freedom from law should be a freedom for order and for fraternal service; it "is the servant of love and of neighbor" (WA 18, 72, 23). Because of one's brothers, especially the weak, one should hold on to such "worldly and indifferent things" as ceremonies (WA, Br 11, 200, 17). Luther repeatedly designates the order of the visible Church as "worldly" (WA, 50, 559, 31), even as "lying outside the Church" (WA, Br 3, 211, 96). It was natural, therefore, to regard the secular government as competent in this regard. The reformer himself was probably not of this view but of the opinion that the Church had to take herself in hand in the ordering of her worldly affairs.[17] Therefore, he even referred to the territorial lords as "emergency bishops,"[18] who were to render

---

[15] Ruth Götze, *Wie Luther Kirchenzucht übte* (Berlin 1959).

[16] "From this passage [Matt. 16:18; 18:18] they have taken the word 'to bind' and explained it to mean as much as to command or to set up law and prohibition for Christianity. And so they give the pope the power to bind Christians' souls and consciences by laws" (1530; WA 30, II, 465, 20; cf., WA 6, 536, 20; 45, 460, 27; WA, Br 5, 490, 11–492, 27; 493, 38).

[17] J. Heckel, *Kirche und Kirchenrecht nach der Zwei-Reiche-Lehre*, pp. 267–271; F. Lau, *"Äusserliche Ordnung" und "Weltlich Ding" in Luthers Theologie* (Göttingen 1933).

[18] " . . . as our common emergency bishop, because otherwise no bishop will aid us" (WA, Br 8, 396, 14); " . . . as real emergency bishops in such a case, for a chapter takes the wrong track" (WA 53, 256, 3; 255, 5). As emergency bishop, the prince has an ecclesiastical office and is not exercising his secular power. This results from a letter of Luther's of 19 March 1539: "But now our prince must be an emergency bishop and emergency official, because such goods are acquired, not through civic management but from the ecclesiastical ministry. Hence they cannot be under civil law: they are in the hand and the right of the emergency bishop" (WA, Br 8, 15ff.; WA, Tr 4, 378, 25): "Nam nostro electori scripsi, adhortabar, ut ipse vigilaret pro ecclesia, that he was an emergency bishop" (1537).

"first aid" in acute distress. But the development went astray in the direction of even greater secular authority of the prince, although nothing further in the way of an emergency was to be noticed.

In the twenty-three Nürnberg visitation articles, which were accepted at Schwabach on 14 June 1528, we find:

> The Church is empowered only to choose ministers and to employ Christian excommunication and to arrange that the needy be provided with alms. . . . . All other power belongs either to Christ in heaven or to the secular authority on earth.[19]

Melanchthon decisively fostered the development into the princely Church government. He attributed to the authority the "custodia primae tabulae" and hence the supervision of the worship of God. To it belonged also the prohibition of false doctrine and ungodly worship.[20] According to Melanchthon, knowledge of the true doctrine pertains to the whole Church, priests and laity, and, among the latter, especially to princes. They have to make the Gospel respected in public life and carry out the judgments of synods. Hence the secular power is "minister and executive organ of the Church" (CR 3, 472). Its supervision of the ecclesiastical order no longer appears here as an emergency measure. The prince's special position and obligation in the Church result from his character as "foremost member"[21] of the new visible Church. Just as in civil life princes lead the way for their subjects, so also in the service of the Church and of her reform:

> With their authority they are to support the true Church, remove blasphemous teachers, and install pious preachers.

> Before all others, the outstanding members of the Church, kings and princes, should aid and care for the Church, in order that errors may be eliminated and consciences may be rightly instructed.

Thus did he write in the treatise De potestate papae, which was accepted at Schmalkalden in 1537 as a statement of creed.[22]

As members of the Church, then, the territorial lords took charge of the nomination to office, summoned synods, ordered visitations, and issued Church ordinances. Considering the strong tendency toward the

[19] Sehling, XI, 1, 132.
[20] CR 3, 225; 2, 711; "Loci" of 1535, CR 21, 553; Studienausgabe II, 2, 727.
[21] " . . . praecipua membra in externa societate" (De iure reformandi, 1537; CR 3, 251, 244).
[22] Bekenntnisschriften, p. 488.

territorial Church—already in existence since the late Middle Ages—it was natural soon to attribute to the secular authority as such what princes or the *pius magistratus* should do as a matter of first aid and out of love, because of their membership in the Church.

CHAPTER 19

The Completion of the Lutheran Community

Luther was disappointed in his hope that the constructing of congregations of real Christians would be effected solely by the preaching of the Gospel. His ideal proved to be impracticable. His expectations were ruined more than ever in the storm of the year 1525. His complaints about the "unspeakable scorn for the word and the dreadful ingratitude of men in regard to the benefit of the Gospel" became ever more serious and bitter. The preaching of justification by faith and of the freedom of the Christian had not produced the anticipated results in the moral life of his followers. On the contrary, according to Luther's own expressions, a moral deterioration and a disregard of the Sacrament and of Sunday worship seem to have crept in. His sermons bitterly complained of these developments.[1] Evangelical freedom was abused, and even preachers and pastors retained "of the Gospel only such a lazy, pernicious, shameful, carnal freedom" (*WA* 30, I, 125, 24).

Not only disillusionments of this sort, but also the spread of the Reformation and the related destruction of the old Church urgently called for new institutions. In the course of time and with the expansion of the area affected by the new doctrine it became obvious that the reconstruction must not be left to free development and that at least the broad mass were in need of the aid of ceremonies and could not manage without ecclesiastical discipline and the preaching of the law. At stake were the regulation of ecclesiastical property, the liturgy, visitations, and Church order.

Regulation of Church Property

The suppression of the monasteries, the secularization of Church property, and the cessation of foundation Masses and other ecclesiastical rites endowed with stipends caused a series of difficulties. The secular

[1] H. Werdermann, *Luthers Wittenberger Gemeinde wiederhergestellt aus seinen Predigten* (Gütersloh 1929).

lords—high and low—and the cities were very much inclined to appropriate Church property. Whoever had obligations to monasteries and
other spiritual institutions was happy to be freed of them so easily.
Foundation Masses and stole fees disappeared, but the Church's ministers had to live as before, except that now they also had to support wife
and children. Hardly any of those who benefitted by Church property
were ready to assume the expenses of the liturgy, the support of the
preachers, the care of the poor and the sick. According to Luther it was
important to take care that "the goods of such vacant foundations
did not disappear into *Rappuse* [that is, did not become spoil for
everybody], and that everyone did not struggle for something to
snatch" (WA 12, 11, 30). Therefore, like Karlstadt's Church order for
Wittenberg of 1521, Luther demanded that the property be gathered
into a "common chest." According to the "Order of a Common Chest"
for Leisnig (1523), for which Luther wrote the preface and which was
regarded as a model for other congregations, all Church revenues should
go into a common chest, from which should be drawn the expenditures
for the clergy, sexton, and plant, for schools and teachers, and for the
needy of every sort. Administration should be taken care of by a board
of trustees, consisting of two nobles, two councilors, three townsmen
and three peasants from the surrounding villages. All the townsmen and
peasants should meet three times a year to receive a report and to pass
resolutions. Luther had feared that few would follow his suggestion,
because "avarice is a disobedient and unbelieving scoundrel" (WA 12,
12, 9). As a matter of fact, the order did not attain its goal because the
city council was unwilling to turn over to the "chest" the foundations
under its control, and the elector shrank from forcible intervention.
Thus the "chest" lacked means for the intended purposes.

Luther complained vigorously and repeatedly over the congregations'
lack of a spirit of sacrifice.

> Once upon a time we gave much money and property to the
> papists. But now that we should help the ministers of the Church
> and the Gospel with a few pennies, we have nothing.[2] Where
> formerly 300 monks were supported, today not one preacher can
> find bread. [WA 14, 342, 7] It will come to this, that teachers,
> pastors, and preachers devote themselves to a craft and let the
> word go. [WA 15, 361, 2] Almost all congregations . . . want to
> call their pastors . . . and give nothing and support no one. Who-
> ever wants to have the power and the right to call should be
> obliged and bound to support. [WA, Br 4, 135, 10]

[2] WA 29, 94, 11f., 18f. (1529); similarly, WA 14, 341, 23.

This situation called for a tribunal superior to the local congregations, and, since the Church had none, for regulation by the territorial prince. Since all the monasteries and foundations, so Luther argued,

> fell into the hands [of the elector] as their supreme head, there also devolved upon him the duty and burden of ordering such things, since otherwise no one takes charge or can or should take charge of them. Because now such goods . . . are instituted for the divine service, it is only right that they should first of all serve for this. [WA, Br 4, 133f.]

The visitation of 1529 resulted in the elector's ratifying of the common chest for Leisnig (WA 12, 7). Later articles of visitation and Church orders adopted this institution, but its character as an autonomous ecclesiastical institution was long in jeopardy, in so far as the city councils sought to take over its administration or even to treat the chest as common property.

Liturgy

The liberty which Luther had allowed to the individual congregations and his dread of binding forms led to a rank growth and an ever greater fragmentation of liturgical forms. As late as 1524 Luther had rejected suggestions for the convoking of a council of his followers for the creation of a uniform liturgy (WA, Br 3, 373, 16; 384, 108). However, the events of 1525—the impulses of the "mobsters" and the Peasants' War—convinced him of the necessity of establishing uniform ceremonies (WA, Br 3, 582, 6). Together with councilors and choir directors of the principality, he put together a "Mass for the Laity in the Vernacular" (WA, Br 3, 591, 8). Thus finally, on 29 October 1525, a completely German Mass could be celebrated for the first time in the Wittenberg parish church. After it had been tested in practice, the "German Mass and Order of Divine Service" appeared in print at the beginning of 1526 and thus could be introduced elsewhere also.

However, according to Luther's preface, the German Mass was not to be the only form of the Evangelical liturgy in Wittenberg, but rather only one of three. Apart from those "who are already Christian" and need no order, because they have "their worship in spirit," Luther envisages the community, that is, "those who are so far becoming Christian or should become stronger," as divided into three groups. The first comprises the young: for them the Latin "Formula Missae" of 1523 should remain binding. The second are "the simple lay folk."

> Among these are many who do not yet believe or are not yet Christian; the greater number among them just stand there and

gape . . . just as though we were celebrating the liturgy in a public square or field among Turks and pagans. [*WA* 19, 74]

Here it is not at all a question of an ordered "gathering in which one can rule Christians according to the Gospel, but there is an open inducement to the faith and to Christianity" (ibid.).

The third group consists of those "who seriously wish to be Christians and profess the Gospel with hand and mouth." For them a simple order is enough; "there is no need for much and long singing" (*WA* 19, 76). They are a confessional community; they meet in one house expressly for prayer, scriptural reading, reception of the Sacrament, and other Christian work. Whoever "does not behave as a Christian" is punished or excommunicated. Luther did not want to establish any order for this narrow circle, for as yet people for it were lacking. If this *elite* community had only been formed, "the orders and methods would soon have followed."

Accordingly, Luther also saw the possibility of finding a place for the circle of the resolute, the confessional Church, "in the common heap," in the people's Church. But in actuality this "Christian gathering" did not materialize and Luther remained content with the liturgy for the "people" who are not yet seized by the spirit of the Gospel and must still be led to the seriousness of justification by faith.[3] But if there is question "for this reason of enlightening and leading the people" (*WA* 19, 97), then an instruction in worship is inevitable. Accordingly, the Eucharistic Preface became an "exhortation" to the participants in the Sacrament, the "Our Father" became an explication, the "Sanctus," an historical report. No longer was there a realization by the community that it was progressing "to the city of the living God, to the heavenly Jerusalem, to countless hosts of angels" (Heb. 12:22). Rather, the community was instructed in regard to what "happened to Isaiah the Prophet" (*WA* 19, 100, 6).

Actually the German Mass followed the Roman. But the Roman psalmody was replaced by popular hymns. Most important of all, it was reduced from the viewpoint of the doctrine of justification or the rejection of sacrifice. The Roman Mass adopted by Luther was the private form of celebration, itself only a curtailed form. A creative liturgical achievement could hardly be expected in that period, with its deficient grasp of worship as a re-presentation of salvation history, even from Luther himself, if we abstract from his linguistic power of expression.

---

[3] Cf. K. Müller, *Kirche, Gemeinde und Obrigkeit nach Luther* (Tübingen 1910), pp. 39f., with the concluding sentence: ". . . it remains in the community of the great heap." (p. 40).

And so it is not to be wondered at that the German Mass, with its pedagogical tendency, was in some respects only a torso and left "parts of the old liturgy . . . side by side, quite unexpectedly, . . . as unconnected rubble."[4]

Criticism from outside and his own new knowledge induced Luther to revise and make more rigid the baptismal liturgy, already published in 1523. It appeared in the autumn of 1526 under the title of *Das Taufbüchlein verdeutscht, aufs neue zugerichtet* and was widely circulated as a supplement to the small catechism of 1529. Because the pastors proved incapable on their own of preparing a nuptial rite corresponding to the reformed views, Luther composed a *Traubüchlein für die einfältigen Pfarrherren,* which appeared in April 1529 and was also added to the small catechism, which was published in book form soon after. In the remarks with which it was preceded Luther briefly explained his idea of marriage. Already in *De captivitate* (1520) he had refused to regard it as a Sacrament. There he wrote:

> It is contrary to all Scripture to regard matrimony as a Sacrament.
> . . . We nowhere read that he who takes a wife obtains any grace from God. The sign in matrimony was also not instituted by God.
> . . . The married state of the ancestors was no less holy than ours; the marriage of unbelievers is no less right than that of believers. [WA 6, 550]

Consequently, in the *Traubüchlein* it is concluded that, because "matrimony and the married state are a worldly matter, it in no way pertains to us priests and ministers to order or regulate them" (*WA* 30, III, 74, 3). However, "though it is a worldly state," it is still a "divine work and command" (*WA* 30, III, 74, 16–23), and so it is right to ask the blessing of the priest or bishop. Hence only prayers and blessing belong to the Church. Marriage itself is a civil act. If the Church officiates at marriage, she does so in the name of the secular authority. In conformity with Luther's *Traubüchlein,* the marriage ceremony took place outside the church, the proclamation of the word and blessing at the altar. This separation of the marriage ceremony, which took place at home or outside the church building, from the ecclesiastical celebration—in the pre-Reformation situation this was especially the nuptial Mass—was not

---

[4] F. Rendtorff, *Die Geschichte des christlichen Gottesdienstes unter dem Gesichtspunkt der liturgischen Erbfolge* (Giessen 1914), p. 42. Similar criticism in: J. Gottschick, *Luthers Anschauungen vom Gottesdienst* (Freiburg (1887), p. 72; *Leiturgia. Handbuch des ev. Gottesdienstes* I (Kassel 1954), 60. The contrary in: "Luthers Deutsche Messe und die Rechtfertigungslehre," *LuJ* 10 (1928), 170–203; id., "Luthers Reform der Abendmahlsfeier in ihrer konstitutiven Bedeutung," *Schrift und Bekenntnis,* ed. V. Herntrich–T. Knolle (Hamburg 1950), pp. 88–105.

unusual at that time. In the pre-Tridentine Church it was legitimate because the bride and bridegroom administered the Sacrament to each other; to Luther, on the other hand, it was legitimate because marriage was not properly a religious act.

Completion of the Ecclesiastical Constitution

Matters did not end with the mere publishing of liturgical books and catechisms. A tribunal was needed to introduce them as an obligation and thereby, as with other disciplinary measures, to put an end to the anarchy in the ecclesiastical system. In the absence of an ecclesiastical office beyond the local congregation, only the secular power was qualified for this.

The Recess of the Diet of Speyer of 1526 had left the execution of the Edict of Worms to the judgment of the territorial princes. Even though no *ius reformandi* was thereby given them, they claimed it in practice. To the extent that they inclined to the Reformation, they proceeded to enforce the uniform practice of religion in their territories, that is, to liquidate what was left of the Catholic organization and to set up or consolidate the new by the arranging and implementing of visitations.

Meanwhile, Luther had been forced to the recognition that the word alone did not suffice; human authority had to create at least the external preconditions and remove opposition. Like Nikolaus Hausmann, pastor at Zwickau before him, he had written to the Elector Johann on 31 October 1525 that, in view of the wretched condition in the parishes, "a bold order and stately maintenance of churches and lecture chairs" must be undertaken by the elector (*WA, Br* 3, 595). The elector hesitated but said that Luther should "compose an order" which should be established.

Luther thereupon proposed an ecclesiastical visitation. It was started at the beginning of 1526 in a few areas by two officials and the priests Spalatin and Myconius, but soon came to a stop. Luther, however, insisted. The visitation was resumed in the spring of 1527, this time with Melanchthon participating. On 16 June 1527 the elector issued an instruction for it.[5] In this he prescribed the visitation as prince and had it conducted by officials and theologians, who had "power and command" from him (p. 142). The visitation was concerned not only with Church property and the salary of the clergy and with public morality, but first of all with the true doctrine. No pastor should dare to teach, to preach, and to administer the Sacraments except according to God's word, "as this has been accepted by us and ours at the time when God has done

[5] Sehling, I, 142–148.

and given his grace" (p. 143). The elector intends, indeed, compels no one to the faith, but he will forestall "dangerous sedition" and tolerate no sectarianism or schism in his territory. Anyone who is unwilling to accept such a "Christian instruction" offered by the authority should sell all his property "and move out of our territory" (p. 144). Here there is no question that the elector is acting in spiritual matters differently from the way he acts as territorial prince. In other words, "with this instruction the territorial Church government was present."[6]

Melanchthon took part in the visitation especially as a theologian. Luther played no role, but the reports of the visitation were sent to him for his examination. Adequate instructions for the visitors were lacking, and so the implementation of a uniform Church order was not realized.

For this reason Melanchthon worked out an order of visitation, to which Luther contributed a number of improvements. In September 1527 it was discussed by the visitors—to whose number Spalatin had been added—with recourse to Luther and Bugenhagen. Meanwhile, the visitations and a preliminary work of Melanchthon's that had appeared without his knowledge, the *Articuli de quibus egerunt per visitatores* (1527), had caused a stir, and "visitationis rumores" (*WA, Br* 4, 232, 4) had spread. On the Catholic side it was thought that in the visitation a *rapprochement* with the doctrine and practice of the "old faith" could be established,[7] while in the Protestant camp the Saalfeld pastor, Kaspar Aquila, accused Melanchthon of returning to "papism." In particular, the director of the school at Eisleben, Johannes Agricola, was the spokesman for those who felt that the Wittenberg theologians "were creeping back" (*WA, Br* 4, 265, 6), that is, reverting to the old Church system. In his view an excessive scope was given to the preaching of the law at the expense of the freedom of the Gospel. Penance must begin, not with servile fear, but with faith and love for justice.[8] Melanchthon, on the other hand, had concluded his *Articuli* with the sentence that the people would be lulled into security without the preaching of the law and that they imagined they had justice from faith, although "faith can exist only in those whose hearts have been made contrite by the law" (*CR* 26, 28).

For this reason the elector again issued invitations to conferences on the order of visitation at Torgau on 25 November 1527. Here a compromise was discovered. "In order that adversaries might not be able to

---

[6] K. Holl, "Luther und das landesherrliche Kirchenregiment," *Gesammelte Aufsätze* I (Tübingen, 6th ed. 1932), 373.

[7] In his *Christenliche underrichtung . . . über ettliche Puncten der Visitation* (1528) Bishop J. Fabri wrote: "hettestu also gelert szo wolt ich dir mit leib und gutt beygestanden sein" (L. Hebling, *Dr. Johann Fabri* Münster 1941, p. 39).

[8] J. Rogge, *Johann Agricolas Lutherverständnis* (Berlin n.d.), p. 105.

say that there had been a disavowal" of the doctrine thus far defended, there was added to the first chapter, "On the Doctrine," the following sentence: Nothing should be taught previous to faith, except that "penance follows from and according to faith."[9] Besides, the necessity of preaching the law was insisted on. It would be a curtailing of the Gospel to speak one-sidedly of the remission of sins but to say nothing or only little of penance. "Without penance, however, there would be no remission of sins" and it could not be understood. The result would be that people would think they had already obtained remission of their sins and hence they would be secure and without fear. This would be a greater error and a greater sin than ever before. For the sake of the "common, uneducated man such articles of faith should be left alone under the name of penance, commandment, prayer, fear, and so forth, for otherwise the common man could be in error in regard to the word 'faith' and raise useless questions."[10] The frequent reference to the "common man" makes clear the danger of pedagogism or moralism in regard to the Gospel in the Lutheran national Church as it was then developing.

The printing of the "Instruction of the Visitors to the Pastors" was protracted till the end of March 1528. The text is mainly Melanchthon's. Luther wrote the preface, in which he stressed that it was the function of the bishop to be overseer and visitor and that he had "been glad to see it restored again, as something very badly needed" (WA 26, 197, 15). Where the bishops had failed, he said, it would have been natural that the reformers should have taken their place. "However," he reported, "because none of ours had been called to this or had any positive command," he had applied to the elector with the request that several qualified men should be called and appointed to this office. Luther made his request to the territorial prince, but not as a secular authority, which had "not been commanded to teach and to rule spiritually" (WA 26, 200, 29), but for the sake of the "office of charity, which is common and necessary to all Christians" (WA 26, 197, 20). It is the business of the secular authority to break malicious opposition, for it must "see to it that discord, mobs, and sedition not be stirred up among the subjects" (WA 26, 200, 30). With this distinction between what the elector was to do as authority and what he was to do "out of Christian charity" as a member of the Church, on the occasion of visitations, Luther was apparently seeking to maintain the autonomy of the Church. Hence the preface has "the meaning of a certain correcting or of a tacit protest"[11] against the elector's instruction of 1527 and the princely

[9] Sehling, I, 152.
[10] Ibid.
[11] K. Holl, op. cit., p. 374.

ecclesiastical government claimed by it. A protest, to be sure, which was ineffective.

In accord with the instruction of 1527, suitable pastors were named as "superintendents" to carry out the visitation. They were to exercise supervision over their fellow officials in a district, and these fellow officials could have recourse to them in difficult cases. Contrary to Luther's expectation, marriage cases especially soon turned out to be such. Pastors whose conduct, discipline, and teaching gave ground for objections and in regard to whom the admonitions of the superintendents were of no avail were, according to the "Instruction of the Visitors," to be reported to the magistrate for denunciation to the elector.[12] There was no higher ecclesiastical office. If one could apply temporarily to the visitation commissions or to Luther, this was still no solution in the long run. And so there ensued the forming of consistories. In this matter also Electoral Saxony gave the example. The need for matrimonial courts provided the first impulse. In 1538, by order of the Elector Johann Frederick, Justus Jonas elaborated an expert opinion, together with Bugenhagen, Melanchthon, and jurists, in 1538: "Der Theologen Bedenken von wegen der Konsistorien, so aufgerichtet werden sollen." When the discussions on the subject were protracted, the consistory was set up on an experimental basis and undertook operations at the beginning of 1539. A consistorial order was not drawn up until 1542.[13]

If the superintendents can be regarded as holders of an ecclesiastical office, then the consistory took the place of the bishop, though in reality it was an institution of the territorial prince. He summoned it, nominated its members, determined its order of business, and in all things had the final decision. The consistory was composed of electoral advisers who were experts in law and of theologians. The theologians were often only of secondary importance and were only called upon from case to case. In the course of time the consistory became competent for the administering of ecclesiastical discipline and excommunication, for the total administration of the territorial Church, and for decisions in marriage cases and other ecclesiastical disputes, such as patronage and tithes. The princely ecclesiastical government found in this body its corresponding organ and its definitive establishment.

Schools and Religious Instruction

The destruction of the old ecclesiastical system also had involved schools and universities. "The first effects of the Reformation on the

---

[12] Sehling, I, 171.
[13] Ibid., pp. 200–209.

educational system were of a destructive character."[14] Church and school were too intimately connected, not merely in theory but also in actuality, for one to be able to destroy the structure of the former without also striking at the latter. Furthermore, teaching and scholarship needed quiet and peace, which were impossible in the heat of polemics and in the convulsions of the Peasants' War. And finally, there were circles like Karlstadt, which justified by the Bible a rejection of education and schools. All this led to a decay of the schools and a strong falling off in the number of students. In 1528 Erasmus complained to Pirckheimer: "Wherever Lutheran teaching prevails, there is the collapse of scholarship."[15] For Luther, as for Melanchthon, teaching was basically secular in character; it was spiritual only in so far as it was in the service of the word. It was the duty and right of the secular power to set up and maintain the school system.

The treatise *An die Ratsherren aller Städte deutschen Lands, dass sie christliche Schulen aufrichten und halten sollen* (1524) had its origin in the fact that "everywhere schools have been allowed to disappear" (*WA* 15, 28). It was a summons to the city government to establish Latin schools and not to excuse themselves with subterfuges such as: "If we are only able to teach the Bible and the word of God in German, this is sufficient for salvation" (*WA* 15, 36). Luther regarded schools as necessary for service to the Gospel as well as to the world. For, even if

> the Gospel came only through the Holy Spirit and so comes daily, it has come however by means of languages and it has grown in the same way and so it must be preserved in the same way. [*WA* 15, 37] And let this be said, that we will not receive the Gospel without languages. . . . They are the chest in which this jewel is carried. . . . Therefore, it is certain that, where languages do not remain, the Gospel must finally perish. [*WA* 15, 38]

Hence schools constituted a vital question for real Christianity. But the secular government also needed "good schools and scholars" and care had to be taken that "cultured and capable persons" should take an interest in the world.

> If right now there was no soul and no need of schools and languages for the sake of Scripture and God, still this reason alone would be sufficient for setting up the very best schools for both boys and girls everywhere—that the world, in order to maintain externally its worldly condition, needs cultured and capable men and women. [*WA* 15, 44]

[14] F. Paulsen, *Geschichte des gelehrten Unterrichts* I, 184.
[15] Letter of 20 March 1528 in Allen, VII, 366, 40, no. 1977.

Here the parents have the most pressing obligations, but this task goes beyond their strength. Nothing is to be expected from the princes. "And so, dear councillors, I want it to continue in your hands alone. You have the capacity for it, better than princes and lords" (*WA* 15, 45).

While Luther specified the several fields of instruction, he did not lay down a curriculum. Rather, this was Melanchthon's job. He had already cooperated in the establishing of the school at Eisleben in 1525. In the last section of the "Instruction of the Visitors" (1528) he submitted his ideas on the carrying out of educational instruction in more detail. In this he had in mind the modest circumstances in Saxony and hence he renounced the teaching of Greek and Hebrew from the outset. In fact, in the interests of concentration, "in order [not] to burden the poor children with so much variety,"[16] no German should be taught either. With Melanchthon and with the contemporary schools there was concern only for the Latin language. The primer was already Latin; German did not appear at all.

The school was to be organized in three stages. In the first the children learned to read and write; in the second, grammar; in the third, also prosody, dialectics, and rhetoric. One day, Saturday or Wednesday, was devoted to "Christian instruction." "To learn nothing but Scripture" was to be tolerated as little as "to learn nothing from Scripture."[17] The Our Father, the Creed, the Ten Commandments, and a group of psalms should be learned and explained. From the New Testament, the Gospel according to Matthew should be "grammatically explained." Otherwise, at most the explanation of the Epistles to Timothy, of the First Epistle of John, and of Proverbs was envisaged for the older youths. Pedagogical considerations prevented the treating of other books of the Bible, "for it is not profitable to burden the young with difficult and sublime books," such as Isaiah, the Epistles to the Romans, and the Gospel according to John.[18] Contemporary school regulations, such as those of Wittenberg of 1533, of Braunschweig and Hamburg of 1528, and of Schleswig-Holstein of 1542, show that the basic principles of the "Instruction of the Visitors" were established in Electoral Saxony and became models for other districts. New was the admitting of religious instruction into the school curriculum. But this was so only in the cities and even there not for a long time in all of them. Hence the religious education of youth could not be turned over to the visitors alone. Consequently, on Sunday afternoon, because then "the farmhands and young folk come to church . . . the Ten Commandments, the articles of faith, and the

[16] Sehling, I, 172.
[17] Ibid., p. 173.
[18] Ibid., p. 168.

Our Father should be preached and explained in order."[19] In this connection there should "also be sermons intentionally on the Sacraments of baptism and of the altar" (p. 169). "For the sake of the children and of other simple and unlettered folks, [the texts should] be recited word for word" (ibid.).

The visitations had revealed a great ignorance in the congregations and among the preachers. Melanchthon encountered a pastor who did not even know the Ten Commandments. Suitable textbooks were urgently needed. Luther had already emphasized in the German Mass: "Now then, in God's name, what is needed first in the German liturgy is a thick, plain, simple, good catechism" (WA 19, 76, 1). Here he meant a catechism in the broad sense, oral instruction in the five chief points—commandments, faith, Lord's prayer, baptism, Lord's Supper. But no less imperative was a book in which this instruction should be set down for pastors and fathers of families, who should "present" the truth to their children and workers. Luther set to work to supply this urgent need.

Others before him had already shown an interest in this task. "Between 1522 and 1529 about thirty such efforts at composing a catechism had been published, some of which were printed in many editions."[20] In addition to Melanchthon and Bugenhagen, Johannes Brenz especially had compiled such a booklet for the religious instruction of the young at Schwäbisch Hall. He titled it *Fragestücken des christlichen Glaubens* (1527f.). Andreas Althammer at Ansbach gave his book of religion the title *Catechism, or Instruction in the Christian Faith* (1528). From 1516 Luther had often delivered catechetical sermons. From this practical activity there came several explanations of the Ten Commandments and the Our Father which had a powerful impact.[21] After the disturbances at Wittenberg the catechetical sermon became a fixed institution in the local parish church. As the substitute for Johannes Bugenhagen, Luther himself in 1528 once again delivered these series of sermons on the five principal points in three cycles during the Ember weeks in May, September, and December. Before the third he had taken part in the visitation, and his experiences in this connection determined him to compose a catechism. The catechetical sermons pro-

---

[20] J. M. Reu, *D. Martin Luthers Kleiner Katechismus. Die Geschichte seiner Entstehung, seiner Verbreitung und seines Gebrauches* (Munich 1929), p. 14.

[21] "Eine kurze Erklärung der 10 Gebote" (1518; WA I, 250–256); "Eine kurze Form der 10 Gebote. Eine kurze Form des Glaubens. Eine kurze Form des Vaterunsers" (1520; WA 7, 204–229); "Eine kurze Form, das Paternoster zu verstehen und zu beten" (1519; WA 6, 11–19); "Eine kurze und gute Auslegung des Vaterunsers vor sich und hinter sich" (1519; WA 6, 21f.); "Auslegung deutsch des Vaterunsers für die einfältigen Laien" (1519; WA 2, 80–130).

vided the material. It was to be a book "for the barbarous pagans" (*WA, Br* 5, 5, 22), that is, for the common uneducated people. But it became too bulky, and so Luther seems to have decided, while he was still composing it, to write another quite brief catechism. This small catechism appeared early in 1529, at first, following the late medieval usage, on tablets which could be hung up in church, school, and home, so that the text could more easily be committed to memory. The large catechism was published in April 1529 as *Deutsch Katechismus Martin Luther* (*WA* 30, I, 125–238). Then on 26 May appeared *Der kleine Katechismus für die gemeine Pfarrherr und Prediger* (*WA* 30, I, 264–339). Whereas the large catechism presents the individual items in detail, in the form of a sermon or lecture, the small catechism is drawn up in the form of question and answer. Through it and through his hymns Luther became the great religious moulder of the people. His two catechisms acquired the status of norms quite early. In 1580 they were accepted into the *Book of Concord* and described in the "epitome" of the formula of concord as "the Bible of the laity," "in which everything is included which is dealt with in scattered parts of Scripture and must be known by a Christian as necessary for salvation."[22]

[22] *Bekenntnisschriften*, p. 769.

CHAPTER 20

Clement VII and Charles V

Cardinal Giulio de Medici, a firm partisan of the Emperor and candidate of the imperial faction, emerged from the two-months-long conclave on 19 November 1523 as Clement VII, but as Pope he was soon to pursue entirely different paths. He declined to renew the defensive alliance concluded by Adrian VI with the Emperor and soon established secret contacts with France. His mind was concerned solely with freeing the Papal State from its encirclement by the Habsburg world power which was ruling Naples and Milan. If his own resources did not suffice to expel all "barbarians" from Italy, then at least a political balance should be established by assisting King Francis I of France to gain Milan. In this way Clement VII intended also to profit the interests of his family and to assure the rule of the Medici in Florence. His ideas were first of all political, not, however, in the sense of a universal papacy but as the ruler of an Italian dynasty. But this was too weak an ambition to exert decisive weight in the conflict of the great powers. Furthermore, Clement VII did not possess the character and stability of a great politician. He was, it is true, intellectually alert and conscientious in carrying out his official duties and in regard to his life style he was an improvement over his thoughtless and prodigal cousin, Leo X. "To this were added a dreadful indecision, vacillation and timidity, so that amid endless negotiations and half-measures he let slip his best opportunities and ended by earning for himself from friend and foe alike a reputation for unreliability."[1]

Vis-à-vis this Pope Emperor Charles V was a ruler who was filled with the notion of a universal emperor, on whose awareness it had been impressed in 1523 by his great political mentor and chancellor, Gattinara, in a memorandum: "Your affairs are those of the whole of Christendom and, in a sense, of the whole world."[2]

Initially the Pope exerted himself for peace among the Christian powers, rendered urgent by the Turkish threat. But his intervention failed. After a series of defeats Francis I succeeded on 26 October 1524 in again acquiring Milan. Impressed by this success, the Pope on 12 December allowed himself to be won to an alliance with France and Venice which granted the French troops passage through the Papal State and promised the Pope the possession of Parma and Piacenza and the assurance of Medici rule in Florence. To the Emperor, angered at his treachery, Clement VII wrote on 25 January 1525, that he had had to yield to the French "unwillingly and under compulsion." But with the overwhelming defeat of the French at Pavia on 24 February 1525 and the captivity of Francis I, the Pope's cleverly intended calculations were ruined. He saw himself constrained to seek again the protection of Emperor Charles V, who was able to dictate to France the Peace of Madrid (14 January 1526) and apparently to attain the fulfillment of all his desires. Francis renounced, among other areas, Naples, Milan, and Genoa, and also his rights in Flanders and Artois. He promised to cede Burgundy and its dependencies and, as a token of enduring friendship, to marry Charles' sister, Eleonor. And his two older sons became hostages to guarantee the execution of the treaty.

Francis I had, however, in a notarial protest declared the peace null because it had been extorted by means of imprisonment and he did not intend to abide by it. And so, in the last analysis, the Emperor had succeeded only in bringing his old opponents closer together out of fear of Habsburg predominance in a new alliance. England, previously on his side, concluded a separate peace with France and promoted the League of Cognac, formed on 22 May 1526 by Francis I, Venice, Florence,

---

[1] Jedin, I, 177 (English trans.: *A History of the Council of Trent* I, 221).

[2] K. Brandi, *Berichte und Studien* IX, *Eigenhändige Aufzeichnungen Karls V. aus dem Jahre 1525. Der Kaiser und sein Kanzler,* NGG, phil.-hist. Kl., 1933 (Berlin 1933), pp. 243f.

Francesco Sforza, and the Pope. In his letter of 23 June 1526 to the Emperor, the Pope claimed to have been determined to this step by his solicitude for peace in Christendom, the freedom of Italy, and the security of the Holy See, while Charles V was disturbing the peace and repaying with ingratitude a vast number of acts of kindness. The Emperor, on the other hand, uttered a very strong protest in a state paper of 17 September 1526. He maintained that in Germany he had made himself the protector of the Apostolic See. He still desired peace; if the Pope were to lay down his arms, all others would follow his example, and the strength of Christendom could be directed against heretics and Turks. Otherwise, he was no father but an enemy, no shepherd but a wolf. The memorandum concluded with the threat of a council:

> For, since we see the entire ecclesiastical order and the Christian religion disturbed for the reasons cited and others, and our interests as well as those of Christendom jeopardized, we regard it as appropriate to summon the Holy General Council.[3]

The Emperor urged the cardinals for their part to summon a general council if the Pope refused to do so. Clement VII abhorred and dreaded a council for many different reasons. The conciliarism of the fifteenth century had not been really overcome; it had merely been crippled by means of the papal policy of concordats. At the moment a council could not fail to effect a strengthening of the Emperor's central authority, which the Pope feared as much as did France. Finally, the illegitimate scion of the Medici could expect a reform council to be critical of his person or even to call into question his legitimacy as Pope.

The threat of a council did indeed impress the Pope, but not to the extent of making him give up his alliance with France and England. This would result only from the military occurrences that overtook Rome and the Pope in the next months. The Colonna family, led by Cardinal Pompeo Colonna, made a surprise attack on Rome and plundered the Leonine City. However this was only the prelude to worse. Jörg von Frundsberg had crossed the Alps in the late autumn and reinforced the Spanish troops with his mercenaries. In February 1527 he joined Charles of Bourbon. But there was no money with which to pay the soldiers. Fatigue and hunger led to mutinies, with which Frundsberg was unable to deal. Then he suffered a stroke. The insubordinate troops headed for the Eternal City, where they assured themselves they would acquire rich booty and revenge themselves on the Pope, the Emperor's

---

[3] J. Le Plat, *Monumenta ad historiam concilii Tridentini spectantia* II (Louvain 1781), 247–288, 9; K. Brandi, op. cit., I, 216; H. Jedin, "Die Päpste und das Konzil in der Politik Karls V.," P. Rassow (ed.), *Karl V. Der Kaiser und seine Zeit* (Cologne 1960), pp. 104–117 (especially p. 106).

enemy. In addition, the old and deep-seated anti-Roman sentiment of the Germans and the new talk about the Antichrist in the Roman Babel stirred the desire of punishing rich and wicked Rome. Charles of Bourbon fell at the very start of the attack on the Eternal City on 6 May 1527, with the result that the murder and pillage on the part of the leaderless soldiery became all the more unrestrained.

The *Sacco di Roma* became a judgment on Renaissance Rome. The Pope had taken refuge in Castle Sant'Angelo but had to surrender on 5 June and for the next six months he was the prisoner of the imperial troops. By agreeing to the occupation of important cities in the Papal State, paying a considerable indemnity, and promising neutrality, he was able to purchase his freedom on 6 December. Until October 1528 he stayed away from ruined and depopulated Rome. Meanwhile, the Emperor's troops were successful in North Italy and in the Kingdom of Naples. The Pope saw that his interest lay on the Emperor's side. When he was assured absolutely that the Emperor would not insist on a council and that there were other ways of dealing with the Protestants, such as a court of arbitration made up of scholars or a religious colloquy, he was ready for peace, which was signed at Barcelona on 29 June 1529. The Emperor promised the restoration of Medici rule in Florence and the retrocession of cities such as Ravenna, Modena, and Reggio to the Papal State. In return he was again invested with Naples and obtained the disposal of benefices in the kingdom. Pope and Emperor made a defensive alliance against the Turks, then advancing on Vienna, and bound themselves to common action against heretics. Since peace with France was also being negotiated—it became a reality on 3 August 1529, in the Ladies' Peace of Cambrai between Margaret of Parma and Louise of Savoy, mother of Francis I—Charles V was able to undertake the long announced journey to Italy.

He met the Pope at Bologna on 5 November 1529. For four months he lived next door to the Pope, seeking in private conversations to win him over to a council. He was unable to overcome Clement's misgivings and obtained only a conditional assent. The Pope wanted guarantees that peace was assured and schisms—here he had France especially in mind—were out of the question.[4]

On 24 February 1530, his birthday and the anniversary of the Battle of Pavia, Charles V received the imperial crown from the Pope at San Petronio in Bologna. The old unity of Emperor and Pope seemed restored, the precondition for the peace of Christendom reestablished. This coronation, the last that a Pope was to perform, was, however, rather a conclusion than a new start. A real understanding between

---

[4] Jedin, I, 195f. (English trans.: I, 244).

Emperor and Pope, that would have been so necessary for defense against the Turkish peril and for overcoming the religious split in Germany, failed to materialize. His dynastic concerns and dread of the Emperor's predominance in Italy brought Clement VII to a new *rapprochement* with France. In October 1533 he went to Marseilles to marry his great-niece, Catherine de Medici, to Henry of Orleans, the second son of the French King. The conversations with Francis I on this occasion remained secret, and so they could only feed the Emperor's suspicions all the more. In the last years of Clement VII's pontificate occurred also the decisive phase of the divorce of Henry VIII and thus the withdrawal of England from the Church. On 24 March 1534 the Pope issued the judgment which declared the validity of Henry's marriage with Catherine of Aragon. Clement did not live to see the final break— the Act of Supremacy of 3 November 1534. He died on 25 September 1534, called by von Ranke "probably the most calamity-ridden of all the popes who ever occupied the Roman See." It was especially mischievous that he took no decisive step toward renewal of the Church, but rather refused the overdue council and felt that the unity of the Church could be assured by political means, by a subtle diplomacy.

CHAPTER 21

*The Speyer Protest
and
The Marburg Religious Colloquy*

The Edict of Worms had been suspended *de facto* at the Diet of Speyer in 1526. The Emperor was fully occupied with the war in Italy, while King Ferdinand had to devote himself to the Turkish danger and the struggle for Hungary, that is, for what was left of the kingdom, claimed by him in the name of his brother-in-law, Louis II, who had perished at the battle of Mohacs in 1526. The princes who inclined to the Reformation, Electoral Saxony and Hesse at their head, were able to utilize the opportunity to construct and consolidate the new ecclesiastical organization in their lands. Just the same, there was a growing feeling of insecurity, and the mutual distrust became deeper. Hence people began to look for allies. Especially active was Philip of Hesse, who was little troubled by scruples in political matters. His efforts were directed toward restoring Duke Ulrich of Württemberg to his territory and, by destroying the Swabian League, to gain the South German cities for an evangelical alliance. Both aims were intended to weaken the Habsburgs and to place the adherents of the Reformation in a position to defend themselves against future unfavorable decrees of a diet.

These far-reaching plans of Philip the Magnanimous very nearly led to war because of the "Pack Affair." In February 1528, Otto Pack, a secretary of Duke Georg of Saxony, made known to Philip that King Ferdinand, Duke Georg of Saxony, the Elector Joachim of Brandenburg, and other Catholic princes had concluded an offensive alliance with the Bishops of Mainz, Salzburg, Würzburg, and Bamberg in Breslau in order to extirpate heresy and to deprive the princes of Electoral Saxony and Hesse of their authority. Philip thereupon united with the Elector Johann of Saxony for a preventive war and allied with France, Denmark, and Zapolya, Ferdinand's rival in Hungary. First of all, the bishoprics of Würzburg and Bamberg were to be occupied. Luther and the Wittenberg theologians had scruples about an offensive war for the Gospel and stressed the duty of obedience by the estates to the Emperor. Moreover, the Pack documents turned out to be forgeries, and so the military expedition collapsed at its start. Nevertheless, Philip obtained from the Franconian bishops compensation for the costs of mobilization and from the Archbishop of Mainz the renunciation of spiritual jurisdiction in Hesse.

The Diet of Speyer in 1529

The plans in regard to an alliance acquired a fresh stimulus by means of the Diet of Speyer, which began on 15 March 1529. Charles V had become reconciled with the Pope and peace was about to be concluded with France. Hence the Emperor could think about a regulation of the situation in the Empire. At the beginning of the discussions his proposal was not yet ready. The suggestions submitted by Ferdinand were more rigorous and far-reaching.[1] Aid against the Turks preempted the stage. Nevertheless, the religious question was energetically discussed. Under penalty of outlawry it was to be forbidden to deprive anyone of his authority and property "because of his faith" or to force him to embrace another faith. The Recess of the Diet of 1526 was declared null because it had given occasion to misunderstandings and caprice.

The advisory committee made the proposal stricter. Nevertheless, the innovations were permitted to continue; but the Mass had to be tolerated everywhere, and the Sacramentarians and Anabaptists were proscribed.[2] The evangelical estates, however, issued on 19 and 20 April the solemn protest that gave them the name "Protestants."[3] Without

[1] *RTA* VII, 1129–36.
[2] Testimonial of 15 April (*RTA,* VII, 1140–43).
[3] *RTA* VII, 1262–65, 1274–88.

regard for this, the Recess of the Diet was signed on 22 April. In it the Emperor was requested to propose to the Pope the convoking of a "free general council in Germany." It should be summoned within one year to meet at Metz, Cologne, Mainz, Strasbourg, or some other German locality and, at the latest, begin its work after another year, "so that the German nation can be united in the holy Christian faith and the impending schism can be discussed."[4] Otherwise, "a general gathering of all the estates of the German nation," a sort of national council then, should take place.[5] The Edict of Worms should remain in force where it was hitherto observed. Where the new doctrine had been introduced and could not be eliminated without tumult henceforth any further innovation should be prevented until the future council could be convened. Above all, teachings and sects which attacked the Sacrament of Christ's body and blood—Zwinglians and Anabaptists—must not be allowed, and the Mass must not be abolished. "Even in places where the other doctrine has taken root and is maintained, it must not be forbidden to hear Mass nor must anyone be hindered from doing so."[6] All "Anabaptists and the rebaptized, men and women of the age of reason, are to be put to death by fire, the sword, or the like . . . without any previous inquiry by the spiritual judges."[7] Finally, it was stated:

> We, electors, princes, prelates, counts, and estates, have unanimously agreed and loyally promised one another that no one of a spiritual or a secular estate is to offer violence to another or compel or attack him because of faith or deprive him of rents, taxes, tithes, or goods.[8]

No notice was taken officially of the protest of the evangelical estates. Hence they presented it, in an expanded form, as an appeal to the Emperor on 25 April.[9] Now fourteen cities with Sankt Gallen, including the Free Cities of Strasbourg, Nürnberg, Ulm, and Constance, declared their adherence to the protest of the princes. In addition to the Elector of Saxony and the Landgrave of Hesse, Duke Ernst of Lüneburg, Margrave Georg of Brandenburg, and Prince Wolfgang of Anhalt had signed. The dilemma facing the religious question became clear in the protest. People demanded toleration but were not prepared to grant it. They resisted majority decrees in questions of conscience— "in matters relevant to God's honor and the soul's salvation everyone

[4] Ibid., 1299.
[5] Ibid., 1142.
[6] Ibid., 1143.
[7] Ibid., 1299.
[8] Ibid., 1301.
[9] Ibid., 1346–56.

must stand alone before God and give an account"[10]—but appeared to recognize the authority of a general council. They were convinced that they "had the word of God without any doubt, pure, undefiled, clean, and right."[11] Therefore, to grant that the evangelical doctrine would only be tolerated where it had thus far been introduced would amount to "denying . . . our Lord and Saviour Christ and his holy word [not only] tacitly but publicly."[12] On the other hand, only to tolerate the Mass would mean to give the lie to the doctrine of evangelical "preachers which we regard as Christian and reliable." In fact, if "the papal Mass were not against God and his holy word, it must still no longer be retained,"[13] because two kinds of worship in one locality is intolerable and must lead "to disagreeableness, tumult, revolt, and misfortune of every sort" among the common people, particularly when they are serious about God's glory.

Even if neither the Emperor nor King Ferdinand was in a position to implement the Recess of the Diet, the Protestants felt impelled to be concerned for their own protection and to look around for allies. On the very day of the Recess, Electoral Saxony, Hesse, Nürnberg, Strasbourg, and Ulm entered into a secret defensive alliance against eventual attacks. But the plans of Philip of Hesse went still further, envisaging a widespread war alliance against the Habsburg. It was promoted by Zwingli's efforts to expand the "Christian citizenship" into an anti-Habsburg coalition, but the controversies over the Eucharist presented an obstacle. These were taken very seriously by the Wittenberg theologians, to whom a confession of faith was more important than a league. Luther had made clear the chasm between him and Zwingli in his solemn *Grosses Bekenntnis vom Abendmahl Christi* (WA 26, 261–509), and he had rendered an understanding difficult by his violent polemics and even his defamatory tactics. Philip of Hesse endeavored to mediate. At the Diet of Speyer he had successfully prevented the Lutherans from cutting themselves off from the South German cities which inclined to Zwingli's doctrine. Hence the cities had been able to agree to the protest. On 22 April when the league of Protestants came into existence at Speyer and the "Christian Union" between the Catholic cantons of Switzerland and Austria was ratified at Waldshut, the Landgrave wrote to Zwingli that he should attend a meeting with Luther and Melanchthon in order "to reach an agreement [in regard to the Eucharist] on the basis of Holy Scripture." For at the Diet the

---

[10] Ibid., 1277.
[11] Ibid., 1280.
[12] Ibid.
[13] Ibid., 1281.

papists had profited by the lack of union among those "who adhered to the pure word of God" to promote their "villainy" (ZW 10, 108f.). The discussion did not take place until October, for while Zwingli enthusiastically accepted the plan (ZW 10, 117f.), people at Wittenberg had political and theological hesitations.

Zwingli's Eucharistic Doctrine

In the epitome of the First Disputation of Zurich (29 January 1523) Zwingli had rejected the Sacrifice of the Mass in a lengthy explanation, in which he referred to the "once for all" of Hebrews 7:27. The Mass implied a "diminution and defamation" of the one perfect Sacrifice of Christ. It was merely a "memorial" of it and an "assurance of the redemption which Christ achieved for us" (ZW 2, 119, 26). While Zwingli attacked the refusal of communion under the species of wine, he ascribed no decisive importance to it. Anyone who, from ignorance or compulsion, is content with the species of bread receives Christ. Lastly, one does not need the Sacrament at all, for one finds salvation in faith in Christ, even if both species should be denied.[14] The doctrine of transubstantiation was, for Zwingli, a speculation of theologians. "What theologians have concocted in regard to the transubstantiation of wine and bread does not bother me" (ZW 2, 144, 13f.).

He wanted John 6:53–56 understood in faith with reference to John 6:63: "It is the Spirit that gives life; the flesh profits nothing."

> As his flesh or body, which suffered death for us, and his blood, which was shed for us, has redeemed us poor creatures, no more powerful food can come to man's soul than that it surely believe this. For thus his death and the shedding of his blood become the life and joy of the soul [ZW 2, 142, 19–23].

If we believe that Christ's body was done to death and his blood was shed for us in order to redeem us and to reconcile us with God, "our soul is given food and drink with the flesh and blood of Christ" (ZW 2, 143, 15f.).

Zwingli did not yet question the real presence. But it was only an aid to the faith of the uneducated. In order that "the covenant might be more easily grasped" in its essence, Christ gave his body the appearance of food, and hence they should be "assured in faith by a visible action." But just as immersion in baptism is of no use without faith, so too the body of Christ is of no use if we do not entirely abandon ourselves to him as our salvation.

---

[14] ZW 2, 134, 18. Cf. Luther's *De captivitate Babylonica* (WA 6, 507, 15).

For Zwingli the words of institution were as yet no problem. Against a "shameless Dominican" he emphasized:

> "This is my body." Is this not a clear, brief, sure, express word of God? How could God have spoken more briefly or really more exactly? [*ZW* 2, 154, 5ff.] For what can be said more clearly than "This is my body"? [*ZW* 2, 154, 21f.]

Two years later, in the *Commentary on the True and False Religion* (1525), the reformer formally retracted his profession of faith in the real presence. If the progress of the Reformation outside Zurich had contributed to this change and if Zwingli had obtained the theological arguments for his new view from outside, nevertheless it was entirely in keeping with his thought. In his humanist-oriented spiritualism he understood *spiritualis* not as "spiritual," as a reality given in the Holy *Pneuma,* but as "intellectual" in contrast to "bodily and material." And so he saw no possibility of a spiritual sacramental presence of the Sacrifice of the Cross—historically unique—in the Mass, but only that of a "memorial," that is, of a making present in thought, in the awareness of the congregation. The intellectual and the material are mutually exclusive. God is a spirit, and he who wants to rise to him must leave behind all that is visible. Ceremonies have their meaning at most as incentives for the unlettered, as pedagogical means on the perimeter of the "true religion." Only spirit can attain to spirit. Worship is accomplished in "spirit and in truth" (John 4:24). It is unworthy of God when we seek to get into contact with him by material means or even to influence him, and, conversely, assume that he wants to communicate himself to us in material signs. Thus our achieving an understanding of the Incarnation, of the Sacrament, and even of the word to which the Spirit of God is bound is greatly obstructed.

Zwingli says that he had made up his mind on the metaphorical nature of the words of institution even before the appearance of Karlstadt, except that he did not know "which word was the metaphor."[15] This did not dawn on him until two "pious and learned men"—Heine Rhode and Georg Saganus—had brought him the letter from the Netherlander, Cornelis Hoen. "In it I found the precious pearl: that the 'is' is to be understood as 'signifies'" (*ZW* 4, 560, 28).

The connection, gained in conjunction with the treatise on the Eucharist by his fellow countryman, Wessel Gansfort (d. 1489), that the copula "is" in the words of institution must be understood as "signifies," had been communicated by the lawyer, Cornelis Hoen of The Hague, in a letter to rector Heine Rhode at Utrecht. Rhode had taken it to

---

[15] *Reply to Johannes Bugenhagen's Letter,* 23 October 1525 (*ZW* 4, 558–576, p. 560, 21).

Luther at Wittenberg in 1521 but had been repulsed. It was accepted by Oecolampadius and Zwingli, whom he and Georg Saganus sought out in 1523–24.[16] In Hoen's letter Zwingli found a clarification of his notion of the Eucharist and in 1525 he published this work, so significant for him, anonymously. Meanwhile Karlstadt had published five treatises on the Eucharist at Basel at the end of October or the beginning of November 1524. Their crude form made them repulsive. When their content was connected with Zwingli, he had to fear for his reputation. Hence he sought to enlighten his friends by writing a detailed letter on the Lord's Supper in November 1524 to the pastor of Reutlingen, Matthäus Alber, who favored Luther.[17] It was at first circulated in manuscript with a request for secrecy and did not appear in print until March 1525, when "more than 500 of the brethren" (ZW 4, 558, 23) had become acquainted with it. Thus Zwingli's alienation from Karlstadt had become known in the circle of his adherents months before the position he had taken in it against Luther caused disturbances at Wittenberg. But Luther's judgment on Zwingli was clearly made on the basis of oral information. To him Zwingli, like Karlstadt, was a fanatic and a Sacramentarian. Luther wrote on 17 November 1524: "Zwingli of Zurich, together with Leo Jud, in Switzerland holds the same views as Karlstadt."[18] While Zwingli is not named in *Wider die himmlischen Propheten,* he is certainly meant.

Simultaneously with the printing of the letter to Alber appeared Zwingli's great systematic work, *De vera et falsa religione commentarius* (ZW 3, 628–911), which, like Calvin's later *Institutio,* was dedicated to King Francis I. What is by far the longest of the twenty-nine chapters deals with the Eucharist. Here again Zwingli proceeds, not from the words of institution, but from the sixth chapter of Saint John. "Faith is the food that Christ discusses so forcibly in this entire chapter" (ZW 3, 776, 30). He satiates the soul with food and drink so that nothing is ever lacking to it. He who believes in Christ remains in God. "Hence it is a spiritual food" [782, 16] of which Christ is speaking. "If he says, 'The flesh profits nothing' [John 6:63], then human audacity should not dispute about an eating of his flesh" (782, 26ff.). To the objection that we are redeemed from death by Christ's flesh Zwingli replies: "Christ's flesh profits everywhere very much, yes, enormously, but . . . as put to death, not as eaten. Put to death, it saves us from death; eaten, it profits

---

[16] A. Eekhof, *De Avondmaalsbrief van Cornelis Hoen* (Facsimile; The Hague 1917); ZW 4, 512–519. English translation in H. A. Oberman, *Forerunners of the Reformation* (New York 1966), pp. 268–278.

[17] *Ad Matthaeum Alberun de coena domini epistola* (ZW 3, 335–354).

[18] *WA, Br* 3, 373, 11; cf. the letter of 19 July 1525 to Johannes Hess (*WA, Br* 3, 544, 3f.).

absolutely nothing" (*ZW* 3, 782, 30ff.). The flesh that brings salvation is enthroned in heaven at the Father's right hand since the Ascension and cannot at the same time be in the bread.

As already stated, Zwingli did not understand the reference to the special, sacramental, and nonhistorical manner of Christ's presence and of the eating of his flesh and blood. He was able to grasp "spiritual" only as "intellectual" in his body-spirit pattern. For him it made no sense to say: "We indeed eat the true and physical flesh of Christ but in a spiritual manner."[19] Those who speak in this way do not see

> that "to be in a body" and "to be eaten spiritually" are incompatible concepts. Body and spirit are opposed to each other. . . . Hence "to eat material flesh in a spiritual manner" is nothing other than to assert that body is spirit. [387, 6–13]

Faith "does not move in the realm of the material and physical; it has nothing in common with this" (787, 19f.).

The "insipid," "silly," and "dreadful" opinion of a physical eating, proper only "to cannibals," cannot be supported by the words of institution (789). They too must be understood in the light of "the flesh profits nothing." "This means: 'This is my body' must not or cannot possibly be understood of bodily flesh or of the physically perceptible body" (792, 10f.). But the "symbolic sense" is not to be found in the "this," as Karlstadt thought. He did "not take hold of the matter in the passage where the victory was to be achieved" (817, 2). The "hoc" can refer also to a masculine word, to *panis,* and it does not thereby exclude the Catholic interpretation. At stake is the meaning of "est." "For in more than one passage in Scripture this word stands for *significat*" (795, 11f.). The words of the Last Supper are hence to be understood thus: "This, namely, what I present to you for eating, is the symbol of my body, given for you, and this that I now do you should do for the future in memory of me" (798, 37f.).

Like the Jewish Passover, the Lord's Supper is the great memorial feast of the Redemption.[20] Hence it is

> nothing else than a calling to mind: those who firmly believe that they are reconciled with the Father by Christ's death and blood proclaim in the Supper this life-giving death; that is, they consider themselves fortunate and glorify it. It follows that he who meets for this custom or feast in order to recall the Lord's death, that is, to

---

[19] *ZW* 3, 787, 5f.; here Zwingli has in mind arguments of Cardinal Cajetan. Cf. W. Köhler, *Zwingli und Luther* I, 161.

[20] "redemptionis commemoratio, festivitas aut celebritas" (803, 26f.).

proclaim it, testifies by so doing that he wishes to be a member of the one body, that he wishes to be bread. [807, 12–18]

The Eucharist is not a real memorial in the sense that Christ by the action of the Church makes his sacrifice present. It is a recalling of the Sacrifice of the Cross, which continues to belong to the past, and a Sacrament, or "oath of allegiance," a binding testimony to membership in Christ and profession of faith by the community.

Johannes Bugenhagen in August 1525 took a narrow and strict position against Zwingli's Eucharistic doctrine.[21] He was the first member of the Wittenberg circle to express himself. Luther did not make known his reaction until the middle of 1526 in the preface to a translation of the *Syngramma* of Swabian preachers (WA 19, 457–461). Luther and Zwingli then exchanged a series of polemics. Luther began with the *Sermon vom Sakrament des Leibes und Blutes Christi wider die Schwarmgeister* (1526). There followed *Dass diese Worte, "das ist mein Leib" noch feststehen* (1527) and *Das grosse Bekenntnis vom Abendmahl* (1528). Zwingli defended himself with *Amica Exegesis* (1527), *Freundliche Verglimpfung über die Predigt Luthers wider die Schwärmer* (1527), *Dass diese Worte, "das ist mein Leib," ewig den alten Sinn haben werden* (1527), and *Über Luthers Buch, "Bekenntnis" genannt* (1528). Their opposition became deeper in the course of this controversy. Mutual insults further envenomed the atmosphere. Thus it was no easy undertaking when Philip of Hesse tried to bring the two reformers to the discussion table; it could only be even more difficult to move them to a common profession, which was regarded by the Wittenberg theologians as the preliminary to forming a league.

The Marburg Religious Colloquy

On 1 July Philip of Hesse sent the official invitation to Luther and Melanchthon, Zwingli, Oecolampadius, Andreas Osiander at Nürnberg, and Jakob Sturm to convene at Marburg on 30 September 1529. Sturm was to bring along Bucer and another preacher from Strasbourg, but only as observers. Only the two Swiss and the two from Wittenberg were to engage in the disputation.

Luther and Melanchthon came armed with a confession in seventeen articles, comprising their entire faith. Persons had met at Torgau at the middle of September by command of the Elector of Saxony to draw up this creed. From the use later made of them, they were called the "Articles of Schwabach."

After a friendly greeting on 30 September, on Friday, 1 October,

[21] *Contra errorem de sacramento corporis et sanguinis domini nostri Iesu Christi epistola.*

Luther and Oecolampadius and Zwingli and Melanchthon received a mandate for a discussion, each group in private. The next day at six in the morning the decisive discussion began in a private room next to the Landgrave Philip of Hesse's bedroom in the presence of a select group of at most fifty to sixty persons. Luther wanted to start from the beginning and submitted seven points in which the Swiss differed from him: the Trinity, the doctrine of the two natures, original sin, baptism, justification, the doctrine of the function of the word, and purgatory. So long as they were not agreed on these, he said, "they would discuss in vain the true value of the Eucharist."[22] The Swiss objected that they had met because of the Eucharist. Luther gave in and at the outset wrote with chalk the words "This is my body" on the table and covered them with the velvet table cloth. He thereby defined the thesis of the disputation but at the same time he stressed that he "rejected carnal proofs and geometrical arguments entirely" and demanded submission to the word of Scripture. On Saturday and Sunday, 2 and 3 October, the debate went on from morning to evening. Melanchthon intervened only once in the conversation. Oecolampadius submitted arguments from Scripture and the Fathers, whereas Zwingli discussed the dogmatic questions. The presence of the Landgrave served to temper the tone of the dispute. Nevertheless, sharp outbreaks were not lacking.

Luther admitted that in Scripture there were figures of speech and metaphors but said that the presence of such had to be proved for each particular case. In referring to the Spirit that gives life, he said, Christ did not intend to exclude physical eating but only to enlighten the people of Capharnaum "that he was not eaten, like bread and flesh, in a dish, or like roast pork."[23]

Luther referred again and again to Holy Scripture. "Those words, 'this is my body,' hold me captive." "Do away with the text for me and I am satisfied."

> If he would command me to eat dung, I would do it, since I well know: it is good for me. The servant does not meditate on his master's will. One must close one's eyes. . . . Do away with the text for me and I am satisfied.[24]

The humanist Zwingli, on the other hand, stressed that antitheses are for the "flesh and spirit."

---

[22] W. Köhler, *Das Marburger Religionsgespräch 1529. Versuch einer Rekonstruktion* (Leipzig 1929), pp. 54, 8.
[23] Ibid., p. 11.
[24] Ibid., p. 13.

God is true and the light. He does not lead us into darkness. Hence he does not say "This is my body" essentially, really, corporeally. . . . The soul is spirit, the soul does not eat flesh, spirit eats spirit.[25]

Luther, on the contrary, would even eat "rotten apples" spiritually, if God offered them to him. "For wherever the word of God is, there is spiritual use." But it does not exclude the material. "The mouth receives Christ's body, the soul believes the words while it is eating the body."

At issue was not only the Eucharist but the means of grace in general. According to Zwingli, the material cannot communicate salvation. God operates directly. He must not be removed to external things. This is as true of the Sacrament as of the word, but it does not stop before the humanity of Christ. Oecolampadius urged Luther: "Do not hang so much to Christ's humanity and flesh, but raise your mind to Christ's divinity!" Luther retorted: "I know no God except him who became man, and I do not want any other."[26]

Not a single truth of faith was disputed, but the basic structure was different. Luther perceived this and expressed it to Bucer: "Our mind and your mind do not make sense to each other, but it is obvious that we do not have the same mind."[27]

It was all the more amazing that a far-reaching agreement was arrived at in the end. At the urging of Philip of Hesse, Luther on 4 October assembled fifteen articles for a concord. The "Articles of Schwabach" served as his model. However, he treated the Eucharist last. Zwingli and Oecolampadius obtained several changes in form. Agreement was reached on the first fourteen of these basically Lutheran articles and on five points of the fifteenth. There was unanimity against the Catholic doctrine and practice in the demand for the Eucharist under both species, in the rejection of the Sacrifice of the Mass, and in the statements that "the Sacrament of the altar is a Sacrament of the true body and blood of Jesus Christ," that there is question "chiefly" of a spiritual nourishment, and that the Eucharist was instituted in order to move weak consciences to faith.

At the conclusion they say: "Although we are not in agreement this time whether the true body and blood of Christ are physically in the bread and wine, still each should show Christian charity to the other in so far as each conscience can permit, and both parties diligently ask

[25] Ibid., p. 15.
[26] Ibid., p. 27.
[27] Ibid., p. 129.

Almighty God to give us the right understanding through his Spirit."[28] Zwingli's signing the essentially Lutheran Articles of Marburg has been presented as a concession from political considerations. Each side probably interpreted the articles in its own sense and was mistaken as to the unanimity. In the expression "Sacrament of the true body and blood" the Lutherans emphasized "true body," whereas Zwingli stressed "Sacrament," understanding Sacrament as a mere sign.[29] Thus the Articles of Marburg would be "an apparent concord in the sense that each of the partners in the colloquy only signed what he had already known until then and erroneously assumed that the other signed the same as he did."[30] And hence disillusion did not fail to appear. Each side quickly charged the other with breach of faith, and the polemics flared up again. On 16 October, scarcely two weeks after the colloquy at Marburg, Electoral Saxony and Brandenburg again tried at Schwabach to gain the South German cities and Hesse for the "Schwabach Articles," and to separate them from the Swiss. They were again unsuccessful.

Zwingli's Death and Succession

Zwingli and Philip of Hesse pursued further their anti-Habsburg league policy in Europe. Strasbourg entered the citizenship on 12 January 1530. The Landgrave allied with Zurich on 30 July. On 18 November there came into being a "Christian understanding" between him, Zurich, Basel, and Strasbourg, "only for defense and safety" in the event of an attack "because of God's word." The Protestant inclinations of Margaret of Navarre, sister of the French King, awakened in Zwingli the hope of winning France, not only for his political plans, but also for his faith. In the early summer of 1531 he composed a second statement of belief, *Fidei expositio,* for Francis I.

The reformer's fate was decided, however, not by his worldwide coalition policy, but by the domestic confrontation in Switzerland. The conflict was due to the "common governments" of Protestant and Catholic cantons, whose officials rotated after agreed terms and while in power tried to impose their creed, while the other party complained of moral constraint. "Zwingli saw a violation of the Peace of Kappel in every proceeding of the five cantons against an evangelical canton, but was unwilling to concede freedom of conscience to the Catholics in his

---

[28] *BSLK,* p. 62.
[29] His marginal gloss on this sentence reads: "Sacramentum signum est veri corporis, etc. Non est igitur verum corpus." Quoted from S. Hausammann, "Die Marburger Artikel—eine echte Konkordie?" *ZKG* 77 (1966), 288–321, p. 318.
[30] Ibid., p. 291.

sphere."[31] He urged war, and this time the religious split was to win out over the ties of nationality. True, Zurich was still alone when it demanded war at the *Tagsatzung* on 24 April 1531. When the city continued to demand, it was constrained to be content with a blockade instead of war. On 28 May an embargo on provisions was laid on the five Catholic cantons, which depended on the importing of corn from Alsace and South Germany. They mobilized for defense in order to break the oppressive ring and on 9 October declared war. In Zurich leadership was lacking. Not until the five cantons assumed the offensive on 11 October did mobilization get under way, and then only seven hundred men, instead of twelve thousand, took the field. Finally, two thousand five hundred men of Zurich faced an enemy eight thousand men strong. On 11 October 1531 Zwingli fell as a soldier at Kappel in a war he had passionately wanted. In the Second Peace of Kappel[32] Zurich had to renounce its policy of foreign alliance. Thereby the progress of the Reformation in German Switzerland was slowed down.

On 9 December 1531, the Zurich city council named Heinrich Bullinger (1504–75) as Zwingli's successor. The new *antistes* and all pastors were for the future to confine themselves to the proclaiming of the word of God and not mix in "worldly matters." Bullinger, born on 18 July 1504 at Bremgarten, the son of the local dean and pastor, was twenty-seven when he took up Zwingli's legacy. He succeeded in mastering the crisis relatively quickly and in stabilizing the Church organization in Zurich. In 1532 he created the Zurich Synodal Order. In 1536 he composed the first Swiss Confession for union discussions with the Germans, which collapsed. However, he did achieve agreement with Calvin on the Eucharistic question in the *Consensus Tigurinus* of 1549. He thereby put Zwinglianism, which he could not bring to worldwide recognition, at least into intimate connection with powerfully rising Calvinism.

[31] W. Köhler, *Huldrych Zwingli,* p. 248.
[32] Text in E. Walder, *Religionsvergleiche des 16. Jahrhunderts* I (Bern, 2nd ed. 1960), 5–14.

CHAPTER 22

The Imperial Diet of Augsburg

When, after he had made peace with France and with Pope Clement VII, Italy had become somewhat calm, Emperor Charles V was able to think of devoting himself to German affairs. It was important to restore unity in faith and to assemble the political forces for defense against the Turkish peril in the East. Influenced by the Erasmians, his chancellor Gattinara at their head, the Emperor was optimistic in regard to an agreement with the Protestant estates. He counted especially on the effect of the personal impression of his imperial dignity and power. Accordingly, the proclamation of the Diet for 8 April 1530, which went out even before the imperial coronation at Bologna on 21 January, was drawn up in very conciliatory and friendly language. It did proceed from the Edict of Worms but sought a new start of discussion. The Diet was to take measures for defense against the danger from the Turks. Furthermore, it was to discuss the method of proceeding in regard to "the differences and schism . . . in the holy faith and the Christian religion." For the sake of unity people should refrain from all discord, leave "past errors" to God, and try hard to listen to the opinion of the other side and to understand it. Whatever "on both sides has not been correctly explained and done" should be ignored. It is important for "all to accept and hold one single and true religion." and as "all are and fight under one Christ," so also should "all live in one community of the Church and unity."[1]

Among the Protestant estates Luther's prince, the Elector Johann of Saxony, took the religious question very seriously but was not prepared, without more ado, to go along with Protestants "of another mind," that is, the Zwinglians. On the other hand, he was intent upon reconciliation with the Emperor, from whom he awaited investiture with the electoral dignity. From this point of view he strove to present the religious differences of opinion as unessential and was inclined to regard an understanding in the question of religion as possible through the Emperor.

The Landgrave Philip, on the other hand, was much more political in his thinking. He feared that a successful Diet would mean a weakening of his anti-Habsburg policy. Consequently, he subordinated the Protestant movement and in its interest he worked for an adjustment of the doctrinal differences within Protestantism and for a coalition against the Emperor. He would have preferred most of all to remain away from the Diet, for he feared a condemnation of the Swiss. He therefore denied the competence of Emperor and Diet in the religious question and hoped, by recourse to a council, to gain time for his plans.[2]

Like the Emperor, the Papal Legate Lorenzo Campeggio underesti-

---

[1] K. E. Förstemann, *Urkundenbuch zu der Geschichte des Reichstages zu Augsburg im Jahre 1530* I (1833; reprinted, Osnabrück 1966), 7f.

[2] Cf. the instruction for the Hessian envoys (W. Gussmann, *Quellen und Forschungen* I, 1, 326ff.).

mated the intransigence of the Protestant estates. While holding basically to the Edict of Worms, he held out hopes for the effort to gain the princes by concessions or to intimidate the cities. He alone counted seriously on the use of force, even if as the *ultima ratio.*

The Diet met much later than planned. The Wittenberg theologians exploited the time thus allowed them in order to formulate their own religious standpoint, both to be ready for a discussion and to arm themselves against blame. Thus originated the *Confessio Augustana.*

Construction of the Creed

The drawing up of creeds within Protestantism was motivated by confrontations of Lutherans with the fanatics and the Zwinglians and also by the self-assurance vis-à-vis the Imperial Governing Council, which was pressing for an implementation of the Edict of Worms. As early as 1528 Luther had added a "confession" to his great work, *Vom Abendmahl Christi* against Zwingli. It begins:

> Because I see that the longer there are mobs and error, the more there will be no stopping of Satan's raging and raving, so that no more, during my lifetime or after my death, will some have anything to do with me and would like to show up my writings as false in order to confirm their errors, as the Sacramentarian and Anabaptist fanatics are beginning to do, I wish therefore, by this work, to confess my faith, bit by bit, before God and the whole world. [WA 26, 499]

In this "confession" Luther further expounded the doctrine of sin, redemption, justification, and Christian perfection (Article 2). In Article 3 he discussed in detail the doctrine of the Church and the Sacraments and sharply rejected the abuses of fanatics and papists.

The seventeen "Articles of Schwabach" go back to this document. They were the first confession to which a group of Lutherans—Electoral Saxony, Brandenburg-Ansbach, and Nürnberg—adhered at Schwabach in Franconia on 16 October 1529 and which they submitted to the envoys of the South German cities. On them the league with the South German "Sacramentarians" was wrecked. The Wittenberg theologians and Electoral Saxony regarded these Schwabach Articles as their confession. Shortly after the opening of the Diet of Augsburg they appeared in print in that city and, together with those of Torgau, served as model in topics and construction for the Augsburg Confession. They were directed, not least of all, against the Zwinglians, who understood them thus. Jakob Sturm (1489–1553) of Strasbourg wrote to Zwingli on 31

May 1539: "I am sending also the articles which Luther earlier tried to force down our throats" (CR 97, 602, 8).

To prepare for the Diet of Augsburg on 14 March 1530, the Elector Johann of Saxony summoned the Wittenberg theologians to Torgau. Here on 27 March they discussed an opinion which has gone into history as the "Articles of Torgau" and which was taken along to Augsburg as working material. In an effort to demonstrate to the Emperor the purity of ecclesiastical usages in Electoral Saxony, doctrines were less discussed in the articles than were the controverted ceremonies. For "now dissension springs especially from several abuses, which were introduced by men into doctrine and laws."[3]

At Augsburg the Lutherans saw themselves facing two fronts and hence in the presence of a twofold task. On the one side they had to repulse the fanatics and Zwingli or keep aloof from them; on the other side they had to convince the Emperor that nothing else was represented by them than the old, pure doctrine of the Catholic Church, as handed down by the Fathers and that they had nothing in common with Anabaptists and Sacramentarians and recognized authority. These two tendencies lay at the basis of the Augsburg Confession. The Catholics had also prepared for the confrontation at the Diet. Probably because of a request by the Bavarian Dukes to the University of Ingolstadt, Johannes Eck had set to work to compile for the Emperor a list of the errors of the Protestants—Lutherans, Zwinglians, and fanatics. Without further elaboration he added up "404 Articles for the Diet of Augsburg."

In these he presented the Bull "Exsurge Domine" (Articles 1–41), the conclusions of the Disputations of Leipzig (Articles 42–54) and Baden (Articles 55–64), and heresies compiled expressly for the Diet. These, Eck said, were only a selection from three thousand heretical statements in his possession. What mattered to Eck was to unmask the Protestants as heretics. The question arises to what extent he was concerned for the clarity that was necessary and, in the final analysis, salutary in view of the far-reaching doctrinal confusion or whether he did not commit the Protestants to error and obstruct the road to an understanding. In any event, the method by which he split up the truth into single sentences and used these without regard for the context and the concerns of the other side, like arguments in a criminal trial, was inadequate for the situation.

On his arrival at Augsburg Melanchthon encountered Eck's 404 Articles and sensed the necessity of formulating as one harmonious confes-

---

[3] K. E. Förstemann, op. cit., I, 69; T. Kolde, *Die Augsburger Konfession* (Gotha 1896), p. 128.

sion the doctrinal and ritual material that he had brought along. Hence he drew the doctrinal Articles of Schwabach and the ceremonial Articles of Torgau into an *apologia,* first conceived only in the name of Electoral Saxony. In the version of the end of May the first article began: "In the Electoral Principality of Saxony it is unanimously taught."[4]

The draft was sent to Luther on 11 May for his objections. As an outlaw he could not appear at the Diet and remained behind at the castle of Coburg. On 15 May he declared his agreement with the draft. He said he was unable to improve on anything in it. He wrote to Johann of Saxony that that "would not be fitting, since I cannot step so easily and lightly" (*WA, Br* 5, 319, 7). The question arises whether Luther on this basis of "stepping lightly" was criticizing a falsification or watering down of the reform problem by Melanchthon or whether he only intended, as on numerous other occasions,[5] to call attention to Melanchthon's pleasing and courteous style. In any event, he would have been unable, in view of his prince's hopes for agreement at Augsburg, to allow himself any language that was too sharp. At first he expressed himself in regard to the *Confessio Augustana* in a thoroughly positive sense.[6] His later criticism was, to be sure, not related to the doctrine of justification and other central articles of faith. But Luther gave the lie to Melanchthon's "untrue sentence."[7] At the conclusion of the first part, "Tota dissensio est de paucis quibusdam abusibus," when on 21 July 1530 he wrote to Justus Jonas that the *Confessio Augustana* conceals the articles on purgatory, the veneration of saints, and, above all, the Pope as anti-Christ. At the same time he again spoke of "stepping lightly."[8]

The *Confessio Augustana* includes twenty-eight articles and is divided into two parts. Part I (Articles 1–21) deals with the "Articuli fidei praecipui." Part II treats of abuses that later crept in but had now been abolished or replaced by other institutions, such as communion under both species (22), marriage of priests (23), the Mass (24), confession (25), regulations in regard to foods (26), religious vows (27), and epis-

---

[4] T. Kolde (ed.), *Die älteste Redaktion der Augsburger Konfession mit Melanchthons Einleitung* (Gütersloh 1906), p. 11.

[5] Cf. *WA* 30, II, 68; *WA, Tr* 3, 460, no. 3619.

[6] 3 July 1530: "placet vehementer" (*WA, Br* 5, 435, 4); 6 July: "publice est praedicatus confessione pulcherrima" (ibid., 442, 14); 9 July: "gloriosa confessione declamatus est" (ibid., 458, 13). If he wrote on 29 June "Pro mea persona plus satis cessum est in ista Apologia" (ibid., 405, 19), this must be understood as the reply to Melanchthon's inquiry as to how far the opponent must still be given in to.

[7] H. Bornkamm, *RGG* I, 735.

[8] "Scilicat Satan adhuc vivit, et bene sensit Apologiam vestram leise treten et dissimulasse articulos de purgatorio, de sanctorum cultu, et maxime de antichristo Papa" (*WA, Br* 5, 496, 1–3).

copal power (28). Other "abuses," such as indulgences, pilgrimages, and the abuse of excommunication, are only mentioned at the end. For ecclesiastical unity, it is stressed, it suffices to agree on the central points of the teaching of the Gospel, as these are professed in Part I. Variety can prevail in the ecclesiastical usages discussed in Part II. From diplomatic motives and genuine concern for the unity of the Church Melanchthon had enjoined great discretion vis-à-vis the Catholic side. But he set the limits all the more strictly "toward the left," the Swiss and the fanatics.

Consequently the South German cities—Strasbourg, Constance, Lindau, and Memmingen—saw themselves forced, because of the controverted doctrine of the Eucharist, to submit a confession of their own, the *Tetrapolitana,* on 9 July. Zwingli had not come to Augsburg but had sent there his confessional work, the *Fidei ratio ad Carolum imperatorem.* It was handed to the Emperor on 8 July.

The Course of the Diet

The Emperor did not reach Augsburg until 15 June. Before this Johann of Saxony had exerted himself to arrive at an agreement with the Emperor on the religious question by means of private negotiations without Philip of Hesse. He had sent several embassies to him at Innsbruck and had declared that he would visit him there but was met with a refusal and with disapproval that he had allowed his pastors to preach Lutheranism at Augsburg.

The Emperor's negative attitude moved the Elector to exert himself all the more for a common confession of Protestants.

On the very day of the solemn entry into Augsburg[9] tension occurred because the Emperor wanted the Protestant princes to take part on the next day in the Corpus Christi procession and forbade Lutheran preaching. The princes stayed away from the procession. A compromise was reached in the question of preaching in so far as it was entirely forbidden to disturb the discussions by polemics from the pulpit. On both sides there was a readiness for an understanding. Even before the opening of the Diet on 20 June there were talks between Melanchthon and the Emperor's secretary, Alfonso Valdes.[10] In these Melanchthon defended the view that the Lutheran affair was not so misguided as the Emperor had been made to believe; the split, he said, had to do merely

---

[9] Cf. the description in Valentin von Tetleben, *Protokoll des Augsburger Reichstages,* edited by H. Grundmann (Göttingen 1958), pp. 59ff.

[10] G. Müller, "Um die Einheit der Kirche. Zu den Verhandlungen über den Laienkelch während des Augsburger Reichstages 1530," *Reformata Reformanda* I, 395ff.

with communion under both species, the marriage of priests, and private Masses (CR, II, 122).

The Papal Legate Campeggio did not avoid the efforts for an arrangement. In his report of 26 June he apparently granted the prospect of union negotiations. On the lay chalice, the marriage of priests, and the changing of the Canon of the Mass he referred to a council as the demand of the Protestants. In return, he said, they were prepared to yield in the question of purgatory, episcopal jurisdiction, and much else.[11]

The readiness for peace found expression in the Protestants' participation in the opening Mass on 20 June. In regard to the order of business they obtained a change in the agenda whereby the discussion of the religious question should precede that of aid against the Turks. But they did not succeed in getting the Catholics to submit their viewpoint in writing since they were unwilling to be pushed into the role of a religious faction and to cooperate in turning the Diet into something of a national council. The Catholics called for a committee of twelve spiritual and secular princes which should receive the Protestants' confession and report to the Emperor. To him, as *advocatus* and supreme protector of the Christian faith, should be left the final decision. From anxiety that the clear Catholic majority would carry its confession in the voting there arose among the Protestants the plan to have the *Confessio* read publicly.

Meanwhile, other Protestant estates had adhered to the *Confessio.* In addition to Johann of Saxony, it was signed by the Margrave Georg of Brandenburg-Ansbach, Dukes Ernst and Francis of Braunschweig-Lüneburg, Prince Wolfgang of Anhalt, the Free Cities of Nürnberg and Reutlingen, and finally the Landgrave Philip of Hesse. The last named failed to carry the modification of the article on the Eucharist in the Zwinglian sense, but he did succeed in substituting for the foreword, drawn up by Melanchthon as an appeal to the Emperor's good will, one written by Chancellor Bruck of Electoral Saxony. In this the legal standpoint was more strongly emphasized and the appeal to a council, expressed at Speyer in 1519 in the event of the failure of agreement, was renewed. The German text was read on 25 June by the Saxon chancellor, Christian Beyer.

While the Catholic theologians were working on a refutation of the *Confessio Augustana,* Melanchthon proceeded further along the path of negotiation. On 4 July he implored Campeggio to accord peace to the Protestants.

---

[11] *NBD* 1. Abt., 1. ErgBd, 1530–31, ed. G. Müller (Tübingen 1963), 70.

He said there was no reason for the use of force. We have no dogma that deviates from the Roman Church. . . . We are ready to obey the Roman Church if, in the mildness she has exercised in regard to all peoples, she overlooks or tolerates trifles that we can no longer change, even if we wished to. . . . Moreover, we most devotedly honor the authority of the Roman Pontiff and the entire Church leadership. [CR 2, 170]

In this "infamous letter" has been seen "a denial of the Gospel."[12] Be that as it may, it proves Melanchthon's far-reaching desire for peace. In retrospect it can be said that he made the dogmatic differences unimportant. In any event, the legate Campeggio agreed to the intervention and on 5 July sent for Melanchthon. In a testimonial requested from him, Melanchthon asked only for the lay chalice and the marriage of priests; he was willing to retain public Masses and hoped that, after the restoration of episcopal authority, the remaining questions could be regulated.[13] In a letter of 7 July to Campeggio, or rather to his secretary, Melanchthon was so accommodating that he asked only for toleration of the lay chalice and the marriage of priests until the council should meet and held out the prospect of eliminating the difficulties relevant to the Mass and of restoring episcopal authority. Meanwhile the legate had probably got a glimpse of the first draft of the *Confutatio,* in which the profound doctrinal differences were made clear. He now declined any further private negotiations, for, he said, the questions affect the whole nation and, in fact, all of Christendom.

The *Confutatio*

In view of the tendency of the *Confessio Augustana* to push doctrinal differences into the background, there loomed for the Catholic reply the question whether only the questions posed by the Protestants' confession should be discussed or whether other reform writings should be considered and the controverted points should be mentioned and proved heretical by a substantiated exposition of Catholic doctrine. The legate Campeggio defended this second opinion against the Emperor. Charles V appointed a commission of twenty theologians, including Eck, Cochläus, and Fabri, but it worked too ponderously. Hence the task of composing a Catholic reply was turned over to Eck, who could have recourse to his *Enchiridion,* his "404 Articles," and other works. The quickly finished first version was debated in the commission of

---

[12] J. von Walter, "Der Reichstag zu Augsburg," *LuJ* 12 (1930), 68.
[13] *CR* 2, 246ff.; according to G. Müller, "Um die Einheit der Kirche," loc. cit., p. 402, footnote 5, not of 8 August but of 5 July 1530.

theologians, approved by the legate, and submitted to the Emperor on 12 July as *Catholica et quasi extemporalis Responsio.* He rejected it as too long and too polemical. Cochläus and Arnold Haldrein of Cologne sought to comply with his intentions in their *Brevis ad singula puncta Confessionis . . . responsio.* But on 22 July the Emperor commissioned the drawing up of a *Confutatio* which was to be issued in his name. The *Catholica Responsio* was thereupon reduced to one-third its size by Eck, its tone was softened, and its content was restricted to what appeared in the *Confessio Augustana.* After repeated examination, reduction, completion, and correction it was read in German to the imperial estates on 3 August, but was not handed to the Protestants.[14] That this was a testimonial of theologians had become a viewpoint of the Emperor, which was shared by electors, princes, and cities. The label *Responsio Pontificia* is thus misleading. The *Confutatio* sought to argue on the basis of Scripture and provided for justified criticism. In itself it is an important witness of the confessional discussion but not a complete reply to the controverted questions, because the *Confessio Augustana* was not a full statement of the Protestant idea. Its effect was jeopardized from the outset because the willingness for an understanding, especially on the part of the princes, was not so great as it seemed to be in the assertions and the real possibility of peace was less than the Emperor assumed. He held that the *Confutatio* had refuted the *Augustana* and expected submission without further discussion. Thus, when the Protestants declared that they did not feel convinced by the *Confutatio,* the effort to clarify the doctrinal questions by means of an imperial award collapsed. The Emperor could hardly implement his threat at the end of the *Confutatio* to do his duty as *advocatus* and protector of the Church in the event that the Protestants rejected it, for the Turkish peril did not permit the use of force.

The prospect of settling the religious quarrel by a council was now worse than ever. The letter in which Charles V on 14 July, with reference to the talks at Bologna, had asked the Pope for an immediate announcement of a general council was answered by Clement VII on 31 July with a "yes" that was so involved in conditions that it amounted to a "no." The Curia seemed more prepared to make concessions to the Protestants than to convoke the so greatly feared council. In the circumstances the Emperor again approved negotiations for a compromise. These took place from 16 to 21 August in a Committee of Fourteen, to which each of the parties sent two princes, two canonists, and three theologians. The negotiations foundered on the very question of the lay

---

[14] Latin and German text in *CR* 27, 81–228; T. Kolde, *Die Augsburger Konfession,* pp. 140–169; Mirbt . . .

chalice on which till now an arrangement had been regarded as attainable. The Protestants were unwilling to be content with a mere toleration of the lay chalice and of the marriage of priests. Furthermore, the theological arguments had not been decisive for a long time, even if they were still in the foreground. Nontheological factors, especially political interests, became very prominent. Thus the Protestant estates were often less ready for an understanding than were the theologians. They, and in particular the Free Cities, were decidedly opposed to a restoring of episcopal jurisdiction, which for them was intimately bound up with the restoration of Church property. On 29 August 1530 Melanchthon wrote to Luther:

> We incur great blame from our people because we give jurisdiction back to the bishops. For the rabble, which is used to freedom and has shaken off the yoke of the bishops, is unwilling to assume that old burden again, the Free Cities in particular hate that authority. They are not concerned about doctrine and religion but only about power and liberty.[15]

Even a committee reduced to six members—one jurist and two theologians from each side—did not achieve the goal. It broke up on 30 August without having come to an agreement in regard to the lay chalice, the Canon of the Mass, the marriage of priests, Church property, and religious vows. And so the negotiations were wrecked on "abuses." More profound differences, especially in the doctrine of the Church, certainly underlay these. "They are termed abuses, which is not the only abuse," wrote Johannes Cochläus in his judgment of the *Confessio Augustana*.[16] But this does not alter the fact that agreement was achieved concerning the doctrinal articles.[17] It is all the more tragic that the *de facto* wrecking of the negotiations determined further developments, rather than this unanimity. For in the confrontations in the succeeding years it was not the agreement arrived at that was the starting point for discussion. Instead, both sides again had recourse to the polemics of 1517–1525.

---

[15] *CR* 2, 328; cf. the letters to Veit Dietrich (*CR* 2, 328) and to Joachim Camerarius (*CR* 2, 329 and 324). Not weakness but anxiety because of a "horribilis confusio dogmatum et infinita Ecclesiarum dissipatio" induced Melanchthon to stand up for the jurisdiction of the bishops. He wrote in October, after the collapse of the negotiations: "Episcopos praestare convenit, ut propagetur ad posteros pura Evangelii doctrina, hoc praecipue postulatur ab isto ordine" (*CR* 2, 433).

[16] *Summarium der kaiserlichen Antwort auff nechstgehalten Reichstag* (Dresden 1531), printed in E. J. Cyprian, *Historia der Augspurgischen Confession* (Gotha 1730), pp. 196–201; quotation on p. 199.

[17] Cf. Johannes Eck's report to Campeggio of 22–23 August 1530, in G. Müller, "Joh. Eck und die Confessio Augustana," *QFIAB* 38 (1958), 239.

On 22 September the draft of the Recess of the Diet, in so far as it touched the religious questions, was submitted to the estates.[18] The Protestants rejected it and sought to present to the Emperor the *Apologia* which Melanchthon had meanwhile composed against the assertion that the *Confessio Augustana* was refuted by Scripture. The Emperor declined to accept it. The Elector of Saxony left Augsburg the next day, and many Protestant estates gradually followed his example. Thus, as at Worms, the Recess of the Diet[19] was issued on 19 November in the absence of most of the Lutheran estates. In order to maintain peace and unity for the good of the Empire the adherents of the *Confessio Augustana* were given time for reflection in regard to the "unsettled articles" until 15 April 1531 (para. 1). Until then they must not introduce other novelties or hinder the practice of the old religion (para. 3). They were to cooperate in prosecuting Sacramentarians and Anabaptists (para. 4). Within six months "a common Christian council" was to be proclaimed "for Christian reformation" and to be held within a year thereafter (para. 5). Monastic and ecclesiastical property that had been taken by force was to be restored. The Emperor, as supreme *advocatus* of Christendom, and the "obedient electors, princes, and estates" had decided on the implementation of the Edict of Worms and desired "to allow no change [before] a decision of the next general council" (para. 10). The old ecclesiastical organization was placed under the protection of the territorial peace (para. 65), and the Imperial Supreme Court, then reorganized at Augsburg, was to proceed against the disobedient (para. 67). Thereby the Protestants incurred the danger of being prosecuted as breakers of the peace. But the very concession of a half-year's moratorium showed how impracticable were the terms of the Recess, severe though they might be.

The *Apologia*

The *Confutatio* had been read to the Protestants on 3 August but not given to them. Hence when, in view of the collapse of the negotiations for a compromise, Melanchthon set about composing a rejoinder, he could rely only on his memory and notes. The Saxon chancellor, Bruck, tried without success to present to the Emperor at Augsburg the resulting *Defense of the Augsburg Confession*. This refusal gave Melanchthon the opportunity to revise his work thoroughly and to expand it. Indirectly, by way of Nürnberg (*CR* 2, 415), he finally came into possession of a

---

[18] K. E. Förstemann, op. cit., II, 474–481.
[19] E. A. Koch, *Neue und vollständigere Sammlung der Reichstagsabschiede* II (Frankfurt 1797), 306–332.

copy of the *Confutatio* and could use it for the expanded version of the *Apologia,* which appeared in print in April–May 1531. In the fall of that year Justus Jonas prepared a German translation, or, more exactly, a free rendition in German. The *Apologia* was at first the private work of Melanchthon. It was only by virtue of its being signed at Schmalkalden in 1537 that it became a confession alongside the *Augustana.* It stressed the doctrinal differences more sharply than did the *Augustana.* Article 4 on justification occupies almost one-third of the entire work. This "important monograph of the reform doctrine of justification," as H. Bornkamm calls it, furthered the one-sided forensic understanding of justification as a mere judgment. It is also said that justification signifies rebirth and new life[20] and gives us the Holy Spirit,[21] and that we become God's children and coheirs of Christ.[22] But what was decisive for the further development and the doctrine of justification of Lutheran orthodoxy were not these statements, but others, which speak of a forensic, merely putative declaration of righteousness.[23] The

> expression of Melanchthon in the *Apologia,* that justification also means making righteous, is too singular; it has had only inadequate consequences in the totality of the reform message. We may understand psychologically and in view of the situation of struggle that the Catholic doctrine of works was rejected. But it should not have been rejected without professing the notion of reward, which is biblical, and attributing to this the proper space.[24]

It was more pernicious that Melanchthon, instead of accepting the authors of the *Confutatio* as real partners in dialogue and confronting them with their doctrine of justification, attacked the "scholastici," of whom there were none in 1530, and combated doctrines which were represented by the nominalists of the late Middle Ages but not by the contemporary Catholic theologians.[25]

The *Confutatio* had expressly condemned the teaching that man can merit eternal life by his own powers without grace and emphasized that "every good gift and every perfect gift comes from above" (James 1:17) and that "all our sufficiency [is] from God" (2 Cor. 3:5). But the

---

[20] IV, 64, 65, 116, 125, 132.

[21] IV, 116, 132.

[22] IV, 195.

[23] IV, 307, 72, 252. Cf. F. Loofs *ThStK* 57, I (1884), 613–688, and the later literature cited in *BSLK* 158, footnote 2; H. Fagerberg, *Die Theologie der lutherischen Bekenntnisschriften von 1529 bis 1537* (Göttingen 1965), pp. 156–161.

[24] H. Asmussen, *Warum noch lutherische Kirche?* (Stuttgart 1949), p. 80.

[25] Cf. IV, 9, 17, 27, 63, 79, 81, 162, 289, and *passim.*

Apologia did not start with this or with the far-reaching agreement in regard to the doctrine of justification that had been established at Augsburg.

CHAPTER 23

The Politicizing of the Reform Movement to the Collapse of the Religious Colloquies

The Diet of Augsburg had exposed the disunity of the Protestants since three different confessions had been laid before the Emperor. In this connection the adherents of the *Confessio Augustana* had striven to hold clearly aloof from the Swiss and the South German cities. But the Recess of the Diet also threatened them with the Supreme Court as breakers of the peace, and so a league for common military resistance suggested itself. In this way the reform movement was further politicized. As early as 23 September, the day after the reading of the draft of the Recess, the Elector Johann of Saxony brought before the representatives of the South German cities at Augsburg his plan for a league "of all Protestant princes and Free Cities."

Right of Resistance

With the coming together for armed defense the question of the right of resistance became acute. Discussions on the subject took place at Torgau in October 1530 between the theologians, led by Luther, and the Elector's legal advisers. Till now Luther had conceded to the princes as individuals only passive disobedience. They might, in fact they had to, deny the Emperor their military service in a religious war against the Lutheran estates.[1] Now the reformer was receptive to the argument of the jurists, who allowed the Imperial Estates a right of armed defense against a violation of the constitution by the Emperor. It was not the business of theologians, he said, to lecture the jurists in regard to their interpretation of the law of the Empire, "for the Gospel does not teach contrary to secular law" (*WA, Br* 5, 662, 7). The Elector Johann was acting as a political person and not as a Christian, he wrote in January 1531 to Nürnberg, where, under the leadership of Lazarus Spengler, people were further questioning a right of resistance to the Emperor. His being a Christian gave the prince no title to armed action

---

[1] *WA* 30, II, 197, 7–10 (military sermon against the Turks, 1529).

but could at most induce him to renounce his right.[2] These reflections did not have as their point of departure the Emperor's position as superior of the princes also. In the course of further developments Luther was to adhere to the jurists, who held the viewpoint that, in accord with the corporate structure of the Empire, the electors were not to be regarded as subjects of the Emperor. They were called to govern the Empire together with the Emperor, just as, in Luther's version of the conciliar idea, the bishops ruled the Church with the Pope and under his guidance as equal members, *iure divino*, of the hierarchy. But if Emperor and princes were on an equal footing in law, then an armed action against them was not an official executive act but war. Since now in the matter of religion the secular authority had no power of command, a war by the Emperor against the Lutheran estates would be an ordinary raid against their possessions. Lastly, so Luther argued in 1539, in this the Pope was the commander-in-chief and the Emperor was his flunkey.

> If it is permitted to wage war against the Turk and to defend oneself against him, it is all the more permitted against the Pope, who is worse. Hence, if the Emperor should mix with the warriors of the Pope or of the Turk, he should be prepared for the fate appropriate to such a military service. [*WA, Br* 8, 367, 20–23]

The League of Schmalkalden

Because of his frequent absence from the Empire, Charles V wanted to provide his lieutenant and brother, Ferdinand, Archduke of Austria and King of Bohemia and Hungary, with greater authority and to have him elected as King of the Romans. He won a majority of the princes over to this plan at Augsburg. But Johann of Saxony aligned himself against it with the anti-Habsburg Catholic Dukes of Bavaria. He replied to the Emperor's invitation to the meeting of electors at Cologne on 29 December, by inviting the Protestant estates to a Diet at Schmalkalden on 22 December to discuss the threatened action by the Supreme Court in the matter of the Reformation and the election of a King of the Romans. Representatives of the South German cities appeared at the Diet, headed by Jakob Sturm of Strasbourg, in addition to the signatories of the *Confessio Augustana*.

Apart from Brandenburg-Ansbach and Nürnberg, which had conscientious scruples about the right of armed resistance, the participants

---

[2] "Quod princeps ut princeps sit politica persona et sic agens non agat ut Christianus, qui nec est princeps nec masculus nec quicquam in mundo personarum. Si igitur principi ut principi liceat resistore Caesari, illorum sit et indicii et conscientiae. Christiano certe nihil licet, ut qui mundo sit mortuus" (*WA, Br* 6, 17, 9–11).

agreed on 31 December to provide common assistance if the Supreme Court should proceed against one of them on the basis of the Augsburg Recess. The formal treaty of alliance was dated 27 February 1531.[3] Entering it were the Elector Johann of Saxony, Duke Philip of Braunschweig-Grubenhagen, Duke Ernst of Braunschweig-Lüneburg, the Landgrave Philip of Hesse, Prince Wolfgang of Anhalt-Bernburg, Counts Gebhard and Albrecht of Mansfeld, and eleven cities— Strasbourg, Ulm, Constance, Reutlingen, Memmingen, Lindau, Biberach, Isny, Lübeck, Magdeburg, and Bremen. Still other cities— Braunschweig, Göttingen, Esslingen, Goslar, and Einbeck—joined by the beginning of 1532. Membership had been offered to the Zwinglian cities of Zurich, Bern, and Basel with the stipulation of the recognition of Bucer's *Tetrapolitana,* but Zwingli managed to thwart this. The treaty of alliance itself made no declaration of the condition. With Zwingli's death in the battle of Kappel on 11 October 1531, the South German cities ceased to be concerned for Switzerland. Nothing now prevented their seeking support from the adherents of the League of Schmalkalden. The treaty of alliance was signed for six years and in 1537 was extended for ten years. Lengthy negotiations were needed before the twenty-three members of the league agreed on a constitution. This was decided only on 2 July 1533 at Schmalkalden and was not finally accepted by all members until 23 December 1535. As early as the autumn of 1536 it was replaced by a second constitution of the League. According to the "Constitution for Urgent Safety and Defense,"[4] the League was directed by two League Captains, the Elector of Saxony and the Landgrave of Hesse, who alternated every six months in the conduct of business. At the Diet the decrees were made by nine spokesmen, of whom two each were named by Electoral Saxony, Hesse, the North German and the South German allied cities, and one by the other princes and counts. The new war councilors, who had the decision in case of war, were determined according to the same ratio. The League army was to be recruited in case of need; however, two months' pay for two thousand horsemen and ten thousand troopers was to be kept in readiness. The Elector of Saxony was to have the supreme command in campaigns in North Germany; the Landgrave of Hesse, in West and South Germany. The League of Schmalkalden became the center of the anti-Habsburg forces. How little it was a question only of the "pure word of God" was made obvious by diplomatic relations with France and England and an understanding with Bavaria not to recognize the election of the Archduke Ferdinand as King of the Romans in October

---

[3] Text in E. Fabian, *Die Entstehung des Schmalkaldischen Bundes,* pp. 349–353.
[4] Text, ibid., pp. 358–376.

1531 and to provide assistance if one of them was attacked for this reason.

The Nürnberg Armistice

The Emperor could not even think of proceeding with force and of carrying out the Augsburg decrees. The Turks swarmed into Hungary, and to repulse them the Emperor had once again to purchase the assistance of the Protestants by an armistice. In the Nürnberg Armistice, or religious peace, of 23 July 1532, the members of the League were promised the suspension of all processes by the Supreme Court in religious affairs until the council or, if it did not meet within a year, until the next Diet, and all use of force because of religion and faith was forbidden. The Emperor went in person to Vienna to lead the great army that had been assembled from all his states in the Turkish campaign. But meanwhile the danger had been eliminated. The small West Hungarian fortress of Güns on the frontier of the Burgenland had heroically withstood the onset of the Sultan's troops from 7 to 29 August. This resistance and the reported strength of the imperial army induced Suleiman II to withdraw, with frightful devastation, through Styria, where the German troops were successful in a battle at Graz. The troops of the Empire could not be induced to pursue the Turks more deeply into Hungary and to procure victory for King Ferdinand's cause against the Hungarian claimant, Zapolya. Again the Turkish peril had been exorcised only temporarily; the paralyzing threat to the Empire persisted. The Emperor hurried via Italy to his Spanish kingdoms and was to be away from the Empire for almost ten years.

Introduction of the Reformation in Württemberg and Other Territories

The Protestants had not only held their ground, but they had gained powerfully in self-confidence. Encouraged by the League of Schmalkalden and under cover of the Nürnberg Armistice, which was *de facto* extended also to new members, a group of cities, including Augsburg, Hanover, Frankfurt an der Oder, and Hamburg, and principalities such as Pomerania, Anhalt-Dessau, and Liegnitz and Brieg in Silesia went over to the Reformation.

The fusion of politics and religion became especially clear in connection with the introduction of the new ecclesiastical system in Württemberg. Since the expulsion of Duke Ulrich (1487–1550) by the Swabian League in 1519, the Duchy had been under Austrian administration and at the Diet of Augsburg it had been conferred on the Archduke Ferdinand as an imperial fief. While activating the anti-Habsburg powers France and Bavaria, Philip of Hesse urged the restoration of the Duke, who had found refuge with him. The Landgrave first managed to prevent the renewal of the Swabian League, the prop of the Habsburg policy. In January 1534 he met the French King and obtained a promise of the necessary subsidies in exchange for a mortgage on the County of Mömpelgard near Belfort in Württemberg. Ferdinand was far too preoccupied elsewhere to take serious measures for the possession of Württemberg when the attack from Hesse occurred. The Austrian army was defeated without difficulty at Lauffen on the Neckar on 12–13 May 1534. In the Peace of Kaaden near Eger on 29 June Ferdinand granted Württemberg to Duke Ulrich as an Austrian rear-fief and conceded to him directly the right to introduce the new ecclesiastical system. In return he obtained the recognition of his royal title and the promise of aid against the Turks.

The Reformation, which was introduced immediately, was under the auspices of a liaison of Zwinglianism and Lutheranism. The people of Strasbourg proposed the Zwinglian Ambrosius Blaurer of Constance as reformer; Philip of Hesse, the Lutheran Erhard Schnepf. An effort was made to eliminate the difficulties in the doctrine of the Eucharist by the so-called Stuttgart Accord. The formula of union proposed by the Lutherans at Marburg was taken as its basis. Despite the division of the territory into two areas of the Reformation, the situation remained tense. The pastors were obliged to the *Confessio Augustana*. The Duke ruthlessly confiscated Church property to cover his debts. In 1537 he established the Tübingen *Stift* for the training of spiritual and secular officials. The University of Tübingen did not become Protestant until Johannes Brenz (1499–1570), the reformer of the Free City of Schwäbisch Hall (1522), was summoned there as professor from 1537 to 1538. In 1535 his small catechism was attached to Duke Ulrich's Church order. If the Protestant Church in Württemberg and in South Germany in general obtained a Lutheran stamp, it was due to the influence of Brenz. Under Duke Christoph (1550–68), as provost in Stuttgart, he became the director of the Württemberg Church and composed the *Confessio Virtembergica* and the *Grosse Kirchenordnung* of 1559.

The Wittenberg Accord

The Württemberg Reformation had again displayed the split among the Protestants and at the same time had indicated the way to union. It had been shown that the *Confessio Augustana* and the Stuttgart Accord did not suffice as the basis for unity. The theologians sought to arrive at

negotiations for an accord and approached Philip of Hesse as mediator. After a compromise between Bucer and Melanchthon at Kassel in December 1534 and an arrangement between Luther and the city of Augsburg, which in April 1536 was admitted to the League of Schmalkalden, the negotiations for the accord took place at Wittenberg from 22 to 29 May 1536. Meanwhile the Swiss and the city of Constance had declined and did not appear. Bucer acknowledged that the bread is truly the body of Christ and is given by the minister to all recipients, if the words of institution are not adulterated. Because, in his opinion, such adulteration takes place by means of the lack of faith in the recipient, there resulted the old problem of *manducatio impiorum.* Here Bugenhagen suggested that it may be "said that the unworthy, as Paul says, receive the body of the Lord." Luther was satisfied with this. The text drawn up by Melanchthon reads thus:

> Accordingly, they hold and teach that, with the bread and wine, the body and blood of Christ are truly and substantially present, administered, and received. And although they do not hold transubstantiation, neither do they hold that the body and blood of Christ are enclosed in the bread *localiter* or are otherwise permanently united with it, apart from the use of the Sacrament. However, they admit that, by sacramental unity, the bread is the body of Christ; that is, they hold, the bread is so administered that then the body of Christ is at the same time present and truly administered, and so forth. For, apart from the use, . . . they do not hold that the body of Christ is present.[5]

In addition to the formula *manducatio indignorum* instead of *impiorum,* the expression *unio sacramentalis* involved an intentional ambiguity. Nevertheless, the Wittenberg Accord had importance as a bridge to Lutheranism for the South German cities, making possible their adherence to the League of Schmalkalden.[6] It was later accepted into the *Solida Declaratio* of the Formula of Concord (VII, 12–16) and thereby again recognized as Lutheran.

Protestant Refusal to Participate in the Council

Until this time the Emperor and the Catholic Protestant estates had demanded a council in a united front, and the postponing of the question of faith till its convocation had been again and again a welcome way

---

[5] E. Bizer, *Studien zur Geschichte des Abendmahlsstreites im 16. Jahrhundert,* pp. 117ff.; *BSLK,* pp. 977f.

[6] To W. Köhler, *Luther und Zwingli* II, 453, "the whole Accord [was] a pretense," because persons on the two sides had a different understanding of the "unworthy."

out of the difficulties. It had not become clear that the ideas on the nature, summoning, and place of the council were very divergent also. But this situation changed decisively when on 2 June 1536, Pope Paul III called for a general council to meet at Mantua in May 1537.

The Elector of Saxony objected that nothing was said about the freedom, Christian character, and impartiality of the council and that it was to take place at Mantua. A council, he said, was a court of arbitration; if a person accepted the invitation, he was bound by the award. He demanded a pretext for refusing to participate from his councilors and theologians, he even considered a plan for a Lutheran countercouncil. Luther was to set down on which articles of his current teaching he intended "to stand and to persevere and . . . not yield." The reformer complied and on 28 December 1536 submitted to a conference of theologians his *Articles of Christian Teaching,* known as the *Articles of Schmalkalden.* To Melanchthon their statements in regard to the Pope were too severe. "For the sake of peace and unity" he was prepared to recognize the Pope's superiority over the bishops *iure humano.* Nevertheless he, with the other Wittenberg theologians, signed the articles, which were sent to the Elector on 3 January 1537 and accepted by him. The three parts of unequal length comprise: articles in which there was no need to yield because they were uncontested, such as the doctrine of the Trinity and of the two natures; articles in which there could be no yielding—atonement and justification by Jesus Christ, the Sacrifice of the Mass and the papacy as divine institutions; and articles which could be discussed with scholars and wise men, such as sin, penance, confession, baptism, ordination and marriage of priests, religious vows, and so forth. Luther expressed himself in particular fullness and with alarming severity on the Mass as the "greatest and most horrible abomination" in the papacy, as though in the meantime there had been no clarifying statement uttered or written on the Catholic teaching of the Mass. He concluded:

> This article on the Mass will be in its entirety in the council. For if it were possible that they should yield all the other articles to us, still they could not yield this article. As Campeggio said at Augsburg: he would sooner let himself be torn to pieces than abandon the Mass. Likewise, I will sooner let myself, with God's help, be reduced to ashes than allow a Mass slave with his work, be he good or bad, be equal to or higher than my Lord and Saviour Jesus Christ. Hence we are and we remain eternally separated and opposed. They rightly feel that where the Mass decays, so does the papacy. Before they would let that happen, they would kill all of us, wherever they could. The dragon's tail, the Mass, has brought

forth on all this much vermin and the filth of various superstitions [*WA* 50, 204, 3–28].

In other respects too Luther, who repeatedly denounced "enthusiasm," the source of all heresy and even of the devilry of the fanatics and of the Pope, did not exactly use a language restrained by God's word. With regard to the imminent council he wrote: There "will we stand not before the Emperor or the secular authority, . . . but before the Pope and the devil himself, who does not intend to listen but to damn abruptly, to murder, and to force to superstition" (*WA* 50, 220, 4–16). At the *Bundestag* at Schmalkalden in February 1537, which was attended by numerous princes, envoys of the cities, and some forty theologians, Luther became ill and could not personally defend his "articles." From dread of a new quarrel over the Eucharist and probably also because of Luther's intransigent language, Melanchthon prevented the articles from being officially submitted to the gathering. The theologians were commissioned to examine the *Confessio Augustana* and to supplement it with articles on the power of the Pope. The formulation was left to Melanchthon. His *Tractatus de potestate papae* received the approval of all and became the official statement of the League by being accepted into the Recess. Luther's "articles," on the other hand, were published as a private work. But they soon enjoyed great esteem and were eventually adopted in the *Book of Concord* of 1580, thus becoming a confessional document of the Lutheran Church.

The gathering at Schmalkalden strictly declined to take part in the council. Acceptance of the invitation would mean to consent to their own condemnation and to accept the Pope as judge in his own case. The bull of invitation to the council was not even taken from the papal legate, Peter van der Vorst. Melanchthon, however, was of the opinion that the invitation should not be bluntly rejected. The Pope, he said, did not indeed have a right to act as judge but he did have the right to summon the council. Melanchthon clearly saw as "the most sad thing of all" the fact "that such discord would continue down to posterity" (*CR* 3, 293). This did not prevent him from composing, by official mandate, the *piece justificative: Weshalb die Fürsten sich dem vom Römischen Papst Paul III. angekündigten Konzil verweigert hoben* (*CR* 3, 313–325).

The Emperor's representative at Schmalkalden was the vice-chancellor, Matthias Held. In accord with his mandate he sought to recruit for the council and rejected the complaints against the Supreme Court but came out more sharply than the Emperor had intended. He faced the harsh reality that the princes insisted on the rejection of the council that had been so vehemently demanded much more than did the theologians. Instead of seeking new paths to an understanding and sounding out the possibilities in the event that no council took place, he pressed for the establishing of a Catholic league. Without this, so he reported to the Emperor in the fall of 1537, everything would collapse, since the heretics were firmly determined to attack the Catholics from the rear, as they did in Württemberg. He found support in King Ferdinand. Consequently, on 10 June 1538 the League of Nürnberg, a defensive alliance between Charles V, Ferdinand, the Dukes of Saxony, Bavaria, and Braunschweig, and the Archbishops of Salzburg and Magdeburg came into existence and lasted for eleven years. With so slight a membership—no elector and scarcely any bishop was involved—and in view of the unclear attitude of Bavaria, the League was in itself not strong. It was soon further weakened by the death of Duke Georg of Saxony in 1539 and the subsequent reformation of his territory.

The Frankfurt Armistice

Even if the League of Nürnberg was not a serious threat to the members of the League of Schmalkalden, the latter felt themselves threatened. This motivated them to bind themselves more closely together. Because of a defeat near Esseg on 9 October 1538 in the Turkish war and the risk of again jeopardizing the ten-years' armistice just concluded at Nice on 18 June 1538 between a league of the Protestants and France, the Emperor could not seriously consider the use of force. In addition, the renewed postponement of the convoking of the council caused him and his contemporaries to doubt the Pope's sincere determination to take hold of the inner problems of the Church. In his effort to restore the unity of faith and of the Empire, Charles V was thus again thrown back upon German resources. He had no choice but to seek peace and aid against the Turks by means of negotiations and to hope to free the way for inner German religious colloquies. At the end of 1538 he appointed as the suitable agent for this the exiled Archbishop of Lund, Johann of Weeze. Prolonged negotiations led on 19 April 1539 to the Frankfurt Armistice. It granted, over and above the Nürnberg peace, an interval of six months to all current adherents of the *Confessio Augustana*. During that time the trials of the Supreme Court were to be suspended and no one was to be attacked because of religion. Peace for fifteen months was offered in the event that the members of the League of Schmalkalden were ready to accept no new members and to renounce any further secularizations. But they could not come to a decision. The Protestants promised to attend the Diet of Princes at Worms to determine the amount of aid needed against the Turks and to implement it. In particular the peace was to facilitate the religious colloquies. These were to take place independently of the council and without the participation of a papal legate in order "to treat of an honorable Christian union." The Elector Joachim II of Brandenburg especially advocated such colloquies. He was in the process of setting up in his own territory a church which occupied a remarkable middle position between the old and the new ecclesiastical system. Since the council was long in coming, he proceeded to introduce the reform as he waited for the council. In August 1539 he ordered debate on a Church order on which Georg Witzel (1501–1573) collaborated and which was decreed in March 1540. It adopted the Lutheran catechism but retained much of the old forms of worship. Luther thought that he could acquiesce in it because the article on justification and orthodox preaching were guaranteed (WA, Br 8, 624). Joachim II stressed that he wanted to be neither "Roman" nor "Wittenberger" but "Catholic." A violation of the Frankfurt Armistice occurred with the introduction of the Reformation in the Duchy of Saxony during the summer of 1539, following Duke Georg's death on 14 April. The members of the League of Schmalkalden kept their troops armed that they had recruited before the Frankfurt Armistice until Georg's brother, Duke Heinrich (d. 1541), had taken possession of his inheritance and introduced the Reformation. On Pentecost a Protestant service was held at Leipzig at which Luther himself preached.

The Religious Colloquies of 1540–41

The colloquy arranged for August 1539 at Nürnberg was postponed by imperial order and did not take place. The agreement that no papal legate should take part in the negotiations for a compromise could not but confirm the Curia's distrust of the imperial policy of union. What was here under way was scarcely different from a national council, so dreaded by Rome. The Protestants were hoping in this way to get a recognition of their confession in imperial law—a recognition which would do away with the need to submit the confession to the future council. Intensive papal diplomacy, however, could not deter the Emperor from his union policy. He promised that the Pope should take part in the projected religious colloquy, and people were invited to come to Speyer for it on 6 June. An epidemic forced its transfer to Hagenau. The chiefs of the League of Schmalkalden—the Elector of Saxony and the Landgrave of Hesse—refused to appear, and attendance by other princes and bishops was very meager. Not only King Ferdinand but also the adviser of the Catholics, the nuncio Morone, who was present, complained of the tardiness of the bishops. On 15 June 1540 he wrote to Cardinal Farnese:

> The spirit of the bishops is really, as His Majesty says, womanish in matters in which it ought to be manly, such as resistance to the opponents of our faith, and masculine in matters in which it ought to be feminine, such as drinking and keeping concubines.[7]

An exception was the Bishop of Vienna, Johann Fabri, who, together with Johannes Cochläus, Friedrich Nausea, Julius von Pflug, Johann Gropper, and especially Johannes Eck, acted as the Catholic spokesman. Melanchthon was taken sick en route and hence Wittenberg was represented only by Kaspar Cruciger, Friedrich Myconius, and Justus Menius. Other Protestant theologians present were Martin Bucer, Wolfgang Capito, Andreas Osiander, Johannes Brenz, U. Rieger, and Jean Calvin. King Ferdinand, who was in charge, wanted to take the Augsburg discussions for a compromise as the basis and to allow discussion only of the articles not agreed upon at Augsburg. The Protestants refused and demanded the *Confessio Augustana* as the basis. The fact that they were unwilling to be pinned down by concessions possibly made earlier, and indeed their mere presence, made clear the changed situation since 1530. They now represented a strongly consolidated Church organization, behind which stood the League of Schmalkalden, then the only close-knit political power in the Empire.

At Hagenau no progress was made beyond the discussion of the method of negotiation. Since there was no unity on the *modus conciliandi,* King Ferdinand announced to the members on 16 July that the religious colloquy had to be adjourned to another meeting. This was appointed for Worms on 28 October in the recess that was published on 28 July. But the imperial minister, Granvella, was not able to open the proceedings until 25 November, a month later than had been provided for. The papal legate, Thomas Campeggio, was only an observer and wanted to come forward as messenger of peace and reconciliation. Morone too was present. Once again there were long preliminary discussions on the *modus procedendi,* especially the voting. It had been decided at Hagenau that each side should have eleven speakers or votes respectively. But the Catholics were not sure of the theologians of Cleves, Brandenburg, and the Palatinate and were afraid of being outvoted on important questions and sought to prevent voting according to individuals. The Protestants, on the contrary, insisted on the proceedings decided at Hagenau and would have nothing to do with a written transaction. It was only on 5 January that it was agreed that there should be one speaker on each side.

The colloquy, engaged in by Eck and Melanchthon, began on 14

[7] Pastor, pp. 187f.; Lammer, *Mon. Vat.,* pp. 275f.

January with the *Confessio Augustana* as its basis. At the start Eck referred to the not inconsiderable deviations in the text of the *Augustana,* the *Variata,* that had been submitted, from that of 1530; these concerned especially the Eucharist. For three days they discussed original sin, especially to what extent the "penalty" remaining after baptism can itself be called sin. In Granvella's residence on 17 January a compromise formula came into existence, worked out by Mensing, Auxiliary Bishop of Halberstadt, Eck, Melanchthon, and Bucer. It was approved by both sides.[8] At the same time an imperial instruction arrived whereby the colloquy was to be transferred to the Imperial Diet appointed for Regensburg. The Emperor was hoping to promote the faltering discussions by his personal presence. Furthermore, during the not very promising discussions at Worms, Granvella had been concerned for a basis of negotiations in the form of a compromise draft. At his urging Gropper and the imperial councilor, Gerhard Veltwyk, had had secret talks with Capito and Bucer at Worms independently of the main discussion. Bucer was encouraged in this by Philip of Hesse. The Landgrave was eager for an arrangement with the Emperor, since he was in a state of bigamy which was threatening to become an embarrassing matter. The basis of these secret talks were Gropper's *Artikall, vor Christlich und der gesunden katholischen Lehr gemäss erkannt,* as completed and corrected by Bucer.[9] There was quick agreement on original sin and justification. Difficulties arose out of the compromise between the principle of Scripture and the recognition of ecclesiastical tradition, including the Mass and the veneration of saints. Bucer himself, however, took a positive view of the usages of the ancient Church because there had "been one Christendom from the Apostles down to the age of the holy Fathers." Hence he felt he could make concessions in regard to ceremonies and the Mass itself, if only the preaching of the Gospel were allowed. He was able to take much of the formulation that he suggested from the draft for the Leipzig colloquy of 1539, which he had elaborated with Witzel. The compromise draft that thus appeared was accepted on 31 December.[10] It represented the original form of the *Regensburg Book.* Even before the start of the Diet Granvella tried to gain as many of the princes as possible for it. Philip of Hesse was in agreement and Joachim II of Brandenburg enthusiastically sent it on to the Elector of Saxony. But skepticism was expressed by Luther (*WA, Br 9,* 333f.; *CR* 4, 96).

---

[8] *CR* 4, 32f., 89.

[9] Printed in J. Gropper, *Wahrhafftige Antwort* (Cologne 1545), fol. 8a–20a.

[10] Text in M. Lenz, *Briefwechsel Landgraf Philipps des Grossmütigen von Hessen mit Bucer* III (Leipzig 1891), 39–72.

At Regensburg the Worms compromise draft, after a few modifications approved by Contarini, Morone, and the Catholic cospeakers, Pflug, Gropper, and Eck, was approved as the basis of negotiations,[11] submitted at the opening of the colloquy on 27 April 1541 and accepted also by the Protestant spokesmen, Melanchthon, Bucer, and Pistorius. Important for the conciliatory mood of the Regensburg religious colloquy was the participation of Cardinal Contarini as papal legate. On the basis of his own religious experience and relying on Paul and Augustine, he was "convinced that the religious starting point of Luther's doctrine of salvation, but not its theological formation and the consequences drawn from it, was primitively Catholic."[12] He felt that, with good will on both sides, with charity and humility, the split could be healed. "Now he was to learn that they alone were not enough."[13] There was surprisingly rapid agreement on the first four articles of the *Regensburg Book:* the original state of man, free will, the cause of sin, and original sin. On the second day, 28 April, the participants turned to Article 5, on justification. Melanchthon and Eck rejected the version at hand. After a discussion of several days, however, they again had recourse to it but in a considerably abbreviated form,[14] and on 3 May it was possible to declare that there was agreement on this article. All were filled with joy and hope. Contarini sent the formula of union to Rome,[15] and the Emperor was confident that now "an understanding would be reached also in the other questions."[16] The conflict had blazed forth on justification, which was thus felt to be the "articulus stantis et cadentis ecclesiae." According to the formula of union, the sinner is "justified by a living and effective faith." This faith is a "movement of the Holy Spirit," whereby the penitent is oriented to God and attains the mercy, forgiveness of sins, and reconciliation promised in Christ. With him is "simultaneously infused charity, which heals the will," so that he can begin to fulfill the law.

> Hence that is a living faith which obtains mercy in Christ and believes that Christ's righteousness will be imputed to it by grace; at the same time it receives the promise of the Holy Spirit and charity. Thus, justifying faith is faith which operates through charity. [CR 4, 199]

[11] Text in CR 4, 190–238; Le Plat, III, 10–44.

[12] Jedin, I, 305.

[13] Ibid., 306.

[14] Jedin, Bizer, and Stupperich say 2 May; Pastor, p. 245, footnote 2, and Lipgens, p. 127, speak of 3 May.

[15] ZKG 5 (1882), 593; F. Dittrich, *Regesten und Briefe des Cardinals G. Contarini* (Braunsberg 1881), p. 177.

[16] NBD 1, VII, p. XVI.

The article seeks to take into account the fact that, on the one hand, we are justified for Christ's sake, his righteousness becomes ours, and we are reconciled with God, and, on the other hand, the new righteousness does not yet have full power over us, "the renewal is still imperfect, and a tremendous weakness still clings to the reborn." "Because of the righteousness inherent in us we are called righteous, for we indeed do what is right and, according to John, he is righteous who does righteousness." We will not, however, place our confidence in this activity of ours, but only in the justice of Christ, just as, on the other hand, we do not doubt our weakness. For this reason no one is excluded from the grace of Christ (CR 4, 200). There is no question of a "twofold righteousness," but of the one righteousness of Christ the Mediator, which produces full grace, favor, and reconciliation with the Father and renews and sanctifies man but has not yet come here fully into effect.

In the further course of the religious colloquy, however, it was to appear that not justification, but the Church and her office in the interpretation of Scripture and in the administration of the Sacraments constituted the articles that were really at the basis of the split. Contarini managed, in opposition to Eck, to have Articles 6 and 9, on the Church and her full authority in interpreting Scripture, postponed. Otherwise, the discussions would have foundered. There was agreement on Articles 10 to 13, the teaching on the Sacraments in general, orders, baptism, and confirmation. There were crucial difficulties with regard to Article 14, on the Eucharist. The question of transubstantiation was struggled with for almost eight days. No understanding was reached on it nor on Article 15, on penance, but there was agreement on matrimony (Article 16) and the anointing of the sick (Article 17). With Article 19, on the hierarchical order of the Church, and Article 20, on the Mass and the veneration of the saints, it finally became plain to all that the colloquy had broken down. On 31 May the Protestants submitted a summary of their divergent views relevant to the Church, the Eucharist, and penance (CR 4, 348–376). The Emperor's policy of union failed utterly when he did not even obtain an understanding that the articles on which there was agreement should be recognized as settled and that patience should be exercised in regard to the others until the council convened.

Meanwhile, it had turned out that the unity over justification was only superficial. On 10 or 11 May Luther had labeled the article a "botched job," "a new piece of cloth patched on to an old coat, so that the rent becomes worse" (WA, Br 9, 407, 20f.). On 29 June he termed the compromise a "papist fraud" (WA, Br 9, 460, 4). On the Catholic side the union formula was charged with being ambiguous. As early as 25

May Contarini defended himself in the *Epistola de iustificatione* against accusations of this sort.[17] The Curia refused its approval. However, when its rejection reached Regensburg on 8 June, the union was already in ruins and it had become clear for the future how complicated an agreement was. Inner Church reform was thus all the more urgent. To the assembled bishops Contarini directed a pressing admonition to fulfill their pastoral duties, to see especially to preaching and the education of the young, and to avoid all scandal in their own persons and in their retinue. For their part the bishops implored the legate to labor without delay for the convoking of the council; otherwise, all Germany would soon be Lutheran. The council seemed about to become a reality. The Pope had had the Emperor informed that he was determined to lift the suspension of the council and to convoke it at once.[18] Of course, this had come too late to prevent the schism in the Church, as is proved by the repeated rejection of a papal council as a binding tribunal by the Protestants (*CR* 4, 517f.).

In the Recess of the Diet on 29 July 1541, the Nürnberg peace was extended for eighteen months.[19] Within that time a general council or, if necessary, a national council should take place. For the sake of aid against the Turks the Emperor, in a secret declaration, assured the Protestants the possession of the secularized Church property, allowed them to hold the explanation of their theologians in the adjusted articles, and promised them equality in the Supreme Court.

[17] *CCath* VII, 23–34.
[18] *CT* IV, 195f.
[19] *CR* IV, 625–630; Contarini's report of 27 July in *HJ* 1 (1880), 498f.; of 26 July in *ZKG* 3 (1879), 183f.

CHAPTER 24

The Breakdown of Universalism
and
The Religious Peace of Augsburg

The Emperor and the Protestants on the Brink of War

The religious colloquies had failed, and once again the Emperor had had to give in to the Protestants. He familiarized himself even more with the idea of a forcible solution. On the other hand it must be counted as a success when, during the Diet of Regensburg in 1541, he managed to weaken the impact of the League of Schmalkalden by paralyzing the activity of Philip of Hesse. While his lawful wife, the mother of his nine children, was still alive, the Landgrave had married a lady-in-waiting. In a *Beichtrat*[1] Luther, Melanchthon, and Bucer had given their approval and they were even present at the wedding in March 1540. The bigamy could not be kept secret and because of it the reformers suffered a painful embarrassment. According to the *Carolina,* the imperial law that he himself had proclaimed, Philip had incurred the death penalty. He tried to evade it by a *rapprochement* with the Emperor. In a treaty of 13 June 1541 he bound himself to prevent an alliance of the League of Schmalkalden with France and England and the admission of the Duke of Cleves to the League and to support the Emperor's claims to Gelderland. The Emperor promised not to attack him on religious grounds unless he had to wage war against all the Protestants. Thus a restoration of religious unity by armed force was envisaged by the Emperor as in the realm of the politically possible, but out of the question for the moment due to external political pressures. Charles V went to Italy and at Lucca on 12 to 18 September 1541 he met Pope Paul III, whom he hoped to gain for a council on German soil, effective aid against the Turks, and support against France. The result was disheartening.

Meanwhile, the peril from the Turks was again great. Zapolya, the King of Hungary, had died in 1540. But, on account of the opposition of the Magyar nobles, King Ferdinand was unable to take up the succession promised him in the Treaty of Grosswardein in 1538. The national Magyar circles invited the Sultan Suleiman II into the country but were not a little astonished when, after occupying Buda on 2 September 1541, he installed a pasha as governor and thus made Hungary a Turkish province. The Emperor's desperate diversionary measure against the Muslim danger through an attack on Algiers in October 1541 failed completely because of stormy weather. At the same time the already critical situation with regard to France became worse, making the ten-years' armistice of 1538 illusory. And so, once again ecclesiastical problems had to yield to political cares. The Diet opened at Speyer by King Ferdinand on 9 February 1542 was overshadowed by the Turkish question. The Protestants made their assistance dependent on their recognition in imperial law by means of the adoption of the Regensburg Declaration in the Recess of the Diet and demanded a visitation of and new personnel on the Supreme Court. This time too the King had recourse to an additional declaration. A visitation of the Supreme Court was

[1] Cf. *CR* 3, 849–865; *WA, Br* 8, 638–644, no. 3423.

indeed introduced but as early as June it was again suspended by the Emperor. Thus the Nürnberg Diets of July–August 1542 and January–April 1543 faced the same problems, to which was added in the second the military confrontation with France and Cleves. If the Emperor could not expect any help here either, at least it was a success that the League of Schmalkalden did not come to the aid of the Duke of Jülich-Cleves-Berg, who was beaten in September 1543. He had to annul the Reformation and turn over Gelderland to the Emperor. This meant a strengthening of the northwestern German sees of Münster, Paderborn, and Osnabrück, which, like Cologne, were then in danger of going over to the Reformation.

Progress of the Reformation

The Reformation continued to make great advances. After several years' strife the chiefs of the League of Schmalkalden, the Elector of Saxony and the Landgrave of Hesse, occupied the territory of the Catholic Duke Heinrich of Braunschweig-Wolfenbüttel in July–August 1542, gave it a provisional government, and had the Reformation introduced by Bugenhagen and Corvinus. The Wittenberg theologians had spoken in favor of these proceedings and against the return of the territory to its legitimate ruler on the ground that one "cannot acquiesce in the restoration of unorthodox doctrine, superstition, and persecution in the country" (*WA, Br* 10, 471, 80f.). When the Duke managed to gain back his territory, but only to be taken captive by Philip of Hesse in 1545, Luther felt that he should be kept in prison: To prevent him from further exercising his "tyranny, blasphemy, and impiety" was to practice mercy to him.[2]

The obliging of a Lutheran prince to hinder idolatry or the abomination of papal "abuses" served territorial interests in a no less questionable manner in the new choice of an occupant of the see of Naumburg. Following the death of the bishop on 6 January 1541 the cathedral chapter, without consulting the Elector of Saxony, had elected the provost of the Zeitz chapter, Julius von Pflug. The Elector, who for some time had been trying to end the political autonomy of the bishopric, in September entrusted the secular administration to an official of the diocese whom he appointed. Since Pflug did not yield and the chapter declined to elect a creature of the Elector, the last named brought about the election of Nikolaus von Amsdorf by the Lutheran estates of the

[2] *An Kurfürsten zu Sachsen und Landgrafen zu Hessen von dem gefangenen Herzog zu Braunschweig* (1545), *WA* 54, 389–411, p. 399, 10.

diocese. Contrary to their original conviction, the Wittenberg theologians had assented to these proceedings. Luther wrote to the diocesan estates that a cathedral chapter which did not make a proper election or clung to a persecutor of the Gospel forfeited its rights. "For the command to teach the right doctrine and to celebrate correct worship takes precedence over all other commands" (WA, Br 9, 598, 21). "Since the worldly property is furnished for the sake of the spiritual ministry, it must follow the right bishop" (WA, Br 9, 598, 60). The control of the worldly property, he said, disappeared with the spiritual power. "Its superstition and its secular power and property" were inseparably united. Luther personally performed the "consecration" of Nikolaus von Amsdorf by the imposition of hands and prayer,[3] "without any chrism . . . and whatever else of the same great sacredness there is" (WA 53, 231, 5), and the enthronement. The next day the council and citizenry of Naumburg did homage to the new bishop at the town hall. But Amsdorf was not to find much joy in his office of Lutheran bishop. He was himself in a "miserable situation"—left to the caprices of the Elector's official in secular matters and in full dependence on the electoral government in the spiritual sphere, without obtaining from the government the necessary support. In addition, the legitimacy of his episcopacy was still disputed. Pflug did not renounce his claims and in March 1542 complained to the Diet of Speyer. The Emperor took his part but was unable formally to invest him with the bishopric until 8 August 1545, after much hesitation. The investiture thus represented the Elector's procedure as robbery. War alone brought a decision favorable to Pflug.

In the bishopric of Meissen the Elector of Saxony also claimed sovereignty. But when he occupied the district of Wurzen in order to guarantee the payment of the Turkish tax and tried to introduce the Reformation, he came into conflict with his Protestant cousin, Duke Maurice, who likewise intended to assert rights of sovereignty, by arms if necessary. While the intervention of Philip of Hesse led to a compromise, it was unable to prevent the intensifying of the opposition between the two branches of the Wettin Dynasty and with it an increased reserve on the part of Duke Maurice toward the League of Schmalkalden.

In Palatinate-Neuburg the Count Palatine Otto Heinrich confiscated Church property and in 1543 proclaimed a Protestant Church Order. In the Electoral Palatinate the Elector Frederick II (1544–56), who was only superficially religious, inclined to the Reformation. In April 1546

---

[3] *Exempel, einen rechten christlichen Bischof zu weihen* (1542), WA 53, 231–260.

he went over to it publicly and had the Mass abolished. The Catholic majority in the Electoral College was thereby imperiled, for at the same time the Electorate of Cologne was in danger of embracing the Reformation.

The Archbishop of Cologne, Hermann von Wied (1515–47), whose grasp of theology was far too inadequate to enable him to evaluate the import of the differences between the Catholic notion of the Church and Protestantism, had in February 1542 invited Bucer to have religious discussions with him and Johann Gropper. The provincial Diet encouraged the archbishop and on 10 March 1542 gave him extensive powers. When, toward the end of the year, Bucer was invited again and preached in the Bonn Minster, there were lively protests at Cologne from the cathedral chapter, the university, the lower clergy, and the city council, and Bucer's departure was demanded. The theological opposition was carried on by the Carmelite Eberhard Billick, the Carthusian Gerhard Kalkbrenner, and especially Johann Gropper. Gropper broke off his connection with Bucer and on 27 January 1543 transmitted to the archbishop a Catholic reform program. Hermann von Wied rejected it and authorized Bucer to draw up an order of Reformation. With the support of other reformers, who, headed by Melanchthon, had meanwhile been enlisted, Bucer put together the "Cologne Reformation." Simultaneously there began the implementation of the Reformation in the archbishopric. By a brief issued in June 1543 the Pope called upon the Elector to return to the Church.

The intervention of Charles V in connection with the War of the Gelderland Succession in August and September 1543 retarded the reform exertions for a while. In a counterreport Gropper attacked the "Cologne Reformation" as not Catholic. Even Luther opposed it and stigmatized its doctrine of the Eucharist as "fanatical." The Archbishop's declaration of January 1544 that he would be satisfied with the preaching of the Gospel, the lay chalice, and baptism and hymns in German did not suffice to overcome the Cologne opposition. The Catholic circles obtained an effective strengthening from the Jesuits, who settled at Cologne in 1544. In the autumn of that year they energetically demanded that the Archbishop annul the innovations and appealed to both Emperor and Pope. A series of polemics, testimonials, and replies testifies to the passionately fought struggle. Hermann von Wied was excommunicated on 16 April 1546 and soon after deposed by the Pope. But it was only in February 1547 that his successor, the former coadjutor Adolf von Schaumburg, could, with imperial support, force him to yield.

The Schmalkaldic War

The successful Gelderland-Cleves campaign of 1543 confirmed Charles V's conviction that power, employed at a given time and properly, is an entirely fit means for mastering "arrogance."[4]

This applied to the Protestants as well as to the French. Hence it was by no means agreeable to him when the Cardinal Legate, Alessandro Farnese, sought at Kreuznach in January 1544 to gain him to peace or at least to an armistice for the sake of the council—in other words to induce him to renounce Milan and Savoy. The Pope favored France and was silent in regard to France's offer of an alliance with the League of Schmalkalden—so ran the bitter words of reproach. At the Diet of Speyer Charles V obtained military help against the Turks and France from the Protestants, who were themselves not united and impressed by the Emperor's success against Cleves. Of course, he had to be quite accommodating in regard to their ecclesiastical demands.[5] He held out to them the prospect of a diet in the coming fall or winter. It was to produce a "Christian reform" because of the religious dispute." Until then no one was allowed to resort to power and force in religious matters. The processes in the Supreme Court and the Recesses of Diets against the Lutherans were to be suspended. Ecclesiastical property was to remain in the hands of those who held it at the moment. For the sake of a momentary success the Emperor here, for the first time, publicly abandoned important positions. As Jedin says, "He offered his hand for a future arbitrary, total regulation of the ecclesiastical situation" by a German diet, a regulation "which, in the situation, could and perhaps had to lead to the complete Protestantization of Germany." The Curia reacted with an admonition of 24 August 1544 to the effect that, by his promise to regulate Church affairs at a diet and by his disposal of Church property, the Emperor had become guilty of a serious invasion of canon law.[6] He should revoke the concessions to the Protestants and, by arranging peace, facilitate the way for the council. In Jedin's words, the brief meant "the taking of a position in principle against the Emperor's religious and conciliar policy." But it was neither officially presented nor published. This did not stop its circulation. Calvin published

---

[4] In his *Commentaires* (edited by Kervyn de Lettenhove [Brussels 1862], p. 100; K. Brandi, *Karl V* II, 339), the Emperor wrote: "L'expérience de ce qui se passait ouvrit les yeux de l'empereur et éclaira son entendement de sorte, que non seulement il ne lui parut impossible de dompter par la force un tel orgueil, mais tout au contraire, cela lui sembla très facile en l'entreprenant dans de circonstances et par des moyens convenables."

[5] Jedin, I, 397f.

[6] Text in *CT* IV, 364-373; Jedin, I, 602.

it and was not sparing in his cutting scorn.[7] Luther lost control of himself in one of his last and most extravagant polemics, *Wider das Papsttum zu Rom, vom Teufel gestiftet* (1545; *WA* 54, 206–299). The Emperor did not react but created new facts by a rapid and successful campaign against France. In the Peace of Crépy the French King had to promise aid against the Turks and, in addition, he had to oblige himself in a secret treaty of 19 September 1544 to cooperate in the elimination of abuses and the return of apostates and to participate in the council that was to meet at a time specified by the Emperor at Trent, Cambrai, or Metz.[8] He also declared that he agreed the aid promised against the Turks could be used against heretics also in case it should be necessary to proceed forcibly against them.

When the Pope finally summoned the Council to meet at Trent on 15 March 1545, in the Bull "Laetare Jerusalem," published on 30 November 1544, the Emperor acquiesced. But he did not desist from his plan of first overcoming the League of Schmalkalden by military might and then of forcing the Protestants to recognize and attend the Council. To this he directed all his strength. Besides, he reckoned on a delay, if not on further obstruction to the opening of the Council. For the present he continued along the route of compromise that had been traveled at Speyer in order to lull his opponents into security. At first this was still the situation at the Diet of Worms, which, because of the Emperor's illness, did not meet on 1 October 1544, but at the end of March 1545 under King Ferdinand. According to the Emperor's wish the aid against the Turks and other political questions were to be urgently dealt with and the religious problems left chiefly to the Council. But the Protestants, who were not ready to recognize the Council, demanded the implementation of the assurances given at Speyer in 1544.

On 17 May, one day after the Emperor, Cardinal Farnese arrived at Worms as papal legate. Discussion of a procedure against the Protestants prepared the way at the end of June for an alliance between Emperor and Pope. The latter promised for the war against the League of Schmalkalden 200,000 ducats, 12,500 auxiliary troops for four months, one-half the revenues of the Spanish Church, and permission to convert up to a half-million ducats into ready cash by alienation of Spanish ecclesiastical property. The opening of the Council was to be delayed. The Emperor continued the Diet in order to gain time and to prevent the Protestants from preparing for war. In the Recess of the Diet on 4 August a religious colloquy was even called for at Re-

---

[7] *CR* 35, 253–288.

[8] Text in A. Hasenclever, "Die Geheimartikel zum Frieden von Crépy vom 19. 9. 1544." *ZKG* 45 (1926), 418–426.

gensburg. In order to safeguard his rear for the war against the Protestants, King Ferdinand in October 1545 concluded an eighteen-months' armistice with the Turks, ceded the lost parts of Hungary to them, and bound himself to pay tribute. Delegates arrived at Regensburg for the religious colloquy on 27 January 1546, even though the Council of Trent had already begun its work on 13 December 1545. In order not to give rise to any rivalry the Emperor assigned the colloquy a purely informational task for the sake of the Diet that had also been summoned to Regensburg. Out of an understandable mistrust the Protestant side demanded that all talks be recorded in the minutes. This troublesome procedure did not allow any free exchange of views, and the Emperor rejected it. The Protestants broke off the discussions on justification, which had scarcely begun, on 10 March and ten days later they secretly left the city. The Diet, for which the Emperor arrived on 10 April, could only be opened on 5 June. The leading Protestant princes did not attend in person. Religion, peace, and law were to be the subjects of discussion, but in reality everyone counted on war. The Catholics recognized the Council of Trent, while the Protestants demanded a free, Christian council in Germany. In the background the Emperor was diligently trying to isolate the members of the League of Schmalkalden. Bavaria bound itself to a benevolent neutrality. The marriage of the heir to the Duchy with Ferdinand's oldest daughter, Anna, was to end the old Habsburg-Wittelsbach rivalry. Maurice of Saxony entertained hopes of obtaining the Saxon Electoral dignity and let himself be gained to a treaty on 19 June 1546. In it he was promised the protectorate of the bishoprics of Magdeburg and Halberstadt. For his part, he promised to recognize the Council and send representatives to it. On 7 June the Emperor signed a treaty alliance with the Pope. Charles gave the sign for war when, responding to an inquiry by the Protestants about the aim of his warlike preparations, he said that he had taken action against disobedient princes according to law and by virtue of his authority. On 9 June he had written to his sister Mary:

> If we did not intervene now, all the estates of the Empire, including the Netherlands, would be in danger of abandoning the faith. After I had considered all this again and again, I decided to start war against Hesse and Saxony as violators of the peace in regard to the Duke of Braunschweig and his territory. And although this pretext will not cover up for long that it is a question of religion, at first anyway it will serve to separate those who have deviated.[9]

[9] Brandi, *Karl V* I, 471.

Accordingly, the Emperor wanted to avoid the impression of a religious war and to have the war viewed in the framework of imperial law. The declaration of outlawry against Electoral Saxony and Hesse contributed to this. Charles intended to wage the war in these principalities, but before he obtained control of the troops from the Netherlands and of the papal auxiliary corps his opponents seized the initiative. Thus the territory south of the Danube became the first arena. The field commander of the League of Schmalkalden, Sebastian Schertlin von Burtenbach, moved against the Ehrenberger Klause on the upper Lech with the intention of obstructing the Emperor's principal force from Innsbruck and the approach of the papal troops. But the League's war council called him back to the Danube. There was also no determined attack by the still preponderant League on Regensburg. The "greatest military confrontation which Germany had hitherto experienced" was at first an endless maneuvering in the area around Ingolstadt, a cautious probing of the opponent without risking a decisive blow.[10] This was to the Emperor's advantage. He was able to assemble his forces and strengthen his at first weaker position. But in time the ineffectual moving about exhausted the financial resources on both sides and desire for a fight seized the troops. In the late fall the Italians especially had to endure rain and cold. There was not even any decisive action on the Emperor's part when the intervention of Maurice of Saxony of itself brought a change. Together with King Ferdinand and the latter's Bohemian troops, he invaded Electoral Saxony, forcing the Schmalkaldic chiefs to leave the South German theater of operations. The Emperor rejected a request made by Philip of Hesse on 14 November for a truce and he was soon master of South Germany. Charles demanded contributions but left the Count Palatine his electoral dignity and Ulrich of Württemberg his principality and, above all, did not interfere with the religious situation so long as the important outcome had not been decided. And now it was the Pope himself who jeopardized that. He feared that the Emperor's complete success would mean his strong preponderance and, influenced by antiimperial forces, he recalled his troops at the end of January 1547, thereby greatly embittering Charles V. This was all the more dangerous when hitherto neutral North German Protestantism came to the aid of the Elector of Saxony. Maurice of Saxony fell into serious trouble. Severely tormented by gout and bladder trouble, the Emperor hurried to Saxony and there, relentlessly unsparing of himself, at Mühlberg on the Elbe on 24 April 1547, he

[10] E. Hassinger, *Das Werden des neuzeitlichen Europa 1300–1600* (Braunschweig 1959), p. 236.

won the single battle that he ever took part in. The Elector Johann Friedrich was taken prisoner and condemned to death for *lèse majesté* and heresy. There was no intention of carrying out this judgment; it was intended rather to lend force to the subsequent negotiations. In the Wittenberg Capitulation of 19 May Johann Friedrich had to renounce his principality and the electoral dignity. He firmly refused to recognize the decrees of the Council and remained in prison. The same fate befell Philip of Hesse when on 19 June he asked the Emperor's pardon at Halle.

Henry VIII of England had died on 28 January 1547, and Francis I of France on 31 March. Martin Luther had preceded them to the grave a year earlier, on 18 February 1546. Charles V seemed left alone as victor on the stage of history. What could now stop him from setting about establishing the new order of Europe in the sense of his own universal imperial idea and of restoring the unity of faith? But this was denied him especially by the one person whose help he had most need of—the Pope. "The dissension that now broke out between the Pope and the Emperor was the salvation of the German Protestants in their extreme distress."[11]

The Violent Diet and the *Interim*

According to the Emperor's plan the Protestants were to be mastered in the field and then brought to participate in the Council at Trent. The first item had succeeded but in the meantime the second had been made impossible by the Council itself with the consent of the Pope. On 11 March it had decreed its tranfer to Bologna. The Protestants were certainly not to be induced to attend a council in a city of the Papal State and to accept the decrees issued there. At the Curia, however, the Catholic Church in Germany had already been written off and the Council's task was seen as predominantly the preservation and reform of the Church in lands that were still Catholic.

After the Emperor's victory at Mühlberg Paul III was all the more fearful of the Spanish-Habsburg pincer movement and of the Emperor's universal power. The bitterness produced by the murder of his son, Pierluigi Farnese, on 10 September 1547, at Piacenza and the occupation of that city by imperial troops quickly envenomed the Pope's relations with Charles V.

The "imperialist" Council Fathers had not gone to Bologna but had stayed on at Trent. The Pope could not be induced to transfer the

[11] Jedin, II, 376.

Council back there, but eventually, not wanting to risk a schism, he had to order a cessation of conciliar activity on 3 February 1548.

In view of this development there remained to the Emperor no other possibility than to try to lead the religious affair to a solution within the German framework and without the Pope. This was the central problem of the "Violent Diet" that opened at Augsburg on 1 September 1547. It was the more urgent when the Emperor's other concern, the reorganization of the Empire—a consolidation of the imperial central power—encountered massive resistance. The Emperor envisaged an Imperial League on the model of the Swabian League that, despite everything, had functioned for almost fifty years, from 1487 to 1533, for the management of South Germany and as an instrument of Habsburg policy. Such a league would have offered the possibility of incorporating the Netherlands, Milan, and Savoy and tying the Empire more closely together with the other lands of the Habsburgs. But the days of an imperial reform in the direction of monarchy were past. The princes had become far too powerful through their victories over the knights and the peasants and through the reform movement. As the Elector of Brandenburg had declared, they were not inclined to reduce the Empire "to servitude" to the Emperor by means of a league.

The Emperor was likewise unable completely to regulate ecclesiastical affairs according to his own view, that is, through the return of the Protestants to the ancient Church. He had to content himself with a temporary solution, the *Interim*. At the Emperor's request Julius von Pflug had composed a *Formula sacrorum emendandorum* for the Diet. According to W. Lipgens,[12] it was based on a reform essay of Gropper's. When a committee on religion at the Diet proved to be unsuited for the task, the *Formula* was, at the Emperor's command, debated and revised by Julius von Pflug, Michael Helding, the Spaniards Pedro de Soto and Pedro Malvenda, and others, together with Johannes Agricola, the only Protestant theologian appointed. The outcome of the two-weeks' work of the theologians was a "compromise" confession, to which the Emperor tried to win the Lutheran and the Catholic estates. But Bavaria and the spiritual princes rejected it. In their view the Catholics should simply be ordered to hold to the ancient faith. After much uncertainty the text was published on 15 May 1548 as *Der römisch-kaiserlichen Majestät Erklärung, wie es der Religion halben im Heiligen Reich bis zum Austrag des gemeinen Concilii gehalten werden soll.*[13] It was imposed on the Protestants in the Recess of the Diet on 30 June. On the other hand, the

---

[12] W. Lipgens, *Kardinal J. Gropper* (Münster 1951), pp. 169f.
[13] Text in M. K. T. Hergang, *Das Augsburger Interim* (Leipzig 1855), pp. 20–155; *Neue und vollständigere Sammlung der Reichstagsabschiede* II (Frankfurt 1747), 550–574.

estates that had "hitherto maintained the order and doctrine of the common Christian Church [were] to continue steadfast in them and neither deviate from them nor introduce changes." Hence the concessions made to the Protestants were to have no validity for them until a decision was made by the Council in regard to the marriage of priests and communion under both species. Thus to label the Augsburg *Interim* an "exceptional law for the Protestants" does not quite fit the situation,[14] for nothing was imposed on them which was not also required of the Catholics.

In the foreword it was asserted that "His Imperial Majesty [was] industriously working to effect a reformation" (paragraph 11), and the conclusion stressed the necessity "of removing the scandals from the Church which have given great cause for the disorder of this time." Hence no one will refuse his encouragement and aid to the Emperor in his efforts "to bring about the useful reform of the Church" (Article XXVI, para. 25).

In the twenty-six articles the fundamental truths of faith were treated: the original state, fall, and redemption of man (I–III), his justification (IV–VIII), the doctrine of the Church (IX–XIII), that of the Sacraments (XIV–XXI), and in particular detail that of the Mass (XXII–XXV). The last article (XXVI) dealt with ceremonies and customs.

Justification takes place on the basis of the merit of Christ's passion and means the forgiveness of sins and renewal in the Holy Spirit. The love of God, which is poured into our heart, brings it about that man "desires what is good and right and accomplishes in deed what he desires." But carnal lusts still fight against the Spirit even in those who "have obtained such righteousness from grace." On this earth man cannot achieve the perfection of this "infused righteousness." Christ must always come to the aid of the weakness of the righteous with his own perfection. Much as justification is God's work and not man's, still "the merciful God does not deal with a man as with a dead log, but draws him with his will" (Article VI, para. 1). "Prevenient grace . . . moves the heart to God through Jesus Christ, and this movement is faith" in Holy Scripture and the divine promises. Faith leads to trust and hope and "hope in the promised mercy glorifies God and hence is led to love" (VI, para. 3). Love is fruitful in good works (VII). The Church is the "community and assembly of believers in Christ, in which the Holy Spirit . . . thus unites the reborn so that they may be one house and one body from one baptism and one faith" (IX). It is invisible and yet also visible (IX, para. 5). The canon of Scripture is established by it (XI,

---

[14] E. Bizer, *Reformationsgeschichte Deutschlands bis 1555: Die Kirche in ihrer Geschichte* III, Lieferung K (Göttingen 1964), 152.

para. 1). It decides doubtful questions by a legitimate council summoned in the Holy Spirit (XI, para. 6). It exercises teaching and the priesthood in special offices. "Although it has many bishops, who rule by divine right the people whom Christ has gained by his precious blood, it still has one supreme bishop who is set over all others in order to avert schisms and dissension" (XIII, para. 1). The theology and practice of the Sacraments and Mass are treated in detail. Christ's sacrifice on the Cross is "by itself sufficient . . . to redeem the whole human race" (XXII, para. 7). The relevant question in the Mass is that "all men will participate in this mighty sacrifice, which has perfectly, sufficiently, and superabundantly achieved salvation for all men, and take advantage of it" (para. 8). The sacrifices of pagans and Jews had meaning in so far as the one sacrifice of Christ was announced and expected in them (para. 10). In the Mass we celebrate without interruption the memorial of this sacrifice and share in its benefits (para. 19). The sacrifice of the cross and that of the Eucharist are "one in substance but different in the manner of offering" (para. 30). The traditional ceremonies are to be retained (XXVI). But they should be explained to the people and all that could "give cause for superstition" should be eliminated (para. 6). The marriage of priests (para. 20) and the lay chalice (para. 21) should be allowed where they are already the custom until a decision by the Council. In the *Interim* nothing is said about the restitution of the property taken from the Church. As a confessional formula it presents the doctrine of the Church with no watering down, but it exerts itself to take up the concerns of the Protestants in both content and language and to do justice to them.[15] Hence it was all the more to be regretted that it did not obtain the assent of the Catholic estates. For the Protestants could only gain the impression that they were to be enticed back to a completely pre-Reformation Church system by means of concessions that were basically not seriously meant, but that would later be required of them. The intransigent, including the otherwise conciliatory Martin Bucer, had no great difficulty in mobilizing resistance to this last effort to save religious unity and in presenting all cooperation as cowardice and betrayal. If the *Interim* did not affect the Catholic estates, still they were not for that reason to be freed of the claims of reform. For them the Emperor on 9 July 1548, issued a *Formula Reformationis per Caesaream Maiestatem statibus ecclesiasticis . . . proposita et ab eisdem probata et recepta.*[16]

---

[15] J. Lortz, *Die Reformation in Deutschland* II: 273, thinks otherwise: "This *Interim,* while well meant, was an ambiguous compromise and hence weak in itself."

[16] Text in M. K. T. Hergang, *Das Augsburger Interim,* pp. 232–272. According to Lipgens, *Gropper,* p. 171, it can be "shown with great probability that Johannes Gropper was the author of the *Formula Reformationis."* This is definitely disputed by G. Pfeilschifter, *ARC* II, 121f., footnote 9.

In it the reform of the clergy is presented as urgent. At the beginning we read:

> In order that abuses and scandals . . . may be removed and clergy and people reformed . . . until the general council puts an end to the schism and abuses, it is especially necessary that the spiritual estate be renewed and purified, since through its disorder, confusion, and insecurity the shape of the Church in general has fallen into disorder and is convulsed in various ways.

Accordingly, Article I deals with the formation and trial of candidates for the priesthood and the episcopacy. The pastoral duties of priests and bishops are strongly emphasized. The latter should make it clear by their conduct that they are bishops rather than princes and that their thoughts are directed to heaven rather than to the world (II). The obligation to preach and, as preparation for this, to study Holy Scripture is given special attention. The Sacraments must not become spectacles which are merely watched ("otiosa spectacula"); they should again and again be made clear to the faithful in talks (IX). For example, the texts in the administration of baptism and matrimony may be spoken in the vernacular. All rites and every religious usage must promote genuine piety. The people should be warned about superstitious abuses (XVI). Accumulation of benefices is forbidden (XVIII). Visitations and diocesan and provincial synods are especially mentioned among the methods of reform. "In order that the pious zeal for reformation may not cool through long delays," diocesan synods were to be held by Martinmas and provincial synods by the following Lent. As a matter of fact such reform synods did take place for most German sees[17] and for the provinces of Mainz, Trier, Cologne, and Salzburg.[18] Here an effort was made to apply the imperial reform decree to local circumstances and to make them operative. The decrees enacted in this connection gave the episcopal visitors goals and means in their exertions in regard to doctrine and discipline. Even though a complete success was certainly not achieved, still a new spirit was discernible and a start toward inner reform of the German Church became visible. The ground was thereby made ready to some extent for the reception of the Tridentine decrees.

Both the *Interim* and the *Formula Reformationis* suffered from the fact

---

[17] G. Schreiber, *Weltkonzil von Trient* II (Freiburg 1951).

[18] L. Lenhardt, "Die Mainzer Synoden von 1548 und 1549," *AMrhKG* 10 (1958), 67–111; H. Foerster, *Reformbestrebungen Adolfs III. von Schaumburg 1547–56 in der Kölner Kirchenprovinz* (Münster 1925); Loserth, "Die Salzburger Prov.-Synode von 1549," *Arch. für östr. Geschichte* 85 (1898), 131–357; B. Caspar, *Das Erzb. Trier im Zeitalter der Glaubensspaltung* (Münster 1966), pp. 68–84; H. Molitor, *Kirchliche Reformversuche der Kurfürsten und Erzbischöfe von Trier* (Wiesbaden 1967), pp. 96–99.

that they were not issued by the proper ecclesiastical authority and represented a problematic intervention by the Emperor into the inner ecclesiastical sphere. To be sure, the papal bull of indult of 18 August 1548 can be interpreted as a certain sanction of these religious-political measures.[19] In this, after protracted negotiations, the Pope granted the dispensations requested by Charles V for promoting reunion.[20] They had the same orientation as the *Interim* and the *Formula Reformationis.* The rehabilitation of repentant concubinaries, the ordination of preachers who had not so far received that Sacrament, and the employment of apostate religious in the parochial care of souls were made possible by it. The lay chalice was conceded under definite cautions, and an adjustment with the holders of revenues and wealth from former ecclesiastical property was facilitated.

The *Interim* was difficult to enforce. It was compromised by being the dictate of the victorious power in war and provoked resistance. Also the convictions necessary for realizing its positive potentialities were wanting. There were not enough priests and religious who could have replaced the opposing Protestant preachers. The Jesuits were just beginning to come to Germany. Only in South Germany, in cities such as Augsburg, Ulm, and Constance and in Württemberg did the Emperor have the power to make the *Interim* respected to some extent. In Saxony an attenuated form of it was provided. The Wittenberg theologians, headed by Melanchthon, who was personally ready for an understanding, had laid their hesitations before a Diet at Meissen in July 1548 (*CR* 7, 12–45). In the article on justification, they maintained, "much that was good was said," in particular "that we are freely justified by grace without merit," but also much "pharisaical leaven was intermixed" (16). After further discussions at Pegau and Torgau a new formula was produced at Altzelle. In this were listed the intermediate things (*adiaphora*) on which there could be agreement. This led on 28 December 1548 to the passing of the Leipzig *Interim* (*CR* 7, 258–264). Confirmation and the anointing of the sick were reintroduced, ordination was committed to the bishops, and ceremonies and vestments at Mass and even the feast of Corpus Christi were ordered. The intention was to cling to doctrine and yield in the *adiaphora.* Only an excerpt, the "little Interim" (*CR* 7, 426–428), was published, together with a mandate of the Elector Maurice of 4 July 1549. It obtained no very great importance but evoked among the Wittenberg theologians the momentous quarrel over *adiaphora.* Luther's disciple, Matthias Flacius, came out against it, left Wittenberg, and from Magdeburg, "our Lord God's chancery," together with Nikolaus von

---

[19] Text in Le Plat, IV, 121.
[20] *CT* VI, 767ff.

Amsdorf, led a severe struggle against the *Interim,* which meant for him the *interitus* of the Reformation. In it he heaped mockery and scorn on Johannes Agricola and the dastardly Melanchthon.

Charles V outlawed Magdeburg and commissioned Maurice of Saxony to execute the sentence. This city's effective resistance confirmed the other Protestant cities of North Germany in their rejection of the *Interim.*

The Revolt of the Princes

The Imperial Diet of Augsburg in 1550–51 was influenced by the Council, whose reopening at Trent had been held out by the new Pope Julius III. The Lutheran estates declared their readiness to send delegates but refused to aid in the implementation of the *Interim* and the imperial *Formula Reformationis.* A growing opposition to Charles V was spreading. As early as February 1550 Hans of Küstrin, Albrecht of Prussia, and Johann Albrecht of Mecklenburg had concluded an alliance at Königsberg for the maintenance of Protestantism and the support of Magdeburg. Now the Emperor's exertions to secure the imperial succession to his son Philip became known. They led to a Habsburg family pact on 9 March 1551, according to which Ferdinand was to succeed Charles as Emperor, but at the same time Philip, the heir of Spain, was to become King of the Romans and hence Ferdinand's successor in the imperial office. Ferdinand's son Maximilian was to yield to the Spaniard. The sequel to this arrangement was an estrangement of the brothers, Charles and Ferdinand, and an anxiety among the princes, who believed they had reason to fear "the brutal Spanish servitude."

Maurice of Saxony now made himself the champion of the liberty of the princes. He had, in the interval, found it quite distasteful to be branded by opponents of the *Interim* as a traitor to the Lutheran cause. In addition, the Emperor had not fulfilled the new Elector's hopes for an increase of power nor yielded to his repeated pleas for the liberation of his father-in-law, Philip of Hesse. Maurice also feared that the League of Königsberg might pursue the aim of restoring the former Saxon Electorate with French help, and he undertook an artful double game to prevent it. While entering into negotiations with France, he displayed at the same time his loyalty to the Emperor by executing the imperial sentence of outlawry against Magdeburg, which surrendered on 4 November 1551. He united with the Königsberg allies, from whom in January 1551 he had withdrawn the troops assembled at Verden for the relief of Magdeburg, and with Wilhelm of Hesse. On 15 January 1552, at Chateau Chambord, they signed a treaty with King Henry II of France. The latter promised them financial aid for the attack on the

Emperor and in return was assured the imperial vicariate over the cities of Metz, Toul, and Verdun. Thus was the gateway to the Empire opened for the French and a wedge thrust between the Netherlands and Burgundy. At the same time Henry II strengthened the aims of the Turks for an offense and encouraged the Emperor's opponents in Italy to rebel.

Charles V had disregarded several warnings and was unprepared when, at the end of March, Maurice of Saxony advanced against Augsburg and beyond into Tirol, while Albrecht Alcibiades of Brandenburg-Mulmbach harassed the Franconian bishoprics. Meanwhile, Maurice negotiated unsuccessfully with Ferdinand at Linz from 19 April to 1 May. Before there could be a meeting at Passau for new discussions, the troops of the rebel princes moved via the Ehrenberger Klause against Innsbruck. Charles V saw himself compelled to flee through the Brenner Pass to Villach. At the news of war the Council at Trent had already dispersed on 28 April 1552.

The Emperor was cut to the quick but not broken. The more time he acquired for pushing an energetic countermobilization, the stronger his position became in the negotiations conducted at Passau from May to July 1552. In these King Ferdinand, who was once more in strong difficulties from the Turks, became the spokesman of the neutrals and the mediator between the Emperor and the rebels, who demanded the annulling of the *Interim,* the convoking of a national assembly for an adjustment of the articles of religion, and a lasting religious peace. Church property was to be left in the hands of the current holders. The Emperor scorned any definitive renunciation of a confessional reunion and any binding restrictions on his imperial rights. In the Peace of Passau, which he ratified on 10 August, he again allowed only a truce until the next Diet, at which the religious question and the *gravamina* should be settled.

The Religious Peace of Augsburg

Following the failure of an undertaking against France in the late fall of 1552 and the raising of the siege of Metz in January 1553, Charles V left Germany forever and turned over the Empire to his brother Ferdinand. He saw himself unable to restore religious unity in the Empire and had "scruples" about cooperating in another solution.[21] While he actually summoned the long overdue Diet to Augsburg, he did not

---

[21] In the letter of 8 June 1554 to Ferdinand, "the actual abdication of Charles as German King" (Brandi, op. cit., II, 398), he wrote: "seulement pour le respect du point de la religion, auquel j'ai mes scruples" (K. Lanz, *Correspondenz* III, 624).

intend to appear there in person. The meagerly attended Diet was finally opened on 5 February 1555. At the outset the Emperor lodged a protest against everything whereby "our true, ancient, Christian, and Catholic religion would be in the least injured, insulted, weakened, or encumbered." Since the death of Maurice of Saxony in 1553 the Protestants lacked a leader, but they had asserted their determination to work for an unconditional and perpetual religious peace. Of the Protestant princes only the Duke of Württemberg came to Augsburg in person. The negotiations were conducted by princely councilors, professional jurists, and diplomats. There was a great longing for peace and a general conviction of the need for a compromise. To be sure, the time was not yet ripe for a real religious peace. Even though the Protestants demanded the unlimited exercise of religion for themselves, they were not ready to concede it to Catholics or fanatics in their own territories.[22] On 14 September the Strasbourg delegates, appealing to their consciences, resisted the tolerating of a Catholic minority in their city on the ground that a toleration of Catholicism would be a sin against God.[23]

Of the Catholic estates only the Bishop of Augsburg, Cardinal Otto von Waldburg, defended a consistent, though impracticable idea. He explained that it was impossible for him to approve a division of the one Catholic Church and to acknowledge in the Diet competence for such a decision.[24] But at the news of the death of Pope Julius III on 23 March, he left the Diet with the legate, Cardinal Morone, in order to take part in the conclave. The fact that he did not return and had himself represented by his chancellor was probably due to his insight that he stood alone in his unwillingness for concessions.[25] The Roman Church was at first represented by the Nuncio Delfino, then temporarily by Lippomano, and not at all in the decisive business of the final weeks.

Theological arguments played scarcely a role in the discussions at Augsburg. The princes or jurists decided the fate of the confessions. There was no further thought of a compromise in dogma and liturgy. What was sought was a lasting ecclesiastical peace between imperial estates that differed in religion. In addition to the question of the ownership and usufruct of Church property, difficulties arose from the demand that the bishops should abandon jurisdiction over the subjects

---

[22] "There can be no doubt that [the Protestant estates] were demanding a greater freedom than they were prepared to grant" (A. Druffel–K. Brandi, *Reichsgeschichte* IV, 739, footnote 1).

[23] Ibid., p. 719.

[24] J. Grisar, "Die Stellung der Päpste zum Reichstag und Religionsfrieden von Augsburg 1555," *StdZ* 156 (1954f.), 440–462, p. 444; K. Repgen, *Die römische Kurie* I, 1, 74.

[25] K. Repgen, op. cit., I, 1, 74, footnote 80.

of Protestant princes. There was a severe struggle for the recognition of the "ecclesiastical reservation," whereby a spiritual prince who passed over to the Reformation should lose his office and his rule. The Protestants were unwilling to approve it. When King Ferdinand insisted, stressing that "he had sworn by his honor not to give it up," they made the counterdemand that the ecclesiastical estates should grant "freedom of religion" to the Lutheran knights, cities, and congregations. Ferdinand agreed. He obtained from the Catholics, not its acceptance in the Recess, but only its admission as a subsidiary *Declaratio Ferdinandea.*[26] The "ecclesiastical reservation," on the other hand, was included with the postscript that the Protestants had not approved it.

The Religious Peace of Augsburg was published with the Recess of the Diet on 25 September 1555. It provided that, following so many fruitless efforts for peace, it had been agreed, in an effort to save the fatherland from dissension and ruin, that none of the imperial estates should be attacked by the Emperor or a prince because of its adherence to the *Confessio Augustana* nor suffer any other disadvantage (para. 3). Conversely, the princes of the *Confessio Augustana* were not to inflict any sort of harm on the secular or spiritual estates that clung to the old religion (para. 4). However, all the others which did not belong to the two confessions were to be excluded from this peace (para. 5). The free choice of confession applied only to the imperial estates, not to their subjects, who, in accord with the fundamental principle, "Ubi unus dominus, ibi una sit religio,"[27] had to accept the confession of the authority. If they could not bring themselves to do so, they should have the right to emigrate after selling their property (para. 11). Because the religious factions could not agree in the case of the conversion of an ecclesiastic to the *Confessio Augustana,* the King, by virtue of the imperial authority, decreed that archbishops, bishops, prelates, or other spiritual estates who abandoned the old religion lost their offices and property, and the chapters could elect a successor who held all the property according to old custom (para. 6). Hence spiritual princes should be able to become Protestants only as private persons, without any right to force their subjects to conform, and with the loss of their

---

[26] Text in E. Walder, *Religionsvergleiche des 16. Jahrhunderts* I (Bern, 2d ed. 1960), 68–71.

[27] This statement, frequently made during the negotiations, later became the celebrated formula, "Cuius regio, eius et religio." It first appears in the *Institutiones iuris canonici* (Frankfurt, 2nd ed. 1612) of the Lutheran Joachim Stephani: "ut et ideo hodie religionem religioni cohaerere dici potest, ut cujus sit regio, hoc est ducatus, principatus, territorium seu jus territorii, ejus etiam sit religio hoc est jus episcopale seu jurisdictio spiritalis" (lib. I, cap. 7, no. 52). Quoted from M. Heckel, "Staat und Kirche nach den Lehren der ev. Juristen," *ZSavRG* 42 (1956), 212, footnote 430.

authority. In regard to ecclesiastical property, the situation at the time of the Peace of Passau was taken as decisive (para. 7). Until the definitive religious settlement, spiritual jurisdiction should not be exercised over the estates of the *Confessio Augustana* (para. 8). Knights who were immediate imperial vassals were to be included in the peace (para. 13). Where both confessions existed side by side in the Free Cities, matters should remain thus, and each should leave the other in the peaceful possession of its creed, rites, and property (para. 14). The peace should remain valid until the achieving of a peaceful and definitive settlement of religion. If such a union should not come into existence at a general or national council or at a diet, then it should continue in force as "a steadfast, firm, unconditional peace, lasting for ever" (para. 12).

The Religious Peace, therefore, was understood as only temporary, until the restoration of unity of faith by a council or another authority competent for religion. It was to be permanent only if no better arrangement could be arrived at. In actuality it became something definitive of great historical importance and introduced a period of peace of a duration otherwise unknown in Germany.

The religious cleavage was definitive and the juxtaposition in law of two confessions was created. The principle of equality was established, but only for the Empire as an equilibrium between confessionally complete parts; hence it was an equality based on inequality in the several territories. Thus there could be no question of toleration and freedom of conscience. Quite the contrary: the territorial prince decided the religion of his territory and of his subjects. By recognition of the right of emigration, he merely renounced the implementation of the medieval law on heresy with its consequences for body, honor, and possessions. The arrangement was based on the notion of the modern territorial state, to the consolidation of which confessional unity contributed substantially. The annulling of episcopal jurisdiction in Protestant areas completed the development of the territorial Church and called for the episcopacy of the prince, who, while unable to direct his Church spiritually, had it administered by his jurists. The politicization of religion and the isolation of the confessions intensified their mutual hostility. They knew very little about each other and that only from hearsay in polemical distortions.

The obscurities in the Religious Peace offered much material for conflict. The Protestant estates did not feel bound by the ecclesiastical reservation. They tried in vain to abolish it at later diets. As a matter of fact, the secularization of the sees and chapters in northern and central Germany reached its climax only after 1555: Meissen, Merseburg, and Naumburg in Saxony and Bremen, Lübeck, Schwerin, Camin, Verden, Havelberg, Brandenburg, and Lebus in North Germany. The *Declaratio*

Ferdinandea in regard to the protection of Protestants in the spiritual principalities had, of course, no formal validity in law,[28] but at first it frequently prevented the already insecure Catholic bishops from claiming the right to decide the confessional adherence of their subjects. On the other hand, many Free Cities did not observe the decree for the protection of confessional minorities. The provisional congregations were for the most part again suppressed. Nevertheless, the article on the cities made possible the continued existence of monasteries and chapters in Free Cities with a Lutheran majority. While the peace originally applied only to the adherents of the *Confessio Augustana,* in actuality the Reformed also were soon able to enjoy it, though not without resistance and, until 1648, without any binding force in law. The conversion of the Count Palatine Friedrich III to Calvinism in 1563 contributed decisively to this. Accordingly, the Religious Peace of Augsburg was unable to prevent the split in German Protestantism.

With the abandoning of the exclusive validity of the one, true Catholic faith the concept of the Empire was fundamentally affected. The Empire had been degraded to a mere federation of territorial states. Hence it was more than a coincidence in time that on 12 September 1556 Charles V renounced the imperial throne. The attitude of the Curia, with whose standards the Religious Peace was irreconcilable, can be understood only if one takes into account that under Julius III an interference in the German situation had been avoided because Germany was already regarded as lost[29] and under Paul IV political differences with the House of Habsburg so predominated that "the Religious Peace was not a determining factor."[30] In the entourage of Paul IV there was probably some protest against the Religious Peace, but no more than complaints and accusations in letters to King Ferdinand and others resulted. There was no formal protest and no objection through legal process against the Religious Peace of Augsburg,[31] and, we may say, this was advantageous for the consolidating of the Catholic position in Germany. The Catholic estates, Ferdinand I at their head, were convinced

---

[28] It was neither published nor communicated to the *Reichskammergericht,* and hence for this court it never had validity.

[29] Morone wrote as legate from Augsburg to Rome on 26 March 1555: "To me it seems that the least evil one can do here is to do nothing and to permit matters to collapse of themselves rather than to destroy them by political decrees." Cf. H. Lutz, "Karl V. und die Kurie 1552/56," RSTI 13 (1959), 22–49, pp. 40f.; K. Repgen, *Die römische Kurie* I, 1, 77, footnote 92.

[30] H. Lutz, *Christianitas afflicta,* p. 472.

[31] This is demonstrated against J. Grisar ("Die Stellung der Päpste," *StdZ* 1956 1954f., 461) by H. Lutz (*Christianitas afflicta,* pp. 471–474) and K. Repgen (*Die römische Kurie* I, 1, 82–86).

that at the moment no better solution was possible if one did not want to suffer further losses or put up with further military confrontations. In concepts of his own day, for which that age was not yet ripe, Pius XII grasped the historical reality 400 years later, when he declared concerning the Religious Peace of Augsburg: "The common good of the Empire as well as of the Church, for which it was a question of being or not being within the German frontiers, justified the signing of the Religious Peace by the Catholic princes."[32]

[32] *AAS* 47 (1955), 597.

Europe under the Sign of Confessional Pluralism

CHAPTER 25

The Reformation in Scandinavia

Even to a greater degree than in Central Europe, in the Scandinavian countries the introduction of the Reformation and the constructing of the new ecclesiastical organization were effected under the pressure of political forces. The Scandinavian Kingdoms of Denmark, Sweden, and Norway, together with outlying Iceland and Finland, had been united since 1397 in the Union of Kalmar. This was more a personal union under the Danish King than an organic political unity. National rivalries constantly led to strife. If the King of Denmark sought to exploit the religious innovations as a means of breaking the power of the nobility, especially of the bishops, for Sweden the Reformation was the means of shaking off Danish rule. Norway and Iceland, on the other hand, defended their autonomy against Denmark by the Catholic faith. Ruthlessly and with no effort to gloss matters over, people turned to the confiscation of the well-administered and productive property of churches and monasteries.

Christianity was not yet so deeply rooted in Scandinavia as in southern and central Europe and so people did not know there any "waning of the Middle Ages" with a differentiated and demanding religiosity on the one side and the appearance of decay connected with overripeness on the other. Life went on, as a matter of course and unhindered, in the forms of Catholic piety. The reform exertions of the fifteenth century had had an impact in the North and at times a more lasting effect than in Central Europe. A reformed Catholicism had been active at the beginning of the sixteenth century in the context of humanist zeal for the Bible and the Fathers. It is not always easily distinguished from the Protestant movement.

Alongside the mendicant orders, that of Saint Birgitta displayed a rich life in both the male and female branches. But what has been said of Sweden was true of the Scandinavian countries in general: "Perhaps no country of West European Christendom less needed ecclesiastical Reformation at the beginning of modern times."[1]

[1] H. Holmquist, *Die schwedische Reformation 1523–31* (Leipzig 1925), p. 5.

At the end of the Middle Ages the Scandinavian lands were divided among three ecclesiastical provinces. The Danish, under the Archbishop of Lund, comprised the sees of Aarhus, Börglum, Odense, Ribe, Roskilde, and Viborg. Sweden and Finland constituted the province of Uppsala with the suffragan sees of Linköping, Skara, Strängnäs, Västeras, Växjö, and Abo. To the Norwegian province of Trondheim (Nidaros) belonged the bishoprics of Bergen, Hamar, Oslo, and Stavanger, with Holar and Skalholt on Iceland.

Denmark

In Denmark King Christian II (1513–23), gifted but unbalanced and ruled by his passions, wanted to break the power of nobles and prelates and make the crown hereditary. He managed to gain the middle class and peasantry by progressive measures such as the improving of popular education and of the administration of justice and the promoting of industry and commerce. In 1520 he was able to impose his rule briefly on Sweden by crushing the attempts at independence made by Sten Sture, the administrator of that Kingdom. In the "Stockholm Blood Bath" he tried to get rid of his opponents among the Swedish nobility but thereby incurred such hatred that it was easy for the youthful Gustavus Vasa to win over the people, including leaders among the nobles and churchmen, and to be himself elected administrator in 1521. In the autumn of that year the Danish government had to withdraw and Christian's authority was confined to Denmark, Norway, and Iceland.

In October 1520 Christian had asked Luther's prince, the Elector Frederick the Wise, to send him a preacher of the pure word of God. Thus in June 1521 Karlstadt came to Denmark. But he was unable to realize his radical ideas, for the King, from political motives, including consideration for his brother-in-law, Charles V, was unwilling to go as far as to break with the old Church. Christian II first completed his territorial Church government. He curtailed the rights of bishops and forbade appeal to Rome. He permitted priests to marry. But at the beginning of 1523 he was to fail because of the opposition of the nobles, including a group of bishops. They renounced their fealty to him and raised Duke Frederick of Holstein to the Danish throne. They obliged Frederick to proceed against Luther's disciples and all others who preached against "God, the faith of Holy Church, the Holy Father at Rome, or the Roman Church." But Frederick I (1523–1533) came out more openly in favor of Lutheranism as he saw his position consolidated. In June 1526 he gave his daughter in marriage to Albrecht of Prussia, who had been the first spiritual prince to become a Protestant and had transformed the territory of the Teutonic Order into a secular duchy.

Frederick favored Hans Tausen (1494–1561), the "Danish Luther," a former Hospitaler, who had been gained to the new doctrine as a student at Wittenberg in 1523, and in 1526 made him his court chaplain, even though a charge of heresy had been made against him.

Especially harmful was the Curia's practice of disposing capriciously of the benefices of the Scandinavian Church. For example, it did not confirm the canonically elected and properly qualified Master Aage Jepsen Sparre as Archbishop of Lund, but on 6 February 1520 bestowed the rich see on the curial Cardinal Paul Aemilius Cesi. Thereupon Christian II placed, in succession, three of his confidants in the archbishopric. In 1526 Frederick named Aage Sparre as Archbishop, but papal confirmation was refused. Hence Sparre was unable to receive episcopal consecration and governed as archbishop-elect. Under the influence of this struggle in 1526 the King obtained from the *Herredag* at Odense a law to the effect that henceforth no cleric might ask confirmation or provision from the Pope. The hitherto customary fees were to be used for the defense of the country. In 1532 five of the eight Danish bishops, of themselves Catholic-minded, were not consecrated.

At the *Herredag* at Odense in 1527 the bishops demanded that steps be taken against "the new government and the new teaching," but the King got his way and obtained protection in law for the Lutherans. They won most cities. Only the episcopal cities and the rural folk, with the majority of the nobility, remained Catholic. The Carmelite Paul Helgesen (c. 1485–1534) stood up fearlessly for the old faith. He was stamped with the biblical humanism of Erasmus and hoped for a renewal of the Church from a study of Holy Scripture and patristic theology. The bishops called in from Germany Nikolaus von Herborn (c. 1480–1535), provincial of the Franciscans and preacher at the Cologne cathedral. He composed the declaration of the bishops against the forty-three articles of the *Confessio Hafniensis,* which twenty-one Lutheran preachers, under the leadership of Hans Tausen, had submitted to the *Herredag* at Copenhagen in July 1530, and a *Confutatio Lutheranismi Danici.* King Frederick continued consistently his policy of favoring Lutheranism. After his death in 1533 the bishops wanted to thwart the election of his Lutheran-minded oldest son Christian in favor of the latter's younger brother, still a minor. The younger prince had been raised in reform Catholic circles and gave hopes of a Catholic restoration. At the *Herredag* at Copenhagen it was possible to postpone the election. But a civil war, supported by Lübeck and aiming at the reinstatement of the exiled Christian II, forced the election of Christian III (1534–59). This meant the victory of the Lutheran Reformation in Denmark, together with Norway and Iceland. The bishops were imprisoned and excluded from the secular government and their property was confiscated for the crown. On 30 October 1536 they were deposed by the *Rigsdaag* and replaced by "superintendents," who were really royal officials. Johannes Bugenhagen was called to Copenhagen to construct the new Church organization. He crowned the King, drew up the *Ordinantia Ecclesiastica* on the model of the Saxon Church Order, and ordained seven superintendents. These later assumed the episcopal title, without bothering about apostolic succession. The *Ordinantia Ecclesiastica* was accepted by the *Rigsraad* in 1539 as a provisional solution until the settlement of the religious question by a general council. But, as a matter of fact, it continued in force until 1683 and created a Lutheran national Church under the King's direction. When in 1538 Christian III joined the League of Schmalkalden, the *Confessio Augustana* became the creed of the Danish Church. In 1550 appeared "Christian's Bible," a translation of the entire Scripture into Danish. Resistance to the Reformation was crushed by prison and banishment. King Christian IV (1588–1648) forbade Catholic priests to set foot in Denmark under threat of death. Exile and loss of property remained for centuries the punishment for conversion to Catholicism. Religious liberty was not granted until 1844.

Norway

Christian III introduced the Reformation in Norway at the same time as he did in Denmark. Here Olav Engelbriktsson, Archbishop of Trondheim from 1523 to 1537, had tried to save a remnant of Norwegian autonomy vis-à-vis Denmark along with the ancient faith. But he had been unable to unite the forces of the country against Christian and in 1537 he fled to the Netherlands. Without popular support, the Reformation was imposed in Norway on the Danish model. The bishops were deposed, and ecclesiastical and monastic property was confiscated for the Danish crown.

Assemblies of nobles at Bergen and Oslo, powerfully reinforced by Danish vassals, approved the Danish *Ordinantia Ecclesiastica* in 1539. But out of regard for the people, who were unprepared for Lutheran doctrine, the implementation was carried out with prudence. The Catholic faith continued for decades among the rural folk. Catholic customs, such as pilgrimages and the veneration of the Mother of God and of Saint Olav, persisted far beyond the sixteenth century. An obstacle to bringing the people into a close attachment to Lutheranism was the fact that, in addition to the Danish Bible, the liturgy, hymns, and Luther's *Small Catechism* were available only in Danish, and the Norwegian language survived only as the popular dialect. However, the Lutheran Church Order of 1607 brought the Reformation to a definite conclusion.

Iceland

In Iceland too a living Catholic Church succumbed to the Danish King's desire for power. Lutheranism came there, as it came to Denmark and Sweden, through merchants and young clerics educated in Germany. At first Bishops Ogmundur Palsson of Skalholt (1521–1540) and Jon Arason of Holar (1520–1550) contrived to keep these influences out. On the accession of Christian III Iceland obtained a new governor in Klaus of Merwitz, who demanded that the bishops accept the Danish Church Order. They refused, with their clergy, and in two doctrinal letters warned the people against Luther and his errors. Meanwhile, Gissur Einarsson (1515–1548), who had returned as a Lutheran from his academic career in Germany, had dispelled the hesitations of Bishop Ogmundur and secured the blind old man's confidence. When the bishop resigned in 1540 he recommended that young Einarsson, who in the previous years had made himself indispensable, should be his successor. He was elected and at Copenhagen was confirmed by the King as superintendent. In Iceland he managed at first to keep the conservative circles in the dark as to his intentions. When the old bishop recognized his mistake, he became active, despite his feebleness, in defense of the ancient faith and found support among priests and the people. The Danes resorted to force and in 1541 dragged the old man aboard ship, on which he died shortly after putting out to sea. The Bishop of Holar in northern Iceland, Jon Arason, ecclesiastical prince, poet, statesman, and warrior all in one, was determined to defend the Catholic faith along with Iceland's freedom. He had become a bishop, even though he had four sons, of whom two were priests, and two daughters. Denounced as a rebel and heretic by the Danish King, in the summer of 1550 he proceeded, as a true descendant of Vikings, against the south of the island, captured the Protestant Bishop of Skalholt, and expelled the Danish governor and his adherents. Iceland seemed to be under his control, but on his return to the north he fell by treachery into the hands of his enemies. He was condemned to death and, since he scorned to purchase his life on terms not to be expected of a bishop, he was executed along with his two priest-sons. Now Christian III had an easy time in introducing the Reformation. This meant at the same time the despoiling of the island and the end of its freedom. No wonder that it took so long for Lutheranism to gain access to the hearts of the people. It was only in 1584 that there appeared a complete Bible in Icelandic;

this was followed by a hymnal in 1589 and a book of family devotions in 1594.

Sweden

In Sweden Gustavus Trolle, Archbishop of Uppsala, had joined the Danes against the Swedish nationalist movement. He was deposed in 1517. In 1520 Christian II of Denmark in his campaign for the subjugation of Sweden posed as the defender of the Church's freedom and protector of the Archbishop. He had the leaders of the Swedish opposition put to death in the "Stockholm Blood Bath" of November 1520. The union of the two Kingdoms was thereby gravely weakened and Archbishop Trolle was compromised. The struggle for freedom was thus directed against him and the Church that he embodied. In 1521 Gustavus Erikson Vasa (1496–1560) was elected administrator of the Kingdom at Vadstena and before long he controlled the whole country except for a few strongholds. The Danish government had to yield. With the dethronement of Christian II in Denmark Sweden was to achieve its definite independence. At Pentecost 1523 Gustavus Vasa was elected King at Strängnäs. The local archdeacon, Lars Andersson (1470–1552), became his secretary and chancellor. He guided the royal policy in the direction of the Reformation and managed to make Gustavus Vasa understand the advantages offered by a Lutheran ecclesiastical organization for the royal power and the public treasury. Religion was not a particularly profound concern of the King. What mattered to him was to secure his power by means of a state Church and to take care of the financial needs of his political organization by means of ecclesiastical property without imposing further burdens on the people and the nobility.

In Sweden the Lutheran movement had also become known through merchants who were Germans or had German connections and through theologians who had studied in the land of the Reformation. The most important among them and the real reformer of Sweden, Olav Pedersson (1493–1552), came directly from Luther's school. He had studied at Rostock and Leipzig and, from the late summer of 1516, at Wittenberg. He returned to Sweden in the fall of 1518, full of enthusiasm for Scripture as the supreme authority. He entered the service of the Bishop of Strängnäs and became deacon (1520), master of the cathedral school, and cathedral preacher. When his sermons were challenged, the King created for him in 1524 the position of city secretary and preacher at the main church in Stockholm. He labored zealously there for the Reformation until 1531. He inaugurated his series of numerous, predominantly pastoral writings with *A Useful Instruction*

(1526).[2] This first reform treatise in Sweden is a medley of separate sections with translations of passages from Luther, Bucer, and others. Olav composed hymns, translated the New Testament (1526), and in the *Swedish Chronicle* created the first great work of national history.

Hans Brask, Bishop of Linköping, was the steadfast and methodical champion of the Catholic faith. In 1521 Gustavus Vasa had solemnly promised him that he would protect all the rights and possessions of the Church. He distributed religious writings by means of his own printing press. He pressed for a translation of the New Testament and in pastoral essays came out very sharply against Lutheranism. It is not surprising that in the course of years he came into ever stronger opposition to the King. This was all the more portentous when, in 1523–24, almost all the other sees had become vacant and were now occupied by royal candidates. These were Catholic in sentiment but they had been neither confirmed by the Pope nor consecrated. In November 1523 Gustavus Vasa had applied for the papal confirmation with a demand for a dispensation from the customary fees, threatening that otherwise he would confirm, without the Pope, those elected "a solo et summo pontifice Christo" and have them consecrated. The Curia refused. The Pope confirmed only Peder Mansson (d. 1534), superior of the monastery of Saint Birgitta at Rome, as Bishop of Västeras and had him consecrated.[3] Bishop Brask saw the danger of schism and advocated the King's speedy coronation as well as the confirmation and consecration of the bishops. Gustavus Vasa was not to be hurried; in fact, he was more interested in delay. He aimed to eliminate "episcopal rule" in the country, but the royal coronation involved an oath to respect the privileges of the Church and the position of the bishops, and he wanted to evade this. Furthermore, he had less difficulty with administrators who had been merely elected and not consecrated. He feared that after consecration the bishops intended to recognize no further duties to him, "but only to the Pope at Rome."[4]

The decision as to the fate of the Swedish Church was made at the Diet of Västeras in 1527. By recourse to craft Gustavus Vasa contrived to parry the religious question—he said he did not want to introduce any new religion but only to have the pure word of God and the Gospel preached—and to push the Kingdom's difficulties into the foreground. He was chiefly concerned to strip the Church of power and to divert her

---

[2] On the writings of Olav Pedersson cf. S. Ingebrand, *Olavus Petris reformatoriska Askadning* (Lund 1964), pp. 19–48 (German summary, pp. 348–351).

[3] T. van Haag, "Die apostolische Sukzession in Schweden," *Kyrkohistorisk Arsskrift* 44 (Uppsala 1945), 5ff.

[4] S. Kjöllerström, "Gustav Vasa und die Bischofsweihe (1523–31)," *Festschrift für Joh. Heckel,* ed. S. Grundmann (Cologne–Graz 1959), pp. 164–183.

wealth to the advantage of the unitary state that he was seeking to establish. The passionate appeal of Bishop Hans Brask on behalf of the freedom of the Church and the authority of the Pope produced only a passing impression. In the decree of the Diet the estates completely surrendered the Church to domination by the state. It decided which revenues should continue to accrue to the bishops for their spiritual ministry. The monasteries came under the King's supervision or were turned over to the nobles for spoliation. The external organization of the Church remained, but the King could appoint and depose priests. They had to preach the pure word of God.

Gustavus Vasa had achieved his goal at Västeras. Now his coronation and the consecration of the bishops could bring him only advantages and consolidate his position vis-à-vis the outside and the opposition in the country. He made known to the bishops-elect that the people no longer wanted to be without "consecrated bishops." They had to receive consecration or give up their positions. But they should be bishops "in accord with the word of the Lord, not of the Pope." Consequently they had to take an oath to preach the Gospel, to be content with the revenues necessary for their function, and to be loyal to the King. The Pope was not mentioned. The consecration was performed by the Bishop of Västeras, Peder Mansson, who had himself been consecrated in Rome. The candidates stressed their loyalty to Rome, certifying in writing that, when the opportunity presented itself, they would obtain papal confirmation.[5] A week later, on 12 January 1528 Gustavus Vasa had himself anointed and crowned King by the bishops in the Uppsala cathedral according to the old Catholic rite. But in the coronation oath there was no mention of the protection of Holy Church and of the privileges of bishops. The reformer, Olav Pedersson, preached the sermon.

In February 1529 the synod of Örebro denied to the Pope authority higher than that of bishops but was otherwise reform Catholic rather than Protestant. The break with the papacy became complete when in 1531 the brother of the reformer Olav, Lars Pedersson, who had just finished his studies at Wittenberg, was made Archbishop of Uppsala with no concurrence by Rome. In the same year appeared Olav's *Ordo Missae Sueticae,* a translation and revision of the old order of the Mass in the spirit of the reform. Among other things, the Nürnberg Mass served as its model. As chancellor of King Gustavus Vasa, Olav Pedersson exercised the greatest influence in these years 1531–33. Later he and Lars Andersson fell into royal disfavor. Gustavus Vasa sought the advice of two Germans, the theologian Georg Norman and the jurist Georg

[5] Ibid., p. 180.

von Pyhy, to strengthen his influence over the Church. He placed it under the supervision of a superintendent and to this office he appointed Norman, his sons' tutor, in 1539. Olav Pedersson and Lars Andersson were not submissive to this political caprice; they were condemned to death but then pardoned on payment of a heavy fine. From 1543 Olav Pedersson again worked as chief pastor in Stockholm, where he died in 1552.

Gustavus Vasa's attitude on the religious question was subject to change according to the political situation in the succeeding years. On the whole the construction of the Lutheran Church proceeded quietly but methodically. The external institutions were preserved more than they were elsewhere. Of course, much time was needed to gain the people, especially the rural folk.

Of the sons of Gustavus Vasa, Erik XIV (1560–88) first succeeded to the throne. Highly gifted but extravagant and with no sense for the possible, he provoked the nobility by his attempt to continue or further perfect the absolutist regime of his father and angered the Lutheran clergy by the favor he showed to Calvinism. And yet he urgently needed support by all the forces of the Kingdom because of the seven-years' war with Denmark over Livonia. He was toppled by a rising of the nobles in 1568 and in 1577 poisoned in prison.

His brother and successor, John III (1568–92), gave the Swedish state Church its present form in the Church Order of 1571. It had been composed by Lars Pedersson in 1561 but suppressed by Erik XIV. The revised edition of 1571 was more intimately related to old Swedish tradition, introduced a richer liturgy, and gave the episcopal office more importance and prestige.[6] The episcopal constitution of the Church was completely restored.

John III was himself interested in theology. His marriage with the sister of King Sigismund II of Poland, Catherine, who remained true to her Catholic faith, his own humanist education, and an encounter with the Anglican Church and its liturgy caused him to think of mediating between the Catholic and the Protestant Churches. He was fascinated by the idea of a Church unity based on the common tradition of the patristic age. Union seemed to him to be possible if the marriage of priests, the lay chalice, and the vernacular liturgy were conceded. His "catholicizing" efforts found their expression in the new Church Order of 1575 and in the *Liturgy of the Swedish Church* of 1576, the so-called *Red Book.* Regardless of the opposition, the King held discussions with

---

[6] E. Färnström, *Laurentius Petris handskrivna Kyrkoordning av ar 1561* (Stockholm 1956).

the learned Jesuit Anton Possevino (d. 1611) on reconciliation with Rome.

The forces that offered resistance to reconciliation were organized by the third son of Gustavus Vasa, Duke Charles of Södermanland. On the death of John III, Charles felt that the time was especially favorable for energetic measures against a return to Catholicism. John's son Sigismund (1592–99), who had been King of Poland since 1587, and had labored zealously there for the Catholic faith, intended to do likewise as King of Sweden. Duke Charles made use of the time before the King's assumption of the throne to confront him with a *fait accompli*. The national Synod of Uppsala in March 1593 rejected the liturgy of John III as superstitious and formally ascribed to the *Confessio Augustana* of 1530. The coronation of the new King was made contingent upon his agreeing to these decrees. Sigismund agreed. Later he was not even able to secure the free exercise of religion for his Catholic entourage. Disillusioned, he returned to Poland and committed the government to his uncle, Duke Charles. Only when the latter by his autocratic conduct had run afoul of the higher nobility in the *Riksrad* did King Sigismund try to seize power again by armed force. But Charles retained the ascendancy, took bloody vengeance on his opponents after the Diet of 1560, and in 1604 mounted the Swedish throne as Charles IX (1604–11).

In 1595 the Diet of Söderköping had decreed the expulsion of all Catholics from the country and the suppression of the last monastery, Saint Birgitta's foundation at Vadstena.

Finland

The fate of the Church in Finland was totally determined by the country's dependence on Sweden. The decrees of the Diet of Västeras in 1527 and of the Synod of Örebro in 1529 were authoritative here also. But Canon Peter Sarkilathi (d. 1529) of Abo (Turku), who had studied in Germany, had already spread Lutheran teachings. Marten Skytte, who, as a seventy-year-old man, had been made Bishop of Abo by Gustavus Vasa in 1528, was himself a Catholic, but he fostered the Reformation by sending gifted young men to study in Germany. The most important of these, Mikael Agricola (1508–57), returned to Finland with a letter of recommendation from Luther after a period of study at Wittenberg (1536–39). He became the director of the cathedral school, then coadjutor and in 1554 successor of Bishop Skytte. Agricola not only became the reformer of Finland; at the same time he laid the foundations of the Finnish written language and literature. In 1543 he published a speller, attached to a brief catechism, and the next year, a large prayerbook. His chief work was the translation of the New

Testament in 1548. In addition, he produced parts of the Old Testament (1551–52) and a liturgy modeled on the "Swedish Mass."

In the same year as Agricola (1544), Paul Juusten, who had also studied at Wittenberg (1543–46), became bishop of the newly erected see of Viborg (Viipuri). Learned and gifted in a practical and pastoral sense, he ranks as the "Melanchthon of Finland." He died in 1576 as Bishop of Abo. The efforts of John III for recatholicization found a receptive soil in Finland, but here too they were cancelled by the Uppsala Synod of 1593. Significant for the attaching of the people to the Reformation were the Finnish hymnal of 1605, an improved edition of that of 1580, a catechism in questions and answers (1618), and a two-volume book of sermons (1621).

CHAPTER 26

The Reformation in Eastern Europe

At the beginning of modern times the countries of Eastern Europe were characterized by a plurality of nationalities, social orders, and constitutional forms. The sequel was that the Reformation made its appearance relatively early and easily but, except in Prussia and Livonia, was nowhere established fully nor exclusively in its Lutheran form. The plurality of forces produced an altogether milder religious climate and a juxtaposition of several confessions in one territory. Often the authority did not impose a uniform confession, and the consequence was not only the toleration of Protestantism but its fragmentation. In addition to Lutherans and Calvinists, the Antitrinitarians—Unitarians and Socinians—and the Anabaptists and Bohemian Brethren, expelled from the lands of their origin, had a chance to develop.

Religion and nationality were closely connected. The Germans were Lutherans and remained such until the time of the Counter Reformation. Religion and nationality supported each other in an alien environment. Poles and Magyars, in so far as they did not remain Catholics, turned chiefly to Calvinism.

For the smaller nations and national groups the reform movement meant a cultural event to a far greater degree than elsewhere. The exertions in regard to Scripture and to a vernacular liturgy and preaching led to translations of the Bible and the publishing of hymnals, catechisms, collections of sermons, and a devotional literature. In this way dialects often became literary languages, and literary monuments arose which supplied both expression and support to the national consciousness.

The German population in the cities and the nobility and great proprietors in the country played an important role in the introduction of the Reformation. Because of their endeavors to secure and expand their jurisdiction vis-à-vis the King and the episcopal tribunals they were all open to a confession not held by the monarchy or the authority. As a result, frequently only a small upper stratum was affected by the reform movement, and a later recatholicization made easy progress.

The Duchy of Prussia

By the Second Peace of Torun in 1466 the western part of the lands of the Teutonic Order—Pomerellen and Kulmerland—together with the bishopric of Ermland was incorporated into Poland. East Prussia with Königsberg was left to the grand master of the Teutonic Knights, who, however, had to take an oath of personal fealty to the Polish King. When Albrecht of Brandenburg-Ansbach (1490–1568) was elected grand master of the order in 1511, he, like his predecessor, tried to evade the taking of the oath and to recover the West Prussian territories of the order. The sequel was war with Poland in January 1520. In the truce of Torun the solution of the controverted question was referred to a commission of arbitration. In the matter of the reform of the order and of the administration of its territory, Albrecht's adviser, Dietrich von Schönberg, as early as 1521 wanted to submit the order's rules to Luther for revision. But this was not done until June 1523, after Albrecht had meanwhile been gained for the reform movement by Osiander's preaching at Nürnberg in 1522 (WA, Br 3, 86f.). On 28 March 1523 Luther had already published *An die Herren Deutschen Ordens, dass sie falsche Keuschheit meiden.*[1] In the autumn of the same year Albrecht summoned two Lutheran preachers, Doctor Johannes Briesmann[2] and Johannes Amandus, to Königsberg and at the end of November he met Luther at Wittenberg. Luther advised him to abandon the rules of the order, to marry, and to transform the order's territory into a secular principality (WA, Br 3, 315, 22–25). In December Luther replied to Albrecht's questions: whether Christ had founded his Church on Peter and on the Popes as Peter's successors, whether the Pope had the power, with or without a council, to issue a law over and above the commandments of God, a law whose observance would be important for salvation, and

---

[1] WA 12, 232–244; cf. WA, Br 3, 195.
[2] Cf. R. Stupperich, "Johann Briesmanns reformatorische Anfänge," *Jahrbuch für brandenburgische Kirchengeschichte* 34 (1937), 3–21.

whether Pope and councils could change God's commandments (*WA, Br* 3, 207–219). Through Briesmann, who had already anonymously published theses on justification in September–October 1523,[3] the Bishop of Samland, Georg von Polentz (1478–1550), was won for the reform movement. He delivered a Lutheran sermon in the cathedral at Königsberg on Christmas 1523.[4] Polentz appealed to his episcopal office and intended, as "shepherd and watchman instituted by God" to lead his congregation to the "true and pure word of God" and to confidence in Jesus Christ. He wanted henceforth to use the German tongue in baptism. In an effort to obstruct the progress of the Reformation in his diocese, the new bishop of the neighboring see of Ermland, Mauritius Ferber, issued an edict against the Lutheran heresy on 20 January 1524. Polentz thereupon decreed the introduction of the vernacular in the administration of baptism in a reform mandate for his diocese, issued on 28 January, and recommended the reading of the following works of Luther: the translation of the New Testament, *Von der Freiheit des Christenmenschen, Von guten Werken,* the *Kirchenpostille,* the exegesis of the "Magnificat," and of the psalms. Instructive of his understanding of Reformation is the fact that he does not mention Luther's polemics.[5]

Luther's German brochure on baptism was printed at Königsberg in 1524 as an aid for pastors and in Lent an explication of the "Our Father" was introduced.[6] In the "Salve Regina" "advocate" and "King Jesus" replaced "Mary."[7] At the same time appeared *Ein Sermon von dreyerley heylsamer Beycht* by Briesmann,[8] in which he maintained that auricular confession to a priest was not commanded by God; also an Easter sermon by Bishop Polentz,[9] containing an exhortation to communion under both species. In the two principal churches of Königsberg the

---

[3] *Flosculi de homine interiore et exteriore, fide et operibus,* ed. by P. Tschackert (Gotha 1887). Canon Tidemann Giese, of the neighboring see of Ermland, composed a reply, the *Antilogikon,* "drawn up in a noble spirit" (P. Tschackert, *Urkundenbuch* I, 69), but it was not printed until 1525. Cf. U. Horst, "Reformation und Rechtfertigungslehre in der Sicht Tidemann Gieses," *Zeitschrift für die Geschichts-und Altertumskunde Ermlands* 89 (1960), 38–62.

[4] Cf. P. Tschackert, *Urkundenbuch* (hereinafter *UB*) I, 70–74; 41, no. 154.

[5] *WA* 15, 148, 27–35. Luther, who in 1524 published both episcopal edicts with notes, missed in them only Melanchthon's *Loci.*

[6] Tschackert, *UB* II, no. 184.

[7] Ibid., no. 189; here is found also the prayer, "Christe qui lux es," in German.

[8] Ibid., no. 188; cf. ibid., I, 77f. Cf. also Briesmann's *Etliche Trostsprüche für die Furchtsamen und Herzfeigen,* which appeared at Königsberg in October 1524; it is printed in R. Stupperich, *Reformatorische Verkündigung und Lebensordnung* (Bremen 1963), pp. 121–148.

[9] *UB* II, no. 202; cf. ibid., 79–81.

images of the saints were removed during Lent, and on Easter Monday and Tuesday Johannes Amandus urged the people in sermons to plunder and destroy the Franciscan monastery. The resistance of citizens with Catholic sympathies to the innovations was officially and forcibly suppressed by Polentz, who at this time was still in charge of government business for Albrecht.[10] In order to push the further spread of the Reformation, Polentz sent Lutheran preachers into the cities and village parishes of the territory confided to him and then carried out their installation by recourse to his office as regent even when the people of a city were unanimously opposed to the measure.[11]

Meanwhile, Paul Speratus (1484–1551) was summoned to Königsberg as court-preacher; he arrived around the end of July 1524. There soon arose a dispute between Amandus and Speratus over the value of the episcopal office. Whereas Amandus could see no difference between the episcopal and the preaching offices, Speratus insisted: "We are preachers, not bishops. . . . One only is our Bishop in Christ," namely Polentz. "The power to impart the episcopal function belongs to the Church, not to the people and the local authority."[12] Amandus was banished from Königsberg in the autumn of 1524. Around the end of the year poor laws were decreed in the cities of Königsberg-Kneiphof and Königsberg-Altstadt.[13] At the same time Erhard von Queis, postulated as Bishop of Pomesania by the cathedral chapter of Marienwerder but never confirmed by the Pope, published a reform program entitled *Themata episcopi Riesenburgensis.*[14] In twenty-two points Queis demanded, among other things, the abolition of pilgrimages (point 4), processions (5), Masses for the dead (6 and 8), sacramentals (7), religious orders (9), daily Mass (19), and the reduction of the seven Sacraments to two, the Lord's Supper and baptism (1). Accordingly, "bishops should be and remain not chrism-bishops and not ordination-bishops; but they should preach and teach and explain God's pure word and govern the Church" (10).

Meanwhile, Albrecht had decided to follow Luther's advice and transform the territory of the Teutonic Order into a secular duchy. On 9 April 1525, one day before the armistice agreed to in 1521 expired, he signed the Peace of Cracow, which provided for the suppression of the Teutonic Order in Prussia and the enfeoffment of Albrecht with the

---

[10] Cf. the penal mandate of 15 August 1524 (*UB* II, no. 249).

[11] Cf. *UB* II, no. 224.

[12] Ibid., no. 247. Cf. also Luther's dedicatory preface to the exegesis of Deuteronomy (1525): "Georgio a Polentis vere Episcopo Sambiensis Ecclesiae" (*WA* 14, 497).

[13] *Ordnung eines gemeinen kastens der aldenstadt Königsberg,* Sehling, IV, 143f.; cf. *UB* II, nos. 290f.

[14] Sehling, IV, 29f.

order's Prussian lands as an hereditary secular duchy. On 10 April Albrecht solemnly took the oath of fealty to the Polish King. In August Bishop Polentz relinquished all secular authority in his bishopric to Albrecht, because "it would not be proper for him, as a prelate and bishop, who is obliged to preach and proclaim the word of God, to rule lands and people, to garrison castles, countryside, and cities, but rather to cling to the true and pure word and to carry it out."[15] "But Polentz remained officially what he was—Bishop of Samland—with all the ecclesiastical rights that he had exercised up to now; he retained the right of ordaining the clergy,[16] the right of visitation of all churches in his territory, and jurisdiction over matrimonial cases, just as he had done as Bishop."[17] Erhard of Queis surrendered his secular authority to Albrecht in October 1527. In the summer of 1525 Polentz, Briesmann, and most religious and priests in Prussia married. In the fall, while Duke Albrecht was absent, there were disturbances among the peasants. After they had been forcibly suppressed, Albrecht, who had earlier admitted Briesmann and Johannes Poliander, newly arrived from Wittenberg, into his cabinet as ducal councilors, summoned a Diet for December 1525. At this a territorial ordinance[18] and a Church Order issued by Polentz and Queis were adopted.[19] The annual visitation provided in the latter was first carried out in the spring of 1526.[20] Thereby the Reformation was firmly consolidated in the Duchy of Prussia.

Livonia

The Baltic territories of Kurland, Livonia, and Estonia were under their own master of the Teutonic Order, who was then Wolter von Plettenberg (1499–1535). But he shared the government with the bishops and allowed the cities extensive autonomy. Early on the Reformation got a foothold at Riga, Reval, and Dorpat. Andreas Kopken (b. c. 1468) preached at Riga in the spirit of the Reformation from the late summer of 1521. Having previously been an assistant to Johannes Bugenhagen at Treptow in Pomerania, he went to him a second time in 1519, was gained for the Reformation, and in 1521 returned to Riga. In 1522,

---

[15] *UB* II, no. 356.

[16] Cf. the formula of ordination of 1543 (Sehling, IV, 61).

[17] *UB* I, 113. Later the episcopal constitution of the Church was "abolished only because an independent bishop was inconvenient to the government and cost too much money" (ibid.).

[18] Cf. *UB* II, no. 417; text in Sehling, IV, 38–41.

[19] Sehling, IV, 30–38.

[20] Cf. the visitation instruction of 31 March 1526 issued by the territorial prince and the bishop (Sehling, IV, 41f.).

without regard for the cathedral chapter's right of provision, the city council appointed him and Master Sylvester Tegetmeyer of Rostock as preachers in the city churches.

There is evidence for Lutheran preaching also at Reval, Narva, and Dorpat by 1524 at the latest. In the winter of 1524–25 there were riots directed against the churches and monasteries. The city authorities used these as an opportunity for reorganizing the Church and disposing of much Church property, and not merely, as has been alleged, for the care of the poor and the preachers.

In the summer of 1524 Riga renounced its oath of homage to the archbishop, Johannes Blankenfeld, who energetically championed the old faith, and offered to the master of the Teutonic Order, Wolter von Plettenberg, the suzerainty of the city, to be exercised alone instead of with the archbishop. Otherwise, the city would look for another lord. This was an allusion to Albrecht of Prussia, whose secularizing notions were well known. Thus the master was in a difficult position. On the one hand, he did not want to infringe on the archbishop's rights; on the other, he had to allow Albrecht no pretext for interfering. But when the archbishop, in an effort to maintain himself, allied with the Grand Prince of Moscow, Wolter von Plettenberg had a reason for arresting him for treason and assuming the undivided suzerainty. He definitely rejected the demand to secularize Livonia as Prussia had been secularized, but in September 1525 he was willing to concede to the city of Riga the right of free Lutheran preaching in order to evade the danger of Albrecht of Prussia's intervention. He proved that this was only a concession due to political considerations by his energetic efforts on behalf of the Catholic faith within the order and in its territory. The same end was fostered by the speedy restoration of the archbishop, who subjected himself to him but soon died (1527).

In 1527 the city of Riga summoned the Königsberg reformer, Johannes Briesmann, to become cathedral preacher and also gave him a post corresponding to that of superintendent. He stayed until 1531, elaborating a Lutheran Church Order with Andreas Kopken in 1529. This *Kurtz Ordnung des Kirchendienst*,[21] printed in 1530, contained a liturgy in High German and a hymnal in Low German and was made obligatory by Riga, Reval, and Dorpat in 1533. The efforts of Albrecht of Prussia to make Livonia a secular duchy by means of his brother Wilhelm, who became coadjutor in 1530 and Archbishop of Riga in 1539, and to eliminate the Teutonic Order foundered on the resistance of the order and of its victorious master, Wilhelm of Fürstenberg. But when in 1558 the order, without allies, faced an invasion by the Rus-

---

[21] Sehling, V, 11–17.

sians and succumbed to their superiority, Livonia broke up. The last master of the order, Gotthard Kettler, received Kurland and Semgallen from Poland as a secular vassal duchy and led it to the Reformation. Ösel fell to Denmark, Estonia to Sweden, while the rest of the order's territory, with the archbishopric of Riga, came under Polish rule in 1561. But King Sigismund II Augustus granted the German cities extensive autonomy and assured them the free exercise of religion according to the *Confessio Augustana*.

Poland

Pre-Reformation currents, the ideas of conciliarism, the impact of Hussitism, and the spirit of humanism also prepared the soil for the Reformation in Poland.

The influence of the royal court, above all that of the Renaissance Queen, Bona Sforza, was harmful to the Catholic Church, especially in the matter of nominations to bishoprics. For example, it was possible for Jan Latalski, called "Bacchus" by the people because of his addiction to strong drink, to purchase the see of Poznan in 1523 for twelve thousand florins. In this country of a predominantly agricultural economy and an aristocratic society the nobility played a great role. Its struggle against episcopal jurisdiction and for extensive autonomy favored the spread of Protestantism.

The reform movement was introduced and propagated by students who had studied abroad, by merchants' sons who were sent to Nürnberg, Augsburg, or Leipzig for training, and by Luther's writings. The humanist Andrzej Modrezewski (1503–72), who had himself studied at Wittenberg in 1531–32 and from 1547 was secretary of the royal chancery, reported: "Luther's books were brought to us from Germany and were sold openly at the University of Cracow. They were hailed and approved by many . . . and even our theologians took no offense."[22] As early as 1520 King Sigismund I (1506–48) saw himself compelled to issue an edict, which was made more strict in 1523, against the introduction of Luther's writings. In 1534 and 1540 attendance at heretical universities was forbidden, but the effect of this decree was not too great.

Luther's treatise on the Ten Commandments had already been printed at Danzig in 1520. Jakob Hegge, Doctor Alexander Svenichen, and Matthias Binewald preached there in the spirit of the Reformation. As almost everywhere else, enthusiasm for the new teaching was con-

---

[22] R. Stupperich, "Der Protestantismus auf seinen Wegen nach Osteuropa," *Kirche im Osten* 1 (1958), 28.

nected with social demands, such as that for a reduction of taxes and for a public statement of the household accounts. In 1524 an attack on monasteries and rioting occurred. The old city council had to yield. In January 1525 five preachers of the new doctrine were appointed and in the *Articles of the Community* of 23 January poor laws that had been demanded were provided.[23] In May 1525 Luther sent Michael Meurer of Heinichen to Danzig. Meanwhile, the overthrown mayor, Eberhard Ferber, appealed for help to King Sigismund I. After the Diet, which had been summoned to Piotrkov, and the provincial Diet, convoked at Marienburg for Polish Prussia, had promised the King support, he restored the old order at Danzig, thus stopping for the moment the progress of the Reformation.

Under Sigismund I there were as yet no reform congregations established, but the Reformation gained many adherents among the nobility. The humanist Christoph Hegendörfer was active at the Poznan Academy from 1529 until his banishment in October 1535. In 1530 Andrzej Gorka, castellan of Poznan, had Lutheran services celebrated in his castle.

Before the middle of the sixteenth century Cracow and Königsberg were the most important centers for the spread of the Reformation. At Cracow from 1542 a group of scholars, nobles, and priests met regularly under the direction of the Franciscan Francesco Lismanini, confessor of the Queen and later a Calvinist, to acquaint themselves with the reform movement outside Poland. A Polish translation of Luther's small catechism was printed at Königsberg as early as 1530. The Church Order of the Duchy of Prussia of 1544 appeared not only in German and Latin but also in Polish.[24] Andrzej Samuel and Jan Seklucian (1500–70) fled from Poznan to East Prussia in 1543. Seklucian composed revisions of the catechism in Polish in 1545 and 1547 and published a Polish hymnal at Königsberg in 1547. In 1552 he also published a New Testament at Königsberg,[25] and in 1556 a Polish prayerbook,[26] a free rendering of that of Melanchthon and Spangenberg. Also active at Königsberg[27] were, among others, Stanislaus Murzynowski (1528–1553) and Jan

---

[23] Text in Sehling, IV, 175f.

[24] Text, ibid., 61–72.

[25] In 1561 there appeared at Cracow a Catholic translation of the entire Bible into Polish. The Calvinist "Brest Bible" dates from 1563.

[26] Nicholaus Rej (1505–69) composed the most popular Protestant prayerbook in Polish in 1558; cf. K. Gorski, "Biblia i sprawy biblijne w Postylii Reja," *Reformacja w Polsce* 12 (1956), 62–125; K. Krejci, *Geschichte der polnischen Literatur,* pp. 52–58.

[27] Cf. B. Stasiewski, *Reformation und Gegenreformation in Polen* (Münster 1960), p. 46; K. Volker, *Kirchengeschichte Polens* (Berlin–Leipzig 1930), pp. 179f.

Maletius (d. 1567)—the latter published a catechism[28] in 1546—and the Lithuanians[29] Abraham Culvensis,[30] Stanislaus Rapagelan,[31] and Martin Mosvidius.[32] The University of Königsberg, founded in 1544, contributed significantly to the spread of the Reformation.

Protestantism reached its greatest development in Poland under King Sigismund II Augustus (1548–1572). In 1562–63 some six hundred out of thirty-six hundred parishes were in Protestant hands. In 1569 the Senate counted fifty-eight Protestant members as opposed to fifty-five Catholics, but the latter figure does not include the fifteen bishops. From 1552 to 1565 only Protestants were elected as marshals of the Diet.

The Protestants had great hopes in the King, who corresponded with Melanchthon and Calvin. Calvin dedicated his commentary on Hebrews to him in 1549.[33] Prince Mikolaj Radziwill of Lithuania, a zealous champion of Protestantism, was on friendly terms with the King and as grand chancellor occupied an influential position. But on 12 December 1550 Sigismund II publicly professed the Catholic faith, while at the same time continuing to tolerate the advance of Protestantism.

At Pinczow the local lord, Mikolaj Olesnicki, expelled the Minims, destroyed the images and relics in the parish church, and had Lutheran services celebrated. Similar occurrences took place at Niedzwiedz, Dubiecko, and elsewhere. Sigismund approved the acceptance of the *Confessio Augustana* by the *Landtag* Diet of Polish Prussia in 1559. He likewise assured Livonia, when it came under Polish rule in 1561, the recognition of the *Confessio Augustana*. The Warsaw Confederation of 28 January 1573 guaranteed freedom of religion to every noble.[34]

Despite these successes the impact of Protestantism was weakened by its fragmentation among Lutherans, Calvinists, Bohemian Brethren, and Antitrinitarians. Lutheranism was represented chiefly by the German middle class. About half the congregations in Greater Poland joined in a synodal union. Erazm Gliczner worked as superintendent from 1565. The main body of the Bohemian "Fraternal Unity" consisted of breth-

---

[28] *UB* II, no. 1872.

[29] Cf. S. Kot, "La Reforme dans le Grand-Duche de Lethanie," *Annuaire de l'institut de philologie et d'histoire orientales et slave* 12 (Brussels 1953), 201–261.

[30] T. Wotschke, "Abraham Culvensis," *Altpreussische Monatsschrift* 42 (1905), 153–252.

[31] First professor of theology at the University of Königsberg (WS1544–45; lectures on the psalms; disputation theses, *WA* 39, II, 258–283), he died in May 1545. He was the author of the first hymn in Lithuanian (*UB* I, 289, footnote 1).

[32] Holder of a scholarship at the university and author of the first catechism in Lithuanian (*UB* II, no. 2064).

[33] Cf, *CR* 91, 281–286 (no. 1195).

[34] Text in G. Rhode, *Die Reformation in Osteuropa,* p. 489, footnote 21.

ren who emigrated to Poznan after the Schmalkaldic War.[35] They found a great response both among the nobility—Jakub Ostroróg, Andrzej and Raphael of Lissa—and among the common people. Their centers were Poznan, Kozminek, and Lissa.

Calvinism made great strides after 1550. Its main centers were Lesser Poland (Cracow) and Lithuania; its adherents came chiefly from the Polish population and the nobility. Jan Laski (1499–1560), a highly educated aristocrat, was its most important figure. After his travels had led him throughout the West, he returned to his Polish homeland in 1556 to act as reformer in Calvin's spirit. Prince Mikolaj Radziwill used his own great influence for Calvinism. Wherever he could, he established a Calvinist worship. He brought about a translation of the entire Bible and founded a press specifically for the printing of this "Brest Bible" (1563). Even the center of the Protestantizing Cracow circle of humanists, Francesco Lismanini, devoted himself to the Calvinist confession after a visit to Geneva at the beginning of the 1550s. With Jan Laski he worked to unite all the Protestants in Poland and to create a strict ecclesiastical system on the Geneva model. But they were unable to overcome the fragmentation and, after Laski's death, Lismanini himself went over to the sect of the Antitrinitarians.[36]

In 1565, under the leadership of the Cracow pastor, Gregor Pauli (Pawel), the Antitrinitarians separated from the Calvinist Church as the "Ecclesia minor." They had taken over the rejection of the dogma of the Trinity from Italian refugees for their faith, such as Giorgio Biandrata and Valentino Gentile. Faustus Sozzini (c. 1537–1604) became their leading theologian. They were later called Socinians after him, though he himself did not join their community. After 1600 Rakow became their intellectual and organizational center, and in that city in 1605 appeared the *Rakow Catechism,* based on preliminary studies by Sozzini.

At Kozminek in 1555 a union of the Calvinists of Lesser Poland and the Bohemian Brethren of Greater Poland was formed. The *Consensus* of Sandomir in 1570 led to a fraternal union which included the Lutherans.[37] But it broke up again in 1645. In addition to the fragmentation

---

[35] Whereas the old Utraquists again sought the communion of the Roman Catholic Church, the new Utraquists and the Bohemian Brethren followed the Reformation. In 1538 Luther published the 1535 confession of the Brethren (cf. *WA* 50, 374–380). Of importance for the new Czech literary tongue was the Kralitz Bible (1579–93), Cf. B. Stasiewski, *Reformation und Gegenreformation,* pp. 46–48; E. Benz, *Wittenberg und Byzanz,* pp. 129–140.

[36] Cf. Stasiewski, *op. cit.,* pp. 52–59; *RGG* VI, 207–210; *LThK* IX (2d ed.), 928–931; P. Wrzecionko, "Die Theologie des Rakower Katechismus." *Kirche im Osten* 6 (1963), 73–116; id. "Humanismus und Aufklärung im Denken der polnischen Brüder," ibid., 9 (1966), 83–100.

[37] Test in Sehling, IV, 257–259.

and the lack of educational institutions, the weakness of Polish Protestantism lay especially in its failure to win the broad masses of the people. It remained the affair of a thin upper stratum and of the nobility.

> The broad masses of the rural population were virtually untouched by the religious forces of the Reformation. They took part in the worship as modified in accord with the orders of the manorial lord . . . , but nevertheless had no inner sympathy for it.[38]

Hungary

At the close of the Middle Ages Hungary was engaged in a close cultural interchange with its western neighbors.[39] And so Luther's writings were circulated in Hungary too, especially among the German population. At the royal court in Buda the Reformation found a promoter in the Margrave Georg of Brandenburg-Ansbach-Kulmbach (1484–1543). He had lived there with his royal uncle since 1506 and in 1516 became tutor of the still underage King Louis II (1516–1526) and a member of the government. He represented German interests[40] in opposition to the Magyar faction under John Zapolya.

The young Queen, Mary of Habsburg, sister of Charles V, read Luther's writings enthusiastically[41] and maintained close contact with the humanists, Simon Grynaeus (1493–1541), then rector of the University of Buda and later (1529) successor of Erasmus at Basel, and Vitus of Windsheim. Conrad Cordatus (1476–1546) labored for the Reformation as court preacher in 1521–22; he later planned the first collection of Luther's *Table Talk*.[42] Johannes Henckel, his successor, served the same cause.[43] And Paul Speratus, who had to give up his post of cathedral preacher at Würzburg in 1520 after his marriage, also received a call to Buda.

As early as 1521 the Archbishop of Esztergom was moved to have the bull excommunicating Luther read in the churches of the kingdom. The

---

[38] K. Volker, *Kirchengeschichte Polens,* p. 159.

[39] The sermons of the Hungarian Franciscan Ladislas Pelbartus of Temesvar (d. 1504) were printed in Nürnberg, Lyons, Hagenau, Basel, and Strasbourg. Of these, the series "De Sanctis" alone went through ten editions at Hagenau in 1499–1516. The well-known collection of sermons, *Biga salutis,* was published by a Hungarian Franciscan, Oswald of Lasko (d. 1531), and printed at Hagenau.

[40] Cf. L. Neustadt, *Markgraf Georg als Erzieher am ungarischen Hofe* (Breslau 1883).

[41] In 1526 Luther dedicated to her the exegesis of the four psalms of consolation; cf. *WA* 19, 542–615; *WA, Br* 4, 126.

[42] Cf. *WA, Tr* 2, XXIFF.; *WA, Br* 4, 139, footnote 1.

[43] Cf. A. Hudak, "Der Hofprediger Johannes Henckel und seine Beziehungen zu Erasmus von Rotterdam," *Kirche im Osten,* 2 (1959), 106–113.

Diet of Buda in 1523 decided to apply the paragraph on heretics to the Lutherans also. An edict of 1525 threatened them with burning at the stake. The higher nobility urged the removal of the Lutheran court preacher. Conrad Cordatus was imprisoned, but in 1524 he was able to escape to Wittenberg, to which Grynaeus had earlier betaken himself.

Decisive importance attaches to the battle of Mohács, where on 29 August 1526, in addition to King Louis II, two archbishops and five bishops fell in the struggle against the Turks. Following the Turkish victory Hungary was divided into three parts: the "Kingdom of Hungary," comprising the northern and western parts, came under Habsburg rule; the Turkish province, which included the Pusta, the low plain in the area of the Danube and the Theiss; and the "Principality of Transylvania," where Zapolya (1526–40) maintained himself as vassal of the Sultan and which, after his death, fell, despite the Peace of Grosswardein (1538), not to King Ferdinand but to Zapolya II.

The ecclesiastical property in the widowed bishoprics was seized by the higher nobility, while Ferdinand let part of it be expropriated by his generals, most of whom were inclined to Lutheranism, in payment of his war debts. The rivalry between Ferdinand and John Zapolya prevented any proceedings against the nobles and the Lutherans, since neither wanted to lose adherents, and Ferdinand in particular was dependent on the German faction, which was for the most part friendly to Luther.

The sequel was that in the following years both Ferdinand and Zapolya each named a bishop for the same see, so that some of them, for example Csanad, Weissenburg, Eger, and Grosswardein, at times had two claimants. There was no nomination by the Curia until 1539.

The school of Bartfeld acquired a special importance for the further spread of the Reformation in the German part of the population. Leonhard Stöckel (1510–60) took charge of this in 1539. He had studied at Kaschau, Breslau, and from 1530 Wittenberg and in 1536–37 he directed the school at Eisleben. The majority of the future statesmen of Hungary went through the humanist-oriented school of Bartfeld,[44] from which proceeded nearby schools and printeries. The five royal Free Cities of Bartfeld, Eperies, Kaschau, Klein-Zeben, and Leutschau joined the Reformation in 1549 by adopting the *Confessio Pentapolitana* composed by Stöckel. This confession, stamped with a humanist spirit and recognized even by Ferdinand because of its dogmatic moderation, became the basis of the confession of the seven hill towns of Lower

---

[44] Cf. the *Leges scolae Barthphensis* (1540), composed by Stöckel. Other important works by Stöckel are: *Catechesis pro iuventute Barthphensi* (1556), *Apologia ecclesiae Barthphensis* (1558); *Historia von Susanna in Historien Tragoedien Weise gestellet . . .* (1559), a commentary on Melanchthon's Loci (1561), and volumes of sermons.

Hungary as well as of the fraternity of the twenty-four towns in the Zips.

Johannes Honter (1498–1549), who had studied at Vienna, is regarded as the reformer of the Germans in Transylvania. When after 1529 the Transylvanian cities passed to Zapolya, Honter, as a partisan of Ferdinand, had to flee from his native Kronstadt. Following a stay at Cracow and Basel, he was called back home in 1533 and there he conducted a private school and established the first printery in the country. The prefaces to two works of Augustine[45] that he printed in 1539 were early testimonies to his reform outlook. After his friend Johannes Fuchs had assumed the government of Kronstadt in 1541 and even the clergy had been gained for the Reformation, Valentin Wagner was sent to Wittenberg to establish closer relations with Melanchthon. The liturgy was reformed at Kronstadt in the autumn of 1542. The approval by the city of the Reformation brochure[46] that Honter published in 1543 meant the introduction of the Reformation. To defend it, Honter wrote an Apologia for the Diet at Weissenburg.[47] He was intrigued by the idea of a Reformation within the Catholic Church. This found expression in the fact that as late as 1543 he recognized the Archbishop of Esztergom and the Bishop of Weissenburg. The word of God, he held, had to be the supreme guideline of every reform. Hence the Mass as a sacrifice should be abolished and the Eucharist under both species introduced. On this point Honter appealed to discussions at Regensburg in 1541 for a compromise. Rebaptism was rejected on the basis of the *Decretum Gratiani.* In the doctrine of justification Honter, following Melanchthon and Major, stressed the necessity of good works against the perils of a justification by faith alone.

The example of Kronstadt was soon followed by Hermannstadt, where the city pastor, Matthias Ramser, himself introduced the Reformation, and by Mediasch, Schässburg, and Bistriz.

> In this context there everywhere appeared the effort to remain externally still in the unity of the old Church. At first the Reformation affected merely the form of the liturgy, not the Church organization.[48]

---

[45] Printed in O. Netoliczka, *Johannes Honterus' ausgewählte Schriften*, pp. 3–10; cf. Melanchthon's preface to the edition of the Reformation brochure, published by him in 1543, in *CR*, 5, 172–174.

[46] Netoliczka, op. cit., pp. 11–28.

[47] Ibid., pp. 29–46.

[48] K. Reinerth, *Die Reformation der siebenbürgisch-sächsischen Kirche* (Gütersloh 1956), p. 43.

The *Reformatio ecclesiarum Saxonicarum in Transsylvania*,[49] a Church Order based on Honter's Reformation brochure and valid for the entire Saxon area of settlement, appeared in 1547; it was commissioned by the *Universitas Saxorum,* the political organ of the Saxon element in the population. Its aim was to maintain order against fanatics. The power of the keys and excommunication were again more closely linked with the spiritual function. James 2:17 was cited as the chief proof in the doctrine of justification. Even a censorship of books was provided. The Eucharistic teaching was oriented to Wittenberg. This Church Order was made a law in 1550, a year after Honter's death. During the vacancy of the see of Weissenburg Paul Wiener was elected bishop in 1553. His successor, Matthias Hebler (1556–71), had to defend the Lutheran character of the Church against Calvinists and Antitrinitarians. In 1557 the Diet of Torda conceded to the three confessions equality with the Catholic confession, which was itself forbidden by law in 1566.

The Magyars were won to the Reformation, partly by Germans, for example in Transylvania by Kaspar Heltai and Ferenc Dávid, who had conformed to the Magyar culture, or by a few itinerant preachers, most of whom had studied at Wittenberg. Melanchthon's pupil, Johannes Sylvester (c. 1504–1552), directed the school or Ujsziget near Sarvar at the end of the 1530s. After a printery had been opened there in 1537–38, Sylvester published a grammar of the Magyar language and in 1541 the first complete Magyar translation of the New Testament. Mátyás Devai Bíró (c. 1500–45) preached at Buda and Kaschau and on the estates of the noble families of Nadasdy, Perenyi, and Dragffy. After his studies at Vienna, Cracow, and Wittenberg—in the last of which he took his degree in 1544—Stephan Szegedi Kis (1502–72) was schoolmaster at Csanad, Gyula, Cegled Mako, and from 1548 at Temesvar.[50] After the death of Zapolya in 1540 this area was administered by Peter Petrovics, who was entrusted by the widow Queen with the guardianship of the Prince. Petrovics was a zealous promoter of the Reformation and hence the congregations of this territory could be organized as a unit in 1549–1550 and Mátyás Gönzi elected Bishop. When in 1551 Petrovics had to surrender the frontier castle of Temesvar to the Catholic-minded Losonczy, Szegedi moved into the Turkish-occupied area and became head of the school at Tolna and pastor at Lasko and Kalmancsa and, eventually, after being imprisoned by the Turks, pastor and general superintendent at Rackeve. Testimony of his theological

---

[49] O. Netoliczka, op. cit., pp. 56–125.
[50] Cf. M. Skaricza, *Vita Stephani Szegedini* (introduction to Szegedi's *Theologiae sincerae loci communes*) (Basel 1585).

formation and of his Calvinistic theology is provided by his works, printed in Switzerland after his death.[51]

Mikael Sztarai (c. 1500–75) was also active for the Reformation in the Turkish-occupied territory as preacher, teacher, and author of hymns and plays. By 1551 he had founded 120 congregations. Imre Ozorai composed the first printed treatise in the Magyar tongue, a work on Christ and Antichrist (Cracow 1535). Stephan Galszecsi and Stephan Bencedi Szekely each had hymnals printed in 1536 and 1538 respectively. Two important centers of the Reformation arose through the favor of the noble family of Torok in Papa and Debrecen.

By 1560 the greatest part of the nobility and, since the manorial lord could appoint Lutheran pastors by virtue of the right of patronage, of the rural folk had been gained for the Reformation.

In the Slovene and Croatian border areas the noble families of Zrinyi, Erdeody, and especially Ungnad supported the Reformation. Johann Ungnad, Baron of Sonneck (1493–1564), the leading official in Styria, after embracing Protestantism went to Württemberg and on his estate at Urach arranged the printing of Bibles, catechisms, primers, and prayer-books in Slovene and Croatian.[52]

The leaders in cultivating the Slovene language for the sake of the Reformation were: Primoz Trubar (1508–86), who published, among other things, a catechism and a speller in 1550 and between 1555 and 1577 the entire New Testament and writings of Melanchthon and Luther; Sebastian Krelj (1538–67), with his children's Bible of 1566 and prayerbook of 1567; Jurij Dalmatin (1547–89), who translated the Old Testament; and Adam Bohoric (c. 1520–c. 1600), who published the psalter, hymns, some school texts, and in 1584 a Slovene grammar.

Stephan Consul was occupied with translating into Croatian. It was due principally to Georg Zrinyi, who set up a printery at Nedelisce, that the Kajkavisch dialect of the northern Croats became a literary tongue. On the Catholic side there appeared at Graz in 1574 the Slovene catechism of Leonhard Pacherneker. But real literary activity only began early in the seventeenth century with the publishing of a catechism, the Gospels, a prayerbook, and a hymnal by Bishop Thomas Hren (1560–1630).

While the German portion of the population remained Lutheran, the Magyar element, especially in the 1550s and 1560s, adhered to Cal-

---

[51] Cf. *Assertio vera de Trinitate* (1573); *Theologiae sincerae loci communes* (manual of the theology controversy, 1581); *Speculum romanorum pontificum* (history of the Popes, 1584); *Tabulae analiticae* (sermon book, 1592).
[52] E. Benz, "Hans von Ungnad und die Reformation unter den Südslawen," *Wittenberg und Byzanz* (Marburg 1949), pp. 141–246.

vinism. The leading Calvinist theologians were Kalmancsehi, Szegedi Kis, Peter Melius, Gregor Szegedi, and Kaspar Karolyi.

At the end of 1559 appeared the first written Hungarian confession, the *Eucharistic Confession of Neumarkt,* in which the Magyar part of Hungary agreed on the Calvinist view of the Last Supper. Antitrinitarianism became a great danger for Calvinism. It was chiefly represented by Stancaro (1501–74), Biandrata (1514–ca. 1590), physician of King Johann Sigismund, and Ferenc Dávid (ca. 1510–79), Calvinist bishop of Transylvania. A synod met in 1567 at Debrecen, the intellectual center of the Calvinists, for defense against the Antitrinitarian currents. It accepted, in addition to two confessions drawn up by Melius (ca. 1536–72), Bullinger's *Confessio Helvetica Posterior* and a Church Order.

On behalf of the Catholics Georg Utjesenovich, called Martinuzzi (d. 1551),[53] especially tried to stop the advance of the Reformation. He was the most intimate adviser of Zapolya, after whose death in 1540 he was entrusted with the regency of Transylvania. After his assassination by some of Ferdinand's people, altars were eliminated in Grosswardein and several Catholic priests were banished. Matthias Zabardy, from 1553 Bishop of Wardein, managed to push back Calvinism temporarily. After his death in 1557, however, monasteries were destroyed in Grosswardein and the Franciscans were expelled. Earlier, in 1556, P. Bornemisza, who had become Bishop of Weissenburg in 1554,[54] had had to flee. The estates of Transylvania prevented the filling of the see, which thus remained vacant until 1716. There were no bishops in the Turkish-occupied areas. In 1543 the Metropolitan of Esztergom transferred his residence to Tyrnau. From 1554 the Archbishop was Nikolaus Olahus (1493–1568), friend of Erasmus and former secretary of Queen Mary of Hungary. He worked for the restoration of Church property, called the Jesuits to Tyrnau in 1561, and in 1566 opened there the first seminary in the country. When he insisted on the observance of celibacy, many married priests went over to Lutheranism.

Whereas Maximilian II (1564–76) sympathized with the Reformation and in 1564 forbade the publication of the Tridentine decrees, Stephen Bathory, Prince of Transylvania from 1571, promoted the Catholic faith and fought the radical wing of the Antitrinitarians, led by Ferenc Dávid. He confided the direction of the Klausenburg Academy to the Jesuits in 1579, but they were expelled in 1595.

---

[53] Cf. K. Juhasz, "Kardinal Georg Utjesenovich (d. 1551) und das Bistum Tschanad," *HJ* (1961), pp. 252–264.
[54] *Hierarchia catholica* III (Münster 1923), 101.

It was especially through the work of the Jesuits and of Archbishop Peter Pazmany (1570–1637) of Esztergom, himself from a noble Calvinist family, that Hungary eventually became once again a predominantly Catholic land.

CHAPTER 27

Schism and Reformation in England

As in the Scandinavian countries, so in England the Reformation was introduced and carried out "from above"—under the decisive influence of the government. It began as schism under Henry VIII. Under Edward VI Protestantism forced its way into worship and doctrine. And, following the collapse of the Catholic restoration under Mary I, the Anglican Church acquired its definitive form in the reign of Elizabeth I.

Under Henry VII (1485–1509) the Church in England had notably recovered from the devastating effects of the Wars of the Roses. Without possessing a formal right of nomination, the King saw to it that his candidates, usually jurists who had proved themselves in the royal service, obtained the bishoprics in both ecclesiastical provinces: Canterbury, with twenty suffragans, and York, with three. William Warham, Archbishop of Canterbury (1503–33), well known as the patron of Erasmus, was far surpassed in political influence in the reign of Henry VIII (1509–47) by the ambitious and unscrupulous Thomas Wolsey, Archbishop of York (1514–30) and Cardinal since 1515. As Lord Chancellor, Wolsey was director of domestic and foreign policy, and as Papal Legate from 1518 he also ruled the English Church in virtual independence. By suppressing the smaller monasteries he procured the means for richly endowing his Oxford foundation, Cardinal College, now called Christ Church College. He adopted strict measures to prevent the entry of Lutheranism. The morals of the parish clergy seem, so far as we can learn from pre-Reformation visitations, such as that of 1515–19 in the diocese of Lincoln, to have provided fewer occasions for censure than was the average on the continent. But the humanist permeation of Oxford under John Colet and of lay circles especially under Thomas More did not take the place of the missing theological education. Only one out of 349 books printed in England between 1468 and 1530 had a strictly theological content. Fifty-eight were liturgical, 106 were devotional manuals. English translations of the Bible had been forbidden since the suppression of Wyclifism, but Lollardy had by no means ceased as an undercurrent. Popular devotion was zealous but not really healthy—Parker terms it "fervent rather than solid piety." A certain anticlericalism found an outlet in the House of Commons, but because of the protection set up by *Praemunire* against the fee system of the Curia there could scarcely be any question of anti-Romanism. During the Western Schism England had adhered to the Roman obedience; during the conflict between Eugene IV and the Council of Basel, it had upheld the Pope. But the serious danger which the Church in England concealed within itself became visible in the second half of the reign of Henry VIII.

The Marriage Case of Henry VIII

Henry VIII's education, unusual for a prince in that period and including theology, had enabled him to come forward in the *Assertio septem sacramentorum* (1521) in refutation of Luther's *De captivitate Babylonica*. In return Leo X had honored him with the title of "Defender of the Faith." It was the unrestrained sensuality of the crafty and brutal monarch that occasioned his break with the papacy. Appealing to Leviticus 18:16 and 20:21, he claimed that his marriage with Catherine of Aragon was invalid because she had previously been married to his older brother Arthur, who had died at the age of fourteen. He said that the dispensation granted by Julius II on 26 December 1503 violated the divine law; that a brief of dispensation of the same date, which was drawn up more clearly in several points, had been falsified;[1] and, finally, that before contracting marriage with Catherine he had declared that the marriage was against his will. Despite this, he had consummated the marriage and had had seven children by Catherine, but only Mary, the future queen, survived. Conscientious scruples in regard to the validity of his marriage did not actually occur to the King until Anne Boleyn, a maid-of-honor with whom he was in love, declined to belong to him except as his wife.[2] Catherine denied the consummation of her first marriage with Arthur and the nullity of her second marriage with Henry. At first probably in ignorance of the King's ultimate intentions, Wolsey was prepared to seek from the Pope a declaration of nullity of Henry's marriage by a court of special competence for this case. Edward Fox and Stephen Gardiner, sent by him as emissaries to Orvieto, where

[1] Ehses makes it credible that it was intended for the Court of Aragon, to satisfy its demands in regard to Catherine's interests, and was first produced by her nephew, Charles V, in 1528.

[2] The existence of conscientious scruples of this sort in Henry is denied by many authors but is not excluded by Thieme (see footnote 4) and others. One motive was certainly the desire for a male heir to the throne.

Clement VII was staying since the *Sacco di Roma,* succeeded in having Wolsey and the highly esteemed jurist Cardinal Lorenzo Campeggio, who had already lived in England as legate in 1518–19, authorized on 8 June 1528 to conduct the canonical trial in England. The Pope promised to confirm their judgment and granted in advance a dispensation for a new marriage in the event that the declaration of nullity should materialize.

But the process, conducted in London, did not result in the judgment desired by the King. At its very opening on 18 June 1529, Catherine appealed to the Pope. The Bishops of Rochester and Saint Asaph upheld the validity of the marriage, but Campeggio observed in regard to the prejudiced conduct of the case: "In another's house one cannot do all that one would like."[3] Hence the Pope, who had meanwhile been set free again by the conclusion of the Peace of Barcelona and who had come under pressure from Catherine's nephew, Charles V, transferred the case to Rome on 19 July 1529. Wolsey had promised too much and had played a double game. He fell from power and died on 29 November 1530, en route to London to be tried for high treason.

In order to influence the Roman proceedings according to his wishes, Henry VIII, upon the advice of Thomas Cranmer, the next Archbishop of Canterbury, gathered legal opinions from universities and individual professors of law, for which he paid handsomely. Favoring the nullity of the King's marriage with Catherine, in addition to the English universities Oxford and Cambridge, were also those of Paris, over the protest of forty-three doctors, Orléans, Angers, Bourges, Toulouse, Bologna, Siena, Padua, Pavia, and others. The opposite opinion was held by those of Louvain, Naples, Salamanca, Alcalá, Granada, and others. At Salamanca Francis de Vitoria in his *Relectio de matrimonio* dealt with the "Causa Regis Angliae." At Wittenberg, where the King urged his case through his emissary Robert Barnes, Luther also spoke out for the validity of the marriage.[4]

The Act of Supremacy

While Clement VII was postponing his decision, Henry VIII was arranging another sort of solution—one without the Pope. On 11 February 1531 the Convocation of the Clergy, under strong royal pressure, voted to hand over 100,000 pounds to the king as "Protector and Supreme Head of the English Church and Clergy," but with the

---

[3] Ehses, *Römische Dokumente zur Geschichte der Ehescheidung Heinrichs VIII.,* p. 119.
[4] H. Thieme, *Die Ehescheidung Heinrichs VIII. und die europäischen Universitäten* (Karlsruhe 1957).

addition, at the suggestion of John Fisher, Bishop of Rochester, of "in quantum per Christi legem licet." All the bishops and likewise Thomas More, who was then still Lord Chancellor, assented to the ambiguous formula. It was the first step toward apostasy. Parliament forbade any appeal to Rome. On 23 May 1533 the complaisant Archbishop of Canterbury declared Henry's marriage with Catherine null; this was a belated and shabby justification of Henry's marriage to Anne Boleyn, which had already taken place secretly in January.

It was only now that Clement VII intervened. In the consistory of 11 July 1533, he announced that the King would incur excommunication if he did not dismiss Anne by the end of September and take back Catherine as his lawful wife. The decision issued in the canonical trial on 23 May 1534 confirmed the validity of Henry's marriage with Catherine.[5] It upheld the sanctity and indissolubility of marriage. But it can hardly be questioned that the Pope's original effort to be accommodating, determined by political considerations, aroused in Henry hopes impossible to realize, and that the long delay of the final decision made it easier for the King to prepare for the schism.

Already in June 1533 an antipapal pamphlet, *The Glasse of the Truthe,* composed by order of the King, had conditioned public opinion for the coming measures. In the *Articles,* circulated at the end of the year, "the Bishop of Rome, whom some call pope," was branded as "usurper of God's law and infringer of general councils," and, in addition, an enemy of England. In the spring of 1534 Parliament passed five laws which made ready the break with Rome. These laws gave to the King the nomination of bishops; forbade the obtaining of dispensations at Rome and the paying of fees there and subjected all exempt monasteries to the King; made the clergy subject to the civil laws; required the acceptance under oath of the royal succession of the children born of the marriage of Henry with Anne Boleyn (first Succession Act); and, in the Heresy Act, declared that no statement against the primacy of the Bishop of Rome was to be regarded as heresy.

In sermons and pamphlets the content of these laws was made clear to the people and thereby the way was prepared for the final event—the Act of Supremacy of 3 November 1534.[6] By it the title of "the only supreme head on earth of the Church of England" was conferred on the King, and his power was also extended to maintaining the purity of doctrine. A second Act of Succession required of all officials and ecclesiastics an oath to uphold the succession of Anne's children, while

---

[5] Text in Ehses, op. cit., pp. 215f.
[6] Text in Ceble, *Statutes,* p. 436; also Gee-Hardy, *Documents,* pp. 243ff.

the Treason Act branded as high treason the refusal or questioning of the new royal title.

The break with the papacy had thereby been definitively accomplished. For even if the definition of the primacy by the Council of Florence was not universally regarded then as binding, it was still beyond any doubt that the Pope was, by divine law, the visible head of the Church and that a secular ruler, even if he claimed imperial rights, as Henry VIII then did, could not be the "head" of the Church in his country, bearer of the power of teacher and shepherd.

The first victims of the Act of Supremacy were the three Carthusian priors, John Houghton, Augustine Webster, and Robert Lawrence. Together with the learned Richard Reynolds, they were hanged at Tyburn on 4 May 1535, in their religious habits, and hence without having been previously degraded. On 22 June 1535 followed the glory of the English episcopate, Bishop John Fisher of Rochester. Before being beheaded he addressed the spectators: "Christian people, I die for the faith of the holy Catholic Church of Christ." Almost identical was the profession of the former Lord Chancellor, Thomas More, before his execution on 6 July 1535. In the legal proceedings he had characterized the Act of Supremacy as "directly repugnant to the laws of God and his holy Church."[7] The nonjurors, however, constituted a decreasing minority. Except for Fisher, all functioning bishops took the oath, surrendered their papal bulls of nomination, and asked and obtained the *licentia regia ad exercendam iurisdictionem episcopalem.* Earlier the overwhelming majority of the diocesan and regular clergy had signed the declaration: "The Bishop of Rome has by divine law in this Kingdom of England no greater jurisdiction than any other foreign bishop." The question arises: How was it possible that the clergy of an entire country submitted almost unanimously to the King's will and denied the doctrine of the papal primacy?

In replying to this depressing question it must be remembered that the episcopate, standing in complete dependence on the crown, led the way and the rest of the clergy followed. Neither group possessed the theological insight that the papal primacy, far from being a theory of curial canonists, was firmly rooted in the Church's awareness of the faith. What were seriously discussed, even by Church-minded theologians and canonists, were merely its extent and its relations to the Church and the episcopate. Significantly, the *Defensor Pacis,* the most

---

[7] Hughes, *The Reformation in England* I, 281; More's moving letters to his daughter Margaret Roper, in *The Correspondence of Sir Thomas More,* ed. E. Frances Rogers (Princeton 1947), pp. 501–565.

radical denial of the divine right of the primacy to date, was now printed in English at the expense of the King, with the omission, to be sure, of the passages on the so-called sovereignty of the people. In direct dependence on Marsilius' doctrine, Edward Fox published a pamphlet on the two powers. Though he had long shown Lutheran sympathies, he was soon after named Bishop of Hereford. A book by Bishop Gardiner of Winchester in defense of the royal supremacy, composed immediately after the beheading of the martyrs Fisher and More, bore the significant title of *De vera obedientia.* On the other hand, a book *On the Defense of the Unity of the Church,* printed at Rome in 1538, exercised no influence in England, but gained for its author, Reginald Pole, a relative of the King and a resident in Italy, Henry's hatred. Pole's mother, Margaret, was imprisoned and executed in 1541.

The Suppression of the Monasteries

Resistance on the part of the people did not show itself until the king, following the advice of the Lord Chancellor Cromwell, had a general visitation of the monasteries made in 1535–36 by a commission named by him and consisting of two priests, Layton and London, and two laymen, Legh and Rice. Its chief aim was to get control of the extensive monastic property in order to assure the King of defense against any eventual attacks, to fill his privy purse, and to gain support among the nobility. At the same time the religious life was to be defamed by disclosing moral failings. Relying on the reports of the visitors, which were full of accusations against the conduct of the religious, the King, with the consent of the accommodating Parliament, decreed on 4 April 1536 the suppression of 291 lesser monasteries—191 of men and 100 of women—which had an annual income of less than 200 pounds, and confiscated their real estate and moveable property. The material support of the members left much to be desired, but the numerous complaints do not admit of generalization.[8] However, since the confiscation, and to some extent the squandering, of the monastic properties was a severe financial blow not only to their peasants and servants but also to the inhabitants of the adjoining areas, and the procedure of the visitors stirred up popular indignation, risings occurred, first in Lincolnshire and then in North England. In the latter area Robert Aske, leader of the "Pilgrimage of Grace," declared that the suppression of the monasteries meant the ruin of religion in England and that the royal supremacy was contrary to the law of God. With 9000 men he marched on York and

[8] Knowles, *The Religious Orders in England* III, 402ff.; cf. also G. Baskerville, *English Monks and the Suppression of the Monasteries* (London 1950).

brought expelled monks and nuns back to their monasteries. Since he was willing to negotiate and gave credence to a promise of amnesty, the King gained time for a countermove. The rising was suppressed in blood and Aske was executed.

The first tide of suppression had involved only the lesser monasteries. Between 1537 and 1540 the larger monasteries of the monastic order were also dissolved, mostly by means of "voluntary" surrender to the King, frequently accompanied by and based on the members' acknowledgment of guilt. The houses of the mendicant orders were suppressed at the same time. "Thus, without noise or outcry, almost without a whimper, a familiar class of men disappeared from English life."[9] The account reported at the end of the reign of Henry VIII by the royal treasurer in regard to the sale of monastic property or the revenue realized from it amounted to the then immense sum of 1.3 million pounds.[10]

Alliances and Creeds

Apart from the doctrine of the papal primacy, the Schism of 1534 had not yet attacked the substance of the Catholic faith. This occurred only when the King, basing himself on the authority attributed to him in matters of faith, in agreement with the docile episcopate, accommodated the faith of his subjects to his foreign policy and the question of a council. Between 1534 and 1547 he prescribed no fewer than four norms of faith—the Ten Articles of 1536, the Bishops' Book of 1537, the Six Articles of 1539, and the King's Book of 1543. In them the Protestant ideas which had meanwhile spread in England came to the surface more or less, in adjustment to the political situation of the moment.

Despite the existing book banning, reform writings had come to England as early as the 1520s from the Netherlands and Germany through active commercial relations. Groups had probably been formed for this purpose, but no real congregations. William Tyndale, who in 1524 had left the circle of theologians sympathetic with Luther at Cambridge, had his English translation of the New Testament printed on the continent in 1526. From here it returned secretly to the island along with other works from his pen, anticlerical rather than strictly Lutheran pamphlets. In *The Obedience of a Christian Man* he championed unconditional subordination to the King, who "may at his lust do right or wrong." During his stay at Wittenberg Robert Barnes accepted the

[9] Knowles, op. cit., III, 365.
[10] Gasquet, *Henry VIII and the English Monasteries* II, 438f.

Lutheran doctrine of justification. Recalled by Cromwell, he acted as agent in the King's matrimonial case and in arranging his marriage with Anne of Cleves, but then he lost the royal favor and was burned as a heretic in 1540.[11] A circle of theologians favorable to innovation, which had been formed at Cardinal College, Oxford, was broken up by Wolsey in 1528. Its most important member, John Frith, fled to Marburg and published at Antwerp, under the title of *De Antichristo,* an English revision of Luther's reply to Ambrosius Catharinus. On 24 May 1530 a list of 251 erroneous propositions which were said to be in the writings of English authors was submitted to the King,[12] who warned against propagating them. When Frith, relying on the imminent break with Rome, returned to England in 1533, he was executed for his teaching on purgatory and the Eucharist. The literary war against Lutheranism proceeded along a parallel line. Fisher's *Confutatio* (1523) belongs with the best examples of pre-Tridentine Catholic controversial writings. Later, Bishop Gardiner of Winchester, who had taken the oath of supremacy, was the chief of the middle party, which did not want to surrender any other doctrine of the Catholic faith. But, despite the position of political trust which he enjoyed with the King, he could not prevail over the Protestant-minded primate, Cranmer, whose suppleness was able to adapt itself to the changes in the royal ecclesiastical policy, which in turn followed the law of *raison d'etat.*

The text of the bull of the major excommunication against Henry VIII was ready on 30 August 1535. But the new Pope, Paul III, hesitated to publish it, because he wanted to assure himself of the cooperation of the great powers in putting the ecclesiastical censures into effect, and for this a projected general council seemed to be the most appropriate means. To prevent its realization became the unchanging goal of Henry's policy. For this reason he joined in discussions with German Protestants. An agreement was arrived at, in the event that the Council, contrary to expectations, should actually meet, for a common protest, but an alliance with the League of Schmalkalden did not materialize, since the discussions of theologians on fundamental questions, held at Wittenberg at the beginning of 1536, did not result in union. The Wittenberg theologians refused to recognize divorce, while Henry would not accept the *Confessio Augustana.*[13]

These fruitless discussions, the convoking of the Council to Mantua, and the disturbances provoked by the suppression of the monasteries constitute the background of the Ten Articles of Faith, prescribed by

---

[11] On Barnes' vacillations in regard to the versions of his "supplication" of 1531 and 1534, see Clebsch, *England's Earliest Protestants,* pp. 58–77; on Frith, ibid., pp. 78–136.
[12] Text in Hughes, op. cit., II, 331–346.
[13] F. Prüser, *England und die Schmalkaldener 1535/40* (Leipzig 1929).

the King on 12 July 1536.[14] Though ambiguous in many places, they betray the effort to meet the Wittenberg theologians halfway. The principle of Scripture as the sole rule of faith was admitted, justification was described according to Melanchthon's *Loci,* only three Sacraments—baptism, Eucharist, and penance—were expressly named, the veneration of saints and images, though not forbidden, was viewed as the cause of many abuses, and prayer for the dead was permitted, though it was denied that purgatory has a scriptural basis.

The *Institution of a Christian Man,* published in 1537 and referred to as the *Bishops' Book* because it was signed by twenty bishops, was a compromise between the Protestant-minded and the conservative wings of the episcopate. After the manner of a large catechism it treated the traditional points of doctrine, the Creed, the Sacraments, the Commandments, the Our Father, and also the Hail Mary. It mentioned the four Sacraments that had been omitted in the Ten Articles, but did not refer to the Mass as a sacrifice. Gardiner, who had not contributed to it, referred to it as a storehouse where everyone deposited what suited him. At the same time the King saw to it that the general Council that had been summoned by the Pope was attacked in several pamphlets.[15]

A new approach to the German Protestants seemed to be under way at the beginning of 1539 when Charles V and Francis I allied against Henry VIII. The English King sent an envoy, Christopher Mount, to Electoral Saxony and arranged to marry Anne of Cleves. Lutheran theologians appeared in London. They became witnesses, however, not of a doctrinal *rapprochement* but of a Catholic reaction. The Six Articles, submitted in the House of Lords by the bishops and assented to by the King on 28 June 1539 commanded under severe penalties the doctrine of transsubstantiation, communion under one species, clerical celibacy, monastic vows, the lawfulness of private Masses, and the necessity of auricular confession.[16] This surprising turn was occasioned by a renewal of ties between France and England. Henry no longer needed the Protestant allies against a threatening coalition of the great powers and

---

[14] Reproduction of the text and evaluation in Hughes, op. cit., I, 349ff., II, 29f.; ibid., II, 30–46, with a detailed discussion of the *Bishops' Book,* whose actual title is: *The Institution of a Christian Man, containing the Exposition or Interpretation of the Common Creed, of the Seven Sacraments, of the Ten Commandments, and of the Pater Noster and the Ave Maria, Justification and Purgatory.*

[15] For the state papers of 1537, see *CT* XII, 767–774; on two other treatises against the Council, see P. A. Sawada, "Two Anonymous Tudor Treatises on the General Council," *JEH* 12 (1961), 197–214. On Henry VIII's entire policy in regard to the Council, see Jedin, *Geschichte des Konzils von Trient* I, 244ff. (*History of the Council of Trent* I, 303ff.); also P. A. Sawada, "Das Imperium Heinrichs VIII. und die erste Phase seiner Konzilspolitik: *Reformata reformanda* I, 476–507.

[16] Gee-Hardy, *Documents,* pp. 303–319.

wished to be regarded as a "Catholic prince." The Lord Chancellor Cromwell fell out of favor and was beheaded, Barnes was burned, and two Protestant-minded bishops, Latimer and Shaxton, resigned. Cranmer, however, maintained his position. A Catholic restoration according to the teaching of the Six Articles did not occur.

The equilibrium between old and new doctrine continued to be the norm governing religious policy even in the last years of the reign, when Henry was allied with the Emperor against France. The *King's Book* of 1543,[17] regarded as a catechism for the laity, showed in its teaching on justification a relationship to the Wittenberg Articles of 1536, but stressed the necessity of good works, and warned "not in this lifetime to presume upon the said benefits of Christ, or take occasion of carnal liberty or security." The freedom of the will was maintained, absolute predestination was denied. The ecclesiology continued to be Anglican. The papal primacy was branded as a human invention. The guardian of the orthodox faith was the King, who was bound "to conserve and maintain the true doctrine of Christ," which is found in Scripture, the three ancient creeds, the first four councils, and the exegesis of the Fathers. In his preface the King spoke of the period preceding the Schism as "the time of darkness and ignorance."

Nevertheless, the change in the substance of faith as a matter of fact already went deeper than the two last-mentioned norms of faith indicate. Hitherto Tyndale's translation of the Bible had been strictly forbidden. But in the revision by John Rogers, who hid behind the pseudonym of Thomas Matthew, the prohibition was removed on Cranmer's urging in 1537 and, as "Matthew's Bible," it was ordered purchased by every parish church the following year. A homiliary composed by Cranmer provided a suitable explanation. Gardiner, conservative in ecclesiastical matters and a long-time political adviser of the King, lost the royal favor shortly before Henry's death on 28 January 1547 and was excluded from the council of guardians of the nine-year-old King Edward VI.

The Upsurge of Protestantism under Edward VI (1547–53)

Protestant ideology invaded the life of the Church of England on a broad front during the regency, which was dominated by the King's uncle, the Duke of Somerset. The practical sense of the English was taken into account in that the new doctrines were not so much prescribed as formulations of faith but rather were introduced under the

---

[17] *A Necessary Doctrine and Erudition for Any Christian Man, set forth by the King's Majesty of England* (London 1543); cf. Hughes, op. cit., II, 46–60.

guise of a new liturgy, which, however, retained some traditional forms, such as vestments and candles. Just as on the continent, so too in England the abolition of the Mass struck at the center of the Catholic concept of the Church. The process moved forward step by step. At the end of 1547 communion under both species was allowed and Mass endowments were confiscated by the crown. The Catholic doctrine of the Eucharist and of the Mass was attacked in pamphlets and sermons. An English Communion rite, composed by Cranmer and prescribed on 8 March 1548 was modeled on the "Cologne Reformation," composed chiefly by Bucer, whose Strasbourg colleague Fagus and Vermigli, a refugee from Italy, came to England. A year later (1549) appeared the *Book of Common Prayer*.[18] This not only altered forms, such as the introduction of English as the liturgical language, it also changed the doctrinal content of the liturgy in specific points. Only two Sacraments, baptism and the Lord's Supper, were instituted by Christ. In the rite of the Lord's Supper the sacrificial character was suppressed and any clear acknowledgment of the real presence was lacking. The place of daily Mass was taken by a liturgy of the word, in the constructing of which Cranmer used the Holy Cross breviary of Cardinal Quinonez; the entire psalter was prayed or sung within a month. The ordination rite introduced in 1550 was based on the texts of Bucer's *De ordinatione legitima ministrorum ecclesiae revocanda* (1549). Contrary to Bucer, the ordinations of bishops, priests, and deacons were distinct, but the consecrating prayers accompanying the imposition of hands were changed. At the same time the prohibition of marriage for priests was abolished. A royal decree of 24 November 1550 commanded the removal of consecrated altars; their place was taken by wooden tables. For refusal to execute the decree the Bishop of Chichester was imprisoned and deposed. In the revised form of the Prayer Book, which went into effect on All Saints' Day of 1552, the rite, maintained till now, of the anointing of the sick, the anointings at baptism, and prayers for the dead at their burial disappeared. Participation in the new liturgy was obligatory. Whoever took part in another rite was punished with six months in prison for the first offense, a year for the second, and life imprisonment for the third. Only at the end of the reign of Edward VI was the new statement of faith, summarized in the Forty-two Articles drawn up by Cranmer, prescribed.

Neither the fall of Somerset in 1549 nor the opposition of individual

---

[18] *The booke of the common prayer and administration of the Sacramentes, and other rites and ceremonies of the Churche after the use of the Churche of England* (London 1549); cf. F. Procter–W. H. Frere, *A New History of the Book of Common Prayer* (London 1951); n.ed. E. S. Gibson (London 1960); further bibliography in *LThK*, 2nd ed., II, 604; also, E. R. Rathcliff, "The Liturgical Work of Archbishop Cranmer," *JEH* 7 (1956), 189–203.

bishops, particularly to the new rite of ordination, nor the passive attitude of a great part of the parochial clergy was able to stop this evolution. When the Prayer Book was introduced in Devonshire, the people in many parishes opposed it and ridiculed the new liturgy as a "Christmas game," but without success. The confiscation of Church treasures, such as chalices and monstrances, which had begun under Henry VIII but was only now completed, was endured, even though with bitterness. People lamented the disappearance of works of charity, which had earlier been provided by ecclesiastical foundations, and the loss of many parish schools. Nevertheless, the essence of the faith, as hitherto maintained, faded irresistibly with the liturgical forms that had protected it. The loss was so serious that the restoration under Mary I and Cardinal Pole was unable to make it good again.[19] It came too abruptly, was too brief, and was imposed by the government. The clergy, high and low, who had submitted to the Church laws of Henry VIII and Edward VI, headed by Gardiner, as Lord Chancellor, were in no position to gain confidence and above all were not zealous executors of the new laws. The strictness with which Queen Mary proceeded against Cranmer, executed on 21 March 1556, and other opponents of her regime gained it no sympathy. The *Book of Martyrs* by John Fox, published soon after Mary's death—in Latin in 1559 and in English in 1563—glorified them. Emigrants returning from Frankfurt, Strasbourg, and Zurich became the instruments for expanding the Anglican Church under Elizabeth I.

Ecclesia Anglicana under Elizabeth I (1558–1603)

Elizabeth I (1558–1603), the well-educated and clever daughter of Anne Boleyn, first made sure of her throne by an extremely cautious foreign policy. From the start there was no doubt about the direction of her Church policy at home. A new Act of Supremacy and Uniformity in 1559 again put into effect ten Church laws of Henry VIII and Edward VI that had been annulled under Mary and, in addition, the Prayer Book of 1552.[20] The bishops, appointed under Mary and opposed to these measures, were deposed and replaced by new prelates, who were ready to take the Oath of Supremacy. At their head was Matthew Parker, new Archbishop of Canterbury. The penalties decreed for re-

---

[19] "England, surely, was no longer a Catholic country by 1553," says Hughes, op. cit., II, 302. Numerous examples of the dispersal of Church treasures, based on the inventories of 1552, in H. B. Walters, *London Churches at the Reformation* (London 1939). On the Catholic restoration under Queen Mary I, see below, Chaper 36.

[20] Cf. J. E. Neale, "The Elizabethan Acts of Supremacy and Uniformity," *EHR* 65 (1950), 303–332.

fusing the oath were, however, mitigated—loss of office and, in the event of a relapse into the crime of defending the papal primacy, death. Attendance at the liturgy on Sundays and feasts was prescribed under a fine of twelve pence for each absence. The few monasteries that had been restored under Mary were suppressed. The dividing line was thus clearly drawn against the defenders of the old faith. But a relentless persecution of them did not begin until Pius V had pronounced the major excommunication and deposition of the Queen. On the other hand, the still numerous members of clergy and laity who rejected the new order or were indifferent to it were consciously spared. The Thirty-nine Articles, drawn up by the Convocation of 1563, were a revision of Cranmer's Forty-two Articles of 1552.[21] They breathed a Calvinist rather than a Lutheran spirit. The *Apologia ecclesiae Anglicanae* by the Bishop of Salisbury, John Jewel, which appeared in Latin in 1562 and in English in 1564, justified the new faith and the new order. The *Book of Homilies* (1562) was prescribed for the use of parish priests. Episcopal visitations, which took place from 1568, saw the removal of everything that still recalled the Catholic past. The clergy were strictly supervised by making use of Church wardens and school teachers. The episcopal structure, the cathedral chapters, and the office of archdeacon continued under the shelter of the royal supremacy. When the Calvinist Cartwright at Cambridge advocated the introduction of the Geneva Presbyterian system, John Whitgift sharply opposed him. In 1583 Whitgift became Archbishop of Canterbury. Toward the close of the Elizabethan Age Richard Hooker in his *Laws of Ecclesiastical Polity* (1593) summarized the doctrine and constitution of the now firmly established Anglican Church.[22] The formation of a new type among the Reformation Churches was thereby achieved.[23] An official translation of the Bible, however, was published only under James I.[24]

---

[21] Comparison of the two in Hughes, op. cit., 111, 152ff.

[22] P. Munz, *The Place of Hooker in the History of Thought* (London 1952).

[23] A graphic description, provided with abundant details, of the ecclesiastical conditions is given by A. L. Rowse, *The England of Elizabeth. The Structure of Society* (London 1950), pp. 386–437. Despite his favorable judgment of Elizabethan Church policy, which is represented as tolerant and liberal, he comes to the conclusion (p. 420) that: "The old observances lingered on in country places, in some areas long and tenaciously." In the chapter on the minorities, Catholics and Puritans (pp. 438–488), he explains the harshness of the persecution of Catholics from the time of Pius V by stating that, during the difficulties with Spain, they constituted a "fifth column." Important for the intellectual life is P. H. Kocher, *Science and Religion in Elizabethan England* (San Marino, Cal. 1953).

[24] D. Daiches, *The King James Version of the English Bible. An account of the development and sources of the English Bible of 1611, with special reference to the Hebrew Tradition* (Chicago 1941).

CHAPTER 28

The Struggle over Lutheran Orthodoxy

When, following Luther's passionate protest within the One Church, there gradually developed a particular ecclesiastical system outside and in opposition to the ancient Church, there arose the question of what was distinctive, of what was "reformed." There loomed the task of providing a special, positive profession of the right doctrine for the new reformed congregations. It no longer sufficed to apply corrections and protests to the tradition; now one had to admit into the profession the presuppositions that had, of course, hitherto been accepted as the basis. On the other hand, it appeared that the original outline, alluring in its one-sided emphasis on the reform preoccupation, had to be safeguarded against misunderstandings and extended and corrected.

Luther's struggle against the Pope for the freedom of the Gospel was often understood as a license for revolt, the plundering of monasteries, and laxity of morals. "Now no fear of God is any longer a means of discipline, because the Pope's authority has become obsolete. And everyone does what he wants to" (*WA, Br* 4, 133, 11f.) and that "on the pretext of the Gospel" (*WA* 32, 219, 28). Melanchthon admitted: "The papists charge us with much, not without reason" (*CR* 4, 960). He clearly recognized the moral deterioration, and in 1527 he declared those responsible who, "out of a colossal hatred of the Pope, curse everything, good as well as bad, in the same way" (*CR* 4, 959). In his *Instruction for the Visitors* he intended to bring up "the matter without bitterness."

> I had many reasons for such a restraint. I did not want to nourish the fury of Aureus and like-minded companions, who think that to teach the Gospel means only to upbraid, with the utmost polemics and bitterness, those who think otherwise than ourselves, as though they were carters. I well know how much hatred this discretion of mine earns for me with certain people. But it is far more important to me to look at what pleases God than at how I can appease those greedy accusers, by whom I am now treated as a heretic and a fanatic. [*CR* 1, 898f.]

Melanchthon was afterwards often charged with pusillanimity and cowardice. "But I do not regret this moderation of mine, even if our courtesy is sometimes interpreted as pusillanimity and cowardice," he wrote to Cruciger in October 1536 (*CR* 3, 179). Melanchthon did not understand reformation as a merely negative criticism. His anxiety was for the unity of the Church. In 1527 he wrote to Casper Aquila:

I ask you, through Christ, to teach moderately, to have care for the harmony of the Church, to overcome opponents by forbearance, and not so to fight against slanderers that you yourself be guilty of slander. . . . Thanks to divine grace, much is now taught better in the Church than formerly. But once some taught some things better than unlearned Lutherans now do. Your task is to heal souls, both those of the opponents and those of your own people, and not to nourish faction hatred. [CR 1, 960]

But Melanchthon did not merely rebuke the excessive zeal of some complainants. He also had the courage and the sense of responsibility to apply essential corrections to his own theology. In 1530 he would no longer recommend to his pupils his *Loci* of 1521, which Luther had then declared to be worthy of canonization. He said he had decided to change much in them that was too crude. Instead, he referred to his exegesis of the Epistle to the Colossians of 1527 (CR 2, 457). Likewise, in 1532 he published his commentary on the Epistle to the Romans in order to suppress the transcript of his lectures of 1521.[1] The various versions of his *Loci* were the expression of this change in his theology. The several "Philippist" controversies are to be viewed against this background.

The Antinomian Controversy

As early as 1524 Lutheran preachers had defended at Tetschen the thesis that "The Law was given to the Jews, not to the heathens. And so the Law or the Ten Commandments do not apply to us" (WA 15, 227, 5f.). Vis-à-vis such preachers, who "speak presumptuously about Christian freedom" (St.A. I, 235, 12), Melanchthon stressed that:

All who teach in the churches may cautiously communicate the doctrine on the Law. If the doctrine of faith without Law is handed on, countless scandals will result. The people become assured and imagine that they have the righteousness of faith, because they do not know that faith can be only in those who have contrite hearts by means of the Law. (CR 26, 28) Now it is customary to speak about faith, and yet what faith is cannot be understood unless penance is first preached. They are clearly pouring new wine into old skins who proclaim faith without penance, without the doctrine of the fear of God and of the Law, and accustom the people

[1] Studienausgabe (St.A.) V, 26, 5–8.

> to a certain carnal security. This security is worse than all the errors previously under the Pope. [CR 26, 9]

This notion that preaching about the Law must first produce penance and contrition before faith scandalized Johannes Agricola of Eisleben (1499–1566). He drew up a condemnation (CR 1, 915) of Melanchthons's articles of visitation (CR 26, 7–28). Melanchthon reported thus:

> He finds fault that I do not teach that penance finds its beginning with love for righteousness, that I am far too much attached to the preaching of the Law, that I have sometimes perverted Scripture in the usual way, that in some passages I have violated Christian freedom. He makes me a double papist. [CR 1, 920]

Agricola saw in the Law merely an expression of God's anger. It was abolished for Christians by the revelation of God's grace in the Gospel. Christ, he held, preached the Ten Commandments only to the Jews. "But since we are freed from the Law, the decalog is not to be preached" (CR 1, 916). Moses "does not concern the heathens."[2] Thus, penance must begin, not with the preaching of the Law, but with love for righteousness. Agricola felt that with this notion of his he had to defend Luther against Melanchthon, who "was creeping back" (cf. WA, Br 4, 265).

At the end of November 1527 the electoral court convened a theological meeting to Torgau. Through Luther's mediation there was effected a temporary agreement between Melanchthon and Agricola.[3]

Agricola came out against Luther himself in the second Antinomian Controversy. At Christmas of 1536 the Elector had held out to him the prospect of a position at the University of Wittenberg, and Agricola immediately moved there. With his family he was taken into Luther's house and was frequently asked to represent him. But soon the old controversy, which had seemed to be forgotten, was to blaze forth again. In a collection of sermons, published in June, Agricola defended the thesis of a "twofold revelation: a first one of grace, a second of wrath" (CR 3, 386).

God as Judge, if he has any place as such in Agricola's thought, is first made known through the Gospel. Here God's anger is revealed, not indeed for all who are guilty before God, but only toward all those who,

---

[2] Agricola, *130 gemeine Fragstücke* (Wittenberg 1528), in F. Cohrs, *Die evangelischen Katechismusversuche vor Luthers Enchiridion* II (Berlin 1900), 293, 17f.

[3] Cf. the formula of compromise which Melanchthon inserted in the instruction for the visitors (*St.A.* I, 222, 14–27; *WA*, 26, 202f.).

out of false security, deride and ridicule the first revelation of grace.[4] At the same time Agricola circulated a collection of theses in which he sought to play off the young Luther against the later Luther. He "denied that the decalog is to be taught in the Church and made a collection of authentic and unauthentic passages relating to the the decalog from Luther's and my writings," wrote Melanchthon to Brenz at the middle of July 1537 (*CR* 3, 391; cf. *CR* 3, 386).

While Luther had not taken the quarrel of 1527 too seriously, now he was dismayed by Agricola's stand: "This should not be begun in our lifetime by our people!" (*WA, Tr* 3, 405, 6). In a sermon of 30 September 1537 (*WA* 45, 145–156) he stated his own idea of Law and Gospel in opposition to Agricola. The latter endeavored to pacify his teacher[5] and was still concerned for a compromise. But an open quarrel broke out when, at the end of October, he sent his summaries of the Gospels to the printer.[6] Luther learned of the work and brought about the suppression of the pages already printed (*CR* 3, 454).

Together with his opposing theses (*WA* 39, I, 342–354) he published Agricola's above-mentioned collection of Antinomian theses and had the first Antinomian disputation take place on 18 December 1537 (*WA* 39, I, 360–417). As dean of the theological faculty, Luther, on 8 January 1538, withdrew Agricola's *venia legendi* (*WA, Br* 8, 186).

The mediation of Agricola's wife brought about another reconciliation between him and Luther. In order to make it public, persons arranged a second public disputation on 12 January (*WA* 39, I, 418–485). But the real points of controversy were not settled there, and so the conflict broke out again in a third Antinomian disputation on 6 September.[7] Luther now demanded of Agricola a definite recantation, and the court threatened to cut off his salary. Agricola thereupon composed a "form of revocation," which he submitted to Melanchthon as arbiter and which the latter revised. At the same time Agricola turned to Luther himself: "the doctor should himself present him with a form" (*WA* 50, 465). Luther agreed and wrote the treatise *Wider die Antinomer* (*WA* 50, 468–477) in the form of an open letter to the Eisleben preacher, Caspar Güttel. From Agricola Luther demanded in January 1539 theses for

---

[4] J. Rogge, *Johann Agricolas Lutherverständnis* (Berlin 1960), pp. 140f.; cf. *WA* 22, 86, 32ff.

[5] Cf. "Johann Agricolas Verzeichnis, was er bisher gelehrt habe," *ZKG* 4 (1881), 304f.

[6] K. E. Förstemann, *Neues Urkundenbuch zur Geschichte der evangelischen Kirchenreformation* I (Hamburg 1842), 296ff.; cf. *WA* 51, 431, 33–432, 24; J. Rogge, of. cit., pp. 156–164.

[7] *WA* 39, I, 486–584; cf. J. Rogge, op. cit., p.187.

another disputation, which he appointed for 1 February.[8] In this way there arose further dissension. Agricola complained of Luther to the Elector (cf. *WA* 51, 425–444) and during the very discussions he fled to Berlin, where he accepted a post as court preacher to the Elector Joachim II.

Luther explained the question of the meaning of the Law in his *Von den Konziliis und Kirchen* of 1539 (*WA* 50, 599, 5ff.) and in a series of theses of September 1540 (*WA* 39, I, 358).

At stake in the Antinomian Controversy was the correct understanding of Luther. Agricola thought that Luther in his writings taught two different ways of justification: "the one way is through Law and Gospel; the other, only through the Gospel, without the Law." Hence he desired a decision as to which way is correct, "so that the Church which will come after us will not be in perplexity when she sees that both are said and taught."[9] He tried to solve the problem by extracting expressions of the young Luther for a uniform system. Luther was distressed by the controversy which flared up over his legacy in his own lifetime. His struggle was so harsh and pitiless because he dreaded laxity and caprice as the consequences of Agricola's doctrine: "Then sweet grace becomes useless, for there will follow a great and unending wantonness and villainy, which it will be impossible to control."[10]

The Synergist Controversy

Agricola had played off the earlier Luther against the later. In the doctrine of the sole operation of grace in the awakening of justifying grace and of the will's lack of freedom in regard to salvation Melanchthon was accused of deviating from Luther. Melanchthon wrote to Veit Dietrich on 22 June 1537:

> You know that I speak a bit less crudely in regard to predestination, the consent of the will, the necessity of our obedience, and mortal sin. In all these matters I know that Luther thinks essentially as I do, but the imprudent are all too fond of certain of his over-subtle expressions, though they do not see in what context they belong. [*CR* 3, 383]

Luther, like Melanchthon, had represented a strict determinism in 1520–21:

[8] Text in *ZKG* 4 (1881), 313ff.; *WA, Br* 12, 277ff.
[9] *WA, Br* 8, 279,5f., 14f.; J. Rogge, op. cit., pp. 165f., dates the letter December 1537.
[10] *WA, Tr* 4, 452, 14f.; cf. 468, 16; 513f.

Everthing happens of absolute necessity. This is what the poet meant when he said: "Everything exists according to a definite law."[11] God even performs bad works in the godless. [WA 7, 144, 34]

Concerning faith, Luther had said that it was the "work of God in us without us" (WA 6, 530). But in practice Luther had always appealed to man's personal activity, and consequently he had probably taught that God is all-effective while not consistently teaching that he is uniquely effective.

From 1527 Melanchthon tried to free himself from determinism, from Stoic notions, as he later expressed it.[12] In accord with the Fathers, he emphasized the free will of man as the "ability to turn to grace" (St.A. II, 245, 30f.). If God, according to 1 Timothy 2:4, wills that all men be saved, then the reason why some are saved and others are lost must lie with man. Whereas Luther tried to weaken this passage by translating it as "who wishes that all men become better or healthy,"[13] Melanchthon was unable to escape the force of the passage. "Since we must proceed from the [revealed] word and since the promise is universal, we conclude that a cause of the election lies in us: an instrumental cause to lay hold of the promise."[14] If Melanchthon also represents the human will which assents to the promise as a real factor (cf. CR 21, 658), there is question here not of an autonomous human will, but of a will which, supported by the Holy Spirit, accompanies prevenient grace (CR 12, 481; St.A., II, 243, 20–244, 11; CR 9, 970). Accordingly, three causes cooperate in conversion: God's word, the Holy Spirit, and the human will, which assents to the word and does not resist it (CR 21, 658; St.A. II, 243, 14–17).

Borrowing from the *Interim* of Augsburg (VI, para. 1), the *Interim* of Leipzig stated:

> Although God does not justify man through the merit of the special works which man does . . . . , nevertheless the merciful God does not operate with man as with a log but he draws him so that his will also cooperates, if he is of an age to understand. [CR 7, 51]

---

[11] *Assertio* 1520 in *WA* 7, 146, 7ff.; cf. *Loci* 1521 in *St.A.* II, 10, 11ff.

[12] Cf. *CR* 21, 652; *CR* 9, 766; "In Luther's lifetime and afterwards I rejected these Stoic and Manichaean follies. Luther and others have taught that all works, good and bad, must operate in this manner in all, good and bad. Now it is clear that this saying is contrary to God's word and is harmful to all discipline and blasphemous" (1559).

[13] Cf. E. Hirsch, *Hilfsbuch zum Studium der Dogmatik* (Berlin 1964), p. 157.

[14] "Disputatio de sententia: Deus vult omnes homines salvos fieri," 1537, in *CR* 12, 481.

In 1549 the Hamburg senior minister, Johannes Äpinus (1499–1553), who at this very time caused a controversy over Christ's descent into hell,[15] took offense at this teaching. He stated that "Man is as little able to come to the Gospel and to Christ's Kingdom through his free will as is a log through its inability to move or a hog through its lack of reason." Matthias Flacius (1520–75) and Nikolaus Gallus (1516–70) had seen in the formulation of the Leipzig *Interim* the "burying of a papist *meritum de congruo.*"[16] Melanchthon's pupils, Georg Major (1502–74), Victorin Strigel (1524–69), and later Johannes Pfeffinger (1493–1573), expressly taught the necessity of the cooperation of free will in justification. Pfeffinger was a professor at Leipzig from 1544. In two disputations in 1555 he defended, in dependence on Melanchthon, the thesis that, in conversion, the consent of our will is required. In this connection he spoke of a certain *synergia* of the will. Although, according to him as well as to Melanchthon, the will is here dependent on the help of the Holy Spirit, Nikolaus von Amsdorf accused Pfeffinger of teaching, together with his "gang," that man can fit himself for grace and prepare for it by the natural powers of his free will.[17] For his part Amsdorf maintained that "man's will is, before God, nothing but clay, stone, or wood."[18] Flacius and Gallus wrote in a similar vein.[19]

In the *Weimar Confutation Book,* which, inspired by Flacius, appeared in 1559, Pfeffinger's so-called Synergism was condemned in Article 6. Victorin Strigel, professor at Jena and until now a friend of Flacius and opponent of the Philippists, opposed the introducing of the *Confutation Book* and hence was imprisoned for several months. After his liberation there took place at Weimar a public disputation between him and Flacius from 2 to 8 August 1560 on the freedom of the will. Here the question found its theological precision. After this disputation Flacius in 1566 defended the notion that original sin is man's *forma substantialis.* The Religious Colloquy of Altenburg, held from 21 October 1568 to March 1569 at the instigation of the Elector August and Duke Johann Wilhelm of Saxony, was fruitless. What made the acceptance of the Catholic idea impossible also prevented an agreement among the Lutherans. The "and" in "grace and free will" was understood as an additive and not as something conclusive, while the divine activity in grace and the releasing of man's will for freedom were envisaged as two self-sufficient causes, moving concurrently on the same plane.

---

[15] Cf. E Vogelsang in *ARG,* 38 (1941), 107–119.
[16] O. Ritschl, *DG* II, 375f.
[17] Ibid., 432.
[18] Ibid., 433.
[19] Cf. the enumeration of the individual polemics, ibid., 424, footnote 4.

The Majorist Controversy

A similarly embittered struggle blazed up over the relationship between justification and good works. From the Wittenberg professor Georg Major (1502–74), who stirred up the quarrel after Luther's death, it is referred to as the Majorist Controversy. It too was based on a problem left unsettled by Luther, that of the inner relation of justification and sanctification, of grace and gift, and the significance or necessity of love in regard to salvation. Luther had laid emphasis on faith and felt that from it good works proceeded naturally. He loved to stress that the good tree produces good fruit. But he shrank from continuing, in accord with Matthew 7:19, that "Every tree that does not bear fruit is cut down and thrown into the fire."[20] The more narrowly Luther's pupils presented justification in their public utterances and the more the concept of inner renewal for good works was pushed into the background or even denied, the more difficult it became to establish the necessity of good works, which were to follow justification.

Melanchthon came more and more to stress the biblical imperative, but without adequately showing its basis in the indicative, in the new being of the one justified.[21] He was moved by pastoral and pedagogical viewpoints: "In all men there is such a natural weakness that, when we hear the doctrine of the account that will freely follow, we become more careless about good deeds, and our carnal security is consolidated."[22] Hence, Melanchthon, following the Gospels and Paul, speaks of God's command and of the necessity of good works:

> Nevertheless, the righteousness of works must necessarily follow. For it is God's command that we render this obedience, because Christ clearly enjoins, "Do penance". . . I do not see why I should shrink from the word "command," since Christ also says [John 15:2], "This is my command," and Paul [Romans 8:12], "We are debtors." Besides, the necessity is so great that Paul clearly says of adulterers, lechers, murderers, and others [Galatians 5:21], "They

[20] Cf. P. Manns, "Fides absoluta—Fides incarnata. Zur Rechtfertigungslehre Luthers im Grossen Galater-Kommentar," *Reformata Reformanda. Festgabe für Hubert Jedin* I (Münster 1965), 265–312, p. 306 especially.

[21] In a testimonial on the Majorist Controversy in 1555 Melanchthon wrote retrospectively: "And this disputation was caused by many previous wicked speeches of the past twenty years. Some will not tolerate this statement, "good works are necessary," or hence "one must do good works." They are unwilling to accept the two words *necessitas* and *debitum*. . . . However, *necessarium* and *debitum* do not mean, first of all, *extortum coactione*, but the eternal, immutable order of divine wisdom, and the Lord Christ and Paul themselves use these words, *necessarium* and *debitum*" (*CR* 8, 411; cf. *CR*, 8, 842).

[22] *Commentary on the Epistle to the Romans* of 1544 (1540), *CR* 15, 634; something similar earlier in the exposition of 1532 (*St.A.* V, 199, 1ff.).

who do such things will not attain the Kingdom of God." [*Loci*, 1535: *CR* 21, 432]

Nikolaus von Amsdorf reported to Luther in a letter of 14 September 1536 from Magdeburg:

> It is said here that the contrary is taught at Wittenberg. That man [Melanchthon] is urging powerfully and to excess in the school that works are necessary for eternal life. [*WA, Br* 7, 540, 5ff.]

Already on 20 August and 8 September 1536, Konrad Cordatus, then pastor at Niemegk, had turned on Caspar Cruciger (1504–48), who had been professor at Wittenberg since 1528, and attacked him because, he alleged, in his lectures he was presenting a "sophistical and papist" faith and deviating from Luther, "the only man through whom we believe in Christ" (*CR* 3, 159, note; cf. 193). The quarrel concerned whether repentance is a *causa sine qua non* of justification and whether the new obedience is necessary for salvation.[23] Melanchthon backed Cruciger. "You rightly say," he wrote to Cordatus, "that Cruciger's affair touches me. . . . I am glad to take the whole business upon myself" (*CR* 3, 345).

When Justus Jonas, rector of the University of Wittenberg, dismissed his complaint (*CR* 3, 348f.), Cordatus on 17 April 1537 turned to the Electoral Chancellor, Brück, and complained that there was at "Wittenberg opposition to the dear doctrine of that pious man Luther." Philip, he said, had written to him yesterday: "On my own I have bettered much in my books, and I rejoice that I have done so" (*CR* 3, 353; cf. *CR* 3, 344).

For his part Luther urged Cordatus to be calm (*WA, Br* 8, 79) and utilized the promotion disputation of 1 June 1537 to clarify the question (cf. *WA* 39, I, 202–257; cf, *CR* 3, 385). He concurred with Melanchthon in the matter to the extent of quoting Augustine: "He who created you without your cooperation will not save you without your cooperation" (*WA* 39, I, 209, 20f.; cf. 121, 29f.). But he expressed himself against "necessary for salvation," because, he said, it implied something merited (*WA* 39, I, 256, 23ff.).

Thus did this point of controversy come to rest for the time being. But Flacius and Gallus again took umbrage at the formulation of the Leipzig *Interim* of 1548 to the effect "that these virtues, faith, charity, hope, and others must be in us and are necessary for salvation" (*CR* 7,

---

[23] *CR* 3, 159–161; *WA, Br* 7, 541–545; 579–581 (*CR* 3, 179); *WA, Br* 7, 600f.; *CR* 3, 182, 185; *WA, Br* 7, 615f. (*CR* 3, 206); *CR* 3, 206f.; *CR* 3, 365f. (*WA, Br* 7, 81–84), 372, 383, 385. On the term "causa sine qua non" cf. *WA, Br* 7, 542; *CR* 3, 180, 593ff., 602, 634, *CR* 13, 674.

63), since it was designed "for the benefit of the papists." Open controversy ensued when Melanchthon's pupil and friend, Georg Major, wrote against Amsdorf in 1552:

> I admit that I have hitherto taught and still teach and will hereafter teach, throughout my life, that good works are necessary for salvation. I say publicly, clearly, and unambiguously that no one becomes holy through evil works and also that no one becomes holy without good works, and I say further that if anyone teaches otherwise, even an angel from heaven, let him be anathema.[24]

Nikolaus von Amsdorf thereupon declared Major to be a "Pelagian, Mameluke, apostate Christian, and twice papist."[25] Against the written attacks of Amsdorf, Flacius, and Gallus, Major defended himself in the sense that he in no way intended to belittle justification by grace alone through Christ and that salvation is not merited by good works. But, he asserted, these are necessary so that salvation can be maintained and not lost again.[26] Melanchthon had taught something similar in his *apologia* in accord with 2 Peter 1:10:

> Do good works so that you may continue with the Gospel, with your heavenly call, so that you may not again fall away, become cold, and lose spirit and gifts which come to you from grace through Christ and not because of the subsequent works. [*BSLK* 316, 18ff.]

Agricola, with whom Amsdorf was closely allied, had rejected 2 Peter 1:10 in the Antinomian theses: "Peter did not know Christian liberty" (*WA* 50, 345, 9f.). In 1559 Amsdorf published a work of his own under the title: *That the Proposition* ["Good works are prejudicial to salvation"] *is a Correct, True, Christian Proposition, Taught and Preached by the Saints, Paul, and Luther.* In the wider Majorist Controversy between the "Gnesiolutherans" (cf. *CR* 3, 453), Amsdorf, Flacius, and Gallus, and the "Philippists," namely Melanchthon's adherents, Major and Justus Menius (1499–1558), the last named tried to be conciliatory and, to avoid the misunderstanding of being thought of as papists, they declared themselves ready to drop the addition: necessary "for salvation or for eternal life."[27] However, no real compromise ensued. Flacius and his

---

[24] Major, *Antwort auff des Ehrenwirdigen Herren Niclas von Ambsdorff schrifft* (Wittenberg 1552), Bl. C^{vf}. Cited from O. Ritschl, *DG* II, 377.

[25] O. Ritschl, *DG* II, 377.

[26] Major, "Sermon on the Conversion of Saint Paul," according to O. Ritschl, *DG* II, 378.

[27] *CR* 8, 336, 411, 842; 9, 39, 142, 370, 469, 470, 473, 496–499; cf. Major, *Bekenntnis von dem Artikel der Justification* (Wittenberg 1558), Bl. 3B; the revocation formula (1556) of Menius, printed in O. Ritschl, *DG* II, 380, footnote 4.

friends were not satisfied with a mere dropping of the proposition; they wanted it to be condemned as false (*CR* 9, 474f.). Melanchthon, for his part, declared:

> In sum, to conclude briefly and finally, we say clearly that we cannot abandon this proposition: new obedience is necessary in all the converted. If anyone will not endure this, we regard him as an Antinomian and an enemy of God. [*CR* 9, 552]

In order to justify his position Melanchthon appealed, in addition to Romans 8:12 and 10:10, 1 Corinthians 6:9, 2 Corinthians 7:10, 1 Timothy 1:18, and other places, also to Philippians 2:12: "Work out your salvation with fear and trembling" (*CR* 9, 475). As opposed to this the Gnesiolutherans wanted to maintain the full assurance of salvation and security of conscience. If works were somehow necessary, then salvation depended on man, who could not even be sure of himself. From this viewpoint follows the oversubtle claim of Nikolaus von Amsdorf that good works are prejudicial to salvation, for they seduce man into placing his confidence of salvation in something in himself rather than exclusively in the grace of God. In this way the Gnesiolutherans—in their theology become ideology, their bias, and their "endless revolving around the I, its temptations, and its consolations"—were absolutely not qualified to advance in love beyond themselves to God and neighbor. "If the chief interest of the new man in ethics, as Flacius describes it, proceeds to the point of acquiring feelings of comfort, then there is not much time left for the business whose center is the neighbor."[28]

The Adiaphora Controversy

If behind the outward form of Melanchthons's doctrine of justification, which involved the Antinomian, Synergist, and Majorist Controversies, there lay the problem of protecting men from a false security and from carelessness, Melanchthon's attitude in the Adiaphora Controversy must be understood from the viewpoint of his concern for the right order and the unity of the Church. In a testimonial on the *Interim* he wrote on 1 April 1548:

> I sincerely wanted to advise peace and unity, and many years ago I proposed several serious articles on unity in my teaching, as many wise persons know, and I have never taken pleasure in quarreling

---

[28] L. Haikola, *Gesetz und Evangelium bei Matthias Flacius Illyricus* (Lund 1952), p. 336; cf. O. Modalsli, *Das Gericht nach den Werken* (Göttingen 1963), p. 192; R. Bring, *Das Verhältnis von Glauben und Werken in der lutherischen Theologie* (Munich 1955), p. 100.

about unnecessary and unimportant matters. I am now so old that I well know that great division and destruction follow useless squabbling. Also, God has forbidden it and punishes it, as Solomon says: "He is an abomination before God who causes disunity among brothers."

Melanchthon and the other theologians who had assembled at Torgau to discuss the *Interim* stated in their testimonial of 13 April 1549 that it was "criminal obstinacy and confusion" to brand as papist whatever one does not wish to retain.[29] Many would quarrel "more about their own freedom than about high and necessary articles of Christian doctrine and aboug right and false appeal and good discipline" (*CR* 7, 365, cf. 624). Answering the charge of idolatry in the Mass they insisted: And even this form which we retain in the Mass was observed one thousand years ago, as Dionysius clearly testifies" (*CR* 7, 366).

Apart from political grounds,[30] a developed confessionalism was also important to Flacius, who rejected any community with the opposing side and for whom there were no *adiaphora,* because Church customs under the papacy were the "seat of godlessness and superstition."[31]

Osiander was of the same opinion when he wrote:

To accept and agree to the *Interim* is nothing other than to come to terms, in externals, with Antichrist and hence to help to cover up, palliate, excuse, strengthen, and maintain all his sins, abuses, errors, seductions, superstitions, and blasphemies and abominations, whereby consciences are defiled and God's anger, which has already condemned the Antichrist and damned him to the eternal fire of hell, is incurred.[32]

---

[29] "And is not the papacy concerned that persons approve of ceremonies which existed in the early Church in the time of the Apostles, such as Christmas, Easter, Ascension, Pentecost, the Sunday, and so forth, many of which we have retained until the present? And if we were unwilling to retain them, we said that these were papal, that such barbarity was a criminal obstinacy and a disorder, which operated among the people to impede discipline and doctrine" (*CR* 7, 364).

[30] "The fact that Melanchthon now entered his [Maurice of Saxony's] service and even became at once one of his most esteemed theological advisers could not but have alienated many who could not forgive Maurice for his attitude in the last years" (O. Ritschl, *DG* II, 335).

[31] R. Seeberg, *Lehrbuch der DG* IV, 2, 485; cf. Melanchthon (1558): "But because Illyricus and his adherents so aggravate this, one should undertake nothing to please the papists, whether it is a middle thing in itself, it is also harshly intensified. For if the bishops thus willed to accept Christian doctrine and wanted equality in some intermediate ceremonies, this does not mean that such equality should be condemned" (*CR* 9, 476).

[32] Work on the *Interim,* extract in W. Möller, *A. Osiander* (Elberfeld 1870), pp. 323f.

The Osiander Controversy

Philippists and Gnesiolutherans stood together in a common front in the controversy with Andreas Osiander (1498–1552) concerning justification. In cooperation with Lazarus Spengler, Osiander had won Nürnberg for the Reformation. He had been lector at the Augustinian monastery there in 1520 and in 1522 had become preacher at Sankt Lorenz. He had compiled a list of twenty-three questions and doctrinal articles for the Nürnberg ecclesiastical visitation.[33] On behalf of the city he had taken part in the Marburg Religious Colloquy of 1529 and in 1530 he had composed a work on justification for the Diet of Augsburg.[34] Together with Johannes Brenz he had drawn up the Brandenburg-Nürnberg Church Order of 1533.[35] In this connection there had been difficulties with the people of Nürnberg, because in their model Osiander and Brenz had expunged public guilt (general confession) and the general absolution following the admonition to the Lord's Supper in order to restore private confession to prominence.[36] Osiander was opposed in principle to general absolution. For it is to be understood either conditionally ("if you do penance"), and then it is neither a Sacrament nor absolution, or unconditionally, and then it is the most ridiculous sacrilege thus to cast pearls before swine. Osiander argued further:

> If this is really absolution, no excommunication can maintain a place in the Church, for every excommunicated person can immediately have absolution, since no one can forbid him to listen to preaching. One key cannot be opposed to the other, so that it can thereby be hindered from carrying out its function according to Christ's institution.[37]

Summoned to Palatinate-Neuburg by the Count Palatine Otto Heinrich, Osiander in 1543 had drawn up the Church order for the Palatinate. In November 1548 he had abandoned Nürnberg as a protest against the *Interim* and in 1549 he had accepted a professorship at the

---

[33] Sehling, 11, 128–134.
[34] W. Gussmann, *Quellen und Forschungen zur Geschichte des Augsburgischen Glaubensbekenntnisses* I, 1 (Leipzig–Berlin 1911), 297–312.
[35] Sehling, 11, 140–205.
[36] Cf. W. Möller, op. cit., pp. 177ff. G. T. Strobel, "Beytrag zur ältesten Beichtegeschichte Nürnbergs vom Jahre 1531," *Neue Beyträge zur Litteratur besonders des 16. Jahrhunderts* II (Nürnberg 1791), 175–390.
[37] W. Möller, op. cit., p. 179; cf. the testimonials of the Wittenberg theologians who were seeking a compromise: in *WA, Br* 6, no. 2008; 2010 (*CR* 2, no. 1108); 2052 (*CR* 2, no. 1133); 2053; 2054; *CR* 3, no. 1477; *WA, Br* 7, no. 3104; 3108 (*CR* 3, no. 1489).

University of Königsberg that had been offered him by Albrecht of Brandenburg-Ansbach.

He began his teaching activity on 5 April 1549, with a disputation on the Law and the Gospel (cf. *CR* 7, 402) and then lectured on the first chapters of Genesis. There soon ensued controversies over penance, the meaning of Christ's Incarnation, and the attitude to the *Interim,* which Osiander had sharply criticized.[38] His authoritarian appearance contributed to the intensification of the friction. A public quarrel broke out over Osiander's "Disputation on Justification by Faith" of 24 October 1550. As he had already done in regard to the doctrine of justification in the *Interim,*[39] he now publicly attacked that of Melanchthon as one-sided: "They are teaching something colder than ice who teach that we are to be regarded as justified only for the forgiveness of sins and not also because of the righteousness of Christ, who dwells in us through faith."[40] Osiander wanted to bring into prominence that man is really justified and to stress against a one-sided emphasis on Christ's vicarious atonement his life-renewing activity in man. Christ alone is righteous, but not so much because he fulfilled the Law as because

> he was born from all eternity, a righteous Son, from the righteous Father [John 17:25]. Hence it is this righteousness of the Father and the Son and the Holy Spirit whereby he who is himself righteous justifies the godless, that is, the righteousness of God, which is precisely the righteousness of faith.[41]

In the works *Whether the Son of God would have Become Flesh Even If Sin Had Not Come into the World. And on the Image of God: What It Is* (1550) and *On the Sole Mediator Jesus Christ and Justification by Faith* (1551) Osiander expounded his idea in more detail.

He explained the creation of Adam as the image of God thus:

> Hence there dwelt in Adam through grace the Word, the Son of God, and consequently also the Father and the Holy Spirit. Thus, as our Lord Jesus Christ was by nature God and man, Adam was man by nature but by grace he was a sharer in the divine nature and participated in it.[42]

[38] Cf. Osiander's work *Von dem neugeborenen Abgott und Antichrist zu Babel* (1550).

[39] "Then the *Interim* does not teach an agreed word about the correct and true righteousness, which is the proper and essential righteousness of God and his son Jesus Christ and is brought, given, and imputed to us through the faith whereby Christ dwells in us" (W. Möller, op. cit., p. 327).

[40] Thesis 73, cited from R. Seeberg, *Lehrbuch der DG* IV, 2, 497; cf. W. Möller, op. cit., pp. 385f.; H. E. Weber, I, 1, 258; cf. *CR,* 9, 469.

[41] Cited from W. Möller, op. cit., p. 383.

[42] Ibid., p. 392.

Christ's righteousness consisted in his divine nature. The original right-eousness of the justified consists in his participation in the divine nature. Proceeding from this notion Osiander explained 1 John 4:2, the coming of Christ in the flesh, simply as the indwelling of the Word in us.[43] It is said of the justified that both natures are in them, just as in Christ.[44] Accordingly, justification is the reproducing of the Incarnation of the essentially divine righteousness in the individual man: "The ontological 'indwelling' of the essential 'righteousness' of Christ in the believer is what is primary, and only on the basis of this does God declare him to be righteous."[45] In his emphasis on the essential righteousness of God in us, in contradistinction to righteousness *extra nos,* Osiander appealed to Luther. Melanchthon, whose doctrine of justification Osiander attacked, tried at first to mediate (cf. *CR* 7, 775), but finally was induced in 1552 to publish a *Reply to the Book of Master Andreas Osiander on the Justification of Man.*[46]

In this he first alluded to the distinction between grace and gift and then insisted:

> And so we clearly profess and have always taught, as all the churches can testify, that it is true that a change must occur in us and that certainly God, Father, Son, and Holy Spirit, effect conso-lation and life in us in conversion and hence are in us and dwell in us to the extent that the Gospel is accepted with faith, whereby the Eternal Word, the Son of God, operates and gathers to himself one Church. [*CR* 7, 894f.; *St.A.* VI, 455, 24–30]

He said there was no quarrel over this presence of God in us (*CR* 7, 895; *St.A.* VI, 456, 10–13). However, it is not the basis of our confi-dence. Faith is based on the God-Man Jesus Christ, on his merits and his intercession (*CR* 7, 898). Even after rebirth man is still in need of the forgiveness of sins. He obtains it through the Mediator, Jesus Christ, who is to be distinguished from the Father and the Holy Spirit. If Osiander had censured the superficiality of Melanchthon's doctrine of justification and felt that "this teaching makes people secure" (*CR* 7, 898), Melanchthon referred to the salvific function of Christ's humanity

---

[43] Testimonials on the *Interim;* cf. W. Möller, op. cit., p. 329. "Disputatio de ius-tificatione," Thesis 67; cf. H. E. Weber, I, 1, 279.

[44] H. E. Weber, I, 1, 279f.

[45] E. Kinder, "Die evangelische Lehre von der Rechtfertigung," *Quellen zur Konfes-sionskunde,* Reihe B, Heft 1 (Lüneburg 1957), 7.

[46] *CR* 7, 892–902; *St.A.* VI, 453–461; cf. *CR* 8, 608–612, to which Osiander replied with the *Widerlegung: Der ungegründeten, undienstlichen Antwort Philippi Melanchthonis* (1552).

and to his historical work of redemption, which came off badly in Osiander's mystical doctrine of justification.

In the declaration of theologians that he drew up at the Naumburg assembly of 23 May 1554, he thus accused Osiander:

> He nowhere makes a distinction between the Son and the Holy Spirit; he likewise makes no distinction between the presence of the divine nature in Christ and in other saints. . . . Likewise [he maintains] that only the divinity is righteousness; Christ's obedience is not righteousness.[47]

Friedrich Staphylus (1512–71) had again become a Catholic at Breslau in 1552. In 1546 he had been summoned to Königsberg on Melanchthon's recommendation (CR 6, 145) and in 1552 he had composed a work against Osiander at Danzig.[48] He now passed a similar judgment, maintaining that Osiander underestimated the importance of Christ's humanity, saw the basis of justification in charity, righteousness, and wisdom rather than in faith, and made it one with the essence of God.[49]

Flacius, Menius, Amsdorf, and Mörlin (1514–71) at Königsberg also wrote against Osiander. And Franciscus Stancarus, opposing him, went the other extreme, teaching that Christ justifies man only by virtue of his human nature.[50] The *Formula of Concord* rejected both the doctrine of Osiander and that of Stancarus.[51]

---

[47] CR 8, 286; cf. CR 8, 541: "What confusion there is, if only this is said: men are justified by the indwelling of the Father, the Son, and the Holy Spirit, and if Father, Son, and Holy Spirit are not distinct, and the obedience and intercession of the Mediator are not distinct from his activity, and the atonement is not distinct from the subsequent sanctification, and the old saying, that the Holy Spirit is never given without the Son, is not explained." Cf. CR 8, 426f., 555–563, 623; cf. CR 12, 5–12; CR 8, 589.

[48] *Synodus Sanctorum Patrum Antiquorum contra nova dogmata Andreae Osiandri* (Nürnberg 1553).

[49] Cf. *Lutheranae trimembris Theologiae Epitome* (1558) (p. III, *catalogus sectarum inter Confessionistas* III): "Osiander's followers have this in common with those of Schwenkfeld: that love, righteousness, and wisdom (but not love), by which man is made righteous and wise by God, are themselves the essence of God. Peculiar to Osiander's adherents is the doctrine that Christ justifies man only according to his divine nature, and likewise that man, since he is the image of God, becomes entirely the same image of God that Christ, Son of God and of Mary, is."

[50] Cf. *Apologia contra Osiandrum* (1552). *De trinitate et mediatore domino nostro Iesu Christo* (1562). Melanchthon (CR 23, 87–102; St.A. VI, 260–277) and Calvin (OC, 9, 333–358) composed refutations.

[51] Cf. BSLK 913, 10ff., 935, 15ff.

The Second Eucharistic Controversy

While the Lutherans were fighting among themselves over the *Interim,*
Calvin and Bullinger reached agreement on the Eucharist at Zurich in
the *Consensus Tigurinus,* as will be related in Chapter 29. Calvin had
made concessions for the sake of unity. Bread and wine are still only
signs of the spiritual community (actual communion) with Christ's flesh
and blood. In this way was jeopardized the common understanding with
Lutheranism, which had been declared at least in form by the signing of
the *Confessio Augustana Variata* in 1541. Furthermore, it had not been
made clear whether the *Variata* was a binding Lutheran confession. The
Zurich agreement was first sent to the other Swiss churches for their
acceptance, and hence its publication in print was delayed until 1551.
German Lutheranism then saw itself faced with a growing influence of
Calvin's theology and an encroachment by Calvinism on German soil.
Thus the quarrel now erupting over the real presence of Christ in the
Eucharist acquired a special violence and a more strongly confessional
tone, which injected controversy into the congregations to a far greater
extent than earlier. The division did not run clearly between the Calvinists and the Lutherans. Instead, many in the ranks of the latter,
especially the educated, showed themselves to be accessible to the Calvinist teaching on the Eucharist. They opposed the then incipient Lutheran orthodoxy and the dogma of ubiquity which it represented. For
this reason, following Melanchthon's death in 1560, they were labeled
Cryptocalvinists and attacked.

The Hamburg pastor Joachim Westphal (1510–74) began the struggle in 1552 with a work entitled *Farrago.*[52] It was especially a summons
to the Lutherans in view of the menacing danger. He followed this up
the next year with his *Recta fides de coena Domini.* The extent of the
chasm separating the Protestant confessions became clear when in 1553
Jan Laski (1499–1560), in flight from England with his Calvinist congregation, sought refuge in Germany. They met rejection and even
hatred from the North German Lutherans. Westphal called them martyrs of the devil, and Bugenhagen had them told that he would sooner
support papists than them.[53] They were finally received at Danzig and
Emden. Laski composed a catechism at Emden in 1554. Thereupon
strife broke out at Bremen (cf. *CR* 8, 336) between Melanchthon's
pupil Albert Rizaeus Hardenberg (1510–47), whom Laski had gained
for the Reformation in 1542 and who had been cathedral preacher at
Bremen since 1547, and Johannes Timann, called Amsterodamus (d.

---

[52] *Farrago confuseanarum et inter se dissidentium opiniorum de coena Domini* (Magdeburg
1552).
[53] E. Bizer, *Studien zur Geschichte des Abendmahlstreits im 16. Jahrhundert,* p. 275.

1557). Timann's polemic[54] was answered by Laski.[55] Westphal denied to the Calvinists the right to appeal to Augustine.[56] Calvin himself did not intervene in the quarrel until January 1555, with a *Defense of the Doctrine of the Sacraments.*[57]

Westphal refuted this in his *Legitimate Defense against the False Accusation of a Certain Sacramentarian* (1555). To Calvin's annoyance (*OC* 16, 53f.) it was printed at Frankfurt-am-Main. Laski had gone there with his fugitive Calvinist congregation. Referring to the Religious Peace of Augsburg, the Lutheran clergy demanded agreement with the *Confessio Augustana,* which Laski tried hard to demonstrate.[58] Calvin dedicated his *Second Defense of the Devout and Right Faith,*[59] of the beginning of 1556, to the pastors of Saxony and Lower Germany, stressing that he was not fighting against them, but was only defending himself against Westphal's attacks. He represented Westphal as a disturber of the peace and an outsider. To favor Westphal's activities or in any way to agree with him was

> to regard as of no importance [the agreement of faith], which was clearly the work of God, and to create a schism among those who followed the same Lord of hosts. This is a heartless and godless severing of the members of Christ. [*OC* 9, 50]

This summons to unity was answered by a series of very sharp rejoinders. In 1556 Erhard Schnepf (1495–1558) published at Jena a *Profession on the Eucharist.* Westphal replied with a *Letter Containing a Brief Retort to Jean Calvin's Squabbling* [printed in *OC* 9, XVIII–XXI] *and to Jan Laski's Work in Which he Recasts the Augsburg Confession into Zwinglianism.* He also composed a *Confession of Faith in Which the Ministers of the Saxon Church . . . Expound the Presence of the Body and Blood of Our Lord Jesus Christ in the Holy Supper . . .* (*OC* 9, XXI–XXIII). Calvin replied in 1557 with a *Last Admonition to Joachim Westphal* (*OC* 9, 137–252). A year previously there had also occurred a dispute over the doctrine of the Eucharist (cf. *CR* 8, 662) between the Lutheran Georg Buchholzer (1503–66) at Berlin and Crato of Crafftheim (1519–85) at Breslau.

---

[54] *Farrago sententiarum consentientium* (Frankfurt 1555).

[55] *Forma ac ratio tota ecclesiastici ministerii* (Frankfurt 1555).

[56] *Collectanea sententiarum D. Aurelii Augustini de Coena Domini* (Regensburg 1555).

[57] *Defensio sanae et orthodoxae doctrinae de sacramentis* (*OC* 9, 4–36; cf. *OC* 15, 272–296, 304–307; *OS* II, 263–287).

[58] *Purgation oder nothwendige christliche Verantwortung der frembden Kirchen-Diener zu Franckfurt am Mayn* (1556).

[59] *Secunda defensio piae et orthodoxae de sacramentis fidei contra Joachimi Westphali calumnias* (1556) (*OC* 9, 41–120).

At Heidelberg Tilemann Hesshusen (1527–88),[60] professor and Bishop of the Palatinate, defended the Lutheran position against his deacon, Wilhelm Klebitz, whom he finally excommunicated. In this dispute the new Elector Frederick III (1559–76) turned to Melanchthon for an opinion. Melanchthon agreed that the Elector should impose silence on both factions and felt that, after the removal of those who were contentious, a common formula could be found for the others (St.A. VI, 484, 15–20). Melanchthon was probably thinking of an all-German synod. This manner of evading a decision was condemned by the senior minister at Regensburg, Nikolaus Gallus.[61] He had earlier severely criticized Melanchthon's view that Christ is present merely at the moment of reception. Now he published Melanchthon's testimonial with sharp marginal glosses. In these he accused Melanchthon of falsifying the written confessions in order to create a doctrine acceptable to all. Gallus abetted Calvinism and even agreed with Calvin in the question of the Eucharist. According to him, it was not the Gnesiolutherans who were the sources of discord; they were only defending themselves and the pure doctrine and guarding Luther's legacy. Hesshusen himself reacted to Melanchthon's testimonial with a very sharp Responsio (1560). He had had to leave Heidelberg, but he continued the struggle against the Calvinist doctrine of the Eucharist at Bremen and Magdeburg. He accused Hardenberg of having turned the Bremen cathedral into a den of cut-throats. Calvin replied to his work On the Presence of Christ in the Lord's Supper against the Sacramentarians (Jena 1560) with his own Clear Explanation of the Sound Doctrine . . . (1561; OC 9, 457–524).

The key figure in this dispute, conducted with great bitterness by both sides, was Melanchthon.[62] Lutherans and Calvinists appealed to him. Westphal sought to prove that Melanchthon did not agree with Calvin.[63] Calvin, on the other hand, claimed him for himself but accused him of favoring, by this silence, "unlearned, restless characters," who had again started the dispute over the Sacrament. "For," he wrote on 23 August 1554, "however insolent their stupidity may be, no one doubts that if you decided to admit publicly your opinion, it would be easy for you to calm their rage, at least to some extent."[64]

Here, as in the other controverted questions, Melanchthon was not

---

[60] Iudicium de controversia de coena Domini (1560) (St.A. VI, 482–486).

[61] R. Stupperich, Der unbekannte Melanchthon (Stuttgart 1961), pp. 123–126.

[62] Calvin himself felt, differing from Bullinger, that Westphal had been treated more roughly than was intended (OC 15, 359), but he remarks in the letter to the Saxon pastors that there was nothing left to him "but to drop a violent thunderbolt on a thick head" (OC 9, 47).

[63] Clarissimi viri Ph. Melanchthonis sententia de coena domini (1557).

[64] OC 15, 216; cf. OC 9, 52, 107; 16, 430.

the one to assume leadership. In the effort to avoid a dispute he had only made it worse through his reserve.

The Eucharistic doctrine which he represented was from the outset more different from Luther's than both of them realized. From the start Melanchthon stressed the sacramental action: it, the eating and drinking, was the sign to a greater degree than were the elements.[65] Instead of the presence of Christ's body "in" the bread, he spoke of its presence "with" the bread in the course of his controversy with the Swiss. This allowed him to cling to the real presence without attaching it to the bread and giving occasion to spatial notions. In the *Confessio Augustana Variata* he had contributed the diluting formula: "that with bread and wine Christ's body and blood are truly administered to those who eat of the Lord's Supper."[66] In this Melanchthon had far greater possibilities of a connection with Bucer, Bullinger, and Calvin than with Luther. He did not expressly deny the reception of the body of Christ by the unworthy, but probably out of regard for Luther he did not mention the subject. At first he also passed over in silence the doctrine of ubiquity, but from about 1531 he attacked it as a false understanding of the *communicatio idiomatum.* "We must take care not to stress the divinity of Christ's humanity so much that we destroy his true corporeality" (*CR* 7, 780). The ancient Church rejected "this thesis that Christ is everywhere in his body" (*CR* 7, 780), and we must not introduce any new dogma (*CR* 2, 824).

> This talk [that Christ's body is in all places, in stone and wood] is new in Christianity; from the beginning to this day it has been rejected even by papists. For, while this thesis is true, that Christ is everywhere on the basis of the *communicatio idiomatum,* as he says "I in them" and "I am in their midst," it has a meaning different from this thesis, that his body is everywhere. [*CR* 9, 470]

The confession drawn up by Johannes Brenz at the Stuttgart Synod of 1559, in which it is said that all men, and hence unbelievers and the unworthy, received with their mouths the true body of Christ and that the humanity of Christ impregnates all things in a heavenly way, inaccessible to reason, was stigmatized by Melanchthon as "Hechingen Latin."[67] For him Christ, by his ascension, has occupied a place he did not previously have (*CR* 7, 884f.). But this did not mean, as Zwingli thought (*CR* 1,1100), that Christ could be only in heaven in his body;

---

[65] Already in the *Loci* of 1521 it is said: "Signum gratiae certum est participatio mensae domini, hoc est, manducare corpus Christi et bibere sanguinem" (*CR* 21, 221); cf. H. Gollwitzer, *Coena Domini* (Munich 1937), p. 65.

[66] *BSLK* 63, footnote 2; *St.A.* VI, 19, 31–33.

[67] *CR* 9, 1034, 1046.

rather it meant that Christ is present where he wished to be. Melanchthon emphasized the mystery. Instead of a presence in many places, he preferred to think that the many places are present as one point to the person of Christ and, by means of the person, to the body of Christ also (*CR* 2, 222). In relation to his notion of the "intended presence" of Christ[68] Melanchthon also rejected a presence apart from the action instituted by Christ ("extra usum institutum") and an adoration of the elements (artolatry): "What is left after the celebration is not a Sacrament" (*CR* 7, 872; 8, 598). Melanchthon did not undertake a careful exegesis of the scriptural passages that speak of the Eucharist. He referred less to the narrative of the institution than, again and again, to 1 Corinthians 10:16, in which he saw the best formula of union. He understood it to mean: the bread is the distributing of the body of Christ. Paul, he held, did not say "the bread is God," but "it is that by which arises communion with the body of Christ."[69] Melanchthon was profoundly distressed by the many theological quarrels which were destroying the unity of the Church and especially by the fact that they flared up over the Eucharist. He sought to restore unity in the Eucharistic controversy by reference to the ancient and devout Church (cf. *CR* 2, 824; 7, 543), but he would have much preferred not to dispute at all "over the manner of the presence" (*CR* 3, 511).

But Luther had already denied the doctrine of transsubstantiation as an inadmissible speculation and wanted to leave the "how" of the presence uninvestigated. However, the very necessity of a confrontation with adherents of the Reformation had caused him to seize upon the *theologoumenon* of the ubiquity of Christ's humanity, which brought with it far greater difficulties. Despite all his protestations of being satisfied with the fact of the presence as the pledge of the divine promise, Melanchthon could not do otherwise.

The quarrels continued after his death. His son-in-law, the Elector's physician Kaspar Peucer (1525–1602), the councillor Georg Cracow (1525–75), the theologian Christoph Pezel (1539–1604), and others even more sharply disavowed Luther's doctrine of ubiquity and developed Melanchthon's views still further in the direction of Calvinism. These were frequently not theologians but humanistically trained physicians, jurists, and men of letters, "who concealed their free thinking in regard to religion and life under the guise of Philippism and spread it under such protection."[70] If the educated then subscribed to a Crypto-

---

[68] *CR* 23, 751; 4, 264; 7, 877, 887.

[69] *CR* 8, 538, 660; *St.A.* VI, 484 (*CR* 9, 962); cf. H. Gollwitzer, op. cit., p. 83.

[70] J. Moltmann, *Christoph Pezel (1539–1604) und der Calvinismus in Bremen* (Bremen 1958), p. 11.

calvinism, this was because the particular formulas offered were open to a humanistic spiritual understanding. Paul Eber (1511–64) and Paul Crell (1531–79), on the other hand, stressed the real presence more strongly and tried to mediate between the Gnesiolutherans and the Philippists. Their Cryptocalvinism was made clear to all the world with the appearance of the *Exegesis perspicua et ferme integra de Sacra Coena* (1574), composed by Joachim Curaeus (1532–73) but published anonymously.[71] In it ubiquity was rejected as a monophysitic heresy and Luther's sacramental realism was criticized. Toleration was again demanded for the Swiss on the basis of the *Consensus Tigurinus,* until an international synod should have formulated a common Protestant doctrine. The strictly Lutheran Elector August I (1553–86) felt that he had been imposed upon by his theologians. Peucer, Cracow, the court preacher Schütz, and the senior minister Stössel were imprisoned. Others, like Pezel, were banished and thereafter urged Hesse, Nassau, Bremen, and Anhalt to mediate between Wittenberg and Geneva. Strict Lutheranism was restored in Electoral Saxony by the ecclesiastical power of the prince. The route back to the Lutheran position was found in the Torgau Eucharistic Confession of 1574 and at the same time the way was prepared for the doctrinal consensus of the adherents of the *Confessio Augustana* in the *Formula of Concord* of 1577. Article 7 of the *Concord* states: "Nevertheless they hold and teach that, with the bread and wine, the body and the blood of Christ are truly and essentially present, given, and received." Just the same, Crypotocalvinism revived in Electoral Saxony under the weak Elector Christian I (1586–91) and his domineering chancellor, Nikolaus Krell, until the latter was imprisoned in 1591 and, following a ten-year trial, was beheaded in the Dresden marketplace on 9 October 1601.

[71] Edited by W. Schaffler (Marburg 1853).

CHAPTER 29

Jean Calvin
Personality and Work

Youth, Studies, and Early Writings (1509–36)

The Reformed Church of Western Europe bears the stamp of the personality and work of Jean Calvin. Born on 10 July 1509, at Noyon in Picardie, he was the son of Gerard Cauvin, manager of the properties of the local cathedral chapter. As such, Calvin's father had probably had many a glimpse into all the human frailties which only too often accompanied the linking together of money or economic interests and religion. Because of a suit against the cathedral chapter he was excommunicated in 1528 and died under the censure in 1531. We must expect that these circumstances may have prejudiced Calvin against the traditional ecclesiastical life. It is significant that the other Geneva reformer, Guillaume Farel, was also the son of the manager of a cathedral chapter's property. If from his father Calvin had inherited a legalistic mind and a sober critical sense, through his Flemish mother he was connected with the intensity of late medieval piety. However, he lost his mother while still a boy.

A benefice at Noyon opened up for young Calvin the way into the clerical state, but first of all it provided him especially with the means to commence his studies. He obtained his earliest education with the sons of a friendly noble family, and with them he went to Paris in 1523, at the age of fourteen. He arrived there in August, the very month in which the Augustinian Jean Vallière was burned outside the gates of the city because of his Lutheran agitation—the first Frenchman to die in this cause. Calvin was admitted to the College de la Marche and in 1524 into the College Montaigu, which was steeped in tradition. Erasmus had already complained of the strictness and scholastic narrowness of the Montaigu. There nominalism was the prevailing approach, and Natalis Beda (d. 1537) played a major role. He was the soul of the opposition to the Lutheran currents in Paris, but he also saw a danger to the Church in humanist reformers such as Lefèvre d'Etaples and Erasmus. In 1528 Calvin obtained the licentiate in the liberal arts. But he did not continue his studies in theology. Apart from the fact that, during his arts courses, he became acquainted with the Fathers and with theological problems—his teacher in this faculty was the Scotsman John Mair (Major)—he never studied theology as such and earned no degree in it. His impressive later knowledge of it was due to private study.[1]

At the wish of his father, then on the outs with the Noyon canons, he studied law at Orléans under Peter de l'Estoile and later (1529) at Bourges under Andreas Alciati, and in 1532 obtained the licentiate.

---

[1] F. W. Dankbaar, *Calvin* (Neukirchen 1959), pp. 5, 26. According to K. Reuter, *Das Grundverständnis der Theologie Calvins* (Neukirchen 1963), however, Calvin is supposed to have been introduced by John Major in 1524–28 to a "new concept of anti-Pelagian and Scotist theology and to a revived Augustinianism" (pp. 21, 36). From John Major he is supposed to have taken, independently of Luther, the doctrine of Gregory of Rimini on God, providence, and sin (pp. 168, 202; cf. pp. 148, 158). The first edition of the *Institutio* gives no indication of this. At the Montaigu Calvin was from fourteen to eighteen years old.

During his studies at Orléans and Bourges he was in contact with the Swabian Melchior Volmar, a reform-minded humanist (born at Rottweil in 1496, died at Tübingen in 1556). Volmar introduced him to Greek.[2] After his father's death in 1531, Calvin went to Paris, where he concentrated especially on the humanities. The fruit of this interest was a commentary on Seneca's *De clementia* (1532), which shows a familiarity with the classical authors and the Church Fathers. It also has a strong political and ethical tone and exhibits its author as a humanist reformer of a juristic stamp. Calvin was still under the spell of biblical reform humanism, whose chief at Paris was Lefèvre d'Etaples (ca. 1450–1536). But the young reformer was too much a man of clarity, of precise commitment, and of ecclesiastical order to be satisfied with the humanist "Nicodemitism." It cannot be exactly determined when he turned to Protestantism. According to the second *apologia* against Westphal, he had already read Luther's writings before 1529 and had "begun to emerge from the darkness of the papacy,"[3] but in the foreword to his commentary on the psalms of 1557 he speaks of a "subita conversio" to the Reformation. It states:

> . . . and although I had so obstinately submitted myself to the papal superstition that it was very difficult to be extricated from so deep a morass, still God, by a sudden conversion to docility (*subita conversione ad docilitatem*), subdued my heart and made it submissive, even though in view of my age, it was only too obdurate in such matters.[4]

If we follow this late testimony of Calvin and accept a sudden change, it must have occurred at the end of 1533. But in that case it is still doubtful whether Calvin, who always defended himself most fiercely against the charge of having split the Church, at that time regarded his conversion as a break with Rome or instead as a summons to "reestablish prostrate religion"[5] or to the "honorable function of preacher and minister of the Gospel."[6] In any event, his conversion, unlike Luther's, did not spring from an anxious wrestling for his own salvation and was not to the same degree experienced by him as a fundamentally new understanding of the Gospel. For Calvin the reform of the Church was much more prominent. He was concerned for *vera religio* against the idolatry of the contemporary Church and, as a layman, he intended to

[2] Dedication of the exegesis of Second Corinthians, 1546 (*OC*, 12, 364f.).

[3] *OC* 9, 51.

[4] Ibid., 31, 21; cf. P. Sprenger, *Das Rätsel um die Bekehrung Calvins* (Neukirchen 1960), pp. 9ff.

[5] Letter to Sadoleto (*OC* 5, 410).

[6] Preface to the commentary on the Psalms (*OC*, 30, 21).

aid *pietas* against the *impii*. The decisive turning points of his life were determined by experiencing that God had laid his hand upon him and destined him for the service of the Church. He was unable to withhold himself. He stated that, "For a person must be cruel and without piety, to be able to behold with dry eyes the Church in our time. But whoever could heal her and fails to do so—such a person is the embodiment of inhumanity."[7]

Thereafter, Calvin led a wandering life. Among other places, he stayed at Angoulême with Canon Louis du Tillet, and perhaps it was here that he began the preliminary work on his chief literary production, *Institutio Christianae Religionis*. Via Poitiers he went to Orléans, where he composed his first theological work, *Psychopannychia*.[8] In it he took issue with the humanist and fanciful doctrine of the sleep of the souls of the dead until the resurrection of the body. He made abundant use of Scripture—more than two hundred quotations on fifty-one pages—and proved a good knowledge of the Church Fathers. In May 1534 Calvin's benefices in Noyon were distributed to others, and this is generally seen as his final separation from the old Church. At the end of that year or early in 1535 he went via Strasbourg to Basel. Here he met not only the Basel reformers Simon Grynaeus (1493–1541) and Oswald Myconius (1488–1552), but also Heinrich Bullinger (1504–75) of Zurich, who was continuing Zwingli's life work, and Martin Bucer (1491–1551) and Wolfgang Capito (c. 1480–1541) of Strasbourg.

In the summer of 1535 he finished the *Institutio,* which was printed in 1536. This first edition contained a brief compendium of the teachings of the Gospel and at the same time an *apologia* for the French Protestants with a dedicatory note to King Francis I. The King had taken measures against the Protestants when lampoons attacking the Mass had been posted in several parts of Paris and even in the royal Chateau Amboise on the Loire. In a letter to the German Protestant princes he had represented his action as directed against Anabaptists and anarchists. Against this, Calvin intended to plead "the common cause of all the pious, the very cause of Christ himself." For, according to him, the godless have achieved their purpose in that the truth of Christ, if it is not dying scattered and banished, at least remains buried and neglected, and the *paupercula ecclesia* is either carried off by horrible murders or is driven into exile, or, discouraged by threats and terrors, no longer dares to open its mouth.[9] This "poor little" persecuted Church is the one

---

[7] *Institutio* of 1536, chap. 5, *OS* I, 215f.

[8] *Psychopannychia,* 1542, ed. W. Zimmerli (Leipzig 1932).

[9] Dedication to Francis I (*OC* 1, 11); Schwarz, *Briefe* I, 36.

Church of Jesus Christ, which cannot be "seen with bodily eyes" and cannot be "circumscribed by borders." For Calvin, who sharply defended himself against the reproach of schism and sectarianism, the dispute arose because his opponents "claimed, first, that the Church was constantly present and was visible in her external form, and, second, that they fixed the form of the Church in the Roman See and the hierarchy of their bishops."[10] "The Church can also exist without a visible form," or at least her essence does not depend on it. Her marks are "the pure preaching of the word and the legitimate dispensing of the Sacraments."[11] The *gloria Dei,* Calvin's main concern, is often stressed in this letter. The Church founded on the word of God finds its *raison d'etre* in his glory. It is a question of "how God's glory is to be inviolate on earth, how God's truth is to maintain its dignity, how Christ's kingdom is to be well established and supported among us."[12]

The *Institutio* of 1536 shows how in Basel Calvin's theological thought acquired its definitive form. Probably decisive were his status as a fugitive, life in the reform congregation of this city, and the profound study here possible to him. His studies comprised especially the Bible and Luther's writings, chiefly his catechisms, the *Freiheit eines Christenmenschen,* and *De captivitate Babylonica.* The locally prevailing theology—Zwingli's—seems to have been less influential on him. Whereas the 1536 edition of the *Institutio* offered only a brief summary of Christian doctrine in six chapters, Calvin constantly enlarged the work, and the edition of 1559–60 finally became a comprehensive treatise on dogma in four books and eighty chapters.

First Activity in Geneva (1536–38)

After a short stay at Ferrara and at his old home, Calvin, prevented by the war from going to Strasbourg, went to Geneva in July–August of 1536. The Reformation had been established here a short time before, and, as frequently in Switzerland, its introduction took the form of the city's struggle for freedom, even of a patriotic rising against foreign rule. In October 1533 the citizens had expelled Bishop Pierre de la Baume (d. 1544), who was merely the puppet of the Duke of Savoy. Thereafter the bishop and the cathedral canons had resided at Annecy.

Guillaume Farel had appeared in Geneva as a preacher as early as

---

[10] *OC* 1, 20; Schwarz, *Briefe* I, 44.
[11] *OC* 1, 21; Schwarz, *Briefe* I, 44.
[12] *OC* 1, 11; Schwarz, *Briefe* I, 36.

1532.[13] The opposition of the canons, however, had forced him to leave the city, but at the end of 1533 he was back. The reform currents found powerful support in Geneva's ally, Bern. Following a disputation between Catholic and reformed theologians, lasting from 30 May to 24 June 1535, the struggle was decided in favor of the latter, and in May 1536 the city council and the people solemnly resolved "to live according to the Gospel." When Calvin arrived there in the summer of that year, everything was, as he expressed it, topsy-turvy.[14] Farel needed his help, especially his talent for organization, and hence urged him to stay. Calvin wrote later: "It was as though God had stretched out his hand from above and laid it on me in order to stop me."[15] He first ministered not as preacher or pastor but under the title of a "lecturer on Holy Scripture."[16] He interpreted the Epistle to the Romans and preached only occasionally. It was only at the end of 1536 that he was appointed preacher and pastor of the Church of Geneva.[17] Early in October, at a disputation in Lausanne between Catholics and reformed theologians, he had displayed the force of his religious conviction and his wide knowledge of the Bible and of theology. In the same year he drafted the rules of organization for the congregation. Much as Geneva needed it, it met with little approval among the citizens, for large segments of the populace had gone over to the Reformation, not for the sake of the Gospel, but to shake off the rule of the bishop and of the Duke of Savoy. Not a few mistook evangelical freedom for political independence or even for license.

The *Articles concernant l'organisation de l'Eglise,*[18] submitted to the city council "by Master Guillaume Farel and other preachers" on 16 January 1537 were largely Calvin's work. As was stressed from the outset, governing laws for the congregation and ecclesiastical discipline were necessary for the dignified celebration of the Lord's Supper. "It is certain that a congregation cannot be regarded as well ordered and managed, if the Lord's holy Supper is not often celebrated and received in it."[19]

---

[13] Guillaume Farel was born at Gap in Dauphine in 1489. Through his studies in Paris (1509) he came into contact with Lefèvre d'Etaples. He worked for the Reformation from 1521. Flight brought him to Basel and Strasbourg. He had much success for the Reformation at Montgeliard (1524), Aigle, Bern, and especially Neuchâtel (1529). Again and again he returned to Neuchâtel from Geneva. He died on 13 September 1565. Cf. *Guillaume Farel (1489–1565). Biographie nouvelle* (Neuchâtel-Paris 1930).

[14] *OC* 9, 892; *OS* II, 401.

[15] Cf. the preface to the explanation of the Psalms (1577), *OC* 31, 26; J. Cadier, *Calvin* (Zollikon 1959), p. 78.

[16] *OC* 21, 30; 21, 126.

[17] Ibid., 5, 386.

[18] *OS* I, 369–379.

[19] Ibid., I, 369.

Exclusion from the Sacrament— excommunication—is needed in order to keep out the unworthy and preserve the Church spotless. "Those who will not submit voluntarily and in all obedience to the holy word of God after friendly exhortation" should be punished and taught by means of such Church discipline.[20] Because of the profit to believers, who thereby "really share in the body and blood of Christ, in his death, his life, his spirit, and all his gifts,"[21] communion should be celebrated every Sunday as a praiseworthy demonstration of the divine wonders and gifts of grace and as an encouragement to a Christian life in peace and in the unity of the body of Christ. For "Jesus did not institute this Sacrament so that we might celebrate it two or three times a year as a memorial meal, but that we might strengthen and exercise our faith and love through a frequent celebration."[22] However, because of the ignorance of the people, Calvin would agree to a monthly celebration. The city council would not accept even that and decreed that the celebration of Communion be held only four times a year. This became the rule, contrary to the reformer's intention.

In all sections of the city expressly appointed men of strong and incorruptible character were to keep a watchful eye on the behavior of their fellow citizens. If they ascertained improper conduct or vice in anyone, they were to discuss this with a pastor so that he might admonish the guilty and urge them fraternally to mend their ways.[23] Here were the origins of the later *presbyterium.* In the second section of the "articles" directions are given for the congregational psalmody. The third deals with the instruction of children. With the aid of a catechism they should be made capable of confessing the faith.

As soon as the articles had been adopted by the council, Calvin brought out a catechism in French,[24] but not yet in the form of question and answer, which he would do later. In brief chapters it deals with the commandments, the Creed, the Lord's Prayer, the Sacraments, and spiritual and secular authority. To this catechism is added a Creed, "which all the citizens and inhabitants of Geneva and all subjects of the region were to bind themselves on oath to observe and uphold."[25] Comprising twenty-three articles, it begins: "We confess that, as the rule of our faith and of our religion, we will follow only the Holy Scripture, without the addition of any human ideas whatsoever." Whoever refused to accept this Creed was to lose his citizenship and "go elsewhere to

---

[20] Ibid.
[21] Ibid., I, 370.
[22] Ibid.
[23] Ibid. I, 373.
[24] *Instruction et Confession de Foi dont on use en l'Eglise de Genève* (OS I, 378–417).
[25] *OS* I, 418.

live." The ecclesiastical officials were to see to it that everyone lived according to the Creed, and the council was to punish those who refused. The council had prevented the forming of a court independent of the civil authorities, with the result that the Church government was to a great extent dependent on the secular power. This should be kept in mind in speaking of a theocracy at Geneva. At most, at that time, a theocracy existed only in so far as public affairs were to be regulated according to the word of God and the authorities had to supervise religion.

Even in this mitigated form the implementation of the articles encountered opposition. The rigorous measures resorted to against those of evil life, such as the pillory, met with scant approval. After all, not for this had the yoke of the bishop and of the Duke of Savoy been thrown off. Nevertheless, on 13 March 1537 the "small council" decided that the Church organization was to be obeyed in full. On 29 July the council secretary Michael Roset mounted the pulpit and read aloud the Creed and the city ordinance. The "presidents of the tenths," or heads of the city districts, were to bring the inhabitants of their territories to the cathedral of Saint-Pierre, where all would bind themselves under oath to the Creed. But many stayed away or refused, and on 12 November the order was renewed. Whoever did not take the oath was to incur the loss of all rights in Geneva. But this was easier said than done. Opposition to the council grew, and the animosity against the French pastors increased more and more.

Calvin did not budge. At the beginning of January the reformers told the council that they would exclude from communion everyone who had not taken the oath to the Creed. But the council, viewing developments with some alarm, decreed that admittance to the Lord's Supper was to be denied to no one.[26] When, in February 1538, men hostile to Calvin and Farel were elected to the council and the opposition obtained a majority, the council forbade the reformers to mix in political affairs and instituted an inquiry into remarks made by Calvin in sermons.[27] The reformers, on the other hand, tried to preserve the independence of religion when Bern urged that the customs it had retained—the baptismal font, unleavened bread, and holy days apart from Sunday, such as Christmas, New Year's, and the Ascension—should be reintroduced at Geneva. On 11 March 1538 the Council of Two Hundred voted its acceptance of ceremonial agreement with Bern and ordered the pastors to comply. They declined to do so.[28] Calvin and

[26] OC 21, 219f.
[27] Ibid., 21, 222.
[28] Ibid., 21, 224f.

Farel refused to administer communion on Easter 1538, on the ground that, with so much unrest, mockery, and mob activity, it would be a sacrilege. Despite a prohibition, they mounted the pulpit. On Easter Tuesday, 23 April the council decreed the banishment of Calvin and Farel, who had to leave the city within three days.[29] At the news Calvin said: "If we had served men, this would be a poor recompense. But we serve a great Lord, who will not withhold his reward from us."[30] His bitterness over the wrong did not keep him from admitting that he himself had made a few wrong turns. He wrote to Farel in September 1538:

> Even though we intend to confess before God and his people that, because of our lack of experience, our carelessness, our neglect, and our mistakes, at least partly it has come about that the Church entrusted to us has collapsed so wretchedly, nevertheless it is our duty to assert our purity and innocence against those by whose deceit and malice, dishonesty and shamelessness such a debacle occurred.[31]

Strasbourg (1538–41)

On 25 April 1538 Calvin left Geneva and went to Basel, intending to live there as a private scholar and to revise his *Institutio.* At the time he seems to have entertained doubts as to his pastoral calling. But Bucer, Capito, and Sturm asked him to come to Strasbourg. When Calvin hesitated to undertake again a pastoral office, Bucer threatened him with the anger of God, with reference to the Prophet Jonah. And Calvin wrote in the preface to his commentary on the psalms:

> Martin Bucer called me forcibly to my new post with an adjuration similar to that once employed by Farel at Geneva. The example of Jonah, with which he reproached me, overcame me and I again took up the office of teacher.[32]

Calvin went to Strasbourg in September 1538. He assumed the function of preacher in the French refugee community and at the same time was made lecturer in Scripture at the secondary school conducted by the humanist Johannes Sturm. Here he composed the second, much enlarged and revised, edition of the *Institutio,* which appeared in Latin in 1539 and in French in 1541. But the Strasbourg period was more

[29] Ibid., 21, 226.
[30] Ibid., 21, 226f.
[31] Ibid., 10, II, 246; cf. *OC,* 10, II, 253.
[32] Ibid., 31, 28.

decisive for his development by providing him with an apprenticeship in practical theology. His fate at Geneva had indeed shown how difficult it was to develop a newly born community and how very much he had lacked patience and experience. Now he learned from cooperating with Bucer and Capito how to build up a community and its order of worship and thus found his complete formation as a reformer.

A "German Mass," composed by the pastor Theobald Schwarz, had been celebrated in Strasbourg as early as 1524. Bucer had further elaborated it. Calvin was able to utilize these works in a liturgy for his French congregation at Strasbourg; in 1540 issuing a formulary for the liturgy of the word, communion, and baptism. Already in 1539 he had compiled in French a psaltery, containing eighteen psalms, the Apostles' Creed, the canticle of Simeon, and the Ten Commandments in hymn form. He had himself put five psalms in poetic form; the others were done by the French court poet, Clement Marot. For these texts the reformer adopted Strasbourg melodies. Bucer had also done the spade work in Church discipline. In Strasbourg Calvin did not have to fear difficulties similar to those in Geneva because his little refugee congregation was under the scrutiny of the city council to a lesser degree. In Idelette de Bure, widow of an Anabaptist, he found a wife who became also a helper in his life's work.

By participating in religious discussions at Frankfurt (1539), Hagenau (1540), Worms (1540–41), and Regensburg (1541), Calvin became acquainted with religious conditions in Germany and came into contact with leaders of German Protestantism, especially Melanchthon. Luther and Calvin never met; they knew each other only through their respective Latin writings. Their differences in personality added to their differing theological interpretations, notably in regard to communion. Luther's sentimental ways and fits of anger could not but be repugnant to Calvin's clear rationalism. On 25 November 1544 the latter wrote to Heinrich Bullinger of Zurich:

> I hear that Luther recently made a fearful verbal attack, not only on you, but on all of us. . . . I do not know whether Luther was provoked by any of your writings; but even if a nature such as his, which is not only irritable but downright soured, goes into a rage for a trivial reason, he certainly could have no adequate grounds for such a storm and uproar. I now hardly dare to ask you to keep silent; for it would not be right to let the innocent be treated so shamefully and to deny them the opportunity to justify themselves; it would also be hard to say whether it would be good to keep silent. But this is my desire: that you keep in mind how great a man Luther is, with what extraordinary spiritual gifts he is

endowed, how bravely and unshakeably, how skillfully, how learnedly and effectively he has always hitherto labored for the destruction of the rule of Antichrist and for the spread of the doctrine of salvation. I have already often said: if he were to call me the devil, I would still do him the honor of regarding him as a most outstanding servant of God, who, it is true, suffers from great defects, just as he is rich in brilliant virtues. If only he had exerted himself to control better his impetuous nature, which explodes everywhere! If only he had constantly turned his innate passion against the enemies of truth instead of letting it flare up against the Lord's servants![33]

Calvin participated in the Regensburg Colloquy of 1541 as delegate of Strasbourg. He had several reservations in regard to Bucer's conciliating method and the unclear formulae of the *Regensburg Book*. Still, he accepted the concept of twofold justice and defended it against Farel.[34] But he would not be satisfied "with half a Christ" for the sake of union. He expressed himself very critically in regard to the negotiations on the doctrine of the Eucharist: "Philip Melanchthon and Bucer drew up ambiguous and fine sounding theses on transubstantiation in an attempt to satisfy their opponents without really yielding anything. The plan does not please me."[35] Calvin firmly opposed the treatment of the Mass and departed before the colloquy foundered on this subject. Soon after, on 13 September 1541, Calvin returned to Geneva.

There was a prelude to his return. In Geneva the situation had become ever more confused, and pastors and mayors were in no position to reestablish orderly life. The partisans of Calvin and Farel, called "Guillermins," raised their heads again, but a not inconsiderable segment of the population pressed for a return to the old Church. In this situation Cardinal Jacob Sadoleto, Bishop of Carpentras, at the suggestion of an episcopal conference at Lyons, published an open letter to the city of Geneva, inviting it to come back to the bosom of the Church, which "for now fifteen centuries has found unanimous acceptance and approval."[36] The learned, Erasmian-minded cardinal wrote "as a friend and brother" and showed his anxiety over the dissension that was destroying the city. The reformers in their midst, he stated, had led the Genevans astray and sown discord out of mere striving for personal power and honor. After treating of justification by faith alone, of the Sacraments, and of the invocation of the saints, he concluded:

---

[33] Ibid., 11, 774; Schwarz, *Briefe* I, 285.
[34] Ibid., 11, 215; Schwarz, *Briefe* I, 190f.
[35] *OC* 11, 217.
[36] *OS* I, 441–489.

Return to the unity which is guaranteed only in the venerable, ancient, Catholic Church. For she is guided always and everywhere by the Spirit of Christ. Only thus can we appear with confidence before the judgment seat of God. But he who separates himself from this Church has no champion at the Last Judgment, and the outer darkness awaits him. Therefore, attach yourselves again to the Catholic Church and its spiritual leaders, for Scripture says, "Do what they say." We have only your salvation in view.[37]

This letter made an impression, and the Geneva pastors were at a loss what to do. A request for a rejoinder was sent to Calvin at Strasbourg. The *Reply to Sadoleto* was composed in six days and is signed: Strasbourg, 1 September 1539.[38] It deals mainly with the Church, justification, and the Sacraments. The Church is based, not on the approval of the centuries, but on the word of God. She proves that she is the true Church by her doctrine, organization, Sacraments, and correct worship. In a sort of psalm of vengeance Calvin solemnly calls God to witness that he did not split the Church nor withdraw from her.

> In what people are careful to blame on me as apostasy from the Church, I am aware of nothing evil in myself. Or is one to be regarded as a deserter who again holds aloft the leader's standard where he sees soldiers collapsed and, pale with anxiety, leaving their ranks, and calls them back to their positions? . . . In order to gather them out of this chaos I have not put them under a strange banner but under your only banner, which we must follow if we wish to belong to your people.[39]

The letter again won Geneva for the Reformation. The people became all the more aware of the inability of their pastors, and the desire to have Calvin back grew. Furthermore, in February 1539 mayors had come into office who were sympathetic to radical reforms. Calvin was called back, but he declined. In October 1540 an official petition from the "small council" reached him. It was seconded by friends such as Farel. But for Calvin the will of man was not the determining factor. He consulted his conscience and tried to determine the will of God. On 24 October he wrote to Farel:

> I present my heart to the Lord as a sacrifice. I want the brethren at Strasbourg to consider only what is best for God's glory and the

---

[37] Ibid., I, 455.
[38] *OC* 5, 356–416; *OS* I, 457–489.
[39] *OS* I, 482. German translation by G. Gloede, *Musste Reformation sein? Calvins Antwort an Kardinal Sadolet* (Göttingen n.d.).

welfare of his Church. You do not need to be concerned for me. Even though I am not very ingenious, I would probably have excuses which would make it seem to men as though the matter had gone astray without me. But I know that I must deal with God, who brings such falsehood to light. Therefore, I have bound my mind and handed it over into obedience to God. And because I do not know how I must decide, I submit myself to the guidance of those through whom, I hope, God will speak to me.[40]

Participation in the religious colloquies granted time for delay, and in a letter of 1 March 1541, he sighed to the impatiently importunate Farel:

The lightning flashes with which you so surprisingly thunder against me—why I do not know—have utterly confused and frightened me. For you know that I have dreaded a call back, but I have not shirked it. Why must you inveigh so violently against me that you almost call an end to our friendship?[41]

When Calvin finally left Strasbourg on 4 September 1541 he was probably thinking only of a temporary stay in Geneva, for he did not take his family.

The Organization of Church Authority in Geneva (1541–64)

Calvin went to Geneva in the spirit of his motto, *prompte et sincere*. On 13 September 1541 he entered the council hall and was treated with the greatest politeness and was told he would be well provided for materially. He avoided acting harshly and in any way taking his opponents to task. All the same, serious struggles over the independence of the spiritual power from the city government were still in store for him. He immediately set about organizing the congregation, and already on 20 November 1541, *Les ordonnances ecclésiastiques,*[42] modeled on those of Strasbourg, were accepted by the councillors. There soon followed a liturgy (*Forme des prières et chants ecclésiastiques,* 1542) and the catechism (1542–45). From Bucer at Strasbourg Calvin adopted the system of four ecclesiastical offices—pastors, doctors, elders, and deacons.

Pastors were to preach the word of God and administer the Sacraments. Those of the three city churches and of the surrounding villages constituted the *Vénérable compagnie des pasteurs.* Every week it was to meet for the study of Scripture and consultation on pastoral matters. In

[40] *OC* 11, 100; *ep.* 248.
[41] *OC* 11, 169f.; *ep.* 286.
[42] *OS* II, 325ff.; W. Niesel, *Bekenntnisschriften* (Zollikon-Zurich), pp. 42–64.

differences of opinion as to correct doctrine it was to decide according to God's word what was to be believed. Every three months the mutual, fraternal "censorship," a criticism of conduct was to take place. The *compagnie* was to nominate new pastors, but the sole power of selection rested with the council. It presented them to the congregation, which could only assent to the choice of the council after the event. Calvin wanted to retain the imposition of hands in ordination as an apostolic custom, but he was only too ready to accommodate himself to the city council on the grounds that, out of consideration for the current superstition, it was perhaps better to give up the imposition of hands—as though an abuse could be a sufficient reason for abolishing an apostolic custom. Hence there was preserved the remark that pastors should be inducted into office without any superstitious ceremonies, with only instruction on the office and prayer.

Doctors, as teachers of theology, were to deliver lectures on the Old and New Testaments. They also had to supervise candidates for the office of pastor. In the secondary school they were to teach the biblical languages and impart a general education. The council named them after consulting the pastors.

The elders, or presbyters, had to supervise the behavior of the members of the congregation. Together with the five to ten pastors they formed the Church council or consistory. In Geneva the "elder" was no purely ecclesiastical official but rather an agent of the city council. The twelve elders were selected by the "small council," in agreement with the pastors, from among the membership of the council and confirmed by the "great council." A mayor was chairman of the consistory. Calvin was unable to achieve the full independence of the Church. As preaching and the administration of the Sacraments were the duty of the pastor, so the direction of the Church pertained to the consistory. The elders had to supervise the conduct of the congregation by means of, among other things, regular visits to homes. Whoever was guilty of gossiping, drunkenness, usury, immorality, brawling, card playing, and so forth, was brought before the consistory each Thursday by a city official. In criminal cases the city council had competence. Stubborn contemners of the Church order had to be excommunicated after three warnings and denounced to the council. Thus ecclesiastical justice was largely subject to the civil law. Calvin had to fight a prolonged battle in order to reserve at least the admission to communion to the spiritual tribunal. If we speak of theocracy or bibliocracy maintained by the reformer at Geneva, we must not forget to what an extent the secular officials interfered in ecclesiastical life and that Calvin was unable for the most part to carry out what he held to be right. In the definitive version of *Les ordonnances ecclésiastiques* of 1561 he was, it is true, able to gain more prominence for his idea of the congregation.

Deacons were stewards of ecclesiastical institutions or took direct charge of the poor and the sick.

Following the organization of the Church, Calvin compiled a catechism in November 1541. This "Geneva Catechism" of 1542 differed in form and arrangement from that of 1537. It was no longer a treatise but consisted of questions and answers. It also abandoned the arrangement of Luther's small catechism. Whereas the latter treated the law before the Creed, the order in the Geneva catechism of 1542 was: faith, law, prayer, Sacraments. In this is expressed a new concept of the law and the Gospel. The law is not only a "disciplinarian," its meaning lies not merely in convicting man of sin; but as the regulation of the covenant it gives the baptized the rule of Christian life. "The law shows us the goal for which we must strive in order that each, in proportion to the grace which God has given him, may ceaselessly exert himself to reach it and may advance day by day" (Question 229).

The community organization at Geneva could be realized only after drawn out struggles. When a start was made of imposing a strict Christian manner of life, many again regarded this as an unpleasant limitation of personal freedom. It was easy to mobilize the local patriotism of the established Geneva families against the overmighty influence of the outsider Calvin and against the French refugees who suported him. These opponents of Calvin called themselves patriots, but his friends called them "libertines," because they stood for a more liberal concept of morals and for the right to a gayer life. The center of the opposition was the family of the mayor, Amié Perrin, who had at first been one of the enthusiastic adherents of Farel and Calvin. But when his father-in-law, Francois Favre, had been denied communion because of immoral conduct; his brother-in-law had been jailed for eight days because of unseemly behavior at a wedding; and his wife had been rebuked for dancing at a wedding, Perrin joined the strong opposition to the pastorate. The question arose as to the limits of the consistory's power. For years Calvin had to put up with various restrictions and affronts. But in the elections of January 1555 the "libertines" suffered a decisive defeat. The new mayors and a majority of the council were on Calvin's side. When his opponents allowed themselves to engage in demonstrations and even in an armed uprising, their fate was finally sealed. The rioters were either executed or banished.

Calvin was now able to give the congregational idea greater importance. The ecclesiastical council obtained more freedom from the secular government. According to the definitive Church organization of

1561 a mayor, when acting as president of the Church council, was to dispense with his staff of office in order to make clear the difference between secular authority and spiritual leadership. Furthermore, the new citizens—the French refugees—were also to be eligible for office and the members of the congregation might express their reservations in regard to candidates.

When, after 1555, Calvin was certain of the support of council and citizenry, he turned to the realization of his old plan, the founding of a university. At Strasbourg in 1556 he sought the advice of the great teacher, Johannes Sturm. The academy finally opened in 1559 with two departments. In addition to elementary instruction, Latin, Greek, and philosophy were taught in the "Schola privata," a continuation of the earlier Latin school. On this was based the "Schola publica," in which lectures were given in Greek, Hebrew, the branches of the liberal arts—that is, philosophy and literature—and in theology, especially exegesis and dogma. Calvin found a rector for the academy in Theodore Beza (1519–1605). Beza and Peter Viret (1511–71) had come from Lausanne, where they had been relieved of office because of difficulties with the officials of Bern. The new university exercised a very strong attraction on students far beyond the boundaries of Switzerland and contributed decisively to the transplanting or the consolidating of the Reformed Church in other European countries—including Kaspar Olevianus (1536–87), the Trier reformer and later professor at Heidelberg; Philip Marnix de Sainte-Aldegonde (1540–98), organizer of the reform in Holland; and John Knox (c. 1515–72), the reformer of Scotland; all of whom studied there.

Until December 1559 Calvin was not even a citizen of Geneva, and hence could act in political commissions at the most as an adviser. But then the council spontaneously offered him citizenship as a "recognition of the many valuable services that Calvin [had] rendered since the Christian Reformation of the republic." By an extensive correspondence Calvin exercised influence beyond the walls of Geneva on the organization of the churches of France, Belgium, the Palatinate, Poland, Hungary, and many other countries. He forced an enormous amount of work on his weak and almost always ailing body until his death on 27 May 1564.

Basic Outline of Calvin's Theology

As a second generation reformer and because of his own intellectual make-up and his education, Calvin was much more a systematizer than Luther was. He avoided narrow positions and sought to bring together his ideas and his knowledge. In the *Institutio* he has left us a compact treatment of dogma, but we must not forget that in it he intended only "to introduce the theology candidate to the reading of the divine word" and to equip him "to establish what he should principally seek in Scripture and to what goal he should relate its content."[43] Calvin wished above all to be an exegete, and hence his numerous exegetical works must be related to the exposition of his theology.

What the theologian was able by himself to say about God and man was "vain folly." He must let himself be instructed by God himself in Scripture. "No one acquires even the slightest understanding of the correct and salutary doctrine unless he first becomes a student of Scripture" (*Institutio* I, 6, 2). Scripture "bears its proof within itself"; by virtue of the illumination of the Holy Spirit it is recognized by us as the word of God (I, 7, 5). The Holy Spirit alone is the proper interpreter of Scripture. He "who spoke by the mouth of the prophets must penetrate our heart" (I, 7, 4) and open it up to the word which lies hidden in the words of Scripture. The determining idea in Calvinist theology is the glory of the sovereign God—*soli Deo gloria.* The glory of God is the meaning of creation and of the redemption of the elect as well as of the punishment of the damned. Calvin's strongly developed doctrine of the Trinity has a soteriological character. He staunchly defended the truth of the Trinity against the heresy of Servetus and others because he wanted to assure the true divinity of Jesus Christ. "No one will really accept Christ as his God in his heart if he does not comprehend the various divine persons in the unity of nature."[44] Calvin strongly emphasized divine providence against the fatalism of the Renaissance and against deistic currents (I, 16–18). The course of things is determined, not by any fate, but by God, Lord of the world. God maintains the creature in existence, gives it its sphere of activity, and guides everything to its goal. "It follows that providence consists in his *works,* and so it is unwise for persons to chatter about a mere *foreknowledge*" (I, 16, 4).

God's special concern is for man, his noblest creature. But in the human realm the greatest importance belongs to the Church. "Because God has chosen the Church as his dwelling, he undoubtedly displays with special testimonies his fatherly concern in supervising her." (I, 17, 6). God's providence does not take away man's responsibility. On the other hand, the active government of the world by God will not allow us to speak, in regard to evil, of his merely permitting it. "As though God were sitting in peaceful contemplation and waiting for things to happen by chance!" (I, 18, 1). Here we confront the mystery which we must not seek to unravel and which is especially impenetrable in the Cross. "And

---

[43] Preface, *OS* II, 6.
[44] *OC* 9, 331; cf. W. Niesel, *Die Theologie Calvins* (Munich, 2nd ed. 1957), p. 56.

indeed if Christ had not been crucified by the will of God—from where would our redemption come?" (I, 18, 3). God does not force man to evil. "He guides all of man's acts in so marvelous and incomprehensible a way that man's will is left unhampered" (*OC* 36, 222). Here "our wisdom [can] consist in nothing else than in this—that we accept, humbly but eagerly, everything without exception that is proclaimed to us in Scripture" (I, 18, 4).

Even more impenetrable to Calvin is the mystery of predestination, "the eternal choice whereby God has destined one for salvation, another for damnation" (III, 21, 1). Prying curiosity has as little place here as does a fearful concealing of God's word. Calvin warns against an overly speculative treatment of this question. He himself had, of course, succumbed to this danger in the course of his controversy with his opponents. To keep silent about the mystery of predestination was "to lessen God's glory."[45] For only when "God's eternal election has been made known" to us do we become aware that our salvation issues from the spring of the unmerited mercy of God. Calvin's definition is as follows:

> By predestination we understand God's eternal order by virtue of which he decrees in himself what, according to his will, is to happen to every individual human being. For men are not all created with the same destiny. To some eternal life is assigned; to others, eternal damnation. Accordingly then, as the individual is created for the one or the other goal, he is, we say, predestined to life or to death. [III, 21, 5][46]

To look for a reason over and above the divine good pleasure, such as the foreknowledge of man's merits, would be to make God's will dependent on external causes.

> This decree is, we assert, based in regard to the elect on God's unmerited mercy, without any regard for human worthiness. But in regard to those whom he delivers over to damnation—he locks up the entrance to life according to his own just and irrevocable but incomprehensible judgment. [III, 21, 7] Hence we can cite only one reason why he allots mercy to his own—because it so pleases him. But by the same token we have for his rejection of others no reason other than his will. [III, 22, 11]

The basis of our predestination to salvation and at the same time of our assurance of salvation is Jesus Christ. In him God has sealed the covenant of life with us.

[45] III, 21, 1; cf. Commentary on John 6:40 (*OC* 47, 147) and catechism of 1537 (*OS* I, 391).
[46] III, 21, 5; *OC* 51, 259; 26, 520; 47, 297; 51, 149; 55, 353.

Therefore, it is said of those whom God has accepted as his children, not that they have been chosen in themselves, but in his Christ [Eph. 1:4]. For only in him could he love them. . . . But if we have been chosen in him, we will not find the assurance of our election in ourselves nor even in God the Father, if we imagine him by himself alone, without the Son. Accordingly, Christ is the mirror in which we are to behold our election and in which we can do so without any deception. [III, 24, 5]

The sign of our election is acceptance of the preaching about Christ and fellowship with him in faith and in communion. Even works, as "fruits of the calling," can have a certain significance for this recognition of our salvation, but only by inference. "Hence, if the conscience is established, supported, and strengthened, the consideration of works also serves to strengthen it, because they are evidence that God dwells and rules in us" (III, 14, 18). The teaching that the number and success of our works are proof of our election occurs only later in Calvinism—*syllogismus practicus*—and does not correspond to Calvin's own tendency. The stronger he stresses that grace is irresistible in the elect and that they are unable to lose salvation, the darker becomes the mystery of reprobation. How is it that Christ is not active in all? Should he be so powerless that he is unable to win to himself all who resist him?[47] Here Calvin sees himself, like Paul, before the unfathomable secret of the will of God. "The Apostle confesses that God's judgments are so deep that every human intellect is swallowed up by them when it seeks to penetrate them" (III, 23, 5).

In his doctrine of justification and sanctification Calvin starts with Jesus Christ. He asks: "In what way do we now participate in the grace of Christ? . . . How do the treasures which the Father has confided to his only-begotten Son reach us?" (III, 1, 1). The answer—that we attain to them by faith—does not satisfy Calvin. It is necessary "to seek more deeply" and to confess that "the Holy Spirit is the bond whereby Christ effectively joins us to himself" (III, 1, 1). In him Christ takes hold of us and he effects in us the "yes" of faith, which is the orientation to Christ brought about by the Holy Spirit.

Through fellowship with him we receive principally a twofold grace. On the one hand, by his innocence we are reconciled to God, so that he is now no longer our judge . . . and on the other hand, we are sanctified by his Spirit. [III, 11, 1]

We distinguish justification and sanctification.

---

[47] Cf. W. Niesel, *Die Theologie Calvins,* p. 169.

> But Christ bears both of them inseparably in himself. Do you, then, wish to attain to justice in Christ? Then you must first possess Christ. But you can in no way possess him without simultaneously sharing in his sanctification. For he cannot be torn to pieces. [III, 16, 1; 11, 6]

Although sanctification is the result of justification, in the *Institutio* Calvin treats it first in order from the start to dispose of the misconception that faith, through which alone we are justified by grace, is sterile and without works. By sharing in Christ's death and resurrection we die and rise "to a new life which corresponds to the justice of God" (III, 3, 9). This rebirth has as its goal the restoration of our being the image of God, which by Adam's sin "was as good as effaced." However, renewal does not occur "in a moment," and we are not at once in full possession of freedom; but we must "spend our entire life in penance" (III, 3, 9). Hence, sanctification is a slow process; the believer remains a sinner, but sin must not prevail in him (III, 3, 13). Accordingly, if sanctification can be partially realized and if it can be increased, justification on the contrary must come to us as a whole. "A fragment of justification would not soothe the conscience until it had been determined that we are pleasing to God, because without reservation we are justified in his sight" (III, 11, 11). But, on the other hand, justice does not become essentially imminent in us, but is imputed to us. Justification meant for Calvin "the acceptance whereby God receives us in grace and has us pass for justified . . . it is based on the remission of sins and the imputing of the justice of Christ" (III, 11, 2). Calvin sharply attacks Osiander's "monstrous doctrine" of an essential justice and an essential indwelling of Christ in us. Against such an "uncouth mixture" Calvin emphasizes the "spiritual relationship" with Christ (III, 11, 10). Through the power of the Holy Spirit we grow together with Christ, our head (III, 11, 5). Thus our justification is outside us, that is, in Christ, and at the same time it is our own,

> because we have put on Christ and have been incorporated into his body; in short, because he has condescended to make us one with himself, and hence we glory that we have the fellowship of justice with him. [III, 11, 10]

Because of this union with Christ, not only are we ourselves justified, but our works too are regarded by God as justified, "because all the infirmities in them are buried by the purity of Christ and hence are not imputed" (III, 17, 10).

Doctrinal Trials

"Christ's spiritual kingdom and the civil order" were, for Calvin, "two entirely different things" (IV, 20, 1). But this does not imply that Church and state stand side by side and unrelated. In Christ both have the same Lord, and for his earthly life the Christian needs the state. For Calvin the state was reckoned among the "external means" whereby "God summons us to fellowship with Christ and preserves us in it" (IV, 1, 1). The secular authority has to protect the preaching of the Gospel and to take care "that idolatry, blasphemy against God's name, calumny against his truth, and other scandals relating to religion may not flaunt themselves publicly" (IV, 20, 3). The rulers are also bound by the word of God, since there is no sphere which stands outside God's claims. It is not the task of the authorities to do the actual preaching of the Gospel. It is an evil if the civil authority seizes the Church government and makes itself judge in matters of doctrine and of spiritual authority. Accordingly, throughout his life Calvin worked to place ecclesiastical discipline in the hands of spiritual officials and to guarantee the independence of the consistory vis-à-vis the power of the state. But he did not hesitate to urge the city council to proceed against his theological opponents.

Sebastian Castellio (1515–63), to whom the Geneva school system was greatly indebted, was disqualified from the office of pastor because of his biblical criticism and his concept of Christ's descent into hell and had to give up his position as rector of the Latin school. He went to Lausanne in 1544 and to Basel in 1545. At Basel he became professor of Greek, translated the Bible, and appealed for freedom of conscience.[48]

The former Carmelite friar, Jérôme Bolsec (d. 1584), practiced as a physician after embracing the Reformation. But he retained his interest in theological questions and took part in the weekly meeting of the *Compagnie des pasteurs.* He opposed Calvin's doctrine of predestination and charged that he was not a true interpreter of the Bible. Following the meeting of the *Compagnie* in which he had engaged in a violent dispute with Calvin, Bolsec was arrested. For Calvin, as for Aquinas, idolatry was treason and heresy was punishable. Whoever corrupted the soul was more guilty than one who injured the body, and, like the second, the first crime could be punished by the secular court. It was of no avail to Bolsec that he based his claim on Melanchthon and that the

---

[48] *De haereticis, an sint persequendi* (1554, Latin and French); new edition by Sape van der Woude (Geneva 1954).

congregations of Bern and Zurich, when asked for an opinion, called for moderation in so difficult a question. On 23 December 1551 Bolsec was banished from Geneva by a judgment of the court. He later returned to Catholicism and avenged himself on Calvin by a very polemical biography of the reformer. It appeared at Lyons in 1577 under the title: *History of the Life, Dying, Morals, Deeds, Teachings, Steadfastness, and Death of John Calvin, former Pastor of Geneva.*

The trial for heresy of the physician Michael Servetus caused a great sensation and severe criticism of Calvin even to our own day. He was burned on 27 October 1553, in compliance with the sentence of the Geneva city council. Born at Villanueva in Aragon on 29 September 1511, he was the son of a Spanish father and a French mother. He studied law, theology, and medicine and discovered, among other things, the pulmonary circulation of the blood. As early as 1531 he attacked the doctrine of the Trinity in a brief work, *De erroribus trinitatis.* For him it was a question, not of three Persons in God, but of three forces or manners of operation. Around 1546 he carried on a correspondence with Calvin which really made clear the gulf between them. In 1553 he published at Lyons a collection of various treatises. The title *Christianismi Restitutio* already discloses his polemic against Calvin or the latter's *Christianae Religionis Institutio.* The attention of the Lyons Inquisition was directed to Servetus by Guillaume de Trie, a French refugee living in Geneva. Calvin himself contributed original letters whereby Servetus could be unmasked as author of the *Restitutio.* But he escaped from prison and, *in absentia,* was condemned to death by burning. Fleeing, he came to Geneva, where he was accused before the city council by Calvin's secretary, Nicolas de Fontaine, and then arrested.

The trial began on 15 August and was dragged out for weeks. In many respects it took the form of theological discussions between Calvin and Servetus. The Swiss cities whose opinion was sought—Bern, Basel, Zurich, Schaffhausen—all declared Servetus guilty. On 26 October 1553 the council decided that Servetus should be burned alive and his books consigned also to the flames. Calvin had demanded the death penalty. But he and other pastors sought to have the sentence mitigated by asking for decapitation instead of the pyre. His intervention, however, was fruitless. The sentence was in keeping with the convictions and practice of the time. So discreet a person as Melanchthon wrote later to Calvin:

> I have read your essay in which you refuted the horrible blasphemies of Servetus and I thank the Son of God, who was judge in your struggle. The Church too is now and hereafter in your debt. I

am in complete agreement and at the same time I acknowledge that your authority has acted rightly in condemning the blasphemer to death, after a legitimate trial.[49]

The mention of the practice of the time certainly does not imply any justification, least of all for the reformer who claimed for himself the right, by virtue of his understanding of Scripture, to disregard the traditional teaching. For Calvin appeal to his conscience meant at the same time the guarantee of a prophetic commission and the demand that all agree with him. On 6 October 1552 he had written to the Geneva council:

> As for me, my lords, in my own conscience I am sure that what I have taught and written did not arise in my head, but I have it from God and I must hold it fast, if I do not wish to become a traitor to the truth.[50]

Calvin's Doctrine of the Eucharist and his Efforts for Ecclesiastical and Sacramental Fellowship among the Protestants

In his proceedings against "heretics"—Castellio, Bolsec, Servetus—Calvin is clearly a man of intolerance, determined to preserve the unity of the Church at any cost and to assure it with all the means provided by Church discipline, including recourse to the power of the state. Not entirely without cause has he been frequently presented by polemicists as a ruthless fanatic. Calvin's thinking was more decidedly ecclesiological than was Luther's. His basic question is not, "How do I find a merciful God?" but "How does one arrive at the power of God over mankind?"[51] God's universal rule becomes concrete in the visibly constituted Church. Calvin treats this in detail in the fourth book of his *Institutio,* according to which the Church is one of the "external means whereby God invites us to fellowship with Christ." In Chapter I, "On the true Church with which we must maintain unity, because she is the mother of all the devout," he discusses in nineteen out of twenty-nine sections the unity which the Christian must maintain with the Church. Powerfully as Calvin stresses the congregational idea, still, for him, the Church does not grow out of an amalgamation of believers, but she is an institution planted from above. He often quotes Cyprian's saying that no one can have God for his father who does not have the Church for his

---

[49] Letter of 4 October 1554 (*CR* 8, 362).

[50] *OC* 14, 382; Schwarz, *Briefe* II, 608.

[51] ". . . quomodo regnum Christo sartum tectumque inter nos maneat" (*ep.* to Francis I [1536]: *OS* I, 23).

mother (IV, 1, 1; 1, 4). His concept of the Church is organic, conceived according to the Pauline image of the body of Christ. Corresponding to this, the Church is visible and necessarily one. Already in the first edition of the *Institutio* (1536) he had written:

> We believe the holy Catholic Church . . . : that there is one Church and one fellowship and one people of God, whose ruler and supreme head is Christ our Lord, like the head of a body. . . . This fellowship is Catholic, or universal, since there cannot be two or three, but instead the elect of God are all united and held together in Christ, so that, as they depend on one head, they grow into one body and mutually support one another as members of one body.[52]

According to Calvin the Holy Scripture speaks of the Church in a twofold manner. First, she is the community of all the elect since the very beginning of the world. I must believe this "Church, visible only to God's eyes." In the second meaning the Church comprises the flock scattered throughout the world, consisting of those who confess Christ, who "are equipped by baptism for faith in him, and by partaking of the Eucharist testify to their unity in the true doctrine and charity" (IV, 1, 7). There is no genuine faith in the Church without esteem for this visible Church and without readiness for fellowship with her (IV, 1, 7). She becomes visible "where God's word is truly preached and heard and the Sacraments are administered according to Christ's institution" (IV, 1, 9).

For Calvin Reformation means restoration of the original Church, shattered by the papacy, and of her real unity. Calvin admits *vestiga* or *reliquiae* of the true Church even in the papal Church, especially in baptism (IV, 2, 11), but this Church lacks "the true and legitimate organization which is found on the one hand in the fellowship of the Sacraments as signs of confession, but on the other hand especially in the fellowship of doctrine" (IV, 2, 12). In regard to the true Church, which can be concretely experienced, Calvin again distinguishes between the universal Church spread throughout the world (*ecclesia universalis*) and the local churches (*singulae ecclesiae*). He is chiefly concerned with the Universal Church. Absolute unity in regard to doctrine and Sacraments must be preserved in her. But, apart from specified central points of doctrine, "differences of opinion" among the individual churches can prevail without any injury to unity in faith. Correspondingly, we see the reformer prepared for compromise in his exer-

---

[52] *OS* I, 86; cf. *Inst.* IV, 1, 7.

tions for unity to an extent that we should not expect in view of his practice in Geneva.

This especially appears in the controversy among the reformers over the Sacrament of unity and peace, the Eucharist. Theologically, Calvin had derived his views from Luther, but before 1536 he had already become acquainted also with Zwingli's *Commentarius de vera et falsa religione.*[53] On 22 September 1537 he took part on behalf of Geneva in a synod at Bern. It had been called at the urging of Martin Bucer to settle the controversy between Zwinglians and Lutherans in regard to the Eucharist. The Swiss charged that Bucer, by consenting to the Wittenberg agreement of May 1536 with its vague notion of the "unio sacramentalis" of the bread and the body of Christ,[54] had sacrificed the Bern Disputation of 1528 and was seeking the union of Lutherans and Swiss at the cost of truth. At the Bern synod of 1537 Bucer intended to clear himself of this suspicion and put an end to distrust. When the violent discussions between him and the Bern preacher and teacher Kaspar Megander (1495–1545) led to no result, Calvin, Farel, and Viret were asked to draw up a *Confessio fidei de Eucharistia.* It was composed by Calvin and signed by the Strasbourg theologians as a sign of their consensus with the Swiss.

According to this confession,[55] Christ offers us in the signs of bread and wine a real participation in his flesh and blood. But this does not mean local presence, which we are deprived of through Christ's ascension. His spirit, however, is in no way limited in its activity. It is the bond of sharing and nourishes us with the substance of Christ's body and blood. Thus Calvin occupies a position between Luther and Zwingli. Against Luther he rejects local and historical and bodily presence. Against Zwingli he so emphasizes the reality of the fellowship in Christ's body and blood that he does not even shy away from the word "substance." In May 1539 Calvin wrote to an opponent of the efforts for unity:

> By no means do I concede that in Zwingli's doctrine there is nothing questionable. For it is easy to see that he, too much preoccupied with eradicating superstition about the bodily presence of Christ, at the same time discards the true force of union [with Christ] or at least obscures it. But especially this point must be brought into the light more.[56]

[53] A. Lang, "Die Quellen der Institutio von 1536," *EvTh* 3 (1936), 100–112 (especially p. 107).

[54] E. Bizer, *Studien zur Geschichte des Abendmahlstreites* (Darmstadt, 2nd ed. 1962), p. 118.

[55] *OS* I, 435f.

[56] *OC* 10, II, 356; Schwarz, *Briefe* I, 117f.

Calvin made a special gesture of good will by signing the *Confessio Augustana* at the Regensburg Religious Colloquy of 1541. This was not the *Confessio* of 1530, but the *Confessio Augustana Variata,* a version drawn up by Melanchthon in 1540 with a view to an understanding with the Swiss. At first the *Variata* encountered no opposition from Lutherans and was actually tacitly tolerated by Luther himself. The difference had to do especially with the doctrine of the Eucharist. Whereas the version of 1530 met the Catholics half-way and seemed to teach even transubstantiation, the *Variata* showed consideration to the Swiss. Article 10 reads: "Concerning the Lord's Supper they teach that, with bread and wine, the body and blood of Christ are really given to those who partake."[57] Instead of "under the appearances of bread and wine" it has now "with bread and wine;" instead of "is present," "are given to those who partake." This admitted an interpretation in Calvin's sense. And in later controversies he could refer to his having signed the *Confessio Augustana* without having disavowed his view.

If in the *Variata* Calvin had assented to a confession that had been composed without him, in the agreement with the people of Zurich, the *Consensus Tigurinus* of 1549, he was one of the authors, or even the real driving force. As a result of Luther's *Kurzes Bekenntnis vom heiligen Sakrament* (1544), the dispute with the Swiss over the Sacraments had flared up again. In his "boundless, lightning-hurling anger," as Calvin described it,[58] Luther had also attacked Zwingli, now fourteen years in his grave. The next year Heinrich Bullinger defended his predecessor Zwingli and the Zurich Eucharistic doctrine in the rejoinder, *Wahrhafte Bekenntnis der Diener der Kirche zu Zürich . . . insbesondere über das Nachtmahl.* Earlier, on 25 November 1544, Calvin had asked Bullinger not to let himself be provoked by Luther's harshness and to keep silent. On this occasion he had expressed the desire to treat orally some time with Bullinger their differences in regard to the Eucharist. He wrote to Bullinger:

> If we were able to discuss the matter some time for only half a day, we would, I hope, easily agree, and not only in regard to the matter itself but even in regard to its formulation. Meanwhile, this small disagreement should not prevent our maintaining a brotherly friendship in the Lord.[59]

Though harmony was not destined to be achieved so quickly, still Calvin succeeded, in his serious efforts for unity over a period of three

---

[57] *Die Bekenntnisschriften der evangelisch-lutherischen Kirche* (Göttingen, 5th ed. 1963), pp. 65, 45.
[58] A letter of 28 June 1545 to Melanchthon; *OC* 12, 98; Schwarz, *Briefe* I, 308.
[59] *OC* 11, 775; Schwarz, *Briefe* I, 286.

years, in gaining Bullinger's confidence. In 1547 Bullinger submitted his *De sacramentis* to Calvin for an opinion. In a letter of 25 February 1547,[60] Calvin discussed the work critically and again expressed his desire for a personal conversation. He received no answer at first and then, at the end of 1547, a very unfriendly one. On 1 March 1548 Calvin stressed that, if he taught a more intimate union with Christ in the Sacrament than did Bullinger, still they did not cease to have the same Christ and to be one in him. "Perhaps it will some day be granted to us to come together in complete harmony."[61] A visit by Calvin and Farel to Zurich in May 1548 did not accomplish much. In a letter of 26 June 1548, containing "all the thoughts of his heart,"[62] Calvin once again explained his opinion in detail.[63] In July he sent his *Propositiones de sacramentis* to Bullinger,[64] who answered them in November with his *Annotationes*. Further comments passed back and forth, but an agreement was not yet forthcoming. Then in April 1549 Bullinger surprised Calvin with the report that now very little stood in the way of a general Swiss confession. Calvin journeyed happily to Zurich, although Bullinger stated rather reservedly that the matter could be arranged by writing. From all this it becomes clear "that it was not Bullinger and the people of Zurich who pressed for the agreement, but Calvin, who for this purpose traveled several times to Zurich."[65] The accord, in twenty-six articles, was drawn up at the end of May 1549. It was, however, not printed until 1551,[66] because the consent of the other Swiss congregations was awaited.

The twenty-six articles deal almost exclusively with the doctrine of the Sacraments in general and with the Eucharist. The Sacraments are to be understood only in relation to Christ, Priest and King (1–4). This Christ communicates himself to us, makes us one with himself, through his Spirit. The Gospel and the Sacraments testify this (5–6). Through the Sacrament God makes present and seals his grace. This happens also through the word. But it is a great thing that living images are represented to our eyes and thus our senses are more strongly impressed (7). A distinction must be made between sign and thing signified, and still sign and reality must not be separated. All who, in faith, take hold of the promises held out in the sign receive Christ spiritually with all his

---

[60] *OC* 11, 481; Schwarz, *Briefe* I, 370.

[61] *OC* 12, 666; Schwarz, *Briefe* II, 412f.

[62] *OC* 12, 731; Schwarz, *Briefe* II, 424.

[63] *OC* 12, 727f.; Schwarz, *Briefe* II, 421ff.

[64] *OC* 12, 726ff.

[65] H. Grass, *Die Abendmahlslehre bei Luther und Calvin* (Gütersloh, 2nd ed. 1954), p. 210.

[66] *OS* II, 247–253.

spiritual graces. If union with him already exists, then it is continued and renewed (9). Hence more attention should be paid to the promise than to the sign. For it is not water, bread, and wine that are able to make us sharers in spiritual gifts, but only faith in Christ's promise (10). Of themselves the Sacraments effect nothing. God alone acts through his Spirit.[67] If, in so doing, he makes use of the Sacraments, this does not mean that he, as it were, infuses his power into them and they operate independently of him (12–15). Hence not all who receive the Sacraments share in their grace, but only the elect. Accordingly, it cannot be said that all those receive grace who do not present the obstacle of mortal sin. God does indeed offer grace to all, but only believers are capable of laying hold of it. The Sacraments give nothing which faith would not already have received, but they strengthen and increase faith (19).

Articles 21 to 26 deal specially with the Eucharist. Any notion of bodily presence must be eliminated. Christ as man is to be sought only in heaven and indeed only in spirit and in the knowledge of faith (*mente et fidei intelligentia;* 21). To enclose him within the elements of this world is a wicked and infamous superstition. The words of institution, "this is my body," are to be understood figuratively. The thing signified is transferred to the sign. Bread and wine are termed that for which they are signs (22).

This formulation was subsequently too weak for Calvin. He was especially concerned that there was no mention of the eating of the flesh. And so he asked Bullinger to agree to the insertion of the following Article 23, "De manducatione carnis Christi."[68] The eating of his flesh and the drinking of his blood, represented in the sign, mean that Christ nourishes our souls in faith in the power of his Spirit, but any "intermingling or interpenetration of substance" must be excluded. Article 24 even more strongly attacks "transubstantiation and other absurdities." In it are to be rejected, along with this papal invention, all "crass fancies and idle sophistries" which "either detract from his heavenly glory or are not in full harmony with the truth of his human nature." It is indeed regarded as no less absurd to localize Christ in the bread or to confine him to bread than to change the bread into his body. According to Article 25, Christ's body is in heaven as in a place and as such it is to be sought only there. In this way the distance in space is to be expressed and emphasized.

> For even though, philosophically speaking, there is no place beyond the heavens, yet Christ's body is finite in accord with the

---

[67] "Deus enim solus est, qui spiritu suo agit," Article 12.

[68] *OC* 13, 305; Schwarz, *Briefe,* II, 477.

nature of a human body and is inclosed by heaven as by a place; hence it is necessary that he be separated from us by so great a spatial interval as is heaven from the earth.

If our imagination, then, must not confine Christ in bread and wine, it is also "even less permitted to adore him in the bread" (26). Bread and wine are signs of union with Christ. As signs they are not the thing itself nor do they contain this within themselves nor unite it with themselves. "Hence they make of it an idol who direct their senses to the sign in order to adore Christ in it" (26).

For the sake of unity Calvin had made several concessions in the *Consensus Tigurinus,* among other things in regard to the efficacy of the Sacraments.[69] Nevertheless, the *Consensus* can be regarded as his view. He himself so declared when he was reproached because of it.[70] The development of the Calvinist doctrine of the Eucharist from the first edition of the *Institutio* in 1536 to the *Consensus Tigurinus* of 1549 or the *Institutio* of 1559 is characterized by a steadily decreasing mention of an inner connection between the signs of bread and wine and union with Christ's body and blood. If in 1536 and 1543 it is still said that bread and wine are sanctified, in the *Consensus Tigurinus* and in the 1559 *Institutio* they are only signs of partaking of the body and blood, which takes place, by the power of the Holy Spirit, on the occasion of celebrating communion.[71] With Calvin there can be no question of the real presence, but of real communion with the body and blood of Christ. The believer to whom bread and wine are given at communion really shares in the fellowship of Christ's body and blood. But they are not tied to bread and wine—to say nothing of being inclosed in them. This is impossible because of Christ's true humanity, which, locally circumscribed, is enthroned in heaven and will not come to us until the *parousia.* The divine Word "is united with the nature of man in one person but is not confined in it," so that it still has reality outside it (II, 13, 4; *Extra calvinisticum*). On the other hand, the true humanity of Christ forbids our attributing to it properties such as ubiquity, which belong to the divinity alone. Calvin regards this as assumed in both the Lutheran and the scholastic doctrine of the real presence. The Holy Spirit effects communion with the life-giving flesh of Christ.

---

[69] Cf. the letter of October 1549 to Bucer; *OC* 13, 439; Schwarz, *Briefe* II, 497.
[70] *OC* 13, 534f.; Schwarz, *Briefe* II, 514f.
[71] 1536: "sacramentum est panis in Christi corpore sanctificatus et vinum in eius sanguine sanctificatum" (*OS* I, 136). 1543: "signa sunt panis et vinum, quae in Christi corpore et sanguine sanctificantur, ut invisibilem eorum communionem re praesentent" (*OS* V, 342, note c; *OC* 1, 991, note 2, 1). 1559: "signa sunt panis et vinum, quae invisibile alimentum, quod percepimus ex carne et sanguine Christi, nobis repraesentant" (IV, 17, 1; *OS* V, 342).

The Lord grants us through his Spirit the favor of becoming one with him in body, mind, and soul. The bond of this union is, accordingly, the Spirit of Christ. [IV, 17, 12; 17, 33]

He makes it possible

that Christ's flesh can, despite so great a separation in space, reach us in order to become our food. . . . What is separated in space, is united by the Holy Spirit in truth. [IV, 17, 10]

If the local presence of Christ in heaven prevents his descending to us and being present on the altar, still Calvin does not find the reverse difficult, that is, that Christ, through the Holy Spirit, "leads us up to him" (IV, 17, 31), and, accordingly, he understands the summons to prayer, *Sursum corda,* quite literally. Calvin's idea becomes fully clear in its practical consequences. Since the body and blood of Christ are in no way united to the bread and wine, the veneration of the Sacrament is forbidden. We must direct our mind, not to the sign, but to the signified, to Christ in heaven. Calvin also rejects the *manducatio impiorum.* The Sacrament is offered to all, but unbelievers receive only the sign, while the union with the life-giving flesh of Christ, affected by the Holy Spirit, does not take place. For "they who are devoid of the Spirit of Christ cannot eat the flesh of Christ" (IV, 17, 33).

The *Consensus Tigurinus* saved the unity of the Swiss and Reformed Protestantism while making definitive the break with Lutheranism. This became evident in the disputes of Calvin and the Calvinists with Joachim Westphal (1510–74) and Tilmann Hesshus (1527–88) in the so-called Second Eucharistic Controversy.

CHAPTER 30

The Spread of Calvinism in Western Europe

In contradistinction to Luther, who was concerned about the "merciful God" and personal justification, Calvin's question was: "How does one arrive at God's dominion over mankind?"[1] If he saw the Reformation as the establishing of the Kingdom of God, then he could not limit himself to Geneva. The community there was in his view only the cornerstone of a worldwide Church. In his extensive correspondence Calvin maintained contact with the decisive personalities of Europe. He intervened

[1] " . . . quomodo Dei gloriae sua constet in terris incolumitas, quomodo suam dignitatem Dei veritas retineat, quomodo regnum Christo sanctum tectumque inter nos maneat"; preface to the *Institutio* on 1536, letter to Francis I (*OC* 1, 11; *OS* I, 23).

wherever he saw a door opened for his movement and acted with a sound political sense and great tenacity. Like Calvin, Calvinism showed itself to be active, militant, and at times ruthless. The reformer demanded that his adherents translate their faith into action and realize it, not only in private, but also in public life. They were to carry their confession into the world and set up Reformed congregations wherever they went. He not infrequently gave them detailed instructions as to where and how this should be done and managed to inspire them with a readiness to be a witness to their doctrine—a witness that did not shrink from even death. To this goal of realizing the Kingdom of God on earth they had to subordinate even political exertions. It goes without saying that Calvin claimed the authority of the state for his aims, and, wherever it was denied him, he turned on the opposing forces. For a prince who attacked the Church that had been reformed in accord with God's word—in other words, the only valid form of Christianity, prescribed by God—was failing in his duty and thereby ceased to be a prince. Orderly "resistance" to him was permitted. The estates, the lesser authorities, and the princes were the ones especially charged with leading such resistance. Differing from the Lutheran, a Calvinist who was not in agreement with the religious policy of his ruling authority had in his very religion a legal basis for resistance, if necessary by armed force. The religious wars in the West, which aroused Frenchmen, Dutchmen, Englishmen, and Scotsmen against their monarchs, were thus partly inspired by Calvin's spirit.

France

Calvin's relations with France, his native land, were especially close. Many French refugees found a home at Geneva and from there preachers were sent to French cities in order to foster the establishing of congregations.

King Henry II (1547–59) continued the anti-Protestant religious policy of his father, Francis I. In this he was assisted by the mutually rival forces which tried to exert influence on the weak monarch: the chief minister, the Connétable Montmorency; the Guise brothers, Duke Francis and Cardinal Charles of Lorraine; and the Queen, Catherine de Médicis. Catherine only became important when, after thirteen years of marriage, she presented the King with sons. In October 1547 Henry obtained from the *parlement* the establishing of a special court for heresy cases, the *Chambre ardente*. There were then throughout the country groups of adherents of the Reformation, who were referred to as Lutherans, though they were really oriented to Strasbourg and at first sought their preachers there. They recruited from all strata of the population, including the higher nobility, but practiced their faith secretly, had their children baptized in the old Church, and often even participated in the Mass in order to escape persecution.

Calvin was to mould congregations out of these groups of people who regarded themselves as converts to the Gospel, congregations which were prepared, for their part, to convert their environment. He sharply attacked "Nicodemism." Anyone who could not hold himself aloof from the "defilements of the papacy" should emigrate. If he cannot belong to the number of the elect to whom God grants the strength and the honor of martyrdom, then he should at least withdraw to where he can find God's word, a genuine Church, and the pure Sacraments. One must have the courage "to separate from idolatry and all superstition, which are contrary to serving and confessing God."[2] The administration of baptism and the celebration of the Lord's Supper, Calvin advises, should wait until a stable community has been founded on the basis of the assembly for prayer and preaching. For baptism

> at least a small flock, which represents the Church, must be collected, and the one baptizing must be acknowledged as pastor. . . . Hence it is necessary that the child be baptized in a community which has permanently separated from the defilements of the papacy.[3]

For the distribution of communion one must

> be unanimously chosen and elected as pastor. And for this it is necessary that there be an organized ecclesiastical community.[4]

Despite persecution congregations were formed in many places from 1555 based on the Geneva model. At first the gatherings took place in secret, but in 1558 Calvinists dared to sing psalms publicly in Paris. From 1555 to 1562 the Geneva *Compagnie* sent eighty-eight pastors to France. They often exchanged places in order to evade persecution. At an assembly in Poitiers in 1558 it was decided to hold a synod at Paris the next year in order to define the confession of faith and the Church Order. Representatives from fifty congregations met in this first Calvinist National Synod on 25 May 1559. Calvin sent envoys, to whom he gave a confession of faith. The synod added several articles to it. The definitive version, the *Confessio Gallicana,* had, like the appended

[2] Letter of 12 October 1553 (*OC* 14, 638).
[3] Letter of 11 October 1554 (*OC* 15, 265).
[4] Letter of 19 June 1554 (*OC* 15, 174).

Church Order, the *Disciplina,* forty articles.[5] The first treated of the authority of Scripture. It alone is authoritative and the

> most sure rule of our faith, not so much through the general agreement and conformity of the churches as through the testimony and the inner persuasion of the Holy Spirit, who lets us distinguish it from the other ecclesiastical books.

The real, though spiritual, community with the body and blood of Christ in the Lord's Supper is clearly stressed. But it is shared only by believers and a real presence in the bread and wine is not accepted.

> As already stated, we believe that God actually gives us in both the Eucharist and baptism what he represents in them. Therefore we connect with the signs the true possession and enjoyment of that which is there offered us. And consequently all who bring to Christ's holy table a pure faith, as to a vessel, really receive what the signs there attest: namely, the body and blood of Jesus Christ serve the soul as food and drink no less than bread and wine serve the body [1 Cor. 11:24f.; John 6:56] [37].

The secular authority has to punish by the sword crimes against the first panel of the Ten Commandments, and hence heresy and the like (39). One must be subject, "with a good and free will," even to an unbelieving authority, "provided that God's dominion remains intact (Acts 4:17ff.)" (40). A right of resistance is here formulated only cautiously and *ad casum,* if indeed it is actually formulated at all.

Calvinism found adherents, or at least sympathizers, even in circles in the higher nobility and in the royal house itself. Jeanne d'Albret, Queen of Navarre, her husband, Anthony of Bourbon, his brother, Prince Louis de Condé, the Coligny brothers—Admiral Gaspard, infantry general Francois d'Andelot, and Cardinal Odet de Coligny—and other influential persons were among Calvin's adherents. The more they became aware of their strength and political motives, such as the safeguarding of the rights of the nobility against the absolute crown, and these actually became predominant, the more the religious movement developed into a faction.

Henry II died in 1559 of an injury received in a tournament, just as he was beginning to act still more energetically in the struggle to maintain religious unity in his country. In the reign of his sickly fifteen-year-old son, Francis II (1559–60), the Guise brothers took control.

---

[5] Text in *Bekenntnisschriften und Kirchenordnungen der nach Gottes Wort reformierten Kirche,* ed. W. Niesel (Zurich, 3rd ed. n. d.), pp. 66–79.

The *coup de main,* attempted at Chateau Amboise with the aim of removing the King from the influence of these advisers, failed and cost many Protestants their lives. From that time they were known as Huguenots (*hugenauds*), a word probably derived from *Eidgenossen* or *aiguenots,* the term for the adherents of the Reformation in Geneva, who were rebels against Savoy.[6]

The Queen-Mother, Catherine de Médicis, now took the business of state into her own hands. She pushed aside the Guise brothers and summoned their protégé, Michel de L'Hôpital (1503–73), to the chancellorship. As an Erasmian, he was opposed to force in religious matters, just as Catherine, for political reasons, was intent upon *détente.* She assumed the regency for Charles IX (1560–74), brother of the deceased Francis II. She intended to effect a compromise by means of a religious colloquy, which she arranged at Poissy. In his opening speech on 31 July 1561, the chancellor, L'Hôpital, termed the gathering a national council. Such a synod could, better than a general council, provide a remedy, he said, in France's difficulties by reform of morals and doctrine. But the bishops repudiated a national council; they would have nothing to do with any discussion of doctrine but only with the problem of abuses. Nevertheless, the assembly turned into a religious colloquy, in which Theodore Beza from Geneva confronted the Cardinal of Lorraine and the Jesuit general, Lainez. The question of the Eucharist showed how profound the division was.

The number of Calvinists grew. Coligny offered the Queen the assistance of more than two thousand congregations. In January 1562 the Edict of Saint-Germain-en-Laye allowed the Huguenots to hold synods and to celebrate their liturgy outside of cities and private devotions inside them. A triumvirate, consisting of the Duke of Guise, the Connétable Montmorency, and the Marshal Saint-André, was formed to save the Catholic faith; it actively opposed the government's policy of toleration. On the other hand, the concessions did not satisfy the Huguenots. Coligny tried to induce the Queen to an anti-Spanish policy; the Catholic party sought in turn to involve Spain and the Pope. The *parlement* of Paris refused to register the Edict of Saint-Germain.

The overture to the eight Wars of Religion, which were to devastate France until 1598, was sounded by the Massacre at Vassy on 1 March 1562. Francis of Guise caused the breaking up of a service of worship, which was taking place in the city, contrary to the edict. In the skirmish seventy-four participants were killed and around a hundred wounded. The Huguenots, led by the Prince de Condé and Coligny, flew to arms.

---

[6] H. Naef, " 'Huguenot.' Le procès d'un mot," *Bibliothèque d'Humanisme et Renaissance* 12 (1950).

Massacres, profanation of churches, and acts of retaliation convulsed the country. Catherine de Médicis turned for help to the Duke of Savoy, the Pope, and King Philip II, while the Huguenots asked aid from Queen Elizabeth of England. Her assistance arrived too late. Condé was defeated and taken prisoner by the Duke of Guise, who, however, was ambushed and killed by a Huguenot noble in February 1563. The Edict of Amboise in 1563 put an end to the first war. It conceded the free exercise of religion to the nobility; in addition, Calvinist worship was to be permitted in one city of each *baillage,* except Paris. Since neither side was satisfied, the implementation of the edict led to new difficulties. Condé brought on the second war (1567–68), allegedly to free the King from his mother's control. The plan to surprise the court at Meaux miscarried. Catherine de Médicis saw the collapse of her policy of reconciliation. Condé was killed in the third war (1568–1570) and Coligny became the sole leader of the Huguenots. Fearful of the power of the Guises and of Spain, Catherine again showed herself accommodating to the Huguenots and granted them liberty of conscience in the Peace of Saint-Germain (8 August 1570). Calvinist worship could be held where it had taken place before the war and, in addition, in the castles of the nobility and the suburbs of two cities in a province. And four fortified towns were granted to the Huguenots for two years.

The engagement of the King's sister, Margaret of Valois, to Henry of Navarre, the future Henry IV, who had fought on the Huguenot side, appeared to strengthen the compromise. In 1571 the Huguenots were able to hold a national synod at La Rochelle, where the confession and Church Order of 1559 were revised to strengthen the position of the pastors.

Coligny gained ascendancy over Charles IX and persuaded him to go to war against Spain in support of the Protestants of Belgium. A defeat of the French troops gave heart to Coligny's opponents. Catherine de Médicis sought to exploit the situation to reestablish her influence and exclude Coligny. Four days after the marriage of her daughter Margaret with Henry of Navarre, at which the Huguenot nobility was strongly represented, she arranged an attempt to assassinate the admiral, who, however, was only wounded. An investigation ordered by the King in search of the guilty threatened to expose Catherine. She convinced her son of the necessity of getting rid of Coligny and the other Huguenot leaders. From three to four thousand men in Paris alone are said to have fallen victim in the subsequent massacre of Saint Bartholomew's Day, 23–24 August 1572, that was thereupon perpetrated by agents of the Guises. The carnage was continued for weeks in the provinces, with the cooperation of the mob. Not religion but an alleged conspiracy against the King and his court was the pretext for the slaughter. This was the explanation sent to the Curia.[7] The Huguenots were now without leaders but they did not give up and successfully defended themselves in La Rochelle. Under Henry III (1574–89) they again obtained religious liberty throughout the kingdom, apart from Paris, in the Peace of Beaulieu (6 May 1576). The Catholic League was established to oppose them with the aim of maintaining the interests and liberties of the estates against royal absolutism as well as of defending the Catholic faith.

With the death of the Duke of Alençon, the youngest brother of the childless Henry III, in 1584, Henry of Navarre, leader of the Huguenots, became heir presumptive. In view of the danger thereby presented of a Protestant succession to the throne, Henry of Guise assumed the direction of the League. An alliance was concluded with Philip II of Spain and, by means of a popular tumult, the King was compelled in the Edict of Nemours in 1585 to repudiate all concessions to the Protestants and to forbid their liturgy under penalty of death. Pope Sixtus V declared that Henry of Navarre, as a relapsed heretic, was excommunicated and had forfeited all claim to the throne. The Eighth War of Religion was initiated by the League in the autumn of 1585 and before long it became an open opposition to Henry III. A popular rising in May 1588 compelled him to leave Paris, which favored the League. King Henry III tried to ward off the threatening might of the Guises by having Duke Henry assassinated on 23 December 1588 and the Duke's brother, Cardinal Louis, on the following day. The League's opposition was thereby strengthened and on 7 January 1589 the Sorbonne declared that the King's subjects were released from their oaths of loyalty. Henry III sought to ally with Henry of Bourbon-Navarre but this only intensified the hatred against him and led to the assassination of the "tyrant" by a fanatical adherent of the League, the Dominican Jacques Clement, on 1 August 1589.

The mortally wounded King had designated Henry of Navarre as his successor. The latter, as Henry IV (1589–1610), proclaimed on 4 August that he would not injure the Catholic religion and that he wished to submit to the decision of a free general or national council. This did not satisfy the League. But its policy threatened to lead to the decisive influence of Spain in France, something that was contrary to French tradition as well as to the Pope's ideas. The danger made Catholic circles ready for negotiations with Henry IV. On 17 May 1593 the King declared to the Archbishop of Bourges his willingness to become a Catholic and on 25 July he repudiated Calvinism at Saint-Denis at the

---

[7] On Gregory XIII's attitude see p. 514.

tombs of the Kings of France. After being anointed at Chartres he was able to enter Paris in March 1594. The struggle with Spain had now lost its character as a religious war, especially after the King had been absolved by Pope Clement VIII in the fall of 1595. The remaining Catholic opposition in the country gradually disappeared. Peace with Spain was finally granted to the exhausted land in May 1598 through the Pope's mediation.

A few weeks earlier, on 13 April 1598, Henry IV in the Edict of Nantes had given his former coreligionists a position in the state, which, while not complying with all their demands, certainly far exceeded what people were then inclined to concede to a minority in the way of religious and political rights.[8] At the time the number of Huguenots was about 1.2 million, so that they constituted a good twelfth of the population.

The Catholic religion was recognized as the prevailing faith in the state. Catholic worship had to be reinstituted where it had been suppressed, and buildings and property that had been withdrawn from it had to be given back. The adherents of what was called the "religion prétendu réformée" obtained liberty of conscience in the entire country and freedom of worship in places where they had actually exercised it in 1596–97 and, in addition, in the country seats of the nobility and in one place in each *baillage,* with the exception of Paris. They were permitted to hold consistories and synods, to lay out cemeteries, to institute schools and printeries in the places where they had the right of free worship. In regard to admittance to the universities, schools, and hospitals, Calvinists were not to be discriminated against. For their part they were to respect Catholic holy days and, like Catholics, they were subject to the prohibition of marrying close blood relatives. Even more farreaching were the concessions in civil law and in politics. The Huguenots were competent in law without restriction and had access to all offices. Mixed tribunals, made up of Catholics and Calvinists on an equal footing, were to be established to decide their dispute. As guarantee they received more than a hundred fortified towns for eight years. Their commandants were to be Calvinists and the garrisons were to be supported by the state. Such a concession of a private army within the state could have been made by the government only under compulsion. It was to be expected that it would be annulled as soon as the crown felt itself strong enough to take this step.

When the Pope expressed his consternation the King maintained the political necessity of the edict for the restoration of the Kingdom. The

[8] Text in E. Walder, *Religionsvergleiche des 16. Jahrhunderts* II, 13–11; E. Mengin, *Das Edikt von Nantes,* pp. 21–56.

parlements, the supreme courts, procrastinated about registering the edict and thereby giving it force. The *parlements* of Aix and Reims did not agree to do so until the fall of 1605.

The Netherlands

Due to its clear dogmatic line, its strict organization, and its political theory, Calvinism made rapid progress in the Netherlands, answering as it did to the efforts for independence in the area. It soon counted adherents in all classes and even the nobles professed it in great numbers. Thus Calvinism became the confession of the national revolution.

The political situation proved to be especially favorable to its spread. Emperor Charles V, it is true, was concerned for a good administration in Flanders and Holland and thus had the Netherlands governed by regents beloved by the *bourgeoisie,* first by his aunt, Margaret of Austria, and later by his sister Mary. However, this was no substitute for the lack of religious liberty.

> Influenced by the current theory that the peace and strength of a nation were based on unanimity of religion among all its members and fearful that the Protestant-inclined Netherlands could expose his flank to France and the Lutheran imperial estates, Charles proceeded along with the Church against heresy.[9]

A decree of 25 September 1550 stated that: "No one was to print, transcribe, reproduce, keep, conceal, sell, buy, or give any book or writing of Martin Luther, Johannes Oecolampadius, Ulrich Zwingli, Martin Bucer, Jean Calvin, or any other heretic condemned by Holy Church."[10] Further the Emperor forbade private and public gatherings, "in which adherents of the above-mentioned heretics" spoke. Anyone under even a general suspicion of heresy must not be lodged and aided by the citizenry.

> If anyone should be found guilty of transgressing the aforementioned points, he is to be punished as a disturber of our state and of the general peace as follows: men are to be killed by the sword and women are to be buried alive, if they do not persist in their errors; if they do persist in them they are to be put to death by fire. In both cases their property is to be subject to confiscation by the crown.[11]

---

[9] W. Durant, *The Age of the Reformation.*
[10] L. Motley, *Der Abfall der Niederlande und die Entstehung des Holländischen Freistaats* I (Dresden 1857), 245ff.
[11] Ibid.

This edict was intended, among other things, to destroy the Calvinists in the Netherlands, but as a matter of fact the activity of the Calvinist preachers and congregations was intensified. Even the officials in the Netherlands only supported the execution of the edict very reluctantly. They were by no means willing to have anything to do with the Inquisition, which they regarded as a Roman affair and hence a means of suppression by Spaniards. Thus, in a pernicious way, the religious was fused with the political and national. In addition there existed a special sympathy for Calvin, who always displayed a great understanding for the religious situation in the Netherlands. He came from neighboring Picardie, and his mother was from Cambrai. He thus called himself a Belgian.[12] He had come into contact with Anabaptists at Strasbourg and had married one of them, the widow Idelette de Bure. Soon afterwards (from Geneva) he had made contact with Belgian reformers.

The most important representatives of the new teachings in the Netherlands were the teacher Johannes Sturm (1507–89); the historian Johannes Sleidan (1506–56); the noble Jacques de Bourgogne; the ex-Dominican Pierre Brully (d. 1545); and Guy de Bray (1522–67). Sturm and Sleidan, both of whom came from Schleiden in the Eifel, were at first connected with the Brethren of the Common Life. The Protestant congregation at Strasbourg exercised a great influence on the development of Calvinism in the Netherlands, especially in the French-speaking parts. Sturm owed his renown to the renewal of the *Gymnasium* there. Sleidan became the political agent and later the historian of the League of Schmalkalden. Pierre Brully, formerly a Dominican at Metz, was Calvin's successor as preacher for the French refugee congregation at Strasbourg. In 1544 he was sent by Bucer to the Calvinists at Tournai and Valenciennes, who had requested a preacher. After a few months he was arrested and, following an ecclesiastical trial, handed over to the secular powers and condemned to death at the stake (19 February 1545). He was not the only victim of the more severe Church policy adopted by Charles V after his victory over the Duke of Cleves in 1543 and the Peace of Crépy in 1544. Five other executions occurred at Tournai, six at Ghent, three at Brussels, and two at Bruges. In the same year the first Flemish translations of Calvin's writings were published and his name appeared on the Liège *Index.*

Calvinism gained strength in the Netherlands in spite of severe persecution by the Inquisition, and many Netherlanders went to Geneva to learn there the pure doctrine. The new teaching spread more and more in the Flemish area through the activity of French congregations. Some Calvinists were rash and fanatical. Bertrand Le Blas, for example, had to

[12] L. E. Halkin, *La Réforme en Belgique sous Charles-Quint,* p. 96.

pay with his life at Tournai for a dramatic spectacle directed against "idolâtrie papistique." He dared to wrest the Host from the hands of the priest who was celebrating the High Mass in the Tournai cathedral on Christmas of 1554. As the punishment for so unprecedented an act he was condemned, after a four-days' trial, by the city court in the presence of imperial councillors. Both his hands were struck off and he was burned.

Georges Kathelyne gave a similar example of religious provocation at Ghent. Having gone over to the Flemish Calvinist Church, he once heard a sermon by a Dominican in the Ghent church of Saint-Michel. He suddenly interrupted the preacher with the words, "O faux prophète."[13] The people covered Kathelyne's escape but a few days later he was arrested. After long discussions between the prisoner and the Dominicans on the real presence, the veneration of saints, purgatory, and the authority of the Pope, on all points of which he professed the Calvinist belief, he was finally condemned to death and in 1555 executed outside Saint-Michel.

The most important Calvinist in the Netherlands and the best preacher was Guy de Bray. Born at Bergen in Hainault, he is regarded as the "Reformer of the Netherlands." Following his conversion to Calvinism, he spent some time in England and at Lille and Frankfurt. He studied at Geneva and Lausanne and preached at Doornik, Sedan, and Antwerp. Finally he was preacher at Valenciennes; with the capture of this city he was executed on 31 May 1567. He was the author of the *Confessio Belgica* of 1561;[14] in composing it he adhered strictly to the Huguenot confession, "but in an entirely independent spirit."[15] "The special character of the Netherlands confession" lies, "on the one hand, in the detailed recourse to the doctrinal forms of the ancient Church in an effort to renew orthodoxy, and, on the other hand, in the telling use of scriptural passages in the text itself."[16] Especially informative is the definition of the true and the false Church in Article 29. Against the "false Church" de Bray launched the charge that it attributed greater validity to its institutions than to the word of God. "It is based on men rather than on Jesus Christ and persecutes those who live a holy life according to God's word and who reproach its vices, such as avarice and idolatry."[17] The organization of the Netherlands Church is explained in Articles 30 to 32. Elders and deacons constituted, with the pastors, the council of the congregation, by which the "ministers of the word of

---

[13] Ibid., p. 107.
[14] P. Jacobs, *Reformierte Bekenntnischriften und Kirchenordnungen*, p. 154.
[15] Ibid.
[16] Ibid.
[17] Cf. ibid., p. 168.

God" were to be chosen. Calvin exercised a direct influence on the numerous writings of de Bray, the "minister of the word of God in the Netherlands."[18]

When Guy de Bray was at the height of his activity, Philip II (1556–98) assumed the government of the Netherlands. Despite his stern exertions against the Reformation, he was unable to stop the expansion and consolidation of Calvinism. His champions were the University of Louvain and the Prince-Bishop of Liège, Eberhard of Mark. Philip was soon confronted by a powerful opposition, headed by the Prince of Nassau-Orange, governor of the provinces of Holland, Zeeland, and Utrecht, by Count Egmont, governor of Flanders, and by Admiral Hoorne. Egmont, protagonist of the independence of the Netherlands but himself not a Calvinist, and Hoorne were executed in 1586. The considerable increase in the number of dioceses, made by Paul IV in 1559, gave offense; it was intended to make possible an energetic attack on heresy. Philip II's conflict with the Calvinists split the Netherlands in two. His half-sister, Margaret of Parma, was governor-general from 1559. During her regency there was formed at Brussels in 1565 a league of the lesser nobility for the struggle against the Inquisition. These nobles were termed *Gueux,* beggars, by their opponents. The revolt by the Gueux and the constant progress of Calvinism induced Philip to send the Spanish Duke of Alba to Brussels with full powers. Immediately after his arrival, Alba established the "Council of Troubles," which passed many death sentences. Many Calvinists sought religious freedom in London, Wesel, Emden, Geneva, Strasbourg, and Frankfurt. These congregations of emigrants, "the Church under the cross," provided themselves with a definite order at the Assembly of Wesel (1568) and the Synod of Emden (1571). At Emden an effort was made to realize a "Church reformed in accord with the word of God," which should be united with the state but not dependent on it. The synod worked out a plan for the government of all the churches in the Netherlands and thus united them into a national Church. The *Confessio Belgica* was adopted, and the Geneva Catechism was made obligatory for the French-speaking districts, the Heidelberg Catechism for the Flemish-speaking.

Alba's measures brought about a struggle for freedom; the Prince of Nassau-Orange emerged as its leader. He had converted to Calvinism in 1573, but at first he had very little interest in religion. During his contest with Spain Calvinism consolidated itself especially in the provinces of Holland and Zeeland. In 1575 the University of Leiden was founded and soon became the scholarly center of Calvinism. In the

---

[18] W. F. Dankbaar, *Hoogepunten uit het Nederlandsche Calvinisme in de zestiende eeuw,* pp. 5–40.

"Pacification of Ghent" in November 1576 all the provinces united for the expulsion of the Spanish. The more the political struggle contributed to the spread of Calvinism, the more the Catholic provinces—Walloon Flanders, Artois, and Hainault—feared for their existence. They joined for the defense of the Catholic faith in the Union of Arras on 6 January 1579 and recognized Philip II as their lord. Spain honored this by withdrawing its troops from the provinces of the Union.

The Calvinists' reply to the Union of Arras was the federation of the provinces of Holland, Zeeland, and Utrecht and of the "Ommelanden" around Groningen, together with John of Nassau, governor of Gelderland, in the Union of Utrecht. Of itself it was supposed to have no confessional features, and it expressly guaranteed religious liberty. But in reality the Catholic liturgy was regarded as criminal in the Union's sphere of influence.

Calvinism had conquered the northern Netherlands, but the southern provinces, thanks not least of all to the skill of Alessandro Farnese (1578–92), remained in the Catholic Church. By agreement with Spain the establishing of a Dutch Republic was effected in 1609. Once external peace had been achieved for the Calvinist Church of the Netherlands, serious inner theological conflicts erupted over predestination. "Supralapsarianism" defended a predestination independent of the commission of sin, whereas "Infralapsarianism" saw it as sin's consequence.

The national Synod of Dordrecht (1617–18), attended by representatives of almost all the Calvinist churches of Europe, meant the definitive consolidation of the Reformed Church in the Netherlands. At it were laid down the basic theological doctrines of Calvinism, especially an unconditional predestination. The lively intellectual development of the succeeding decades can be ascribed only partially to Calvinism, for the "orthodox" Calvinists were less tolerant than the Catholics before them.[19]

Germany

Calvinist communities appeared on the lower Rhine when, around the turn of the years 1544–45, Walloons and Flemings moved there for economic reasons and as a consequence of Charles V's more rigorous religious policy in the Netherlands. They met with a good reception especially at Wesel, which from 1540 was regarded "abroad as a city of the *Confessio Augustana*.[20] Not the least compelling reason for their

---

[19] J. T. McNeill, *The History and Character of Calvinism*, p. 267.
[20] A. Wolters, *Reformationsgeschichte der Stadt Wesel*, p. 80.

acceptance was the fact that people felt they would promote the local textile industry. Because of language difficulties they were allowed their own service of the word of God, but for the sake of unity in the practice of religion the city council required them to participate in the Lord's Supper in the city churches. However, the Calvinist-trained foreigners took offense at the choir dress in use there and at other Catholic ceremonies. They applied to Strasbourg, which sent the French noble, Valerand Poullain, to assume charge of their spiritual needs.

On the accession of Mary the Catholic to the English throne in 1553 many Protestants who had emigrated there left the country again and sought a new shelter, among other places, at Emden, Frankfurt-am-Main, and on the lower Rhine. A rather large group came again to Wesel. The denial of their own celebration of the Last Supper and the demand to accept the *Confessio Augustana* led, in the case of this relatively closed group, to a much greater resistance than was earlier true of the Walloons. They wanted to maintain their confessional standing in congregations of their own. The question was discussed in 1556 with Calvin and Jan Laski at Frankfurt, where similar problems had arisen. Calvin had already written: "It would greatly sadden us if the French Church which could be established at Wesel would be destroyed because we could not adapt ourselves to special ceremonies."[21] He now advised that ceremonies should be overlooked for the sake of the unity of the Church. But the quarrel extended to the doctrine of the Eucharist. When the foreigners were not prepared to sign a confession of the real presence in the sense of *manducatio oralis,* they were expelled in 1557. The victorious Lutheran faction, inspired by Tilemann Hesshusen, in its zeal for the pure doctrine, went to such extremes that it antagonized the city council; the result was a reaction at Wesel. This encouraged the willingness to receive the stream of refugees from the Netherlands, pouring into German territory from 1567, when the Duke of Alba became Spanish governor at Brussels. These emigrants were decided Calvinists. Wherever they arrived, among other places at Emmerich, Rees, Cleves, Gennep, Goch, Duisburg, and Wesel, they established congregations or got the upper hand in existing communities by virtue of their activity and their quite strong confessional stamp. At that time Wesel became a Calvinist city. The number of Calvinists on the lower Rhine had increased to such a degree by 1568 that it was possible to consider giving them an organization. Thus on 3 November numerous pastors and elders and some nobles gathered in synod, the "Wesel Assembly."[22] In accord with Paul's instruction that in the Church every-

[21] Letter of 13 March 1554 (*OC* 15, 80); cf. *OC* 16, 286ff. (1556), 19 619ff. (1563).
[22] Minutes in A. Wolters, op. cit., pp. 335–358.

thing should be arranged and proceed with propriety recommendations were elaborated for uniting the refugees into congregations and classes. The synodal organization in use in France and the Netherlands was applied to the new situation. Three years later the guidelines of the Wesel Assembly were declared binding at the general Synod of Emden (4–14 October 1571) and further details relevant to discipline were enacted. This synod was the affair of the scattered Dutch congregations. The local church council played no role, either in its preparation or in its implementation. People at Emden were at that time not yet Calvinist but belonged to an intermediate, Melanchthonian tendency. It was only under Menso Alting (1541–1612) that Emden became the "Geneva of the North."

Nevertheless, beyond the Netherlands and the lower Rhine "the congregations of the continent" were united through the Emden Synod "into a Church with a common confession and common order."[23] The laity were much used in the service of the Church. Together with the preachers (*ministri*), the elders and deacons constituted the consistory, which was to meet weekly (Article 6). "In places where the service of the word could not be carried out" lecturers, elders, and deacons were to be instituted so that congregations could be assembled (41). Hence, in times of persecution, the congregations could, if necessary, get along without preachers. Several congregations formed a "class," which was to hold its own assembly every three or six months (7). Thus the individual congregation found support in the larger unity. The "Wesel Class," in which the congregations of the lower Rhine were amalgamated, met pretty regularly between 1573 and 1609. It not only held together the "Dutch churches under the Cross" on the lower Rhine, but gradually brought the native Protestants into its group or, where there were no refugee congregations, worked for the founding of Calvinist congregations of natives. The Calvinism of the lower Rhine felt itself bound to the Church of the Netherlands and long remained closely united with it. It was not until 1610 that the congregations of Cleves, Mark, Jülich-Berg, and Ravensberg established in Duisburg their own general synodal union. By the Treaty of Xanten in 1614 Cleves, Mark, and Ravensberg fell to Brandenburg. Shortly before this the Elector Johannes Sigismund of Brandenburg had gone over to Calvinism. In 1655 the founding of a Calvinist university for Brandenburg-Cleves finally took place in Duisburg, the chief center of the Calvinist confession.

On the lower Rhine and in East Friesland Calvinism had arisen from below by the founding of congregations and had built itself into a

---

[23] W. Niesel, *Bekenntnisschriften und Kirchenordnungen*, p. 277; ibid., pp. 279–290, the synodal acts.

synodal union on the French and Netherlands model. The situation was different where it was introduced from above, by the decision of a prince or of a city government. In these cases the authority sought to retain control of Church administration and hence the congregational organization, created by Calvin, was subject to some restriction. The first German prince to accept the Calvinist creed and introduce it in his territory was Friedrich III of the Palatinate (1559–76). His most important assistants in introducing Calvinism were Melanchthon's Silesian pupil, Zacharias Ursinus (1534–83), and Kaspar Olevianus of Trier (1536–87). Olevianus had made contact with Calvinist congregations as a law student at Paris, Orléans, and Bourges. He took it upon himself to gain his homeland for the Reformation and from 1558 studied theology at Geneva and Zurich. He was sent by Calvin to Trier around 1559. Here he obtained the position of teacher of Latin from the council but was soon active as a preacher of the Reformation. His reform endeavors foundered on the opposition of the elector and of the majority of the city council, and he took refuge at the court of the Elector Palatine at Heidelberg.

The Elector Friedrich III had, shortly before, succeeded the childless Otto Heinrich (1556–59). His wife, Mary of Hohenzollern, daughter of Margrave Kasimir of Brandenburg-Kulmbach, had gained him for Lutheranism. In his religious and ethical seriousness he inclined to rigorism and was intolerant of Catholics, Jews, and, later, of Lutherans. He regarded his purpose in life as the struggle "with Christ" against "the devil and his apostle, the Pope."[24] Concerned for the unity of Protestantism, he was personally involved in the Eucharistic quarrel between the pugnacious Lutheran, Tilemann Hesshusen, called to Heidelberg by Otto Heinrich, and university circles, represented chiefly by the deacon Klebitz, who had received his degree there. The Elector was indignant at the strife of theologians, especially at Hesshusen's fanaticism and, for his own part, intended to arrive at a solution through prayer and the study of Holy Scripture. He declared the Eucharistic formula of the *Confessio Augustana Variata* to be obligatory. According to this version, "the body and the blood of Christ are really administered," not in or under, but "with the bread and wine."[25] In this way one could profess Calvin's view and at the same time be included in the protection afforded by the Religious Peace of 1555 as an adherent of the *Confessio Augustana*. Hesshusen was allowed no peace and was finally dismissed as superintendent. His place was taken by a church council of three theologians and three laymen. A testimonial from Melanchthon of 1

[24] A. Kluckholn (ed.), *Briefe Friedrichs des Frommen* I, 517.
[25] *BSLK* 65, 45.

November 1559, and a disputation at Heidelberg on 3–6 June 1560, urged by Friedrich's Gnesiolutheran son-in-law, Duke Johann Friedrich II of Saxony, made the Elector Palatine incline more than ever to the Calvinist viewpoint. On 12 August 1560 he issued an edict whereby ministers who were unwilling to accept Melanchthon's Eucharistic formula had to leave the principality. At the same time Calvinists driven from their homelands, such as Kaspar Olevianus from Trier, Zacharias Ursinus from Breslau, and Wenceslaus Zuleger from Bohemia, acquired great influence at the Electoral court. Despite his youth—he was only twenty-nine—Zuleger was appointed president of the church council. Olevianus became professor and pastor; Ursinus, professor and director of the *Collegium Sapientiae,* the theological school which was separated from the university. When his efforts to assure the unity of Protestantism by again acquiring signatures for the *Confessio Augustana Variata* failed at the Naumburg Diet of Princes in 1561, Friedrich III went over definitively to Calvinism. But he hesitated to adopt the Geneva Catechism, which would have signified an open break with the *Confessio Augustana,* so he commissioned the drawing up of a special catechism. The resulting Heidelberg Catechism of 1563 was essentially the work of Ursinus; that Olevianus made a considerable contribution or revised the German text is improbable.[26] In 129 questions the catechism provides a systematic and carefully composed theology. Following the Introduction—"What is your single consolation in life and in death? That one is the property of Christ his Saviour"—come three parts: I. "On Man's Misery" (sin, which is recognized by virtue of Christ's twofold commandment of love of God and neighbor); II. "On Man's Redemption" (questions 12 to 85: the Creed, baptism, the Lord's Supper); III. "'On Gratitude" (questions 86 to 129: works, the decalog, the Lord's Prayer). The Calvinist doctrine of predestination and any polemic against the Lutheran teaching on the Eucharist are abandoned. All the more sharply is the Catholic Mass repudiated, from the third edition, in Question 80: "And thus the Mass is basically nothing less than a denial of the unique sacrifice and suffering of Jesus Christ and a damnable superstition." Hence the clarification of the doctrine of the Mass that had meanwhile been made by the Council of Trent was completely ignored. The fourth and definitive edition of the catechism was published, along with the Church Order, in November 1563 for the dominions of Friedrich III of the Palatinate. Beyond this area it won, among other places, Nassau-Orange, the lower Rhineland, the County

---

[26] Cf. W. Hollweg, "Bearbeitete Caspar Olevianus den deutschen Text zum Heidelberger Katechismus?" *Neue Untersuchungen zur Geschichte und Lehre des Heidelberger Katechismus* (Neukirchen 1961), pp. 124–152.

of Mark, and especially the Netherlands. It was translated into Dutch as early as 1563 and at the Dordrecht Synod of 1618–19 it was declared to be the symbolic book whereby the way into the entire Calvinist world was opened up.

The Church Order dealt with preaching and the administration of the Sacraments. Exclusion from the Sacraments was provided for. But, so that no abuse could creep into the matter of excommunication, as happened under the papacy, it was to lie, not in the power of the ministers, but in that of the entire Christian congregation.[27]

Swiss influence became especially apparent in the cessation of all ceremonies. Eventually the Church Order regulated the eleemosynary system, dress, marriage cases, the care of the sick and of prisoners, and burial. Ecclesiastical life was to be supported from without by a strict police organization. The Church council acquired a new order in 1564. It had to exercise authority over the territorial Church as one of the prince's administrative offices. Also, ecclesiastical districts were subject to it, each headed by its superintendent. Olevianus instituted Church discipline on the Geneva model, whereby it was entrusted rather to the congregation or to a court selected by it. He was able to see his plans realized at least partially when in 1570 the Elector issued a disciplinary order for the Church council. According to this the council had the means of calling to account every deviation in doctrine or too outspoken notion. Two pastors, inclined toward anti-Trinitarianism, were enabled to experience what this meant. One of them, Adam Neuser, contrived to flee to Constantinople, where he became a Muslim; the other, Johannes Sylvanus, superintendent of Ladenburg, was, despite recantation, executed in the public square in the presence of his wife and children.

The appearance of the Heidelberg Catechism brought Friedrich III into new difficulties with imperial law. The Lutheran Dukes Christoph of Württemberg and Wolfgang of Zweibrücken, King Maximilian II, and the Emperor Ferdinand I accused him of sectarianism. In a letter of 13 July 1563 the Emperor stated that the Calvinist Lord's Supper was not in accord with the *Confessio Augustana* and hence the Electoral Palatinate was excluded from the Religious Peace of 1555.[28] Then and in 1566 at the Diet of Augsburg, when the accusations were repeated, it was argued by the champions of the Palatinate that they were in agreement with the *Confessio Augustana* as properly understood and in accord with the teaching of great foreign Protestant churches. In addition, the Elector in 1563 requested a testimonial from Bullinger; and in 1565 he

[27] W. Niesel, op. cit., pp. 194, 34–45.
[28] A. Kluckhohn, op. cit., I, 420f.

again asked him for literary assistance in view of the coming Diet. These difficulties led to the printing and approving of a profession of faith which Bullinger, for personal reasons, had put in writing in 1562 in the expectation of his death. It was printed in 1566 as the *Confessio Helvetica Posterior* and sent to Heidelberg.

This temporarily threatening situation did not keep Friedrich III from again proceeding forcibly against Lutheranism and especially from suppressing Catholic worship and faith. Almost forty monasteries and chapters had thus far maintained themselves in the Palatinate. The route of a peaceful Reformation, which the Elector had probably first wanted to travel, proved to be all the less successful as Catholicism began to display signs of a regeneration. It was extirpated by brute force. Friedrich III did not even shrink from suppressing monasteries in areas of condominion where he shared rule with Catholic princes, showing a disregard of their rights and from staging iconoclastic outbreaks in churches. He who had appealed to his own conscience at the Diet of 1566 was not prepared to concede this right to Lutherans and Catholics. For, so he argued, it is one thing to force a person to the good, to God's word and truth, and quite another thing to force him to idolatry and lies.

After his death Lutheranism was restored for five years by his son and successor, Ludwig VI (1578–83), who had recourse to the same state-police methods. Olevianus, who had warned from the pulpit that the wolves, the Lutherans, were on the point of tearing to pieces the sheep, the Calvinists, was the first to have to leave the country. He went to Berleburg to become tutor of the princes and then in 1584 to Herborn as pastor and professor of theology.

There, in Nassau, Count John VI (1559–1606), a brother of William of Orange, favored Calvinism; he was confirmed in this by his close connections with the Netherlands. In 1568 he summoned Gerhard Eobanus Geldenhauer from Hesse and in 1572 appointed him superintendent. When the Calvinist theologians were expelled from the Palatinate and the Cryptocalvinists from Wittenberg, they obtained a public reception in Nassau in 1577. On 8–9 July 1578 the Synod of Dillenburg adopted the Nassau Confession,[29] which was composed chiefly by Christoph Pezel. A *presbyterium* was instituted in the same year. The General Assembly of 1581 adopted the Palatinate Church Order and the Heidelberg Confession. The Johannea University, established at Herborn in 1584 on the model of the Geneva Academy, acquired a great reputation through its important teachers, Kaspar Olevianus, Johann Piscator, Georg Pasor, Johann Alsted, Johann Althusius, and others, and became, after Geneva and Leiden, a center of Calvinist

---

[29] Text in E. F. K. Müller, *Die Bekenntnisschriften der reformierten Kirche*, pp. 720–739.

theology. At the general synod in Herborn in 1586 a superterritorial synodal Church of the counties of the Wetterau was founded at the suggestion of Johann VI and his theologians. In 1648 it had to give way again to the territorial Church system. The Herborn Order,[30] an effort to unite the Geneva presbyterial-synodal system with the territorial institution of superintendents, continued to operate until the Rhenish-Westphalian Church Order of 1835.

In Bremen Philippism had gained influence through Hardenberg. In an effort to mediate between the Zwinglians, represented by Molanus, and the Lutherans, by Jodocus Glanaeus, the city council in 1570 summoned the Melanchthonian Marcus Mening. In 1572, when he was superintendent, an "Agreement on the Chief Points of Christian Doctrine" was accepted. The influence of Calvinism also grew at Bremen from the downfall of Philippism in Electoral Saxony. Christoph Pezel was active in the Hansa city from 1580. A confession that he composed, the Consensus Bremensis,[31] was signed on 2 May 1595, by all members of the Church officialdom and in 1644 it was declared by the council to be the valid creed. In comparison with the Nassau Confession, it was enlarged by, among other points, a section on predestination and it represented a strict Calvinism.

Simon VI (1554–1613) assumed control of the government of the County of Lippe in 1579. He had studied at Strasbourg in 1567–69, together with his teacher, the Philippist Thodenus, who had been banished from Wittenberg. Simon maintained good relations with the Calvinists of the Netherlands. He gradually filled the parishes of his county with Calvinist clerics. While the Lutheran Church Order of 1571 was not formally annulled, the three superintendents introduced a Calvinist Lord's Supper on the basis of the consistorial ordinance of 1600. Luther's small catechism was replaced by one composed by Anger (1547–1607). The Heidelberg Catechism was introduced in 1618. Apart from Lemgo, which successfully resisted and in 1617 obtained extensive autonomy, the County of Lippe became a Calvinist principality. Then in 1684 Count Simon Henry introduced a new Calvinist Church Order in place of that of 1571.

Prince Joachim Ernst of Anhalt (1546–86) brought all parts of the principality under his rule from 1570. While inclined to Lutheranism, he could not be induced to sign the *Formula of Concord*. Wolfgang Amling (1542–1606), called by him to Zerbst in 1578 to become superintendent, opposed to the *Formula of Concord* a *Confessio Anhaltina* and an *Apologia Anhaltina*. Without having been authorized, he had preachers

---

[30] Text in W. Niesel, op. cit., pp. 290–298.
[31] Text in E. F. K. Müller, op. cit., pp. 739–799.

ordained in accord with these writings of a private character. Some clerics who had been driven from Saxony under the suspicion of Cryptocalvinism were welcomed in Anhalt. Because of his mediating attitude Prince Joachim Ernst was accused of being a Calvinist. In 1585 he had his theologians draw up a "Brief and True Profession of the Lord's Holy Supper," which all clergymen of his territory had to sign. His successor, Johann Georg I, through his marriage was in close connection with the Electoral Palatinate; his brother, Christian, was married to a daughter of the Calvinist Count of Bentheim. In 1596 they both decreed that the tablets and wooden crucifixes on and over altars, the candles, and the vestments were abolished. Altars were to resemble tables, and the clergy were to break bread behind the table and facing the congregation.[32] In all this it was maintained that these changes meant no modification of doctrine. But as early as 1599 Johann Georg commissioned his superintendent Amling to draw up a liturgy. The outline,[33] sketched by Amling and some theologians, did not meet with the Prince's approval, for, as he said, it did not resemble enough the Palatinate liturgy. With the coming of age of Johann Georg's brothers the principality was divided in 1603 into Dessau, Bernburg, Zerbst, and Köthen. The confessional basis of the corresponding territorial Churches consisted of the *Confessio Augustana Variata,* the Palatinate liturgy, and the Heidelberg Catechism.

Thus around 1600 the formation of the Calvinist territorial Church in Germany was completed. A leading role in this had been played by pupils of Melanchthon, some of whom had had to give way to Lutheran orthodoxy at Wittenberg. They proclaimed their passage to Calvinism as a "second Reformation."[34] In their eyes, Lutheranism, with its "papist" relics, was a preliminary step; Melanchthon, with his theology of mediation, was the transition; Calvinism, on the other hand, with its liturgy, its ecclesiastical discipline, and its idea of Christian authority, was the consistent completion of the Reformation. In contradistinction to the "Reformation of doctrine" that was carried out by Luther, in Calvinism was seen the "Reformation of life."

Scotland and England

In 1549 the Scottish National Synod stressed two reasons for the deterioration of the Church in Scotland:[35] the immorality and the defective

---

[32] Sehling, II, 533–580.

[33] Ibid., 536f., 581.

[34] J. Noltmann, *Christoph Pezel (1539–1604) und der Calvinismus in Bremen,* pp. 76–81; H. E. Weber, *Reformation, Orthodoxie und Rationalismus* I, 2 (Darmstadt, 2d ed. 1966), 326f.

[35] *A Source Book of Scottish History* II, 147–148.

formation of the clergy. The Church required, among other things, that priests should be capable of explaining Scripture and that pastors and bishops should preach at least four times a year. It also forbade the spending of ecclesiastical revenues on illegitimate children. An improvement in the manner of life of the clergy was everywhere called for, so that "those who show others the way might not themselves be at fault."[36] From a report made by Cardinal Sermoneta to Pope Paul IV in 1556,[37] it appears that none of these demands of the synod were carried out. This climate created a good soil for the reception of the new teaching, and even the political situation was favorable. James V of Scotland died in 1542, when his successor, Mary, Queen of Scots, was only a week old. The struggle over the regency between the Archbishop of Saint Andrews, Cardinal David Beaton (1539–46), and the Earl of Arran, heir presumptive to the throne, ended in the victory of the latter. The outcome was an encouragement of Protestantism. For, like many other nobles, the Earl favored the Reformation in the expectation of thereby acquiring a part of the property of the Church.

Under these conditions George Wishart (c. 1513–46) found it easy to gain adherents for Protestantism.[38] Wishart, called "the martyr of the Scottish Reformation," spent a short time in Switzerland and Germany, where he got to know Calvinism and Lutheranism in their pure forms. From 1544 he was closely associated with John Knox. He died at the stake, as a heretic, in Edinburgh on 1 March 1546.[39] In return, Cardinal David Beaton was assassinated by a group led by John Knox.[40]

From then on, Knox (c. 1505–72) was the chief figure in the Scottish Reformation. He carried on the work of his friend and teacher much more decisively and even more fanatically and thus became the "Reformer of Scotland." When, following a two-years' absence abroad— from 1547 to 1549 he was in detention on a French galley—he returned to Scotland, the Scottish court was under the domination of Mary Stuart's mother, Mary of Guise, Francophile and Catholic. Knox was able to stir up the Protestants, who had been forced into the background, to new activity. At the Scottish provincial synod in 1552 it was decided to publish a catechism in the Scottish tongue as an aid for the clergy in explaining the Bible. This "Hamilton's Catechism"[41] accepted a Protestant ideology, especially in the teaching on predestination:

---

[36] W. C. Dickinson, *A New History of Scotland* I, 313.
[37] *A Source Book of Scottish History* II, 150f.
[38] J. Knox, *History of the Reformation in Scotland* I, 60ff.
[39] Cf. *A Source Book of Scottish History* II, 136f.
[40] Ibid., 138–142.
[41] Ibid., 148–150.

In short, we must entrust ourselves entirely to God. Our salvation, our trust, our confidence rest on his help, his support, goodness, and merciful providence in all our needs, dangers, every misfortune, every weakness. In everything [we must] give up our own will and in obedience entrust everything to God's gracious will.[42]

The Covenant of 1557 constitutes a climax in the development of the Scottish Reformation. In this the Scottish nobility swore to defend the "congregation of Christ" and to annihilate the "congregation of Satan."[43] From now on the Catholics were confronted by a compact array of influential men. Meanwhile, Knox had spent a year (1554–55) at Geneva, where he became a definite follower of Calvin. His chief aim hereafter was to combat Catholics and Catholicism with all his energy. He preached, with Calvinist severity, resistance to "unrighteous authority," as well as the destruction of images, churches, and monasteries. He knew how to captivate the masses. As an example may be cited his libel, *Against the Monstrous Regiment of Women,* composed in 1558. The persecution of Protestants in England by Queen Mary I was attributed to this work, which thus understandably aroused resentment in the persecuted against Knox. When Calvin chided the English Protestants because of this "unfraternal attitude" of theirs toward Knox, they retorted:

> We can assure you that this outrageous libel has added much fuel to the flames of persecution in England. For not one of our brethren suffered death before its publication, but as soon as it was put on sale, many distinguished men were sent to the stake.[44]

This example makes clear how the more radical bent of John Knox, stamped by Calvinism, differed from the more moderate English Protestants and what course Scotland would hereafter follow. The marriage of Queen Mary Stuart with the future Francis II of France in 1558 was unfortunate for the Catholics of Scotland, for the Protestants would have much preferred an alliance with Protestant England. Because of the marriage distrust and discontent between Catholics and Protestants grew to such an extent that finally civil war broke out in 1559. The immediate reason was the support given to the Ancient Church by Mary of Guise. The Protestants managed to maintain themselves with the help of English troops. Though outlawed by the regent, Knox from now on displayed an extremely active agitation against Catholic "idolatry."

In 1560, after the death of Mary of Guise, an assembly of spiritual and secular lords met in Edinburgh, at the urging of John Knox. Three

[42] Ibid., 150.
[43] Ibid., 162.
[44] A. Zimmermann, "Zur Reformation in Schottland," *RQ* 25 (1911), 39.

important decisions were taken, almost unanimously, by this meeting of the estates: the authority and jurisdiction of the Pope were abolished, the Mass and all else that was opposed to the Protestant confession were forbidden, and the *Confessio Scotica* was declared in force. This *Scottish Confession* was composed by a committee of six on the initiative of Parliament. The leading spirit was here again John Knox.

> The *Confession* makes us aware of his spirit in each section: namely, in the unflinching justification of every single statement of belief on the sole authority of Holy Scripture. It thereby ranks on a level of equality with the other Church confessions of the Age of the Reformation, especially those of the churches influenced by Calvin.[45]

The assembly which enacted the *Confessio Scotica* is called the "Reformation Parliament." It was attended by a large number of members of the lesser nobility, all of whom were enthusiastic Protestants. Their vehemence went so far that anyone taking part in the celebration of the Catholic liturgy was threatened with the death penalty. Mary Stuart, who, following the death of her husband, assumed the government of Scotland in 1561, never signed this *Confession of Faith and of Doctrine.* Under her, a convinced Catholic, the religious question remained unsolved. Vis-à-vis the Calvinists she adopted a very liberal position, but she was nevertheless regarded by them as a danger for their faith. On the first Sunday after her return to Scotland the Queen had Mass celebrated for herself and her court. The upshot was a rising of the Calvinists against her. She had to promise by proclamation to maintain the status quo, that is, to accept Protestantism as the state religion, as it had been since 1560. The Queen's privy councilors even promised to support the Calvinist Church; this meant that one-third of the Church property was confiscated. The Calvinists obtained one part of this; the remainder went to the Queen. The fact that the Calvinists' share became in the course of time ever less and the Queen's all the greater gave occasion to Knox's remark: Two parts of all Church property belong to the devil; the third part is divided between God and the devil.[46] In view of the activity of Knox's adherents, Mary could not dare to uphold those of her own faith, especially since Knox more and more emphasized that the Calvinists must not be forced to concur with the "idolatrous Queen."

Mary's second marriage, to Henry Darnley, in 1565 did nothing to improve her position. On the contrary: when this incompetent man was murdered on 10 February 1567, the Queen was accused of complicity,

---

[45] P. Jacobs, *Reformierte Bekenntnisschriften und Kirchenordnungen,* p. 128.
[46] W. C. Dickinson, op. cit., I, 335.

since three months later she married the Protestant Earl of Bothwell who had taken part in the crime. Knox ranted against the Queen and demanded her execution. In July 1567 there was nothing left for her except to abdicate in favor of her infant son, James VI, who was later to become James I of England. He was educated as a Calvinist.

More so than elsewhere, in Scotland the Reformation was a lay movement,[47] lacking so theologically distinctive a leader as Luther, Calvin, Zwingli, or Cranmer. John Knox is in a different category from the reformers just mentioned; he was a fanatical Church Leader rather than a theologian. But he did not succeed in fully realizing the plans and hopes which he had set forth in his *First Book of Discipline* in 1560.[48] For the Scottish Lords regarded the Church Order advocated by him, the proposal of an earthly republic which was to prepare for heaven, from quite another viewpoint than his own and "refused to consider an independent system of canon law, in which the Church ruled the state, took over the schools, and provided for the sick and weak."[49] Knox envisaged an intimate cooperation between Church and state. In his *Book of Discipline* he protested, in agreement with Calvin, against Church festivals; they were human institutions and hence to be abolished. Here he meant not only the feasts of Apostles, martyrs, and other saints, but also Christmas, the Circumcision, the Epiphany, "and other feasts of our Lady. . . . "[50] A further section had to do with church buildings. Worship was permitted only in parish churches or schools, not in monasteries and abbeys. The place of worship had to be properly equipped. Knox devoted himself in great detail to the "admission of ministers."[51] Every congregation had the right to elect its own clergy. The prerequisite was a definite educational level; ordination and imposition of hands were repudiated. Readers and exhorters were assigned to churches which had no permanent minister. The requirement for this appointment was a religious life and intellectual ability. After their trial period, readers and exhorters could advance to the regular clerical state. A comprehensive support of the families of ministers in which there was a definite need was demanded; attention to the education of the children and the maintenance of the widows was especially stressed. Knox required that the poor in general be supported, but only those who could not really help themselves, not those "who followed the profession of

---

[47] A. Zimmermann, loc. cit., 38.
[48] *A Source Book of Scottish History* II, 171–180.
[49] A. Zimmermann, loc. cit., 113.
[50] *A Source Book of Scottish History* II, 171.
[51] Ibid., 172f.

begging."[52] These demands and proposals point to the modern welfare state.

Knox's remarks on the use of superintendents give an insight into the organization of the Church.[53] The entire country was to be divided into ten or twelve provinces, and each province was to receive a superintendent. Their duties were to establish congregations and institute clergymen. They were responsible for the order and morals of the congregations and their ministers. The prerequisite of this function was a two-years' ministry in a parish. The Church was also responsible for the education of the people. Every congregation in the city had to appoint a schoolmaster who was able to teach grammar and Latin. In the country instruction in the catechism, in accord with the *Book of Common Order,* had to be provided for children and adolescents. "Colleges" were to be founded in the larger cities, in particular in the superintendent's seat, and in these the arts and languages were to be taught. In addition, three universities—St. Andrews, Glasgow, and Aberdeen—were demanded for all of Scotland. It was made possible for pupils and university students to obtain scholarships; the deciding factors here were the intellectual ability of the candidate and the financial situation of his parents. Clergymen, the poor, the schools, and the teachers had to be provided for out of ecclesiastical revenues and property.

The "Kirk Session"—a tribunal of laymen and ministers—was to be of great importance for the ecclesiastical organization of the Church.[54] At its annual session took place the election of deacons and elders. It was the duty of the elders to assist and supervise the pastor. Unworthy pastors were to be deposed by the elders with the approval of the Church and the superintendent; here the presbyterial system was already making its appearance. Knox also clearly expressed his ideas on public and family piety.[55]

As far as possible, baptism was to be administered only on Sunday, following the sermon; the Lord's Supper was to be celebrated four times a year—on the first Sunday of March, June, September, and December. The requirement for reception was to be a knowledge of the "Our Father," of the Creed, and of the ten commandments. Every church had to possess an English Bible. The faithful were to be obliged to listen to the Bible and its explanation. Every head of a family had to instruct the members of his household in Christian doctrine. All the faithful were to

---

[52] Ibid., 174.
[53] Ibid., 174–176.
[54] Ibid., 179.
[55] Ibid., 179f.

learn psalms and practice so as to be able "to sing along mightily" at worship. According to this *First Book of Discipline,* people and rulers are subjects of the same God. Church and state are the two pillars for God's Kingdom on earth. But the repudiation of this book in Scotland shows that there people were still far from the "perfect city of Geneva."

If, with the deposition of Mary Stuart in 1567, Protestantism flourished again and the *Confession of Faith* and the *Book of Discipline* were recognized, no practical consequences really resulted from this approval. Knox remarked in this regard: "Greed does not allow this depraved generation to accept the aims of pious ministers."[56] The Catholic bishops and priests were at first left undisturbed in their positions, but they no longer had any influence on the faithful. There thus existed, side by side, two Churches; the one was reduced to silence, but wealthy, while the other was active, but poor. Meanwhile, the Calvinist Church was completing its institutions at synods. When positions became vacant, they were given to Calvinist preachers. The bishops were treated in the same way. From 1572, on the basis of the Concordat of Leith, they were no longer nominated by the crown but were examined and accepted by Calvinist preachers, and they were subject only to the General Assembly, the general synod of the Scottish Church.

Andrew Melville found this "tolerant" attitude of the Scottish Calvinists when in 1574 he returned from Geneva to become Knox's successor. He thus felt called upon for a *Second Book of Discipline.*[57] Like the *First Book,* he claimed to be merely going back to the word of God. Like Knox, he wanted all the possessions of the Church to be turned over to Calvinist ministers, schools, the poor, and other ecclesiastical institutions. But the demand for the equality of ministers was a departure from the *First Book.* The episcopal organization was superseded by the presbyterian. Church discipline was to be guaranteed not only by clerics but by tribunals of laymen and ministers. These were called the "Kirk Session," "Presbyter Synod," and "General Assembly," and had authority to give decisions in regard to laymen and clerics in ecclesiastical matters. At the beginning of the book it is explained that the Church has a "power of its own," which is given directly by God. It has no head on earth, its only head being Christ. If the secular power offends in matters of conscience and religion, it is subject to Church law. It is the Church's duty to prescribe to the secular power how it is to bring its activities into harmony with the word of God. Here was the initial step toward a Church that could determine the policy of the state. What

---

[56] W. C. Dickinson, op. cit., I, 349.
[57] *A Source Book of Scottish History* III, 22–31.

meaning could a secular Parliament still have, if the Church claimed to be in direct "counsel with God"?

King James VI (1567–1625) was intelligent enough to recognize the danger in this development. It was to be feared that the General Assembly would soon control every aspect of royal authority. Melville, in fact, maintained that the authority of the Church stood, not merely alongside, but above that of the state. In 1584 he made it known to the King's secret council that it was a usurpation to control the ambassadors and envoys of a King who was far above him, the earthly King. This led to the declaration by James VI that Scottish Presbyterianism was as compatible with the monarchy as were God and the devil, and that he was guided by the axiom: "No bishop, no king." Thus one can understand the King's proceedings against Melville and the Scottish Church. James wanted an episcopal system; he wanted bishops who would be named by the crown. In this he saw the sole possibility of being master in his country. Melville, on the contrary, worked for a presbyterial system, independent of the state and actually over it.

With the arrival of Erné Stuart, Lord d'Aubigny, came new difficulties. He was suspected of being a papist agent. In an effort to end this suspicion James VI, Lord d'Aubigny, who had meanwhile become Earl of Lennox, and the entire royal family signed the "King's Confession" in 1581. It was also called the "Negative Confession," because in it every religion and doctrine that was not in harmony with the *Confessio Scotica* of 1566 was rejected. Two months later all Scotland had to subscribe to this document.

> This so-called "Confessio Negativa" of 1581 was brought about by the agitation of the Counter-Reformation, which made itself felt in Scotland. Hence in a quite special way it bears an expressly anti-Roman character in that it mentions and rejects individually the errors and superstitious usages of the Church of Rome. Its author was the chaplain of the royal household, John Craig, who was entrusted with the work by the King himself.[58]

In August 1582 the King, by whose orders the "Confessio Negativa" had been drafted, was imprisoned because he was still regarded as a danger to true religion. After James' escape Melville was charged with treason against the country, but he fled to England. The King, embittered by his imprisonment, now turned against everything that Melville had demanded for the Church. The so-called "Black Acts"[59] were

[58] P. Jacobs, op. cit., p. 128.
[59] *A Source Book of Scottish History* III, 39–43.

enacted in May 1584 as measures of retaliation. They stated that Parliament and Council were above all spiritual and temporal estates and sanctioned them as such. Supervision of the lower clergy and of ecclesiastical government in general was to continue with the bishops and "commissioners," who were now responsible to the King and not, as formerly, to the General Assembly. Meetings of the clergy were forbidden except with the King's express consent. It was declared that this decree was directed especially against Presbyterianism. The King now claimed jurisdiction over clergy and laity. All decrees of the Church that lacked his ratification were invalid for the future. This was unacceptable to the Calvinists. In order to achieve a compromise it was recommended by representatives of the Church in 1586 that the King should suggest the names of bishops to the General Assembly; but this never became effective in practice, for the "Magna Charta of the Church of Scotland" meant the repudiation of the "Black Acts" by the King. In it he confirmed all privileges of the Calvinist Church and again promised it the right to convoke general assemblies, synods, and presbyterial meetings. He even declared that the "Black Acts" were not to oppose the "privilege which God has given to spiritual officials in the Church."[60] Despite these concessions the equality of all clergymen was for the King the cause of all evil, or "mother of confusion"; hence his change was a purely external one. His diplomatic skill soon enabled him to give the episcopal form the predominance again over the presbyterian form.

In sum, it can be said of the development in Scotland: In organization and doctrine the Scottish Church was Calvinist. It was not yet Presbyterian under Knox, who never called for the equality of all clerics. It was only his successor, Melville, who pushed the development further in this direction and realized a full Presbyterianism. In James VI it discovered a great opponent. An so in the period that followed there was a continual struggle between King and Presbyterianism for the leadership of the Church.

In England Calvinists were long unable to establish themselves. For the most part they were refugees from France or Englishmen who had become acquainted with Knox's ideas in Scotland. Having become used to the simplicity of the Calvinist worship, they regarded as too much to approve the "Romish" rite of the Anglican Church. And the royal control of the Church was for them a relic of "papist domination." Thus the Calvinists were in conflict with the Anglican Church. They had no possibility of developing an ecclesiastical system of their own, however, for the Act of Uniformity, issued under Queen Elizabeth I in 1559, prescribed a uniform Anglican liturgy.

---

[60] Cf. Dickinson, op. cit., I, 362–370.

The Calvinists did not stop demanding a "pure" Church, "in accord with Scripture," thereby acquiring the name "Puritans" around 1566. The middle class especially favored them. At first they represented a group with a particular intellectual outlook within the Anglican Church; a really passionate attachment to the letter of Scripture was proper to them. When the state Church would not go along with their demand, they separated from it and instituted their own congregations in 1567. They gave themselves a democratic Church organization and thus became Presbyterians. Following this their opposition to the Anglican High Church became notorious and severe persecutions ensued. Many "Dissenters" went to prison, but they could not be exterminated. Many left England. In 1620 one group, the "Pilgrim Fathers," sailed for North America on the *Mayflower* and established a new home for themselves in Massachusetts. Their idea of the autonomous congregation under Christ as its unique head contributed substantially to the American notion of democracy as the political form of government most in accord with God's will.

Puritans were also persecuted in England under Charles I (1625–49). In particular Archbishop Laud of Canterbury (d. 1645) tried to restore unity of worship and proceeded sternly against Puritanism and Presbyterianism in Scotland. This led to civil war. The King's defeat in 1645–46 and execution in 1649 meant the temporary end of the Anglican Episcopal Church and the victory of Presbyterianism.

CHAPTER 31

The Development of Denominations in the Sixteenth and Seventeenth Centuries

When the division of the Western Church had long been a sad reality and there was already a multiplicity of religious communities which differed substantially in doctrine, worship, and law, people were still in no sense aware of the full import of these facts. Only relatively late were there denominations in the sense of ecclesiastical communities, whose members knew they were united in professing clearly defined truths of faith and by means of a common worship and common norms of moral conduct and that they were separated from other groups. Denominational formation took place in a slow process of more than a century and in a manner quite different according to countries and even localities. In Catholic territories it was ordinarily much more protracted than in Protestant lands. Acceptance of the Reformation by a state or a city did not mean, of course, that the masses also took this step from their own convictions. If the reformers did not intend to found a new Church, *a fortiori* their adherents were not thinking of any schism in faith and Church. People wanted "preaching according to Scripture," they professed the "pure doctrine," and, in short, intended to take reform seriously. When Christendom was actually split into denominations, each of them thought of itself as universal, as the true Church, and accordingly considered all others as heretical. People clung to the traditional notion of the unity of the Church and of its teaching, which could be formulated in obligatory dogmas. To deviate from them was to become guilty of wicked heresy.

The situation was complicated but also mitigated by the fact that not only Catholics and Protestants were in opposition. For Protestants soon split into various groups, bitterly hostile to one another, and again had to defend themselves, together with the Catholics, against Anabaptists, fanatics, and Spiritualists. Then all groups, more or less, found it necessary to be more firmly united. This process of clarifying and acquiring awareness from within and of stabilization and differentiation from without, which we call denominational formation, was not only and not even most powerfully urged and supported by religious forces but also by cultural and social and especially by political strength. Undoubtedly, Lutheran preaching was only in its beginnings from 1520 in broad areas of Germany and Switzerland. But the destruction and rebuilding of the ecclesiastical organization that it had called for could as yet be regarded only as the long overdue and longed-for reform of the Church. The formation of an autonomous Lutheran Church came about not only by means of the "German Mass" of 1526 and the Catechism of 1529 but also through the visitations arranged by the political authority and the Church Order decreed by it.

At Augsburg the Protestants were invited by the Emperor to present their viewpoint. The result was the *Confessio Augustana* and its *Apologia*. But these were intended as a confession of the "Catholic Church"[1] and endeavored to show that what was sought was not a new Church but only the abolition of abuses. Discussions and agreements were made, not by ecclesiastical communities among themselves, but by political powers—by the Emperor and the estates in the Empire, by the cantons in Switzerland. Of course, they regarded themselves as bound by a confession; accordingly, the then already customary notion of "religious factions" correctly describes the situation.[2] The unity of religion with a

[1] Apol. VII, *BSLK* p. 235, 27 and frequently.
[2] F. Dickmann, "Das Problem der Gleichberechtigung der Konfessionen," *HZ* 201 (1965), 265–305 (especially p. 267).

particular political sphere was still taken for granted by all concerned. According to Luther, no contrary preaching should be tolerated in a principality or city, for the sake of peace. Hence he was unwilling that Lutheran preachers should sneak into Catholic communities and preach there uninvited.[3]

When religious unity could no longer be preserved for the Empire, it was assured for the individual territories by awarding to the princes the right to decide the confession of their subjects. The princes made a powerful contribution to the formation of denominations after the 1555 Religious Peace of Augsburg by striving to create in their territories a distinct and uniform religious situation. They tried to eliminate other creeds and to consolidate their own by various means. Where authority made no use of its right to determine the religion of its subjects the process of denominational formation was longest drawn up. This was the case, for example, on the lower Rhine, where the Dukes of Jülich-Cleves-Berg favored reform in the spirit of Erasmus, without adopting Protestantism and without fighting it energetically. They were happy with reform but hostile to novelty. For decades they allowed free rein to the religious currents and thereby fostered Protestantism without intending to do so.

Consequently, the relationship of the political authority to the Church in its territory was in no sense everywhere the same. "Cuius regio eius et religio" was, of course, universally in force as a principle, but it was not everywhere made use of in the same way. Partly the political power of the princes did not suffice to impose their religion. Resistance came, not from the masses of the people, but from the leading circles of the cities and from the rural nobility, which asserted its independence from state authority by means of a religion different from that of the prince. This was seen above all in Bohemia, Hungary, and Poland. The rural estate and the cities often favored another creed out of opposition to the prince's religious policy. In the Swiss Confederation and in some Imperial Free Cities political necessity produced a juxtaposition of confessions. In Austria and France the *raison d'état* at times required a giving in. In 1598 the French crown conceded extensive privileges to the Protestants of the country by the Edict of Nantes, but it modified them and finally withdrew them when it felt strong enough.[4]

---

[3] "Denn es ist nicht gut, das man ynn einer pfarr odder kirchspiel widderwertige predigt yns volck lesst gehen, denn es entspringen daraus rotten, unfried, hass und neid auch ynn andern, welltlichen sachen" (*WA* 31, I, 209, 28). Cf. H. Bornkamm, "Die religiöse und politische Problematik im Verhältnis der Konfessionen im Reich," *ARG* 56 (1965), 209–218 (especially p. 213).

[4] H. Lutz, "Die Konfessionsproblematik ausserhalb des Reiches und in der Politik des Papsttums," *ARG* 56 (1965), 218–227 (especially p. 220). See *supra*, p. 397.

Economic viewpoints could also motivate the tolerating and even the granting of privileges to denominational minorities.[5] Difficulties easily occurred in areas of condominium, when lords belonging to different religions held the territorial sovereignty. Thus the Elector Palatine Frederick III introduced Calvinism in districts in which he shared rule with the Prince Bishops of Worms and Speyer, without concerning himself for his partners' rights of sovereignty.[6] The Catholic congregation of Kröw on the Moselle could put to flight the Lutheran pastor sent to it by the government of Zweibrücken because it had the support of the Archbishop-Elector of Trier, who shared authority there with the Dukes of Palatinate-Zweibrücken and the Margrave of Baden.[7]

The manner and degree in which the secular power influenced the religious situation differed according to denomination. Lutheranism allowed the greatest amount of influence to the the state. Calvinism sought to gain the authority of the state for itself but at the same time to preserve its independence in the sphere of dogma, worship, and ecclesiastical discipline. The Catholic Church also claimed the secular arm for the organizing of Church life and in return had to permit some interference in the spiritual sphere. In principle she made decisions independently in matters of doctrine, worship, and canon law, and she did so from central headquarters without regard for political boundaries. This was felt as irksome by some governments and led to conflicts between the spiritual and the secular power. A Protestant authority issued ecclesiastical decisions without anyone seriously lecturing it; a Catholic authority, on the other hand, had to reckon with the objections of the competent bishop, of the legate, or of a religious superior with international connections, and to take these into consideration.[8]

How did the population react? How did it accept the control of its religious confession by its lord? It is difficult to find a universally valid answer. The response would differ according to particular areas and decades. At the beginning of the seventeenth century people were no longer as ready as they had been at the middle of the sixteenth century to change their religion along with their prince. This was the result of a better religious formation and of the increased denominational awareness. Examples are not wanting of resistance by the population to the introduction of a novel ecclesiastical organization and to changes in worship. The rural folk especially clung to traditional customs. Monasteries and collegiate chapters often resisted the introduction of the

---

[5] E. Hassinger, "Wirtschaftliche Motive und Argumente für religiöse Duldsamkeit im 16. und 18. Jahrhundert," *ARG* 49 (1958), 226–245.

[6] L. Stamer, *Kirchengeschichte der Pfalz* III, 1 (Speyer 1955), 52.

[7] V. Conzemius, *Jakob III. von Eltz* (Wiesbaden 1956), pp. 53–65.

[8] E. W. Zeeden, *Die Entstehung der Konfessionen* (Munich 1965), p. 96.

Reformation by the authority and yielded only to force. On the whole, however, change of religion as decided by the political power was effected rather smoothly.

The most flagrant example is the Palatinate, where within a span of thirty years the people changed their creed four times along with the prince. Under the Elector Otto Heinrich (1556–59) a visitation instituted by the prince introduced Lutheranism. The Elector Friedrich III (1559–76) made his territory Calvinist in 1563. His son, Ludwig VI (1576–83), forcibly suppressed Calvinism in favor of Lutheranism, while the Count Palatine Johann Kasimir, who headed the regency for his underage nephew, Friedrich IV, from 1583–92, again imposed the Heidelberg Catechism. When Lutheranism became the territorial creed in 1576, the Calvinist congregations in great numbers asked to be permitted to retain their pastors and their customary ecclesiastical life. Because this was refused, several hundred families, mostly of pastors and teachers, emigrated. Since they had no Lutheran successors, it was not easy to establish Lutheranism solidly. Nevertheless, seven years later, when Johann Kasimir restored Calvinism, the same congregations defended their Lutheran faith and asked for its preservation, as they had previously requested the preservation of Calvinism.

> Hence, in this case a period of seven years sufficed, not only to turn a people from the faith they had formerly practiced, but to accustom them so strongly to a newly introduced form that they desired to retain it and opposed a return to the previous form. The expulsion of pastors and teachers seems to have been decisive in both cases.[9]

The masses were mostly uneducated and often unaware of the change of faith. This was possible especially in the sphere of Lutheranism, where the retention of ceremonies was allowed so generously that it almost amounted to a deception of the congregations. The elevation of the Host, for example, was retained at Wittenberg until 1542. The fact that great portions of the Canon, which was in any event prayed silently, had been dropped did not necessarily attract the notice of those in attendance. In northern and eastern Germany the retaining of the Catholic organization and usages went especially far. This involved the liturgical vestments, feasts of Our Lady and the saints, candles on the altar, private confession with absolution. In some places the Latin choir office, the "Angelus" and the weather bell, processions, elevation of Host and chalice, bells, incense, Mass servers, and much else continued in use.

A visiting Catholic bishop from Poland, who attended the worship in

[9] Ibid., p. 70.

the Berlin collegiate church, said that he found no difference between it and the Catholic liturgy.[10] How, then, should the common folk have noticed the distinction? The ease with which entire populations of subjects were led to the Reformation or back to Catholicism is all the more understandable.

In addition to legitimate Catholic traditions that had been accepted in the Church Orders, some practices were maintained which were irreconcilable with a Protestant ideology but which the people, especially the rural folk, were unwilling to give up. Even at the close of the sixteenth century visitations found cause to take measures against pilgrimages and the blessing of water, salt, herbs, candles, and so forth.[11] A Lutheran "First Mass" was celebrated according to a missal of 1514 at Frankfurt an der Oder in Electoral Brandenburg in 1591.[12] Denominational uncertainty, frequent change, and the circumstance that pastors suitable for the religion decreed from above were not available fostered indifference and increased the number of those who no longer went at all to church and the Sacraments. Complaints were heard.

> The people are now becoming more Epicurean, and one religion is as important to them as another, a blaspheming papist, Jew, or Turk as an honest Christian. To them everything is something in between. They are good fellows and boon companions with everyone.[13]

The Lutheran superintendent of Ulm stated bitterly that gradually there had arisen a new, third crowd, which went to no church, neither the Lutheran nor the papist, nor to the Sacraments.[14]

Crass ignorance in matters of faith, neglect of religion, and immorality characterized the situation in the second half of the sixteenth century cutting across all denominations. Massive superstition, curiosity for marvels, astrology, and the witchcraft delusion also flourished where people boasted of the pure Gospel. They especially spread in the now Protestant northeast of Europe, where Christianity had up to then

---

[10] N. Müller, "Zur Geschichte des Gottesdienstes der Domkirche zu Berlin 1540–98," *Jahrbuch fur Brandenb. Kirchengeschichte* 2–3 (1905f.), 342; J. Mörsdorf, "Das erste Domkapitel und die erste Domkirche zu Berlin," *Wichmann-Jahrbuch* 8 (1954), 88–109 (especially p. 101).

[11] For example, Instr. Magdeburg 1583; Schling, II, 424.

[12] H. Grimm, "Die liturgischen Drucke der Diözese Sebus," *Wichmann-Jahrbuch,* 9–10 (1956), 45–51 (especially p. 51).

[13] According to E. W. Zeeden, op. cit., p. 71.

[14] J. Endriss, *Die Ulmer Kirchenvisitationen der Jahre 1557–1615* (Ulm 1937), p. 34.

scarcely established itself against paganism and the gloomy forces of blood and earth.

And so, together with the clarifying and deepening of the awareness of the particular denomination, it was important for Christianity in general to send new roots into the masses as doctrine and life. In this what routes were traveled? What help was at hand?

First of all, by means of formulated "confessions," catechisms, and textbooks an effort was made to end the uncertainty about what the doctrine was and the arbitrary way it was proclaimed. Assent to the true teaching became the distinctive mark of belonging to a denomination.

In the *Confessio Augustana* Lutheranism had started the practice of defining a particular standpoint by means of a denominational book. But it had turned out to be inadequate in the doctrinal strife within Lutheranism, and meanwhile a differentiation in regard to Calvinism had become necessary. On the initiative of several princes, in particular of the Elector August of Saxony, several discussions occurred with the aim of ending the doctrinal quarrels and of restoring unanimity in the confession. Jakob Andreä (1528–90), chancellor of the University of Tübingen, especially worked for doctrinal unity. After years of struggle, the result was the *Formula Concordiae* of 1577. On 25 June 1580, fifty years after the presentation of the *Confessio Augustana,* the *Book of Concord*—the collection of Lutheran confessional documents ending with the *Formula of Concord*—was published at Dresden. The Concord was signed by fifty-one princes, thirty-five cities, and more than eight thousand theologians.

From the outset Calvinsim had followed the path of clear creedal formulae and of systematic exposition of doctrine. Jean Calvin had set the example with the Geneva Catechism of 1542–45 and the *Institutio Religionis Christianae* (1536; 4th edition 1559). There followed official formulae of faith on a national basis: the *Confessio Gallicana* (1559), *Scotica* (1560), *Belgica* (1561), *Helvetica posterior* (1566), and the Heidelberg Catechism of 1563. In accord with the Calvinist ideas of the Church, these confessions also contained instructions in regard to congregational organization and discipline.

In the Catholic Church an end was put to what Jedin calls the "doctrinal confusion" by the decrees of the Council of Trent. The *Catechismus Romanus* of 1566, based on them, provided clergy and people with a compendium of Christian doctrine. The *Professio fidei Tridentina* had to be sworn to by all bishops and, on the urging of Peter Canisius, also by professors of theology. King Ferdinand I ordered the composing of a compendium of Catholic doctrine. He fostered the work of Canisius on the catechism, prescribed it for his territories, and issued detailed instructions on the manner of using it.[15] The formulae of faith and the catechisms put an end to the dogmatic uncertainty but at the same time necessarily restricted the area of free discussion and produced a polemical discrimination vis-à-vis other ideas.

Second, in addition to the clear formulation of doctrine, a Church Order was of great importance for the introduction and consolidation of a denomination. This regulated worship, law, education, salaries of pastors and teachers, administration, and the care of the poor for the Church in a territory, a city, a lordship, and, in certain circumstances, in a mere district. In the period 1550–1600 the number of such Church Orders increased to the hundreds.[16]

The fact that Duke Wilhelm V (1539–92) of Cleves-Jülich-Berg could not make up his mind to enact a new Church Order and that the discussions on the subject were prolonged from 1545 to 1567 shows the denominational uncertainty that characterized the lower Rhine area.

To enforce the Church Orders and to see to it that the territorial religion was also practiced by the subjects was the business of the periodic visitations. The records of visitations gave a picture of the religious situation and were the reason and the motive for further political and pastoral measures. On the Catholic side, visitations, following diocesan or provincial synods, were the means of assembling forces that had become uncertain and disoriented and of implementing the Tridentine reform.

Third, if the defective formation of clergy and people was the chief reason for the uncertainty and confusion in matters of faith, the establishing of educational institutions and the care for the formation and social security of pastors was the best means of creating a clear denominational situation. In the struggle against Cryptocalvinism the consistories took pastors and students to task and examined them in regard to their orthodoxy. In this way a group of students were expelled from Wittenberg in 1594. At the instigation of the Margrave of Ansbach the theologians and jurists of the University of Tübingen were arrested and banished because of too mild a punishment of the court preacher, who had been convicted of Calvinism. They had proposed life-imprisonment, with separation from wife and child. Lutheran officials also set up an index of forbidden books in defense of the unity and purity of the denominational Church and had the book trade supervised by inspectors.[17] The concern for a better formation of the clergy had

---

[15] Text of the order of 14 August 1554, in O. Braunsberger (ed.), *Beati P. Canisii epistulae et acta* I (Freiburg 1896), 752–754; J. Broderick, *Peter Canisius* I (Vienna 1950), 325–328.

[16] Cf. Sehling, I-XIIIff.

[17] E. W. Zeeden, op. cit., pp. 115f.

tangible success from 1600, but of course the situation still differed from one locality to another. These efforts to educate the clergy and for the development of schools were to be observed in all denominations toward the close of the sixteenth century. On the Catholic side the profession of teacher and tutor in secondary schools, universities, and seminaries was the chief activity of the Jesuits. Apart from transmitting the treasures of education, their instruction aimed at winning the youth for the Church and strengthening them in the Catholic creed and life. In this the religious drama played an important role at Jesuit and Benedictine schools. "All of pedagogy was geared to the practice of Christianity in the sense of denominations."[18]

Fourth, the appearance of Calvinism at the end of the 1550s eventually contributed powerfully to the formation of denominations and the defining of fronts. Its very consciousness of election, its organizational strength, and its aggressiveness had as their consequence a well developed denominational awareness. On the lower Rhine it helped to make clear that the age of Erasmian efforts at mediation was over and an unambiguous confession was the order of the day.

The effort to distinguish itself denominationally from Calvinism led in Lutheranism to an emphatic love of ceremonies and to the restoration of Catholic institutions, such as Mass vestments and the elevation of Host and chalice.[19] If denominational differentiation here produced a certain degree of enrichment, the contrary was normal. As soon as definite usages and ceremonies became characteristic of one denomination, they were thereby forbidden to the others, even if, in themselves, they were *adiaphora* and had nothing or only remotely to do with differences of doctrine. In fact, the less people were aware of the really distinctive differences, the more "ceremonies" became marks of the differences among denominations. If the sign of the cross or the "Angelus" was "Catholic," then it was for that reason no longer to be practiced by Lutherans. A visitation at Coburg in 1554–55 forbade the bell for the "Salve," even though this had been recommended by many Lutheran Church Orders, "for the sake of foreign and neighboring peoples, so that we will not be regarded as papists."[20] While at the middle of the

---

[18] Ibid., p. 125.

[19] The general superintendent of Electoral Brandenburg, Andreas Musculus (d. 1581), a stern champion of Lutheranism against Calvinism, had himself portrayed with breviary and rosary (*Wichmann-Jahrbuch,* 9–10 [1956], 51; cf. footnote 12) and urged pastors not to abolish the elevation (Schling, III, 236). The Elector Johann Georg ordered all pastors of the Neumark to reintroduce the elevation "zu mehrerer bekreftigung unseres glaubens von der wahren kegenwertigkeit des leibes und blutes Christi" (Sehling, III, 27).

[20] Sehling, I, 544.

sixteenth century it still seemed possible by the concession of the lay chalice to preserve for the Catholic Church large groups in Bavaria, Austria, and the lower Rhineland, who desired Communion under both species, the form of administering Communion soon became so much a question of denominational distinction that the granting of the chalice merely caused confusion. Thus, Communion under both species, introduced in Bavaria in 1565 by virtue of an indult of Pius IV, was again abolished as early as 1571. Similarly, the reform demand for the vernacular in the liturgy brought it about that in the minds of Catholics the Latin language acquired the special character of orthodoxy and the initial steps taken in the Middle Ages toward a more careful regard for the vernacular were not followed up. In view of the Protestant denial of an official priesthood, this was pushed so powerfully to the foreground by the post-Tridentine Church that the priesthood of all Christians, based on baptism and confirmation, was almost forgotten. In view of Luther's doctrine of the hidden Church, the Church as a visible community and institute of salvation was so greatly stressed that her inner mystery as the mystical Body of Christ was hardly seen any more, and Cardinal Robert Bellarmine (d. 1621) could say of the Church that she is as visible and tangible as the Republic of Venice.[21] On the one hand, the Church, as the bride of Christ, as the mother of the faithful, as the protector of the truth and minister of the life of grace, became herself the object of devotion; on the other hand she risked succumbing to the appeal of a superficial triumphalism. Compared with the Protestant communities as churches of the word, the Catholic Church became a narrow Church of the Sacrament.

Thus the form and rise of the denominations were greatly influenced by the "anti" to the other. People were in danger of overlooking the common inheritance because of the emphasis on differences and even of becoming impoverished and narrow. Denominational complacency contained an obstinate and militant trait. Processions obtained the character of demonstrations, and accordingly the opposition took a very dim view of them and resisted them. Controversy and polemics took up much room in theology; exasperation, vast prejudices, and various tricks were the result in wide circles of people who had no insight into the real doctrinal differences. A popular song of the Lutheran Cyriacus Spangenberg (1528–1604) began: "Keep us, Lord, in your word and arrange the murder of Pope and Turk." The poet and theologian Paul Gerhardt (1606–76), by whose hymns all denominations today feel themselves enriched, in his strict Lutheran orthodoxy said in the pulpit:

[21] *De controversiis christianae fidei* III, 2, *Opera omnia* (Naples 1858), II, 75b.; cf. ibid., III, 12.

"I cannot regard the Calvinists, *quatenus tales,* as Christians."[22] All this constituted the negative side, weighing heavily on the future of the formation of denominations, a process that, as such, was necessary for clarifying and solidifying, after the Reformation had finally led to a split instead of to the reform of the one Church.

[22] E. W. Zeeden, op. cit., p. 140.

PART TWO

Catholic Reform and Counter Reformation

The Historical Concepts

Both concepts, "Catholic Reform" and "Counter Reformation," presuppose the term "Reformation" as an historical definition of the Protestant separation from the body of Catholic believers. By "Counter Reformation" the Göttingen lawyer Pütter (1776) understood the forcible restoration to the Catholic faith of territories that had become Protestant. Ranke, after first speaking of Counter Reformations (in the plural), soon acknowledged the unity of the movement and, as its root, the "restoration, the new planting, so to speak, of Catholicism." Moritz Ritter's *Deutsche Geschichte im Zeitalter der Gegenreformation* (1889ff.) popularized the term outside Germany also (*contre-réforme*, Counter Reformation, *contrariforma, contrarreforma*), but it encountered an almost unanimous rejection in Catholic historiography, because the expression seemed to interpret the recovery of the Catholic Church merely as a counteraction to the schism and seemed to imply the use of force in religious matters. Hence, L. Pastor, J. Schmidlin, and others preferred the designation "Catholic Restoration," which, however, did not adequately express either continuity with the Middle Ages or the new elements accruing from the Tridentine reform.

Meanwhile, following von Ranke, W. Maurenbrecher had coined (1880) the term "Catholic Reformation" to describe the self-renewal of the Church, especially in Spain and Italy, which was the continuation of late medieval reform efforts. He had been preceded by the Catholic writers Joseph Kerker ("Catholic Reform" 1859) and Constantin Höfler ("Roman Reformation," 1878). We prefer the designation "Catholic Reform," because it avoids the term "Reformation" in the sense of "Protestant Reformation"—an expression that is subject to certain misgivings but is in general use—while on the other hand it indicates the continuity of the efforts for the reinvigoration of the Church from the fifteenth to the sixteenth centuries, without excluding, as does the term "Restoration," the new elements and the influence of the schism on the progress of the movement. However, it requires the additional concept "Counter Reformation," for the Church, inwardly renewed and strengthened, did actually proceed after the Council of

Trent to a counterattack and recovered lost territory, in association, to be sure, with confessional absolutism, the importance of which Eder has made clear. Hence both concepts are justified, as signifying not separate but intimately correlated movements. Also, Catholic authors, such as Paschini and Villoslada, hold that the term "Counter Reformation" is permissible for the entire movement of renewal and counteraction. Only when the terms "Catholic Reform" and "Counter Reformation" are used in conjunction can they be considered epoch-making in Church History. How far the extension of the term "Counter Reformation" to the succeeding centuries, including the very transition to the present age, as has become usual since the Second Vatican Council, is justified will be shown at the end of Section Five.

Origin and Breakthrough of the Catholic Reform to 1563

CHAPTER 32

Preliminary Steps in Italy and Spain

The Catholic Reform drew its strength from the late medieval endeavors for religious renewal, which were able to maintain themselves in Italy and Spain without being interrupted by schism. Its further development became possible only when, under Paul III, the reform movement gained a footing in Rome, when it began to eliminate obstacles inherent in the practices of the Curia, and when it finally affected the whole Church through the Council of Trent. Its growth and its breakthrough to Rome, which became apparent in the papal elections of 1555, occurred under the pressure and influence of the defections in northern Europe, which showed that an interior renewal of the Church was absolutely necessary. In substance Catholic Reform meant an orientation toward the apostolate and active *Caritas,* an orientation which came about through Christian self-realization. Not only did the religious points of departure vary, but the emphasis which the individual proponents of this reform assigned to these three elements also differed. In several instances, laymen and secular powers participated in the beginnings, but it was of decisive importance that the episcopate and the papacy initiated the necessary steps for the reform of the diocesan and the regular clergy.

Reform Efforts in Italy

The amply developed system of religious confraternities in Italy produced, apart from numerous "Compagnie," which were run like ordinary clubs, a tendency in the fifteenth century toward a more profound inwardness and an uncommon devotion to charitable goals. The regulations of the Brotherhood of Saint Dominic of Bologna, set up before 1443, offered a complete introduction to the spiritual life. The Brotherhood of Saint Jerome, founded at Florence in 1442 with the cooperation of Saint Antoninus, devoted itself to the relief of the deserving poor, as did the Brotherhood of Saint Nicholas, which was established in Bologna in 1495, also under the direction of the Dominicans. Bergamo had a "Schola disciplinatorum divini amoris." In 1494 Saint Bernardino of Feltre founded at Vicenza an "Oratory of Saint Jerome," twelve of whose members visited the sick and twelve took care of the poor every week. In 1506 it took charge of the hospital of the Misericordia. A Brotherhood of Saint Jerome, with a similar purpose, was established at Orvieto in 1510 by the Canon Thomas di Silvestro. All these brotherhoods consisted of lay persons, some under the direction of the mendicant Orders, some subject to the local bishop.

In the "Fraternitas divini amoris sub divi Hieronymi protectione," established at Genoa in 1497, the layman Ettore Vernazza (ca. 1470–1524), influenced by Saint Catherine of Genoa, effected a combination of self-sanctification and apostolate. According to its statutes, it admitted no more than thirty-six laymen and four priests. Its aim was "to implant in hearts the love of God, that is, Caritas." "Whoever wishes to join it must be humble of heart and center all his thought and hope on God." Striving for perfection, common religious exercises, and serving the sick were closely bound together.[1] The brotherhood maintained a hospital, started by Vernazza, for the incurable sick, the prototype of similar institutions established from the turn of the century at Savona, Bologna, Rome, and Naples.

Vernazza was certainly responsible for the Brotherhood of the Divine Love in Naples (1518), where he gained for the management of the hospital the widow Maria Laurenza Longo. On the other hand, it is uncertain who founded the Venetian brotherhood associated with a hospital for the incurable. Little is also known of the Milan "Oratory of Divine Wisdom." All of these were surpassed in importance by the Roman brotherhood, usually called the "Oratory of Divine Love." Founded before 1515 under the patronage of Saint Jerome, it bound its sixty members, lay and clerical, to daily attendance at Mass, at least monthly confession and communion, assiduous prayer, visiting the sick, and service in the hospital of the incurable, entrusted to them by Leo X in 1515. Once a week they gathered for Mass and community prayers in the parish church of Santa Dorothea in Trastevere, whose pastor, Julian Dati, was a member. The statutes and activity of the brotherhood were to be kept secret. A list of members compiled in 1524 includes, among fifty-six members, fourteen "laymen," so expressly termed, and also six bishops and several high curial officials.[2] Among them are the founders of the Theatine Order, but not, as was formerly assumed, Sadoleto, Aleander, Giberti, and Contarini. After 1527 the Oratory ceased to

---

[1] Statutes in Tacchi Venturi, I/2, 25–38.
[2] Cistellini, *Figure,* pp. 282f.

exist. Though short-lived and inconspicuous, it was a deeply earnest cell of Christian renewal in Medicean Rome.

In 1521 a member, the curialist Bartolomeo Stella, left Rome and founded a hospital for the incurable in Brescia and in 1525 an Oratory, which obtained the approval of Clement VII and was patterned after the one in Rome. The members designated themselves as an "amicitia," as did also a circle at Cremona, in which Zaccaria, who later founded the Barnabites, used to give talks. Stella was in close contact with the Augustinian canoness and mystic of Brescia, Laura Mignani (d. 1525), the Dominican nun Stefana Quinzani (d. 1530), and Saint Angela Merici; later he joined the circle of Cardinal Pole. Probably associated with him and a group of pious folk at Salò on Lake Garda was the diocesan priest Francesco Cabrini (d. 1570), who started at Santa Maria della Pace a society of diocesan priests. In 1619 it was incorporated into the Oratory of Saint Philip Neri.

Independent of and uninfluenced by these brotherhoods, the young Venetian patrician, Paolo Giustiniani (1476–1528), gathered around himself in Venice a circle of like-minded men who had become acquainted at the University of Padua. In a house of his on the island of Murano they studied together the Bible and the Fathers of the Church, not out of a purely humanistic interest but as a means to Christian perfection. The only priest was the humanist Egnazio. The others were laymen: Vincenzo Quirini (1479–1514), for a time Venetian ambassador at the courts of Philip the Fair of Burgundy and the Emperor Maximilian I; Gasparo Contarini; and Nicolò Tiepolo. Contarini was Venetian ambassador at the Diet of Worms in 1521; Tiepolo, at that of Augsburg in 1530. After a visit to the Holy Land, Giustiniani determined to renounce the world completely and entered the hermitage of Camaldoli near Arezzo. He was soon followed by Quirini and Sebastian Giorgi but not by Contarini, who, after a hard inner struggle, deliberately sought a Christian way in the world. The experience of justification, which he describes in a letter of 24 April 1511 to Giustiniani, resembles Luther's tower experience and explains his later appreciation of Luther's religious concern. As Camaldolese, Giustiniani and Quirini rescued their monastery from the maladministration of the general, Delfino, Savonarola's former adversary, and presented to Leo X a memorandum, intended for the Fifth Lateran Council, on the reform of the Church, which anticipated some basic ideas of the Tridentine reform and contained suggestions for union with the Eastern Churches and the missions in the New World.[3] It had no sequel. Quirini died in Rome,

[3] Text in Mittarelli-Costadoni, *Annales Camaldulenses* IX (Venice 1773), 612–719; cf. J. Schnitzer, *Peter Delfin* (Munich 1926), pp. 227–249; for the section on the missions see *NZM* 2 (1946), 81–84.

nominated a cardinal; Giustiniani founded after 1520 the Congregation of Hermits of Monte Corona.[4]

The importance of these reform circles becomes clear when one considers their cross-connections, in both personnel and ideas, with the founding of new religious institutes and with the Tridentine reform.

New Orders

The founding of the Theatine Order was the work of two members of the Roman Oratory. Both Saint Cajetan of Thiene (c. 1480–1547) and Gian Pietro Carafa (d. 1559 as Paul IV) sought the spiritual renewal of the clergy. Cajetan, born at Vicenza, had attained the rank of protonotary in the Curia when in 1516 he was ordained a priest. The Neapolitan Carafa, patronized by his uncle, Cardinal Oliviero Carafa, had been Archbishop of Chieti (*Theate*) in the Abruzzi since 1505 and had been entrusted with several diplomatic missions. In the spirit of the Oratory Cajetan, during a passing stay in his native district, established hospitals in Vicenza, Venice, and Verona on the model of that in Rome. Back in Rome, together with the priests Boniface di Colle and Paolo di Siglieri, he founded in 1524 a society of clerics on the basis of the so-called Augustinian Rule. Carafa joined them. The society was to have neither real estate nor fixed income but neither was it to live by begging, as the mendicant Orders did. Its support was to be left to divine providence. It was approved by Clement VII on 24 June 1524, with Carafa as its first superior. Pride of place was assigned to the careful fulfillment of all priestly duties: the praying of the Office, the worthy celebration of Mass, preaching, and every sort of pastoral activity. After they had been dispersed from Rome in 1527, Venice and Naples were, for some time, their only centers. Their recovery began with Carafa's election as Pope. He called upon them for the reform of the breviary and promoted one of them, Bernardino Scotti, to the College of Cardinals. At the end of the sixteenth century and during the seventeenth the Order was a nursery of good bishops but it flourished little outside Italy.[5]

A native of Cremona, Saint Antonio Maria Zaccaria (1502–37) was ordained a priest in 1528 after the completion of his medical studies at Padua and, with the jurist Ferrari and the mathematician Morigia, established at Milan in 1533 a society of priests, the Clerics Regular of Saint Paul, who were to imitate the Apostle of the Gentiles. They were known as Barnabites after the monastery of San Barnabà had been given

---

[4] Confirmation by Pope Clement VII in *Bull Rom* VI, 117ff.
[5] St. Cajetan in Munich 1675; houses earlier in Prague and Salzburg.

to them. For them the apostolate held the first importance. They especially stressed missions among the people, in which they were assisted by a community of women, the Angelicals, established in 1530 by Luisa Torelli, and the deepening of devotion to the Eucharist through the introduction of the Forty Hours' Prayer. Their rule was approved by Gregory XIII in 1579 after it had been examined by Saint Charles Borromeo, who made use of it in the reform of his diocese.

Works of charity held the first place among the Somaschi. Their founder, Saint Jerome Aemiliani, shortened to Miani (1481–1537), captured while defending the fortress of Castelnuovo, had undertaken the education of orphans in Venice after his liberation, and in Verona, Brescia, and Bergamo had established orphanages, partly with the active assistance of the members of the Oratory. Later in Somasca, between Milan and Bergamo, he founded a large institution for the education of orphans, but also for the care of the poor and sick. The society, approved in 1540, was responsible for its support. After a temporary union with the Theatines (1547–55) it was confirmed as an Order by Pius IV in 1568.

Closely associated with the pious circles of Brescia was Saint Angela Merici (1474–1540), from Desenzano on Lake Garda, when in 1535 she founded there, with twenty-eight companions, the "Company of the Servants of Saint Ursula," a society for the education of neglected girls. Though at first it did not practice the common life, its statutes obtained episcopal approval in 1536 and papal confirmation in 1544. The common life and simple vows were introduced by Saint Charles Borromeo in 1572 on the authority of Gregory XIII. The Ursulines became an Order with strict inclosure and solemn vows after their establishment in France (1612), where they were especially strong until the French Revolution. Individual convents were at times combined into a union, but they were never centrally administered.

Reform of the Mendicant Orders

Parallel to the rise of these new institutes ran efforts for the renewal of the mendicant Orders. From the end of the fifteenth century their generals were frequently drawn from the Observant branches, which had gained the right to exist in the canonical form of congregations alongside the provinces in all the mendicant Orders, though in the course of time they had lost something of their original austerity. Their aims were essentially the same: suppression of all private ownership, restoration of the common life, more careful training of novices, and improvement of theological studies. These were called for in visitations and in the decrees of general chapters, but as a rule were achieved only slowly and imperfectly. For those in dread of reform it was easy to obtain, by approaching the Sacred Penitentiary, authorization to live outside the monasteries (*licentia standi extra*) and thereby to escape the claustral discipline. Conditions could not improve until this source of much evil was eliminated by a reform of the Curia.

In the Order of Preachers success attended the reform work of the generals, Thomas de Vio of Gaetà (1506–18), together with his general procurator, Nikolaus von Schönberg, and García de Loaysa (1518–24). All three were later made cardinals.[6] In Aegidius of Viterbo (1506–18) the Hermits of Saint Augustine acquired a general of outstanding spirituality and a zealot for reform, whose instructions constituted the basis for the renewal of the Order during Seripando's term as general.[7] Between 1523 and 1562 the reform of the Carmelites was in the hands of the Cypriot Nicholas Audet, who continued the work of the most zealous promoter of the observance in the fifteenth century, John Soreth. However, during the first years of his office he was hampered by a schism that occurred in France. Among the Franciscans the General Chapter of 1517 had consummated the separation of the two branches, Conventuals and Observants, without providing a solution to the centuries-long dispute over the Order's ideal. Although the Observants obtained a scholarly general in Francesco Lichetto (1518–20) and earnest reforming superiors in Francisco Quiñones (1523–27) and Vincenzo Lunelli (1535–41), the Capuchin Order was founded as a third branch of the Franciscan religious family.

Matteo da Bascio and Ludovico da Fossombrone, ascetics belonging to the Observance but dissatisfied with it, obtained from Clement VII in 1528, through the intercession of Catherine, Duchess of Camerino, authorization to follow the Franciscan Rule in its original austerity and to wear a habit of coarse material with an angular capuche. At first limited to the Marches of Ancona and Umbria, the movement established for itself at the Chapter of Albacina (1529) a preliminary constitution envisaging the eremitical ideal and lay activities, such as manual labor and the care of the sick.[8] Despite powerful opposition the number of members grew—there were thirty-five houses in 1535. It was the Vicar General Bernardino d'Asti who, through the constitutions which

[6] Acts of the General Chapters at Rome (1508), Genoa (1513), Naples (1515), Rome 1518), Valladolid (1523), and Rome (1525) in *MOP*, IX (Rome 1917), 81–216; R. Creytens, "Les vicaires généraux de la Congrégation dominicaine de Lombardie 1459–1531," *AFP*, 32 (1962), 285–326.

[7] The acts of the General Chapters of Naples (1507), Viterbo (1511), and Rimini (1515) have not been preserved; cf. *AAug* IX (Rome 1918f.), 171–182.

[8] *MHOMC*, V, 158–171; the statutes of 1536 were printed under the title *Costituzioni de li frati Minori detti Capuccini* (Naples 1537).

he drew up in 1536, prescribing the care of souls and preaching, gave to the originally ascetic movement the character of an Order dedicated to pastoral work and thereby became its real founder. Matteo and Ludovico departed. The approval of the vicar general continued to be reserved to the general of the Conventuals by virtue of the confirmation given by Paul III in 1536. Vittoria Colonna had exerted her influence to obtain it. When the most renowned preacher of the new Order, Bernardino Ochino of Siena,[9] accused in Rome of teaching Lutheran ideas, fled to Geneva in 1542, the Capuchins were for a time forbidden to preach. The restriction of the Order to Italy lasted until 1574.

Cardinals and Bishops

Although the College of Cardinals had received a thoroughly secular tone as a result of the creations of Sixtus IV, there sat in the Senate of the Church a few outstanding individuals, even under Julius II and the two Medici Popes. Oliviero Carafa (d. 1511) had a share in the reform gesture of Alexander VI. Included in the great creation of 1517 were the generals of the Dominicans and the Augustinian Hermits, Thomas de Vio and Aegidius of Viterbo, who had been prominent at the Fifth Lateran Council. The former was an unsurpassed commentator on Saint Thomas and an original exegete; the other, a Platonist and humanist, who in a "keynote" sermon at the opening session of the Council had formulated the guiding principle of the Catholic Reform: "Men must be transformed by the holy, not the holy by men." Adrian VI found an expert adviser for his reform undertakings in Lorenzo Campeggio (d. 1539),[10] who did not enter the clerical state until after more than ten years of married life.

Not only in the College of Cardinals but also in the Italian episcopate there were at hand individuals favorable to a Catholic Reform, though not very many. The overwhelming majority was not concerned for reform in the first third of the sixteenth century. All the great sees belonged to absentee cardinals or, through resignation, to their relatives or intimates, so that they have been labeled by Tacchi Venturi "fiefs of the great noble families." The proper care of souls was therefore greatly neglected. Bishops of a really spiritual life and of genuinely pastoral activity were rare. The pastoral tradition of the fifteenth century, maintained by Saint Lorenzo Giustiniani (d. 1455), Saint Antonio of Flor-

---

[9] R. H. Bainton, *B. Ochino* (Frankfurt am Main 1940); B. Nicolini, "B. Ochino Capuccino," *Atti dell'Academia Pontaniana*, NS 6 (1956f.), 1–19; id., "G. Muzio e B. Ochino," *Biblion* 1 (1947), 9–45. On Ochino's connections with Bologna and Lucca see B. Nicolini, *Aspetti di vita religiosa e letteraria del Cinquecento* (Bologna 1963).

[10] Campeggio's memorandum of 23 March 1522 for Adrian VI in *CT* XII, 5–17.

ence (d. 1459), John di Tossignano, Bishop of Ferrara (d. 1446), and Antonio Bertini, Bishop of Foligno (d. 1486), would have to be regarded as interrupted, had not Pietro Barozzi, Bishop of Padua (1487–1507), provided the living model of the ideal bishop, which the layman, Gasparo Contarini, wrote about in 1516 for his friend, Pietro Lippomani, just promoted to the see of Bergamo:[11] The self-sanctification and the spiritually oriented conduct of the bishop form the basis for his function as teacher and shepherd, which Barozzi exercised not only as a preacher and a pastor concerned with individuals, but also through the reform statutes of a diocesan synod (1488). He was under the influence of the Christian humanists, Guarino and Francesco Barbaro.

Although the opening up of the archival sources is as yet only in its beginnings, it may be held that good bishops were not entirely lacking. Claude de Seyssel, once a French court bishop, who had exchanged the see of Marseilles for that of Turin (1517–20), measured up to the episcopal ideal which he sketched in his treatise *On the Threefold State of Pilgrimage* (1518).[12] Gian Pietro Carafa, as Archbishop of Chieti in the Abruzzi, exerted himself for the reform of his diocese before participating in the founding of the Theatine Order. The Cistercian Jerome Trevisani of Cremona (1507–23) and John Peter Grassi of Viterbo (1533–38) were regarded as zealous bishops. Cardinal Ercole Gonzaga, engrossed in politics and for a time regent of the Duchy of Mantua, had his see of Mantua visited from 1535 by his excellent vicar general, Francesco Marno. Andrea de Novellis, Bishop of Alba, issued for his diocese such splendid statutes that his successor in the Tridentine period, the humanist Jerome Vida, needed only to re-enact them.

The model of the future Tridentine reform on the diocesan level was Giovanni Matteo Giberti, Bishop of Verona (1524–43).[13] From 1527, when he left Rome for his diocese, following the fiasco of his pro-French diplomacy, he systematically improved the care of souls despite numerous obstacles. He began by assuring a higher quality among the clergy through an association of priests and the providing of lectures for their further education, the development of an existing boarding school into a seminary, the drawing up of registers of households in the parishes, the organization of preaching and of the instruction of adults

[11] G. Contarini, *Opera omnia* (Venice 1589), pp. 401–431.

[12] P. Broutin–H. Jedin, *L'évêque dans la tradition pastorale du XVIe siècle* (Louvain 1953), pp. 26–37.

[13] The constitutions for the diocese of Verona (1542) with other documents on the diocesan reform as well as the *Vita* of Giberti, by Fr. Zini, with the significant title "Boni Pastoris Exemplum," are contained in *I. M. Giberti, Opera,* ed. P. and H. Ballerini (Ostiglia 1740); there is given Giberti's motto, *Commisso gregi prodesse non praeesse.* On Giberti's influence at the Council of Trent and on Charles Borromeo, see chaps. 37–38.

and children, and the establishing of a charitable society (*Societas Caritatis*) in which the bishop and the pastor cooperated with the laity. The entire work of reform was in 1542 condensed in printed constitutions. Soon after, Giberti's secretary, Zini, sketched the bishop's life under the title *Example of a Good Shepherd*. A new episcopal ideal was forming and was being described in writing. Absenteeism, hitherto so lightly regarded, was more and more understood to be incompatible with it.

A stimulus toward religious renewal made itself felt in the domain of the Eucharist itself from the close of the fifteenth century. In almost all the larger cities of Italy arose confraternities devoted to promoting the cult of the Eucharist. Out of their own means the members saw to the worthy reservation of the sacred species and the maintenance of the perpetual light. They provided an escort when the Sacrament was carried to the sick. The founding of an archconfraternity of the Eucharist at Santa Maria sopra Minerva in Rome by Paul III gave these confraternities a center.[14]

The Fifth Lateran Council

On the eve of the schism the single attempt at a general reform of the Church, the Fifth Lateran Council, had, it is true, produced salutary results in the mendicant Orders, which were forced to defend themselves against the attacks of the bishops by means of self-reform, but otherwise its success was meager. No abuse was really eradicated, no reform decree was consistently carried out. The reform constitutions of 1513–14 abolished abuses in the curial system of taxation and provisions, but did not eliminate their cause, the venality of offices and pluralism. The decree on preaching, favorable to the exempt Orders, was an adjustment of jurisdiction rather than a genuine reform. As formerly, preaching was essentially restricted to the great cycles of Advent and Lent, and the sermons were given almost exclusively by mendicant friars. The introduction of the censorship of printed matter would perhaps have prevented much future mischief if it had been really enforced.

Lacking consistency, the feeble gesture of reform grew even weaker. In order to cut the ground from under the legitimate complaint that at Rome ordinations were conferred on clerics of foreign dioceses without the necessary examination of the candidates, without the consent of the proper Ordinarios, and, secretly or publicly, in a manner smacking of

---

[14] Bull "Dominus Noster" of 30 November 1539, in *Bull Rom* VI, 275ff., according to Tacchi Venturi (I/1, 223) an "epoch-making document."

simony, Gian Pietro Carafa was in 1524 appointed examiner of candidates for ordination and given extensive authority.[15] But a definite improvement did not occur until the appointment of Filippo Archinto as Vicar of Rome (1542) and the examination of candidates by the Jesuits. The colleges established by Cardinals Capranica (1475) and Nardini (1484) for future priests touched only a slight fraction of the candidates and can be regarded only in a very restricted sense as forerunners of the Tridentine seminaries. The reform decrees of Clement VII for the Jubilee of 1525 likewise brought very little change in the situation. Only the catastrophe of the *Sacco di Roma,* which was almost universally considered to be a judgment on Renaissance Rome, produced in the papacy a change of heart or at least an awareness that things could no longer go on as they had.

France and Germany

North of the Alps, in France and Germany, were there no efforts for a Catholic Reform? There too, on the eve of the schism, were bishops who were concerned for improving the quality of the clergy and for the care of souls. Parochial pastoral activity was in general superior to that in Italy, and the duty of residence was less neglected. But neither the plan of the Fleming Standonck for the reform of the French diocesan clergy (1493) nor the initial efforts for a synodal self-reform, notably in the province of Salzburg—the Provincial Council of 1512 and the Mühldorf Reform Council of 1522—nor the encouragement proceeding from the northern version of the current Christian humanism were of immediate advantage to the Catholic Reform. They were all overwhelmed by the schism before sustaining support came from the Church's center, from the papacy. A decisive impulse for reform flourished only in the Iberian Peninsula. It differed from all the other movements thus far mentioned.

Spain

Whereas in Italy the sources of the Catholic Reform were found in small communities of clerics and lay persons, from which proceeded several new religious institutes and eventually some strong personalities, in Spain even before the turn of the century the episcopate and the monas-

---

[15] The letter of appointment of 2 May 1524 (Pelliccia, *Preparazione,* pp. 462f.) gives an idea of the meager demands made of the candidates for ordination, when it confers on Carafa the authority (not the obligation): promotos in regulis, more et norma celebrationis et recitationis missarum, horarum canonicarum et aliorum divinorum officiorum ac ministerio sacramentorum docendi et imbuendi."

tic and mendicant Orders became, with the active encouragement of the Catholic Kings, the representatives of religious and ecclesiastical renewal. While in the rest of Europe the crusading idea had long since lost its force, in the Iberian Peninsula the *Reconquista*—the total expulsion of the Muslims—remained a political and religious goal. It was achieved when in 1492, under Ferdinand and Isabella, the united kingdoms of Castile and Aragón succeeded in taking Granada, the last Islamic stronghold. The missionary task thereby imposed did not find the Spanish Church unprepared.

Earlier, at the national Council of Seville (1478), an agreement had been reached between the Catholic Kings and the bishops, under the presidency of the "Great Cardinal," Pedro González de Mendoza, that crown and episcopate should promote the reform of the Spanish Church together and ward off any possible interference from outside.[16] Bishops and other benefice-holders were to be bound to residence for at least six months of the year, papal provisions and the privileges of exempt Orders were to be curtailed, and abbeys were not to be given to diocesan clerics. The close cooperation between the spiritual and the secular powers promoted the reform in that the pious and energetic Queen Isabella, influenced by her director, the Hieronymite Hernando Talavera, named efficient prelates, zealous for reform, to several Castilian sees. Among them was the Bishop of Burgos, Paschal de Ampudias, who continued the reform work of the *conversos*, Paolo and Alfonso of Burgos. Talavera himself, as first Archbishop of reconquered Granada (1493–1507), untiringly shared in the administration of the Sacraments and preaching—on all Sundays and holy days—and instituted farsighted organizational measures. These included the building of about one hundred churches, the employment of Arabic-speaking missionaries, the founding of a seminary for future priests, of houses for *conversos* and orphans, and the preparing of a "Breve Doctrina" for popular instruction. He was thus a direct forerunner and model of a bishop of the Catholic Reform. His apostolic activity was continued a generation later (from 1529) by Blessed Juan de Avila and then by Archbishop Pedro Guerrero.

Even more far-reaching was the activity of Cardinal Ximenes de Cisneros, Archbishop of Toledo (1495–1517). Originally a jurist and vicar general of Cardinal Mendoza in Sigüenza, in 1484 he had joined the Observant Franciscans and as provincial worked for the reform. Finally he was promoted to the primatial dignity by his spiritual daugh-

---

[16] The acts of the synod (*Boletino de la Real Academia de Historia*, 22 [1893], 215–250) give an accurate picture of the cooperation of throne and episcopate: the Catholic Kings propose sixteen reform decrees; the prelates reply and make counter-suggestions; agreement is reached on eight reform proposals.

ter, Queen Isabella. He enforced the reform of the diocesan and regular clergy with a firm and at times hard hand and in the University of Alcalá, which he founded, created a center for humanism and positive theology; its supreme achievement was the Complutensian Polyglot (1514–17). At his suggestion the *Imitation of Christ* was translated into Spanish; the *Exercitatorium Spirituale* of his nephew García was also influenced by the *Devotio moderna*. As Abbot of Montserrat (1493–1510), García brought the famed monastery into the reform Congregation of Valladolid and established there a printing press.[17]

The typically Spanish cooperation of crown and episcopate was confirmed again when on 17 December 1511 Ferdinand the Catholic summoned several prelates to Burgos for consultation in preparation for the Fifth Lateran Council. In the advice which they gave to the King, as well as in his instructions for the delegates to the Council, ideas emanating from the days of the reform councils were evident.[18] Bishop Ampudias of Burgos was opposed to any modifying of the decrees of the Council of Constance in regard to papal elections and the general reform of the Church by Pope and cardinals, and maintained that the theory that the Pope cannot commit simony, whereby the practice of the *Dataria* was justified, should be condemned as heretical. The Grand Inquisitor, Archbishop Deza of Seville, traced the disorder in the Church to frivolously granted papal dispensations from the common law. Both were agreed that papal reservations were to be curbed, taxes reduced, and the hamstringing of ecclesiastical jurisdiction through appeals to Rome ended. Almost all the abuses which were later discussed at the Council of Trent were enumerated, but the positive program of reform was not so fully developed. Deza advocated the introduction of the concursus for nomination to parishes, following the model of the diocese of Palencia, thanks to which that see had more properly educated clerics (*clérigos letrados*) than all the other bishoprics of Castile combined. In his instruction for the delegates to the Council the King called for the formal abrogation of the decrees of Constance in regard to conciliar supremacy but for the ratification of the decree "Frequens" and other reform measures of the Councils of Constance and Basel. Concern for Church reform was expressed along with national reform; it was agreed that the current reform of the Spanish Church could not achieve its goal without a general Church reform.

In the Spanish branches of the mendicant Orders the Observants

---

[17] A. Albareda, "La imprente de Montserrat," *Analecta Montserratensia* 2 (1918), 11–166.

[18] The views of the bishops together with the instruction for the conciliar delegates in J. M. Doussinague, *Fernando el Católico y el cisma de Pisa* (Madrid 1946), pp. 521–543.

experienced progress unequaled elsewhere. The Franciscan Recollects, who saw Pedro de Villa Creces as their spiritual father, were greatly aided by Ximenes, who was one of them. The reformed provinces of the Augustinian Hermits were as distinguished for fidelity to the rule as were the Observants, but frequently caused difficulties for the central authority in the Order on account of their highhandedness. The Spanish Dominican provinces were united with the Observants at the Chapter of Burgos (1506) under the guidance of Father Diego Magdaleno, after an earlier effort by Deza (1500) had miscarried. The ascetical and reform ideas of Savonarola entered Spain through Dominico de Mendoza and greatly stimulated the spiritual life, but also gave rise to strife in regard to the visionary María de Piedrahita and the ultra-reformer Juan Hurtado de Mendoza. The assignment of the Dominican Francisco de Vitoria to Salamanca made this university the starting point of the renewal of scholastic theology. Vitoria made the *Summa theologiae* of Saint Thomas the basis of his enthusiastically attended lectures and treated also the pressing questions of colonial ethics and international law, reform and council, according to Thomas's concepts. Without making concessions to the conciliar theory, he called for assurances against papal disregard of the decrees of ecumenical councils.[19] From his school proceeded the great Spanish theologians of the Council of Trent—Dominico Soto and Andrés de Vega—and outstanding bishops of the reform era.

Spanish Church reform suffered a setback during the first years of the reign of Emperor Charles V because of the political disturbances then current—the Comunero Revolt. Charles encountered violent criticism from Paolo de León (*Guía del cielo,* composed before 1527) and Juan Maldonado (*Pastor Bonus,* written in 1529). At the same time Spain was invaded by the ideas of Erasmus, for which the University of Alcalá had become the port of entry ever since the Conference of Valladolid took place. Their chief proponents were the brothers Juan and Alfonso Valdéz, both in the service of Charles V.[20] Juan's *Dialogue on Christian Doctrine* (1529) was an Erasmian catechism with a spiritualistic bent, which was later emphasized in his brother Alfonso's writings. Erasmus's thought permeated even the hierarchy. Cardinal López de Mendoza,

---

[19] The Relectio VII of 1534 bears the striking title: "Utrum concilium generale possit facere decreta et leges condere, quas nec Summus Pontifex possit immutare vel per dispensationem vel prorsus per abrogationem?"

[20] Domingo de Sta. Teresa, *Juan Valdés. Su pensamiento religioso y las corrientes espirituales en su tiempo* (Rome 1957); J. Méseguer, "Nuevos datos sobre los hermanos Valdés: Alfonso, Juan, Diego y Margarita," *Hispania* 17 (1957), 369–394; J. I. Tellechea, "Juan de Valde y Bartolome de Carranza. Sus normas para leer la Sagrada Escritura," *RET* 22 (1962), 373–400.

Bishop of Burgos (1529–37), protected Erasmus from Stunica. Though the anti-Erasmian reaction begun as early as 1530 with the trial of the Greek specialist Juan Vergara, Erasmian ideas continued to affect both preaching and popular instruction until they were definitively suppressed by the Inquisition in the middle of the 1550s. This Spanish "Evangelism" was a branch of a European movement, which as such was not assimilated by the Catholic Reform, but was definitively expelled from it. Spain's contribution to Catholic Reform lay in its episcopate, desirous of and experienced with reform, and in the theology of the Salmanticenses. These had a vital share in determining the image of the Council of Trent because behind them stood the Spanish world power. Finally, Spain also gave birth to the most effective reform Order, the Society of Jesus.

CHAPTER 33

Ignatius Loyola and His Order to 1556

The Society of Jesus became the most effective agent of the Catholic recovery. In the person and the work of its founder the fundamental principles of the Catholic Reform clearly emerge, obtain a new character, valid for centuries, and become of the greatest historical significance.

The Founder

Iñigo López de Loyola, born in 1491 in the ancestral castle (province of Guipúzcoa) of one of the ten great families of the Basque country, received the tonsure and a family benefice when still a boy, but was trained as a knight at court and, probably from 1507, was in the service of the Grand Chancellor of Castile, Juan Velásquez, at Arévalo, where he not only learned courtly manners but was also deeply impressed with the moral worth of loyalty to the ancestral dynasty. Heeding his impulses for adventure, he became an officer in the service of the Duke of Nájera and was seriously wounded at the siege of Pamplona by the French on 20 May 1521. While the healing of his shattered leg long confined him to his sick bed, he read the Franciscan Ambrose Montesa's Spanish translation of the *Life of Christ* by Ludolf of Saxony and a Spanish translation of the *Lives of the Saints* (*Flos Sanctorum*) of Jacobus a Voragine. When he found that this literature produced in him an inner peace, whereas the courtly romances were disquieting, he longed "to do great things in God's service" instead of seeking the warlike deeds of heroism that were denied him, and above all "to accomplish great external works of the sort mentioned [works of penance], because the saints had accomplished such for the honor of God."[1] After a general confession in the monastery of Montserrat upon his recovery, he hung up his dagger and sword before the miraculous image of the Mother of God, put aside his clothes, assumed the dress of a pilgrim, and kept a night vigil at the altar. Then he went to nearby Manresa, where, preoccupied with reading the *Imitation of Christ,* between March 1522 and February 1523 he experienced a mystical transformation and put into writing the first part of his *Exercises.* The visions which he had in the beginning revealed themselves as having been inspired by the devil. After a period of despair, during which he sought forcibly to acquire peace of soul by extravagant penitential practices and long hours of prayer, he received in new visions, principally in one at the chapel of Saint Paul on the Cardoner River, such an illumination in regard to the reality and the relationship of the mysteries of faith that later, whenever he was approached for decisions by his companions, he would refer to the insights acquired at that time. To dedicate himself entirely to the service of God and the salvation of souls was henceforth his life's goal: "In the mystical transformation of Manresa," says H. Rahner, "from Iñigo, the pilgrim and penitent, emerged Ignatius the churchman." But which road he would have to take toward this goal was still not clear to him. He remained a seeker for more than a decade.

A pilgrimage took him in 1523 *via* Rome to Jerusalem, but his plan of settling permanently in Palestine was vetoed by the Custos. On his return home he applied himself at Barcelona to a study of the rudiments of Latin and at Alcalá (1526–27) began the Arts course. Since, assisted by like-minded people, he began to engage in the spiritual direction of ladies, he came under suspicion as an *alumbrado,* was questioned three times by the Inquisition and the episcopal court respectively, and was imprisoned for forty-two days. After a similar experience while continu-

---

[1] The chief source is the autobiography, based on the oral account given by the saint and written down by González, superior of the Roman house of the professed, in 1553 and 1555; it ceased after 1538. The original text, in Spanish, from Chapter 79 in Italian, with a Latin translation by Coudray in *MHSI, Fontes Narr.* I, 353–507; it is supplemented by a letter of Lainez of 16 June 1547 (ibid., pp. 70–145), notes of Polanco and Nadal, and especially the diary of González for 1555 (ibid., pp. 527–752). Criticism of the sources: J. Šusta, "Ignatius' von Loyola Selbstbiographie," *MIÖG* 26 (1905), 45–106. The *Spiritual Diary* (*MHSI, Const.* I, 86–158) is extraordinarily jejune, especially in the later parts; extract: A. Feder, *Aus dem Geistlichen Tagebuch des Ignatius von Loyola* (Regensburg 1922); *Ignatius von Loyola, Das geistliche Tagebuch,* ed. A. Haas–P. Knauer (Freiburg 1961); P. de Leturia, "La Conversión de S. Ignacio," *AHSI* 5 (1936), 1–35.

ing his studies at Salamanca, he departed for Paris in 1528,[2] and there he lived in the College of Saint Barbara. He earned his livelihood by begging on journeys as far away as Flanders and England. Once again he fell under suspicion for having conducted spiritual exercises for his fellow-students. He took the degree of master of arts and at Montmartre on 15 August 1534, with six companions—Lainez, Salmerón, Bobadilla, Francis Xavier, Rodrigues, and Faber—vowed poverty, chastity, and a pilgrimage to Jerusalem, as well as work for the care of souls. At the renewal of vows in 1536 Lejay, Broët, and Condure joined the group. In order to carry out the planned pilgrimage to Jerusalem the companions met in Venice on 8 January 1537. Prevented from sailing, they engaged in pastoral work and in hospital service there and in the vicinity, and on 24 June 1537, Ignatius received the priesthood.

After a year they decided to offer their services to the Pope. With Lainez and Faber, Ignatius proceeded to Rome in November 1538, encouraged shortly before arrival by Christ's promise, made during prayer in a chapel at La Storta: "I will be gracious to you."[3] In Rome "the windows were shut tight" at first and Ignatius was even charged again with heresy. The case ended in his acquittal. Because of the good impression made by the apostolic activity of the small community, the atmosphere became favorable, and Ignatius then definitely decided in the spring of 1539 to found an Order.

A petition, presented to the Pope on 3 September 1539 through the good offices of Cardinal Contarini, contained the *Formula Instituti,* that is, the fundamental idea of the foundation. What was new in it was that, in addition to the vows of poverty and chastity, a vow of obedience to the Pope was to be taken. Once the hesitations of especially Cardinal Guidiccioni, who was very close to Pope Paul III, and of the conservative Cardinal Ghinucci had been overcome, the Society of Jesus was confirmed on 27 September 1540 by the Bull "Regimini Militantis Ecclesiae."[4] Its aim was "to fight for God under the standard of the Cross and to serve only the Lord and the Roman Pontiff, his Vicar on earth," by preaching, teaching, and works of *Caritas.* The members took the three customary vows and also a fourth—to obey without

---

[2] R. G. Villoslada, *La Universidad de Paris durante los estudios de Francisco de Vitoria* (Rome 1938); G Schurhammer, *Franz Xaver* I (Freiburg 1955), 71–261.

[3] T. Baumann, "Die Berichte über die Vision des hl. Ignatius bei La Storta," *AHSI* 27 (1958), 181–208. Sources for the charges of 1538 in *MHSI, Fontes Narr.* I, 500ff.

[4] Text in Mirbt, no. 430, with the documents; *MHSI, Const.* I, 1–32. The term "Compagnia," earlier usually interpreted as "troop," and hence of a military connotation, is traced by T. Baumann to the Italian use of "compagno" to mean "comrade," in "Compagnie de Jésus. Origine et sens primitif de ce nom," *RAM* 37 (1961), 47–60.

hesitation ("sine ulla tergiversatione aut excusatione") every command given by the Pope for the salvation of souls and the spread of the faith. Their number was limited to sixty. Ignatius was elected superior (*Praepositus*) on 8 April 1541 and a solemn profession followed at San Paolo on 22 April.

The founder lived thereafter in Rome, from 1544 in the house of the professed near the little church of Santa Maria della Strada, preoccupied with composing the constitutions and consolidating the Society. The *Formula Instituti* of 1539 was the basis of the constitutions,[5] in the formulation of which Ignatius consulted not only Lainez but also his most intimate coworker, Nadal, and his secretary, Polanco. The first edition of 1541 was completely revised after Ignatius had made a thorough study of the monastic and mendicant rules and had sought the views of his first companions on specific points, and in 1550 it was prescribed for a trial period. Repeatedly altered in the succeeding years, the constitutions were essentially in final form at Ignatius's death and were put in force by the General Congregation of 1558. They devote special attention to the reception and the studies of the members. Simple vows are made only after a two-years' novitiate. The study of philosophy and theology, lasting at least seven years, is interrupted by practical activity as teacher and tutor; during this period the "scholastic" is a member of the Society but he can be dismissed at any time. After being ordained, he completes a third year of novitiate (tertianship). Then, depending on aptitude, he is admitted to perpetual simple profession of the three vows as a "spiritual coadjutor" or, after additional years of trial, to the solemn profession of the four vows—the fourth being that of obedience to the Pope—as a "professed" in the strict sense. The "professed" constitute the real heart of the Order; they alone occupy the higher offices.

The constitution of the Order is strongly monarchical. The general (*Praepositus generalis*) is elected for life by the General Congregation and has virtually unlimited authority. He names all superiors, and they are required to make regular reports to him. In the government of the Order he is aided by the assistants, to whom several provinces are assigned at a time. The General Congregation meeting after the general's death is composed of the vicar general elected for the interregnum, the assistants, the provincials, and two elected delegates of each province. It exercises the supreme legislative authority. The strong centralization promotes the Society's goal of acting in military uniformity and strict obedience for the cause of Christ and the Church. In Ig-

---

[5] For the origin of the constitutions see the introduction to Volume I of the edition in the *MHSI:* edition of 1541, ibid.

natius's eyes obedience is the concrete realization of the surrender to the will of God and self-renunciation.[6] In his last will he lays down the rule: "In all that is not sinful I must follow the superior's will and not my own," for "God speaks through every superior." When he continues: "I must regard myself as a corpse which has neither will nor feeling," he is speaking of ascetical and perfect obedience, not of blind and abject obedience.

It is disputed whether the "Rules for cultivating the mind of the Church" are anti-Reformation or anti-Erasmus.[7] The strong rejection of Erasmus by Ignatius finds, in any case, its deepest motive in the Erasmian criticism of the Church and her display of piety. Luther appears only once in Ignatius's letters; it is regarded as certain that he had read none of Luther's books,[8] and not even an inclination to engage in controversial theology is evident. When his biographer, Ribadeneira, draws out certain parallels in the lives of Luther and Ignatius, it cannot be inferred from them that the founder of the Society of Jesus considered himself to be an "Anti-Luther" and established his Order as a battle corps for the war against Protestantism. Defense against Protestantism soon became more and more the center of attention, because the crisis in the Church required the effort on this front. But Ignatius's primary goal continued always to be inner renewal, promoted by the *Exercises,* and a worldwide apostolate.

The forgoing of a special religious habit and of choir service, customary until then in all Orders, and above all the election of the general for life encountered strong criticism from Pope Paul IV, who, since his conflict with Ignatius at Venice, had been hostile to him and characterized him as a "tyrant." He forced the Order to make appropriate changes in the constitutions, but after his death they were annulled by Pope Pius IV. The position of Protector of the Society, which Cardinal Rodolfo Pio of Carpi had exercised from about 1544 to 1564, was not filled after his death;[9] here too the Order went its own way. The establishment of a female branch of the Jesuits, imposed on the founder by a

---

[6] P. Blet, "Les fondements de l'obéissance Ignatienne," *AHSI* 25 (1956), 514–538; B. Schneider, "Zum historischen Verständnis des Papstgehorsams-Gelübdes," *AHSI* 25 (1956), 488–513; K. D. Schmidt, *Die Gehorsamsidee des Ignatius von Loyola,* (Göttingen 1935).

[7] J. Salaverri, "Motivación histórica y significación teológica del ignaciano sentir con la Iglesia," *EE* 31 (1937), 139–171; P. de Leturia, "Sentido verdadero en la Iglesia militante," *Gr* 23 (1942), 137–168; R. G. Villoslada, "S. Ignacio de Loyola y Erasmo de Rotterdam," *EE* 16 (1942), 235–264, 399–426; 17 (1943), 75–103.

[8] H. Wolter, "Gestalt und Werk der Reformatoren im Urteil des hl. Ignatius von Loyola," Lortz F, I (Baden-Baden 1958), 43–67.

[9] J. Wicki, "R. P. da Carpi, erster und einziger Kardinalprotektor der Gesellschaft Jesu," *Misc. Hist. Pont.* 21 (Rome 1959), 243–267.

decree of Pope Paul III which had been obtained by Ignatius's former benefactress, Isabel Roser of Barcelona, was, with papal permission, cancelled after one year (1 October 1546). Ignatius wrote to the deeply disappointed lady: "I have come to the conclusion, in harmony with my conscience, that it is not compatible with the commitments of our Society to undertake expressly the direction of women bound by the vow of obedience."[10] After an irritating struggle and a lawsuit brought by Isabel's nephew in regard to monetary gifts which Ignatius had received from her, she acquiesced and returned to Barcelona. The saint's decision was doubtless influenced by the many difficulties which at that very time the mendicant Orders were experiencing from the spiritual direction of the convents of nuns affiliated with them. Nevertheless, on 3 January 1555 he admitted the Infanta Joanna, daughter of Charles V, to the profession of the so-called "scholastic vows" under a pseudonym and thereby received her temporarily into the Order.[11]

When Ignatius died on 31 July 1556 the Order was in a serious external crisis, brought about by the hostility of Paul IV toward Spain and Spaniards, which led to the Carafa War against Spain. Just as soon as he had received news of the election of the Carafa Pope, Ignatius, according to his own admission, trembled in his whole body. On the outbreak of the war the Roman house of the professed was searched for weapons; none were found. There was further suspicion when the Spanish fathers suggested that the General Congregation be held outside Rome. The Vicar General Lainez won his point that it should take place in Rome (August–September 1558). It was due to his good sense and prudent tactics that the Order came safely through the difficult period of the Carafa pontificate.

In his lifetime Ignatius had refused to sit for his portrait. The source of the later portraits, for example that by Coello, is the death mask taken by an unknown person. Just the same, we are relatively well informed in regard to his external appearance. He was short (5'2") and of a delicate rather than a strong constitution. His head, with its high forehead and aquiline nose, was dominated by piercing eyes; the serene facial expression was that of a man united to God. The Fleming Coster described his external appearance on 29 May 1553:

> The old man went through the garden, supported by a cane. His face radiated piety; he is gentle, amiable, and charming and converses with the learned and the unlearned, with the great and the lowly.

---

[10] H. Rahner, *Ignatius von Loyola, Briefwechsel mit Frauen*, p. 332.
[11] Informative is the memorandum of 26 October 1554, in H. Rahner, op. cit., pp. 62ff.

Ignatius combined cold reason with mystical devotion to Christ, the military rigor of his idea of obedience with great liberty in the shaping of the interior life, imperturbable foresight in regard to the worldwide tasks of the Society with a tender sympathy for the individual person, the courtesy of a man of the world with the practical good sense of the Basque peasant. Constantly maintaining an aristocratic reserve, he was never on familiar terms with even his closest associates. He made a point of considering his decisions long and carefully, of listening to others' advice, of seeking divine guidance in prayer, and then, when the decision had been reached, of enforcing it without respect for people and even with severity. In his *Exercitia Spiritualia* he shows himself to be one of the great teachers of the spiritual life, thoroughly familiar with human nature, and a master in the handling of men.[12]

The title of his work is not original; the adherents of the *Devotio moderna* referred to their spiritual maxims as *exercitia,* and in 1500 Abbot Cisneros of Montserrat had published an *Exercitatorium spirituale.* But in content and construction the *Exercises* are undeniably Ignatius's work, the fruit of his own searching for God. After being examined by the Cardinal of Burgos, the vicar general of Rome, Archinto, and the Master of the Sacred Palace, Egidio Foscarari, they received papal approval on 31 July 1548. "It has long been established by history that the spirit and thought of Ignatius Loyola acquired their clearest expression in the book of *The Spiritual Exercises* and that his Order emanated from the deliberations of this book and continues to come forth from it." "With the help of the two most important meditations of this book—'On the Kingdom of Christ' and 'On the Two Standards'—we can summarize in a single sentence the basic organization of the perfect life: Man has been created to wage war in the Church Militant against Satan in loyal service to the majesty of the Triune God through assimilation to the crucified Man Jesus and thus to arrive at the glory of the Father." What was peculiar to this ideal of perfection and made it appropriate to its age was its intimate relationship to the visible Church: "From the union of love that bursts everything open with his being tightly compressed into the body of the Church is released that vast power which we can establish as historically certain in his work."[13] Though eminently personal traits are not wanting, such as the explanation of the Kingdom of Christ in terms of a worldly kingdom in whose

---

[12] Critical edition in *MHSI (supra);* besides the literature there cited, P. de Leturia, "La devotio moderna en el Montserrat de S. Ignacio," *RF* lll (1936), 371–386; M. Batllori, "Montserrat i la Campanyia de Jesus," *Miscellania Anselm Albareda* I (Montserrat 1962), 89–100.

[13] H. Rahner, op. cit., pp. 11f.

service Ignatius had grown up, the book of *Exercises* is full of the basic thought of traditional theology. When on the fourth day of the second week of the *Exercises* he poses the question under which of the two standards (*banderas*), Christ's or the devil's, one desires henceforth to fight, he is taking his stand on the Augustinian theology of the two Cities. The older characteristics of the Christian ideal of perfection, which he had seen at first only in the opaque light of medieval legends, especially those of Onufrius, Francis, and Dominic, he later grasped more exactly through study of the great religious rules and fused them into his new ideal, which was different from them but was filled nevertheless with the spirit of the tradition. The blending of ascetical tradition and personal experience made the *Exercises,* in the words of H. Böhmer, a "book of destiny for mankind." "The work of Ignatius is unequalled in its ability to transform, in the spirit of its author, the men who came upon it."[14]

Spread of the Society

The two great books, *Constitutions* and *Exercises,* radiate the strength of Ignatius's personality and constitute the basis of the astonishing expansion of the Order in the very first decades after its establishment. Until about 1550 the individual effort of the members in the care of souls and in teaching was in the foreground, but thereafter the Order was consolidated by the erection of an increasing number of foundations—houses of the professed, colleges, residences—and the development of the organization. The limitation of the number of members to sixty was abandoned as early as 1544. Already in 1539 Father Araoz had gone to Spain. In 1540 the Order was established in Paris. In the same year Father Faber set out for Germany in the company of the imperial diplomat Ortiz, who had earlier made a retreat under Ignatius, and, soon after, Peter Canisius was won for the Society. Fathers Lejay and Bobadilla went in 1542 to Regensburg to strengthen Catholicism there. At the request of King John III of Portugal, Francis Xavier and three companions sailed to the East Indes in April 1541. Lainez and Salmerón took part, as papal theologians, in the first period of the Council of Trent. At the beginning of 1548 Jesuits were entrusted at Rome with the examining of candidates for the priesthood. The requests by bishops and other highly placed people to the general to put Fathers at their disposal became so numerous that all of them could by no means be satisfied. But there was also opposition.

In the Spanish realm, from which the majority of the first members came, neither Charles V nor his successor Philip II was well disposed

[14] K. Holl, "Die geistlichen Übungen des Ignatius von Loyola," *Gesammelte Aufsätze zur Kirchengeschichte* III (Tübingen 1928), 285–301; the quotation, p. 285.

toward the Society,[15] and the Dominican Melchior Cano, highly esteemed as a theologian and at court, was its bitter enemy. It found strong support, though, in Francis Borgia, Duke of Gandía and Viceroy of Catalonia, who received seven Jesuits at Gandía in 1545 and in 1546 entered the Society. The excessive asceticism of Borgia and other Spanish members, however, endangered the uniform development of the Spanish branch for a time. Founded in 1547, the province was already divided seven years later into three provinces—Castile, Aragón, Andalusia—which, out of regard for Spanish national pride, were grouped under Borgia as deputy. In Granada Archbishop Guerrero, a good friend of the Society, made possible the founding of a college, and about the same time colleges were established in Zaragoza, Seville, and Medina del Campo. In Portugal the Society experienced a downright spectacular growth because of Rodrigues, who was highly esteemed by King John III. The first foundation arose at Lisbon in 1541; in 1542 a college was established at Coimbra; in 1546 Rodrigues became first provincial of Portugal. The number of members grew so fast that their thorough inner formation could not keep pace. Since Rodrigues did not correct abuses, he was deposed in 1552. The new provincial, Miron, dismissed 130 members, retaining only 105.

In Italy the founding of colleges at Messina (1548) and Palermo (1549) was followed by the establishment of the Roman College (1551), which developed as the Order's principal educational institute. In 1556 colleges had already been founded or were coming into existence in twenty Italian cities, including Naples, Florence, Bologna, Modena, Ferrara, Venice, and Genoa. On the other hand, in France the Order encountered the opposition of the *Parlement* of Paris and the Sorbonne. Father Doménech was expelled from Paris in 1542 and went to Louvain. Although a French province had been established in 1552, it was not until 1556 that, thanks to the assistance of the Bishop of Clermont, the first college could be opened at Billom. After the successful appearance of Lainez at the Religious Colloquy of Poissy (1561), the *Parlement* of Paris gave its consent for further foundations, whereupon there followed at close intervals those in Tournon, Rodez, and Paris. The establishment of colleges in the Low Countries was at first delayed by the refusal of the States General to grant the Order legal recognition as a corporation; not until 1562 were colleges founded at Brussels and Tournai.

Nadal's saying, "Vae nobis, si non iuvemus Germaniam," expresses the importance attributed by Ignatius to the crisis in Germany. The

---

[15] M. Batllori, "Carlos V y la Compañia de Jesús," *Cuarto centenario del emperador Carlos V. Estudios carolinos* (Barcelona 1959), pp. 131–148.

Order's chief promoters were Cardinal Otto of Augsburg, the Dukes of Bavaria, and King Ferdinand I. But the soul of the movement was Peter Canisius, who from 1549 was active at the University of Ingolstadt as professor and spiritual director. He began the erection of colleges at Vienna (1552) and Ingolstadt (1556) and in 1556 became provincial of the Upper German Province, from which a Lower German Province branched off. The colleges at Munich (1559), Trier (1560), and Dillingen (1563)—the last named grew to be a university—developed into strongholds of the gravely threatened Catholicism of Germany.

The ever increasing number of colleges founded from the mid-1550s was the sequel to an expansion of the Order's activity which was to be of the greatest importance. While not ceasing to be pastorally oriented, it became increasingly a teaching Order, because the formation of a new generation was recognized as the most urgent task. The colleges, which were originally intended for the training of the Order's recruits at existing universities and hence were permitted to possess fixed revenues and real estate, proceeded to accept externs who did not plan to join the Order. The college of Messina became the model of this new type. Thus, in the constitutions of 1550 there appeared colleges offering public instruction in addition to those, chiefly at universities, intended for the Jesuit recruits. In the definitive edition of the constitutions the emphasis had already shifted: the colleges were "rather for externs" and served also for the education of recruits.[16]

Although Ignatius himself had recognized the necessity of this change, Lainez may be regarded as the chief promoter of the new role of the colleges. Probably the Order's keenest theological mind, during his generalship (1558–65) he fostered the move toward a teaching Order and obtained from Pius IV the right to confer academic degrees. In 1563 there originated at the Roman College the first Marian Congregation, which aimed to further religiously and ascetically the pick of the best. Though Lainez was essentially of an imperious nature and hence had been sternly handled by Ignatius, as general he ruled with great mildness. The Order grew at an ever faster tempo. At the founder's death (1556) it had had about 1000 members in twelve provinces; when Lainez died on 19 January 1565, it counted 3500 members in eighteen provinces. Jesuits were active in all parts of the Portuguese colonial empire, but not yet in the Spanish. After 1549 there was a province in India, with its headquarters at Goa; after 1553 a Brazilian province; in 1555 Nuñez Barreto became the first Jesuit to set foot in China; after 1562 there was a foundation in Macao.

---

[16] L. Lukács, "De origine collegiorum externorum deque controversiis circa eorum paupertatem obortis," *AHSI* 29 (1960), 189–245; 30 (1961), 1–89.

The Beginnings of the Catholic Reform in Rome under Paul III

The self-reform of the members, as realized in the Italian reform groups and the new Orders proceeding from them, in the Spain of the Catholic Kings, and above all in the Society of Jesus, could not extend throughout the Body of the Church until it had first gained the Church's Head. Its advance on Rome made strides in the pontificate of Paul III, not only because of its inherent strength but because of the pressure of the seemingly irresistible progress of the schism, which at that very moment was consolidating itself in Germany as a distinct Church and was beginning to spread throughout Europe. While Paul III (1534–49) cannot be regarded as the first Pope of the Catholic Reform, he was its forerunner.

From a conclave lasting only two days (11–13 October) came forth as Pope the oldest and most intellectual of the cardinals, the Dean of the College, Alessandro Farnese. A product of the Renaissance and formed by it, he not only owed the red hat, conferred by Alexander VI in 1493, to the depravity of that era, but in his own personal life he had paid tribute to it. His children, Pierluigi and Costanda, born out of wedlock before his promotion to higher Orders, and his grandsons, Alessandro the Younger and Ottavio, seriously compromised his pontificate. The exaltation of his family and its admission among the dynasties of Italy through the bestowal of the Duchies of Parma and Piacenza on Pierluigi and even further designs on Milan had a disastrous influence on both the political and the ecclesiastical decisions of the Pope. His policy of neutrality between the two great powers, the Habsburgs and France, at times served his dynastic interests no less than those of the Church. Nevertheless, his pontificate marks a new start. Paul III had understood that the policy of Clement VII, opportunistic and almost exclusively diplomatic, could only founder, because it failed to recognize the predominant forces of that era and that the papacy had to extend its hand to the agencies of renewal, if it wanted to halt the progress of the schism. A Catholic Reform had to confront the Protestant Reformation. In the consciousness of the age, reform and council were inseparably linked; they became the essential components of Paul's program of government.

The establishment of the Roman Inquisition served the purpose of defense rather than of reconstruction. The points of entry of the new doctrine into Italy were Milan and Venice, which were closely bound to southern Germany and Switzerland through commercial relations; but communities of dissidents were found also in Central Italy (Modena and Lucca) and at Naples. Devotional writings, such as the little book *On the Favor of Christ,* disseminated a piety which only trained theologians could recognize as no longer Catholic. Lay persons interested in religion crowded into lectures on the Pauline Epistles and argued about problems of justification, grace and freedom, and predestination. Italy's greatest woman poet, Vittoria Colonna, and the greatest artist of the age, Michelangelo Buonarroti, were affected by the movement of "Evangelism," which contained many positive merits as well as serious dangers. From the end of the 1530s it increasingly happened that preachers, especially mendicant friars, occasioned strife and scandal, but because of the conflicts of jurisdiction between religious superiors, bishops, and local inquisitors they were called to account either tardily or not at all.[1]

Hence, through a brief of 14 January 1542, the Pope annulled for Italy every exemption in matters within the competence of the Inquisition and by the Bull "Licet ab initio" of 21 July 1542 he entrusted responsibility for maintaining the purity of the faith and investigating and punishing all doctrinal errors on both sides of the Alps to a commission of six cardinals—Carafa, Toledo, Parisio, Guidiccioni, Laurerio, and Badia—whose powers included the infliction of the death penalty on "obstinate heretics"; judgment on those willing to recant was reserved to the Pope.[2] In keeping with the Pope's attitude, the procedure of the new institution was relatively mild during his pontificate. It became stricter as the influence of Carafa, the spiritual father of the new foundation, grew; at his suggestion the Dominican Michele Ghislieri was appointed general delegate (1551). As early as 1543 the Roman Inquisition forbade any introduction of Protestant books into Italy; the enforcement of the prohibition naturally depended on the secular arm. Aleander, nuncio at Venice, was unable to prevent the smuggling of forbidden books. The nuncios to the imperial court, to King Ferdinand I, and to France were also instructed to keep an eye on the press. Morone and Tommaso Campeggio submitted lists of controversial German theologians,[3] but they received inadequate support from Rome. The significance of the press for the spread of Protestantism and for the Catholic Reform was not sufficiently appreciated until later.

More important than these defensive measures was the strengthening

---

[1] Fundamental are: B. Fontana, "Documenti Vaticani contro l'eresia lutherana in Italia," *ASR* 15 (1892), 71ff.; H. Jedin, "Ein Streit um den Augustinismus vor dem Tridentinum," *RQ* 35 (1927), 351–368; P. Paschini, *Venezia e l'Inquisizione Romana da Giulio III a Pio IV* (Padua 1959), pp. 3–29.

[2] *Bull Rom* VI, 344f.

[3] *NBD* I/2, 68; I/6, 293ff.

of the reform element at the Curia through the nomination of strongly Church-minded cardinals and the fostering of reform in the Orders. Even in the High Renaissance the Senate of the Church had not been entirely lacking in men zealous for reform. Oliviero Carafa, Francesco Piccolomini, Egidio of Viterbo, and Cajetan had maintained the great tradition of the fifteenth century, but they could not prevail against the powerful *nepoti,* the worldly minded scions of Italian princely families, and the crown cardinals of the great powers. And yet only a purified College of Cardinals could elect a reform Pope. Paul III began by creating two youthful *nepoti,* Alessandro Farnese and Guido Ascanio Sforza, but the next creation (21 May 1535) included, in addition to the martyr-bishop John Fisher, the future leader of the reform party at the Curia, Gasparo Contarini (1483–1542). Deeply imbued with the spirit of Giustiniani's circle, as Venetian ambassador at the imperial court (1521–25) Contarini had witnessed the beginnings of the schism and, though a layman, had exerted himself as a theologian. He became the soul of the Catholic Reform in Rome and of contact with the Lutherans.[4] In the following years the purple was bestowed upon Carafa, cofounder of the Theatines; the humanist Sadoleto;[5] Aleander,[6] well informed on the events in Germany; and the Englishman Pole, highly esteemed for his deep piety. Later followed Marcellus Cervini, destined to mount the throne of Peter as the first reform Pope; Morone, long active in Germany; the Dominican Badia and the Benedictine Cortese,[7] both distinguished for piety and scholarship. If one takes into account that even among the new cardinals selected from curial posts and among the crown cardinals, especially the Spanish, there were men who were convinced of the need of Church reform, such as the canonists Guidiccioni,[8] Ghinucci, and Sfondrato, and the Spaniard Juan Alvarez de Toledo, then it does not seem to be an exaggeration to speak of a renewal of the College of Cardinals.

[4] F. Dittrich, *G. Contarini* (Braunsberg 1885); *id., Regesten und Briefe des Card. G. Contarini* (Braunsberg 1881); "G. Contarinis gegenreformatorische Schriften," ed. F. Hünermann, *CCath,* 7 (1923); H. Jedin, *Contarini und Camaldoli* (Rome 1953); further literature: *DHGE* XIII, 771–784; *LThK* 2nd ed., III, 49f.; also A. Casadei, "Lettere del Cardinale G. Contarini durante la sua legazione de Bologna 1542," *AstIt* (1960), pp. 77–130, 220–285; H. Mackensen, "Contarini's Theological Role at Ratisbon in 1541," *ARG* 51 (1960), 36–57; A. Stella, "La lettera del Card. C. sulla predestinazione," *RSTI* 15 (1961), 411–441.
[5] S. Ritter, *Un Umanista teologo: J. Sadoleto* (Rome 1912).
[6] G. Müller, "Die drei Nuntiaturen Aleanders in Deutschland," *QFIAB,* 39 (1959), 222–276; cf. ibid., pp. 328–342.
[7] *Opera,* 2 vols. (Padua 1774).
[8] H. Jedin, "Concilio e riforma nel pensiero del Card. B. Guidiccioni," *RSTI* 2 (1948), 33–60.

Of course, the reform cardinals did not constitute a homogeneously oriented group; they were agreed on the goal but not on the choice of means. Contarini and Carafa were convinced that profound and radical interventions in the organization of the curial offices, the Orders, and the diocesan clergy were necessary; the conservatives, mainly consisting of curial canonists, felt that reform of the Church could be effected not through new laws but through a return to the "old law," that is, the observance of the canonical rules. Opposed to any change in the status quo was the organized curial bureaucracy, whose revenues were threatened by reforms.[9] Through certain administrative chiefs, for example, the Grand Penitentiary Pucci, this group was assured of firm support. That Paul III allowed full scope to all three tendencies was in keeping with his breadth of mind, but also indicated the limitations of his desire for reform.

The renewal of the College of Cardinals was not without effect on the reform of the mendicant Orders, in whose charge lay, at least in Italy, theology, preaching, and urban pastoral work. As their protectors, the reform cardinals were able to promote the reform element in this important field. Far-reaching plans for the unification of the various kinds of Orders, such as had been suggested from the time of the reform councils and most recently by Cardinal Guidiccioni, were put aside— Benedictines and Cistercians as the only monastic Orders, Dominicans and Franciscans as the only mendicant Orders, and, in addition, one military Order, and also Carafa's proposal to suppress the Conventual branches of the mendicant Orders.

Following the retirement of the excellent generals Cajetan and Loaysa, the Dominican Order suffered at first from frequent change in administration and the weakness of the generals Butigella and Du Feynier, and its protectors, Pucci and Salviati, were indifferent to reform. The general Romeo (1536–52), from the convent of San Marco in Florence, and his successor, Usodimare (1553–58), were the first to take it in hand, supported by the protector, Juan Alvarez de Toledo,[10] himself a Dominican. In the Franciscan religious family, whose two branches had been separate since 1517, the Conventuals at first continued to suffer from the decay of discipline, though they still produced capable theologians, such as Giovanni Antonio Delfino. In Lunello (1535–41) and Calvi (1541–47) the Observants acquired distinguished minister generals, who were seconded by the protectors, Cardinals

---

[9] W. v. Hofmann, *Forschungen zur Geschichte der kurialen Behörden vom Schisma bis zur Reformation,* 2 vols. (Rome 1914), especially I, 243–329.

[10] Acts of the General Chapters at Rome (1539, 1546, 1553) and Salamanca (1551) in B. M. Reichert, *Acta cap. gen. OP* IV, 266–361; Walz, pp. 257ff.

Quiñones and Carpi. The Augustinian Hermits, especially imperiled by Luther's apostasy, elected Seripando as general at the General Chapter of Naples (1539), on the personal initiative of the Pope, and commissioned him to restore morals and orthodoxy.[11] When he resigned in 1551 after an excellent administration, he saw to it that the reform would be continued under his successor by having Cervini named protector. As regards the Carmelites, Audet, general from 1523 to 1562, balanced the accounts for Maffei, who became protector in 1550: out of thirty provinces, six in northern Europe were destroyed, while the others had either been already reformed or had at least been persuaded to reform.[12] Among the Servites improvement was brought about in the generalships of Laurerio (1535–42), who became a cardinal, and Bonuccio (1542–53), prominent at Trent.[13]

Without prejudice to the diversity of constitutions, these reformers pursued essentially the same goals: restoration of the common life, abolition of private ownership, and greater attention to the admission and training of recruits. They used the same means: extended journeys of visitation for the enforcement of the decrees of general chapters and designation of energetic provincials. The authority of the generals was strengthened, and in the mendicant Orders there was a definite tendency toward centralization, as realized in the Society of Jesus. As the progress of the reform became more evident, the special position of the Observant branches seemed less justified; among the Augustinian Hermits and the Carmelites the virtually autonomous Observant congregations were, after a tiresome struggle, again subjected to the general's authority. The Pope encouraged this development in the interest of reform, but could not bring himself to eliminate the influence that was especially harmful to religious discipline—that of dispensations and privileges all too easily issued by the Curia, and chiefly by the Sacred Penitentiary, and, particularly, the flagrantly abused permission to live outside the community and to receive benefices, whereby those dreading reform escaped being reformed. Like the reform endeavors of individual bishops, the pre-Tridentine reform of religious institutes encountered an obstacle that was to be removed only by reform of the Curia.

"Purga Romam, purgatur mundus"—this challenge directed to Adrian VI was still valid. Beginnings of a reform of the curial offices had

---

[11] *Analecta Augustiniana* IX (1921), 277: "ut ordo vester quandoque restauretur ac suae integritati pristinoque suae sanctimoniae candori restituatur"; acts of the General Chapters at Naples (1539), Rome (1543), Recanati (1547); ibid., pp. 271–381, X, 117–166.
[12] A. Staring, *Der Karmelitengeneral Nikolaus Audet und die katholische Reform des 16. Jahrhunderts* (Rome 1959), pp. 427–431.
[13] P. Soulier, *Constitutiones antiquae et recentiores Serv. S. Mariae* (Brussels 1905) (General Chapter at Butri [1548]). For the sequel cf. chap. 36 and 38.

been made since the days of the reform councils by Pius II, Sixtus IV, Alexander VI, and at the Fifth Lateran Council, but none were carried through. On the contrary, the number of salable official posts had been constantly increased for financial reasons. They were made lucrative by raising and multiplying the fees, many of which were not fixed but were determined by the *Datarius* in an arrangement with the parties. Every reform curtailed the income of the officials and the Pope.

At first Paul III did not go beyond the reform gestures that had by now become almost routine. Soon after his election he set up a commission of cardinals for a "reform of morals," and on 23 August 1535, the commission, activated and expanded, was operating in the traditional manner. It was only the impending Council that moved the Pope to summon to Rome in the fall of 1536 eight independent and uncommitted men, from whose deliberations emanated a reform statement, the "Consilium de emendanda Ecclesia." On 9 March 1537 this was submitted to the Pope and commented on by Contarini.[14] With admirable candor it designated as the root of all evils the exaggerated growth of the papal theory and avarice; it called for a ruthless correction of the curial procedures in regard to dispensations, a restriction of exemptions, a greater care in the conferring of ordinations, a new and sincerely Christian countenence for the city of Rome.

The memorandum did not remain secret. It was printed, first in Italy and then in Germany, and misused as an alleged confirmation of the charges raised earlier by the opponents of the papacy.[15] The conservative Guidiccioni saw in it an unjust attack on the centuries-old curial procedure, which he said was to be spared, but even he did not actually deny the necessity of reform.[16] Symptomatic of the fate of the bold attack was the struggle fought in 1537–38 in regard to the *Dataria*. Contarini and Carafa did not prevail against the canonists Ghinucci and Simonetta; the "compositions" of the *Dataria*, openly branded as simony in the memorandum, found defenders among theologians, and the Pope shrank from putting up with the threatened loss of a considerable part of his income. At the end of 1537 an observer reported: "The reform of the *Datarius* has gone up in smoke." In the succeeding years, a similar fate befell efforts to reform the Chancery, the *Camera,* the

[14] *CT* XII, 131–145, with the signatures of Contarini, Carafa, Sadoleto, Pole, Ridolfi, Aleander, Giberti, Cortese, and Badia; excerpt in Mirbt, no. 427.
[15] E.g., by Luther (*WA* I, 288ff.) and J. Sturm; against the latter J. Cochläus wrote his "Aequitatis discussio super Consilio delectorum cardinalium" (1538), ed. H. Walter, *CCath* 17 (1931).
[16] *CT* XII, 226–256. An attempt at a chronological arrangement of the partly undated documents is made by H. Jedin, *A History of the Council of Trent* I (St. Louis 1957), 429, footnote 2.

Penitentiary, and the Rota, chiefly because the corporations of functionaries utilized the opportunity to defend their alleged "legitimate rights." Some individual abuses were removed, but complete success was not achieved because the Pope was only lukewarm in his support for the authors of the memorandum.

Of all the abuses in the pre-Tridentine Church the worst was the neglect of the duty of residence on the part of those responsible for the proper care of souls—bishops and parish priests. Absenteeism sprang from the view that the right to a benefice and its revenues was distinct from the personal fulfillment of the official duties connected with it. Cardinals possessed bishoprics which they had never seen; dozens of bishops lived permanently in Rome and Venice who scarcely ever visited their dioceses and had them administered by vicars. Neglect of residence by parish priests is less easy to ascertain by statistics.[17] In this matter also Paul III initiated some improvement. On 13 December 1540 he called upon eighty bishops present in Rome to go to their dioceses. They defended themselves by pointing to the manifold hindrances to episcopal activity from above, from below, from outside.[18] they cited the numerous exemptions of individual persons, Orders, and corporations, their own scant influence on the nominations to benefices, the abetting of reform-shy elements by appeals to the Roman tribunals, and the many interferences on the part of the secular power with the exercise of jurisdiction and the administration of ecclesiastical property. The demands of the bishops were at least partially met in a reform bull, drafted early in 1542 but not enforced.

Convocations of the Council

Undeniably, the greatest service of Paul III to the Catholic Reform was convoking the Council of Trent. Long convinced that the delaying tactics of his predecessor were ill-advised, he fixed his eyes from the start on the organizing of a general council. He was aware, and became increasingly more conscious, of the risk connected with it for the papacy since the emergence of conciliarism and in the face of the widespread

---

[17] Outstanding in its methodical approach is J. Absil, "L'absentéisme du clergé paroissial au diocèse de Liège au XVe et dans la première moitié du XVIe siècle," RHE 57 (1962), 5–44 (neglect of the duty of residence not synonymous with pastoral neglect). Cf. also F. W. Oediger, "Niederrheinische Pfarrkirchen um 1500," AHVNrh 135 (1939), 132f. (of 143 pastors of the archdeaconry of Xanten, around 1500, some 60 paid the tax on absentees). According to P. Hughes, The Reformation in England I (London 1952), 103, in the 1088 parishes of the see of Lincoln visited in 1518–19 there were 247 absentee pastors; in 1530 the ratio was 585 to 43.

[18] CT IV, 481–485.

anti-Romanism. The difficulties had increased with the long delays in the calling of a council. Papal promises of a council were regarded by Protestants as altogether insincere and were not taken at face value even by many Catholics. A council that was supposed to be attended by representatives from all parts of Christendom required the concurrence of the Christian princes and kingdoms, for whom it was at the same time a political event of the first importance. In regard to the rival great powers, the Habsburg Emperors and France, the Pope was determined to remain neutral, but how was this compatible with the fight against the apostasy? The Pope's policy in regard to a council can be understood only against the backdrop of all these circumstances, and its sincerity was often called into question.[19]

In the spring of 1535 the Pope announced the imminent summoning of the Council through his nuncios in Germany (Vergerio), France (Carpi), and Spain (G. Guidiccioni) and proposed as the meeting place Mantua, his first choice, and then Turin, Piacenza, and Bologna. France declined, fearing from the council a weakening of the Protestant opposition to the Emperor and a corresponding increase in the power of its chief foe. It relented when the Pope in a personal meeting with Emperor Charles V had obtained his consent to Mantua without yielding his own fundamental neutrality in the impending war with France. The Bull "Ad Dominici Gregis Curam," of 2 June 1536, summoned the council to Mantua and listed as its tasks the condemnation of heresies, the reform of the Church, and the restoration of peace among Christian princes for defense against the Turkish threat.

Three causes conspired to frustrate this first summons. On 24 February 1537, the League of Schmalkalden firmly declined the invitation delivered by the Nuncio Peter van der Vorst; Francis I announced that Mantua, situated within the Emperor's sphere of influence, was unacceptable; and the Duke of Mantua demanded that the Pope maintain a force of from five thousand to six thousand to protect the council. After the announced opening date, 23 May 1537, had passed, Paul III saw himself compelled to substitute Vicenza for Mantua. The three legates, Cardinals Campeggio, Simonetta, and Aleander, went there, but the bishops did not appear, and so the opening had to be postponed a second time. On 21 May 1539 it was prorogued to an unspecified date.

Although the war between Charles V and Francis I had in the meantime been ended by the armistice of Nice, the plan for a council was for

---

[19] P. Leturia, "Paolo III e il Concilio di Trento nelle memorie di Carlo V," *CivCatt* 97/II (1946), 12–23. The question of the imperial conciliar policy was again opened up by G. Müller, "Zar Vorgeschichte des Tridentinums. Karl V. und das Konzil während des Pontifikates Clemens' VII.," *ZKG* 74 (1963), 83–108.

a time laid aside, since the negotiations initiated by the Emperor for reunion with the German Protestants seemed to indicate that another solution of the religious crisis was within the realm of possibility. Its dramatic climax, the Religious Colloquy of Regensburg in 1541, proved the impossibility of bridging the gap. The division in the Church was already a fact which could not be disposed of even by the exceptional willingness of the Papal Legate Contarini to come to an understanding. The failure of Regensburg, coinciding with alarming reports of the invasion of Italy by Protestantism, determined the Pope in the summer of 1541 to take up again the plan for a council.

During a meeting with the Pope at Lucca (September 1541) the Emperor proposed Trent as the place of the council, for, situated in imperial territory, it satisfied the demand for a council "on German soil." The Pope at first insisted on Mantua (besides Ferrara and Cambrai) but finally approved the agreement of the Nuncio Morone with the Imperial Estates in regard to Trent and by the Bull "Initio Nostri Huius Pontificatus" of 22 May 1542 summoned the council to meet there on 1 November 1542. This second summons was also fruitless, for in the summer the war between Charles V and Francis I broke out again. The Pope was again neutral, but France declined to send delegates, and the Emperor regarded the convocation of the council as an insincere gesture. His minister, Granvella, sent as his deputy to Trent early in January 1543, ascertained that, except for the Legates Parisio, Morone, and Pole, almost no bishops were present; in May, despite numerous summonses from the Pope, there were only ten. A meeting at Busseto near Parma (June 1543) produced no agreement. The Pope refused to give up his neutrality; the Emperor declined to transfer Milan to the Farnese as urged on him especially by the *nepote,* Alessandro Farnese. Since the unsettled situation in Trent could not continue without of loss of prestige, the Pope on 29 September 1543 ordered the suspension of the council.

The tension between him and the Emperor increased when the latter, in order to obtain the assistance of the estates against France at the Diet of Speyer (1544), made considerable concessions to the Protestants and proposed for the next diet a reform of the Church without the Pope's participation. In a brief of reprimand (24 August 1544) the Pope lodged a solemn protest and renewed his offer of a council. This again became a possibility unexpectedly fast by the conclusion of the Peace of Crépy (18 September 1544). Not only did it eliminate the principal obstacle which had obstructed the success of this first convocation of the Council to Trent, but it also contained a secret clause whereby Francis I dropped his opposition to Trent and declared his willingness to participate in a council to be held there or in Cambrai or Metz. Thus the Emperor had seized the initiative in the matter of settling the question of the council. He carefully explored his great plan of forcibly crushing the religious and political opposition of the League of Schmalkalden and of then inducing the Protestants to accept the hitherto rejected invitation to the council, where the existing doctrinal differences were to be authoritatively decided and a general reform of the Church resolved. Without entering upon further negotiations with the powers, the Pope, in the Bull "Laetare Jerusalem" (30 November 1544), thereupon annulled the suspension of the Council and appointed Laetare Sunday, 15 March 1545, as the opening date. On 22 February Cardinals Del Monte, Cervini, and Pole were named as legates.

When, on 13 March, they arrived at Trent and were welcomed by the local bishop, Cardinal Christoforo Madruzzo, not a single other bishop was there except the papal deputy Sanfelice. Because the viceroy of Naples had designated four bishops of the kingdom to represent the entire Neapolitan episcopate and had directed the others to grant them full powers of attorney, the Pope on 17 April 1545 forbade the naming of proxies without sufficient reason. While the bishops who had meanwhile arrived in Trent were impatiently awaiting the signal for the opening, an understanding between Pope and Emperor was reached in regard to concerted action together with the Council against the German Protestants. It had been prepared through dispatch of Alessandro Farnese to Charles V at Worms. The Pope bound himself to furnish an auxiliary corps and to contribute a subsidy; the Emperor, to promote attendance at the council after victory had been achieved. The beginning of the war had to be deferred to the following year, for the Emperor was not yet prepared for the attack, and a new colloquy with Protestants, organized at Regensburg, stirred new misgivings at Trent. Unhappy over the delays, the legates discussed a transfer of the Council to Rome or Ferrara, without realizing that the change of place imperiled the great plan as a whole. The Emperor firmly rejected the suggestion of a transfer when the papal private secretary, Dandino, broached it to him at the beginning of October. Giovio wrote from Rome to Trent: "The key [to the opening] of the council has fallen into a deep well, and the blind Archbishop of Armagh is not likely to find it."[20] The Pope, however, disregarded all misgivings and appointed the third Sunday of Advent, 13 December, for the opening in Trent. In addition to the three legates and Madruzzo, four archbishops, twenty-one bishops, and five generals of Orders took part in the first session.

[20] *CT* X, 216.

CHAPTER 35

The Council of Trent under Paul III and Julius III

"Now the gate is open," the Augustinian general Seripando wrote happily in his diary.[1] But the deliberations got under way slowly, the delay arising from three causes. The number of participants was meager. There was as yet no order of business nor clearly drawn up program. And, whereas the Emperor, seeing the Council in the framework of his great plan and looking forward to the eventual participation of the German Protestants, favored postponing questions of doctrine until Church reform had been achieved, the Pope insisted that priority belonged to matters of faith.

Due to the constantly repeated admonitions addressed by the Pope to the bishops of Upper Italy and to those staying in Rome and Venice, the number of the voting members rose by 17 June to sixty-six; it dropped to about fifty in the autumn, and at the beginning of 1547 again reached almost seventy.[2] In addition to the Italians, who constituted approximately three-fourths, only the Spaniards were present in any number. They were represented by outstanding bishops—those of Astorga, Calahorra, and Badajoz—and, led by Cardinal Pacheco of Jaén, formed with the bishops of Naples, Sicily, and Sardinia, a compact group in political questions. France was represented by three bishops; Germany, following the departure of Helding, Auxiliary Bishop of Mainz, in January 1546, only by the proxies of the Archbishops of Mainz and Trier.

Agreement as to the right to vote in the general congregations was reached at the end of December: Entitled to vote were all bishops, including auxiliaries, the generals of the mendicant Orders, and two abbots from each of the monastic congregations. All plural voting was excluded. The indult granted to the German bishops and abbots on 5 December 1545, whereby they could be represented by voting proxies, was modified by the legates to mean only a consultative vote. The conciliar officials—the auditor Pighino, the promotor Severoli, the abbreviator Boncompagni—were named by the Pope. As secretary of the Council, in place of Ludovico Beccadelli, who withdrew, Angelus Massarelli, was selected on 1 April 1546, who till then had been secretary of

---

[1] *CT* II, 409.

[2] The list of all participants in the first period (*CT* V, 1037–1041) comprises twelve archbishops, seventy-four bishops, three abbots, six generals of Orders, and two proxies; with the three legates and Cardinals Madruzzo and Pacheco, the number is about 100.

the Legate Cervini. In its second session (7 January 1546) the Council prescribed its regimen; the order of seating was based on the dates of appointment as bishop. The decision of 22 January, which called for the considering of dogma and reform at the same time,[3] encountered the Pope's opposition and was not published in the third session (4 February), but it was actually observed throughout the duration of the Council. The right of proposition, that is, of deciding the program and the daily order of business, was claimed and exercised by the legates as deputies of the Pope. However, on 20 May 1546, the president, Del Monte, expressly stated that freedom of speech was not thereby curtailed.[4]

In order to acquaint the Fathers with the theological problems proposed for discussion, the plenary sessions of the Fathers entitled to a vote (general congregations) were, from 20 February 1546, preceded by particular congregations, in which the theologians delegated by the Pope (the Jesuits Lainez and Salmerón) and the theological advisers of the participants, mostly mendicant friars, discussed questions formulated by the legates or propositions from the writings of the Reformers and their confessional books. These were followed by full debate in the general congregations, in which each qualified member cast his vote. The proposed rough drafts of decrees were drawn up either by selected committees or by the legates, with the assistance of expert prelates and theologians. They were debated in the general congregations, often in several readings, and correspondingly revised until acceptance in the solemn session was secured. In regard to the deliberations on reform, on 23 March 1546 the Pope agreed in principle to the treatment of abuses connected with the curial offices,[5] but reserved to himself the carrying out, on his own authority, of the reform of these offices, an attempt that had broken down before the beginning of the Council. Dread of conciliarism induced the legates not to admit into the decrees the designation of the Council as "universalem Ecclesiam repraesentans," which was again and again called for by the Spaniards and some Italians.

Although the Emperor repeatedly (2 May and 16 June) besought the legates through his second ambassador, Francisco de Toledo—the first, Diego Hurtado de Mendoza, was usually absent—to postpone dogmatic decisions for the present, namely, until the end of the war, the Council, during the period from February to June 1546, issued dogmatic as well as reform decrees, in conformity with the decision of 22 January. Fundamental for all later doctrinal definitions was the decree of the fourth

[3] *CT* IV, 569–572.
[4] *CT* V, 152.
[5] *CT* X, 427.

session (8 April) on the sources of revelation.[6] The Canon of Holy Scripture includes also the deuterocanonical books; the books of both Testaments, having for their author the one God, and the apostolic traditions concerning faith and morals, insofar as they have been preserved through the uninterrupted succession in the Catholic Church, are accepted with the same, and not merely "similar," respect. The opinion advocated by the Bishop of Chioggia and the Servite general Bonuccio, that revelation is in its entirety contained in Holy Scripture and that "tradition" is only the interpretation of it as given authoritatively by the official teaching office, led to a slight change in the original draft of the decree (substitution of "et . . . et" for "partim . . . partim"), but there is hardly any doubt that the overwhelming majority of the Fathers understood the apostolic traditions as a stream of revelation complementing Scripture.[7] The adoption of the decree on the Vulgate was preceded by a spirited debate on the lawfulness and appropriateness of translating the Bible into the vernacular. Cardinal Madruzzo of Trent advocated it, Pacheco opposed it. The "vetus et vulgata editio" of the Bible was declared "authentic," that is, free from doctrinal error, and suitable for scholarly and practical use. The correction of the Vulgate text, acknowledged as necessary, was carefully considered; study of the original languages of the Bible and versions in the vernacular were not forbidden. Just the same, the decree occasioned hesitations in Rome, but without resulting in an alteration of its text.

During the discussions of Original Sin, following the fourth session, Seripando and other theologians of the Augustinian school advocated the view that the removal of guilt by baptism does not prevent the survival of a concupiscence that is in some degree sinful, and Pacheco sought to obtain the definition of the Immaculate Conception. Neither view prevailed. Canon 5 specified the remission of sin in every respect ("totum id, quod veram et propriam peccati rationem habet"); concupiscence, it states, is at times labeled sin in Saint Paul because it issues from it and lures to it. The Council declared that it did not intend to include the Mother of God in the decree on Original Sin; the constitu-

---

[6] *CT* V, 91f.; the draft of 22 March *CT* V, 31f. Bibliography in Jedin, *A History of the Council of Trent* II (St. Louis 1961), 52f. For the treatise, not given there, of the Carmelite general Audet on the Canon, see *E Carm* 4 (1950), 337–355.

[7] Opposed to the interpretation of the decree as expounded by J. R. Geiselmann (*Una Sancta* 11 [1956], 131–150, and by M. Schmaus, *Die mündliche Überlieferung* [Munich 1957], pp. 123–206) are F. Lennerz, *Gr* 40 (1959), 38–53, 624–635; J. Beumer, *Scholastik* 34 (1959), 249–258; G. Rambaldi, *Antonianum* 35 (1960), 88–94; cf. also H. Holstein, "La Tradition d'après le Concile de Trente," *RSR* 47 (1959), 367–390; Y. Congar, *La tradition et les traditions* (Paris 1960); R. Geiselmann, *Schrift und Tradition* (Freiburg 1962).

tions of Sixtus IV concerning the dispute between Dominicans and Franciscans over the Immaculate Conception were to remain in force.

A reform decree dealing with the establishing of prebends of lectorships in cathedral and collegiate churches sought in this traditional manner to improve the defective instruction of the clergy. During the debate over the reorganization of preaching Bishop Martelli of Fiesole attacked the exemption of the mendicants and demanded that, even for preaching in their own churches, they should have to seek the permission of the local bishop. The mendicants resisted successfully, but the right and the duty were enjoined on bishops of taking steps, regardless of exemption, against preachers who disseminated error or caused other kinds of scandal. The bishop was personally obliged to the preaching of the faith; parish priests, to vernacular sermons on all Sundays and holy days. An attempt by the Emperor's supporters to deal also in this connection with the duty of residence on the part of bishops and parish priests was rejected by the majority.

The Decree on Justification

With the simultaneous publication of the two reform decrees and the decree on Original Sin in the fifth session (17 June),[8] the Council was confronted with its most difficult assignment: the definition of the doctrine of justification. The opinions propounded by the thirty-four conciliar theologians (22–28 June) on six proposed questions—nature of justification, faith and works, grace and freedom—reflected the views of the three great theological schools represented at the Council—Dominican, Franciscan, and Augustinian. The proposal on which the general debate (30 June–23 July) was based distinguished three stages (*status*) of justification: the conversion of the sinner; the increase of justification; its recovery following the loss of grace. The first draft, submitted on 28 July and formerly attributed incorrectly to the Franciscan Andrés de Vega,[9] was so severely criticized that it had to be withdrawn. The simultaneous outbreak of the Schmalkaldic War and the advance of the Protestant army against the Ehrenberger Klause having occasioned a panic in Trent, the legates considered the transfer of the Council to Bologna, which, situated within the Papal State, conformed

[8] Decrees of Session V in *CT* V, 238–243; bibliography on the decree on Original Sin in Jedin, op. cit., II, 132f; on the decree on preaching, Jedin op. cit., II, 105f.; also E. Feyaerts, "De evolutie van het predikatie-recht der Religieuzen," *StC*, 25 (1950), 117–190, 225–240.

[9] *CT* V, 384–391. A Mobilia, *Cornelio Musso e la prima forma del decreto sulla giustificazione* (Naples 1960), argues for the authorship of Cornelio Musso, Bishop of Bitonto.

to the Pope's original plan as to the place of the Council. Though they had received full authority from the Pope in this regard, they lost precious time by making an inquiry at Rome and missed a favorable opportunity, since the military situation soon stabilized itself. It was not until 23 September that they perforce again took up the thread of the discussions. At Cervini's suggestion, they submitted a new draft composed by Seripando,[10] which complemented the "canones" by a positively stated "doctrina." "Even if all the universities of the world and the Lutherans were here," wrote Bishop Lipomani of Verona, impressed by the general debate on this second draft (27 September–12 October), "the subject could not have been better discussed."[11]

The Emperor's faction, now firmly held together, sought to delay the conclusion. In order to meet them halfway and to gain time in which to arrange the contemplated suspension of the Council, the legates called for particular congregations (15–26 October) on two problems which had come to the foreground in the course of the debate: the question, open since the Regensburg Religious Colloquy of 1541, of twofold justification (justification by the justice of Christ and that by grace immanent in man); and the possibility of attaining certainty on the state of grace (Luther's certainty of faith and the Scotist view on the efficacy of the Sacraments). Both questions were argued in the general congregations from 9 November to 1 December together with the "November draft" of the decree,[12] with the result that the doctrine of a twofold justification was rejected but not formally condemned. As for the certainty of grace, the Council confined itself to striking out against Luther's certainty of faith. Here, as in other matters, the Council adhered to the principle of not deciding differences of opinion within Catholic theology. Throughout December the form of the decree was polished by a committee (*Praelati theologi*); the definitive wording (the fifth) was approved on 11 January 1547, and two days later unanimously accepted in the sixth session.[13] In sixteen dogmatic chapters and thirty-three canons, it defined the responsibility of grace for justification in all its stages, its nature as sanctification and renewal of the inner man, the necessity of a preparation, and the importance of faith in the process

[10] *CT* V, 420–427; Seripando's preliminary drafts, *CT* V, 821–833; bibliography in Jedin op. cit., II, 168ff., 239; also J. I. Tellechea, "El Articulus de iustificatione de fray Bartolome de Carranza," *RET* 15 (1955), 563–635. Of the older works listed by me, op. cit., the most important are those by H. Rückert and E. Stakemeier.
[11] *CT* X, 675.
[12] *CT* V, 510–518.
[13] *CT* V, 791–799; perhaps too far-going in its harmony is the interpretation in H. Küng, *Rechtfertigung. Die Lehre Karl Barths und eine katholische Besinnung* (Einsiedeln 1957), pp. 105–276.

of justification; the increase of justification, its restoration, and the possibility of merit; and eternal life as grace and reward.

The length of the debate on justification was due not only to the subject but also to political considerations. In late autumn the Bishop of Fano, intimate with the Emperor's party, had brought forward a plan for a temporary suspension of the Council in order to do away with the discrepancy between the Emperor's delaying tactics and the legates' efforts for acceleration. In an agreement on 16 November between Cardinal Farnese and the first imperial ambassador, Mendoza, it was proposed to suspend the Council for six months and to complete the debate on justification, but not to publish the decree. But when the Emperor refused to ratify this agreement of Trent, the legates proceeded to promulgate the decree.

Whereas the acceptance of the decree on justification was unanimous, the reception of that on the duty of residence of bishops and parish priests, promulgated in the same sixth session of 13 January 1547, was greatly divided. During a first, brief debate on 9 and 10 June the Spaniards had demanded not only punishment for neglect of residence but the elimination of its causes: dispensation from the duty, only too easily obtained from the Curia; impeding of episcopal control through privileges of exemption granted by the Pope and on the part of the secular powers; and the frequent exclusion of the bishops in the successive steps of judicial appeals. At the prompting of the legates, bishops had submitted lists of these "impedimenta residentiae."[14] But the draft proposed by Del Monte on 29 December removed the whole set of hindrances. Pacheco expressed his opinion thus: "No reform is better than this sort!" The amended draft of 11 January 1547, the work of a committee of canonists (*Praelati canonistae*), went farther than the "little solution" of the presidential draft by annulling dispensations from residence obtained for an unspecified period and obliging those in possession of limited dispensations to make them known to the bishops, who were then to see to the appointment of qualified vicars. Bishops obtained also the right, by apostolic authority, to visit and correct exempt cathedral canons, but only in person. These concessions, however, did not satisfy the episcopal opposition; on the other hand, they seemed to be too extensive to high curial officials, such as T. Campeggio, Cicada, Pighino, and Archinto. Members of both factions qualified their *placet* in the session with so many stipulations that the approval of the decree appeared doubtful. The legates were obliged to broach once more the problem of residence.

---

[14] *CT* XII, 578–597 (six memoranda in full and two summaries).

A reform proposal of 3 February 1547,[15] prepared by the commission of canonists, already contained the basic features of a new law dealing with ordination and appointments to office. It gave to the bishop concerned the responsibility for ordination, including control of dimissorial letters issued by the Curia, and recognized the principle that office and benefice were inseparable by forbidding pluralism and requiring definite personal qualifications in those designated to become bishops and parish priests. Del Monte designated as the goal of the whole reform the restoration of pastoral care ("animabus providere"). In an effort to meet the demands of the opposition halfway, the Pope had at the beginning of the year transmitted to the legates the sketch of a reform bull in which the position of the bishops was strengthened, for example, by a limitation of exemptions and by the so-called alternation in the conferring of benefices. By a consistorial decree of 18 February he forbade the cardinals to hold more than one see.[16] Hence in the general congregation of 25 February 1547, after careful examination of the votes cast in the session, the acceptance of the decree on residence could be proclaimed. Bishops of every rank, including cardinals, who failed to fulfill the duty of residence for six successive months were deprived of one-fourth of their revenues; if the absence continued for a year, they lost another fourth. The climate of the reform discussions had so greatly improved that the new reform proposal, which had meanwhile been extended to include statements opposing the union of benefices and dealing with the bishops' right of visitation, was accepted in the seventh session on 3 March 1547 by a large majority.[17]

The preparation of the thirty canons on the Sacraments in general, baptism, and confirmation, promulgated in the same session, had begun on 17 January when a collection of thirty-five erroneous propositions, extracted from the writings of the reformers, was submitted for evaluation by the theologians of the Council. The current rivalries among the schools in regard to the causality of the Sacraments and a certain insecurity as to the nature of the sacramental character did not prevent complete unanimity with reference to the nature and sevenfold number of the Sacraments. In the general debate (8–21 February) the Council decided to limit its definition strictly to the condemnation of the concepts of the reformers and not, as proposed by Bishop Archinto of Saluzzo, to draw up a doctrinal decree of a positive nature, modeled on

---

[15] *CT* V, 871f.

[16] The reform bull of 31 December 1546, in *CT* IV 504–512; the consistorial decree of 18 February 1547, in *CT* V, 981f.

[17] *CT* V, 984ff.

the *Decretum pro Armenis* of 1439, nor to condemn the reformers by name along with their writings, as demanded by two Spanish bishops. The last-mentioned decision was in accord with the policy suggested by Cardinal Farnese at the beginning of the Council: that doctrines and not persons be condemned. On 25 February he again impressed this policy on the Council and added as a reason that otherwise the reformers ought to be summoned to the Council and heard by it.[18] The canons accepted in the seventh session defined the sevenfold number of the Sacraments and their institution by Christ. The Council described their nature as efficacious signs by having recourse to the scholastic terms added only during the concluding debate on 1 March: *gratiam non ponentibus obicem conferre* or *ex opere operato conferre*. The importance of faith was only negatively stated: The Sacraments were instituted not only for the strengthening of faith and operate not only through faith in the word of promise. Rebaptism was condemned and the bishop was designated as the ordinary minister of confirmation.

Transfer to Bologna

During February the theologians had discussed the doctrine of the Eucharist. It had just been referred to the full Council when several cases of typhus fever, presumably brought to Trent from the German theater of operations in the war, provided the grounds for the decision reached on 11 March in the eighth session, by a vote of thirty-nine to fourteen (with five doubtful), to transfer the Council to Bologna. The epidemic was not invented, as opponents of the transfer claimed; the expert opinion drawn up by the Council physician, Fracastoro, is medically incontrovertible.[19] However, it is equally certain that the legates and the Italian majority had long aimed at the transfer and felt that they were thereby complying with the Pope's desire, but a direct charge to the legates is not demonstrable. The imperial minority regarded the decree of transfer as not binding and remained at Trent. The long-existing tension led to a rupture just at the moment when the Council seemed to have assumed the function of restoring Church unity.

For, since the turn of the year 1546–47, a victory of the Emperor over the Schmalkaldic League was in prospect. The army of the League had had to evacuate South Germany, and several Free Cities, the Duke of

---

[18] *CT* X, 291, 826f.
[19] *CT* V, 1014f. On the author, see F. Pellegrini, *G. Fracastoro* (Verona 1948); H. Jedin, "Laientheologie im Zeitalter der Glaubensspaltung: Der Konzilsarzt Fracastoro," *TThZ* 64 (1955), 11–24.

Württemberg, and the Count Palatine had submitted to the Emperor. However, instead of now negotiating, as Paul III desired, with the still unconquered leaders of the League, the Elector Johann Friedrich of Saxony and the Landgrave Philip of Hesse, and their secret patron, France, Charles V aimed at total victory, which he obtained at Mühlberg on 24 April. In a brief of 22 January the Pope had ended his alliance with the Emperor and had recalled his troops. His aim in the war was the subjugation of the Protestants, not the revival of the imperial power in Germany and the consolidation of Charles V's universal monarchy. Considering the Spanish supremacy in Italy, it was not without reason that he feared becoming dependent upon Charles V. Incensed by this change in papal politics, the Emperor showered the Nuncio Verallo with reproaches.[20] The transfer of the Council to Bologna frustrated his great plan completely and wrecked the understanding laboriously established two years earlier between the two leaders on whom the plan depended. Charles demanded that the Pope annul the transfer of the Council, but the Pope refused on the ground that it was the business of the Council alone. However, the gathering in Bologna stipulated as a condition to any discussion of a return to Trent that first the minority that had remained there must submit to the decree of transfer and move to the new place of meeting. Finally, the personal relations of Paul III with the Emperor were irreparably contaminated when, on 10 September 1547, Pierluigi Farnese was murdered at Piacenza at the instigation of the imperial governor of Milan, Ferrante Gonzaga, and the city was occupied by imperial troops. Nevertheless both parties made serious efforts to avoid a complete break. The Pope allowed the Council at Bologna to discuss but not to publish any decree; the Emperor established a provisional ecclesiastical settlement for the Empire without the direct participation of the Pope but with his tacit toleration.

In the ninth session (21 April 1547) the Council had constituted itself officially at Bologna and during May the debate begun at Trent on the Eucharist had been resumed. But the eight canons on the Real Presence,[21] already completed, were not published in the tenth session (2 June) for the reason just mentioned. The same fate befell the canons discussed in June on the Sacrament of penance[22] and those on the anointing of the sick, holy orders, and matrimony, which engaged the general congregations and the then very prominent theological commis-

[20] Verallo's report of 7 February 1547, in *NBD* I, 9, 462–469.
[21] *CT* VI, 166f.
[22] *CT* VI, 196, 218f.

sion (*Praelati theologi*) during July, August, and September.[23] The Council theologians, whose number rose at times to eighty and never fell below fifty, were preoccupied with the doctrine of purgatory and indulgences in June and July, with the Sacrifice of the Mass in August. The reform commission appointed on 6 June drew up as a program for the discussion of reform the abuses in the administration of the Sacraments, and, after preparatory work in the commission of canonists, these abuses were debated in the plenary sessions during the autumn and winter (26 September 1547 to 30 January 1548).[24] On 28 November a new commission was formed to codify abuses in the celebration of Mass, in indulgences, and in religious Orders.[25] On 10 December two more commissions were appointed—one to compile a list of abuses on the part of the secular powers, the second to deal with other abuses not yet discussed.[26] But their assignments were not completed.

Though in its sessions at Bologna the Council did not issue a single reform decree, this period was important for almost all the subsequent decrees in that their topics were now for the first time thoroughly discussed. The view previously put forward at Trent, that the improvement of pastoral activity was the Council's central concern, was brought into clearer focus; once again the need to strengthen the position of the bishops was affirmed, and consideration was given to the arrangement of provincial and diocesan synods, the preparation of a catechism, and the liturgy.

After the Emperor's final move, through the dispatch of Cardinal Madruzzo to Rome to induce the Pope to restore the Council to Trent, had failed, he lodged a formal protest against the transfer in Bologna on 15 January 1548 and in Rome on 23 January. Imperial circles were already weighing the continuation of the Council by means of the minority that had remained in Trent.[27] To avoid the threatened schism,

---

[23] V. Heynck, "Contritio Vera. Zur Kontroverse über den Begriff der contritio vera auf der Bologneser Tagung des Trienter Konzils," *FStud* 33 (1951), 137–179; P. Fransen, "Ehescheidung im Falle von Ehebruch. Der fundamental theologisch-dogmatische Ertrag der Bologneser Verhandlungen von 1547," *Scholastik* 27 (1952), 526–556; *id.*, "Réflexions sur l'Anathème au Concile de Trente (Bologne 10–24 septembre 1547)," *EThL* 29 (1953), 657–672.

[24] T. Freudenberger, "Der Kampf um die radikale Abschaffung der Stolgebühren während der Bologneser Periode des Trienter Konzils," *MThZ* 1 (1950), 40–53.

[25] *CT* VI, 611.

[26] *CT* VI, 630.

[27] H. Jedin, "Der kaiserliche Protest gegen die Translation des Konzils von Trient nach Bologna," *HJ* 71 (1952), 184–196; F. de P. Sola, "Manuscritos Tridentinos en el Archivo de Protocolos de Barcelona," *Estudios historicos y documentos de los Archivos de Protocolos* 3 (Barcelona 1955).

the Pope on 1 February decreed the suspension of discussions at Bologna and requested the Council to defend the legality of the transfer before a tribunal set up at Rome; the minority in Trent also received the invitation to send a deputation to Rome.[28] It declined. The deputies from Bologna were heard by the tribunal in the summer of 1548, but no verdict was reached.

Meanwhile, the Emperor had undertaken to settle the religious affairs of Germany, regardless of the Council, by means of the *Interim* of Augsburg and the "reform" simultaneously published for the Catholic estates. These were not authorized by the Pope, but their realization was indirectly furthered by him when he sent two reform nuncios to the Empire, Pighino and Lippomani, with extensive faculties for the reconciliation of Protestants. The *Interim* foundered on Protestant resistance. The Augsburg "reform" led to a series of provincial and diocesan synods but could effect no thorough Church renewal because the forces of regeneration were still too weak. The death of Paul III on 10 November 1549, however, opened up the prospect of reactivating the Council of Trent and hence of resuming the original "Great Plan."

Second Period of Sessions

Though the new Pope, Julius III, had, as Council president, brought about the transfer to Bologna, he conceded to the Emperor the return of the Council to Trent on the assumption that the Protestant estates, in conformity with the Recess of the Diet of 30 June 1548, would submit to it. The assumption proved to be wrong, for their submission, given under pressure of military defeat, was bound up with two conditions: that the Council should not be under the Pope's direction and that it should reopen for discussion the doctrinal decrees promulgated during the first period of sessions, taking as a starting point the Protestant principle of Scripture. The Emperor and even the Pope, who was at first inadequately informed of this state of affairs, acted as though an unconditional surrender were at hand. The Bull "Cum ad Tollenda" of 14 November 1550, reconvoking the Council to Trent, maintained the view held by the Curia that the transfer had been legitimate by speaking of "resuming" (*reductio*), but at the same time it met the Emperor halfway by designating the new meeting at Trent as a "continuation" of the earlier. France, having recognized the transfer, declined to participate.

The Legate Marcellus Crescenzio, in association with co-presidents Pighino and Lippomani, who were previously active in Germany as reform nuncios, opened the meeting on the appointed day, 1 May 1551,

---

[28] *CT* VI, 739ff.

but discussions did not get under way until September. The character of the gathering differed from the earlier one, for the imperial minority, which had held out in Trent after the transfer, had been increased during the fall and winter by thirteen bishops from Germany and Switzerland, including the three Ecclesiastical Electors,[29] and the previous predominance of the Italians had been broken. Among the Council theologians there were now present, in addition to the great Spaniards (D. Soto, M. Cano, and A. de Castro), representatives of the University of Louvain (R. Tapper, Hessels, and Ravesteyn) and the German theologians Johann Gropper, Eberhard Billick, and Ambrosius Pelargus. And, above all, there appeared for the first and only time ambassadors of the Protestant imperial estates: Brandenburg, Württemberg, Strasbourg, and Electoral Saxony, among them the historian Johannes Sleidanus.

The ten articles on the Eucharist which were submitted on 2 September were related to the articles of Trent of 3 February 1547, rather than to the canons formulated in Bologna, but, thanks to the preliminary work accomplished in Bologna and to the complete agreement on this article of faith, the debate was relatively brief (particular congregations of 8 to 16 September and general congregations of 21 September to 10 October). The decree on the Eucharist was soon ready for promulgation; it was accepted on 11 October 1551, in the thirteenth session.[30] It defined the Real Presence and the notion of transubstantiation as suitable (*aptissime*) for designating the substantial change and condemned the teaching that Christ is present only at the moment of reception. A decision in regard to communion under both species was deferred.

Likewise, the twelve articles on the Sacrament of penance and the four on the anointing of the sick were not identical with the Bologna canons. Debate occurred in particular congregations from 20 to 30 October, in general congregations from 6 to 15 November. Contrary to Luther's teaching that penance consists in a recalling of baptism and is essentially a penitential attitude, the Council defined penance as a Sacrament, consisting of three elements: contrition, confession, and satisfaction. Confession of all serious sins committed after baptism is required by divine law, and priestly absolution is a judicial act. The anoint-

---

[29] More precise information on the German participants in Schreiber, II, 1–265, 295ff.; H. Ries, "Vorboten und Gefolge des Kurfürsten Johann V. von Trier auf seinem Zug zum Konzil von Trient im Sommer 1551," *TThZ* 60 (1951), 281–289. A list of the documents and books taken to the Council by Archbishop Heusenstamm of Mainz, published by A. Bruck in *AMrhKG* 5 (1953), 301–310; H. Jedin, "Das konziliare Reformprogramm Friedrich Nauseas," *HJ* 77 (1958), 229–253.

[30] *CT* VII, 111–229.

ing of the sick is no mere ceremony adapted for the relief of those who are ill, but a Sacrament instituted by Christ and promulgated by the Apostle James. As in the case of the Eucharist, the Canons relative to penance were complemented by a "doctrina," but only at the last moment.

Less satisfactory was the progress of the discussions on reform. The reform decree of Session XIII regulated the successive appeals in criminal trials; that of Session XIV amended the law on ordination and appointment (Chapters 12 and 13 governed the *patronatus*). Spaniards and Germans agreed that reform was not being adequately pursued. When the Bishop of Verdun complained that the conferring of monasteries *in commendam* was not being entirely abolished, Crescenzio rebuked him so sharply that the Archbishop of Cologne blurted out, "Is this still a free Council?"[31] In December and January, during the debates on the Mass and holy orders, the negotiations with the ambassadors of the Protestant imperial estates, which were conducted by means of the imperial representatives, Count Montfort and Francisco de Toledo, made no progress. The envoys of Württemberg and Electoral Saxony were received in the general congregation of 24 January 1552, and on the next day, in the fifteenth session, obtained the amended safe-conduct that they had demanded. But a theological discussion failed to materialize, for the Protestants insisted on their earlier stipulations relative to recognizing the Council. "For both sides," said Bizer,[32] "it is clearly a question of principle, in which to yield would have meant to surrender."

At the same moment there arrived alarming reports concerning the military activity of the Elector Maurice of Saxony, who was allied to France. The German archbishops took their departure, the Legate Crescenzio fell gravely ill, and the suspension of the Council seemed inevitable. But the Emperor, approached for instructions by his envoys at the Council, strenuously resisted any admission that his great plan had definitely collapsed and commanded that the suspension be opposed.[33] When the rebel princes took the initiative in April and compelled the Emperor to flee from Innsbruck, no alternative remained. On 28 April 1552, in the sixteenth session, the Council decided to adjourn indefinitely. After the dissolution a Spaniard wrote, with resignation: The suspension has revealed the futility of the Council; neither have the heresies that arose in Germany and elsewhere been liquidated, nor has the Church been reformed, nor has peace been restored among Chris-

---

[31] *CT* XI, 710, 713.

[32] Bizer, *Confessio Virttembergica*, p. 40.

[33] Instruction for the treasurer Vargas and the Emperor's reply of 17 February in *CT* XI, 994–1003.

tian princes.[34] Disappointment obstructed the view of what had really been achieved, but it was incontestable that the Council presented itself as a torso: Its doctrinal decrees embraced only a part of the disputed teachings, the reform decrees eliminated some but in no sense the most crying abuses, and they had no binding force, because they had not yet been confirmed by the Pope.

[34] H. Jedin, "Ein spanischer Epilog zur zweiten Tagungsperiode des Konzils von Trient," *Gr* 31 (1950), 100–113.

CHAPTER 36

The Breakthrough of the Catholic Reform (1551–59)

The decade 1549–59 witnessed the breakthrough of the Catholic Reform in Rome. In 1555 two of its leaders mounted the Throne of Peter in rapid succession.

Julius III, as nephew of Cardinal Antonio Del Monte, who was much esteemed under Leo X and Clement VII, had risen high in the curial career and was an outstanding canonist. After a long conclave (29 November 1549 to 7 February 1550) he was elected as a result of an understanding between Cardinals Guise and Alessandro Farnese, after the zealous reformer Pole, one of the Emperor's candidates, had failed by one vote to obtain the required two-thirds majority. Though not inclined toward the Emperor, he necessarily promoted the imperial policy in restoring the Council to Trent. Furthermore, he was impelled to the Emperor's side by the war against Ottavio Farnese, who refused to surrender the Duchies of Parma and Piacenza to the Church and was supported by France. When both undertakings had miscarried, Julius declared his official neutrality in the struggle for Siena, which broke out in the summer of 1552 on the expulsion of its Spanish garrison. But the two peace envoys, sent in the spring of 1553—Dandino to the Emperor, Capodiferro to Henry II—accomplished nothing. The Sienese, supported by France, lost their freedom to Cosimo I of Florence, and Spanish predominance in Italy was finally consolidated. The Pope came to terms with it, on the advice of Dandino, favorable to France, and of Ricci, inclined to the imperial side. Ricci had undertaken the virtually impossible task of rescuing the finances from the chaos produced by the *nepoti* policy of Paul III. The costly Parma War and the preparations for the defense of the Papal State, rendered necessary by the Siena War, deepened the financial distress. Just the same, the Pope laid out a sumptuous villa before the Porta del Popolo and eagerly superintended its construction.

The most important event of his pontificate, the Catholic Restoration in England, fell into Julius III's lap without his participation. On 19 July 1553, Mary, daughter of Catherine of Aragon, was proclaimed Queen of England. Resolved from the start to lead the nation back to the Roman obedience, she proceeded cautiously in the question of religion, advised by her cousin, Charles V, and mindful of the strong opposition she had to overcome even after her accession. The religious laws of Edward VI were repealed, Catholic worship was restored, and on 1 April 1554 Bishop Gardiner, whom she had appointed Lord Chancellor, consecrated six bishops to replace those deposed. The Queen herself applied to the Pope for their confirmation.

But Cardinal Pole, named as Papal Legate, was not permitted to set foot in England until the end of November 1554, after the marriage arranged by the Emperor of Charles V's son Philip to Mary had taken place. On 30 November 1554, the legate solemnly pronounced the absolution from schism in the presence of the Queen and Parliament. Demands for the return of alienated Church property were dispensed with and the current holders were confirmed in possession on 24 December. The Provincial Council of Canterbury, presided over by Pole (4 November 1555 to 10 February 1556), was to institute the rebuilding of the Church in England and was in accord with the spirit of the Catholic Reform in its concern for obliging bishops to reside in their dioceses and to preach, the organizing of groups of preachers to take the place of the mendicants, and the decree on the founding of seminaries for boys, which became the direct model of the Tridentine decree on seminaries.

The task of reconstruction was hampered by the fact that half the bishops in office had been compromised by the schism, that there were not enough priests on hand, and above all that after twenty years of schism a great part of the faithful were estranged from the papacy and Catholic worship. The acts of the visitations of the dioceses of Lincoln and Canterbury make clear how thoroughly the Catholic tradition had been liquidated—as late as 1557 sixty churches in the archiepiscopal see of Canterbury had no crucifix at the high altar.[1] The judicial proceedings against schismatics and Protestants, normally instituted by the secular judge, frequently aroused popular resentment, because a number of the ecclesiastical judges themselves had cooperated with the earlier system. Among the 273 persons put to death were, it seems very likely, many Anabaptists, who had been persecuted by the Anglican Church as

[1] W. Sharp–L. E. Whatmore, *Archdeacon Harpsfield's Visitations 1557* (London 1950f.).

well as by the Catholic Church. The flight of Protestant-minded preachers to the continent, from fear of the Queen, prepared the collapse of the restoration.

The most pressing, but so far deferred, task of the papacy continued to be the reform of the Roman Curia. In the autumn of 1550 Julius III had summoned to Rome three resolute members of the reform party, Cervini, Pole, and Morone, and through them, and a little later through still other cardinals, he expanded the reform commission which had been formed soon after his election. But, like Paul III, he had not carried out his original purpose of anticipating the impending reconstitution of the Council by a papal reform of the Curia. On the suspension of the Council there emerged the plan of entrusting the reform to an international gathering of bishops who were to meet in Rome. But because of the opposition raised by the Emperor's faction it was dropped.[2] Still, during the winter of 1552–53, Cervini and Maffei pushed so zealously the reform of the conclave, the consistory, the *Signatura,* and the Sacred Penitentiary, taking into consideration old and new opinions, that Andreas Masius, agent of the Duke of Cleves, expected the "reformation of the Roman Court in a few days."[3] The Tridentine reform decrees, completed by a "reform of the princes" and modified in several points, were to be put in force by a great reform bull.

The driving force sprang out of events in Spain and Portugal, where many bishops, supported by the secular powers, were beginning to carry out certain reform decrees of the Council, notably Chapter 4 of Session VI concerning the visitation of exempt capitulars, though these still lacked papal confirmation and hence were without the force of law. The Pope reacted with great firmness. On 15 January 1554 he referred the King of Portugal to the forthcoming reform bull; in Spain he intervened in favor of the exempt cathedral canons of León, Astorga, Segovia, and Calahorra and categorically demanded that the bishops withdraw the orders issued against them.[4] He thereby rejected the view that conciliar decrees possessed validity as "directives of the Holy Spirit for the good of souls" without papal confirmation and at the same time squarely faced the Erastian tendency to play them off against the papacy. In the introduction to the projected reform bull (spring of 1554) was expressed the intention of conferring the force of law through it on the conciliar decrees together with the newly drafted reform chapters. The bull was

[2] For the view of the Spanish diplomat Francis Vargas against this plan, see *CT* XIII/1, 178–182.

[3] M. Lossen, *Briefe von Andreas Masius* (Leipzig 1886), p. 119.

[4] In addition to the evidence in *HJ* 54 (1934), 411ff., cf. C. Gutiérez, "Una edición española en 1553 de los decretos conciliares tridentinos," *EE* 28 (1954), 73–105.

submitted to the cardinals for their consideration at the beginning of December 1554,[5] but before it could be given a final polishing Julius III died on 23 March 1555.

Seripando's judgment, that Julius neither promised nor achieved Church reform ("nec dixit nec fecit"), sprang from the disappointment of a reform zealot, but it is too severe.[6] Numerous notes in the acts of reform, in the Pope's own hand, testify to his personal interest. Among the twenty cardinals he created were such splendid men as Puteo, Dandino, Bertano, and the Pope's nephew, Nobili, but there was also the totally unworthy adopted son of his brother Baldovino, Innocenzo Del Monte. Julius had encouraged reform bishops by grants of full apostolic authority. At the beginning of 1554 he issued a list of only fourteen bishops who, needed for service in the Curia, were permitted to remain in Rome; the others were to go to their dioceses. But to reform circles these measures seemed inadequate; they expected more.

On the death of Julius III the reform party proved to be strong enough to take advantage of the approximately equal balance between the two political factions in the College of Cardinals and thus to secure the tiara for one of their own. Neither the imperialists nor the French could expect to rally the two-thirds majority for one of their candidates. Furthermore, the leading candidate of the French, Ippolito d'Este, who was wholly a Renaissance figure, damaged rather than promoted his own candidacy through his intrigues. Hence the imperialist faction, led by Sforza, contrived to carry the election, after a four days' conclave (6–10 April 1555), of the most ardent of all the reform cardinals, Cervini, who was all along acceptable to the French.

Marcellus Cervini, born at Montepulciano near Siena in 1501, was a Christian humanist and patristic scholar, and as tutor of Paul III's nephews had been raised to the purple as early as 1539. Though not in continuous residence, he had conscientiously cared for his sees (first Nicastro, then Reggio-Emilia, and finally Gubbio). As legate at the Council he had retained the Pope's confidence, even after he had fallen out with Alessandro Farnese over the latter's unscrupulous family politics. In his decision not to change his name and to be known as Marcellus II is discerned his wish to remain as Pope what he had been before. In a suggestion for his administration, which he had solicited, appeared the deeply moving sentence: "For twenty years people have talked about reform and openly admitted that it is necessary, but nothing has

---

[5] For the final redaction of the Bull "Varietas Temporum," with the views of the cardinals, see CT XIII/1, 291–312.

[6] CT II, 449; cf. H. Jedin, *Seripando* II (Würzburg 1937), 34f.

resulted."[7] Marcellus II was resolved to take vigorous action; hence he is the first Pope of the Catholic Reform. His directives to the *Signatura* and the Penitentiary to render no decisions until the reform bull should appear demonstrate his firm will to act. But he died on 30 April, "shown rather than given" to the Church. However, the breakthrough had been achieved.

In the next conclave (14–23 May 1555) the same constellation within the College of Cardinals produced a similar result. The election of Puteo, pushed by the imperialists, misfired and in his place was chosen a declared enemy of the Spaniards, the dean of the College, Gian Pietro Carafa, a man of irreproachable life but dreaded for his severity. Paul IV, born in 1476, belonged to one of the great baronial houses of the Kingdom of Naples. Through the efforts of his uncle, Oliviero Carafa, of decisive influence in the reform deliberations under Alexander VI, he had obtained as early as 1505 the archiepiscopal see of Chieti and had discharged the duties of nuncio in England and Spain. Then, having renounced his benefices, he had founded the Theatine Order with Cajetan of Thiene. A judgment drawn up in Venice in 1532 on defense against Protestantism in Italy and certain proposals of the "Consilium de emendanda Ecclesia," notably with regard to the establishment of the Roman Inquisition, presented his radical views, wholly different from the thought of the humanistic reform movement.

Despite his advanced age the tall, ascetic, but passionate Neapolitan was in full possession of his physical and mental powers. Profoundly conscious of the majesty of his office and an adherent of the papal theory in its most extreme form, an autocrat by character and conviction, he abandoned the political neutrality maintained by his predecessors and sought, without regard to the changed situation, to rule Christendom after the manner of a Pope of the High Middle Ages. The unilateral nature of his reform measures, curiously incompatible with his blind nepotism, lessened their efficacy and provoked a reaction harmful to the progress of the Catholic Reform.

By family tradition and his own observations a violent opponent of Spanish rule in Naples and of Spanish ascendancy in Italy, he permitted himself to be led into an alliance with France and a war against Spain by Carlo Carafa, his energetic and ambitious, but morally worthless nephew. The war laid bare the military and political impotence of the Papal State, led to defeat near Paliano, and ended with the Peace of Cave on 12 September 1557. When England entered the war against

---

[7] *CT* XIII/1, 315. G. M. Monti, *Studi sulla Riforma Cattolica,* pp. 38ff., attributes the memorandum to an unknown Theatine.

France on the side of the Emperor, Paul deprived Pole of his position as legate for England and replaced him with the Franciscan Petow, who, however, declined the post.

The death on 17 November 1558 of Pole and of Mary the Catholic and the accession of Elizabeth I brought a sudden end to the Catholic Restoration in England. Though long since determined to renew the schism, the new Queen deferred the break with Rome until her throne was firm. In February 1559 she recalled her ambassador from Rome, on 23 March the bill concerning the royal supremacy—with "head" replaced by "governor of the Church of England"—was accepted against the opposition of the bishops, especially of Archbishop Heath of York, and in the summer of 1559 the Anglican liturgy was reintroduced. All the bishops, except the Bishop of Llandaff, refused to recognize the new establishment and were deposed. But still Paul IV pronounced no ecclesiastical censure on Elizabeth.

The situation of the Church in Poland was likewise threatened. The Nuncio Luigi Lippomani found the existence of Catholicism in great danger, for a part of the higher nobility, headed by Prince Radziwill, were Protestant-minded, the greater number of the bishops, apart from such praiseworthy exceptions as the Primate Dzierskowski of Gniezno, were compliant or even, like Bishop Uchanski of Chelmno, suspected of leaning toward Protestantism, and King Sigismund Augustus was powerless. The royal demands for the marriage of priests, the lay chalice, Mass in the vernacular, and a national council were flatly rejected by the Pope. A provincial council held in Lowicz banished, at least for the moment, the danger of a national council. At the Diet of Petrikow (1558) Lippomani's successor, Mentuato, in whose retinue was Peter Canisius, managed to prevent the issuing of resolutions directed against the Catholic religion but not to stop the continuation of Protestant propaganda. The Pope had to be content with appealing to the King's conscience through a letter of admonition.

In Germany the Protestant estates of the Augsburg Confession gained recognition by imperial law through the Religious Peace of Augsburg of 25 September 1555. To replace the Nuncio Delfino, who had been recalled to Rome, the Pope had sent Lippomani to Augsburg with instructions to do all in his power to prevent the ratification of the Peace of Passau. Since the Emperor was known to be opposed to the Passau concessions, the nuncio sought to induce him to restrict the power transferred to his brother Ferdinand. These measures were inadequate. That the Pope misjudged the situation of the Church in Germany in general as well as the significance of the Religious Peace is made clear by his charge to the Nuncio Delfino, returning to Germany, to induce King

Ferdinand I and the Duke of Bavaria to withdraw their consent. The expected papal protest was not lodged.[8] The Pope's exasperation with the Habsburg brothers was so intense already in 1556 that their deposition was discussed in all seriousness. When, following his brother's abdication, Ferdinand I had himself crowned at Frankfurt and assumed the title of "Roman Emperor elect," without having obtained the Pope's consent or even having admitted the Nuncio Antonio Agustín, Bishop of Alife, to the election proceedings, the Pope denied him recognition, alleging as his reason, derived from medieval canon law, that both the resignation of Charles V and the election of Ferdinand I were subject to papal scrutiny, and that the election was invalid because of the participation of three Protestant Electors.[9] Before Ferdinand I was able to refer the quarrel to the Diet of Augsburg and thereby introduce into a totally changed world the medieval struggle between *Sacerdotium* and *Regnum*, the Pope died.

As in politics, so also in the ecclesiastical sphere Paul IV followed paths different from those of his predecessors. For him the resumption of the Council of Trent was out of the question. Instead of taking up the almost completed reform bull of Julius III, he appointed a commission of some sixty cardinals, bishops, and curial officials in the spring of 1556 and considered settling, by a doctrinal decree on the question of simony, the theological considerations which under Paul III had served as a pretext for impeding the reform of the *Dataria,* the chief item in the reform of the Curia;[10] a later expansion of the commission into a papal council, on the model of the Fifth Lateran Council, was contemplated. At the same time three newly created cardinals, Scotti, Rebiba and Reumano—all in the Pope's confidence—were entrusted with the reform of the *Dataria,* and a new *Datarius* was named who seemed to give promise of finally realizing the reform of this office. But the outbreak of the Carafa War interrupted the execution of these projects, and after the Peace of Cave they were not taken up again.

The Theatines Scotti and Isacchino and the papal librarian Sirleto busied themselves at the Pope's orders with the reform of the breviary and the missal, an old concern of Paul IV and the Theatines. The reformed breviary compiled by Cardinal Quiñones, known as the "Holy Cross Breviary" from his titular church of Santa Croce and consisting

---

[8] J. Grisar, "Die Stellung der Päpste zum Reichstag und Religionsfrieden von Augsburg 1555," *StdZ,* 156 (1955), 440–462, regards a condemnation of the Religious Peace, pronounced in the Consistory of 22 August 1556 as equivalent to a protest.

[9] Cf. J. I. Tellechea Idigoras, "La renuncia de Carlos V y la elección de Fernando de Austria," *Scriptorium Victoriense,* 7 (1960), 7–78, 207–283.

[10] Acts in *CT,* XIII/1, 327–364; also *RQ* 43 (1935), 128–156.

almost exclusively of Scriptural texts, was forbidden.[11] In time the Pope proceeded ever more exclusively to extirpate with Draconian severity the grievances against which he had earlier inveighed in vain, above all to check the advance of Protestantism through stern measures of repression.

The presenting of monasteries to secular clerics *in commendam* was forbidden. Severe penalties were visited on "apostates," religious who had abandoned the common life without authorization or with a surreptitiously obtained indult. Any who were apprehended in Rome were taken into custody. Public immorality and acts of violence, once an everyday occurrence, were suppressed by excessively severe decrees of the governor of the city. Renaissance Rome changed its image. In an effort to impose a halt to the spread of Protestantism, at least where the Church's arm reached, Paul created and sharpened two weapons: the Index of Forbidden Books and the Inquisition.

The preventive censorship prescribed by the Fifth Lateran Council had proved to be ineffective. State as well as ecclesiastical authorities began, in view of the annually swelling flood of publications of the religious innovators, to forbid books that had already appeared, individually or by drawing up lists. Between 1544 and 1556 the Sorbonne published four such catalogs; the most painstaking was that of the theological faculty of Louvain, issued at the Emperor's command in 1546. The Louvain catalog contained a list of forbidden versions of the Bible in Latin, Greek, German, and French, an alphabetically arranged index of Latin books, and finally lists of German and French books. Because of its rich contents it was adopted and expanded by the Spanish Inquisition in 1551. For Venice the Nuncio Giovanni della Casa had drawn up a similar catalog in 1549. On 21 December 1558, Paul IV withdrew all previously granted licenses for the reading of forbidden books, commanded that they be surrendered, and the next year published the first Papal Index of Forbidden Books. In arrangement and content it was modeled on the Louvain catalog, but in severity it far surpassed it. In addition to the writings of the reformers, all the works of Erasmus, whatever their content, were forbidden, all works on occult sciences (palmistry, geomancy, etc.), all publications issued in the preceding forty years without the name of the author or publisher, and finally, regardless of content, all products of sixty-one printers specified by name, fourteen of whom were from Basel alone.[12] The great ma-

---

[11] J. A. Jungmann, "Warum ist das Reformbrevier des Kardinals Quiñonez gescheitert?" *ZKTh* 78 (1956), 98–107.

[12] Text in H. Reusch, *Die Indices Librorum prohibitorum des 16. Jh.* (reprint, Nieuwkoop 1961), pp. 176–208, preceded by the most important earlier lists; M. Scaduto, "Lainez e l'Indice del 1559," *AHSI* 24 (1955), 3–32.

jority of editions of the Bible and of the Fathers fell under the prohibition, and many scholars saw themselves deprived of their scientific tools. From Germany Peter Canisius wrote: "Even the best Catholics disapprove of such rigor."[13]

Almost passionately the Pope addressed himself to the improvement of the Roman Inquisition.[14] It acquired precedence over all other offices and its general delegate Ghislieri had the same powers as the cardinals of the Inquisition. Its jurisdiction was extended to embrace moral lapses of the greatest variety. The doctrinal tribunal became a bureau of morals. Death sentences were passed more frequently than before, and no one was safe. Cardinal Morone, highly meritorious because of Church reform and the Council, was cast into the Castel Sant'Angelo on suspicion of heresy. As time went on, the Pope's interest was more exclusively focused on the Inquisition, whose sessions he never missed.

The Pope was rudely aroused from the most serious self-deception when, early in 1559, the Theatine Isacchino apprised him of the scandalous doings of his nephews, the Cardinal Carlo Carafa and his brother, who, following the downfall of the Colonna, had been made Duke of Paliano. Paul IV banished them from Rome, but the moral damage could not be repaired. He had refused to pay any heed to the wishes of the great powers in his creations of cardinals. But the more he had enriched the college with such distinguished men as Ghislieri, the Theatines Rebiba and Reumano, and his great-nephew Alfonso Carafa, so much the more flagrant appeared the crimes of his nephews.

The Pope was lacking in moderation. He took such pains with the nomination of bishops that in October 1558 no fewer than fifty-eight sees were vacant. The undeniable tightening of all ecclesiastical standards, noticeable, for example, in the dispensation procedures of the *Signatura*,[15] was a great forward step on the road of Catholic Reform, but the narrow-mindedness and harshness of his measures and his prolonged blindness in regard to his nephews made his pontificate a great disappointment. After his death (18 August 1559) the repressed hatred for the Pope and his family exploded in the destruction of the headquarters of the Inquisition and the abuse of his statue on the Capitol.

---

[13] *P. Canisii Epp. et Acta,* ed. O. Braunsberger, II, 377; an instruction for the drawing up of the Index, issued in February 1559, edited by A. Mercati in *Miscellanea Hist. Pont.* 19 (Rome 1945), 95–102.

[14] The Jesuit Bobadilla had recommended this reorganization; cf. P. Leturia, "Los recuerdos presentados por el Jesuita Bobadilla al recién elegido Paulo IV," *Miscellanea A. De Meyer* II (Louvain 1946), 855–869.

[15] Examples in *RQ* 42 (1934), 311–332. According to a statement of the Venetian Ambassador Soranzo, the revenues of the *Dataria* dropped as a consequence from between 30,000 and 40,000 ducats per month to 6,000: E. Alberi, *Relazioni degli ambasciatori veneti* II, 4, 87.

The success of the reform movement in the papal elections of 1555 did not yet mean definitive victory over the crisis. The apostasy was making apparently irresistible progress. England was about to be lost to the papacy once more. The Religious Peace of Augsburg had been concluded in the Empire. In France and Poland the position of the Church was shaky. She still held her own, unchallenged, only in the two southern peninsulas, thanks to the support furnished by the secular arm. But the very relations of the papacy with Spain, which became the leading European power in the Peace of Câteau-Cambrésis in 1559 between Spain, England, and France and regarded itself as the protector of the Church, were almost ruptured. Only one relatively small remnant of the Western Christian Family of Nations felt itself bound with its head. The Catholic Reform had now reached this head; the resumption and conclusion of the Council of Trent enabled it to embrace the members.

CHAPTER 37

Pius IV and the Conclusion of the Council of Trent

The first two periods of the Council of Trent were occasioned by the German religious split and were oriented to it. Their dogmatic decrees were the reply of the Church's teaching authority to the doctrinal concepts of Luther and Zwingli and the ecclesiastical communities based on them. Their reform decrees were an as yet inadequate endeavor to meet the Protestant Reformation with a Catholic Reform. Politically, both sittings constituted a part of the great plan, projected by Emperor Charles V and approved and supported by Paul III and Julius III, of rendering the German Protestants impotent. The third and final period of the Council was motivated by ecclesiastical events in France, where Calvinism seemed about to gain for itself the most heavily populated country of the West, the one that had been the intellectual leader into the late Middle Ages. Had this goal been achieved, the Catholic Church would have been definitely confined to the two southern peninsulas of Europe.

After a dramatically developing conclave of over three months (5 September to 26 December 1559), in which the three about evenly matched factions of Spanish, French, and Carafa cardinals confronted one another, the Milanese Gianangelo Medici, candidate of Duke Cosimo of Florence, was elected. Pius IV, who had been employed mostly in the administration of the Papal State and made a cardinal by Paul III in 1549, was not an outstanding politician, and in his entire previous career he had not belonged to the reform party. His closest adviser was Cardinal Morone, just liberated from Sant'Angelo, and in matters of high politics he usually followed the counsels of the crafty Duke Cosimo, who had come to terms with the Spanish power in Italy. Affairs of government were conducted by the Pope himself and not by his still youthful nephew, Carlo Borromeo, whom he elevated to the cardinalate on 31 January 1560. It was not until after the death of his brother Federigo on 19 November 1562, which profoundly affected him, that Carlo became the chief promoter of reform at the papal court. The Pope's "new course" implied a break with the Carafa regime and a return to the Church policies of Paul III and Julius III. Yielding to the bitterness against the Carafas, he had proceedings instituted against Cardinal Carlo Carafa and his brother, the Duke of Paliano, and had them put to death on 5 March 1561. Numerous repressive measures of Paul IV were annulled and the paths laid out by his predecessors were again followed. Not a reform assembly at Rome but the continuation of the still suspended Council of Trent lay in the administrative program of the new Pope.

His very first contacts with the great powers made it clear that two basically different views confronted each other. Philip II of Spain, undeniably the mightiest monarch in Europe since the Peace of Câteau-Cambrésis, regarded the envisaged Council as the continuation of the two earlier sittings, whose decrees, even though they had not yet been ratified by the Pope, might not be changed. The Emperor and France, on the other hand, wanted a new council: Ferdinand I, out of regard for the German Protestants, who feared a continuation of Trent would endanger the permanence of the Religious Peace of Augsburg; France, in the hope of finding in a new council, in default of other means, a settlement with the rising Huguenot faction. The Bull of Convocation, "Ad ecclesiae regimen," of 29 November 1560,[1] favored the first view by referring to the lifting of the suspension, without excluding the second in using the expression "announcement" (*indictio*). None of the parties was satisfied and all hesitated in accepting the bull.

The Protestant estates, meeting at Naumburg, gave the Nuncio Commendone another flat refusal. Ferdinand I replied ambiguously to the Nuncio Delfino, who had been sent to him and to South Germany, and in this he was supported by France, where, since the death of Francis II and the downfall of the Guises, the Queen Mother, Catherine de Médicis, was acting as regent for her second son, Charles IX. This niece of Clement VII, to maintain herself in power, was playing off the two religious factions and their political exponents against each other

---

[1] *CT* VIII, 104–107.

and, advised by the Chancellor Michel de L'Hôpital, was seeking an accommodation. While as yet no definitive acceptance had been given by the powers, the Pope in February and March 1561 named five legates for the Council: the highly cultured and politically experienced Ercole Gonzaga, who in the last conclave had come close to gaining the tiara; the canonist Puteo; the one-time general of the Augustinians, Seripando, now Archbishop of Salerno; Stanislaus Hosius, expert in controversial theology, Bishop of Warmia, and nuncio to the Emperor; and the curial canonist Ludovico Simonetta, who possessed the Pope's full confidence. Later the papal nephew Sittich von Hohenems was substituted for the ailing Puteo.

Though Gonzaga and Seripando were in Trent from 16 April 1561, it was not certain that the Council would actually meet until the autumn. To be sure, Philip II, once he had obtained the Pope's assurance in a secret brief of 17 July that the Council was to be regarded as the continuation of the earlier sittings, had commanded the Spanish bishops to prepare for the journey. And Ferdinand I had finally promised to appoint envoys. But events in France decided the issue. The assembly of the clergy at Poissy in August–September 1561—really a national council—and the religious discussion there with the Calvinists under the leadership of Theodore Beza made clear the danger of the country gradually drifting toward Calvinism. The Pope did not allow himself to be deceived by the palliating reports of the Cardinal Legate Hippolytus d'Este and exerted himself to have the Italian bishops go to the Council. The first Spaniards also made their appearance at the end of the year. It was possible to have the opening on 18 January 1562, in the presence of 109 cardinals and bishops, four abbots, and four generals of Orders. Compared with this numerous gathering, said Seripando, the opening session of 1545 was like that of a diocesan synod.

The legates endeavored to put aside the continuing controversy concerning the relationship to the earlier sittings by submitting on 11 March twelve reform articles which were inspired by a memorandum of some of the Italian bishops.[2] Article 1 took up the still unsettled problem of the duty of residence; in the meantime a vigorous literary controversy concerning its basis had blazed forth.[3] In the course of the debate, which began on 7 April a minority, consisting of Spaniards and

[2] *CT* VIII, 378f. The ninety-three Italian reform articles in *CT* XIII/1, 607–612. L. Castano, "Pio IV e la Curia Romana di fronte al dibattito tridentino sulla residenza," *Miscell. Hist. Pont.* 7 (1943), n. 12.

[3] The Dominicans B. Carranza and D. Soto, following Cajetan, and the future Jesuit Francis Torres spoke in favor of the *ius divinum;* opposed were A. Catharinus and T. Campeggio. A collection of all relevant treatises appeared at Venice in two volumes in 1562; cf. *CT,* XIII/1, 655.

reform-zealous Italians, declared that the obligation of residence on the part of the bishops is of divine law and hence not an object of the Pope's dispensing power. The other side vigorously attacked this *ius divinum* argument as prejudicial to the papal primacy. When the legates brought this main point to a vote in the general congregation of 20 April, sixty-seven Fathers expressed themselves in favor of the *ius divinum,* thirty-five against it, and thirty-four left the decision to the Pope.[4] Alarmed by the reports of the Legate Simonetta, the Pope on 11 May forbade the continuation of the debate on residence, rebuked Gonzaga and Seripando for opening the question, and considered recalling them.

The "residence crisis," basically a crisis of confidence among the legates and in their relations with the Pope, produced a rather long standstill in the conciliar discussions. In the nineteenth session on 14 May the Council received the "orators" of the King of Spain, the Republic of Venice, and Duke Cosimo; in the twentieth session on 4 June, the ambassadors of France and of the Catholic Swiss cantons. Those of the Emperor had been in Trent since spring. On 6 July these last presented to the legates the Emperor's carefully prepared reform project, which, among other things, asked for the grant of the chalice to the laity and the marriage of priests.[5] The conciliar discussions again got under way only after Gonzaga had held out the prospect of a resumption of the debate on residence in connection with the consideration of holy orders. The Pope dropped his plan of recalling the two senior legates but never again gave them his full confidence. The conciliar crisis had not really been overcome, but only postponed.

The decision for the continuation, which the Spanish Ambassador Pescara had again demanded, was actually made through the decree of the twenty-first session, 16 July 1562, on Communion under both species;[6] it reflected the Eucharistic decree of 1551. The petition for the grant of the lay chalice, now supported by Duke Albrecht of Bavaria,[7] was referred to the Pope after a long debate and over the strong opposition of the Imperial Ambassador, Bishop Draskovich of Pécs.

In the succeeding debate on the sacrificial character of the Mass, its relationship to the Sacrifice of the Cross was worked out. The chief point of controversy was whether the Last Supper was a propitiatory sacrifice. The "August draft,"[8] submitted on 6 August, suppressed the

---

[4] S. Ehses, "Eine bewegte Abstimmung auf dem Konzil von Trient," *Miscellanea Franz Ehrle* III (Rome 1924), 224–234.

[5] *CT,* XIII/1, 661–685.

[6] *CT,* VIII, 698ff.

[7] A. Knöpfler, *Die Kelchbewegung in Bayern unter Herzog Albrecht V* (Munich 1891), pp. 106ff.

[8] The August draft in *CT* VIII, 751–755; the September draft, *CT* VIII, 909–912.

passage on the subject in the schema of 1552. But as the opponents of this doctrine—including Seripando, the Archbishops of Granada and Braga, and the Bishop of Modena—continued to constitute a minority in the debate, it was restored in the "September draft" and passed into the definitive wording of the decree on the Mass, which was approved in the twenty-second session on 17 September 1562.[9] The Sacrifice of the Mass is the reenacting and recalling of the Sacrifice of the Cross and the applying of its fruits, a propitiatory offering for the living and the dead, offered by the same Christ who offered the Sacrifice of the Cross (*una eademque hostia, idem nunc offerens*) but by means of priests and performed in a different manner. The Canon of the Mass is free of error. It is allowed to celebrate Mass in honor of the saints, though of course the Sacrifice is offered to God alone. Private Masses are lawful, and the use of the vernacular in the Mass is not practicable (*non expedire*). A corresponding reform decree abolished some of the many abuses listed by a conciliar commission.[10] The second reform decree of Session XXII was directed against abuses in the diocesan sphere but it did not seriously take into account the reform memoranda which the Spanish and Portuguese bishops had been submitting since spring nor the Emperor's reform project.[11] The ambassadors accredited to the Council by the secular powers, except those sent by Venice and Florence, entered a protest with the legates on 16 September against the prevailing manner of handling the question of reform.

The lingering crisis of the Council became acute when on 13 November Charles de Guise, the "Cardinal of Lorraine," arrived in Trent with thirteen French bishops. After a briefing on the position of the conciliar business he espoused the side of the opposition and became its leader. The discussions initiated on the Sacrament of holy orders in the general congregation of 13 October and the new decree on residence,[12] submitted on 6 November, converged on the problem of primacy-episcopacy. The institution of the episcopal office *de iure divino,* contained in the schema of 21 January 1552, had been suppressed in the proposal given

---

[9] *CT* VIII, 959–968.

[10] *CT* VIII, 916–921, extraordinarily informative for the pre-Tridentine Mass procedure.

[11] In addition to the Italian reform articles (cited in footnote 2) and the Emperor's reform project (footnote 5) there were on hand a reform memorandum of the Spanish bishops, presented at the beginning of April 1562 (*CT* XIII/1, 624–531); a memorandum composed at the same time by the Portuguese Ambassador Mascarenhas (ibid., pp. 632f.); a petition of Portuguese bishops of 6 August (ibid., pp. 725ff.); a request of the Archbishops of Granada and Braga in regard to the conferring of benefices of 17 August (ibid., pp. 727–730).

[12] *CT* IX, 135ff.

to the theologians on 18 September,[13] and the new decree on residence traced the obligation to divine *and* human law. The French and Spanish opposition, supported by a part of the Italians, urged "episcopalism"[14] to solve the problem, while the *zelanti,* encouraged by Rome and supported in the body of legates by Simonetta, aimed at a strictly curialist decision. Though Gonzaga and Seripando exerted themselves from December 1562 to February 1563 to discover compromise formulas,[15] the opposing camps became so adamant that the Council was disabled, the Catholic powers began to intervene, and the collapse of the Council seemed a distinct possibility. To keep the Council busy, the legates inaugurated particular congregations on the Sacrament of matrimony on 9 February 1563. Cardinal Guise, extremely bitter over the obstinacy of the *zelanti,* obtained from the Emperor, during a visit to Innsbruck, a serious letter of admonition to the Pope not to resist reform by the Council and to impose restraint on the *zelanti.* The conflict, hitherto constantly avoided, over the relation of the Pope to the Council, seemed at hand.

The great crisis in the Council was not overcome until, following the deaths of Cardinals Gonzaga (2 March) and Seripando (7 March), a new president was acquired in Morone, who enjoyed the Pope's full confidence. Hurrying to Innsbruck, he first pacified the Emperor. In Trent he pushed aside the collateral government of Simonetta and the *zelanti,* ignored a *Practica* for the settlement of the crisis which the former nuncio to France, Bishop Gualterio of Viterbo, had devised along with the French ambassador to the Council, Ferrier, and finally, in a way not fully clarified, won Cardinal Guise to a compromise which was accepted in a conference of Council notables on 6 July. Previously, in an autograph of 1 April, the Pope had convinced the King of Spain of his determination to continue the Council and lead it to a conclusion and of the sincerity of his reform intentions.

Now, after an interruption of almost ten months, it was possible to hold on 14 July 1563 the twenty-third session,[16] which became the turning point of the Council. The compromise proposed by Cardinal Morone and accepted by the opposition amounted to this, that the Council limited itself to rejecting, in canons 6 to 8 on holy orders, the Protestant teaching on the episcopal office while avoiding a definition of

---

[13] *CT* IX, 6.

[14] The term "episcopalism" is used here in a broad sense to denote the strengthening of the authority of bishops; hence it does not imply a denial of the papal primacy.

[15] A classification of the compromise formulas then discussed, in *CT* IX, 226–241.

[16] *CT* IX, 620–630. For its antecedents: G. B. da Farnese, *Il sacramento dell'Ordine nel periodo precedente la Sessione XXIII di Trento* (Rome 1946); F. García Guerrero, *El Decreto sobre residencia de los obispos en la tercera asamblea del Concilio Tridentino* (Cádiz 1943).

the papal primacy. In the remaining canons and in the appended doctrinal chapters were defined the institution of the priesthood of the New Law by Christ and the distinction of major and minor orders. The new decree on residence increased the penalties for neglect of the obligation and left the *ius divinum* unmentioned. No less important was the final chapter (chap. 18) of the reform decree: the bishops were obliged to establish seminaries for the training of future priests.[17]

On 30 July 1563 Morone handed to the orators of the powers for their comments a reform proposal in forty-two articles, prepared chiefly by the Uditore Paleotti. It took into account numerous postulates from the reform memoranda under consideration by the Council, including the French petition of 3 January 1563, but so constructed that none of the current claims of the Curia were abandoned in principle. In the general congregations from 11 September to 2 October twenty-one articles,[18] taken from this schema but slightly revised, were debated. Previously, during July and August, in the debate on matrimony, the declaration of the nullity of clandestine marriages and the question, relevant to the practice of the Greeks, of divorce by reason of adultery had evoked spirited arguments.[19] The fourteenth session on 11 November 1563, embraced three decrees, the significance of which cannot be too highly esteemed. A dogmatic decree affirmed the sacramental nature of matrimony, its indissolubility, and the Church's right to establish matrimonial impediments. The reform decree "Tametsi" made the validity of future marriages dependent upon the observance of the *forma tridentina,* the exchange of the marriage promises before the authorized parish priest and two or three witnesses; it also ordered priests to keep registers of baptisms and marriages.[20] The general reform decree, in twenty-one chapters, contained norms for the method of nominating bishops, including the conducting of processes for obtaining information,[21] for the holding of triennial provincial councils and annual diocesan synods and for episcopal visitations, and finally for

---

[17] J. A. O'Donohoe, *Tridentine Seminary Legislation. Its Sources and Its Formation* (Louvain 1957). H. Jedin, "Domschule und Kolleg. Zum Ursprung der Idee des Trienter Priesterseminars," *TThZ* 67 (1958), 210–223.

[18] *CT* IX, 748–759.

[19] The eleven canons on matrimony of 20 July in *CT* IX, 639f; the twelve revised canons of 5 September, ibid., pp. 760ff.

[20] H. Jedin, "Das Konzil von Trient und die Anfänge der Kirchenmatrikeln," *ZSavRGkan* 32 (1943), 419–494; H. Börsting, *Geschichte der Matrikeln von der Frühkirche bis zur Gegenwart* (Freiburg 1959) 94–104; M. Simon "Zur Entstehung der Kirchenbücher," *ZBKG* 28 (1959) 129–142 (on the Nürnberg plan for a church book in the 14th cent.)

[21] H. Jedin, "Die Reform des bischöflichen Informativprozesses auf dem Konzil von Trient," *AkathKR* 116 (1936), 389–413.

cathedral canons and appointments to parishes. Throughout, where pastoral considerations required, the rights of bishops were extended at the expense of exempt Orders and corporations by grant of apostolic authority.

Even after Cardinal Guise, most of the Spaniards, and the imperialists had been won to Morone's policy of reconciliation, an increasingly dwindling minority of Spaniards, notably the Bishop of Segovia,[22] held firm in their opposition and were supported by Count Luna, who had been introduced on 21 May 1563 as ambassador of Philip II. Luna was against the legates' exclusive right of proposition[23] and Morone's exertions for a quick conclusion of the Council; the reform project introduced by the president, he said, neither satisfied the Spanish postulates of reform nor took sufficient consideration of the German situation. Cardinal Morone overcame these and other obstacles adduced by the powers against a speedy closing of the Council when he threatened the consideration of a proposed "reform of the princes," that is, the complaints of the bishops against the interference of the secular powers in the ecclesiastical domain.[24] During November the rest of the great reform schema was discussed.

The final session was set for the middle of December, but at the news that the Pope was ill it was advanced to 3 December and continued on 4 December (the twenty-fifth session).[25] It included decrees on controverted doctrines not so far considered: purgatory, the veneration of saints and their relics, images,[26] and indulgences, all of which could be debated only briefly on 2 and 4 December. The reform of the Orders, sketched under Julius III, preserved the character of a skeleton law which did not annul their existing constitutions but merely modified them in specific points. It contained norms for the acceptance of new members and on the novitiate, poverty, and the inclosure of nuns.[27] Despite the bristling opposition of Alessandro Farnese and other cardi-

---

[22] H. Jedin, "Die Autobiographie des Don Martin Perez de Ayala," *Spanische Forschungen* I/11 (1955), 122–164.

[23] The brief of 8 May 1563 (*CT*, IX, 956, n. 8), in which the Pope had declared his willingness to drop the legates' exclusive right of proposition, was not executed because of Morone's energetic remonstrances (Šusta, IV, 71f.); in Session XXIV the legates explained that the formula "proponentibus legatis" of the decrees did not limit the freedom of speech permitted up till then at ecumenical councils.

[24] L. Prosdocimi, "Il progetto di Riforma dei principi al Concilio di Trento," *Aevum* 13 (1939), 3–64.

[25] *CT* IX, 1077–1110.

[26] H. Jedin, "Entstehung und Tragweite des Trienter Dekrets über die Bilderverehrung," *ThQ* 116 (1935), 143–188, 404–429.

[27] H. Jedin, "Zur Vorgeschichte der Regularenreform Trid. Sessio XV," *RQ* 44 (1936), 231–381.

nals,[28] the cardinals too were included in this session's second reform decree, which in chapter 1 sketched the duties of bishops. In addition, it contained directions for the conducting of the visitation (chap. 6) and the administration of the Church's hospitals,[29] a reorganization of the *ius patronatus* (chap. 9) and of the proceedings against concubinaries (chap. 14). The revision of the Index of Paul IV, for which a conciliar commission had been appointed early in 1562, the reform of the missal and the breviary, also dealt with, and the drawing up of a catechism for parish priests could not be brought to completion. The Council decided to turn over to the Pope the preliminary work "so that it can be finished and put into effect by his authority."

After all the decrees of the two earlier periods under Paul III and Julius III had been once more read aloud, all the bishops present confirmed their acceptance over their own signatures. The decrees were signed by six cardinals, three patriarchs, twenty-five archbishops, 169 bishops, seven abbots, and several generals of Orders. At the close of the session Cardinal Guise proposed acclamations in honor of the three Popes of the Council, Emperors Charles V and Ferdinand I, and all who had contributed to the success of the work. All present cried out, "We are resolved always to profess the faith of the Sacred Ecumenical Council of Trent, always to observe its decrees!"

The importance of the Council of Trent in ecclesiastical and secular history is based on two achievements. First, it precisely defined the Catholic deposit of faith against the reform doctrines, though not in every controverted point, for the definition of the papal primacy and of the concept of the Church, the most violently challenged teachings, was prevented by episcopalism and Gallicanism. The Council did not aspire to settle theological differences of opinion within the Church. Second, to confront the Protestant Reformation the Council set up a Catholic Reform. Not a *reformatio in capite et membris* in the late medieval sense, it admittedly disregarded many postulates of the reform movement—it bypassed the reform of the Curia—but it did eliminate the most crying abuses on the diocesan and parochial levels and in the Orders, effectively strengthened the authority of the bishops, and gave priority to the demands of pastoral care.

However, the Council's reform achievement could become operative only if the papacy took charge of the execution of the decrees. In accord with the resolution contained in the last session, Morone sought papal

---

[28] J. Birkner, "Das Konzil von Trient und die Reform des Kardinalskollegiums unter Pius IV," *HJ* 52 (1932), 350ff.

[29] H. Jedin, "Zwei Konzilsdekrete über die Hospitäler," *Atti del primo congresso italiano di Storia Ospitaliera* (Reggio–Emilia 1957), pp. 376–385.

confirmation of the conciliar decrees. This was given orally on 26 January 1564, and, after strong curial resistance had been overcome, in writing on 30 June by the Bull "Benedictus Deus," antedated 26 January. To prevent the exploitation of the Council against the Pope, Pius IV reserved to himself the interpretation of the decrees and on 2 August 1564 instituted a congregation of cardinals for their authentic interpretation and enforcement. They were made of obligation outside Rome from 1 May 1564.[30] By the end of March they were available in print in the official version edited by Paul Manutius, but the plan of also publishing the conciliar acts was dropped. Peter Canisius delivered texts of the decrees with accompanying papal briefs to the German bishops. In Italy the enforcement began when on 1 March 1564 the Pope urged the bishops present in Rome to take up residence in their dioceses. At the same time the first diocesan synods and episcopal visitations were held, as prescribed by the Council, and the mendicant Orders brought their constitutions into conformity with the regulations of Session XXIV. In the Bull "Dominici gregis," of 24 March 1564, the Index of forbidden books, prepared at the Council, was published.[31] The Pope complied with the petition for the lay chalice by allowing it, with certain reservations, to the bishops of the six provinces of Germany, the provinces of Esztergom and Prague, and several exempt dioceses on 16 April 1564.[32] A brief summary of the dogmatic results of the Council, the "Professio Fidei Tridentinae," was prescribed on 13 November 1564, to be taken by bishops, religious superiors, and doctors. Thereby the Council made a distinct impression in the domain of belief.

Paul III had begun but not pushed the reform of the Curia as a result of the Council, but with the breakthrough of 1555 a longer reprieve was clearly impossible. Since Pius IV insisted that the reform of the administration was not within the competence of the Council, he had to take up the task himself. In 1561 and 1562 appeared in rapid sequence decrees on the reform of the Rota, the Sacred Penitentiary, the Chancery, and the *Camera,* and thus on 29 June 1562, the Pope could assert: "We have announced and accomplished a strict reform of Our court."[33] A bull of 9 October 1562 was directed against abuses that had occurred

---

[30] On the beginnings of the Congregation of the Council cf. P. Prodi, *Paleotti,* pp. 193ff. (the older literature is there given) and S. Tromp, "De primis secretaris S. Congr. Concilii," *Gr* 40 (1959), 523–527.

[31] New material concerning the procedure in A. Rotondo, "Nuovi documenti per la storia dell' Indice dei libri prohibiti 1572–1638," *Rinascimento* II/3 (1963), 145–211.

[32] G. Constant, *Concession à l'Allemagne de la Communion sous les deux espèces,* 2 vols. (Paris 1923).

[33] Sickel, *Röm. Berichte* II, 118.

in the last conclave.[34] The chief representative of the new spirit was the Cardinal-Nephew Borromeo, concerning whom Soranzo, the Venetian ambassador, reported: "He in his own person does more good at the Roman Court than all the decrees of the Council together." In actuality, the renewal of the papacy formed the basis for the enforcement of the Tridentine decrees, which in turn led to the successful self-assertion of the Church in the Counter Reformation. The forces of renewal now began to operate, but the crisis had by no means been surmounted.

[34] *Bull Rom* VII, 230ff.; cf. *RQ* 42 (1934), 306–311.

The Papacy and the Implementation of the Council of Trent (1565–1605)

CHAPTER 38

Personality and Work of the Reform Popes from Pius V to Clement VIII

A glance at the contemporary religious map of Europe makes clear the gravity of the crisis in which the Church found herself at the conclusion of the Council of Trent. Only the inhabitants of the Italian and Iberian peninsulas had remained positively Catholic. In Western Europe the Calvinist offensive threatened to sever France from Rome, as it had already succeeded in doing with Scotland. In Rome there was still reluctance to admit that England, by renewing the schism, had definitely entered the ranks of the Protestant powers. The Scandinavian North was gone; in Poland kingship and Catholicism were wavering. In the Empire the Religious Peace of Augsburg had not stopped the progress of Protestantism: in North Germany the last footholds of the ancient Church were lost, in the South and West she was asserting herself with difficulty in the ecclesiastical states and under the protection of the houses of Wittelsbach and Habsburg, but Austria, Bohemia, and Hungary remained exposed, and the Swiss Confederation continued to be split on the question of religion.

That the Church overcame the crisis and at the end of the century stood forth renewed and strengthened is due to the carrying out of the Council of Trent by the papacy. Because of the efforts of three outstanding Popes its decrees did not remain a dead letter but permeated the life of the Church. The methods employed by them were as different as their personalities, but the goal was identical: the regeneration of the Church in the spirit of the Catholic Reform.

Pius V

In the conclave following the death of Pius IV (20 December 1565 to 7 January 1566), which was, according to Pastor, "freer from external influences than any other in the memory of man," Cardinal Borromeo prevented the election of Ricci, skillful in business and favored by Duke Cosimo, and of Alessandro Farnese, and, after the rejection of the candidates whom he promoted (Morone and Sirleto), succeeded, in an understanding with Farnese, in having the Dominican Michael Ghislieri elected, who was, in the judgment of the Spanish Ambassador Requesens, "the pope demanded by the times."[1] A remarkable opinion, if it is borne in mind that the new Pope Pius V owed his rise to that enemy of Spain, Paul IV. But it was an accurate appraisal, for he differed from his patron by thinking and acting in all spheres from the religious viewpoint and shunning both the blind nepotism and the pomp of the Carafa. His court was as austere and frugal as was the Pope himself. In the severity of his measures against blasphemy, immorality, and the profanation of holy days and in his zeal for the Inquisition he did not yield place to the Carafa Pope. It was said of him that he sought to turn Rome into a monastery. The sentences of the Inquisition were made known and carried out in public *autos-da-fe*.[2] Among the "obstinate" and the relapsed who were condemned to death were Clement VII's former private secretary, Pietro Carnesecchi, and the humanist Aonio Paleario, both of whom had been acquitted under Pius IV. The number of Inquisition processes soared; in Venice alone eighty-two were carried out under Pius V. The Bull "In Coena Domini," to be read aloud on Holy Thursday, in which the ecclesiastical censures reserved to the Pope were listed, was given a new and stricter form in 1568.[3]

These repressive measures, in comparison with the work of positive reconstruction, are of meager importance in the total picture. The catechism for parish priests, begun by the Council of Trent, was brought to completion chiefly by the Dominicans Egidio Foscarari, Leonardo Marini, and Francisco Foreiro, put into classical Latin by the humanist Giulio Poggiani, and, following another revision by Cardinal Sirleto, appeared in print in September 1566.[4] The reformed Roman breviary (1568) and the Roman missal (1570), on which had cooperated, besides Marini and Sirleto, the Theatine Scotti and Paul IV's great-nephew, Antonio Carafa, were prescribed for use in all dioceses and Orders

---

[1] A *mi juicio es el Cardenal que en los tiempos de agora convendria que fuese papa* (J. J. I. Döllinger, *Beiträge* I, 579). The comprehensive report (ibid., pp. 571–588) provides an excellent characterization of the whole College of Cardinals.

[2] Relevant extracts from the diary of the master of ceremonies Firmanus in Pastor, XVII, 400–404.

[3] K. Pfaff, "Beiträge zur Geschichte der Abendmahlsbulle vom. 16.–18. Jh.," *RQ* 38 (1930), 23–76.

[4] P. Paschini, *Il Catechismo romano del Concilio di Trento* (Rome 1923; reprinted in P. Paschini, *Cinquecento romano e riforma cattolica* [Rome 1958], pp. 33–89).

which had not had breviaries and missals of their own for the preceding 200 years.[5]

But far more decisive than these supplements to the Council was the Pope's will of steel to enforce the Trent reform decrees and to tolerate no return to the former lax procedure in regard to dispensations, which would have detracted from their validity. A reform of the Sacred Penitentiary, restricting its competence to the internal forum, definitely sealed off this source of limitless abuses.[6] Observing the Tridentine regulation, the Pope visited the Roman patriarchal basilicas in person; he entrusted the visitation of the parishes to a commission to which Borromeo's vicar, Ormaneto, belonged. The "Confraternity of Christian Doctrine," transplanted from Milan to Rome, received such a powerful impetus from Philip Neri and his companion Pietra that people designated "the Roman Reform as the daughter of the Milanese."[7] In an effort to push the Tridentine Reform energetically, at least in Italy, in 1571 the Pope appointed apostolic visitors for the bishoprics of the Papal State and the Neopolitan Kingdom,[8] while Marini was given a corresponding assignment for twenty-four dioceses of Central and North Italy, and, later, Ragazzoni and Castelli for the Adriatic sees. Convinced that the Tridentine reform decrees were the instrument of Church renewal throughout the world, he took pains to have them published also in mission lands, as far as Mexico, Goa, and the Congo.[9] Numerous provincial and diocesan synods applied the decrees on the diocesan level, many seminaries were founded, and the rules of Trent's

---

[5] H. Jedin, "Das Konzil von Trient und die Reform des Römischen Messbuchs," *Liturgisches Leben* 6 (1939), 30–66; also, the supplement of B. Opfermann in *E Lit* 72 (1958), 214f.; H. Jedin, "Das Konzil von Trient und die Reform der liturgischen Bücher," *E Lit* 59 (1945), 5–38; E. Focke–H. Heinrichs, "Das Kalendarium des Missale Pianum," *ThQ* 120 (1939), 383–400, 461–469; A. P. Frutaz, "Contributo alla storia del Messale promulgato de San Pio V nel 1570," *Problemi religiosi*, pp. 187–214.

[6] E. Göller, *Die päpstliche Poenitentiarie* II/2, 98ff.; *Bull Rom* VII, 750ff.

[7] A. Monticone, "L'applicazione de Concilio di Trento a Roma," *RSTI* 7 (1953), 225–250, 8 (1954), 23–48; G. Franza, *Il Catechismo a Roma dal Concilio di Trento a Pio VI nello zelo dell'Archiconfraternita della Dottrina Christiana* (Alba 1958).

[8] With the statements of Pastor (XVII, 218ff., and XIX, 76ff.) compare P. Villani, *La Visita Apostolica di Tommaso Orfini nel Regno di Napoli 1566–1568* (Rome 1957); later: A. Bason, "La diocesi di Aquileja secondo la Visita Apostolica dell'anno 1584," *Studi Aquileji offerti a G. Bus* (Aquileia 1953), pp. 433–451; G. Vitezic, *La Prima Visita Apostolica post-tridentina in Dalmazia (1579)* (Rome 1957); on the visitations of the Jesuit Possevino in the lands of the Gonzaga, cf. M. Scaduto, *Arch. stor. lombardo* VIII/10 (1960), 336–410.

[9] C. Bayle, "El Concilio de Trento en las Indias espanolas," *RF* 131 (1945), 257–284.

decree on regulars were made even stricter in regard to the inclosure of nuns.[10]

The pattern of a vigorous and effective application permeating all aspects of Church life was furnished by Charles Borromeo through his activity at Milan (1565–84). By his personal efforts, his visitations, and his legislation at eleven diocesan and six provincial synods (1565, 1569, 1575, 1579, 1582), he became, in Pastor's words, "the paragon of a Tridentine bishop." The regulations he issued for the daily routine and manner of life of his household[11] were evidence of the new spirit: a *praefectus spiritualis* took charge of the spiritual life of the group. A seminary was established in Milan for the training of priests with several minor seminaries attached, among them one for late vocations. He intensified and improved the care of souls by dividing the extensive diocese into twelve districts, each under a trusted deputy. The Jesuits and the Theatines obtained colleges; the schools of Christian Doctrine, organized by the priest Castellino da Castello, counted more than twenty thousand pupils in 1595. Borromeo visited in person even the most remote Alpine valleys of his diocese and still found time to travel from place to place in his suffragan sees, such as Bergamo, in his capacity as apostolic visitor. When in 1582 the *Acta Ecclesiae Mediolanensis*—a condensation of the entire work of reform—appeared, one hundred copies were ordered in Lyons, eleven in Toledo. The eagerness of the tireless archbishop, expending himself in the apostolate to christianize all facets of life in his diocese, led to serious conflicts with the Spanish viceroys Requesens and Ayamonte, so that for a while it appeared doubtful that the Pope, now Gregory XIII, would support him vis-à-vis the Spanish state Church. His presence in Rome, where the measures of the "zealot" of Milan had many opponents, restored the situation. The acts of the fourth provincial council were ratified and a papal brief vindicated the archbishop before the Milanese who chafed under his strictness.

Borromeo was not the unique embodiment of the Tridentine episcopal ideal. A decade after his death Cardinal Valier of Verona cautioned Borromeo's successor Federigo against copying the example of his great model in all things.[12] Cardinal Paleotti pursued different paths in his see of Bologna; and eventually Francis De Sales, whose

---

[10] The list of synods (Pastor, XVII, 215f.), as Pastor himself remarks, needs to be revised, for the zenith of synodal activity occurs in the pontificates of Gregory XIII and Sixtus V. For the Bull "Circa Pastoralis Officii" on inclosure, see *Bull Rom* VII, 447–450.
[11] *Acta Eccl. Mediol.* II (Milan 1599), 811–825.
[12] A. Valerius, "De cauta imitatione sanctorum episcoporum," Mai S, VIII, 89–117; P. Prodi, "Lineamenti dell'organizzazione diocesana in Bologna durante l'episcopato del Card. Paleotti," *Problemi religiosi*, pp. 323–394.

activity in Geneva belongs to the following century (1599–1622), set up a new episcopal ideal of humanistic breadth. But it is doubtful that the mountain of abuses could have been leveled without Borromeo's "steely consistency," capable of being intensified into hardness.

Pius V blazed a new trail in the nomination of bishops by instituting a commission of his own for examining candidates. Among the twenty-one cardinals he created were such distinguished men as Antonio Carafa, Santorio, the Dominican general Giustiniani, the Franciscan Felice Peretti, the Theatine Burali. But what was decisive was that Pius V excluded the slightest vacillation in affirming the Tridentine Reform. The Pope's death on 1 May 1572 was suffused with the glory of the victory over the Turks at Lepanto on 7 October 1571, achieved by the fleet of the Holy League with Spain and Venice which he had laboriously brought into being in 1570. He was beatified in 1672 and canonized in 1712.

Gregory XIII

His successor, the canonist Ugo Buoncompagni, originally a curial official, did not possess the ascetical severity and unflinching consistency of his predecessor, but his long pontificate (1572–85) was no less significant for the carrying out of the Council of Trent, in which he had taken part, and the consolidating of the Catholic Reform. Gregory XIII owed his unusually speedy election on 13 May 1572 to the intervention of Philip II. But his frank recognition of Spanish hegemony did not prevent him from defending, with moderation, ecclesiastical jurisdiction in Milan and Naples and even in Spain against the Spanish state Church.[13] In 1576 he concluded, with a mild verdict, the trial of Archbishop Carranza of Toledo, indicted by the Spanish Inquisition, whom Pius V already had summoned to Rome.[13a] Jealously concerned for his independence, he allowed only a restricted influence on his decisions to even his most intimate adviser, his private secretary, Toloemo Galli, the "Cardinal of Como." In the application of the Tridentine norms he was more open than his predecessor to considerations of ecclesiastical politics. In order to bind the dynastic interests of the House of Wittelsbach to the

---

[13] P. Prodi, "San Carlo Borromeo e le trattative tra Gregorio XIII e Filippo II sulla giurisdizione ecclesiastica," *RSTI* 11 (1957), 195–240, with information on the earlier literature.

[13a] A comprehensive collection of sources is Fray Bartolomé Carranza, *Documentos Históricos,* ed. I. I. Tellechea Idigoras, 3 vols. (Madrid 1962–1966); in addition there are numerous detailed studies by the author, of which, "Melchior Cano y Bartolomé Carranza, dos Dominicos frente a frente" *HS* 15 (1962) 5–93, touches upon a particularly critical point.

security of Catholic property rights in Northwest Germany he allowed the worldly Ernst of Bavaria to accumulate eventually five bishoprics, in flagrant violation of the Tridentine prohibition of pluralities.

Gregory's chief merit was to have transformed the nunciatures into instruments of Church reform. They had in the past never been exclusively diplomatic agencies, but now their ecclesiastical duties moved so far into the foreground that a generation later it could be claimed: "On them depends to a great extent the restoration of religion, worship, and ecclesiastical government."[14] To the existing permanent nunciatures at the Catholic courts—the Emperor, Spain, France, Portugal, Poland, Venice, Florence, Savoy—were added nunciatures, expressly for reform, in Upper Germany (Ninguarda and Porzia), Switzerland (Bonhomini), and Lower Germany (K. Gropper), which carried out duties like those of the apostolic visitors in Italy and were the origin of the permanent nunciatures in Lucerne (1579), Graz (1580), and Cologne (1584). The view, widespread under Paul III and his successors, that Germany was lost to the Church, was now abandoned. The "German Congregation," formed by Pius V and comprising experts on German affairs, such as Cardinals Otto of Augsburg, Madruzzo, Morone, Delfino, and Commendone, acquired a clear picture of conditions and from 1573 coordinated relevant measures.

Since the enforcing of the Tridentine decree on seminaries encountered serious difficulties in the imperiled lands, Gregory XIII encouraged the expanding of existing Roman colleges to care for the training of clerics and founded new ones. The Jesuits' Roman College was accommodated in an imposing new structure and richly endowed; it still bears his name. The Collegium Germanicum was united with the Hungarian College and through generous donations enabled to support 100 students, from whom were to emerge capable leaders for the German Church, still suffering from a serious lack of priests. Like the German College, the English College, founded in 1579, was entrusted to the Jesuits. The Greek Collegio Sant'Atanasio, a Maronite, and an Armenian college were intended to provide a center in Rome for the Eastern Churches in communion with the Holy See. By virtue of these educational foundations Gregory XIII inaugurated a development of incalculable significance: Rome, long a center of ecclesiastical administration, became likewise a center of theological scholarship and of the training of clerics for the Universal Church.

Finally, identified with the name of Gregory XIII is the reform of the Julian Calendar, projected long before under Sixtus IV, Leo X, and Clement VII. Now, after the views of numerous scholars had been

---

[14] Cf. Pastor, XIX, 59–65.

obtained, agreement was reached by a commission under Sirleto's presidency on the basis of the proposals of the brothers Giglio, and on 24 February 1582 the work was concluded in the papal Villa Mondragone near Frascati.[15] The synchronization of the astronomical with the calendar year was assured by dropping ten days (5–14 October 1582) and introducing a new rule for leap years. The introduction of the Gregorian Calendar indicated the extent of papal authority. The Catholic states accepted it. The Protestant states did not follow suit for more than a century, despite the support of the astronomers Brahe and Kepler; the Greek Orthodox world waited until the twentieth century.

Sixtus V

Like that of 1565–66, the conclave after the death of Gregory XIII (4 April 1585) was virtually free from the influence of the great powers. Cardinal Medici, supported by the French against Farnese, succeeded in having the Friar Minor Felice Peretti of Montalto elected on 24 April 1585, and thereby brought a towering personality to the highest office in the Church. Sixtus V (1585–90) combined in himself the strictly ecclesiastical outlook of Pius V, who had raised him to the purple in 1570, with the statesmanlike gifts of a Paul III, which the papacy needed even more than in Paul's day if it was to maintain its independence. His inflexible sovereign will impressed its features on the Roman Curia and on the City of the Popes for centuries. Persuaded that the papacy's worldwide activity presupposed order in the Papal State, he ruthlessly suppressed the brigand disorder that had flourished in the time of Gregory XIII and so successfully restored the papal finances that he left in Castel Sant'Angelo a treasure of some four million gold *scudi*. His most important contribution to the Catholic Reform was the reorganization of the Roman Curia.

Yielding to the firm wishes of the Popes, the Council of Trent had waived the *reformatio capitis*. But the existing organs of government—the plenary meeting of the cardinals (Consistory) and the central administrative offices handed down from the Middle Ages (Chancery and *Camera*)—though meanwhile purged of the grossest abuses, were no longer adequate for the mounting tasks of the reform Popes. Ever since the Catholic Reform had gained a foothold in Rome, the Popes had proceeded to depute the weightiest tasks to commissions of cardinals, several of which—the Roman Inquisition (1542), the Congregation of the Council (1564), the Congregation of the Index (1571), the Congregation of Bishops (1572)—had, because they were permanent, already

[15] *Bull Rom* VIII. 386ff.: Pastor. XIX. 283–296.

acquired administrative authority, whereas others were dissolved on the completion of their assignments. By a bull issued on 22 January 1588, Sixtus V created fifteen permanent congregations of cardinals with carefully circumscribed competence and administrative character. Six directed the government of the Papal State. The others tended to the business of the Universal Church—Inquisition, Index, the Council, Bishops, Regulars, the Consistory, the *Signatura Gratiae,* Rites, and Vatican Printing Press.[16] From 1588 on the participation of the cardinals in the government of the Church was discharged in the congregations. The Consistory declined in importance, as did the Chancery, which functioned henceforth only as a dispatching office. The claim to corule, pressed by a numerically small oligarchy of cardinals in the late Middle Ages and even under the Renaissance Popes, was definitively destroyed. At the same time the number of cardinals, limited to twenty-four by the Council of Constance, was fixed at seventy—six cardinal bishops, fifty cardinal priests, fourteen cardinal deacons—and a new list of titular churches and deaconries was drawn up.[17] The Pope filled the vacancies by creating thirty-three new cardinals.

The closer union of the members with the head was promoted by the new arrangement of the visit to Rome on the part of bishops (*visitatio liminum*), dated 20 December 1585.[18] The bishops of Italy, the adjacent islands, Dalmatia, and Greece were obliged to make their report in Rome every three years; for most of the other countries of Europe, in particular the Empire, France, and Spain, the interval was set at four years, for those farther away at five, and for those overseas at ten years. On the occasion of the visit a report on the state of ecclesiastical life (*Relatio status dioecesis*) was to be submitted in a definitely prescribed form. The "status reports," presented in increasing numbers from the turn of the century, provide, though frequently in colors too rosy, many particulars for diocesan statistics that would not otherwise be available. At that time they frequently constituted the point of departure for papal reform instructions. In this way the steps taken by the Pope became a "turning point and permanent factor of the Catholic Reformation" (Schmidlin).

Obsessed with a passion for building, Sixtus V undertook to make Rome, by means of imposing buildings and of a carefully supervised city

---

[16] *Bull Rom* VIII, 985ff.; Pastor, XXI, 247ff.

[17] *Bull Rom* VIII, 808ff. (3 December 1586). Jerome Manfredus, *De perfecto cardinali S.R.E.* (Rome 1584) sketched a likeness of a cardinal and dedicated it to Gregory XIII.

[18] J. Schmidlin, *Die kirchlichen Zustände in Deutschland vor dem Dreissigjährigen Kriege nach den bischöflichen Diözesanberichten an den Heiligen Stuhl,* 3 parts (Freiburg 1908–10), on the Bull "Romanus Pontifex," I, XVIIIff.; further literature in Fink, *Vat. Archiv.* 120.

planning, the most beautiful city in Europe and at the same time the center of the world. The cupola of Saint Peter's was completed by Giaconio della Porta; together with the obelisk set up in the Piazza San Pietro and the palace designed by Domenico Fontana, it is still for every Roman pilgrim the distinctive landmark of the Eternal City. The tortuous complex of buildings at the Lateran Basilica, though sacred because of a millennium of history, had to make way for a new construction. The principal church of the Jesuits, the Gesu, begun in 1568 and erected according to the plans of Vignola and Giaconio della Porta, was consecrated on 25 November 1584, the first great monument of Roman Baroque architecture. The Chiesa Nuova of the Oratorians was under construction. The medieval city, hitherto confined to the bend of the Tiber, reached out again to the hills which had been built up in Roman imperial days but now lay desolate. On the Quirinal Gregory XIII had begun to construct in a more healthy location a new residence, which was finished by Paul V a generation later, and he had a new street built to connect the Lateran with Santa Maria Maggiore. Sixtus V laid out a connecting street from the Pincio to Santa Maria Maggiore, where he erected a grandiose burial chapel for himself and his patron, Pius V. Other newly laid out streets facilitated the pilgrimage to the seven principal churches, a custom revived by Philip Neri. The crowning of the columns of Trajan and Marcus Aurelius with the statues of the Apostles Peter and Paul symbolized the Pope's aims for the construction of a new Baroque Rome, which quickly made the plans sketched by Bufalini (1551) and Du Perac (1577) obsolete. Rome had become a "new city," whose progress in the epoch of the Catholic Reform left far behind all other cities of Europe.[19]

The limits to the creative aims of this great Pope, to whom are due also the new construction of the Vatican Library and the establishment of the Vatican Press, became apparent in his solution of a scholarly task which the Council of Trent had planned but had not achieved—the revision of the Vulgate Bible. For decades the learned Sirleto had been doing preliminary work for the revision of both the Greek and the Latin texts of the Bible. The commission set up by Sixtus V for the revision of the Vulgate, to which, among others, Cardinal Carafa belonged, took great pains but proceeded too slowly to suit the impatient Pope. He had them turn over the data to him and through arbitrary manipulations so

---

[19] Delumeau, *Vie économique et sociale de Rome* I, 358. The description of the building activity of Sixtus V in Pastor, XXII, 202–312, is to be compared with the section "Rome at the close of the Renaissance" in Pastor, XIII, 356–427. For the publisher Franzini's guides to Rome, appearing from 1588 in numerous editions and embellished with woodcuts, cf. L. Schudt, *Le guide di Roma* (Vienna–Augsburg 1930), pp. 31ff.

altered the sacred text that the edition, which appeared in print on 2 May 1590, had to be recalled after the Pope's death on 27 August 1590, though it had already been sent to twenty-five princes and the accompanying bull of introduction had been published.[20] A new commission, set up by Gregory XIV and headed by Cardinal Colonna, eliminated the crudest blunders. At Robert Bellarmine's suggestion the edition thus rectified was published by Clement VIII in 1592 as the *Sixto-Clementina*.

The Tridentine generation died out with three popes who followed one another in rapid succession; all of them had personally taken part in the Council. Urban VII (15–27 September 1590), Gregory XIV (5 December 1590–16 October 1591), and Innocent IX (29 October–30 December 1591) had cooperated actively, as bishops or nuncios, in the carrying out of the Council decrees: Gian Baptist Castagna as Archbishop of Rossano and nuncio at Madrid under Pius V, Miceolò Sfondrato as Bishop of Cremona, Gian Antonio Facchinetti as Bishop of Nicastro and nuncio at Venice. The pious but ailing Gregory XIV continued the Council's reform work by regulating the procedure for determining the qualifications of candidates for the episcopacy, but, influenced by his inexperienced nephew, Paul Emilio Sfondrato, he squandered a considerable part of the treasure amassed by Sixtus V through hopeless subsidies to the French Catholic League.

Clement VIII

Like the three preceding ones, the conclave of 10–30 January 1592 was strongly influenced by Spain. Though unable to carry the election of its preferred candidate, the intellectually outstanding but harsh Santorio,[21] it did achieve that of Ippolito Aldobrandini, who was equally acceptable though far weaker. Clement VIII (1592–1605) disappointed Spanish hopes, however, when, after much hesitation, he granted absolution to Henry IV of France despite the powerful opposition of Philip II. Thereby the papacy recovered its political freedom of movement, was enabled to act as mediator in the arranging of the Franco-Spanish Peace of Vervins (1598), and, on the extinction of the direct line of the House

---

[20] The thesis that the bull was really published was defended by P. M. Baumgarten, *Neue Kunde von alten Bibeln*, 2 vols. (Krumbach 1922–1927) against C. A. Kneller and again in the essay "Die Bibelbulle Sixtus' V," *ZKTh* 52 (1928), 202–224; 59 (1934), 81–101, 268–290, and may be regarded as proved. The earlier literature (Le Bachelet, Amann, Höpfl) is in Seppelt, IV, 521, and also in P. Paschini, *G. Sirleto ed il Decreto tridentino sull'edizione critica della Bibbia* (Lecco 1923).

[21] The informative *Autobiografia di Mons. G. A. Santori*, ed. G. Cugnoni (Rome 1890).

of Este, recovered the papal fief of Ferrara and incorporated it into the Papal State.[22]

In his person Clement VIII embodied the episcopal ideal of the Catholic Reform. He led the austere life of a devoted priest and zealous bishop, made a monthly pilgrimage on foot to the seven principal churches, heard confessions in Saint Peter's for hours at a time during the Jubilee Year, made the visitation of the patriarchal basilicas and of several monasteries and hospitals. He chose Baronius as his confessor and honored Philip Neri as a father. Nevertheless, in his pontificate the movement of renewal began to lose verve and the universal character which it had received from Pius V and his two immediate successors. A new revision of the Index of Forbidden Books (1596) omitted Bellarmine's works but it struck heavily at Jewish literature. In 1593 the Republic of Venice surrendered the apostate Dominican Giordano Bruno to the Roman Inquisition, which sent him to the stake on 17 February 1600, following his relapse into his views, which were contrary to Catholic doctrine and which he had repeatedly recanted, as late as 5 April 1597[23] The quarrel which had erupted between Dominicans and Jesuits on the question of grace Clement left undecided, and he was unable to make up his mind in regard to promulgating the new collection of decretals, which was completed and was supposed to bear his name. Though as a former nuncio in Poland he was in no sense politically inexperienced, the conscientious but indecisive Pope abandoned the conduct of affairs almost entirely to his nephews, Cincius and Peter Aldobrandini, and threw the papal finances into disorder by excessive gifts to his family.

Despite these weaknesses of the Aldobrandini Pope the Jubilee Year of 1600 turned out to be a triumph for the regenerated papacy. The previous Jubilee of 1575 had drawn hundreds of thousands of pilgrims to Rome, especially from all over Italy, and renowned preachers, such as the Jesuit Francisco de Toledo, the Capuchin Lupus, and the Friar Minor Panigarola, had given the pilgrimage the character of a popular mission. When, on 31 December 1599, Clement VIII opened the Holy Door, 80,000 persons were present. The total number of pilgrims was estimated at 1.2 million. In order to accomodate at least a portion of the teeming masses, the Hospice of Santa Trinita dei Pellegrini, founded by Philip Neri, was enlarged. In order to gain the indulgence fifteen churches had to be visited by the foreign pilgrims, thirty by the Ro-

---

[22] B. Barbiche, "La politique de Clément VIII a l'égard de Ferrare en Novembre et Décembre 1597 et l'excommunication de César d'Este," *MAH* 74 (1962), 289–328.
[23] The extract taken before the summer of 1597 from the acts of the trial in A. Mercati, *Il Sommario del processo di G. Bruno* (Citta del Vaticano 1942); ibid., pp. 46–53, a well-balanced judgment of Bruno's personality.

mans. The Pope made sixty visits, frequently washed the feet of poor pilgrims, and invited them to his table. He received processions of pilgrims in the Cortile del Belvedere. All classes of society were represented: the Dukes of Bavaria and Lorraine, the viceroy of Naples, Cardinals Andreas of Austria and Dietrichstein. How a German prelate found the new Rome a few years later (1612–13) is clearly described in the *Raiss uf Rom* by Bishop Aschhausen of Bamberg.[24]

A generation had sufficed to change the face of the Church. Following the close of the Council of Trent the Popes had carried its decrees like a banner and had gathered and encouraged the religious forces at hand. The papacy's authority was restored, if not throughout the medieval *Respublica Christiana,* at least within the peoples that had remained Roman Catholic. The restoration of papal power by means of the Council of Trent was not, as claimed by Vergerio, Sarpi, and other anticurial writers,[25] a sly trick of power-hungry curialists, but the natural result of the Catholic Reform, sought sincerely though not always with strict consistency and complete success.[26] The new centralization, replacing the fiscally oriented late medieval centralization, was based on religious and spiritual foundations. The papacy had given the norms of Trent validity. One Bible, the Vulgate; one liturgy, the Roman; one Law Code guaranteed unity and effected a far greater uniformity of Church life than the pre-Tridentine Church had known. But the Tridentine Reform was no mere restoration of the Middle Ages. In almost all its manifestations it displayed anti-Reformation characteristics. From the affirmation of its own special nature it drew the strength for self-renewal and self-assertion.

[24] Pastor, XIX, 197–214, XXIV, 269–280; Ch. Hautle, *Des Bamberger Fürstbischofs J. G. von Aschhausen Gesandtschaftsreise 1612–13* (Tübingen 1881).

[25] P. P. Vergerio maintained this view in the fictitious "Consilium quorundam episcoporum Bononiae congregatorum" (1553) and in the "Actiones duae secretarii pontificii (1556)," in F. Hubert, *Vergerios publizistische Tätigkeit* (Göttingen 1893), pp. 284f., 299f. P. Sarpi developed it in his *Istoria del Concilio Tridentino* I/1; cf. Jedin, II, 3ff.

[26] Bellarmine's sharp criticism of the imperfect enforcement of the Council of Trent is found in the memoranda in Le Bachelet, *Auctarium Bellarminianum* (Paris 1913), pp. 513–518 and 518ff. (1600–1601) and 533ff. (1612).

CHAPTER 39

Self-Assertion of the Church in Western and Eastern Europe

From the close of the Council of Trent the Catholic Reform had been canalized and coordinated—it was virtually identical with the enforcement of the Tridentine decrees under papal leadership. Proceeding from the medieval view that the secular arm must cooperate, the Popes exerted themselves, though not always to the same degree, to secure the acceptance of the Council by the state, successfully in Spain, the Spanish Netherlands, and Poland, unsuccessfully in France. The two "religious wars" of the period, in which political as well as religious power struggles were decided—the Huguenot Wars and the Revolt of the Netherlands—ended at the turn of the century. The French monarchy and the southern Netherlands were saved for the Church; the northern Netherlands were lost. The Anglican state Church was consolidated in England, Calvinism in Scotland; only in Ireland did the majority of the people remain Catholic. The return of the Swedish King John III and his son Sigismund to the Church cost the latter his throne. In Poland, recently recovered, Catholic Reform made progress and raised hopes of a union with the Russian Orthodox Church.

Spain and the Netherlands

Under Philip II (1556–98), sincerely religious and conscientious but indecisive and aloof, Spain was the Church's strongest support and the leading European power. It was only after detailed consideration that he decided to accept the Council's decrees, with the restrictive clause "without prejudice to the rights of the crown." These included the *placet* for papal dispensations, the *recursus ab abusu*—the right to appeal to the secular power against abuses of the spiritual power—the autonomy of the Spanish Inquisition, and the *patronato* in the colonies. It would, however, be unfair to condemn the "ecclesiastical establishment" of Philip II for its numerous interventions in the sphere of Church jurisdiction and to disregard entirely the King's zeal in effecting the Catholic Reform when this work encountered resistance, chiefly from exempt canons and Orders, and sought support in Rome. The papal nuncios, who included Castagna (later Pope Urban VII), Ormaneto, and Speciano—the last two were colleagues of Borromeo[1]—were in a difficult position

[1] N. Mosconi, *La Nunziatura di Spagna di Cesare Speciano 1586–1588* (Brescia, 2nd ed. 1961), pp. 25ff.

whenever they had to champion papal complaints about state interference with the Church.

Even though the Tridentine reform decrees by no means complied with all the desires of the Spanish episcopate, the bishops, at the royal command, set a good example to all other countries by promulgating them in provincial and diocesan synods. Provincial councils were held at Toledo, Salamanca, Granada, Zaragoza, and Valencia as early as 1565–66. For that of Toledo Juan de Avila composed a bulky memorandum in which the modifications desirable for Spain were proposed. Naturally, the enforcement of the decrees was a slower process. For example, the diocese of Pamplona did not obtain a "ley fundamental" until the diocesan synod of 1590,[2] and in Coria, where a reform synod of 1537 continued to have validity, the enactments of the synod of 1606 constituted "la major fuente de restauracion tridentina hasta dos siglos mas tarde." Several Tridentine seminaries, the founding of which started early in Spain,[3] could not be maintained because those liable for contributions opposed giving them. Thus the seminary of Coria, founded in 1579, obtained a sound financial basis only through a grant by Bishop Galaza in 1603. The unreformed Orders had to put up with serious interference based on Pius V's briefs of 2 December 1566 and 16 April 1567. The Conventual Franciscans were forced to adopt the Observance. The Mercedarians, Trinitarians, and Carmelites accepted the papal decrees. The Premonstratensians successfully resisted a forced union with the Hieronymites.[4] The monasteries of the Benedictine Congregation of Tarragona were subjected to apostolic visitations but resisted the reform bull of 1592.[5] The close union of Church and state acquired an impressive expression in the Hieronymite monastery of the Escorial, built by Philip II in 1563–84, in which the King's cell overlooked the high altar.

Long before the ecclesiastical organization of the mother country had been carried further,[6] three new ecclesiastical provinces had been established in the Spanish Netherlands on 12 May 1559, at the request of Philip II: Cambrai, with Tournai, Arras, Saint-Omer, and Namur as suffragans; Mechlin, with Antwerp, 'sHertogenbosch, Ghent, Bruges,

[2] J. Goni Gaztambide, *Los Navarros en el Concilio de Trento y la Reforma tridentina en la diocesis de Pamplona* (Pamplona 1947), pp. 181–301; F. S. Pedro Garcia, "La Reforma del Concilio de Trento en la diocesis de Coria," *HS* 10 (1957), 273–299.

[3] D. Mansilla, "El seminario conciliar de S. Jeronimo de Burgos," *HS* 7 (1954), 3–44, 359–398; for Coria, *HS* 10 (1957), 286f.

[4] J. Goni Gaztembide, "La Reforma de los Premonstratenses espanoles del Siglo XVI," *HS* 13 (1900), 5–96.

[5] R. Auge, "La bulla de Clemente VIII per la Reforma de la Congregacion claustral tarraconense," *Catalonia Monastica* 2 (1929), 259–283.

[6] D. Mansilla, "La reorganizacion eclesiastica espanola del Siglo XVI," *Antologica annua* 4 (1956), 97–238.

Ypres, and Roermond; Utrecht, with Haarlem, Middelburg, Leeuwarden, Deventer, and Groningen. The imperial bishopric of Liège remained in the province of Cologne. Of the eighteen sees fourteen were new. The task of filling them was somewhat drawn out or, as in the North, became impossible, for the revolt of the Netherlands impeded the reconstruction.

The national opposition to Spanish rule was bound up with religious opposition, chiefly Calvinist. While Margaret of Parma was governor, the "Geusen" (so called from *gueux,* the beggars) had demanded the mitigation of Charles V's edicts on religion (the "placards"), the abolition of the Inquisition, and the convocation of the States General. A barbaric iconoclasm in 1566 destroyed irreplaceable works of Christian art. The "Council of Troubles," set up by the Duke of Alba, could not suppress the revolt, but the statesmanship of the governor Alessandro Farnese, Margaret's son, succeeded in having the almost wholly Catholic southern provinces break away from the Pacification of Ghent (1576). The mostly Protestant northern provinces, allied in the Union of Utrecht (1579), proclaimed their independence in 1581 and, at first under William of Orange (assassinated in 1584) and then under his son Maurice (1585–1625), carried on the war against Spain until the truce of 1609. In the States General all Catholic worship had been forbidden since 1574. The care of the still numerous Catholics was provided in an insufficient manner under the direction of a vicar apostolic in Utrecht.

The Council of Trent had been accepted by the governor, Margaret of Parma, on 11 July 1565, with the same reservations as in Spain, but the political confusion, together with the not infrequent resistance of the clergy, delayed enforcement. Definite progress came only in the governorship of the Archdukes Albrecht and Isabella.[8]

France

In France, too, the Church was engaged in a struggle for existence which was not conducive to the progress of the Catholic Reform. Like

[7] M. Dierickx, *De oprichting der nieuwe bisdommen in de Nederlande onder Filips II 1559–1570* (Antwerp 1950); for the relevant *acta* see the summary of the literature.

[8] In addition to Willcox (see the summary of the literature): G. Rolin, "L'esprit du Concile de Trente dans le statut organique de l'Archevêché de Malines en 1561," *Miscellanea De Meyer,* II, 881–894; E. Voosen, "Exécution du Concile de Trente dans la diocèse de Namur," *Revue diocésaine de Namur* 9 (1954), 321–349; E. Brouette, "La vie religieuse dans le Comté de Namur au siècle de la réforme," *Revue du Nord* 35 (1953), 233–251; H. J. Elias, *Kerk en Staat in de zudelijke Nederlanden onder de Regeering der Aartsherzogen Albrecht en Isabella 1598–1621* (Antwerp 1931). For Liège: H. Dessart, "La visite du diocèse de Liège par le nonce A. Albergati 1613–1614," *Bulletin de la Commission Royale d'hist.* 114 (1949), 1–135. E. Donkel, "Luxemburger Gutachten zu den Trienter Reformdekreten," *Rhein. Vierteljahrsbll.* 19 (1954), 119–134.

the revolt of the Netherlands, the Huguenot Wars (1562–98) were never purely a religious conflict, even while Catherine de Médicis was regent for Charles IX (1560–74), and under Henry III (1574–89) they became more and more a power struggle between the Houses of Bourbon and Guise, with Spain intervening on the side of the Catholics, England and the States General of the Netherlands on the side of the Calvinists. Correspondingly, the papal policy was straightforward when the preservation of Catholicism and the suppression of Calvinism was or seemed to be in question, but cautious vis-à-vis the political power groups, especially the League of Henry of Guise, Charles of Bourbon, and Philip II, established in 1576 and revived in 1584.

The Edict of Amboise (1563), which ended the First Huguenot War, granted Calvinists the right of worship in one town of each *baillage*. When, not satisfied with this success and supported by English money and German troops, they again took up arms, Pius V sent subsidies and a military force, only to be disillusioned when the Huguenots, several times defeated, were accorded freedom of religion in the Peace of Saint-Germain (1570). In an effort to shield her son, Charles IX, from the influence of the Huguenot leader, Admiral De Coligny, Catherine de Médicis sought to remove the latter by assassination. When this proved unsuccessful, she tried to conceal the crime by a still greater one, the Massacre of Saint Bartholomew's Day, 24 August 1572. Misled by euphemistic and misleading reports, Gregory XIII saw in this damnable act, proceeding from an unscrupulous greed for power, the thwarting of a treasonable attempt against the King and a victory over Calvinism. He prescribed a Te Deum and personally attended a thanksgiving service in the French national church of San Luigi. He played no part in the preparation and execution of the crime, which claimed between five thousand and ten thousand victims.[9]

The opposition of the Huguenots became even more bitter. In the Fifth Religious War they obtained from the weak Henry III in the Peace of Beaulieu (1576) almost complete religious freedom, but in the following year it was again restricted by the Edict of Poitiers. The danger that the French crown would devolve on a Calvinist became acute when, on the death of the younger brother of the childless Henry III, the Bourbon Henry of Navarre was recognized as his successor by the King and also by many Catholics. Though Sixtus V did not actually join the Catholic League formed against Henry of Navarre, he forever excluded him from the succession in 1585 as a relapsed heretic. The League

---

[9] The older literature in regard to Saint Bartholomew's Day (till 1923) in Pastor, XIX, 482–518; H. Hauser, loc. cit. nos. 2099–2173; S. L. England, *The Massacre of St. Bartholomew* (London 1938); P. Erlanger, *Le massacre de la Saint-Barthélemy* (Paris 1960).

gained military ascendancy and in 1588 forced Henry III to issue the Edict of Rouen, which envisaged the suppression of Calvinism. To rid himself of pressure from the League, the King a half year later procured the murder of its leaders, Henry and Louis of Guise, at Blois and allied himself with Henry of Navarre, only to be himself stabbed to death by the Dominican Jacques Clément on 1 August 1589. Charles of Bourbon, raised up as rival King by the League, died on 9 May 1590. Henry of Navarre, who as Henry IV had very quickly promised to protect the rights of the Catholic Church and who also had a strong Catholic following, found a steadily increasing recognition, particularly after he had returned to the Church on 25 July 1593. Gregory XIV and at first Clement VIII supported the League in its opposition. But when it was quite certain that Henry IV maintained the upper hand and, when, though remaining indifferent to religion ("Paris is worth a Mass"), he approached the Pope, Clement VIII condescended to absolve him under specific conditions. By the Edict of Nantes (30 April 1598) Henry IV granted to the Calvinists unrestricted freedom of conscience, access to political office, the right to worship publicly in all places where this was allowed in 1596–97 and in two places in every *bailliage,* and finally possession of 200 strongholds for eight years. These were quite extraordinary rights, but the crown and the vast majority of the people remained Catholic and once again France was a Catholic power. In politics Sixtus V had felt that in regard to Spain he was impotent, "like a fly facing an elephant." But now the papacy had again achieved a limited political independence.

The reception of the Council of Trent in France ran into strong opposition from the partly Huguenot, partly Gallican-minded, jurists of the highest tribunals, the *parlements*, in which every law valid in France had to be registered. The Calvinists Du Moulin and Gentillet denied the binding force of both the dogmatic and the reform decrees; the Gallicans Ranchin and Thou rejected only the reform measures.[10] A petition of the clergy, seconded by the Nuncio Salviati, to the Estates of Blois (1577–78), to the effect that the King might promulgate and carry out the decrees (*publier et inviolablement garder*) without prejudice to the Gallican Liberties, was unavailing, as was its renewal by the assembly of the clergy of Mélun in 1579. When the League adopted the reception of the Council in its program and the Papal Legate Morosini, at the command of Sixtus V, demanded its unconditional publication, Henry III gave in only when his cause was already lost and the assassination of

[10] A survey of the anti-Tridentine journalism so far as the historical material is concerned in V. Martin, *Le Gallicanisme et la réforme catholique* XXIIIff. (Paris 1919), and H. Jedin, *Überblick*, pp. 66–79.

Cardinal Louis of Guise excluded any agreement with the Pope. To what extent the publication of the Council by order of the state was a sign of the King's religious conviction is evident from the advice given to Henry IV by Cardinal Gondi, Archbishop of Paris: "Publish the Council of Trent!"[11] Although the clergy again presented a petition, the King, influenced by the Gallicans Harlay and Thou, did not in 1600 live up to the promise he had given through his proxies before his absolution. Gallican anti-Trent journalism—Ranchin, Thou, Ribier, Richer—was strong enough to bring about the definite denial of acceptance by the state at the Estates General of 1614.

Meanwhile, the bishops, left to themselves, had begun to carry out the Council. Shortly after his return from Trent Cardinal Charles Guise had taken the lead with the Provincial Council of Reims (1564). The assembly of the clergy at Mélun set up guidelines, on the basis of which eight provincial councils were held between 1580 and 1590. That of Aix (1585), guided by Archbishop Canigiani, was to the greatest extent under Milanese influence. Bishop La Rochefoucauld of Clermont (1585–1610), following Borromeo's example, exerted himself for the improvement of his clergy.[12] The reform will of bishops and clergy finally proved sufficiently strong to proceed without regard to the state. At the assembly of the clergy in Paris on 7 July 1615, three cardinals, forty-seven archbishops and bishops, and thirty deputies of the rest of the clergy swore to accept (*recevoir*) and to carry out (*observer*) the Council of Trent. This decision produced a powerful reform wave and formed the prelude to the steep ascent of the French Church in the next generation. Until this moment there had been, despite isolated and usually short-lived foundations, "a search for a solution of the seminary problem."[13] It was not only the known opposition to financing it that had delayed the realization of the Tridentine decree on seminaries, but also the rivalry of the universities and the Jesuit colleges and the absence of a clearly formulated ideal. In the course of the seventeenth century France finally became the leader in this field through its development of various types of priestly formation—Bourdoise, the Sulpicians, the Eudists.[14]

---

[11] V. Martin, op. cit., p. 279.
[12] Rochefoucauld composed a guide for the priestly seeking of perfection, *De la perfection de l'état ecclésiastique* (Lyon 1597, 1628); cf. Broutin, I, 44ff.; P. Gouyon, *L'introduction de la réforme disciplinaire du Concile de Trente dans la diocèse de Bordeaux* (Paris 1945).
[13] Broutin, II, 181.
[14] A. Degert, "Les premiers seminaires français," *RHEF* 2 (1911), 24–38, 129–144; G. Bonnenfant, *Les seminaires Normands du XVI au XVIII siècles* (Paris 1915); P. de Lattre, "Les Jésuits et les seminaires," *RAM* 20 (1953), 161–176.

England

By means of the Act of Uniformity of 1559—slightly mitigated by substituting "Supreme Governor" for "Supreme Head"—Elizabeth I of England had effectively renewed the Anglican Schism; the reintroduction of the *Book of Common Prayer* and the Thirty-Nine Articles of 1563 had restored the creed and liturgy of Edward VI in the English state Church. Of the sixteen bishops who had functioned under Mary the Catholic, fifteen were deposed for rejecting the Oath of Supremacy and for the most part replaced by clerics who had taken refuge on the continent during the Catholic Restoration. The overwhelming majority of the parish clergy took the oath,[15] and the laity were encouraged by the threat of considerable fines to frequent the Anglican worship. Just the same, the Queen, who was well versed in all diplomatic tricks and was supported at Rome by Spanish efforts of pacification, knew how to ward off the menacing blow until such time as her throne was secured against every assault from within.

It was not until 25 February 1570 that Pius V pronounced the major excommunication against Elizabeth I and her deposition.[16] The bull of excommunication aggravated the situation of the English Catholics all the more in that Mary Stuart, a prisoner in England since 1568, was regarded as the Catholics' claimant to the throne, and hence, on the outbreak of war with Spain, they came under suspicion of high treason. From 1581 death was the penalty for celebrating Mass, administering the Sacraments, and sheltering priests. One hundred and twenty-four priests and sixty-one lay persons were executed, including the Jesuit Campion. Another Jesuit, Gerard, was released after a long imprisonment.[17] A college was established at Douai (1568) by William Allen (cardinal in 1587, died 1594) to train priests for the extremely dangerous ministry to the English Catholics, who continued to exist despite all measures of suppression. The Jesuit Persons founded similar institutes at Valladolid and at Eu and Saint-Omer, and there were English colleges in Rome and Reims.[18] The efforts to maintain the care of souls in England were compromised by the opposition between the "Spanish" wing, whose chief was the Jesuit Persons, and the "Scottish" under Lewis. After the diocesan priests working in England had acquired a

---

[15] A list of sixty-one "recusants" of 1561 in P. Hughes, *The Reformation in England* III, 422–427.

[16] *Bull Rom* VII, 810ff.; Mirbt, n. 491.

[17] E. Waugh, *E. Campion* (London 1935); *The Autobiography of an Elizabethan* [John Gerard], ed. P. Charaman (London 1952); C. Devlin, *The Life of Robert Southwell, Poet and Martyr* (London 1956).

[18] P. Guilday, *The English Catholic Refugees on the Continent* I (London 1914); M. Hayle, *William Allen* (London 1914).

superior without episcopal consecration in the person of the Archpriest George Blackwell, who maintained good relations with the Jesuits, an anti-Jesuit minority, the "Appellants," opposed him and maintained that it was lawful to take the oath of loyalty to the Queen.

The Anglican Church was consolidated under the Archbishops of Canterbury, Parker (1559–76) and Whitgift (1583–1604). The Elizabethan establishment, attacked by the Presbyterian Cartwright, was justified and defended in the eight books of Richard Hooker's *Laws of Ecclesiastical Polity*.[18a]

The ruin of the Catholic Church in Scotland was sealed in the enactments of the Parliament of Edinburgh in 1560. The religious discussions of Aberdeen and Edinburgh and Ninian Winzet's literary defense (1562) could do nothing to alter the *fait accompli*. Queen Mary Stuart, a Catholic but morally vulnerable and finally completely isolated, was powerless against it. Archbishop Beaton of Glasgow resided in France from 1560 and the other bishops were deprived of their jurisdiction. After 1565 the Queen named the outstanding John Sinclair as Bishop of Brechin and in the following year sent an envoy to express her obedience to Pius V. But the Nuncio Laureo, dispatched by the Pope, was not allowed on Scottish soil. Following the Queen's forced but not undeserved abdication in 1567, the suppression of Catholics gained in intensity. Four priests were condemned to death for having celebrated Mass, and on 5 April 1571 the last Archbishop of Saint Andrew's, John Hamilton, was hanged for high treason. The care of the few remaining Catholics was exercised mostly by priests who had fled from England. Gregory XIII's plan to arrange that Mary's son, James VI, who had been baptized a Catholic, should be brought up as one proved to be impossible. When James took over the reins of government, he tried without success to substitute an episcopal system for the presbyterian constitution of the Scottish Church, which he detested. His cleverly feigned inclination toward Catholicism and his wife's conversion did not keep him from further increasing the penal laws against Catholics after his accession to the English throne as James I (1603–25).[19]

Only the Irish successfully resisted the introduction of the Anglican Church in the Emerald Isle. Their attachment to the ancestral faith, kept alive by native priests and by missionaries sent from Rome, was identified with the struggle against England. A landing expedition of Earl Fitzmaurice, with the support of Gregory XIII, miscarried in 1579.

[18a] See H. Marot, "Aux origines de la théologie Anglicane," *Irenikon* 33 (1960), 321–343.

[19] On James' attempts at contact with Gregory XIII and Clement VIII see Pastor, XXIV, 49–80.

Clement VIII congratulated the Catholic leader O'Neill after the victory at Blackwater (1598). Though the Catholic nobility was almost wholly exterminated and replaced by English landowners, the impoverished and repressed people held fast to the Church.

Poland, Sweden, and Russia

King Sigismund II Augustus of Poland (1548–72), whose wavering attitude had made possible the progress of Lutheranism and later of Calvinism and the anti-Trinitarians, accepted the Tridentine decrees at the urging of the Nuncio Commendone in 1564, but the "Warsaw Confederation" of the mainly Protestant nobility interceded in favor of the equality of the dissidents with the Catholics (1573). The Catholic renewal got under way with King Stephen Bathory (1575–86). Deeply Catholic, yet tolerant, and inspired by bold projects, he had the cooperation of the Nuncios Caligari and Bolognetti. The Provincial Council of Piotrkow (1577) repudiated the Warsaw Confederation and accepted the Council of Trent. Hosius, his successor Martin Cromer, Archbishop Uchanski of Gniezno, and Bishop Konarski of Poznan championed its enforcement. Bishop Karnkowski of Wloctawek founded the first Tridentine seminary. The Jesuit College at Vilna became an academy. The Jesuit Skarga made many conversions, including Prince George Radziwill, who became Bishop of Vilna and a cardinal. Jesuit colleges in Riga and Dorpat worked to recover Livonia for the Church.

The prospect of the restoration of Catholicism in Sweden seemed to be favorable when King John III (1586–92) became a Catholic in 1578, influenced by his Polish wife Catherine and also hoping to win the Polish throne. The liturgy which he introduced, the Red Book of 1576, was modeled on the Roman missal but was rejected by the Protestant clergy. The Jesuit Antonio Possevino, sent to Sweden as nuncio, realized that the recovery of the country would be impossible if the concessions demanded—marriage of priests, the chalice for the laity, Mass in the vernacular—were granted by Rome, which they were not. John's son Sigismund, raised a Catholic, had to confirm on oath before his coronation (1594) the exceptional laws demanded by the assembly of the clergy at Upsala in 1593 against Catholics, including the prohibition of public worship and exclusion from offices of state. After his departure for Poland the last traces of Catholic ritual disappeared, such as the elevation after the consecration. The nuns of the Birgittine convent of Vadstena were expelled. When Sigismund had tried without success to put down the revolt led by his uncle Charles, he was deposed (1599) and the profession of the Catholic faith was severely penalized. The great hopes connected with the conversion of the House of Vasa crumbled.[20]

The same fate befell an approach directed toward Russia. Hard pressed by the victorious Polish King, Czar Ivan the Terrible in 1581 sent an embassy to Rome to ask mediation for peace and promised to participate in the war against the Turks. Possevino did indeed negotiate a truce between Poland and Russia but in talks with Ivan he discovered no leaning toward union. The Pope, declared the Czar, was "not a shepherd but a wolf." During his stay in Moscow Possevino was kept from any other contacts by a "guard of honor." A second embassy from the Czar, in the company of which Possevino returned to Rome, confined itself to an exchange of courtesies. Disappointed by this failure, Sixtus V now supported Bathory's far-reaching plans: the conquest of Russia, which, after Ivan's death (1584), was weakened by internal dissensions, and then a concentrated assault on the Turkish Empire. They became pointless when Bathory died at the age of only fifty-four and Sigismund Vasa established himself as King against the Curia's candidate, Archduke Maximilian of Austria.

During the long reign of Sigismund III (1587–1632) Polish Catholicism grew progressively stronger.[21] About half the lost churches became Catholic again. A new elite of clergy and laity was formed in the Jesuit colleges of Poznan, Braunsberg, Vilna, Polock, and Lublin, and at the same time popular missions extended the field. The Jesuit Wujek produced a Polish translation of the Bible and a *Catholic Prayer Book* which was used for three centuries, and his confrere Skarga (d. 1612) was active as a preacher and author.[22] His book *On the Government and Unity of the Church of God under one Shepherd and the Greek Schism* contrasted the prosperity of the Church in Poland with the decline of the Orthodox Church, which was predominant in Lithuania and the Ukraine. Its intellectual center was the Academy of Ostrog, founded by Prince Constantine Ostrogski; from it came the "Ostrog Bible" in Ukrainian, of a decidedly Protestant tendency. Two synods, which the Ecumenical Patriarch Jeremias II held in connection with his journey to Moscow for the consecration of the patriarch (1589), were unable to

---

[20] Especially in the *Relatio* of Malaspina, composed in 1594–98; see Pastor, XXIV, 544ff.

[21] In the final report of Cardinal Caetani, who had lived in Poland as legate in 1596–1597, it is said: "Religio Catholica in Polonia . . . fructificat et crescit et novis quotidie haereticorum conversionibus et animarum lucris augetur" (Pastor, XXIV, 117, footnote 1).

[22] A. Berga, *Un prédicateur de la Cour de Pologne sous Sigismond III* (Paris 1916); Sommervogel, VII, 1263–1287; T. Glemma, *Piotr Kostka 1532–1595* (Thorn 1959).

settle the disputes among the Orthodox bishops. This situation is the key to the origin and fortune of the Union of Brest (1596).

As early as 1590 the four Orthodox bishops of Tuck, Chelmno, Lwow, and Przemysl had declared their readiness, under specific conditions, to break with the Metropolitan of Kiev and attach themselves to Rome. But the declaration had no sequel. A new statement of Bishops Terlecki of Tuck and Pociej of Vladimir, in Torczyn at the end of 1594, which had been preceded by conversations with Maciejowski, Latin Bishop of Tuck, was followed by discussions with the representative of the nuncio in Cracow. Even before a settlement had been reached, Prince Ostrogski's violent opposition decided the King to send Terlecki and Pociej to Rome, where on 23 December 1595 they returned to the Union of Florence. The Bull of Union allowed the Ruthenians to retain their rite; bishops were to be named by the metropolitan, who was himself to be elected by the bishops. The Synod of Brest (6–10 October 1596) accepted the union; a countersynod, held at the same time and comprising, among others, the Bishop of Przemysl and lay deputies, excommunicated the Uniates. In addition to Ostrogski, the union was resisted by a group of theologians, notably the future Ecumenical Patriarch Kyrill Lukaris, who was under Calvinist influence, and the lay brotherhoods, which had been ignored during discussions of the Synod. Their participation in the revolt (Rokosz) of 1606–08 led to their being suppressed by the state, but they were revived after the Patriarch Theophanos of Jerusalem, supported by the Cossacks, had erected a new schismatic hierarchy in 1620. Saint Josaphat Kuncewicz, Catholic Bishop of Potock, fell victim to their hatred in 1623.[23]

Recognized as such by the King alone, but not, like the Latin bishops, admitted into the Senate, the Uniates held their own under the guidance of the zealous Metropolitans Pociej and Rudzki. But they were unable to prevent persons from going over to the Latin Rite, favored by the Polish side, though this had been forbidden by the Congregation of Propaganda since 1624. The reform of the Basilians, pursued by Rudzki, went much too far in assimilating this Order to those of the Latin Rite. The Religious Colloquy of Torun, organized by King Vladislav IV in 1645 and aiming at a new union which should include the Orthodox, only deepened the estrangment. Alongside the constantly expanding Church of the Latin Rite, the Uniate Church declined more and more in importance. Its status found no improvement until the accession of the Orthodox bishops of Galicia to the union in 1681.

Shortly after the conclusion of the Union of Brest there again appeared hopes of gaining a foothold in Russia. Misled by reports of the

---

[23] E. Unger-Dreiling, *Josafat* (Vienna 1960).

Nuncio Rangoni, Paul V supported the "False Demetrius," who claimed to be a son of Ivan the Terrible and had become a Catholic. His murder on 27 May 1606, terminated the adventure. Antipathy for the Roman Church was stronger than before and became even worse when the accession of Michael Romanov to the throne in 1613 brought an end to Russia's internal troubles.

CHAPTER 40

Crisis and Turning Point in Central Europe

As the Council of Trent was finishing its work, the Catholic Church in Germany seemed to be on the point of total dissolution. The Religious Peace of Augsburg had not halted the Protestant movement. The majority of the secular princes and the great Free Cities had joined it; a large part of the nobility and of the cities in the Catholic territories had done the same. Episcopate and clergy had by no means overcome their defeatism; slight was their concern for self-reform, and their will for self-defense was weak. The more precise doctrinal clarification effected at Trent was the first step toward recovery and the prerequisite for taking the second step, which was much more difficult, namely, the implementation of the Council's reform measures, enacted virtually without the cooperation of the German episcopate and hence not adapted to the German situation.

The determining of confessional allegiance was settled by the Religious Peace of Augsburg; it was definitively and by law taken away from Emperor and Empire and transferred to the states; thus making acceptance of the Council of Trent by the Empire an impossibility. Commendone, sent as legate to the Augsburg Diet of 1566, had to content himself with an oral declaration, given in the name of the Catholic estates, that the Council's decrees would be carried out as far as possible. Nothing of the sort could be expected from the Protestant-minded, "enigmatic emperor," Maximilian II (1564–76). However, at the Regensburg Diet of 1576, to which Cardinal Morone had been sent as legate, it was possible to prevent ratification of the *Declaratio Ferdinandea,* which would have undermined both the principle contained, but not expressly formulated, in the Religious Peace—"Cuius regio, eius et religio"—and the Ecclesiastical Reservation. The significance of these for the preservation of Catholicism revealed itself even more clearly. To avoid the appearance of violating the Religious Peace, the Catholic estates maintained a cool reserve in regard to the Council.

Furthermore, even public opinion was unfavorable to Trent. Against the massive onslaught of the Lutheran Martin Chemnitz in his *Examen Concilii Tridentini*[1] only a feeble response was attempted.[2] The nobly born cathedral canons, eager before all else to maintain their privileges, and the great majority of the parochial clergy, among whom marriage or concubinage was widespread, offered passive resistance. A new kind of leadership, which would in itself embody the Tridentine ideal of the shepherd of souls, had to develop and implant the ideal in others. Hence, apart from a few starts, the Tidentine Reform made general progress only from the turn of the century. This process took place amid the formation of denominations and the struggle for self-assertion.

The delimitation of the "confessions" was much slower and required much more time than was formerly thought. Only by having people make the Tridentine Profession of Faith, "will it be possible to ascertain who is of the Catholic Religion and who is opposed to it,"[3] declared the Würzburg Cathedral Chapter in a resolution to this effect of 3 March 1570. The determining factor, in accord with the Religious Peace, was the right of the territorial state to determine religious adherence, but in practice there were barriers of different kinds, such as consideration for neighboring princes of another creed and the opposition of the estates.

Nevertheless, the territorial state first fixed the clearly changing ecclesiastical map of the Empire. Where there existed an impossibility or an unwillingness to adopt a definite viewpoint, odd mixtures resulted, as on the Lower Rhine. At the court of Duke Wilhelm V of Jülich-Cleve-Berg (1539–92) Catholics and Lutherans were referred to as "the two Catholic factions," and under the influence of the irenical Witzel and Cassander an ecclesiastical order inspired by the spirit of Christian antiquity was sought. In Minden the Protestant canons regularly took part in the Mass and processions of the Catholic canons.[4] Into the seventeenth century it is at times impossible exactly to determine from reports of visitations to which denomination the pastors belonged. Because the indult granting the chalice to the laity obliterated the frontier between denominations, it fell into disuse in Bavaria, on the Lower Rhine, and elsewhere. The attitude of the laity toward the officially imposed religion differed from place to place. Religious ignorance encouraged adaptation all the more when the Protestant authorities and

---

[1] First complete edition, Frankfurt 1574; the last, personally supervised by Chemnitz himself in 1578, was reedited by E. Preuss (Berlin 1861).

[2] W. Lindanus, *Stromata* (Cologne 1575); Kaspar Frank, *Rettung und Erklärung des tridentinischen Concils* (Cologne 1582); Andrada's *Defensio Tridentinae fidei* was reprinted in Cologne (1580) and Ingolstadt (1580 and 1592).

[3] Schreiber, II, 85.

[4] H. Nottarp, *Zur Communicatio in Sacris cum Haereticis* (Halle 1933), p. 16.

pastors respected Catholic traditions, as was the general rule in the North and East. But on both sides there were convinced and loyal believers, who remained steadfast in the midst of an alien religious environment or emigrated elsewhere. Repeated shifts of religious allegiance on the part of the government, as in the Margraviate of Baden-Baden and in the Upper Palatinate, led not infrequently, of course, to insecurity of faith and to indifference.

The Tridentine Reform took hold first of all in the ecclesiastical province of Salzburg, where, since the beginning of the religious cleavage, the reform efforts of the bishops had never been entirely broken off. At the provincial council of 1569, which was under the influence of Ninguarda, the Tridentine reform decrees were applied to German conditions in sixty-four constitutions. A second provincial council (1573) ordered the decrees to be printed, but they were not promulgated until after the diocesan synod of Salzburg (1576), under pressure from the Nuncio Portia. All clerics were obliged to make the Tridentine Profession of Faith and to observe celibacy; in addition, the Cardinal Legate Morone issued a reform mandate in the same year.[5] These measures and the diocesan synods had only meager success. Ninguarda, the soul of all efforts for the implementation of the Council, returned to Italy in 1583 without seeing the realization of the principal items of reform—the general visitation of all dioceses and the founding of seminaries. Even willing bishops, such as Urban von Trennbach of Passau (1561–98), were unable to succeed against their cathedral canons and the passive resistance of their clergy. Dietrich von Raitenau, Archbishop of Salzburg (1587–1612), proceeded vigorously against the Protestants of his see, but his own unclerical conduct prejudiced the internal reform. The friction between the bishops and the Dukes of Bavaria, Albrecht V (1550–79) and Wilhelm V (1579–97), which had already hurt the pre-Tridentine reform efforts, was lessened by a concordat in 1583. The "definitive victory of the Tridentine renewal" (Oswald) was not achieved until after the turn of the century, when shepherds of souls in the spirit of the new episcopal ideal assumed leadership—Hausen in Regensburg (1600–13), Gebeck in Freising (1618–51), Lodron in Salzburg (1619–53). Passau, from 1598 to 1664 dominated by Habsburg archdukes, obtained capable administrators. In the Austrian part of this extensive bishopric the dynasty decided the issue anyway.

[5] *QFIAB* 4 (1900), 123–137; K. Schellhas, *Der Dominikaner Felician Ninguarda und die Gegenreformation in Süddeutschland und Österreich 1560–1583*, 2 vols. (Rome 1930–39); J. Oswald, "Die Tridentinische Reform in Altbayern," Schreiber, II, 1–37.

The strength of Protestantism in Upper Austria was gradually broken after the suppression of a peasant uprising by the "General Reformation" (1597–1602) decreed by Emperor Rudolf II; from 1600 Jesuits were active in Linz. In the Lower Austrian part of the diocese of Passau and in the dioceses of Vienna and Wiener Neustadt Maximilian II had allowed to the nobles, in the "Religious Concession" (1568), the free exercise of religion in their castles and domains. During a demonstration before the Castle of Vienna in 1579 the cry was heard, "We are asking for the Gospel." Only the firm stand of Rudolf II and of his brother Ernst, supported by the energetic action of the *officialis* of Passau, Melchoir Klesl (1580–1600), secured the continuance of Catholicism. At the Diet of 1572 the Archduke Charles had granted religious freedom to the Protestant nobles of Inner Austria—Styria, Carinthia, Carniola—but in 1580 he had refused it to the cities. His son, Ferdinand, later Emperor, expelled the Protestant preachers—twenty-seven in Klagenfurt alone. These stern measures would have had scarcely any success if they had not been supplemented by internal ecclesiastical renewal, especially on the part of Bishops Brenner of Seckau (1585–1615) and Stobaeus of Lavant (1584–1618). In Tirol Bishop Spaur of Brixen (1600–13) became the "great reformer of the see" (Wodka) through his visitations, a diocesan synod, and the founding of a seminary.[6]

In Franconia leadership was assumed by the city of Würzburg under Julius Echter von Mespelbrunn (1574–1617), equally outstanding as bishop and statesman.[7] A Jesuit college, with a seminary attached, had already been founded by his predecessor, Bishop Wirsberg (1558–73). Without binding himself strictly to the letter of the Tridentine decrees and always maintaining a certain independence even toward Rome, von Mespelbrunn combined the internal renewal of the diocese, through visitations and by establishing the university, with the reconversion of the, since 1585, mostly Protestant subjects of his see. His activity is the

[6] E. Tomek, *Kirchengeschichte Österreichs* II (Innsbruck 1949), 301–326; J. Wodka, *Kirche in Österreich* (Vienna 1959), pp. 195–240, with indication of the literature, pp. 433–436; T. Wiedemann, *Geschichte der Reformation und Gegenreformation im Lande unter der Enns,* 5 vols. (Prague 1876–87); K. Eder, *Glaubensspaltung und Landstände in Österreich ob der Enns 1525–1602,* 2 vols., (Linz 1936); J. Loserth, *Reformation und Gegenreformation in Innerösterreich* (Stuttgart 1898): V. Bibl, *Erzherzog Ernst und die Gegenreformation in Niederösterreich* (Vienna 1901); J. Stadlhuber, "Die Tridentinische Priesterbildung unter dem Brixener Fürstbischof J. Ch. v. Spaur," *ZKTh* 81 (1959), 351–368; J. Rainer, "Quellen zur Gesch. der Grazer Nuntiatur," *Rom. hist. Mitteilungen* 2 (1959) 72–81.
[7] G. Frh. v. Pölnitz, *Julius Echter von Mespelbrunn* (Munich 1934); A. Biglmair, "Das Konzil von Trient und das Bistum Würzburg," Schreiber, II, 39–91 (with copious bibliography).

classical example of combining the Catholic Reform with Counter Reformation. If his procedure against Abbot Dernbach of Fulda, who was overzealous, on bad terms with the estates of his principality, and threatened by his Protestant neighbors, must be judged unfortunate, the neighboring see of Bamberg, where little in the way of reform had occurred under the unclerical Bishop Würtzburg, found in him a strong support. In 1586 Bishop Mengersdorf opened there a seminary and in 1594 his successor, Thüngen, organized a visitation and issued a decree on religion. But it was only after a severe setback under the concubinary Gebsattel that the Tridentine principles were realized through Aschhausen (1609–22), an alumnus of the Collegium Germanicum.[8] Eichstätt, weakened through the loss of 209 parishes in the Protestant parts of the diocese, was in a relatively satisfactory state: the seminary founded by Bishop Martin von Schaumberg in 1564–65 was the first on German soil. In 1614 it was given to the Jesuits.[9]

Events in Augsburg and Constance show how dubious was the purely formal introduction of the Tridentine decrees. The diocesan synod of Dillingen (1567), at which the reform decrees of Trent were, almost in their entirety, declared in force, "was denied any lasting success," (Zoepfl), largely because its organizer, Cardinal Otto Truchsess von Waldburg, more zealot than zealous, soon went to Rome (1573).[10] The Jesuit College he had founded at Dillingen (1563) and the university, soon after given to the Jesuits, exerted influence beyond the boundaries of the bishopric of Augsburg, but Bishop Heinrich von Knoeringen (1598–1646) was the first to refashion his see in the Tridentine pattern through the synod of 1610 and the founding of a seminary at Dillingen. In Constance Cardinal Mark Sittich von Hohenems had adopted the Tridentine decrees at a diocesan synod in 1567. The visitation then prescribed was, however, only carried out at irregular intervals, partly through the deans, and, like the later visitations, for example, that of the vicar general Pistorius in 1591, produced no significant result, while the constantly discussed project for a seminary was unrealized. A new era

---

[8] W. Hotzelt, *Veit II von Würtzburg, Fürstbischof von Bamberg 1561–1577* (Freiburg 1919); J. Kist, "Bamberg und das Tridentinum," Schreiber, II, 119–134; L. Bauer, "Die Kurie und J. Ph. v. Gebsattel, Bischof von Bamberg," *QFIAB* 40 (1960), 89–115.

[9] F. X. Buchner, "Das Bistum Eichstätt und das Konzil von Trient," Schreiber, II, 93–117.

[10] F. Siebert, *Zwischen Kaiser und Papst. Kardinal Truchsess von Waldburg und die Anfänge der Gegenreformation in Deutschland* (Berlin 1943); G. Frh. v. Pölnitz, "Petrus Canisius und das Bistum Augsburg," *Festgabe Spindler* (Munich 1955), pp. 352–394; O. Bucher, "Marquard von Berg, Bischof von Augsburg 1575–1591," *ZBLG* 20 (1957), 1–52; J. Spindler, *Heinrich V. von Knoeringen, Fürstbischof von Augsburg 1598–1646* (Dillingen 1911); F. Zoepfl, "Die Durchführung des Tridentinums im Bistum Augsburg," Schreiber, II, 135–169.

dawned with Bishop Jakob von Fugger (1604–26) in the diocesan synod of 1609. The statutes of the synod were printed and later repeatedly renewed and reprinted, and a visitation was made by the bishop.[11]

Of the Rhenish archbishoprics only Trier under Jakob von Eltz (1567–81), energetic both as a bishop and as a territorial prince, was exposed relatively early to the reform, which was actually carried out by Archbishop Johann von Schönenberg (1581–99).[12] Daniel Brendel, Archbishop of Mainz (1555–82), also showed his good will toward achieving the Tridentine Reform. He required the cathedral canons to make the Tridentine Profession of Faith and, through the agency of Nikolaus Elgard, alumnus of the Germanicum, reconverted Eichsfeld, which belonged to the see. Jesuit colleges were established in Mainz in 1568 and Heiligenstadt in 1581. But Brendel refused to summon a provincial council for the promulgation of the Tridentine decrees. His successor, Dalberg, would not publish the Bull "In Coena Domini" and only because of Rome's unrelenting pressure agreed to organize a general visitation and to compile a ritual in the spirit of the Tridentine decrees (1598). Under Schweikard von Cronberg, another alumnus of the Germanicum, the Rhenish part of the see was brought back to Catholicism; his "Order of Reformation" (1615) could be regarded as a substitute for a Tridentine diocesan synod. The realization of the Tridentine Reform, "for which efforts had been made in Mainz for a century without real success" (Brück), fell to the lot of the great Johann Philip von Schönborn after the Thirty Years' War.[13]

That the most serious danger to the stability of the prince-bishoprics was internal is indicated by events in Strasbourg and Cologne. In Johann von Manderscheid (1569–92) the see of Strasbourg had had a zealous reform prelate.[14] Nevertheless, after his death a Protestant-minded

[11] K. Schellhas, *Gegenreformation im Bistum Konstanz im Pontifikat Gregors* XIII (Karlsruhe 1925); K. Holl, *Fürstbischof Jakob Fugger von Konstanz (1604–1626) und die Katholische Reform in der Diözese im ersten Viertel des 17. Jh.* (Freiburg 1898); H. Tüchle, "Das Bistum Konstanz und das Konzil von Trient," Schreiber, II, 171–191.

[12] V. Conzemius, *Jakob III. von Eltz, Erzbischof von Trier 1567–1581* (Wiesbaden 1956); L. Just, "Ein Bericht des Kölner Nuntius O. M. Frangipani über die Durchführung der Tridentinischen Reformen in Trier 1595," Lortz F, I, 343–367.

[13] A. L. Veit, *Kirche und Kirchenreform in der Erzdiözese Mainz 1517–1618* (Freiburg 1920); A. P. Brück, "Das Erzstift Mainz und das Tridentinum," Schreiber, II, 193–243. A. Dolle, "Erzbischof D. Brendel von Mainz und die Gegenreformation auf dem Eichsfelde," *Universitas. Festschrift für A. Stohr* II (Mainz 1960), 110–125; L. Drehmann, *Der Weihbischof Nikolaus Elgard, eine Gestalt der Gegenreformation* (Leipzig 1958).

[14] K. Hahn, *Die katholische Kirche in Strassburg unter dem Bischof Erasmus von Limberg 1541–1568* (Frankfurt a. M. 1940); id. *Die kirchlichen Reformbestrebungen des Strassburger Bischofs J. von Manderscheid* (Strasbourg 1913); also L. Pfleger, *AElsKG* 9 (1934), 97ff.

minority in the cathedral chapter elected Johann Georg von Brandenburg. The Catholics chose the Cardinal Charles II of Guise, who established himself with French aid and obtained imperial investiture with
the see after he had accepted as his coadjutor the Archduke Leopold. In
Cologne under the successors of Adolf von Schaumburg, who was well
disposed toward reform, Protestant infiltration made great progress, and
the cathedral chapter entered into negotiations with the rebel Dutch for
the secularization of the see. Archbishop Friedrich von Wied, a nephew
of the apostate Hermann von Wied, openly refused to make the Tridentine Profession of Faith. The visitation of the Rhenish part of the see
(1569–70), ordered by Salentin von Isenburg, was rather an inventory
than the beginning of a vigorous reform. Catholic-minded but without
higher orders, Salentin resigned in order to perpetuate his family.
Gebhard Truchsess von Waldburg, confirmed as his successor only after
the conquest of serious scruples, broke with the Church in his "Christian Declaration" of 1583, married the canoness Agnes von Mansfeld,
and sought to secularize the see. With Cologne the remnants of Catholicism in North Germany, in fact the very continuance of the Catholic
Empire, were in danger; the loss of Cologne would have meant the loss
of the remaining archiepiscopal sees of North Germany and would have
assured the Protestants a majority in the Electoral College. Deposed on
1 April 1583, Gebhard was expelled by Bavarian troops with Spanish
assistance in the "War of Cologne." He was succeeded by the worldly
Ernst of Bavaria (1583–1612), under whom the nuncios at Cologne,
Bonhomini, and Frangipani, "laid the foundations for all later reform
activity" (Franzen), though they were unable to achieve the promulgation of Trent at the diocesan synod of 1589. Only the decree on matrimony, "Tametsi," was published by Frangipani in 1590. Ferdinand of
Bavaria (1612–50), accepted as coadjutor in 1595, can be regarded as
the first Tridentine reform bishop in the Rhenish metropolis. He personally visited the see, at least in part, held five diocesan synods, obliged
the pastors to make the Tridentine Profession of Faith, and out of his
own resources founded a modest seminary (1615), which lasted only
thirty years.[15] In this work of reconstruction, which proceeded in the

---

[15] M. Lossen, *Der Kölnische Krieg,* 2 vols. (Gotha 1882); P. Weiler, *Die kirchliche Reform
im Erzbistum Köln 1583–1615* (Münster 1931); A. Franzen, *Der Wiederaufbau des Kirchlichen Lebens im Erzbistum Köln unter Ferdinand von Bayern 1612–1650* (Münster
1941); id. "Innerdiözesane Hemmungen und Hindernisse der kirchlichen Reform im
16. und 17. Jh.," *Festgabe Wilhelm Neuss* (Cologne 1947), pp. 163–201; *idem, Die Kölner
Archidiakonate in vor- und nachtridentinischer Zeit* (Münster 1953); id., *Die Durchführung des Konzils von Trient in der Diözese Köln,* Schreiber, II, 267–294; A. Brecher,
*Die kirchlichen Reform in Stadt und Reich Aachen von der Mitte des 16. bis Anfang des 18.
Jh.* (Münster 1957); A. J. Herkenrath, *Die Reformbehörde des Kölner Kirchenrates 1601–
1615* (Düsseldorf 1960).

face of uninterrupted disputes with the cathedral chapter and the archdeacons, he was aided from 1601 by an "Ecclesiastical Council" and later by his capable vicars general, Gelenius, Binius, and Stravius. The last named was, after Ferdinand's death, the soul of the diocesan synod of 1662, at which Trent was formally promulgated.

In Münster, where Bishop Hoya (1566–74) and the zealous dean of the chapter, Raestel, had prepared the ground, Ferdinand of Bavaria created "an environment in which Trent could enjoy free operation" (Schroer). He accomplished this through the visitation of 1611–16 and the five great reform decrees connected with it. Only after the Thirty Years' War was the reform completed here by Bishop Galen.[16] The fate of Hildesheim would have been virtually sealed by the Lutheran-minded Friedrich von Holstein, but Bishop Oberg (1557–73) and his successors, the Bavarian princes Ernst and Ferdinand, at least saved the bishopric. On the other hand, Osnabrück, where in 1570 Bishop Hoya had promulgated Trent, fell for a half-century (1575–1623) into Protestant hands. The Catholic restoration under Cardinal Eitel Friedrich von Hohenzollern and Franz Wilhelm von Wartenberg was not lasting. The Peace of Westphalia called for the odd arrangement of alternating Catholic and Protestant bishops, and the see itself, with seventeen Protestant parishes out of forty-five, continued to be divided as to denomination.[17]

Definitely lost in North Germany through the chapter election of Protestant administrators were the archbishoprics of Magdeburg and Bremen and the prince-bishoprics of Minden, Halberstadt, Verden, and Lübeck. Magdeburg was incorporated into Brandenburg after the confirmation, surreptitiously obtained, of the Hohenzollerns Friedrich and Sigismund, sons of Joachim II. Georg von Braunschweig was the last Archbishop of Bremen to be confirmed by a Pope (1561); Heinrich von Sachsen-Lauenburg, elected by the chapter, secularized the see. Halberstadt was annexed by Heinrich Julius of Braunschweig-Wolfenbüttel to that duchy, while Minden, where the cathedral canons long maintained Catholic worship in an entirely Protestant environment, was added to Braunschweig by Hermann von Schaumburg in 1582. The cathedral chapter of Lübeck, designated as Catholic by the papal agent Trivius under Gregory XIII, was unable to withstand Bishop Holle,

[16] L. Keller, *Die Gegenreformation in Westfalen und am Niederrhein,* 3 vols. (Leipzig 1881–95); A. Schröer, "Das Tridentinum und Münster," Schreiber, II, 295–370; W. Stüwer, "Das Bistum Paderborn in der Reformbewegung des 16. und 17. Jh.," Schreiber, II, 387–450; H. Kramer, "Abt Leonhard Ruben," *Westfal. Zeitschr.,* 103–104 (1954), 271–333.

[17] H. Hoberg, "Das Konzil von Trient und die Osnabrücker Synodaldekrete des 17. Jh.," Schreiber, II, 371–386.

who, though confirmed by Pius IV, had gone over to Protestantism. He also secularized the see of Verden. The Saxon bishoprics of Naumburg, Merseburg, and Meissen were regarded as lost under Gregory XIII. They were confiscated by their Protestant territorial lords, as were the mediatized sees of Brandenburg, Mecklenburg, and Pomerania.[18]

Not until the struggle over the Religious Peace of Augsburg and the carrying out of the Tridentine Reform in the last third of the sixteenth century was it decided that the South and West of Germany would remain mostly Catholic. To be sure, one can speak of a "carrying out of the Tridentine Reform" only within limits; it was indeed attempted, but until the turn of the century it was realized only to a very slight degree. None of the three distinguishing marks by which the reform is usually measured is ascertainable in all places—reform synods on the basis of Trent, episcopal visitations according to its norms, and the founding of Tridentine seminaries. Only in the ecclesiastical province of Salzburg were provincial councils held; they were convoked in no other province. It is doubtful whether under existing conditions they would have had the expected success, for even the comparatively few diocesan synods, for example, at Augsburg and Constance, were ineffectual. Trent had ordered the personal visitation of the diocese by the bishop; where visitations were made in Germany they were usually conducted by deputies, with the participation, as a rule, of civil officials in the secular territories, and in some instances by papal reform legates. In many cases they effected no thorough-going improvement of conditions, because, due to the existing shortage of priests, it was impossible to remove unorthodox or concubinary pastors. The establishment of seminaries was frustrated in most dioceses by the refusal of the cathedral canons to contribute to their founding and support. While their importance in educating a Catholic elite is undisputed, scholarship endowments and the Jesuit colleges springing up in all metropolitan sees and Catholic territories provided no real substitute for the training of a uniformly prepared diocesan clergy.

Not until toward the end of the century did a new class of ecclesiastical leadership appear. The cathedral chapters, which decided the choice of the bishops and which regarded themselves as coowners and corulers of the sees, were, partly through papal provision, interspersed with elements zealous for reform, especially from the Collegium Germanicum. While the bourgeois were not excluded, preference was shown to students of noble birth, out of regard for the current capitular statutes, with the result that, of the 800 students who had entered the college by 1600, six became bishops and eight auxiliary bishops. In

<hr>

[18] Synopsis in K. Müller, *Kirchengeschichte* II/2, 277.

Breslau, because of the personal policies of the Bishops Gerstmann and Jerin, of the twenty-one canons who met for an episcopal election in 1599 twelve were alumni of the Germanicum. Mainz, the highest ranking bishopric in the Empire, had from 1604 to 1647 three archbishops who had come from the Germanicum.

The Tridentine ideal of the bishop as shepherd of souls was found in only a few individuals, and in none of these to a very high degree. The prince-bishop had to prove himself as a prince. Only with the prestige stemming from his status of territorial lord could he maintain the Catholic character at least of his own see. The struggle forced upon the Church for her very existence led to a flagrant violation of the Tridentine prohibition of pluralism. In order to preserve Cologne for the Church, and the even more seriously exposed North German sees of Paderborn and Hildesheim, as well as Liège, threatened by its Dutch neighbors, these bishoprics were given to Bavarian princes; thereby ecclesiastical interests were joined to dynastic, so that for almost two hundred years there existed on the Lower Rhine a sort of Bavarian secundogeniture.[19] The same motive led, somewhat later than at Cologne, to the episcopal pluralism of the Habsburg Archdukes Leopold and Leopold Wilhelm in the sees of Passau, Strasbourg, Breslau, and Olmütz. In these cases of pluralism, tolerated rather than encouraged by the Popes, was revealed the importance of the Wittelsbach and Habsburg dynasties in maintaining Catholicism and the Tridentine Reform. Wherever re-Catholicization of territories almost or completely lost was undertaken, such as in the Margraviate Baden-Baden, it was done upon the initiative of the territorial lord, that is, the estate. It was Philipp II, a Wittelsbach, educated at Ingolstadt, who after 1577, aided by Ingolstadt's secular councilors, suppressed non-Catholic doctrines and rejuvenated the spiritual estate.[19a]

Inner renewal in the spirit of Trent came to the German Church not from its own strength but through the use of existing political means and through help from abroad. Not bishops but secular princes, the Bavarian Wittelsbachs, led the way with the strict implementation of the right to determine religious allegiance as guaranteed to the territorial prince by the Religious Peace. In all Germany there was no succession of princes so resolutely Catholic as Albrecht V, Wilhelm V, and Maximilian I of Bavaria. The Habsburgs followed them only a generation later, after overcoming strong opposition from their estates.

---

[19] G. v. Lojewski, *Bayerns Weg nach Köln. Geschichte der bayr. Bistumspolitik in der 2. Hälfte des 16. Jh.* (Bonn 1962).

[19a] *Der Geistliche Rat zu Baden-Baden und seine Protokolle 1577/84,* ed. H. Steigelmann (Stuttgart 1962).

It is difficult to imagine how the Tridentine Reform could have made progress if the Popes had not kept the episcopate under unrelenting pressure through nuncios. Its more rapid progress in the South than in the West is explained by the fact that in the South there were fewer "episcopalian" hindrances to be dealt with than in the Rhenish archbishoprics. The lack of suitable personnel for education and the care of souls was somewhat remedied by the introduction of the Orders, especially of those originating in the course of Catholic Reform—the Society of Jesus and the Capuchins.

The network of Jesuit colleges, in which the future Catholic elite was formed, became ever more widespread between 1564 and 1618, particularly in the Habsburg territories (for example, Hall, Krems, Graz, Klagenfurt, Laibach), but also in the West and North, where they proved to be the strongest centers of the renewal—Koblenz, Cologne, Münster, Paderborn, Heiligenstadt. Naturally, the occasional endowment of the colleges with the buildings and property of sparsely occupied or defunct monasteries of other Orders caused resentment in these.

No oil was poured on troubled waters by the court confessors, such as Blyssem and Viller in Graz and Mengin in Munich, whose presence was at first resented by their superiors, but who were in a position to contribute to the direction of the ecclesiastical policies of the courts. However, their influence has often been overestimated. Far more effective and influential were others: Peter Canisius, as organizer of his Order in Germany, as agent of the Popes in matters of ecclesiastical policies, as teacher, preacher, and writer; with him in Cologne were Kessel and Rethius, both murdered in 1574 by a mentally deranged confrere; in South Germany Paul Hoffaeus (d. 1608), successor of Canisius as South German provincial and later a dreaded visitor; in Austria Georg Scherer (d. 1605), an important preacher. The undeniable success of the Jesuits explains the hate they inspired in Protestants. The Count Palatine Ludwig called them "spiritual locusts" and "scorpions in Christendom";[20] the libel of the apostate Hasenmüller, *Historia Jesuitici Ordinis* (1593), found wide circulation.

Shortly before the turn of the century the Capuchins entered the lists on the side of the Jesuits as popular preachers, confessors, and missionaries in Tirol (Innsbruck, 1593), Salzburg (1596), and Bavaria (Munich, 1600). In South Germany there arose six Capuchin provinces in addition to the two Rhenish provinces, which were founded from Flanders. Significantly, the three outstanding Capuchins who were active in Central Europe in the first decades of the seventeenth century

[20] A. Kluckhohn, *Briefe Friedrichs d. Frommen* II (Braunschweig 1872), 811.

were Italians—Laurentius of Brindisi (d. 1619), Hyacinth of Casale (d. 1627), and Valerian Magni (d. 1661).

As in the Empire, in Switzerland also Tridentine Reform and self-assertion in the face of Protestantism went hand in hand; and the forces and counterforces in action were similar. The implementing of the Council began in the Catholic central parts of Switzerland and was supported by the lay authorities when the bishops of Constance, whose responsibility it was, failed to act. In the name of the seven Catholic cantons their former envoy to the Council, Melchior Lussy, on 3 March 1564, accepted all the Tridentine decrees. Harsh measures were taken against concubinary clerics, but all efforts to found a local seminary failed. Here too help from abroad was decisive; specifically, the activity of the nuncios to Lucerne—Bonhomini, Santonio, Paravicini, and finally Borromeo, who visited Switzerland in 1570 and founded the Helvetian College in Milan. In Lucerne there was a Jesuit College from 1574. In its mayor, Ludwig Pfyffer, this Catholic center possessed an energetic leader. The Capuchins were almost more active than the Jesuits. Between 1581 and 1589 they established themselves in Altdorf, Stans, Lucerne, and Schwyz, and in 1595 in Zug. After 1589 the Swiss monasteries constituted a separate province.

The Abbots of Einsiedeln and Sankt Gallen, Joachim Eichhorn and Othmar Kunz, were able to boast at the diocesan synod of Constance in 1560 that they had "fully observed and carried out" the Council.[21] Internally regenerated, the two great abbeys fortified a consciousness of the faith in all of Catholic Switzerland. When the pilgrimage to Einsiedeln was resumed, Stoyb, diocesan priest of Schwyz, wrote: "The Almighty has reserved to Himself seven thousand and more who have not apostatized from the faith." In the diocese of Basel Bishop Blarer (1575–1608) began the Tridentine renewal at the diocesan synod of 1581. The Treaty of Baden (1583) with the city of Basel assured financial compensation for the valuable episcopal property that had been lost there, and gave a free hand for the maintenance of Catholicism in Blarer's territorial domain. In the Valais, which had not joined the Catholic cantons, Bishop Riedenstein of Sion (1565–1604) was too weak to prevent the further progress of Protestantism and to carry out the Tridentine Reform in earnest. In the see of Chur the reform of the clergy was begun with the liturgy of 1590 and the diocesan statutes of 1605. However, when Bishop Flügi (1601–27) took vigorous action, the Nuncio d'Aquino wrote in 1613: "the bishop moves in constant

---

[21] R. Tschudi, *Das Kloster Einsiedeln unter den Äbten Ludwig II Blarer und Joachim Eichhorn 1526–1569* (Einsiedeln 1946), p. 195; Stoyb's remark, ibid., p. 155.

danger to his life from the Protestant confederates; in his see city there is not a Catholic apart from the episcopal curia."[22] The see of Lausanne had shrunk substantially to the Canton of Fribourg. Here the Jesuit College, founded in 1580, and Peter Canisius supported the reform.

The self-assertion of the Church in Central Europe and the progress of the Tridentine Reform, together with the ending of the Huguenot Wars, the continuing union of the southern Netherlands with Spain, and the consolidation of Catholicism in Poland, made it possible after the turn of the century to regard the crisis of the religious cleavage, if not as overcome, at least as definitely checked. Contributing not a little to this outcome was the weakening of the Protestant front resulting from the conflict between Calvinists and Lutherans. The deepest cause, however, lay in the reinvigoration of the spiritual and intellectual substance of ecclesiastical life, which was manifested in the flowering of theology, of religious life, and of piety.

[22] J. G. Mayer, *Das Konzil von Trient und die Gegenreformation in der Schweiz,* II, 310f.

Religious Forces and Intellectual Content of the Catholic Renewal

CHAPTER 41

The Revival of Scholasticism, Michael Baius and the Controversy over Grace

Just as in the Middle Ages the flowering of scholasticism was intimately connected with the rise of the universities, so now its revival was associated with the formation of new centers in the development of the European universities. Now, as before, the University of Paris maintained its great authority in doctrinal decisions; this was impaired only by the university's Gallicanism and its opposition to the aspiring Society of Jesus. Alongside Paris new centers of theological activity sprang up from the second third of the sixteenth century. In Louvain, which through Latomus, Driedo, and Tapper had very early joined Cologne in opposing Luther and had strengthened its reputation through the presence of its professors at Trent in 1551–52, Augustinianism received a new stimulus at the hands of Baius, Hessels, and the older Jansenius. The revival of scholasticism, which stamped its character on the era, did not, however, proceed from these universities situated on the very battlefield of religious innovation, but from Spain, whose universities at the time of the Council of Trent and until the turn of the century exercised a leadership similar to that of the Spain of Philip II in high politics.

At Salamanca the Dominican Francisco de Vitoria, as holder of the first theological chair at the university, the *Catedra de prima,* founded a theological school which spread not only in Spain and Portugal but even to Rome and Germany. Of the seven chairs of theology, six were reserved for speculative theology, and for these the Dominicans of the Colegio San Esteban competed with members of the other mendicant Orders. In addition, there were four chairs of Greek and two of Hebrew. Even more keenly was positive theology pursued at Alcalá, in keeping with the aim of Ximenes, the founder; here the Colegio San Ildefonso held a predominant place, similar to that of San Gregorio at Valladolid. At Coimbra theology and canon law were taught in the convent of San Agustín. The Spanish Benedictines founded their own university at Zaragoza, or, more properly, Irache.

In the last third of the century Rome overtook the Spanish universities through the brilliance at the Jesuits' Roman College of stars of the first magnitude, all of them Spaniards, except Bellarmine: Francisco de Toledo, Maldonado, Suarez, Vazquez, Ruiz. They made Rome what it had never been in the Middle Ages or in the Renaissance—a stronghold of theological study. Theologians of the rising Society of Jesus carried the revitalized scholasticism to the German universities of Ingolstadt and Dillingen, the "citadels of the Catholic counter-offensive in the Empire" (Willaerts). Among their professors were many Spaniards and Dutch, at their head Gregorius of Valencia, whose work was continued by the Germans Gretser and Tanner.

How did the spirit and method of this reinvigorated scholasticism differ from the content and teaching method of the late medieval theological schools?

Whatever the answer to the question of Luther's nominalism, the fact is that this school of thought had scarcely any champions left at the Council of Trent. There the Franciscans had numerically the strongest representation, but the Dominicans were best able to undertake the defense of the Church against Protestantism. Neither of these schools was entirely able to free itself from the influence of Humanism, which was strongest in the Augustinian School led by Seripando. Above all, the fact that the Protestants asserted the sufficiency of Scripture and invoked the authority of the Fathers on behalf of the new doctrines forced upon Catholics an intensive preoccupation with the Bible and the witness of Tradition, which were not only given more weight than formerly and consulted at first hand in systematic theology but also led to the establishment of an autonomous domain of positive theology. Both revived scholasticism and controversial theology were committed to positive theology. Four new approaches resulted from this return to the positive data of revelation contained in Scripture and Tradition.

First, the new scholasticism proceeding from Salamanca sought, like the medieval, to reconcile *fides* and *ratio* but dispensed with the ballast, amassed in the late Middle Ages, of oversubtle questions amounting to dialectical acrobatics and took as its standard the classical period of scholasticism and especially Thomas Aquinas. Thus the reproof of the humanists—*Perdunt nugis tempora*—was no longer applicable and once more theology became simpler, clearer, and more relevant to life. Second, attacked by humanist and reformer alike, it reexamined the method of theological proof. Third, as controversial theology, it grappled with the theological problems raised by the religious cleavage, but also sought answers to the ethical and juridical questions which became acute with the colonizing activity of the Iberian peoples in the New World. Fourth, in the pastoral spirit of the Council of Trent, it was much concerned with popular religious instruction and preaching. All five Doctors of the Church who lived at this period were eminently practical theologians: Canisius and Bellarmine as compilers of catechisms, John of the Cross as a mystic, Francis de Sales as a teacher of the spiritual life, Lorenzo of Brindisi as a preacher.

Revival of Scholasticism

The "Golden Age of Scholasticism" was inaugurated by the Dominican Francisco de Vitoria (d. 1546). He was introduced to the study of Saint Thomas by another Dominican, Petrus Crockaert, at the University of Paris, but he was also familiar with the investigation of the sources that was going on at Louvain. After his change in 1526 to Salamanca as holder of the first theological chair he based his teaching very largely on the *Summa* of Aquinas. His dynamic lectures, above all on questions of moral theology, and his celebrated conferences (*Relectiones*) had an extraordinary effect on his large audiences, sometimes numbering as many as one thousand people, even though not one of his books was printed in his own lifetime. The *Summa sacramentorum*, compiled by one of his pupils and first printed in 1560, went through more than thirty-three editions and became "the manual of pastoral theology most used by the Spanish clergy in the sixteenth century" (Stegmüller). Thomistic in his basic approach, Vitoria was not narrow-minded. His moderate views on the relationship between Pope and Council determined the attitude of many Spanish bishops at the Council of Trent. His analysis of the ethical and juridical problems of the Spanish Colonial Empire entitles him to be considered the founder of modern international law. Hugo Grotius is heavily indebted to him.

Among the sixty-six doctors of Salamanca who attended the Council of Trent were many bishops and theologians who had sat at Vitoria's feet. His pupil and successor in the chair, the Dominican Melchior Cano (d. 1560), became, through his *De locis theologicis* (1563), the founder of theological methodology.[1] Following the Humanist Rudolf Agricola instead of the Topics of Aristotle in the definition of *loci* (sources), Cano distinguished ten such *loci* (or *domicilia*, as he also called them) from which theological arguments are drawn: Holy Scripture, Apostolic

---

[1] Last edition in *Opera* I–II (Rome 1890). A. Lang, *Die Loci theologici des M. Cano und die Methode des dogmatischen Beweises* (Munich 1925) demonstrated the dependence on Agricola, contrary to A. Gardeil, "La notion du Lieu théologique," *RSPhTh* 2 (1908), 51–73, 246–276, 484–505; J. Beumer, "Positive und spekulative Theologie," *Scholastik* 29 (1954), 53–72; E. Marcotte, *La nature de la théologie de M. Cano* (Ottawa 1949), along with G. Thils in *EThL* 26 (1950), 409ff.; F. Pelster, "Eine Kontroverse über die Methode der Moraltheologie aus dem Ende des 16. Jh.," *Scholastik,* 17 (1942), 385–411.

Tradition, the *magisterium* of the Universal Church, the councils, the *magisterium* of the Roman Church, the Fathers, the scholastics and canonists, natural reason, the philosophers, and history. This work made Cano the "father of theological methodology" (Lang). His reputation was tarnished by his passionate attacks on his fellow Dominican Carranza[2] and on the Jesuits.

Though the groundwork for this revival had been laid at the very beginning of the sixteenth century by the great commentators Cajetan and Koellin, Thomism received a powerful stimulus and a wide dissemination from the Salamanca School. In 1567 Pius V proclaimed Aquinas a Doctor of the Church. His *Summa theologiae* gradually supplanted the *Sentences* of Peter Lombard as a textbook. But in the last third of the century a differentiation was beginning to show. The Spanish Dominicans Bartolomeo of Medina (d. 1580) and Dominico Báñez (d. 1604) were developing the "classical Thomistic School" (Grabmann), that is, strict Thomism; while the Jesuit School, increasingly prominent, went its own way in both method and doctrine.

Jesuit Theology

The Jesuit theologians at the Council of Trent, Lainez and Salmeron, had still adhered to a certain eclecticism. The general congregation of 1593 prescribed Thomas as the guide of the Society's theologians, allowing them to depart from him only in exceptional cases and for good reasons (*gravate admodum et rarissime*). The voluntarist and activist tendency of the Society, however, soon made itself felt in theology, both in Spain (Molina) and in Rome and Germany.

Gregorius of Valencia (d. 1603), who had been educated at Salamanca, combined a sound grasp of scholasticism with a humanist attitude and remarkable talent for exposition. As professor at Ingolstadt (1575–97), he contributed to a large degree through the training of numerous pupils—hence his title of *Doctor Doctorum*—to restoring the good name of scholasticism in Germany, where it had been most exposed to contempt by the criticism of humanists and reformers.[3] His

[2] For the literature, see *LThK* 2nd ed. II, 957; J. I. Tellechea Idigoras, *B. Carranza Arzobispo* (San Sebastian 1958); *Fray B. Carranza. Documentos historicos,* ed. J. I. Tellechea Idigoras, so far 2 vols. (Madrid 1962).

[3] His chief work, *Commentarii theologici,* 4 vols. (Ingolstadt 1591–97), had twelve editions in twenty years; see Sommervogel, VIII, 388–400, IX, 897, W. Hentrich, *G. von Valencia und der Molinismus* I (Innsbruck 1928); cf. *Scholastik* 4 (1929), 91–106; id. *G. von Valencia und die Erneuerung der deutschen Scholastik,* (Regensburg 1930); J. Esposa, *Arch. teol. Granadino* 8 (1945), 99–123; H. Wolter, "Die Kirche im Religionsgespräch zwischen Gregor v. V. und Lucas Osiander," *Sentire ecclesiam,* ed. J. Danielou and H. Vorgrimler (Freiburg 1961), pp. 350–370.

pupil and successor, Jakob Gretser (d. 1625), wrote all his numerous theological, philological, and historical works in the form of controversial theology,[4] as did Adam Tanner (d. 1632), who taught in Munich, Ingolstadt, Prague, and Vienna.[5] Tanner encouraged von Spee in his opposition to witchcraft trials.

Clearly decisive for the further growth of the new scholasticism were its spread to Rome and its development by the great Jesuit theologians, Francisco de Toledo, Bellarmine, Suarez, and Vazquez. Important also as an exegete, Francisco de Toledo (d. 1596),[6] a pupil of Soto, taught from 1559 at the Society's Roman College; in 1593 he became the first Jesuit cardinal. The most profound and most prolific of these men, both in philosophy and in theology, was the *Doctor Eximius,* Francisco Suarez (d. 1617).[7] Also trained at Salamanca, he taught at times at Rome (1580–85), only to return to Spain and to Alcala, Salamanca, and finally Coimbra (1598–1616) where he reached the climax of his creative work. Here he produced his works on grace and law—"summing up the achievements of sixteenth-century Spanish theology in natural law, international law, and political philosophy" (Stegmüller)—as well as a large-scale defense of religious Orders and of the Society of Jesus. On several occasions he intervened in the dispute concerning grace to contribute his expert opinion, and Protestant universities also paid attention to his philosophy. Like Suarez, Gabriel Vazquez (d. 1604) was active only briefly (1586–91) at Rome and then returned to Spain.[8] His relationship to Suarez has been compared to that of Scotus to Thomas. An extremely keen-sighted theologian, dreaded as a fiery debater, Vazquez, who had studied under Báñez at Alcalá, became famed among his contemporaries as a "second Augustine" because of his knowledge of the Fathers of the Church; he entered the dispute over grace as a strict Molinist.

[4] Important for history is *De Cruce Christi,* 3 vols. (Ingolstadt 1598); his 234 printed works, including Latin plays, in Sommervogel, III, 1743–1809.

[5] W. Lurz, *A. Tanner und die Gnadenstreitigkeiten* (Breslau 1932); his chief work is *Universa theologia scholastica,* 4 vols. (Ingolstadt 1626f.); Sommervogel, VII, 1834–1855.

[6] His chief work, the commentary on the *Summa,* last edited by J. Paiva, 4 vols. (Rome 1869–70); Sommervogel, VIII, 64–82.

[7] His works are in 23 vols. (Lyons–Mainz 1630); latest complete edition in 28 vols. (Paris 1856–61); Sommervogel, VII, 1661–87; P. Mugica, *Bibliografía Suarenciana* (Granada 1948); R. De Scoraille, *Fr. Suarez,* 2 vols. (Paris 1912–13); F. Stegmüller, *Zur Gnadenlehre des jungen Suarez* (Freiburg 1933); G. Ambrosetti, *Il diritto naturale della Riforma cattolica. Una giustificazione storica del sistema di Suarez* (Milan 1951); J. Giers, *Die Gerechtigkeitslehre des jungen Suarez* (Freiburg 1958). Survey of the most recent literature in *AHSI* 30 (1961), 471f.

[8] Commentary on Saint Thomas (1608–15); Sommervogel, VIII, 513–519.

The brightest star of the Jesuit School and the systematizer of controversial theology was Robert Bellarmine (1542–1621). A nephew of Pope Marcellus II, he had already occupied himself with the Protestant concepts as a teacher at Louvain (1570–76), where he distinguished himself as a preacher. Appointed professor of controversial theology at the Roman College (1576–88) and in 1592 its rector, then consultor of the Holy Office and theological adviser to Clement VIII, he won such esteem that the Pope in 1599 made him a cardinal. Because of differences with the Pope over the controversy on grace, he was removed from Rome by his appointment as Archbishop of Capua in 1602, but returned after the death of his former patron and under Paul V took part in all the great disputes in which the papacy was involved: the quarrels with Venice and James I of England and the Galileo Case. His *De potestate Pontificis in rebus temporalibus*, composed at this time (1610), which enlarged on the teaching he had already championed in the *Controversies* in regard to the merely indirect power of the Pope in the temporal sphere, met with violent opposition from the advocates of the *potestas directa*, as well as from the Protestants. At the peak of his scholarly activity and finally as a cardinal, Bellarmine remained as devoted to pastoral activity as he had always been: his small catechism (1597), with its 400 editions, almost equalled that of Canisius; the larger catechism (1598) was intended for catechists. In the last years of his life Bellarmine, who was the friend of Baronius and Francis de Sales, composed ascetical works, for example, *De arte bene moriendi* (1620). His cause was introduced in 1627 but was suspended by Benedict XIV. He was beatified in 1923 and canonized in 1930; the next year he was declared a Doctor of the Church.

Bellarmine's chief work, the *Disputationes de controversiis fidei* based on his Roman lectures and usually called *The Controversies*, is a synthesis of the Catholic controversial theology of the sixteenth century. Though by no means original, it is inspired by a consistent fundamental concept and enriched by an astonishing command of literature. It far surpasses the earlier controversial manuals of Johannes Eck, Albert Pigge, Stanislaus Hosius, and Ruard Tapper[9] through its assimilation of all the material amassed in countless monographs, and it had a natural advantage over them in being able to build on all the decrees of the Council of Trent. Whereas the Council, because of the opposition of Gallicans and "episcopalists," had avoided a declaration on the concept of the Church,

---

[9] S. Hosius, *Confessio catholicae fidei christiana* (1551); L. Bernacki, *La doctrine de l'église chez le card. Hosius* (Paris 1936); J. Lortz, *Kard. St. Hosius* (Braunsberg 1931). R. Tapper, *Explicatio articulorum ven. facultatis . . . Lovaniensis circa dogmata ecclesiastica ab annis XXXIV controversa* (1555); *Opera* (Cologne 1582).

Bellarmine, after a discussion of the sources of revelation—Scripture and Tradition—placed the doctrine of the Church at the beginning (Book I) and only then passed on to the Sacraments (II) and to the doctrine of grace and justification (III). His predecessor in this arrangement of controversial theology was the Englishman Thomas Stapleton (d. 1598), who had rightly attributed the limited success of the contemporary controversial theologians to the fact that they had not started with the teaching office of the Church.[10]

Michael Baius

At the Council of Trent the moderate Augustinian School led by Seripando had been unable to carry the day.[11] Even before the Council was finished Augustinianism in its strictest form found scholarly and stubborn representatives in the Louvain professors Michael Baius (d. 1589) and Johannes Hessels (d. 1566). When one of their pupils, the Franciscan Sablons at Nivelles, defined the freedom of the will as freedom from external compulsion and expressly declared that Calvin's teaching on the subject was correct,[12] twenty of his propositions were censured by the University of Louvain at the beginning of 1560; both professors concurred with the judgment on eighteen of them. In the summer of the same year the Sorbonne likewise censured eighteen theses of the Franciscan. The Nuncio Commendone demanded the intervention of the Pope, who imposed silence on both parties. Baius and Hessels traveled to Trent in 1563; but the Council, then at its worst crisis, did not take up the matter. Baius himself explained his teaching on man's original state, justification, freedom of the will, merit, and also on Sacrifice and Sacraments in a collection of treatises (1563–64). Numerous propositions extracted from this work were, at the request of Philip II, censured on 31 March 1565 by the University of Alcalá, and

---

[10] *Principiorum fidei doctrinalium demonstratio methodica* (composed 1579), *Opera* I (Paris 1620), 1–503. N. Sander, *De visibili monarchia ecclesiae* (Louvain 1571), was composed as a defense of the Primacy, with exclusive concern for the English situation. On all these, see G. Thils, *Les notes de l'Eglise dans l'apologétique catholique depuis la Réforme* (Gembloux 1937). J. B. Bicunas, *Doctrina ecclesiologica S. Roberti Card. Bellarmini cum illa Jo. Card. Turrecremata comparata* (Rome 1963); M. R. O'Cormell, *Thomas Stapleton and the Counter-Reformation* (New Haven 1964).

[11] H. Jedin, *G. Seripando*, I, 354–426, II, 239–268; id., "Agostino Moreschini und seine Apologie Augustins," *Augustinus-Festschrift* (Cologne 1931), pp. 137–153.

[12] M. Roca, "Documentos ineditos en torno a Miguel Bayo," *Anthologia annua* 1 (1953), 311: "Calvinus bene scripsit de libero arbitrio, nec erat reprehendendus, nisi in aliis errasset;" the concurrence of the two professors, ibid., p. 318.

on 8 August 1565 by the University of Salamanca.[13] The University of Louvain then asked Rome for a judgment on 26 November 1566. After the expanded new edition of the offending book had been censured once more by the University of Alcalá, Pius V in the Bull "Ex omnibus afflictionibus" of 1 October 1567, condemned seventy-nine of the 120 propositions rejected by the Spanish censors in the sense intended by the author, although some of them could have been interpreted in an acceptable sense.[14] Baius submitted to the bull, which had not been made public, later (1569) formally repudiated the errors attributed to him, and in 1575, under oath, professed the faith of the Council of Trent.

Nevertheless, the dispute grew in intensity. A case brought before the Holy Office ended in 1580 with a new condemnation by Gregory XIII. Baius accepted this too in the presence of Francisco de Toledo, who had been dispatched to Louvain, and the Louvain Faculty committed itself to an anti-Baian formulary. As the unquestionably sincere submission of Baius to the several papal judgments shows, his basic attitude was Catholic, but the difficulty of reconciling the decisions of the *magisterium* with the conclusions to which his studies had led him created a genuine conflict of conscience. Convinced that it must vindicate the Augustinian teaching on grace, the Louvain Faculty, with the cooperation of Baius, in 1587 censured thirty-four theses of Leonard Lessius (d. 1623), a Jesuit teaching at the Louvain College, on the inspiration of Holy Scripture, grace, and predestination; by order of Sixtus V the Nuncio Frangipani had again to enjoin silence on both parties. The Louvain disputes were, however, soon eclipsed by the great Molinist conflict over grace described below, though they did break out again with full force in the Jansenist Quarrel of the seventeenth century.

Controversy over Grace

In 1588 there appeared in Lisbon, with the approval of the censor of the Inquisition, the Dominican Ferreira, the Jesuit Luis de Molina's book, *Liberi arbitrii cum gratiae donis, divina praescientia, providentia, praedestinatione et reprobatione concordia,* which undertook to explain the compatibility of the universal efficacy of grace with the free will of man by virtue of God's foreknowledge, and which was expressly directed against the Thomistic teaching presented in the commentary on Saint

[13] M. Roca, op. cit., pp. 322ff., 329ff.
[14] D. 1001–1080. By changing the punctuation (Comma Pianum), the Baianists gave to the formula the meaning: "Although some of them might be maintained in the sense intended by the author."

Thomas published just previously (1584) by the Dominican Báñez. Molina's *Concordia* was, for this reason, suppressed for three months by the Portuguese Inquisition, but after its release it was at once reprinted by leading publishers in Lyons, Antwerp, and Venice. When Báñez tried to bring it before the Spanish Index, Molina replied with the charge that his opponent's teaching on physical predestination and on efficacious grace agreed with Luther and Calvin and contradicted Trent. On the other hand, the Dominican Nuño, at a disputation arranged by the Jesuits at Valladolid on 5 March 1594, termed some of their theses erroneous and heretical; the Jesuits either defended these or denied that Molina held them.

In order to put an end to the scandalous quarrel, behind which the rivalry of the two great Orders was now apparent, Clement VIII in an instruction of 28 June 1594 to the nuncio at Madrid, Gaetani, withdrew the case to Rome; the nuncio forbade any further dispute over efficacious grace. Both parties objected to the imposition of silence. Báñez, in a memoir to the Pope, maintained that he was only expressing the teaching of Augustine and Aquinas; Bellarmine, in an opposing opinion, denied this claim and the assertion that the Jesuits were "innovators." Thereupon, the order of silence was canceled for both parties by the Roman Inquisition on 26 February 1598.

In the same spring of 1598 the case, which had meanwhile been brought to Rome, took a turn which seemed to bring victory within the grasp of the Dominicans. The theological commission appointed by the Pope had been directed to examine, not the disputed point as such, namely, the teaching of both parties, but only Molina's teaching. It decided on 13 March 1598 that the book and the doctrine were to be forbidden and renewed this decision after weighing the exhaustive expositions of both schools, in which the most eminent theologians on both sides took part, the opinions of the Universities of Salamanca, Alcalá, and Sigüenza, and the views of five Spanish bishops and four Spanish theologians. A report drawn up by the secretary of the commission, the Augustinian Coronel, which was presented to the Pope on 12 March 1599, proposed that sixty theses of Molina be condemned. Thus far Molina himself had not been directly heard, although he had requested a hearing in a petition to the Pope. In order to permit the Jesuits to have a better opportunity to speak, Clement VIII, at the intercession of Philip III of Spain and other highly placed patrons of the Society, had the two generals, Beccaria and Acquaviva, each assisted by eminent theologians—among others, the Dominican Diego Alvarez and the Jesuit Michael Vazquez—define orally and in writing their viewpoint in the controversy. The Dominicans resisted any side-tracking of the real issue, which in their opinion concerned only the teaching of

Molina. The Jesuits insisted on discussion of the entire problem, including Báñez's teaching on the *praemotio physica;* in any case, they said, Molina's teaching was not that of the Society. They won their point, despite the protests of the Dominicans.

The success was only a brief one. When the Theological Commission, enlarged by three members, resumed its activity at the Pope's command, it again decided against Molina, by a majority of nine to two, and rejected twenty propositions contained in his works. On 5 December 1601 it submitted all its documents to the Pope, who exclaimed when he saw the mass of paper: "A year may have been sufficient for you to write all this, but a year is not sufficient for me to read it."[15] In Spain the rumor was already spreading that Molina, who had died in 1600, had been condemned and his effigy burned, when the Jesuits, by means of a memoir handed to the Pope on 12 February 1602, succeeded in obtaining another postponement. Clement VIII decided to hear both parties himself and to pass sentence personally. All the same, the prospects of the Jesuits were as bad as ever, because the Pope was angry with them. The Jesuit College of Alcalá had held a disputation on the subject of whether it was a truth of faith that the reigning Pope was the lawful successor of Peter! Once again the two generals and their theologians, in the presence of the Pope, of Cardinals Arigoni and Borghese, and of the Theological Commission, further strengthened by four members, debated only Molina's teaching, comparing it with Augustine and Cassian and also with Trent. Although the disputations—a total of sixty-eight— and the succeeding deliberations of the cardinals and consultors were continued for almost three years (1602–5), the Pope felt unable to reach a decision. Bellarmine had clearly been right in warning him not to try to settle so weighty a question himself but to refer it to a council or to trained theologians. Clement VIII was inclined to favor the Dominicans; his confessor, Cardinal Baronius, admitted to being an opponent of Molina but a friend of the Jesuits. At the Pope's death nothing had been settled.

Paul V had both sides present their views to him concisely and in writing. But nevertheless, on 2 September 1605, he again convened the commission which had been investigating Molina and had shortly before been sharply attacked by the Jesuit Bastida. On 14 September 1605 the disputations were resumed over the documentary evidence which it had not been possible to consider at the beginning of the year because of the illness of Clement VIII. Their course convinced Pope Paul V that in this manner no progress was possible. He ordered that only the fundamental question should be considered: how the efficacy of grace on the free will

---

[15] Pastor, XXIV, 336.

is to be understood. Thus the doctrine of Molina, which had been generally fixed as the point at issue under Clement VIII, was put aside and the Pope now yielded to the original demand of the Jesuits. These endeavored to refute the Thomistic doctrine of the *praemotio physica* and to prove that it was akin to the Calvinist theory of grace.

After the conclusion of the disputations the consultors were directed to answer four questions: 1. Which propositions on grace should be defined; 2. Which should be condemned; 3. Where lay the difference between the Catholic and the heretical views; 4. Whether a bull should be issued on the subject. The opinion of the consultors, rendered at the end of November 1606, was that forty-two propositions of Molina were to be censured; only one consultor, the Carmelite Bovio, counseled against any decision because the question was not ready for a final judgment. This was also the view of Francis de Sales and Cardinal Duperron, whose advice the Pope sought. Of the nine cardinals whom he questioned on 28 August, four advocated further discussion; two recommended a judgment, but without indicating in what sense; the Dominican Cardinal Bernerio called for the condemnation of Molina's forty-two propositions; Cardinals Bellarmine and Duperron asked for the contrary. In these circumstances the Pope refrained from a decision, saying that the teaching of the Dominicans was quite different from that of Calvin, the teaching of the Jesuits, different from Pelagianism; so that no definition was necessary. The *Congregatio de Auxiliis* was dissolved and silence concerning the discussions was enjoined on all participants. The Inquisition, on 11 December 1611, decreed that, for the future, writings published on the subject of grace would require its previous approbation.

Molina barely had escaped condemnation, but the Society of Jesus, accused with him, had held its own. No definition concluded the greatest dogmatic controversy which had ever broken out within Catholic Theology, over what is, in the final analysis, an almost insoluble problem, and which had kept in suspense not only the Catholic but also the Protestant world. The issue remained officially undecided and probably had to, because the mystery of the collaboration between divine grace and man's free will defies ultimate clarification by human reason. The antagonism between the two schools, Thomists and Molinists, has begun to diminish only quite recently.

CHAPTER 42

The Rise of Positive Theology

Humanism's slogan, "To the sources," had riveted attention on the Bible and the Fathers. Now the confrontation with the Protestant doctrinal system on the basis of Scripture and Tradition, defined at Trent as the sources of revelation, together with the defense of the Church institutions that were under attack, led to the construction of historical theology.[1] While at first Spaniards and Italians played the leading role in the Catholic Reform, toward the close of the period under discussion the French joined them with distinguished achievements.

The Tridentine decree on the Vulgate did not prevent work on the Hebrew and Greek texts of the Bible. By order of Philip II Arias Montanus (d. 1598) supervised the "Royal Polyglot"[2] based on the Complutensian text. The Parisian philologist Robert Estienne revised four of Erasmus' editions of the Greek New Testament, the last of which (1551) introduced the verse arrangement. The *textus receptus* of the Leiden book dealer Elzevir (1633) enjoyed the greatest esteem. The edition of the Septuagint, prepared under the direction of Cardinal Antonio Carafa, appeared in Rome in 1587. The most popular text of the Vulgate until the release of the Sixto-Clementina was the often reprinted Louvain edition of the Dominican Johann Henten (1547), which was later improved by Luke of Bruges (d. 1619).

Despite Trent's contrary attitude, the Bible was translated into the vernacular, especially in countries threatened by Protestantism. The German translations of Dietenberger and Eck were unsatisfactory; the one begun in 1614 by Caspar Ulenberg,[3] but not completed until after his death by Heinrich Francken-Sierstorff (1630), continued in use into the eighteenth century as the "Mainz Catholic Bible," so called because of revisions by theologians of Mainz. The French Bible going back to Jacques Lefèvre d'Etaples was placed on the Index in 1546, but after being revised by Louvain theologians it was reprinted at least two hundred times.

Biblical exegesis was not outdistanced by textual criticism. Whereas the exegetical works of the Jesuit Francisco de Toledo, important also as

---

[1] This expression already occurs in A. Possevino, *Bibliotheca selecta* (Rome 1593), p. 151.

[2] Eight volumes (Antwerp 1569–72). B. Rekers, *Benito Arias Montano 1527–98* (Gronigen 1961).

philosopher and preacher, are only a part of his total achievement, Juan de Maldonado (d. 1583)[4] became the most celebrated exegete of the period with his commentary on the Gospels (posthumously published in 1596) and those on the Old Testament. Both men came from the Salamanca school. But in the extent of exegetical accomplishment both were surpassed by Cornelius a Lapide (van Steen, d. 1637),[5] who commented on almost all the books of the Bible during his long teaching career at Louvain. Sixtus of Siena (d. 1569) established the "introduction" to Scripture on a scientific basis. After his conversion from Judaism he had been condemned to death for alleged heresy, pardoned through Ghislieri's intervention, and admitted to the Dominican Order. His *Bibliotheca Sancta*[6] contained not only the most complete introduction to Scripture up to that time but also a critical history of biblical interpretation.

Church Fathers and Councils

The Fathers of the Church, the knowledge of whom had been so greatly promoted by Erasmus' complete editions, became the arsenal of controversial theology. It was necessary to produce witnesses for the antiquity of the Mass and the Real Presence, for the official priesthood and the papal primacy, for ceremonies and the veneration of saints. John Fisher and Hieronyumus Emser had already had recourse to them. For purposes of controversial theology Cochläus published writings of Cyprian, Optatus of Milevis, Gregory Nazianzen, and Chrysostom. Guglielmo Sirleto submitted evidence to the Council of Trent from the Vatican manuscripts, especially those of the Greek Fathers.[7] Although he published little, he was a pioneer of Greek patrology. Athanasius, Basil the Great, Gregory Nazianzen, and Chrysostom were first termed Doctors of the Church in the breviary of Pius V. The early complete editions had provided their works only in Latin translation; after the turn of the century editions in both Greek and Latin appeared in rapid

---

[3] J. Solzbacher, *Kaspar Ulenberg* (Münster 1948), pp. 61–66 [*KLK* 8].

[4] Sommervogel, V, 403–412.

[5] Sommervogel, IV, 1511–26; last edition in 22 vols. (Paris 1859ff.) G. Boss, *Die Rechtfertigungslehre in den Bibelkommentaren des Kornelius a Lapide* (Münster 1962) [*KLK* 20].

[6] Two volumes (Venice 1566); best edition by T. Milante (Naples 1742); J. W. Montgomery, "Sixtus of Siena and Roman Catholic Scholarship in the Reformation Period" in *ARG* 54 (1964), 214–234.

[7] Extracts for 1545–47 in *CT* X, 929–955; cf. S. Merkle, "Ein patristischer Gewährsmann des Tridentinums," *Festgabe A. Ehrhard* (Bonn 1922), pp. 342–358.

succession.[8] The most prominent scholar active in this work was the French Jesuit Fronton du Duc (d. 1624). The Basel complete editions of Augustine (by Amerbach in 1506, by Erasmus in 1528f.) were replaced by the Louvain editions (1577); the Basel editions of Erasmus' texts of Jerome (1516–20) and Ambrose (1527), by the Roman editions (Jerome in 1565–72 and Ambrose in 1579–87). About the same time the Sorbonne professor Marguerin de la Bigne (d. 1589), in his *Bibliotheca Sanctorum Patrum,* published writings of more than 200 ancient and medieval authors in order to provide material for refuting the Magdeburg Centuriators.[9] The authenticity of the *Apostolic Canons* and of the pseudo-Isidorean decretals was defended by the Spaniard Franciscus Torres (d. 1584) against the Centuriators but disproved by the *Pseudo-Isidorus et Turrianus Vapulantes* (1628) of the Calvinist Blondel. The *Apostolic Constitutions,* first published in 1563, also by Torres, and to an even greater degree the researches of the Augustinian Hermit Onofrio Panvinio (d. 1564) on the Roman stational churches, titular churches, and deaconries, the origin of the College of Cardinals, and the iconography of the Popes "lighted the fire of the science of Christian antiquity" (De Rossi), which culminated in the rediscovery of the catacombs.

Individual catacombs had indeed been accessible during the Middle Ages and had been visited by pilgrims, for example, San Sebastiano, San Pancrazio, San Callisto. But the way was really paved for their exploration by the devotion to the Church of the Martyrs enkindled by Philip Neri. Accidentally, in the summer of 1578, the hitherto entirely unknown Catacomb of the Giordani on the Via Salaria was discovered; it was at first believed to be the Catacomb of Santa Priscilla. Its paintings and inscriptions were catalogued by Alphonse Chacon, Philip de Vighe, and John Makarios. The systematic exploration of the old and the recently discovered catacombs began in 1593 with Antonio Bosio (d. 1629), of whose grand-scale *Roma sotteranea* only a part was published, posthumously, in 1632.[10] The reawakened interest in Christian antiquity was further stimulated by fortunate discoveries, such as that of the well-preserved remains of Saint Cecilia by Cardinal Sfondrato in 1599.

The conflict over the Council had brought forth the first complete

---

[8] Athanasius, Heidelberg 1601; Basil, Paris 1618 (preceded by a Greek edition [Basel 1532]); Gregory Nazianzen, Paris 1609–11; Gregory of Nyssa, Paris 1615; Epiphanius of Salamis, Paris 1622 (by Petavius); Chrysostom, Paris 1609–33 (by Fronton du Duc).

[9] Nine volumes (Paris 1575–89).

[10] A. Ferrua, "Le tre Rome sotterranee," *CivCatt* II (1938), 399–412; C. Marcora, "Il Card. Federigo Borromeo e l'archeologia cristians" in *Mélanges E. Tisserant* V (Citta del Vaticano 1964), 115–54.

editions of the ancient councils by Merlin (1524) and Crabbe (1538). They were thereafter continually enlarged. Crabbe's second edition (1551) comprised three volumes; the next, by the Carthusian Surius (1567), four; and Bini, a canon of Cologne, enlarged it in 1606 to five volumes. But all these were far surpassed by the Roman edition in four volumes (1608–12), ordered by Sixtus V but not completed until the pontificate of Paul V. It not only gave better texts; it was the first to give the Greek.[11] Later in the seventeenth century the French took the lead in this field. Bartolomé Carranza composed a much used and often printed compendium of the history of the councils.[12]

To facilitate a general survey of Christian literature, which in the course of the sixteenth century had increased enormously, most of all through the abundant publication of sources, the Augustinian Hermit Angelus Rocca (d. 1620) composed an *Epitome,* at first for his own convenience but published in 1594 with a dedication to Clement VIII.[13] It contained, though not yet in chronological order, a summary of editions of the Bible and exegetes, the works of the great Latin and Greek Fathers, of the great scholastics, and of selected modern writers. Of a similar origin but far more satisfactorily arranged in chronological order was Bellarmine's brochure of 1613 on ecclesiastical authors.[14] Much more detailed than both was Possevino's alphabetically arranged *Apparatus sacer,* with an attached guide to ecclesiastical libraries.[15] The old catalogues of authors by Jerome, Gennadius, Sigebert of Gembloux, and others had been reedited in 1580 by the Frisian Suffridus Petri (d. 1597). The Belgian historian Miraeus (Le Mire, d. 1640), to whom we owe several works on Church statistics, continued the last medieval catalogue of authors, that of Johannes Trithemius, by means of two appendices, one of which appeared in his lifetime (1639), the second and more copious after his death (1649).[16]

---

[11] S. Kuttner, *L'édition Romaine des Conciles généraux et les actes du premier Concile de Lyon* (Rome 1940) [*Misc. Hist. Pont.* III, 5]; C. Leonardi, "Per la storia dell'edizione romana dei Concili ecumenici 1608/12" in *Mélanges E. Tisserant* VI (Citta del Vaticano 1964), 583–637; V. Peri, "Due protagonisti dell'editio romana dei Concili ecumenici: P. Morin ed A. d'Aquino," ibid., VII, 131–232; on the importance of the edition for the enumeration see id., *Aevum* 37 (1963), 430–501.

[12] *Summa conciliorum et pontificum* (Venice 1546), often reprinted. On the compiler, see chapter 41, note 2.

[13] *Bibliothecae theologicae et scripturalis epitome sive index* (Rome 1594).

[14] *De scriptoribus ecclesiasticis* (Rome 1613). The first draft, composed in Louvain in 1569–76, in Le Bachelet, *Auctarium Bellarminianum,* pp. 339–357.

[15] Three volumes (Venice 1606).

[16] *Notitia episcopatuum orbis christiani* (Antwerp 1613). *Politia ecclesiastica* (Cologne 1609) on the mission territories; *Geographia ecclesiastica* (Lyons 1620).

Church History

Even more important than these advances in Christian literary history were those in Church history, which, literally refounded at this time, at once displayed a monumental achievement. The *Catalogus testium veritatis* (1556) and to a much greater extent the Church history by Matthias Flacius Illyricus and his associates, known as the *Centuries,*[17] which set for itself the goal of establishing the "integram ecclesiae Christi ideam" but in reality was an historial defense of orthodox Lutheranism drawn up with great scholarship, had evoked rebuttals by Conrad Braun, Peter Canisius, and Gilbert Génébrard,[18] whose scholarly equipment, however, was inadequate for this task. A satisfactory reply had to wait for the *Annales ecclesiastici* of the Oratorian Caesar Baronius (1538–1607). The *Annales* grew out of the lectures which Baronius, at the request of Philip Neri, had delivered since 1558 at the Roman Oratory. After he had repeated the course seven times and, constantly revising it, had assembled a vast amount of material, "Especially against the innovators of today in defense of the antiquity of the sacred traditions and of the authority of the Roman Church,"[19] Neri induced him "to make for that immensely broad sea" and undertake the composition of a Church history based on the sources, which, in spite of its annalistic arrangement and its fundamentally apologetic tendency, is outstanding as a sincere searching for truth.[20] Tirelessly the always unassuming but strong-principled scholar, who was raised to the purple in 1596, continued his work through twelve volumes to 1198. The rejoinder of the Calvinist Isaac Casaubonus (1614) did not prevent the *Annales* and their later continuations, especially by Raynald and Laderchi, from remaining to the present as a standard work in Church history.[21]

---

[17] *Ecclesiastica historia . . . secundum singulas centurias* (1559–74); principal collaborators were J. Wigand and M. Judex. W. Preger, *M. Flacius Illyricus und Seine Zeit,* 2 vols. (Erlangen 1859–61); L. Haikola, *Gesetz und Evangelium bei M. Fl. Ill.* (Lund 1952); P. Polman in *RHE* 27 (1931), 27–73.

[18] C. Braun, *Liber adversus Centurias Magdeburgenses* (Dillingen 1565); P. Canisius, *De verbi Dei corruptelis* (Dillingen 1571); *idem, De Maria Virgine incomparabili Dei genitrice* (Ingolstadt 1577); G. Génébrard, *Chronographiae libri IV contra Centuriatores Magdeburgenses* (Paris 1580).

[19] Dedicatory letter to Sixtus V: "praesertim contra novatores nostri temporis, pro sacrarum traditionum antiquitate ac S. Romanae Ecclesiae potestate."

[20] Ibid.: "cum nihil periculosius sit in historia, quam cuivis scribenti de quacumque re fidem habere."

[21] This judgment does not hold for Baronius's first continuator, the Dominican Abraham Bzovius, whose extremely biased treatment of Ludwig the Bavarian led to a conflict with Bavaria. A. Kraus, "Die Annales ecclesiastici des A. Bzovius und Maximilian I. von Bavern," *Reformata reformanda* II, 253–303.

As the Magdeburg *Centuries* unintentionally contributed to the development of general Church history, so did the history of the Council of Trent by the Servite Paolo Sarpi stimulate research into this fundamental event of the entire era.[22] Sarpi's seemingly sober and objective presentation was in reality only an attack on the post-Tridentine papacy, and he not infrequently bridged gaps in his sources by conjectures. The writers whom Urban VIII summoned to refute it were to some extent unqualified or they were drowned in their material, for example, the Jesuit Terenzio Alciati (d. 1651). The latter's confrere, Sforza Pallavicino (d. 1667), succeeded in producing a history of the Council that would be the standard Catholic work into the nineteenth century. He availed himself of the rich source materials amassed by his predecessor and considerably augmented by himself. By his own avowal, he intended it as an historical defense, and that is what it was.[23]

The Protestant rejection of the cult of the saints was met by the hagiographers Lippomani and Surius with their collections of lives of saints. The *Vitae sanctorum priscorum Patrum* of Luigi Lippomani (d. 1559 as Bishop of Bergamo) contained, among other items, the first translation of the lives of Byzantine saints by Simon Metaphrastes and John Moschus;[24] the Frenchman Hervet and Sirleto collaborated with him. The Carthusian Laurentius Surius (d. 1578), meritorious as editor of the councils and also for a contemporary history and his translations of the works of Suso, Tauler, and Ruysbroeck, received from Lippomani a third of his material, chiefly Metaphrastes, but often had recourse to the original sources, including those in manuscript. The reproach hurled at him, that he arbitrarily altered various *vitae,* or rather the critical texts, can be verified in only a few cases, but he frequently changed expressions and suppressed passages that might have offended Catholic readers.[25] These defects were to some extent rectified in the third edition (1618). Surius' work was the chief forerunner of the *Acta*

---

[22] H. Jedin, "Survey," pp. 83–93, is corrected by G. Cozzi, "Fra P. Sarpi, l'Anglicanesimo e la Historia del Concilio Tridentino." *RSIT* 68 (1956), 559–619, thus: The publication of the work took place with Sarpi's knowledge and consent, and it was marked by a Calvinist bias. The manuscript was supplied only by fascicles (*a puntate*) in the course of printing. In regard to M. A. de Dominis, apostate Archbishop of Spalato, until recently termed a go-between, and his theory of the Church, cf. D. Cantimori, "Su M. A. de Dominis," *ARG* 49 (1958), 245–258; id. "L'utopia ecclesiologica di M. A. de Dominis," *Problemi di vita religiosa in Italia nel Cinquecento* (Padua 1960), pp. 103–122.

[23] H. Jedin, *Der Quellenapparat der Konzilsgeschichte Pallavicinos* (Rome 1940).

[24] Vols. I–V (Venice 1551–56); VI–VIII (Rome 1558–60); an abridged edition in 2 vols. (Louvain 1564).

[25] *De probatis sanctorum historiis,* 6 vols. (Cologne 1570–75); second edition, *ibid.,* 1576–81. P. Holt, "Die Sammlung von Heiligenleben des Laurentius Surius," *NA* 44 (1922), 341–364.

Sanctorum, which, first projected by the Jesuit Heribert Rosweyde in 1607, appeared in its initial volumes in 1643. The *Martyrologium Romanum,* compiled by Cardinal Sirleto with the assistance of Baronius at the order of Gregory XIII, was prescribed for liturgical use in 1584.[26]

The apologetic tone of not only hagiography but of other aspects of historical theology gradually lessened and the historico-critical method asserted itself. The Jesuit Dionysius Petavius (1593–1652)[27] directed his energies in his writings, saturated with historical material, on the special priesthood (1639) and on the hierarchy (1643) against Grotius and Salmasius and also against the Jansenists. His main work, *Dogmata theologica,* is regarded as the foundation of the history of dogma. His *Doctrina temporum,* the first scientific chronology, inaugurated a long series of French contributions to the establishment of auxiliary sciences of history and the historical method, culminating in the works of Mabillon and Montfaucon.

Canon Law

A trend toward the positive historical method is seen, finally, in canon law. Of the Spanish triple constellation, Martin de Azpilcueta (d. 1586) and his pupil Diego de Covarruvias (d. 1577 as Bishop of Segovia) were systematizers.[28] The first named, the "Doctor Navarrus," after a long teaching career in Salamanca and Coimbra, moved to Rome and from the time of Pius V was looked upon as an oracle even in difficult questions of moral theology. On the other hand, Antonio Agustin (d. 1586 as Archbishop of Tarragona), who had been educated at Alcalá and Salamanca, applied the historico-critical method during his stay in Italy first to Roman and then to canon law under the influence of the jurist Andrea Alciati. His textual criticism of the Decree of Gratian, based on preliminary studies of the ancient collections of decretals, indicated numerous errors in the new edition of 1582, ordered by Gregory XIII. Agostino Barbosa (d. 1649) was the outstanding Italian canonist by virtue of his extensive acquaintance with the law and the canonical literature. The growing influence of canon law in the domain of moral casuistry is clearly discernible in the Jesuit Paul Laymann (d. 1635). The

---

[26] H. Lämmer, *De Martyrologio Romano* (Regensburg 1878).

[27] *Dogmata theologica,* 4 vols. (Paris 1644–50); *Doctrina temporum,* 2 vols. (Paris 1627).

[28] F. Merzbacher, "Azpilcueta und Covarruvias. Zur Gewaltendoktrin der spanischen Kanonistik im Goldenen Zeitalter," *ZSavRGkan* 46 (1960), 317–344; on pp. 318ff., complete list of the literature on both these canonists; id. "Kard. Juan de Lugo als Rechtsdenker," *Spanische Forschungen,* 19 (1962), 269–280; *Martin de Azpilcueta,* Commentario resolutorio de cambios, ed. A. Ullastres–J. M. Perez Prendes–L. Perena (Madrid 1965) [-Corpus Hispanorum de Pace IV].

founders of modern Gallicanism, Pierre Pithou (d. 1596) and Edmund Richer (d. 1631), belong to this period but can only be understood against the background of the ecclesiastico-political and ecclesiological development of seventeenth-century France.

The progress of historical theology did not yet include, on the Catholic side, the introduction of Church history into the theological curriculum. Whereas at most Protestant universities universal history—still treated from the viewpoint of salvation history—and Church history became fields of study, the perceptible trend at some Catholic universities toward academic instruction in history disappeared. Such a trend could have led to instruction in Church history, under the influence of the Jesuit *Ratio Studiorum,* which dominated all studies.[29] The plan of the Jesuit general Acquaviva to establish a sort of academy of Church history was unrealized.[30]

Printing Houses and Libraries

Connected with the rise of positive theology was the growth of efficient printing presses and of well-equipped ecclesiastical libraries. Of the printing centers, Basel, where Erasmus' editions of the New Testament and of many Church Fathers had appeared, had become Protestant, while Paris and Lyons were severely handicapped by the Huguenot Wars. Now, alongside Venice, reformed Rome became the place where excellent works were published. In 1561 Pius IV summoned the Venetian printer and philologist Paul Manutius to Rome[31] for the express purpose of using his talents as a qualified printer and publisher. In 1587 Sixtus V founded the Vatican Printing Press, which brought out, among other works, Baronius' *Annales* and the Roman conciliar collection. And the Propaganda Fidei Printing Press, set up in 1626, had Arabic and Armenian fonts as well as Latin and Greek.[32] The prosperity of the Plantin family of Antwerp sprang from the printing of the Tridentine breviary.[33] The Quentel heirs—Gerwin Calenius is counted as one of them—Johann Birckmann, and Maternus Cholinus, printed many

---

[29] E. C. Scherer, *Geschichte und Krichengeschichte an den deutschen Universitäten* (Freiburg 1927), pp. 52–131.

[30] P. Leturia, "L'Insegnamento della storia ecclesiastica nella Roma dell'Umanesimo e del Barocco," *CivCatt* IV (1945), 393–402.

[31] F. Barberi, *P. Manuzio e la stamperia del Popolo romano* (Rome 1942); A. M. Giorgetti Vichi, *Annali della stamperia del Popolo romano 1570–98* (Rome 1959).

[32] Pastor XXII, 199ff., XXIX, 216.

[33] R. M. Kingdom, "The Plantin Breviaries." *Bibliothèque d'Humanisme et de Renaissance* 22 (1960), 133–150.

Catholic works at Cologne,[34] while in South Germany the houses of Weissenhorn and Eder made Ingolstadt the leading publishing center. Four hundred and sixty-five printings from the Dillingen firm of Sebald Mayer are known for the years 1550–76; after 1620 the Jesuit college at Dillingen had its own press.[35] A survey of new publications was rendered easier after 1564 by the Frankfurt book catalogues, which on the eve of the Thirty Years' War recorded more than fifteen hundred titles a year. Occasionally they were accompanied by indexes of Catholic books, compiled at the instigation of the Jesuits, as counterparts of the Index of Forbidden Books.[36]

The *Ratio Studiorum* ordered for each college the preparation of a library budget, because the Fathers would otherwise be "unarmed soldiers." Peter Canisius could sooner imagine a college without a church than one without a library.[37] The importance of libraries was also clearly grasped at Rome. Under Cervini, the first cardinal librarian, and his successors, Sirleto, Antonio Carafa, and Baronius, the Vatican Library grew enormously.[38] For it Sixtus V raised the building still in use, which, it is true, bisected Bramante's Belvedere Cortile but architecturally inaugurated the series of Italian library complexes. Its manuscript and book collections were enriched by the gift of the Heidelberg Palatina, made to the Pope by the Elector Maximilian of Bavaria. The Biblioteca Angelica, so called from its founder, Angelus Rocca, was a public library. Cardinal Francesco Barberini's collection of books and manuscripts became, under the direction of Luke Holstenius (after 1636), the richest of all Roman libraries next to the Vatican. In Milan Cardinal Federigo Borromeo founded the Ambrosian Library in 1602. By 1669

[34] H. Schrörs, "Der Kölner Buchdrucker Maternus Cholinus," *AHVNrh* 85 (1908), 147–165. On the printer Franz Behem, who was related to Cochläus and who between 1540 and 1580 printed works of Cochläus, Witzel, Braun, Hosius, and others at Mainz cf. S. Widmann, *Eine Mainzer Presse der Reformationzeit im Dienste der kath. Literatur* (Paderborn 1889).

[35] D. Bucher, *Bibliographie der deutschen Drucke des XVI. Jahrdunderts,* I: *Dillingen* (Bad Bocklet–Vienna 1960), lists 796 printed works of the Dillingen firm.

[36] Cf. also W. Brückner, "Die Gegenreformation im politischen Kampf um die Frankfurter Buchmessen," *Archiv für Frankfurts Geschichte und Kunst* 48 (1962), 67–86.

[37] O. Braunsberger, "Ein Freund der Bibliotheken und ihrer Handschriften," *Miscellanea F. Ehrle* V (Rome 1924), 455–472.

[38] P. Batiffol, *La Vaticane de Paul III a Paul V* (Paris 1890); Pastor, XXII, 291ff., XXVII, 243ff.; P. Petitmengin, "Recherches sur l'organisation de la Bibliothèque Vaticane à l'époque des Ranaldi 1547–628.

Italy had eighty libraries, the Netherlands fifty, France twenty-seven, Germany twenty-three, and England eleven.[39]

[39] J. W. Montgomery, *A Seventeenth-Century View of European Libraries* (Berkeley–Los Angeles 1962). A survey for Spain is provided by A. Schott, *Hispaniae bibliothecae seu de academiis ac bibliothecis,* 3 vols. (Frankfurt 1608).

CHAPTER 43

Spiritual Life, Popular Devotion and Art

Ascetical and mystical literature leads to the sources of the Church's renewal. The connection of this literature, in regard to both its content and the persons involved, with the reinvigorated theology makes apparent its relevance to life. Luis de León stated as its aim "to explain the sound doctrine which rouses souls and conducts them to the way of virtue." It proceeded from Spain and in Spain culminated in the Carmelite mystics. Until about the mid-century people were content with guides to the interior life and prayer and to a virtuous life. Erasmus' polemic against extraversion of piety and certain abuses in worship and popular devotion was insignificant in the light of positive suggestions; in 1546 his *Modus orandi* was translated into Spanish, and Luis of Granada followed the rules of life of the *Enchiridion.*[1] The Dominican John of the Cross, not to be confused with the Carmelite, in his *Dialogo* (1555) defended vocal prayer and ritual. The influence of Savonarola, predominant in the Spanish Dominican reform, is evident in the *Guia del cielo* (1527) of the Dominican Pablo de León and in the most popular ascetical works of the Catholic Reform, the *Libro de la oracion y meditacion* and the *Guia de precadores* of Luis of Granada (d. 1588). The latter's real model was his director, Juan de Avila (d. 1569), the "Apostle of Andalusia."[2] In the last years of his life, when physically broken as a

[1] V. Beltran de Heredia, *Las corrientes de espiritualidad entre los Dominicos de Castilla* (Salamanca 1941), rejected the overemphasis of Erasmian influence on Spanish piety in the French original of Battaillon (1937); the Spanish edition of Battaillon took these objections into account to some extent.
[2] *Obras,* ed. J. Cuervo, 14 vols. (Madrid 1906–8); M. Llaaneza, *Bibliografia del Ven. P. L. de Granada,* 4 vols. (Salamanca 1926–28); M. Battaillon, *Erasmo y Espana* II, 191ff. (with the literature); Fidele de Ros, "Los misticos del Norte y Fray L. de Gr.," *AIA,* 7 (1941), 5–30, 145–165; R. L. Oechslin, *L. de Granada ou La reconte avec Dieu* (Paris 1954); J. I. Tellechea Idigoras, "Aprobacion de la Guia de Pecadores de Fray L. de Granada en el Concilio de Trento," *HS* 12 (1959), 225ff.; A.Huerga, "El proceso inquisitorial de la Monja de Lisbon y Fray L. de Granada," *HS* 12 (1959), 333–356; id., "Fray L. de Granada y S. Carlos Borromeo. Una amistad al servicio de la restauracion catolica," *HS* 11 (1958), 299–347.

consequence of overexertion in preaching and pastoral activity, Juan had his *Audifilia* printed (1557)—a guide to the spiritual life intended for Doña Sancha Carillo—and thereafter devoted himself to the direction of souls. His spiritual letters are the fruit of this preoccupation.[3] The Portuguese Dominican Bartholomaeus a Martyribus (d. 1590 as Archbishop of Braga), in his *Stimulus pastorum* (1567), composed at Borromeo's request, sketched the episcopal ideal of the Tridentine Reform, that of the Good Shepherd, drawn to a great extent, like his *Compendium doctrinae spiritualis* (1582), from Scripture and the Fathers.[4]

In Francisco de Osuna (d. 1540 or 1541) the Franciscan school had produced an outstanding master of the spiritual life, whose *Abecedario espiritual* (6 parts, 1527–54) led Teresa of Avila to interior prayer. Peter of Alcántara (d. 1562, canonized in 1669), highly esteemed as a spiritual director but, as founder of the Franciscan Recollects, excessively strict with himself and others, wrote a *Treatise on Prayer and Contemplation*—its relationship to Luis of Granada's work of the same title is disputed—which developed still further the doctrine of interior prayer. With Perez de Valdivia (d. 1589), he completed the tendency toward mysticism, which realized in Juan de los Angeles (d. 1610) its most subtle psychological depths under the influence of Tauler and Ruysbroeck.[5]

Alonso de Orozco (d. 1591), the most prolific ascetical writer of the Spanish Augustinian Hermits, also betrays a mystical trend in his many treatises.[6] But the Augustinians' "most read, most often translated, and most often commented" author was Luis de León (d. 1591), who received from Domingo Soto the position of professor of Scripture at Salamanca. His exposition of the fourteen biblical names of Christ (*De*

---

[3] *Obras Completas* (Madrid 1588); critical edition by L. Sala Balust, 3 vols. (Madrid 1952ff.); the spiritual letters, edited by V. Garcia de Diego, also in *Clasicos Castellanos* XI (Madrid 1912); good character sketch by J. M. de Buck in *NRTh* 55 (1928), 30–49; on the Inquisition proceedings in which Juan de Avila was involved in 1532f., see C. M. Abad in *MCom* 6 (1946), 95–167; A. Berengueras de Nilar in *Verdad y vida* 17 (1959), 75–96; for his reform memorandum see chapter 35.

[4] *Opera Omnia,* ed. M. d'Inguimbert, 2 vols. (Rome 1734f.); H. Jedin–P. Broutin, *L'évêque dans la tradition pastorale du 16e siècle* (Paris 1953), pp. 84–103.

[5] Fidele de Ros, *Un maitre de S. Therese: Le Père François d'Osuna* (Paris 1937); S. Piat, *Le maitre de la mystique S. Pierre d'Alcantara* (Paris 1960); Vicente de Peralta, "El doctor Perez de Valdivia," *Estudios Franciscanos* 27 (1931), 177–225; for Valdivia's stay in Barcelona, see J. M. Madurell y Marimon in *Anal. S. Tarracon.* 30 (1957), 343–371. *Juan de los Angeles, Obras Misticas* ed. J. Sala, 2 vols. (Madrid 1912–17); further literature in *LThK* 2nd ed., V, 998.

[6] T. Camara, *Vida y escritos del B. Alonso de Orozco* (Valladolid 1882); later bibliography in D. Guttierrez, *S. Augustinus vitae spirit. Magister* II, 173ff.

los nombres de Cristo, 1583) and his *La perfecta casada* (1583), intended for his cousin, Maria Varela, showed him to be a poet of real inspiration (K. Vossler) and a master of language, who fused theological depth with practical sense.[7] Not his least merit is to have made possible the printing of the works of Teresa of Avila by his judgment "de muy sana y catolica doctrina."

Carmelite Mysticism

After the mid-century the cultivation of contemplative prayer brought forth the flower of mysticism in Carmel. Teresa of Avila, actually de Ahumada y Cépeda (1515–82, canonized in 1622), surpassed the late medieval German mystics in blending the most refined psychological observation and mystical experience with a truly Spanish practicality and tireless activity for the reform of her Order. The story of her interior life to the beginning of her reform activity (1562) is contained in her autobiography, recorded at the command of the Toledo Inquisitor and completed in 1565. The exquisitely refreshing *Libro de las fundaciones* narrates the establishing of eighteen reformed houses between 1567 and 1582, accomplished after overcoming strong opposition. Intended for her nuns was the *Camino de perfección,* composed about 1565 at the request of her confessor, the Dominican Báñes. The most complete of her mystical writings is *El castillo interior* (1577), in which she describes her progress to mystical union with God in seven stages. A knowledge of her truly great personality is provided by her less mystical writings (*Exclamaciones, Avisos,* and others) and above all by her 440 letters, while the constitutions approved by the chapter of 1581 show her activity in the Order. She profited by her careful reading of spiritual works—Augustine's *Confessions,* the German mystics, Osuna—to describe correctly her own mystical experiences concerning whose divine origin she was long troubled, and to express them without affectation in classical Spanish. Patiently and with fortitude she finally vanquished all her opponents, including the papal Nuncio Sega, who regarded her as an adventuress.

Associated with Teresa from 1568 was John of the Cross (1542–91, canonized in 1726, declared a Doctor of the Church in 1926), who had made his theological studies at Salamanca. As spiritual director of the convent of the Incarnation (1572–77), of which Teresa was superior, he seconded her endeavors, only to be thrown into prison himself by the

---

[7] *Obras Completas,* ed. F. Garcia (Madrid 1944); K. Vossler, *Luis de Leon* (Munich 1946); S. Munoz Iglesias, *Fray L. de Toledo teologo* (Madrid 1950); R. J. Welsh, *Introduction to the Spiritual Doctrine of Fray L. de Leon* (Washington 1951).

opponents of reform. When the autonomy of the reformed branch of the Order had been achieved, he occupied posts in the Order at Baeza and Segovia and died in Ubeda, misunderstood and shamefully treated but purified by suffering. In his chief works, *Subida del Monto Carmelo* (1579) and *Noche oscura del alma* (1579), he describes the active and passive purification of the soul and outlines a system of mystical theology: The night of the senses and the night of the spirit must be overcome in order to mount "far above all limitations of knowledge" to union with God in the essence of the soul. The *Cantico espiritual* and the *Llama de amor viva,* composed during his imprisonment in Toledo, are genuinely poetic, expressing a never surpassed exclamation of the soul, cleansed by suffering and united with God.

Italy and France

Italy too produced mystics, such as Catherine Ricci (d. 1592), influenced by Savonarola, and the ecstatic Maria Magdalena dei Pazzi (d. 1607, canonized in 1669).[8] The most influential ascetical work, after and alongside the *Exercises* of Saint Ignatius, was, however, the *Combattimento spirituale* (single and unrevised edition: Venice 1589) of the Theatine Lorenzo Scupoli (d. 1610). The Jesuit school of spirituality, after some hesitation while Borgia was general, adhered to the sober and psychologically sound asceticism of the founder. Some authors, A. Cordeses, P. Sánchez, B. Rossignoli, followed the traditional plan of the three stages in the ascent to God. Based entirely on the manner of life in the Order, and hence unsystematic, was the teaching of Alonso Rodríguez (d. 1616) on prayer and the virtues in his *Ejercicio de perfección y virtudes cristianas* (3 vols., 1609–16). Alvarez de Paz (d. 1620) developed a theory of meditation culled from Scripture. Luis de la Puente (d. 1624),[9] a pupil of Francisco Suárez and Balthasar Alvarez, in his *Meditaciones de los misterios de nuestra Santa fé* (1605) and even more in his commentary on the Canticle of Canticles (1622) and the *Sentimientos* (published posthumously in 1670), makes it clear that he "was blessed with the gift of mystical prayer" (Guibert).

From the turn of the century the French school became increasingly

---

[8] Ermanno del SS. Sacramento, "Y manoscritti originali di S. Maria Maddalena de' Pazzi," *ECarm* 7 (1956), 323–400; *Tutte le opere di S. Maria Maddalena* I (Florence 1960); M. Petrocchi, *L'estasi nelle mistiche italiane della riforma cattolica* (Naples 1958), pp. 76f.; other literature in *LThK* 2nd ed., VII; biographies by F. van der Kley (Chicago 1957) and Alberto de la Virgen del Carmen (Madrid 1957).

[9] *Obras espirituales,* 5 vols. (Madrid 1690); C. M. Abad, "Doctrina mistica de V.P.L. de la P.," *EE* 3 (1924), 113–137, 4 (1925) 43–58, 251–273. On the whole subject see Guibert, *Spiritualite,* pp. 198ff., 237–270.

prominent. Even before then the reform-minded Benedictine Abbot Louis de Blois (Blosius, d. 1566), shunning certain harsh aspects of Spanish asceticism, had designated the cultivation of interior prayer, humility, and charity as the pillars of the virtuous life.[10] Francis de Sales (1567–1622, canonized in 1665, proclaimed a Doctor of the Church in 1877), very successful as a missionary and as Bishop of Geneva, promoted a realistic asceticism in his *Introduction à la vie dévote* (1608, usually known as *Philothea*) and his *Traité de l'amour de Dieu* (1616, also called *Theotimus*). His correspondence with Jane Frances de Chantal (d. 1641, canonized in 1767) is a monument of understanding and firm spiritual direction. His *Humanisme dévote* is much indebted to the mystic Barbe Acarie (d. 1618), who, married and the mother of six, established the Discalced Carmelites in France and, after her husband's death, joined them. It owes even more to the Oratorian Pierre de Bérulle (1575–1629, a cardinal in 1627), founder of the French Oratory (1611) and influential in Church politics, who is to be considered the real founder of the French school of spirituality. Educated in the Jesuit College de Clermont, in his youth Bérulle was influenced by the German and then by the Spanish mystics. Beginning in 1601 with his *Discours de l'état et de la grandeur de Jésus* there was formed in him a strictly Christocentric piety, which he spread as director of souls and which was still further developed by Charles de Condren (d. 1641), his pupil and successor in the government of the Oratory. The Oratory became the nursery for the leaders of the French spirituality of the *Grand Siècle*—Olier, Eudes, and others.

Preaching of the Faith

The stream of spiritual literature was indeed broad, but not broad enough to touch the uneducated classes. This duty was fulfilled by means of preaching and popular catechetical instruction, which the Council of Trent made obligatory for parish priests on all Sundays and holy days. In the Latin countries, as earlier, the Advent and Lent series, given mostly by preachers of the mendicant Orders, continued in practice. But the mission and apologetic sermons favored by the Jesuits and Capuchins were a new development. The present state of research does not provide a comprehensive or even adequate picture. In Italy, where between 1530 and 1550 entire books of the Bible, above all the Pauline Epistles, had been expounded in public lectures, Scriptural preaching, as carried out, for example, by Seripando and as Bishop Florimonte of

[10] *Opera* (Louvain 1568); reprinted in Cologne (1572) and Paris (1622); literature in *DSAM* I (1937), 1730–1738.

Sessa had sought to promote it in his collection of patristic homilies, later yielded again to topical preaching, causing the Conventual Cornelius Musso (d.1574) to indulge in bombast.[11] The three most renowned preachers around 1580 were thus characterized: Toledo (the Jesuit Francisco de Toledo) instructs, Panigarola (a Franciscan who died in 1594 as Bishop of Asti) is applauded, Lupus (a Spanish Capuchin who died in 1593) thrills hearts.[12] Lorenzo of Brindisi (1559–1619, canonized in 1881, declared a Doctor of the Church in 1959)[13] kept close to Scripture even in his topical sermons. In Germany the defense of the faith was served by the sermons of Eck, Hoffmeister, and Wild based on the Scriptural passage of the liturgy and even more by the topical sermons of Tintzmann, a pastor of Neisse.[14] The Lenten and Eucharistic sermons of Simon Vigor (d. 1575 as Archbishop of Narbonne) were published in several editions. French pulpit eloquence did not reach its climax, however, until the seventeenth century, with Vincent de Paul and Lejeune.

The clergy had at hand far more and far better tools for catechetical instruction than had been the case before Trent. In addition to the *Roman Catechism,* Peter Canisius' *Summa doctrinae christianae* (1554) for catechists and Bellarmine's *Dichiarazione* (1598) and the corresponding popular catechisms—Canisius' *Parvus catechismus* (1558) and *Catechismus minimus* (1556) and Bellarmine's *Dottrina cristiana breve* (1597)—

[11] H. Jedin, *Seripando* II, 63–84; for Florimonte's patristic homilies, ibid., II, 294; for Musso as a preacher see *RQ* 41 (1933), 252ff.

[12] Hurter, III, 249; P. M. Sevesi, "S. Carlo Borromeo e il P. F. Panigarola," *AFrH* 40 (1947), 143–207; G. Pozzi, "Intorno alla Predicazione del Panigarola," *Problemi religiosi* . . . (Padua 1960), pp. 315–323.

[13] The *Opera Omnia* (15 vols., Padua 1928–56) contain mostly sermons, including three for Lent. Literature in *Lex Cap,* pp. 925–930. For the Capuchin method of preaching see Arsenio d'Ascoli, *La predicazione dei Capuccini nel Cinquecento in Italia* (Loreto 1956), Bonaventura von Mehr, *Das Predigtwesen in der kölnisch-rheinischen Kapuzinerprovinz im 17. und 18. Jh.* (Rome 1945); Melchoir a Pobladura, *Hist. ord. Cappuccinorum* I, 247–264.

[14] Sermon books most used in Germany were those of: John Eck (5 vols.; Vols. I–III treat the scriptural readings of Sundays and feasts; Vols. IV–V deal with the Sacraments and the Decalog; editions *CC,* 16, n. 68); Johannes Hoffmeister, O.E.S.A. (for the twelve editions of his homilies on the Gospels for 1547, see N. Paulus, *J. Hoffmeister, O.E.S.A.,* pp. 388f.); Johann Wild, O.F.M. (4 vols. 1552–55); H. Pöhlein, *Wolfgang Seidel 1492–1562, Benediktiner aus Tegernsee, Prediger zu München* (Munich 1951); H. Jedin, "Das Breslauer Kanonikus und Pfarrer von Neisse N. Tintzmann (d. 1616) als Prediger," *ArSKG* 5 (1940), 142–151 (six complete annual courses of pastoral sermons, 1589–96, in which, among other items, the sermons of the Auxilliary Bishop Feucht of Bamberg and Stapleton's *Promptuarium* are used).

found a wide circulation.[15] Within eight years 42,000 copies of the Auger Catechism (1563) were sold in France. The *Doctrina cristiana* (1607) of the Jesuit Astete was much used in Spain. If the early catechisms, for example those of Dietenberger and Witzel, were strongly influenced by Luther and Erasmus, the later ones testified to more independence but were frequently lacking in clarity.[16] The Confraternity of Christian Doctrine, introduced in Milan by Borromeo, spread in and beyond Italy. The catechist César de Bus founded at Aix the Congregation of Priests of Christian Doctrine, which was confirmed by Clement VIII in 1598.[17] The Piarists of Joseph Calasanctius acquired an importance in elementary education analogous to that of the Jesuit colleges in higher education.

Like the acceptance and implementation of the Tridentine reform decrees, the introduction of the reformed breviary and missal of Pius V made very slow progress outside Italy.[18] Diocesan feasts were included in appended "propers."[19] Though not prescribed, the *Rituale Romanum* (1614) acquired great prestige for the administration of the Sacraments.[20] It utilized Cardinal Santori's ritual, printed in 1584 but not official, and also no fewer than fourteen other diocesan rituals, supplanted the older pastoral manuals in common use, such as the

---

[15] P. Canisius, *Catechismus lat. et germ.,* ed. F. Streicher, 2 vols. (Munich 1932–36); editions of Bellarmine's *Catechism* in Sommervogel, I, 1127–1178.

[16] C. Moufang, *Katholische Katechismen des 16. Jh. in deutscher Sprache* (Mainz 1881); R. Padberg, *Erasmus als Katechet* (Freiburg 1956); id., "Zum katechetischen Anliegen G. Witzels," *ThG1,* 43 (1953), 192–200; L. Pralle, "Die volksliturgischen Bestrebungen des G. Witzel," *Jahrbuch f. d. Bistum Mainz* 3 (1948), 224–242; E. Feifel, *Grundzüge einer Theologie des Gottesdienstes, Motive und Konzeption der Glaubensverkündigung Michael Heldings* (Freiburg 1960); F. Brand, *Die Katechismen des E. Augerius* (Fribourg 1917).

[17] A. Tamborini, *La compagnia e le scuole della dottrina cristiana* (Milan 1939); F. Pascucci, *L'Insegnamento religioso in Roma dal Concilio di Trento ad oggi* (Rome 1938); G. Franza, *Il Catechismo a Roma dal Concilio di Trento a Pio VI nello zelo dell'Arciconfraternita della dottrina cristiana* (Alba 1958). V. Sempels, "Het catechismusonderricht te Brussel gedurende de Contra-Reformatie," *Miscellanea De Meyer* II, 928–940; A. Berz, *Geschichte des Katechismus im Bistum Basel* (Fribourg 1959). L. Volpicella, *Il pensiero pedagogico della controriforma* (Florence 1960), gives text with introduction.

[18] The acceptance of Pius V's reformed breviary and missal needs to be further investigated; the most important tool is W. H. J. Weale-H. Bohatta, *Catalogus missalium ritus latini* (London 1928).

[19] E.g., the Breslau Diocesan Synod of 1592 prescribed the *Breviarium Romanum,* but it was not definitively adopted in the cathedral until 1653, and the *proprium* was approved in 1662; see *ArSKG* 5 (1940), 198f.

[20] B. Löwenberg, *Das Rituale des Kard. J. A. Sanctorius. Ein Beitrag zur Enstehungsgeschichte des Rituale Romanum* (Munich 1937); id. "Die Erstausgabe des Rituale Romanum von 1614," *ZKTh* 66 (1942), 141–147.

Sacerdotale Romanum (1523) of Alberto Castellani, and promoted the standardization of the rites, but of course repressed the vernacular tongues. Although people took pains to defend and explain "ceremonies" in areas exposed to Protestantism and the good screen between clergy and people gradually disappeared from the churches, popular participation in the liturgy was neither sought nor achieved. German Church hymns, held back rather than stimulated by the Protestant example, recovered ground only after much hesitation (Ulenberg's *Psalms* of 1582; the Mainz *Cantuale* of 1603; the Constance *Gesangbuch* of 1613; and F. Spee, *Trutznachtigal* of 1649).

Administration of Sacraments

The rite of administering the Sacraments and the frequency of reception still differed greatly from region to region. At the beginning of the sixteenth century annual Easter Communion was the almost invariable rule. Reception three or four times a year, prescribed in the Third Orders and the confraternities, was interpreted as a sign of religious zeal in the laity. But from the middle of the sixteenth century reception became much more frequent, especially under the influence of the new Orders—Theatines, Barnabites, Jesuits, and Capuchins—and in consequence of the general rise of devotion to the Eucharist. In many Italian confraternities monthly Communion was prescribed, while the Jesuits recommended weekly Communion for those seeking Christian perfection. However, the students of the Eichstätt seminary were encouraged to receive only five times a year—on Christmas, Easter, Pentecost, Assumption, and All Saints. The Easter Time in which Communion was of obligation and which was restricted by Eugene IV in 1446 to Holy Week and the Octave of Easter and in some places still further reduced, was again extended in certain dioceses, such as Salzburg in 1616.

As a rule Communion was preceded by confession. The confessional, hitherto usually open and moveable and in most churches close to the altar or the choir inclosure, was gradually replaced from the turn of the century under the influence of the *Rituale Romanum* by one that was stationary and provided with a wooden screen. In the Baroque period (beginning about 1550) the confessional in three sections, often artistically decorated, became a fixture of church equipment. The anointing of the sick was seldom requested in Germany, according to the records of visitations. The Constance synod of 1609 complained that in a large part of the diocese it had become obsolete. Confirmation slowly became more common in connection with visitations. When in 1586 it was first administered in Paderborn after a lapse of forty years, only 200 Catholics appeared. In the bishopric of Augsburg, where according to

Ninguarda's reports (1579) it had fallen into disuse many years before, 30,000 Catholics were confirmed in two months according to the *realatio* of 1597. The rite of contracting marriage exhibited, as previously, very great differences, but, due to the decree "Tametsi," there was a tendency to specify the reception of the Sacrament in the exchange of consent before the parish priest or in the blessing given by him.

Popular Devotion

Popular devotions, processions, and pilgrimages, frequently arranged by the again flourishing confraternities, became genuine expressions of popular piety. What was new in this post-Tridentine piety was its emphasis on specifically Catholic doctrines and forms of worship; it became anti-Protestant and hence a confessional piety. The Eucharistic confraternities, going back to the fifteenth century and having as their model the *Confraternità del SS. Sacramento* at Santa Maria sopra Minerva, which had been confirmed by Paul III in 1539, promoted devotion to the Eucharist in addition to communion, in particular the maintenance of the perpetual light and the providing of an escort for the taking of communion to the sick.[21] The Forty Hours' Prayer during Holy Week, originally lasting from Holy Thursday to Holy Saturday, was introduced in Milan by Borromeo in 1577 and by the Nuncio Frangipani in Cologne in 1591. In Rome it was extended as the Perpetual Prayer in 1592.[22] The Corpus Christi procession, recommended by Trent, was celebrated with great solemnity in several Catholic districts of Germany (Munich Processionals, 1582–1611).[23] In Spain the *Fiesta del Corpus* became during the second half of the sixteenth century the "highest of all Church feasts" and was enhanced by special performances, the *autos sacramentales*. Gradually the altar tabernacle replaced the receptacle situated to one side.

Devotion to Mary was intensified. The Marian Congregation, established by the Fleming Johannes Leunis in 1563 for the students of the Roman Jesuit College, made it the starting point of self-education and the fostering of an apostolic attitude. Introduced into almost all Jesuit colleges, by 1576 it numbered already 30,000 members. It was con-

[21] P. Tacchi Venturi, *Storia della Comp. di Gesu in Italia* 2nd ed., I, 217–290.
[22] J. A. Jungmann, "Die Andacht der 40 Stunden und das Hl. Grab," *LF* 2 (1952), 184–198.
[23] A. Mitterweiser, *Geschichte der Fronleichnamsprozession in Bayern* (Munich 1930); G. Matern, *Zur Vorgeschichte und Geschichte der Fronleichnamsfeier* (Münster 1962).

firmed by Gregory XIII in 1584.[24] The Marian place of pilgrimage, Loreto, was visited by many Romans, and the Litany of Loreto, traceable there back to 1531, was approved in 1589 by Sixtus V. The rosary acquired its present form and was promoted by rosary confraternities. And in thanksgiving for the victory at Lepanto Pius V instituted the feast of the rosary. In Germany the pilgrimages to miraculous Marian shrines, which had slackened during the religious cleavage, were revived at Altötting and Einsiedeln; many new ones arose, for example Kevelaer and Werl, and were encouraged by Catholic territorial princes in order to prevent "leakage" into foreign states. Reports of favorable answers to prayers were recorded in miracle books.

At the end of the sixteenth century the gild, predominant in the Middle Ages and based on considerations of rank and status, was outstripped by the confraternity of prayer, which stood above class lines.[25] The book of family devotions, the private prayerbook, and the devotional picture became popular.[26] The example given by the courts of the Catholic Habsburg and Wittelsbach dynasties was imitated in popular devotion.[27] Spanish and Italian forms of piety and the saints popular in those countries were especially made known by religious Orders—Ignatius and Francis Xavier by the Jesuits, Anthony of Padua by the Franciscans, devotion to Saint Joseph by Teresa of Avila. Religious folklore increased in the course of the seventeenth century, and so did superstition. If it is certain that post-Tridentine piety preserved or resumed many pre-Reformation characteristics, it cannot be denied that it stressed new, anti-Reformation ideas and aimed to revive a Catholic consciousness of the faith and arouse enthusiasm for it. But in our period it must not be termed "Baroque piety" without qualification.

[24] P. Löffler, *Die Marianischen Kongregationen* (Freiburg 1924); J. Stierli, *Die Marianischen Kongregationen,* 2 vols. (Lucerne 1947); J. Wicki, *Le P. Leunis* (Rome 1951); the devotional book used in the Marian Congregations, F. d. Coster, *Vitae christianae institutiones* (Cologne 1576), went through sixteen editions to 1616. H. Rahner, *Die geistesgeschichtliche Bedeutung der Marianischen Kongregationen* (Augsburg 1954).

[25] E.g., the St.-Anna-Bruderschaft, originating in Koblenz around 1500, at first comprised only jurists of the electoral court; in 1589 it was reestablished as a religious confraternity. A. Schmidt in *Veröffentlichungen des köln. Geschichtsvereins* 25 (1960), 285–342.

[26] G. Achtern-H. Knaus, *Deutsche und niederländische Gebetbuch-handschriften der Hessischen Landesbibliothek Darmstadt* (Darmstadt 1959); A. Schrott, "Das Gebetbuch in der Zeit der Katholischen Restauration," *ZKTh* 61 (1937), 1–28, 211–257; A. Spamer, *Das Kleine Andachtsbild vom 16. bis 20. Jh.* (Munich 1930).

[27] A. Coreth, *Pictas Austriaca. Ursprung und Entwicklung barocker Frömmigkeit in Österreich* (Munich 1959).

Arts and Literature

The same precaution against glib terminology is necessary in regard to the relationship of "mannerism" and of the Baroque to religious and ecclesiastical development during the seventeenth century.[28] The following facts are to be borne in mind. The Tridentine decree on images had as its aim to defend the lawfulness of sacred images and their veneration against the Calvinist iconoclasm in France and to eliminate abuses, but not to determine the canons of artistic production. In his *De imaginibus* (in Italian, 1582; in Latin, 1594) Cardinal Paleotti required in religious art a strict imitation of the *realta naturale e storica*, rejected the representation of pagan divinities and myths and the merging of this world and the next, and insisted that the principles of the Tridentine decree on images should be supplemented by detailed orders for their execution and strictly carried out. But he found no approval in Rome.[29] The first large church buildings of the Jesuits, the *Gesù* in Rome and St. Michael in Munich, in which the style of the Renaissance is little changed, coincide in time with the climax of the Catholic Reform; along the Rhine and in the Low Countries the Jesuits at first built in the Gothic style.[30] The history of the construction of the new Saint Peter's reflects the gradual turning away from Renaissance concepts and the return to the traditional plan, but at the same time it represented the breakthrough of the Baroque style by the architects Maderna and Bernini. The beginning of Baroque art in Rome corresponds to the papal assumption of leadership in the implementation of the Council of Trent and of Church renewal. On the other hand, Roman Baroque arrived at a

[28] Against W. Weisbach, *Der Barock als Kunst der Gegenreformation* (Berlin 1921), N. Pevsner, "Gegenreformation und Manierismus," *Report, für Kunstwiss.* 46 (1925), 243–262, sought to prove that "Manierismus" corresponds to "Counter Reformation," i.e., to the Church renewal lasting till about 1600; later observations of both authors, ibid., 49 (1928), 16–28, 225–246. H. Lützeler, "Der Wandel der Barockauffassung," *DVfLG* 11 (1933), 618–636; W. Hager, "Zur Raumstruktur des Manierismus," *Festschrift M. Wackernagel* (Cologne 1958), pp. 112–140; W. Friedländer, *Mannerism and Antimannerism in Italian Painting* (New York 1958); R. Stamm, *Die Kunstformen des Barockzeitalters* (Bern 1956); A. L. Mayer, "Liturgie und Barock," *JLW* 15 (1941), 67–154.

[29] Paleotti's memorandum of 1596 in P. Prodi, "Ricerche sulla teoria delle arti figurativa nella riforma cattolica," *Archivio per la storia della pieta* 4 (1962); on the whole subject see H. Jedin, "Das Tridentinum und die bildenden Künste," *ZKG* 74 (1963).

[30] J. Braun, *Die belgischen Jesuitenkirchen* (Freiburg 1907); id., *Die Kirchenbauten der deutschen Jesuiten*, 2 vols. (Freiburg 1918); *id., Spaniens alte Jesuitenkirchen* (Freiburg 1913); P. Pecchiai, *Il Gesu di Roma* (Rome 1952); P. Perri, *Giovanni Pristano e i primordi della architettura gesuitica* (Rome 1955); P. Moisy, *Les églises des Jésuits de l'ancienne assistance de France* 2 vols. (Rome 1958).

new climax under Urban VIII (1623–44) and his successors, when the Catholic Reform was already declining in internal strength and the Counter Reformation came to a halt. The zenith of German Baroque proceeded side by side with the reestablishment of the Church and the carrying out of the Tridentine Reform after the Thirty Years' War. The effect of Trent on iconography is unequivocal. Painting and sculpture favored the controverted subjects defined at Trent. They aspired to strengthen Catholic awareness of the faith and to stir up devotion.

The legend started by Agazzari (1609) that the Council of Trent's contemplated prohibition of polyphonic music was dropped because of Palestrina's "Missa Papae Marcelli" is historically true to the extent that this Mass, presumably produced during the Council (1562), and the conciliar prayers composed by the Dutchman Otto Kerle realized the demands of the reformers—textual integrity and moral purity.[31] As Palestrina (d. 1594) in his choral compositions combined classical proportions and deep feeling, so too did the extremely productive Orlando di Lasso (d. 1594), court composer for the Duke of Bavaria at Munich. The compositions of the Spaniard Thomas de Vitoria (d. 1613) were also in the spirit of Palestrina. The Medicean edition of the *Graduale Romanum,* so called because it was produced in the Medici Press, was published in 1614–15 at the command of Paul V. It altered the Gregorian melodies in accord with humanist principles.

If the Spanish national literature of the *Siglo de Oro* is unthinkable apart from Spain's leading role in the ecclesiastical sphere, the relationships are more complicated in Italy and France and even more so in Germany, where antibourgeois, courtly, and absolutist tendencies are bound up with the anti-Reformation trends. Certainly from the religious background came the Jesuit theater, which culminated in the dramas of Jakob Bidermann (d. 1639), the "Cenodoxus" and the martyr plays "Adrianus" and "Philemon Martyr."[32] According to Kindermann, "it is one of the chief glories of the European stage in the seventeenth century."

---

[31] The older view, defended by F. Y. Haberl and K. Weinmann, "Zur Geschichte von Palestrinas Missa Papae Marcelli," *Jb. der Musikbibliothek Peters* 22 (1916), 23–42, that there is no direct connection with the Council of Trent, has been corrected by O. Ursprung and K. Jeppesen (in the works listed *supra* under "Literature").

[32] *Ludi theatrales sacri* (Munich 1666); "Philemon Martyr," Latin and German, ed. M. Wehrli (Cologne 1961). A. Dürrwächter, *Jacob Gretser und seine Dramen* (Freiburg 1912); K. W. Drozd, *Schul-und Ordenstheater am Kollegium SJ Klagenfurt 1604–1773* (Klagenfurt 1965); C. Zander, *Jesuitentheater u. Schuldrama als Spiegel trierischer Geschicte:* Kurtrier Jb. 5 (1965), 64–88; J. Seidenfaden, *Das Jesuitentheater in Konstanz* (Stuttgart 1963).

CHAPTER 44

The New and the Old Orders

The fundamental motives of the Catholic Reform—first, self-sanctification, then the apostolate and works of charity—which had been basic to the new pre-Tridentine foundations, continued to operate in the religious life of the post-Tridentine period. The most powerful impulses came from Spain and Italy and, with the turn of the century, from France.

The idea of the apostolate is found in probably its purest form in the Oratory of Philip Neri (1515–95, canonized in 1622).[1] After being ordained in 1551, this affable and humorous "Apostle of Rome," beloved by high and low, began to gather young men, chiefly students, at San Girolamo della Carita for spiritual conferences, often with musical interludes. The society of diocesan priests, founded in 1564 and soon joined by the future Cardinals Baronius and Tarugi, was formally established in 1575. Its constitution was confirmed by Paul V in 1612. Its headquarters were at Santa Maria in Vallicella; other houses arose in Naples, Palermo, Lucca, and elsewhere in Italy. In 1611 Pierre de Bérulle transplanted the Oratory to France, where it received a fresh impetus.

The Oblates of Saint Ambrose were a society of diocesan priests, founded at Milan by Borromeo in 1578. Their single vow obliged the members to be at the disposal of the Archbishop of Milan in the care of souls and instruction.[2] The Regular Clerics of the Mother of God, living according to the Augustinian Rule, were founded at Lucca in 1574 by Gionvanni Leonardi (d. 1609, canonized in 1938) and later moved to Rome.[3] Among them the education of poor children gradually assumed

---

[1] The older literature in Heimbucher, II, 562ff.; *Il primo processo per S. Filippo Neri nel Cod. Vat. lat. 3798*, ed. G. Incisa della Rocchetta–N. Vian–C. Gasbarri, 3 vols. (Citta del Vaticano 1957–60), containing the acts of the process of beatification (1595–1601). Older biographies: A. Capecelatro, *Vita di S. F. N.* 2 vols. (Rome, 3rd ed., 1889–92); L. Ponnelle–L. Bordet, *S. F. N. e la Societa romana del suo tempo* (Florence 1932; Paris, 2nd ed. 1958); A. Dupront, "Autour de S. P. N.," *MAH* 49 (1932), 219–259; id. "D'un Humanisme chrétien en Italie à la fin du XVIe siècle," *RH* 175 (1935), 296–307; C. Gasbarri, *Il riformatore di Roma* (Rome 1937); P. Hofmeister, "Die Verfassung des Oratoriums Ph. Neris," *Festschrift J. Heckel* (Cologne and Graz 1959); G. de Libero, *Vita di S. Filippo Neri, Apostolo di Roma* (Grottaferrata 1960); M. Jouhandeau, *P. Neri* (Paris 1957).

[2] Heimbucher, II, 560f.

[3] Heimbucher, II, 113f.; F. Ferraironi, *S. G. Leonardi e Propaganda Fide* (Rome 1938).

primary importance, and it became the real aim of the Piarists, called in Italy the *Scolopi,* an abbreviation of *scuole pie.*[4] The Aragonese Joseph Calasanctius (1556–1648, canonized in 1767), who, on settling in Rome in 1592, had first been active in the Confraternity of Christian Doctrine, opened there in 1597 the first free elementary school and gathered his coworkers into a community with simple vows (1617). The constitutions were confirmed in 1622. The Order had already spread from Italy to the Habsburg lands and Poland when the founder was brought before the Inquisition and deposed from the generalship (1643); his foundation was reduced to a mere society without vows. Alexander VII restored it as an Order. Its field of activity continued to be elementary education.

The Society of Jesus was, and became even more so, the most influential Order in education. Following its tempestuous growth at the beginning, it experienced under the generals Borgia (1565–73) and Mercurian (1573–80) a period of internal consolidation, which was completed by the intellectually distinguished Claudius Acquaviva (1581–1615). The order of the day and manner of life of the members was fixed, a *directorium* for the conducting of the Exercises was drawn up, and, after long preparation, the *Ratio Studiorum* was put in force (1599). Their ultimate goal in education was "to stimulate the knowledge and love of our Creator and Redeemer." Following the "Paris Method," a mastery of written and spoken Latin (to a lesser extent, of Greek) was systematically aimed at; on it was built the philosophical and finally the theological training. The pupils' ambition was incited by competition, and plays and dramatic presentations open to the public forged a bond between students and parents, while youthful saints—Stanislaus Kostka (d. 1568), Aloysius Gonzaga (d. 1591), and John Berchmans (d. 1621)— were held up as models. Following the uniform instructional plan of the *Ratio Studiorum,* the 372 colleges which the Society maintained in 1616 were training an ecclesiastical and secular elite which shaped Church and world more effectively than any other factor. In the Parisian province alone some thirteen thousand students were enrolled in eighteen colleges in 1643.

The Society found and maintained its definitive frame and reached the height of its influence during the late sixteenth and early seventeenth centuries. Popes Pius V and Sixtus V, both from mendicant Orders, sought without success to remodel it along mendicant lines by introduc-

---

[4] *Epistolario di S. Giuseppe Calasanzio,* ed. L. Picanyol, 8 vols. (Rome 1950–55); G. Santha, *S. Jose de Calasanz* (Madrid 1956); C. Vila Pala, *Fuentes inmediatas de la pedagogia calasancia* (Madrid 1960). L. Picanyol, *Brevis conspectus historico-statisticus ordinis scholarum piarum* (Rome 1932); other literature in M. Escobar, *Ordini e Congregazioni religiose* I, 855–870.

ing the choral office and having solemn profession precede ordination and even to change its name. Gregory XIII, favorably disposed, curtailed the hitherto predominant Spanish influence on the government of the Society by procuring in 1573 the election of the Belgian Mercurian in place of Polanco, who had long been the Society's secretary. Efforts of Spanish Jesuits with the support of Philip II to obtain a general deputy for the Spanish Empire or to transfer the general to Spain were unavailing. Acquaviva publicly disavowed the intervention in politics of such prominent members as Auger in France and Skarga in Poland. In conflicts with his critics, for example the German Assistant Hoffaeus, he demonstrated both firmness and moderation. The number of members, about 3500 in 1563, rose to more than 13,000. Under Acquivava's mild and sensible successor, Mutius Vitelleschi (1615–45), the Order obtained in 1622 the canonization of its founder and greatest missionary, Francis Xavier, and in 1640 celebrated the first century of its existence with great pageantry. The magnificent *Imago primi saeculi Societatis Iesu* documented its achievement.

Though the Jesuits, in the spirit of their founder, rendered great service as preachers and confessors in the pastoral care of all classes through their conducting of the Exercises and of popular missions, as exemplified in Saint John Francis Regis (d. 1640) in Languedoc, still, in works for the masses they were at least equalled by the Capuchins from the close of the sixteenth century. Once Gregory XIII had removed the restriction of this new branch of the Franciscans to Italy in 1574, it spread extraordinarily fast in France, Spain, the Low Countries, and the German-speaking world. When in 1621 Paul V freed it from dependence on the general of the Conventuals, it already numbered 15,000 members. The greater the number of preachers trained in higher institutions—Saint Bonaventure became the Order's Doctor in 1578—the more attention they devoted to itinerant preaching and popular missions, in addition to the customary sermons of the Advent and Lent cycles, and they became the favorite guides and confessors of the people. Matthias of Salo (d. 1611),[5] prominent as organizer and preacher, promoted the Forty Hours' Prayer. Fidelis of Sigmaringen, prior at Feldkirch, was slain at Seewis in 1622 by Calvinist peasants before beginning his mission preaching; he was canonized in 1746.[6] Lorenzo of Brindisi, general from 1602–5, did much to establish the Order in the Habsburg and Wittelsbach territories while he was general

---

[5] His not entirely reliable *Historia cappuccina,* edited by Melchior a Pobladura, 2 vols. (Rome 1946–50); other literature in *Lex Cap* pp. 1078ff.

[6] Festschrift on the occasion of the bicentennial of his canonization (Lucerne 1946); *Lex Cap,* pp. 585ff.

deputy.[7] Even though his share in the founding of the League was of benefit to the Catholic cause, the "Gray Eminence," Joseph of Paris (d. 1638), an austere religious and devoted director of souls, still allowed himself to be used by Richelieu as an instrument of his power politics.

Jesuits and Capuchins, their apostolic zeal and their new pastoral methods, are as integral to the picture of the sixteenth-century Catholic renewal as were the then new mendicant Orders to that of the thirteenth century. And once again the mendicants showed their vitality. They now adapted their constitutions to the Tridentine decree on Regulars. The effort for a strict observance of the rule led in some Orders to the founding of houses of Recollects within the provinces, in others to the formation of new branches with a "stricter" and a "most strict" observance. Among the Franciscans, the Alcantarines, so called from their founder, Peter of Alcántara, but also known as Discalced, and widespread in the Spanish empire, surpassed, because of their penitential strictness and their extreme poverty, the "Riformati," who had originated at Fonte Colombo near Rieti and were very popular in Italy and South Germany; they also surpassed the French Recollects, who first united at Nevers after the Huguenot Wars. The Alcantarines described themselves as "of the strictest observance," the others, as "of the more strict observance," but all of them remained within the Order of the Observance. This was also true of the Spanish Discalced Augustinians, who from 1601 constituted a separate province of the Augustinian Hermits. In 1621 this was divided into four provinces and even obtained its own vicar general. More loose still was the dependence on the general of the Order among the Italian Discalced, who spread from Sicily as far as Austria and Bavaria, and also the French Congregation, which held its first general chapter at Avignon in 1617. Several reform congregations of the Dominicans were changed into provinces, but new Observant congregations, such as that of Saint Louis in France (1629), also arose.

On the other hand, the Carmelite general Rossi did not succeed in leading back the reformed houses of friars and nuns that had been established in Spain by Teresa of Avila and John of the Cross "to a less austere observance and to obedience to the superiors of the Order," in accord with the decree of the general chapter of Piacenza in 1575. In 1580, with the permission of Gregory XIII, secured by Philip II, the reformed set up a province of their own with statutes which stressed strict observance of the rule and the cultivation of interior prayer. When in 1593 they obtained the right to elect their own general, they became

---

[7] Cf. chapter 70, footnote 12; also, Lazaro de Aspurz, "Personalidad y mision de S. Lorenzo de Brindisi," *Estudios Franciscanos,* 61 (1960), 175–201.

an independent Order. These Discalced Carmelites had a house in Rome from 1597 and spread to Poland (Cracow, 1605), France (Paris, 1611), Germany (Cologne, 1613, and Vienna, 1622), and Ireland (Dublin, 1625). In 1631 Urban VIII approved their revised constitutions, which brought them close to the penitential monastic Orders of Carthusians and Camaldolese through the extremely strict manner of life they prescribed—prohibition of meat, fasting from 14 September to Easter, two hours of meditation a day, and perpetual silence in the convents of hermits. The *Collegium Complutense Philosophicum* (Alcalá, 1624) and the *Cursus Theologicus* of the Order's theologians at Salamanca (1631) gave them a great reputation for scholarship. Thomas of Jesus (d. 1627) was instrumental in the founding of the Congregation of Propaganda by means of his *De procuranda salute omnium gentium* (1613), a work on mission theology.[8]

A glance at statistics, naturally not complete, indicates the continuing importance of the two great mendicant Orders in the life of the Church. In 1573 the Dominicans had 920 houses in twenty-nine provinces, five congregations, and four vicariates; the number of members was considerably more than 7,000.[9] In the Franciscan family there were in 1682 some 15,000 Conventuals in thirty-one provinces and 952 houses; around 1585 the Observants counted 2,113 houses in eighty-eight provinces. Since the number of members was given as 30,000 at the time of the separation from the Conventuals in 1517 and as 60,000 in 1680, it was at least 40,000 in the Tridentine period.[10]

Whereas the enforcing of the regular observance in the centralized mendicant Orders frequently produced centrifugal tendencies, the concern of the Benedictine reforms continued to be to protect the individual monastery from isolation and decay by organization in a larger union. The Council of Trent in its reform of Regulars had prescribed the federation of exempt monasteries either in provincial chapters or in congregations. Italy and Spain already had the great congregations of Montecassino and Valladolid. The Congregation of Flanders, founded in 1564, and the "Great Gallican" Congregation in France, from which that of Saint-Denis split in 1617, satisfied the letter of the Tridentine requirement but did little for reform because many monasteries were still, as earlier, the property of commendatory abbots and had only a few monks. The Abbey of Liessies, reformed by Blosius, influenced

---

[8] Reprinted at Rome in 1940; on the sources, see P. Charles, *Scientia missionum ancilla* (Nijmegen 1953), pp. 46–53. On the activity of Calced Carmelites in Germany, see G. Mesters, *Die rheinische Karmeliterprovinz während der Gegenreformation* (Speyer 1958).
[9] Walz, pp. 421f. Cf. also S. Forte, "I Domenicani nel carteggio del Card. Scipione Borghese, Protettore dell'Ordine 1606–1613," *AFP* 30 (1960), 351–416.
[10] Holzapfel, pp. 415ff., 596f.

nearby monasteries by its example but established no congregation. A new flowering of Benedictine monasticism was first effected by the Congregation of Saint-Vanne, to which abbeys of Lorraine and Burgundy belonged from 1604 to 1670; also important were the Belgian Congregation, formed by Abbot Fanson of Saint-Hubert in 1629 after violent struggles with the episcopate, and especially the Maurist Congregation, confirmed in 1621. The Maurists, finally comprising 178 monasteries, gave themselves, on the model of the Montecassino Congregation, a strict organization under a triennial general, residing at Saint-Germain-des-Prés, with a general chapter, a strictly regulated visitation, and a common novitiate in each of the six provinces. In it there came to maturity in the succeeding epoch the great works on the history of the Benedictine Order and patristic editions that are not outdated even today. The Maurists also perfected the historico-critical method in these provinces.

Despite great losses, the Union of Bursfeld in northern and western Germany had weathered the storms of the Reformation.[11] In South Germany, following the failure of several moves for apostolic visitations, the Swabian Congregation was formed in 1603 under the leadership of Abbot Georg Wegelin of Weingarten;[12] the Swiss Congregation had originated in 1602. Somewhat later was the Austrian Congregation, which was confirmed in 1625; but it was set up for defense of its privileges rather than for reform. The project of amalgamating all the German Congregations into a single one foundered on the opposition of the bishops. A resolution to that effect, passed by a meeting of abbots at Regensburg in 1631, was annulled by Urban VIII. But success crowned the effort of the German Benedictines to create a center of scholarship in the university of Salzburg, founded in 1617 by Archbishop Mark Sittich and incorporated into the Order.

Among the Cistercians too the pre-Tridentine trend toward merging reformed monasteries into congregations continued. New congregations arose in Portugal (1567), Poland (1580), Upper Germany (1595), Aragon (1616), Rome (1623), and Calabria (1633). A reform of the entire Order, suggested by Louis XIII and entrusted to Cardinal Rochefoucauld by Gregory XV, came to nothing. The Cistercians of the Strict Observance were separated as the Trappist Order in the following period.

[11] For the 1597 reform plan of the Cologne Nuncio Garzadoro, see P. Volk, *Urkunden zur Geschichte der Bursfelder Kongregation* (Bonn 1951), pp. 150ff.
[12] R. Reinhardt, *Restauration, Visitation, Inspiration. Die Reformbestrebungen in der Benediktinerabtei Weingarten 1567–1627* (Stuttgart 1960).

The strengthening of the episcopal control of the hospital institutions by Trent could not impede their progressive secularization.[13] However, the physical and the spiritual needs of the sick, especially during epidemics,[14] were attended to, sometimes with heroic risks, and two new Orders dedicated themselves exclusively to this work. John of God (1495–1550, canonized in 1690),[15] having been converted as a result of a sermon delivered by Juan de Avila, in 1540 founded at Granada a hospital, which, provided with new accommodations with the help of Archbishop Guerrero, also received the insane. The community, consisting of helpers whom John of God had attracted, received the Augustinian rule from Pius V in 1572; Sixtus V approved its constitutions in 1586. Under Urban VIII the Brothers Hospitallers had seventy-nine hospitals in the Spanish Empire under a general resident at Granada. The houses founded in Italy (from 1571), France (from 1602), and Austria (from 1605) had after 1592 their own general, who lived in Rome. Shortly before, in 1584, Camillus of Lellis (1550–1614, canonized in 1746)[16] had founded in Rome the Clerics Regular for the Aid of the Sick, especially the dying. Also called "Camillians," they distinguished themselves during plagues in Rome and Naples and from the time of Gregory XV bound themselves to this ministry by a fourth vow. At the founder's death the Order had sixteen houses in Italy.

Although Trent's strict regulations on inclosure at first constituted an impediment, communities of religious women began to engage in the Church's works of social charity. In addition to the Ursulines,[16a] the Visitandines and the English Ladies devoted themselves to the education of young girls. The Visitandines, founded at the suggestion of Saint Francis de Sales by the widow Jane Frances Fremiot de Chantal (1572–

---

[13] Synopsis of the ecclesiastical legislation in: E. Nasalli Rocca, *Il diritto ospedaliero nei suoi lineamenti storici* (Milan 1956), pp. 131ff.; Benedetto da Alatri, *Le ospedali di Roma e le bolle pontificie* (Viterbo 1950); M. Vanti, *Bernardino Cirillo, Commendatore e Maestro generale dell'ordine di S. Spirito 1556–1575* (Rome 1936).

[14] E.g., Donato da S. Giovanni in Persiceto, "I cappuccini e la peste a Bologna nel 1630," *Atti del primo Congresso italiano di Storia Ospedaliera* (Reggio-Emilia 1957), pp. 228–246.

[15] Heimbucher, I, 600f.; biographies by L. Ruland (Frankfurt a. M. 1949) and J. Cruset (Barcelona 1958); *Per il IV Centenario della morte di S. Giovanni da Dio* (Rome 1950); C. Salvadori, *Incontri con S. Giovanni da Dio* (Rome 1959); A. Chagny, *L'Ordre hospitalier de St. Jean de Dieu en France* I (Lyons 1951).

[16] Heimbucher, II, 114ff.; biographies by M. Fischer (Freiburg 1935), R. Svoboda (Linz, 5th ed. 1946), and M. Vanti (Milan, 2nd ed. 1958).

[16a] See M. de Chantal Gueudré, *Les monastères des Ursulines sous l'Ancien Régime 1612–1788* (Paris 1960).

1641, canonized in 1767),[17] were at first occupied in the service of the poor and the sick. But after they had become an Order with the Augustinian rule in 1618, they took up the training and instruction of young girls in boarding schools, out of regard for the Tridentine prescription of inclosure. At the death of de Chantal the Order had eighty-six independent convents, all in French-speaking countries. At about the same time an English woman, Mary Ward (d. 1645),[18] had founded at Saint-Omer in 1609 a community, the Institute of the Blessed Virgin Mary, which was supposed to conform to the rule of the Jesuits but forego the Tridentine inclosure. The request for papal confirmation was denied for this reason, the community was dissolved in 1631, and Mary Ward herself was for a time imprisoned on flimsy charges. Thanks to the protection of Maximilian I of Bavaria, the Institute, whose members were popularly known as the English Ladies, was established at Munich in 1626–27 for teaching in girls' schools and became the source of many new foundations in South Germany. Only Vincent de Paul succeeded in founding a female Order for the care of the sick. The Daughters of Charity, directed from 1634 by Louise de Marillac (d. 1660, canonized in 1934), took the place of the associations of women organized by Vincent for the care of the poor and the sick and in 1656 were approved as an Order by Innocent X.[19] Together with the Borromeans of Nancy (1652), they blazed the trail for the grand-scale development of the modern congregations of women, without which the Church's social work in the nineteenth century could not be imagined.

---

[17] Sources in *Ste. J. F. de Chantal, sa vie et ses oeuvres,* 8 vols. (Paris 1874–79); biography by H. Waach (Eichstätt 1957); M. Müller, *Die Freundschaft des hl. Franz von Sales mit der hl. J. F. von Ch.* (Regensburg 1924); D. Mezard, *Doctrine spirituelle de Ste. J. F. de Ch.* (Paris 1928).

[18] M. Oliver, *M. Ward* (London 1959); J. Grisar, *Die ersten Anklagen in Rom gegen das Institut M. Wards* (Rome 1959); id., "Vani tentativi di M. Ward di fondare scuole femminili a Napoli 1623–28," *Studi in onore di R. Filangieri* II (Naples 1959), 525–549.

[19] Bibliography by L. Gebsattel in *Car* 61 (1960), 158ff., 200f.; J. Guy, *L. de Marillac* (Paris 1960).

The Springtime of the Missions in the Early Modern Period

CHAPTER 45

The Missions under Spanish Patronage

The discovery of the Canary Islands (1312–41) may be considered the prelude to the great discoveries of the fifteenth and sixteenth centuries.[1] What followed set the example for all missionary activity in the so-called Age of Discovery. As early as 1351 Pope Clement VI appointed the Carmelite Bernard as Bishop of the "Happy Islands,"[2] and in 1368 Urban V directed the Bishops of Barcelona and Tortosa to send missionaries there. But these early endeavors were unsuccessful. Thirteen missionaries are said to have been slain by the inhabitants in 1391. Only the conquest of the islands by the Spaniards created more favorable conditions. In 1404 the bishopric of the Canary Islands was established as the new diocese of Rubicon,[3] and in 1424 Fuertaventura became the second see.[4] Besides Dominicans and Augustinians, it was especially Franciscans—Saint Diego of Alcalá (d. 1463) and Alfonso of Bolano—who labored for the conversion of the presumably Berber islanders. Their work was seriously hampered by the encroachments of the Spanish conquerors and merchants, and Pope Eugene IV had to protect the neophytes from exploitation and enslavement and defend their human rights.[5] But, contrary to what has been frequently claimed, the native population was not exterminated. In fact, within scarcely a

[1] R. Henning, *Terrae incognitae* III (Leiden 1938), 136–143, following Petrarch, *De vita solitaria* II, Chapter 3.

[2] K. Eubel, "Der erste Bischof der canarischen Inseln," *RQ* 6 (1892), 237–240; Lütolf, "Zur Entdeckung und Christianisierung der westafrikanischen Inseln," *ThQ* 59 (1877), 319–332.

[3] Streit, XV, 354f.; on the whole question cf. *Historia de la Religion en Canarias* (Santa Cruz de Tenerife 1957); J. Zunzunegui, "Los origenes de las misiones en las Islas Canarias," *RET* 1 (Madrid 1940), 361–408; I. Ormaecheverria, "En torno a las misiones del archipielago Canario," *Missionalia Hispanica* 14 (Madrid 1957), 539–560.

[4] Streit, XV, 390f.

[5] Ibid., pp. 400, 409; cf. J. Wölfel, "Bericht über eine Studienreise in die Archive Roms und Spaniens zur Aufhellung der Vor- und Frühgeschichte der Kanarischen Inseln," *Anthropos* 25 (1930), 711–724.

century it had become a civilized European nation.[6] By 1476 the majority of the islanders were Catholics, and in 1483 Las Palmas became the episcopal see for the entire archipelago.

The marriage of Isabella of Castile to Ferdinand of Aragon paved the way for Spanish national unity, and the victory at Granada in 1492 completed the *reconquista*. In the same year Spain entered into competition with Portugal in the field of exploration. The Genoese Christopher Columbus (1451–1506), in the service of Spain, discovered America, which he thought to be a part of Asia and hence called the "West Indies." To counter Portuguese claims, the Spanish royal pair secured from Pope Alexander VI the recognition of their right to the newly discovered regions and the drawing of a line of demarcation 100 leagues west of the Azores and the Cape Verde Islands: All lands discovered on the far side of the line were to belong to Spain, all lying on the other side of the line were to belong to Portugal.[7] In 1494 this imaginary line was advanced some 270 leagues farther to the west, at the request of Portugal, in the Treaty of Tordesillas—perhaps proof that Portuguese sailors had already acquired knowledge of the new world before Columbus. In any case, on the basis of this revision, Portugal could legally claim possession of Brazil, occupied by Cabral in 1500. Following the first circumnavigation of the globe and the discovery of the Philippines by Ferdinand Magellan (1480–1521) there broke out a protracted struggle for a corresponding line of demarcation in the Pacific. This quarrel was to be of great importance in the missionary history of the Far East. It concerned not only the Philippines but eventually Japan and China. And the fact that the Spanish missionaries had to go to Asia via America (Mexico) is noteworthy.

Passions have been frequently aroused by Pope Alexander VI's award, referred to as the "partition of the world" and the "Donatio Alexandrina." Its importance is discussed even today.[8] It seems clear that it granted a national monopoly of the missionary work in specified regions, for, in return for the "donation," the Spanish King assumed the

---

[6] Cf. E. Fischer, *ZE* 62 (Braunschweig 1931), 258–281; J. Wölfel, ibid., pp. 282–302.
[7] Cf. the two Bulls "Inter Caetera" of 3 and 4 May 1493 and the Bull "Eximiae Devotionis" of 4 May 1493; also P. Leturia, "Las grandes bulas misionales de Alejandro VI (1493)," *Bibliotheca Hispania Missionum* 1 (Barcelona 1930), 209–251; M. Gimenez Fernandez, "Las bulas alejandrinas de 1493," *Anuario de Estudios Americanos* 1 (Sevilla 1944), 171–429; A. Garcia Gallo, *Las Bulas de Alejandro VI y el Ordenamiento Juridico de la Expansion Portuguesa y Castellana en Africa e Indias* (Madrid 1958).
[8] E. Staedler, "Die 'donatio Alexandrina' und die 'divisio mundi' von 1493," *AkathKR* 117 (1937), 363–402; id., "Die westindischen Lehnedikte Alexanders VI (1493)," ibid., 118 (1938), 377–417; J. Leclercq, "Autour de la 'donation' d'Alexandre VI (1493)," *Etudes* 237 (1938), 5–16, 195–208.

obligation of promoting the spread of Christianity in the new lands; thereby laying the basis for the royal *patronato*. Responsibility for missionary work implied corresponding rights in the ecclesiastical sphere and these were given to the Spanish crown in 1508 by Julius II's Bull "Universalis Ecclesiae."[9] To the duty of supporting the clergy, churches, and dioceses was added the right to found dioceses and to name all benefice-holders, even bishops.

From its mission mandate Spain deduced the right of conquest and annexation. The *conquista* became a war against paganism, as the *reconquista* had been a war against Islam—it was waged for the faith. "The sword in one hand, they held out the Gospel with the other."[10] The force taking possession of an area sometimes issued a *requerimiento*[11] whereby, under threat of the most severe penalties, the inhabitants were called upon to accept Chrisitanity and to recognize the dominion of the Spanish King. Whoever refused lost his freedom or was killed. The conquerors took the land as a royal fief (*encomienda*)[12] and had the right to force the Indians to work it. The missionaries who accompanied the troops, being men of that era, usually approved this procedure. They were not prepared for their missionary work and had absolutely no knowledge of peoples of a strange culture. They felt that exotic peoples could become genuine Christians only if their views, customs, and worship were first destroyed ("method of *tabula rasa*"). To this end, recourse to force was at times necessary, but from this it is not to be inferred that the Spanish missionaries knew only compulsory methods. Such a conclusion is contradicted by the fact that, clearly due to the work of the missionaries, in most Latin American countries the Indian population has maintained itself to this day and the native languages survive to some extent.

The overall view of the age contained a theological bias which did not keep pace with the problems raised by the widening of the world horizon. Thus, the unsolved question concerning the salvation of pagans and the nature and extent of the faith necessary for salvation led to the too speedy conferring of baptism,[13] producing many new Christians but only a superficial christianization. How little people were aware of the new situation is revealed by the fact that at Trent the Fathers hardly

[9] Streit, II, 54.

[10] Quoted in Schmidlin, M, 290, footnote 3, from Baluffi, *L'America sotto l'aspetto religioso* I (1845), 159.

[11] B. Biermann, "Das requerimiento in der spanischen Conquista," *NZM* 6 (1950), 94–114.

[12] S. A. Zavala, *La encomienda indiana* (Madrid 1935).

[13] F. Rousseau, *L'idée missionaire aux XVIe et XVIIe siècles* (Paris 1930); V. Carro, *La teologia y los teologos-juristas españoles ante la conquista de America* (Seville 2nd ed. 1951).

mentioned the overseas lands, let alone seriously discussed them. Hence Church life in the missions retained its pre-Tridentine stamp long after 1561. The home situation was transferred just as it was to areas of very different culture where closed and exclusively Latin-European dominions were established under the rule of the "Catholic" King of Spain.[14]

Spanish discoverers made rapid strides in the sixteenth century. In 1513 Vasco Núñez de Balboa, having crossed the isthmus of Panama, reached the Pacific, which he called the "South Sea." By 1519 the northern coast of the Gulf of Mexico was traversed; by 1526 the southern outlines of South America had been determined. Discovery was followed by conquest, and in a little more than a half-century America from Chile to Oregon was claimed to be under Spanish rule. This achievement is explained not only by might and technical superiority: It finds its causes also in the discords and the internal deterioration of the ancient American empires. Spain's ability to retain these vast regions for centuries is due to the strictly organized administration which was set up immediately after the conquest and before the *conquistadores,* often acting on their own, succumbed to the temptation to establish independent empires. Thus arose clearly distinct administrative areas: the Antilles, Mexico (New Spain), Peru, and New Granada, with corresponding ecclesiastical divisions. Hence it is proper to present the missionary history of Spanish America with regard to this geographical arrangement.

The Antilles

It can be regarded as almost certain that Columbus was not accompanied by any priest on his first voyage.[15] On the second voyage a motley group of twelve or thirteen diocesan and regular priests went to the new world under the direction of Fray Bernard Boyl, but the expedition was fruitless and by the end of 1494 Boyl had returned to Spain. Missionary work in America really began with the departure of a group of Franciscans in 1500. Already in their first letter they were able to report 3000 baptisms.[16] The erection of an archdiocese and two suffragan sees for the Antilles, decreed in 1504 by Julius II, foundered on King Ferdinand's objection that his rights had been disregarded. Only when these had been assured (1508) could the sees of Santo Domingo

---

[14] In *Il Concilio di Trento* I (Rome 1942), 35–43, P. Leturia investigates why the American bishops did not attend the Council.

[15] B. Biermann, "Die ersten Missionen Amerikas," *Festschrift 50 Jahre katholischer Missionswissenschaft* (Münster 1961), pp. 115–120; D. Olmedo, "La primera evangelizacion en America 1494–1504," *Abside* (Mexico 1953), pp. 35–67.

[16] Streit, II, 37.

and Concepción de la Vega on Hispañiola (Haiti) and San Juan on Puerto Rico be established in 1511. The first diocese on the American continent, Santa María Antigua del Darién (Panama), followed in 1513.

In the meantime Dominicans also had come to America in 1509–10, inaugurating a new epoch in the scarcely opened missionary history of America—the age of the struggle for the freedom and for the procedure of evangelization.Decrees in favor of the Indians had indeed already been issued,[17] but they were ignored by the Spaniards. Even Columbus carried Indians to Spain as slaves. Forced labor, sicknesses connected with exposure to the diseases of the Europeans, and acts of violence decimated the population. Frightful epidemics of suicide completed the work of depopulation. As early as 1501 the import of Negro slaves from Africa was allowed in order to counteract the depopulation. Scarcely more than twenty years of colonization sufficed to reduce the population of the Antilles from millions to 14,000 and finally to a few hundred.[18] From 1517 Negroes were systematically settled on Haiti, and very soon they constituted two-thirds of the island's population.

The abuses induced the Dominicans to intervene. Antonio de Montesino was the first to make a violent protest. To his aid came Bartolomé de Las Casas (1474–1566), who was a diocesan priest at that time but became a Dominican in 1522. Las Casas crossed the ocean seven times to implore the king to protect the Indians deprived of their rights. He obtained the righting of the worst abuses and exercised a decisive influence on Spanish legislation in favor of the Indians. He forced the theologians and lawyers of his time to face squarely the still unsettled questions as to the human rights of the Indians, the lawfulness of war against infidels, and Spain's claim to have a legitimate title to the occupation of America. Nevertheless, history's judgment on Las Casas has not yet been rendered. Some regard him as an unflinching champion of freedom and justice, or even as a divinely sent leader, while others consider him a dangerous fanatic, a mad genius, or even a wanton and conscious falsifier of history and a libeler. Certainly Las Casas was guilty of unjustified generalizations and exaggerations; he was concerned to denounce wrongs. As accuser, he had to produce proof of guilt, and nothing else interested him. Thus, in a sense, he is the source of the *leyenda negra,* which discredited the whole colonizing and christianizing activity of the Spaniards abroad and contributed to the judgment, hardened by tradition, on the Spanish methods. In this he was, in the final analysis, neither more nor less than one of the authentic representatives of the Christian conscience of Spain in the New World.

[17] In 1497, 1501, 1503, 1509. Cf. Streit, II, 33f. 38, 42, 56.
[18] Las Casas speaks of 3 million on Haiti, others of 1 million.

Mexico

By arbitrarily changing his mandate to explore, Hernando Cortés (1485–1546) quickly put an end to the Aztec empire in Central America (1519–1521). Montezuma II (1502–20) was killed, the capital, Tenochtitlán, was razed, and in its stead Mexico City was founded. The complete pacification of the country, however, was not achieved until about 1550.

Cortés was typical of the *conquistadores*. Violent and excessively cruel, at the same time he was zealous for the spread of the Christian faith. Everywhere he set up crosses, forbade human sacrifice, and destroyed idols. The reports he constantly sent to Charles V testify to his zeal.[19] He always had priests in his army to preach the faith. The Mercedarian Bartolomé de Olmedo especially distinguished himself on Cortés' first expedition, but the real missionary work was begun by Franciscans. The first three came from the southern Netherlands; the best known of these, Peter of Ghent, labored in Mexico for fifty years. In 1524 they were followed by twelve Spanish Franciscans, the "Twelve Apostles of Mexico." Among them was Toribio de Benavente, called by the Mexicans "Motolinía," the poor man, because he selflessly gave away all that he had. The Franciscans were joined by Dominicans in 1526 and Augustinians in 1533. The Spanish religious houses were emptied in behalf of the new overseas provinces of the Orders. In 1559 in Mexico alone the Franciscans numbered 380 members in eighty houses, the Dominicans 210 and the Augustinians 212 in forty houses each.

From Mexico proper the missionaries spread over the areas to the north and the south of New Spain subject to the Viceroy of Mexico. In 1525 one of the three Flemish Franciscans went to Guatemala, and missionary work began in Honduras in 1527, Yucatán in 1534, and New Mexico in 1540. The success of conversion corresponded to the supply of missionaries. The sources speak of millions of neophytes and extol their faith. Many a conversion may have been merely external. The mass baptisms—as many as 14,000 a day!—betray a hurried and superficial procedure and the numerical data in regard to destruction of temples and idols refer to the use of force. Still, the Indians' conversion must have been genuine and sincere on the whole. The rapid establishment of the hierarchy testifies to the development of Christian life. The see of Tlaxcala was founded in 1525, Tegucigalpa in 1527, Mexico City in 1530, Honduras in 1531, Anteguera in 1535, Michoacán in 1536, Chiapas in 1538, Guadalajara in 1548, Yucatán in 1561. In 1546 Mexico City became the metropolitan see of New Spain, with all the

---

[19] Streit, II, 187ff., 194; cf. p. 466.

other dioceses as its suffragans. The Franciscan Juan de Zumárraga was Mexico City's first and most important bishop (1530–48).[20]

Recent historical investigation of the methods of evangelization indicate that the Spanish missionaries have been seriously maligned. They not only adapted themselves to the native languages and customs but through their scholarship made noteworthy contributions to the philology, ethnology, and historiography of America. The extant catechisms, prayer books, and devotional treatises, together with their grammars, provide irreplaceable sources for modern research. Let it suffice to mention only Bernardin of Sahagún, whose works are being reprinted today.[21]

It is, then, understandable if the Franciscans quickly exerted themselves for the education of the Indians. In 1523 Peter of Ghent set up a school in which, together with religion, reading, writing, and arithmetic were taught and trades and skills were imparted. In 1536 Bishop Zumarraga even started a college of higher studies, presumably for the training of a native clergy,[22] but this goal was not achieved. However, the college sent forth a supply of splendidly educated people from whom Sahagún selected his assistants in his scholarly undertakings. The Jesuits, who did not arrive until 1572, created nothing new in this regard. They devoted themselves at first chiefly to the care of souls and instruction of the Spanish city dwellers. From 1584 they too turned to missionary work, and in 1609 forty-four of them were tending four missions of their own. The Carmelites and the Mercedarians followed the Jesuits. All together, there were about 400 religious houses in New Spain at the turn of the century. Mexico had become a Catholic country, and the stage of direct missionary work was over.

The essence of missionary work was regarded as the conferring of baptism. Of the other Sacraments only confession and matrimony were stressed. For decades serious hesitations existed in regard to allowing the Indians to receive communion[23] and even more so in regard to ordaining them. In 1555 the First Council of Mexico forbade the conferring of major orders on Indians, *mestizos,* and mulattoes.[24] This pro-

---

[20] J. Garcia Icazbalceta, *Don Fray J. de Zumarraga, primer obispo y arzobispo de Mexico* (Mexico City 1881); F. de J. Chauvet (Mexico City 1948).

[21] *Colloquios y doctrina cristiana, Quellenwerke zur alten Geschichte Amerikas, aufgezeichnet in den Sprachen der Eingeborenen,* 3 (Stuttgart 1949).

[22] R. Ricard, *5e Semaine de Missiologie de Louvain 1927* (Louvain 1927), pp. 83–89.

[23] J. de Lugo (d. 1660) treats the question in his *Disputationes scholasticae et morales* IV (Paris 1869), but answers it in favor of the Indians.

[24] See J. Specker, "Der einheimische Klerus in Spanisch-America im 16. Jh., *"Der einheimische Klerus in Geschichte und Gegenwart* (Festschrift für L. Kilger) (Schöneck-Beckenried 1950), pp. 73–97; for Mexico, pp. 75–83.

hibition remained in force throughout the sixteenth century and was influential still later. Perhaps here lies one reason for the prevailing shortage of priests throughout Latin America[25] Into the nineteenth century the Church maintained the appearance of a foreign institution.

Peru

Between 1532 and 1536, starting with a force of only 180, Francisco Pizarro (1475–1540) undertook to conquer the Inca empire, extending from southern Colombia to northern Chile and northwest Argentina, which had already been weakened by the rivalry between the cities of Cuzco and Quito. The Inca Acahualpa received the Spaniards in a friendly manner but was made prisoner and, despite the surrender of his treasury gold and the reception of baptism, was executed. The collapse of the Inca empire was thereby sealed, though the conquest of the vast territory was not completed until 1572. Power-struggles among the *conquistadores,* strong protests against the laws aimed at protecting the Indians (*nuevas leyes*), and the elimination of the "Pizarro Dynasty" by the royal government long disturbed the peace of the largest viceroyalty in Latin America. Lima, the "City of Kings," founded by Pizarro in 1535 and made a diocese in 1541 and an archdiocese in 1546, was so much the political and ecclesiastical center that the history of all of South America, except Brazil, can be read in its story.

Missionary work in Peru was begun by the Dominicans,[26] whose first representative, Vincent Valverde, came in 1531. In 1539 Paul III erected the Peruvian Dominican province and in 1544 it had about fifty-five members. It provided in Jerome de Loaysa the first Bishop of Cuzco and the first Archbishop of Lima (1541–81). The Franciscans came next and spread across the land. Their most prominent missionary was Saint Francis Solano (1549–1610),[27] the "miracle-worker of the New World." They were joined by Augustinians and Mercedarians and in 1568 by the first Jesuits. In 1570 there were forty-four Jesuits in Peru, in 1575 sixty, in 1581 the number had risen to 110, in 1592 to 242, and in 1607 to 376. The early Jesuits worked almost exclusively in the larger cities; thus, in 1575 of the total of sixty there were forty-three in Lima and fourteen in Cuzco.

The religious Orders determined the history of the missions and of

---

[25] Cf. J. Höffner, *Christentum und Menschenwürde,* p. 296.

[26] B. Biermann, "Die Anfänge der Dominikanertätigkeit in Neuspanien und Peru,"*AFP,* 13 (1943), 5–58.

[27] Streit, II, 1437; also, O. Maas (Leutesdorf 1938) for the literature; F. Royer (Paterson, N.J. 1955).

the Church in the viceroyalty. In their presence the diocesan clergy, predominantly Spaniards and Creoles, could maintain themselves only with difficulty. However, along with the Dominicans, Franciscans, and Augustinians, they also provided prelates for the numerous sees which were suffragans of Lima—Panama (1513), León in Nicaragua (1534), Cuzco (1536), Quito (1545), Popayán in Colombia (1546), Paraquay (1547), Charcas in Bolivia (1551), Santiago de Chile (1561), Imperial in Chile (1563), Santiago de Estero (1570), Arequipa (1577), Trujillo (1577), and Buenos Aires (1582).

The internal development of the Church kept pace with its expansion. The Archbishops of Lima, especially Saint Toribio Alfonso de Mogrovejo (1581–1606),[28] the Apostle of the Indians, exerted themselves to lay a firm foundation at the numerous provincial councils, held in 1552, 1567,[29] 1583, 1591, and 1601. Though the conciliar acts betray the prevailing defects in methods of evangelization, they also certify a clear insight into the necessity of thorough reforms. Thus the Council of 1567 warned against hasty baptism and insisted on the obligation of systematic instruction of catechumens and neophytes. The establishing of the so-called *doctrinas,* meaning both "instruction" and "community," was intended to meet this need. Not only the parish priests (*doctrineros*) but also the *encomenderos* were responsible for this work twice a week.

The same council made obligatory the study of the native languages and strictly forbade the hearing of confessions through an interpreter. The Church festivals were celebrated in great splendor, if not with pomp, but it was soon discovered that pagan customs often were concealed by ecclesiastical ceremonies. Hence the method of eradication (*tabula rasa*) was advocated, the too ready admission of Indians to the reception of communion was disapproved, and their very ability to become priests was flatly denied. It was not until the Tridentine decrees on the qualifications for the priesthood had become known overseas that a more conciliatory view became evident in theory.[30] In practice, however, the admission of Indians, *mestizos,* and mulattoes to the priesthood was closed into the seventeenth century, even though in 1576 Gregory XIII had allowed ordination to persons of illegitimate birth in

---

[28] C. Garcia Irigoyen, *S. Toribio,* 4 vols. (Lima 1906f.); V. Rodriguez Valencia, *S. Toribio de Mogrovejo,* 2 vols. (Madrid 1956f.); A. Oyarzun, *La organizacion eclesiastica en el Peru y en Chile durante el pontificado de Sto. Toribio de M.* (Rome 1935); P. de Leturia, *I grandi missionari* II (Rome 1940), 69–117.

[29] F. Mateos, *Los dos Concilios Limenses de Jeronimo de Loaysa* (Madrid 1947).

[30] A. Pott, "Das Weihehindernis für Indianer im 3. Konzil von Lima," *NZM* 12 (1956), 108–118.

order to obtain priests conversant with the vernaculars.[31] This measure led to so many abuses that caution in regard to it can be detected already at the Provincial Council of 1583.

The implementation of the conciliar decrees was seriously impeded by the vast extent of the province of Lima. Other obstructions were the inadequate means of communication, the difficult geographical and climatic conditions in the widely varying altitudes, and the sparse and widely scattered Indian settlements. Saint Toribio needed six years for his first missionary journey, four for his second. In order to overcome the difficulties he would have needed a numerous clergy of more than average moral and intellectual stature. Thus the danger always remained that the newly won Christians would reassert their pagan customs.

From Peru proper Christianity spread through all the neighboring areas. In Chile,[32] in spite of the strong and centuries-long resistance of the Araucanians to the Spanish colonists, cities, churches, and monasteries could be erected and many conversions could be realized. Here too the first sees arose very soon—Santiago in 1561 and Imperial in 1563. In the La Plata districts christianization made evident progress when in 1547 the connection with Peru was established by means of El Gran Chaco. At the close of the sixteenth century Paraguay and Uruguay were also included in the missionary zone and the whole region was divided into dioceses.

New Granada

Colombia, conquered for Spain by Quesada in 1536 and united with Venezuela in 1549 to form the Audiencia of New Granada, was evangelized chiefly by Dominicans. Contrary to what had occurred in Mexico and Peru, here the Dominicans did not establish any monasteries at first, but merely isolated missions and schools. It was not until 1551 that the individual enterprises were gathered into a congregation, which in 1569 included eighteen priories, forty *doctrinas,* and 100 Indian villages. The Dominican province of New Granada was canonically erected in 1577. The outstanding missionary was Saint Louis Beltrán (1526–81),[33] who in a few years brought tens of thousands of Indians to the Christian faith, though he constantly encountered obstacles in the

---

[31] L. Lopetegui, "El Papa Gregorio XIII y la ordinacion de mestizos hispano-incaicos," *Miscellanea Hist. Pont.* 7 (Rome 1943), 180ff.

[32] Gazulla, *Los primeros Mercidarios en Chile* (Santiago 1918); R. Ghigliazza, *Historia de la provincia dominicana de Chile* (Concepcion 1898); F. Enrich, *Historia de la Compania de Jesus en Chile,* 2 vols. (Barcelona 1891); Maturana, *Historia de los Agustinos en Chile,* 2 vols. (Santiago 1904).

[33] B. Wilberforce, *Vie de St. Louis Bertrand* (Paris 1904).

excesses of the Spaniards. The Franciscans too had to defend their neophytes against the *conquistadores,* and this they did so ardently that they were charged with having destroyed the *conquista.* Around the mid-century the Augustinians also joined the ranks of the missionaries. Due to the efforts of all of these Orders, the population became Christian within a few decades. Santa Fe de Bogotá became an episcopal see in 1562 and in 1564 it obtained metropolitan status, with Popayán and Santa María as suffragans.

Venezuela, also belonging to the viceroyalty of New Granada, had been evangelized at the beginning of the sixteenth century from the Antilles. But success on the continent was more and more frustrated by the outrages of the licentious Spanish soldiers, for whose misdeeds the missionaries had to pay with their lives in various places. And the attempt of Bartolomé de Las Casas to make a settlement in this region (Cumaná in 1521) foundered as a result of atrocities committed by a punitive expedition against the Indians. When in 1528 Venezuela was assigned by Charles V to the Augsburg business house of Welser as holder of the monopoly for the importation of Negro slaves, matters hardly changed. Of course, the German mercenaries brought missionaries into the country, but they must have behaved in a worse manner than the Spaniards. In 1546 the grant to the Welser was withdrawn and in 1549 the Spanish viceroyalty of New Granada was erected.

The first great theorist of the missions in modern times, the Jesuit José de Acosta (1540–1600),[34] in his *De procuranda Indorum salute* (Salamanca 1588), gives a detailed report on the success of the South American missions and on the shortcomings of the methods employed. Here the lack of qualifications in the clergy is presented as the reason for the symptoms of decay. However, de Acosta expresses himself as opposed to admitting Indians and colonists' sons to the priesthood.[35]

The Jesuit Reductions in Paraguay

An especially characteristic undertaking of the Latin American missionary endeavor is provided by the so-called Reductions, villages where

---

[34] L. Lopetegui, *El P. Jose de Acosta y las Misiones especialmente americanas del siglo XVI* (Madrid 1942); id., "Notas sobre la actividad teologica del P. Jose de Acosta," *Gr* 21 (1940), 527–563; id., "I: Como debe intenderse la labor misional de P. Jose de Acosta," "II: Bibliografia misional del P. Jose de Acosta," *StMis* 1 (Rome 1943), 115–136; L. Kilger, "Die Peru-Relation des J. de Acosta 1576 und seine Missionstheorie," *NZM* 1 (1945), 24–38.
[35] A. Pott, "Der Acosta-Text vom Weihehindernis für Indianer," *NZM* 15 (1959), 167–180.

Christian Indians, segregated from the Spanish immigrants, lived under the more or less patriarchal authority of the missionaries. Best known are the Jesuit Reductions in Paraguay, but they were neither peculiar to this country nor to the Society of Jesus. In fact, such Christian villages were begun in the very first years of South American mission history. As early as 1503 an instruction laid down regulations for Indian settlements of this sort, and Las Casas experimented with this method of colonization and evangelization. In a sense, the *doctrinas* (like the *aldeas* in Portuguese missionary territory) were forerunners or variations of the reductions. But the system existed on the largest scale and in its most typical fashion in the Jesuit missions of Paraguay.

Invited into the country in 1585 by the Dominican Bishop Vittoria of Tucumán to evangelize the Indians who had retreated before the Spaniards into the inaccessible forests of the Pampas and the Gran Chaco, the first Jesuits conformed to the then prevailing methods of the itinerant mission. But the conversions thus made were not lasting, and the Jesuits were considering abandoning the work as a failure when their general Claudius Acquaviva, on the basis of a report of a visitation made by Father Stephen Paez, ordered the erection of permanent settlements in which the Indians should live shielded as far as possible from outside influences. The mere spreading of the word, he said, was not enough; the seeds must also be tended. This project of isolation and concentration met with the approval of the Spanish crown, despite the colonists' opposition. The still unoccupied Paraná territory was turned over to the Jesuits with the full authority to gather all Christian Indians, independently of any other supervision and far from contact with the outside world. The execution of the mandate began in 1610. In four decades of assiduous work the missionaries pushed forward to the Brazilian province of Tape and united the Indians of the Guaraní and Chaco peoples into a Christian Indian state. There was no lack of resistance on the part of Church and state. Finally, the Indians had to be equipped with firearms in order to repulse raids made by *mestizo* kidnappers from Brazil. In the wars with the so-called *Paulistas* or "Mamelukes," thousands of neophytes were carried off and several reductions destroyed, but some thirty reductions, with about 150,000 Christian Indians, were victorious in 1641.

Through the centuries the "Paraguay Jesuit State" has had friends and foes and has evoked a vast quantity of literature. Against the censures, justified and unjustified, there rises the objection that the reductions were a relative necessity and a legal self-defense against the danger, threatening from all sides, of exploitation and extermination. The pure motives of most of the missionaries are beyond question. Problems of evangelization and of colonization, as they presented themselves, were brilliantly solved. In spite of a few drastic educational methods, such as beatings and imprisonment, there is no question of terror or violence but at most of too strict a tutelage. The later catastrophe in no way implies a merely apparent success. On the contrary, the reversion to savagery rather shows how necessary was the authoritarian and strictly organized direction of the unstable and helpless Indians. Whether the Jesuits regarded the reductions as a stage of transition to adulthood cannot be determined, but it seems to be refuted by the painful fact that no native priest came out of the Jesuit reductions.

The Mission in the Philippines

With the Portuguese Ferdinand Magellan, who in Spanish service discovered the Philippines in 1521, there also landed Spanish Augustinian Hermits, who together with the crew proclaimed the Gospel to the natives. On Easter Magellan had Mass celebrated and a cross set up, to which the island Kings had to do reverence and homage. A village which refused was reduced to ashes. This act of violence caused a rising in which Magellan was murdered, and the crew and missionaries only escaped with difficulty.

For the moment Spain could not take possession of the newly discovered islands because the Pacific line of demarcation, drawn in 1529, assigned them to Portugal. But Portugal displayed no interest in the archipelago; in any event, Spain was able to undertake various attempts from her settlements in America at bringing the Philippines under her occupation. It was only in 1564 that the Augustinian Andrea de Urdaneta succeeded in doing so.[36] He was a former fleet admiral, who regarded the treachery of the natives against Magellan as cause for declaring war in the event that they should oppose an effort at conversion. In 1569 Spain formally took possession of the islands, regarding them as an extension of her American holdings and as outposts of the continent of Asia. The road from Madrid to Asia went via Mexico and the Philippines. Attention was directed almost exclusively at China, and this is the reason why missionary work on the islands was taken up only reluctantly. Manila was founded in 1571; in 1583 the Audiencia Manila was made subject to the viceroy of New Spain (Mexico).

Here too there began a downright migration of Spanish friars. Twenty-four Augustinian Hermits landed on Luzón in 1575 and were followed by the first Franciscans in 1577. Manila was made a see in 1579, and the first bishop, the Dominican Dominic de Salazar, wanted his confreres to play a role in the evangelization. His exertions in this

[36] Streit, IV, 1134, 1138.

regard make clear the dangers a journey overseas involved at the time. Of the twenty friars whom the bishop brought along, eighteen died en route, while only fifteen of thirty-two Dominicans who sailed from Spain in 1586 reached Manila. Still, the influx of new missionaries did not cease. Into the beginning of the seventeenth century 450 religious are said to have embarked for the Philippines; these included Jesuits (1581) and Augustinian Recollects (1606). The Franciscan province of Saint Gregory arose in 1586,[37] the Dominican province of the Holy Rosary in 1592, the Jesuit province in 1606.

From the islanders, who practiced a primitive animism, the evangelists encountered almost no resistance. Only in the Islamic principalities on Jolo and Mindanao in the south of the archipelago was a barrier raised against their endeavors. On the other islands they could find gratification in abundant success. The number of Christians was 400,000 as early as 1585, and it increased to almost 700,000 in 1595 and to more than 2 million in 1620. In scarcely more than a half-century the mass of the inhabitants had become Christian. The Philippines obtained its own hierarchy in 1595, the sees of Cebu, Nueva Segovia, and Nueva Caceres being suffragans of Manila.[38]

From the viewpoint of method, the Philippine missions occupy an exceptional position within the history of the Spanish missions and *patronato,* the reason being the special status of the Philippines in the Spanish Colonial Empire. The islands could be reached only by way of Mexico. This so impeded commerce with the mother country that, in comparison with missionary work, it withdrew completely into the background. The missionaries seem to have recognized this exceptional situation, and they profited by it to avoid and prevent the mistakes that had been made in America. What had been impossible to a Las Casas could be realized here. There was no slavery and no forced labor. The missionaries had themselves named as protectors of the "Indians" and were able to shield them from all excesses of the whites. The consideration and gentleness shown to the natives did not fail to produce an effect. The Filipinos remained loyal to Spain and to their missionaries, with whom they maintained the colonial empire during 150 years against all attacks by Moros, Chinese, and Dutch.

The success of the undertaking meant a new Catholic nation, the only one in the Far East. To be sure, the population completely lost its own character and became Spanish, but it took part in the intellectual and spiritual life of Catholic Spain. The educational system flourished, with schools and colleges everywhere. In 1611 the Dominicans established

[37] Streit, IV, 1240f.
[38] Streit, IV, 1315, 1318f.

the Colegio Santo Tomás,[39] which became a university in 1645.[40] A direct result of this intensive educational activity was that soon there were native priests, who in the course of time took charge of almost half the parishes.[41] It was only the decline of the Spanish world power that was to make the first change in this favorable picture.

[39] *Algunos documentos relativos a la Universidad de Manila* (Madrid 1892), pp. 5–20.
[40] Bull "In Supereminenti" of Innocent X (20 November 1645) in Streit, V, 863.
[41] A. Huonder, *Der einheimische Klerus in den Heidenländern* (Freiburg 1909), pp. 47–56.

CHAPTER 46

The Missions under Portuguese Patronage

The transfer to the Portuguese kings of the rights of the *Militia Christi*[1] and Alexander VI's award to Portugal of all territories to the east of the line of demarcation constituted the basis of Portuguese *padronado*. In the lands recently discovered and still to be discovered the Portuguese Crown had not only the duty of spreading the Christian faith but the right to nominate suitable incumbents to sees, churches, and benefices.[2] "By this fact the Church in the Portuguese colonies was for all time delivered over to the state" and "thus the dignity of grand master of the *Militia Christi* became the source of state absolutism in Portuguese missionary areas."[3]

When Columbus discovered the "West Indies" for Spain in 1492, Portuguese caravels in search of the Indies had already occupied the key positions of the African coast and under Bartolomeo Diaz in 1486–87 they had sailed around the "Cape of Storms," which John II (1481–95), overjoyed to be so near his goal, renamed the "Cape of Good Hope." In 1498 Vasco da Gama pushed up the East African coast and from there, aided by Arab pilots, reached India. In 1500 Pedro Alvares Cabral discovered Brazil; from there he sailed around the southern tip of Africa to India and brought the first cargo of Indian spices to Lisbon. The Arab spice monopoly had been broken; it was ruined by the capture of Ormuz, Aden, and Diu. The approaches to the "Spice Islands" proper, or Moluccas, were in Portuguese possession by 1511. The taking of Malacca was celebrated in Lisbon as a victory for Christianity over Islam. And not entirely without justification: in the same year the Kings

[1] Cf. Chapter 9.
[2] Leo X's Bull "Dum fidei constantiam" (7 July 1514) in *Bull Patr* I, 98f.
[3] A. Jann, *Die katholischen Missionen in Indien, China und Japan* (Paderborn 1915), pp. 65f.

of Sumatra and Java, of Siam and Pegu (Burma) entered into friendly relations with Portugal, and in 1512 the Negus of Ethiopia sent an embassy to arrange peace and friendship with King Manuel I (1495–1521) of Portugal.

King Manuel at once took up the question of Portuguese missions. He had informed Alexander VI of his decision to send diocesan and regular priests as missionaries to the lands discovered since 1499 and had obtained by the Bull "Cum sicut maiestas" of 26 March 1500 the right to subject the region from the Cape of Good Hope to India inclusively to an apostolic delegate, who, like the grand prior of the *Militia Christi,* was to be given quasi-episcopal jurisdiction. Julius II encouraged these missionary endeavors by granting Portugal spiritual advantages[4] and all of Manuel's missionaries a plenary indulgence.[5] In the interests of a more efficient direction of the regions, which could be hardly supervised from Portugal, the urgency of erecting an overseas bishopric more and more imposed itself. For this purpose Manuel suggested to the Pope the capital of Madeira, Funchal. Leo X thereupon suppressed the jurisdiction of the *Militia Christi* and by the Bull "Pro excellenti praeeminentia" (12 June 1514) erected the diocese of Funchal, to comprise all conquered islands and lands from the southern border of Mauretania to the Indies in the East and Brazil in the West.[6] Simultaneously King Manuel had all lands conquered and to be conquered adjudged as his inalienable possession.[7]

It was not until 1534, at a time when Spain already had seven missionary jurisdictions in her overseas territories, that, in the interests of a further division of the vast diocese, Funchal was raised to metropolitan rank and given as suffragans Santiago de Cabo Verde, São Tomé, São Salvador de Angra (Azores), and Goa.[8] But even this new arrangement was inadequate, for Goa embraced the entire area from the Cape of Good Hope as far as the Japanese islands, limited of course to the boundaries of the Portuguese colonial holdings, a restriction that was later to become extraordinarily significant. Just the same, the elevation of Goa to diocesan status made possible a development in keeping with local circumstances.

The question why Portugal, in contrast with Spain, was so slow to

---

[4] Constitution "Orthodoxae fidei" (12 July 1505) in *Bull Patr* I, 62–69.

[5] "Romanus Pontifex" (12 July 1506) in *Bull Patr* I, 76.

[6] *Bull Patr* I, 100f.

[7] "Praecelsae devotionis" (3 November 1514) in *Bull Patr* I, 106f.

[8] By the Bull "Aequum reputamus" of Paul III (3 November 1534), confirmed as authentic by "Romani Pontificis" (8 July 1539), in *Bull Patr* I, 148–152, 170–173.

divide her mission territory into dioceses must not be answered by suggesting that the Portuguese Kings were excessively parsimonious. It is only fair to consider the reasons which can be deduced from the inner structure of the Portuguese colonial possessions and which created an entirely different situation from that encountered by Spain in her territories. Most important of all is the fact that Portugal, except in Africa, faced countries and empires moulded by highly developed cultures and vigorous religious systems. Hence it was not possible for Portugal to create a colonial empire with areas linked together; she could only establish trading posts. This meant that the missions, which thrived only in the area under the influence of Portuguese power, acquired the character of ecclesiastical colonies. They did not gain populations but merely religious minorities. Christianity continued to be something imported from Europe, and native Christians were suspected of having given up their nationality when they accepted the faith. Hence they ceased to have any influence in favor of Christianity on their pagan countrymen.

And just as Portugal did not succeed in displacing the native rulers, so too Christianity was unable to absorb native religions and cultures. To make matters worse, the selfishness of the Portuguese merchants and settlers made the preaching of the missionaries untrustworthy and at times even impossible. The government itself frequently preferred its commercial interests to the spreading of the faith. This was invariably true of Africa, regarded merely as an intermediate stop en route to India. An so Portugal made absolutely no effort to penetrate beyond a more or less extensive coastal strip into the interior of the continent. And even here she possessed mere bases serving and protecting trade. The names given to the various coastal strips—Pepper Coast, Ivory Coast, Gold Coast, Slave Coast—indicate what Portugal expected from Africa. Most lucrative was the commerce in "black ivory," or slaves, who were annually exported by the tens of thousands to the West Indies. That even priests, biased in favor of the opinions of the day, took part in this commerce is the clearest proof of how little they were aware of their missionary responsibility toward unfamiliar peoples.

When Portugal, toward the close of the sixteenth century and in the course of the seventeenth, ceased to be a world power and was losing one colonial area after another to the Dutch and the English, she was no longer able to fulfill the duties of her patronage completely. The personal union with Spain (1580–1640), resulting from the extinction of the Dynasty of Aviz, eventually affected missionary work. Prolonged vacancies in the overseas dioceses resulted and hence led to the decay of what had been so laboriously built up in the missionary lands.

Africa

West Africa to the mouth of the Congo, included under the name "Guinea" in contemporary reports, was entrusted by Pius II in 1462 to the Franciscans under the leadership of Afonso of Bolano.[9] Dominicans were also active in West Africa from 1486, especially on the Bight of Benin and from 1489 among the Wolof in Senegambia. But there were no enduring successes to be recorded except in the neighborhood of the Portuguese strongholds. The Cape Verde Islands and São Tomé became the points of departure for repeated missionary endeavors, and hence in 1534 were made episcopal sees.

In the *Congo,* reached by Diogo Cão in 1482, the victory of the Infante Afonso over the pagan opposition led by his brother inaugurated a period which held out hope of the Christianization of the entire Congo. King Afonso himself preached to his subjects and, when his requests for missionaries went unanswered, sent his own son with several companions to Lisbon to be educated there as priests. It seems that Afonso's letters were falsified by interpreters or were suppressed by the local Portuguese authorities. Finally, "since he could no longer trust any Portuguese,"[10] Afonso had a Congolese student write to entreat Manuel I "by the Saviour's Passion" to help him; in the letter he likens the whites in Africa, including the priests, to the Jews who crucified Christ.[11] Finally, he had the consolation of receiving back his son Henry as titular Bishop of Utica (1521). Afonso expected great things of him for the Christianization of his Empire. He would have liked to see his capital, São Salvador, raised to the status of a diocese, but in 1534, São Tomé obtained the honor and a European bishop. Afonso, greatly disappointed, thought of refusing his consent to the appointment,[12] but his son, Dom Henry, was in chronic ill health after his return from Europe and his anxious father did not let him out of his sight. Consequently, Bishop Henry did not comply with a summons to go to Rome and to the Council of Trent.[13] It may be that by that time he was no longer alive. There is no news of him after 1534, and a letter written by his father in 1539 speaks of him as dead. King Afonso himself died in 1541, having suffered the cruel experience that a priest sought to murder him during the Easter Mass.

King Afonso of the Congo is one of the most tragic figures in the history of Europe's encounter with lands beyond the seas. He asked for

[9] Streit, XV, 550.
[10] Ibid., p. 757.
[11] Ibid., p. 811.
[12] "Facta fide de expeditione Episcopatus non posse concedi" (Streit, XV, 993).
[13] Ibid., p. 972.

bread and received stones. Manuel I of Portugal thus instructed his envoys to him: "Although our efforts are directed first of all to the greater glory of God and the satisfaction of the King, still you must explain to the King of the Congo, as if you were speaking in my name, what he has to do in order to fill our ships with slaves, copper, and ivory."[14] Three centuries later David Livingstone found on the left bank of the Congo River, 160 kilometers from its mouth, an inscription hewn into a rock in which the King professes his Christian faith and announces that there are twelve churches in his empire and that to a distance of 200 leagues from the coast thousands of his subjects can read.[15]

Under Afonso's grandson Diogo the first Jesuits came to the Congo in 1548. They found a greatly decayed Christianity. Their remonstrances, which did not spare even the King, so enraged him that he ordered all whites to quit his Empire. It was no longer possible for the missionaries to exert a beneficent influence, and after scarcely seven years the Jesuit mission was closed. All attempts to begin again were failures. A group of Spanish Carmelites perished by shipwreck, another fell into the hands of English pirates. A third group, which finally arrived in the Congo in 1584, could only confirm the fact that the few priests in the country "sought slaves rather than souls."[16] Hence they left in 1587 to seek new instructions and their superior did not let them go back. At last Philip II, who had worn the Portuguese crown since 1580 and was much preoccupied with details of the missions in the Portuguese demarcation zone, succeeded in detaching the Congo from the diocese of São Tomé. In 1596 Clement VIII made São Salvador an episcopal see, suffragan of Lisbon.[17] But this measure did not help the Congo mission. One of the first bishops was murdered shortly after he had taken possession of his see, causing his successors to reside at Loanda and shun the Congo.

Angola, explored by the Portuguese as early as 1520, did not establish contacts with Portugal until 1558. Included was the establishing of a mission which Francis Borgia undertook for the Society of Jesus. In a letter announcing the departure of the first missionaries it is expressly noted that the Gospel had not hitherto been preached in Angola.[18] And even then it was not going to be done for some time, as the Jesuits were thrown into prison. One of them contrived to go to Portugal in 1575,

---

[14] Cf. J. Cuvelier, *L'Ancien Royaume de Congo* (Brussels 1946), p. 131.
[15] G. Renault, *Die Karavellen Christi* (Wiesbaden n. d.), pp. 96f.
[16] Streit, XV, 2016.
[17] Bull "Super specula" (20 May 1596).
[18] *MHSI* 5 (1925), 519–525.

shortly before the new missionary expedition arrived. Again matters went awry. The Angolese bitterly resisted the occupation of their country and it was not till 1581 that the Portuguese won a victory and the missionaries their first converts. In the annual report for 1590–91 they counted 25,000 Christians.[19] At the same time the Portuguese governor was announcing that from 1575 to 1591 the number of slaves exported from Angola was 52,053.[20] No wonder that thereafter there was no end to reports of revolt and war. Not until the Bishops of São Salvador took up residence at Loanda in 1626 could the mission be stabilized.

East Africa. Authenticated information on missionary activity on the east coast of Africa does not antedate 1559. The priests in the fortified port cities labored exclusively among the Portuguese soldiers and traders. Even Saint Francis Xavier, passing through Mozambique, had to be content with preaching to Portuguese Christians.

In 1559 a report reached the Jesuits in Goa that a son of the King of Inhambane (Zambesi) had had himself baptized and in his father's name was asking for missionaries. The Jesuits accepted the mission, since Inhambane had not yet been touched by Islam. Furthermore, from there they hoped to find access to the Gold Emperor of Monomotapa. The mission was entrusted to Father Gonçalo da Silveira.[21] In Inhambane he achieved initial success, baptizing the King and 400 of his people. And in 1561 he was able to baptize the Emperor of Monomotapa, thereby arousing a strong movement toward Christianity. This alerted the Muslims, who feared for their trade and influence. They accused the missionary of espionage and magic and were so successful that the Emperor had Father Gonçalo strangled. In Inhambane, too, things became so difficult that the missionary who had remained there decided to return to India. The East Africa mission had collapsed, and the Portuguese traders in Mozambique, with an eye to their trade, opposed its continuance. In 1571 the Portuguese government organized a punitive expedition to avenge the death of Father Gonçalo, but it ended miserably. At length Dominicans resumed their missionary work in 1577 and Jesuits in 1607. Around 1624 the two Orders maintained some twenty stations and forty-five missionaries. In 1612 the area was detached from Goa as the vicariate of Mozambique and organized as an autonomous jurisdiction.[22]

---

[19] Streit, XV, 2095.

[20] Ibid., p. 2097.

[21] H. Chadwick, *Life of the Ven. Fr. Gonçalo da Silveira, Proto-Martyr of South Africa* (London 1910); B. Leite, *D. Gonçalo da Silveira* (Lisbon 1946).

[22] Constitution "In supereminenti" (21 January 1612) in Streit, XVI, 2405.

Asia

India. The early missionary age in India was inaugurated by diocesan priests and the older Orders, chiefly Franciscans and Dominicans. Coming with the explorers and conquerors, they built monasteries and churches or destroyed temples and replaced them with churches. But their activity among the natives was limited by their ignorance of the languages and their faulty methods. Baptism was the goal of their preaching; once it was achieved, the missionaries moved on, without taking sufficient care for the absorption of Christian doctrine. There was no dearth of successes so far as numbers go, though the figures for the early period must be regarded with caution. Many conversions to Christianity were obtained by the sword, others were purchased by worldly benefits. Thus the 10,000 to 20,000 Paravas of the Fishery Coast became Christians because they expected Portuguese protection from the Muslims. Successes could be obtained even among the schismatic "Saint Thomas Christians" of South India. However, missionary efforts were seriously hindered by the wicked lives of the Portuguese and by the Hindu caste system. Christians came almost exclusively from the lowest strata of the population.

In the matter of jurisdiction, from 1506 to 1534 India was subject to an apostolic delegate[23] and his vicar general, though in 1514 Goa had been incorporated into the diocese of Funchal. In 1534 Goa became a suffragan see of Funchal. Its first bishop, the Franciscan John d'Albuquerque (1537–53),[24] exerted himself tirelessly for a better organization of his extensive territory. Under him the College of the Holy Faith was founded at Goa in 1541 for the training of a native clergy; a second, for the Saint Thomas Christians, was established at Cranganur.[25]

The second period of India's missionary history began with the entrance of the Jesuits into evangelization. Ignatius Loyola, approached by John III for some members of the Society, which had just obtained papal confirmation, selected Francis Xavier (1506–52) for India. Paul III named him legate in 1541 and provided him with the fullest authority. Francis Xavier bacame the Apostle of India and of the entire Far East and is the greatest missionary of modern times.

Francis waived his legatine authority and placed himself at the disposal of the Bishop of Goa. At the beginning of his career he differed

---

[23] See p. 590. The apostolic delegates for India and East Africa were Duarte Nuñez, O. P. (1514–17), Andrea Torquemada, O. F. M. (1520–22), Martinho (1522–30?), and Fernando Vaqueiro, O. F. M. (1531–32).

[24] Paul III's Bull "Regimini universalis" (April 11, 1537) in *Bull Patr* I, 278–181.

[25] Cf. A. Huonder, *Der einheimische Klerus in den Heidenländern* (Freiburg 1909), pp. 56ff., 65.

from the other missionaries only in his extraordinary zeal. His method, like theirs, was determined by tradition. His first care was for the Portuguese colonists, whose moral and religious life had hopelessly deteriorated. Only then did he turn to the conversion of the pagans. He visited the existing congregations on the Paravas and Malabar coasts, worked to organize them, preached, and baptized. In 1545 he undertook a missionary exploration of the Portuguese colonial area. His journey carried him beyond Cochin and Malacca to the Moluccas (Amboina, Ternate) and then back to Malacca, where his attention was directed to Japan. In Japan (1549–51) he conceived the plan of extending his activity to China; but entry was denied him. Alone and forsaken, he died on the night of 2–3 December 1552 on the rocky island of Sanch'uan near Canton.

Francis Xavier's merit does not lie in his having shown the methods of the modern mission in the Far East. Far more important for the missions among the highly cultured peoples of Asia was the realization that, if the missionaries wanted to gain foreign and unfamiliar peoples for Christianity, they must adapt themselves to them. Questions about the successes of the saint, who was canonized by Gregory XV in 1622, about his miracles and the gift of tongues attributed to him, should therefore pale before the appraisal of his understanding of method. The number of those he baptized, including many children of Christian parents, may have amounted to 30,000 people. Reports of miracles appeared only after his death, and in his letters he complained of the difficulties in communication because of language. What made him a great missionary was the saint's power to attract. His example and his letters inspired many to missionary work in the succeeding period.

In 1557–58 Goa became the metropolitan see of all of East Asia, with the dioceses of Cochin and Malacca as its suffragans.[26] Later the sees of Angamale (1600)[27] and Mailapur (1606)[28] were added in India. This early granting of autonomy to the Church in India was of great importance for missionary procedure. At numerous provincial councils in Goa (1567, 1575, 1585, 1592, 1606) steps were taken against the use of force and against state interference and a more convincing method of conversion was recommended.

An especially difficult problem presented itself in regard to the schismatic Saint Thomas Christians of the Malabar Coast.[29] Jurisdiction over them was disputed among the Nestorian Patriarch of Mosul, the

[26] Streit, IV, 825ff., 839ff.; *Bull Patr* I, 191–198.
[27] Clement VIII's Constitution "In supremo militantis" (4 August 1600) in Streit, V, 6; *Bull Patr* I, 260f.
[28] Paul V's Cedula Consistorialis of 9 January 1606 in Streit, V, 83, *Bull Patr* II, 4ff.
[29] Jann, op. cit., pp. 142–173.

Chaldean Patriarch of Amida, and the Archbishop of Goa. Matters were aggravated by the fact that both patriarchs sought to install in the sees of the Saint Thomas Christians men of their respective obediences, while the Portuguese Franciscans, active in Malabar for a half-century, wanted a Latin bishop at Angamale. The attendant scandalous political intrigues made the situation confused.

At the Provincial Council of Diamper in 1599 all disputed points were to be definitively settled and the reunion of the Saint Thomas Christians formally ratified.[30] The Syro-Chaldean Rite was to be maintained; the liturgical books were purged of heretical elements; and a catechism in the Malayalam language was intended to increase and deepen the Saint Thomas Christians' knowledge of the faith. The Syriac archbishopric of Angamale was divested of its metropolitan rank and made a suffragan of Goa.[31] The Jesuit Francisco Roz was named as bishop. He was fluent in Syriac and Malayalam and had worked for years among the Saint Thomas Christians. But Angamale's reduction in rank was not accepted quietly. Actual riots put the union in serious danger. Rome relented and in 1608 Angamale recovered its former status.[32] In 1609 the see was moved to the Portuguese citadel of Cranganur for reasons of safety.[33]

Elsewhere in India Christianity spread very slowly. For a time it seemed that the Emperor Akbar (1556–1605) would embrace the faith, but this hope was unfulfilled.[34] An even more promising endeavor was undertaken by the Italian Jesuit, Roberto de Nobili (1577–1656).[35] He realized that the transfer of Western usages and institutions deprived Christianity of any prospect of lasting success. Hence he decided to adapt himself to the Hindus' manner of life and viewpoints. He studied Tamil, Telugu, and Sanskrit and dressed and lived as a penitential monk. His neophytes were allowed to retain Hindu customs in so far as these were not pagan in character. This method proved to be very effective with the Brahmins, who had hitherto rejected Christianity. In 1609 he had to build a church for them. De Nobili did not escape opposition, but his method was finally approved by Gregory XV.[36] At de Nobili's death the Madura mission counted 40,000 faithful.

---

[30] Acts of the Diocesan Synod of Diamper in *Bull Patr,* Appendix I, pp. 148–357; cf. J. Thaliath, *The Synod of Diamper* (Rome 1958).

[31] Streit, V, 6; *Bull Patr* I, 260f.

[32] Streit, V, 106; *Bull Patr* II, 8f.

[33] Streit, V, 127; *Bull Patr* II, 10f.

[34] A good complete presentation (with bibliography) in A. Camps, *Jerome Xavier, S. J., and the Muslims of the Mogul Empire* (Schöneck–Beckenried 1957).

[35] Streit, V, 91 (works and literature).

[36] "Romanae Sedis Antistes" (31 January 1623) in Streit, V, 254, *Bull Patr* II, 32ff.

Franciscan missionaries reached Ceylon as early as 1517. However, they did not take up the work in large numbers until 1540, when they had much success in the kingdoms of Cotta and Kandy. At the beginning of the seventeenth century Jesuits also settled on the island.

Malay Archipelago. The goal of the Portuguese seafarers' commercial policy was the "Spice Islands," the source of the cloves so much desired by Europe. In 1511 they were discovered in the Moluccas. In accordance with the attitude of the age, the merchants felt obliged to spread the faith in the islands they had discovered. They sought to win the chiefs, and, if successful, left there the religious who had made the voyage with them. It was in this way that the first Christian communities arose on Amboina, Ternate, and other islands. However, since most of the inhabitants were Muslims, the Christians and their missionaries were persecuted, as on Ternate in 1534. As early as 1521 the Portuguese had erected a fortress on Ternate for the protection of their commerce. The island had to be reconquered and "reconverted" after 1534. Francis Xavier visited the Moluccas in 1546–47.[37] He was followed by other Jesuits, who were tending forty-seven congregations in 1556 and in 1569 close to 80,000 Christians. Eventually the Dutch gained possession of the islands and the missions fell into ruin. In 1644 the number of Christians had dropped to 3,000.

The first missionary efforts on Celebes (1525) were fruitless. But in 1548 the Franciscans arrived and their preaching of hell-fire converted whole princedoms in South Celebes; elsewhere too the concept of hell is said to have impressed the Muslims far more than tidings of paradise. Christianity was unable to penetrate North Celebes until Jesuits arrived there in 1563. They are supposed to have baptized a quarter of the population. But communities of any size were not established on Celebes until 1641, when the Bishop of Malacca, expelled by the Dutch, set up his see in Makassar.

The other large Sunda Islands, despite their proximity to India, were scarcely affected by evangelization. The lack of missionaries, the resistance of the Muslim sultans, and the inaccessibility of the interior of the islands may have been the reasons. Only in East Java did Jesuits have some success among the as yet non-Islamic population.

The small Sunda Islands, discovered by Spaniards in 1522 during the first circumnavigation of the globe, were, however, successfully evangelized by the Dominicans. Their chief center was the island of

---

[37] C. Wessel, *De geschiedenis der R. K. Missie in Amboina vanaf har stichting door de H. Franciscus Xaverius tot har vernietiging door de O. I. Compagnie, 1546–1605* (Nijmegen 1926).

Solor,[38] from which Christianity spread to the other islands, and before long more than fifty thousand believers were counted. But Muslim opposition and Portuguese blunders almost wiped out the successes. In spite of the Dutch conquest of the islands, the Dominicans continued their work and were even able to induce a new flowering of Christianity. The Solor missions managed to survive into the eighteenth century.

Japan was accidentally discovered by the Portuguese in 1542–43, when a vessel, driven off course by a typhoon, landed there instead of in Siam. In 1548–49 the Portuguese undertook the first expedition to establish commercial relations with Japan. Francis Xavier, having met three Japanese in Malacca, had become interested in the island empire of the Far East and went there with them in 1549. He landed on Kagoshima, where he established the first Christian community. His aim was to win the Emperor to the faith and through him and the Buddhist monasteries to convert the people. But he soon had to acknowledge that the Mikado was only the nominal ruler of the country. In fact, Japan was in a state of anarchy; the island empire had dissolved into some fifty petty states and the territorial princes, or Daimyos, did as they pleased. To gain access to them, Francis decided henceforth to proceed as papal legate in great splendor and he directed that future missionaries should seek to win the people by their public appearance, among other things by observing the Japanese rules of etiquette. The encounter with the high culture of the Japanese induced the saint to abandon the traditional Europeanizing method and to urge a far-reaching accommodation. In his religious discussions with Buddhist monks he unhesitatingly accepted their religious concepts,[39] for example the term *Dainichi* for God. But when he discovered that *Dainichi* denoted, not a personal being, but the original substance of all things, he resumed the Latin *Deus*. (In a revision of his catechism in 1556 some fifty Buddhist terms had to be replaced by Portuguese-Latin terms.)

Francis Xavier returned to Goa in 1551, entrusting to his companion, Father Cosmas de Torres, three Christian communities with approximately 1000 neophytes, all of them from the lower classes. The first Daimyo was not baptized until 1563, but so many others soon followed that their conversion became the special mark of the early Japanese mission.[40] Their example attracted many Samurai and Bonzes and finally

---

[38] B. Biermann, "Die alte Dominikanermission auf den Solorinseln," *ZMR* 14 (1924), 12–48, 269–273; *id.,* "Frei Luis de Andrada und die Solormission." *ZMR,* 43 (1959), 176–187, 261–274.

[39] G. Schurhammer, *Das kirchliche Sprachproblem in der japan. Jesuitenmission des 16. und 17. Jh.* (Tokyo 1928).

[40] M. Steicher, *Les daimyos chrétiens ou un siècle d'histoire religieuse et politique du Japon 1549–1650* (Hongkong 1904).

the people. In certain parts of Japan regular mass conversions occurred. In 1570 the young Christendom counted from 20,000 to 30,000 faithful, among whom worked thirty Jesuit priests and brothers, aided by lay Japanese. Since in Japan the mission could not, as was the case elsewhere, claim the assistance of the Portuguese state, these successes cannot be overestimated. In most cases the conversions were genuine, without any selfish motives.

Of course, the missionaires had to support themselves. This unfortunately induced them to participate in the Portuguese silk trade and to lease houses which they had received as gifts. This would have been permitted if disagreements in regard to procedures had not arisen among the missionaries. De Torres' successor, Francisco Cabral, was opposed to any accommodation and insisted on the Europeanizing missionary method traditional among the Portuguese. This produced tension within the Christian communities, especially among Christians of the higher classes. Still, the number of Christians grew and reached 150,000 while Cabral was in charge (c. 1580). In 1576 Japan was detached from the diocese of Malacca and placed under the new see of Macao.[41]

The internal crisis was exorcised by the arrival as visitor of Father Alessandro Valignano (1539–1606).[42] This farsighted and intelligent man quickly carried out a reform of the mission in accord with Xavier's principles of accommodation, prescribed a thorough study of the language by the missionaries, and, with the construction of two seminaries, laid the foundation for a native diocesan and regular clergy. On his departure he took along a Japanese embassy to the Pope and the King of Spain. The embassy not only caused a sensation in Europe (1582–90) but aroused a keen interest in the Japanese mission.[43]

Meanwhile a reaction had taken place in Japan's internal politics. Following the restricting of the arbitrariness of the Daimyos by the Commander-in-Chief Nobunaga between 1564 and 1568, Hideyoshi acquired as regent of the Mikado an almost unlimited authority in the early 1580s. Originally friendly to the Christians, he became suspicious because of the indiscretions of the mission superior Coelho and was turned into a foe of Christianity. In 1587 he issued an order for the expulsion of all missionaries. Though the order was not carried out, the work had to be done much more circumspectly. Still, between 1587 and 1597 the Jesuits gained 65,000 additional converts. In 1588 Japan became a separate diocese, with Funai as the episcopal residence.[44]

---

[41] "Super specula" of Gregory XIII (23 January 1576) in Streit, IV, 1525.

[42] J. F. Schütte, *Valignanos Missionsgrundsätze für Japan,* I, 1–2 (Rome 1951–58).

[43] L. Frois, *La première ambassade du Japon en Europe 1582–1592.* Première partie: "Le voyage en Europe (1582–1586), ed. J. A. A. Pinto et al. (Tokyo 1942).

[44] Sixtus V's Cedula Consistorialis of 19 February 1588 in Streit, IV, 1701.

In the missionary sphere too an entirely new situation had arisen in Japan. After the union of the Portuguese and Spanish crowns in 1580 Spanish missionaires from the Philippines sought to enter the Portuguese missionary area, though in 1585 Gregory XIII had granted the Society of Jesus the exclusive right to evangelize the Far East.[45] In 1593 Franciscans under the leadership of Pedro Bautista began missionary work in Japan. Having gained the good will of Hideyoshi, they displayed great zeal and, though adhering to the traditional Spanish method, had considerable success. But the national antipathies of Portuguese and Spanish were more fundamental than the differences in method and the rivalry of the Orders. Hideyoshi skillfully exploited these by subtle trickery and finally discovered a pretext for striking at Christianity. This was provided by the celebrated and still sharply debated remark of the pilot of the *San Felipe*,[46] that the Spaniards sent merchants and missionaries in order to conquer foreign lands with their assistance. The sequel was the first mass martyrdom of Nagasaki, where the six Spanish Franciscans, three Japanese Jesuits, and seventeen other Japanese Christians suffered death on 5 February 1597.[47] Despite this, the Franciscans resumed the work in Japan in 1598 and, following the annulment of the Jesuits' privilege,[48] Spanish Dominicans and Augustinians also arrived. The number of Christians continued to grow in spite of the persecution and in 1614 amounted to about three hundred thousand. The first Japanese priests were ordained in 1601. At the close of the early Japanese missionary age there were fifty of them—nine diocesan priests, thirty-two Jesuits, three Dominicans, and one each of the Franciscan and Augustinian Orders. Twenty-one of them died as martyrs.[49]

On Hideyoshi's death in 1598, wars raged again between rival army commanders. The victor, Tokugawa Ieyasu, established a military dynasty that lasted until 1868. The seizure of political power by an absolute dictator was something so unprecedented that the Daimyos appeared to be completely paralyzed. That the Christians among them might, perhaps with outside aid, unite against the central government was sufficient cause for Ieyasu to declare war on Christianity. The commercial intrigues of the European powers, aggravated by the denomina-

---

[45] Brief "Ex pastorali officio" of 28 January 1585 in Streit, IV, 1647.

[46] Cf. also the articles of J. Laures in *NZM* 7 (1951), 184–203; J. F. Schütte in *ZMR* 36 (1952), 99–116; and L. Alvarez-Talandriz in *Missionalia Hispanica* 10 (Madrid 1953), 175–195; and also F. J. Schütte in *ZMR*, 38 (1954), 328–331.

[47] L. Frois, *Relacion del Martirio 1597* (Rome 1935); G. Huber, *Kreuze über Nagasaki* (Werl 1954).

[48] "Onerosa pastoralis officii" of Clement VIII (12 December 1600) in Streit, V, 987.

[49] A. Brou, "Le clergé japonais au XVIIe siècle." *RHM* 9 (1932), 475–505.

tional opposition of Portuguese and Spaniards on the one hand and Dutch and English on the other, made him see in the religion of the West a national danger for Japan. The Christian Daimyos failed in the trial of strength forced upon them. The first Christian generation had completely disappeared and the second was not inspired with the early ardor. From 1603 one family after another apostatized. In 1613 Ieyasu issued an edict against Christians, which was followed in 1614 by a decree of banishment.[50] Only eighteen Jesuits, seven Dominicans, six Franciscans, five diocesan priests, and one Augustinian remained. Every year many Christians died as martyrs. In the second mass martyrdom 100 died together, including eighteen missionaries from the four Orders. The persecution grew in intensity. After 1623 every Japanese had to declare publicly his religious adherence every year. From 1627 the so-called *efumi*, or "image-trampling," prevailed, for the persecutors desired to make apostates rather than martyrs. By 1630 the number of those who had died for their faith amounted to 4,045.[51] The persecution found its final climax in the Shimabara Revolt of 1637–38, in which 30,000 Christians were put to death. Japan shut itself off more and more from the outside world; trade relations with Spain and Manila were broken off in 1624, with Portugal in 1639. The Dutch alone, under conditions not entirely honorable, were able to conduct a modest trade on the island of Deshima until 1854. To achieve this, they had cooperated in putting down the Shimabara Revolt. Christianity had thereafter to lead a catacomb existence in Japan but did maintain itself into the nineteenth century.

China. Francis Xavier's death at the very gates of China was the reason prompting the Jesuits to seek admission to the sealed off Middle Empire, which had been known to the Portuguese since 1514–15. But the Portuguese did not succeed in establishing relations with China until 1554. They acquired the Gozan peninsula and there founded the city of Macao, which was to be the focal point of European interests in the Far East for 300 years. The city soon became also the base and refuge of missionaries, but all efforts from 1555 on to set foot in China failed. Macao became an episcopal see in 1576,[52] and, to satisfy the Spaniards, Manila had to be given the same honor in 1581. Thus in the Far East there were two centers from which efforts were made to obtain access to China. Many difficulties of the China mission derived from the fact that

[50] H. Cieslik, "Das Christenverbot in Japan unter dem Tokugawa Regime," *NZM* 6 (1950), 175–192, 256–272; 7 (1951), 24–36.

[51] J. Laures, "Die Zahl der Christen und Martyrer im alten Japan," *Monumenta Nipponica* 7 (1951), 84–101.

[52] "Super specula" of Gregory XIII (23 January 1576) in *Bull Patr* I, 243–245.

missionaries of different nationalitites took up their activities in the Middle Empire from different starting points. Here too the personal union of the two Iberian empires made itself felt. The Spanish Jesuit Alonso Sanchez even defended the right to procure entry by armed force and offered plans relevant to a military conquest of China.[53]

Finally in 1583 two Jesuits, Michele Ruggieri and Matteo Ricci (1552–1610),[54] succeeded in obtaining authorization to reside in China. They settled at Chao-ch'ing near Canton and began their work dressed as Buddhist monks. They eagerly learned Chinese and studied the writings of Confucius and other Chinese sages. Compared with the statistics then in use, their success was slight. By 1586 they had gathered no more than forty converts. An effort to extend their sphere of activity brought forth a prohibition of remaining longer in Chao-ch'ing, but they were permitted to settle in another place in the same province. There they changed their dress, for they had discovered that the Buddhist monks were not highly regarded. From then on they appeared in the robes of scholars and were able to use their knowledge of the profane sciences for the spread of the faith. Ricci's two philosophical works, *On Friendship* and *The Art of Recollection* were from this period (1595). From his discussions with Chinese scholars came his *The True Doctrine of God*, a brochure later admitted among the Chinese classics.

The missionaries had quickly learned that everything depended on gaining the good will of the Emperor. Ricci sought in every way to be admitted to the Court at Peking. His efforts led to the founding of settlements at Nan-ch'ing and Nanking, where Ricci himself took up residence in 1598. Here he produced the famous "Map of Ten Thousand Empires," a map of the world on which Ricci, to avoid hurting the feelings of the Chinese, made China literally the "Middle Empire" in the very center of the map.[55] It was here that Ricci gained his most important convert, the scholar Hsu Kuang-ch'i, who, as Paul Hsu, was to play a notable role in China's mission history.

In 1601 Ricci was able to settle in Peking. The Emperor himself presented the Jesuits with a house and allowed them to erect a church.

[53] Cf. Streit, IV, 329, nn. 31, 32, 34.

[54] In addition to the old biographies by D'Orleans (1693), Sainte Foi (1859), and Werfer (1870), see particularly Ricci-Ricardi, *Il d. Matteo Ricci* (Florence 1910); J. Brucker, "Le P. M. Ricci," *Etudes,* 124 (Paris 1910), 5–7, 185–208, 751–779; P. Tacchi Venturi, *L'apostolato del P. M. Ricci in Cina secondo i suoi scritti inediti* (Rome, 2nd ed. 1910); H. Bernard, *Le P. M. Ricci et la société de son temps (1552–1610),* 2 vols. (Tientsin 1937; P. D'Elia, "Il P. M. Ricci, S. J., fondatore delle moderne missioni della Cina," *I grandi missionari* I (Rome 1939), 127–176.

[55] J. Brucker, "Note sur une carte supposee du P. Ricci," *Atti e Memorie di Geografi-Orientalisti* (Macerata 1911), pp. 85ff.; P. E'Elia, *Il mappamondo del P. M. Ricci, commentato, tradotto e annotato* (Citta del Vaticano 1938).

Ricci developed an extensive teaching and gained influential members of the imperial court and the learned world for the faith. There are said to have been more than 200 Christians in Peking in 1605. In 1608 a settlement was made in Shanghai also. The total number of Christians was given in the same year as 2500, many of them of rank and position. When Ricci died in 1610 at the age of fifty-eight, exhausted by his tireless activity, he left his confreres, in his own words, "before a gate that can be opened to the advantage of all but not without toil and danger."

Soon after Ricci's death his liberal accommodation[56]—that the Chinese Christians might continue after baptism to honor their ancestors and Confucius—caused scandal and later gave rise to the so-called Dispute over Rites and Accommodation. About one thing there is no room for doubt: Ricci was a man of apostolic outlook and a capable missionary, who destroyed prejudices against the Christian religion and won important scholars for the faith. It may be that he was misled in regard to the meaning and importance of the Chinese rites, which he interpreted as purely civil. Several things were later attributed to him which can definitely not be ascribed to him, for example, preserving secrecy about or even falsifying Christian doctrines in essential points. If this had been the case, his converts would not have endured so heroically the persecutions that soon overtook them. In spite of all difficulties, Christianity in China rose from 5,000 in 1615 to 38,200 in 1636.

Johann Adam Schall von Bell (c. 1591–1666) of Cologne was Ricci's real and effective successor for the period from 1630 to 1666.[57] He skillfully brought the mission through the troubles of his day. Spanish-Portuguese power was more and more violently shaken in the Far East during this period. The destruction of the Spanish Armada had only now begun to make itself felt. The Dutch had established themselves in the Indian Ocean since 1601, and in 1639 the remainder of the trade with Japan passed into their hands. In 1640 the national revolution of the Braganza destroyed the loose union of Portugal with Spain. The Manchus invaded China and toppled the Ming Dynasty in 1644.

The political confusion was aggravated by the tension among the Christians, which had been produced by missionaries from the Spanish

---

[56] A. Brou, "Les tâtonnements du P. M. Ricci," *RHM* 15 (1938), 228–244; J. Bettray, *Die Akkommodationsmethode des P. M. Ricci in China* (Rome 1955).

[57] A. Väth, *Joh. Adam Schall von Bell SJ, Missionar in China, kaiserlicher Astronom und Ratgeber am Hofe von Peking, 1592–1666* (Cologne 1933).

Philippines.[58] In 1631 the Dominican Angelus Cocchi landed at Fukien; in 1633 the Dominican Juan Baptist de Morales and the Franciscan Antonio de Santa María Caballero followed, eventually bringing many of their confreres. So far as the Church was concerned, they could count on approval of their undertaking. (As a matter of fact, Urban VIII in 1633, at the urging of the Congregation of Propaganda, permitted all Orders to do missionary work in East Asia. In order to assure a unified effort, they were supposed to base their preaching on the Tridentine Catechism and Cardinal Bellarmine's *Doctrine christiana*.[59])

The appearance of the Spanish missionaries, who showed very little consideration for the missionaries already active in the country, caused much perplexity among the faithful. They went about in their habits, preached publicly, cross in hand, and made clear to the faithful their opposition to the worship of ancestors and of Confucius. The conflict in method was to grow into the disastrous Disputes over Rites, which will be considered in detail later. By way of anticipation it may be said that the solution of the conflict is not to be sought in the success or failure of the various methods, for the Dominicans and Franciscans had successes to record similar to those of the Jesuits. Around the middle of the seventeenth century the China mission experienced a new flowering in spite of all the internal and external confusion. In 1651 the Congregation of Propaganda was already considering a plan to erect a patriarchate in Peking and to subject to it two or three archbishoprics and twelve bishoprics.[60] But matters were to take an entirely different course.

Indochina. From 1511 Malacca served as the point of departure for mission work in Indochina. It was an almost fruitless effort because of the deplorable example of the Portuguese, although Franciscans, Dominicans, Jesuits, and Augustinians had monasteries and churches in the city and in 1557–58 Malacca had been made a diocese.

Toward the close of the sixteenth century missionaries were admitted to Burma, the ancient Pegu, as chaplains for the Portuguese mercenaries and Goan prisoners of war, who, having married Burmese wives, established Catholic village communities.

Siam witnessed various missionary endeavors of Dominicans and Franciscans, but not a few of them paid for their boldness with their lives. They did not have any success until a commercial treaty with Portugal had been concluded at the beginning of the seventeenth century.

[58] B. Biermann, *Die Anfänge der neueren Dominikanermission in China* (Münster 1927); O. Maas, *Die Wiedereröffnung der Franziskanermission in China in der Neuzeit* (Münster 1926).

[59] Streit, V, 1489; *Collectanea S. Congreg. de Propaganda Fide* I (Rome 1907), 72.

[60] F. Schwager, *ZMR* 2 (1912), 207f., according to the Propaganda materials.

A Portuguese Dominican labored in Cambodia from the middle of the sixteenth century. At the time of the personal union of Portugal and Spain, Spanish Franciscans from the Philippines established themselves in this part of the Portuguese sphere of demarcation.

The Church's most promising mission field lay to the east, in the empires of Annam, Cochin-China, and Tongking. But here too the work of the Portuguese Franciscans was made more difficult by their Spanish confreres from Manila. The Jesuits were the first to succeed in establishing stable communities (from 1615). The most successful was the French Jesuit, Alexandre de Rhodes (1591–1660), who worked here from 1624. In Tongking in four years he gained almost 7,000 converts, among them 200 priests and the King's sister. In spite of a royal prohibition (1630), the number of Christians continued to mount, thanks to native lay catechists. In 1639 there were 82,000 Tonkinese Christians.

Having been expelled from Tongking in 1640, de Rhodes returned to Cambodia, where by himself he cared for 30,000 faithful. In order to obtain help with the work, he established a catechists' school. From among the pupils he formed a religious community of catechists, who lived celibate lives and bound themselves by oath to a lifetime of service in the congregations. In 1645 de Rhodes was expelled from here also. He returned to Europe to seek assistants for the missions and to submit plans to Rome for the formation of a native clergy and hierarchy.

Brazil

From the time of its discovery by Europeans in 1500 Brazil saw numerous but isolated missionary endeavors, made by Portuguese, Spanish, and Italian Franciscans of the various branches of the Order.[61] As a consequence of the cruelty of Portuguese soldiers, traders, and colonists, these undertakings had little permanent success. Enduring missionary activity had to await the arrival of the Jesuits, who came in 1549 with the governor, Tomé de Souza. Their leader, Father Manuel da Nóbrega (1519–70),[62] urged above all else the erection of a Brazilian bishopric, which was established as early as 1551 in the capital at that

[61] A. Jaboatam, *Novo Orbe Serafico Brasilico ou Chronica dos Frades Minores da Provincia do Brasil* (Lisbon 1761; Rio de Janeiro, 2nd ed. 1858f., in two parts); V. Willeke, "Die franziskanische Missionspraxis unter den Indianern Brasiliens (1585–1619)," *ZMR* 42 (1958), 133–139; D. Romag, *Historia dos Franciscanos no Brasil, 1500–1659* (Curitiba 1940); B. Roewer, *A Ordem Franciscana no Brasil* (Petropolis, 2nd ed. 1947); id., *Paginas de Historia Franciscana no Brasil* (Petropolis, 2nd ed. 1958); O. van der Vat, *Principios da Igreja no Brasil* (Petropolis 1952).
[62] A. Peixoto, *Cartas Jesuiticas* I: *Manuel da Nobrega, Cartas do Brasil, 1549–1560* (Rio de Janeiro 1931), which contains the dialogue "Conversao do gentio."

time, São Salvador (Bahia).[63] But the first bishop, Pedro Fernandes Sardinha, could not cope with the situation. The insubordination of his own priests threatened to cancel out their labors as missionaries. In 1556 the bishop fell into the hands of pagan Indians, who ate him.[64]

In 1506 there arose in Bahia the Colegio de Jesus, which was destined to become the famous center for the training of the Brazilian clergy and a model for all similar institutions in the larger cities of Brazil. Its importance becomes clear from the curious fact that in the Portuguese colonial sphere of influence in America there was not a single university or printing press.

The Jesuits' educational activity was entirely geared to the service of the missions among the Indian population. The missionaries, who within a few years pushed forward to the extreme south of the country and began their Guarani mission, to become so famous, along the Portuguese-Spanish border, sought to acquire the local languages, instructed the children in reading and writing, and translated prayers and catechisms. In regard to missionary methods it is significant that the Jesuits were very cautious about conferring baptism. They required a long period of preparation and carefully selected the neophytes from the number of catechumens. They were even slower in allowing the new Christians to receive communion. The first ones were not admitted to Easter Communion until 1573 and they had to prepare for it by fasting and mortification. This procedure explains why the Jesuits did not accept a single Indian into the Society or let any be ordained.

The work of the missionaries was obstructed by the colonists, above all by the mulattoes known as "Mamelukes." Before long the Jesuits in Brazil were filling a role analogous to that of Las Casas in Spanish America. To protect the Indians, they gathered them into communities called *aldeas* or *doutrinas* or into reductions. In 1609 they succeeded in doing away with Indian slavery, but the Portuguese colonists were able to render the law inoperative by introducing forced labor.

The Jesuits of Brazil were constituted a separate province of the Society in 1553. Though forty Jesuits were sunk by Huguenot pirates while at sea,[65] and twelve more were captured and killed a year later, the Brazilian province counted 142 members in 1584 and about 180 in 1622. But not all of them were Portuguese; they came from various European countries. Portugal, which then had about 1,500,000 inhabitants, could never have carried out its tasks in its gigantic colonial empire

[63]Julius III's Bull of 25 February 1551 in *Bull Patr* I, 177f.

[64] Pastor, XIII, 293.

[65] M. G. de Costa, *Inacio de Azevedo* (Braga 1946); A. Rumeau de Armas, "La expedicion misionera al Brasil martirizada en aquas do Canarias (1570)," *Missionalia Hispanica* 4 (Madrid 1947), 329–381.

without outside help. The burden of the mother country was heavy enough besides. For example, in 1572 Pope Pius V decreed that two-thirds of all Church revenue in Portugal must be applied to the missions of Brazil and Japan.[66] In 1627 North Brazil became the autonomous Jesuit province of Maranhão. Missionary work had been very quickly carried ever deeper into the interior. The stimulus to this came from José de Anchieta (1534–97),[67] a native of the Canary Islands, who earned for himself the title of Apostle of Brazil by his tireless zeal. By 1584 the number of Indian Christians is said to have mounted to 100,000.

Toward the end of the sixteenth century other Orders also entered the field. Carmelites came in 1580[68] Benedictines in 1581,[69] and a bit later Augustinians and Oratorians. When the competing French broke into Latin America at the beginning of the seventeenth century and founded a colony of their own at Maranhão in North Brazil, they obtained Capuchin missionaries for their district.[70] France was preparing to enter the contest with the Iberian colonial powers.

Entry of France into the Mission Field

North America. Francis I of France (1515–47) was not inclined to stand aloof from the partition of the world. He assisted Giovanni de Verrazzano, a Venetian in French service, who sighted the Hudson in 1523, and Jacques Cartier, who in 1534 took possession of Canada for France. Francis also, either from conviction or from political considerations, looked upon discovery and conquest as a means for the conversion of the "savages." But possession of Canada remained unexploited. French failure in Brazil—in 1557 they were driven from the Bay of Rio de Janeiro which they had occupied two years before—made them recognize *de facto* the division of the world by Alexander VI. Later Henry IV (1589–1610) managed to secure in the Treaty of Vervins of 1598 the

[66] Streit, II, 1301.

[67] A. Peixoto, *Cartas Jesuiticas* III; *Cartas, informacoes, fragmentos historicos e sermoes do P. Joseph de Anchieta, S. J., 1554–1594 (Rio de Janeiro 1933);* S. Leite, A primeira *biografia inedita de Jose de Anchieta, apostolo do Brasil* (1934); S. Lopez Herera, *El P. J. de Anchieta* (Madrid 1954); works in Streit, II, 1239, pp. 339–342.

[68] P. A. Prat, *Notas historicas sobre as Missioes carmelitas no extremo norte de Brasil. Seculos XVII–XVIII* (Recife 1948).

[69] D. J. Luna, *Os mongos beneditinos no Brasil* (Rio de Janeiro 1947); G. Muller, *Os Beneditinos no Brasil* (Bahia 1947).

[70] C. D'Aberville, *L'arrivée de Pères Capucins en l'Inde Nouvelle, appelée Maragnon . . .* (Paris 1612); cf. Streit, II, 2370; *Suite de l'histoire des choses plus mémorables advenues en Maragnon . . .* (Paris 1615); cf. Streit, II, 2378.

right to annex territory north of an east-west line which intersected the Canary Islands.

Following the isolated efforts of two Jesuits in Acadia (1611–13), four Franciscan Recollects settled in 1615 at Quebec, founded in 1608 by Samuel de Champlain.[71] In 1625 the first Jesuits arrived in Canada under Father Charles Lalemant to evangelize the Hurons and other Indian tribes. But England seized the colony in 1628 and the missionaries had to leave. Not before 1632 could a third group of Jesuits undertake a new effort under Father Paul Le Jeune.[72] Jean de Brébeuf followed with a mission among the Hurons in 1633.[73] It seemed that the spell was broken, and as early as 1637 there were twenty-nine Jesuits in Canada. The first female religious came in 1639, among them the Ursuline Marie de l'Incarnation.[74]

But terrible reverses soon occurred. The wars between the Iroquois and the Hurons exacted bloody sacrifices from the Jesuits. Jean de Brébeuf, Gabriel Lalemant, Isaac Jogues, and five others suffered martyrdom between 1642 and 1649; they were beatified in 1925 and canonized in 1930.[75] The Huron mission was wiped out and the surviving missionaries returned to Quebec.

The Near East. France was chiefly interested in gaining influence in the Near East, and to this end Louis XIII (1610–43) and his minister, Cardinal Richelieu (1585–1642), made special use of the Capuchins. Their most eager assistant was Father Joseph of Paris,[76] born François

---

[71] O. Jouve, *Les Franciscains et le Canada* I: *L'établissement de la foi, 1615–1629* (Paris 1915).

[72] J. Bouchard, *Le R. P. Paul Le Jeune S. J. et la fondation des missions des Jésuites en Nouvelle France, 1632–1642* (Rome 1958).

[73] R. Latpurelle, *Etude sur les écrits de S. Jean de Brébeuf*, 2 vols. (Montreal 1952f.); F. X. Talbot, *Saint Among the Hurons* (New York 1949).

[74] *Ecrits spirituels et correspondance de Marie de l'Incarnation*, ed. by A. Jamet, 3 vols. (Paris 1928–35); 4 vols. (Quebec 1929–39); H. Bremond, *Histoire littéraire du sentiment religieux en France* IV (Paris 1926), 1–76; P. Renaudin, *Une mystique française au XVIIe siècle: Marie de l'Incarnation, ursuline de Tours et de Quebec* (Paris 1935); G. Goyau, "La première francaise missionnaire: La vocation canadienne de Mère Marie de l'Incarnation," *Et* (1936), 145–168; id., *L'Eglise en marche* V (Paris 1936), 95–125; *Le témoignage de Marie de l'Incarnation, O. S. U.* (Paris 1943); Marie-Emmanuel, *Marie de l'Incarnation, d'après ses lettres* (Ottawa 1946); *Les Ursulines de Quebec*, 4 vols. (Quebec 1863–66).

[75] G. Goyau—G. Rigault, *Martyrs de la Nouvelle France, XVIIe et XVIIIe siècles. Extraits des relations et lettres des missionnaires Jésuites* (Paris 1928); H. Fouqueray, *Martyrs du Canada* (Paris 1930); J. A. O'Brien, *The American Martyrs* (New York 1953).

[76] G. Fagniez, *Le P. Joseph et Richelieu*, 2 vols. (Paris 1894); L. Dedouvres, *Politique et apôtre, Le P. Joseph de Paris*, 2 vols. (Paris 1932); G. Goyau, *L'Eglise en marche* V (Paris 1936), 63–94; G. de Vaumas, "L'activité missionnaire du Père Joseph de Paris," *RHM* 15 (1938), 336–359; G. de Vaumas, *Lettres et documents du P. Joseph de Paris concernant les missions étrangères, 1619–1638* (Lyon 1942).

Le Clerc du Tremblay, Baron de Maffliers (1577–1638), in whom was a strange blend of crusading ardor and diplomatic finesse. Within a short time he managed to have 100 of his confreres sent to the Near East under a French protectorate.

Hence France's entry into the mission field took place despite the Portuguese and Spanish rights of patronage. And from the beginning it was clear how deeply national interests were involved. Thus was the ground prepared for the French protectorate of the missions that was destined to play a fateful role in their future history.

CHAPTER 47

The Sacred Congregation for the Propagation of the Faith

Into the seventeenth century the history of the missions was determined almost exclusively by the partition of the world into Portuguese and Spanish spheres of influence and the related rights of patronage. But it became increasingly more apparent that the two powers were far more concerned for their rights than for their duties. The view was even expounded that the Pope in granting the right of patronage had renounced his own rights over the missions. His instructions and decisions were subjected to a royal *placet,* without which they were not valid. In mission affairs the Kings were no longer regarded as merely the Pope's vicars but as the direct representatives of God.[1]

This development and the resulting abuses in mission lands called for the taking of decisive action by Rome, especially since the reform Popes had just taken the first steps to recover leadership in missionary work. Thus in 1568 Pius V established a Congregation of Cardinals for the Conversion of Infidels, and its activity is discernible in many mission briefs of the Pope. But presumably this was intended only as a temporary institution, for the systematic revamping of the Curia by Sixtus V involved no special department for the missions. It was not until Clement VIII that a specific Congregation of the Missions was constituted, which met several times at the turn of the century and had Cardinal Sanseverino as its *spiritus rector.*[2]

[1] Cf. J. Solorzano Pereira, *De Indiarum iure* (Madrid 1629); also A. de Egana, "La funcion misionera del poder civil segun Juan de Solorzano Pereira (1575–1655)," *StMis* 6 (1950–51), 69–113.

[2] P. Tacchi Venturi, *Diario concistoriale di Antonio Santori, Cardinale di Santa Severina* (Rome 1904); J. Schmidlin, "Eine Vorläuferin der Propaganda unter Klemens VIII.," *ZMR* 11 (1921), 232–234.

The view that a congregation of this sort must form part of the permanent set up of the Curia made steady progress and found literary expression in the *De procuranda salute omnium genitum* of the theorist of the missions, the Carmelite Thomas of Jesus (1564–1627).[3] In Book III the institution of a Roman Congregation for the Propagation of the Faith was urged. Gregory XV took up the suggestion and before the end of the first year of his pontificate established the *Sacra Congregatio de Propaganda Fide* on Epiphany 1622. Thirteen cardinals,[4] two prelates, and a secretary were assigned to it. It held its first meeting on 14 January, and on 22 June the Pope signed the bull of institution, "Inscrutabili divinae providentiae arcano,"[5] which claimed for the Pope in the fullest degree the duty and right to spread the faith as the chief task of the papal role of shepherd of souls. In this way the new congregation was to prepare for the change "from the colonial mission to the purely Church mission" (Kilger). Hence the entire mission system was to be subordinated to the Roman central authority; all missionaries were to depend on it in the most direct manner possible and be sent out by it, missionary methods were to be regulated, and mission fields to be assigned by it.

To carry out this task it was important first of all to clarify the status of the missions. For this purpose the earth was divided into twelve provinces, which were allotted to the respective nuncios in Europe and to the patriarchal vicars in the Near East. The nuncios were to compile information from their districts and then to report to Propaganda. In actual fact, the first reports came in from the missionary Orders.[6] Relying on them, the first secretary of the congregation, Francesco Ingoli (1622–49), composed three important memoranda in which he exposed the shortcomings and hindrances in missionary work and indicated remedies that would eliminate them.[7] Almost everywhere missionary activity was the victim both of jurisdictional quarrels between the local bishops and the religious and of the opposition between the older Orders and the Jesuits. Similarly, nationalist rivalries among missionaries and a mania to feather their own nest during residence overseas con-

---

[3] Antwerp 1613; Rome 1940.

[4] Among them was Cardinal Eitel Friedrich von Zollern, Bishop of Osnabrück (1623–25).

[5] *Coll* I, n. 3.

[6] Propaganda archives: *Scritture antiche* 189, fol. 13f., 20–23 (Jesuits); 33–38 (Dominicans); 206–211 (Observant Franciscans); 220f. (Augustinian Hermits). In addition, a letter of the Bishop of Malacca (ibid., fol. 228), the report of the *collettore* in Portugal, Anthony Albergati (1623: Congr. Part. I, fol. 315–318), and the report of the Franciscan Gregory Bolivar on Spanish American (*Scritt. ant.* 189, fol. 62–74).

[7] 1625: *Scritt. ant.* 189, fol. 279–281; 1628: ibid., 189, fol. 153–155; 1644: ibid., 192, fol. 1–5.

tributed to making their work ineffectual. Hence Ingoli felt that a clear distinction of missionary areas according to membership in the Orders and nationality was the first achievement to be sought. In addition, the sees were to be increased in number and assigned as far as possible to members of the diocesan clergy. An on the spot supervision of missionary work should be realized by the dispatching of papal legates or nuncios. In order to stop the mercantile activities of the missionaries, all departing missionaries had to be checked in regard to their pure intentions, and to guarantee this Ingoli wanted branches of Propaganda to be set up in Seville and Lisbon. He regarded as particularly urgent the formation of a native clergy, which should share in the work and in the direction of the missions on an equality with the foreign missionaries. Through the realization of these proposals Ingoli hoped to free the missions from the colonial powers and from direction by European religious superiors and, as a result, to have them become autonomous.

A cursory glance at the *Collectanea S. Congregationis de Propaganda Fide* is sufficient to show that these guidelines had existence not only on paper. The first care was for the training of missionaries, and as early as 15 April 1622 a special committee for the Roman seminaries and national colleges was set up. The various generals of Orders were admonished to establish schools for teaching languages to future missionaries (no. 7), and Propaganda itself erected seven schools of apologetics for the education of missionaries destined for work among heretics.[8] In 1627 Urban VIII, in the Constitution "Immortalis,"[9] set up a special College of Propaganda, which was soon accepting candidates from the missions. On missionary bishops was imposed the obligation of admitting qualified youths to the priesthood.[10] As arguments Propaganda adduced the practice of the Apostles and of the early Church, the greater confidence which a native priest would enjoy among his fellow countrymen, and his familiarity with their language, customs, and inclinations. Before long Propaganda was in a position to carry out its principles. A young Christian Brahman, Matteo de Castro Mahalo, had come to Rome in 1625 because in India he had not been permitted to enter the priesthood. He took degrees in philosophy and theology, became a priest, and in 1631 returned home as protonotary apostolic and Propaganda missionary to realize the aims of Propaganda in the

[8] *Jus Pont.* II/1, no. 2.
[9] Of 1 August 1627 in *Jus Pont.* I, no. 87. Cf. N. Kowalsky, *Pontificio Collegio Urbano de Propaganda Fide* (Rome 1956).
[10] Thus, according to *Coll* I, no. 1002, p. 543, as early as 1626 for Japan and, according to *Coll* I, no. 62, in 1630 for India.

Mughal Empire and educate a native clergy. In spite of the hostility of the Portuguese and of the missionaries of the patronage, he contrived to gather a few priests from among the Brahmins into a sort of Oratory.[11]

Many things which are today taken for granted in missionary efforts were first proposed at that time, even though they could not be immediately realized. Such are: the duty of submitting an annual report (no. 22); the prohibition of giving up the mission without authorization (no. 41); the determining of the conditions in which missionaries may act as physicians (no. 42); the distinction between religious superiors and mission superiors (no. 46); the granting of special faculties to missionaries (nos. 88f.); and regulations on Church music (no. 107). All this vindicates von Ranke's judgment that Propaganda "sought to fulfill its function on a grand scale . . . , perhaps most successfully at its beginning."[12]

Not unexpectedly, this activity of the Propaganda Congregation encountered lively opposition from the powers enjoying patronage. Portugal especially, which had suffered painful losses of power in its East Indian possessions because of the union with Spain, defended its patronage in order thereby to retain influence overseas at least in the spiritual domain. But in the final analysis, the Congregation of Propaganda was concerned less with power than with an entirely new concept of the missions. The patronage powers had after all proved that it was their aim to assimilate the newly gained Christians to themselves in every respect, that in fact they were transplanting European Christianity overseas. But the Propaganda represented more than ever before the contrary idea. By means of a clergy recruited from the mission countries an indigenous Christianity was to be developed and a Church in complete harmony with it was to be founded. The renunciation of Europeanism was clearly expressed some decades after the erection of the new Congregation.[13]

The Spanish patronage power also resisted the claims made by Propaganda in regard to the papacy's exclusive right over the missions. Although Juan de Solorzano Pereira's *De Indiarum iure* had been put on the Index in 1642, in the Spanish colonial territories it continued to be an authoritative statement of prescriptive law for the local administra-

---

[11] T. Ghesquière, *Mathieu de Castro, premier Vicaire Apostolique aux Indes* (Lophem-Bruges 1937); also, J. Schmidlin in *ZMR* 27 (1937), 243–250; F. Combaluzier in *RHE* 39 (1943), 132–151.

[12] *Die römischen Päpste in den letzten vier Jahrhunderten* II (Leipzig 1874; Munich 1938), 299.

[13] Cf. the instruction for the vicars apostolic in 1659 in *Coll* I, no. 135.

tions; the condemnation was not published overseas.[14] The Catholic powers stubbornly refused to accept Propaganda's claim to the exclusive right to issue orders in regard to the missions.

The Congregation had openly made this claim to the superiors of Orders.[15] These, however, knew how to escape direct control by Propaganda by again procuring privileges which enabled them, as before, to decide on the sending or recalling of their members. It was clear that the new Congregation could not assert itself vis-à-vis the competence of the other congregations and the administrative routine. The Orders had recourse, according to circumstances, to the department from which they expected a favorable decision in strife produced by rivalry or even in strictly missionary questions. Even the Pope failed to place himself squarely on the side of the supreme mission authority and, after all missions had been subjected to Propaganda in principle, allowed himself to be persuaded to renew the privileges of the Orders.

Hence it should cause no surprise that Propaganda sought to deal in another way with the difficulties arising from the patronage powers and the Orders by establishing missions outside the patronage lands and entrusting them to religious communities which had hitherto done little or hardly any missionary work, such as the Carmelites and the Capuchins. Since France had long sought, for reasons easy to understand, to open up overseas colonial areas of its own and to maintain missions in them, Propaganda obtained the opportunity it wanted. To be sure, the national opposition of the new European great powers to the older Iberian world powers contained new explosives. When Portugal withdrew from the personal union with Spain in the Braganza Revolt of 1640 and the Pope, under pressure from His Catholic Majesty, had to deny recognition to the new King, there arose in the Portuguese colonial empire a situation urgently calling for a solution. For soon almost all the dioceses in the Portuguese patronage area were vacant. In 1649 Brazil and Africa were without bishops, as were the East Indian sees of Cochin, Mailapur, Macao, and Funai. The course adopted by Rome in an effort to liquidate this state of affairs introduced a new period in the history of Catholic missions.

[14] Cf. P. de Leturia, "Antonio Lelio de Fermo y la condanacion del 'De Indiarum iure' de Solorzano Pereira," *HS* 1 (1948), 351–385; 2 (1949), 47–87; *id.*, "El regio vicariato de Indias y los comienzos de la Congregacion de Propaganda," *Spanische Forschungen der Görres-Gesellschaft* 1. Reihe: *Gesammelte Aufsätze zur Kulturgeschichte Spaniens* II (Münster 1930), 133–177.

[15] 5 December 1640 (*Coll* I, no. 101).

European Counter Reformation and Confessional Absolutism (1605–55)

CHAPTER 48

Paul V, Gregory XV and the Beginnings of the Central European Counter Reformation

Sustained by the religious and intellectual forces of the Tridentine Reform, the papacy under Paul V and Gregory XV attained a position which can be compared only with that of the High Middle Ages. Its neutrality between the rival Catholic great powers, Spain and France, did not as yet work against Catholic interests, because France's relations with the rising Protestant powers of the North, the rebel Netherlands, England, and Sweden, had not yet been solidified into alliances for war. Hence the active Catholic faction in the Empire, the League, and Emperor Ferdinand II succeeded in defeating the disunited Protestants and in pushing the restoration of lost lands to the Catholic Church. But since Urban VIII was unwilling and perhaps not in a position to thwart Cardinal Richelieu's policy of alliance with Protestants, the defeat of the Catholics in the Empire sealed the end of the Counter Reformation and of the papacy's position of political leadership. From the Peace of Westphalia in 1648 its influence subsided irresistibly and the spirit of the Catholic Reform weakened. Religious and intellectual leadership within the Church passed from Italy and Spain to France, but also the secularization of European thought announced itself.

Sixty cardinals took part in the conclave of 14 March to 11 April 1605, following the death of Clement VIII. Cardinal Aldobrandini, leader of the strongest faction, was allied with the French; Cardinal Montalto, with the Spaniards. Cardinals Medici and Baronius, favored by France, met the resolute opposition of the Spaniards—Baronius because of his criticism of the *Monarchia Sircula*. Just the same, Baronius lacked only eight votes on 30 March. Since, however, not he but Zacchia was Aldobrandini's real candidate, the French Cardinal Joyeuse succeeded in carrying the election of Medici. As ambassador of Cosimo I in Rome, Leo XI had become the favorite disciple of Saint Philip Neri and was highly esteemed for his piety and integrity. But on 27 April

1605 he died as a result of a chill which he had caught when taking possession of the Lateran.

In the next conclave (8–16 May 1605) the fronts changed to the disadvantage of Aldobrandini. The election of Bellarmine foundered on Spain's veto. After vehement confrontations Aldobrandini and Montalto agreed on the fifty-two-year-old Camillus Borghese, hardly noticed until now. Paul V came from a family of lawyers that had moved to Rome from Siena and had himself risen from auditor of the *Camera* to the cardinalate in 1596. At first lacking in political experience, he conscientiously familiarized himself with matters of state, and little influence was exercised by the Cardinal Nephew, Scipione Borghese. His political advisers were first Cardinal Arigoni, later Millini, formerly nuncio in Spain, and Maffeo Barberini, formerly nuncio in France. He continued until 1613 the division of the Secretariate of State into two departments, introduced by Clement VIII, with one chief secretary for each (*Secretarius domesticus in capite, Secretario intimo*), although in 1609–11 Margotti, promoted to the purple, had conducted the business by himself. After 1613 Feliciani was the sole chief secretary.

Paul V's policy was based on the principle of neutrality vis-à-vis the tension between Spain and France. Ubaldini, nuncio to Henry IV, and Coton, the King's Jesuit confessor, urged a Habsburg-Bourbon marriage alliance, but the project was frustrated by Henry's refusal to give up his support of the rebel Netherlands and his urging of the claims of Brandenburg and Palatinate-Neuburg to the Jülich-Cleves inheritance. In an effort to prevent the threatened war from breaking out, Cardinals Millini and Barberini were dispatched as peace envoys to Spain and France, but before they were able to carry out their commission Henry IV was assassinated on 14 May 1610 by a fanatic, Ravaillac, who had not been instigated by the Jesuits, as was once claimed. The impending European war was averted, but the pernicious rivalry of the two great powers continued even though the dynastic alliance desired by the Curia was effected by the marriage in 1616 of the Bourbon Louis XIII to Anne of Austria, daughter of the Habsburg Philip III.

Conflict with Venice

The conflict of Paul V with the Republic of Venice very nearly led to a European war, which would necessarily have acquired the character of a religious war. Even before the Pope's accession the Venetian *Signoria* had forbidden the erecting of churches, monasteries, and hospitals and the acquiring of real estate by the Church without the permission of the state and, without regard to the *privilegium fori,* had brought two unworthy clerics to trial and had imprisoned them. In briefs of 10 December 1605 and 26 March 1606, Paul V condemned these procedures and, on the republic's declining to cancel its measures, sent an ultimatum threatening excommunication and interdict on 17 April 1606. On the advice of its official theologian, the shrewd and fluent Servite Paul Sarpi (1552–1623), the *Signoria,* protesting its divine right, forbade the publication of the papal censures under pain of death. After the expiration of the four weeks' respite allowed, the censures became effective but were ignored by the republic as invalid. A majority of the clergy obeyed the state and disregarded the interdict. All diocesan and regular priests who observed it, headed by the Jesuits, were banished. In his *Treatise on the Interdict*[1] and numerous other polemics Sarpi denied its validity on the ground that the Pope was abusing his authority and whoever obeyed him was guilty of sin. The conflict over Church policy was escalated to a conflict of principle over the relations of the spiritual to the secular power. As early as 1607 the Jesuit Gretser counted twenty-eight polemical writings favoring Venice and thirty-eight upholding the Pope, among these last being works by Bellarmine, Baronius, and Suarez. The apostasy of Venice from the Church and even a European war were distinct possibilities, especially when England, through its ambassador, Wotton, held out to the *Signoria* the prospect of support by the Protestant powers.

It was only after Cardinal Joyeuse, acting on instructions from Henry IV, had ascertained in the spring of 1607 how far the *Signoria* was prepared to yield that the Pope also gave in. The two imprisoned ecclesiastics were surrendered to Joyeuse. The *Signoria* promised not to repeal the laws in dispute, but not to enforce them, and the Kings of France and Spain vouched for this. Also, except for the Jesuits, priests who had been expelled for observing the interdict were allowed to return to Venice. On 21 April 1607 Joyeuse absolved the *Signoria* from the ecclesiastical censures it had incurred; thus the *Signoria* tacitly acknowledged their existence. The Pope's defeat was only thinly veiled: he lifted the interdict without requiring the *Signoria* to make adequate satisfaction or to abandon the principle at stake. The demanded surrender of Sarpi and of his partisans, Micanzio and Marsiglio, was refused and for almost fifty years the Jesuits were excluded from Venetian territory. Responsibility for a murderous attempt on Sarpi was blamed on the Curia because the culprits had taken refuge in the Papal State. Sarpi's *History of the Council of Trent,* printed in London in 1619, was inspired by hatred of the papacy and greatly damaged its prestige. However, his effort to propagate Calvinism in Venice misfired, as did his

---

[1] *Istoria dell'Interdetto e altri scritti editi e inediti,* ed. M. D. Busnelli–G. Gambarin, II, 1–41.

plans to overthrow the papacy with the aid of a coalition of Protestant powers.[2]

Loyal to his principle of neutrality, Paul V refused financial support to the Catholic Grisons (the easternmost canton of Switzerland) against the Protestants because he was unwilling to lay himself open to the reproach of furthering the involved strategic interests of Spain in a territorial connection between Milan and Tirol. To preserve peace, Paul's successor even agreed to have papal troops occupy the strongholds of the Valtellina.

Paul V's death was followed by a brief conclave on 8 and 9 February 1621. The choice fell on Allessandro Ludovisi, beloved for his kindness, esteemed for his knowledge of law, but in poor health. In memory of Gregory XIII, his fellow Bolognese, he styled himself Gregory XV. His right arm was the Cardinal Nephew, Ludovico Ludovisi, very much like him in character and a gifted statesman, whose many-faceted intellectual interests are demonstrated by the construction of Sant'Ignazio, the layout of the Villa Ludovisi on the Pincio, and his collections of antiques. "Let the fear and love of God be your political wisdom," was the Pope's admonition to his nephew.[3] According to Pastor, "Probably never has a short pontificate left such deep traces in history."

In the bull on the papal election, 15 November 1621,[4] the so-called election by adoration—or unanimous quasi-inspiration—which had taken place in several recent elections, was not excluded, but the secret written vote was prescribed as the rule. Subsequent "accession" was for the future to be allowed only in writing and only once after each of the two daily scrutinies. The greatness of the Ludovisi pontificate was revealed most clearly in the establishment of the Congregation for the Propagation of the Faith on 22 June 1622 as already noted. Financially well endowed and furnished with exceptional authority, it was conceived as the organ for the coordination of the missions in America, Asia, and Africa and as the counterpoise of the patronage exercised by the Spanish and Portuguese crowns. But since relations with the Eastern Churches and the spread of the Catholic faith in the parts of North Europe that had become entirely or mostly Protestant were assigned to

---

[2] Sarpi's innermost conviction remains a puzzle. I still adhere to the view of Gallican influence on his history of the Council, even though, according to Ulianich, his concept of the Church was far more radical than the Gallican.

[3] "La vostra dottrina politica, i precetti di ragione di stato e gl'intimi consiglieri siano il timore e l'amore di Dio." H. Laemmer, *Zur Kirchengeschichte des XVI. und XVII. Jh.* (Freiburg 1863), p. 23.

[4] *Bull Rom,* XII, 619–627; further details are provided by a second bull of 12 March 1622 (ibid., p. 662ff.).

it, it developed into the headquarters of the Counter Reformation.[5] Its presupposition was the continuance of the Catholic Reform, in which were concentrated the forces for the self-assertion of the Church in the struggle against Protestantism, and no less the political and military successes of the Catholic powers at the beginning of the Thirty Years' War.

Successes and Failures

The implementation of the reform decrees of the Council of Trent was the chief concern of both Paul V and Gregory XV. The duty of residence was again enjoined on the bishops, and titular rather than residential bishops began to be appointed nuncios. The exertions of the Nuncios Barberini and Ubaldini to achieve the acceptance of Trent by France finally collapsed at the Estates General of 1614–15 because of the resistance of the Third Estate and of the *Parlement* of Paris, but on 7 July 1615 the clergy voted the publication of the reform decrees in provincial councils. In the Spanish Netherlands the decrees of the Provincial Council of Mechlin (1607) and of the diocesan synods following were declared binding by the government. In 1621 the Cologne Nuncio Albergati wrote that "the salvation of Germany depends" on the publication and observance of Trent.[6] In the conviction that the Catholic renewal was based not merely on the enforcement of laws but equally on the strength of ideals, the great sixteenth-century champions of renewal were raised to the honors of the altar. Charles Borromeo was canonized in 1610. Paul V had beatified Ignatius Loyola in 1609, Teresa of Avila in 1614, Philip Neri in 1615, and Francis Xavier in 1619; on 12 March 1622 the four of them were canonized in a single ceremony which in brilliance surpassed all previous celebrations.

But setbacks were not lacking. When on 5 November 1605 it was discovered that a group of English Catholics planned to blow up Parliament in order to kill King James I, suspicion of complicity fell on the Jesuit Garnet, who had acquired knowledge of the "Gunpowder Plot" under the seal of confession but had sought to stop the crime. Garnet's trial, legally open to attack, was exploited to charge the Pope and the Jesuits with high treason and immoral principles; Garnet was executed.[6a]

---

[5] The nuncios acted as connecting links: Brussels kept an eye on England, Holland, Denmark, and Norway; Cologne, on North Germany; the nuncio in Poland, on Sweden and Russia (Pastor, XXVII, 135f.).

[6] "Ex illo sc. Concilio Tridentino pendet salus Germaniae" (Pastor, XXVII, 318).

[6a] In addition to Pastor, XII, 405–428, see H. R. Williamson, *The Gunpowder Plot* (London, 1951).

New laws aggravated the situation of the English Catholics. An oath was required of them to the effect that James I was the lawful King of England and that the Pope had no power to depose him. The Archpriest Blackwell and many of the laity took the oath, though it had been condemned by Paul V, but sixteen priests and two lay persons who refused it were executed. The attitude to the oath of loyalty split the English Catholics into two factions.

In the Habsburg hereditary states the dissension between the incompetent Emperor Rudolf II and his brothers resulted in far-reaching concessions to the Protestants, which raised apprehension of serious losses to the Church. The Calvinist estates of Hungary obtained religious liberty in the Peace of Vienna (1606), as did the adherents of the Bohemian Confession in the "Letter of Majesty" of 9 July 1609. King Matthias extended the rights of the Hungarian Calvinists and in 1609 granted religious liberty to the Protestant estates of Upper Austria, a move synonymous with the suppression of Catholicism in their lands.

Despite these reverses the Catholics' self-assurance was so strengthened that they ceased to be satisfied with merely preserving what they held and considered the pushing back of Protestantism and the reconquest of lost areas. A plan to seize Geneva, the "Babylon of heresies," and to restore it to the Church again surfaced. The concessions to the Huguenots in the Edict of Nantes seemed to the Curia to be excessive. The Nuncio Barberini was to explain to Henry IV that reasons of state called for a confessionally unified state; at least the Protestants should be excluded from the highest functions of government, as Simonetta, nuncio in Poland, was successfully urging. Thus the Counter Reformation sought the aid of Poland, where the political disunion of the Catholics had been surmounted through the establishing of the League, while in Emperor Ferdinand II the House of Habsburg acquired a leader for whom the defense and propagation of the Catholic religion was a matter of conscience.[7]

Start of the Thirty Years' War

The execution by Duke Maximilian I of Bavaria of the ban against the Free City of Donauwörth, which had violated the Religious Peace, and the unlawful imposition of Catholicism on the city led to the bolting of the Diet of Regensburg by the Protestant estates and to the forming of a league, the Union (16 May 1608), led by the Calvinist Elector Palatine.

[7] Ferdinand had declared that "he would sooner lose his kingdoms and lands than knowingly let pass an opportunity to promote the true faith." *ARG* 49 (1958), 259.

The reply to this was the concluding a year later of a Catholic defensive alliance, the League, at the prompting of Maximilian I. At first it comprised, besides Bavaria, only the most seriously menaced spiritual princes—Würzburg, Constance, Augsburg, and Regensburg—and after 30 August 1609, the three spiritual electors, but not the Habsburgs, who were quarreling among themselves. The Pope hesitated to enter into a formal treaty with the League and made his financial support contingent upon proof that there existed a general Protestant union directed against the Catholics; legalist that he was, he did not wish to be suspected of violating the Religious Peace.[8] It was not until 1610 that he promised subsidies, while at the same time he urged the inclusion of the Emperor in the League. For its part, the Union acquired powerful support through alliances with England (1612) and Holland (1613).

While Emperor Matthias, under the influence of his advisor Klesl, Bishop of Vienna and in 1616 a Cardinal, was inclined to yield to Protestant demands in the Empire, such as permitting the Protestant administrator of Magdeburg to sit in the Diet, his successor, Ferdinand II, elected King of Bohemia in 1617 and King of Hungary in 1618, was opposed to any compromise. The revolt of the Protestant nobles in Bohemia and the election as anti-King of the Count Palatine Friedrich V set off the long-threatening religious war. Both Ferdinand II and the reinvigorated League obtained considerable subsidies from the Pope from 1620 onward. The "Winter King," left in the lurch by his allies, was defeated in the Battle of the White Mountain on 8 November 1620. To enable Ferdinand II and the League to make the most of their victory, Gregory XV in just two and one-half years contributed subsidies in the amount of about 1,239,000 florins in sound money and of about 700,000 florins in bad money, depreciated through inflation.[9] The transfer of the dignity of Elector Palatine to Bavaria was energetically pushed by the Pope, by, among other measures, the dispatch of the Capuchin Hyacinth of Casale. These military and political successes formed the basis for the Counter Reformation now getting under way, first of all only in the Habsburg states.

At the instigation of the energetic and circumspect nuncio, Carlo

---

[8] "Dixit nuntius quod S. Stas cupiat religionem Augustanae Confessionis et talia compactata illaesa." *Briefe und Akten zur Geschichte des 30jährigen Krieges* IX (Leipzig 1903), 312.

[9] Cf. Albrecht, "Zur Finanzierung des Dreissigjährigen Krieges. Die Subsidien der Kurie für Kaiser und Liga 1618-35," *ZBLG* 19 (1956), 534–567. Paul V had contributed around 650,000 florins in the last two and one-half years of his pontificate and in addition imposed a tithe on the German clergy.

Carafa,[10] Protestant ministers and teachers were expelled from Bohemia. At the start only those who had taken part in the revolt were affected, but later all were included on the basis of the King's right of reformation. Mixed commissions under military protection restored the churches and introduced Catholic pastors. Resistance, especially from the urban middle class and from the peasants, who were unwilling to forego the lay chalice, was quashed by military force. In order to avoid oppressive billeting, expected to force conversions, many Protestants emigrated. Recourse to these measures of force was not mitigated until 1626 and then without abandoning the fundamental requirement of return to the Catholic Church.

The soul of the rebuilding of Catholicism was Cardinal Harrach, Archbishop of Prague (1624–67), advised by the Capuchin Valerian Magni. At his urging, the role of the state's means of pressure gradually yielded to pastoral action. The chief source of difficulty was the lack of diocesan priests, and thus the lion's share of the immensely heavy burden fell to the Orders, most of all to the Jesuits and the Capuchins, but also to the older institutes. The University of Prague was entrusted to the Jesuits. Corresponding to Harrach in Prague was Cardinal Dietrichstein in his bishopric of Olmütz. In Silesia, where the "Letter of Majesty" continued in force, the Counter Reformation was carried out only in the principalities directly under the King and in the territory of the see of Breslau, which was held by Habsburg archdukes from 1608 to 1665. In Upper Austria on 12 October 1624 the Protestants were given until Easter of 1626 to return to the Church. In Lower Austria, where Ferdinand II had assured religious liberty to the nobles adhering to the Augsburg Confession, the authorities were content with expelling the Calvinist preachers. In Styria, Carinthia, and Carniola the Protestant nobles too were banished (1628). The restoration of Catholicism in Hungary was almost entirely the work of Cardinal Pázmány, Archbishop of Esztergom (1616–37).[11]

As early as 1621, opinions concerning the anti-Reformation measures

---

[10] Carafa's final report of 1628, edited by J. G. Müller in *Archiv für Kunde österreichischer Geschichtsquellen* 23 (1860), 103–450, is based on several preliminary studies; cf. J. Pieper, *HJ* 2 (1881), 388–415; Pastor, XXVII, 229f.; H. Jedin, *RQ* 39 (1931), 411ff. His *Commentaria de Germania sacra instaurata* (Antwerp 1630; Cologne 1639; etc.) is the most important contemporary exposition of the Counter Reformation in the Habsburg hereditary states and in the Empire.

[11] His *Opera Omnia,* Series lat., 6 vols. (Budapest 1894–1904); Series Mugarica, 7 vols. (Budapest 1910–11); latest bibliography: L. Polgar, *Bibliographica Soc. Jesu* (Rome 1957)n. 1150–1416. Pázmány is viewed highly as a Hungarian stylist.

to be adopted[12] recognized both the urgency and the questionable character of the Church's use of secular means of compulsion. Success, it was felt, depended on the intensification of the care of souls. The political postulate of denominational unity continued to be admitted. The extending of the Counter Reformation to the Empire belongs in the pontificate of Urban VIII.

[12] Larmormaini's opinion, composed after 1 October 1621, in J. Kollmann, *Acta S. Congregationis de Propaganda Fide res gestas Bohemicas illustrantia* I, 17–36; H. Jedin, "Eine Denkschrift über die Gegenreformation in Schlesien aus dem Jahre 1625," *ArSKG* 3 (1938), 152–171 (composed by Christoph Weller, S.J.). The memorandum *De missionibus Germanicis* (composed around 1600) also points in this direction; it will be found in Döllinger-Reusch, *Geschichte der Moralstreitigkeiten* II (Nördlingen 1889), 390–393.

CHAPTER 49

Urban VIII, Innocent X and the End of the Counter Reformation

In the conclave of 19 July to 6 August 1623, the small Ludovisi faction was so reinforced by the adherents of Aldobrandini, the German Cardinals Zollern and Klesl, and the Princes Farnese and Medici that it was almost equal to the followers of Borghese and was able to prevent the election of Millini, which Borghese was urging. The illness of a number of the cardinals hastened an agreement by the two party leaders on the person of the Florentine Maffeo Barberini, who, to the delight of the Romans, called himself Urban VIII. Only fifty-five years of age, he had acquired valuable political experience that qualified him to participate personally in the conduct of affairs.[1] He did so, at least in the first third of his pontificate, proving his skill in dealing with diplomats and his keen self-assurance. He had a dislike of Spain and a partiality for France that went back to the period of his nunciature in the latter kingdom (1604–07). More given to nepotism than any other Pope of the century, he bestowed the purple on his brother Antonio and his nephews Francesco and Antonio the Younger and enriched his family so prodigally that on his death bed he felt remorse of conscience. His extravagance toward the Barberini family presented a painful contrast to his

[1] "All business," said the Venetian Ambassador P. Contarini in 1627, "passes through the hands of His Holiness, and without his knowledge and instructions no political or other important decision is rendered" (N. Barozzi–G. Berchet, *Le relazioni della Corte di Roma lette al Senato degli ambasciatori veneti nel sec. XVII* I, 212).

niggardly contributions for the support of the Catholic side in the Thirty Years' War. At the urging of his nephews he had the papal fief of Castro occupied on the ground that its holder, Duke Odoardo Farnese of Parma, was not satisfying his creditors in Rome. But since the duke found support in France and formed a league with Venice, Tuscany, and Modena against the Pope, the "Castro War" ended with the Pope's defeat. The Papal State, enlarged by the territory of Urbino following the renunciation of claims by the last duke, della Rovere, suffered severely from the devastation of large areas and disordered finances.

A connoisseur of both ancient and modern literature, owner of a large library, and himself an accomplished stylist, the Pope personally took part in the reform of the breviary of 1631, rewriting a number of the hymns. The reform commission, headed by Cardinal Gaetani and including the Franciscan Luke Wadding, the Jesuit Terenzio Alciati, the Dominican Niccolò Riccardi, and the Barnabite Bartolomeo Gavanti, contented itself with trifling changes in the lives of saints and the homilies. The corrections in the missal (1634) and pontifical (1644) were of no importance. Liturgical centralization found its culmination in the constitution of 5 July 1643, in which beatification and canonization were reserved to the Pope and every liturgical cult of a saint was forbidden which had not been in effect for at least a century with proper ecclesiastical approval. In 1630 Urban VIII granted cardinals the title of "Eminence." In an effort to deal with the pressure from the Catholic powers to consider their candidates, he preferred Italians even more than his predeccessors had in the creation of new cardinals. In nine promotions he bestowed the purple on seventy-eight men.

Church Policy during the Thirty Years' War

Von Ranke's view, that Urban VIII, from antipathy to Spain and preference for France, favored Cardinal Richelieu's anti-Habsburg policy and thus indirectly saved German Protestantism, simplifies the situation too much. Following the principle, correct in itself, that the papacy must stand above the rivalry of the great powers and intervene for the preservation of peace, he was unable and perhaps not really willing to thwart Richelieu's superior and crafty diplomacy, which, without regard for the interests of the Church, aimed at the destruction of the power of the Habsburg lands and at French hegemony in Europe. He failed to grasp that the defeat of the Emperor and of the League involved the ruin of the Counter Reformation which his predecesors had promoted. The question whether in this he let himself be influenced by the view that recourse to political and military means for religious ends was obsolete and restriction to the religious strength of the Church was necessary cannot be solved in the present state of research. The Pope's policy of neutrality must be evaluated from this standpoint.

He took no effective measures to prevent the expulsion of the papal troops from the fortresses of the Valtellina by Swiss in French pay. After the unsuccessful peace delegation of the Cardinal Nephew Francesco Barberini (1625), the affair was finally settled by the Treaty of Monzon in 1626. On the other hand, he refused to enter the anti-Spanish League promoted by France in the War of the Mantuan Succession (1628), although he regarded the claims of the Duke of Nevers as strongest and was opposed to a further extension of Spanish preponderance in Italy. He participated as mediator in the concluding of the Peace of Regensburg in 1630. When in 1631 France allied with Gustavus Adolphus of Sweden in the Treaty of Bärwalde, Urban trusted in Sweden's promise to maintain Catholic worship in the conquered territories and expected that the Franco-Bavarian alliance arranged with the cooperation of Bagno, nuncio at Paris, would deter Richelieu from joining the German Protestants. Both hopes were disappointed. When after Gustavus Adolphus' victory at Breitenfeld it was made clear that he had been deceived by Richelieu, the Pope made nothing stronger than paper protests and refused the Habsburg side the adequate financial help which could have brought relief to the seriously threatened Catholics.[2] Only when the victories of the Swedish King aroused fears of an invasion of Italy did he propose an Italian defensive league, which, however, found no favor. The tale that on the news of the death of Gustavus Adolphus he celebrated a Requiem Mass was long ago disproved.[3]

It was the interlacing of political and religious interests that made Urban's position so difficult. In Spain there was talk of convoking a general council, while Richelieu threatened schism. But when France's open entry into the war in 1635 compelled Ferdinand II to make concessions to the Protestants in the Peace of Prague, the Emperor was severely blamed, whereas Richelieu received merely an admonition to peace. The peace congress convoked to Cologne was sabotaged by Richelieu, but the Pope drew no conclusion from this attitude. It is hard

---

[2] According to D. Albrecht, "Zur Finanzierung des Dreissigjährigen Krieges," ZBLG 19 (1956), 548–562, virtually only what was left of the amount earlier promised was paid out until 1631 and from then until 1635 about 550,000 thalers. In regard to the scene with Cardinal Borgia on 8 March 1632, described by Pastor (XXVIII, 286ff.), it is to be borne in mind that Cardinal Ludovisi, highly esteemed by Pastor, was on Borgia's side and the far more moderate Cardinal Pázmány had no support from Urban VIII.

[3] S. Ehses, "Papst Urban VIII. und Gustav Adolf," HJ 16 (1895), 336–341; J. S. Schnitzer, "Urbans VIII. Verhalten bei der Nachricht vom Tode des Schwedenkönigs," Festschrift Camposanto (Freiburg 1897), pp. 280–283.

to avoid the impression that Urban VIII's policy of neutrality actually amounted to a patronage of France. Its inescapable sequel was the cessation of the Counter Reformation in the Empire and heavy damage to Catholic interests.

Counter Reformation in the Empire

From the beginning of the seventeenth century the Catholics had held the initiative in the Empire. Following the conversion of Wolfgang Wilhelm of Palatinate-Neuburg in 1613, his territories had become again at least partly Catholic, Bamberg was assured by Aschhausen, and at the same time Bishop Jakob Fugger was effective in Constance. In North Germany also progress was to be noted. The Calvinist council was expelled by Spanish troops from the Free City of Aachen (1614). The Tridentine reform was carried out in the see of Münster by Ferdinand of Bavaria, Elector of Cologne, who was also able to profit by the measures of his predecessor Fürstenberg in the bishopric of Paderborn. But here and throughout the North there was no real change in the situation until the victories of Tilly and Wallenstein. The return of the prince-bishoprics and abbeys that had become Protestant since 1552 was begun. Montorio, nuncio at Cologne, sent missionaries to Bremen, Magdeburg, and Halberstadt. The convert Johann von Leckow and, later, Jesuit missionaries were active in the Margraviate of Brandenburg.

The legal basis for a large-scale operation was to be furnished by the Imperial Edict of Restitution of 6 March 1629. It was prepared by the *Pacis Compositio* of the same year, whose authors, the Jesuits Forer and Laymann, upheld the view that the Religious Peace of Augsburg did not formally annul the Edict of Worms and established merely a temporary emergency law which did not entitle the Protestants to further "reformations" beyond the position of 1552.[4] The Edict of Restitution decreed: 1) the return of the two archbishoprics, twelve bishoprics, and numerous monasteries, direct imperial fiefs, that had been alienated since the Treaty of Passau; 2) the return of mediatized sees and monasteries and their property, alienated in the same period; 3) by means of the abrogation of the *Declaratio Ferdinandea,* the equalizing of the Catholic estates with the Protestant in the "right of reformation." Defensible in law, the edict was a serious political mistake, for it united German Protestantism by threatening its very existence.[5]

---

[4] M. Heckel, "Autonomia und Pacis compositio. Der Augsburger Religionsfriede in der Deutung der Gegenreformation." *ZSavRGkan,* 45 (1959), 141–248.
[5] Text in M. C. Lundorp, *Acta Publica* II (Frankfurt a. M. 1668), 1048.

Imperial delegates were appointed to carry it out. In Lower Saxony the energetic Bishop of Osnabrück, Franz Wilhelm von Wartenberg,[6] obtained the sees of Verden and Minden; Bremen, Magdeburg, and Halberstadt were entrusted to the Archduke Leopold Wilhelm. By the end of 1631 two archbishoprics, five bishoprics, two prince-abbeys, and 150 churches and monasteries were again in Catholic hands. But before the execution of the edict was completed and the interior permeation of the newly won lands had passed beyond the initial stage, the preconditions for distribution of power for the counteroffensive were offset. Wallenstein was toppled, and the victories of Gustavus Adolphus and his advance into South Germany involved the loss of all gains in the North and of most of the South, especially in Württemberg. In the Peace of Prague with Saxony (1635) the Emperor was forced to renounce the Edict of Restitution and concede for forty years to those adherents of the Augsburg Confession who assented to the peace the ecclesiastical lands they had occupied from the Treaty of Passau until 12 November 1627.

The Peace of Westphalia

The Pope's endeavor to mediate between the chief opponents—the two Habsburg powers and France—through the Cardinal Legate Ginetti at the Peace Congress of Cologne came to nothing. Matters did not progress beyond formalities (1636–40). Meanwhile, year after year, the military situation of the Catholic party in the Empire deteriorated. Ferdinand III and his advisors understood that peace was impossible without great concessions in the ecclesiastical sphere. Fabio Chigi, nuncio at Cologne, was sent to the Peace Congress at Münster with instructions to intervene only between Catholic states. Whereas Count Trautmannsdorf, the Emperor's plenipotentiary, and the Elector Maximilian of Bavaria regarded broad concessions to the Protestants as unavoidable, a closed group whose public spokesman was the Jesuit Wangnereck, under the leadership of Cardinal Wartenberg and Bishop Knöringen of Augsburg, came forward against the surrender of ecclesiastical rights and claims as a matter of principle. But their efforts were in vain.

The peace signed on 24 October 1648,[7] contained three provisions

---

[6] G. Schwaiger, *Kardinal Franz Wilhelm von Wartenberg als Bischof von Regensburg* (Munich 1954).

[7] The *Instrumentum Pacis Osnabrugense* and *Monasteriense* are most readily found in K. Zeumer, *Quellensammlung zur Geschichte der deutschen Reichsverfassung in Mittelalter und Neuzeit* (Leipzig 1904), pp. 332–379; the acknowledgment of the protest by Innocent X in *Bull Rom* XV, 603ff.

which solidified the religious cleavage in the Empire, defined the property of the denominations, and brought the Counter Reformation to an end: 1) The Religious Peace of Augsburg was extended to include the Calvinists; 2) Except in the Austrian hereditary states, the standard year for deciding the practice of religion and the ownership of Church property was computed as 1 January 1624; 3) The "right of reformation" of the estates and the Ecclesiastical Reservation, which had hitherto been assailed by the Protestants, were both recognized. Against these stipulations, so injurious to the Church, but not against the peace as such, Chigi on 14 October 1648 lodged a protest long before prepared, and about twenty Catholic imperial estates associated themselves with it. It was confirmed, though to no purpose, by a papal brief of 26 November 1648. In the Peace of Westphalia a new age proclaimed itself; the system of European states freed itself from papal controls. Urban VIII's successor, by whom the protest was made, could do nothing to arrest this development.

In the conclave of 9 August to 14 September 1644, Sacchetti, at first the most promising candidate of the nephews of Urban VIII and of the French, incurred the veto of Spain. Thereupon both factions united to elect Gianbattista Pamfili, though he was not acceptable to the French and the Spanish minister-in-charge Olivarez had earlier opposed the elevation of the former nuncio in Spain to the cardinalate. More to the point than any other characterization of Innocent X is the portrait by Diego Velazquez from 1650: a majestic appearance, intelligent, reserved, even distrustful, hence slow, sometimes vacillating in reaching decisions, intent on right and order. His pontificate, termed by Pastor "neither brilliant nor fortunate," was overshadowed by his tyrannical and venal sister-in-law, Olimpia Maidalchini, to whom he allowed far too much influence in secular matters and in personal politics. However, her son, the Cardinal Nephew Camillo Pamfili did not become secretary of state. This post went to Cardinal Panciroli, who was succeeded in 1651 by the former nuncio at Cologne, Chigi. When the Barberini were to be called to account for squandering Church money, Cardinal Antonio fled to France and placed himself under French protection. Overawed by the French prime minister's threats, the Pope submitted to a pardon for him.

The continuing war between France and Spain forced Innocent X "to tread a silk thread," to quote Pastor. Though inclined toward Spain, he could not disregard France, rising to the position of leading power in Europe, and its prime minister during the minority of Louis XIV, the Italian Jules Mazarin (d. 1661). Portugal had broken away from the Spanish crown in 1640 and elected a native King, John IV of the House of Braganza. Like Urban VIII, Innocent X refused to recognize him and to fill vacant sees with bishops nominated by him. During the Masaniello Revolt of 1647 he declined to uphold Spanish rule in the Kingdom of Naples but, contrary to Mazarin's wishes, did not exploit the confusion to extend the Papal State on the plea of the papal right of suzerainty. In the north the Papal State was rounded off by the confiscation of the Farnese fief on the Lake of Bolsena. The still strained relations with Venice improved when the Pope restored the inscription removed by Urban VIII from the Sala Regis. This was a representation of the Peace of Venice of 1177, which mentioned that Pope Alexander III had recovered his position through the aid of Venice. But when the *Signoria* continued to infringe ecclesiastical immunity, Innocent X gave it only meager support in its war with Turkey over the island of Candia (Crete).

England's Hegemony among Protestant Powers

In England the marriage of Charles I to Henrietta Maria, daughter of Louis XIII of France, did not bring the expected alleviation of persecution to the Catholics. The promises made when the dispensation was obtained were not honored when Parliament raised opposition. To replace the archpriest hitherto functioning there, a vicar of episcopal rank was named in 1623. But strife with the Jesuits induced the second holder of the office to leave England, and thus the approximately one hundred fifty thousand Catholics were without a head. Catholic worship continued to be proscribed, while absence from the Anglican service was punishable by a fine. Under the influence of the King, who inclined personally to the Catholic Church, and of the Queen the persecuting laws were more mildly enforced and even the possibility of reunion was discussed,[8] but Charles' absolute rule and, in the ecclesiastical sphere, the greater emphasis on the episcopalian constitution, which his father had gradually reintroduced in Scotland, and the communion rite, closer to the Catholic tradition, which he himself had prescribed there in 1637, encountered powerful opposition in Parliament and among the Presbyterians and Independents respectively. Although on the outbreak of the Civil War in 1642 he was supported by the Catholic nobility and eventually by the Irish, he was defeated and executed (1649). The fanatically anti-Catholic Lord Protector, Oliver Cromwell, abolished the

---

[8] H. R. T. Brandreth, "Grégoire Panzani et l'idéal de la rèunion sous le règne de Charles I. d'Angleterre," *Irenikon* 21 (1948), 32–47, 179–192; M. Nedoncelle, *Trois aspects du problème anglo-catholique au 17e siècle* (P 1951); the reunion writing of the convert C. Davenport of 1634 is discussed in R. Rouse–S. C. Neill, *Geschichte der ökumenischen Bewegung* I (Göttingen 1957), 191ff.

fine for non-attendance at Anglican worship (1650), but the religious toleration granted by him was of slight benefit to Catholics as "idolators." Anyone who rejected the oath of abjuration, demanded of laity and clergy from 1655—repudiation of the papal primacy, of transubstantiation, and of the veneration of saints and images—lost twothirds of his property and almost all his civil rights, and priests had to leave the country under pain of death.

The English revolution annihilated also the hope of an alleviation of the lot of the harshly suppressed Irish Catholics. Their at first victorious rising against English rule had been supported by Urban VIII through money and the sending of nuncios. The Treaty of Kilkenny (1645), in which the royal agent Glamorgan had guaranteed them religious liberty, was not ratified by Charles I and it was not until shortly before his fall that he granted it to them in return for an assurance of armed assistance in the struggle with Parliament.[8a] The concession came too late. With cruel severity Cromwell subjected the country to his control and by means of an act of settlement expropriated a great part of the property of Catholic landowners. A decree of 6 January 1653 prescribed that all Catholic priests had to leave the country under penalty of high treason. The Catholics were decimated, partly through deportation to the West Indies, partly through emigration and famine.

Cromwell made England the greatest Protestant power in Europe. The Netherlands obtained the definitive recognition of their sovereignty in the peace with Spain. Sweden, though unable long to maintain the position of a great power gained by Gustavus Adolphus, still dominated the Baltic Sea through its bridgeheads on imperial soil and forced Poland to make peace. The Protestant powers, in which the Catholic faith was virtually exterminated,[9] were in the ascendancy. Spain, the former Catholic power, was defeated by the France of Richelieu who was unwilling to accept Philip II's role of protector of Catholic interests. The Counter Reformation had come to a stop in Central Europe, but the Tridentine reform had not. Like his predeces-

---

[8a] According to H. F. Kearney, "Ecclesiastical Politics and the Counter-Reformation in Ireland 1618–1648," *JEH* 11 (1960), 202–212, the Irish episcopate was divided between a moderate faction, in favor of a reconciliation with England, and a radical one, favoring Spain; the Curia after 1640 supported the former.

[9] *Romeinische Bronnen voor den kerkelijken Toestand der Nederlanden onder de Apostolische Vicarissen* I, ed. J. D. M. Cornelissen ('s Gravenhage 1932), sources from 1592 to 1651; J. Metzler, *Die Apostolischen Vikariate des Nordens* (Paderborn 1919); I. Hansteen-Knudsen, *De Relationibus inter Sanctam Sedem et Norvegiam* (Rome 1946); on the Jesuits' fruitless missionary efforts in Denmark and Sweden, see Duhr, II, 2, 75ff.

sors, Innocent X worked for it and, soon after the conclusion of peace, set in motion in the Empire a wave of Church renewal.[10]

In condemning five propositions from the *Augustinus* of Cornelius Jansenius (d. 1638 as Bishop of Ypres) on 31 May 1653, Innocent X delivered the most momentous official doctrinal decision of the century. It can be appreciated only in connection with the quarrel over the Augustinian doctrine of grace, which had broken out again under Urban VIII. This controversy continued the quarrel over Baius and Molinism but, in contrast to them, it affected almost all facets of Church life far into the eighteenth century.

Under Innocent X occurred a change still operative in regard to the highest political office in the Holy See: the respective Cardinal Nephew was supplanted as chief minister by the secretary of state. In the pontificate of his predecessor the Cardinal Nephew Francesco Barberini, who at first had been overshadowed by the secretaries of state Magalotti and Azzolini, had contrived to secure a predominant influence at the side of and in fact ahead of the secretary of state, Ceva, whom the Pope regarded as a counterpoise, and finally (1643) obtained this post for his creature, Spada. But this enhancement of the political importance of the cardinal nephew was no more than an episode. Camillo Pamfili and Astalli, nephews of Innocent X, never played a leading role. This went instead to the secretaries of state, Panciroli and after 1651, Chigi, with whom begins the series of cardinal secretaries of state. "For the first time in the history of the secretariate of state the nuncios and legates sent their correspondence directly to the secretary of state; for the first time the secretary of state alone signed letters and instructions" (Hammermayer). And Chigi became the first secretary of state to ascend the Throne of Peter.

The paralysis of the Catholic counteroffensive did not involve that of artistic powers. On 18 November 1626, Urban VIII had consecrated the new Saint Peter's, for which his architect, Bernini, executed the bronze baldachin over the *confessio* and the tomb of the Barberini Pope.[11] Numerous churches of martyrs, such as Santa Bibiana and Santi Cosma e Damiano, were restored by him, his nephews, and other cardinals. The rebuilding of the Seven Hills, started by Sixtus V, was continued with the laying out of new streets and the erection of a splendid family palace, and the appearance of the city was enhanced by the

---

[10] Encyclical of 4 April 1652, mentioned in *Deutsche Geschichtsblätter* 16 (1915), 10.

[11] Pastor, XXIX, 455–544; XXX, 381–411; L. Schudt, *Le guide di Roma* (Vienna 1930), pp. 40ff.; O. Pollak, *Die Kunsttätigkeit unter Urban VIII (Augsburg 1928); R. Wittkower, *Bernini, the Sculptor of the Roman Baroque* (London 1955).

installation of numerous fountains. The guides to Rome by Mancini and Celio, Baglione and Totti were no longer pilgrims' guides to the sanctuaries and relics but experts on the artistic monuments of pagan and Christian Rome from antiquity to the present. Under the prosaic and thrifty Innocent X Bernini was for a time out of favor. The belfrey of Saint Peter's that he had erected was again torn down but the interior decorations were completed and thus the estimated seven hundred thousand pilgrims of the Jubilee Year 1650 viewed the church in essentially its present form. The same holds for the Lateran Basilica, restored by Borromini, and the Baroque churches of Sant' Ignazio and Sant' Andrea della Valle, finished after a long period of construction. The jewel of all the Roman squares, the Piazza Navona, where arose the Pamfili family palace, received its final form with Bernini's Fontana dei Fiumi. Baroque Rome was now completed. In the march of the Catholic Reform its universities and colleges had made it a center of ecclesiastical scholarship. Now it became the goal of cultural journeys.

CHAPTER 50

Denominationalism and Secularization

The strict doctrinal and territorial separation between Catholics, Lutherans, and Calvinists, "confessionalization," and the resulting doctrinal quarrels are the outstanding characteristics of the century between the Council of Trent and the Peace of Westphalia. But the very violence of the opposing polemics and the blood-letting of the wars of religion gave rise to a new longing for religious peace and Church unity. While it is true that the ever more numerous conversions around the turn of the century and a series of religious colloquies led to renewed strife, nevertheless the hazards of irenicism were embraced, though only by individualists. When it became clear that religious unity within the state could no longer be enforced, the idea of toleration made progress, but, except in the France of Henry IV, it was unable to carry the day.

Strictly speaking, conversions to the Catholic Church presupposed the strict differentiation of the Catholic doctrine from the Protestant by the Council of Trent. This concept does not cover the return of entire territories on the basis of edicts issued by territorial lords, though, for example among the figures reported by the Jesuits,[1] a large number of genuine conversions based on conviction is found. The series of German

---

[1] Duhr, II,2, 66ff. J. Schacher, "Luzerner Akten zur Geschichte kath. Konvertiten 1580–1780," *ZSKG* 57 (1963), 1–36, 165–220, 303–41.

converts of princely rank began in 1590 with the Margrave Jakob of Baden-Hachberg, later followed by the Count Palatine Wolfgang Wilhelm, Count Johann Ludwig of Nassau-Siegen, Margrave Christian Wilhelm of Brandenburg, Landgrave Friedrich of Hesse, and, in the years immediately after the Peace of Westphalia, Duke Ulrich of Württemberg, Duke Johann Friedrich of Braunschweig-Lüneburg, and Landgrave Ernst of Hesse-Rheinfels. It is obvious that in some of these conversions political and opportunistic motives played a part. For the conversion of scholars the disunity of the Protestants and the diversity of their doctrinal concepts were frequently given as motives, while the uniformity of the Catholic doctrinal system and the beauty of its worship exercised a powerful attraction. Outstanding among the large number of scholarly converts were: Friedrich Staphylus (d. 1563), former professor at Königsberg; the Hessian Johannes Pistorius (d. 1608), whose pamphlet *Anatomia Lutheri* (1595–98) enraged Protestants; the Marburg Jesuit Helferich Hunnius (d. 1636); the philologist Lukas Holstenius (d. 1661) of Hamburg, whose change of mind went back to the period of his Leiden activity and who, only after his conversion in Paris, was employed by Cardinal Francesco Barberini as librarian.

The religious conversations of the age varied from place to place. The colloquy arranged by Emperor Ferdinand I at Worms from 11–20 September 1557 was a straggler of the talks called for by Charles V to overcome a dilemma. Ferdinand's colloquy was sterile, for the Jena theologians, Flacius at their head, could not agree with the majority of the Protestant speakers led by Melanchthon, and these last refused to condemn doctrinal opinions not in accord with the original *Confessio Augustana*.[2] The Religious Colloquy of Baden (1589) had been summoned by the Margrave Jakob of Baden-Hachberg, the future convert. Its chief topic was the doctrine of justification. The Protestant spokesmen were Jakob Andreä and Jakob Heerbrand; the Catholic, the convert Pistorius and the Jesuit Busaeus. Pistorius was excluded from the Colloquy of Emmendigen, arranged the next year to discuss the doctrine of the Church.[3] The prospect of conversion was also the basis of the Regensburg Religious Colloquy of 1601, jointly convoked, after careful preparation, by Maximilian I of Bavaria and the strongly Lutheran Philip Ludwig of Palatinate-Neuburg. The topic was the relationship of Scripture and Tradition. In addition to Philip Ludwig, theologians from Württemberg, Electoral Saxony, and Brandenburg upheld the

---

[2] *P. Canisii Epp. et Acta* II, 125–180; ibid., p. 791, the list of the Catholic participants. Bishop Pflug of Naumburg presided. Further literature in Janssen, IV, 21–31.

[3] *Acta des Colloquii zu Baden* (1950); cf. A. Kleinschmidt, *Jakob III., Markgraf zu Baden-Hachberg, der erste regierende Konvertit in Deutschland* (Frankfurt a. M. 1875).

Protestant side; the Jesuits Gretser and Tanner, the Catholic view. No less than fifty-five controversial works came out of this discussion.[4] King Ladislaus of Poland summoned the Religious Colloquy of Torun in 1645 in the hope of ending the altercations going on within his country. In the number of participants—twenty-six Catholics, twenty-eight Lutherans, twenty-four Calvinists—it surpassed all earlier discussions, but it foundered at the outset on the question of the order of business.[5] Effective incentives for mutually drawing closer did not emanate from any one of these meetings, but came from elsewhere.

The humanist irenicists around the middle of the sixteenth century always started from the Erasmian distinction between the fundamental articles of faith, concerning which there was or at least could be agreement, and theological doctrinal opinions, which were to be left to free discussion; in them the traditional consciousness of the one Christianity lived on. However, there were not unimportant variations. Georg Witzel aspired to restore Christian unity by reform of the present Church and return to the ancient Church. His work on unity, *Via regia,* appeared posthumously in 1564.[6] Georg Cassander (d. 1566) became the most influential representative of this "Old Catholic" orientation. In his *De officio pii et publicae tranquillitatis vere amantis Viri,* composed on the occasion of the Religious Colloquy of Poissy (1561), he declared that all who accept the Apostles' Creed belong to the Church of Christ. The *Consultatio de articulis inter Catholicos et Protestantes controversis* (1564), ordered by Emperor Ferdinand I, specified as the sole practicable road to reunion a return to the faith and the institutions of the ancient Church, which for him was identified with the Age of Constantine and of the great Fathers of the Church.[7] But neither Witzel nor Cassander were regarded by Peter Canisius as real Catholics (*vere et integre catholici*), because they did not observe the decrees of the Council of Trent and the norms of a sound theology, and occasionally even deviated from the Catholic faith.[8] The influence of Erasmus continued predominant in the Pole Andreas Frycz Modrzewski (d. 1572), who as secretary of King

---

[4] W. Herbst, *Das Regensburger Religionsgespräch von 1601* (Gütersloh 1928).

[5] K. E. Jordt Jorgensen, *Ökumenische Bestrebungen unter den polnischen Protestanten bis zum Jahre 1645* (Copenhagen 1942); H. Schüssler, *Georg Calixt. Theologie und Kirchenpolitik* (Wiesbaden 1961), pp. 122–133.

[6] W. Trusen, *Um die Reform und Einheit der Kirche. Zum Leben und Werk Georg Witzels* (Münster 1956), pp. 77ff.

[7] M. E. Nolte, *Georgius Cassander en zijn oecumenisch streven* (Nijmegen 1951).

[8] *P. Canisii Epp. et Acta* VII, 553 (8 August 1580). According to Reusch, *Der Index* I, 361, Cassander's edition of ancient Church hymns was put on the Index of Trent, but not his work on union.

Sigismund Augustus influenced the latter's religious policy,[9] and in Michel de L'Hôpital (d. 1573), Catherine de Médicis's chancellor, who bridged humanist irenicism and the idea of state toleration and the group of *politiques* seeking an understanding with the Huguenots.[10] Cassander's ideas were taken up a half-century later by two Protestant irenicists, Grotius and Calixt.

The Dutchman Hugo Grotius (d. 1645), while he was imprisoned for having attacked the dominant strictly Calvinist line and for high treason (1619–21), developed the theological principles of his later efforts to bring closer especially the Protestant denominations, the Anglicans, and the Orthodox. Though as a boy he had sought to induce his Catholic mother to apostatize, because she "was too intelligent to remain a papist," toward the close of his life he drew nearer the Catholic Church by championing the apostolic succession, the hierarchy, and the Catholic concept of the Sacraments. He declared that the solution of the religious split, which with Erasmus he regarded as unnecessary and pernicious, was possible on the basis of the *Confessio Augustana* and, in the midst of the Thirty Years' War, outlined the ideal of a reconciled *Magna Universitas Christianorum,* headed by the supreme priest, the Pope.[11]

Whereas, on the side of the Reformed—partly from ecclesiastico-political motives, since Calvinism was not yet recognized in imperial law—exertions for the union of Protestants were never broken off, for example, the efforts of Philippe de Mornay Duplessis, Franz Junius, and John Dury, on the Lutheran side the "Old Catholic" tendencies present in Melanchthon were suppressed by orthodoxy and only reappeared with the Helmstedt theologian Georg Calixt (d. 1656). The principle of tradition, which at first (1629) he had sought to exploit against the Catholic Church, became the basis of his irenicism, which consciously made use of Cassander. Apostolicity and the universal consensus of the ancient Church on the fundamental articles of Christian faith constituted for him the only possible basis for reunion.[12] His viewpoint was violently attacked from the strict Lutheran side in the *Anatomia Calixtina* (1644), but some of his ideas recurred in the Mainz Plan of Union

[9] *De republica emendanda* (Basel 1559); cf. G. Schramm, "Modrevius-Forschungen," *Jahrbücher fur Geschichte Osteuropas,* NF 6 (1958), 352–373 (report on the literature).
[10] A. Buisson, *Michel de L'Hôpital* (Paris 1950), with excellent bibliography.
[11] *Via ad pacem ecclesiasticam* (Paris–Amsterdam 1642); to the works of J. Schlüter, R. Voeltzelt, and P. Polman (listed in *LThK* 2nd ed., IV, 1244) add J. Spörl, "Hugo Grotius und der Humanismus des 17. Jh.," *HJ* 55 (1935), 350–357; J. Cornelissen, "H. de Groot op den Index," *Miscell. historica in honorem L. van der Essen* II (Brussels 1947), 757–768; K. Repgen, "Grotius papizans," *Reformata reformanda* II, 370–400.
[12] E. L. T. Henke, *Georg Calixt und seine Zeit,* 2 vols. (Halle 1853f.); H. Schüssler, *Georg Calixt. Theologie und Kirchenpolitik* (Wiesbaden 1961).

of 1660, which was probably connected with the efforts of Johann Philip von Schönborn, Elector of Mainz, to achieve a *rapprochement* of the denominations. This sought a reunion of the Lutherans, not of the Calvinists, with the Catholic Church on the basis of the *Confessio Augustana,* the marriage of priests, the lay chalice, and certain dogmatic and disciplinary concessions. As "reformed Catholics" they were to return to the obedience of the Pope.[13] The Elector remained aloof, and in Rome the project was presumably never given serious consideration.

Antipapal rather than irenic in tone was the project of union of the apostate Marcantonio de Dominis:[14] United in faith in Christ and in apostolicity, an Episcopal Church was to include the Protestants, without prejudice to certain doctrines proper to them; the Pope was the external symbol of unity but he must first restore their original rights to the members of the Church.

Different in principle from the efforts of the irenicists, though resembling them in their results, were the discussions on the lawfulness of toleration by the state. While the postulate that only one religion or denomination should prevail within a state remained essentially undisputed, it could not be maintained in practice. During the Huguenot Wars the *politiques*—the sons of the Connétable Montmorency, Cardinal Bellay, Maurillac, and others—advocated cooperation with and toleration of the Calvinists. According to Bodin (d. 1596), the monarch is obliged to preserve the religious unity of his country if it exists, but it must not be restored by force. Later Bodin inclined to the view that it is best to allow to each his own personal religion.[15] After Henry IV had granted religious liberty to the Huguenots in the Edict of Nantes, the English and the Dutch Catholics asked in vain for the same concession.[16] In Germany the Jena theologian Johann Gerhard (d. 1637) characterized unity of faith within a state as a desirable but scarcely realizable ideal. In the denominationally mixed state the prince might tolerate individuals of other faiths but not public worship for fear of serious

---

[13] A. P. Brück, "Der Mainzer Unionsplan aus dem Jahre 1660," *Ehrengabe A. Schuchert* (Mainz 1960), pp. 148–162.

[14] D. Cantimori, "L'utopia ecclesiologica di M. A. de Dominis," *Problemi di vita religiosa in Italia nel Cinquecento* (Padua 1960), pp. 103–122; on p. 111 the passage: "Neque componi potest dissensio neque partes ad concordiam possunt redire nisi restitutio fiat in integrum."

[15] J. Lecler, *Histoire de la tolérance au siècle de la réforme* I, 91ff., 153ff. E. Benz, "Der Toleranzgedanke in der Religionswissenschaft. Über den Heptaplomeres des J. Bodin," *DVfLG* 12 (1934), 540–571.

[16] R. Persons, *Treatises tending to Mitigations towards Catholic Subjects in England* (1607); cf. J. Lecler, op. cit., II, 383f.; H. Witte, *Die Ansichten Jacobs I. v. England über Kirche und Staat mit besonderer Berücksichtigung der religiösen Toleranz* (Berlin 1940).

disorders; excepted from toleration were Anabaptists and Unitarians.[17] And the Jesuit Martin Becanus (d. 1624), contradicting Bellarmine, knew a series of cases in which a Catholic prince may tolerate heretics in his territory: if they are in the majority or are more powerful than the Catholics or are supported by outside powers, and also if the use of force would impede their conversion.[18]

Theories of State and Absolutism

In these theological exchanges over the permissibility of toleration by the state is reflected the power shift in the relations of state and Church since the religious cleavage. Earlier, during the Great Schism and the struggle against conciliarism, the papacy had had to court the secular powers. Now it was the princes first of all, and individuals only in the second place, who determined adherence to religion and creed. The Council of Trent took place in agreement with the princes, and only with their cooperation could it be enforced and implemented. To an even higher degree the Counter Reformation was their work. The power shift proceeded hand in hand with a change in the structure of the state, from a feudal to a modern bureaucratic state, with the development of princely absolutism and modern theories of government in which the way was prepared for its secularization.

Machiavelli's idea of the autonomous power state, subject to its proper law, the reason of state, slowly gained ground. In his *apologia* against Henry VIII Cardinal Pole had clearly recognized the threatening danger. Later writers, such as Giovanni Botero, for a time in Borromeo's service, believed it possible to transform Machiavelli's idea into a Christian one and thereby to neutralize it.[19] Bodin did not question the religious obligations of the prince, but subordinated the form and laws of the state to the concept of the sovereignty and the natural conditions of nations and individuals, in the final analysis to the welfare of the state.[20] Friends and enemies of Machiavelli derived arguments from Tacitus. Justus Lipsius, who revived him (though in 1591 he returned to the University of Louvain and to the Catholic Church) openly championed Machiavelli and his *Politica* (1589) was translated into five

---

[17] J. Lecler, op. cit., I, 289ff.; J. Wallmann, *Die Theologiebegriff bei Johann Gerhard und Georg Calixt* (Tübingen 1961).

[18] J. Lecler, op. cit., I, 292ff. On the penetration of Machiavellian ideas into England see G. Mosse, *The Holy Pretence* (Oxford 1957).

[19] *Della ragion di stato* (1589), n.ed. L. Firpo (Turin 1948).

[20] J. Bodin, *Six livres de la république* (1576); A. Schmitz, *Staat und Kirche bei J. Bodin* (Leipzig 1939); J. H. Franklin *J. Bodin and the XVIth Century Revolution in the Methodology of Law and History* (New York–London 1963).

languages.[21] The Duke of Rohan, a coworker of Richelieu, made the statement that princes command peoples and interest commands princes.

The roots of princely absolutism reach back into the late Middle Ages, but its refinements, differing widely according to countries and people, were incontestably furthered, in both the Protestant and the Catholic area, by the religious split and its consequences. Considerable power accrued to the Protestant territorial princes through the formation of the territorial Church and the secularization of Church property. The Catholic princes not only made use of their right to determine the religion of their subjects; while protecting the Church and promoting reform and even reconquering lost territory for her, they extended their own authority in the ecclesiastical sphere, frequently with the consent or at least the toleration of the papacy. Roles were reversed: the state no longer afforded help to an imperiled Church, but the Church, even unconsciously and often unwillingly, aided a state that was becoming absolute.

The intrusion of the modern state into the ecclesiastical field is essentially different from the ascendancy of the lay power in the early medieval Western Christian family of nations. Now for the first time there arose a genuine Church establishment. The papacy defended the freedom and independence of the Church particularly against the claims of the dominant Catholic powers, Spain and France, but in most cases without any outstanding success. Papal decrees were subject to the royal *placet;* clerical privileges, such as the *privilegium fori* and the right of asylum, were curtailed; Church property was taxed, with or without papal authorization and in France by means of clerical contributions voted by the national assembly; the Inquisition and ecclesiastical censure of books were impeded or, as in Spain, nationalized. Even after the adjustment of the conflict with Rome, Venice tolerated the propaganda proceeding from the Dutch and English embassies, refused to readmit the Jesuits, and acted as protector of monasteries whose reform was demanded by the Curia. The Church was forced into a defensive position.

The doctrine of the right of resistance and of tyrannicide is to be explained by the increasing pressure of princely absolutism. In the last third of the sixteenth century assassinations of princes increased in number, and Bodin declared tyrannicide lawful. Nevertheless it created a sensation when the Spanish Jesuit Juan Mariana in his *De rege et regis*

---

[21] G. Oestreich, "J. Lipsius als Theoretiker des modernen Machtstaates," *HZ* 181 (1956), 31–78; id., "J. Lipsius in sua re," *Festgabe Fritz Neubert* (Berlin 1956), pp. 291–311. Other literature in *LThK* 2nd ed., VI, 1072.

institutione (1599), dedicated to King Philip III, expounded the theory that a usurper may be killed by anyone, but a legitimate prince only if, in the general opinion (*si vox populi adsit*), he is destroying the state, despising religion and laws, and there is no other way of inducing him to cease from tyranny. These rules, unobjectionable in regard to content, were intended as a warning to princes who ruled in an absolutist manner, but since they were related to a thinly veiled approval of the assassination of Henry III of France the Sorbonne, on the basis of the decree of Constance against John Petit, condemned Mariana's book, and the Society's general, Acquaviva, disavowed it and forbade further debate.

Secularization of Thought

Even more portentous than absolutism and Church establishment, or than the rising secularization of the concept of the state, were the beginnings of the secularization of European thought in both the arts and the sciences. It must not only be assessed negatively as a natural process of maturation. It must also be regarded as a reaction to the extreme claims of theologians and their quarrels, to the recourse to ecclesiastical and political means of power in the religious sphere, and to the luxuriant growth of superstition. Skepticism and incredulity became a problem. A growing number of religious individualists, abandoning the central doctrines of the Christian faith, were rejected by the Catholic Church as well as by the Protestant denominations. And religious splintering proceeded noticeably. Unrelated to theology, there arose the "natural system of intellectual knowledge" (W. Dilthey). The natural sciences, with no regard for authority, based themselves on empirical observation and mathematical computation, but in the "Galileo Case" they encountered the Church's opposition.

In the "century that wanted to believe" superstition proliferated. Astrology was held in reverence, illness in man and beast was traced to magic, devils and witches were portrayed in the theater. The most frightful aberration of superstition, the witch trials, claimed thousands of innocent victims in both Catholic and Protestant Germany. In Gerolshofen, belonging to the see of Würzburg, ninety-nine witches were put to death in the year 1616; in Ellwangen, 167 in 1612; in Trier and its vicinity the witchcraft delusion required 306 victims in less than seven years from 1587 to 1593; in the Canton of Bern more than 300 within the decade 1591–1600. Only with great exertion did Johannes Kepler save his mother from the pyre. Duke Heinrich Julius of Braunschweig-Wolfenbüttel (1589–1613) enjoyed the dubious fame of a zealous burner of witches.[22] Denunciations and the ruthless resort to torture to extort confessions released the basest instincts; not infrequently piety led to the suspicion of witchcraft. Although according to Janssen, "not a single example is known of Jesuits' having brought the ill-starred persons to the attention of the authorities or of ever having advocated their being burned," they were frequently accused of having instigated the trials. And in fact a majority of Jesuits, like the rest of their contemporaries, were under the spell of the witchcraft delusion, which they connected with diabolical possession; for example, Georg Scherer, Delrio, and Stengel. On the other hand, the moral theologians Tanner and Laymann warned against the illegal and inhuman conduct of the trials, and Friedrich von Spee (1591–1635), who, as confessor of many of the accused, knew at first hand their deep distress and despair, summoned the courage to brand the absurdity and the injustice of the trials as crying out to heaven, comparing them to the methods of Nero's persecution of Christians.[23] Within his own Order he met stiff resistance and was urged to leave it. Von Spee's Christian conscience was roused to indignation against the witch trials but he could not end them. It was inevitable that the reaction against the excesses perpetrated would one day bring into question the belief in a spiritual world.

The resort to ecclesiastical and political means of compulsion for the preservation of orthodoxy had already led, with Sebastian Castellio (d. 1563) and Jacobus Acontius (d. 1566–67), to the repudiation of any external force in the religious sphere. Religious individualists and groups, repelled and suppressed by the prevailing denominations, demanded freedom of conscience and of teaching; for example, the Arminians in Holland. Some even attacked the central dogma of the Trinity, especially Italians who had broken with the Christian faith and had fled from the Inquisition, usually into Switzerland. They had taken refuge,

---

[22] Still of value are J. Hansen, *Zauberwahn, Inquisition und Hexenprozess im MA und die Entstehung der grossen Hexenverfolgungen* (Leipzig-Munich 1900); N. Paulus, *Hexenwahn und Hexenprozess vornehmlich im 16. Jh.* (Freiburg 1910); Janssen, VIII (Freiburg, 15th ed. 1924), 531–751; F. Merzbacher, *Die Hexenprozesse in Franken* (Munich 1957); W. Kramer, *Kurtrierische Hexenprozesse im 16. und 17. Jh.* (Munich 1959); H. Klein, "Die älteren Hexenprozesse im Lande Salzburg," *Mitt. der Gesellschaft für Salzburger Landeskunde,* 97 (1957), 17–50; popular and taking into account also France and England is K. Baschwitz, *Hexen und Hexenprozesse* (Munich 1963); other literature in *LThK* 2nd ed., V, 316–319.

[23] *Cautio criminalis* (Rinteln 1631) anonymous; German translation by J. F. Ritter (Weimar 1939); H. Zwetsloot, *Friedrich Spee und die Hexenprozesse. Die Stellung und Bedeutung der Cautio criminalis in der Geschichte der Hexenverfolgungen* (Trier 1954); E. Rosenfeld, *F. Spee von Langenfeld* (Berlin 1958); K. Honselmann, "F. von Spee und die Drucklegung seiner Mahnschrift gegen die Hexenprozesse," *Westfäl. Zeitschrift* 113 (1963), 427–54.

some in western, some in eastern Europe. Celio Secundo Curione lived in Basel until his death in 1569; Bernardino Ochino died in Moravia in 1565; Lelio Sozzini, who had attacked the dogma of the Trinity in his commentary on the prologue of the Fourth Gospel,[24] closed his turbulent wandering life at Zurich in 1562. Whereas the earlier anti-Trinitarians, such as Adam Pastoris, had drawn their objections from the Bible, the later ones were more rationalistic in their approach; for example, the Padua jurist Matteo Gribaldi, Giovanni Gentile (beheaded at Bern in 1566), and the physician Giorgio Blandrata, who drew from his Unitarianism the conclusion that, differing from Christianity, Judaism and Islam had preserved the true doctrine of the "One and Supreme." Poland became a refuge of anti-Trinitarians; as early as 1556 Papal Nuncio Lippomanni dealt with them in a report but without distinguishing between the different tendencies—Tritheists and Unitarians.

Unitarianism established itself between 1560 and 1568—Peter Gonesius constitutes a transitional stage. The "Polish Brethren" were partly inclined to Anabaptism, and hence the leader of the anti-Trinitarians, Fausto Sozzini (d. 1604), Lelio's nephew, prevailed only slowly. His catechism appeared in Polish in 1605. The sect's intellectual center was Rakow near Sandomir, where the general synod met annually and a secondary school flourished. But it was suppressed in 1638 and in 1658 the adherents of the sect were expelled from the country. Part of them took refuge in Holland; the historian of the Unitarians, Stanislaus Lubiniecki, found it in Hamburg.

In France François de Rabelais (d. 1553) had already posed the problem of unbelief. The skeptical outlook of Montaigne (d. 1592) was directed especially at the existing authorities and was compensated by a fideism, to which his friend, Pierre Charron (d. 1603), also subscribed in his *Trois Vérité* (1593), a defense of Christianity. Jean Pierre Camus, friend of Saint Francis de Sales, saw in Montaigne an ally against the rigid dogmatism of the Calvinists and defended him. The Jesuit Garasse recognized the mortal danger of skepticism and warned against it.[25] For René Descartes (d. 1650) methodical doubt was the beginning of

---

[24] Text in D. Cantimori–E. Feist, *Per la storia degli Eretici italiani del secolo XVI in Europa* (Rome 1937), pp. 61–78; A. Stella, "Ricerche sul Socianesimo," *Bolletino dell'Instituto di storia della societa e dello Stato veneziano* 3 (1961), 77–120. Written from a Marxist viewpoint and inadequate in content is A. Pirnat, *Die Ideologie der Siebenbürger Antitrinitarier in den 1570er Jahren* (Budapest 1961); cf. *RHE* 57 (1962), 602ff.; J. Tazbir, *Stanislaw Lubiniecki, przywodca arianskie j emigrac ji* (Warsaw 1961). For the Unitarian movement as a whole see E. M. Wilbur, *History of Unitarianism*, 2 vols. (Cambridge, Mass. 1945–52).

[25] R. H. Popkin, "Scepticism and the Counter-Reformation in France," *ARG* 51 (1960), 58–87; J. Lecler, "Un adversaire des libertins au début du XVIIe siècle, le P. François Garasse," *Etudes 209 (1931)*, 553–572.

philosophizing. His awareness of the sovereignty of constructive thought places him at the head of modern philosophy, emancipated from theology.

Though dependent on modern scholasticism in his doctrine of rights, and in particular on Francisco de Vitoria and Suarez, Hugo Grotius had preceded Descartes in understanding law as "an effective function of life, based on natural law and reason" (E. Wolf). The ethical foundation of law lies in man's social nature. Hence law is spiritually autonomous; its connection with theological and philosophical assumptions is not entirely broken but it is loosened. To this extent Grotius is the founder of modern natural and international law.

The rising independence of the arts, including history, was in itself a natural maturing of the European mind. It did not necessarily have to lead to conflict with the faith and with theology, no more than the constructing of a natural science on empirical observation and mathematical computation had to. The reason why the systems of natural philosophy, suspected of Pantheism, of the ex-Dominican Tommaso Campanella (d. 1639) and Giordano Bruno were, together with their creators, condemned by the Church lay in the nature of things and in the attitude of their representatives.

Far more momentous was Galileo's encounter with the Inquisition. Nicholas Copernicus (d. 1543) had dedicated to Paul III his *De revolutionibus orbium coelestinum,* which had endeavored to prove by mathematical arguments the motion of the earth around the sun. Since that time the "Copernican World System" had, like its preliminary steps in the Parisian natural philosophy of the fourteenth century, encountered no hostility from the Church. After 1594 the University of Salamanca made the text of Copernicus the basis of instruction. Luther, Melanchthon, Osiander, and the University of Tübingen attacked the Copernican system as contradicting Scripture. Nevertheless, it was further developed around the turn of the century. Johannes Kepler, court astronomer of Rudolf II, discovered the laws of planetary motion. Galileo Galilei (1564–1642), active in Florence from 1610, found confirmation of the Copernican system by observing the heavenly bodies, such as the moons of Jupiter. With the help of a telescope he constructed and defended it against objections drawn from Scripture (Josh. 10:12f., Ps. 103:5).[26] Following denunciation by the Dominican court preacher Lorini, Galileo was summoned before the Roman Inquisition. Until then he had enjoyed the greatest esteem in Rome's ecclesiastical circles and in 1611 had been admitted to the Papal Academy. But by his vehement

---

[26] Galileo to the Benedictine Castelli on 21 December 1613; *Opere,* ed. A. Favaro, V, 279–288.

efforts to demonstrate the compatibility of his system with a correct interpretation of Scripture, he so provoked the consultors of the Inquisition that on 24 February 1616 it declared his propositions on the standing of the sun and the movement of the earth as heretical or erroneous and forbade him to defend them in the future. He was not obliged to abjure them or to cease his investigations, and Pope Paul V granted him an audience and assured him of his protection. Just the same, on 5 March 1616 the work of Copernicus and all books that defended his system were placed on the Index. After the accession of Urban VIII Galileo, relying on the Pope's benevolence, dedicated to him his reply to a criticism by the Jesuit Grassi and, following a visit to Rome, was extolled "as the man whose fame shines forth in the sky and permeates the world." But when, confident of the Pope's favor, he published, with the *Imprimatur* of Riccardi, Master of the Sacred Palace, his *Dialogues on the two most important World Systems* in 1632, the Inquisition again summoned him on 23 September 1632, for having violated the earlier prohibition of 1616. Though during the second trial he declared that interiorly he did not adhere to the Copernican system, he was condemned on 22 June 1633 to abjuration and to life-imprisonment. He recanted and the imprisonment was commuted to a mild detention on his estate of Alcetri near Florence. The sequel to the Galileo trial was that his mathematico-physical concept of the world was not accepted by the Church and his chief work, *Discorsi e dimostrazioni matematiche intorno a due nuove scienze* (1638), the "first text in physics" (Von Laue), had to be printed in Leiden. Galileo's personal fate was determined by his taking into his own hands the resolving of the apparent contradiction between his conclusions from his study of natural science and scriptural revelation, instead of leaving it to theologians.

A new epoch in Church history begins in the mid-seventeenth century. The Peace of Westphalia definitely settled denominational rights in the Empire and put a stop to the Counter Reformation as an ecclesiastico-political activity. It brought to a close the age of the Wars of Religion and at the same time shifted political powers. The Peace of the Pyrenees (1659) decided the struggle for European hegemony in favor of France, and a decade later the recognition of the English Navigation Acts by the States General of the Netherlands put the seal on England's maritime supremacy. Innocent X's protest against the religious articles of the Peace of Westphalia fell on deaf ears, and the papacy could not assert, even vis-à-vis the remaining Catholic powers, its authority as guarantor of supranational order. The already long-faded idea of *Christianitas* completely lost its significance in practical politics. However, the Church had been interiorly renewed since the Council of Trent and had overcome the crisis of the religious schism. She was asserting herself and was even able to recover lost ground, but to restore the unity of the Church had proven clearly impossible. Confessionalization divided the Christian peoples of the West into three sharply defined and quarrelling bodies—Catholics, Lutherans, and Calvinists—and lessened the convincing force of Christian thought. Forced into a defensive position, the Church was unable to master the religious and intellectual forces pressing to the surface, some of them released by the split, others having their roots deep in the late Middle Ages. She lost command, and a new crisis, the supreme crisis of the European mind, announced itself.

Parallel to, and often intertwined with, this changing relationship to the "world" were structural changes within the Church. Defense against Protestantism and inner renewal of the Church from the time of the Council of Trent were possible only because the papacy sharply tightened the reins of the central authority and, in a new centralization, very different from the medieval, strengthened the threatened members who were themselves too weak, by means of nuncios, controlled the bishops through the *visitatio liminum,* and in the congregations that were becoming stabilized and being organized as offices created an effective instrument, which, unlike the chancery and *camera* of the late Middle Ages, did not pursue a mainly financial end. The "Episcopalist" currents, which, becoming ever stronger in the course of the seventeenth and eighteenth centuries, resisted this tendency, left themselves open to suspicion because in part they attenuated or denied the Pope's primacy of jurisdiction, in part they relied on the protection of the national estate, as in France and Spain, or on secular means of power, as in the Holy Roman Empire. From the time of Bellarmine ecclesiology put the doctrine of the papal primacy in the center and caused the function of the college of bishops to withdraw into the background. After Trent no general council was summoned for more than three centuries.

The Tridentine doctrinal system and reform work, to which the Church owed her renewal and self-assertion, impressed their stamp on the Church's life and well-nigh became its unique form. The post-Tridentine Church was anti-Protestant and became anti-reform. Theological schools which had been unattacked in the Middle Ages, such as Augustinianism, were hard put to maintain themselves. Gratian and the older canon law lost their importance. And the historical picture of the Church which could have been obtained from the flourishing study of patrology and Church history became ineffectual. Just as liturgy in its post-Tridentine form hardened into rubricism, so canon law became formalistic and remained so for three whole centuries. Is one justified, then, in extending the "Tridentine epoch" of Church history or the

"Counter Reformation" into the nineteenth century or even to the present?

It is not to be denied that certain characteristics of the post-Tridentine Church—her anti-Protestant orientation in doctrine and piety, her centralization and formalism—remained active after the time limit here treated, the middle of the seventeenth century. Nevertheless, it is misleading and ruinous to any effort to obtain an insight into the real historical process if the centuries that have elapsed since Trent are studied from the one viewpoint of the present, of ecumenism and the openness to the world as displayed by the Second Vatican Council, while the influence of the Enlightenment and of the great upheavals since the French Revolution—to cite only these examples—are treated as of little significance. It is no less one-sided, as our presentation has shown, to regard the schism in the Church as a tragedy only, while overlooking the deepening and activating of the religious life which it had as a consequence, the wealth of values which came to light in the Catholic Reform, in new and old Orders, in asceticism and mysticism, in piety and art, in missionary expansion on three continents. In the hard crust that was forming there lay hidden a precious kernel, a specific, not to be mistaken kernel, encountered only in this epoch. To throw it away as worthless, not to recall that every period of Church history stands directly before God, is unhistorical and presumptuous: unhistorical, because one cannot see the limits and possibilities of the pilgrim Church; presumptuous, because it means forgetting that even we are not in possession of the perfect. Instead we are awaiting it—and only then will we dispose of the standards for judging fairly.

BIBLIOGRAPHY

GENERAL BIBLIOGRAPHY

I. SOURCES FOR THE HISTORY OF THE REFORMATION AND COUNTER REFORMATION

1. GENERAL AIDS, DICTIONARIES AND REFERENCE-WORKS

A. v. Brandt, *Werkzeug des Historikers* (Stuttgart[2] 1958; with bibliography); G. Wolf, *Einführung in das Studium der neueren Geschichte* (Berlin 1910); H. O. Meisner, *Aktenkunde. Ein Handbuch für Archivbenutzer mit besonderer Berücksichtigung Brandenburg-Preussens* (Leipzig[2] 1952; with bibliography); A. Brennecke–W. Leesch, *Archivkunde* (Leipzig 1953); K. Haebler, *Handbuch der Inkunabelkunde* (Leipzig 1925); M. Geisberg, *Der deutsche Einblattholzschnitt in der l. Hälfte des 16. Jahrhunderts* (Munich 1923–30); Ch. Du Cange, *Glossarium ad scriptores mediae et infimae latinitatis,* 10 vols. (Niors 1883–88); M. Lexer, *Mittelhochdeutsches Hand-Wörterbuch,* 3 vols. (Leipzig 1872–78); id., *Mittelhochdeutsches Taschen-WB* (Leipzig[24] 1944); A. Goetze, *Frühneuhochdeutsches Glossar* (Berlin[5] 1956); H. Rössler–G. Franz, *Biographisches Wörterbuch zur Deutschen Geschichte* (Munich 1952); id., *Sachwörterbuch zur Deutschen Geschichte* (Munich 1958); E. Haberkern–J. F. Wallach, *Hilfswörterbuch für Historiker* (Bern-Munich 1964); H. Rudolph, *Vollständig geographisch-topographisch statistisches Ortslexikon von Deutschland,* 2 vols. (1859–68; including Austria); J. Penzler, Ritter's *Geographisch-Statistisches Lexikon,* 9th reprint, 2 vols. (1905–6); J. G. Th. Graesse, *Orbis Latinus oder Verzeichnis der wichtigsten lat. Orts-und Ländernamen,* revised ed. by F. Benedict (Berlin 1922); W. Maurer, *Namenliste zur deutschen Geschichte des 16. Jahrhunderts,* Part I: A-E (Leipzig 1941); A. Cappelli, *Lexicon abbreviaturarum. Dizionario di abbreviature latine ed italiane* (Milan[6] 1961); id., *Cronologia, Cronografia e Calendario perpetuo. Dal principio dell'Era Christiana ai giorni nostri* (Milan 1930); *Dictionary of National Biography* (London 1885f.); G. Strauss, *Sixteenth Century Germany: Its Geography and Topography* (Madison, Wis. 1959); C. T. Martin, *The Record Interpreter: A collection of Abbreviations* (London 1949); M. S. Giuseppi, *A Guide to the Manuscripts Preserved in the Public Record Office* (London 1923–24), 2 vols. (supercedes F. S. Thomas, *Handbook to the Public Records* (London 1853); S. Scargil-Bird, *Guide to the Principal Classes of Documents in the Public Record Office* (London 1891, 1896, 1908); a new guide to the Public Record Office is in preparation; R. Hale, *Guide to Photocopied Historical Material in the United States* (Ithaca 1961); P. Haner (ed.), *A Guide to the Archives and Manuscripts in the United States* (New Haven 1961); D. H. Thomas–M. L. Case (eds.), *Guide to the Diplomatic Archives of Western Europe* (Philadelphia 1959); G. F. Howe et al., *The American Historical Association's Guide to Historical Literature* (New York 1961).

2. SOURCES AND BIBLIOGRAPHY

P. Herre, *Quellenkunde zur Weltgeschichte* (Leipzig 1910); Dahlmann-Waitz, *Quellenkunde der deutschen Geschichte,* ed. H. Haering, 2 vols. (Leipzig[9] 1930–31; new edition in preparation); A. W. Pollard–G. R. Redgrave, *A Short-Title-Catalogue of Books Printed in England, Scotland and Ireland, and of English Books Printed Abroad, 1475–1640* (The Bibliographical Society 1926); F. Schnabel, *Deutschlands Quellen und Darstellungen in der Neuzeit* I: *Das Zeitalter der Reformation 1500–1550* (Leipzig 1931); G. Wolf, *Quellenkunde der deutschen Reformationsgeschichte,* 3 vols. (Gotha 1915, 1916 and 1922, two parts 1923); suppls. in *Mitteilungen aus der historischen Literatur* 45 (1916), 46 (1918), 51 (1923), 52 (1926), 55 (1927), 56 (1928), 57 (1929); L. Hain, *Repertorium bibliographicum,* 2 vols. (Stuttgart 1826–38; reprint Milan 1948); W. A. Coppinger, *Supplement zu Hains Repertorium Bibliographicum* Part I, II: 1, 2 (Milan 1950); G. W. Panzer, *Annalen der älteren deutschen Literatur,* 2 vols. (Nürnberg 1788–1805; reprint Hildesheim 1961); J. Weller, *Repertorium typographicum. Die Deutsche Literatur im ersten Viertel des 16. Jahrhunderts* (Nördlingen 1864; reprint Hildesheim 1961); *Gesamtkatalog der Wiegendrucke,* published by the Kommission für den Gesamtkatalog der Wiegendrucke (I–VII A-Ei) (1925–38); Th. Bestermann, *Early Printed Books to the End of the Sixteenth Century* (Geneva 1961); G. Franz, *Bücherkunde zur deutschen Geschichte* (Munich 1951); id., *Bücherkunde zur Weltgeschichte* (Munich 1956); W. Trillmich, *Kleine Bücherkunde zur Geschichtswissenschaft* (Hamburg 1949); G. Franz, *Historische Kartographie, Forschung und Bibliographie* (Bremen 1955); M. Arnim, *Internationale Personalbibliographie,* 3 vols. (Stuttgart 1952–63); G. M. Dutcher, *Guide to Historical Literature* (New York 1949; mainly Anglo-Saxon literature); H. Planitz-T. Buyken, *Bibliographie zur deutschen Rechtsgeschichte* (Frankfurt a. M. 1952) with index volume (to 1500; considers also legal ecclesiastical conditions); I. Dagens, *Bibliographie Chronologique de la Litterature de Spiritualité et de ses sources* (1501–1610) (Paris 1952); K. Schottenloher, *Bibliographie zur deutschen Geschichte im Zeitalter der Glaubensspaltung 1517–85,* 6 vols. (Leipzig² 1956–58); VII, writings from 1938 to 1960 (Stuttgart 1966); *Bibliographie de la Réforme, 1450–1648:* I. Allemagne, Pais-Bas (Leiden 1958); II. Belgique, Suède, Norvège, Danemark, Irlande, Etats-Unis d'Amérique (ibid. 1960); III. Italie, Espagne, Portugal (ibid. 1961); IV. France, Angleterre, Suisse (ibid. 1963); H. J. Hillebrand, *Bibliographie des Täufertums 1520–1630* (Gütersloh 1962); A. Goetze, *Die hochdeutschen Drucker der Reformationszeit* (Strassburg 1905); A. Kuczyński, *Verzeichnis einer Sammlung von nahezu 3000 Flugschriften Luthers und seiner Zeitgenossen* (Nieuwkoop 1955); *Antiqua literarum monumenta autographa Lutheri aliorumque celebrium virorum ab A. 1517 usque ad A. 1546* (Brunswig 1690); *Bibliotheca Missionum* of Robert Streit, continued by Johannes Dindinger: I. Grundlegender und allgemeiner Teil (Münster 1916); II. Amerikanische Missionsliteratur 1493–1699 (Aachen 1924); IV. Asiatische Missionsliteratur 1245–1599 (Aachen 1928); V. Asiatische Missionsliteratur 1600–99 (Aachen 1929); XV. Afrikanische Missionsliteratur 1053–1599 (Freiburg 1951); XXI. Missionsliteratur von Australien und Ozeanien 1525–1950 (Freiburg 1955); Continued by Johannes Rommerskirchen and Josef Metzler: XXII. Grundlegender und allgemeiner Teil 1910–35 und Nachtrag zu Band I (Freiburg 1963); XXIII. Grundlegender und allgemeiner Teil 1936–60 (Freiburg 1964); S. Delacroix, *Histoire Universelle des Missions Catholiques,* 4 vols. (Paris 1956); L. Vriens–A. Disch (eds.), *A Critical Bibliography of Missiology* (Nymegen 1960).

3. SOURCES

GERMANY: J. Ch. Lüning, *Teutsches Reichs-Archiv* 22 (Leipzig 1719); *Neue und vollständige Sammlung der Reichs-Abschiede, welche von den Zeiten Kayser Conrads des II bis jetzo auf den Teutschen Reichs-Tagen abgefasst worden sammt den wichtigsten Reichs-Schlüssen,* 2 vols. (Frankfurt a. M. 1747); K. Lanz, *Staatspapiere zur Geschichte des Kaisers Karl V. aus dem*

Königlichen Archiv und der Bibliothèque de Bourgogne zu Brüssel (Stuttgart 1845); id., *Correspondenz des Kaisers Karl V.*, 3 vols. (Leipzig 1846); J. Fiedler, *Die Relationen der Botschafter Venedigs über Deutschland und Österreich im 17. Jahrhundert* (Vienna 1866) (=Fontes rerum Austriacarum); J. J. I. Döllinger, *Beiträge zur politischen, kirchlichen und Culturgeschichte der sechs letzten Jahrhunderte* I: *Dokumente zur Geschichte Kaiser Karls V., Philipps II. und ihrer Zeit. Aus spanischen Archiven* (Regensburg 1862), III (Vienna 1882); *Politische Korrespondenz der Stadt Strassburg im Zeitalter der Reformation*, 5 vols. (Strassburg–Heidelberg 1882–1933); A. V. Druffel, *Beiträge zur Reichgeschichte*, 3 vols. (Munich 1873–82), Vol. 4 ed. K. Brandi (Munich 1896); *Deutsche Reichstagsakten, Jüngere Reihe*, ed. the Historischen Kommission bei der Bayerischen Adademie der Wissenschaften: I. A. Kluckhohn, Kaiserwahl 1519 (Gotha 1893); II. A. Wrede, Reichstag zu Worms 1520–21 (Gotha 1896); III. id., Nürnberger Reichstag 1522 u. 1523 (Gotha 1901); IV. id., Nürnberger Reichstag 1524 (Stuttgart 1905); VII. J. Kühn, 1. u. 2. anberaumter Reichstag zu Regensburg 1526–27; *Schwäbische Bundestage 1527–28. Reichstag zu Speier 1529* (Stuttgart 1935); *Acta Pacis Westfalicae*, ed. M. Braubach–K. Repgen (Münster 1962f.); *Briefe und Akten zur Geschichte des Dreissigjährigen Krieges*, ed. the Bayerischen Akademie der Wissenschaften, 11 vols.: 1596–1613 (Leipzig 1870–1908); n. ed. 1618–51, Part II: 1–3: 1623–27 (Leipzig 1907f.); 4:1628–29 (Munich 1948).

FRANCE: *Collection des documents inédits relatifs à l'histoire de France*, to date 290 vols. (Paris 1836f.); *Correspondance de Réformateurs dans les pays de langue française*, ed. A. L. Herminjard, 9 vols. (Geneva–Paris 1866–7; reprinted Nieuwkoop 1966).

THE NETHERLANDS: L. P. Gachard, *Collection des voyages des souverains des Pays-Bas* (Brussels 1874); *Bibliotheca Reformatoria Neerlandica*, ed. S. Cranier–F. Pijper, 10 vols. ('s-Gravenhage 1903–4); *Documenta Reformatoria*, ed. J. N. Bakhuizen van den Brink et al., 2 vols. (Kampen 1960–62); G. Brom–A. H. L. Hensen, *Romeinsche Bronnen voor den Kerkelijk-staatkundig toestand der Nederlanden in de 16de eeuw* (Rijks geschiedkundige Publikatien . . . Groote serie 52) ('s-Gravenhage 1922); J. D. M. Cornelissen, *Kerkelijken Toestand der Nederlanden onder de apostolische Vicarissen 1592–1727*, Part 1, 1592–1651 ('s-Gravenhage 1932); *Bibliotheca catholica Neerlandica impressa 1500–1727* (The Hague 1954).

ENGLAND: *Calendar of State Papers Relating to English Affairs*, ed. J. M. Rigg, 2 vols. (London 1961–62).

SPAIN: *Colleción de documentos inéditos del Archivo general de la Corona de Aragón*, 41 vols. (Barcelona 1847–1910).

REPORTS OF PAPAL NUNCIOS

GERMANY: *Nuntiaturberichte aus Deutschland nebst ergänzenden Aktenstücken*, Section I: 1533–59, 14 vols., ed. the Preussische Historische Institut in Rome (Gotha 1892–1912); more recently XIII: 1552–53, ed. H. Lutz (Tübingen 1959), XVI: 1550–54, ed. H. Goetz (Tübingen 1965); Erg. I: 1530–31, ed. G. Müller (Tübingen 1963); Section II: 1560–72, 7 vols. (1897–1953); Section III: 1572–85, 4 vols. (1894–1909); Section IV: 17th Century, 3 vols. (1895–1913); *Nuntiaturberichte aus Deutschland nebst ergänzenden Aktenstücken 1585–1604*, Section 2 with 6 vols., ed. the Görres-Gesellschaft (Paderborn 1895–1919); Editions of the Görres-Gesellschaft in addition to the Series "Nuntiaturberichte aus Deutschland" are: 1539–40; 1573–76 (*Quellen und Forschungen aus dem Gebiete der Geschichte* I (1892), V (1898); Details of the nuncio reports from Germany: H. Lutz, "Nuntiaturberichte aus Deutschland. Vergangenheit und Zukunft einer 'klassischen," Editionsreihe: *QFIAB* 45 (1965) 321–324.

BOHEMIA: *Epistulae et Acta nuntiorum apostolicorum apud imperatorem 1592–1628 curis Instituti historici Bohemoslovenici* (Rome–Prague 1932–46), III, IV, 1–312.

SWITZERLAND: *Nuntiaturberichte aus der Schweiz,* Part I, 1579–81, 3 vols. (Solothurn 1906–29).

FRANCE: *Acta Nuntiaturae Gallicae,* ed. the Gregoriana and the Ecole Française in Rome, 1535–46 and 1583–86, 3 vols. (Rome–Paris 1961–63), particulars in ZKG 75 (1964) 347–354.

BELGIUM: *Analecta Vaticano Belgica.* 2d series, ed. the Belgian Historical Institute in Rome, 1–10: 1596–1642 (=Nuntiatur in Flanders) (Brussels-Paris 1924–55; Section B, 1: 1634–39 (=Nuntiatur in Cologne) (Brussels-Rome 1956); 3: 1606–74 (Brussels-Rome 1958).

ITALY: *Nunziature di Napoli,* ed. the Instituto storico italiano per l'età moderna e contemporanea, I: 1570–77, revised by P. Vallani (Rome 1962); Nunziature di Venezia, I: 1533–35 revised by F. Gaeta, (Rome 1958); 2: 1536–42 (Rome 1960); *Nunziature di Savoia,* I: 1560–73, revised by F. Fonzi (Rome 1960).

SPAIN: *Legaciones y nunciaturas en España* I: 1466–86, ed. the Instituto español de historia eclesiastica, revised by A. J. Fernandez (Monumenta Hispaniae vaticana, 2 Secc.: Nunciatura I) (Rome 1963).

POLAND: *Monumenta Poloniae Vaticana IV–VI,* Series Nuntiaturae Poloniae, I: 1578–81 (1915), II: 1581–82 (1923–33), III: 1583 (1938).

REFORMATION: V. E. Löscher, *Vollständige Reformations-Akta und Dokumente 1517–19* (Leipzig 1720–29); J. E. Kapp, *Kleine Nachlese einiger zur Reformationsgeschichte nützlicher Urkunden* (Leipzig 1727–33); Ch. G. Neudecker, *Urkunden der Reformationszeit* (Kassel 1836); *Neues Urkundenbuch zur Geschichte der evangelischen Kirchenreformation* I (Hamburg 1842); H. Laemmer, *Monumenta Vaticana historiam ecclesiasticam saeculi XVI illustrantia* (Freiburg 1861); O. Schade, *Satiren und Pasquille aus der Reformationszeit* 1–3 (Hanover ²1863); P. Balan, *Monumenta reformationis lutheranae* (Regensburg 1881–84); *Flugschriften aus der Reformationszeit,* 19 vols. (Halle 1877–1928); *Flugschriften aus den ersten Jahren der Reformation,* ed. O. Clemen, 4 vols. (Halle 1906–11); *Flugschriften aus der Reformationszeit in Facsimiledrucken,* ed. O. Clemen (Leipzig 1921); *Acta reformationis catholicae ecclesiam Germaniae concernentia saeculi XVI.* The negotiations of the German episcopate on reform from 1520–70, I: 1520–32, II: 1532–42, ed. G. Pfeilschifter (Regensburg 1959–60); *Schriften zur Kirchen- und Rechtsgeschichte,* ed. E. Fabian, to date 31 vols. (Tübingen 1956f.); B. J. Kidd (ed.), *Documents Illustrative of the Continental Reformation* (Oxford 1911).

4. OLD DOCUMENTS WITH LISTED SOURCES

S. Franck, *Chronica, Zeitbuch und Geschichtsbibell von anbegyn biss in diss gegenwertig iar verlangt* (Ulm 1536); J. Cochlaeus, *Commentaria de actis et scriptis Martini Lutheri* (Mainz 1549); J. Sleidanus, *De Statu religionis et reipublicae Carolo quinto Caesare Commentariorum libri XXVI* (Strassburg 1555); O. Reginaldus (Reynald) and J. Laderchi, *Caesaris Baronii Annales Ecclesiastici* 31–37: 1513–71 (Paris 1878–83); L. v. Seckendorf, *Commentarius historicus apologeticus de Lutheranismo sive de Reformatione religionis ductu D. Martini Lutheri . . .* (Frankfurt–Leipzig 1688); Ch. A. Salig, *Vollständige Historie der Augspurgischen Confession und derselben Apologie,* 3 vols. (Halle 1730–35); P. Sarpi, *Istoria del Concilio Tridentino* (London 1619). Critical edition by S. Sambaria, 3 vols. (Bari

1935); P. Sforza Pallavicino, *Istoria del Concilio di Trento,* 2 vols. (Rome 1656–57); best edition by F. A. Zaccaria, 5 vols. (Faenza 1792–96); *Texte zur Kirchen-und Theologiegeschichte,* ed. G. Ruhbach, II: The beginning of the reformation historical writings (Melanchthon, Sleidanus, Flacius, and the Magdeburg Centuries) (Gütersloh 1966); J. Sandar, *De Origine ac Progressu Schismatis Anglicani* (Cologne 1585); T. Stapleton, *Vita Thomae Morae in Tres Tomae* (Cologne 1612); S. Cattely, ed. *The Acts and Monuments of John Foxe,* 8 vols. (Oxford 1837–41).

5. THEOLOGY

H. Hurter, *Nomenclator literarius theologiae catholicae* II–III (Innsbruck 1906–7); Ch. Du Plessis d'Argentré, *Collectio judiciorum de novis erroribus,* 3 vols. (Paris 1724–36); *Spicilegium Sacrum Lovaniense. Etudes et documents pour servir à l'histoire des doctrines chrétiennes dupuis la fin de l'âge apostolique jusqu'à la clôture du concile de Trente:* Université Catholique et Collèges O. P. et S. J. de Louvain, Paris, 28 vols. (Louvain 1922ff.); *Corpus Reformatorum* (the works of Melancthon, Calvin, and Zwingli; to date 101 vols.) (Halle 1834ff.; Braunschweig 1853ff.; Berlin 1905; Leipzig 1908ff.; Zurich 1959ff.); *D. Martin Luthers Werke. Kritische Gesamtausgabe* ("Weimarer Ausgabe"), 58 vols. (Weimar 1883ff.); id., *Die Deutsche Bibel,* 12 vols. (Weimar 1906–61); id., *Tischreden,* 6 vols. (Weimar 1912–21); id., *Briefwechsel,* 12 vols. (Weimar 1930–67); *Luthers Werke in Auswahl,* ed. O. Clemen–E. Vogelsang–H. Rückert–E. Hirsch, 4 vols. (Berlin 1966) and 4 suppls. (Berlin 1959ff.); *Klassiker des Protestantismus,* ed. Ch. M. Schröder, I: *Wegbereiter der Reformation,* ed. G. A. Benrath (Bremen 1967), II: *Der Glaube der Reformatoren,* ed. F. Lau (Bremen 1964), III: *Reformatorische Verkündigung und Lebensordnung,* ed. R. Stupperich (Bremen 1963), IV: *Der Linke Flügel der Reformation,* ed. H. Fast (Bremen 1962); *Corpus Catholicorum, Werke Katholischer Schriftsteller im Zeitalter der Glaubensspaltung,* ed. J. Greving et al., to date 29 vols. (Münster 1919ff.).

6. COUNCILS, DOCTRINAL AND CANONICAL DECISIONS, CANON LAW

H. Quentin, *J. D. Mansi et les Grandes Collections Conciliaires* (Paris 1900); J. D. Mansi, *Sacrorum Conciliorum Nova et Amplissima Collectio,* 31 vols., to 1440 (Florence, then Venice 1759–98); n. ed. with additions 1902 by J. B. Martin–L. Petit, 60 vols. (Paris 1899–1927); J. Hardouin, *Acta Conciliorum et Epistolae Decretales ac Constitutiones Summorum Pontificum,* 12 vols. (Paris 1714–15); *Conciliorum Oecumenicorum Decreta,* ed. Centro di Documentazione Bologna (Freiburg i. Br. 1962); J. Le Plat, *Monumentorum ad Historiam Concilii Tridentini Potissimum Illustrandam Spectantium Amplissima Collectio,* 7 vols. (Louvain 1781–87); *Concilium Tridentinum, Diariorum, Actorum, Epistularum, Tractatuum Nova Collectio,* ed. the Görres-Gesellschaft, to date 13 vols. (Freiburg 1901ff.); J. Doellinger, *Ungedruckte Berichte und Tagebücher zur Geschichte des Concils von Trent,* Abt. I–II (Nördlingen 1876); J. Sirmond, *Concilia Antiqua Galliae,* 3 vols. (Paris 1926) with suppl. by P. Delande (Paris 1966); J. Sáenz de Aguirre, *Collectio Maxima Conciliorum Omnium Hispania et Novi Orbis,* 4 vols. (Rome 1693); 2nd ed. by J. Catalanus, 6 vols. (Rome 1753–55); D. Wilkins, *Concilia Magnae Britanniae et Hiberniae,* 4 vols. (London 1737); J. Hartzheim, *Concilia Germaniae,* 11 vols. (Cologne 1759–90); H. Denzinger–A. Schönmetzer. *Enchiridion Symbolorum, Definitionum et Declarationum de Rebus Fidei et Morum* (Barcelona–Freiburg 1965); *Corpus Confessionum, Die Bekenntnisschriften der Christenheit, Sammlung Grundlegender Urkunden aus Allen Kirchen der Gegenwart,* ed. C. Fabricius (Berlin 1931ff.); *Quellen zur Konfessionskunde:*

Reihe A. Römisch-katholische Quellen, I, ed. D. Schmidt–W. Sucker (Lüneburg 1954–57). *Reihe B. Protestantische Quellen,* ed. K. Kinder et al., Heft I–VII (Lüneburg 1957–61); *Die Bekenntnisschriften der Evangelisch-Lutherischen Kirche,* ed. the Deutsche Evangelische Kirchenausschuss (Göttingen ⁵1963); *Die Bekenntnisschriften der Reformierten Kirche,* ed. E. F. K. Müller (Leipzig 1903); *Bekenntnisschriften und Kirchenordnungen der Nach Gottes Wort Reformierten Kirche,* ed. W. Niesel (Zurich 1948); *Reformierte Bekenntnisschriften und Kirchenordnungen in Deutscher Übersetzung,* ed. P. Jacobs (Neukirchen 1949); W. Gussmann, *Quellen und Forschungen zur Geschichte des Augsburgischen Bekenntnisses,* 2 vols. (Leipzig 1911, Kassel 1930); *Corpus Juris Canonici,* the best edition of *Editio Romana Iussu Gregorii XIII* (Rome 1582); E. Friedberg, 2 vols. (Leipzig 1879–91); *Codis Juris Canonici Fontes,* ed. Petrus Card. Gasparri, since VII by Justinianus Card. Serédi, I–VIII and IX: Tabellae (Rome 1923–39); A. U. Richter, *Die Evangelischen Kirchenordnungen des 16. Jahrhunderts (1846); E. Sehling, Die Evangelischen Kirchenordnungen des 16. Jahrhunderts.* I–V (Leipzig 1902–13); VIff. (Tübingen 1955ff.); *Bullarium Romanum, Editio Taurinensis* by A. Tomassetti, 24 vols. (Turin 1857–72); C. Mirbt, *Quellen zur Geschichte des Papsttums und des Römischen Katholizismus* (Tübingen 1934); 6th ed., ed. K. Aland, I (Tübingen 1967); A. Mercati, *Raccolta dei Concordati su Materie Ecclesiastiche tra la S. Sede e le Autorità Civili* (1908–54), 2 vols. (Rome 1954).

7. CHURCH HIERARCHY

A. Ciaconius, *Vitae et Res Gestae Pontificum Romanorum et S. R. E. Cardinalium* III (Rome 1677); P. B. Gams, *Series Episcoporum Ecclesiae Catholicae* (Regensburg 1873; suppl. 1879–86 Graz 1957); C. Eubel, *Hierarchia Catholica Medii et Recentioris Aevi* II: 1431–1503, III: 1503–92, IV: 1592–1667 (Münster 1914–35).

8. HAGIOGRAPHY

Acta Sanctorum, ed. J. Bolland˙ and his followers (Antwerp–Brussels–Tongerloo–Paris 1643ff., Venice 1734ff., Paris 1863ff.); H. Quentin–H. Delehaye (eds.), *Martyrologium Hieronymianum* = Acta SS Nov. II, 2 (Brussels 1931); H. Delehaye et al. (eds.), *Martyrologium Romanum, Propylaeum ad Acta SS Decembris* (Brussels 1940).

9. ORDERS

H. Urs v. Balthasar (ed.), *Die Grossen Ordensregeln* (Einsiedeln ²1961); L. Holstenius–M. Brockie (eds.), *Codex Regularum Monasticarum et Canonicarum,* 6 vols. (Augsburg 1759); A. M. Zimmermann, *Kalendarium Benedictinum,* 4 vols. (Vienna 1933–38); J. M. Canivez (ed.), *Statuta Capitulorum Generalium Ordinis Cisterciensis 1116–1786,* 9 vols. (Louvain 1933); N. Backmund, *Monasticon Praemonstratense,* 3 vols. (Straubing 1949ff.); J. Le Paige, *Bibliotheca Ordinis Praemonstratensis* (Paris 1633); *Bullarium Franciscanum* I–IV (Rome 1759–68), V–VII (Rome 1898–1904), VIII (Quaracchi 1929), IX–X (ibid. 1939–49). Suppl. I (Rome 1780); suppl. II (Quaracchi 1908); *Acta Ordinis Fratrum Minorum,* I–V (Rome 1882–86), VIff. (Quaracchi 1887ff.); L. Wadding, *Annales Ordinis Minorum,* 30 vols. (Quaracchi 1931ff.); id., *Scriptores Ordinis Minorum* (Rome³ 1906); suppl., 4 vols. (Rome 1906–36); *Bullarium Ordinis Fratrum Praedicatorum,* 8 vols. (Rome 1729–49); *Epitome Bull. OP* (Rome 1898); *Monumenta OP Historica,* 14 vols. (Rome 1896–1904); cont'd (Paris 1931ff.); J. F. Ossinger, *Bibliotheca Augustiniana historica* (Ingolstadt–Augsburg 1768); J. Lanteri, *Eremi Sacrae Augustinianae,* 2 pts. (Rome 1874–75); id., *Postrema Saecula Sex Religonis Augustinanae* I–II (Tolentino

1858–59), III (Rome 1860); N. Crusenius, *Pars Tertia Monastici Augustiniani* I (Valladolid 1890); *Acta Ordinis Eremitarum Sancti Augustini* (Rome 1956ff.); Daniel a V. Maria, *Speculum Carm.*, 2 vols. (Antwerp 1680); E. Monsignani, *Bullarium Carm.*, 4 vols. (Rome 1715–68); B. Zimmermann, *Monumenta Hist. Carm.* I (Sérius 1905–07); G. Wessels, *Acta Capit. General.*, 2 vols. (Rome 1914–34); C. de Villiers, *Bibliotheca Carm.*, 2 vols. (Rome 1927); *Annales Ordinis Servorum Mariae*, 3 vols. (Lucca 1719); *Monumenta Ordinis Servorum Mariae* (Brussels–Rome 1917ff.; to date 20 vols.); *Bibliotheca Scriptorum Ordinis Minorum S. Francisci Capuccinorum* (Venice 1747); Appendix 1747–1852 (Rome 1852); *Bullarium OFM Cap.* I–VII (Rome 1740–52), VIII–X (Innsbruck 1883–84); *Monumenta Historica OFM Cap.*, 8 vols. (Assisi–Rome 1937); *Monumenta ad Constitutiones OFM Cap.* (Rome 1916); *Constitutiones OFM Cap.* (Rome 1926); *Ordinationes Capitulorum Gen. OFM Cap.* (Rome 1928); *Monumenta Historica Societatis Jesu*, to date 70 vols. (Madrid 1894ff., Rome 1932ff.); C. Sommervogel, *Bibliothèque de la Compagnie de Jésus*, 9 vols. (Brussels–Paris 1890–1900); X-suppl. by E. M. Rivière (Toulouse 1911).

10. Missions

Bullarium Patronatus Portugalliae Regum in Ecclesiis Africae, Asiae et Oceaniae . . . , ed. L. M. Jardão et al. 1–3 (Lisbon 1868–79) (=Bull. Patr.); *Collección de Documentos Inéditos Relativos al Descubrimiento, Conquista y Colonización de las Posesiones Españolas en América y Oceania*, 42 vols. (Madrid 1864–84); 2nd Series, 13 vols. (Madrid 1885ff.); P. Hernáez, ed., *Colección de Bulas, Breves, y Otros Documentos Relativos a la Iglesia de America y Filipinas* (Brussels 1879); *Cuerpo de Documentos del Siglo XVI Sobre los Derechos de España en las Indias y las Filipinas*, ed. L. Hanke-Millares Carlo (Mexico 1943); R. Ricard, *Études et Documents pour l'Histoire de l'Espagne et du Portugal* (Louvain 1931); *Bullarium Pontificii de Propaganda Fide Pars Prima*, ed. R. de Martinis, I (Rome 1888). *Collectanea S. C. de Propaganda Fide* I (Rome 1907).

II. NARRATIVE ACCOUNTS

1. General

Historia Mundi, ed. F. Valjavek, 10 vols. (Bern 1952–61), VIII: *Übergang zur Moderne* (1957); *Handbuch der Weltgeschichte*, ed. A. Randa, 2 vols. (Olten–Freiburg 1954–55); *Propyläen-Weltgeschichte*, ed. G. Mann–A. Heuss, 12 vols. (Berlin 1961ff.), VIII: *Von der Reformation zur Revolution* (1964); *Histoire Générale des Religions*, ed. R. Goree–R. Mortier, 5 vols. (Paris 1948–51), IV: *Christianisme Medieval–Réforme Protestante;* J. Pirenne, *Les Grands Courants de l'Histoire Universelle*, 6 vols. (Neuchatel 1939), revised (1944–58); *The New Cambridge Modern History*, ed. G. R. Elton, I–II: *The Reformation (1493–1559)* (Cambridge 1957–58); A. Ballesteros y Beretta, *Historia de España*, 9 vols. (Barcelona 1920–36), I–III in 2, revised (Barcelona 1943–48), IV on Hapsburg Spain (Barcelona 1926–27); J. Janssen, *History of the German People at the Close of the Middle Ages*, 8 vols. (London 1896–1925); O. Brandt–A. O. Meyer, *Handbuch der Deutschen Geschichte* II (Potsdam 1935–41), newly edited by L. Just, II (Constance 1953), incomplete; B. Gebhardt–H. Grundmann, *Handbuch der Deutschen Geschichte* II: *Von der Reformation bis zum Ende des Absolutismus* (Stuttgart 1955); H. Holborn, *A History of Modern Germany* I: *The Reformation* (New York 1959).

2. Handbooks of Church History

K. Müller, *Kirchengeschichte* II, 1–2 (Tübingen ³1923); K. Bihlmeyer-H. Tüchle, *Church History* III (Westminster, Md., 1966); G. Krüger, *Handbuch der Kirchengeschichte für Studierende* III: H. Hermelink–W. Maurer, *Reformation und Gegenreformation* (Tübingen 1931); K. Heussi, *Kompendium der Kirchengeschichte,* (Tübingen 1960); A. Fliche–V. Martin, *Histoire de l'Église* 17: L. Christiani, *L'Église à l'Époque du Concile de Trente* (Paris 1948); 18: *Après le Concile de Trente. La Restauration Catholique (1563– 1648)* (Paris 1960); R. G. Villoslada–B. Llorca, *Historia de la Iglesia Católica* III: *La Iglesia en la Época del Renacimiento y de la Reforma Católica* (Madrid 1961); K. D. Schmidt-E. Wolf, *Die Kirche in ihrer Geschichte* III, K: F. Lau-E. Bizer, *Reformationsgeschichte Deutschlands bis 1555* (Göttingen 1964); L. J. Rogier et al., *The Christian Centuries* III: H. Tüchle, *Reformation und Gegenreformation* (Einsiedeln 1965).

3. Accounts from the Middle Ages to the Reformation

J. Haller, *Papsttum und Kirchenreform. 4 Kapitel zur Geschichte des Ausgehenden Mittelalters* (Berlin 1903); R. Stadelmann, *Vom Geist des Ausgehenden Mittelalters* (Halle–Saale 1929); W. E. Peukert, *Die Grosse Wende. Das Apokalyptische Saeculum und Luther* (Hamburg 1948; new impression, Darmstadt 1966); J. Huizinga, *The Waning of the Middle Ages* (New York 1937); *The Cambridge Medieval History.* vol. VIII, *The Close of the Middle Ages,* ed. by C. W. Previté-Orton–Z. N. Brooke (Cambridge 1936); W. K. Ferguson, *Europe in Transition 1300–1520* (Boston 1962); S. H. Thompson, *Europe in Renaissance and Reformation* (New York 1963); G. Leff, *Heresy in the Later Middle Ages,* 2 vols. (Manchester 1966); W. Andreas, *Deutschland vor der Reformation. Eine Zeitwende* (Stuttgart–Berlin⁶ 1959); L. Spitz, *The Renaissance and Reformation Movements* (Chicago 1971); A. G. Dickens, *The Age of Humanism and Reformation* (Englewood Cliffs, N. J., 1972).

4. Accounts of the Reformation and of the Counter Reformation

L. von Ranke, *Deutsche Geschichte im Zeitalter der Reformation* (Berlin 1839–47). Akadamie-Ausgabe, ed. P. Joachimsen, 6 vols. (Munich 1925–26); I. Doellinger, *Die Reformation, ihre innere Entwicklung und ihre Wirkung im Umfange des Lutherischen Bekenntnisses,* 3 vols. (Regensburg 1848); W. Maurenbrecher, *Geschichte der Katholischen Reformation* I (Nördlingen 1880); G. Egelhaff, *Deutsche Geschichte im 16. Jahrhundert bis zum Augsburger Religionsfrieden,* 2 vols. (Stuttgart 1889–92); Friedrich von Bezold, *Geschichte der Deutschen Reformation* (Berlin 1890); M. Ritter, *Deutsche Geschichte im Zeitalter der Gegenreformation und des Dreissigjährigen Krieges,* 3 vols. (Stuttgart 1889–1907); P. Imbert de la Tour, *Les Origines de la Réforme,* 3 vols. (Paris 1905–14), vol. I was reprinted in 1944; J. Menyz, *Deutsche Geschichte im Zeitalter der Reformation, Gegenreformation, und des 30jährigen Krieges* (Tübingen 1913); E. Fueter, *Geschichte des Europäischen Staatensystems von 1492–1559* (Munich–Berlin 1919); G. Schnürer, *Katholische Kirche und Kultur in der Barockzeit* (Paderborn 1937); L. E. Binns, *The Reformation in England* (Hamden ²1966); J. Lortz, *The Reformation in Germany,* 2 vols. (New York 1968); T. W. Windsay, *A History of the Reformation,* 2 vols. (Edinburgh 1948); T. Janelle, *The Catholic Reformation* (Milwaukee, Wis., 1949); K. Eder, *Die Geschichte der Kirche im Zeitalter des Konfessionellen Absolutismus (1555 bis 1648)* (Freiburg–Vienna 1949); G. Ritter, *Die Neugesaltung Europas im 16. Jahrhundert. Die Kirchliche und Staatliche Wandlung im Zeitalter der Reformation und der Glaubenskämpfe*

(Berlin 1950); A. Hymna, *From Renaissance to Reformation* (Grand Rapids, Mich., 1951); P. Joachimsen, *Die Reformation als Epoche der Deutschen Geschichte,* ed. Otto Schottenloher (Munich 1951); R. H. Bainton, *The Reformation of the Sixteenth Century* (Boston 1952); F. H. K. Green, *Renaissance and Reformation* (London 1952); M. Benediscioli, *La Riforma Protestante* (Rome 1952); id., *La Riforma Cattolica* (Rome 1958); H. J. Grimm, *The Reformation Era (1500–1650)* (New York 1973; extensive literature); E. H. Harbison, *The Age of Reformation* (New York 1955); H. Rössler, *Europa im Zeitalter von Renaissance, Reformation, und Gegenreformation (1450–1650)* (Munich 1956); K. Brandi, *Deutsche Geschichte im Zeitalter der Reformation und Gegenreformation* (Munich³ 1960); E. G. Léonard, *Histoire Générale du Protestantisme,* 2 vols. (Paris 1961), vol. I in English translation, *The Reformation* (London 1965); H. E. van Gelder, *The Two Reformations in the 16th Century* (The Hague 1961); W. Durant, *The Reformation* (New York 1957); R. Rousse–S. C. Neill, *History of the Ecumenical Movement* (London 1954); G. R. Elton, *Reformation Europe 1517–59* (London 1963); H. Lutz, *Christianitas Afflicta. Europa, das Reich und die Päpstliche Politik im Niedergang der Hegemonie Kaiser Karls V* (Göttingen 1964); E. Hassinger, *Das Werden des Neuzeitlichen Europa, 1300–1600* (Braunschweig 1964); A. G. Dickens, *Reformation and Society in Sixteenth Century Europe* (London 1966); O. Chadwick, *The Reformation* (Grand Rapids, Mich., 1965); H. Koenigsberger–G. Mosse, *Europe in the Sixteenth Century* (New York 1968); G. Swanson, *Religion and Regime: A Sociological Account of the Reformation* (Ann Arbor, Mich., 1967); J. P. Dolan, *History of the Reformation. A Conciliatory Assessment of Opposite Views* (New York 1965); F. Braudel, *The Mediterranean and the Mediterranean World in the Age of Philip II,* 2 vols. (New York 1972).

5. Papal and Conciliar History

L. von Ranke, *History of the Popes,* 3 vols. (London 1873); L. von Pastor, *History of the Popes from the Close of the Middle Ages,* 40 vols. (London 1891), esp. vols. VIII to XXX; F. X. Seppelt, *Geschichte der Päpste* IV–V, revised by G. Schwaiger (Munich 1957–59); C. J. Hefele–H. Leclercq, *Histoire des Conciles* VIII: *1472–1536* (Paris 1917–21); IX: *Concile de Trente* (Paris 1930–31); X: *Les Décrets du Concile de Trente* (Paris 1938); H. Jedin, *Ecumenical Councils of the Catholic Church,* (St. Louis 1960); id., *A History of the Council of Trent* I: *Council and Reform from the Council of Basle to the Lateran Council;* II: *The First Sessions at Trent 1545–47* (Freiburg 1951); id., *Das Konzil von Trient. Ein Überblick über die Erforschung seiner Geschichte* (Rome 1948); K. Repgen, *Die Römische Kurie und der Westfälische Friede. Idee und Wirklichkeit des Papsttums im 16. und 17. Jahrhundert* I: *Papst, Kaiser, und Reich 1521–1644,* 2 parts (Tübingen 1962, 1965).

6. Legal and Constitutional History

G. Phillips, *Kirchenrecht,* 7 vols. (Regensburg 1845–72); VIII by F. Vering (ibid. 1889); F. v. Schulte, *Geschichte der Quellen und Literatur des Canonischen Rechts* (Stuttgart 1877–80; new impression, Graz 1956); P. Hinschius, *System des katholischen Kirchenrechts* I–VI (Berlin 1869–97; new impression, Graz 1959); R. Sohm, *Kirchenrecht,* 2 vols. (Leipzig 1892–1923); J. B. Sägmüller, *Lehrbuch des kath. Kirchenrechts,* 2 vols. (Freiburg i. Br. 1914); J. Freisen, *Verfassungsgeschichte der katholischen Kirche Deutschlands in der Neuzeit* (Leipzig–Berlin 1917); G. Holstein, *Die Grundlagen des evangelischen Kirchenrechts* (Tübingen 1928); E. Sehling, *Geschichte der protestantischen Kirchenverfassung* (Leipzig–Berlin 1930); B. Kurtscheid, *Historia iuris canonici,* 2 vols. (Rome 1941–43); F. Hartung, *Deutsche Verfassungsgeschichte vom 15. Jahrhundert bis zur Gegenwart* (Stuttgart 1959); H. E. Feine, *Kirchliche Rechtsgeschichte. Die katholische Kirche*

(Cologne–Graz 1964; Lit.); E. Wolf, *Ordnung der Kirche. Lehr- und Handbuch des Kirchenrechts auf ökumenischer Grundlage* (Frankfurt 1961); H. Dombois, *Das Recht der Gnade. Ökumenisches Kirchenrecht* I (Witten 1961); W. Plöchl, *Geschichte des Kirchenrechts* III: *Das katholische Kirchenrecht der Neuzeit* (Vienna 1959).

7. Religious Orders

P. Hélyot, *Histoire des ordres monastiques, religieux et militaires,* 8 vols. (Paris 1714–19); M. Heimbucher, *Die Orden und Kongregationen der kath. Kirche,* 3 vols. (Paderborn 1933–34); G. G. Coulton, *Five Centuries of Religion,* 4 vols. (Cambridge 1923–50) (from the eleventh cent. on); M. Escobar, *Ordini e Congregazioni religiose,* 2 vols. (Turin 1951–53); D. Pflanzer (ed.), *Orden der Kirche,* to date 4 vols. (Fribourg 1955ff.); J. Hasenberg-A. Wienand, *Das Wirken der Orden und Klöster in Deutschland* (Cologne 1957); Ph. Schmitz, *Histoire de l'ordre de Saint Benôit,* 6 vols. (Maredeous I–II; III–VI 1948–49); dt.: *Geschichte des Benediktinerordens,* 5 vols. (Einsiedeln 1947ff.); St. Hilpisch, *Geschichte des benediktinischen Mönchtums* (Freiburg 1929); id., *Geschichte der Benediktinerinnen* (St. Ottilien 1951); E. Martène, *Histoire de la Congrégation de St-Maure,* 9 vols. (Ligugé–Paris 1928–43); B. Grassl, *Die Prämonstratenserorden* (Tongerloo 1934); L. Lekai–A. Schneider, *Geschichte und Wirken der weissen Mönche* (Cologne 1958); A. M. Rossi, *Manuale di Storia dell'Ordine dei Servi di Maria* (Rome 1956); H. Holzapfel, *Handbuch der Geschichte des Franziskanerordens* (Freiburg 1909); Th. Ferrée, *Histoire de l'ordre de S. François* (Reims 1921); Lázaro de Aspurz, *Manual de historia franciscana* (Madrid 1954); A. Mortier, *Histoire des maîtres généraux do l'ordre des frères prêcheurs* (Paris 1903ff.); A. Walz, *Compendium historiae ordinis Praedicatorum* (Rome² 1948); D. A. Perini, *Bibliographia Augustiniana,* 4 vols. (Florence 1929–35); P. Cuthbert–J. Wildlöcher, *Die Kapuziner* (Munich 1931); Bernardinus a Colpetrazzo, *Historia ordinis fratrum minorum Capuccinorum 1525–93,* 3 vols. (Rome 1939–41); Melchior a Pobladura, *Historia generalis ordinis fratrum minorum Capuccinorum,* 2 vols. (Rome 1947–48); Th. Graf, *Zur Entstehung des Kapuzinerordens* (Olten 1940); id., *Die Kapuziner* (Fribourg 1957); B. Duhr, *Geschichte der Jesuiten in den Ländern deutscher Zunge,* 4 vols. (Freiburg 1907–28); T. Sévérin, *L'épopée des Jesuits* (Liege ²1946); P. Tacchi Venturi, *Storia della Compagnia di Gesù in Italia* (Rome 1950); R. G. Villoslada, *Manual de Historia de la Compagnia de Jesús* (Madrid 1954); H. Becher, *Die Jesuiten* (Munich 1961); O. Kapsner, *Catholic Religious Orders* (Collegeville, Minn., 1948); P. Kunkel, *The Theatines in the History of the Catholic Reform Before the Establishment of Lutheranism* (Wash., D. C. 1941); C. Hess, *The Capuchins* (New York 1929); Sr. M. Monica, *Angela Merici and Her Teaching Idea,* (London 1927); M. Jounandeau, *St. Philip Neri* (New York 1961); J. de Guibert, *The Jesuits: Their Spiritual Doctrine and Practice* (Chicago 1964); R. Huber, *A Documented History of the Franciscan Order, 1182–1517* (Wash., D. C. 1941); L. Lekai, *The Cistercians* (Kent State, Ohio 1977); W. Hinnebusch, *The History of the Dominicans* I (New York 1966).

8. History of Education, Universities, Schools, Culture

E. Paulsen, *Geschichte des gelehrten Unterrichts an den deutschen Schulen und Universitäten vom Ausgang des Mittelalters bis zur Gegenwart,* 2 vols. (Leipzig 1919–21); J. van den Driesch–J. Esterhues, *Geschichte der Erziehung und Bildung,* 2 vols. (Paderborn 1956–57); A. C. Crombie, *Augustine to Galileo. The History of Science 400–1560* (London 1957); St. de Irsay, *Histoire des universités françaises et étrangères des origines à nos jours,* 2 vols. (Paris 1933–35); P. Féret, *La faculté de théologie de Paris et ses docteurs les plus célèbres, Époque moderne,* 7 vols. (Paris 1890–1909); Th. Muther, *Aus dem Universitäts-und*

Gelehrtenleben im Zeitalter der Reformation (Erlangen 1866); G. Kaufmann, *Zwei katholische und zwei protestantische Universitäten vom 16–18. Jahrhundert* (Ingolstadt–Wittenberg–Helmstedt–Freiburg i. Br.) (Munich 1920); H. Rückert, *Die Stellung der Reformation zur mittelalterlichen Universität* (Die Universität, Stuttgart 1933); L. Petry, "Die Reformation als Epoche der deutschen Universitätsgeschichte. Eine Zwischenbilanz" *Festgabe J. Lortz*, ed., E. Iserloh–P. Manns (Wiesbaden 1958), II: *Glaube und Geschichte,* 317–353; E. Bonjour, *Die Universität Basel. Von den Anfängen bis zur Gegenwart 1460–1960* (Basel 1960); M. Curtis, *Oxford and Cambridge in Transition, 1558–1642* (Oxford 1959); H. Porter, *Reformation and Reaction in Tudor Cambridge* (New York 1959); H. Barycz, *Historja Uniwersytetu Jagiellonskiego w epoce Humanizmu* (Cracow, 1935); N. Wood, *The Reformation and English Education* (London 1931). For art history of the period: *The Pelican History of Art:* A. Blunt, *France, 1500–1700* (London 1953); H. K. Gerson–E. H. Kuile, *Belgium, 1600–1800* (London 1960); E. Hempel, *Central Europe, 1600–1800* (London 1965); G. Kubler–M. Soria, *Spain and Portugal, 1500–1800* (London 1959); J. Rosenberg, *Dutch Art and Architecture, 1600–1800* (London 1966); J. H. Summerson, *Britain, 1530–1830* (London 1953); R. Wittkower, *Italy, 1600–1750* (London 1958). On Music: *The New Oxford History of Music: Ars Nova and the Renaissance, 1300–1540,* III; *The Age of Humanism, 1540–1630,* IV (Oxford 1954–1968). H. Rashdall, *The Universities of Europe in the Middle Ages,* (n.ed. in 3 vols. by F. Powicke–A. Emben) (Oxford 1958).

9. The History of Dogma and Theology

L. Maimbourg, *Histoire du Lutheranisme,* 2 vols. (Paris 1680); G. J. Planck, *Geschichte der Entstehung, der Veränderungen und der Bildung unseres protestantischen Lehrbegriffs vom Anfang der Reformation bis zur Einführung der Concordienformel,* 6 vols. (Leipzig 1791–1800); id., *Geschichte der protestantischen Theologie von der Konkordienformel an bis in die Mitte des 18. Jahrhunderts* (Göttingen 1831); J. A. Möhler, *Symbolik oder Darstellung der dogmatischen Gegensätze der Katholiken und Protestanten nach ihren öffentlichen Bekenntnisschriften* (Mainz 1832), critical edition by J. R. Geiselmann, 2 vols. (Cologne 1958–61); H. Laemmer, *Die vortridentinische-katholische Theologie des Reformations-Zeitalters* (Berlin 1858; new impression, Frankfurt a. M. 1966); K. Werner, *Geschichte der apologetischen und polemischen Literatur der christlichen Theologie,* 5 vols. (Schaffhausen 1861–67); id., *Geschichte der kath. Theologie seit dem Trienter Concil bis zur Gegenwart* (Munich–Leipzig 1889; new impression, Hildesheim 1965); J. A. Dorner, *Geschichte der protestantischen Theologie, besonders in Deutschland* (Munich 1867; new impression, Hildesheim 1965); O. Ritschl, *Dogmengeschichte des Protestantismus,* 4 vols. (Göttingen 1908–27); A. v. Harnack, *Lehrbuch der Dogmengeschichte,* 3 vols. ([1885–89] Tübingen 1931–32); F. Loofs, *Leitfaden zum Studium der Dogmengeschichte* ([1889] Tübingen 1959); R. Seeberg, *Textbook of the History of Doctrines,* 2 vols. (Philadelphia 1905); P. Wernle, *Der evangelische Glaube nach den Hauptschriften der Reformatoren,* 3 vols. (Luther, Zwingli, Calvin) (Tübingen 1918–19); E. Troeltsch, *The Social Teaching of the Christian Churches,* 2 vols. (New York 1949); W. Elert, *Morphologie des Luthertums* I: *Theologie und Weltanschauung des Luthertums hauptsächlich im 16. und 17. Jahrhundert,* II: *Soziallehren und Sozialwirkungen des Luthertums* (München [1931], 1952–53). English trans. of Vol. 1: *The Structure of Lutheranism: The Theology and Philosophy of Life of Lutheranism,* (St. Louis 1962); M. Grabmann, *Die Geschichte der katholischen Theologie seit dem Ausgang der Väterzeit* (Freiburg 1933); H. E. Weber, *Reformation, Orthodoxie und Rationalismus,* 2 vols. in 3 parts (Gütersloh 1937–40–51; new impression, Darmstadt 1966); C. Giacon, *La seconda scolastica,* 3 vols. (Milan 1946–50); W. Koehler, *Dogmengeschichte. Von den Anfängen bis zur Reformation* (Zurich 1951); id., *Dogmengeschichte. Das Zeital-*

ter der Reformation (Zurich 1951); E. Hirsch, *Geschichte der neueren evangelischen Theologie im Zusammenhang mit den allg. Bewegungen des europ. Denkens,* 5 vols. (Gütersloh 1964); M. Werner, *Der protestantische Weg des Glaubens,* 2 vols. (Bern 1955–62); M. Schmaus–J. R. Geiselmann–A. Grillmeier, *Handbuch der Dogmengeschichte* (Freiburg 1951ff.); P. Jacobs, *Theologie reformierter Bekenntnisschriften in Grundzügen* (Neukirchen 1959); H. A. Oberman, *The Harvest of Medieval Theology* (Cambridge, Mass., 1963); F. Stegmüller, *Geschichte des Molinismus* I (Munich 1935).

10. HAGIOGRAPHY AND ICONOGRAPHY

R. Aigrain, *L'Hagiographie. Ses sources, ses méthodes, son histoire* (Paris 1953); P. Peeters, *L'oeuvre des Bollandistes* (Brüssel 1961); F. Doye, *Heilige und Selige der römisch-katholischen Kirche. Deren Erkennungszeichen, Patronate und lebensgeschichtliche Bemerkungen,* 2 vols. (Leipzig 1929); J. Baudot et Chaussin, *Vies des Saints et des Bienheureux selon l'ordre du calendrier avec l'historique des fêtes,* 13 vols. (Paris 1935–59); J. Torsy, *Lexikon der deutschen Heiligen* (Köln 1959); P. Manns (ed.), *Die Heiligen in ihrer Zeit* (Mainz 1967); *Bibliotheca Sanctorum,* ed. Istituto Giovanni XXIII, to date 8 vols. (A-Mar) (Rome 1961–67); K. Künstle, *Iconographie der christlichen Kunst,* 2 vols. (Freiburg 1926–28); J. Braun, *Tracht und Attribute der Heiligen in der deutschen Kunst* (Stuttgart 1943); L. Réau, *Iconographie de l'art chrétien,* 3 vols. (Paris 1955–58).

11. LITURGY

Liturgisch Woordenboek, ed. L. Brinkhoff et al., 2 vols. (Roermond 1962ff.); L. Eisenhofer, *Handbuch der katholischen Liturgie,* 2 vols. (Freiburg i. Br.² 1941); J. A. Jungmann, *The Mass of the Roman Rite, History of the Liturgy,* Vol. I trans. F. A. Brunner (New York 1951); M. Righetti, *Manuale di storia liturgica,* 4 vols. (Milan: I, 1950; II, 1955; III, 1964; IV, 1955); A. G. Martimort, *Handbuch der Liturgiewissenschaft* I (Freiburg 1963); Th. Klauser, *Kleine abendländische Liturgiegeschichte. Bericht u. Besinnung* (Bonn 1965); *Leiturgia, Handbuch des evangelischen Gottesdienstes,* ed. K. F. Müller–W. Blankenburg, 4 vols. (Kassel 1954–61); P. Graff, *Geschichte der Auflösung der alten gottesdienstlichen Formen in der evangelischen Kirche Deutschlands,* 2 vols. (Göttingen 1937–39); Ph. Wackernagel. *Das dt. Kirchenlied von der ältesten Zeit bis zu Anfang des 17. Jahrhunderts,* 5 vols. (Leipzig 1864–77); W. Bäumker, *Das katholische deutsche Kirchenlied in seinen Singweisen von den frühesten Zeiten bis gegen Ende des 17. Jahrhunderts,* 4 vols. (Freiburg 1883–1911).

12. MISSIONS

J. Schmidlin, *Katholische Missionsgeschichte* (Steyl o. J. [1925]); *Histoire universelle des missions catholiques* I–II, ed. S. Delacroix (Paris 1956–57); K. S. Latourette, *A History of the Expansion of Christianity* III (New York–London 1939); A. Mulders, *Missionsgeschichte. Die Ausbreitung des katholischen Glaubens* (Regensburg 1960); A. Jann, *Die Katholischen Missionen in Indien, China und Japan. Ihre Organisation und das portugisische Patronat vom 15. bis 18. Jahrhundert* (Paderborn 1915); R. Aubenas–R. Ricard, *L'Église et la renaissance:* Fliche-Jarry XV (Paris 1951).

BIBLIOGRAPHY TO INDIVIDUAL CHAPTERS
Part One
The Protestant Reformation

SECTION ONE

Martin Luther and the Coming of the Reformation
(1517–25)

1. Causes of the Reformation

LITERATURE

G. v. Below, *Die Ursachen der Reformation* (Munich 1917); J. Haller, *Die Ursachen der Reformation* (Tübingen 1917); J. Hashagen, *Staat und Kirche vor der Reformation* (Essen 1931); W. Andreas, *Deutschland vor der Reformation* (Stuttgart 1932, 1948); J. Lortz, *Die Reformation als religiöses Anliegen heute* (Trier 1948); id., *Wie kam es zur Reformation?* (Einsiedeln 1955); id., *Zur Problematik der kirchlichen Missstände im Spätmittelalter* (Trier 1950: SD from *TThZ* 58, 1949); H. Rückert, "Die geistesgeschichtliche Einordnung der Reformation" *ZThK* 52 (1955) 43–64; R. Post, *Kerkelijke verhoudingen voor de Reformatie* (Utrecht 1955); L. Spitz, *The Reformation: Material or Spiritual* (Boston 1962) selections of recent interpretations; H. J. Grimm, "Social Forces in the German Reformation" *CH* XXXI (1962) 3–13; H. A. Oberman, *Forerunners of the Reformation* (New York 1966).

2. Martin Luther: The Early Years

SOURCES

The first edition of Luther's collected works appeared during his own lifetime at the insistence of the Saxon Elector Johann Friedrich and his friends. This Wittenberg edition appeared in German in fifteen volumes between 1539 and 1559 and a Latin edition in seven volumes appeared between 1545 and 1557. The Jena edition, more complete and reliable, appeared between 1555 and 1558, eight volumes in German and four in

Latin. J. Aurifaber edited a "Comprehensive Eisleben" addition to the Jena volumes in 1564–1565. Meanwhile, the ten-volume Altenburg edition with a better chronological order and an index appeared. This was enlarged in 1702 by J. G. Zeidler in his Halle Supplement. The Altenburg, Eisleben, and Halle volumes formed the basis for the twenty-two-volume Leipzig edition which appeared between 1728 and 1734. Johann Georg Walch published the twenty-four-volume Halle edition between 1740 and 1753 which included introductory material as well as other reformatory writings including those of the opponents of Luther. The Latin works were translated into German. In 1826 Johann Georg Plochmann and Johann Konrad Irmischer began the Erlangen edition. The German section contains some sixty-seven volumes of which volumes 1–20 and 24–26 were revised by E. L. Enders (1862–85). The Latin section remained incomplete with thirty-eight volumes. To this was added the correspondence in nineteen volumes (Frankfurt, 1884–1932) edited by E. L. Enders, G. Kawerau, and P. Fleming. Due to the great advances made in Luther studies, the Erlangen edition was outdated before its completion. Hence J. F. K. Knaake during the jubilee year of 1883 began the new critical Weimar edition (*Martin Luthers Werke, Kritische Ausgabe*). After completing the first two volumes himself he was forced to call upon the assistance of collaborators among philologists and theologians. The project consists of the chief writings, sermons, lectures, and disputations arranged in chronological order with critical footnotes. By 1921 the *Table Talk* was finished in six volumes; the Works fill an entire sixty-nine volumes; the Letters comprise eleven volumes and the German Bible ranges over twelve volumes. The first part of volume 58, released in 1948, is an index of previous volumes. The first, Lectures on the Psalms (1513–15) WA 3 and 4, was revised and other volumes have been photographically reproduced; vol. 32 in 1963; 33 in 1961; vol. 40, 1st and 2nd sections, in 1962. The new editions do not contain the emendations, supplements, citations, and indices, rather they are found in additional revisions published separately. The Berlin student edition "Luthers Werke in Auswahl" (four vols. Berlin [6]1966) and a compendium 1950–55 by O. Clemen, E. Vogelsang, and E. Hirsch is based upon the Weimar edition.

ENGLISH EDITIONS: The "Philadelphia Edition" *Works of Martin Luther,* ed. by H. E. Jacobs, 6 vols. (Philadelphia 1915–43). *Luther's Correspondence* (selections), ed. by P. Smith, 2 vols. (Philadelphia 1913–18). An American edition of *Luther's Works in English* (LW) St. Louis, 1955ff. by J. Pelikan is in the process of completion. As planned it will include fifty-five volumes. The first thirty volumes are to contain Luther's expositions of various Biblical works, the remaining volumes will contain his Reformation writings and other occasional pieces. The final volume will be an index, quotes, proper names, topics, and a glossary of technical terms. Volume 26 (1963) contains Luther's lectures on Galatians (1535) chaps. 1–4. The Library of Christian Classics also contains a number of Luther's works in translation, including his Lecture on Romans, Scholea vol. XV (Philadelphia 1961) and vol. XVI (Philadelphia 1962). Early Theological Works containing Lectures on the Epistle to the Hebrews 1517–18, disputation against "Scholastic Theology" 1517, Heidelberg Disputation, 1518, and Answer to Latomus (poor translation) appeared in *Works of Martin Luther* (WML, Philadelphia 1965).

GUIDE TO LUTHER'S WORKS AND EDITIONS: G. Kawerau, *Luthers Schriften* (SVRG 147) (Leipzig [2]1929); K. Aland, *Hilfsbuch zum Lutherstudium* (Berlin [2]1958); H. Volz, *RGG* IV ([3]1960) 520–523 (lit.); G. S. Robert, "A Checklist of Luther's Writings in English" *Concordia Theological Monthly* XXXVI (1965) 772–792; K. Hagen and J. Bigane, *Annotated Bibliography of Luther Studies, 1967–1976* (Sixteenth Century Bibliography, No. 9) (St. Louis 1977).

LITERATURE

1. BIOGRAPHIES AND GENERAL WORKS: J. Köstlin–G. Kawerau, *Martin Luther. Sein Leben und seine Schriften*, 2 vols. (Berlin ⁵1903); H. Denifle, *Luther und Luthertum*, 2 vols. and 2 suppl. (Mainz 1904–9); Grisar, 3 vols. (Freiburg 1924–25) English trans. 6 vols. (London 1913–17); id., *Martin Luthers Leben und sein Werk* (Freiburg 1927); K. Holl, *Gesammelte Aufsätze KG* I: *Luther* (Tübingen 1948); G. Ritter, *Luther* (New York 1963); R. Thiel, *Luther* (1933–35, Berlin–Stuttgart 1952); J. Lortz, *Reformation* (Westminister, Md. 1964); P. J. St. Reiter, *Martin Luther's Umwelt, Charakter und Psychose*, 2 vols. (Copenhagen 1937–41); R. H. Bainton, *Here I Stand. A Life of Martin Luther* (New York 1950); H. Bornkamm, *Luther's World of Thought* (London 1958); id., *Das Jh. der Reformation* (Göttingen 1961); H. Fausel, *Martin Luther. Sein Werden im Spiegel eigener Zeugnisse* (Stuttgart 1955); F. Lau, *Luther* (Philadelphia 1963); J. Mackinnon, *Martin Luther and the Reformation*, 4 vols. (London 1925–30); H. Boehmer, *Road to Reformation* (St. Louis 1946); R. H. Fife, *The Revolt of Martin Luther* (New York 1957); G. Rupp, *Luther's Progress to the Diet of Worms* (New York 1964); E. S. Schweibert, *Luther and His Times* (St. Louis 1950); V. H. H. Green, *Luther and the Reformation* (London 1964).

2. LUTHER'S THEOLOGY: Th. Harnack, *Luthers Theologie mit besonderer Beziehung auf seine Versöhnunge- und Erlösungslehre*, 2 vols. (1862–86, new printing, Munich 1927); J. Köstlin, *Luthers Theologie in ihrer geschichtlichen Entwicklung und ihrem inneren Zusammenhang*, 2 vols. (Stuttgart 1901); R. Seeberg, *Dogmengeschichte* IV, 1 (Leipzig 1933, new printing, Basel 1953); E. Seeburg, *Luthers Theol.* I: *Die Gottesanschauung* (Göttingen 1929), II: *Christus* (Stuttgart 1937); id., *Luthers Theologie in ihren Grundzügen* (Stuttgart 1950); W. v. Loewenich, *Luthers Theologia crucis* (Munich 1954); Ph. S. Watson, *Um Gottes Gottheit. Einf. in Luthers Theologie* (Berlin 1952); R. Hermann, *Gesammelte Studien zur Theologie Luthers* (Göttingen 1960); R. Prenter, *Spiritus Creator, Studien zu Luthers Theologie* (Munich 1954); E. Seeberg, *Textbook of the History of Doctrine* (Grand Rapids, Mich. 1964) 221–306; W. Ebert, *The Structure of Lutheranism* (St. Louis 1962); J. Pelikan, *Obedient Rebels* (New York 1964); J. Dillenberger, *God, Hidden and Revealed* (Philadelphia 1953); J. M. Headley, *Luther's View of Church History* (New Haven 1963); P. Althaus, *Die Theologie M. Luthers* (Gütersloh 1963); id., *Die Ethik M. Luthers* (Gütersloh 1965); L. Pinomaa, *Sieg des Glaubens, Grundlinien der Theologie Luthers* (Göttingen 1964); I. Asheim (ed.), *Kirche, Mystik, Heiligung und das Natürliche bei Luther* (Göttingen 1967).

3. LUTHER STUDIES: H. Boehmer, *Luther im Lichte der neueren Forschung* (Leipzig 1906, 1918); E. Wolf, "Über neuere Lutherliteratur u. den Gang der Lutherforschung" *Christentum und Wissenschaft* 10 (1934) 6–21, 203–219, 259–273, 437–457; H. Hermelink, "Die neuere Lutherforschung" *ThR NF* 7 (1935) 63–85, 131–165; V. Vajta, *Lutherforschung heute* (Berlin 1958) contains summaries of research in various countries, presented at first International Congress for Luther Research at Arhus, Denmark, 1956; D. Löfgren, "Verschiedene Tendenzen in der neueren Lutherforschung" *KuD* 5 (1959) 146–164; G. Müller, "Neuere Lit. zur Theologie des jungen Luther" *KuD* 11 (1965) 325–357; W. Pauck, "The Historiography of the German Reformation in the Past Twenty Years" *CH* IX (1940) 305–340; J. Dillenberger, "Major Volumes and Selected Periodical Literature in Luther Studies, 1956–1959" *CH* XXX (1961) 61–87; H. Grimm, "Luther Research Since 1920" *Journal of Modern History* XXXII (1960) 105–118; id., *The Reformation in Historical Thought* (New York 1946).

4. HISTORY OF THE UNDERSTANDING OF LUTHER: H. Stephan, *Luther in den*

Wandlungen seiner Kirche (1907, Berlin 1951); O. Wolff, *Die Haupttypen der neueren Lutherdeutung* (Stuttgart 1938); A. Herte, *Das kath. Lutherbild im Bann der Lutherkommentare des Cochläus,* 3 vols. (Münster 1943); E. W. Zeeden, *Martin Luther and the Reformation in the Estimation of the German Lutherans* (London 1954) id., "Die Deutung Luthers und der Reformation" *ThQ* 140 (1960) 129–162; H. Bornkamm, *Luther im Spiegel dt. Geistesgeschichte* (Heidelberg 1952); English trans. *Luther's World of Thought* (St. Louis 1958); W. Seibel, *Martin Luther. Wandlungen des Lutherbildes* (Kevelaer 1962); *Wandlungen des Lutherbildes, Stud. u. Ber. d. kath. Akad. in Bayern,* ed. K. Foster, H. 36 (Würzburg 1966). E. Carlson, *The Reinterpretation of Luther* (Philadelphia 1948).

5. THE YOUNG LUTHER: O. Scheel, *Martin Luther. Vom Katholizismus zur Reformation,* 2 vols. (Tübingen 1921–30); id., *Dokumente zu Luthers Entwicklung* (Tübingen 1929); H. v. Schubert, *Luthers Frühentwicklung bis 1517* (Leipzig 1916); E. Wolf, *Staupitz und Luther* (Leipzig 1927); id., "Johann v. Staupitz und die theol. Anfänge Luthers" *LuJ* II (1929) 43–86; H. Boehmer, *Road to Reformation* (Philadelphia 1946); K. A. Meissinger, *Der kath. Luther* (Munich 1952); M. Werner, "Psychologisches zum Klostererlebnis Martin Luthers" *Schweizer Zschr. für Psychologie* 7 (1948) 1–18; F. Lau, "Luthers Eintritt ins Erfurter Augustinerkloster" *Luther* 27 (1956) 49–70; E. Iserloh, "Luther-Kritik oder Luther-Polemik?" *Festgabe J. Lortz* I (Baden-Baden 1958) 15–42; E. H. Erikson, *Young Man Luther* (New York 1962); H. Strohl, *Luther jusqu'en 1520* (Paris ²1962); S. Rupp, *Luther's Progress to the Diet of Worms* (New York ²1962); J. von Rohr, "The Sources of Luther's Self-despair in the Monastery" *Journal of Bible and Religion* XIX (1951) 6–11; R. Bainton, "Luther's Struggle for Faith" *CH* XVIII, 193–206.

6. LUTHER AND THE THEOLOGY OF THE LATE MIDDLE AGES: F. Benary, *Zur Geschichte der Stadt und Universität Erfurt* ("via antiqua" and "via moderna" at the German universities of the Middle Ages with special attention to the University of Erfurt) (Gotha 1919); H. Rommel, *Über Luthers Randbemerkungen* (Diss., Kiel 1931); A. Hamel, *Der junge Luther und Augustin,* 2 vols. (1934–35); P. Vignaux, *Luther: Commentateur des Sentences* (Paris 1935); id., "Sur Luther et Ockham" *FStud* 32 (1950) 21—30; E. Vogelsang, "Luther und die Mystik" *LuJ* 19 (1937) 32–54; W. Kohlschmidt, *Luther und die Mystik* (Diss., Hamburg 1936); W. Link, *Das Ringen Luthers um die Freiheit der Theologie von der Philosophie* (Munich 1955); R. Weijenborg, "La Charité dans la première théologie de Luther" *RHE* 45 (1950) 617–669; A. Gyllenkrok, *Rechtfertigung und Heiligung in der frühen ev. Theologie Luthers* (Uppsala 1952); W. Jetter, *Die Taufe beim jungen Luther* (Tübingen 1954); B. Hägglund, *Theologie und Philosophie bei Luther und in der occamistischen Tradition* (Lund 1955); E. Iserloh, *Gnade und Eucharistie in der philos. Theologie des W. v. Ockham* (Wiesbaden 1956); H. Beintker, "Neues Material über die Beziehungen Luthers zum ma. Augustinismus" *ZKG* 68 (1957) 144–148; E. Bizer, *Fides ex auditu* (Neukirchen 1958); L. Grane, *Contra Gabrielem* (Byldendal 1962); R. Schwarz, *Fides, spes und caritas beim jungen Luther* (Berlin 1962); K. Bauer, *Die Wittenberger Universitätstheologie und die Anfänge der Reformation* (Tubingen 1928); A. Zumkeller, "Die Augustinertheologen Simon Fidati von Cascia u. Hugolin von Orvieto u. M. Luthers Kritik an Aristoteles" *ARG* 54 (1963) 15–36.

7. LUTHER'S JOURNEY TO ROME: H. Boehmer, *Luthers Romfahrt* (Leipzig 1913); R. Weijenborg, "Neuentdeckte Dokumente im Zshg. mit Luthers Romreise" *Antonianum* 32 (1957) 147–202.

8. LECTURE ON PSALMS: Text: *WA* 3; 4; Selection *Cl* V, 38–221; *LW* vols. 12, 13, and 14. Literature: A. W. Hunzinger, *Luthers Neuplatonismus in der Psalmen-Vorlesung von 1513–16* (Leipzig 1906); K. A. Meissinger, *Luthers Exegese der Frühzeit* (Leipzig

1911); H. Thomas, *Zur Würdigung der Psalmen-Vorlesung Luthers von 1513–15* (Weimar 1920); H. Boehmer, *Luthers 1. Vorlesung* (Leipzig 1924); J. Ficker, "Luthers 1. Vorlesung -welche?" *ThStk* 100 (1927–28) 348–353; E. Vogelsang, *Die Anfänge von Luthers Christologie nach der 1. Psalmen-Vorlesung* (Berlin–Leipzig 1929); H. Lang, "Die Rechtfertigungslehre in Luthers 1. Psalmen-Vorlesung" *NKZ* 40 (1929) 549–564; F. Huck, "Die Entwicklung der Christologie Luthers von der Psalmen- zur Römervorlesung" *ThStK* 102 (1930) 61–142; A. Hamel, *Der junge Luther und Augustin,* 2 vols. (Gütersloh 1934–35); W. Wagner, "Die Kirche als Corpus Christi mysticum beim jungen Luther" *ZKTh* 61 (1937) 29–98; F. Hahn, "Faber Stapulensis und Luther" *ZKG* 57 (1938) 356–432; id., "Die Hl. Schrift als Problem der Auslegung bei Luther" *EvTh* 10 (1950) 407–424; G. Ebeling, *Ev. Evangelienauslegung. Eine Untersuchung zu Luthers Hermeneutik* (Munich 1942); id., "Die Anfänge von Luthers Hermeneutik" *ZThK* 48 (1951) 172–230; id., "Luthers Psalterdruck vom Jahre 1513" *ZThK* 50 (1953) 43–99; id., "Luthers Auslegung des 14.(15.) Ps in der 1. Psalmen-Vorlesung im Vergleich mit der exegetischen Tradition" *ZThK* 50 (1953) 280–339; H. Volz, "Luthers Arbeit am lateinischen Psalter" *ARG* 48 (1957) 11–56; U. Saarnivaara, *Luther Discovers the Gospel* (St. Louis 1951); J. Pelikan, *Luther the Expositor* (St. Louis 1959); A. Brandenburg, *Gericht und Evangelium* (Paderborn 1960); Also, E. Iserloh, "Existentiale Interpretation" in "Luthers 1. Psalmen-Vorlesung?" *ThRv* 59 (1963) 73–84; R. Prenter, *Der barmherzige Richter. Iustitia dei passiva in Luthers Dictata super Psalterium 1513–15* (Copenhagen 1961); S. Raeder, *Das Hebräische bei Luther bis zum Ende der 1. Ps-Vorlesung* (Tübingen 1961); G. Müller, "Ekklesiologie u. Kirchenkritik beim jungen Luther" *NZSTh* 7 (1965) 100–128.

9. LECTURE ON THE EPISTLE TO THE ROMANS: Text: *WA* 56; Selection *Cl.* V, 222–304; German Translation by: E. Ellwein (Munich 1957); Italian-German Edition: 2 vols. (Darmstadt 1960); English: W. Pauck, *Christian Classics* XV. Literature: K. Holl, "Die Rechtfertigungslehre in Luthers Vorlesung über den Römerbrief" *Gesammelte Aufsätze* I, 111–154; F. W. Schmidt, "Der Gottesgedanke in Luthers Römerbrief-Vorlesung" *ThStK* 93 (1920–21) 117–248; H. Lang, "Die Bedeutung Christi für die Rechtfertigungslehre in Luthers Römerbrief-Vorlesung" *NKZ* 39 (1928) 509–547; R. Hermann, *Luthers These "Gerechte und Sünder zugleich"* (1930, new printing Gütersloh 1960); A. K. Wood, "The Theology of Luther's Lecture on Romans" *Scottish Journal of Theology* 3 (1950) 1–18, 113–126; J. Hilburg, *Luthers Frömmigkeit in seiner Vorlesung über den Römerbrief* (Diss., Marburg 1951); P. Althaus, *Paulus und Luther* (Gütersloh 1958); H. Beintker, "Glaube und Handeln nach Luthers Verständnis des Römerbriefs" *LuJ* 28 (1961) 52–85; J. Lortz, "Luthers Römerbrief-Vorlesung" *TThZ* 71 (1962) 129–153, 216–247; M. Lienhard, "Christologie et humilité dans la Theologia du commentaire de l'Épître aux Romains du Luther" *RHPhR* 42 (1962) 304–315; W. Grundmann, *Der Römerbrief . . . und seine Auslegung durch M. Luther* (Weimar 1964); H. Hübner, *Rechtfertigung und Heiligung in Luthers Römerbrief-Vorlesung* (Witten 1965).

10. LECTURE ON THE EPISTLE TO THE GALATIANS: Text: *WA* 57, II; Selection *Cl* V, 327–343. Literature: H. v. Schubert–K. A. Meissinger, *Zu Luthers Vorlesungstätigkeit* (Heidelberg 1920); J. Ficker, "Zu Luthers Vorlesung über den Galaterbrief 1516–17" *ThStK* 88–89 (1926) 1–17; L. Grane, "Lov og nåde in Luthers Galaterbrevsforelæsning 1516–17," *Svensk teologisk kvartalskrift* 50 (1954) 107–122; H. Volz, "Eine neue studentische Nachschrift von Luthers 1. Galaterbrief-Vorlesung" *ZKG* 66 (1954–55) 72–96.

11. LECTURE ON THE EPISTLE TO THE HEBREWS: Text: *WA* 57, III; Selection *Cl* V, 344–374; E. Hirsch–H. Rückert, *Luthers Vorlesung über den Hebräerbrief* (Berlin–Leipzig

1929); J. Ficker, *Luthers Vorlesung über den Hebräerbrief* (Leipzig 1929); trans. E. Vogelsang (Berlin–Leipzig 1930); trans. G. Helbig (Leipzig 1930); *Library of Christian Classics,* vol. 16, contains Disputation against Scholastic Theology, etc. Literature: E. Vogelsang, *Die Bedeutung der neuveröffentlichten Hebräerbrief- Vorlesung Luthers von 1517–18* (Tübingen 1930); E. Ellwein, "Die Entfaltung der Theologia crucis in Luthers Hebräerbrief-Vorlesung" *Theologische Aufsätze, K. Barth zum 50. Geburtstag* (Munich 1936) 382–404.

12. REFORMATION EXPERIENCE: IUSTITIA DEI: E. Stracke, *Luthers grosses Selbstzeugnis 1545* (Leipzig 1926); H. Bornkamm, "Luthers Bericht über seine Entdeckung der iustitia dei" *ARG* 37 (1940) 117–128; id., "Iustitia Dei in der Scholastik und bei Luther" *ARG* 39 (1942) 1–46; id., "Zur Frage der Iustitia beim jungen Luther" *ARG* 52 (1961) 16–29, 53 (1962) 1–59; E. Bizer, *Fides ex auditu* (Newkirchen 1966); G. Pfeiffer, "Das Ringen des jungen Luthers um die Gerechtigkeit Gottes" *LuJ* 26 (1959) 25–55; A. Peters, "Luthers Turmerlebnis" *Neue ZSTh* 3 (1961) 203–236; E. Hirsch, *Initium theologiae Lutheri: Lutherstudien* II (Gütersloh 1954) 9–34; E. G. Rupp, *The Righteousness of God* (London 1953); F. E. Cranz, *An Essay on the Development of Luther's Thought on Justice, Law and Society* (Cambridge, Mass. 1959); K. Aland, *Der Weg zur Reformation* (Munich 1965); O. Pesch, "Zur Frage nach Luthers reformatorischer Wende" *Catholica* 20 (1966) 216–243, 264–280.

3. *The Indulgence Controversy*

LITERATURE

LThK ²I (1957) 46–54; N. Paulus, *Geschichte des Ablasses im Mittelalter vom Ursprung bis zur Mitte des 14. Jh.,* 3 vols. (Paderborn 1922–23); B. Porschmann, *Der Ablass im Lichte der Bussgeschichte* (Bonn 1948); id., *Penance and the Annointing of the Sick* (London–New York 1964).

THE INDULGENCE CONTROVERSY: N. Paulus, *Johannes Tetzel, der Ablassprediger* (Mainz 1899); W. Köhler, *Dokumente zum Ablassstreit von 1517* (Tübingen 1934); E. Göller, *Der Ausbruch der Reformation und die spätmittelalterliche Ablasspraxis* (Freiburg i. Br. 1917); A. Schulte, *Die Fugger in Rom 1495–1523,* 2 vols. (Leipzig 1904); G. v. Pölnitz, *Jakob Fugger,* 2 vols. (Tübingen 1949–51); H. Volz, *Martin Luthers Thesenanschlag und dessen Vorgeschichte* (Vienna 1959) (lit.); E. Iserloh, *Luthers Thesenanschlag. Tatsache oder Legende?* (Wiesbaden 1962); English: *The Theses Were Not Posted* (Boston 1968; id., *Luther zwischen Reform und Reformation* (Münster 1966); K. Aland, *Martin Luthers 95 Thesen* (Hamburg 1965); English: *Martin Luther's Theses* (St. Louis 1967); K. Honselmann, *Urfassung und Drucke der Ablassthesen M. Luthers und ihre Veröffentlichung* (Paderborn 1966); F. Lau, "Die gegenwärtige Diskussion um Luthers Thesenanschlag," *LuJ* 34 (1967) 11–59; H. Bornkamm, *Thesen und Thesenanschlag Luthers* (Berlin 1967).

4. *Rome's Proceedings against Luther and the Leipzig Disputation*

LITERATURE

THE PROCESS: K. Müller, "Luthers römischer Prozess" *ZKG* 24 (1903) 46–85; P. Kalkoff, *Forschungen zu Luthers römischem Prozess* (Rome 1905); id., "Zu Luthers römischem Prozess" *ZKG* 25 (1904), 31 (1910), 32 (1911), 33 (1912); id., *Zu Luthers römischem Prozess. Der Prozess des Jahres 1518* (Gotha 1912); id., *Luther und die Ent-scheidungsjahre der Reformation* (Munich–Leipzig 1917); suppl. *ZKG* 44 (1925) 213–225; Kalkoff's researches are summarized in E. G. Schwiebert, *Luther and His Time* (St. Louis 1950) 481f.; N. Paulus, *Johannes Tetzel, der Ablassprediger* (Mainz 1899); J. Atkinson, *The Trial of Luther* (New York, 1971).

ON THE RELATIONSHIP OF LUTHER TO FREDERICK THE WISE: P. Kalkoff; *ARG* 14 (1917) 249–262; *ZKG* 43 (1924) 179–208; *HZ* 132 (1925) 29–42; P. Kirn, *Friedrich der Weise und die Kirche* (Leipzig 1926); A. Koch, "Die Kontroversen über die Stellung Friedrichs des Weisen zur Reformation" *ARG* 23 (1926) 213–260; I. Höss, *Georg Spalatin* (Weimar 1956); F. Lauchert, *Die italienischen literarischen Gegner Luthers* (Freiburg i. Br. 1912); J. F. Groner, *Kardinal Cajetan* (Fribourg 1951); H. A. Creutzberg, *Karl v. Miltitz* (Freiburg i. Br. 1907); P. Kalkoff, *Die Miltitziade* (Leipzig 1911); K. Brandi, *Die Wahl Karls V* (Göttingen 1925).

THE LEIPZIG DEBATE: *WA* 2, 250–383; O. Seitz, *Der authentische Text der Leipziger Disputation* (Berlin 1903); H. Emser, "De Disputatione Lipsicensi" *CCath* 4 (1921); J. Lortz, "Die Leipziger Disputation 1519" *BZThS* 3 (1926) 12–37; F. Schulze, *Aus Leipzigs Kulturgeschichte* (Leipzig 1956) 41–70; H. Barge, *Andreas Bodenstein v. Karlstadt, 2* vols. (Leipzig 1905); S. Harrison Thomson, "Luther and Bohemia" *ARG* 44 (1953) 160–181; E. Kähler, "Beobachtungen zum Problem von Schrift und Tradition in der Leipziger Disputation von 1519" *Hören und Handeln, Festschrift f. E. Wolf* (Munich 1962) 214–229.

5. *Luther's Reform Writings of 1520*

LITERATURE

H. Dannenbauer, *Luther als religiöser Volksschriftsteller 1517–1520* (Tübingen 1930); O. Clemen, *Die Lutherische Reformation und der Buchdruck* (Leipzig 1939); H. v. Campenhausen, "Reformatorisches Selbstbewusstsein und reformatorisches Geschichtsbewusstsein bei Luther, 1517–1522" *ARG* 37 (1940) 128–150; H. Volz, "Die ersten Sammelausgaben von Lutherschriften und ihre Drucker (1518–1520)" *Gutenberg-Jb.* (1960) 185–202; W. Köhler, "Zu Luthers Schrift an den christlichen Adel deutscher Nation" *ZSavRGkan* 14 (1925) 1–38; W. Maurer, *Von der Freiheit eines Christenmenschen* (Göttingen 1949); H. Asmussen, "Glaube und Sakrament. Zwei Abschnitte aus 'De captivitate'" *Begegnung der Christen* (Stuttgart 1959) 161–178.

6. *The Excommunicated Friar before the Diet of Worms*

SOURCES AND LITERATURE

A) THE BULL OF EXCOMMUNICATION: Cf. Chap. 4; "Exsurge Domine": *BullRom* V 748–757; D. 741–781; "Decet Romanum Pontificem": *BullRom* V 761–764; Schottenloher I 12043–56; V 47670a–71; H. Roos, "Die Quellen der Bulle Exsurge Domine" *Festschrift Schmaus* (Munich 1957) 909–926; A. Schulte, "Die römischen Verhandlungen über Luther 1520" *QFIAB* 6 (1904) 32–52, 174ff.; J. Greving, "Zur Verkündigung der Bulle Exsurge Domine durch Dr. J. Eck 1520" *RGStT* 21–22 (Münster 1912) 196–221; G. Müller, "Die drei Nuntiaturen Aleanders in Deutschland" *AFIAB* 39 (1959) 222–276.

THE BURNING OF THE BULL OF EXCOMMUNICATION: Schottenloher I 14107–15, VII 55923–27; J. Luther–M. Perlbach, *SAB* V (1907) 95–102; O. Clemen, *ThStK* 81 (1908) 460–469; H. Boehmer, *LuJ* 2–3 (1920–21) 3–53; J. Luther, *ARG* 45 (1954) 260–265.

B) THE DIET OF WORMS: *Deutsche Reichstagsakten unter Karl V* (=RA), II (Gotha 1896); Th. Brieger, *Aleander und Luther 1521. Die vervollständigten Aleander-Depeschen I. Abt* (Gotha 1884); P. Kalkoff (trans.), *Die Depeschen des Nuntius Aleander vom Wormser Reichstag* (Halle ²1897) id., *Briefe, Depeschen und Berichte über Luther vom Wormser Reichstage* (Halle 1898); J. Cochlaeus, "Colloquium cum Luthero Wormatinae olim habitum" *Flugschriften aus den ersten Jahren der Reformation* IV (Leipzig 1910) 177–218; Schottenloher I 14281–346, III 27923–50; H. v. Schubert, "Die Vorgeschichte der Berufung Luthers auf den Reichstag zu Worms 1521" *SAH* (1912); H. Grisar, *Luther zu Worms* (Freiburg 1921); Paul Kalkoff, *Der Wormser Reichstag von 1521* (Munich 1922); E., Kessel, "Luther vor dem Reichstag in Worms 1521" *Festgabe für Paul Kirn,* ed. E. Kaufmann (Berlin 1961) 172–190.

7. *Luther at the Wartburg and the Reform Movement in Wittenberg*

LITERATURE

G. Kawerau, *Luthers Rückkehr von der Wartburg nach Wittenberg* (Halle 1902); H. Barge, *Andreas Bodenstein von Karlstadt,* 2 vols. (Leipzig 1905); id., "Luther und Karlstadt in Wittenberg" *HZ* 99 (1907) 256–324; id., *Frühprotestantisches Gemeindechristentum in Wittenberg und Orlamünde* (Leipzig 1909); id., *Aktenstücke zur Wittenberg Bewegung Anfang 1522* (Leipzig 1912); K. Müller, *Luther und Karlstadt* (Tübingen 1907); N. Müller, *Die Wittenberger Bewegung 1521 und 1522* (Leipzig ²1911); W. Köhler, *GGA* 174 (1912) 505–550; Th. Knolle, *Luther und die Bilderstürmer* (Wittenberg 1922); H. v. Campenhausen, "Die Bilderfrage in der Reformation" *ZKG* 68 (1957) 96–128; I. Höss, *Georg Spalatin* (Weimar 1956); P. Graff, *Gesch der Auflösung der alten Gottesdienstformen in der evangelischen Kirche Deutschlands* I (Göttingen ³1937); L. Fendt, *Der lutherische Gottesdienst im 16. Jh.* (Munich 1923); V. Vajta, *Die Theologie des Gottesdienstes bei Luther* (Göttingen ²1952); B. Lohse, *Mönchtum und Reformation* (Göttingen 1963); H. B. Meyer, *Luther und die Messe* (Paderborn 1965).

8. *The Reformers in Luther's Circle*

LITERATURE

R. Stupperich (ed.), *Reformatorische Verkündigung und Lebensordnung* (Bremen 1963).

NIKOLAUS VON AMSDORF: *Ausgewählte Schriften,* ed. O. Lerche (Gütersloh 1938); E. O. Reichert, *Amsdorf und das Interim. Erstausg. seiner Schriften zum Interim mit Kommentar und hist. Einl.* (Diss. Halle–Wittenberg 1955); O. H. Nebe, *Reine Lehre. Zur Theologie des Niklas von Amsdorff* (Göttingen 1935); H. Stille, *Nikolaus von Amsdorf, sein Leben bis zu seiner Einweisung als Bischof von Naumburg (1483–1542)* (Diss. Leipzig 1937); O. Lerche, *Amsdorf und Melanchthon* (Berlin 1937); P. Brunner, *Nikolaus von Amsdorf als Bischof von Naumburg* (Gütersloh 1961).

JUSTUS JONAS: Th. Pressel, *Justus Jonas. Leben und ausgewählte Schriften* (Elberfeld 1862); *Briefwechsel des Justus Jonas,* ed. G. Kawerau, 2 vols. (Halle 1884–85); Supp. by

W. Delius: *ARG* 31 (1934) 133–136, 42 (1951) 136–145; M. Schellbach, *Justus Jonas* (Essen 1941); W. Delius, *Lehre und Leben. Justus Jonas* (Berlin 1952); id., *Reformationsgeschichte der Stadt Halle* (Berlin 1953); H. Abe, *Der Erfurter Humanismus und seine Zeit* (Diss. Jena 1953); F. W. Krapp, *Der Erfurter Mutiankreis und seine Auswirkungen* (Diss. Cologne 1954). M. Lehmann, *Justus Jonas, Loyal Reformer* (Minneapolis, Minn. 1963).

JOHANNES BUGENHAGEN: G. Geisenhof, *Bibliotheca Bugenhagiana I, Bibliographie . . . des Johannes Bugenhagen* (Leipzig 1908); *Briefwechsel,* ed. O. Vogt (Stettin 1888); G. Buchwald (ed.), *Predigten Bugenhagens* (Halle 1885); id., *Johannes Bugenhagens Katechismuspredigten* (Leipzig 1909); id., *Ungedruckte Predigten Bugenhagens* (Leipzig 1910); id., "Bugenhagens Katechismuspredigten vom Jahre 1534" *ARG* 17 (1920) 92–104; K. A. T. Vogt, *Johannes Bugenhagen Pomeranus* (Elberfeld 1867); H. Hering, *Dr. Pomeranus Johannes Bugenhagen* (Halle 1888); E. Wolf, *Johannes Bugenhagen. Gemeinde und Amt. Peregrinatio* (Munich, 1962) 257–278; W. Rautenberg (ed.), *Johannes Bugenhagen, Beiträge zu seinem 400. Todestag* (Berlin 1958) (lit.); R. Stupperich, "Dr. Pomeranus. Zum 400. Todestag des Reformators Johannes Bugenhagen" *Luther* 29 (1958) 49–60; additional articles on Johannes Bugenhagen: *NDB* III, 9f.

GEORG SPALATIN: I. Höss, *Georg Spalatin* (Weimar 1956); id., "Georg Spalatins Traktat 'De sacramento venerabile eucharistiae et de confessione' vom Jahre 1525" *ARG* 49 (1958) 79–88; id., "Georg Spalatins Verhältnis zu Luther und die Reformation" *Luther* 31 (1960) 67–80; H. Volz, "Bibliogr. der im 16. Jh. erschienenen Schriften Georg Spalatins" *Zschr. für Bibliothekswesen und Bibliogr.* 5 (1958) 83–119; W. Ulsamer, "Spalatins Beziehungen zu seiner fränkischen Heimat" *Jb. für fränkische Landesforschung* 19 (1959) 425–479.

PHILIP MELANCHTHON: Works: *CR* 1–28 (Halle-Braunschweig 1834–60); *Epistolae iudicia, consilia etc.,* ed. E. Bindseil (Halle 1874); *Supplementa Melanchthoniana,* 6 vols. (Leipzig 1910–26); Selected Works (text for study), ed. R. Stupperich (Gütersloh 1951f.); P. Fraenkel, "Fünfzehn Jahre Melanchthonforschung (lit)" *Bibliothèque d'Humanisme et Renaissance* 22 (1960) 582–624, 23 (1961) 563–602, 24 (1962) 443–478; C. L. Hill (ed.), *The Loci Communes of Philip Melanchthon* (Boston 1944); id., *Selected Writings* (Minneapolis, Minn. 1962); C. Schmidt, *Philipp Melanchthon, Leben und ausgewählte Schriften* (Elberfeld 1861); A. Herrlinger, *Die Theologie Melanchthons* (Gotha 1879); K. Hartfelder, *Philipp Melanchthon als Praeceptor Germaniae* (Berlin 1889); G. Ellinger, *Philipp Melanchthon* (Berlin 1902); O. Ritschl, "Die Entwicklung der Rechtfertigungslehre Melanchthons bis zum Jahre 1527" *ThStK* 85 (1912) 518–540; P. Joachimsen, "Loci Communes" *LuJ* 8 (1926) 27–97; H. Engelland, *Melanchthon, Glauben und Handeln* (Munich 1931); F. Hübner, *Natürliche Theologie und theokratische Schwärmerei bei Melanchthon* (Gütersloh 1936); Cl. Bauer, "Die Naturrechtsvorstellungen des jüngeren Melanchthon" *Festschrift G. Ritter* (Tübingen 1950) 244–255; id., "Melanchthons Naturrechtslehre" *ARG* 42 (1951) 64–98; id., "Melanchthons Wirtschaftsethik" *ARG* 49 (1958) 115–160; P. Schwarzenau, *Der Wandel im theologischen Ansatz bei Melanchthon von 1525–35* (Gütersloh 1956); W. H. Neuser, *Der Ansatz der Theolgie Philipp Melanchthons* (Neukirchen 1957); W. Maurer, "Melanchthons Anteil am Streit zwischen Luther und Erasmus" *ARG* 49 (1958) 89–115, and in *Melanchthon-Studien* (Gütersloh 1964) 137–162; id., "Die Loci Communes als wiss. Programmschrift" *LuJ* 27 (1960) 1–50; A. Sperl, *Melanchthon zwischen Humanismus und Reformation* (Munich 1959); G. Urban (ed.), *Philipp Melanchthon. Gedenkschrift zum 400. Todestag* (Bretten ²1960); H. Bornkamm, *Philipp Melanchthon* (Göttingen ³1960); P. Meinhold, *Philip Melanchthon. Der Lehrer der Kirche* (Berlin 1960); W. Elliger (ed.),

Philipp Melanchthon. Forschungsbeiträge (Göttingen 1961); V. Vajta (ed.), *Luther und Melanchthon* (Göttingen 1961); R. Stupperich, *Melanchthon* (Berlin 1960); id., *Der unbekannte Melanchthon* (Stuttgart 1961); R. Schäfer, *Christologie und Sittlichkeit in Melanchthons frühen Loci* (Tübingen 1961); P. Fraenkel, *Testimonia Patrum. The Function of the Patristic Argument in the Theology of Philip Melanchthon* (Geneva 1961); H. Lieberg, *Amt und Ordination bei Luther und Melanchthon* (Göttingen 1962); E. Bizer, *Theologie der Verheissung, Studien der theol. Entwicklung des jungen Melanchthon (1519–24)* (Neukirchen 1964); F. Hildebrandt, *Melanchthon: Alien or Ally?* (New York 1946); C. L. Manschreck, *Melanchthon, the Quiet Reformer* (New York 1958); M. Greschat, *Melanchthon neben Luther* (Witten 1965); H.-G. G. Geyer, *Von der Geburt des wahren Menschen* (Neukirchen 1965).

9. The Pontificate of Adrian VI

SOURCES

L.-P. Gachard, *Correspondance de Charles-Quint et d'Adrien VI* (Brussels 1859); H. J. Reusens, *Syntagma doctrinae theologicae Adriani Sexti* (Louvain 1862); A. Mercati, *Dall'Archivio Vaticano* II: *Diarii di concistori del pontificato di Adriano VI* (*SteT* 157) (Rome 1951).

LITERATURE

C. v. Höfler, *Papst Adrian VI.* (Vienna 1880); M. v. Domarus, "Die Quellen zur Geschichte des Papstes Hadrian" *HJ* 16 (1895) 70–91; P. Kalkoff, "Kleine Beiträge zur Gesch. Adrians VI." *HJ* 39 (1918–19) 31–72; L. v. Pastor, *Gesch. der Päpste* IV, 2, pp. 3–157; E. Hocks, *Der letzte dt. Papst* (Freiburg 1939); E. Göller, "Hadrian VI. und der Ämterkauf an der päpstl. Kurie" *Abhh. aus dem Gebiete der mittleren und neueren Gesch. Festgabe H. Finke* (Münster 1925) 375–407; H. W. Bachmann, *Kuriale Reformbestrebungen unter Adrian VI.* (Diss. Erlangen 1948); E. van Eyl, "Keizer Karel V en de pauskeuze van Adriaan VI" *SE* 1 (1948) 277–298; P. Brachim, "Adrian VI et la devotio moderna" *Etudes Germaniques* 14 (1959) 97–105; *EThL* 35 (1959) 313–629 (with bibliography); J. Posner, *Der dt. Papst Adrian VI.* (Recklinghausen 1962); P. Berglar, *Verhängnis und Verheissung* (Bonn o. J.).

SECTION TWO

The Struggle over the Concept of Christian Freedom

10. The Knights' War

LITERATURE

KNIGHTHOOD: Schottenloher 41521a–41534; K. Schottenloher, *Flugschriften zur Ritterschaftsbewegung des Jahres 1523* (Münster 1929); R. Fellner, *Die fränkische Ritterschaft von 1495–1524* (Berlin 1905); G. Lotz, "Der fränkische Adel und dessen Einfluss auf die Verbreitung der Reformation" *Zschr. für die gesamte luth. Theologie und Kirche* 29 (1868) 465–486; G. Knetsch, *Die landständische Verfassung und reichsritterschaftliche Bewegung im Kurstaate Trier, vornehmlich im 16. Jh.* (Berlin 1909); O. Brunner, *Adeliges Landleben und europäischer Geist* (Salzburg 1949)

SICKINGEN AND THE TRIER AFFAIR: Schottenloher 20010–20067; 49329–49339a; 58243–58254; H. Ullmann, *F. v. S.* (Leipzig 1872); id., *ADB* 34, 151–158; E. Göller, "Sickingen u. seine Beziehungen zur Reformation: Bl. für Pfalz." *KG* 2 (1926) 36–46; K. H. Rendenbach, *Die Fehde F. v. Sickingens gegen Trier* (Berlin 1933); G. Franz, "F. v. S." *Saarpfälz. Lebensbilder* 1 (1938) 61–74; E. Kilb, *F. v. S.* (Metz 1943); W. R. Hitchcock, *The Background of the Knight's Revolt 1522–1523* (Berkeley 1958).

ULRICH V. HUTTEN: Schottenloher 9157–9301; 47021–47043; 65068–65071; 55286–55308; *Werke,* ed. E. Böcking, 5 vols. and 2 suppl. vols. (Leipzig 1859–70); *Deutsche Schriften,* ed. S. Szamatolski (Strassburg 1891); F. Walser, *Die politische Entwicklung Huttens* (Munich–Berlin 1928); P. Held, *Hutten, seine geistige Auseinandersetzung mit Katholizismus, Humanismus und Reformation* (Leipzig 1928); H. Holborn, *Ulrich v. Hutten and the German Reformation* (New Haven 1937); H. Fechter, *Ulrich v. Hutten* (Pähl 1954); K. Kleinschmidt, *Ulrich von Hutten* (Berlin 1955).

E. Bock, *Der Schwäb. Bund u. seine Verfassungen 1488–1534* (Breslau 1927); G. Truchsess v. Waldburg: Schottenloher 21459–21463; 60985–60988; F. Siebert, *Zwischen Kaiser und Papst* (Berlin 1950).

11. *The "Fanatics" Karlstadt and Müntzer*

LITERATURE

KARLSTADT:**Works:** E. Freys and H. Barge, "Verz. der gedr. Schriften des Andreas Bodenstein von Karlstadt" *ZblB* 21 (1904; reprinted Nieuwkoop 1965); *Von Abtuhung der Bilder,* ed. H. Lietzmann, *Kleine Texte 74* (Berlin 1911); E. Kähler, *Karlstadt und Augustin, Der Kommentar des Andreas Bodenstein von Karlstadt zu Augustins Schrift De spiritu et litera. Einführung und Text* (Halle 1952); *Schriften aus den Jahren 1523–25,* ed. E. Hertzsch, 2 vols. (Halle 1956–57); "Karlstadts Sabbat-Traktat von 1524," ed. R. Stupperich: *Neue Zschr. für systematische Theologie* 1 (1959) 349–375. **Literature:** similar to Chap. 35: H. Barge, *Andreas Bodenstein von Karlstadt,* 2 vols. (Leipzig 1905); E. Hase, "Karlstadt in Orlamünde" *Mitt. der geschichts- und altertumsforschenden Ges. des Osterlandes* 4 (1858) 42–125; W. Friedensburg, "Der Verzicht Karlstadts auf das Wittenberger Archidiakonat" *ARG* 11 (1914) 69–72; M. Wähler, *Die Einführung der Reformation in Orlamünde* (Erfurt 1918); E. Hertzsch, *Karlstadt und seine Bedeutung für das Luthertum* (Gotha 1932); id., *Luther und Karlstadt: Luther in Thüringen,* compiled by R. Jauernig (Berlin 1952) 87–107; E. Kähler, "Karlstadts Protest gegen die theologische Wissenschaft" *450 Jahre Martin-Luther-Universität Halle-Wittenberg* I (Halle 1952) 299–312; G. Fuchs, "Karlstadts radikal-reformatorisches Wirken und seine Stellung zwischen Müntzer und Luther" *Wiss. Zschr. der Martin-Luther-Universität Halle-Wittenberg* 3 (1953–54) 523–551; *NDB* II 356f.; *RGG* III 1154f.; G. Rupp, "Andrew Karlstadt and Reformation Puritanism" *JthS NS* 10 (1959) 308–326; J. Seuppel, *Schwenckfelk, Knight of Faith* (Pennsburg, Pa. 1961).

MÜNTZER: **Works:** G. Franz, "Bibliographie der Schriften Th. Müntzers" *Zschr. des Vereins für Thüring. Gesch. u. Altertumskunde NF* 34 (Jena 1940) 161–173; H. J. Hillerbrand, *Bibliographie des Täufertums* (Gütersloh 1962) 21011–21050; *Thomas Müntzers*

671

Briefwechsel, ed. H. Böhmer–P. Kirn (Leipzig 1931); *Thomas Müntzer, sein Leben und seine Schriften,* ed. O. H. Brandt (Jena 1933); O. J. Mehl, *Thomas Müntzers deutsche Messen und Kirchenämter* (Grimmen 1937); Sehling I; *Thomas Müntzers politische Schriften,* ed. C. Hinrichs (Halle 1950); *Die Fürstenpredigt,* ed. by and with introduction by S. Streller (Leipzig 1958). **Literature:** O. J. Mehl, "Thomas Müntzer als Liturgiker" *ThLZ* 76 (1951) 75–78; C. Hinrichs, *Luther und Müntzer* (Berlin 1952); H. S. Bender, "Thomas Müntzer und die Täufer" *ThZ* 8 (1952) 262–278; A. Meusel, *Thomas Müntzer und seine Zeit* (Berlin 1952); M. Schmidt, "Das Selbstbewusstsein Thomas Müntzers" *Theologia viatorum* 6 (Berlin 1954–58) 25–41; M. M. Smirin, *Die Volksreformation des Thomas Müntzer und der grosse Bauernkrieg* (Berlin ²1956); M. Steinmetz, "Zur Entstehung der Müntzerlegende" *Beiträge zum neuen Geschichtsbild. Zum 60. Geburtstag von A. Meusel* (Berlin 1956) 35–70; id., *Das Müntzerbild in der Geschichtsschreibung von Luther und Melanchthon bis zum Ausbruch der französischen Revolution* (Jena 1956); cf. R. Schmid, "Thomas Müntzer im Geschichtsbild des Dialektischen Materialismus" *Deutsches Pfarrerblatt* 65 (1965) 258–262; G. Franz, *Der deutsche Bauernkrieg* (Darmstadt ⁴1956) 248–270; H. Goebke, "Neue Forschungen über Thomas Müntzer" *Harz-Zschr* 9 (Bad Hatzburg 1957) 1–30; G. Baring, "Hans Denck und Thomas Müntzer" *ARG* 50 (1959) 145–181; W. Elliger, *Thomas Müntzer* (Berlin 1960); id. *LuJ* 34 (1967) 90-116; *RGG*³ IV 1183f.; E. Iserloh, "Zur Gestalt und Biographie Thomas Müntzers" *TThZ* 71 (1962) 248–253.

12. The Peasants' War

BIBLIOGRAPHY

Dahlmann-Waitz 9891–9902; 9976–9981; 10065–10080; Schottenloher 34765–35241; 51510–51531; 62311–62366; *Bibl. de la Réforme* I, Reg. p. 77.

SOURCES

L. Baumann, *QQ zur Gesch. des Bauernkrieges in Oberschwaben* (Tübingen 1876); id., *Akten zur Gesch. des Bauernkrieges aus Oberschwaben* (Freiburg 1877); H. Wopfner, *QQ zur Gesch. des Bauernkrieges in Dtl.* I (Innsbruck 1908); H. Brandt, *Der grosse Bauernkrieg* (Jena 1925); *Akten zur Gesch. des Bauernkrieges in Mittel-Dtl.,* ed. O. Merx–G. Franz–W. P. Fuchs, 3 vols. (Leipzig–Berlin 1923–1941); G. Franz, *QQ zur Gesch. des Bauernkrieges* (Munich 1963).

LITERATURE

G. Franz, *Der dt. Bauernkrieg* (Darmstadt ⁴1956); R. M. Radbruch–G. Radbruch, *Der dt. Bauernkrieg zwischen MA u. Neuzeit* (Göttingen 1962); H. v. Schubert, *Revolution u. Reformation im 16. Jh.* (Tübingen 1927); H. Hantsch, *Der dt. Bauernkrieg* (Würzburg 1925); W. Stolze, *Bauernkrieg und Reformation* (Leipzig 1926); A. Rosenkranz, *Der Bundschuh,* 2 vols. (Heidelberg 1927); E. Bohnenblust, *Luthers Verhalten im Bauernkrieg* (Bern 1929); A. Waas, *Die grosse Wende im dt. Bauernkrieg* (Munich–Berlin 1939); id., *Die Bauern im Kampf um Gerechtigkeit 1300–1525* (Munich 1964); I. Schmidt, *Das göttl. Recht* (Diss. Jena 1939); M. M. Smirin, *Die Volksreformation des Th. Müntzer u. der grosse Bauernkrieg* (Berlin 1956); H. Kamnitzer, *Zur Vorgesch. des dt. Bauernkrieges* (Berlin 1953); W. Andreas, *Der Bundschuh* (Karlsruhe 1953); P. Althaus, *Luthers Haltung im Bauernkrieg* (Tübingen 1952); H. Michaelis, *Die Verwendung und Bedeutung der Bibel in den Hauptschriften der Bauern von 1525–26* (theol. diss.

Greifswald 1954); F. Lau, "Der Bauernkrieg und das angebliche Ende der lutherischen Reformation als spontaner Volksbewegung" *LuJ* 26 (1959) 109–134; M. Greschat, "Luthers Haltung im Bauernkrieg" *ARG* 56 (1965) 31–47; J. S. Schapiro, *Social Reforms and the Reformation* (New York 1909); H. Kirschner, *Luther and the Peasant's War* (Philadelphia, 1972); A. Holmio, *The Lutheran Reformation and the Jews* (Hancock, Mich., 1949).

13. *Luther's Rejection of Humanism—Erasmus' Later Years*

LITERATURE

F. Kattenbusch, *Luthers Lehre vom unfreien Willen und von der Prädestination nach ihren Entstehungsgründen untersucht* (Diss. Göttingen 1875); K. Zickendrath, *Der Streit zwischen Erasmus und Luther über die Willensfreiheit* (Leipzig 1909); H. Jedin, *Des Johannes Cochläus Streitschrift De libero arbitrio hominis* (1525) (Breslau 1927); E. Schott, "Luthers Lehre vom servum arbitrium in ihrer theologischen Bedeutung" *ZSTh* 7 (1929) 399–430; W. Maurer, "Humanismus und Reformation" *ThR NF* 3 (1931) 49–74, 104–145; R. Hermann, "Zu Luthers Lehre vom unfreien Willen" *Greifswalder Studien zur Lutherforschung und neuzeitlichen Geistesgeschichte* 4 (1931) 17–38; A. Renaudet, *Études érasmiennes (1521–1529)* (Paris 1939); E. Schweingruber, *Luthers Erlebnis des unfreien Willens* (Zürich 1947); L. Schauenburg, *Luthers Lehre vom verborgenen, alleinwirksamen Gott und von der Unfreiheit des Willens* (Diss. Göttingen 1949); E. Erikstein, *Luthers Prädestinationslehre geschichtlich dargestellt bis einschliesslich "De servo arbitrio"* (Diss. Göttingen 1957); M. Werner, *Erasmus und Luther: Glaube und Aberglaube* (Bern–Stuttgart 1957) 50–65; H. Bandt, *Luthers Lehre vom verborgenen Gott* (Berlin 1958); H. Bornkamm, "Erasmus und Luther" *LuJ* 25 (1958) 3–22; W. Maurer, "Melanchthons Anteil am Streit zwischen Luther und Erasmus" *ARG* 49 (1958) 89–115; id., *Melanchthonstudien* (Gütersloh 1964) 137–162; C. Reidijk, "Das Lebensende des Erasmus" *Basler Zschr. für Gesch. u. Altertumskunde* 57 (1958) 23–66; K. H. Oelrich, *Der späte Erasmus und die Reformation* (Münster 1961); O. J. Mehl, "Erasmus contra Luther" *LuJ* 29 (1962) 52–64; J. Boisset, *Erasme et Luther* (Paris 1962); E. F. Winter, (ed.), *Erasmus-Luther-Discourse on Free Will* (New York 1961); E. W. Kohls, *Die Theologie des Erasmus* (Basel 1966); J. P. Dolan, *The Essential Erasmus* (New York 1964); H. Holeczek, *Humanistische Bibelphilologie als Reformproblem bei Erasmus von Rotterdam, Thomas More und William Tyndale* (Leiden, 1975); J. Rouschausse, *Erasmus and Fisher: Their Correspondence, 1511–1524* (Paris 1968); The first volume of the new edition of the complete works of Erasmus appeared in 1969, the five-hundredth anniversary of his birth: *Opera Omnia Desiderii Erasmi Roterodami recognita et adnotatione critica instructa notisque illustrata* (Amsterdam 1969ff.).

14. *Zwingli and the Beginnings of the Reformation in German Switzerland*

SOURCES

Die Eidgenössischen Abschiede aus dem Zeitraume von 1521–28 (The Confederate Secession of 1521–1528), *Der Amtlichen Abschiedesammlung* IV, la, revised by J. Strickler (Bruges 1873); W. Oechsli, *Quellenbuch zur Schweizergeschichte*, n.s., (Zurich 1893); id., *Quellenbuch zur Schweizergeschichte, Kleine Ausgabe* (Zurich 1918); *Actensammlung zur Schweizerischen Reformationsgeschichte in den Jahren 1521–1532*, revised and edited by J. Strickler, 5 vols. (Zurich 1878–83); *Actensammlung zur Gesch. der Zürcher Reformation in den Jahren 1519–1533,* ed. E. Egli (Zurich 1879); *Actensammlung zur Gesch. der Berner Reformation 1521–1532,* ed. R. Steck–G. Tobler (Bern 1923); *Actensammlung zur Geschichte der Basler Reformation in den Jahren 1519–1534,* ed. E. Dürr–P. Roth, 6 vols. (Basel 1921–1950); *Heinrich Bullingers Reformationsgeschichte,* ed. J. J. Hottinger–H. H. Vögeli, 3 vols. (Frauenfeld 1838–1840); *Die Chronik des Bernhard Wyss 1519–1530,* ed. G. Finsler (Basel 1901); *Johannes Stumpfs Schweizer- und Reformationschronik,* 2 parts, ed. E. Gagliardi–H. Müller–F. Büsser (Basel 1952–55); *Gerold Edlibachs Chronik,* ed. J. M. Usteri (Zurich 1847); *Valentin Tschudi's Chronik der Reformationsjahre 1521–33,* ed. Joh. Strickler (Bern 1889); B. Sprüngli, *Beschreibung der Kappelerkriege,* ed. W. Weiss (Zurich 1932); *Reformation und kath. Reform 1500 bis 1572, Quellenhefte zur Schweizergeschichte* 5, revised A. Bucher–W. Schmid (Aarau 1958).

ZWINGLI, Works: First complete edition, ed. M. Schuler–J. Schultheiss, 8 vols. (Zurich 1828–42); *Huldreich Zwinglis sämtliche Werke: Corpus Reformatorum* 88–92; 93–98, 100–101 (Berlin 1905, Leipzig 1908, 1935, Zurich 1959ff.) (=ZW 1–14), cf. *Zwingliana* 12 (1964) 1–9; Ulrich Zwingli, *Eine Auswahl aus seinen Schriften,* trans. and ed. G. Finsler–W. Köhler–A. Rüegg (Zurich 1918); Zwingli, *Hauptschriften,* revised by F. Blanke–O. Farner–O. Frei–R. Pfister, 11 vols. (Zurich 1940–63); *Huldrych Zwingli. Auswahl seiner Schriften,* ed. E. Künzli (Zurich 1962); *Aus Zwinglis Predigten,* 2 vols., ed. O. Farner (Zurich 1957).

LITERATURE

J. Dierauer, *Gesch. der Schweizer Eidgenossenschaft 1516–1648* (Gotha 1907); E. Gagliardi, *Gesch. der Schweiz,* 2 vols. (Zurich 1934–37); H. Nabholz et al., *Gesch. der Schweiz* (Zurich 1932–38); Th. Schwegler, *Gesch. der kath. Kirche in der Schweiz* (Stans² 1945); E. Egli, *Schweizerische Reformationsgeschichte* I (1519–25) (Zurich 1910); B. Fleischlin, *Schweizerische Reformationsgeschichte,* 2 vols. (Stans 1907–09); W. Hadorn, *Die Reformation in der deutschen Schweiz* (Frauenfeld–Leipzig 1928); R. Pfister, *Kirchengeschichte der Schweiz* I (Zurich 1964); G. Gerig, *Reisläufer und Pensionenherren in Zürich 1519–32* (Zurich 1947); O. Vasella, *Reform und Reformation in der Schweiz* (Münster 1958); W. Oechsli, *History of Switzerland* (Cambridge 1922).

ZWINGLI: **Bibliography and research reports:** G. Finsler, *Zwingli-Bibliographie* (1897, new printing Nieukoop 1962); G. Locher,: "The Change in the Understanding of Zwingli in Recent Research" *CH* 34, 3–24 (1965); L. v. Muralt, "Probleme der Zwingli-Forschung" *Schweizerische Beiträge zur Allgemeinen Gesch.* 4 (Aarau 1946) 247–267; R. Pfister, "Die Zwingli-Forschung seit 1945" *ARG* 48 (1957) 230–240; id., "Neue Beiträge" *Zwingliana* 9 (1952) 445–452; J. v. Pollet: *RevSR* 28 (1954) 155–174, 37 (1963) 34–59, 38 (1964) 294–298; P Hauri, *Die Reformation in der Schweiz im Lichte der neueren Geschichtsschreibung* (Zurich 1945); G. W. Locher, "Wandlungen des Zwingli-Bildes" *Vox Theologica* 32 (Assen 1962) 169–182; F. Büsser, *Das katholische Zwingli-Bild von der Reformation bis zur Gegenwart* (Diss. Zurich 1964). **Biographies:** R. Staehelin, *Huldreich Zwingli. Sein Leben und sein Wirken,* 2 vols. (Basel 1895–97); W. Köhler, *Huldrych Zwingli* (1943, Stuttgart 1952); O. Farner, *Huldrych Zwingli,* 4 vols. (Zurich 1943–60); id., *Zwingli the Reformer* (New York 1952); J. Courvoisier, *Zwingli* (Geneva 1953); J. v. Pollet, *Huldrych Zwingli et la Réforme en Suisse* (Paris 1963); id., *LThK* X 1433–41; F. Schmidt-Clausing, *Zwingli* (Berlin 1965); F. Blanke, *Aus der Welt der Reformation* (Zurich 1960); Th. Pestalozzi, *Die Gegner am Grossmünsterstift* (Zurich 1918); J. Figi, *Die innere Reorganisation des Grossmünsterstiftes in Zurich 1519–31* (Phil. Diss. Zurich 1951); O. Vasella, "Die Wahl Zwinglis als Leutpriester von Glarus" *ZSKG* 51 (1957) 27–35; id., *Österreich und die Bündnispolitik der kath. Orte* (Fribourg 1951); J. Rogge,

Zwingli und Erasmus (Stuttgart 1962); J. Rilliet, *Zwingli, Third Man of the Reformation* (Philadelphia 1964); M. Haas, *Zwingli und der l. Kappeler Krieg* (Diss. Zurich 1962); cf. *Zwingliana* 12 (1964) H. 1, 93–136; 2, 35–68; L. v. Muralt, "Zwingli als Sozialpolitiker" *Zwingliana* 5 (1929–33); W. Köhler, *Zürcher Ehegericht und Genfer Konsistorium*, 2 vols. (Leipzig 1932–40); K. Kildenmann, *Die Organisation des Zürcherischen Ehegerichtes zur Zeit Zwinglis* (Zurich 1946); R. Ley, *Kirchenzucht bei Zwingli* (Zurich 1948); A. Farner, *Die Lehre von Kirche und Staat bei Zwingli* (Tübingen 1930); Erik Wolf, "Die Sozialtheologie Zwinglis" *Festschr. Guido Kisch* (Stuttgart 1955) 167–188; S. Rother, *Die religiösen und geistigen Grundlagen der Politik Zwinglis* (Erlangen 1956); J. F. G. Goeters, *L. Hätzer* (Gütersloh 1957); S. M. Jackson, *Huldreich Zwingli* (New York 1901). J. Walton, *Zwingli's Theocracy* (Toronto 1968). **Theology:** F. Blanke, "Zwinglis 'Fidei ratio' (1530). Entstehung und Bedeutung" *ARG* 57 (1966) 96–101; J. Courvoisier, *Zwingli: A Reformed Theologian* (Richmond 1963); E. Künzli, "Zwingli als Ausleger des AT" *ZW* 14, 871–899; id., *Zwingliana* 9 (1952) 185–207, 253–307; 10 (1957) 488–491; G. Krause, "Zwinglis Auslegung der Propheten" *Zwingliana* 11 (1960) 257–265; L. v. Muralt, *Zwinglis dogmatisches Sondergut* (Zurich 1932); A. Rich, *Die Anfänge der Theologie H. Zwinglis* (Zurich 1949); R. Pfister, *Das Problem der Erbsünde bei Zwingli* (Leipzig 1939); id., *Die Seligkeit erwählter Heiden bei Zwingli* (Zurich 1952); H. Schmid, *Zwinglis Lehre von der göttlichen und menschlichen Gerechtigkeit* (Zurich 1959); G. W. Locher, *Die Theologie H. Zwinglis im Lichte seiner Christologie,* 1st part: *Die Gotteslehre* (Zurich 1952); id., "Das Geschichtsbild Zwinglis" *ThZ* 9 (1953) 275–302; id., "Die Prädestinationslehre H. Zwinglis" ibid. 12 (1956) 526–548; W. Tappolet, *Das Marienlob der Reformatoren* (Tübingen 1962); G. W. Locher, "Inhalt und Absicht von Zwinglis Marienlehre" *Kirchenblatt für die reformierte Schweiz* 107 (1951) 34–37; K. Federer, "Zwingli und die Marienverehrung" *ZSKG* 45 (1951) 13–26. **Eucharistic Doctrine:** F. Blanke, "Zwinglis Sakramentsanschauung" *ThBl* 10 (1931) 283–290; C. C. Richardson, *Zwingli and Cranmer on the Eucharist* (Evanston, Ill., 1949); W. Köhler, *Zwingli und Luther. Ihr Streit über das Abendmahl nach seinen politischen und religiösen Beziehungen,* 2 vols. (Leipzig 1914, Gütersloh 1953); H. Gollwitzer, "Zur Auslegung von John 6 bei Luther und Zwingli" *In Memoriam E. Lohmeyer* (Stuttgart 1951) 143–168; H. Rückert, "Das Eindringen der Tropuslehre in die Schweizer Auffassung vom Abendmahl" *ARG* 37 (1940) 199–221; J. Courvoisier, "Vom Abendmahl bei Zwingli" *Zwingliana* 11 (1962) 415–426; J. Schweizer, *Zur Ordnung des Gottesdienstes in den nach Gottes Wort reformierten Gemeinden der deutschsprachigen Schweiz* (Zurich 1944); id., *Reformierte Abendmahlsgestaltung in der Schau Zwinglis* (o. J.); F. Schmidt-Clausing, *Zwingli als Liturgiker* (Berlin 1952); id., "Johann Ulrich Surgant, ein Wegweiser des jungen Zwingli" *Zwingliana* 11 (1961) 287–320; id., "Zwingli und die Kindertaufe" *Berliner Kirchenbriefe* 6 (1962) 4–8; G. W. Locher, *Im Geist und in der Wahrheit. Die reformatorische Wende im Gottesdienst zu Zurich* (Neukirchen 1957); M. Lenz, "Zwingli und Landgraf Philipp" *ZKG* 3 (1879); R. Hauswirth, "Landgraf Philipp v. H. und Zwingli" *Zwingliana* 11 (1962) 499–552. C. Richardson, *Zwingli and Cranmer on the Eucharist* (Evanston, Ill., 1949).

Leo Jud: Leo Jud, *Katechismen,* compiled by O. Farner (Zurich 1955); id., *Vom Leiden, Sterben und Auferstehen des Herrn,* revised by O. Farner (Zurich 1955); Schottenloher 9528–34f., 36656, 55341–48; L. Weiss, *Leo Jud, Ulrich Zwinglis Kampfgenosse* (Zurich 1942); O. Farner, "Leo Jud, Zwinglis treuester Helfer" *Zwingliana* 10 (1955) 201ff.

Constance: A. Willburger, *Die Konstanzer Bischöfe Hugo v. Landenberg, Balthasar Merklin, Johann v. Lupfen (1496–1537) und die Glaubensspaltung* (Münster 1917); C. Gröber, "Die Reformation in Konstanz von ihrem Anfang bis zum Tode Hugos von

Hohenlandenberg (1517–32)" *FreibDiözArch* 46 (1919) 120–322; Th. Gottlob, *Die Offiziale des Bistums Konstanz im MA* (Limburg 1951); O. Vasella, *Das Visitationsprotokoll über den Schweizer Klerus des Bistums Konstanz von 1586* (Bern 1963); L. Helbling, *Dr. Johann Fabri und die schweizerische Reformation* (Einsiedeln 1933).

ST. GALLEN: Th. Müller, *Die St. Gallische Glaubensbewegung* (1520–30) (St. Gallen 1913); P. Staerkle, *Beiträge zur spätmittelalterlichen Bildungsgeschichte St. Gallens* (St. Gallen 1939); G. Thürer, *St. Gallen Geschichte,* 1st vol. (St. Gallen 1953), cf. *HJ* 76 (1956) 518; K. Spillmann, *Zwingli und die Zürcherische Politik gegenüber der Abtei St. Gallen* (St. Gallen 1965).

VADIAN: Schottenloher 21628–56, 58615–40; J. Ninck, *Arzt und Reformator Vadian* (St. Gallen 1936); W. Näf, *Vadian und seine Stadt St. Gallen,* 2 vols. (St. Gallen 1944–57) (lit.); *Vadianstudien. Untersuchungen und Texte,* ed. W. Näf, 1–7 (St. Gallen 1945–62); C. Bonorand, "Stand und Probleme der Vadianforschung" *Zwingliana* 11 (1959 bis 1963) 586–606; id., "J. Vadian und die Täufer," *Schweizer Beiträge zur allg. Gesch.* 2 (1953) 43–72.

TOGGENBURG: O. Frei, *Die Reformation im Toggenburg* (Zurich 1920).

GRAUBÜNDEN: E. Camenisch, *Bündnerische Reformationsgeschichte* (Chur 1920); id., *Gesch. und Reformation und Gegenreformation in den italienischen Südtalern Graubündens* (Chur 1950); O. Vasella, "Bauernkrieg und Reformation in Graubünden 1525 bis 1526" *ZSKG* 20 (1940) 1–65; id., *Abt Theodul Schlegel von Chur und seine Zeit* (Freiburg, Switz. 1954) (lit.).

APPENZELLERLAND: J. Willi, *Die Reformation im Lande Appenzell* (Bern 1924).

SCHAFFHAUSEN: J. Wipf, *Reformationsgeschichte der Stadt und Landschaft Schaffhausen* (Zurich 1929).

BASEL: Schottenloher 23706–58, 59189–59219; Wackernagel, *Gesch. der Stadt Basel,* 3rd vol.: *Humanismus und Reformation* (Basel 1924); E. Staehelin, *Das Buch der Basler Reformation* (Basel 1929); K. Gauss, "Basels erstes Reformationsmandat" *Basler Jahrbuch* 50 (1930) 185–224; P. Roth, *Die Reformation in Basel,* 1st part: *Die Vorbereitungsjahre* (1525-28): Neujahrsblatt 114 (Basel 1936); id., *Durchbruch und Festsetzung der Reformation in Basel* (Basel 1942); P. Burckhardt, *Gesch. der Stadt Basel von der Zeit der Reformation bis zur Gegenwart* (Basel ²1957); W. Brändly, "Oswald Myconius in Basel" *Zwingliana* 11 (1959–63) 183–192.

OECOLAMPADIUS: E. Staehelin, "Oekolampad-Bibliographie" *Basler Zeitschrift für Gesch. und Altertumskunde* 17 (1918) 1–119; id., *Briefe und Akten zum Leben Oekolampads* I: 1499–1526 (Leipzig 1927), II: 1527–1593 (Leipzig 1934) (lit.); id., *Das theologische Lebenswerk Joh. Oekolampads* (Leipzig 1939); H. W. Frei, "Johannes Oekolampads Versuch, Kirchenzucht durch den Bann zu üben" *Zwingliana* 7 (1939–43) 494–503; A. Moser, "Die Anfänge der Freundschaft zwischen Zwingli und Oekolampad" *Zwingliana* 10 (1958) 614–620.

BERN: *Gedenkschrift zur Vierjahrhundertfeier der bernischen Kirchenreformation,* 2 vols. (Bern 1928); W. Koehler, *Zwingli und Bern* (Tübingen 1928); O. E. Strasser, *Capitos Beziehungen zu Bern* (Leipzig 1928); H. Specker, *Die Reformationswirren im Berner Oberland 1528* (Freiburg, Switz. 1951); R. Feller, *Gesch. Berns,* 2nd vol.: *Von der Reformation bis zum Bauernkrieg 1516–1653* (Bern 1953); K. Guggisberg, *Bernische Kirchengeschichte* (Bern 1958).

THE DISPUTATION AT BADEN: Schottenloher 41283c-97; A. Baur, "Zur Vorge-schichte der Disputation von Baden" *ZKG* 21 (1901) 91–111; L. v. Muralt, *Die Badener Disputation* (Leipzig 1926); A. Weiss, "Das Kloster Engelberg unter Abt A. Bürki" *ZSKG Beiheft* 16 (1956); Th. Platter, *Lebensbeschreibung,* ed. A. Hartmann (Basel 1944).

THE DISPUTATION AT BERN: Text: E. F. K. Müller, *Die Bekenntnisschriften der Reformierten Kirche* (Leipzig 1903); Schottenloher 41299–311; F. Schlachter, *Das Evangelische der Reformation am Berner Religionsgespräch 1528* (Bern 1909); K. Lindt, "Der theologische Gehalt der Berner Disputation" *Gedenkschrift zur Vierjahrhundert-feier* I: 301–344; L. v. Muralt, "Zwinglis Mitwirkung an der Berner Disputation" *ZW* 6: 1202–225.

15. *Anabaptists and Spiritualists*

LITERATURE

GENERAL: **Bibliography:** H. J. Hillerbrand, *A Bibliography of Anabaptism* (Elkart 1962); Schottenloher 44213a–44512, 52181–52191, 64167–64431. **Sources:** Hillerbrand 2683–3542; *Quellen zur Geschichte der Wiedertäufer* (in late vols, *Täufer*): Vol. 1, *Württem-berg,* ed. G. Bossert (Leipzig 1930): Vol. 2, *Bayern I,* ed. K. Schornbaum (Leipzig 1934): Vol. 3, *Glaubenszeugnisse oberdeutscher Taufgesinnter,* ed. L. Müller (Leipzig 1938); Vol. 4, *Baden und Pfalz,* ed. M. Krebs (Gütersloh 1951); Vol. 5, *Bayern II,* ed. K. Schornbaum (Gütersloh 1951); Vol. 7–8, *Elsass 1–2,* ed. M. Krebs–H. G. Rott (Gütersloh 1959–60); *Quellen zur Geschichte der Täufer in der Schweiz:* I., *Zürich,* ed. L. von Muralt and W. Schmid (Zurich 1952); *Urkundliche Quellen zur Hessischen Reformationsgeschichte:* IV., *Wiedertäuferakten 1527–1626,* ed. G. Franz (Marburg 1951); *Urkunden zur Geschichte des Bauernkrieges und der Wiedertäufer,* ed. H. Böhmer (Berlin 1933); *Spiritual and Anabaptist Writers,* ed. G. H. Williams (Philadelphia 1957); *Der linke Flügel der Reforma-tion. Glaubenszeugnisse der Täufer,* ed. H. Fast (Bremen 1962) (=H. Fast); *Bibliotheca Reformatoria Neerlandica,* ed. S. Cramer–F. Pijper (Gravenhage 1903–14) (=BRN); *Documenta Reformatoria 1,* ed. J. N. Bakhuizen van den Brink et al. (Kampen 1960). **Literature:** *The Mennonite Quarterly Review* (Goshen, Ind., 1927f.) (=*MQR*); *Men-nonitisches Lexikon* (Frankfurt–Karlsruhe 1913–58 (=*ML*); *The Mennonite Encyclopedia,* 4 vols. (Scottdale, Pa. 1955–59); W. Wiswedel, *Bilder und Führergestalten aus dem Täufer-tum* III (Kassel 1952); S. Hirzel, *Heimliche Kirche. Ketzerchronik aus den Tagen der Refor-mation* (Hamburg 1953); F. H. Littel, *The Anabaptist View of the Church* (Boston 1958); H. A. E. van Gelder, *The Two Reformations* (The Hague 1961); G. H. Williams, *The Radical Reformation* (Philadelphia 1962); J. C. Wenger, *Die dritte Reformation* (Kassel 1963); G. F. Hershberger, *Das Täufertum* (Stuttgart 1963); K. Holl, "Luther und die Schwärmer" *Gesammelte Aufsätze* I (Tübingen 1923) 420–467; H. S. Bender, "Die Zwickauer Propheten, Thomas Müntzer und die Täufer" *ThZ* 8 (1952) 262–278; R. Stupperich, "Melanchthon und die Täufer" *KuD* 3 (1957) 150–170; H. J. Hillerbrand, "Anabaptism and the Reformation: Another Look" *CH* 29 (1960) 404–423; U. Bergfried, *Verantwortung als theologisches Problem im Täufertum des 16. Jh.* (Wuppertal 1938); F. Heyer, *Der Kirchenbegriff der Schwärmer* (Leipzig 1939); W. Wiswedel, "The Inner and the Outer Word" *MQR* 26 (1952) 171–191; F. H. Littell, *Von der Freiheit der Kirche* (Bad Nauheim 1957); G. Rupp, "Word and Spirit in the Reformation" *ARG* (1958) 13–26. C. Clasen, *Anabaptism: A Social History* (Ithaca, N.Y. 1972).

1. THE SWISS BRETHREN AND THE LOWER GERMAN ANABAPTISTS: *Ausbund, das ist: Etliche schöne christliche Lieder, Wie sie in dem Gefängnis zu Passau . . . von den*

Schweizer-Brüdern . . . gedichtet worden (Lancaster County, Pa. 1935). Literature: E. Bernhofer, *Täuferische Denkweisen und Lebensformen im Spiegel mittel-und oberdeutscher Täuferverhöre* (Diss. Freiburg 1967); G. Zschäbitz, *Zur mitteldeutschen Täuferbewegung nach dem grossen Bauernkrieg* (Berlin 1958); H. W. Schraepler, *Die rechtliche Behandlung der Täufer in der deutschen Schweiz, Südwestdeutschland und Hessen 1525–1618* (Tübingen 1957); H. J. Hillerbrand, *Die Politische Ethik des oberdeutschen Täufertums* (Leiden–Cologne 1962); Ch. H. Hege, *Die Täufer in der Kurpfalz* (Frankfurt 1908); E. F. P. Güss, *Die kurpfälzische Regierung und das Täufertum* (Stuttgart 1960).

THE SWISS BRETHREN: W. Köhler, "Die Zürcher Täufer" *Gedenkschrift zum 400jährigen Jubiläum der Mennoniten oder Täufgesinnten 1525–1925,* ed. C. Neff (Ludwigshafen 1925) 48–64; F. Blanke, "Beobachtungen zum ältesten Täuferbekenntnis" *ARG* 37 (1940) 240–249; O. Vasella, "Zur Geschichte der Täuferbewegung in der Schweiz" *ZSKG* 48 (1954) 179–186; P. Peachy, *Die soziale Herkunft der Schweizer Täufer in der Reformationszeit* (Karlsruhe 1954); F. Blanke, *Brüder in Christo: Die Geschichte der ältesten Täufergemeinde* (Zurich 1955); J. Yoder, *Täufertum und Reformation: I, Die Gespräche zwischen Täufern und Reformierten in der Schweiz 1523–1548* (Karlsruhe 1962).

CONRAD GREBEL: Hillerbrand 1484–1508; H. Fast 9–27; H. S. Bender, *Conrad Grebel (c. 1498–1526): The Founder of the Swiss Brethren* (Goshen 1950).

FELIX MANTZ: Hillerbrand 1840–1847; H. Fast 27–35; E. Krajewski, *Leben und Sterben des Zürcher Täuferführers Felix Mantz* (Kassel 1958); id., "The Theology of Felix Mantz," *MQR* 36 (1962) 76–87.

JÖRG BLAUROCK: Hillerbrand 1190–1199; J. A. Moore, *Der starke Jörg* (Kassel 1955); *NDB* II: 292.

MICHAEL SATTLER: Hillerbrand 2276–2285; Schottenloher 57954–57969; H. Fast 58–77; *ML* 4 (1959) 29–38.

WILHELM REUBLIN: Hillerbrand 2216–2221; H. Fast, "Neues zum Leben Wilhelm Reublins" *ThZ* 11 (1955) 420–426; *ML* 3 (1958) 477–481.

BALTHASAR HUBMAIER: Hillerbrand 1602–1640a; Schottenloher 9057–9075, 46993–46998, 55259–55266a; *Hubmaiers Schriften,* ed. G. Westin–T. Bergsten (Gütersloh 1962); H. Fast 35–58; C. Sachsse, *D. Balthasar Hubmaier als Theologe* (Berlin 1914); W. Wiswedel, *Balthasar Hubmaier* (Kassel 1939); *ML* 2, 353–363; T. Bergsten, *Balthasar Hubmaier* (Kassel 1961).

HANS DENCK: Hillerbrand 1350–1402; *Schriften* I (with bibliog.), ed. G. Baring (Gütersloh 1955); II (with bibliog.) and III, ed. W. Fellmann (Gütersloh 1956–60); O. E. Vittali, *Die Theologie des Wiedertäufers Hans Denck* (Offenburg 1932); J. J. Kiwiet, "The Life of Hans Denck" *MQR* 31 (1957) 227–259; id., "The Theology of Hans Denck" *MQR* 32 (1958) 3–27; G. Baring, "Hans Denck und Thomas Müntzer in Nürnberg 1524" *ARG* 50 (1959) 145–181; W. Fellmann, "Der theologische Gehalt der Schriften Dencks" *Leibhaftigkeit des Wortes. Festgabe für Adolf Köberle* (Hamburg 1958) 157–165; id., "Irenik und Polemik bei Hans Denck" *LuJ* 29 (1962) 110–116.

LUDWIG HÄTZER: Hillerbrand 1528–1549a; J. F. G. Goeters, *Ludwig Hätzer* (Gütersloh 1957).

HANS HUT: Hillerbrand 1648–1659; H. Fast 79–99; W. Neuser, *Hans Hut* (Berlin 1913); H. Klassen, "The Life and Teaching of Hans Hut" *MQR* 33 (1959) 171–205; id., "Hans Hut und Thomas Müntzer" *MQR* 267–304.

BIBLIOGRAPHY

2. THE HUTTERIAN BRETHREN: Hillerbrand 221–336; *Die älteste Chronik der Hutterischen Brüder,* ed. A. J. F. Zieglschmid (Ithaca, N.Y. 1943); *Das Kleingeschichtsbuch der Hutterischen Brüder,* ed. A. J. P. Zieglschmid (Philadelphia 1947); F. Hubry, "Die Wiedertäufer in Mähren" *ARG* 30–32 (1935) 1–36, 1–40, 61–102, 170–211; R. Friedmann, "The Christian Communism of the Hutterite Brethren" *ARG* 46 (1955) 196–209; G. Mecenseffy, "Die Herkunft des oberösterreichischen Täufertums" *ARG* 47 (1956) 252–259; G. J. Neumann, "Nach und von Mähren" *ARG* 48 (1957) 75–90; P. Hofer, *The Hutterian Brethren and their Beliefs* (Starbuck Man 1955); V. J. Peters, *A History of the Hutterian Brethren, 1528–1558* (Diss. Göttingen 1960); R. Friedmann, *Hutterite Studies* (Goshen, Ind. 1961).

JAKOB HUTTER: H. F. Fischer, *Jakob Hutter* (Diss. Vienna 1949–Newton 1956); R. Friedmann, "Jakob Hutter's Last Epistle to the Church in Moravia 1535" *MQR* 34 (1960) 37–47. Z. Zeman, *The Anabaptists and the Czech Brethren in Moravia* (The Hague 1969).

3. THE ANABAPTISTS IN THE LOW COUNTRIES AND IN NORTH GERMANY: Hillerbrand 877–1094; Schottenloher 44213a–44513, 52181–52188, 64314–64324; W. J. Kühler, *Geschiedenis der nederlandsche Doopsgezinden* I–III (Haarlem 1961); N. van der Zijpp, *Geschiedenis der Doopsgezinden in Nederland* (Arnheim 1952); A. F. Mellink, *De Wederdopers in de Noordelijke Neerlanden 1531–1544* (Groningen–Djakarta 1954); A. L. E. Verheyden, *Geschiedenis der Doopsgezinden in de zuidelijke Nederlanden in de XVIe eeuw* (Brussel 1959); J. F. G. Goeters, "Die Rolle des Täufertums in der Reformationsgeschichte des Niederrheins" *Rheinische Vierteljahresblätter* 24 (1959) 217–236; H. Stiasny, *Die strafrechtliche Verfolgung der Täufer in der freien Reichsstadt Köln 1529–1618* (Münster 1962).

MELCHIOR HOFMANN: Hillerbrand 1570–1593; H. Fast 196–318; W. I. Leendertz, *Melchior Hofmann* (Haarlem 1883); F. O. zur Linden, *Melchior Hofmann* (Haarlem 1885); P. Kawerau, *Melchior Hof(f)man als religiöser Denker* (Haarlem 1954); E. W. Kohls, "Ein Sendbrief Melchior Hofmanns aus den Jahre 1534" *ThZ* 17 (1961) 356–365.

THE MÜNSTER ANABAPTISTS: Hillerbrand 513–767; Bahlmann: *Zschr. für vaterländische Gesch. u. Altertumskunde* 51 (1893) 119–174; off print with additions (Münster 1894); K. Löffler, "Zur Bibliographie der münsterischen Wiedertäufer" *ZblB* 24 (1907) 116–118; H. Detmer, "Ungedruckte Quellen zur Geschichte der Wiedertäufer in Münster" *Zschr. für vaterländische Gesch. u. Altertumskunde* 51 (1893) 90–118; C. A. Cornelius, *Berichte der Augenzeugen über das Münsterische Wiedertäuferreich* (Münster 1853); *Hermanni a Kerssenbroch Anabaptistici furoris . . . narratio,* ed. H. Detmer, 2 vols. (Münster 1899–1900); *Die Wiedertäufer zu Münster 1534–35. Berichte, Aussagen und Aktenstücke von Augenzeugen und Zeitgenossen,* ed. K. Löffler (Jena 1923). **Literature:** C. A. Cornelius, *Geschichte des Münsterischen Aufruhrs,* 2 vols. (Leipzig 1855–60); L. Keller, *Geschichte der Wiedertäufer und ihres Reichs zu Münster* (Münster 1880); F. Blanke, "Das Reich der Wiedertäufer zu Münster 1534–35" *ARG* 37 (1940) 13–37; H. Rothert, *Das Tausendjährige Reich der Wiedertäufer zu Münster 1534–35* (Münster 1947); R. Stupperich, *Das Münsterische Täufertum* (Münster 1958); H. Neumann, *Masse und Führer in der Wiedertäuferherrschaft in Münster* (Diss. Freiburg 1959); K. H. Kirchhoff, "Die Wiedertäufer in Coesfeld" *WZ* 106 (1956) 113–174.

BERNHARD ROTHMANN: Hillerbrand 2254–2270; R. Stupperich, *Die Schriften der münsterischen Täufer und ihrer Gegner* 1: *Die Schriften Bernhard Rothmanns* (Münster

1968); H. Fast 340–360; F. J. Wray, "The 'Vermanung' of 1542 and Rothmann's 'Bekenntnisse' " *ARG* 47 (1956) 243–251.

OBBE PHILIPS: *BRN* 7; H. Fast 318–340; B. Stroman, *Obbe Philipsz, oudste der Doopers* (Hilversum 1935); J. A. Brandsma, "Is Obbe Filips wer Roomsk wurden?" *It Breaken. Tydskrift fan der Fryske Akademy* 22 (1960) 119–121.

DIRK PHILIPS: *BRN* 10; *Enchiridion oder Handbüchlein von der christlichen Lehre und Religion* (Scottdale, Pa. 1920); C. J. Dyck, "The Christology of Dirk Philips" *MQR* 31 (1957) 147–155, 277–295; W. Keeney, *Dirk Philips* (Diss. Hartford Theol. Seminary 1957); id., *MQR* 32 (1958) 171–191, 298–306; J. ten Doornkaat Koolman, "Een onbekende brief van Dirk Philips (1550)" *Nederlands Archief voor Kerkgeschiednis* 43 (1959) 15–21; id., *Dirk Philips* (Haarlem 1964).

MENNO SIMONS: Hillerbrand 1893–2002e; Schottenloher 15370–15580a, 48248–48254, 57026–57046; C. Krahn, "Menno Simons Research (1910–1960)" *CH* 30 (1961) 473–480; *Opera omnia theologica* (Amsterdam 1681); *The Complete Works,* 2 vols. (Elkhart 1876–81); *The Complete Writings,* trans. L. Verduin, ed. C. Wenger, with a biography by H. S. Bender (Scottdale, Pa. 1956); H. Fast 147–169. **Literature:** C. H. Smith, *The Story of the Mennonites,* 3rd rev. ed. C. Krahn (Newton 1957); F. H. Littell, *A Tribute to Menno Simons* (Scottdale, Pa. 1961); H. W. Meihuizen, *Menno Simons* (Haarlem 1961); J. A. Brandsma, *Menno Simons* (Kassel 1962) (from the Dutch); I. B. Horst, *A Bibliography of Menno Simons* (Wieuwboop 1962).

4. SPIRITUALISM:

KASPAR SCHWENCKFELD: Schottenloher 19575–19720, 49233–49247, 58077–58140. Works: *Corpus Schwenckfeldianorum,* 19 vols. (Leipzig 1907ff.); H. Fast 204–217. **Literature:** G. Wolf, *Quellenkunde der deutschen Reformationsgeschichte* II/2 (Gotha 1922) 171–183; S. G. Schultz, *Caspar Schwenckfeld von Ossig* (Norristown, Pa. 1946); H. Urner, "Die Taufe bei Caspar Schwenckfeld" *ThLZ* 73 (1948) 329–342; H. J. Schoeps, *Vom Himmlischen Fleisch Christi* (Tübingen 1951); K. Ecke, *Kaspar Schwenckfeld* (Gütersloh 1952); P. G. Eberlein, "Schwenckfelds Urteil über die Augsburger Konfession" *Jahrbuch für die Schlesische Kirche und Kirchengesch.* NF 34 (1955) 581–586; G. Maron, *Individualismus und Gemeinschaft bei Caspar von Schwenckfeldt* (Stuttgart 1961); J. H. Seyppel, *Schwenckfeld, Knight of Faith* (Pennsburg, Pa. 1961); R. Pietz, *Der Mensch ohne Christus. Eine Untersuchung zur Anthropologie Schwenckfelds* (Diss. Tübingen 1956); W. Knörrlich, *Kaspar von Schwenckfeld und die Reformation in Schlesien* (Diss. Bonn 1957); T. Bergsten, "Pilgram Marbeck und seine Auseinandersetzung mit Caspar Schwenckfeld" *Kyrkohistorik Arsskrift* 57 (1957) 39–100, 58 (1958) 53–87; P. L. Maier, *Caspar Schwenckfeld on the Person and Work of Christ* (Assen 1959); R Pietz, *Die Gestalt der zukünftigen Kirche. Schwenckfelds Gespräch mit Luther 1525* (Stuttgart 1959); W. Knoke, "Schwenckfelds Sakramentsverständnis" *ZRGG* 11 (1959) 314–327.

SEBASTIAN FRANCK: Hillerbrand 1453a–1457; Schottenloher 6472–6536, 46321–46334, 54608–54623; H. Fast 217–248; B. Becker, "Nederlandsche vertalingen van Sebastiaan Francks geschriften" *Nederlands Archief voor Kerkgeschiedenis* 21 (1928) 149–160; A. Hegler, *Geist und Schrift bei Sebastian Franck* (Freiburg 1892); W. E. Peuckert, *Sebastian Franck* (München 1943); E. Teufel, *"Landräumig." Sebastian Franck* (Neustadt a.d. Aisch 1954); K. Räber, *Studien zur Geschichtsbibel Sebastian Francks* (Basel 1952); J. Lindeboom, *Een Franc-tireur der Reformatie, Sebastian Franck* (Arnheim 1952); S. L. Verheus, *Kroniek en Kerugma. Een theolog. studie over de Geschichtsbibel van Sebastiaan Franck* (Arnheim 1958).

16. The Catholic Literary Opponents of Luther and the Reformation

TEXTS

Corpus Catholicorum (=*CCath.*) *Werke kath. Schriftsteller im Zeitalter der Glaubensspaltung,* to date 29 vols. (Münster 1919–67). For the origins of this series see H. Jedin, *Jos. Greving (1868–1919)* (Münster 1954).

LITERATURE

K. Werner, *Geschichte der apologetischen und polemischen Literatur der christlichen Theologie* IV (Schaffhausen 1865); H. Laemmer, *Die vortridentinischkatholische Theologie des Reformationszeitalters* (Berlin 1858); F. Falk, "Das Corpus Catholicorum" *Der Katholik* 71/1 (1891) 440–463; N. Paulus, "Kath. Schriftsteller aus der Reformationszeit" *Katholik* 72/1 (1892) 544–564; 73/2 (1893) 213–223; id., *Die deutschen Dominikaner im Kampf gegen Luther (1518–63)* (Freiburg 1903); F. Lauchert, *Die italienischen literarischen Gegner Luthers* (Freiburg 1912); G. Wolf, "Die kath. Gegner der Reformation vor dem Tridentinum und Jesuitenorden" *Quellenkunde der dt. Reformationsgeschichte* II ²(Gotha 1922) 206–262; P. Polman, *Die polemische Methode der ersten Gegner der Reformation* (Münster 1931); id., *L'élément historique dans la controverse religieuse du XVIᵉ siècle* (Gembloux 1932); H. Jedin, "Die geschichtl. Bedeutung der kath. Kontroversliteratur im Zeitalter der Glaubensspaltung" *HJ* 53 (1933) 70–97; id., *The Council of Trent* (St. Louis 1957) 355–409; J. Lortz, *The Reformation in Germany* (New York 1968) 175–223; E. Iserloh, *Der Kampf um die Messe in den ersten Jahren der Auseinandersetzung mit Luther* (Münster 1952); *Acta Reformationis catholicae ecclsiam Germaniae concernantia,* ed. G. Pfeilschifter, I: 1520–1532 (Regensburg 1959), II: 1532–42 (1960); J. P. Dolan, "The Catholic Literary Opponents of Luther" *Journal of Ecumenical Studies* II (1974) 447–466;

JOHANNES ECK: List of Writings: J. Metzler, *CCath* 16 (1930) LXXI–CXXXI. New editions: *CCath* 1 (1919), 2 (1921), 6 (1923), 13 (1928), 14 (1929); W. Friedensburg, "Dr. Johannes Ecks Denkschriften zur dt. Kirchenreformation 1523" *Beitr. zur bayer, Kirchengesch.* 2 (Erlangen 1895–96) 159–196, 222–253; id., Letters, *ZKG* 19 (1899) 211–264, 473–485; J. Greving, *Eck als junger Gelehrter* (Münster 1906); id., *Ecks Pfarrbuch für U. L. F. in Ingolstadt* (Münster 1914); H. Schauerte, *Die Busslehre des Johannes Eck* (Münster 1919); W. Gussmann, *Des Johannes Eck 404 Artikel zum Reichstag von Augsburg 1530* (Kassel 1930); H. Rupprich, *Der Eckius Dedolatus und sein Verf.* (Vienna 1931); G. v. Pölnitz, "Die Beziehungen des Johannes Eck zum Augsburger Kapital" *HJ* 60 (1940) 685–705; Th. Wiedemann, *Dr. Johannes Eck* (Regensburg 1865); H. G. Assel, *Das kanon. Zinsverbot und der 'Geist' des Frühkapitalismus in der Wirtschaftsethik bei Eck und Luther* (unpublished Diss., Erlangen 1948); E. Iserloh, *Die Eucharistie in der Darstellung des Johannes Eck* (Münster 1950); F. Zeopfl, *Johannes Eck: Lebensbilder aus dem Bayer. Schwaben* (Münich 1958) 186–216; Gerh. Müller, "Johannes Eck und die Confessio Augustana. Zwei unbekannte Aktenstücke vom Augsburger Reichstag 1530" *QFIAB* 38 (1958) 205–242.

HIERONYMUS EMSER: Works: L. Enders, *Luther und Emser. Ihre Streitschriften aus dem Jahre 1521,* 2 vols. (Halle 1890–91); *De disputatione Lipsicensi (1519), A venatione Luteriana assertio (1519),* ed. X. Thurnhofer; *CCath* 4 (Münster 1921). Letters: *RGStT* 3 u. 40; 5 *Messopferschriften 1524–25,* ed. Th. Freudenberger; *CCath* 28 (Münster 1959). Literature: P. Mosen, *Hieronymus Emser* (Halle 1890); G. Kawerau. *Hieronymus Emser* (Halle 1898); F. Gess, *Akten und Briefe zur Kirchenpolitik Herzog Georgs von Sachsen,* 2 vols. (Leipzig 1905–17); F. Jenssen, *Emsers N. T. in niederdt. Übertragung* (Schwerin

1933); G. Reichel, *Herzog Georg der Bärtige und Erasmus von Rotterdam* (Diss. Leipzig 1947); O. Vossler, "Herzog Georg der Bärtige und seine Ablehnung Luthers" *HZ* 184 (1957) 272–291.

JOHANNES COCHLAEUS: List of Writings: M. Spahn, *Johannes Cochlaeus* (Berlin 1898) 341–373 New editions: *Flugschriften aus den ersten Jahren der Reformation* IV (Leipzig 1910) 177–218; *CCath* III, XV, XVII, XVIII; *CT* XII, 166–208. Letters: *ZKG* 18 (1898); *RGStT* 3 (1907) 14–18, 44–51, 53ff., 57, 59–65; 7 (1909) 32ff., 45ff., 51ff., 58–62; 21–22 (1912) 248–252; *RQ* 35 (1927) 447–451 with additional letters; ArSKG 5 (1940) 216–220. Literature: M. Spahn, *Johannes Cochlaeus* (Berlin 1898); H. Jedin, *Des Johannes Cochlaeus Streitschrift de libero arbitrio hominis (1525)* (Breslau 1927); id., *Schlesische Lebensbilder* IV (Breslau 1931) 18–28; A. Herte, *Die Lutherkommentare des Johannes Cochlaeus* (Münster 1935); id., *Das kath. Lutherbild im Bann der Lutherkommentare des Cochlaeus,* 3 vols. (Münster 1943); K. Kastner, "Cochlaeus und das Priestertum" *ArSKG* 10 (1952) 84–105.

JOHANNES FABRI: Works: *Opuscula* (Leipzig 1537); *Opera* (Cologne 1537–41); *Malleus in haeresim Lutheranam,* ed. A. Naegele; *CCath* 23–26 (Münster 1941–52); *CT* IV: 10–23. Literature: A. Horawitz, "J. Heigerlein (gen. Fabri) bis zum Regensburger Convent" *SAW* 107 (1884) 83–220; K. Czerwenka, *Johannes Fabri als Generalvikar von Konstanz* (Diss. Vienna 1903); L. Helbling, *Johannes Fabri* (Münster 1941, with further lit. and ref. to sep. works).

FRIEDRICH NAUSEA: Letters, ed. W. Friedensburg: *ZKG* 20 (1900) 500–545; 21 (1901) 537–594; *Acta Reformationis Catholicae* II (Regensburg 1960) 547–555; "Reformgutachten" *CT* XII: 364–426, 428–431. Literature: J. Metzner, *Friedrich Nausea* (Regensburg 1884); J. G. Mayer, "Bischof Nausea auf dem Konzil von Trient" *HJ* 8 (1887) 1–27; H. Gollob, *Friedrich Nausea* (Vienna 1952); H. Jedin, "Das konziliare Reformprogramm Friedrich Nauseas" *HJ* 77 (1958) 229–253; J. Wodka, *Kirche in Österreich* (Vienna 1959) 201–205.

BERTHOLD VON CHIEMSEE: *Tewtsche Theologey,* ed. W. Reithmeier (Munich 1852); F. X. Remberger, "Die Lehre von der Kirche in der 'Tewtschen Theologey'" *MThZ* 9 (1958) 97–109.

LOUVAIN UNIVERSITY: H. De Jongh, *L'ancienne faculté de théologie de Louvain* (Louvain 1911); E. de Moreau, "Luther et l'université de Louvain" *NRTh* 54 (1927) 402–435; R. Guelluy, "L'évolution des méthodes théologiques à Louvain d'Erasmus à Jansenius" *RHE* 37 (1941) 52–71; J. Étienne, *Spiritualisme érasmien et théologiens louvanistes* (Louvain 1956); K. Blockx, *De Veroordeeling van Maarten Luther door de Theol. faculteit de Leuven in 1519* (Brussels 1958).

JAMES LATOMUS: *Opera Omnia* (Louvain 1550); "De Primatu Romani Pontificis (1525)" *Bibliotheca reformatoria neerlandica* III, ed. F. Pijper (The Hague 1905) 111–195; J. Étienne, *Spiritualisme érasmien* 163–186 (works and lit.).

ALBERT PIGGE: H. Jedin, *Studien über die Schriftstellertätigkeit Albert Pigges* (Münster 1931); L. Pfeifer, *Ursprung der kath. Kirche und Zugehörigkeit zur Kirche nach Albert Pigge* (Würzburg 1938); J. Feiner, *Die Erbsündenlehre Albert Pigges* (Zurich 1940); M. E. Kronenberg, "Albert Pigge zijn geschriften en zijn bibliotheek" *Het Boek* 28 (1944) 107–158, 226; R. Bäumer, *Die Unfehlbarkeitslehre Albert Pigges* (Diss. Bonn 1956); id., "Die Auseinandersetzung über die römische Petrustradition in den ersten Jahrzehnten der Reformationszeit" *RQ* 57 (1962) 20–57.

HENRY VIII: *Letters and Papers of the Reign of Henry VIII,* ed. J. S. Brewer, 21 vols.

BIBLIOGRAPHY

(London 1861–1910); C. S. Meyer, "Henry VIII burns Luther's Books, 12 May 1521" *JEH* 9 (1958) 173–187; P. Hughes, *The Reformation in England*, 3 vols. (London 1951–54); E. Koermberg, *Henry VIII and Luther* (Stanford 1961); H. E. Jacobs, *The Lutheran Movement in England* (Philadelphia 1894); L. B. Smith, *Tudor Prelates and Politics* (Princeton 1953); E. F. Pollard, *Henry VIII* (London 1913); H. Thieme, *Die Ehescheidung Heinrichs VIII. und die europäischen Universitäten* (Karlsruhe 1957).

JOHN FISHER: *Opera*, ed. G. Fleischmann (Würzburg 1597); *English Works*, ed. J. B. Mayor (London 1876). Suppl. (London 1921); *Sacerdotii defensio: CCath* 9 (Münster 1925); T. E. Bridgett, *Life of blessed John Fisher* (London 1888, 1922); J. Grisar, "Der hl. Martyrer John Fisher" *StdZ* 129 (1935) 217–230; F. P. Bellabriga, *De doctrine beati Joannis Fisher in operibus adversus Lutherum* (Rome 1934); V. McNabb, *St John Fisher* (London 1935); O. Hendriks, *John Fisher. Bissehop en martelaar* (Nijmegen 1947).

THOMAS MORE: *Opera Omnia latina* (Frankfurt–Leipzig 1689; n. ed., Frankfurt 1963); *English Works*, ed. W. Rastell (London 1557), re-edited by W. E. Campbell, 2 vols. (London 1931). Literature: *Moreana 1478–1945*, ed. F.–M. P. Sullivan (Kansas City–Los Angeles 1946); T. E. Bridgett, *Life and Writings of Sir Thomas Morus* (London 1892); E. M. G. Routh, *Sir Thomas Morus and his Friends* (London 1934); *AAS* 27 (1935) 159–162, 201–208; R. W. Chambers, *Thomas Morus* (London 1935), German (Munich 1946, lit.); W. E. Champbell, *Erasmus, Tyndale and More* (London 1949); P. Huber, *Traditionsfestigkeit und Traditionskritik bei Thomas Morus* (Basel 1953); E. Flesseman van Leer, "The Controversy about Scripture and Tradition between Thomas Morus and W. Tyndale" *Ned. Archief voor Kerkgesch. NS* 43 (The Hague 1959) 143–164; id., "The Controversy about Ecclesiology between Thomas Morus and W. Tyndale" ibid. 44 (1960) 65–86; H. de Vocht, *Acta Thomae More* (Louvain 1947); G. J. Donnelly, *A Translation of Sir Thomas More's Responsio ad Lutherum* (Washington 1962); E. F. Rogers, ed., *The Correspondence of Sir Thomas More* (Princeton 1947); id., *Selected Letters* (New Haven 1961); E. E. Reynolds, *St. Thomas More* (London 1953); T. Stapelton, *Thomas Mori. in Tres Thomae* (Cologne 1612); L. Bradner–C. A. Lynch, *The Latin Epigrams of Thomas More* (Chicago 1953); R. W. Gibson, *St Thomas More: A Preliminary Bibliography* (New Haven 1961); G. Marchadour, *L'Univers de Thomas More* (Paris 1963); R. Ames, *Citizen Thomas More and his Utopia* (Princeton 1949); E. L. Surtz, *The Praise of Pleasure* (Cambridge, Mass. 1957); id., *The Praise of Wisdom* (Chicago 1957); J. H. Hexter, *More's Utopia* (New York 1965); J. P. Dolan and W. Greene, *The Essential Thomas More* (New York 1967); J. M. Headley, "Thomas Murner, Thomas More, and the First Expression of More's Ecclesiology" *Studies in the Renaissance* XIV 73–92; A. Prévost, *Saint Thomas More, contribution a l'histoire de la pensée religieuse* (Diss. Lille 1945).

SILVESTER PRIERIAS: F. Lauchert, *Die it. literarischen Gegner Luthers* (Freiburg 1912) 7–30.

THOMAS DE VIO CAJETANUS: *Opera Omnis*, 5 vols. (Lyon 1639); *Opuscula Omnia* (Lyon 1558); *De divina institutione Pontificatus Romani*, ed. F. Lauchert: *CCath* 10 (Münster 1925); J. F. Groner, *Kard. Cajetanus* (Freiburg 1951) (lit.).

AMBROSIUS CATHARINUS: *Apologia*, ed. J. Schweizer: *CCath* 27 (Münster 1956); J. Schweizer, *Ambrosius Catharinus* (Münster 1910); F. Lauchert, *Die it. literarischen Gegner Luthers* (Freiburg 1912) 30–133; *ECatt* IX 1686f. (lit.).

JAKOB VAN HOOGSTRAETEN: *Bibliotheca reformatoria neerlandica* III, ed. F. Pijper (The Hague 1905); *De veneratione sanctorum* (1524), *De Purgatorio* (1525), *Disputationes contra Lutheranos* (1526); N. Paulus, *Die dt. Dominikaner im Kampf gegen Luther* (Freiburg 1903) 87–107.

JOHANNES MENSING: N. Paulus, *Die dt. Dominikaner* 16–45; A. Warko, *Johannes Mensings Lehre von der Ebrsünde und Rechtfertigung* (Diss. Breslau 1963); E. Iserloh, *Der Kampf um die Messe* (Münster 1952) 46–52.

JOHANNES FABER, OP: N. Paulus, *Die dt. Dominikaner* 292–313; Th. a Dillis, "Johannes Faber" *Lebensbilder aus dem bayerischen Schwaben* 5 (1956) 93–111.

JOHANNES FABRI, OP: N. Paulus, *Die dt. Dominikaner* 232–266; P. Siemer, *Gesch. des Dominikanerklosters St. Magdalena in Augsburg* (Vechta 1936) 107–114.

AMBROSIUS PELARGUS, OP: N. Paulus, *Die deutschen Dominikaner,* 190–212; A. Keil, "Ambrosius Pelargus" *AMrhKG* 8 (1956) 181–223; W. Mann, "Eine humanistische Schrift über die Messe," *AMrhKG* 13 (1961) 197–233; P. Mohr, *Der Opfercharakter der Messe in der Apologia und im Hyperaspismus des Ambrosius Pelargus* (Speyer 1965).

JOHANNES DIETENBERGER: Ch. Moufang, *Kath. Katechismus des 16. Jh.* (Mainz 1881) 1–105; N. Paulus, *Die dt. Dominkaner* 186–189; H. Wedewer, *Johannes Dietenberger* (Freiburg 1888).

AUGUSTIN VON ALVELDT: *CCath* 11 (Münster 1926); *Wyder den wittenbergischen Abgot (1524) u. Erklärung des Salve Regina (1527);* L. Lemmens, *P. Augustin von Alveldt* (Freiburg 1899); id., *FStud* 5 (1918) 131–134; G. Hesse, "Augustin von Alveldt, Verteidiger des Apostolischen Stuhles" ibid. 17 (1930) 160–178.

KASPAR SCHATZGEYER: *Omnia Opera* (Ingolstadt 1543); *Scrutinium,* ed. U. Schmidt: *CCath* 5 (Münster 1922); N. Paulus, *Kaspar Schatzgeyer* (Freiburg 1889); O. Müller, *Die Rechtfertigungslehre nominalistischer Reformationsgegner* (Breslau 1940); V. Heynck: *FStud* 28 (1941) 129–151, 29 (1942) 25–44; H. Klomps, *Kirche, Freiheit und Gesetz bei . . . Kaspar Schatzgeyer* (Münster 1959); E. Komposch, *Die Messe als Opfer der Kirche. Die Lehre Kaspar Schatzgeyers über das eucharistische Opfer* (Diss. Munich 1962).

NIKOLAUS HERBORN: *Enchiridion,* ed. P. Schlager: *CCath* 12 (Münster 1927), *Confutatio Lutheranismi danici (1530),* ed. L. Schmidt (Quaracchi 1902); E. Kurten, *Franz Lambert von Avignon und Nikolaus Herborn* (Münster 1950).

GASPARO CONTARINI: *Opera* (Paris 1571; Venice 1578, 1589); *Gasparo Contarinis Gegenreformatorische Schriften,* ed. F. Hünermann: *CCath* 7 (Münster 1923); "Reformgutachten" *CT* XII 131–145, 153f., 208–215; F. Dittrich, *Gasparo Contarini* (Braunsberg 1885); id., *Regesten und Briefe* (Braunsberg 1881); H. Rückert, *Die theol. Entwicklung Gasparo Contarinis* (Berlin 1926); H. Jedin, *Kard. Contarini als Kontroverstheologe* (Münster 1949); id., *Contarini und Camaldoli* (Rome 1953); id., "Ein 'Turmerlebnis' des jungen Contarni" *HJ* 70 (1951) 115–130; id., *Gasparo Contarini e il contributo veneziano alla Riforma Cattolica: La Civilta Veneziana del Rinascimento* (Florence 1958) 105–124; R. M. Douglas, *Jacopo Sodaleto* (Cambridge, Mass. 1959).

JOHANNES GROPPER: W. van Gulik, *Johannes Gropper* (Freiburg 1906); W. Lipgens, *Kard. Johannes Gropper* (Münster 1951, lit.); H. Lutz, "Reformatio Germaniae. Drei Denkschriften Johannes Groppers" *QFIAB* 37 (1957) 222–310; R. Stupperich, "Briefe und Merkblätter Johannes Groppers aus den Jahren 1542–1549" *WZ* 109 (1959) 97–107; H. Jedin, "Das Autograph Johannes Groppers zum Kölner Provinzialkonzil von 1536" *Spiegel der Gesch. Festgabe für M. Braubach* (Münster 1964) 281–292.

JULIUS PFLUG: A. Jansen, "Julius Pflug" *Neue Mitteilungen aus dem Gebiet hist. antiquarischer Forschung* X/1 (Halle 1863) 1–110; X/2 (1864) 1–212; W. Offele, *Ein Katechismus im Dienst der Glaubenseinheit* (Essen 1965) (lit.).

MICHAEL HELDING: N. Paulus, "Michael Helding" *Katholik* 74, II (1894) 410–430, 481–502; E. Feifel, *Grundzüge einer Theologie des Gottesdienstes, Motive und Konzeption der Glaubensverkündigung Michael Heldings* (Freiburg 1960) (lit.); id., *Der Mainzer Weibischof Michael Helding zwischen Reformation und kath. Reform* (Wiesbaden 1962).

GEORG WITZEL: G. Richter, *Die Schriften Georg Witzels bibliographisch bearb.* (Fulda 1913; new edition, Niewkoop 1963); *Apologia* (1533); A. Räss, *Die Convertiten seit der Reformation* I (Freiburg 1872) 156–184; H. Volz (ed.), "Drei Schriften gegen Luthers Schmalkaldische Artikel von Cochläus, Witzel und Hoffmeister" *CCath* 18 (Münster 1932); L. Pralle, "Die volksliturgischen Bestrebungen des Georg Witzel" *Jb. für das Bistum Mainz* 3 (1948) 224–242; R. Padberg, "Zum katechetischen Anliegen Georg Witzels" *ThGl* 43 (1953) 192–200; id., "Georg Witzel der Ältere, ein Pastoraltheologe des 16. Jh.s." *ThQ* 135 (1955) 385–409; J. P. Dolan, *The Influence of Erasmus, Witzel and Cassander in the Church of Ordinances . . . of the United Duchies of Cleve* (Münster 1957); id., "Witzel et Erasme a propos des sacrements" *RHE* LIV 1 (1959); id., "Georg Witzel: Liturgiker und Kirchenreformer" *Una Sancta* XI, IV, 196–204; id., *N. Cath. Enc.* XIV: 984–985; W. Trusen, *Um die Reform und Einheit der Kirche. Zum Leben und Werk Georg Witzels* (Münster 1957).

STANISLAUS HOSIUS: *Opera*, 2 vols. (Cologne 1584); *Die dt. Predigten und Katechesen*, ed. F. Hipler–V. Zakrzewski (Krakau 1879–88); E. M. Wermter (ed.), *Kard. Stanislaus Hosius und Herzog Albrecht von Preussen. Ihr Briefwechsel über das Konzil von Trient* (Münster 1957) (lit.); *Bibliographia Hosiana*, ed. J. Smoczynsky (Peplin 1937); H. Eichhorn, *Der ermländische Bischof und Kard. Stanislaus Hosius,* 2 vols. (Mainz 1854); J. Lortz, *Kard. Stanislaus Hosius* (Braunsberg 1931); L. Bernacki, *La doctrine de l'église chez le Card. Hosius* (Paris–Posen 1935); F. J. Zdrodowski, *The Concept of Heresy according to Card. Hosius* (Washington 1947).

REGINALD POLE: *Epistolae*, 5 vols. (Brescia 1744–57); M. Haile, *Life of Reginald Pole* (New York 1910); W. Schenk, *Reginald Pole, Cardinal of England* (London 1950).

JACOPO SADOLETO: *Omnia Opera*, 4 vols. (Verona 1737; Rome 1760–64); *Epistulae* (Cologne 1590; Rome 1767); F. C. Church, *The Italian Reformers, 1534–1564* (New York 1932); A. Cistellini, *Figure della Riforma pretridentina* (Brescia 1948); S. Ritter, *Un Umanista teologo Jacope Sadoleto* (Rome 1912); G. Schultess-Reckberg, *Der Kardinal Jacope Sadoleto* (Zurich 1909); R. M. Douglas, *Jacope Sadoleto: Humanist and Reformer* (Cambridge 1959); F. Benoit, *La Légation du cardinal Sadolet auprès de François I en 1542* (Paris 1928); P. McNair, *Peter Martyr in Italy* (Oxford 1967).

SECTION THREE

The Reform in the German Principalities

17. *The Confessional Leagues. The Imperial Diets of Nürnberg (1524) and Speyer (1526)*

LITERATURE

Deutsche Reichstagsakten. Jüngere Reihe. IV, compiled by A. Wrede (Stuttgart 1905)= *RTA; Acta Reformationis Catholicae*, ed. G. Pfeilschifter, I (Regensburg 1959)=*ARC;* W.

Friedensburg, "Der Regensburger Convent von 1524," *Hist. Aufsätze dem Andenken v. G. Waitz* (Hannover 1886) 502–539; id., *Zur Vorgeschichte des Gotha-Torgauischen Bündnisses der Evangelischen* (Marburg 1884); id., *Der Reichstag zu Speier im Zusammenhang mit der politischen und kirchlichen Entwicklung Deutschlands im Reformationszeitalter* (Berlin 1887); id., "Die Reformation und der Speierer Reichstag von 1526" *LuJ* 8 (1926) 120–195; J. K. Seidemann, "Das Dessauer Bündniss vom 26. Juni 1525" *ZHTh* 17 (1847) 638–655; E. Cardinal, *Cardinal L. Campeggio, Legate of the Courts of Henry VIII and Charles V* (Boston 1935); Schottenloher 41253–57 (Regensburg Konvent); 27957a–60a (Nürnberg 1524); 27960b–74 (Speyer 1926).

18. Luther's Concept of the Church and Doctrine of the Two Kingdoms

SOURCES

CONCEPT OF THE CHURCH: "Von dem Papsttum zu Rom wider den hochberühmten Romanisten zu Leipzig" (1520; *WA* 6: 285–324); "Ad librum . . . Ambrosii Catharini . . . responsio" (1521; *WA* 7: 705–778); "Dass eine christliche Versammlung oder Gemeine Recht und Macht habe, alle Lehren zu urteilen und Lehrer zu berufen, ein- und abzusetzen" (1523; *WA* 11: 408–416); "De instituendis ministris ecclesiae ad senatum Pragensem Bohemiae" (1523; *WA* 12: 169–196).

DOCTRINE OF THE TWO KINGDOMS: "Von weltlicher Oberkcit, wic weit man ihr Gehorsam schuldig sei" (1523; *WA* 11: 245–281); "Wider die himmlischen Propheten . . ." (1525; *WA* 18: 62–125); "Ob Kriegsleute auch in seligem Stande sein Können" (1526; *WA* 19: 623–662); "Vom Krieg wider die Türken" (1529; *WA* 30/II: 107–148); "Eine Heerpredigt wider den Türken" (1529; *WA* 30/II: 160–197).

LITERATURE

CONCEPT OF THE CHURCH: J. Köstlin, *Luthers Lehre von der Kirche* (Stuttgart 1853); P. Drews, *Entsprach das Staatskirchentum dem Ideale Luthers?* (Tübingen 1908); K. Müller, *Kirche, Gemeinde und Obrigkeit nach Luther* (Tübingen 1910); M. Rade, "Der Sprung in Luthers Kirchenbegriff" *ZThK* 24 (1914) 241–260; K. Holl, "Die Entstehung von Luthers Kirchenbegriff" *Ges. Aufsätze* I (Tübingen 1932) 288–325; id., "Luther und das landesherrliche Kirchenregiment" loc. cit. 326–380; F. Kattenbusch, "Die Doppelschichtigkeit in Luthers Kirchenbegriff" *ThStK* 100 (1927–28); E. Kohlmeyer, "Die Bedeutung die Kirche für Luther" *ZKG* 47 (1928) 466–511; E. Rietschel, *Das Problem der unsichtbar-sichtbaren Kirche bei Luther* (Leipzig 1932); H. J. Iwand, "Zur Entstehung von Luthers Kirchenbegriff" *Festschr. für G. Dehn* (Neukirchen 1957) 145–166; K. G. Steck, "Ecclesia-creatura verbi" J. Beckmann et. al., *Von Einheit u. Wesen der Kirche* (Göttingen 1960) 40–56; E. Kinder, *Der evangelische Glaube und die Kirche* (Berlin 1960) 57–144 (lit.).

DOCTRINE OF THE TWO KINGDOMS: R. Sohm, *Kirchenrecht* I (Leipzig 1892); Harold Diem, *Luthers Lehre von den beiden Reichen* (Munich 1938); G. Törnwall, *Geistliches und weltliches Regiment bei Luther* (Munich 1947); E. Kinder, *Luther und die Politische Frage* (Neukirchen 1950); F. Lau, *Luthers Lehre von den beiden Reichen* (Berlin 1953); J. Heckel, *Lex charitatis. Eine juristische Untersuchung über das Recht in der Theologie M. Luthers* (Munich 1953); id., *Im Irrgarten der Zwei-Reiche-Lehre* (Munich 1957); id., "Kirche und Kirchenrecht nach der Zwei-Reiche-Lehre" *ZSavRGkan* 48 (1962) 222–284; Gunnar Hillerdal, *Gehorsam gegen Gott und Menschen. Luthers Lehre von der Obrigkeit und die moderne evangelische Staatsethik* (Göttingen 1955); P. Althaus, "Luther Lehre von den beiden Reichen im Feuer der Kritik" *LuJ* 24 (1957) 40–68 (lit.); id., *Die Ethik Martin Luthers* (Gütersloh 1965) 49–87; Sigfrid Grundmann, "Kirche und Staat nach der Zwei-Reiche-Lehre Luthers: Im Dienste des Rechts" *Festschr. Franz Arnold* (Vienna 1963) 38–54; E. Wolf, "Königsherrschaft Christi und lutherische Zwei-Reiche-Lehre" *Peregrinatio* II (Munich 1965) 207–229; *EKL* III, 1927–47 (opposing interpretations of Luther's doctrine by P. Althaus and Joh. Hechel). **Melanchthon:** R. Nürnberger, *Kirche und weltliche Obrigkeit bei Melanchthon* (Diss. Würzburg 1937); A. Reuter, "Luther und Melanchthons Stellung zur jurisdictio episcoporum" *NKZ* 36 (1925) 549–575; A. Sperl, *Melanchthon zwischen Humanismus und Reformation* (Munich 1959); F. Lau, "Melanchthon und die Ordnung der Kirche" *Philipp Melanchthon. Forschungsbeiträge,* ed. W. Elliger (Göttingen 1961) 98–115.

19. The Completion of the Lutheran Community

SOURCES

E. Sehling (ed.), *Die evangelischen Kirchenordnungen des 16. Jh.* (Tübingen 1955–56), 1–5 (1902–13), 6–8, 11–13 (1955–66).

CHURCH PROPERTIES: "Ordnung eines gemeinen Kastens" (Leipzig 1523; *WA* 12: 11–30).

DIVINE SERVICES: "Deutsche Messe und Ordnung des Gottesdiensts" (1526; *WA* 19: 72–113); "Das Taufbüchlein verdeutscht, aufs neue zugerichtet" (1526; *WA* 19: 537–541); "Das Taubüchlein für die einfältigen Pfarrherrn" (1529; *WA* 30/III: 74–80).

VISITATION: "Unterricht der Visitatoren an die Pfarrherren im Kurfürstentum Sachsen" (1528) *CR* 26: 51–96; *WA* 26: 195–240; *Melanchthons Werke in Auswahl* I (1959) 215–271; Sehling, I: 149–174.

SCHOOLS: "An die Ratsherren aller Städte deutschen Landes, dass sie christliche Schulen aufrichten und halten sollen" (1524; *WA* 15: 27–53); "Eine Predigt, dass man Kinder zur Schulen halten solle" (1530; *WA* 30/II: 517–588); R. Vormbaum, *Die evangelishcen Schulordnungen des 16. Jh.* (Gütersloh 1860); S. Hendrix, "Luther and the Climate for Theological Education" *Lutheran Quarterly* 26 (1974) 3–11.

CATECHISM: *WA* 30/I: Sermons on the Catechism 1528 and the Text of Luther's Catechism with introduction, bibliography, and philological notations, by O. Albrecht, O. Brenner, G. Buchwald and J. Luther (1910); *BSLK* 501–733; F. Cohrs, *Die Evangelischen Katechismusversuche vor Luthers Enchiridion,* 5 vols. (Berlin 1900–7).

LITERATURE

CHURCH PROPERTIES: A. Schultze, *Stadtgemeinde und Reformation* (Tübingen 1918); F. H. Löscher, *Schule, Kirche und Obrigkeit im Reformations-Jahrhundert* (Leipzig 1925); H. Werdermann, *Luthers Wittenberger Gemeinde wiederhergestellt aus seinen Predigten* (Gütersloh 1929); H. Lehnert, *Kirchengut und Reformation* (Erlangen 1935).

DIVINE SERVICES: H. Jacoby, *Die Liturgik der Reformatoren,* 2 vols. (Gotha 1871–76); P. Drews, "Studien zur Gesch. des Gottesdienstes IV–V" *Beiträge zu Luthers liturgischen Reformen* (Tübingen 1910); J. Smend, *Die Deutschen Messen bis zu Luthers deutscher Messe* (Göttingen 1896); H. Waldenmaier, *Die Entstehung der evangelischen Gottes-*

dienstordnungen Süddeutschlands im Zeitalter der Reformation (Leipzig 1916); L. Fendt, *Der lutherische Gottesdienst des 16. Jh.* (Munich 1923); A. Allwohn, *Gottesdienst und Rechtfertigungsglaube* (Göttingen 1926); E. Reim, "The Liturgical Crisis in Wittenberg 1524" *Concordia Theological Monthly* 20 (1949) 284–292; W. Jensen, "Von der ev. Mess" *Festgabe für K. Schornbaum* (Neustadt a. d. Aisch 1950) 61–100; V. Vajta, *Die Theologie des Gottesdienstes bei Luther* (Göttingen 1959); A. Boes, "Die Reformatorischen Gottesdienste in der Wittenberger Pfarrkirche von 1523 an" *JLH* 4 (1958–59) 1–40; H. B. Meyer, *Luther und die Messe* (Paderborn 1965).

VISITATION: C. H. Burkhardt, *Geschichte der sächsischen Kirchen- und Schulvisitationen 1524–1545* (Leipzig 1879); E. Sehling, *Geschichte der protestantischen Kirchenverfassung* (Leipzig 1914); K. Eger, "Grundsätze evangelischer Kirchenverfassung bei Luther" *ThStK* 106 (1934–35) 77–123; M. Schmidt, "Die Reformation Luthers und die Ordnung der Kirche" *Im Lichte der Reformation* II (Göttingen 1959) 5–31.

SCHOOLS: F. Paulsen, *Geschichte des gelehrten Unterrichts an den deutschen Schulen und Universitäten* I (Leipzig 1919); G. Mertz, *Das Schulwesen der deutschen Reformation im 16. Jh.* (Heidelberg 1902); F. H. Löscher, *Schule, Kirche und Obrigkeit im Reformations-Jahrhundert* (Leipzig 1925); O. Scheel, "Luther und die Schule seiner Zeit" *LuJ* 7 (1925) 141–175; F. Falk, "Luthers Schrift an die Ratsherrn . . . und ihre gesch. Wirkung auf die deutsche Schule" *LuJ* 19 (1937) 55–114; Th. v. Sicard, *Luther und die Schule* (Gütersloh 1947); G. Mertz, "Luther über die Schule" *Schule und Leben* I (1950) 289–296; E. Lichtenstein, "Luther und die Schule" *Der ev. Erzieher* 7 (1955) 2–13; E. Reimers, *Recht und Grenzen einer Berufung auf Luther in den neueren Bemühungen um eine evangelische Erziehung* (Weinheim 1958); I. Asheim, *Glaube und Erziehung bei Luther* (Heidelberg 1961) (Bibliography).

CATECHISM: O. Albrecht, *Luthers Katechismen* (Leipzig 1915); D. J. M. Reu, *D. Martin Luthers Kleiner Katechismus* (Munich 1929); J. Meyer, *Historischer Kommentar zu Luthers Kleinem Katechismus* (Göttingen 1929); K. Aland, *Der Text des Kleinen Katechismus in der Gegenwart* (Gütersloh 1954); Appraised by G. Dehn: *ThLZ* 79 (1954) 719–724; G. Hoffmann, "Der kleine Katechismus als Abriss der Theologie M. Luthers," *Luther* 30 (1959) 49–63; E. V. Wills, "Joh. Brenz's Catechismus of 1528 and 1535" *Lutheran Church Quarterly* 19 (1946) 271–280.

20. *Clement VII and Charles V*

LITERATURE

Pastor, X (London 1938) Chaps. 1–8; T. Pandolfi, "Giovan Matteo Giberti e l'ultima difesa della libertá d'Italia negli anni 1521–1525" *AS Romana* 34 (1911) 131–237; E. Rodonachi, *Les pontificats d'Adrien VI et de Clément VII* (Paris 1933); K. Brandi, *The Emperor Charles V* (New York 1939); P. Rassow, *Die Kaiser-Idee Karls V.* (Berlin 1932); id., *Die politische Welt Karls V.* (Munich 1947); M. Salomies, *Die Pläne Karls V. für eine Reichsreform* (Helsinki 1953); J. Calmette, *Charles V* (Paris 1945); R. Tyler, *The Emperor Charles the Fifth* (London 1956); *Karl V: Der Kaiser und seine Zeit,* ed. P. Rassow–F. Schalk (Cologne 1960); I. Ludolphy, *Die Voraussetzungen der Religionspolitik Karls V.* (Stuttgart 1965).

21. *The Speyer Protest and the Marburg Religious Colloquy*

THE PACK AFFAIR: Schottenloher 40566a–91; J. Kühn, "Über die Verantwortlichkeit an der Entstehung des politischen Protestantismus" *Festschr. W. Goetz* (Leipzig 1927); id., "Landgraf Philipp von Hessen, der politische Sinn der Packschen Händel" *Festschr. E. Brandenburg* (Leipzig 1928); K. Dülfer, *Die Packschen Händel,* 2 vols. (Marburg 1958).

DIET OF SPEYER: *Deutsche Reichstagsakten unter Karl V.,* VII, revised by J. Kühn (Stuttgart 1935); *Die Appellation und Protestation der ev. Stände auf dem Reichstag zu Speier,* ed. J. Ney (1906; Neudruck Darmstadt 1967); J. Kühn, *Die Gesch. des Speyrer Reichstages 1529* (Leipzig 1929); J. Boehmer, "Protestari und protestatio, protestierende Obrigkeiten und protestantische Christen" *ARG* (1934) 1–22.

RIGHT OF RESISTANCE: See Chap. 23.

THE MARBURG COLLOQUY: See Chapter 14; H. Heppe, *Die fünfzehn Marburger Artikel vom 3. Oktober 1529* (Kassel ²1854) (facsimile); M. Lenz, "Zwingli und Landgraf Philipp" *ZKG* 3 (1879) 28–62, 220–274, 429–463; id., (ed.), *Briefwechsel Landgraf Philipps des Grossmütigen von Hessen mit Bucer,* 3 vols. (Leipzig 1880, 1887, 1891); R. Hauswirth, "Landgraf Philipp von Hessen und Zwingli" *Zwingliana* 11 (1959–63) 499–552; H. v. Schubert, *Bekenntnisbildung und Religionspolitik 1529–30* (Gotha 1910); id., *Anfänge ev. Bekenntnisbildung bis 1529–30* (Leipzig 1928); W. Köhler, *Das Marburger Religionsgespräch 1529. Versuch einer Rekonstruktion* (Leipzig 1929); id., *Zwingli und Luther* II (Gütersloh 1953); E. Bizer, *Studien zur Gesch. des Abendmahlsstreits im 16. Jh.* (Gütersloh 1940); H. Köditz, "Die gesellschaftlichen Ursachen des Scheiterns des Marburger Religionsgesprächs 1529" *Zschr. f. Geschichtswiss.* 2 (1954) 37–70; J. Staedtke, "Eine neue Version des sog. Utinger-Berichtes vom Marburger Religionsgespräch 1529" *Zwingliana* 10 (1954–58) 210–216; F. Büsser (ed.), *Beschreibung des Abendmahlstreites von Johannes Stumpf* (Zurich 1960); H. W. Neuser, "Eine unbekannte Unionsformel Melanchthons vom Marburger Religionsgespräch" *ThZ* 21 (1965) 181–199; Chr. Gestrich, *Zwingli als Theologe, Glaube und Geist beim Zürcher Reformator* (Diss. Zurich 1966); S. Hausammann, "Die Marburger Artikel–eine echte Konkordia?" *ZKG* 77 (1966) 288–321.

HEINRICH BULLINGER: **Works:** *Reformationsgeschichte,* ed. J. J. Hottinger–H. H. Vögeli, 3 vols. (Frauenfeld 1838–40); *Diarium,* ed. E. Egli (Basel 1904); *The Decades of Heinrich Bullinger,* ed. T. Harding, 4 vols. (Cambridge 1849–52); *Das höchste Gut,* ed. J. Staedtke (Zurich 1955); *Das 2. helvetische Bekenntnis,* ed. R. Zimmermann–W. Hildebrandt (Zurich 1936); G. W. Bromily (ed.), *Zwingli and Bullinger* (Philadelphia 1953) (Contains Bullinger's *Of the Holy Catholic Church*). **Literature:** Schottenloher 2049–2122, 45237–46, 52997–53032; C. Pestalozzi, *Heinrich Bullinger. Leben und ausgewählte Schriften* (Elberfeld 1858); A. Bouvier, *Heinrich Bullinger réformateur et conseiller oecuménique* (Neuchâtel 1940); F. Blanke, *Der junge Bullinger* (Zurich 1942); W. Hollweg, *Heinrich Bullingers Hausbuch* (Neukirchen 1956); P. Walser, *Bullingers Lehre von der Prädestination* (Zurich 1957); H. Fast, *Heinrich Bullinger und die Täufer* (Weierhof 1959); J. Staedtke, *Die Theologie des jungen Bullinger* (Zurich 1962) (Bibliography to 1528 and literature); *Glauben und Bekennen, 400 Jahre Confessio Helvetica Posterior* (Zurich 1966).

22. The Imperial Diet of Augsburg

SOURCES

Schottenloher 28011–67, 34504–687a, 36895; 62221–50; G. Brück, *Geschichte der Handlungen in der Sache des heiligen Glaubens auf dem Reichstage zu Augsburg im Jahre 1530,* ed. K. E. Förstemann (Halle 1831); K. E. Förstemann, *Urkundenbuch zu der Geschichte des Reichstages zu Augsburg im Jahre 1530,* 2 vols. (Halle 1833–35; new imprint Osnabrück 1966); *Monumenta Vaticana historiam ecclesiasticam saeculi XVI illustrantia,* ed. H. Laemmer (Freiburg 1861); F. W. Schirrmacher, *Briefe und Akten zu der Geschichte des Religionsgespräches zu Marburg 1529 und des Reichstages zu Augsburg 1530* (Gotha 1876); *Die Ratschläge der evangelischen Reichsstände zum Reichstag von Augsburg,* ed. W. Gussmann: *Quellen und Forschungen zur Geschichte des Augsburgischen Glaubensbekenntnisses* I, 1 and 2 (Leipzig–Berlin 1911); *J. Ecks 404 Artikel zum Reichstag von Augsburg 1530,* id.: ibid. II (Kassel 1930); V. Tetleben, *Protokoll des Augsburger Reichstages 1530,* ed. H. Grundmann (Göttingen 1958); St. Ehses, "Kardinal Lorenzo Campeggio auf dem Reichstag von Augsburg 1530" *RQ* 17–21 (1903–07); J. Walter, *Die Depeschen des venez, Gesandten N. Tiepolo* (Berlin 1928); *Nuntiaturberichte aus Deutschland, Erste Abt. 1533–59,* I. ErgBd 1530–31, ed. G. Müller (Tübingen 1963); "Briefwechsel," *CR* 2; *WA, Br* 5.

CONFESSIO AUGUSTANA: *BSLK* 31–137; M. Reu, *The Augsburg Confession* (Chicago 1930).

CONFUTATIO: *Die Konfutation des Augsburgischen Bedenntnisses. Ihre erste Gestalt und ihre Geschichte,* ed. J. Ficker (Leipzig 1891); *CR* 27, 1–243; Th. Kolde, *Die Augsburgische Konfession* (Gotha 1896, 1911) 140–169.

CONFESSIO TETRAPOLITANA: E. F. K. Müller, *Die Bekenntnisschriften der reformierten Kirche* (Leipzig 1903) 55–78; Zwingli, *Fidei ratio (1530):* ibid. 79–94.

APOLOGIA: *CR* 27, 244–378; *BSLK, 139–404.*

LITERATURE

L. Pastor, *Die kirchlichen Reunionsbestrebungen während der Regierung Karls V.* (Freiburg 1879); J. Walter, *Die Depeschen des venez. Gesandten N. Tiepolo* (Berlin 1928); id., "Der Reichstag zu Augsburg 1530" *LuJ* 12 (1930) 1–90; R. Hermann, "Zur theol. Würdigung der Augustana," ibid. 162–214; H. Schubert, "Luther auf der Koburg" ibid. 109–161; id., *Der Reichstag zu Augsburg im Zusammenhang der Reformationsgeschichte* (Leipzig 1930); W. A. Nagel, *Luthers Anteil an der Confessio Augustant* (Gütersloh 1930); W. Köhler, *Zwingli und Luther* II (Gütersloh 1953); F. W. Kantzenbach, *Das Ringen um die Einheit der Kirche im Jahrhundert der Reformation* (Stuttgart 1957); G. Müller, "Johann Eck und die CA" *QFIAB* 38 (1958) 205–242; H. Grundmann, *Landgraf Philipp von Hessen auf dem Augsburger Reichstag 1530* (Gütersloh 1959); W. Maurer, "Studien über Melanchthons Anteil an der Entstehung der Confessio Augustana" *ARG* 51 (1960) 158–207; id., "Melanchthon als Verfasser der Augustana," *Luth. Rundschau* 10 (1960–61) 164–179; E. Honée, "Die Vergleichsverhandlungen zwischen Katholiken und Protestanten im August 1530" *QFIAB* 42–43 (1963) 412–434; G. Müller, "Um die Einheit der Kirche. Zu den Verhandlungen über den Laienkelch während des Augsburger Reichstages 1530" *Reformata Reformanda, Festgabe H. Jedin,* ed. E. Iserloh–K. Repgen, I (Münster 1965) 393–427; K. Honselmann, "Otto Beckmanns

Vermittlungsversuch beim Reichstag zu Augsburg 1530" ibid. 428–444; K. Thieme, *Die Augsburgische Konfession und Luthers Katechismen auf theologische Gegenwartswerte untersucht* (Giessen 1930); E. Schlink, *Theologie der lutherischen Bekenntnisschriften* (Munich 1948); H. Asmussen, *Warum noch lutherische Kirche* (Stuttgart 1949); F. Brunstäd, *Theologie der lutherischen Bekenntnisschriften* (Gütersloh 1951); M. Lackmann, *Katholische Einheit und Augsburger Konfession* (Cologne 1959); H. Fagerberg, *Die Theologie der lutherischen Bekenntnisschriften von 1528–1537* (Göttingen 1965); H. Bornkamm, *Das Augsburgische Bekenntnis* (Hamburg 1965); L. Fendt, *Der Wille der Reformation im Augsburgischen Bekenntnis,* 2 revised by B. Klaus (Tübingen 1966); B. Moeller, "Augustana-Studien" *ARG* 57 (1966) 76–95; F. Blanke, "Zwinglis 'Fidei ratio' (1530), Entstehung und Bedeutung" ibid. 96–101.

23. The Politicizing of the Reform Movement to the Collapse of the Religious Colloquies

LITERATURE

1. THE RIGHT OF RESISTANCE: L. Cardauns, *Die Lehre vom Widerstandsrecht des Volkes gegen die rechtmässige Obrigkeit im Luthertum und im Calvinismus des 16. Jh.* (Diss. Bonn 1903); K. Müller, "Luthers Äusserungen über das Recht des bewaffneten Widerstandes gegen den Kaiser" *SAM* 1915, VIII (Munich 1915); H. Lüttge, "Melanchthons Anschauung v. Recht des Widerstandes gegen die Staatsgewalt" *ZKG* 47 (1928) 512–542; J. Heckel, *Lex charitatis* (Munich 1953) 184–191; id., "Widerstand gegen die Obrigkeit?" *Zeitenwende* 25 (1954) 156–168; E. Wolf, "Widerstandsrecht" *RGG* VI 1681–92.

2. THE LEAGUE OF SCHMALKALD: Schottenloher 41646–71; 52101f; 64018–26; O. Winckelmann, *Der Schmalkaldische Bund und der Nürnberger Religionsfrieden* (Strassburg 1892); E. Fabian, *Die Entstehung des Schmalkaldischen Bundes und seiner Verfassung* (Tübingen 1962 lit.); id., *Die Schmalkaldischen Bundesabschiede 1530–32* (Tübingen 1958); Chr. Glitsch, *Die Bündnispolitik der oberdt. Städte des Schmalkaldischen Bundes unter Einfluss von Strassburg und Ulm 1529–32* (Diss. Tübingen 1960); St. Fischer-Galati, "Ottoman Imperialism and the Religion Peace of Nürnberg" *ARG* 47 (1956) 160–179; R. Schelp. *Die Reformationsprozesse der Stadt Strassburg am Reichskammergericht z. Z. des Schmalkaldischen Bundes* (Kaiserslautern 1965).

3. THE REFORMATION IN WÜRTTEMBERG: Schottenloher 34046d–62; 61983–62018; J. Wille, *Philipp der Grossmütige von Hessen und die Restitution Ulrichs v. Wirtemberg 1526–35* (Tübingen 1882); J. Rauscher, *Württembergische Reformationsgeschichte (1500–1559)* (Stuttgart 1934); H. Hermelink, *Gesch. der ev. Kirche in Württemberg von der Reformation bis zur Gegenwart* (Stuttgart u. Tübingen 1949); W. Köhler, *Zwingli u. Luther* II (Gütersloh 1953).-J. Brenz: W. Köhler, *Bibliographia Brentiana* (Berlin 1904); J. Brenz, *Anecdota Brentiana,* ed. Th. Pressel (Tübingen 1868); "Brentiana," ed. W. Köhler: *ARG* 9–26 (1911–29); *Confessio Virtembergica,* ed. E. Bizer (Stuttgart 1952); *Predigten des Joh. Brenz,* ed. E. Bizer (Stuttgart 1955); A. Hegler, *Joh. Brenz und die Reform in Württemberg* (Freiburg 1899); M. Brecht, *Die frühe Theologie des Johannes Brenz* (Tübingen 1966) (lit.: auch Schottenloher 52867–81).

4. THE WITTENBERG CONCORD: E. Bizer, *Studien zur Geschichte des Abendmahlsstreites im 16. Jh.* (1940, Darmstadt 1962); W. Köhler, *Zwingli u. Luther* II (Gütersloh 1953).

5. THE SCHMALKALDIC ARTICLES: (*Sch. A.*): *BSLK,* 405–468, 1226–1228 (lit.); H. Volz, "Luthers Sch. A. u. Melanchthons Tractatus de potestate papae" *ThStK* 103 (1931) 1–70; E. Bizer, "Die Wittenberger Theologen u. das Konzil" *ARG* 47 (1956) 77–101; id., "Zum geschichtlichen Verständnis von Luthers Sch. A." *ZKG* 67 (1955–56) 61–92; id., "Noch einmal: Die Sch. A." *ZKG* 68 (1957) 287–294; *Urkunden u. Aktenstücke zur Gesch. von M. Luthers Sch. A. (1536–74),* ed. H. Volz (Berlin 1957); H. Volz, "Luthers Sch. A." *ZKG* 68 (1957) 259–286; id., "Zur Entstehungsgeschichte von Luthers Sch. A." *ZKG* 74 (1963) 316–320; A. Ebneter, "Luther und das Konzil" *ZKTh* 84 (1962) 1–48; Chr. Tecklenburg Johns, *Luthers Konzilsidee* (Berlin 1966).

6. THE TREATY OF FRANKFURT: Text: P. Fuchtel, "Der Frankfurter Anstand" *ARG* 28 (1931) 145–206; Le Plat II 625–630; E. Ziehen, "Frankfurter Anstand und deutsch-evangelischer Reichsbund von Schmalkalden 1539" *ZKG* 59 (1940) 324–351; G. Müller, "Zur Vorgeschichte des Frankfurter Anstandes 1539" *QFIAB* 39 (1959) 328–341.

REFORMATION IN SAXONY: O. A. Hecker, *Religion und Politik in den letzten Lebensjahren Herzog Georgs des Bärtigen von Sachsen* (Leipzig 1912); E. Brandenburg, *Herzog Heinrich d. Fr. von Sachsen und die Religionsparteien im Reich* (Dresden 1896); S. Issleib, "Herzog Heinrich als ev. Fürst" *Beitr. zur sächs. KG* 19 (1905) 143–215; H. Bornkamm, *Das Jahrhundert der Reformation* (Göttingen 1961) 142–162; H. Helbig, *Die Reformation der Universität Leipzig im 16. Jh.* (Gütersloh 1953).

BRANDENBURG: P. Steinmüller, *Einführung der Reformation in der Kurmark Brandenburg durch Joachim II.* (Halle 1903); N. Müller, "Zur Geschichte des Gottesdienstes der Domkirche zu Berlin 1540–1598" *Jb. für brandenburgische KG* 2–3 (1906) 337–550; L. Zscharnack, *Das Werk M. Luthers in der Mark Brandenburg* (Berlin 1917); W. Wendland, "Einführung in die Quellen und Literatur zur märkischen Reformations-Gesch." *Jb. f. brandenburgische KG* 34 (1939) 131–163; 35 (1940) 217–227; id., "Die märkische Reformation" ibid. 34 (1939) 33–51; W. Dürks. "Der Beginn der märkischen Reformation i. J. 1539" ibid. 52–87; O. Gross, "Vom Widerstand der Kath. Kirche gegen die Kirchenordnung Joachims II." *Wichmann-Jb.* (1953) 36–52; W. Delius, "Die Reformation des Kurfürsten Joachim II." *Theol. Viatorum* 5 (1954) 174–193; B. Klaus, "Die kurbrandenburgische Kirchenordnung" *JLH* 4 (1958–59) 82–85; E. W. Zeeden, *Katholische Überlieferungen in den luth. Kirchenordnungen des 16. Jh.* (Münster 1959).

7. THE RELIGIOUS COLLOQUIES: Schottenloher 41279f; K. Brandi, *Kaiser Karl V.* II (Münich 1941) 296–306; L. Pastor, *Die kirchlichen Reunionsbestrebungen während der Regierung Karls V.* (Freiburg 1879); L. Cardauns, *Zur Geschichte der kirchlichen Unions- und Reformbestrebungen 1538–42* (Rome 1910); R. Stupperich, *Der Humanismus und die Wiedervereinigung der Konfessionen* (Leipzig 1936); W. Lipgens, *Kardinal J. Gropper 1503–1559* (Münster 1951); H. Jedin, *Kirche des Glaubens-Kirche der Geschichte* I (Freiburg 1966) 361–366.

HAGENAU: Schottenloher 41323a–28; Text of the Abschiedes in L. v. Ranke, *Dt. Gesch. im Zeitalter der Reformation* VI (Munich 1926) 136–145; R. Moses, *Die Religionsverhandlungen in Hagenau und Worms* (Jena 1889); F. Dittrich, *Nuntiaturberichte G. Morones vom dt. Königshofe 1539–40* (Paderborn 1892) 130–179; *NBD* I 420–464; A. Ph. Brück, "Die Instruktion Kardinal Albrechts von Brandenburg für das Hagenauer Religionsgespräch" *AmrhKG* 4 (1952) 275–280.

WORMS: Schottenloher 41404–16; W. Lipgens, "Theologischer Standort fürstlicher Räte im 16. Jh." *ARG* 43 (1952) 28–51; H. Jedin, *Tommaso Campeggio (1483–1564)* (Münster 1958).

REGENSBURG: Schottenloher 28073–82, 41253–57, 41376–89; P. Vetter, *Die Religionsverhandlungen auf dem Reichstage zu Regensburg 1541* (Jena 1889); V. Schultze, "Aktenstücke zur dt. Ref.-Gesch. (Dispatches from Regensburg)" *ZKG* 3 (1879) 150–183, 609–653; L. Pastor, "Die Correspondenz des Card. Contarini . . . 1541" *HJ* 1 (1880) 321–392, 473–500.

SUPPLEMENTS: *NBD* 17 (Berlin 1912); H. Eells, "The Origin of the Regensburg Book" *Princeton Theol. Review* 26 (1928) 355–372; R. Stupperich, "Der Ursprung des Regensburger Buches" *ARG* 36 (1939) 88–116; J. Schattenmann, "Regensburger Religionsgespräche 1541 u. 1546" *Zeitwende* 19 (1947–48) 44–52; H. Mackensen, "Contarini's Role at Ratisbon in 1541" *ARG* 51 (1960) 36–57.

24. *The Breakdown of Universalism and the Religious Peace of Augsburg*

LITERATURE

GENERAL: K. Lanz, *Correspondenz des Kaisers Karl V.* III 1550–1556 (Leipzig 1846); A. v. Druffel, Beiträge zur Reichsgeschichte, [Vol. 1] 1546–51 (Munich 1873), [Vol. 2] 1552 (Munich 1880), [Vol. 3] 1546–52 (Munich 1882), [Vol. 4] 1553–1555, completed and revised by K. Brandi (Munich 1896) [=*Briefe und Akten zur Geschichte des 16. Jahrhunderts Vol. 1–4*]; *Nuntiaturberichte aus Deutschland,* first section 1533–1559, Vol. 7–13, 16 (Vienna, Leipzig, Tübingen 1898–1965); K. Brandi, *Kaiser Karl V.* 2 vols. (Munich 1941, 1959); F. Hartung, *Karl V. und die Reichsstände* 1546–55 (Halle 1910); J. Lecler, *Toleration and the Reformation,* 2 vols. (New York 1963); K. Repgen, *Die Römische Kurie und der Westfälische Friede* I: *Papst, Kaiser und Reich 1521–*1644, 2 parts (Tübingen 1962, 1965); H. Lutz, *Christianitas afflicta, Europa, das Reich und die päpstliche Politik im Niedergang der Hegemonie Kaiser Karls V. 1552–1556* (Göttingen 1964; lit.).

THE EMPEROR AND THE PROTESTANTS IN THE EARLY STAGES OF THE WAR: A. Hasenclever, *Die Politik der Schmalkaldener vor Ausbruch des Schmalkaldischen Krieges* (Berlin 1901); id., *Die Politik Kaiser Karls V. und Ladgraf Philipps von Hessen vor Ausbruch des Schmalkaldischen Krieges* (Marburg 1903); P. Heidrich, *Karl V. und die deutschen Protestanten am Vorabend des Schmalkaldischen Krieges,* 2 vols. (Frankfurt 1911–1912).

THE BIGAMY OF PHILIPP OF HESSE: Schottenloher 30354–30369; W. W. Rockwell, *Die Doppelehe des Landgrafen Philipp von Hessen* (Marburg 1904); W. Köhler, "Die Doppelehe Landgraf Philipps von Hessen" *HZ* 94 (1905) 385–411; Th. Brieger, "Luther und die Nebenehe des Landgrafen Philipp" *ZKG* 29 (1908) 174–196; N. Paulus, "Die hessische Doppelehe im Urteil der protestantischen Zeitgenossen" *HPB1* 147 (1911) 503–517, 561—573; H. Eells, *The Attitude of Martin Bucer toward the Bigamy of Philipp of Hesse* (New Haven 1924); W. Maurer, "Luther und die Doppelehe Philipps von Hessen" *Luther* 24 (1953) 97–120.

THE WAR OF SUCCESSION IN GELDER: Schottenloher 30740a–g, 37186–37201; F. Petri, "Landschaftliche und überlandschaftliche Kräfte im habsburgisch-klevischen Ringen um Geldern und im Frieden von Venlo 1537–1543" *Festschr. F. Steinbach* (Bonn 1960) 92–113.

PROGRESS OF THE REFORMATION: "The Attack on Braunschweig (Brunswick)" Schottenloher 29766–29836; F. Bruns, *Die Vertreibung Herzog Heinrichs von Braunschweig durch den Schmalkaldischen Bund* (Diss. Marburg 1889); E. Brandenburg, *Die Gefangen-nahme Herzog Heinrichs von Braunschweig durch den Schmalkaldischen Bund (1545)* (Leipzig 1894); H. Reller, *Vorreformatorische und reformatorische Kirchenverfassung im Fürstentum Braunschweig-Wolfenbüttel* (Göttingen 1959).

THE DIOCESE OF NAUMBURG: P. Brunner, *Nikolaus von Amsdorf als Bischof von Naumburg* (Gütersloh 1960) (lit.); Julius Pflug: Schottenloher 17222–17232, 31567–31572; F. I. Schwarzius, *Acta Julii Pflugii episcopi Numburgensis in caussa religionis* (Eisenberg 1774); A. Jansen, "Julius Pflug" *Neue Mittheilungen aus dem Gebiet historisch-antiquarischer Forschungen* 10 (1864) I: 1–110, II: 1–212; W. van Gulik, "Zeitzer Beiträge zur Geschichte der katholischen Gegenreformation im 16. Jh., I Julius Pflug und Eberhard Billick, II Julius Pflug und Daniel Mauch" *RQ* 18 (1904) 57–83; E. Hoffmann, *Naumburg im Zeitalter der Reformation* (Leipzig 1900).

COLOGNE: Schottenloher 30837–30880, 51297–51301, 61327–61339; C. Varrentrapp, *Hermann von Wied und sein Reformationsversuch in Köln* (Leipzig 1878); id., "Zur Charakteristik Hermanns von Wied, Bucers und Groppers" *ZKG* 20 (1900) 37–58; W. Lipgens, "Neue Beiträge zum Reformationsversuch Hermanns von Wied aus dem Jahr 1545" *AHVNrh* 149–150 (1950—51) 46–73; J. Niessen, "Der Reformationsversuch des Kölner Kurfürsten Hermann von Wied (1536–1547)" *Rhein. Vierteljahresbl.* 15–16 (1950–51) 298–312; H. Jedin, "Fragen um Hermann von Wied" *HJ* 74 (1955) 687–699; Th. Schlüter, *Die Publizistik um den Reformationsversuch des Kölner Erzbischofs Hermann von Wied aus dem Jahre 1542–1547* (Diss. Bonn 1957); E. Mühlhaupt, "Die Kölner Reformation" *Monatshefte für ev. KG des Rheinlandes* 11 (Düsseldorf 1962) 73–93; M. Köhn, *Martin Bucers Entwurf einer Reformation des Erzstiftes Köln* (Witten 1966).

THE SCHMALKALDIC WAR (=SCH. K.): Schottenloher 41672–41797, 52103, 64027–64029; G. Wolf, *Quellenkunde der dt. Reformationsgeschichte* I (Gotha 1915) 466–476; F. Hortleder, *Der Römischen Keyser- und Königlichen Majesteten, auch des Heiligen Römischen Reichs geistlicher und weitlicher Stände Handlungen und Ausschreiben von den Ursachen des Teutschen Kriegs* (Frankfurt 1617–18, Gotha 1645); A. Stein, *Kaiser und Kurfürst. Historische Erzählung aus dem Sch. K.* (Halle a. S. 1885); A. Schütz, *Der Donaufeldzug Karls V.* (Tübingen 1930); A. Ph. Brück, "Stadt und Erzstift Mainz im Sch. K." *Hessisches Jb. für Landesgeschichte* 4 (1954) 155–185; E. Hühns, "Nationale Propaganda im Sch. K." *Zschr. für Geschichtswissenschaft* 6 (1958) 1027–1248.

THE COLLOQUY OF REGENSBURG: Schottenloher 41390–41398; H. Jedin, II: 165–168, 478 (lit.); H. v. Caemmerer, *Das Regensburger Religionsgespräch im Jahre 1546* (Diss. Berlin 1901); F. Roth, "Der officielle Bericht der von den Evangelischen zum Regensburger Gespräch Verordneten an ihre Fürsten und Obern" *ARG* 5 (1907–8) 1–30, 375–397; V. Schultze, "Das Tagebuch des Grafen Wolrad II zu Waldeck zum Regensburger Religionsgespräch 1546" *ARG* 7 (1909–10) 135–184, 294–347; H. Nebelsieck, "Elf Briefe und Aktenstücke über das Religionsgespräch in Regensburg von 1546" *ARG* 32 (1935) 127–136, 253–283.

THE INTERIM: Schottenloher 38259a–38330a; K. Th. Hergang, *Das Augsburger Interim* (Leipzig 1855); N. Müller, "Zur Geschichte des Interims" (Leipzig 1855); N. Müller, "Zur Geschichte des Interims" *Jb. für brandenburgische KG* 5 (1908) 51–171; "Verteidigung des Augsburger Interims von dem Bischof Julius Pflug, aus einer Handschrift," ed. Ch. G. Müller: *Archiv für alte und neue KG* 4 (1818) 104–148; M. Weigel, "Ein Gutachten des Johann Agricola von Eisleben über das Interim" *ZBKG* 16 (1941)

32–46; W. v. Loewenich, *Das Interim von 1548;* id., *Von Augustin zu Luther* (Witten 1959) 391–406.

REVOLT OF THE PRINCES: K. E. Born, "Moritz v. Sachsen und die Fürsten-verschwörung gegen Karl V." *HZ* 191 (1960) 18–67 (lit.).

THE RELIGIOUS PEACE OF AUGSBURG: Schottenloher 34481–34503, 62198–62220; Text: K. Brandi, *Der Augsburger Religionsfriede vom 25. September 1555* (Göttingen 1927); E. Walder, *Religionsvergleiche des 16. Jh. I* (Bern 1960) 41–68; Ch. Lehenmann, *De pace religionis acta publica* (Frankfurt 1707); A. Druffel–K. Brandi, *Beiträge zur Reichsgeschichte 1553–1555; Briefe und Akten zur Geschichte des 16. Jh.* IV (Munich 1896); K. Brandi, "Passauer Vertrag und Augsburger Religionsfriede" *HZ* 95 (1905) 206–264; G. Wolf, *Der Augsburger Religionsfriede* (Stuttgart 1890); W. Kühns, *Gesch. des Passauischen Vertrages 1552* (Diss. Göttingen 1906); G. Bonwetsch, *Gesch. des Passauischen Vertrages von 1552* (Göttingen 1907); N. Paulus, "Religionsfreiheit und Augsburger Religionsfriede" *HPBl* 149 (1912) 356–367, 401–416; F. Siebert, *Zwischen Kaiser und Papst. Kardinal Truchsess von Waldburg und die Anfänge der Gegenreformation in Deutschland* (Berlin 1943); M. Simon, *Der Augsburger Religionsfriede* (Augsburg 1955); G. Pfeiffer, "Der Augsburger Religionsfriede und die Reichsstädte" *Zschr. des hist. Vereins für Schwaben* 61 (1955) 213–321; H. Tüchle, "Der Augsburger Religionsfriede. Neue Ordnung oder Kampfpause?" ibid. 323–340; H. Lutz, "Aus vatikanischen Quellen zum Augsburger Religionsfrieden 1555" ibid. 389–401; J. Grisar, "Die Sendung des Kardinals Morone als Legat zum Reichstag von Augsburg 1555" ibid. 341–387; id., "Die Stellung der Päpste zum Reichstag und Religionsfrieden von Augsburg" *StdZ* 156 (1954–55) 440–462; L. W. Spitz, "Particularism and the Peace of Augsburg 1555" *CH* 25 (1956) 110–126; M. Heckel, "Staat und Kirche nach den Lehren der ev. Juristen in der ersten Hälfte des 17. Jh." *ZSavRGkan* section 42 (1956) 117–247; id., "Autonomia und Pacis Compositio. Der Augsburger Religionsfriede in der Deutung der Gegenreformation" ibid. 45 (1959) 141–248; id., "Parität" ibid. 49 (1963) 261–420; W. P. Fuchs, "Der Augsburger Religionsfriede von 1555. Ein Literaturbericht" *Jb. der Hessischen Kirchengeschichtlichen Vereinigung* 8 (1957) 226–235; L. Petry, "Der Augsburger Religionsfriede von 1555 und die Landesgeschichte" *Blätter für Deutsche Landesgeschichte* 93 (1957) 150–175; H. Bornkamm, *Der Augsburger Religionsfriede:* id., *Das Jahrhundert der Reformation* (Göttingen ²1966) 242–253.

SECTION FOUR

Europe under the Sign of Confessional Pluralism

25. *The Reformation in Scandinavia*

BIBLIOGRAPHY

Bibliographie de la Réforme (1450–1648). Ouvrages parus de 1940 à 1955, fasc. 2 (Leiden 1960); H. Kellenbenz, "Forschungsbericht über skandinavische Geschichte I" *HZ* 190 (1960) 618–655.

LITERATURE

I. G. Lindhardt, *Den nordiske Kirkes Historie* (Copenhagen 1945); M. Gerhardt–W. Hubatsch, *Deutschland und Skandinavien im Wandel der Jahrhunderte* (Bonn 1950); G. Johannesson, "Die Kirchenreformation in den nordischen Ländern" *XIe Congrès International des Sciences Historiques. Rapports IV* (Göteborg–Stockholm–Uppsala 1960) 48–83; G. Schwaiger, *Die Reformation in den nordischen Ländern* (Münich 1962).

DENMARK: *Acta Pontificum Danica* V–VI, ed. A. Krarup–J. Lindbeck (Copenhagen 1913–1915); J. Danstrup, *A History of Denmark* (Copenhagen 1948); N. K. Andersen, *Confessio Hafniensis (1530)* (Copenhagen 1954); E. H. Dungley, *The Reformation in Denmark* (London 1948); Hal Koch–B. Kornerup, *Den Danske Kirkes Historie* IV (Copenhagen 1959); *Ekklesia,* ed. F. Siegmund–Schultze, II:7 (Leipzig 1937); L. Schmitt, *Der Karmeliter Paulus Heliä* (Freiburg 1893); id., *Joh. Tausen* (Cologne 1894); id., *Die Verteidigung der katholischen Kirche in Dänemark gegen die Religionserneuerung* (Paderborn 1899); id. (ed.), *Nic. Stagefyr seu Herborn, Confutatio Lutheranismi Danici (1530)* (Quaracchi 1902); J. O. Andersen, *Der Reformkatholizismus und die dänische Reformation* (Gütersloh 1934); id., *Paulus Helie I* (Copenhagen 1936); M. Christensen, *Hans Tausen* (Copenhagen 1942); C. T. Engelstoft, *Liturgiens Historie i Danmark* (Copenhagen 1840); J. Schnell, *Die dänische Kirchenordnung von 1542 und der Einfluss von Wittenberg* (Breslau 1927); E. Feddersen, "Philippismus und Luthertum in Dänemark und Schleswig-Holstein" *Festschr. H. von Schubert ARG ErgBd* 5 (Leipzig 1929) 92–114; id., "Die lateinische Kirchenordnung König Christians III. von 1537" *Schriften des Vereins für Schleswig-Holsteinische Kirchengesch.* I:18 (1934) 1–93; O. Kaehler, "Zur Gesch. der dänischen Kirchenordnung von 1537" *Festschr. K. Haff* (Innsbruck 1950) 111–119.

NORWAY: *Diplomatarium Norvegicum,* to date 21 vols. (Oslo 1847ff.); A. Chr. Baug, *Den norske kirkes historie ireformationsaarhundredet* (Oslo 1895); *Ekklesia,* ed. F. Siegmund-Schultze, II:6 (Gotha 1936); J. Welle, *Norges kirkehistorie* (Oslo 1948); O. Garstein, "The Reformation in Norway" *The Month* N.S. 21 (London 1959) 95–103; T. B. Wilson, *History of Church and State in Norway from the 10th to 16th Century* (Philadelphia 1903); K. Larsen, *A History of Norway* (Princeton 1948).

ICELAND: *Diplomatarium Islandicum,* 12 vols. (Copenhagen 1857–1902; Reykjavik 1900–1932); F. Johanneus, *Historia ecclesiastica Islandiae,* 4 vols. (Copenhagen 1772–1778); J. Helgason, *Islands Kirke fra Reformation en til vore Dage* (Copenhagen 1922); *Ekklesia,* ed. F. Siegmund-Schultze, II:7 (Leipzig 1937); T. J. Oleson, "Bishop Jon Arason (1484–1550)" *Speculum* 28 (Cambridge, Mass. 1953) 245–278; cf. ibid. 29 (1954) 535f.

SWEDEN: J Weidling, *Schwedische Gesch. im Zeitalter der Reformation* (Gotha 1882); J. Andersson, *Schwedische Geschichte* (Munich 1950); B. Gustafsson, *Svenk kyrkogeografi* (Malmö 1957); id., *Svenk kyrkohistoria* (Stockholm 1963); J. F. Martin, *Gustave Vasa et al Réforme en Suède* (Paris 1906); Hj. Holmquist, *Die Schwedische Reformation 1523–1531* (Leipzig 1925); S. Kjöllerström, "Kirche und Staat in Schweden nach der Reformation" *ZSavRGkan* 41 (1955) 271–289; id., *Guds och Severiges lag under Reformationstiden* (Lund 1957); id., "Gustav Vasa und die Bischofsweihe (1523–1531)" *Festschr. für Joh. Heckel* (Cologne–Graz 1959) 164–183; H. Yrwing, *Gustav Vasa, kröningsfrågan och Västeras riksdag 1527* (Lund 1956); I. Salvenius, *Gustav Vasa* (Stockholm 1950); E. Färnström, *Laurentius Petris Handskrivna Kyrkoordning av år 1561* (Stockholm 1956); Olavus Petri, *Samlade skrifter,* 4 vols., ed. B. Hesselmann, (Stockholm 1914–17); R. Holm, *Olavus Petri* (Uppsala 1917); C. Bergendoff, *Olavus Petri and the Ecclesiastical*

Transformation in Sweden (1521–1552) (New York 1928); R. Murray, *Olavus Petri* (Stockholm 1952); S. Ingebrand, *Olavus Petris reformatoriska åskådning* (Uppsala 1964); E. E. Yelvertow, *The Manual of Olavus Petri* (London 1951); G. Carlsson, "Preussischer Einfluss auf die Reformation Schwedens" *Festschr. O. Scheel* (Schleswig 1952) 36–48; M. Roberts, *The Early Vasas: A History of Sweden 1523–1611* (Cambridge 1968); J. Kolberg, "Aus dem Leben der letzten katholischen Bischöfe Schwedens" *Vorlesungsverzeichnis der Akademie Braunsberg* (1914); *Briefe von Johannes und Olaus Magnus,* ed. G. Buschbell (Stockholm 1932); Th. v. Haag, "Die apostolische Sukzession in Schweden" *Kyrkohistorisk Arsskrift* 44 (Uppsala 1945) 1–168; J. G. Hoffmann, *La réforme en Suède 1523–1527 et la succession apostolique* (Neuchatel 1945); E. Benz, *Bischofsamt und apostol. Sukzession im dt. Protestantismus* (Stuttgart 1953); Y. Stenström, *Om biskops tjänst och ämbete* (Stockholm 1959); A. A. Stomberg, *A History of Sweden* (New York 1931); H. W. Waddamg, *The Swedish Church* (London 1946).

FINLAND: W. Sommer, *Gesch. Finnlands* (Munich 1938); I. Salomies, *Suomen kirkon historia,* 3 vols. to date (Helsinki 1944–1962); G. Sentzke, *Die Kirche Finnlands* (Göttingen 1963); *Ekklesia,* ed. F. Siegmund-Schultze, II:8 (Leipzig 1938); J. Gummerus, *Michael Agricola, der Reformator Finnlands* (Helsinki 1944); T. Harjunpaa, "Liturgical Developments in Sweden and Finland in the Era of Lutheran Orthodoxy" *CH* XXXVII (1968) 14–36.

26. *The Reformation in Eastern Europe*

LITERATURE

E. Sehling, *Die ev. Kirchenordnungen des 16. Jh.* IV, V (Leipzig 1911–13) (Lit.); E. Benz, *Wittenberg und Byzanz* (Marburg 1949); R. Stupperich, "Der Protestantismus auf seinen Wegen nach Osteuropa" *Kirche im Osten* 1 (1958) 24–40; G. Rhode, "Die Reformation in Osteuropa" *Zeitschrift für Ostforschung* 7 (1958) 481–500; "Gestalten und Wege der Kirche im Osten" *Festgabe für A. Rhode,* ed. H. Kreska (Ulm 1958); R. Stupperich, "Geschichtl. Wandlungen und Lebensbedingungen des slawishcen Protestantismus" *Kirche im Osten* 2 (1959) 80–96; J. Matl, "Reformation und Gegenreformation als Kulturfaktoren bei den Slawen" *Festschr. Karl Eder* (Innsbruck 1959) 101–117; R. Stupperich, "Melanchthons Verhältnis zu Polen und Ungarn: Der Remter" *Zscht. für Kultur und Politik im Osteuropa* 6 (1960) 236–243; *La Renaissance et la Réformation en Pologne et en Hongrie,* ed. G. Székely–E. Fûgedi (Budapest 1963); E. W. Zeeden, *Die Entstehung der Konfessionen* (Munich–Vienna 1965) 153–178; *The New Cambridge Modern History* II (London–Cambridge 1962) 186–204; *Baltische Kirkengeschichte,* ed. R. Wittram (Munich 1956).

PRUSSIA: P. Tschackert, *Urkundenbuch zur Reformationsgesch. des Herzogtums Preussen,* 3 vols. (Leipzig 1890); H. Laag, "Die Einführung der Reformation im Ordensland Preussen" *NKZ* 36 (1925) 845–873; K. Forstreuter, *Vom Ordensstaat zum Fürstentum* (Kitzingen 1951); E. M. Wermter, "Herzog Albrecht von Preussen und die ermländischen Bischöfe" *Zschr. für die Gesch. und Altertumkunde Ermlands* 86 (1957) 198–311; id., "Reformversuche im Ermland vor dem Konzil von Trient" ibid. 87 (1958) 428–437; M. Lackner, "Neuere Lit. zur preussischen Reformationsgesch." *Kirche im Osten* 3 (1960) 195–200; P. Tschackert, *Georg von Polentz* (Leipzig 1888); id., *Paul Speratus von Rötlen* (Halle 1891); R. Stupperich, "Johann Briesmanns reformatorische Anfänge" *Jb. Für brandenburgische Kirchengesch.* 34 (1937) 3–21; E. Roth (ed.), *Vertrau Gott allein. Gebete*

Herzog Albrechts von Preussen (Würzburg 1956); W. Hubatsch, *Albrecht von Brandenburg-Ansbach* (Heidelberg 1960); J. B. Blessing, *Johannes Dantiscus* (Phil. Diss. Hamburg 1959); R. Stupperich (ed.), *Die Reformation im Ordensland Preussen 1523-24. Predigten, Traktate und Kirchenordnungen* (Ulm 1966).

LIVONIA–ESTONIA–CURLAND: L. Arbusow, *Die Einführung der Reformation in Liv-, Est-, und Kurland* (Leipzig 1921); O. Pohrt, *Reformationsgesch. Livlands* (Leipzig 1928); St. Arnell, *Die Auflösung des livländischen Ordensstaates* (Lund 1937); K. D. Staemmler, *Preussen und Livland im ihrem Verhältnis zur Krone Polens 1561–1586* (Diss. Göttingen 1949); R. Wittram, "Die Reformation in Livland" *Baltische Kirchengeschichte* (Göttingen 1956) 35–56; R. Ruhtenberg, "Die Beziehungen Luthers und der anderen Wittenberger Reformatoren zu Livland" ibid., 56–76; E. Treulich, "Die Reformation der kurländischen Kirche unter Gotthard Kettler" ibid., 77–86.

POLAND: Ch. Z. Salig, *Vollständige Historie der Augsburgischen Confession* II (Halle 1733) 515–803 (Poland through 1557); K. Völker, *Kirchengeschichte Polens* (Berlin–Leipzig 1930); G. Smend, *Die Synoden der Kirche Augsburgischer Konfession in Grosspolen* (Posen-Poznan 1930); K. E. Jordt Jorgensen, *Ökumenische Bestrebungen unter den polnischen Protestanten bis zum Jahre 1645* (Copenhagen 1942); A. Rhode, *Gesch. der ev. Kirche im Posener Lande* (Würzburg 1956); A. Schwarzenberg, "Besonderheiten der Reformation im Polen" *Kirche im Osten* 1 (1958) 52–64; E. W. Zeeden, "Calvins Einwirken auf die Reformation in Polen-Litauen" *Syntagma Friburgense. Histor. Studien H. Aubin dargebracht* (Lindau–Konstanz 1956) 323–359; K. Krejci, *Gesch. der polnischen Literatur* (Halle 1958); G. Schramm, "Antitrinitarier in Polen 1556–1658, ein Literaturbericht" *Bibliothèque d'Humanisme et Rennaissance* 21 (1959) 473–511; O. Bartel, "Luther und Melanchthon in Polen" *Luther und Melanchthon* ed. V. Vajta (Göttingen 1961) 165–177; id., "Melanchthon und Polen" *Philipp Melanchthon* (Berlin 1963) 227–236; B. Stasiewski, *Reformation und Gegenreformation in Polen* (Münster 1960); cf. J. Lecler, *Toleration in the Reformation* I (New York 1960) 385–422; H. Holzapfel, *Tausend Jahre Kirche Polens* (Würzburg 1966); A. F. Modrevius, *Opera omnia,* ed. C. Kumaniecki, I–V (Warsaw 1953–60), compare to: J. Lecler; Jan Laski, *Werke,* ed. A. Kuyper, 2 vols. (Amsterdam 1866); O. Bartel, *Jan Laski* I (Warsaw 1955); U. Falkenroth, *Gestalt und Wesen der Kirche bei Johannes von Laski* (Diss. Göttingen 1958); G. Schramm, *Der polnische Adel und die Reformation 1548–1607* (Wiesbaden 1965); O. Halecki, *A History of Poland* (Baltimore 1924); *The Cambridge History of Poland* I, ed. W. F. Reddaway et al. (New York 1950); S. Kot, *Socialism in Poland* (Boston 1957); O. Bartel, *Jan Laski* I (1499–1556) (Warsaw 1955).

BOHEMIA: Schottenloher 62501a–07; P. Rican, *Das Reich Gottes in den böhmischen Ländern* (Stuttgart 1957) (lit.); id., *Die Böhmischen Brüder* (Berlin 1961) (lit); id., "Melanchthon und die böhmischen Länder" *Philipp Melanchthon* (Berlin 1963) 237–260.

HUNGARY: G. D. Teutsch, *Urkundenbuch der ev. Landeskirche Augsburgischen Bekenntnisses in Siebenbürgen,* 2 vols. (Hermannstadt 1862–83); id., *Die Reformation im (siebenbürgischen) Sachsenland* (Hermannstadt 1929); F. Teutsch, *Gesch. der ev. Kirche in Siebenbürgen,* 2 vols. (Hermannstadt 1921–23); A. Schullerus, *Die Augustana in Siebenbürgen* (Hermannstadt 1923); V. Bruckner, "Die oberungarischen Glaubensbekenntnisse und die CA" *Gedenkbuch anlässl. der 400jähr. Jahreswende der CA* (Leipzig 1930) 1–67; B. v. Pukanzsky, *Gesch. des deutschen Schrifttums in Ungarn* (Münster 1931); M. Ödön, *Die Entstehung der ungarischen protestantischen Kirchenverfassung im Reformations-Jh.* (Papa 1942); E. Roth, *Die Reformation in Siebenbürgen,* 2 vols. (Cologne-Graz 1962–64); id., *Die Geschichte des Gottesdienstes der Siebenbürger Sachsen*

(Göttingen 1954); K. Reinerth, *Die Reformation der siebenbürgisch-sächsischen Kirche* (Gütersloh 1956); id., "Studien und Kritiken zu E. Roth, Die Geschichte des Gottes-dienstes" *Jb. für Liturgik und Hymnologie* 4 (1958–59) 73–82; M. Bucsay, *Geschichte des Protestantismus in Ungarn* (Stuttgart 1959) (Lit.); J. Solyom, "Melanchthonforschung in Ungarn" *Luther und Melanchthon,* ed. V. Vajta (Göttingen 1961) 178–188; E. Kovacs, "Melanchthon und Ungarn" *Philipp Melanchthon* (Berlin 1963) 261–269; K. Juhasz, "Kardinal Georg Utjesenovich (+1551) und das Bistum Tschanad" *HJ* 80 (1961) 252–264 (lit.); F. Kidric, *Die protestantische Kirchenordnung der Slovenen im 16. Jh.* (Heidel-berg 1919); G. Stöckl, *Die deutsch-slavische Südostgrenze des Reiches im 16. Jh., ein Beitrag zu ihrer Geschichte, dargestellt an Hand des südslavischen Reformationsschrifttums* (Breslau 1940); id., "Der Beginn des Reformationsschrifttums in slowenischer Sprache" *Südostforschungen* 15 (1956) 268–277; F. Valjavec *Gesch. der deutschen Kulturbeziehungen zu Südosteuropa* II (Munich 1955); A. Slodnjak, *Gesch. der slovenischen Lit.* (Berlin 1958); Johannes Honter, *Ausgewählte Schriften,* ed. O. Netoliczka (Vienna 1898); K. K. Klein, *Der Humanist und Reformator Johannes Honter* (Hermannstadt–Munich 1935); Solyom, "Disticha Novi Testamenti. Ein didaktischer Buchdruck des siebenbürgischen Refor-mators Johannes Honter" *Geschichtswirklichkeit und Glaubensbewährung. Festschr. für R. Müller* (Stuttgart 1967) 192–203; G. Gündisch, "Franz Salicäus, Ein Beitrag zur Reformationsgesch. Siebenbürgens" ibid., 204–219; L. Binder, "Die frühesten Syno-den der ev. Kirche in Siebenbürgen" ibid., 220–244; J. Balazs, *Johannes Sylvester* (1958) (lit.); W. Toth, "Stephen Kis of Szeged" *ARG* 44 (1955) 86–103; N. Rupel, *Primus Truber* (Munich 1965); W. Toth, "Highlights of the Hungarian Reformation" *CH* IX (1940) 141–156; L. Revesz, *History of the Hungarian Reformed Church* (Washington 1956).

27. Schism and Reformation in England

BIBLIOGRAPHY

C. Read, *Bibliography of British History. Tudor Period* (Oxford 1933).

SOURCES

J. S. Brewer–J. Gairdner, *Letters and Papers, Foreign and Domestic, of the Reign of Henry VIII,* 21 vols. (London 1862–1910); J. M. Rigg, *Calendar of St. Paul relative to English Affairs, principally in the Vatican Archives and Library,* 2 vols. (London 1916–26), to 1578; *Calendar of State Papers, Domestic and Foreign, for the Reigns of Edward, Mary and Elizabeth,* see C. Read, nos. 65, 66, 425; N. Pocock, *Records of the Reformation,* 2 vols. (Oxford 1870); J. Keble, *Statutes* (London 1684); H. Gee–W. J. Hardy, *Documents Illustrative of English Church History* (London 1896); G. R. Elton, *The Tudor Constitu-tion, Documents and Commentary* (Cambridge 1960); *Tudor Royal Proclamations* I, ed. P. G. Hughes–I. F. Larkin (New Haven 1964); *The Work of Thomas Cranmer,* ed. J. I. Packer–C. E. Duffield (Appleford 1964); St. Ehses, *Römische Dokumente zur Geschichte der Ehescheidung Heinrichs VIII. von England* (Paderborn 1893).

LITERATURE

GENERAL: J. D. Mackie, *The Earlier Tudors* (Oxford 1952) (Oxford History of England VII); J. A. Williamson, *The Tudor Age* (London ³1964); G. R. Elton, *The Tudor Revolution in Government* (Cambridge 1953); C. H. -K. George, *The Protestant Mind of the English*

Reformation 1570–1640 (Princeton 1961); Opposing the idealization of the character of Henry VIII, especially by A. F. Pollard, *Henry VIII* (London 1951), see G. R. Elton, *Henry VIII. An Essay in Revision* (London 1962); H. Maynard Smith, *Henry VIII and the Reformation* (London 1962); G. Mattingly, *Catharine of Aragon* (London 1942); N. Sanders, *De origine ac progressu schismatis Anglicani* (Köln 1585), the oldest complete description of the English schism; One of the newest accounts: G. Constant, *La réforme en Angleterre*, 2 vols. (Paris 1930–39), to Edward VI; Ph. Hughes, *The Reformation in England,* 3 vols. (London 1950–54), to Elizabeth I; An excellent short account is P. M. Parker, *The English Reformation to 1558* (London 1963), with good literature survey; F. A. Gasquet, *Heinrich VIII. und die englischen Klöster,* 2 vols. (Mainz 1890–91); the work is brought up to date by D. Knowles, *The Religious Orders in England III: The Tudor Age* (Cambridge 1959) and W. C. Richardson, *History of the Court of Augmentation 1536–54* (Baton Rouge, La. 1961); Concerning the penetration of Protestantism: E. G. Rupp, *Studies in the Making of the English Protestant Tradition* (Cambridge 1947); H. C. Porter, *Reformation and Reaction in Tudor Cambridge* (Cambridge 1958); C. Hopf, *M. Bucer and the English Reformation* (Oxford 1946); W. A. Clebsch, *England's Earliest Protestants 1520–35* (New Haven 1964); C. W. Dugmore, *The Mass and the English Reformers* (London 1958); H. C. White, *The Tudor Books of Private Devotion* (Madison 1951); J. K. McConica, *English Humanists and Reformation Politics under Henry VIII and Edward VI* (Oxford 1965); N. S. Tjernagel, *Henry VIII and the Lutherans* (Saint Louis 1965); J. E. Oxley, *The Reformation in Essex* (Manchester 1965); A. G. Dickens, *The English Reformation* (London 1964); T. Mac Caffery, *The Shaping of the Elizabethian Regime* (Princeton, 1968); P. Seaver, *The Puritan Lectureships, The Politics of Religious Dissent 1560–1662* (Stanford 1970); M. Breslow, *A Mirror of England: English Puritan Views of Foreign Nations, 1618–1640* (Cambridge 1970); M. O'Connell, *Thomas Stapelton and the Counter Reformation* (New Haven 1964).

CHURCH GOVERNMENT: E. W. Kemp, *Counsel and Consent. Aspects of Church Government* (London 1961); E. T. Davies, *Episcopacy and the Royal Supremacy in the Church of England* (Oxford 1950); Very detailed for the time of Elizabeth: W. P. M. Kennedy, *Elizabethan Episcopal Administration,* 3 vols. (London 1924); F. Higham, *Catholic and Reformed. A Study of the Anglican Church* (London 1962).

BIOGRAPHIES: A. F. Pollard, *Thomas Wolsey* (London 1953); Ch. Ferguson, *Naked to Mine Enemies. The Life of Card. Wolsey* (London 1958); See *LThK*² III 85 for works concerning Cranmer by A. F. Pollard (²1926), A. C. Deane (1927), G. W. Bromily (1956) and T. Maynard (1956) to the comprehensive biography by J. Ridley, *Thomas Cranmer* (Oxford 1962). For literature concerning J. Fisher and Thomas More which increased greatly after canonization (1935), see *LThK*² IV:159 and VII:628; G. J. Donelly, *A Translation of St. Thomas More's Responsio ad Lutherum* (Washington 1962); G. Marc'Hadour, *St. Thomas More. Lettre à Dorp. La supplication des âmes* (Namur 1962); *Opera omnia* (Frankfurt a. M. 1689), reprinted unaltered in Frankfurt 1963; E. Flessmann–E. van Leer, "The Controversy about Scripture and Tradition between Th. More and W. Tyndale" *NAKG* 43 (1959–60) 143–164; From the extensive literature concerning the *Utopia:* E. Surtz, *The Praise of Pleasure. Philosophie, Education and Communism in More's Utopia* (Cambridge, Mass. 1957); H. Süssmuth, *Studien z. Utopia des Th. M.* (Münster 1967). *Complete Works of St. Thomas More* (New Haven, Ct. 1961ff.).

28. The Struggle over Lutheran Orthodoxy

LITERATURE

GENERAL: Ch. A. Salig, *Vollständige Historie der Augsburgischen Confession* I–III (Halle 1730–1733–1735); G. J. Planck, *Gesch. der Entstehung, der Veränderungen und der Bildung unsers protestantischen Lehrbegriffs vom Anfang der Reformation bis zu der Einführung der Concordienformel* I–VI (Leipzig 1791–1800); H. Heppe, *Gesch. des deutschen Protestantismus* I–IV (Marburg 1852–59); H. R. Frank, *Die Theologie der Concordienformel,* 4 vols. (Erlangen 1858–65); F. Loofs, *Leitfaden zum Studium der Dogmengeschichte* (Halle 1906); P. Tschackert, *Die Entstehung der lutherischen und der reformierten Kirchenlehre* (Göttingen 1910); O. Ritschl, *Dogmengeschichte des Protestantismus* (= DG) I–IV (Leipzig 1908–12, Göttingen 1926–27); R. Seeberg, *Lehrbuch der Dogmengeschichte* IV, 2 vols. (Leipzig ³1920; new imp., ³1959) (Eng. *The History of Doctrines,* #76, #77; Grand Rapids, Mich. 1964); H. E. Weber, *Reformation, Orthodoxie und Rationalismus* T1. I 1.2 (Gütersloh 1937–40; new impression, Darmstadt 1966); P. Meinhold, *Philipp Melanchthon* (Berlin 1960); R. Stupperich, *Der unbekannte Melanchthon* (Stuttgart 1961); F. W. Katzenbach, *Die Reformation in Deutschland und Europa* (Gütersloh 1965); W. Preger, *Matthias Flacius Illyricus und seine Zeit,* 2 vols. (Erlangen 1859–61; reprint Hildesheim–Nieuwkoop 1964); H. Aland, "Die theologische Fakultät Wittenberg während des 16. Jh." *Kirchengeschichtliche Entwürfe* (Gütersloh 1960) 283–394; L. Theobald, "Einiges über die Lebensschicksale des Gallus während seiner Regensburger Superintendentenzeit" *ZBKG* 19 (1950) 67–77, 20 (1951) 100; H. W. Gensichen, *Damnamus. Die Verwerfung von Irrlehre bei Luther und im Luthertum des 16. Jh.* (Berlin 1955); M. Mirkovic, *Matjia Vlac'c Ilirik* (Zagreb 1960); J. Massner, *Kirchliche Überlieferung und Autorität im Flaciuskreis* (Berlin–Hamburg 1964); P. Fraenkel, *Testimonium Patrium: The Function of Patristic Argument in the Theol. of Melanchthon* (Geneva 1961); C. L. Manschreck, *Melanchthon, the Quiet Reformer* (New York 1958).

THE ANTINOMIAN CONTROVERSY: G. Kawerau, "Der Ausbruch des antinomistischen Streites" *ThStK* 53 (1880) 24–48; id., "Briefe und Urkunden zur Gesch. des antinomistischen Streites" *ZKG* 4 (1880–81) 299–324, 437–465; id., "Beiträge zur Gesch. des antinomistischen Streites" *Beiträge zur Reformationsgeschichte, Köstlin gewidmet* (Gotha 1896) 60–80; id., *RE* ³I (1896) 585–592; J. Werner, "Der erste antinomistische Streit" *NKZ* 15 (1904) 801–824, 860–873; G. Hammann, *Nomismus und Antinomismus innerhalb der Wittenberger Theologie von 1524–30* (Diss. Bonn 1952); R. Hermann, *Zum Streit um die Überwindung des Gesetzes* (Weimar 1958); G. Rosenberger, *Gesetz und Evangelium in Luthers Antinomerdisputationen* (Diss. Mainz 1958); J. Rogge, *Johann Agricolas Lutherverständnis* (focuses on Antinomianism) (Berlin 1960).

THE SYNERGISTIC AND MAJORISTIC CONTROVERSY: C. Schlüsselburg, *Catalogus Haereticorum* V (*De Synergistis,* Frankfurt 1611), VII (*De Maioristis,* Frankfurt 1599); Ch. E. Luthardt, *Die Lehre vom freien Willen und seinem Verhältnis zur Gnade in ihrer geschichtlichen Entwicklung dargestellt* (Leipzig 1863); G. L. Schmidt, *Justus Menius,* 2 vols. (Gotha 1867); Kawerau, *RE* ³XIX:229–235 (Synergy); K. D. Schmidt, "Der Göttinger Bekehrungsstreit 1566–70" *Zschr. der Ges. für niedersächsische KG* 34–35 (1929) 66–121; H. Kropatscheck, *Das Problem theologischer Anthropologie auf dem Weimarer Gespräch von 1560 zwischen Matthias Flacius Illyricus und Viktorin Strigel* (Diss. Gottingen 1943); L. Haikola, *Gesetz und Evangelium bei Matthias Flacius Illyricus* (Lund 1952); R. Bring, *Das Verhältnis von Glauben und Werken in der lutherischen Theologie* (Munich 1955); G. Moldaenke, *Schriftverständnis und Schriftdeutung im Zeitalter der Reformation* T1. I: *Matthias Flacius Illyricus* (Stuttgart 1936).

THE ADIAPHORAN CONTROVERSY: C. Schlüsselburg, 13 (1599); H. Ch. Hase, *Die Gestalt der Kirche Luthers. Der casus confessionis im Kampf des Matthias Flacius gegen das Interim von 1548* (Göttingen 1940); C. L. Manschreck, "The Role of Melanchthon in the Adiaphora Controversy" *ARG* 48 (1957) 165–182; H. Scheible, "Melanchthons Brief an Carlowitz" *ARG* 57 (1966) 102–130.

THE OSSIANDRIAN CONTROVERSY: W. Möller, *Andreas Osiander* (Elberfeld 1870); A. Ritschl, "Die Rechtfertigungslehre des Andreas Osiander" *Die christliche Lehre von der Rechtfertigung und Versöhnung* I (Bonn ³1889) 235–255; E. Hirsch, *Die Theologie des Andreas Osiander* (Göttingen 1919); M. J. Arntzen, *Mystieke rechtvaardigingsleer. Een bijtrage ter beorderling van de theologie van Andreas Osiander* (Kampen 1956).

THE EUCHARISTIC CONTROVERSY: A. Ebrard, *Das Dogma vom Abendmahl und seine Gesch.*, 2 vols. (Frankfurt a. M. 1845); A. W. Dieckhoff, *Die evangelische Abendmahlslehre im Reformationszeitalter geschichtlich dargestellt* I (Göttingen 1854); G. L. Plitt, "Melanchthons Wandelung in der Abendmahlslehre" *Zschr. f. Protestantismus und Kirche* NF 56 (1868) 65–101; G. Mönckeberg, *Joachim Westphal und Joh. Calvin* (Hamburg 1865); C. H. W. Sillem, *Briefsammlung des J. Westphal 1530–75*, 2 vols. (Hamburg 1903); R. Calinich, *Kampf und Untergang des Melanchthonismus in Kursachsen* (Leipzig 1866); J. F. A. Gillet, *Crato v. Crafftheim und seine Freunde*, 2 vols. (Frankfurt 1860–61); H. Gollwitzer, *Coena Domini. Die altlutherische Abendmahlslehre in ihrer Auseinandersetzung mit dem Calvinismus dargestellt an der lutherischen Frühorthodoxie* (Munich 1937); E. Bizer, *Studien zur Gesch. des Abendmahlstreites im 16. Jh.* (1940; new impression, Darmstadt 1962); H. Grass, *Die Abendmahlslehre bei Luther und Calvin* (Gütersloh ²1954).

29. John Calvin: Personality and Work

WORKS

Omnia Opera (=OC), 59 vols. CR 29–87 (Braunschweig-Berlin 1863–1900); *Supplementa Calviniana, Sermons inédits* I: *Predigten über 2 Sam.* ed. H. Rückert (Neukirchen 1961); V: *Sermons sur le Livre de Michée*, ed. J. D. Benoît (Neukirchen 1964); *Opera Selecta* (=OS), 5 vols. ed. P. Barth, W. Niesel, D. Scheuner (Munich 1952–62); *Johannes Calvins Auslegung der Heiligen Schrift*, New Series, ed. O. Weber, 20 vols. (Neukirchen 1937f.); *Johann Calvin, Diener am Wort. Predigtauswahl*, ed. E. Mülhaupt (Göttingen 1934); *Der Psalter auf der Kanzel Calvins*, ed. E. Mülhaupt (Neukirchen 1959); *Institution de la religion chrétienne* (1541), ed. J. Pannier, 4 vols. (Paris 1936); A. L. Herminjard, *Correspondance des Réformateurs dans les pays de langue francaise*, 9 vols (Geneva 1866–1897); *Johannes Calvins Lebenswerk in seinen Briefen*, trans. R. Schwarz, 3 vols. (Neukirchen 1961–62); *Bekenntnisschriften und Kirchenordnungen der nach Gottes Wort reformierten Kircher*, ed. W. Niesel (Zollikon–Zurich 1938); *Reformierte Bekenntnisschriften und Kirchenordnungen in dt. Übersetzung*, ed. P. Jacobs (Neukirchen 1949); *Commentaries and Letters*, ed. J. Harovtiwian (Philadelphia 1958); *Institutes of the Christian Religion*, 2 vols., ed. J. T. McNiel (Philadelphia 1961); *Theological Treatises*, ed. J. A. S. Reid (Philadelphia 1954); *A Collation of the Latin Texts of the First Edition of Calvin's Institutes*, ed. W. G. Hards (Baltimore 1958).

LITERATURE

Bibliographia Calviniana: Opera 59, 457–586, new printing (Nieuwkoop 1960); W. Niesel, *Calvin-Bibliographie 1901–1959* (Munich 1961); J. T. McNiel, "Thirty Years of

Calvin Study" *CH* XVII (1948) 207–240; XVIII (1949) 241; E. A. Dowey, "Continental Reformation Reference Works of General Interest. Studies in Calvin and Calvinism since 1955" *CH* XXIX (1960) 187–204.

BIOGRAPHIES: F. W. Kampschulte, *Johannes Calvin, seine Kirche und sein Staat in Genf,* 2 vols. (Leipzig 1869–99); A. Lang, *Johannes Calvin* (Leipzig 1909); E. Doumerque, *Jean Calvin, Les hommes et les choses de son temp.,* 7 vols. (Lausanne–Paris 1899–1927); A. de Quervain, *Calvin. Sein Lehren und Kämpfen* (Berlin 1926); P. Imbart de la Tour, *Les origines de la Réforme IV: Calvin et l'institution chrétienne* (Paris 1935); G. Gloede, *Calvin, Weg und Werk* (Leipzig 1953); W. F. Dankbaar, *Calvin. sein Weg und sein Werk* (Neukirchen 1959); J. Cadier, *Calvin. Der Mann, den Gott bezwungen hat* (Zollikon 1959); E. Pfisterer, *Calvins Wirken in Genf* (Neukirchen 1957); F. Büsser, *Calvins Urteil über sich selbst* (Zurich 1950); J. Moltmann, ed., *Calvin-Studien 1959* (Neukirchen 1960); J. Rogge, ed., *Johannes Calvin (1509–1564)* (Berlin 1963); J. Bohatec, *Budé und Calvin* (Graz 1950); E. W. Zeeden, "Das Bild Martin Luthers in den Briefen Calvins" *ARG* 49 (1958); A. Ganoczy, *Le jeune Calvin* (Wiesbaden 1966).

THEOLOGY: SOURCES: F. Wendel, *Calvin—The Origins and Development of his Religious Thought* (London 1963); B. B. Warfield, *Calvin and Augustine* (Philadelphia 1956); L. Smits, *Saint Augustin dans l'oeuvre de Jean Calvin* (Assen 1957–58); K. Reuter, *Das Grundverständnis der Theologie Calvins* (Neukirchen 1963); W. Neisel, *Theology of Calvin* (Philadelphia 1956); R. C. Hunt, *Calvin* (London 1933).

GENERAL WORKS: P. Wernle, *Der evangelische Glaube* III: *Calvin* (Tübingen 1919); O. Ritschl, *Dogmengeschichte des Protestantismus* III (Göttingen 1926); H. Bauke, *Die Probleme der Theologie Calvins* (Leipzig 1922); H. Weber, *Die Theologie Clavins* (Berlin 1930); E. Mülhaupt, *Die Predigt Calvins* (Berlin 1931); W. Niesel, *Die Theologie Calvins* (Munich ²1957); H. Wendorf, *Calvins Bedeutung für die prot. Welt* (Leipzig 1940); H. Olsson, *Calvin och reformationens theologi* I (Lund 1943).

SPECIAL STUDIES: G. Gloede, *Theologia naturalis bei Calvin* (Stuttgart 1935); T. H. L. Parker, *The Doctrine of the Knowledge of God* (Edinburgh 1952); E. A. Dowey, *The Knowledge of God in Calvin's Theology* (New York 1952); H. H. Wolf, *Die Einheit des Bundes. Das Verhältnis von AT und NT bei Calvin* (Neukirchen 1958); H. Jackson Forstmann, *Word and Spirit. Calvin's Doctrine of Biblical Authority* (Stanford, Calif. 1962); H. Noltensmeier, *Reformatorische Einheit. Das Schriftverständnis bei Luther und Calvin* (Graz–Cologne 1953); P. Brunner, *Vom Glauben bei Calvin* (Tübingen 1952); M. Neeser, *Le Dieu de Calvin* (Neuchâtel 1956); J. F. Jansen, *Calvin's Doctrine of the Word of Christ* (London 1956); W. Kolfhaus, *Christusgemeinschaft bei Johannes Calvin* (Neukirchen 1939); id., *Vom christlichen Leben nach Johannes Calvin* (Neukirchen 1937); S. van der Linde, *De leer van de Heilige Geest* (Wageningen 1943); W. Krusche, *Das Wirken des Heiligen Geistes bei Calvin* (Göttingen 1957); J. Beckmann, *Vom Sakrament bei Calvin* (Tübingen 1926); W. F. Dankbaar, *De Sacramentsleer van Calvijn* (Amsterdam 1941); id., *De tegen woordigheid van Christus in het Avondmaal* (Nijkerk 1950); R. S. Wallace, *Calvin's Doctrine of the Word and Sacrament* (Edinburgh 1953); L. G. M. Alting v. Geusa, *Die Lehre von der Kindertaufe bei Calvin* (Mainz 1963); G. P. Hartvelt, *Verum Corpus* (Delft 1960); W. Niesel, *Calvins Lehre vom Abendmahl* (Munich 1935); W. Boelens, *Die Arnoldshainer Thesen* (Assen 1964); J. Rogge, *Virtus und res. Um die Abendmahlswirklichkeit bei Calvin* (Stuttgart 1965); A. Ganoczy, *Calvin Théologien de l'église et du ministère* (Paris 1964); L. Schummer, *Le ministère pastorale dans l'Institution chrétienne de Calvin* (Wiesbaden 1965); K. Fröhlich, *Gottes Reich, Welt und Kirche bei Calvin* (Stuttgart 1965); W. Nijenhuis, *Calvinus Oecumenicus* ('s Gravenhage 1959); Th.

703

F. Torrance, *Calvin and the Doctrine of Man* (London 1949); H. Quistorp, *Die letzten Dinge im Zeugnis Calvins* (Gütersloh 1941); W. A. Hauck, *Sünde und Erbsünde nach Calvin* (Heidelberg 1938); id., *Calvin und die Rechtfertigung* (Gütersloh 1938); id., *Christusglaube und Gottes Offenbarung nach Calvin* (Gütersloh 1939); id., *Vorsehung und Freiheit nach Calvin* (Gütersloh 1947); id., *Die Erwählten, Prädestination und Heilsgewissheit bei Calvin* (Gütersloh 1950); A. Göhler, *Calvins Lehre von der Heiligung* (Munich 1934); P. Jacobs, *Prädestination und Verantwortlichkeit bei Calvin* (Neukirchen 1937); E. Buess, "Prädestination und Kirche in Calvins Institutio" *ThZ* 12 (1956) 347–361; H. Otten, *Calvins Theologische Anschauung von der Prädestination* (Munich 1938); G. Räcke, *Gesetz und Evangelium bei Calvin* (Diss. Mainz 1953); J. Bohatec, *Calvin und das Recht* (Feudingen 1934); id., *Calvins Lehre von Staat und Kirche* (Breslau 1937, reprinted Aalen 1961); M. E. Chenevière, *La Pensée politique de Calvin* (Paris 1937); J. T. McNiell, *John Calvin on God and Political Duty* (New York 1950); W. A. Mueller, *Church and State in Luther and Calvin* (Nashville, Tenn. 1954); Q. Breen, *John Calvin, A Study in French Humanism* (Grand Rapids, Mich. 1931); R. M. Kingdom, *Geneva and the Coming of the Religious Wars in France 1555–1563* (Geneva 1956); J. T. McNeill, *Calvin and the Reformation* (New York 1962); A. M. Schmidt, *John Calvin and the Calvinistic Tradition* (London 1961); S. G. Craig, (ed.), *Calvin and Augustine* (Philadelphia 1956); W. E. Stuermenn, *A Critical Guide to Calvin's Concept of Faith* (Tulsa 1952); R. W. Battenhause, "The Doctrine of Man in Calvin and in Renaissance Platonism" *Journal of the History of Ideas* IX (1948) 447–471; J. T. McNeill, "The Democratic Element in Calvin's Thought" *CH* XVIII (1949) 153–168; G. L. Mosse, *Calvinism: Authoritarian or Democratic* (New York 1957); J. Baur, *Gott, Recht und weltliches Regiment im Werke Calvins* (Bonn 1965).

HERESY TRIALS: F. Buisson, *S. Castellio, sa vie et son oeuvre*, 2 vols. (Paris 1892); E. Giran, *S. Castellio et la Réforme Calvinienne* (Paris 1914); H. Fazy, *Procès de Bolsec* (Geneva 1866); E. Choisy, *Calvin et Servet* (Neuilly 1926); B. Becker (ed.), *Autour de M. Servet et de S. Castellio* (Haarlem 1953); J. F. Fulton, *M. Servet. Humanist and Martyr* (New York 1953); P. Cavard, *Le procès de M. Servet à Vienne* (Vienna 1953); R. H. Bainton, *Hunted Heretic* (Boston 1953); id., *Concerning Heretics* (New York 1935).

30. The Spread of Calvinism in Western Europe

SOURCES

E. F. K. Müller, *Die Bekenntnisschriften der reformierten Kirche* (Leipzig 1903); W. Niesel, *Bekenntnisschriften und Kirchenordnungen der nach Gottes Wort reformierten Kirche* (Zurich ³1938); P. Jacobs, *Reformierte Bekenntnisschriften und Kirchenordnungen* (Neukirchen 1949); D. C. Fabricius, *Die Kirche von England, ihr Gebetbuch, Bekenntnis und kanonisches Recht* (= *Corpus Confessionum* 17. Abt.) (Berlin-Leipzig 1937); id., *Presbyterianismus* (= *Corpus Confessionum* 18. Abt.) (Berlin 1940).

LITERATURE

E. Knodt, *Die Bedeutung Calvins und des Calvinismus für die protestantische Welt* (1910); H. Wendorf, *Calvins Bedeutung für die protestantische Welt* (Leipzig 1940); A. A. van Schelven, *Het calvinisme gedurende zijn blocitijd in de 16ᵉ en de 17ᵉ eeuw. Zijn uitbreiding en cultuur-historische betecknis* I: *Genève, Frankrijk;* II: *Schotland, Engeland, Noord-Amerika* (Amsterdam 1943–51); H. Rössler, *Der Calvinismus* (Bremen 1951); J. T. McNeill, *The History and Character of Calvinism* (New York 1954); B. S. Warburton,

Calvinism (Grand Rapids 1955); E. G. Leónard, *Histoire générale du protestantisme* II: *L'établissement* (1564–1700) (Paris 1961); E. A. Dowey, "Continental Reformation: Works of General Interest. Studies in Calvin and Calvinism since 1955" *CH* XXIX: 187–204.

FRANCE

SOURCES: H. Hauser, *Les sources de l'histoire de France. Le XVIe siècle* (1494–1610), 4 vols. (Paris 1906–16); *Lettres de Catherine de Médicis,* 10 vols. (Paris 1880 through 1909); Ivan Lontchinsky, *Documents inédits sur la Réforme et la Ligue* (Paris 1857).

LITERATURE: G. v. Polenz, *Gesch. des französischen Calvinismus,* 5 vols. (Gotha 1857–69); Ch. Roulet, *Histoire de l'Église de France,* 3 vols. (Paris 1946–49); J. Viénet, *Histoire de la Réforme française des origines à l'Édit de Nantes,* 2 vols. (Paris 1926–34); P. Imbart de la Tour, *Les origines de la Réforme* IV: *Calvin et l'Institution chrétienne* (Paris 1935); J. Chambon, *Der französische Protestantismus* (Munich 1948); R. Nürnberger, *Die Politisierung des französischen Protestantismus* (Tübingen 1948); S. Mours, "Liste des églises réformées" *Bulletin de la Société de l'Histoire du Protestantisme français* 103 (1957) 37–59, 113–130, 200–216; *Checklist of French Political Pamphlets 1560–1644 in the Newberry Library,* compiled by D. V. Welsh (Chicago 1950); E. Armstrong, *The French Wars of Religion* (Oxford 1904); id., *Geneva and the Consolidation of the French Protestant Movement* (Madison, Wisconsin 1967); R. M. Kingdom, *Geneva and the Coming of the Wars of Religion in France* (Geneva 1956); J. W. Thompson, *The Wars of Religion in France* (Chicago 1909); O. Zeff, *The Huguenots* (New York 1942); J. H. Mitchell, *The Court of the Connetable* (New Haven, Conn. 1947); S. L. England, *The Massacre of St. Bartholomew* (London 1938). **Wars of Religion:** L. Romier, *Les origines politiques des guerres de rélligion,* 2 vols. (Paris 1913–14); id., *Le royaume de Catherine de Médicis: La France à la veille des guerres de religion,* 2 vols. (Paris 1922); id., *La conjuration d'Amboise* (Paris 1923); id., *Catholiques et Huguenots à la cour de Charles IX* (Paris 1924); G. de Lagarde, *Recherches sur l'esprit politique de la Réforme* (Paris 1926); L. R. Lefèvre, *Les Français, pendant les guerres de Religion* (Paris 1949); A. de Lévis-Mirepoiz, *Les guerres de Religion 1559–1610* (Paris 1950); Ph. Erlanger, *Le massacre de la Saint-Barthélemy* (Paris 1960); *The Letters and Documents of . . . Baron di Biron (1524–1592),* 2 vols., ed. J. W. Thompson (Berkeley 1936). **Edict of Nantes:** Text: E. Walder, *Religionsvergleiche des 16. Jh.* II (Bern 1961) 13–71; id., E. Mengin (ed.), *Das Edikt von Nantes* (Flensburg 1963); E. Benoist, *Histoire de l'édit de Nantes,* 5 vols. (Delft 1693–95); J. Pannier, *L'église réformée de Paris sous Henri IV* (Paris 1911); J. Faurey, *Henri IV et l'édit de Nantes* (Bordeaux 1903); id., *L'édit de Nantes et la question de la tolérance* (Paris 1929); J. de Missècle, *L'édit de Nantes et sa révocation* (Colmar 1930); A. Bailly, *La réforme en France jusqu'à l'Édit de Nantes* (Paris 1960); A. Buisson, *Michel de l'Hôpital* (Paris 1950); Jean Héritier, *Catherine de Médicis* (Paris 1941, Lit.); E. Neale, *The Age of Catherine de Medici* (London 1943); H. O. Evenett, *The Cardinal of Lorraine and the Council of Trent* (Cambridge 1930); E. Marcks, *Gaspard de Coligny, sein Leben und das Frankreich seiner Zeit* (Leipzig 1918); Ph. Erlanger, *Henri III* (Paris 1948); P. de Vaissière, *Henri IV* (Paris 1928); Ph. Erlanger, *L'étrange mort de Henri IV* (Paris 1957); M. Reinhard, *Henri IV ou la France sauvée* (Paris 1958).

THE NETHERLANDS

SOURCES: S. Cramer–F. Pijper, *Bibliotheca Reformatoria Neerlandica* I–X (The Hague 1903–14); *Racueil des ordonnances des Pays-Bas,* 6 vols. (1506–1555) (Brussels 1893–

1922); W. Perquin, *Bibliotheca catholica neerlandica impressa 1500–1727* (The Hague 1955); *Recueil des ordonnances de la principauté de Liège I (1507–80)* (Brussels 1869); P. Frederico, *Corpus documentorum inquisitionis haereticae pravitatis Neerlandicae* IV–V (Gent 1900–06); G. Brom–A. H. L. Hensen, *Romeinsche bronnen voor den kerkelijk-staatkundigen toestand der Nederlanden in de 16ᵈᵉ eeuw* (The Hague 1922); J. Lefèvre, *Correspondance de Philippe II sur les affaires des Pays-Bas* (Brussels 1940); M. Dietrick, *Documents, inédits sur l'érection des nouveaux diocèses au Pays-Bas 1521–70*, 3 vols. (Brussels 1960–62).

LITERATURE: **History:** J. W. Motley, *Der Abfall der Niederlande und die Entstehung des Holländischen Freistaats*, 3 vols. (Dresden 1857–60); A. Heune, *Histoire du règne de Charles-Quint en Belgique* (Brussels 1858–60); P. Frederico, *De Nederlanden onder Keizer Karl V.* (Gent 1885); E. Gossart, *L'établissement du régime espagnol dans les Pays-Bas et l'insurrection* (Brussels 1905); G. de Boom, *Charles-Quint, prince des Pays-Bas* (Brussels 1941); M. Dierickx, *De oprichting der nieuwe bisdommen in de Nederlanden onder Filips II 1559–70* (Antwerp–Utrecht 1950); id., *RHE* 59 (1964) 489–499. **Inquisition:** P. Claessens, *L'Inquisition et le régime pénal pour la répression de l'hérésie dans les Pays-Bas du passé* (Turnhout 1886); J. Scheerder, *De Inquisitie in de Nederlanden in de 16ᵈᵉ eeuw* (Antwerp 1944). **Calvinism:** H. Q. Janssen, *De Kerkhervorming in Vlaanderen* (Arnhem 1868); F. L. Rutgers, *Calvijns involved op de Reformatie in de Nederlanden* (Leiden 1899); H. J. Elias, *Kerk en Staat in de zuidelijkjke Nederlanden 1598–1621* (Antwerp 1931); L. J. Rogier, *Geschiedenis van het Katholicisme in Noord-Nederland in de 16ᵉ en de 17ᵉ eeuw*, 3 vols. (Amsterdam 1945–47); W. F. Dankbaar, *Hoogtepunten uit het Nederlandsche Calvinisme in de zestiende eeuw* (Haarlem 1946); J. Lindeboom, *De confessioneele ontwikkeling de Reformatie in de Nederlanden* (The Hague 1946); J. Roelink, *Het calvinisme, Algemene Geschiedenis de Nederlanden* IV (Utrecht 1952); E. de Moreau, *Histoire de l'église en Belgique* V (Brussels 1952); L. E. Halkin, *La Réforme en Belgique sous Charles-Quint* (Brussels 1957, Lit.).

GERMANY

LOWER RHINE: *Die Akten der Synoden und Quartierskonsistorien in Jülich, Kleve und Berg, 1570–1610* (Neuwied 1909); E. Simons (ed.), *Urkundenbuch zur rheinischen KG* I: *Synodalbuch;* A. Wolters, *Reformationsgesch. der Stadt Wesel bis zur Befestigung ihres reformierten Bekenntnisses* (Bonn 1868); J. Hillmann, *Die ev. Gemeinde Wesel und ihre Willibrordkirche* (Düsseldorf 1896); W. Hollweg, "Calvins Beziehungen zu den Rheinlanden" *Calvinstudien,* ed. der reformierten Gemeinde Elberfeld (Leipzig 1909) 126–186; H. Kessel, "Reformation und Gegenreformation im Herzogtum Cleve (1517–1609)" *Düsseldorfer Jb.* 30 (1918–19) 1–160; H. Forsthoff, *Rheinische KG* I: *Die Reformation am Niederrhein* (Essen 1929); D. Coenen, *Die katholische Kirche am Niederrhein von der Reformation bis zum Beginn des 18. Jh.* (Münster 1967); G. Hövelmann u.a., *Niederrheinische KG* (Kevelaer 1965).

PALATINATE: A. Kluckhohn, "Wie ist Kurfürst Friedrich III. von der Pfalz Calvinist geworden?" *Münchener Historisches Jb.* (1866) 432–520; id., *Friedrich der Fromme, Curfürst von der Pfalz, der Schützer der reformierten Kirche 1559–76* (Nördlingen 1876); id., (ed.) *Die Briefe Friedrichs des Frommen,* 2 vols. (Braunschweig 1866–70); R. Lossen, *Die Glaubensspaltung in Kurpfalz* (Heidelberg 1930); E. Mayer, *Pfälzische KG* (Kaiserslautern 1939); L. Stamer, *KG der Pfalz III* 1 (Speyer 1955); H. Müller, "Der Calvinismus am Rhein" *Monatshefte für KG des Rheinlands* (1954) 34–41; E. W. Zeeden, *Kleine Reformationsgesch. von Baden-Durlach und Kurpfalz* (Karlsruhe 1956) (lit.); K.

Sudhoff, *C. Olevianus und Z. Ursinus* (Elberfeld 1857); Ruth Wesel-Roth, Thomas Erastus. *Ein Beitrag zur Gesch. der reformierten Kirche und zur Lehre von der Staatssouveränität* (Lahr 1954); W. Hollweg, *Neue Untersuchungen zur Gesch. und Lehre des Heidelberger Katechismus* (Neukirchen 1961); id., *Der Augsburger Reichstag von 1566 und seine Bedeutung für die Entstehung der Reformierten Kirche und ihres Bekenntnisses* (Neukirchen 1964); J. Staedtke (ed.), *Glauben und Erkennen. 400 Jahre Confessio Helvetica Posterior* (Zurich 1966).

NASSAU: B. Weber, *Cartons aus dem deutschen Kirchenleben* (Mainz 1858) 575–660: Die Reformation in Nassau; H. F. Röttsches, *Luthertum und Calvinismus in Nassau-Dillenburg* (Berne 1954) (lit.); L. Hatzfeld, "Die Reformation in der Grafschaft Nassau-Dillenburg" *AMrhKG* 7 (1955) 77–111; K. Wolf, "Zur Einführung des reformierten Bekenntnisses in Nassau-Dillenburg" *Nassauische Annalen* 66 (1955) 160–193.

BREMEN: O. Veeck, *Gesch. der reformierten Kirche Bremens* (Berlin 1917); J. Moltmann, *Christoph Pezel (1539–1604) und der Calvinismus in Bremen* (Bremen 1958).

LIPPE: W. Butterweck, *Die Gesch. der Lippischen Landeskirchen* (Schötmar 1926); H. Kiewning, *Lippische Gesch.* (Detmold 1942).

ANHALT: R. Specht, *Bibliogr. zur Gesch. von Anhalt* (Magdeburg 1930); supplement 1930–35 (Dessau 1935); H. Wäschke, *Gesch. Anhalts im Zeitalter der Reformation* (Cöthen 1913); H. Duncker, *Anhalts Bekenntnisstand während der Vereinigung der Fürstentümer unter Joachim Ernst und Johann Georg (1570–1606)* (Dessau 1892); C. A. Valentiner, *Das Bekenntnis der Anhaltischen Landeskirche* (Bernburg 1895); G. Schubring, "Die Einführung der reformierten Confession in Anhalt" *Zschr. für die gesamte luth. Theol. u. Kirche* 9 (1848) 291–340; H. Becker, "Der wesentliche Anteil Anhalts an der Festlegung der Bezeichnung 'reformiert' als Kirchenname in Dtl." *ThStK* 74 (1901) 242–269; A. Boes, "Die ev. Landeskirche Anhalts, ihre geschichtliche Entwicklung in Bekenntnis und Verfassung" *Amsblatt der ev. Landeskirche Anhalts* (Dessau 1956) 41–45.

SCOTLAND

SOURCES: *Acts and Proceedings of the General Assemblies of the Kirk of Scotland, from the year 1560*, ed. Th. Thomson, 3 vols. (Edinburg 1839–45); D. Calderwood, *The History of the Kirk of Scotland*, ed. Th. Thomson–D. Laing, 8 vols. (1842–49); R. Keith, *History of Affairs of Church and State in Scotland*, ed. J. Parker Lawson, 3 vols. (1844–50); *Statuta Ecclesiae Scoticanae (Concilia Scoticae)*, ed. Joseph Robertson, 2 vols. (1866); *Papal Negotiations with Mary Queen of Scots during her Reign in Scotland, 1561–67*, ed. John Hungerford Pollen (1901); John Knox, *History of the Reformation in Scotland*, ed. W. C. Dickinson, taken from the works of Knox, I–II (1949); *A Source Book of Scottish History* II (1424–1567), III (1567–1707), ed. W. C. Dickinson–G. Donaldson (Edinburgh 1958).

LITERATURE: A. Lang, *History of Scotland*, 4 vols. (Edinburgh 1903–07); F. H. Brown, *History of Scotland to the Present Time*, 3 vols., II: *From the Accession of Mary Stuart to the Revolution* (Cambridge 1911); G. Donaldsen, *The Scottish Reformation* (Cambridge 1960, Lit.); W. C. Dickinson–G. S. Tryde, *A New History of Scotland*, 2 vols., I: *Scotland from the Earliest Times to 1603* (1961), II: *Scotland from 1603 to the Present Day* (1962) (lit.). **Church History**: A. Bellesheim, *Gesch. der katholischen Kirche in Schottland*, 2 vols. (Mainz 1883); A. R. MacEwen, *A History of the Church in Scotland*, 2 vols. (London

1913–18); D. Nobbs, *England and Scotland 1560–1707* (London 1952); J. H. Burleigh, *A Church History of Scotland* (New York 1960). **Reformation in Scotland:** F. Mitchell, *The Scottish Reformation. Its Epochs, Episodes, Leaders and Distinctive Characteristic,* ed. D. H. Fleming (Blackwood–Edinburgh 1900); D. H. Fleming, *The Reformation in Scotland, Causes, Characteristics, Consequences.* (London 1910); A. Zimmermann, "Zur Reformation in Schottland" *RQ* 25 (1911) 27–41, 110–123; G. Donaldson, *The Scottish Reformation* (Cambridge 1960); J. Girdwood Maggregor, *The Scottish Presbyterian Polity* (Edinburgh 1926); G. D. Henderson, *Religious Life in Seventeenth Century Scotland* (Cambridge 1937); id., *The Claims of the Church of Scotland* (London 1951). **John Knox:** A. Lang, *John Knox and the Reformation* (London 1905); Lord E. Percy, *John Knox* (London 1937); *Works,* ed. D. Laing, 6 vols. (Edinburgh 1895); P. H. Brown, *John Knox* (New York 1905); H. Watt, *John Knox in Controversy* (New York 1950). **Scotch-English Royal Houses:** D. H. Fleming, *Mary Queen of Scots: From her Birth to her flight into England* (London 1898); H. Witte, *Die Ansichten Jakobs I. von England über Kirche und Staat* (Berlin 1940); S. A. Tannebaum, *Mary Stuart, Queen of Scots. A Concise Bibliography,* 3 vols. (New York 1944–46); A. Fraser, *Mary Queen of Scots* (London 1969).

ENGLAND

E. C. E. Boume, *The Anglicanism of William Laud* (London 1947); W. Haller, *The Rise of Puritanism* (New York 1956); J. Marlowe, *The Puritan Tradition in English Life* (London 1957); M. P. Ashley, *Oliver Cromwell and the Puritan Revolution* (London 1958); P. Collinson, *The Elizabethan Puritan Movement* (Berkley 1967); see chaps. 27 and 39; A. Fraser, *Cromwell the Lord Protector* (New York 1974).

31. *The Formation of Denominations in the Sixteenth and Seventeenth Centuries*

SOURCES

E. Sehling (ed.), *Die evangelischen Kirchenordnungen des 16. Jh.* 1–5 (Leipzig 1902–14), 6–8, 11–13 (Tübingen 1955–6); L. Richter (ed.), *Die evangelischen Kirchenordnungen des 16. Jh.* (Weimar 1846); W. Niesel (ed.), *Bekenntnisschriften und Kirchenordnungen der nach Gottes Wort reformierten Kirche* (Zurich ³1938); *Die evangelisch-lutherischen Bekenntnisschriften* (Göttingen 1952).

VISITATIONS: cf. Chap. 19; M. Gmelin, "Die Visitationsprotokolle der Diözese Konstanz 1571–86" *ZGObrh* 25 (1873) 129–204; J. Jungnitz, *Visitationsberichte der Diözese Breslau,* 4 vols. (Breslau 1902–08); W. E. Schwartz, *Die Akten der Visitation des Bistums Münster aus der Zeit Johannes von Hoya 1571–73* (Münster 1913); A. Franzen, *Die Visitationsprotokolle der ersten nachtridentinischen Visitation im Erzstift Köln unter Salentin von Isenburg 1569* (Münster 1960).

LITERATURE

A. Franzen, *Die Kelchbewegung am Niederrhein im 16. Jh.* (Münster 1955); id., "Die Herausbildung des Konfessionsbewusstseins am Niederrhein im 16. Jh." *AHVNrh* 158 (1956–57) 164–209; id., "Das Schicksal des Erasmianismus am Niederrhein im 16. Jh." *HJ* 83 (1964) 84–112; H. Lutz, "Bayern und der Laienkelch" *QFIAB* 34 (1954) 203–235; H. W. Gensichen, *Damnamus: Die Verwerfung von Irrlehre bei Luther und im Luther-*

tum des 16. Jh. (Berlin 1955); H. Nottarp, *Zur Communicatio in sacris cum haereticis* (Halle 1933); E. W. Zeeden, "Grundlagen und Wege der Konfessionsbildung in Deutschland im Zeitalter der Glaubenskämpfe" *HZ* 185 (1958) 249–299; id., *Katholische Überlieferungen in den lutherischen Kirchenordnungen* (Münster 1959); id., *Die Entstehung der Konfessionen* (Munich 1965); J. B. Götz, *Die religiösen Wirren in der Oberpfalz 1576–1620* (Münster 1937); D. Coenen, *Die Katholische Kirche am Niederrhein von der Reformation bis zum Beginn des 18. Jh.* (Münster 1967); A. Zieger, *Das religiöse und kirchliche Leben im Spiegel der Kirchenordnungen von Preussen und Kurland* (Diss. Tübingen 1963); F. Dickmann, "Das Problem der Gleichberechtigung der Konfessionen im Reich im 16. und 17. Jh." *HZ* 201 (1965) 265–305; H. Bornkamm, "Die religiöse und politische Problematik der Konfessionen im Reich" *ARG* 56 (1965) 209–218; H. Lutz, "Die Konfessionsproblematik ausserhalb des Reiches und in der Politik des Papsttums" ibid. 218–227; E. W. Zeeden and H. Molitor, *Die Visitation im Dienst der kirchlichen Reform* (Münster 1967).

Part Two
Catholic Reform and Counter Reformation

The Historical Concepts

LITERATURE

A. Elkan, "Entstehung und Entwicklung des Begriffes Gegenreformation" *HZ* 112 (1914) 473–493; H. Jedin, *Katholische Reformation oder Gegenreformation?* (Lucerne 1946), in addition K. D. Schmidt, *Katholische Reform oder Gegenreformation* (Limburg 1957); E. W. Zeeden, "Probleme und Aufgaben der Reformationsgeschichtsschreibung" *Geschichte in Wissenschaft und Unterricht* 6 (1955) 201–217; G. Villoslada, "La contrarreform, su nombre y su concepto histórico" *Saggi storici intorno al Papato* (Rome 1959) 189–242; B. Croce, *Der Begriff des Barocks und der Gegenreformation* (Zurich 1926).

GENERAL ACCOUNTS

W. Maurenbrecher, *Geschichte der katholischen Reformation* I (Nördlingen 1880); G. Schnürer, *Katholische Kirche und Kultur in der Barockzeit* (Paderborn 1937); K. Eder, *Die Kirche im Zeitalter des konfessionellen Absolutismus* (Freiburg 1949); P. Janelle, *The Catholic Reformation* (Milwaukee, Wisc. 1949); M. Bendiscioli, *La riforma cattolica* (Rome 1958); K. Eder, "Die katholische Erneuerung" *HM* VII (Bern 1957) 114–160; G. H. Tavard, "The Catholic Reform in the XVI Century" *CH* 26 (1957) 275–288; B. J. Kidd, *The Counter Reformation* (London 1933); H. Daniel-Rops, *The Catholic Reformation* (New York 1960); E. M. Burns, *The Counter Reformation* (Princeton 1964).

SECTION ONE

Origin and Breakthrough of the Catholic Reform to 1563

32. Preliminary Steps in Italy and Spain

SOURCES AND LITERATURE

A general work on the sources is lacking; likewise complete descriptions of each of the two countries; for France and Germay see Chapters 39 and 40.

ITALY: P. Tacchi Venturi, *Storia della Compagnia di Gesù in Italia* I:2–3 (Rome 1950); M. Petrocchi, *La contrariforma in Italia* (Rome 1947); P. Paschini, *Tre ricerche sulla storia della Chiesa nel Cinquecento* (Rome 1945) 3–88 (Oratories of Divine Love); id., *Eresia e riforma cattolica al confine orientale d'Italia* (Rome 1951); G. Alberigo, *Contributi alla storia delle Confraternite dei disciplinati e della spiritualità laicale nei secoli XV e XVI* (Perugia 1961); A. Cistellini, *Figure della riforma pretridentina* (Brescia 1948) (B. Stella and the Oratory in Brescia); F. S. da Brusciano, "Maria Lorenza Longo e l'opera del Divino Amore a Napoli" *CollFr* 23 (1953) 166–226; On the Venetian reform group: J. Leclercq, *Le bienheureux P. Giustiniani* (Rome 1951); The ascetic main work G.s: *Secretum meum mihi* (Frascati 1941); H. Jedin, "Contarini und Camaldoli" *Arch. Ital. per la Storia della pietà* 2 (1959) 51–117; id., "Quirini und Bembo" *MisMercati* IV (1946) 407–424; id., "G. Contarini e il contributo veneziano alla Riforma cattolica" *La Civiltà veneziana del Rinascimento* (Florence 1958) 105–125; F. Gaeta, *Il vescovo Barozzi e il trattato de factionibus extinguendis* (Venice–Rome 1958).

ROME AND DIOCESES: G. Pelliccia, *La preparazione ed amissione dei chierici ai santi ordini nella Roma del secolo XVI* (Rome 1946); R. Putelli, *Prime visite pastorali alla città e diocesi [de Mantove]* (Mantua 1934); A. Grazioli, *G. M. Giberti* (Verona 1955).

THEATINES: P. Paschini, *S. Gaetano Thiene, G. P. Carafa e el origini dei Chierici Regolari Teatini* (Rome 1926); P. Chiminelli, *S. Gaetano Thiene, cuore della riforma cattolica* (Vicenza 1948); F. Andreu, *Le lettere di S. Gaetano da Thiene* (Città del Vaticano 1954); R. de Maio, "Un tentativo rifomatore nel Cinquencento. Girolamo Ferro" *Regnum Dei. Collectanea Theatina* 16 (1960) 1–58.

BARNABITES: O. Premoli, *Le lettere e lo spirito religioso di Antonio Maria Zaccaria* (Rome 1909); id., *Storia dei Barnabiti nel Cinquecento* (Rome 1913); G. Chastel, *S. A. M. Zaccaria* (Paris 1930), Italian edition by S. de Ruggiero (Brescia 1933); G. M. Cagni–F. M. Ghilardotti, "I sermoni di S. A. M. Zaccaria" *Arch. Ital. per la Storia della pietà* 2 (1959) 231–284; G. Boffitto, *Scrittori barnabiti* IV (Florence 1937).

SOMASCHI: G. Landini, *S. Girolamo Miani* (Rome 1947); G. Vaira, *G. Miano educatore* (Rome 1960); M. Tentorio, *Ven. P. Francesco Spaur da Trento preposito generale dei padri somaschi* (Rome 1961); P. Bianchini, "Origine e sviluppo della Compagnia dei servi dei poveri" *Rivista dell' Ordine dei PP. Somaschi* 31 (1956) 100–111, 184–192, 229–237; 32 (1957) 11–28, 103–116.

URSULINES: C. Lubieńska, *S. Aniela Merici i jej Dziejo* I (Cracow 1935 with bibl.); P. Guerrini, *S. A. Merici e la Compagnia di S. Orsola* (Brescia 1936); S. M. Monica, *Angela Merici and her Teaching Idea* (S. Martin, Ohio ²1945).

MENDICANTS: H. Jedin, "Zur Vorgeschichte der Regularenreform Trid. Sess. XXV" *RQ* 44 (1936) 231–281; id., *G. Seripando* I (Würzburg 1937) 147–289; A. Ghinato, "I Francescani e il Monte di pietà di Terni" *AFrH* 52 (1959) 204–289; id., "Il b. Michele d'Acqui e il suo apostolato in Verona" *Venezie francescane* 4 (1957) 145–192; L. Saggi, *La Contregazione Mantovana dei Carmelitani sino alla morte del B. Battista Spagnoli 1512* (Rome 1954); A. Staring, *Der Karmelitengeneral Nikolaus Audet und die katholische Reform des 16. Jh.* (Rome 1959); P. Cuthbert-J. Widlöcher, *Die Kapuziner* (Munich 1931); *Monumenta Hist. Ord. Min. Capuccinorum* (since 1937); Melchior a Pobladura, *Historia generalis O. Min. Cap.* I (Rome 1947); Th. Graf, *Die Kapuziner* (Fribourg 1957); G. Abate, "Fra Matteo da Bascio el gli inizi dell'Ordine Cappuccino" *CollFr* 30 (1960) 31–77.

SPAIN: F. Fernández, *F. Hernando de Talavera, confesor de los Reyes y primer arzobispo de Granada* (Madrid 1942); Tarsicio de Azcona, "El tipo ideal de obispo en la Iglesia española antes la rebelión luterana" *HS* 11 (1958) 21–44; id., *La elección y reforma del Episcopado español en tiempo de los Reyes Católicos* (Madrid 1960); L. F. de Retana, *Cisneros y su siglo,* 2 vols. (Madrid 1929); J. M. Doussinague, *Fernando el Católico y el cisma de Pisa* (Madrid 1946); V. Beltrán de Heredia, *Historia de la Reforma de la Provincia de España 1450–1550* (Rome 1936); id., *Las corrientes de espiritualidad entre los Dominicos de Castilla durante la primera mitad del siglo XVI* (Salamanca 1941); *Introducción a los origines de la Observancia en España: Las Reformas de los siglos XIV el XV* (Madrid 1958); M. Battaillon, *Erasmo y España,* 2 vols. (Mexico 1950); C. Sánchez Aliseda, "Precedentes Toledanos de la Reforma tridentina" *Revista española de Derecho Canónico* 2 (1948); J. I. Tellechea Idigoras, *El Obispo ideal en el siglo de la Reforma* (Rome 1963), with special reference to Spanish authors.

33. *Ignatius Loyola and His Order to 1556*

BIBLIOGRAPHY AND SOURCES

A. Carayon, *Bibliographie historique de la Compagnia de Jésus* (Paris 1864); Heimbucher II:130–138; A. de Backer–Ch. Sommervogel, *Bibliothèque des écrivains de la Compagnie de Jésus,* 11 vols. (Paris 1890–1932); Since 1932 a continuous bibliography in *AHSI.* On the origin (1894) and history of the chief source material, *MHSI* cf. P. de Leturia: *AHSI* 13 (1944) 1–61 and *HJ* 72 (1953) 585–604. It was located originally in Madrid, since 1929 in Rome. The first section of the *Monumenta Iganatiana* contains 4 series: I: *Epp. et instructiones,* 12 vols. (1903–11), 6813 letters of the last decade, for the most part not by Ignatius himself, but rather formulated by his assistants. II: *Exercitia spiritualia* (1919), J. Iparraguirre, *Directoria Exercitiorum Spiritualium 1540–1899* (Rome 1955). III: *Constitutiones,* 3 vols. (1934–38) and *Regulae Societatis Jesu* (1948). IV: *Fontes narrativi di S. Ignatio,* 3 vols (1943–60), containing the so-called "Memories of Life," other contemporary testimonies, and the canonization process. Manuscript: *Obras completas de S. Ignacio de L.,* ed. J. Iparraguirre (Madrid 1952); On Ignatius and the establishment of the order the so-called *Chronicon S. J.* written by the secretary of the saint, by J. A. Polanco, *Vita S. Ignatii Loyolae et rerum Soc. Jesu historia,* 6 vols. (1894–97), in addition, *Complementa,* 2 vols. (1916–17) are important. For the history of the establishment of the order the following are useful in addition to the letters in the *MHSI:* The letters of the first members in the *MHSI: Lainii Monumenta,* 8 vols. (1912–17). *Fabri Mon.* (1914). *Epp. Salmeronis,* 2 vols. (1906–07). *Bobadillae Mon.* (1913). *Epp. Hieronymi Nadal,* 4 vols. (1889–1905). The *Epp. mixtae 1537–56,* 5 vols. (1898–1901) are useful also for general Church history.

LITERATURE

IGNATIUS: J. Juambelz, *Bibliografía sobre la vida, obras y escritos de S. I. de L.* (Madrid 1956); J. Iparraguirre, *Orientaciones bibliográficas sobre S. I. de L.* (Rome 1957); F. G. Gilmont–P. Daman, *Bibliographie Ignatienne 1894–1957* (Paris–Louvain 1958). The official life of Ignatius is presented in the *Vita of P. Ribadeneira* (+1611), first appearing in Naples, 1572. Cf. R. G. Villoslada, "La figura histórica de S. I. de L. a través de cuatro siglos" *RF* 153 (1956) 40–70; H. Böhmer, *Ignatius von Loyola,* ed. H. Leube (Leipzig 1941); P. Dudon, *S. Ignace de L.* (Paris 1934); P. de Leturia, *El gentilombre I. López de Loyola* (Barcelona 1949); The numerous preliminary works of the former editor of the *MHSI* for an until now missing biography of large scope are collected in the *Estudios ignacianos,* ed. J. Iparraguirre, 2 vols. (Rome 1957); The 400th anniversary of the death of Loyola produced many biographies of varying worth: G. Papàsogli (Rome 1955), J. Brodrick, A. Guillermon, F. Wulf, R. G. Villoslada (all 1956, Villoslada in second edition 1961); *Commentarii Ignatiani* (Rome 1956), the Jubilee volume of the *AHSI,* with collection of the literature of the Jubilee, 617–629. Because of its insight one biography stands out: H. Rahner, *I. v. L. Briefwechsel mit Frauen* (Freiburg 1956); J. Lewis, *Le gouvernement spirituel selon S. Ignace de Loyola* (Bruges–Paris 1961).

SPIRITUAL EXERCISES: H. Böhmer, *Loyola und die deutsche Mystik* (Leipzig 1921); L. Zarncke, *Die Exercitia Spir. des hl. I. v. L. in ihren geistesgeschichtlichen Zusammenhängen* (Leipzig 1931); A. M. Albareda, "Intorno alla scuola di orazione metodica stabilita a Monserrato dall'abbate Garsias Jimenez de Cisneros" *AHSI* 25 (1956) 254–316. For the originality: A. Codina, *Los orígenes de los Ejercicios espirituales de S. I. de L.* (Barcelona 1926); P. de Leturia, "Génesis de los Ejercicios de S. Ignacio y su influjo en la fundación de la Compañiá de Jésus" *AHSI* 10 (1941) 16–59; H. Rahner, "I. v. L. und die aszetische Tradition der Kirchenväter" *ZAM* 17 (1942) 61–77; id., *I. v. L. und das geschichtliche Werden seiner Frömmigkeit* (Salzburg 1949), fundamental; id., "Zur Christologie der Exerzitien" *GuL* 35 (1962) 14–38, 115–140; id., *The Dynamic Element in the Church,* chap. III (New York 1964); J. Iparraguirre, *Espíritu de S. I. de L.* (Bilbao 1958); F. Charmot, *L'union au Christ dans l'actions selon S. Ignace* (Paris 1959); J. de Guibert, *La spiritualité de la Comp. de Jésus* (Rome 1953); Issac Jogues Iroquois, *Fr. Mission in Canada;* J. de Guibert, *The Jesuits, Their Spiritual Doctrine and Practice* (Chicago 1965): This is the chief work on the subject.

FIRST MEMBERS: F. Cerecéda, *Diego Laínez en la Europa religiosa de su tiempo,* 2 vols. (Madrid 1945); J. Danemarie, *Le bienheureux P. Favre* (Paris 1960); G. Guitton, *Le bienheureux P. Favre* (Lyon–Paris 1960); M. Nicoláu, *J. Nadal* (Madrid 1949); G. Schurhammer, *Franz Xaver* I (Freiburg 1955); O. Karrer, *Der hl. Franz von Borja* (Freiburg 1921); C. de Dalmases–J. F. Gilmont, "Las obras de S. Francisco de Borja" *AHSI* 30 (1961) 125–179; C. Englander, *Ignatius von Loyola und Johannes von Polanco* (Regensburg 1956); J. F. Gilmont, *Les écrits spirituels des premiers Jésuites. Inventaire commenté* (Rome 1961).

HISTORY OF THE ORDER: The order had from the beginning a carefully kept archive (see G. Schurhammer, "Der Ursprung des römischen Archivs der Gesellschaft Jesu" *AHSI* 12 [1943] 89–118) and carefully recorded its history. Older complete descriptions: N. Orlandini, F. Sacchini et. al., *Historia S. J.,* 6 parts (Rome 1614–1859); D. Bartoli, *Dell'istoria della Comp. di Gesù,* 6 vols. (Rome 1650–60); J. Crétineau–Joly, *Histoire religieuse, politique et littéraire de la Comp. de Jésus,* 6 vols. (Paris ³1851), strongly apologetic; E. Rosa, *I gesuiti dalle origini ai nostri giorni* (Rome ³1957); Th. J. Campbell, *The Jesuits* (London 1935); R. G. Villoslada, *Manual de historia de la Compañía de Jésus* (Madrid 1941); H. Becher, *Die Jesuiten* (Munich 1951), best account in German; More detailed, extending only to 1579: J. Brodrick, *The Origins of the Jesuits* (London 1940); id., *The Progress of the J.* (London 1946). Good tabulated synopsis [F. X. Wernz–J. B. Boetstouwers], *Synopsis Historiae Societatis Jesu* (Louvain 1950). Rich in material but of variable worth are the histories of the provinces written at the mandate of the order: B. Duhr, *Geschichte der Jesuiten in den Ländern deutscher Zunge,* 4 vols (Freiburg–Regensburg 1907–28), extends to the suppression of the order, and is indispensable for the general Church history of Germany from the 16th to the 18th centuries; A. Astraín, *Historia de la Compañía de Jesús en la Asistencia de España,* 7 vols. (Madrid 1902–25); P. Tacchi Venturi, *Storia della Compagnia di Gesú in Italia,* 2 vols. (Rome 1930–51), extending only to 1556; H. Fouqueray, *Histoire de la Comp. de Jésus en France,* 5 vols. (Paris 1910–25), to 1645, completed by P. de Lattre, *Les établissements des Jésuites en France,* 4 vols. (Paris 1941–56); A Poncelet, *Histoire de la Comp. des Jésus dans les anciens Pays-Bas* (Brussels 1927–28); F. Rodrigues, *História da Companhia de Jesus na Assistén-*

713

cia de Portugal I (Porto 1931); A. Kröss, *Geschichte der Böhmischen Provinz der Gesellschaft Jesu,* 2 vols. (Vienna 1910–38). For the histories of the overseas provinces see chaps. 45 and 46.

REFERENCE BOOKS AND WORKS ON THE SPIRIT OF THE ORDER: B. Duhr, *Jesuitenfabeln* (Freiburg 1904); L. Koch, *Jesuitenlexikon* (Paderborn 1934); P. Lippert, *Zur Psychologie des Jesuitenordens* (Freiburg 1956); G. Gundlach, *Zur Soziologie der kath. Ideenwelt und des Jesuitenordens* (Freiburg 1928); H. Stoeckius, *Forschungen zur Lebensordnung der Gesellschaft Jesu im 16. Jh.,* 2 parts (Munich 1910–11); M. Mir, *Historia interna documentada de la Comp. de J.,* 2 vols. (Madrid 1913); P. M. Baumgarten, *Ordenszucht und Ordensstrafrecht [der Jesuiten]* (Krumbach 1932); P. v. Hoensbroech, *Der Jesuitenorden,* 2 vols. (Leipzig 1926–28), pamphlet.

ASSESSMENTS OF THE ORDER WRITTEN BY NON-JESUITS: Pilatus [=V. Naumann], *Der Jesuitismus* (Regensburg 1905); R. Fülöp-Müller, *Macht und Geheimnis der Jesuiten* (Lucerne 1929); H. Böhmer, *The Jesuits* (Philadelphia 1928).

34. The Beginnings of the Catholic Reform in Rome under Paul III

SOURCES

BullRom VI:173–401; Raynold, *Ann. Eccl.* XXI:1; NBD, *I. Abt.* 1–11 (Gotha 1892, Berlin 1910); The preliminary Acts of the Council of Trent: *CT* IV (1904); G. Ribier, *Lettres et Mémoires d'Estat sous François I, Henry II et François II,* 2 vols. (Paris 1666); *Acta nuntiaturae Gallicae,* I: *Correspondance des Nonces en France Carpi et Ferrero 1535–40,* ed. J. Lestocquoy (Rome–Paris 1961); id., *G. Alberigo: Critica storica* (1962) 66f.; P. G. Baroni, *La nunziatura in Francia di Rodolfo Pio 1535–37* (Bologna 1962); *Correspondance du Card. de Tournon,* ed. M. Francois (Paris 1946); *Nunziature di Venezia,* ed. F. Gaeta, 2 vols. (Rome 1958–60), cf. also id., *Annuario dell'Instituto storico ital. per l'età moderna e contemporanea* 9–10 (1957–58) 5–281.

LITERATURE

Pastor V; C. Capasso, *Paolo III,* 2 vols. (Messina 1924); L. Dorez, *La cour du Pape Paul III,* 2 vols. (Paris 1932); L. Cardauns, *Von Nizza bis Crépy* (Rome 1923); W. Friedensburg, *Kaiser Karl V. und Papst Paul III.* (Leipzig 1932); K. Brandi, *Kaiser Karl V.,* 2 vols. (Munich 1937–41) Eng. Vol. I (New York 1939); P. Rassow–F. Schalk, *Karl V.: Der Kaiser und seine Zeit* (Cologne 1960) 104–117, the conciliar politics of the Emperor; H. Jedin, *A History of the Council of Trent* I (St. Louis 1957) 245–444, also treats the works of St. Ehses and others used by Pastor; id., "Eine bisher unbekannte Denkschrift Tommaso Campeggios über die Reform der Römischen Kurie" *Lortz F I* (Baden-Baden 1958) 405–417; K. Schnith, "Karl V. in europäischer Sicht. Hinweise auf neuere Arbeiten" *HJ* 80 (1961) 270–285; W. Gramberg, "Die Hamburger Bronzebüste Pauls III" *Festschrift E. Meyer* (Hamburg 1959) 160–172.

ITALIAN EVANGELISM: *Opuscoli e lettere di riformatori italiani del Cinquecento,* ed. G. Paladino, 2 vols. (Bari 1913); E. M. Jung, "On the Nature of Evangelism in Sixteenth-Century Italy" *Journal of the History of Ideas* 14 (1953) 511–527; Bibliography on Vittoria Colonna in the jubilee volume: *V. Colonna, Marchesa di Pescara* (Rome 1947) 126–134; The ambivalent character of Evangelism was often misunderstood due to the numerous defections and the Inquisition, e.g., H. W. Beyer, *Die Religion Michelangelos* (Bonn 1926); P. McNair, *Peter Martyr in Italy* (Oxford 1967).

INQUISITION: G. Buschbell, *Reformation und Inquisition in Italien um die Mitte des 16. Jh.* (Paderborn 1912); P. Paschini, "Episodi della Inquisizione a Roma nei suoi primi decenni" *Studi romani* 5 (1957) 281–301.

35. *The Council of Trent under Paul III and Julius III*

SOURCES

H. Jedin, *Das Konzil von Trient. Ein Überblick über die Erforschung seiner Geschichte* (Rome 1948). The official edition of the *Canones et Decreta* (Rome 1564 by Paulus Manutius) was reprinted innumerable times; expanded to include the most important declarations of the council congregation, ed. E. L. Richter (Leipzig 1853). Phototypic reproduction of an autograph of Massarelli with an introduction about the oldest prints: St. Kuttner, *Decreta septem priorum sessionum Concilii Tridentini sub Paulo III Pont. Max.* (Washington 1945). Because the acts were inaccessible since the end of the 16th century, both of the descriptions of the history of the council, which appeared in the 17th century, were treated into the 19th century almost like source works: the sharply antipapal *Istoria del Concilio Tridentino* by P. Sarpi (London 1619), critical edition by Gambarin, 3 vols. (Bari 1935), and the refutation by P. Sforza Pallavicino, *Istoria del Concilio di Trento* (Rome 1655), best edition by F. A. Zaccaria, 5 vols. (Faenza 1792–96); cf. H. Jedin, *Der Quellenapparat der Konzilsgeschichte Pallavicinos* (Rome 1940). On the reliability of Sarpi see Jedin II 518–21ff. A synopsis of those sources made available up to that time is supplied by J. Le Plat, *Monumentorum ad historiam concilii Tridentini potissimum illustrandam spectantium amplissima collectio,* 7 vols. (Louvain 1781–87); the first, defective edition of the acts A. Theiner, *Acta genuina ss. oecumenici Concilii Tridentini,* 2 vols. (Agram 1874). A critical edition of all comprehensible sources was begun in 1891 after the opening of the Vatican Archives by the Görres-Gesellschaft: *Concilium Tridentinum. Diariorum, actorum, epistularum, tractatuum nova collectio* (Freiburg 1901–61), till now 13 vols. in 4 sections: Diaries, S. Merkle I–III:1; Acts, IV–V (1545–47); VIII–IX (1561–63), ed. St. Ehses; VI:1 (Bologna) and VII:1 (1551–52), ed. Th. Freudenberger; Letters, X–XI, ed. G. Buschbell; Treatises, XIII, ed. V. Schweitzer; XIII:1, ed. V. Schweitzer–H. Jedin. The history of the origin of the collection by Jedin, U. Sufera 195–213.

GENERAL LITERATURE

P. Richard, *Histoire de Concile de Trente,* 2 vols. (Paris 1930–31), suppl. A. Michel, *Les decrets du Concile de Trente (Paris 1938);* L. Cristiani, *L'Église à l'époque du Concile de Trente* (Paris 1948). In addition *RSTI* 2 (1948) 274–284; G. Schreiber, *Das Weltkonzil von Trient,* 2 vols. (Freiburg 1951), there I:11–31 a survey of the literature appearing at the jubilee in 1945.

ON THE PARTICIPANTS: G. Alberigo, "Cataloghi dei partecipanti al Concilio di Trento editi durante il medesimo" *RSTI* 10 (1956) 345–373; 11 (1957) 49–94; H. Jedin, "Die deutschen Teilnehmer am Konzil von Trient" *ThQ* 122 (1941) 238–261; 123 (1942) 21–39; C. Gutiérrez, *Españoles en Trento* (Valladolid 1951); A. Wazl, *I domenicani al Concilio di Trento* (Rome 1961). Further statements about the participants of the orders: Jedin, II:457; J. de Castro, *Portugal no Concilio de Trento,* 6 vols. (Lisbon 1944–46); I. Rogger, *Le nazioni al Concilio di Trento 1545–52* (Rome 1952). On the attitude of the Protestants, comprehensive but not exhaustive, R. Stupperich, "Die Reformation und das Tridentinum" *ARG* 47 (1956) 20–63. A stronger consideration of the sociological factors is demanded by A. Dupront, "Du Concile de Trente. Reflexions autour d'un IVᵉ Centenaire" *RH* 206 (1951) 202f.

FIRST SESSION: "Acts": *CT* IV–V, in addition the later discovered votes on justification by J. Olazarán, *Documentos inéditos Tridentinos sobre la justificación* (Madrid 1957); The diaries of Severoli, Massarelli and the pro-imperial Pratanus: *CT* I–II; The correspondence: *CT* X with suppl. *CT* XI:3–129. Complete description with literature to 1956: Jedin II; newer special literature in the notes. Copious bibliography on the Italian bishops by G. Alberigo, *I vescovi italiani al Concilio di Trento 1545–47* (Florence 1959). H. O. Evennett, *Three Benedictine Abbots at the Council of Trent: Studia monastica* 1 (Montserrat 1959) 343–377.

BOLOGNA: "Acts": *CT* VI:1; the votes follow in VI:2; L. Carcereri, *Storia esterna di Concilio di Bologna* (Montevarchi 1902); id., *Il Concilio di Trento dalla traslazione a Bologna alla sospensione* (Bologna 1910); H. Jedin, "Il significato del periodo Bolognese per le decisioni dogmatiche e l'opera di riforma del Concilio di Trento" *Problemi di vita religiosa in Italia nel Cinquecento* (Padua 1960) 1–10.

SECOND SESSION: "Acts": *CT* VII:1, in addition J. Birkner, "Die Akten des Trienter Konzils für die zweite Tagungsperiode unter Papst Julius III" *QFIAB* 29 (1939) 297–311. The letters of the treasurer Vargas, recorded in the correspondence *CT* XI, the authenticity of which has long been doubted, may now, after recent archival discoveries in England, be considered to be authentic. H. Jedin, "Das Konzilstagebuch des Bischofs Julius Pflug von Naumburg 1551–52" *RQ* 50 (1955) 22–43; E. Bizer, *Confessio Virttembergica* (Stuttgart 1952), with important introduction; C. M. Abád, "Dos Memoriales inéditos para el Concilio de Trento del B. Juan de Avila" *MCom* III (1945), in addition *ZAM* 11 (1936) 124–139; H. Jedin, "Die Deutschen am Trienter Konzil 1551–52" *HZ* 188 (1959) 1–16; J. Birkner, "Kardinal Marcellus Crescentius" *RQ* 43 (1935) 267–285; G. Alberigo, "Un informatore senese al Conc. di Trento 1551–52" *RSTI* 12 (1958) 173–201.

36. The Breakthrough of the Catholic Reform (1551–59)

SOURCES

BullRom VI:401–566; Raynald, *Ann. eccl.* XXI:2; The Reform Decrees of Julius III and Paul IV:*CT* XIII:1; *NBD,* I. Sect. 12 (1901), ed. G. Kupke; Sect. 13 (1959), ed. H. Lutz; R. Ancel, *Nontiatures de France* I (Paris 1909–11), includes the years 1554–57. For the Catholic Restoration in England: *Calendar of Letters, Dispatches and State Papers Relating to the Negotiations between England and Spain. Philip and Mary 1554–58,* ed. R. Tyler (London 1954); The Acts of the Provincial Synod of Canterbury: Mansi XXXV: 475–504; W. Sharp–L. E. Whatmore, *Archdeacon Harpsfield's Visitations 1557* (London 1950–51); J. Tellechea Idigoras, "Pole y Paulo IV" *AHPpont* 4 (1966) 105–154.

LITERATURE

Pastor, VI; Seppelt, ²IV:58–90; H. Lutz, *Christianitas afflicta* (Göttingen 1963).

FOR MARCELLUS II: In addition to the still reliable biography by P. Polidori (Rome 1744): A. Mercati, *Prescrizioni pel culto divino nella diocesi di Reggio-Emilia del vescovo card. M. Cervini* (Reggio–Emilia 1933).

FOR PAUL IV: G. M. Monti, *Ricerche su Papa Paolo IV Carafa* (Benevent 1925); id., *Studi sulla Riforma cattolica e sul papato nei secoli XVI e XVII* (Trani 1941); I. Torriani, *Una tragedia nel Cinquecento romano: Paolo IV e i suoi nepoti* (Rome 1951).

ENGLISH RESTORATION: Ph. Hughes, *Reformation in England* II (London 1954) 184–330; W. Schenk, *Reginald Pole* (London); G. Mattingly, *Catherine of Aragon* (Boston 1941).

OTHER SUBJECTS: H. Jedin, "Kirchenreform und Konzilsgedanke 1550–1559" *HJ* 54 (1934) 401–431; id., "Analekten zur Reformtätigkeit der Reformpäpste Julius' III und Pauls IV" *RQ* 42 (1934) 305–332; 43 (1935) 87–156; id., "Kard. Giovanni Ricci" *Misellanea P. Paschini* II (Rome 1949) 269–358; L. Serrano, "Anotación al tema: El papa Paolo IV y España" *Hispania* 3 (1943) 293–325.

LITERATURE ON POLAND: B. Stasiewski, *Reformation und Gegenreformation in Polen* [=KLK 18] (Münster 1960) 72–78; M. Francois, *Le Card. Francois Tournon* (Paris 1951) [=Bibliothèques des écoles françaises d'Athènes et de Rome, Vol. 173].

37. *Pius IV and the Conclusion of the Council of Trent*

SOURCES

Negotiations: *CT* VIII–IX (St. Ehses); Diaries: *CT* II–III:1 (S. Merkle); Correspondence of the Legates: J. Susta, *Die Römische Curia und das Concil von Trient unter Pius IV.*, 4 vols. (Vienna 1904–14); Most important earlier work: Th. Sickel, *Römische Berichte*, 5 parts (Vienna 1895–1901); Reports of Imperial Ambassadors: Th. Sickel, *Zur Geschichte des Concils von Trient* (Vienna 1872); G. Drei, "La Corrispondenza del Card. Ercole Gonzaga, presidente del Concilio di Trento" *Archivio storico per le provincie Parmensi* 17 (1917) 185–242, 18 (1918) 30–143; H. Jedin, *Krisis und Wendepunkt des Trienter Konzils 1562–63. Die neuentdeckten Geheimberichte des Bischofs Gualterio von Viterbo an den hl. Karl Borromäus* (Würzburg 1941); Survey of important sources for history of last session: H. Jedin, *G. Seripando* II: 121; "Reports of the Nuncios Hosius, Delfino and Commendone to the Imperial Court" *NBD*, II. Abt., 1–3 (Vienna–Graz 1897–1953). E. M. Wermter, *Kard. St. Hosius, Bischof von Ermland, und Herzog Albrecht von Preussen. Ihr Briefwechsel über das Konzil von Trient 1560–62* (Münster 1957) [=RST 82].

LITERATURE

Pastor VII; St. Ehses, "Die letzte Berufung des Trienter Konzils durch Pius IV" *Festschrift G. von Hertling* (Kempen 1913) 139–162; H. Jedin, *G. Seripando* II (Würzburg 1937) 194–238; H. O. Evennett, *The Cardinal of Lorraine and the Council of Trent* (Cambridge 1930); B. Chudoba, "Les relaciones de las dos cortes Habsburgesas en la tercera asemblea del Concilio Tridentino" *Boletín de la R. Academia de la Historia* 103 (1933) 297–368; H. Jedin, "La politica conciliare di Cosimo I" *RSIt* 62 (1950) 345–374, 477–496; G. Constant, *La légation du Cardinal Morone près l'Empereur et le Concile de Trente* (Paris 1922); L. Castano, *Mons. Nicolò Sfrondato, Vescovo di Cremona al Concilio di Trento* (Turin 1939); P. Prodi, *Il Cardinale Gabriele Paleotti* I (Florence 1959).

The Papacy and the Implementation of the Council of Trent (1565–1605)

38. Personality and Work of the Reform Popes from Pius V to Clement VIII

Sources

BullRom VI–IX; L. Serrano, *Correspondencia diplomática entre España y la S. Sede durande el Pontificato de Pio V,* 4 vols. (Madrid 1914); G. Catalano, *Controversie giurisdizionali tra Chiesa e Stato nell'età di Gregorio XIII e Filippo II* (Palermo 1955); for the reports of the Nuncios cf. chap. 39 and 40; A. Sala, *Documenti circa la vita di San Carlo,* 4 vols. (Milan 1857–62); *Acta Ecclesiae Mediolanensis,* ed. A. Ratti, 3 vols. (Milan 1890–96); A. G. Roncalli, *Gli atti della Visita Apostolica di S. Carlo Borromeo a Bergamo,* 5 vols. (Florence 1936–58), also there is the short account of this visitation in *RSTI* 14 (1960), 452–457; P. Guerrini, *Atti della visita pastorale del vescovo Domenico Bollani alla diocesi di Brescia,* 3 vols. (Brescia 1915–40); *Nunziature di Savoia* I, ed. F. Fonzi (Rome 1960); *Nunziature di Napoli* I, ed. P. Villani (Rome 1962); Also, H. Jedin, "Osservazioni della Nunziature d'Italia" *RSIt* 75 (1963) 327–343.

Literature

Basic: Pastor VIII (Pius V), IX (Gregory XIII), X (Sixtus V), XI (Clement VIII); P. Herre, *Papsttum und Papstwahl im Zeitalter Philipps II.* (Leipzig 1907); L. Browne Olf, *The Sword of Saint Michael. The Life of Pius V* (Milwaukee, Wisc. 1943); G. Grente, *Le pape des grands combats* (Paris ²1956); G. Carocci, *Lo Stato della Chiesa nella seconda metà del sec. XVI* (Milan 1961); L. Castano, *Gregorio XIV* (Turin 1957).

Nunciatures: L. Just, "Die Erforschung der päpstlichen Nuntiaturen" *QFIAB* 24 (1933) 244–277; H. Kramer, "Die Erforschung und Herausgabe der Nuntiatur-berichte" *Mitt. des Österr. Staatsarchivs* 1 (1948) 492–514; L. H. Halkin, "Les Archives des Nonciatures" *Bull. de l'Institut Belge de Rome* 33 (1961) 649–700.

Catalogue of Nunciatures: H. Biaudet, *Les nonciatures permanentes jusqu'en 1648* (Helsingfors 1910).

Roman Colleges: P. Paschini, "Le origini del Seminario romano" *Cinquecento romano e riforma cattolica* (Rome 1958) 3–32; R. G. Villoslada, *Storia del Collegio Romano dal duo inizio 1551 alla soppressione della Compagnia di Gesù 1773* (Rome 1954); F. A. Gasquet, *A History of the Ven. English College at Rome* (London 1920); Steinhuber, see chap. 40.

The City of Rome: P. Pechiai, *Roma nel Cinquecento* (Bologna 1949); J. Delumeau, *Vie économique et sociale de Rome dans la seconde moitié du XVIe siècle,* 2 vols. (Paris 1959); H. Siebenhüner, "Umrisse zur Gesch. der Ausstattung von St. Peter in Rom von Paul III. bis Paul V." *Festschrift H. Sedlmayr* (Munich 1962) 229–320; M. Romani, *Pellegrini e viaggiatori nell' economia di Roma dal XIV al XVII secolo* (Milan 1948), there are 323–355 accounts of pilgrims cared for in *S. Trinità dei Pellegrini;* P. M. Baugarten, *Von den Kardinälen des XVI Jh.* (Krumbach 1926).

Catholic Reform in Italy: G. Alberigo, "Studi e problemi relativi all' applicazione del concilio di Trento in Italia" *RSIt* 70 (1958) 239–298, numerous unpublished dissertations are summarized; *Problemi di vita religiosa in Italia nell Cinquecento. Atti del Convegno di Storia della Chiesa in Italia 1958* (Padua 1960). A satisfactory biography of Borromeo does not exist, primarily because his extensive correspondence in the Library Ambrosiana has not been researched. Bibliography: LThK² II: 612; R. Mols, "S. Borromée pionnier de la moderne pastorale" *NRTh* 89 (1957) 600–622, 715–747; M. Grosso–M. F. Mellano, *La Controriforma nella arci diocesi di Torino 1558 bis 1610*, 3 vols. (Vatican City 1957); M. F. Mellano, *La controriforma nella diocesi di Mondovi 1560–1602* (Turin 1955); F. Molinari, *Il card. Teatino B. P. Burali e la riforma tridentina a Piacenze 1568–76* (Rome 1957); R. de Maio, *Le origini del Seminario di Napoli* (Naples 1957); id., *Alfonso Carafa, Card. di Napoli* [SteT 210] (Vatican City 1961); P. Villani, "Una visita apostolica nel Regno di Napoli 1566–68" *Studi in onore di R. Filangieri* II (Naples 1959) 433–466; "Bibliography of the Italian diocesan synods" *Silvino da Nedro, Sinodi diocesani italiani 1534–1878* (Vatican City 1960) [=SteT 207].

39. Self-Assertion of the Church in Western and Eastern Europe

SPAIN AND THE NETHERLANDS

SOURCES: Provincial Synod of Toledo: Mansi 34, 537–570; R. Sánchez Lamadrid, "Un manoscrito inédito del B. Juan de Avila" *Arch. Theol. Granadino* 4 (1941) 137–241, completed by C. M. Abad, "Ultimos inéditos extensos del B. J. de Avila" *MCom* 13 (1950) 13–60. The Provincial Synods of Salamanca, Granada and Saragossa: Aguirre V², 445–463; E. Rodríguez Amaya, *Revista de estudios extremeños* 6 (1951) 235–295. The Statutes of the Provincial Synod of Valencia: Aguirre V, 445–463. **Visitations:** I. I. Tellechea Idiogoras, "El formulario de visita pastoral de B. de Carranza, arzobispo de Toledo" *Anthologica annua* 4 (1956) 385–437; D. Mansilla, "Reacción del Cabildo de Burgos ante las visitas y otros actos de iurisdicción intentados por sus obispos" *HS* 10 (1957) 135–159. **The Religious Policies of Philip II:** Serrano, Catalano and Villani see Chap. 38; For Philip II (early periods): J. de Olarra–M. L. de Larramendi, *Correspondencia entre la nunciatura en España y la S. Sede* I (Rome 1960). **Netherlands:** *Correspondance de Philippe II sur les affaires des Pays-Bas,* ed. L. Gachard, 5 vols. (Brussels 1848–79); *Correspondance de Philippe II sur les affaires des Pays-Bas,* ed. J. Lefèvre (Brussels 1941–53); *Nonciatures de Flandres,* ed. The Belgian Historical Institute in Rome, especially L. van der Essen-A. Louant, *Correspondance d' O. M. Frangipani 1595–1606,* 3 vols. (Rome 1924, 1932, 1942); J. Cleyntjens, *Corpus iconoclasticum,* 4 vols. (Tilburg 1928–34); *Documents relatifs à la jurisdiction des nonces et internonces des Pays-Bas pendant le régime espagnol 1596–1706,* ed. J. Lefèvre (Burssels–Rome 1942); M. Dierickx, *Documents inédits sur l'érection des nouveaux diocèses aux Pays-Bas 1521–70,* 3 vols. (Brussels 1960–62).

LITERATURE: L. Pfandl, *Philipp II* (Munich 1938); R. Konetzke: *HZ* 164 (1941) 316–331; J. M. March, *Niñez y juventud de Felipe II,* 2 vols. (Madrid 1941–42); R. Altamira, *Felipe II, hombre de estado* (Mexico City 1950); G. Mattingly, *The Armada* (Boston 1959); F. Braudel, *La Méditerranée et le Monde méditerranéen à l'époque de Philippe II* (Paris 1949); R. T. Davies, *The Golden Century of Spain 1501–1621* (New York 1961); A. Robb, *William of Orange* I (London 1962); C. V. Wedgewood, *William the Silent* (New Haven 1944); C. J. Cadoux, *Philip of Spain and the Netherlands;* L. van der Essen, *Alexandre Farnèse,* 5 vols. (Brussels 1933–37); B. de Meester, *Le Saint Siège et les troubles des Pays-Bas 1566–79* (Louvain 1934); F. Willcox, *L'introduction des décrets du Concile de Trente dans les Pays-Bas et dans la Principauté de Liège* (Louvain 1929); E. Donckel, "Luxemburger Gutachten zu den Trienter Reformdekreten" *Rhein. Vierteljahrsbll* 19 (1957) 119–134; L. J. Rogier, *Geschiedenis van het Katholizime in Noord-Nederland in de*

16ᵉ en 17ᵉ *Eeuw*, 3 vols. (The Hague 1945–47); A. Pasture, *La restauration religieuse aux Pays-Bas catholiques 1596 bis 1633* (Louvain 1925); J. Scheerder, *Die Inquisitie in de Nederlanden in de XVIᵉ Eeuw* (Antwerp 1944); E. de Moreau, *Histoire de l'Église en Belgique* V (Brussels 1952); C. Petrie, *Philip II of Spain* (New York 1963); I. I. Woltjer, *Friesland in de hervormingstijd* (Leiden 1962).

FRANCE

SOURCES: H. Hauser, *Les sources de l'hist. de France, XVIᵉ siècle* III, IV (Paris 1912–15); *Lettres de Cathérine de Médicis*, ed. H. de la Ferrière-Baguenalt de la Puchesse, 10 vols. (Paris 1880–1909); *Recueil des lettres missives de Henri IV*, ed. Berger de Xivrey et. al., 9 vols. (Paris 1843–76); H. C. Davila, *Historia delle guerre civili di Francia 1559–98* (Venice 1630).——Provincial Councils: Reims 1564: Mansi 33, 1289–1390; Rouen 1581: Mansi 34, 617–682; Reims 1583: Mansi 34, 683–938; Aix 1585: Mansi 34, 937–1014; Toulouse 1590: Mansi 34, 1269–1322; Narbonne 1609: Mansi 34, 1477–1536.——*Girolamo Ragazzoni, évêque de Bergame, nonce en France. Correspondance de sa nonciature 1583–86*, ed. P. Blet (Rome–Paris 1962).

LITERATURE: L. Romier, *Les origines politiques des guerres de Religion*, 2 vols. (Paris 1913–14); id., *Le Royaume de Cathérine de Médicis*, 2 vols. (Paris 1922); id., *Catholiques et Huguenots à la Cour de Charles IX* (Paris 1924); N. Reolker, *Queen of Navare: Jeanne d'Albert, 1528–1572* (Cambridge, Mass. 1968); J. E. Neale, *The Age of Catherine de Medici* (London 1943); A. Bailly, *La réforme en France jusqu' à l'Édit de Nantes* (Paris 1960); R. Nürnberger, *Die Politisierung des französischen Protestantimus* (Tübingen 1948); A. Buisson, *Michel de l'Hôpital* (Paris 1950); Ch. Hirschauer, *La politique de Pie V en France 1566–72* (Paris 1922); V. Martin, *Le Gallicanisme et la réforme catholique* (Paris 1919), chief work, see criticism by Ch. Hirschauer: *RHEF* 9 (1923) 545f.; A. Degert, *Histoire des séminaires français jusqu' à la révolution*, 2 vols. (Paris 1912); L. Serbat, *Les assemblées du Clergé de France 1561–1615* (Paris 1906); V. Carrière, "Le épreuves de l'église de France au XVIᵉ siècle" *Introduction aux études d'histoire eccl. locale* III (Paris 1936) 247–509; J. Lestocquoy, "Les évêques français au milieu du XVIᵉ siècle" *RHEF* 45 (1959) 25–40; J. Cloulas, "Les aliénations du temporel eccl. sous Charles IX et Henri III" *RHEF* 44 (1958) 5–56; id., "Un aspect original des relations fiscales entre la royauté et le clergé" *RHEF* 55 (1960) 876–901; J. Imbert, "Les prescriptions hospitalières du Concile de Trente et leur diffusion en France" *RHEF* 42 (1956) 5–28; R. M. Kingdon, *Geneva and the Coming of the Religious Wars in France* (Geneva 1956); J. R. Mayor, *Representative Institutions in Renaissance France* (Madison 1960); W. C. Grant, *Constitutional Thought in 16th Cent. France* (New York 1947); F. C. Palm, *Calvinism and the Religious Wars* (New York 1932); O. Zoff, *The Huguenots* (New York 1942); S. L. England, *The Massacre of St. Bartholomew* (London 1938); D. Jensen, *Bernardine de Mendoza and the French Catholic League* (Cambridge 1964); R. B. Merriman, *Six Contemporaneous Revolutions* (Oxford 1938); W. F. Church, *Constitutional Thought in 16th Cent. France* (Cambridge 1941); *Bibliography of Cardinal d'Ossat, active in the reconciliation of Henry IV with Rome*, P. Laccade (Tarbes 1937).

ENGLAND

SOURCES: In addition to the older series of State Papers: J. M. Rigg, *Calender of State Papers Relating to English Affairs*, 2 vols. (London 1961–62) (to 1578); J. H. Pollen, *Sources for the History of Roman Catholics in England, Ireland and Scotland* (London 1921);

id., *Unpublished Documents Relating to the English Martyrs* I (London 1908); E. H. Burton–J. H. Pollen, *Lives of the English Martyrs under Elizabeth I 1583–88* (London 1914); L. Hicks, *Letters and Memorials of Father Robert Persons* I (London 1942).——The Act of Uniformity, 1559: H. Gee–W. J. Hardy, *Documents Illustrative of English Church History* (London 1921) 442–458; On the development of the Anglican Church: J. E. Neale: *EHR* (1950) 304ff.; For sources concerning the Establishment of the Anglican Church: Parker Society Publications; For the Inner Consolidation of Anglicanism: *The Works of R. Hooker,* ed. R. W. Church–F. Paget, 3 vols. (Oxford 1888); An Irish source concerning the Flanders Nunciature: *Collectanea Hibernica I,* ed. C. Giblen (Dublin-London 1958).

LITERATURE: J. B. Black, *The Reign of Elizabeth* (Oxford 1959); H. Wilson, *King James VI and I* (London 1956); Ph. Hughes, *The Reformation in England* III (London 1954); A. O. Meyer, *England und die katholische Kirche unter Königin Elizabeth* (Rome 1911) (this is the primary work); J. H. Pollen, *The English Catholics in the Reign of Queen Elizabeth* (London 1920); A. H. Atteridge, *The Elizabethan Persecution* (London 1928); H. S. Lucas, "Survival of the Catholic Faith in the XVIth Century" *CHR* 29 (1943) 25–52; Ph. Caraman, *The Other Face. Catholic Life under Elizabeth I* (London 1960); M. D. R. Leys, *Catholics in England 1559–1829. A Social History* (London 1961); P. McGrath, *Papists and Puritans Under Elizabeth I* (London 1968).

NORTHERN AND EASTERN EUROPE

SOURCES: A. Theiner, *Vetera monumenta Poloniae et Lithuaniae* II (Rome 1861); III (Rome 1863); id., *Schweden und seine Stellung zum Heiligen Stuhl unter Johann III., Sigismund III; und Karl IX.,* 2 vols. (Augsburg 1838–39); The Reports of the Nuncios Caligari (1578–81) and Bolognetti (1581–85): *Monumenta Poloniae Vaticana* IV–VII (Cracaw 1915–50); J. Sawicki, *Concilia Poloniae,* 9 vols. (Cracaw–Warsaw–Breslau 1945–57). Cf. ZSavRGkan 46 (1960) 395–429; M. Olsoufieff, *Le lettere di Ivan il Terribile con i Commentari della Moscovia di A. Possevino* (Florence 1958); *Litterae nuntiorum apostolicorum historiam Ucrainae illustrantes,* ed. A. G. Welykyj, I–IV (Rome 1959–60); *Res Polonicae Elizabetha I Angliae regnante conscriptae ex archivis Londoniarum,* ed. C. H. Talbot (Rome 1961); *Res Polonicae Jacobo I Angliae regnante conscriptae ex archivis Londoniarum,* ed. C. H. Talbot (Rome 1962).

LITERATURE: B. Stasiewski, *Reformation und Gegenreformation in Polen, Neue Forschungsergebnisse* (Münster 1960) (lit.); "The Lists of the Bishops Collected by Z. Szostkiewicz" *Sacrum Poloniae Millenium* I (Rome 1954) 391–608; O. Halecki, "From Florence to Brest" ibid. V (1958) 13–444; St. Polein, *Une tentative d'Union au XVIe siècle. La Mission religieuse du P. A. Possevino en Moscovie 1581–82* (Rome 1957); A. Wolter, "A. Possevino, Theologie und Politik im Spannungsfeld zwischen Rom und Moskau" *Scholastik* 31 (1956) 321–350; J. Lecler, *Histoire de la tolérance au siècle de la réforme* I (Aubier 1955) 363–398 (Concerning tolerance in Poland); E. Winter, *Russland und das Papsttum* I (Berlin 1960); H. Holmquist–H. Pleijel, *Svenska Kyrkans Historia* III:2 (Stockholm 1933); H. Biaudet, *Le St. Siège et la Suède durant la seconde moitié du XVIe siècle* (Paris 1907), with 2 vols. of documents (Paris 1906 and Geneva 1913). O. Garstein, *Rome and the Counter-Reformation in Scandinavia* (Copenhagen, 1963); F. Dvornik, *The Slavs in European History and Civilization* (New Brunswick, N. J. 1962); G. Schramm, *Der polnische Adel und die Reformation 1548–1607* (Weisbaden 1965); I. Revesz, *History of the Hungarian Reformed Church* (Washington, D. C. 1956).

40. *Crisis and Turning Point in Central Europe*

SOURCES

For the background history of the Tridentine reform in Germany the following is basic: *Acta reformationis catholicae ecclesiam Germaniae concernentia saec. XVI (1520–1570)*, ed. G. Pfeilschifter, earlier 2 vols. (Regensburg 1959–60) [=ARC]. *NBD*, section II, 1560–72, ed. the Historical Commission of the Vienna Academy, 7 vols. (Vienna 1897–1953); section III, 1572–85, ed. the Prussian Historical Institute Rome, 1: *Der Kampf um Köln*, ed. J. Hansen (Berlin 1892), 2: *Der Reichstag zu Regensburg 1576 . . .*, ed. J. Hansen (Berlin 1894), 3–5: *Die süddeutsche Nuntiatur des Grafen Portia*, ed. K. Schellhas (Berlin 1899, 1903–09); this portion was completed by W. E. Schwarz, *Die Nuntiaturkorrespondenz Kaspar Groppers 1573–76* (Paderborn 1896). W. E. Schwarz, *Zehn Gutachten über die Lage der katholischen Kirche in Deutschland 1573–76* (Paderborn 1891). The third division closed the undertaking of the Görres-Gesellschaft: *Die Nuntiatur am Kaiserhofe 1584–92* I, ed. R. Reichenberger (Paderborn 1905), II:3, ed. J. Schweizer (Paderborn 1912–19). *Die Kölner Nuntiatur 1584–90* I, ed. St. Ehses and A. Meister (Paderborn 1895), II, ed. St. Ehses (Paderborn 1899). From the fourth section which includes the nuncios' reports of the 17th century, belongs here: *Die Prager Nuntiatur des D. St. Ferreri und die Wiener Nuntiatur des G. Serra 1603–06*, ed. A. O. Meyer (Berlin 1913). From the Czechoslovakian Historical Institute Rome the following is used: *Epistulae et Acta A. Gaetani 1607–08*, ed. M. Linhartova (Prague 1932–37). *P. Canisii epp. et acta IV–VIII*, ed. O. Braunsberger (Freiburg 1905–23).

SYNODS: F. Dalham, *Concilia Salisburgensia* (Augsburg 1788) 348–583 (Salzburg Provincial Synods of 1569 and 1573). Diocesan Synods: Hartzheim, C VII: 498–517 (Lüttich 1585), 873–908 (Breslau 1580), 1057–1077 (Regensburg 1588; VIII), 320–363 (Olmütz 1591), 367–402 (Breslau 1592), 517–536 (Cologne 1598), 822–947 (Constance 1609).

VISITATIONAL REPORTS: M. Gmelin, "Die Visitationsprotokolle der Diözese Konstanz 1571–86" *ZGObrh* 25 (1873) 129–204; J. Jungnitz, *Visitationsberichte der Diözese Breslau*, 4 vols. (Breslau 1902–08); W. E. Schwarz, *Die Akten der Visitation des Bistums Münster aus der Zeit Johanns von Hoya 1571–73* (Münster 1913); A. Franzen, *Die Visitationsprotokolle der ersten nachtridentinischen Visitation im Erzstift Köln unter Salentin von Isenburg 1569* (Münster 1960); J. B. Kaiser, *Der Archidiakonat Longuyon am Anfang des 17. Jh.*, 2 vols. (Colmar 1928–29).

GENERAL LITERATURE

E. W. Zeeden, "Zeitalter der europäischen Glaubenkämpfe, Gegenreformation, Katholische Reform" *Saeculum* 7 (1956) 321–368; Literature of recent research; id., "Das Zeitalter der Glaubenskämpfe" *Gebhardt-Grundmann* II (1955) 105–202; K. Repgen, "Kaiser und Reich als Idee und Wirklichkeit für das Papsttum im Zeitalter der Reform" *Jb. der Görres-Gesellschaft* 1958 (Cologne 1959) 5–15; J. Hashagen, "Das Zeitalter der Gegenreformation und der Religionskrieg" L. Just, *Handbuch der deutschen Geschichte* II (Constance 1956) (with good bibliography); J. Greven, *Die Kölner Kartause und die Anfänge der Kath. Reform in Deutschland* (Münster 1935); Schreiber II (1951); id., "Tridentinische Reformdekrete in deutschen Bistumern" *ZSavRGkan* 38 (1952) 395–442; J. Schmidlin, *Die kirchlichen Zustände in Deutschland vor dem 30 jährigen Kriege*, 3 parts (Freiburg 1908–10); A. Steinhuber, *Geschichte des Collegium Germanicum-Hungaricum in Rom* I (Freiburg 1906); B. Duhr, *Geschichte der Jesuiten in den Ländern deutscher Zunge* I (Freiburg 1907) (rich in material); B. Schneider, "Die

Jesuiten als Gehilfen der päpstlichen Nuntien und Legaten in Deutschland zur Zeit der Gegenreformation" *Miscellanea Hist. Pont.* XXI (Rome 1959) 269–303; Bibliography on Peter Canisius: *LThK*² II, 917.

CONFESSIONALISM: E. W. Zeeden, "Grundlagen und Wege der Konfessionsbildung in Deutschland im Zeitalter der Glaubenskämpfe" *HZ* 185 (1958) 249–299; id., *Katholische Überlieferungen in den lutherischen Kirchenordnungen des 16. Jh.* (Münster 1959); A. Franzen, *Die Kelchbewegung am Niederrhein im 16. Jh.* (Münster 1955); H. Lutz, "Bayern und der Laienkelch" *QFIAB* 34 (1954) 203–235; J. P. Dolan, *The Influence of Erasmus, Witzel and Cassander in the Church Ordinances and Reform Proposals of the United Duchies of Cleve during the Middle Decades of the 16th Century* (Münster 1957); H. Nottarp. *Zur Communicatio in sacris cum haereticis* (Halle 1933).

CONFESSIONAL CHANGES IN THE UPPER PALATINATE: J. B. Götz, *Die erste Einführung des Kalvinismus in der Oberpfalz 1559–76* (Münster 1933); id., *Die religiösen Wirren in der Oberpfalz 1576–1620* (Münster 1937).

SWITZERLAND: K. Fry, *G. A. Volpe. Seine erste Nuntiatur in der Schweiz 1560–64* I (Fribourg 1931), II (Florence 1936), III (Stans 1946), also: *ZSKG* 39 (1945) 1–32, 81–110; F. Steffens–A. Reinhardt, *Die Nuntiatur von G. F. Bonhomini 1579–81,* 3 vols. (Solothurn–Fribourg 1906–29); E. Giddey, "Le nonce Paravicini 1587–91" *Revue Suisse d'hist.* 5 (1955) 369–375; J. G. Mayer, *Das Konzil von Trient und die Gegenreformation in der Schweiz,* 2 vols. (Stans 1902); R. Fischer, *Die Gründung der Schweizer Kapuzinerprovinz 1581–89* (Fribourg 1955), also: *ZSKG* 54 (1960) 257–281; R. Tschudi, *Das Kloster Einsiedeln unter den Äbten Ludwig II Blarer und Joachim Eichhorn 1526–69* (Einsiedeln 1946); W. Brotschi, *Der Kampf J. Chr. Blarers von Wartensee um die religiöse Einheit im Bistum Basel 1575–1608* (Fribourg 1956); A. Chèvre, "La restauration religieuse tridentine dans le diocèse de Bâle" *ZSKG* 42 (1948) 11–22, 107–123; see also 44 (1950), 17–36; 47 (1953), 25–46, 123–148; id., *L'officialité du diocèse de Bâle à Altkirch 1565–1630* (Fribourg 1946); H. Rennefahrt, "Die Verstärkung der Staatsgewalt im Bistum Basel unter Bischof Jacob Christoph 1575–1608" *In memoriam W. Näf* (Bern 1961) 267–310; J. Müller, "Der Kampf um die tridentinische Reform in Disentis" *ZSKG* 42 (1948) 23–65; 43 (1949) 175–202, 259–313; H. Metzger, *Vorstudien zu einer Geschichte der tridentinischen Seelsorgereform im Eidgenössischen Gebiet des Bistums Konstanz* (Basel 1951); H. Andres, *D. Jodocus Knab, Probst von Luzern und Bischof von Lausanne 1593–1658* (Stans 1961).

SECTION THREE

Religious Forces and Intellectual Content of the Catholic Renewal

41. *The Revival of Scholasticism, Michael Baius and the Dispute over Grace*

GENERAL LITERATURE

Grabmann G 158–172; C. Giacon, *La seconda scolastica,* 3 vols. (Milan 1946–50); H. Hurter, *Nomenclator literarius theologiae catholicae* III (Innsbruck ³1907), still indispensable [=Hurter].

UNIVERSITIES: Willaert 183–219; C. Duplessis d'Argentré, *Collectio iudiciorum* II (Paris 1728); P. Feret, *La faculté de théologie de Paris et ses docteurs les plus célèbres* I–IV (Paris 1900–6); J. Urriza, *La preclara facultad de artes y filosofía de la univ. de Alcalá de Henares en el siglo de oro 1509–1621* (Madrid 1942); V. Beltrán de Heredia, "La teología en la univ. de Alcalá" *RET* 5 (1945) 145–178; About Sigüenza: id., *RET* 2 (1942) 409–469; Gonzalo de Arriaga, *Historia del Colegio de S. Gregorio de Valladolid,* ed. M. Hoyos, 2 vols. (Valladolid 1928–40); F. Stegmüller, "Zur Literaturgeschichte der Philosophie und Theologie an den Universitäten Evora und Coimbra im 16. Jh." *Spanische Forschungen* 3 (1931) 385–438, expanded Portugese edition: Coimbra 1959; J. Grisar, "Die Universität Löwen zur Zeit der Gesandtschaft des P. Franciscus Toltus (1580) nach bisher unbenützten Quellen des Vatikanischen Archivs" *Miscellanea De Meyer* II 941–968; K. Eschweiler, "Die Philosophie der spanischen Spätscholastik auf den deutschen Universitäten" *Spanische Forschungen* 1 (1928) 251–325.

VITORIA AND THE SCHOOL OF SALAMANCA: F. Ehrle, *Los Manoscritos Vaticanos de los téologos Salmantinos del siglo XVI* (Madrid 1930); V. Beltrán de Heredia, *Los manoscritos del M. F. de Vitoria* (Madrid 1928); Modern editions of Vitoria's work: *Relecciones teológicas del M. F. de Vitoria,* ed. L. G. Getino (Madrid 1936); *Comentarios a la secunda secundae de Sto. Tomás* (Salamanca 1952); L. G. Getino, *El M. F. de Vitoria* (Madrid 1930) (chief work); F. Stegüller, *F. de Vitoria y la doctrina de la gracia en la escuela Salmantina* (Barcelona 1934); J. I. Tellechea Idigoras, "F. de Vitoria y la reforma católica" *Revista española de derecho canónico* 12 (1957) 65–110; R. G. Villoslada, "Pedro Crockaert OP, maestro de F. Vitoria" *EE* 14 (1935) 174–201.

VITORIA AND INTERNATIONAL LAW: J. Brown Scott, *The Spanish Origin of International Law* (London 1934); J. A. Fernandes-Santamaria, *The State, War and Peace. Spanish Political Thought in the Renaissance, 1516–1559* (Cambridge 1977); E. Reibstein, *Die Anfänge des neueren Natur- und Völkerrechtes* (Berne 1949) on Vasquez; K. Deuringer, *Probleme der Caritas in der Schule von Salamanca* (Freiburg 1959); A. Truyol Serra, *Die Grundsätze des Staats- und Völkerrechtes bei F. de Vitoria* (Heidelberg 1947); id., "Die Grundlagen der völkerrechtlichen Ordnung nach den spanischen Völkerrechtsklassikern" *Heidelberger Jb.* (1958); F. Elias de Tejada, "El concepto del derecho natural en los comentaristas Hispanos de Graciano" *Studia Gratiana* II (Bologna 1954) 230–261; V. Carro, *Domingo Soto* (Salamanca 1931); C. Pozo, *La teoría del progreso dogmático en los téologos de la escuela de Salamanca* (Madrid 1959); J. Btitau Prats, *El pensamiento politico de D. de Soto y su concepción del poder* (Salamanca 1960); A. Dempf, *Christliche Staatsphilosophie in Spanien* (Salzburg 1937).

POLEMICAL THEOLOGY AND BELLARMINE: (Survey) P. Polman, *L'élément historique dans la Controverse religieuse du XVIᵉ siècle* (Gembloux 1932). Bellarmine: last edition of his works in 12 volumes (Paris 1870–76); *Opera oratoria posthuma,* 9 vols. (Rome 1942–44); Sommervogel I:1151–1254. Sources for the history of his life: X. M. Le Bachelet, *Bellarmin avant son cardinalat* (Paris 1911), there 435–466 the controversial autobiography; id., *Auctarium Bellarminianum* (Paris 1913), also suppl. *AHSI* 4 (1935) 132–139; *Scritti politici,* ed. C. Giacon (Bologan 1950); J. Brodrick, *Robert Bellarmine, Saint and Scholar* (London 1961); J. de la Servière, *La théologie de Bellarmin* (Paris 1928). Methodologically correct: G. Buschbell, *Selbstbezeugungen des Kardinals Bellarmin* (Krumbach 1924), and S. Merkle, *ZKG* 45 (1926) 26–73; F. X. Arnold, *Die Staatslehre des Kardinals Bellarmin* (Munich 1934); Further Bibliography: *LThK²* II:160f.; Special Bibliography for Toledo, Suárez, Vázguez in the notes.

BAJUS: *Opera* (Cologne [actually, Amsterdam] 1696), 2nd part contains Documents and is Jansenist inspired; Opposed viewpoint; J.-B. Duchesne, *Histoire du Bainanisme*

(Douai 1731) (anti-Jansenist); M. Roca, "Documentos inéditos en torno a Miguel Bayo" *Anthologica annua* 1 (1953) 303–476; F. -X. Jansen, *Baius et le Baianisme* (Louvain 1927); *DThC* II:38–111, the best treatment is by Le Bachelet; *LThK²* I:1196–1199; Ch. van Sull, *Lessius* (Louvain 1960); J. I. Tellechea Idigoras, "Españoles en Lovaina 1551–58. Primeras noticias sobre el Bayanismo" *RET* 23 (1963) 21–44.

CONTROVERSY CONCERNING GRACE: Critical text of the Concord, ed. J. Rabeneck (Madrid 1953); Older Treatment of the Controversy by the two parties: J. A. Serry OP (under the pseudonym Le Blanc), *Historiae Congregationum de auxiliis divinae gratiae* (Mainz 1699, Antwerp 1709); L. de Meyere SJ (under the pseudonym Eleutherius), *Historiae controversiae de divinae gratiae auxiliis* (Venice 1742); G. Schneemann SJ, *Controversiarum de divinae gratiae liberique arbitrii concordia initia et progressus* (Freiburg 1881); F. Stegmüller, *Geschichte des Molinismus* I (Münster 1935) (chief work); Pastor, XI:513–576, XII:163–183; On Molina: J. Rabeneck, "De vita et scriptis L. Molinae" *AHSI* 19 (1950) 75f.; G. Smith, *Freedom in Molina* (Diss. Toronto 1936); W. Weber, *Wirtschaftsethik am Vorabend des Liberalismus. Höhepunkt und Abschluss der scholastischen Wirtschaftsbetrachtung durch L. Molina* (Münster 1959); *StL⁶* V:805–809 (Stegmüller).

42. *The Rise of Positive Theology*

GENERAL LITERATURE

Still reliable is H. Hurter, *Nomenclator literarius theologiae catholicae* III (Innsbruck ³1907); J. Turmel, *Histoire de la théologie positive du Concile de Trente au Concile de Vaticane* (Paris 1906); P. Polman, *L'Elément historique dans la Controverse religieuse du XVIᵉ Siècle* (Gembloux 1932); R. Snoeks, *L'argument de tradition dans la controverse eucharistique entre catholiques et réformées français au XVIIᵉ siècle* (Gembloux 1951); V. Baroni, *La contreréforme devant la Bible* (Lausanne 1943).

ON THE VULGATE DECREE AND REVISIONS: H. Höpfl, *Compendium introductionis in Sacros utriusque Testamenti libros I* (Rome ³1931) 346–367.

PATROLOGY, CHRISTIAN LITERARY HISTORY, CHURCH HISTORY, AND HAGIOGRAPHY: J. H. Fabricius, *Bibliotheca ecclesiastica* (Hamburg 1718) with Suffridus Petri's and Miraeus' extension of the Catalogue of Trithemius; H. Quentin, *J. D. Mansi et les grandes collections conciliaires* (Paris 1900); C. Baronius, *Annales ecclesiastici,* 12 vols. (Rome 1588–1605) (to 1198).

ON BARONIUS: G. Calenzio, *La vita e gli scritti del Card. C. Baronio* (Rome 1907) (unsatisfactory in spite of using Baronius' own notes); A. Walz, "La storiografia del Baronio e la storiografia de oggi" *Angelicum* 17 (1940) 88–110; A. Roncalli, *Il Card. C. Baronio* (Rome 1961) with bibliography by G. De Luca 47; *Bibliotheca hagiographica Latina* I (Breslau 1898–99), editions of Lippomanis and Surius; P. Peeters, *L'oeuvree des Bollandistes* (Brussels 1961); A. Fabrega Grau, "El P. Pedro Gil SJ (+1622) y su collección de Vidas de Santos" *Analects Sacra Tarracon* 31 (1958) 5–25; For the editor of the *Acta Sanctorum veteris et maioris Scotiae seu Hiberniae* (Louvain 1650) see F. J. Colgan OFM, *Essays in Commemoration of the Third Century of his death,* ed. T. O'Donell (Dublin 1959) 7–40.

CANONISTS: A good survey of canonists in this period in F. Kurtscheid, 278–301; J. F. V. Schulte, *Gesch. der Quellen von der Lit. des Canon. Rechts* III (Stuttgart 1880) though incomplete, is still indispensable; For Azpilcuenta, Antonio Agustin et. al. see footnotes in Pastor, IX 203f. the entire subject is in need of more serious research.

43. *Spiritual Life, Popular Devotion and Art*

LITERATURE

ASCETICISM AND MYSTICISM: M. -J. Dagens, *Bibliographie chronologique de la littérature de spiritualité et de ses sources 1501–1610* (Paris 1952).

PORTUGAL: Survey in I. S. Da Silva Dias, *Correntes de sentimento religioso em Portugal,* 2 vols. (Coimbra 1960)

SPAIN: *DSAM* IV (1961) 1127–1178; C. M. Abád, "Ascetas y misticos españoles del siglo de oro" *MCom* 10 (1948) 27–127; E. Allison Peers, *Studies of the Spanish Mystics* (London 1951); P. S. Rodrigues, *Introduccion a la historia de la literature mistica en Espana,* 4 vols. (Madrid 1927); J. Chuzeville, *Les Mystiques espagnols* (Paris 1952); P. Groult, *Les mystiques des Pays-Bas et la littérature espagnole du XVIe siècle* (Löwen 1927); J. Sanctis Adventosa, *La escuela mística Alemana y sus relaciones con místicos del siglo de oro* (Madrid 1946); D. Gutiérrez, "Ascéticos y místicos agostinos de España, Portugal y Hispano-América" *S. Augustinus spiritualis vitae Magister* II (Rome 1959) 147–238 (lit.); J. Monasterio, *Místicos agustinos españoles,* 2 vols. (El Escorial 1929); *Espirituales españoles,* (Numerous texts), P. Sáinz Rodríguez and L. Sala Balust, eds., 8 vols. (Barcelona 1959f.).

CARMELITE MYSTICISM: *Teresa de Avila, Obras,* ed., Silverius a S. Teresa, 9 vols. (Burgos 1915–24). Popular edition in one volume (Madrid 1948); Comprehensive Biography: Silverio de S. Teresa, *Historia del Carmelo descalzo en España, Portugal y América* I–IV (Burgos 1935–36); E. A. Peers, *A Handbook to the Life and Times of St. Theresa and St. John of the Cross* (London 1954); id., *Complete Works of St. Theresa of Jesus,* 3 vols. (London 1946); id., *The Letters of St. Teresa of Jesus* (Westminster 1950); M. Auclair, *St. Teresa of Avila* (London 1953); H. Flasche, "Syntaktische Untersuchungen zu Santa Teresa de Jesús" *Spanische Forschungen* 15 (1960) 151–174; E. Hamilton, *Saint Teresa* (New York 1959); A. Vermeulen, *Ste. Thérèse en France au XVIIe siècle* (Louvain 1958); S. Juan de la Cruz, *Obras,* ed., J. Vicente de la Eucaristía (Madrid 1957); A. Winklhofer, *Die Gnadenlehre in der Mystik des Hl. Joh. vom Kreuz* (Freiburg 1936); H. Sanson, *St. Jean de la Croix entre Bossuet et Fénelon* (Paris 1953); E. Schering, *Mystik und Tat. Th. von Jesus, Joh. vom Kreuz und die Selbstbehauptung der Mystik* (Munich–Basel 1959); E. A. Peers, *St. John of the Cross* (London 1946); id., *The Complete Works of St. John of the Cross* (Westminster 1949).

ITALY: G. Getto, "La letteratura ascetica e mistica in Italia nell'eta del Concilio Tridentino" *Contributi alla Storia del Concilio di Trento e della Controriforma* (Florence 1948) 51–77; cf. P. de Leturia, *CivCatt* II (1949) 82–98; A. Saba, *Federico Borromeo e i mistici del suo tempo* (Florence 1933); M. Andrews, *Men and women of the Italian Reformation* (New York 1914); F. C. Church, *The Italian Reformers* (New York 1932); P. Misciatelli, *The Mystics of Italy* (New York 1949); M. Jouhandeau, *St. Philip Neri* (New York 1960); L. Ponelle and L. Bordet, *St. Philip Neri and the Roman Society of His Times* (London 1932).

FRANCE: H. Brémond, *Histoire littéraire du sentiment religieux en France depuis la fin des guerres de religion,* 11 vols. (Paris 1916–33); the primary work for our period is in I–III; English trans., *A Literary History of Religious Thought in France,* 3 vols. (New York 1929–1930); L. Cognet, *De la dévotion moderne à la Spiritualité française* (Paris 1958); id., *La Spiritualité française au XVIIe siècle* (Paris 1949). Franz von Sales, *Oeuvres,* 26 vols. (Annecy 1892–1932); Biography by F. Trochu, 2 vols. (Lyon–Paris 1946), H. Waach

(Eichstatt 1955); A. Liuima, *Aux sources du Traité de l'Amour de Dieu de F. d. S.*, 2 vols. (Rome 1959–60); M. de la Bedoyère, *F. de Sales* (London 1960). Pierre Bérulle, *Correspondance*, ed. J. Dagens, 3 vols. (Paris 1937–39); L. Molien, *Le card. de Bérulle*, 2 vols. (Paris 1947); J. Dagens, *Bérulle et les origines de la restauration catholique 1575–1611* (Bruges 1952); J. Orcibal, "Les oeuvres de pitié du Card. Bérulle" *RHE* 57 (1962) 813–862.

PREACHING, SACRAMENTS, AND POPULAR PIETY: Bonaventura von Mehr, "De historica praedicationis, praesertim in ordine Min. Cap. scientifica pervestigatione" *CollFr* 11 (1941) 373–422; 12 (1942) 5–40; A. Valerius, *De rhetorica ecclesiastica* (Venice 1574); F. Borromaeus, *De sacris nostrorum temporum praedicatoribus* (Milan 1632); J. M. Connots, "Homiletic Theory in the Late 16th Century" *AER* 138 (1958) 316–332; B. Fischer, "Predigtgrundsätze des hl. Karl Borromäus" *TThZ* 61 (1952) 213–221; Bonaventura von Mehr, *Das Predigtwesen in der kölnischen und rheinischen Kapuzinerprovinz im 17. und 18. Jh.* (Rome 1945); A. L. Veit–L. Lenhart, *Kirche und Volksfrömmigkeit im Zeitalter des Barock* (Freiburg 1958); G. Schreiber, "Der Barock und das Tridentinum" Schreiber, I:381–425; St. Beissel, *Geschichte der Verehrung Mariens im 16. und 17. Jh.* (Freiburg 1910); H. Aurenhammer, *Die Mariengnadenbilder Wiens und Niederösterreichs in der Barockzeit* (Vienna 1956); C. Flachaire, *La dévotion à la Vierga dans la littérature catholique au commencement du XVIIe* (Paris 1950); M. Petrocchi, "La devozione alla Vergine negli scritti di pietà del Cinquecento italiano" *Problemi di vita religiosa in Italia* (Padua 1960) 281–287.

ART: Ch. de Job, *L'influence du Concile de Trente sur la littérature et les Beaux-Arts chez les peuples catholiques* (Paris 1884); G. Schnürer, *Katholische Kirche und Kultur in der Barockzeit* (Paderborn 1937); F. Würtenberger, *Der Manierismus* (Vienna 1962); C. J. Friedrich, *The Age of the Baroque* (New York 1965); *Trattati d'arte del Cinquecento fra manierismo e controriforma*, ed. P. Barocchi, 2 vols. (Bari 1960–61); B. Croce, *Der Begriff des Barock. Die Gegenreformation* (Zurich 1925); O. Benesch, *The Art of the Renaissance in Northern Europe* (Cambridge, Mass. 1947); E. Kirschbaum, "L'influsso del Concilio di Trento nell'arte" *Gr* 26 (1945) 100–116; E. Mâle, *L'art religieuse après le Concile de Trente* (Paris 1951); B. Knipping, *De iconographie van de Contra-Reformatie in de Nederlanden*, 2 vols. (Hilversum 1939–40); E. M. Vetter, "Der Verlorene Sohn und die Sünder im Jahrhundert des Konzils von Trient" *Ges. Aufsätze zur Kulturgesch. Spaniens* 15 (1960) 175–218; P. Prodi, "Ricerche sulla teoria delle arti figurativa nelle riforma cattolica" *Archivio per la storia della pietà* 4 (1962) 121–212; A. Hauser, *The Social History of Art*, 2 vols. (New York 1950); F. B. Artz, *From the Renaissance to Romanticism* (Chicago 1962).

MUSIC: K. Weinmann, *Das Konzil von Trient und die Kirchenmusik* (Regensburg 1919); K. G. Fellerer, *Palestrina* (Regensburg 1930); id., "Das Kölner Provinzialkonzil von 1536 und die Kirchenmusik" *Festschrift G. Kallen* (Bonn 1957) 327–336; O. Ursprung, "Palestrina und die tridentinische Reform de Kirchenmusik" *Monatschefte für kath. Kirchenmusik* 10 (1928) 210–219; K. Jeppesen, "Marzellusprobleme" *Acta musicologica* 16–17 (1946) 11–38; H. W. Frey, *Die Diarien der Sixtinischen Kapelle in Rom 1560–61* (Düsseldorf 1959) 11–38; W. Boetticher, *Orlando di Lasso und seine Zeit* (Kassel 1958); R. Molitor, *Die nachtridentinische Choralreform zu Rom*, 2 vols. (Leipzig 1901–2); M. F. Bukofzer, *Music in the Baroque Era* (London 1957).

LITERATURE: P. Hankamer, *Deutsche Gegenreformation und deutsches Barock* (Stuttgart 1935); H. Kindermann, *Theatergeschichte Europas* III (Salzburg 1959) 440–484, 679f.; G. Müller, *Das Jesuitendrama in den Ländern deutscher Zunge*, 2 vols. (Augsburg 1930); K. Adel, *Das Jesuitendrama in Österreich* (Vienna 1957); C. M. Haas, *Das Theater der Jesuiten in Ingolstadt* (Emsdetten 1958).

44. The New and the Old Orders

SOURCES AND LITERATURE TO 1933

Heimbucher; additional, M. Escobar, *Ordini e Congregazioni religiose,* 2 vols. (Turin 1951–53); L. Willaert, *La restauration catholique,* (Paris 1960) 95–167.

JESUITS: *Ratio studiorum SJ,* ed. G. M. Pachtler (Berlin 1887, contains the constitutions of 1586, 1599, and 1832). Bibliography: Sommervogel I:487ff.; H. Becher: *Die Jesuiten* (Munich 1961) 108–146; J. Sicard, "La reforma de Clemente VIII y la Comp. de Jesús" *Revista española del derecho can.* 3 (1954) 681–724; B. Schneider, *Paul Hoffaeus* (Rome 1956); id., "Der Konflikt zwischen Acquaviva und P. Hoffaeus" *AHSI* 26 (1957) 3–56; J. Iparraguirre, *Boletín de spiritualité ignatienne 1556–1615* (Rome 1961).

CAPUCHINS: Bernardinus a Colpetrazzo, *Historia ord. fr. min. Capuccinorum 1525–93,* 3 vols. (Rome 1939–41) (with attention to contemporary accounts); Melchior a Pobladura, *Hist. gen. I und II* (Rome 1947–48); Godefroy de Paris, *Les frères mineurs Capucins en France,* 2 vols. (Paris 1937–48); P. Hildebrand, *De Kapucijnen in de Nederlanden en het Prinsbisdom Luik,* 9 vols. (Antwerp 1945–55); A. Jacobs, *Die rheinischen Kapuziner 1611–1725* (Münster 1933); R. Linden, *Die Regelobservanz in der rheinischen Kapuzinerprovinz 1611–68* (Münster 1936); C. von Oberlinsch, "Die Kapuziner in Österreich" *CollFr* 20 (1950) 219–334; Additional literature: *LThK²* V:1332–1339; F. X. Martin, *Friar Nugent. A Study of F. L. Nugent 1567–1635, Agent of the Counter-Reformation* (Rome 1962).

OTHER MENDICANT ORDERS: "Anpassung der Konstitutionen an das Tridentinum bei den Dominikanern" *MOP* X:51ff. (general chapter at Bologna 1564); For the Augustinian Hermits: *Analecta Aug.* IX:423–440 (general chapter from 1564); For the Carmelites: *Acta cap. gen.,* ed. G. Wessels I:462ff.; The Constitutions of the Servites from 1569; *Mon. ord. Serv.* VI:109–158; Additional: Heimbucher and in the histories of the order by Mortier, Walz and Holzapfel.

DISCALCED CARMELITES: B. M. a. S. Cruce [Zimmermann], *Regesta* J. B. Rubei (Rome 1936); Silverio a. S. Teresa, *Historia del Carmel descalzo en España, Portugal y América* IV–IX (Burgos 1935–40) (Chief work, extends to 1650); Higinio a. S. Teresa, *Apuntos para la historia de la Ven. orden tercera del Carmel en España y Portugal* (Victoria 1954).

AUGUSTINIAN: *Bullarium ord. recollectorum S. Augustini,* ed. J. Fernández de S. Corde Jesu, 2 vols. (Rome 1954–61) (extends from 1570 to 1683).

MONASTIC ORDERS: E. Martène, *Histoire de la Congrégation de St. Maure,* 9 vols. (Ligugé–Paris 1928–43), postum; U. Berlière, *Nouveau Supplément á l'hist. litt. de la Congr. de St. Maur,* 3 vols. (Maredsous 1931); Y. Chauny, *Matricula monachorum professorum Congr. S. Mauri* (Paris 1959). List of the numerous letters of the Maurians in *Revue Mabillon* 23–29 (1933–39), 33 (1943); *Die Generalkapitelsrezesse der Bursfelder Kongregation,* ed. P. Volk 11 (Siegburg 1957) (covers the years 1531–1653); Canivez, VII (1939); R. Molitor, *Aus der Rechtsgeschichte benediktinischer Verbände* I (Münster 1928) 319–384 (Post Tridentine Congregations), II (Münster 1932) 37–327 (German attempts at unification), 328–347 (France); Ph. Schmitz-R. Tschudy, *Geschichte des Benediktinerordens* IV (Einsiedeln 1960); St. Hilpisch, *Geschichte des benediktinischen Mönchtums* (Freiburg 1929) 323–350; R. Hesbert, "La Congrégation de St. Maure" *Revue Mabillon* 51 (1961); Additional literature: *LThK²* VII 192; E. Martín, *Los Bernardinos españoles* (Palencia 1951).

SECTION FOUR

The Springtime of the Missions
in the Early Modern Period

45. *The Missions under Spanish Patronage*

SOURCES

Colección de documentos inéditos relativos al descubrimiento, conquista y colonización de las posesiones españolas en América y Oceania, 42 vols. (Madrid 1864–84), Segunda Serie, 13 vols. (Madrid 1885ff.); (P. Hernáez), *Colección de bulas, breves y otros documentos relativos ala Iglesia de América y Filipinas,* 2 vols. (Brussels 1879); *Cuerpo de documentos del siglo XVI sobre los derechos de España en las Indias y las Filipinas,* ed. L. Hanke–Millares Carlo (Mexico City 1943); B. de Las Casas, *Historia general de las Indias,* ed. Millares Carlo, 3 vols. (Mexico City 1951); B. de Las Casas, *Apologética Historia de las Indias,* ed. Serrano y Sanz (Madrid 1909); *The Spanish Tradition in America,* ed. C. Gibson, (Columbia, S.C. 1968); Also the publications of the various orders in their periodicals and collections, e.g. the Franciscans in the Archivo Ibero-Americano and the Americas in the Documentary Series of the Academy of American Franciscan History (Washington, D.C. from 1951), The Archivium Fratrum Praedicatorum (Rome), the Archivium Historicum S. I. and the Monumenta Historica S. I. (Rome).

LITERATURE

Streit II (Aachen 1924); C. Bayle, *España en Indias. Nuevos ataques y nuevas defensas* (Vitoria 1934, Madrid 1944); G. García, *Caracter de la conquista española según los testes de los historiadores primitivos* (Mexico City 1901); L. Hanke, *The Spanish Struggle for Justice in the Conquest of America* (Philadelphia 1949); id., *Colonisation et conscience chrétienne au XVIe s.* (Paris 1957); J. Höffner, *Christentum und Menschenwürde. Das Anliegen der spanischen Kolonialethik im Goldenen Zeitalter* (Trier 1947); P. de Leturia, "Der Heilige Stuhl und das spanische Patronat in Amerika" *HJ* 46 (1926) 1–71; J. Specker, *Die Missionsmethode in Spanisch Amerika im 16. Jh.* (Beckenried 1953); R. Greenleaf (ed.) *The Roman Catholic Church in Colonial Latin America* (New York 1971); A. Ybot León, *La Iglesia y los eclesiásticos españoles en la empresa de Indias* (Barcelona 1954); P. Borges, *Métodos misionales en la cristianización de América s. XVI* (Madrid 1960); A. de Egaña, *La teoría del Regio Vicariato Español en Indias* (Rome 1958); M. Mónica, *La gran controversia del siglo XVI acerca del Dominio Español en América* (Madrid 1952); P. de Leturia, *Relaciones entre la Santa Sede e Hispanoamérica 1493–1835,* 3 vols. (Rome–Caracas 1959).

BARTHLOMÉ DE LAS CASAS: *B. de Las Casas 1474–1566. Bibliografía crítica y cuerpo de materiales, para el studio de su vida . . . ,* ed. L. Hanke–M. Giménez Fernández (Santiago de Chile 1954); L. Hanke, *B. de Las Casas. An Interpretation of his Life and Writings* (The Hague 1951); id., *Bartolome de las Casas: Bookman, Scholar, Propagandist* (Philadelphia 1952); C. H. Haring, *The Spanish Empire in America* (New York 1963) (reprint). B. Biermann, "Lascasiana" *AFP* 27 (1957) 337–358; A. Fabié, *Vida y escritos de D. Fr. B. de Las Casas,* 2 vols. (Madrid 1879). Also the Monographs by A. Freitag (Steyl 1915), M.

Brion (Paris 1927), C. Bayle (Sevilla 1945), M. González Calzada (Mexico City 1948), M. Giménez Fernandez (Sevilla 1953), M. Martínez (Madrid 1955); G. Sanderlin, (ed.) *Bartolomé de Las Casas: A Selection of His Writings* (New York 1971); A. Losada, *Juan Gines de Sepulveda, Democrates segundo o De las justas causas de la guerra contra los indios* (Madrid 1951).

MEXICO

SOURCES: J. García Icazbalceta, *Colección de documentos para la historia de Méjico* (Mexico City 1856–66); *Nueva Collección* (Mexico City 1886–92), there: Jerónimo Mendieta, *Historia Eclesiástica Indiana* (1956), Toribio de Benaventa o Motolinía, *Historia de los Indios de la Nueva España* (1541, Washington, D.C. 1951); F. Zubillaga, *Monumenta Mexicana,* 2 vols. (Rome 1956–59).

LITERATURE: J. García Icazbalceta, *Bibliografía Mexicana del s. XVI* (Mexico City 1886); M. Cuevas, *Historia de la Iglesia en México,* 5 vols. (El Paso 1921–28); R. Ricard, *La "conquête spirituelle" de Mexique* (Paris 1933) Eng. trans. *The Spiritual Conquest of Mexico* (Berkeley 1966); C. Ceccherelli, *El bautismo y los Franciscanos en México* (Madrid 1955); F. J. Alegre, *Historia de la Compañia de Jesús en Nueva España,* 4 vols. (Rome 1956–60); F. Chevalier, *Land and Society in Colonial Mexico* (Berkeley 1963); C. Gibson, *The Aztecs under Spanish Rule: A History of the Indians of the Valley of Mexico 1519–1810* (Stanford, Calif. 1964); F. Cervantes de Salazar, *Life in the Imperial Royal City of Mexico in New Spain and the Royal and Pontifical University* (Austin, Tex. 1953); F. Morales, *Ethnic and Social Background of the Franciscans Friars in Seventeenth-Century Mexico* (Washington, D.C. 1973); J. Jacobsen, *Educational Foundations of the Jesuits in Sixteenth Century New Spain (Berkeley 1938).*

PERU

SOURCES: E. Lissón, *La Iglesia de España en el Perú* (Seville 1943–45); R. Vargas Ugarte, *Concilios Limenses 1551–1772,* 3 vols. (Lima 1951–54); A. de Egaña, *Monumenta Peruana,* 2 vols. (Rome 1954–58).

LITERATURE: F. de Armas Medina, *Cristianización del Perú; 1532–1600* (Seville 1953); R. Levillier, *Organización de la Iglesia y Órdenes religiosas en el Virreinato del Perú en el siglo XVI,* 2 vols. (Madrid 1919); A. Robledo, *La orden Franciscana en la América meridional* (Rome 1948); A. Tibesar, *Franciscan Beginnings in Colonial Peru* (Washington, D.C. 1953); R. Vargas Ugarte, *Los Jesuítas del Perú* (Lima 1941).

THE JESUIT REDUCTIONS IN PARAGUAY

SOURCES: A. Ruiz de Montoya, *Conquista espiritual . . . en Paraguay* (Madrid 1639); id., *Memorial* (Madrid 1643); N. del Techo, *Historia Provinciae Paraquariae* (Liege 1673).

LITERATURE: P. Pastells–F. Mateos *Historia de la Compañía de Jesús en la Provincia del Paraguay,* 8 vols. (Madrid 1912–49); F.-X. Charlevoix, *Histoire du Paraguay,* 6 vols. (Paris 1747); P. Hernández, *El Organización social de las doctrinas Guaraníes,* 2 vols. (Barcelona 1913); M. Fassbinder, *Der "Jesuitenstaat" in Paraguay* (Leipzig 1926); C. Lugon, *La république communiste chrétienne des Guaranis, 1610–1768* (Paris 1949) (with literature); E. Gothein, *Der christlich-soziale Staat der Jesuiten in Paraguay* (Berlin 1883); J. Pfotenhauer, *Die Missionen der Jesuiten in Paraguay,* 3 vols. (Gütersloh 1891–93). R.

Graham, *A Vanished Arcadia: Some Account of the Jesuits in Paraguay* (London 1924); M. Morner, *The Political and Economic Activities of the Jesuits in the Rio de la Plata Region: The Hapsburg Era* (Stockholm 1953); G. O'Neill, *Golden Years on the Paraguay: History of the Jesuit Missions* (London 1934).

MISSIONS IN THE PHILIPPINES

SOURCES: *The Philippine Islands (1493–1898)*, ed. Blair-Robertson, 53 vols. (Cleveland 1903–08); P. Torres y Lanzas, *Catálogo de los documentos relatios a las Islas Filipinas* I–V (Barcelona 1925–29).—For the Mission History of the Orders see Juan de Medina OESA (1630), Diego Aduarte OP (1698), F. Colin SJ (1663), Juan Franc. de S. Antonio OFM (1738–44).

LITERATURE: *Streit* IV–V (1928–29): W. E. Retana, *Catálogo abreviado de La Biblioteca Filipina* (Madrid 1898); Marín y Morales, *Ensayo de una síntesis de los trabajos realizados por las corporacionas religiosas de Filipinas,* 2 vols. (Manilla 1901); F. J. Montalbán, *El patronato español y la conquista de Filipinas* (Burgos 1930); H. Bernard-Maître, *Les Iles Philippines du Grand Archipel de la Chine* (Tientsin 1936); L. de la Costa, *The Jesuits in Philippines, 1581–1768* (Manila 1961).

46. The Missions under Portuguese Patronage

SOURCES

Bullarium Patronatus Portugalliae Regum in Ecclesiis Africae, Asiae et Oceaniae . . . , ed. L. M. Jordão et al., I–III (Lisbon 1868–1879) (-BullPatr.); R. Ricard, *Études et document pour l'histoire de l'Espagne et du Portugal* (Löwen o. J. [1930]).

LITERATURE

A. Jann, *Die katholischen Missionenen in Indien, China und Japan* (Paderborn 1915); J. Godinho, *The Padroado Portugal in the Orient, 1454–1860* (Bombay 1924); B. J. Wenzel, *Portugal und der Heilige Stuhl* (Lisbon 1957); M. de Oliveira, *História ecclesiástica de Portugal* (Lisbon 1960).

1. AFRICA

SOURCES: Paiva Manso, *História do Congo* [-L. M. Jordâo] (Lisbon 1877); A. Brasio, *Monumenta Missionária Africana, Africa Ocidental (1471–1531),* 7 vols. (Lisbon 1952–56).

LITERATURE: E. Weber, *Die portugiesische Reichsmission im Königreich Kongo von ihren Anfängen 1491 bis zum Eintritt der Jesuiten in die Kongomission 1548* (Aachen–Immensee 1924); J. Cuvelier–J. Boon, *Het Oud-Koninkrijk Kongo* (Brügge 1941; French trans. Brussels 1946); J. Cuvelier–L. Jadin, *L'ancien Congo d'après les archives romaines, 1518–1640* (Brussels 1954); L. Kilger, *Die erste Mission unter den Bantustämmen Ostafrikas* (Münster 1917); id., "Die ersten zwei Jahrhunderte ostafrikanischer Mission" *ZMR* 7 (1917) 97–108; P. Schebesta, "Zum ersten Missionsanfang am Sambesi" *ZMR* 14 (1914) 88–99; C. P. Groves, *The Planting of Christianity in Africa,* 4 vols. (London 1948–58).

2. Asia

a) India

SOURCES: *Documentacão para a História das Missões de padroado Português do Oriente. India,* ed. A. da Silva Rego, 12 vols. (Lisbon 1947–58); B. de Tobar, *Compendio Bulario Indico* I (Sevilla 1954); D. Gonçalez, *História do Malavar,* ed. J. Wicki (Münster 1955); S. Gonçalvez, *Primeira parte da História dos Religiosos da Companhia de Jesus . . . nos reynos e provincias das India Oriental,* ed. J. Wicki (Coimbra 1957–60); G. Schurhammer, *Die zeitgenössischen Quellen zur Geschichte Portugiesisch-Asiens und seiner Nachbarländer . . . zur Zeit des hl. Franz Xaver, 1538–1552* (Leipzig 1932, Rome ²1962); G. Schurhammer–E. A. Voretzsch, *Ceylon zur Zeit des Königs Bhuvaneka und Franz Xavers, 1539–1552. Quellen zur Geschichte der Potugiesen sowie der Franziskaner- und Jesuitenmission auf Ceylon,* 2 vols. (Leipzig, 1928); *Epistolae S. Francisci Xaverii aliaque eius scripta,* ed. G. Schurhammer–J. Wicki, 2 vols. (Rome 1944–45); *Die Briefe des Francisco de Xavier, 1542–1552,* ed. E. Gräfin Vitzthum (Munich ³1950); A. Valignano, *Historia del principio y progreso de la Compañís de Jesús en las Indias Orientales, 1542–1564,* ed. J. Wicki (Rome 1944); B. Biermann, "Documenta quaedam initia missionum Ordinis Praedicatorum in India Orientali illustrantia" *AFP* (1940) 132–157.

LITERATURE: G. Correira, *História da Colonizacão Portuguesa na India,* 5 vols. (Lisbon 1948–54); F. Rodriquez, *História da Companhia de Jesus na Assistencia de Portugal,* 4 vols. (Porto 1931–50); M. Müllbauer, *Geschichte der katholischen Missionen in Ostindien von der Zeit Vasco da Gamas bis zur Mitte des 18. Jh.* (Freiburg 1852); A. Jann, *Die katholischen Missionen in Indien, China und Japan. Ihre Organisation und das portugiesische Patronat vom 15. bis 18. Jh.* (Paderborn 1915); G. Schurhammer, *Franz Xaver, sein Leben und seine Zeit* I (1506–1541) (Freiburg 1955); id., *The Malabar Church and Rome During the Early Portuguese Period and Before* (Trichinopoly 1934); E. Tisserant-E. R. Hambye, *Eastern Christianity in India. A History of the Syro-Malabar Church from the Earliest to the Present Day* (London 1957); E. Maclagen, *The Jesuits and the Great Mogul* (London 1932).

b) Malay Archipelago

SOURCES: *Documentacão para a História das Missões do padroado Português do Oriente. Insulindia,* ed. A. B. de Sá, 5 vols. (Lisbon 1954–58).

LITERATURE: B. Visser, *Onder portugeesch-spaansche vlag. De Katholieke Missie van Indonesie 1511–1601* (Amsterdam 1925); A. Mulders, *De Missie in Tropisch Nederland* ('s-Hertogenbosch 1940); *An Introduction to Indonesian Historiography,* ed. Soedja Tmoko (Ithaca, N.Y. 1965); *Historians of South East Asia,* ed. D. G. E. Hall (London 1962) esp. chap. 13–15.

c) Japan

SOURCES: J. Laures, *Kirishitan Bunko. A Manual of Books and Documents on the Early Missions in Japan* (Tokyo 1957); L. Frois, *História do Japão 1549–1578* (Leipzig 1926); *Segunda parte da História de Japan 1578–1582* (Tokyo 1938); *Terza parte da Historia de Japan,* ed. A. Pinto u. a. (Tokyo 1942); *La première ambassade du Japon en Occident (1582–1592),* ed. A. Pinto et al. (Tokyo 1942).

LITERATURE: *Streit* IV–V; H. Haas, *Geschichte des Christentums in Japan* (Tokyo 1902–

04); J. Laures, *Geschichte der katholischen Kirche in Japan* (Kaldenkirchen 1956); C. R. Boxer, *The Christian Century in Japan 1549–1650* (Berkeley 1951); O. Cary, *A History of Christianity in Japan*, 2 vols. (Chicago 1909); J. Jennes, *History of the Catholic Church in Japan, 1529–1873* (Tokyo 1959).

D) CHINA

SOURCES: *Avvisi della Cina* . . . (Milan 1586–1588); *Lettere annue 1601–1611. Fonti Ricciane*, ed. P. D'Elia, 3 vols. (Rome 1942–49); *Cartas de China. Documentos inéditos sobre Misiones Franciscanas de los siglos XVII y XVIII*, ed. O. Maas, 2 vols. (Sevilla 1917); D. Advarte, *Historia de la Provincia del S. Rosario de Filipinas, Japón y China* (Saragossa 1693).

BIBLIOGRAPHY: H. Cordier, *Bibliotheca Sinica*, 4 vols. (Paris 1904–08), suppl. I (Paris 1922); *Streit* IV, V and VII; J. Beckmann, "Neuerscheinungen zur chines. Missionsgeschichte, 1945–1955" *Monumenta Serica* 15 (Tokyo 1956) 378–462.

LITERATURE: K. S. Latourette, *A History of Christian Missions in China* (London 1929); H. Bernard-Maître: *DHGE* XII 693–741; P. M. D'Elia, "Sunto storico dell'attività della Chiesa Cattolica in Cina dalle origini ai nostri giorni (635–1294–1948)" *StMis* 6 (Rome 1951) 3–68; C. Cary-Elwes, *China and the Cross* (New York 1956).

E) INDO-CHINA

SOURCES: Ch. Borri, *Relatione della nuova missione de' Padri di Comp. di Gesù nel Regno di Cochinchina* (Rome 1631); A. de Rhodes, *Relazione de' felici successi della santa fede predicata da' padri della Comp. di Gesù nel regno di Tunchino* (Rome 1650).

LITERATURE: *Streit* IV–V; P. Pachtler, *Das Christentum in Tonking und Cochinchina* (Paderborn 1861); F. Schwager, "Aus der Vorgeschichte der hinterindischen Mission" *ZMR* 3 (1913) 146–156; B. Biermann, "Die Missionen der portugiesischen Dominikaner in Hinterindien" *ZMR* 21 (1931) 305–327; id., "Die Missionsversuche der Dominikaner in Kambodscha" *ZMR* 23 (1933) 108–132.

3. PORTUGUESE-AMERICA: BRAZIL

SOURCES AND LITERATURE: *Streit* II:331–361, 739–753; S. Leite, *Monumenta Brasiliae*, 4 vols. (Rome 1956–60); id., *História da Companhia de Jesus no Brasil* I–II (Lisbon–Rio de Janeiro 1938); A. Lourenco Farinha, *A expansão de fé na Africa e no Brasil* I (Lisbon 1942) 419–542; R. Ricard, "Les Jésuites au Brésil pendant la seconde moitié du XVIᵉ siècle, 1549–1597" *RHM* 1 (1937) 321–366, 435–470; D. Romag, *Compêndio de História da Igreja* (Petrópolis 1952).

4. THE ENTRANCE OF FRANCE INTO THE MISSION FIELD

SOURCES: Ch. le'Clercq, *Premier établissement de la foi dans la Nouvelle France*, 2 vols. (Paris 1691); S. le Tac, *Histoire chronologique de la Nouvelle France, ou Canada*, ed. Réveillaud (Paris 1888); R. G. Thwaites (editor), *The Jesuit Relations and Allied Documents. Travels and Explorations of the Jesuit Missionaries in New France, 1610 to 1791*, 73 vols. (Cleveland 1897–1910; selections [New York 1925]); F.-X. de Charlevoix, *Histoire de la Nouvelle France*, 3 vols. (Paris 1794); *Documents inédits pour servir à l'histoire du christianisme en Orient*, ed. Rabbath, 2 vols. (Beyrouth 1907–10).

LITERATURE: C. de Rochemonteix, *Les Jésuites et la Nouvelle France au XVIIᵉ siècle*, 3 vols. (Paris 1895–96); G. Goyau, *Une épopée mystique. Les origines religieuses du Canada* (Paris 1934); L. Pouliot, *Études sur les Relations des Jésuites de la Nouvelle France* (Brugge 1940); C. de Bonnault, *Histoire du Canada francais, 1534–1763* (Paris 1950); L. Groulx, *Histoire du Canada francais depuis sa découverte* (Montréal 1950); G. de Vaumas, *L'éveil missionnaire de la France au XVIIᵉ siècle* (Paris 1959); *Delacroix* II:70–88, 281–320; H. de Barenton, *La France catholique en Orient* (Paris 1902); Rocco da Cesinale, *Storia delle Missioni dei Cappuccini*, 3 vols. (Rome 1873); Clemente da Terzorio, *Missioni dei Minori Cappuccini* IV–V (Rome 1918–19); F. X. Talbot, *Saint among the Hurons* (New York 1949); J. B. Tyrell (ed.), *Documents Relating to the Early History of Hudson Bay* (Toronto 1931).

47. *The Sacred Congregation for the Propagation of the Faith*

SOURCES

Bullarium Pontificum S. Congregationis de Propaganda Fide, 5 vols. (Rome 1839–41); R. de Martinis, *Juris Pontificii de Propaganda Fide Pars prima . . . ,* 7 vols. (Rome 1888–97), Pars secunda (Rome 1909); *Collectanea S. Congregationis de Propaganda Fide* (Rome 1893 [arranged by subject], ²1907 [2 vols. arranged chronologically]) [=Coll].

LITERATURE

O. Mejer, *Die Propaganda, ihre Provinzen und ihr Recht,* 2 vols. (Leipzig–Göttingen 1852–3); *ZMR* 12 (1922) Heft 1 for the 300th anniversary of the Propaganda with contributions from: J. Schmidlin, "Die Gründung der Propaganda Kongregation (1622)" 1–14, 115; L. Kilger, "Die ersten fünzig Jahre Propaganda—eine Wendezeit der Missionsgeschichte" 15–30; K. Pieper, "Ein Blick in die missionsmethodischen Erlasse der Propaganda" 31–51. Very good material in H. Chappoulie, *Aux origines d'une Eglise. Rome et les missions d'Indochine au XVIIᵉ siècle* I (Paris 1943). Cf. also B. Arens, *Handbuch der katholischen Missionen* (Freiburg 1925) 7–17.

SECTION FIVE

European Counter Reformation and Confessional Absolutism (1605–55)

48. *Paul V, Gregory XV and the Beginnings of the Central European Counter Reformation*

SOURCES

BullRom XI–XII; A. O. Meyer, *Die Prager Nuntiatur des G. St. Ferreri; Die Wiener Nuntiatur des G. Serra 1603–06* (Berlin 1913); L. Linhartova, *Epp. et Acta A. Gaetani 1607–8,* 3 vols. (Prague 1932–37–40); A. Cauchie-R. Maere, *Recueil des instructions générales aux nonces de Flandre 1596–1635* (Brussels 1904); A. Louant, *Correspondance d'Ottavio Mirto Frangipani* III (Brussels 1942); L. van Meerbeeck, *Correspondance des nonces Gésualdo, Morra, Sanseverino avec la Secrétairerie d'Etat Pontificale 1615–21* (Brussels 1937); B. de Meester, *Correspondance du nonce G. F. Guido di Bagno 1621–27* (Brussels 1937); J. Kollmann, *Acta S. Congregationis de Propaganda Fide res gestas Bohemicas illustrantia* I (Prague 1923); *Acta S. C. de Propaganda fide Germaniam spectantia. Die Protokolle der Propagandakongregation zu deutschen Angelegenheiten 1622–49*, ed. H. Tüchle (Paderborn 1962); I. de Olarra Garmendia–M. L. de Larramendi, "Correspondencia entre la nunciatura de España y la Santa Sede durante el reinado de Felipe III" *Anthologica annua* 9 (1961) 495–816 continued to 13 (1965) 395–697.

LITERATURE

Pastor, XII (Paul V.), XIII:1, 27–224 (Gregory XV.); Seppelt, V:243–275.

THE HISTORY OF THE STATE SECRETARIATS: A. Kraus, "Secretarius und Sekretariat" *RQ* 55 (1960) 43–84; id., "Das Päpstliche Staatssekretariat i. J. 1623" *RQ* 52 (1957) 93–122; J. Semmler, "Beiträge zum Aufbau des Päpstlicher Staatssekretariates unter Paul V." *RQ* 54 (1959) 40–80; L. Hammermayer, "Grundlinien der Entwicklung des Päpstlichen Staatssekretariates von Paul V. bis Innocenz X." *RQ* 55 (1960) 157–202; D. Albrecht, *Die deutsche Politik Papst Gregors XV. Die Einwirkung der päpstlichen Diplomatie auf die Häuser Habsburg und Wittelsbach 1621–23* (Munich 1956); id., *Die auswärtige Politik Maximilans I. von Bayern 1618–35* (Göttingen 1962).

CONFLICT WITH VENICE AND SARPI: F. Gaeta, *Origine e sviluppo delta rappresentanza stabile Pontificia in Venezia* (Rome 1958); A. Stella, "La proprietà ecclesiastica nella Repubblica di Venezia dal sec. XV al XVII" *Nuova Riv. storica* 42 (1958) 4–30; P. Pirri, *L'interdetto di Venezia del 1606 e i Gesuiti* (Rome 1959) (many documents); J. M. Pou y Marti, "La intervención española en el conflicto entre Paulo V y Venecia 1605–07" *Misc. P. Paschini* II (Rome 1949) 359–381; M. R. Pazos, "Del conflicto entre Paulo V y Venecia. El embajador de la Serenisima en España y el entredicto" *AIA* 4 (1944) 32–61; A. M. dal Pino, "Fra Fulgenzio da Passirano negli anni di studio e di insegnamento" *Studi storici dell'Ord. dei Servi* 8 (1957–58) 134–151; *Opere di P. Sarpi*, 8 vols. (Helmstat, in reality Verona 1761–68); *Istoria dell'Interdetto e altri scritti editi e inediti*, ed. M. D. Busnelli and G. Gambarin, 3 vols. (Bari 1940); F. L. Polidori, *Lettere di Fra P. Sarpi*, 2 vols. (Florence 1863) (it is surpassed by more recently published collections of letters, especially Busnelli); In opposition to P. Savio, "Per l'epistolario di P. Sarpi" *Aevum* 10 (1936) 1–104; 11 (1937) 3–74, 275–322; 13 (1939) 558–623; 14 (1940) 3–84; 16 (1942) 3–43, 105–138; R. Taucci, *Intorno alle lettere di P. Sarpi ad Antonio Foscarini* (Florence 1939); B. Ulianich, *Paolo Sarpi, Lettere ai Gallicani* (Wiesbaden 1961) (lit.); id., "Considerazioni e documenti per una Ecclesiologia di P. Sarpi" *Lortz F* II (1958) 363–444; V. Buffon, *Chiesa di Cristo e Chiesa Romana nelle opere e nelle Lettere di Fra Paolo Sarpi* (Löwen 1941); C. M. Francescon, *Chiesa e Stato nei consulti di Fra P. Sarpi* (Vicenza 1942); G. Getto, *Paolo Sarpi* (Pisa 1941).

THE BEGINNINGS OF THE THIRTY YEARS WAR AND FERDINAND II: *Briefe und Akten zur Geschichte des 30jährigen Krieges*, 11 vols. (Leipzig 1870–1908); Continued by W. Goetz, *Die Politik Maximilians I. und seiner Verbündeten*, 2 vols. (Munich 1908–1918); Gebhardt-Grundmann II:130f., additional lit.; V.-L. Tapié, *La Politique de la France et le début de la Guerre de Trente ans 1616–21* (Paris 1934); C. V. Wedgewood, *The Thirty Years War* (London 1938); H. Sturmberger, *Aufstand in Böhmen, Der Beginn des 30jährigen Krieges* (Munich 1959); For the characteristics of Ferdinand II—besides F.

Ch. Khevenhiller, *Annales Ferdinandei,* 12 vols. (1716–26) and F. Hurter, *Geschichte Kaiser Ferdinands II.,* 11 vols. (Schaffhausen 1850f.)—B. Dudik, "Korrespondenz Kaiser Ferdinands II. und seiner Familie mit M. Becanus und W. Lamormaini" *AÖG* 54 (1876) 219–350; G. Franz, "Glaube und Recht im politischen Denken Kaiser Ferdinands II" *ARG* 49 (1958) 258–269 (biased); For his confessor Lamormaini: R. Stiegele: *HJ* 28 (1907) 551–569, 849–870; Duhr II:2: 691–713; A. Posch: *MIÖG* 63 (1955) 375–390; F. X. v. Altötting, "Laurentius von Brindisi in der Politik Bayrens 1606–12" *CollFr* 29 (1959) 237–272; Arturo da Camignano, "La part de S. Laurent de Brindes dans le ban de Donauwörth 1607" *RHE* 58 (1963) 460–486; D. Albrecht, *Die auswärtige Politik Maximilians von Bayern 1618–35* (Göttingen 1962) (basic).

49. *Urban VIII, Innocent X and the End of the Counter Reformation*

SOURCES

BullRom XIII–XV; *Le relazioni della Corte di Roma lette al Senato degli ambasciatori veneti nel sec. XVII,* ed. N. Barozzi–G. Berchet, 2 vols. (Venice 1877–79); A. Leman, *Recueil des instructions générales aux nonces ordinaires de France 1620–34* (Paris 1919); Q. Aldea, "España, el Papado y el Imperio durante la guerra de los treinta años, I: Instrucciones a los Embajadores de España en Roma 1631—43" *MCom* 27 (1957) 291–437; A. Malvezzi, "Papa Urbano VIII e la questione della Valtellina. Nuovi documenti" *Nuovo Archivio lombardo* VIII:7 (1957) 5–113; H. Kiewning, *Die Nuntiatur des Palotto 1628–30,* 2 vols. (Berlin 1895–97); V. Kybal–G. Incisa Della Rocchetta, *La Nunziatura di F. Chigi 1640–51,* 2 vols. (Rome 1943–46); W. Friedensburg, "Regesten zur deutschen Geschichte aus der Zeit des Pontifikates Innocenz' X." *QFIAB* 4 (1902) 236–285; 5 (1903) 60–124, 207–222; 6 (1904) 146–173; 7 (1905) 121–138; *Acta Pacis Westfalicae,* ed. M. Braubach–K. Repgen, Series IV, Abt. D., Vol. 1 (Münster 1964).

LITERATURE

Pastor XIII (Urban VIII), XIV:13–299 (Innocent X); Seppelt V:275–321. Pastor's criticism of Ranke and Gregorovius is not without justification, yet he stands too strongly under the influence of Leman in spite of the harsh judgement of Richelieu; See also the unfavorable judgement of J. Grisar, "Päpstliche Finanzen, Nepotismus und Kirchenrecht unter Urban VIII" *Misc. Hist. Pont.* 14 (1943) 205–366; K. Repgen, "Finanzen, Kirchenrecht und Politik unter Urban VIII" *RQ* 56 (1961) 62–74; A. Kraus, "Amt und Stellung des Kardinalnepoten zur Zeit Urbans VIII" *RQ* 53 (1958) 238–243; id., *Die Päpstliche Staatssekretarie unter Urban VIII* (Freiburg 1964); A. Malvezzi, "Papa Urbano VIII e la questione della Valtellina" *Archivio storico lombardo* 84 (1957) 5–113; P. Blet, *Le Clergé de France et la Monarchie* I (Rome 1959); id., "La congrégration des affaires de France de 1640" *Mélanges E. Tisserant* IV:59—105.

EDICT OF RESTITUTION: EARLY HISTORY: Pastor XIII:1, 354f.; K. Repgen, "L. Holstenius als politischer Gutachter in Rom" *QFIAB* 39 (1959) 342–352; H. Günter, *Das Restitutionsedikt von 1629 und die katholische Resauration in Alt-Württemberg* (Stuttgart 1901); For a list of restored church properties: Th. Tupetz, *Der Streit um die geistlichen Güter und das Restitutionsedikt von 1629* (Vienna 1883) 523–566; Comprehensive survey and lit. in K. Repgen, *Die Römische Kurie und der Westfälische Friede* I:157–189 (vide infra).

THE PEACE OF WESTPHALIA: M. Braubach, *Der Westfälische Friede* (Münster 1948); F. Dickmann, *Der Westfälische Frieden* (Münster 1959) (basic); L. Steinberger, *Die Jesuiten und die Friedensfrage 1635–50* (Freiburg 1906) (Wangnereck and his opponent 63f., 78f.); D. Bötticher, "Propaganda und öffentliche Meinung im protestantischen Deutschland 1628–36" *ARG* 44 (1953) 181–203; G. Schmid, "Konfessionspolitik und Staatsräson bei den Verhandlungen des Westfälischen Friedenskongresses über die Gravamina ecclesiastica" *ARG* 44 (1953) 203–222; K. Repgen, "Die Hauptinstruktion Ginettis für den Kölner Kongress 1636" *QFIAB* 34 (1954) 250–287; id., "Fabio Chigis Instruktion für den Westfälischen Friedenskongress" *RQ* 48 (1953) 79–166; id., *Die Römische Kurie und der Westfälische Friede* I (Tübingen 1962); H. Bücker, "Der Nuntius Fabio Chigi in Münster 1644–49" *WZ* 108 (1958) 1–90; S. Cultrera, *Per la pace di Westfalia. Missione alle corti di Francia e di Spagna del P. Innocenzo Marcinò da Caltagirone 1647–48* (Milan 1955); P. Frischauer, *The Imperial Crown* (London 1939); M. Roberts, *The Political Objectives of Gustavus Adolphus in Germany, 1630–32* (London 1957); J. J. Poelhekke, *De Vrede van Munster* (The Hague 1948); E. A. Beller, *Propaganda in Germany during the Thirty Years War* (Princeton 1940).

RICHELIEU AND MAZARIN: G. Hannoteaux, *Histoire du card. Richelieu,* 6 vols. (Paris 1893–1947); C. J. Burckhardt, *Richelieu. Der Aufstieg zur Macht* (Münich 1947); E. Hassinger, "Das politische Testament Richelieus" *HZ* 173 (1952) 485–503; C. V. Wedgewood, *Richelieu and the French Monarchy* (London 1949); L. Dedouvres, *Le P. Joseph de Paris Capucin. L'Éminence grise,* 2 vols. (Paris 1932); U. Silvagni, *Il Card. Mazzarino* (Turin 1928); V. Tornetta, "La politica del Mazzarino verso il papato" *AstIt* 99 (1941) 86–116; 100 (1942) 95–134; R. Derricau-M. Laurain, *La mort du Card. Mazarin* (Paris 1960).

MISCELLANEOUS: G. Marañón-L. Pfandl, *Olivares. Der Niedergang Spaniens als Weltmacht* (Munich o. J. 1939); G. Albion, *Charles I and the Court of Rome* (London 1935); W. Brulez, "La crise dans les relations entre le Saint-Siège et les Pays-Bas au XVIIᵉ siècle" *Bulletin de l'Institut historique belge de Rome* 28 (1953) 63–104; M. J. Havran, *The Catholics in Caroline England* (Stanford 1962); W. M. Southgate, *John Jewel and the Problem of Doctrinal Authority* (Cambridge, Mass. 1962); W. S. Knight, *The Life and Works of Hugo Grotius* (London 1925); J. Laures, *The Political Economy of Juan de Mariana* (New York 1928); C. V. Wedgewood, *A Coffin for King Charles* (New York 1964).

50. *Denominationalism and Secularization*

LITERATURE

IRENICISM AND TOLERANCE: F. W. Kantzenbach, *Das Ringen um die Einheit der Kirche im Jahrhundert der Reformation. Vertreter, Quellen und Motive des "ökumenischen" Gedankens von Erasmus von Rotterdam bis Georg Calixt* (Stuttgart 1957); R. Rouse–St. Ch. Neill, *Geschichte der ökumenischen Bewegung* I (Göttingen 1957); N. Paulus, *Protestantismus und Toleranz im 16. Jh.* (Freiburg 1911); J. Lecler, *Toleration and the Reformation,* 2 vols. (New York 1960); L. Cristiani, "Tolérance et intolérance religieuses au XVIᵉ siècle" *Journal of World-History* 5 (1959) 857–878; E. Hassinger, "Wirtschaftliche Motive und Argumente für religiöse Duldsamkeit im 16. und 17. Jh." *ARG* 49 (1958) 226–245; H. Conrad, "Religionsbann, Toleranz und Parität am Ende des alten Reiches" *RQ* 56 (1961) 167–199; K. Goldammer, "Friedensidee and Toleranzgedanke bei Paracelsus und den Spiritualisten" *ARG* 46 (1955) 20–46, 47 (1956) 180–211; K. Jordan, *The Development of Religious Toleration in England,* 4 vols. (London 1932–40); A. Räss, *Die Convertiten seit der Reformation* I–VI (Freiburg 1866–68) (until 1653); H. Bainton, *The*

Travail of Religious Liberty (Philadelphia 1951); H. Bainton–B. Becker, et al., *Castellioniana, Quatre études sur Sebastien Castellion et l'idee de la tolerance* (Haarlem 1954).

POLITICAL THEORY AND ABSOLUTISM: P. Meinecke, *Die Idee der Staatsräson in der neueren Geschichte* I (Munich 1960); H. Lutz, *Ragione di stato und christliche Staatsethik im 16. Jh.* (Münster 1961); M. Beloff, *The Age of Absolutism* (New York 1962) (a schematic treatment of the period); P. Mesnard, *L'essor de la philosophie politique an XVIᵉ siècle* (Paris 1951); R. v. Albertini, *Das politische Denken in Frankreich zur Zeit Richelieus* (Marburg 1951); L. Firpo, *Il pensiero politico del Rinascimento e della Controriforma* (Milan 1948); T. Bozza, *Scrittori politici italiani dal 1550 al 1650* (Rome 1949) (Bibliography); M. d'Addio, *Il pensiero politico di G. Scioppio e il Machiavellismo del Seicento* (Milan 1958); J. Spörl, *Widerstandsrecht und Grenzen der Staatsgewalt* (Berlin 1955); C. J. Friedrich, *The Age of the Baroque* (New York 1952); J. W. Allen, *A History of Political Thought in the 16th Century* (New York 1928); B. Hamilton, *Political Thought in 16th Century Spain* (New York 1963); R. H. Murray, *The Political Consequences of the Reformation* (London 1926); B. Reynolds, *Proponents of Limited Monarchy in 16th Century France* (New York 1931); H. Butterfield, *The Statecraft of Machiavelli* (London 1940); R. H. Tawney, *Religion and the Rise of Capitalism* (New York 1926). D. Ogg, *Europe in the Seventeenth Century* (New York 1962).

LITERATURE ON ABSOLUTISM: W. Hubatsch, "Das Zeitalter des Absolutismus in heutiger Sicht" *AKG* 33 (1953) 342–371, suppl. M. Schlenke: *AKG* 39 (1957) 112–129; L. Just, "Stufen und Formen des Absolutismus" *HJ* 80 (1961) 143–159; St. Skalweit, "Das Zeitalter des Absolutismus als Forschungsproblem" *DVfLG* 35 (1961) 298–315.

THE SECULARIZATION OF THOUGHT: W. Dilthey, *Weltanschauung und Analyse des Menschen seit Renaissance und Reformation* (Leipzig–Berlin 1914); G. Saitta, *Il pensiero italiano nell'Umanesimo e nel Rinascimento* III (Bologna 1951); H. E. Weber, *Reformation, Orthodoxie und Rationalismus,* 2 vols. (Gütersloh 1940).

PHILOSOPHY: *Ueberweg* III (Darmstadt 1957); F. Copelston, *History of Philosophy* III–IV (London 1958–68). For the Italian emigrants the following works are basic: D. Cantimori, *Eretici italiani del Cinquecento* (Florence 1939); D. Cantimori-E. Feist, *Per la storia degli Eretici italiani del secolo XVI in Europa* (Rome 1937) (Texts). Since the appearance of these works there have been numerous monographs about individual personalities, e.g.: G. Spini, *A. Bruccioli* (Florence 1940); Giacomo Aconcio, *Stratagematum Satana* ll. VIII, ed. G. Radetti (Florence 1946); Ch. Donald O'Malley, *Jacopo Aconcio* (Rome 1955); L. Firpo, *Gli scritti di F. Pucci* (Turin 1957); A. Bertini, "Giovanni Bernardino Bonifacio, Marchese d'Oria" *Archivio Storico napoletano* 76 (1958) 191–265; St. Dunin Borkowski, "Die Gruppierung der Antitrinitarier des 16. Jh." *Scholastik* 7 (1932) 481–523; E. M. Wilbur, *A History of Unitarism* (Cambridge, Mass. 1945); B. Stasiewski, *Reformation und Gegenreformation in Polen* (Münster 1960) 52f.; G. Schramm, "Neue Ergebnisse der Antitrinitarierforschung" *Jahrbücher für Geschichte Osteuropas* NF 8 (1960) 428f.; L. Febvre, *Le problème de l'incroyance au XVIᵉ siècle* (Paris 1942), also the remarks of P. Jourda: *RHEF* 29 (1943) 262–275; id., *Au coeur religieux du XVIᵉ siècle* (Paris 1957); A. Klempt, *Die Säkularisierung der universalhistorischen Auffassung* (Göttingen 1960).

GALILEI: A. Favaro (ed.), *Le Opere di G. Galilei,* 20 vols. (Florence 1890–1909); L. Olschki, *Galilei und seine Zeit* (Florence 1927); A. Koyŕe, *Etudes Galiléennes,* 3 vols.

(Paris 1939); *Nel terzo centenario della morte di G. Galilei.* Saggie conferenze (Milan 1942); F. Dessauer, *Der Fall Galilei und wir* (Frankfurt a. M. 1949).

FOR THE TRIAL PROCEDURE: Pastor, XII:203–214; XIII:1, 616–630; F. A. Yates, *Giordano Bruno and the Hermetic Tradition* (London 1964); G. De Santillana, *The Crime of Galileo* (Chicago 1959).

SUPPLEMENT TO BIBLIOGRAPHY

Part One

Handbuch der Europäischen Geschichte III: *Die Entstehung des neuzeitlichen Europa,* ed. J. Engel (Stuttgart 1971); St. Skalweit, *Reich und Reformation* (Berlin 1967). H. J. Hillerbrand (ed.), *Brennpunkte der Reformation. Zeitgenössische Texte und Bilder* (Göttingen 1967); J. Delumeau, *Naissance et Affirmation de la Réforme* (Paris 1968); J. Lortz–E. Iserloh, *Kleine Reformationsgeschichte* (Freiburg ²1971); R. Stupperich, *Die Reformation in Deutschland* (Munich 1972); R. Kottje–B. Moeller (eds.), *Ökumenische Kirchengeschichte* II (Mainz 1973); K. Kupisch, *Kirchengeschichte* III: *Politik und Konfession. Die Reformation in Deutschland* (Stuttgart 1974); A. Laube, M. Steinmetz, G. Vogler, *Illustrierte Geschichte der deutschen frühbürgerlichen Revolution* (Berlin/DDR 1974).

CHAPTER 1: H. Oberman, *Forerunners of the Reformation* (New York 1960); A. Schroer, *Die Kirche in Westfalen vor der Reformation* (Munster 1967); R. Bäumer, *Nachwirkungen des konziliaren Gedankens in der Theologie und Kanonistik des früben 16. Jahrhunderts* (Münster 1971).

CHAPTER 2: 1. R. Friedenthal, *Luther* (Munich 1967); G. Zschäbitz, *Martin Luther. Grösse und Grenze* I (*1483–1526*) (Berlin 1967); R. García-Villoslada, *Martin Lutero,* 2 vols. (Madrid 1973); G. Ebeling, *Luther* (Tübingen 1974).—2. P. Hacker, *Das Ich im Glauben bei M. Luther* (Graz 1966); F. Gogarten, *Luthers Theologie* (Tübingen 1967); W. Joest, *Ontologie der Person bei Luther* (Göttingen 1967); O. H. Pesch, *Die Theologie der Rechtfertigung bei M. Luther und Thomas v. A.* (Mainz 1967); J. Wicks, *Man Yearning for Grace. Luther's Early Spiritual Teaching* (Wiesbaden 1969); R. Damerau, *Die Demut in der Theologie Luthers* (Giessen 1970); G. Ebeling, *Lutherstudien* I (Tübingen 1971); K. H. Zur Mühlen, *Nos Extra Nos. Luthers Theologie zwischen Mystik und Scholastik* (Tübingen 1972); E. Iserloh, *Luther und die Reformation. Beiträge zu einem ökumenischen Lutherverständnis* (Aschaffenburg 1974).—3. P. Manns, *Lutherforschung heute* (Wiesbaden 1967); H. G. Koch, *Luthers Reformation in kommunistischer Sicht* (Stuttgart 1967); R. Wohlfeil (ed.), *Reformation oder frühbürgerliche Revolution?* (Munich 1972); A. Friesen, *Reformation and Utopia. The Marxist Interpretation of the Reformation and Its Antecedents* (Wiesbaden 1974); M. Bogdahn, *Die Rechtfertigungslehre Luthers im Urteil der neueren katholischen Theologie. Möglichkeiten und Tendenzen der katholischen Lutherdeutung in evangelischer Sicht* (Göttingen 1971).—4. R. Stauffer, *Die Entdeckung Luthers im Katholizismus* (Zurich 1968); W. Beyna, *Das moderne katholische Lutherbild* (Essen 1969); G. Ph. Wolf, *Das neuere französische Lutherbild* (Wiesbaden 1974); K. Aland, *Martin Luther in der modernen Literatur* (Witten 1973); H. Jedin-R. Bäumer, *Die Erforschung der kirchlichen Reformationsgeschichte* (Darmstadt 1975).—5. A. Zumkeller, "Martin Luther und sein Orden" *AA* 25 (1962) 254–290; A. Kunzelmann, *Geschichte der deutschen Augustiner-Eremiten.* Teil V: *Die Sächsich-Thüringische Provinz und die Sächsiche Reformkongregation bis zum Untergang der beiden* (Würzburg 1974).—6. E. Kleineidam, *Universitas Studii Erfordiensis* (Leipzig 1964); E. Iserloh, "Sacramentum et Exemplum. Ein augustinisches Thema lutherischer Theologie" *Reformata* I (Münster 1965) 247–264; G. Baring, "Luther und die "Theologia Deutsch" in der neuesten Forschung" *ThZ* XXIII (1967) 48–62; St. E. Ozment, "Homo Viator: Luther and Late Medieval Theology" *Harv. ThR* 62 (1969) 275–287; H. Hilgenfeld, *Mittelalterlich-traditionelle Elemente in Luthers Abendmahlschriften* (Zurich 1971); K. H. Zur Mühlen, "Zur Rezeption der Augustinischen Sakramentsformel 'Accedit Verbum ad Elementum. et Fit Sacramentum' in der Theologie Luthers" *ZThK* 70 (1973) 50–76.—7. H. Vossberg, *Im Heiligen Rom. Luthers Reiseeindrücke 1510–1511* (Berlin 1966).—8. J. Vercruysse, *Fidelis Populus* (Wiesbaden 1968); S. H. Hendrix, *Ecclesia in Via. Ecclesiological Development in the Medieval Psalms Exegesis and the Dicta Super Psalterium (1513–1515) of Martin Luther* (Leiden 1974).—9. D. Demmer, *Lutherus Interpres. Der theologische Neuansatz in seiner Römerbriefexegese unter besonderer Berücksichtigung Augustins* (Witten 1968); E. Plutta-Messerschmidt, *Gerechtigkeit Gottes bei Paulus. Eine Studie zu Luthers Auslegung von Römer 3–5* (Tübingen 1973).—11. H. Feld, *Martin Luther und Wendelin Steinbachs Vorlesungen über den Hebräerbrief* (Wiesbaden 1971).—12. B. Lohse (ed.), *Der Durchbruch der reformatorischen Erkenntnis bei Luther* (Darmstadt 1968); O. Modalski, "Luthers Turmerlebnis 1515" *StTh* XXII (1968) 51–91; R. Schäfer, "Zur Datierung von Luthers reformatorischer Erkenntnis" *ZThK* 66 (1969) 151–170; O. Bayer, "Die Reformatorische Wende in Luthers Theologie" *ZThK* 66 (1969) 115–150; id., *Promissio. Geschichte der reformatorischen Wende in Luthers Theologie* (Göttingen 1971); A. Franzen (ed.), *Um Reform und Reformation. Zur Frage nach dem Wesen des "Reformatorischen" bei Martin Luther* (Münster 1972).

CHAPTER 3: K. V. Selge, *Normen der Christenheit im Streit um Ablass und Kirchenautorität* (Diss. theol. habil. Heidelberg 1968); R. Bäumer, *Die Diskussion um Luthers Thesenanschlag:* A. Franzen (ed.), *Um Reform und Reformation* (Münster 1968) 53–95.

CHAPTER 4: G. Hennig, *Cajetan und Luther* (Stuttgart 1966); G. Müller, "Die römische Kurie und die Anfänge der Reformation" *ZRGG* XIX (1967) 1–32; U. Mauser, *Der Junge Luther und die Häresie* (Gütersloh 1968); W. Borth, *Die Luthersache (Causa Lutheri) 1517–24* (Lübeck 1970); R. Bäumer, *Martin Luther und der Papst* (Münster 1971); id. (ed.), *Lutherprozess und Lutherbann. Vorgeschichte, Ergebnis, Nachwirkung* (Münster 1972); E. Iserloh, *Aufhebung des Lutherbannes?;* R. Bäumer (ed.), *Lutherprozess und Lutherbann* (Münster 1972) 69–80; D. Oliver, *Der Fall Luthers. Geschichte einer Verurteilung 1517–1521* (Stuttgart 1972); W. Delius, "Der Augustinerorden im Prozess Luthers" *ARG* 63 (1972) 22–42. M. O'Connell, "Cardinal Cajetan: Intellectual and Activist" *The New Scholasticism* L, no. 3 (1976) 310–322.

CHAPTER 5: F. Mann, *Das Abendmahl beim Jungen Luther* (Munich 1971).

CHAPTER 6: E. W. Kohls, *Luthers Entscheidung in Worms* (Stuttgart 1970); F. Reuter (ed.), *Der Wormser Reichstag von 1521. Reichspolitik und Luthersache* (Worms 1971); H. Steitz, *Martin Luther auf dem Reichstag zu Worms 1521* (Frankfurt a. M. 1971); E. W. Kohls, "Die Deutungen des Verhaltens in Worms innerhalb der neueren Historiographie" *ARG* 63 (1972) 43–71; F. T. Bos, *Luther in het orded van de Sorbonne* (Amsterdam 1974).

CHAPTER 7: C. F. Wiesløff, *Abendmahl und Messe. Die Kritik Luthers am Messopfer* (Berlin 1969); F. Pratzner, *Messe und Kreuzesopfer. Die Krise der sakramentalen Idee bei*

Luther und in der mittelalterlichen Scholastik (Vienna 1970); J. Rogge, *Gratia und Donum in Luthers Schrift gegen Latomus. Theolog. Versuche* II (Berlin 1970); E. Iserloh, "Gratia und Donum, Rechtfertigung und Heiligung nach Luthers 'Wider den Löwener Theologen Latomus' (1521)" *Luther und die Reformation* (Aschaffenburg 1974) 88–105.

CHAPTER 8: W. Hammer, *Die Melanchthonforschung im Wandel der Jahrhunderte,* 2 vols. (Gütersloh 1966–68); W. Maurer, *Der Junge Melanchthon,* 2 vols. (Göttingen 1967–69); H. H. Holfelder, *Tentatio et Consulato. Studien zu Bugenhagens "Interpretatio in Librum Psalmorum"* (Berlin 1974).

CHAPTER 9: R. E. McNally, "Pope Adrian VI (1522–23) and Church Reform" *AH Pont* 7 (1969) 253–285; K. H. Ducke, *Das Verständnis von Amt und Theologie im Briefwechsel zwischen Hadrian VI und Erasmus von Rotterdam* (Leipzig 1973).

CHAPTER 11: R. J. Sider, *Andreas Bodenstein von Karlstadt. The Development of His Thought 1517–1525* (Leiden 1974); F. Kriechbaum, *Grundzüge der Theologie Karlstadts* (Hamburg 1967); G. Franz (ed.), *Thomas Müntzer. Schriften und Briefe* (Gütersloh 1968); G. Wehr (ed.), *Thomas Müntzer, Schriften und Briefe* (Frankfurt 1973) (lit.); M. Steinmetz, *Das Müntzerbild von M. Luther bis Friedrich Engels* (Berlin 1971); Th. Nipperdey, "Theologie und Revolution bei Th. Müntzer" *ARG* 54 (1963) 145–181; P. Wappler, *Müntzer in Zwickau und die Zwickauer Propheten* (Zwickau 1908, Neudruck Gütersloh 1966); M. Bensing, *Thomas Müntzer und der Thüringer Aufstand 1525* (East Berlin 1966); H. J. Goertz, *Innere und äussere Ordnung in der Theologie Th. Müntzers* (Leiden 1967); E. W. Gritsch, *Reformer without a Church. The Life and Thought of Thomas Muentzer (1448–1525)* (Philadelphia 1967); G. Goldbach, *Hans Denck und Thomas Müntzer* (Diss. Theol. Hamburg 1969); E. Iserloh, "Revolution bei Thomas Müntzer. Durchsetzung des Reiches Gottes oder Soziale Aktion" *H. J.* 92 (1972) 282–299; G. Wehr, *Thomas Müntzer in Selbstzeugnissen und Bilddokumenten* (Reinbeck 1972); K. Ebert, *Theologie und Politisches Handeln. Thomas Müntzer als Modell* (Stuttgart 1973); H. J. Goertz, "Der Mystiker mit dem Hammer. Die Theologische Begründung der Revolution bei Thomas Müntzer" *KuD* 20 (1974) 23–53; W. Elliger, *Thomas Müntzer. Leben und Werk* (Göttingen 1975).

CHAPTER 12: A. Waas, *Die Bauern im Kampf um Gerechtigkeit 1300–1525* (Munich 1964); H. Angermeier, "Die Vorstellung des Gemeinen Mannes von Staat und Reich im Deutschen Bauernkrieg" *VSWG* 53 (1966) 329–343; A. Franke (ed.), *Das Buch der hundert Kapitel und der vierzig Statuten des sog. oberrheinischen Revolutionärs. Historische Analysen von G. Zschäbitz* (Berlin 1967); H. Buszello, *Bauernkrieg von 1525 als politische Bewegung* (Berlin 1969); K. Kaczerowsky (ed.), *Flugschriften des Bauernkrieges* (Reinbeck 1970); D. W. Sabean, *Landbesitz und Gesellschaft am Vorabend des Bauernkrieges* (Stuttgart 1972); H. Vahle, "Der dt. Bauernkrieg als politische Bewegung im Urteil der Geschichtsschreibung" *GWU 23* (1972) 257–277; R. Endres, "Der Bauernkrieg in Franken" *BDLG* 109 (1973) 31–68; P. Blickle, *Landschaften im Alten Reich* (Munich 1973); id., *Die Revolution von 1525* (Munich 1975); M. Brecht, "Der theologische Hintergrund der zwölf Artikel der Bauernschaft in Schwaben von 1525" *ZKG* 85 (1974) 174–208; R. Wohlfeil (ed.), *Der Bauernkrieg 1524–1526. Bauernkrieg und Reformation* (Munich 1975); W. Lenk (ed.), *Dokumente aus dem dt. Bauernkrieg* (Leipzig 1974) (lit.); G. Seebass, "Bauernkrieg und Täufertum in Franken" *ZKG* 85 (1974) 284–300; W. Becker, *Reformation und Revolution* (Münster 1974); M. Bemsing–S. Hoyer, *Der deutsche Bauernkrieg 1524–1526* (Berlin ³1975); G. Heitz, A. Laube, M. Steinmetz, G. Vogler (eds.), *Der Bauer im Klassenkampf* (Berlin 1975); M. Kabusch–E. Müller, *Der deutsche*

Bauernkrieg in Dokumenten (Weimar 1975); *Flugschriften der Bauernkriegszeit,* ed. Christel Laufer et al. (Berlin 1975).

CHAPTER 13: Lewis W. Spitz, *The Renaissance and Reformation Movements* (Chicago 1971); W. P. Eckert, *Erasmus von Rotterdam: Werk und Wirkung* II: *Humanismus und Reformation* (Cologne 1967); H. J. McSorley, *Luthers Lehre vom unfreien Willen* (Munich 1967); R. D. Jones, *Erasmus and Luther* (Oxford 1968); *Colloquia Erasmiana Turonensia* I–II, *Douzième Stage International d'Etudes Humanistes* (Tours 1969); G. Faludy, *Erasmus of Rotterdam* (London 1970); R. H. Bainton, *Erasmus. Reformer zwischen den Fronten* (Göttingen 1972); A. G. Dickens, *The Age of Humanism and Reformation. Europe in the Fourteenth, Fifteenth, and Sixteenth Centuries* (Englewood Cliffs, N.J. 1972); M. Hoffman, *Erkenntis und Verwirklichung der wahren Theologie nach Erasmus von Rotterdam* (Tübingen 1972); A. Rabil, Jr., *Erasmus and the New Testament. The Mind of a Christian Humanist* (San Antonio, Tex., 1972); H. Holeczek, "Die Haltung des Erasmus zu Luther nach dem Scheitern seiner Vermittlungspolitik 1520–21" *ARG* 64 (1973) 85–112; G. B. Winkler, *Erasmus von Rotterdam und die Einleitungsschriften zum NT* (Münster 1974); W. Hentze, *Kirche und Kirchliche Einheit bei Desiderius Erasmus von Rotterdam* (Paderborn 1974); M. Brod, *Johannes Reuchlin und sein Kampf* (Stuttgart 1965); L. Borinski, *Englischer Humanismus und deutsche Reformation* (Göttingen 1969); *Willibald Pirckheimer 1470–1970, Dokumente, Studien, Perspektiven,* ed. W. Pirckheimer-Kuratorium (Nuremberg 1970); W. P. Eckert–Eh. von Imhoff, *W. Pirckheimer, Dürers Freund, im Spiegel seines Lebens, seiner Werke und seiner Umwelt* (Cologne 1971).

CHAPTER 14: F. Büsser, *Das katholische Zwinglibild* (Zürich 1968); U. Gräbler, "Die Zwingli-Forschung seit 1960" *ThLZ* 96 (1971) 481–490; R. Pfister, *Kirchengeschichte der Schweiz* II: *Von der Reformation bis zum Zweiten Villmerger Krieg* (Zürich 1974); J. Courvoisier, *Zwingli als reformierter Theologe* (Neukirchen 1966); R. C. Walton, *Zwingli's Theocracy* (Toronto 1967); R. Hauswirth, *Landgraf Philipp von Hessen und Zwingli* (Tübingen 1968); M. Haas, *Huldrych Zwingli und seine Zeit. Leben und Werk des Zürcher Reformators* (Zürich 1969); G. W. Locher, *Huldrych Zwingli in neuer Sicht* (Zurich 1969); K. Maeder, *Die Via Media in der Schweizerischen Reformation* (Zurich 1970); W. Jacob, *Politische Führungsschicht und Reformation. Untersuchungen zur Reformation in Zürich 1519–1528* (Zurich 1970); O. Scheib, "Die Theologischen Diskussionen Huldrych Zwinglis, in: *Von Konstanz nach Trient,* ed. R. Bäumer (Munich 1972) 395–417.

CHAPTER 15: *Quellen zur Geschichte der Täufer:* Vol. 11 *Österreich I,* ed. G. Mecenseffy (Gütersloh 1964); Vol. 12 *Glaubenszeugnisse oberdeutscher Taufgesinnter,* ed. R. Friedmann (Gütersloh 1967); Vol. 13 *Österreich II,* ed. G. Mecenseffy; R. Friedmann (ed.), *Die Schriften der Huterischen Täufergemeinschaften* (Graz 1965); H. G. Williams, *The Radical Reformation* (Philadelphia 1962); R. Friemann, "Das Täuferische Glaubensgut" *ARG* 55 (1964) 145–161; C. P. Clasen, *Die Wiedertäufer im Herzogtum Württemberg* (Stuttgart 1965); id., *Anabaptism. A Social History 1525–1618* (London 1972); F. H. Littel, *Das Selbstverständnis der Täufer* (Kassel 1966); W. Schäufele, *Das missionarische Bewusstsein und Wirken der Täufer* (Neukirchen 1966); J. H. Yoder, *Täufertum und Reformation im Gespräch* (Zurich 1968); C. Krahn, *Dutch Anabaptism (1450–1600)* (The Hague 1968); H. D. Schmid, "Das Hutsche Täufertum" *HJ* 99 (1971) 327–344; H. D. Plümper, *Die Gütergemeinschaft bei den Taufen des 16 Jahrhunderts* (Göppingen 1972); E. Geldbach, "Toward a More Ample Biography of the Hessian Anabaptist Leader Melchior Rinck" *MQR* 48 (1974) 371–184; G. H. Williams, "German Mysticism in the Polarization of Ethical Behavior in Luther and the Anabaptists" *MQR* 48 (1974) 275–

304; R. von Dülmen (ed.), *Das Täuferreich zu Münster 1534–1535* (Munich 1974) (lit.); R. Stupperich (ed.), *Die Schriften Bernhard Rothmanns* (Münster 1970); J. W. Porter, *Bernhard Rothmann (1495–1535)* (Diss. Wisconsin 1964); G. Brendler, *Das Täuferreich zu Münster 1534–35* (East Berlin 1966); O. Rammstedt, *Sekte und Soziale Bewegung* (Cologne 1966); K. H. Kirchhoff, *Die Täufer in Münster 1534–35* (Münster 1973); G. List, *Chiliastische Utopie und radikale Reformation* (Munich 1973); C. Bornhäuser, *Leben und Lehre Menno Simons': Ein Kampf um das Fundament des Glaubens* (ca. 1469–1561) (Neukirchen-Vluyn 1973); M. Barbers, *Toleranz bei Sebastian Franck* (Bonn 1964); H. Weigelt, *Sebastian Frank und die lutherische Reformation* (Gütersloh 1972); E. W. Gerdes, "Pietistisches bei Kaspar von Schwenckfeld" *Miscellanea Historiae Ecclesiasticae* (Louvain 1967) 105–137.

CHAPTER 16: J. Lortz, "Wert und Grenzen der Katholischen Kontroverstheologie" A. Franzen (ed.), *Um Reform und Reformation* (Münster 1968) 9–32; F.-J. Kötter, *Die Eucharistielehre in den katholischen Katechismen des 16 Jahrundert* (Münster 1969); P. Fraenkel, "John Eck's Enchiridion of 1525 and Luther's Earliest Arguments Against Papal Primacy" *StTh* 21 (1967) 110–163; id., "Johann Eck und Sir Thomas More 1525 bis 1526," in: *Von Konstanz nach Trient,* ed. R. Bäumer (Munich 1972) 519–545; K. Rischer, *Johann Eck auf dem Reichstag zu Augsburg 1530* (Münster 1968); H. A. Oberman, "Wittenbergs Zweifrontenkrieg gegen Prierias und Eck" *ZKG* 80 (1969) 331–358; G. Epiney-Burgard, *Jean Eck et le Commentaire de la Théologie Mystique du Pseudo-Denys.* Bibliothèque d'Humanisme et Renaissance 34 (1972) 7–29; E. Iserloh, "Die Verteidigung der Bilder durch Johannes Eck zu Beginn des Reformatorischen Bildersturms: Aus Reformation und Gegenreformation" *Würzburger Diözesan-Geschichtsblätter* 35–36 (1974) 75–85; J. Beumer, "Friedrich Nausea und seine Wirksameit zu Frankfurt, auf den Colloquien zu Hagenau und Worms und auf dem Trienter Konzil" *ZKTh* 94 (1972) 29–45; R. Bäumer, "Das Kirchenverständnis Albert Pigges" *Volk Gottes* (Freiburg 1967) 306–322; J. Rouchausse, *La Vie et l'Oeuvre de John Fisher, Évêque de Rochester, 1496–1535* (Nieuwkoop–Angers 1972); E. Surtz SJ, *The Works and Days of John Fisher. An Introduction to the Position of St. John Fisher (1496–1535), Bishop of Rochester, in the English Renaissance and the Reformation* (Cambridge, Mass., 1967); J. Rouchausse (ed.), *Erasmus and Fisher. Their Correspondence, 1511–1524* (Paris 1968); A. Bodem, *Das Wesen der Kirche nach Kardinal Cajetan. Ein Beitrag zur Ekklesiologie im Zeitalter der Reformation* (Trier 1971); M. W. Anderson, "Thomas Cajetan's Scientia Christi" *ThZ* 26 (1970) 99–108; J. P. Massaut, *Josse Clichtove: l'Humanisme et la Réforme du Clergé (1472–1520),* 2 vols. (Paris 1969); G. Chaintraine SJ, "Josse Clichtove: Témoin de l'Humanisme Parisien. Scolastique et Célibat au XVIe Siècle" *RHE* 66 (1971) 507–528; R. Braunisch, *Die Theologie der Rechtfertigung im "Enchiridion" (1538) des Johannes Gropper* (Münster 1974); O. Müller, *Bischof. J. Pflug von Naumburg-Zeitz in seinem Bemühen um die Einheit der Kirche. Beiträge zu Gesch. des Erzb. Magdeburg* (Leipzig 1968) 155–178; Julius Pflug, *Correspondence,* ed. J. V. Pollet, 2 vols. to date (Leiden 1969–73); J. V. Pollet, "Gropper und J. Pflug nach ihrer Korrespondenz" *Paderbornensis Ecclesia* (Paderborn 1972) 223–244; W. Kaliner, *J. Pflugs Verhältnis zur "Christlichen Lehre" des Johann von Maltitz* (Leipzig 1972).

THOMAS MURNER, *Werke* (German), ed. F. Schultz, 9 vols. (Strassburg–Berlin 1918–1928); "Des alten christl. Bären Testament," ed. M. Scherer: *Anzeiger für Schweizer. Gesch.* 50 (Bern 1919) 6–38; "Des Jungen Bären Zahnweh," ed. J. Lefftz: *AElsKG* 1 (1926) 141–167; "Purgatio Vulgaris," ed. J. Lefftz: *AElsKG* 3 (1928) 97–114; *Die gottesheilige Messe,* ed. W. Pfeiffer-Belli (Halle 1928); *M. im Schweizer Glaubenskampf,* ed. W. Pfeiffer-Belli (Münster 1939); "De Immaculata Virginis Conceptione. Eine unvollendete Jugendschr.," ed. F. Landmann: *AElsKG* 15 (1941–42) 73–128.—Lit.: Th. von Liebenau, *Der Franziskaner Dr. Th. M.* (Freiburg 1913); J. Lefftz, *Die Volkstüml. Stilelemente in M.s Satiren* (Strassburg 1915); E. Fuchs, "M.s Belesenheit, Bildungsgang u. Wissen" *FStud* 9 (1922) 70–79; P. Scherer, *M.s Verhältnis zum Humanismus* (Basel 1929); F. Landmann, "M. als Prediger" *AElsKG* 10 (1935) 295–368; M. Sondheim, *M. als Astrolog* (Strassburg 1938); R. Newald, "Wandlungen des M.bildes: Beitr. z. Geistes- u. Kulturgesch. der Oberrheinlande," ed. H. Gumbel (Fr 1938) 40–78; id., *Elsässische Charakterköpfe aus dem Zeitalter des Humanismus* (Colmar 1944) III:185; A. Erler, *M. als Jurist* (Freiburg 1956). P. L. Nyhus, "Caspar Schatzgeyer and Conrad Pellican: The Triumph of Dissension in the Early Sixteenth Century" *ARG* 61 (1970) 179–204; J. Beumer, "Erasmus von Rotterdam und G. Witzel" *Cath* 22 (1968) 41–67; G. Scholtz, *Die Aufzeichnungen des Hildesheimer Dechanten Johan Oldecop (1493–1574). Reformation und katholische Kirche im Spiegel von Chroniken des 16. Jahrhunderts* (Münster 1972).

CHAPTER 17: E. Fabian (ed.), *Quellen zur Gesch. der Reformationshindernisse und der Konstanzer Reformationsprozesse 1529–1548* (Tübingen 1967); O. Scheib, *Die Reformationsdiskussionen in der Hansestadt Hamburg 1522–28* (Münster 1975).

CHAPTER 18: H. Kunst (ed.), *Martin Luther und die Kirche* (Stuttgart 1971); H. W. Krumwiede, *Zur Entstehung des landesherrlichen Kirchenregiments in Kursachsen und Braunschweig-Wolfenbüttel* (Göttingen 1967); H. H. Schrey (ed.), *Reich Gottes und Welt. Die Lehre Luthers von den zwei Reichen* (Darmstadt 1969); U. Duchrow, *Christenheit und Weltverantwortung. Traditionsgeschichte und syst. Struktur der Zwei-Reiche-Lehre* (Stuttgart 1970); A. Hakamies, *Eigengesetzlichkeit der natürlichen Ordnungen als Grundproblem der neueren Lutherdeutung. Studien zur Geschichte der Problematik der Zwei-Reiche-Lehre Luthers* (Witten 1971); G. Ruhbach (ed.), *Die Vorstellung von zwei Reichen und Regimentern bis Luther* (Gütersloh 1972); G. Wolf, *Luther und die Obrigkeit* (Darmstadt 1972); R. Ohlig, *Die Zwei-Reiche-Lehre Luthers in der Auslegung der deutschen lutherischen Theologie der Gegenwart seit 1945* (Diss. Theol. Münster 1974); J. Haun (ed.), *Zur Zwei-Reiche-Lehre Luthers* (Munich 1973) (lit.); K. Trüdinger, *Luthers Briefe und Gutachten an weltliche Obrigkeiten zur Durchführung der Reformation* (Münster 1975); J. Aarts, *Die Lehre Martin Luthers über das Amt in der Kirche. Eine genetisch-systematische Untersuchung seiner Schriften von 1512 bis 1525* (Hämeenliena–Helsinki 1972); P. Manns, "Amt und Eucharistie in der Theologie Martin Luthers," in: *Amt und Eucharistie,* with additions by P. Bläser et al. (Paderborn 1973) 68–173; W. Stein, *Das Kirchliche Amt bei Luther* (Wiesbaden 1974).

CHAPTER 19: P. Johannsen, "Gedruckte deutsche und undeutsche Messen für Riga" *Zschr. f. Ostforschung* 8 (1959) 523–532; E. W. Kohls (ed.), *Evangelische Katechism in der Reformationszeit vor und neben Martin Luthers Kleinem Katechismus* (Gütersloh 1971).

CHAPTER 20: G. Müller, *Die römische Kurie und die Reformation 1523–34. Kirche und Politik während des Pontifikats Clemens VII.* (Gütersloh 1969).

CHAPTER 21: G. Mog (ed.), *Das Marburger Religionsgespräch* (Gütersloh 1970); S. Hausmann, *Römerbriefauslegung zwischen Humanismus und Reformation* (Zurich 1970); Heinrich Bullinger, *Werke. Zweite Abteilung. Briefwechsel. Bd 1 Brr. der Jahre 1524 bis 1531,* updated by Ulrich Gabler and Endre Zsindely (Zurich 1973); J. Staedtke, *Beschreibendes Verzeichnis der gedruckten Werke von Heinrich Bullinger* (Zurich 1972); Ph. Melanchthon, *Apologia Confessionis Augustanae,* ed. H. G. Pöhlmann (Gütersloh 1967).

CHAPTER 22: W. Günther, *Martin Luther und die Reichsverfassung* (Diss. Phil. Freiburg 1972); W. Maurer, "Zur Entstehung und Textgeschichte der Schwabacher Artikel" *The-*

ologie in Geschichte und Kunst. Walter Elliger zum 65 Geburtstag (Witten 1968) 134–151; K. Rischar, *Johann Eck auf dem Reichstag zu Augsburg* (Münster 1968), W. Maurer, "Erwägungen und Verhandlungen über die Geistliche Jurisdiktion der Bischöfe vor und während des Augsburger Reichstags von 1530" *ZSavRGkan* 55 (1969) 348–394; L. Grane, *Die Confessio Augustana* (Wiesbaden 1970); G. Müller, 'Kardinal Lorenzo Campeggio, die Römische Kurie und der Augsburger Reichstag von 1530" *NAKG* 52 (1972) 133–152; E. Honée, "Die Theologische Diskussion über den Laienkelch auf dem Augsburger Reichstag 1530. Versuch einer historischen Rekonstruktion" *NAKG* 52 (1972) 1–96; H. Immenkötter, *Um die Einheit im Glauben* (Münster 1974); M. Bucer, *Opera Omnia.* Ser. I: *Deutsche Schriften.* Vol. 3: *Confessio Tetrapolitana und die Schriften des Jahres 1531,* ed. R. Stupperich (Gütersloh 1969); A. Engelbrecht, "*Abconterfeytung Martin Butzers*" (1546), ed. W. Bellardi (Münster 1974): *CCath* 31; E. W. Kohls, "Martin Bucers Katechismus vom Jahre 1534 und seine Stellung innerhalb der Katechismusgeschichte" *ZBKG* 39 (1970) 83–94; W. P. Steffens, *The Holy Spirit in the Theology of Martin Bucer* (Cambridge 1970).

CHAPTER 23: H. Scheible (ed.), *Das Widerstandsrecht als Problem der deutschen Protestanten 1523–46* (Gütersloh 1969) (lit.); W. von Loewenich, *Duplex Iustitia. Luthers Stellung zu einer Unionsformel des 16. Jahrhunderts* (Wiesbaden 1972); P. Matheson, *Cardinal Contarini at Regensburg* (Oxford 1972).

CHAPTER 24: Hermann von Wied, *Einfältiges Bedenken. Reformationsentwurf für das Erzstift Köln von 1543,* ed. H. Gerhards–W. Borth (Düsseldorf 1972); A. Franzen, *Bischof und Reformation. Erzb. Hermann von Wied in Cologne* (Münster 1972); id., "Zur Vorgeschichte des Reformationsversuchs des Kölner Erzbischofs Hermann von Wied" *HJ* 88 (1968) 300–324; id., "Hermann von Wied, Kurfürst und Erzbischof von Köln" *Der Reichstag zu Worms von 1521* (Worms 1971) 297–315; H. Buck–E. Fabian, *Konstanzer Reformationsgeschichte in ihren Grundzügen* (Tübingen 1965); H. C. Rublack, *Die Einführung der Reformation in Konstanz von den Anfängen bis zum Abschluss 1531* (Gütersloh 1971); B. Caspar, *Das Erzbistum Trier im Zeitalter der Glaubensspaltung* (Münster 1966); M. M. Chrisman, *Strasbourg and the Reform* (New York 1967); H. Stratenworth, *Die Reformation in der Stadt Osnabrück* (Wiesbaden 1971); J. Vögeli (ed.), *Schriften zur Reformation in Konstanz, 1519–38* (Tübingen 1973); Interim: *Acta Reformationis Catholicae* IV (Regensburg 1974) 255–348; J. Mehlhausen (ed.), *Das Augsburger Interim von 1548. Nach den Reichstagsakten Deutsch und Lateinisch herausgegeben* (Neukirchen 1970); H. Jedin, *Interim statt Konzil: Gesch. d. Konzils v. Trient* III (Freiburg 1970) 197–215; H. Rabe, *Reichsbund und Interim. Die Verfassung und Religionspolitik Karls V. und der Reichstag von Augsburg 1547–1548* (Cologne 1971); M. Stupperich, "Das Augsburger Interim als apokalyptisches Geschehnis nach den Königsberger Schriften Andreas Osianders" *ARG* 64 (1973) 225–245; W. Bellardi, "Bucers 'Summarischer Vergriff' und das Interim in Strassburg" *ZKG* 85 (1974) 64–76.

CHAPTER 26: *Ausgewählte Quellen zur Kirchengeschichte Ostmitteleuropas,* ed. Ostkirchenausschuss Hannover (Ulm 1959); B. Geissler–G. Stöckl, in: *Oriente Crux. Versuch einer Geschichte der reformatorischen Kirchen im Raum zwischen der Ostsee und dem Schwarzen Meer* (Stuttgart 1963); K. Juhasz, *Das Tschanad-Temesvarer Bistum im Spätmittelalter 1307—1572* (Munich-Paderborn 1964); P. Kawerau, "Die Reformation in Ost- und Südosteuropa" *Reformation und Gegenwart,* ed. H. Grass (Marburg 1968); C. Bonorand, "Joachim Vadians Beziehung zu Ungarn" *Zwingli* 13 (1969) 97–131; D. Caccamo, *Eretici Italiani in Moravia, Polonia, Transilvania (1558–1611)* (Florence 1970); U. Arnold, "Luther und Danzig" (lit.) *Zschr. f. Ostforschung* 21 (1972) 94–121.

CHAPTER 27: Ph. Hughes, *Theology of the English Reformers* (London 1965); W. P. Haugaard, *Elizabeth and the English Reformation* (London 1968); J. Ridley, *John Knox* (London 1968).

CHAPTER 28: E. O. Reichert, "In Tanta Ecclesiarum Mestitia" *ZKG* 78 (1967) 253–270; *Andreas Osiander d. Ä. Gesamtausgabe Bd. 1. Schriften und Briefe 1522 bis März 1525*, in Zusammenarbeit mit Gottfried Seebass, ed. Gerhard Müller (Gütersloh 1975); J. Seebass, *Bibliographia Osiandrica* (Nieuwkoop 1971); G. Seebass, *Das Reformatorische Werke des A. Osiander* (Nuremberg 1967).

CHAPTER 29: R. Stauffer, *Calvins Menschlichkeit* (Zurich 1964); J. I. Packer, *Calvin the Theologian: Courtenay Studies in Reformation Theology* I (Abingdon 1966) 149–175; Fr. Wendel, *Calvin. Ursprung und Entwicklung seiner Theologie* (Neukirchen 1968); A. Ganoczy, *Ecclesia Ministrans. Dienende Kirche und kirchlicher Dienst bei Calvin* (Freiburg 1968); D. Schellong, *Das Evangelische Gesetz in der Auslegung Calvins* (Munich 1968); J. Staestke, *Johannes Calvin* (Göttingen 1969); D. Schellong, *Calvins Auslegung der synoptischen Evangelien* (Munich 1969); J. Cadier, "La Conversion de Calvin" *Bull-SocHistPrFr* 116 (1970) 142–151; T. W. Casteel, "Calvin and Trent" *HTR* 63 (1970) 91–117; W. Neuser, *Calvin* (Berlin 1971); U. Schmidt (ed.), *Johannes Calvin und die Kirche. Ein Lesebuch* (Stuttgart 1972); T. Stadtland, *Rechfertigung und Heiligung bei Calvin* (Neukirchen 1972); H. Schützeichel, *Die Christologie Calvins* (Munich 1972); id., *Die Glaubenstheologie Calvins* (Munich 1972); W. Bahkle, *Calvijn en de Doperse Radikalen* (Amsterdam 1973); J. Bratt (ed.), *The Heritage of John Calvin. Heritage Hall Lectures 1960–70* (Grand Rapids, Mich. 1973); U. Plath, *Calvin und Basel in den Jahren 1552 bis 1556* (Zurich 1974).

CHAPTER 30: K. J. Seidel, *Frankreich und die deutschen Protestanten* (Münster 1970); J. N. Bakhuizen van den Brink, "De Bartholomeusnacht" *NAKG* 54 (1973) 77–105; J. Railt, *The Eucharistic Theology of Theodore Beza. Development of the Reformed Doctrine* (Chambersburg, Pa. 1972); O. de Jong, "Die Emder Generalsynode vor dem Hintergrund der Westeuropäischen Reformationsgeschichte" *Jb. d. Gesellsch. für Niedersächsische KG* 68 (1970) 9–24; W. Reinhard, *Die Reform in der Diözese Carpentras unter den Bischöfen J. Sadoleto, P. Sadoleto, J. Sacrati, und F. Sadoleto 1517–1596* (Münster 1966); C. A. Tucker, *De Classis Dordrecht van 1573–1609* (Leiden 1965); O. Press, *Calvinismus und Territorial-Staat. Regierung und Zentralbehörden der Kurpfalz 1559–1619* (Stuttgart 1970); M. Schaab, "Die Wiederherstellung des Katholizismus in der Kurpfalz in XVII und XVIII Jh" *ZGObrh* 114 (1966) 147–205; W. Hollweg, *Neue Untersuchungen zur Geschichte und Lehre des Heidelberger Katechismus* II (Neukirchen 1968); G. Güldner, *Das Toleranz-Problem in den Niederlanden im Ausgang des 16. Jahrhunderts* (Lübeck 1968); H. J. Hillerbrand, "The Spread of the Protestant Reformation of the 16th Century" *The South Atlantic Quarterly* 47 (1968) 265–286; H. Schilling, *Niederländische Exulanten im 16. Jahrhundert* (Gütersloh 1972); U. Beyer, *Abendmahl und Messe. Sinn und Recht der 80. Frage des Heidelberger Katechismus* (Neukirchen 1965); *Mélanges d'Histoire du XVIᵉ Siècle: Offers à Henri Meylan* (Geneva 1970); D. Nugent, *Ecumenism in the Age of the Reformation: The Colloquy of Poissy* (Cambridge, Mass., 1974); E. Droz, *Chemins de l'Hérésie: Textes et Documents.* 2 vols. (Geneva 1970–71); N. M. Sutherland, *The Massacre of St. Bartholomew and the European Conflict, 1559–1572* (New York, 1973); P. Bietenholz, *Basle and France in the 16th Century: The Basle Humanists and Printers* (Toronto 1971); H. Salmon, *The French Wars of Religion* (Boston 1967).

CHAPTER 31: E. Hassinger, *Religiöse Toleranz im 16. Jahrhundert* (Basel 1966); F. Schrader, *Die Visitationen der kath. Klöster im Erzbistum Magdeburg durch die evgl. Landesherren 1561–1651* (Münster 1969); id., *Reformation und katholische Klöster* (Leipzig 1973); E. W. Zeeden (ed.), *Gegenreformation* (Darmstadt 1973); H. J. Köhler, *Obrigkeitliche Konfessionsänderung in Kondominaten* (Münster 1975).

Part Two

Basic Ideas and General Descriptions

The two components of the ecclesiastical renewal of the Tridentine Era, "Catholic Reform" and "Counter Reformation," have found in historiography, if not in general, a more univocal significance in so far as, since the Second Vatican Council, one speaks of the end of the Counter Reformation. From the copious body of literature accepting this assumption we list the following selections: F. Molinari, "La Riforma Cattolica" *Scuola Cattolica* 97 (1969) 163ff. (lit.); I. C. Olin, *The Catholic Reformation* (New York 1969); R. Garcia Villada–B. Llorca, *Historia de la Iglesia Católica* III: *Edad Nueva. La Iglesia en la Época del Rinacimiento y de la Reforma Católica* (Madrid 1967); *Sacramentum Mundi* II 1078ff.; M. Marocchi provides evidence for the continuance of reform efforts within the Church in *La Riforma Cattolica, Documenti e Testimonianze*, 2 vols. (Brescia 1970). That Luther and Ignatius of Loyola and the Tridentine Reform really belong to the world of the Middle Ages is the theme of F. Rapp, *L'Église et la Vie Religieuse en Occident à la Fin du Moyen Âge* (Paris 1971). Although the author is close to our position, he nevertheless maintains the traditional distinction: H. D. Evennett, *The Spirit of the Counter-Reformation*, edited by I. Bossy (Cambridge, 1968), lecture on the subject in: I. W. O'Malley, "Recent Studies in Church History 1300–1600" *CHR* 55 (1969) 394–437; the widest survey of bibliography is in *AHPont;* M. B. O'Connell, *The Counter Reformation: 1559–1610* (New York 1974).

SECTION ONE

Origin and Breakthrough of the Catholic Reform to 1563

EARLY PHASES IN ITALY AND SPAIN: Italian reform bishops of the 15th cent.: L. Pesce, *Ludovico Barbo, Vescovo di Treviso 1437–1443*, 2 vols. (Padua 1969); St. Orlandi, *S. Antonino. Studi Bio-bibliografici*, 2 vols. (Florence 1960); id., "Gli Ultimi Otto Anni di Episcopato di S. Antonino secondo il Registro di Entrata e Uscita e Molti Altri Documenti Inediti" *Memorie Domenicane* NS 36 (1960) 169–248; G. Dufner, "Antonio

Bettini, Jesuat und Bischof von Foligno" *RSTI* 18 (1964) 399–428 (B., +1487, personally pious and an active publicist, he was of little importance in Foligno); A. Prosperi, *Tra Evangelismo e Controriforma: G. M. Giberti, 1495–1543* (Rome 1969), presently the most comprehensive biography of the famous bishop; V. Meneghini, "Due Compagnie sul Modello di Quelle del Divino Amore Fondate da Francescani a Feltre e Verona 1499–1503" *AFH* 62 (1969) 518–564; N. H. Minnich, "Concepts of Reform Proposed to the Fifth Lateran Council" *AHPont* 7 (1969) 163–251.—Important for Savonarola's influence: R. Creytens, "Les Actes Capitulaires de la Congregation Toscano-Romaine OP (1496–1530)" *AFP* 40 (1970) 125–230.

CHURCH REFORM IN SPAIN AT THE TURN OF THE FIFTEENTH TO SIXTEENTH CENTURIES: I. Garcia Oro, *La Reforma de los Religiosos Españoles en Tiempo de los Reyes Católicos* (Valladolid 1969); id., *Cisneros y la Reforma del Clero Español en Tiempo de los Reyes Católicos* (Madrid 1971); Tarsicio de Ascona, "Reforma de la Provincia Francescana de la Corona de Aragón en Tiempo de los Reyes Católicos" *EstFranc* 7 (1970) 245–344.—J. P. Massaut, *Josse Clichtove. L'Humanisme et la Réforme du Clergé*, 2 vols. (Paris 1968). On the Bishop of Albi's not too successful efforts to reform the French Carmelites: L. van Wijnen, *La Congrégation d'Albi (1499–1602)* (Rome 1971).

NEW ORDERS: G. Llompart, *Caetano de Thiene. Estudios Sobre un Reformator Religioso* (Wiesbaden 1969); C. Linari, "Il Beato Giovanni Marinoni" *Regnum Dei* (1962) 7–46, biography of the Theatine of Venice; Ph. Caraman, *Sant'Angela Merici. Vita della Fondatrice della Compagnie di Sant'Orsola e della Orsoline* (Bresica 1965); L. Moletta, *La Compagnie di S. Angela Merici a Chiari e le Sue Opere* (Bresica 1966); T. Ledóchowska, *Angèle Merici et la Compagnie de Sainte-Ursule à la Lumière des Documents*, 2 vols. (Rome 1967).

IGNATIUS OF LOYOLA AND THE FOUNDING OF THE SOCIETY OF JESUS: Bibliography *AHSJ* 35 (1966) 420ff. and the following volúmes, finally 43 (1974) 399ff.; I. Iparaguirre, "Desmitificación de S. Ignacio" *AHSJ* 41 (1972) 357–87; A. Jiménez Oñate, *El Origen de la Compañia de Jesús* (Rome 1966).—On the constitutions of the orders: G. Philippart, "Visiteurs, Commissaires, et Inspecteurs dans la Compagnie de Jesus de 1540 à 1615" *AHSJ* 37 (1968).—Important on pedagogical methods: G. Codina, *Aux Sources de la Pédagogie des Jesuites. Le "Modus Parisiensis"* (Rome 1968); the sources in the early period from 1500 to 1556 in the *Monumenta Paedagogica Soc. Jesu* I, edited by L. Lukács (Rome 1965); M. Foss, *The Founding of the Jesuits* (London 1969), in *AHSJ* 43 (1974) 176ff., not adequately evaluated; E. M. Buxbaum, *Petrus Canisius und die kircheiche Erneuerung des Herzogtums Bayern 1459–1556* (Rome 1973).

THE COUNCIL OF TRENT: The edition of the Acts has been continued by Th. Freudenberger VII:2 (1975); Vol. III of Jedin's *Council of Trent,* treating the Bologna period and the second period at Trent, appeared in 1970; Vol. IV, on the conclusion, 1562–63, appeared in 1975; H. Rabe, *Reichsbund und Interim. Die Verfassungs- und Religionspolitik Karls V. und der Reichstag von Augsburg 1547–48* (Cologne 1971).—On the position of the Protestants at Trent, 1551–52, see M. Brecht, "Abgrenzung oder Verständigung. Was wollten die Protestanten in Trient" *Blätter f. Württembergische Kirchengeschichte* 70 (1970) 148–175; F. Schrader, "Die Beschickung des Konzils von Trient durch die Diözesen Magdeburg, Halberstadt, Merseburg, Naumburg und Meissen. Ein Briefwechsel aus den Jahren 1551–52" *AHC* 2 (1970) 303–352.—The debate on the Constitution on Divine Revelation at Vatican II produced a copious body of literature on the subject of the relationship between scripture and tradition, especially by Ortigues,

Congar, Bévenot, and others, cited by J. Ratzinger in: *Das Zweite Vatikanische Konzil* II (Freiburg 1967) 498ff.; M. Midali, "Rivelazione, Chiesa, Scrittura, e Tradizione alle IV Sessione del Concilio di Trento" *Salesianum* 34, 607–650; 35 (1973) 3–51, 179–246.—Other difficult issues, especially in the postconciliar discussions on the sense and importance of the Tridentine decrees were those on original sin (Sess. V); Z. Alszeghy–M. Flick, "Il Decreto Tridentino sul Peccato Originale" *Gregorianum* 52 (1971) 595–635; B. A. Vanneste, *Het Dogma van de Erfzonde* (Utrecht 1969).—On the Eucharist (Sess. XIII), J. Wohlmuth, *Realpräsenz und Transsubstantiation im Konzil von Trient,* 2 vols. (Bern–Frankfurt 1975); G. Fahrnberger, *Amt und Eucharistie auf dem Konzil von Trient,* in: P. Bläser, *Amt und Eucharistie* (Paderborn 1973) 174–207.—On the sacrament of penance (Sess. XIV): H. Jedin, "La Nécessité de la Confession Privée selon le Concile de Trente" *La Maison Dieu* 104 (1970) 88–115; K. J. Becker, "Die Notwendigkeit des vollständigen Bekenntnisses in der Beichte nach dem Konzil von Trient" *Theologie und Philosophie* 47 (1972) 161–228, on canon 3 and 10; Fr. Rodriquez: *Burgense* 13 (1972) 69–84; 14 (1973) 107–136; reaching further back, L. Braekmans, *Confession et Communion au Moyen Âge et au Concile de Trente* (Gembloux 1971).—On the decree on orders (Sess. XXIII): G. Fahrnberger, *Bischofsamt und Priestertum in den Diskussionen des Konzils von Trient* (Vienna 1970); P. F. Franzen, *Das Konzil von Trient und das Priestertum: Priester-Beruf im Widerstreit,* ed. A. Descamos (Innsbruck 1971) 101–137; more on this by I. A. De Aldama, B. Jacqueline, J. Saraiva Martins in: *Teologia del Sacerdocio* V (Burgos 1973); J. Galot, "Le Caratère Sacerdotal selon le Concile de Trente" *NRTh* 93 (1971) 123–946.—The sacrament of marriage and the Tametsi: H. Jedin, *Die Unauflöslichkeit der Ehe nach dem Konzil von Trient:* K. Reinhard–H. Jedin, *Ehe–Sakrament in der Kirche des Herrn* (Berlin 1971) 61–109, 123–135; G. Di Mattia, "La Dotrina sulla Formazione Canonica del Matrimonio e la Proposta per un Suo Esame" *Apollinaris* 44 (1971) 471–522.—Material especially on the origin and implementation of the reform decrees of Trent in: *Il Concilio di Trento. Atti del Convegno Internazionale Trento 2-6 Settembre 1963,* 2 vols. (Rome 1965); H. Jedin, *Kirche des Glaubens—Kirche der Geschichte* II (Freiburg 1966) (this contains the largest collection of essays by the author on the history of the Council of Trent).

SECTION TWO

The Papacy and the Implementation of the Council of Trent (1565–1605)

THE PAPACY, ROME, AND ITALY: H. Jedin, "Nuntiaturberichte und Durchführung des Konzils von Trient" *QF* 63 (1973) 180–213; in the same volume are contributions by H. Lutz, G. Lutz, G. Müller, and H. Goetz on the criticisms and evaluations of the reports of the papal nuncios; of special interest here is K. Repgen, "Die Finanzen des Nuntius Fabio Chigi. Ein Beitrag zur Sozialgeschichte der römischen Führungsgruppe im 17. Jh." *Geschichte—Wirtschaft—Gesellschaft. Festschrift Clemens Bauer* (Berlin 1974) 220–280; J. Krasenbrink, *Die Congregatio Germanica und die Kath. Reform in Deutschland nach dem Tridentium* (Münster 1972) (=RST 105); H. Jedin, *Papst Pius V., die Heilige*

Liga und der Kreuzzugsgedanke: Il Mediterraneo nella Seconda Metà del '500 alla Luce di Lepanto (Florence (1974) 193–213; A. Walz, "S. Tommaso d'Aquino Dichiarto Dottore della Chiesa nel 1567" *Angelicum* 44 (1967) 145–173; P. Hurtubise, "Comment Rome apprit la Nouvelle du Massacre de la Sainte Barthélemy" *AHPont* 10 (1972) 187–210; J. Mieck, "Die Bartholomäusnacht als Forschungsproblem" *HZ* 216 (1973) 73–110; N. Sutherland, *The Massacre of St. Bartholomew and the European Conflict 1559–1572* (New York 1973); H. D. R. Veroliet, "Robert Granjou à Rome 1578–1589. Note Préliminaire à une Histoire de la Typographie Romaine à la fin du XVIᵉ Siècle" *Bull. de l'Institut Belge de Rome* 38 (1967) 177–231; H. Jedin, *Die Autobiographie des Kardinals G. A. Santorio* (Wiesbaden 1969) (=Akademie der Wiss. und der Literatur Mainz, Abh. d. Geistes- und Sozialwiss. Klasse; Jg. 1969, 2); V. Peri, "La Congregazione dei Greci e i Suoi Primi Documenti" *Studia Gratiana* 13:129–256; V. Peri, *Chiesa Romana a "Rito" Greco. G. A. Santoro e la Congregazione dei Greci 1566–1596* (Brescia 1975); J. Krajčar, "The Greek College under the Jesuits for the First Time 1591–1604" *OrChrP* 31 (1965) 85–118; A. Gasparini, *Cesare d'Este e Clemente VIII* (Modena 1960); P. Bartl, "Marciare Verso Constantinopoli. Zur Türkenpolitik Klemens' VIII" *Saeculum* 20 (1969) 44–56.

CHARLES BORROMEO: P. Prodi, "Charles Borromée, Archévêque de Milan et la Papaute" *RHE* 62 (1967) 379–411; G. Alberigo, "Carlo Borromeo come Modello di Vescovo nella Chiesa Posttridentina" *RSIt* 79 (1967) 1031–1052; R. Robres Lluch, "La Congregación del Concilio y S. Carlos Borromeo en la Problemática y Curso de la Contrarreforma 1593–1600" *Anth. An.* 14 (1966) 101–171; a brief compilation with a digest of the canonization decrees and the extensive investigations of E. Cattaneo, C. Marcora, and A. Rimoldi: H. Jedin, *Carlo Borromeo ed il Card. Agostino Valier 1566–84* (Verona 1972), contains the correspondence.

ITALY: Examples of apostolic and episcopal visitations in Marocchi, *La Riforma Cattolica* II:13–44; also S. Tramontin, "La Visita Apostolica del 1581 a Venezia" *St. Ven.* 9 (1967) 453–533; for the Kingdom of Naples: *Nunziature di Napoli* II (1577–1587), ed. P. Villani–D. Veneruso (Rome 1969), and III (1587–1591), ed. B. Bettoni (Rome 1970); D. Fenlon, *Heresy and Obedience in Tridentine Italy: Cardinal Pole and the Counter Reformation* (Cambridge 1972).

SPAIN: B. Llorca, "Acceptación en España de los Decretos del Concilio de Trento" *EE* 39 (1964) 341–360, 459–482; J. L. Santos Diez, *Politica Conciliar Postridentina en España. El Concilio Provincial de Toledo 1565* (Rome 1969); A. Marin Ocete, "El Concilio Provincial de Granada en 1565" *ArchTeolGran* 25 (1962) 23–178; J. Villegas, *Die Durchführung der Beschlüsse des Konzils von Trient in der Kirchenprovinz Peru 1564–1600; Die Bischöfe und die Reform der Kirche* (Cologne 1971); Introduction at the parish level: J. I. Tellechea Idigoras, *La Reforma Tridentina en San Sebastián. El Libro de Mandatos de Visita de la Parroquia de San Vicente 1540–1670* (San Sebastián 1970).

FRANCE: In addition to the *Acta Nuntiaturae Gallicae*, Vol. VII which contains the correspondence of the Nuncio G. B. Castelli, 1581–83, edited by R. Toupin in 1967, the most important accounts are: *Lettres de Henri IV concernant les Relations du St. Siège et de la France 1595–1609*, ed. B. Barbiche (Città del Vaticano 1968) (=*Studi e Testi* 250); R. Mousnier, *The Assassination of Henry IV. The Tyrannicide Problem and the Consolidation of the French Absolute Monarchy in the Early XVII Century* (London 1973).

ENGLAND, SCOTLAND, AND IRELAND: From the ever-growing body of literature on the establishment of the Anglican Church and the fate of the Catholic minority we can

751

offer only a small selection here: W. P. Haugaard, *Elizabeth and the English Reformation. The Struggle for a Stable Settlement of Religion* (Cambridge 1968), on the approval of the 39 Articles; for southern England, R. B. Manning, *Religion and Society in Elizabethan Sussex. A Study of the Enforcement of the Religious Settlement 1558–1603* (Leicester 1969), with many notes on the Catholic recusants; H. Davies, *Worship and Theology in England I: From Cranmer to Hooker 1534–1603* (Princeton 1970).—For the beginning based on the study of the letters of Bentham, see: R. O'Day, "Thomas Bentham" *Journal of Eccl. History* 23 (1972) 137–159; P. MacGrath, *Papists and Puritans under Elizabeth I* (London 1967).—C. Cross, *The Royal Supremacy in the Elizabethan Church* (London 1969), tones down the severity of the execution of the anti-Puritan act and shows that two-thirds of the property of the recusants was not actually confiscated by the Act of 1587, as it was turned over to relatives. *The Welsh Elizabethan Martyrs: The Trial Documents of Saint Richard Gwynn and of the Venerable William Davies,* ed. A. Thomas (Cardiff 1971), Document; *Letters of William Allen and Richard Barret 1572–1598,* ed. P. Renold (London 1967), 120 letters of the first two presidents of the Douay College; *The Seminary Priests. A Dictionary of the Secular Clergy of England and Wales 1558–1850,* Vol. I: *Elizabethan,* ed. G. Anstruthe (Ware–Durham 1969); L. Rostenberg, *The Minority Press and the English Crown. A Study in Repression 1558 to 1625* (Nieukwoop 1971); K. L. Lindley, "The Lay Catholics of England in the Reign of Charles I" *Journal of Eccl. History* 22 (1971) 199–221; R. J. Bradley, *Blacklo and the Counter Reformation. An Inquiry into the Strange Death of Catholic England: Essays in Honour of Garrett-Mattingly,* ed. C. H. Carter (London 1966) 366–370, reaches beyond Jedin's periodization; M. O'Connell, *Thomas Stapleton and the Counter Reformation* (New Haven 1964).

SCOTLAND: The biographies of P. Janton, *John Knox. L'Homme et l'Oeuvre* (Paris 1967) and J. Ridley, *John Knox* (Oxford–New York 1968); L. Hammermeyer, "Herr-schaftlich-staatliche Gewalt, Gesellschaft und Katholizisimus in Irland vom 16. bis 18. Jh. Aspekte des Postreformatorischen Katholizisimus auf den Britischen Inseln während der Penal Times" *Festgabe Karl Bosl* (Munich 1969) 191–218.

EASTERN EUROPE: Rich material on the post-Tridentine synods in Poland in Sawickis *Concilia Poloniae.* An example of a Tridentine visitation in the archdiocese of Cracow in 1599, although there was actually such a visitation in 1565–70: *Materly do Dziejow Kosciola w Polsce* II, ed. Cz. Skowron (Lublin 1965); *Erectici Italiani in Moravia, Polonia, Transilvania 1558–1611,* ed. D. Caccamo (Florence–Chicago 1970); L. Szilas, *Der Jesuit Alfons Carillo in Siebenbürgen 1591–99* (Rome 1966); *Documenta Unionis Berestensis Eiusque Auctorum 1590–1600,* ed. A. G. Welykyj (Rome 1970).

CENTRAL EUROPE, THE EMPIRE, AND THE HABSBURG HEREDITARY LANDS: A great deal of information in the continuing editions of the reports of the Cologne Nunciature by B. Roberg (II:2 and II:3: O. M. Frangipani 1590–1593, Munich 1969–71), K. Wittstadt (IV:1: A. Amalteo 1606–7) and W. Reinhard (V:1: A. Albergati 1610–14, Munich 1972); an excellent summary of this research by W. Reinhard in: *RQ* 66 (1971) 8–65 and by K. Wittstadt in: *Festgabe Franzen* 695–711. The reports of the nuncios at Graz, G. Malaspina and A. Possevino, 1580–82, were edited by J. Rainer (Vienna 1972); he had previously prepared the reports of G. Delfino and G. F. Commendone, from the imperial court, 1571–72 (NB II:8, Graz–Cologne 1967). On the significance of the Peace of Augsburg: M. Heckel, "Autonomie und Pacis Composito. Der Augs-burger Religionsfriede in der Deutung der Gegenreformation" *ZSavRGMan* 45 (1959) 141–248; H. Raab, "Die oberdeutschen Hochstifte zwischen Habsburg und Wittelsbach in der frühen Neuzeit" *Blätter f. Deutsche Landesgesch.* 109 (1973) 69–101.

EXAMPLES OF THE WORKS IN VARIOUS TERRITORIAL HISTORIES ON CHURCH RE-NEWAL: *Julius Echter und seine Zeit,* ed. F. Merzbacher (Würzburg 1974); O. Schaffrath, *Fürstabt Balthasar von Dernbach und seine Zeit. Studien zur Geschichte der Gegenreformation in Fulda* (Fulda 1967); H. G. Molitor, *Kirchliche Reformversuche der Kurfürsten und Erzbischöfe von Trier im Zeitalter der Gegenreformation 1567–1648* (Wiesbaden 1968); E. Camenzin, *Weihbischof Balthasar Würer von Konstanz 1574–1598 und die kirchl. Reformbewegung in den Fünf Orten* (Fribourg 1968); J. Bücking, *Frühabsolutismus und Kirchenreform in Tirol 1565–1665* (Wiesbaden 1972); J. Köhler, *Das Ringen um die Tridentinische Erneuerung im Bistum Breslau vom Abschluss des Trienter Konzils bis zur Schlacht am Weissen Berg* (Cologne–Vienna 1973); *Die Protokolle des Geistlichen Rates in Münster 1601–1612,* ed. H. Immenkötter (Münster 1972).—A hitherto neglected area is covered by U. Eisenhardt, *Die Kaiserliche Aufsicht über Buchdruck, Buchhandel und Presse im Hl. Römischen Reich deutscher Nation 1496–1806* (Karlsruhe 1970); H. Raab, "Apostolische Bücherkommission in Frankfurt a. M." *HJ* 87 (1967) 326–354, where the Index of recommended Catholic books that first appeared in 1614 is mentioned; R. Becker, "Die Berichte des kaiserlichen und apostolischen Bücherkommissars Joh. Ludwig von Hagen an die röm. Kurie 1623–1649" *QF* 51 (1971) 422.

SECTION THREE

Religious Forces and Intellectual Content of the Catholic Renewal

Literature on the rise of Spanish theology by C. Pozo in: *Arch. Teol. Granatino 29* (1966) 87–124; E. Llamas Martinez, "Orientaciones Sobre la Historia de la Teologia Española en la Primera Mitad del Siglo XVI" *Repertorio de Historia de la Ciencias Eclesiásticas en España* I (Salamanca 1967) 95–174; V. Beltran de Heredia, *Domingo Bañez y la Controversia Sobre la Gracia. Textos y Documentos* (Madrid 1968); B. Hamilton, *Political Thought in Sixteenth Century Spain. A Study of the Political Ideas of Vitorio, De Soto, Suárez, and Molina* (Oxford 1963); M. A. Huesbe Llanos, *Henning Arnisaeus 1575–1636. Untersuchungen zum Einfluss der Schule von Salamanca auf das Lutherische Staatsdenken* (Mainz 1965); G. Galeota, *Bellarmino Contro Baio a Lovanio. Studio e Testo di un Inedito Bellarminiano* (Rome 1966), also G. Colombo in: *La Scuola Cattolica* 95 (1967) 307–338; J. Stöhr, *Die theologische Wissenschaftslehre des Juan de Perlin (1569–1638)* (Münster 1967). A survey of the development of the training of the clergy in the late sixteenth and seventeenth centuries in: M. Arneth, *Das Ringen um Geist und Form der Priesterbildung im Säkularklerus des 17. Jhs.* (Würzburg 1970).

SPIRITUALITY: A survey in L. Cognet, *La Spiritualité Moderne* (Aubier 1966) 15–230; F. Chiwaro, *Bernardino Rossignoli SJ (1547–1613). Orientamenti della Spiritualità Post-Tridentina* (Rome 1967). For a biography of St. Theresa of Avila based upon wider sources and more chronologically precise: Efren de la Madre de Dios—O. Stegink, *Tiempo y Vida de Santa Teresa* (Madrid 1968); On the struggle over the reform of the Carmelite Order: O. Steggink, *La Reforma del Carmelo Español. La Visita Canonica del*

General Rubeo y su Encuentro con S. Teresa 1566–67 (Rome 1965); H. J. Prien, *Francisco de Ossuna. Mystik und Rechtfertigung* (Hamburg 1967); A. Barrado Manzano, *San Pedro de Alcántara* (Madrid 1965); A. Cistellini, "S. Filippo Neri e la sua Patriá" *RSTI* 23 (1969) 54–119, on the influence of San Marco and Savonarola: R. Razzi, *Vita di S. Caterina di Ricci* (Florence 1965); *Donna Battista Vernazza da Genova, Commento al Paternoster,* ed. G. J. Scatena (Rome 1968), contains a detailed introduction and bibliography; P. Lopez, *Riforma Cattolica e Vita Religiosa e Culturale a Napoli dalla Fine del Cinquecento ai Primi del Settecento* (Napoli 1964); id., "Le Confraternità Laicali in Italia e la Riforma Cattolica" *Rivista di Studi Salernitani* 4 (1969) 153–238; H. Reifenberg, *Sakramente, Sakramentalien und Ritualien im Bistum Mainz seit dem Spätmittelalter* I (Münster 1971), to 1671; K. Pörnbacher, *Jeremias Drexel. Leben und Werk eines Barockpredigers* (Munich 1965); L. Intorp, *Westfälische Barockpredigten in volkstümlicher Sicht* (Münster 1964); B. Hubensteiner, *Vom Geist des Barock. Kultur und Frömmigkeit im alten Bayern* (Munich 1967); Friedrich Spee, *Guldenes Tugendbuch,* ed. Th. G. M. van Oorschot (Munich 1968).

THE HISTORY OF THE RELIGIOUS ORDERS: From the *Storia della Compagnia di Gesù in Italia* IV on the end of the generalship of Laynez has appeared a comprehensive review of works on the Jesuit theater by M. Scaduto in: *AHSJ* 36 (1967) 194–215; an account of the same in German-speaking lands by R. G. Dimler, "A Geographic and Genetic Survey of Jesuit Drama in German-Speaking Territories 1555–1609" *AHSJ* 43 (1974) 133–146; A. Rodríguez Gutiérrez de Ceballos, *Bartolomé de Bustamente y los Orígenes de la Arquitectura Jesuítica en España* (Rome 1967). For especially wide-ranging and extraordinary literature one might consult the bibliographies in *AHSJ.*—The reform of the Capuchins is placed within the overall reform movement in: Optat de Veghel, "La Réforme de Frères Mineurs Capucins dans l'Ordre Franciscain et dans l'Église" *CollFr* 35 (1965) 5–108; Carmelo de la Cruz, "Derecho Reformatorio de Trento en los Primeros Pasos de su Aplicación a la Reforma Teresiana" *MonteCarm* (Burgos 1965) 49–97; H. Schwendenwein, *Franz von Sales und die Entwicklung neuer Formen des Ordenslebens* (Eichstätt–Vienna 1966); J. Grisar, *Mary Wards Institut vor römischen Kongregationen (1616–1630)* (Rome 1966) (=Misc. Hist. Pont XXVII).

SECTION FIVE

European Counter Reformation and Confessional Absolutism (1605–55)

PONTIFICATE OF PAUL V: J. Semmler, *Das päpstliche Staatssekretariat in den Pontifiken Pauls V. und Gregors XV. (1605–1623)* (Rome 1969); on the Gunpowder Plot see Ph. G. Caraman, *Henry Garnet and the Gun-Powder-Plot* (London 1964); on the conflict with Venice, W. J. Bouwsma, *Venice and the Defence of Republican Liberty. Renaissance Values in the Age of the Counter-Reformation* (Berkeley–Los Angeles 1968); P. Sarpi, *Opere,* ed. G. and L. Cozzi (Mailand 1969). On the editor of Sarpis' *Istoria*: A. Russo, *Marcantonio De Dominis, Arcivescovo di Spalato e Apostata 1560–1624* (Naples 1965); W. Reinhard, "Ein Römisches Gutachten vom Juli 1612 zur Strategie der Gegenreformation im Rhein-land" *RQ* 64 (1969) 168–190; F. Neuer-Landfried, *Die Katholische Liga. Gründung, Neugründung und Organisation eines Sonderbundes 1608–1620* (Kellmunz 1968); E. A. Seils, *Die Staatslehre des Jesuiten Adam Contzen, Beichtvater Kurfürst Maximilians I. von Bayern* (Lübeck–Hamburg 1968).

PONTIFICATE OF CLEMENT VIII: A. Gasparini, *Cesare d'Este Clemente VIII* (Modena 1960); B. Barbiche, (ed.), *Correspondence du Nonce en France Innocenzo del Bufalo, Évêque de Camirno, 1601–04;* id., "L'Influence Française à la Cour Pontificale sous le Regime Henri IV" *MAH* 77 (1965), 277–299; J. de Lamar, *Diplomacy and Dogmatism: Bernardino de Mendoza and the French Catholic League* (Cambridge, Mass., 1964).

PONTIFICATE OF URBAN VIII: A. Springhetti, "Urbanus VIII. P. M. Poeta Latinus et Hymnorum Breviarii Emendator" *AHPont* 6 (1968) 163–190. On the significance of the "Politics of Neutrality" of Urban VIII: G. Lutz, *Kard. G. Fr. da Bagno. Politik und Religion im Zeitalter Richelieus und Urbans VIII.* (Tübingen 1971); A. Kraus, "Der Kardinalnepot Francesco Barberini und das Staatssekretariat Urbans VIII." *RQ* 64 (1969) 191–208; French nuncio reports: *Ranuccio Scotti 1639–41,* ed. P. Blet (Rome 1965). On the case of Galileo: *G. G. Celebrazioni* (Rome 1965); *Galilée. Aspects de sa vie et de son oeuvre* (Paris 1968); G. Galli, "Il Card. Maculano al Processo di Galileo" *Memorie Domenicane* NS 41 (1965) 24–42, 65–101; W. Brandmüller, "Der Fall Galilei—im Konflikt Naturwissenschaft und Kirche?" *StdZ* 162 (1968) 333–342, 399–411; E. Gentili, "Bibliografia Gallileana fra i due Centenari 1942–1964" *SC* 17 (1964) 267–309; P. Blat, (ed.), *Correspondence du Nonce en France Ranuccio Scotti, 1639–41* (Rome 1965); L. von Meerbeeck, (ed.), *Correspondence du Nonce Fabio de Lagonissa, 1627–34* (Brussels 1964); questioning Pastor's interpretation of Urbino's politics of neutrality based on his correspondence is Q. Aldea, "Instrucciones de los Ambajadores en Roma, 1631–43" *Misc. Comillas* 29 (Comillas 1958).

CONVERSIONS: G. Christ, "Fürst, Dynastie, Territorium und Konfession. Beobachtungen zu Fürstenkonversionen des ausgehenden 17. und beginnenden 18. Jh." *Saeculum* 24 (1973) 367–387; H. Tüchle, "Zum Kirchenwesen fürstlicher Konvertiten des 17. und 18. Jh." *Festschrift Ferdinand Maas* (Vienna 1973) 231–247.

WITCHCRAFT IN ITALY: C. Ginzburg, *I Benendanti. Ricerche sulla Stegoneria e sui Culti Agrari Cinquecento e Seicento* (Turin 1966); see also the literature on the subject in: *RSCI* 25 (1971) 231–237. Against the traditional concept "secularization" see: H. Blumenberg, *Säkularisierung und Selbstbehauptung* (Frankfurt 1974).

TOLERANCE AND SECULARIZATION OF THE STATE AND OF THOUGHT: F. Dickmann, "Das Problem der Gleichberechtigung der Konfessionen im Reich im 16. und 17. Jh." *HZ* 201 (1965) 265–305; H. Bornkamm, "Die religiöse und politische Problematik im Verhältnis der Konfessionen im Reich" *ARG* 56 (1965) 209–218; H. Lutz, "Die Konfessionsproblematik ausserhalb des Reiches und in der Politik des Papsttums" ibid. 218–227; E. Hassinger, *Religiöse Toleranz im 16. Jh. Motive, Argumente, Formen der Verwirklichung* (Brussels 1966); F. Raab, *The English Face of Machiavelli: A Changing Interpretation 1500–1700* (London 1964); G. Lewy, *Constitutionalism and Statecraft during the Golden Age of Spain. A Study on the Political Philosophy of Juan de Mariana SJ* (Geneva 1961).

INDEX

INDEX